W9-CDG-957
CCCC
BOOKSTORE
$63.50

Sociology
Micro, Macro, and Mega Structures

Sociology

Micro, Macro, and Mega Structures

Brian J. Jones
Villanova University

Bernard J. Gallagher III
Villanova University

Joseph A. McFalls, Jr.
Villanova University

Harcourt Brace College Publishers
Fort Worth Philadelphia San Diego New York Orlando Austin San Antonio
Toronto Montreal London Sydney Tokyo

Publisher	Ted Buchholz
Senior Acquisitions Editor	Chris Klein
Senior Developmental Editor	Meera Dash
Senior Project Editor	Steve Welch
Senior Production Manager	Tad Gaither
Senior Art Director	Don Fujimoto
Picture Editor	Marty Levick

Cover Image — *Shipping by Western traders at Yokohama;* wood block print, five piece, 1861; by Gountei Teishu. Carl H. Boehringer Collection, Yokohama

On the Cover: *From 1600 to 1850, Japanese rulers kept foreigners and foreign influence out of Japan. But in 1853, four large, black U.S. warships commanded by Commodore Matthew C. Perry arrived to demand the opening of the country to trade. Once the trade treaties were signed, selected treaty harbors rapidly filled with "black ships," as most foreign trading vessels were called. These ships brought traders, missionaries, diplomats, and adventurers of all kinds, and cultural and technological diffusion ensued. This period Japanese print embodies the principle theme of this book: The opening of Japan to trade produced a new international mega structure; the trading companies that sponsored the commerce and colonization were macro structures; and the ships' crews and embarking families were micro structures.*

ISBN: 0-03-029638-2

Library of Congress Catalog Card Number: 94-75159

Address editorial correspondence to:
Harcourt Brace & Company
301 Commerce Street, Suite 3700
Fort Worth, TX 76102

Address for orders:
Harcourt Brace & Company
6277 Sea Harbor Drive
Orlando, FL 32887-6777
1-800-782-4479, or
1-800-433-0001 (in Florida)

Printed in the United States of America

4 5 6 7 8 9 0 1 2 3 032 9 8 7 6 5 4 3 2 1

To my wife Suzanne, and where we came from.
BJJ

To all of the Gallaghers in my life: Michele, Bernard J. IV, Bernard J. Jr., Claire, John W., Mary Lou, John W. Jr., Leah, and Mary Beth. I also want to express my deep gratitude to St. Joseph's Prep for giving me the discipline to do research and write books.
BJG

To my grandparents Joseph and Helen Boyd, and Augustus and Anastasia McFalls.
JAM

PREFACE

Luckily, writing a preface does not require praying to Muses or romantic intoxication. When in need of inspiration, I employ the same device that first served me as a student—sociology. Looking through my disciplinary device, the task of preface writing is transformed. It is an effect quite like using infrared lenses at night: big, obvious things that were there all along appear from the dark. The reason I, Brian Jones, speak for the three of us here is clear in my sociological lenses. It has simply been part of my role in our author team, a collaboration made up of understandings, conversations, frictions, celebrations . . . the stuff of interpersonal relationships. Without this stuff—obvious to me now—there is no team, no book, and certainly no preface. The personal style you are reading is central to our approach. I have tugged on the social bonds with my coauthors to sell them on this approach, but the main selling point is experiential: *Write the way you talk in the classroom.* Since my coauthors are both great teachers with rich experiences inspiring students, they have transplanted that style of communication in this book. It is a style that calls the attention of students to the operation of sociological forces inside their own skins.

The very first time I remember putting on sociological lenses was in reading *The Sociological Imagination* by C. Wright Mills. The author electrified me with a phrase ". . . the imperial reach of social structure into the most intimate parts of one's very self." It is a quote so personally meaningful that it inspired this person-centered style, as well as my personal view of the substance of sociology. Mills's vision of social structure extending outward from the soul led me to give that structure a long, hard, academic look. Of course I had the lenses of academic sociology through which to look, and I have made some adjustments that clarify things for me and my students. Consider our subtitle: "Micro, Macro, and Mega Structures"; it suggests that we sketch social structure in ascending levels proceeding upward from individual experience. Microstructure encompasses social networks and statuses and roles, structures enmeshed in the everyday experience of individuals. Macrostructure encompasses all varieties of groups, from clubs of computer hackers, through organizations such as IBM, all the way up to the supergroup of society itself. Megastructure encompasses structural relations connecting whole societies—a truly sociological depiction of "globalization." This is more than a presentational trick. We have arranged the material on *the* substantive concept of sociology—social structure—into three consecutive chapters mirroring the subtitle.

HIGHLIGHTS OF THE BOOK

To explain how our book inspires students to use the sociological imagination leads us to spotlight ten distinctive traits.

1. Micro, Macro, and Mega Structures
   Our unique approach organizes the idea of *social structure*—the central idea of sociology itself. Concrete human relations are revealed linking individuals (microstructure), groups and organizations (macrostructure), then whole nation–states (megastructure).

   These ascending levels of social structure are evident in the organization, analysis, and terms employed throughout the text. The cumulative effect is to show the shape of the social forces affecting the individual from a student or coworker, to a corporate organization, up through the global economy itself; it is an effect, moreover, reflecting the whole range of human relations, economic and otherwise.

2. Social Networks
Starting with the microstructure, showing the self within a network of relationships that make up the "global village" is a powerful way to uncover the grandeur of social structure.
Virtually every chapter contains a special section devoted to social networks, one of the most rapidly developing areas in sociology. For example, the chapter on Social Class and Stratification presents recent research on the structure of social contacts used in finding jobs.

3. Modern Sociology
We focus on how sociology is actually practiced by working sociologists at the dawn of the twenty-first century. Throughout the book we examine topics such as applied sociology, analysis of large-scale data sets, and global social change. The most concrete illustration is our presentation of a General Social Survey (GSS) table in virtually every chapter. The GSS is *the* most widely used data set in modern sociology. After a careful explanation of table-reading in the chapter on Sociological Research Methods, the other chapters use the GSS tables to enhance substantive points.

4. Objective–Subjective Dimensions
People are often amazed by the realization that what is inside their heads has been conditioned by social forces. But personal opinions about social life (the subjective dimension) are often wildly distorted images of what sociological research reveals (the objective dimension). In contrast to the "myth vs. realities" idea, this fresh, conceptual model explains *why* the subjective and objective dimensions differ. In the Social Class and Stratification chapter, for instance, we explain the factors that shape public opinion about the poor—an opinion in stark contrast to sociological findings about the poverty population.

5. Social Order/Disorder
Our textbook has *two* introductory chapters, the first focusing on patterns of social organization ("order") and the second on social change and social problems ("disorder"). The "making" and the "unmaking" of society are linked principles that have been jointly considered in sociological theory, and both processes resonate with students' life experiences.

6. Gender and Social Change
It is a truism to say that we are living in a period of massive social change. We connect large-scale social shifts directly to the lives of students by spotlighting changing gender roles. In addition to the numerous in-text examples, a feature highlights these changes. A Gender and Social Change box in the chapter on technology, for instance, relates technological innovation to fundamental shifts in women's roles.

7. College Experience
   Many textbooks promise to make a special appeal to the everyday lives of college students; most fail. Student engagement cannot be bought by a few offhand comments about the college scene. Therefore, most chapters provide a feature that digs deeper into a sociological aspect of students' real lives. In the chapter on population, for example, a College Experience box explains that most every U.S. student is a member of either a "Baby Boom" or "Baby Bust" cohort, yielding dramatic differences in "life chances."

8. Sociological Imagination in Fiction
   In most chapters, we excerpt imaginative literature, generally science fiction, fantasy, or novels. It is our experience that carefully drawn selections can be lightning rods for student attention. The advantages for student interest are obvious. When such pieces are carefully blended with the conceptual materials, we have found them to be fascinating case studies of projected futures or alternate realities that demonstrate the breadth of sociological principles on levels that standard studies cannot attain. For example, a Sociological Imagination in Fiction box in the chapter on the macrostructure (groups and organizations) takes a selection from Michael Crichton's familiar *Jurassic Park* and casts it in the unfamiliar, revealing light of sociologist Charles Perrow's concept of "normal accidents."

9. Personal Perspective
   Each chapter opens with a Personal Perspective of the authors, of a student, or of some other person from the undergraduate setting. We have found in our teaching that students actively respond to such pieces, probably because it makes relatively abstract principles come to life. These incidents clearly convey the message that sociological principles operate in the lives of ordinary people such as students—and even sociologists. See the opening of the chapter on Sociological Research Methods for the unsettling experience of a young lecturer whose lecture is being questioned.

10. Presentational Approach
    As you read the book, a distinctive style will be obvious in every passage. The presentational thrust is toward the personalistic involvement of the undergraduate reader, a style that suits the substance of the book right from the first-person accounts of ex-students in Chapter 1.

ORGANIZATION

The arrangement and content of sociological material *is* unique, and that uniqueness pays off in the classroom.

Part One consists of three introductory chapters. The first two are distinctive but also so logical because "Social Order" and "Social Disorder" are complementary processes of social life. Instead of introducing sociology through the usual bios of the field's founders, we organize the insights of classical and contemporary sociologists around the fundamental questions of how society gets organized (Chapter 1), how society gets disorganized (Chapter 2), and how sociologists today study these activities (Chapter 3).

The student–reader is the centerpiece of Chapter 1 ("Social Order: The Making of Society"). The first College Experience box presents autobiographical vignettes of ex-students candidly discussing how sociology has touched their lives (*their* pictures are shown instead of the same old head shots of Durkheim, Marx, and Weber). The material focuses on patterns of social structure reaching into the heart of the self. To dramatize this sociological perspective, Table 1:1 organizes evidence from Chapters 1 to 21 indicating how patterned social inequality influences individual experience. We focus on the complementariness of sociological theories, and establish a framework of Integrating the Theories that we use throughout the text.

Chapter 2 is "Social Disorder: The Unmaking and Remaking of Society." Regarding "unmaking," the authors have developed a conceptual apparatus for understanding social problems and social disintegration both in the professional literature and in the classroom. This apparatus is introduced and applied to three case study issues, then generalized to explain differences between public opinion (the "subjective dimension") and sociological findings (the "objective dimension"); most of the chapters that follow devote a full section to these dual dimensions of social life, as well as a schematic diagram applying the concepts to an issue. The "Remaking of Society" refers to processes of social change that sweep down into the lives of students. This section speaks to the contemporary lives of students.

Chapter 3 introduces "Sociological Research Methods." To put modesty aside for a moment, reviewers have commented collectively that our writing style communicates complex concepts in a rich and lively way. We strove to make this chapter more ambitious *and* more accessible than the usual methods introduction. First, we present the three major "Strategies of Inquiry" in sociology with a clear-eyed view of strengths and weaknesses. Then, we take seriously our mandate to represent "Modern Sociology." We introduce and explain how to read the General Social Survey (GSS) tables. GSS data are used to make crosstabulations quite like those professors use in their own research and, increasingly, students are asked to make on personal computers using SPSS software. We clarify the interpretation of crosstabulations in a section called "The Flow of Sociological Analysis," which presents a series of tables from one coauthor's work-in-progress. After reading this section, students are ready for the GSS tables in subsequent chapters.

Part Two is the most distinctive element of our organization. Social structure—*the* central idea of sociology—is here treated in three full chapters. The chapters are integrated, moreover, to show social structure from the inside out; that is, from the immediate interpersonal world of the self all the way up to the social "world" of globalization.

Chapter 4 ("Microstructure") highlights the self-structure connection in an extensive discussion of the structure and functions of social networks. Network analysis is one of the more rapidly developing areas of the discipline, and we know of no better way to show students sociological forces operating in their own lives. We refocus the traditional status/role material on students' lives, and relate it back to social networks to complete the idea of "Microstructure."

Chapter 5 ("Macrostructure") proceeds into the social world of groups. In keeping with the inside-out approach, the student is walked up structural levels from reference groups, to organizations, to institutions, to the apex of macrostructure—society itself. along the way, special material is developed on network relations within and between bureaucracies, on information processing in groups through Herbert A. Simon's concept of "satisficing," and on Charles Perrow's chilling idea of "normal accidents."

After the application of functionalism, conflict theory, and symbolic interactionism to organizational behavior, "Integrating the Theories" teases out complementary insights from sociology's theories regarding the "downsizing" of the authors' university.

Chapter 6 ("Megastructure") is a thoroughly sociological take on the concept of globalization. Instead of generally summarizing global phenomena, the discussion probes the underlying structural relations—i.e., "megastructures"—linking societies. We have chosen to analyze the worldwide modernization process by using development theory, dependency theory, and world system theory. The discussion of global stratification concludes with a practical demonstration of how social problems flow along the network strands linking First World and Third World societies.

Part Three examines social control processes by which "Social Order" is maintained and the various forms of the breakdown of social control—the "Social Disorder" side of the sociological coin.

Chapter 7 ("Culture") is a refreshing presentation of a topic that looms ever larger with the megastructural framework addressed in Chapter 6. It goes beyond the usual presentation of terms and family arrangements. Even the role of language in cultural development is spiked by a linkage with life on campus. One of the chapter's unique features is its analysis of U.S. values and how they differ from values prevalent elsewhere in the world. The discussion includes the U.S. emphasis on creativity and achievement and how these values permeate even our leisure time. The chapter will be remembered for its "Exotica of Culture," a lively table comparing distinctive cultural traits from around the world, which run the gamut from sex to murder to sports to drunken driving to capital punishment to female circumcision. We believe that the chapter sparks reader interest while reducing ethnocentrism.

Chapter 8 ("Socialization") is one of the most complete chapters of its kind. The chapter uses a wide-angle lens to focus on pure sociological aspects of personality development, as well as well-respected psychological theories such as those of Erik Erikson, Jean Piaget, and Martin Kohlberg. This is in keeping with our personal orientation, which shows how social forces influence people's inner lives. This chapter is a *full* presentation of a whole host of influential agents of socialization including the family, social class, birth order, language, school, peer groups, and the mass media. It also addresses later personality processes, including secondary socialization, resocialization, and desocialization. Interesting examples from the world of work are interspersed throughout the section on occupational socialization. The chapter concludes with a special section on the psychosocial experiences of aging and dying.

Chapter 9 ("Deviance") emphasizes the idea that deviance is both complicated and relative. It includes classic data on Milgram's "shock" studies and brand new data on "whistle blowing." Deviance is not a "black-and-white" issue, but something that varies immensely by time, place, and group. The chapter covers traditional topics such as social control and stigma and extensively discusses the impact of three of the most important forms of deviance (crime, mental disorder, and drug abuse) on U.S. society. It presents the theories needed for a solid understanding, but goes further by explaining how subjective and objective dimensions affect the definition of deviance. The chapter explodes myths of deviant behavior.

Chapter 10 ("Collective Behavior and Social Movements") moves beyond a description of types of crowds and other forms of collective behavior. The subjective/objective analytical framework, for example, works especially well in presenting an explanation of the seeming paradox of riots actually increasing public support for aid to blighted areas. The work of social network theorist Charles Tilly provides an especially enlightening explanation as to how people are recruited into social movements by social contacts. The chapter reads partly like a novel, with past and present items from around the world and a provocative section on urban legends and rumor transmission.

Whereas Part Two presents the conceptual heart of sociology in social structure, *Part Four* presents its substantive heart. Social inequality is *the* most studied subject in the discipline, and the chapters in this section fill out the substance only suggested in Table 1:1.

Chapter 11 ("Social Class and Stratification") focuses on the class system of the United States for a thematic reason: the self-structure connection. Students are shown the structure of social inequality looming above their selves, then offered sociological perspectives on the building of that structure. The personal dimension is emphasized in the latest findings about the involvement of social network ties in students' job prospects. Network analysis also lends itself to illuminating discussions of the different classes, mobility research, human capital, and social capital.

Chapter 12 ("Race and Ethnicity") was challenging to write because the definition of race, for example, is a book in itself. This is not just a chapter about racial tensions in the United States. It spans the complexities of racial and ethnic relations in all parts of the world. A special section discusses the changing racial and ethnic composition of the United States. The subjective/objective analysis proves especially helpful in untangling the contradictory findings on the perceptions and facts about intergroup relations today. We also found humor to be an effective communicator of the complexities of racial and ethnic relations.

Chapter 13 ("Gender") devotes much more attention to theory, current statistics, and examples than do other texts. The subject is especially well-informed by our conceptual distinction between the subjective and objective dimensions. Starting with the important distinction between the concepts *sex* and *gender,* the different arrangement of the material enhances student comprehension. Men and women are compared biologically, psychologically, and cross-culturally. Common forms of gender inequality, including occupational and educational discrimination, as well as the women's movement, are thoroughly explored. Much of the material is strengthened by strong connections to campus life.

Part Five is devoted to the social institutions identified as key elements of "Macrostructure" in Chapter 5.

Chapter 14 ("The Family") focuses on providing the student with a comprehensive, in-depth understanding of modern U.S. families. Basic family concepts that apply the world over are discussed early in the chapter (cross-cultural material on the family appears mainly in Chapters 7 and 19). The discussion focuses on changes, such as lower marriage rates, delayed marriage, less time spent together within marriage, diversity of families, and changes in family life. This chapter benefits very much from the work of Carol DeVita and Dennis Ahlburg on the social, economic, and demographic trends underpinning the changing structure of U.S. families.

Chapter 15 ("Religion") covers all of the major religious issues, but is not much like the religion chapter in any other introductory sociology book. The detailed discussion of Durkheim's theory, for example, makes the ideas more complete. An innovative aspect is the inclusion of civil religion, religious revival, and the electronic church.

Chapter 16 ("Political Economy") jointly considers two social institutions—politics and the economy. These nominally separate institutions are often understood together as constituting a fundamental "type" of society. This chapter's treatment will arm the student with knowledge of *why* they are.

Chapter 17 ("Education") is a comprehensive and often irreverent look at the obvious and non-obvious aspects of education. The discussion focuses on the relationship between education and the "American Dream" of becoming "successful," which, as student readers will discover, is not nearly so obvious as it seems. The chapter also focuses on current sociological theory, research, and policy concerning education.

Part Six collects the special areas of sociology that highlight the social change processes introduced in Chapter 2.

Chapter 18 ("Health and Medicine") explores both the impact of society on health and illness, and the impact of health and illness on society. It also discusses the social institution of medicine and the social aspects of health and illness. Chapter 18 provides students with the most up-to-date sociological framework with which to understand the increasingly important issues related to the American health care system. This chapter was influenced by James F. Fries's conceptualization of the social determinants of life expectancy, illness, and premature death.

Chapter 19 ("The Sociology of Sexuality") focuses on the social causes and consequences of human sexuality. One of the main thrusts is that, while the potential for sexual behavior is provided by human biology, social factors largely determine how that potential is expressed. Another element is the variation between the sexual norms of mainstream U.S. society and such norms of other societies. Sexual deviance and nonconformity are considered. Also included is an in-depth discussion of the sexual revolution as an example *par excellence* of social change. We included a chapter on sexuality because our students have told us that it is their favorite chapter in texts that have one. We also agree with Tom Smith of NORC who writes that sexual behavior is one of the most important human activities. The chapter owes an intellectual debt to John Gagnon, whose pathbreaking book, *Sexualities,* shaped our understanding of the sociology of sexuality.

Chapter 20 ("Population") begins with the basic building blocks of demography—fertility, mortality, and migration—and shows how these forces combine to determine other demographic phenomena like population growth, composition, and distribution. The student thus acquires a command of demographic forces and the ability to understand changing demographic phenomena rather than simply collecting demographic facts. This approach is in keeping with our overall aim of depicting sociology (and its parts like demography) as it is actually practiced in the 1990s.

Chapter 21 ("Technology, Science, and the Environment") introduces students to the idea that technology, whether new or already existing, is not a thing apart from society. The chapter develops the idea that technology has a profound impact on society and is, in fact, one of the most common causes of social change. Further, the chapter shows that technology does not come about in a social vacuum; it is a social creation, which must be understood in terms of its many social and cultural dimensions. The social policy aspects of technology also are explored. This chapter was influenced by the seminal works of Rudi Volti and Robert E. McGinn.

STUDY AIDS IN THE TEXTBOOK

To facilitate the user-friendliness of a textbook that really is different, the following pedagogical aids should prove valuable to students.

- A chapter outline and engaging Personal Perspective open each chapter, and a summary of numbered key ideas ends each chapter.
- General Social Survey (GSS) tables in most chapters illustrate modern sociological analysis. At the bottom of each table is a "Main Point" statement that draws attention to the most important data and conclusions.
- "Integrating the Theories" sections encourage students to derive complementary insights after considering the separate contributions of functionalism, conflict theory, and symbolic interactionism.
- Critical Thinking Questions end all Sociological Imagination in Fiction, Gender and Social Change, and College Experience boxes. These questions focus on applying the sociological theories and concepts and on linking the boxes further to in-text discussion.

- Globe icons highlight the in-text discussions of global social structure starting in Chapter 6. These icons encourage students to go *beyond* the scope of simple cross-cultural comparisons to analyze the social structure of globalization.
- Integrated maps focus on globalization issues and illustrate the levels of micro, macro, and mega structure. The map program also includes U.S. maps showing diversity *within* the United States.
- Thematic charts in the "subjective dimension" sections represent the "subjective dimension" (public opinion), the "objective dimension" (sociological findings), and the concepts that relate them.
- "Social Networks" sections emphasize the flexibility and relevance of networks at the various levels of social structure. A special application of the micro, macro, and mega structures appears on the acetates just prior to Chapter 6, using the example of MADD.
- Comprehensive glossaries of sociological terms appear in the margins, and in alphabetical order at the end of the book. Terms are defined and color-faced in text the first time that they are used.
- An extensive bibliography including more than 1,500 references is distinguished by scholarly currency and the relative prominence of female scholars (some 700 are cited).
- The photographs, drawings, and graphs were carefully developed and selected to operate as part of the pedagogy. The consistent use of fine art should help students to crystallize their understanding.

THE ANCILLARY PACKAGE

Study Guide, by Reba Lewis of James Madison University, includes learning objectives, chapter outlines, review exercises, cultural literacy notes, critical thinking questions, practice tests, and handouts for applying the micro, macro, and mega structure. A bonus section at the start of the study guide discusses various strategies for studying and adapting to testing customs.

Test Bank, also written by Reba Lewis, is available in printed and software versions. The test bank includes more than 100 multiple-choice and essay items per chapter. Each item is classified as "recall" or "application" and keyed to the page number in the textbook and the learning objective in the study guide. Items that come from boxes are so identified. The computerized test bank is available in IBM®, Windows™, and Macintosh® formats. EXAMaster™ software allows instructors to create tests using fewer keystrokes, guided through the process step by step by easy-to-follow screen prompts. EXAMaster™ has three test creation options: EasyTest™, which compiles tests from a single screen based on the instructor's choices;

FullTest™, which includes a larger range of options and editing of items; and RequesTest™, a test compilation service for the instructor who has no computer. EXAMaster™ comes with EXAMRecord™, a customized gradebook software program.

Instructor's Manual, by Karen Cole Smith of Santa Fe (Florida) Community College, includes teaching objectives, lecture outlines, teaching suggestions, video instructor's manual, and many other useful elements. An extensive introduction with course planning suggestions and sample syllabus appears in the manual.

Overhead Teaching Transparencies, a set of 54 full-color transparency acetates, illustrate key sociological concepts. They contain information to supplement (not duplicate) material in the textbook and are accompanied by a manual for suggested use of each transparency.

***Social Issues* Quarterly Report Videos** come from the MacNeil/Lehrer PBS television series, *Social Issues.* Every quarter, excerpts from these programs are selected to keep students engaged in thinking about timely issues. Each quarterly video is organized into four themes: The Global Culture Clash, Crime and Social Justice, Health Care, and The State of American Schools. Contact your local Harcourt Brace representative for details.

***The Sociological Imagination* Video Segments** are twelve 26-minute clips from the Dallas County Community College District introductory sociology telecourse, *The Sociological Imagination.* These segments highlight relevant subject matter in key areas of sociology. See your Harcourt Brace representative for details.

Specialized Videos include *Growing Old In A New Age, Marriage and the Family Videos, The Deadly Deception, Parents and Teenagers, When Families Divorce,* and assorted videos from the Films for the Humanities & Sciences focusing on social issues. Use of all videos is based on the Harcourt Brace policy. See your publisher's representative for details.

Sociology videodiscs include two videodiscs. *Sociological Insights for a Changing World* contains sections of motion video and more than 300 organized still images. The videodisc includes 10 modules that cover diverse topics, from research methods to religion, and comes with *LectureActive* presentation software to facilitate creation of custom lectures. The *Teen Violence Videodisc* is a simpler form of the technology that includes a 29-minute documentary program on homicide as the second leading cause of death for youth ages 15 to 24.

SimCity™: The Sociological Simulator is an educational version of the SimCity™ software game geared to sociology, using environmental, economic, or geographical variables focusing on the "unmaking" of society. In this program, the student becomes mayor of an evolving, growing city, and is forced to take action against disasters, pollution, crime, traffic gridlock, urban decay, and other social problems.

SocialStat Software is an interactive data analysis program that is simple to learn and use. Novices can run frequency distributions, histograms, crosstabulations, scatterplots, and mean charts and have the results in moments. SocialStat Software, an extensively revised version of SocialScene, and its accompanying User's Guide are written by Dean Savage and Jesse Reichler, City University of New York, Queens College.

ACKNOWLEDGMENTS

For reasons arising directly out of the substance and style of this book, it has been conceived—and born—within a special social network. At its center are the co-authors and their core network, without whom this project would have been literally impossible. For reasoned, professional judgment only available beyond our inner circle, we have depended on indispensable "weak ties" (see Chapter 4) to the following reviewers: Christopher Armstrong, Bloomsburg University; Steven Barkan, University of Maine; Matilda Barker, Cerritos College; Steven Beach, Avila College; William Cockerham, University of Illinois; Gerry Cox, Fort Hays State University; Dana Dunn, University of Texas at Arlington; Carol Gunderson, University of Wisconsin–Stout; Frances Hoffman, University of Missouri; Roland Liebert, University of Illinois–Urbana; James C. Miller, Dutchess Community College; Richard Miller, Navarro College; Julie Nash, DeAnza College; Fernando Parra, California State Polytechnic University; Henry Peddle, Elgin Community College; James Ranger-Moore, University of Arizona; Sally Rogers, Montgomery College; Ruth Schaffer, Texas A & M University; Michael Stein, University of Missouri at St. Louis; Carol Stix, Pace University; Lee Taylor, University of Texas at Arlington; Sharron Timmerman, Indiana State University–Terre Haute; Charles Tolbert, Florida State University; Beverly Ullock, Auburn University–Montgomery; Pelgy Vaz, Fort Hays State University; Timothy Wickham-Crowley, Georgetown University; and Ralph Woehle, Southwest State University.

An extra debt of thanks is to be paid to a focus group convened at the 1993 convention of the Midwest Sociological Society. The following participants did, indeed, improve our focus: Nicky Ali, Purdue University–Calumet; Gerry Cox, Fort Hays State University; Roland Liebert, University of Illinois–Urbana; Henry Peddle, Elgin Community College; Steven Vassar, Mankato State University; and Pelgy Vaz, Fort Hays State University.

The sociology of science teaches that ideas are social products. While no intellectual debt can be fully acknowledged, we certainly can thank the following colleagues and experts for explicitly shaping the ideas and particular chapters of the textbook.

The "Remaking of Society" in Chapter 2's title refers to processes of social change. The very term evokes the past (change from *what?*), so we did the right thing: consulted a professional historian. Lisa Ferraro Parmelee, Ph.D, contributed her considerable knowledge, skills, and imagination to our overview of sociological theories of social change. Thanks to her creative touch, what could have been a boring section now speaks to the contemporary lives of students.

Chapter 6 ("Megastructure") would have lost both breadth and depth without the magisterial knowledge or political sociology generously offered by Satya Pattnayak, Ph.D., one of our valued colleagues at Villanova.

Carole Champlin's background as both sociologist and psychotherapist permeates Chapter 8 ("Socialization") with the full meaning of the concept "psychosocial."

Carole Champlin also made a significant contribution to the development of Chapter 10 ("Collective Behavior and Social Movements"). Her creative touch makes the chapter especially interesting to read.

Chapter 15 ("Religion") was also forged with the help of Carole Champlin, and, as such, it reflects the quality of her intellect: comprehensive and superior.

While Chapter 16 ("Political Economy") was in the planning stage, a truly outstanding student came under the tutelage of co-author Brian J. Jones. Monica McDermott, the academic star in question, offered so many sparkling insights while discussing the outline that a thoroughly impressed Dr. Jones encouraged her to draft significant portions of the chapter. Monica is now pursuing her Ph.D. in sociology at Harvard, and we fully expect her to be *cited* in textbooks in the near future. In keeping with the theme of sociology touching individual lives, this is a case in which an extraordinary individual touched the discipline in return.

Our colleague Rick Eckstein helped us enormously in conceptualizing, researching, and writing Chapter 17 ("Education").

Chapter 20 ("Population") has benefited greatly from the generosity of the Population Reference Bureau, which permitted us to use its excellent figures, and from the help of the bureau's editor, Mary Mederios Kent, who helped improve and augment segments of the chapter.

The book's focus on the penetration of social structures into individual lives has led us to people with stories more interesting than our own. The personal experiences of Meghan Byrne, Yana Carter, Yolanda Carter, Janine Ferraro, Nnenna Lynch, Steve McWilliams, Tom Powers, and Stephen Spaeder have immeasurably enriched this book.

The personal linkages of the textbook network have entangled us with the giant "macrostructure" of Harcourt Brace. All such structures are the orchestrations of individual performances that have played some beautiful music for us. "Corporate" sociology editor Chris Klein has offered unfailing "corporate" support and generous doses of common sense. Senior "developmental" editor Meera Dash has shown superb skills in "developing" resources for authors, as well as in handling hard-headed authors. We are especially appreciative of the extraordinary work that she put into our book. Marty Levick secured the excellent photographs that grace the text. Publisher Ted Buchholz has been in our corner from the contract signing to this preface-writing and at all points in between. Steve Welch, Senior Project Editor, took a tedious process, made it smooth, and produced a physical manuscript that is professional in every way. We have also benefitted from the talents of Don Fujimoto, Senior Art Director, and Tad Gaither, Senior Production Manager.

Closer to home at our own "macrostructure" of Villanova University, we extend special appreciation to seven people: Norma Kehoe for helping to manage the process while also managing to keep us sane; Corinne Weaber and Joy Fitzpatrick for the torturous task of typing; Joan Lesovitz for data-crunching and formatting the GSS tables; David Schlosser and Joe Kroart for becoming denizens of the library; and Rachel Levy, who helped at the end with all of these diverse tasks.

BJJ
BJG
JAM

ABOUT THE AUTHORS

Brian J. Jones is Professor of Sociology at Villanova University. He completed professional training in the sociology department and the Fels Center for Public Policy Analysis at the University of Pennsylvania. Dr. Jones has been honored by the Christian R. Lindback Award for Distinguished Teaching, and has been "introducing" students to sociology for twenty years. His area of scholarly expertise is social network analysis, and he has published journal articles on a wide variety of sociological topics. Dr. Jones deeply believes in the real-world relevance of sociology, and he is currently evaluating the effectiveness of drug treatment programs for the state of Pennsylvania.

Dr. Jones resides in Havertown, Pennsylvania, with his wife Suzanne and children Megan and Christopher. One of the themes of the book is the intrusion of social structures into personal lives, a theme well illustrated here; Suzanne's word processing graces every page, one of Megan's drawings appears in Chapter 4, and musical examples inspired by Christopher pop up in several places. Brian's participation in competitive powerlifting through a local club even intrudes upon the opening of Chapter 5.

Bernard J. Gallagher III is Professor of Sociology at Villanova University. He holds an M.B.A. from the Wharton School at the University of Pennsylvania where he also received his Ph.D. in sociology.

Dr. Gallagher's specialty is psychiatric sociology, a field in which he has conducted extensive research on such topics as the causes of schizophrenia, sexual disorders, and criminal and deviant behavior. He is the author of some sixty articles, papers, and books including *The Sociology of Mental Illness,* the leading book in the field. He received Villanova University's Outstanding Faculty Research Award in 1993, and is a perennial finalist for the Lindback Award for Distinguished Teaching.

When he is not writing at his desk, he takes it with him to the South Jersey shore where he spends a lot of time ocean fishing. Until 1987, he was the leader and drummer of a Philadelphia-based rock band called ORION. Dr. Gallagher claims that it was an opportunity for "field research." He is married to Michele, a remarkable woman who has managed to keep him within the boundaries of sanity. Their son, Bernard J. Gallagher IV did not inherit his father's obsessive–compulsive personality traits.

Joseph A. McFalls, Jr., a demographer and sociologist, received an MBA from the Harvard Business School and Ph.D. from the University of Pennsylvania. He is a Professor of Sociology at Villanova University and a Research Associate at the University of Pennsylvania's Population Studies Center. His research interests center on social problems, population infertility, and the demography and sociology of the African-American population. Dr. McFalls is the author of numerous articles and books including *Psychopathology and Subfecundity* (Academic Press), *Frustrated Fertility: A Population Paradox* (Population Reference Bureau), *Disease and Fertility* (Academic Press), and *Population: A Lively Introduction* (Population Reference Bureau).

Dr. McFalls has taught courses in demography and sociology at both the graduate and undergraduate level. He immensely enjoys teaching, and has been nominated for the Lindback Award for Distinguished Teaching at both universities at which he has taught. He loves to get students involved in their own and his research projects, and many have become co-authors with him on journal articles.

Joe McFalls lives in Gladwyne, Pennsylvania, with his wife, Marguerite, their two children, Jeanne Marie and Joe, and their 150-pound Akita,

Jumbo, a neighborhood celeb. Joe McFalls serves as a baseball, soccer, and basketball coach in the neighborhood youth program. His interests include popular films, antique furniture and architecture, audio/video equipment, and O-scale model trains. He is also an avid tennis player, participating in tournaments at the local level.

BRIEF CONTENTS

DETAILED CONTENTS

Sociology

Micro, Macro, and Mega Structures

A rag-tag army of communists, neo-Nazis, and hooligans turned Moscow into an open-air shooting range while trying to restore the old Soviet Union in 1993.

PART ONE

INTRODUCTION TO SOCIOLOGY

Have you ever *seen* society? We intend to show it to you in the ever-clarifying image of modern, scientific sociology.

Have you ever *seen* your self? We intend to show you personal aspects that do not appear in the mirror.

Have you ever *seen* the connection? Sociology reveals the link between the grand edifice of society and the familiar internal landscape that is you. Society organizes that self by orderly routines like your reading of this textbook, and also gives way to the disorderly behaviors that can steal this book from your hand. Part One spotlights both of these processes while introducing the theories and methods of the spotlight itself—sociology.

Chapter 1

Personal Perspective

He looked like a standard college professor: fuzzy old tweeds, a distracted look on his face and a battered briefcase stuffed with papers. While unpacking my own brand-new notepaper, I noticed something odd—the professor was not standing at the podium. Instead of fumbling with lecture notes or sharing nervous conversation with nearby students, he just sat there in the front row. A wave of buzzing swept the audience as other students noticed the same thing, then . . . dead silence. "Who *is* this guy?" I wondered aloud to my boyfriend Jack.

As though my question were a signal, the professor rose from the seat, strode to the door and, very deliberately, slammed it. I sensed several students letting out held breaths as we all settled down to academic business-as-usual. Wait a minute; the mystery lecturer had positioned himself in front of the podium with his back turned to us. The murmuring started to rise. Like a monster doing a slow turn toward victims in a horror movie, he faced us, opened his mouth and said . . .

Nothing. This Ph.D. from Hell loomed silently in front of the class. I watched the hand on the wall clock squeeze out the seconds. Then the head moved. *He was staring directly at me.* It hit like a slap. To hide my embarrassment, I pretended to write something on a perfectly blank notepad. Finally he looked Jack squarely in the face, then at each other student in sequence. It had an effect quite like a breeze rippling across a bed of leaves. His gaze swept the squirming audience for what seemed like hours until, without warning, the Sphinx spoke: "Welcome to sociology class, fellow robots." I flinched, then fought down a rising annoyance as the statement sank in. I actually thought to myself, "Who are *you* calling a robot?"

He said, "I'm calling *you* a robot!"

People giggled uneasily.

"Have I met any of you before?"

No hands went up. This

Social Order: *The Making of Society*

was starting to seem like a magician's parlor tricks . . .

"I'm going to prove that I know you anyway. If some brave soul will tell me one thing—your zip code—I'll tell you about yourself."

My boyfriend, brave soul that he is, called out the five digits.

The professor calmly looked at a map, then read from a list.

"You are a Catholic, both of your parents graduated from high school, you have three siblings, your family subscribes to *Time* magazine, and you are wearing Levi's jeans."

I recognized the flush of surprise rising in Jack's face.

"*Newsweek*," he said meekly.

"Sorry," said the professor, "but I still got 80 percent of you."

There was an audible sigh of relief as he passed out the syllabus.

BJJ

sociology—the scientific study of the relationship between social structure and human behavior.

AN INTRODUCTION TO SOCIOLOGY

This is not a typical textbook. One of the things that makes it atypical is that the pages are like mirrors. You will keep seeing yourself here, much as the professor in the "Personal Perspective" could look right into the private life of the student with only a single clue from that person's social life. This is because social life has a known order, and that order does not stop at your skin. It reaches inside.

The professor cheated. As a sociologist, he had studied the science behind the tricks. One of the ways the social order has burned its image inside of you is in classroom conditioning. You know the pattern right down to its particulars—the subtle differences in demeanor between lecturer and lecturees and especially the requirement that when the former stands facing you, the lecture is supposed to start! The social order extends from your soul outward through the classroom into the world beyond. Sociological research in that world has revealed interconnections of amazing intricacy. Several parts of this pattern are revealed in the zip code trick. Neighborhood is connected to house size which is connected to kids per house which is connected to religion which is connected to educational level . . . The dots signify much more to come. Indeed, the rest of this book is devoted to unraveling such human patterns. Inevitably, you are going to see yourself in them.

A Definition

Sociology is *the scientific study of the relationship between social structure and human behavior.* In many respects, social structure is the idea on which the field is founded. It is an idea better discussed than defined, and most of this chapter has been written just to introduce the idea. Think of any structure at all—a bridge, a building, a pile of blocks—all consist of parts put together in a specific pattern. In fact, the way the blocks are piled up determines what the child has made. The structure is the thing.

Social Structure

Society can be seen the same way. Consider us: The authors have now been linked to you through this book. It is a passive form of communication, but a real link nevertheless. The words you read keep the link alive and, we like to think, will change your behavior—even if it is only to entice you to continue reading. If so, you will learn to see the shape of social structure in human affairs. Speaking of which, an "affair" is a distinctive form

This harmonious social scene from an artist's imagination introduces you visually to images of social order in the sociological imagination, an idea we will explore in this chapter.

of personal relationship. This relationship violates the bond of matrimony with all of its social underpinnings in law, in religion, and in in-laws. However powerful or exotic their personalities, the unfaithful spouse, the wronged spouse, and the outside lover are governed by the *structure* of their interrelationship. This is the well-known "love triangle." Social structure consists of the many and varied geometric forms that make people into a society.

It is natural to resist this idea. Who likes to think that they are bound by their relations to other people, especially in "The Land of the Free"? Walking down the busiest street in the most bustling city, all one sees are individuals. This multitude of persons is not arranged into any structure that is visible to the naked eye. But where are they all going? The mob is

Society often appears to be merely a mob of individuals. What social structures do you think motivate this multitude on a Chinese street?

really an army of social structure, marching to the tunes of corporate organizations, social clubs, churches, families. . . .

Personal Programming

Recall the remark made by the professor calling students (and himself) "robots." Since a robot is a mechanical device programmed like a computer, let us see if the analogy fits human behavior. You get up in the morning (at a time set automatically on the alarm clock) and run your get-ready-for-school program. The sequence of bed-making, toothbrushing, dressing, and cereal-pouring is doubtless quite standardized. The efficiency of this routine—in computerese, a subroutine—is what allows you to leave on time to get to class. You buckle your seatbelt, switch on the radio (automatically tuned to your station), and drive along the same old route to school; if there is a traffic jam (too many people following the same commuting program), you switch to a sequence of familiar, alternate routes. Arriving at school, you park (same spot?), lock the car, then check that you locked it (more than once?). Meeting students on the way to class, you run your conversational program to greet people you know ("How are you doing?" "Fine. How are you?") and systematically ignore strangers. In class, you run the student subroutine—unless some sociology professor disturbs the programming.

Unsettling as it is, we all recognize such behavior patterns in ourselves. They can be found wherever humans are found. On the accompanying page, please find Sociological Imagination in Fiction Box 1:1. This general feature will present a selection from science fiction, fantasy, or horror literature to illustrate the operation of sociological principles across the incredible range of human experience. In this case set at a crossroads of the galaxy in the distant future, one character is being prompted to see human behavior as socially programmed. We have pushed the same provocative insight upon you with the get-ready-for-school routine. No

This picture shows a futuristic social scene from an artist's imagination. What social structures do you think will be operative in the lives of individuals in your society's tomorrow?

BOX 1:1 SOCIOLOGICAL IMAGINATION IN FICTION

Free Will and *Neverness*

What follows is a science-fiction selection depicting the far, far future in which basic questions about human nature are still being argued. The Assassin is trying to provoke the Pilot—a character who can roam the galaxy at will—by saying that all humans are socially programmed.

I [the Pilot] reached into the leg sheath of my kamelaika and removed one of my skate blades. I held it flat in my hand. "I believe I have the freedom to drop this or not, as I wish."

"Free will is illusory," [said the Assassin].

"I will *not* drop it," I said, sliding it back in the sheath. "A free choice, freely made."

"But not so free, after all, Pilot. Why did you choose not to drop it? Because this fine, wood floor is polished so nicely? You wouldn't want to scar the fine floor, would you? You have a respect for finely made things—I can tell. But from where did this respect come? Who programmed it into you? You can't tell me, but I can tell you: It was your mother, years ago when you were a boy. She taught you about beauty in the unspoken ways she appreciated beauty, with the silent language of her eyes and hands. Your mother loves beautiful things, even though she doesn't know of her love, even if she would deny it if you asked her . . ."

"My mother is not a robot, damn you!"

He took a step back and smiled at me. Although he must have known I was trembling to kill him, he seemed quite relaxed. . . .

"The program, Mallory,—you tell me. What makes you run? What runs you?"

I squeezed the skate blade and the edges cut into the new callouses on my palm. "If I knew, if I knew—how can I tell you what I don't know, damn you!"

"We should all know the code of our programs," he said. "Otherwise we can never be free . . ."

Source: David Zindell, *Neverness* (1988). New York: Bantam Books, pp. 367–68, 379–80.

sociological imagination—C. Wright Mills' famous term for the discipline's ability to show the relationship between social and personal patterns.

doubt you, like the fictional character, are straining to think of the ways you express independence from society's program. If so, you are exercising what C. Wright Mills called the **sociological imagination**, ". . . a quality of mind that will help [you] to use information and to develop reason in order to achieve lucid summations of what is going on in the world and what may be happening within [yourself]" (1959, p. 5). It is a "quality of mind" that underlies the concepts, the findings, and the theories of modern sociology.

THE PLACE OF SOCIOLOGY

Science and Nature

To preview this 600-page product of the sociological imagination, we shall pick the brain of Nobel prize-winner Herbert A. Simon about "The Place of Sociology."

In a famous essay, Simon likens the natural world to "A set . . . [which] consists of a box enclosing a second box, which, in turn, encloses a third . . . continuing as long as the patience of the craftsman holds out" (1977, p. 5). Unlike the child's puzzle, nature's systems are not as simple as smaller

FIGURE 1:1 SOCIOLOGY AND THE HIERARCHIES OF NATURE
A depiction of Nobel laureate Herbert A. Simon's idea of the natural world as a set of scientific puzzle boxes; sociology's place is in the top hierarchy.

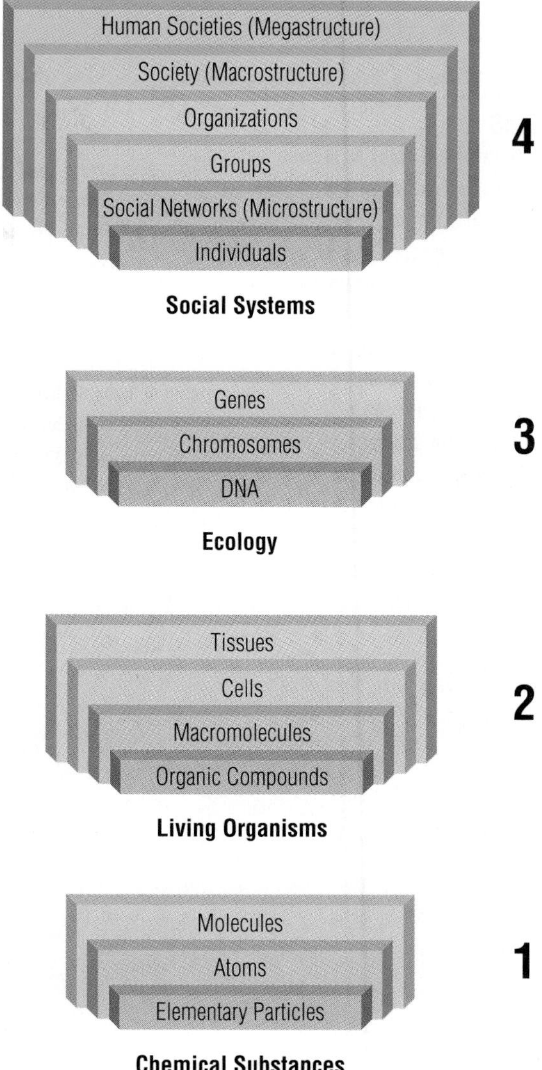

and smaller boxes right down to the essence of matter. Instead, there are four separate sets of boxes—each called a "hierarchy"—which are puzzle-boxlike in that they each contain distinctive levels as illustrated in Figure 1:1. Start at the bottom of Hierarchy 1. Electrons, neutrons, and protons are assembled into atoms. Even if one knows everything about these elementary particles at the subatomic level, once they become hydrogen or oxygen atoms, they have formed a new set of things classified by physicists into the elements of the periodic table. Similarly, the distinct atoms combine into molecules to form substances like gasoline that have properties different enough to be studied by scientists of another discipline—chemists. Hierarchy 2 proceeds upward from organic chemists through cytologists (cell scientists) to biologists. Hierarchy 3 is genetic engineers, geneticists, then ecologists.

Before entering Hierarchy 4—sociology's set of boxes—notice that the levels of the systems have been associated with the types of scientists that study them. The level-science connection is no accident. A specific scientific discipline has grown up at each point *where there is a distinctive phenomenon to investigate.* So, the ecology of organisms inhabiting a pond cannot be understood merely by mapping the genetic material of its native frog (Hierarchy 3). The frog's DNA does not control the distribution of bass and bugs in the frog's food chain, which is, of course, why there are scientists who specialize in ecology.

The Sociological Hierarchy

And now into the social world of Hierarchy 4. Notice that the smallest box contains individual people. Psychologists peek into this box to unlock the secrets of the human psyche. As this chapter has already suggested, sociologists also study this box—but from *above*. Whereas psychology looks at the system of a *person* (personality), sociology studies the systems linking *persons* (social structure). Those systems ascend above individuals in the familiar boxlike levels. **Microstructure** includes the patterns of interpersonal relationships known as social networks (Chapter 4). The next largest box contains such groups as clubs and gangs, and then more formal organizations such as IBM and the CIA. The **Macrostructure** (Chapter 5) of society encloses all of these boxes of social structure. There is still another level to go. Think of the United States as a singular, enormous being. Like human beings, societies have a social life, too. There are patterns of relationship linking the United States to myriad other societies: trade relations,

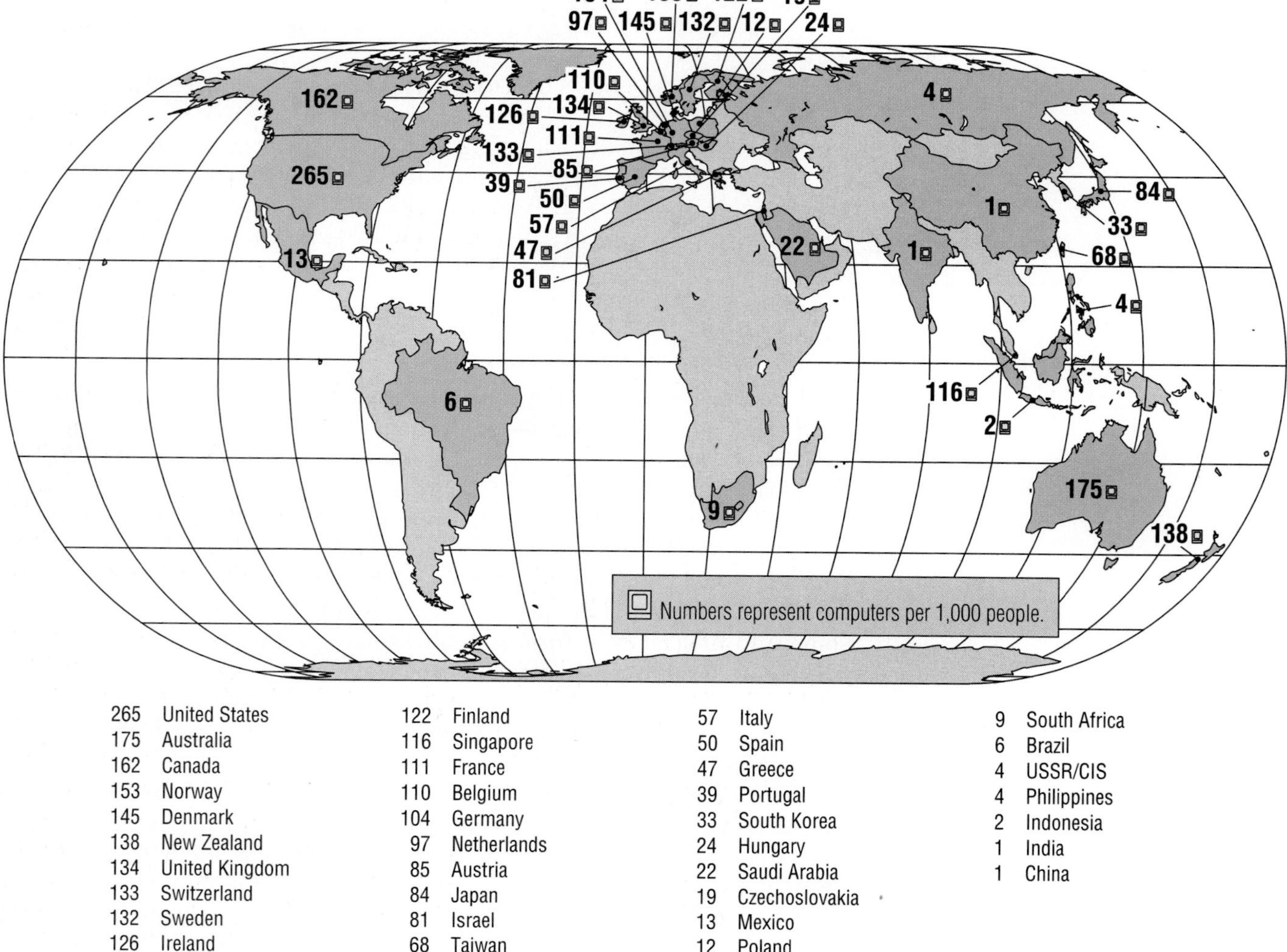

FIGURE 1:2 COMPUTERS AS SOCIAL SYSTEMS

The three major levels of Social Systems from Figure 1:1 are illustrated by the distribution and use of computers. Computers are often connected in person-to-person linkages known as "networks" (Microstructure); they are produced and marketed by corporate organizations (Macrostructure); and they are an increasingly important resource in commercial, military, and cultural exchanges between the societies on the map (Megastructure). Also notice the broad patterns of social inequality in the availability of computer resources, a preview of sociological issues in Chapter 6.

Source: Karen Petska Juliussen and Egil Juliussen, 6th Annual Computer Industry Almanac (Lake Tahoe, Calif.: Computer Industry Almanac, Inc., 1993).

wars, cultural exchanges of college students, etc. **Megastructure** (Chapter 6) defines this highest level of social interaction; if the visions in some of the Sociological Imagination in Fiction selections come to pass, another box could be added for interplanetary interaction. From this planet, Figure 1:2 provides a concrete illustration of the levels of social structure.

Hierarchy 4 is the domain of the social sciences, some of which study only specific pieces of social structure. Political scientists, for example, focus on particular organizations such as political parties and types of government. Economists chart the relations of businesses, the behavior of consumers, the bargaining of trading partners—all relations involving material exchange. Sociologists scrutinize *structure itself,* whatever individuals, groups, organizations, or nations it connects.

SOCIAL STRUCTURE AND PERSONAL EXPERIENCE

Science and You

Sociology is presented here as a scientific discipline. Like any science, it contains both promises and pitfalls. One potential pitfall is abstraction. Sociologists seek laws of human behavior, general principles of social action like $E = mc^2$ in physics. But a general law is *abstract,* meaning it operates over the head of any concrete case. The hazard is that it may be "over the head" of those who would grasp it, the "concrete cases" described in the sociological law such as yourself. Certainly, the schematic drawings at the top of Figure 1:1 are on the abstract side.

As in the natural sciences, the antidote to abstraction is application. Take sociology and apply it to actual cases. We intend to anchor our discipline in the real world in two main ways. First, what immediately follows are boxed personal accounts of the impact of sociology upon individual lives. College Experience Box 1:2 contains a series of autobiographical vignettes in which past and present students candidly discuss the personal relevance of sociology. While the special focus here is on the sociology–self connection, the College Experience feature will return to the relevance-of-the-discipline theme throughout this book by applying sociological insights to the undergraduate setting.

After these accounts of personal fascination with the discipline, we seek to fascinate *you* by presenting selected scientific findings of sociology. The section titled "Inequality and the Inner Self" previews the chapters to follow in a systematic way. Findings reported throughout this book are gathered into Table 1:1 to make a single point: Social class touches virtually every facet of personal life. Since you have a social class position in U.S. society (to be clarified in Chapter 11), reading this table is reading about yourself. We promised you that would happen.

Speaking of promise, sociology has been burdened by spectacular expectations. One of the founders of the field, August Comte (1854), foresaw the emergence of "sociocracy," a sort of sociological royalty that would rule society according to scientific principles. None of your authors has yet been called to such an elevated position. What is it about sociology that elicits grandiose ambitions? For one thing, the discipline offers what any true science offers—understanding. There is inescapable excitement in penetrating human mysteries and revealing their "socio-logic." In addition to the power to know, knowledge is power. Return for a moment to Figure 1:1. A glance up the tiers of the hierarchies is a reminder of wizard-like powers flowing from the wand of science. The singular example at the bottom is

BOX 1:2 COLLEGE EXPERIENCE

Autobiographical Vignettes of Students and Ex-Students

Meoghan Byrne, Ph.D.

In February 1986, as I walked to my sociology class, I heard that the space shuttle *Challenger* had exploded and that Christa McAuliffe and her fellow shuttle astronauts had been killed instantly. Class began in whispers, the stunned speech that always follows unexpected national catastrophe. We spoke in great philosophical abstractions, discomfited by our inability to understand the reasons for such things. On the second day of my first sociology course, students everywhere felt the sting of a teacher's death.

Each day of class, I heard the sociological side of issues familiar to me from the news, from other classes, even from novels—the demographics of poverty, the social perception of "deviants," native and foreign ritual practices—these and other topics began falling into place, revealing discernible patterns within societies. I felt as if I were watching huge puzzles being put together. While in other classes professors explained how specific fields of study could apply to the larger social environment, in my sociology class that environment itself was first given a skeletal outline, gradually fleshed out, then finally made real.

Even in my early years at The University of Delaware's Ph.D. program in literature, my sociological interest kept surfacing. In one failed attempt to come up with an interdisciplinary topic for a paper on Shakespeare, I compared King Lear's withdrawal, aphasia, and apparent regression with the behavior of an autistic child. The professor gently urged me to read through the *Journal of Literature and Psychology* to see how a scholar could successfully combine the fields. Later, I chose Victorian literature as my specialty area. I, like many scholars, was attracted to the grand figure of Charles Dickens, a writer who might be called the first "literary sociologist." Like no other fiction-writer, Dickens was a master painter of social truths. He saw the plight of the overworked and underfed even though it was obscured to many by England's rapidly advancing, highly touted "progress." He obsessively walked the streets of London at night observing the poor, the laboring, the criminal. He witnessed the hangings of murderers and the beatings of prostitutes. Leading an age of reform, Dickens was active in the protection of orphans, the redemption of the disenfranchised, and the criticism of an elite society that ignored what lay under its well-shod feet. During the same century, Thomas Babington Macaulay, Charles Darwin, John Stuart Mill, and Karl Marx rocked British society by renovating economic law; religious, political, and scientific belief; and the entire notion of progress, production, and profit. As a teacher of British literature, I am committed to uncovering for students as many of these social factors as I can, hoping to illustrate the full picture of Victorian life and thought.

A second area I have pursued as a result of my work in both literature and sociology is the teaching of women's studies. Christa McAuliffe, the teacher aboard the *Challenger,* is one of the women we focus on in class. Perhaps because her death is an occurrence I associate with sociology, or perhaps because her career combined traditional with radical new roles for women, I repeat here her oft-quoted remark, "I touch the future, I teach." Because it helped form my career, sociology touched my future. In my own classroom and research, and in the environments we awaken to each day, sociology touches the present in us all.

§

Tom Powers, M.A.

To document why sociology has been important to me, I think in terms of how the discipline is related to the various positions I have been fortunate to achieve

BOX 1:2 COLLEGE EXPERIENCE *continued*

in my 13-year working career. Immediately after graduation, I was an investigator for the Pennsylvania State Department of Corrections. At age 23, I was named Deputy Warden at a major county correctional facility. By age 27, I became one of the youngest prison wardens ever selected in the United States. After progressing to a major administrative position in private corrections in the state of Florida, at 31 I became the state Penitentiary Warden in North Dakota. While serving in that position, I was able to acquire a masters degree, taught adjunct college courses, and consulted in both criminal justice and management. Now, at 35, I am a Vice President and Corporate Officer for a national construction company. I have a wonderful wife and three daughters. God has truly blessed me.

In retrospect, the sociology major and my related experience as a scholarship student-athlete at Villanova University prepared me well. In the first place, sociology taught me about social roles and why we tend to introduce ourselves by reciting them, as I have done above. More formally, sociology taught me about the patterns of criminal behavior that have always existed in our society. Crime is clearly an area worthy of study, and my studies motivated me to help those tangled in its troubled web. More generally, sociology has prodded me to wonder: Why do people behave as they do? and What are the effective agents of social change? The discipline's focus on inter- and intragroup relations forms a useful basis for anyone's transition into the workforce. The world is made up of people, real live human beings, with beliefs, feelings, fears, and trusts. The social scientific approach of sociology taught me to examine all factors motivating a person, to highlight the positive and motivate change away from the negative. From the beginning, it taught me to care.

My current corporate managerial position has stimulated the study of organizational behavior, which is just what makes up a corporation. Sociology's stress on "people skills," that is, the ability to interact with diverse others, has truly been a learned behavior for me. While it has been said that leaders are born, not made, just the opposite is true of an effective manager who must learn in the trenches. Sociological concepts laid the basis for my effective management style. It has also been said that business effectiveness is geared to two major factors: one's ability to communicate orally, and the ability to articulate oneself in writing. I am living proof of that statement. Sociology gently forced me to write many papers, to present them to my peers and my professor, and therein prepared me for opportunities in both the public and private sectors.

Sociology, for me, has been an initial road map to a thus far successful career. While the discipline has had a major impact on shaping social policy, it has also helped shape the career of one individual, who is grateful for the basis it provided for a happy and productive life. I would strongly recommend its study to anyone.

§

Stephen Spaeder, M.B.A.

It is well recognized that accounting finance, marketing, and management are significant components of real-world business. In graduate business school, we seek to develop skills in several of these applied disciplines. Comprehensive knowledge in any one of these areas is a reliable ticket to middle management. That which sets the opportunist, the innovator—let me just say it: the winner—apart from the run-of-the-mill businessperson, however, is the ability to spot trends and capitalize on market imbalance. Critical to this ability is a keen awareness of people and social forces; that is, sociology.

An example of my point becomes evident as I reflect upon

(continued on next page)

BOX 1:2 COLLEGE EXPERIENCE *continued*

the current depressed status of the commercial real estate industry and consider the boom-and-bust cycle of the past ten years. In the United States, the 1980s began with several years of high inflation and high interest rates. What was the impact of these economic conditions on the real estate industry? In the capital-strained financial environment, few real estate firms could afford to undertake new development projects, so the business lagged. Then in 1983, "money value" turned. Inflation fell and capital for investment and growth poured forth. The whole private sector grew rapidly, and, in the boom, women entered the workforce in droves. The demand for office space exceeded supply with willing workers awaiting buildings being built. The number of projects entering the development pipeline was staggering. Suburban business centers grew rapidly, replacing farms and orchards. Even ill-conceived real estate ventures were profitable in the short run due to favorable tax treatment by the federal government and the significant supply/demand imbalance.

With the tax reform act of 1986, real estate development suddenly became less attractive as tax-associated benefits would diminish in the future. However, this did not stop banks from lending and developers from building. In other words, people continued to behave as though the boom were still booming. Even after the demographic shifts associated with suburbanization and the feminization of the workplace had been completed, the speculation continued. Where will the people come from to fill the new offices? What would be the source of this continued demand? These are the questions which an individual who is aware of demographic statistics and general social trends would have asked. The sociologically informed investor recognized the peak values in 1987–1988 and cashed in his or her chips by selling properties. Those not so informed have disappeared from industry directories. The former are now buying property back at 30 percent to 50 percent of what they sold it for in 1988.

In looking to the future, successful real estate companies will continue to respond to the social forces within their markets. With the aging of the "Baby Boomers" there inevitably will be a need for additional health care facilities, congregate care homes, retirement villages, and recreational facilities such as golf courses and country clubs. Let me be blunt: I intend to follow the sociological arrow pointing to these opportunities and make a fortune.

§

Nnenna Lynch

Rhodes Scholar

NCAA Track & Field Champion

Call me a fool, call me egotistical, call me what you will . . . since high school, when people ask me what I want to do, I answer, "Save the world!" Poverty bothers me, violence bothers me, drug and alcohol abuse bother me . . . and I actually want to do something about these problems. I want to change the world we live in—make it a better, more human place for more people. Unfortunately, there's no "How to Save the World" major, so I had to look for something else.

Once I was old enough to question what life was about and had pondered it for a while, I came to the conclusion that love was the most important thing in

life. After all, the extent to which one is able to enjoy one's profession, and even one's material objects is the extent to which one is able to enjoy them with others. Moreover, remove all extraneous things, and what matters the most? Love and intimacy. But since one cannot make a career out of loving family and friends, the next best thing is to love one's larger family—humankind.

So to risk some clichés, after I had questioned the meaning of life, I knew that a worthwhile existence for me involved "making a difference." In order to make a difference, I had to understand people and the wider forces at work in their lives, for if there is one thing that we all can't avoid it's that we are social beings. I considered studying psychology and political science, and, although they are important in understanding ourselves and the world around us, the under-

BOX 1:2 COLLEGE EXPERIENCE *continued*

standing sociology gave seemed to transcend the other social sciences. I saw this in trying to understand many of the big "Why's." Why have we learned to behave in certain ways? Why do we often act like cheerful robots? Why is there inequality? All human problems are essentially social problems, and in trying to address them, we need to understand root causes suggesting real answers, rather than band-aid solutions. Consider drug dealers. Are they simply lacking good moral fiber, or are the opportunities open to them very limited? If it is the latter, why are these opportunities so limited? Does it have to do with the sociological shift to a service economy with fewer chances for personal advancement?

I'm indebted to sociology for showing the world to me through new eyes. It's not so much a body of knowledge that I've accumulated but a new perspective that I've gained. Perhaps the most valuable thing I've learned is not to "psychologize" behavior but always to consider the social circumstances, the human context.

Will I really be able to help save the world? I suppose we shall see, but at least sociology allows me to understand it better. At a minimum, this means a better chance of making my personal part of the world worthwhile.

more than enough. Once the mysteries of atomic physics became less mysterious, they were harnessed to miraculous instruments for human production *or* destruction. But what determines that *or?* It is forces well above the atomic level that push the button, manufacture the uranium, orchestrate the foreign policy . . . in short, it is the workings of social structure. Knowing the laws of social behavior could mean humane control of all of our futures. Grandiose or not, this is the promise of sociology.

Inequality and the Inner Self

And now for a practical demonstration. All of this fancy talk about magic and parlor tricks will presently give way to the elegant simplicity of science. As sciences go, sociology is an infant. Most sociologists trace the origins of the discipline to the middle of the nineteenth century; that means we are at about the same developmental stage as physics circa the fourth century B.C. Despite disciplinary growing pains, sociology has uncovered a treasure trove of data about the social world we all inhabit. The term data signifies information (also called "findings") gathered by scientific study of a phenomenon. This information-gathering process is often referred to as empirical, meaning it is based on the analysis of real-world experience; the empirical approach of science distinguishes it from other modes of knowing such as armchair theorizing, common sense, or artistic inspiration.

data—**the information gathered through a scientific study of a phenomenon.**

empirical—**based on the analysis of real-world experience.**

So, empirical examination of the real social world has yielded a "treasure trove" of data in two literal senses. First, the findings are rich, vast, and surprising insights about social structure and human behavior (the very definition of sociology from p. 5). Second, like any newly discovered treasure, the claims on it, the causes of it, the very *meaning* of the find are as yet undetermined. As you will shortly see, though, there are theories in abundance.

Social Inequality As Social Structure

So you may assess the value yourself, we have reached into a glittering pile of findings and classified them for your consideration in Table 1:1. Observe first the labels on the rows down the left-hand side of the table. They are simply the enumerated chapter titles taken from the table of contents, a

TABLE 1:1 Structured Social Inequality and Individual Lives—Findings from the Text

CHAPTER	INCOME	EDUCATION	OCCUPATION
1. Social Order			
2. Social Disorder			
3. Sociological Research Methods	The urban poor share material resources in networks of strong, reciprocating relationships. The very rich and very poor tend to be undersampled in surveys.	Educational differences can increase researcher visibility in participant observation studies.	Corporate executives are best studied by a "multimethod approach."
4. Microstructure	Upper-income people express greater happiness in surveys than do lower income people.	College students select friends in part based on academic performance. Educational level of self and "closest friend" are related. Educational level is positively associated with the number of one's friends.	Occupational levels of male friends are related. Network relations (and, in particular, weaker relationships) are the most productive sources of job information.
5. Macrostructure	Career salaries produce conformity and ritualism in bureaucracies.	Reference groups change the attitudes and behavior of college students. Educational level is associated with the number of group memberships.	Informal relations affect occupational performance in bureaucracies. Informal relations affect the differential advancement of *Men and Women of the Corporation* (Kanter).
6. Megastructure	There are gigantic differences between First and Third World countries in aggregate income and in the life quality available to their citizens.	Literacy and formal education are very unequally distributed across (and within) countries.	The occupational structures distributing different types of jobs vary enormously from country to country. According to World Systems Theory, richer nations exploit poorer nations by relying on the latter for extractive jobs (removing raw materials).
7. Culture	Subculture membership is more common among the deprived. Impoverished families in some parts of the world sell female offspring.	College students participated heavily in the counterculture of the 1960s. Ethnocentrism is more common among people with lower levels of education.	Acceptance of mainstream American values varies by occupational level.
8. Socialization	Physical abuse of children is more common in impoverished families.	Parents with college degrees especially value children who are considerate and pursue their own interests, whereas parents with low levels of education especially value obedience and manners.	Blue-collar parents stress conformity and obedience in child-rearing, whereas white-collar parents stress responsibility and self-direction.

CHAPTER	INCOME	EDUCATION	OCCUPATION
9. Deviance	Mental illness is more commonly reported in lower income levels. Chances of criminal victimization increase at lower income levels. Chances of suicide increase at upper income levels.	Mental illness is less stigmatized at upper educational levels. Anorexia and bulimia are most common among the highly educated.	Ritualistic behavior is most common among white-collar workers. White-collar criminals receive lesser punishments than do street criminals.
10. Collective Behavior and Social Movements	Slum residents are most susceptible to mob action.	Highly educated respondents are most likely to approve of demonstrations versus the government. College students around the world have often spearheaded antigovernment movements.	Professional women are the most active in the "Women's Movement." The unemployed are most likely to riot.
11. Social Class and Stratification			
12. Race and Ethnicity	Race and ethnicity are significantly related to income level. Race and ethnicity are significantly related to the likelihood of poverty.	Race and ethnicity are significantly related to educational level Race and ethnicity are significantly related to the likelihood of dropping out of high school.	Race and ethnicity are significantly related to occupational level. Race and ethnicity are significantly related to the likelihood of unemployment.
13. Gender	The "gender-gap" in male–female average salaries is 32 percent. Lower income women suffer more sexual and physical abuse than do higher income women.	More educated women are more active in the "Women's Movement." Males and females are exposed to different educational expectations starting in primary school. Female college graduates earn less than males with high school degrees.	Women workers are concentrated in "pink-collar" occupations, such as secretaries and nurses. Women are still underrepresented as college professors, but have made significant recent strides in law and medicine.
14. Family	The higher the wife's income, the more household tasks husbands and children perform. Poverty is associated with relatively high divorce and relatively low remarriage rates.	People tend to marry others of a similar educational level. The higher their level of education, the less likely people are to cohabit rather than marry.	Women with high-status occupations are more likely to divorce than are women in lower status occupations.
15. Religion	Denominational affiliation in the United States is significantly related to income level. Electronic churches are especially appealing to the poor.	Jewish culture places an extremely high emphasis on educational attainment. Amish children attend only primary school.	Occupants of lower level jobs are especially accepting of the idea of an afterlife.

(continued next page)

TABLE 1:1 ***continued***

CHAPTER	INCOME	EDUCATION	OCCUPATION
16. Political Economy	Social networks influence the distribution of income in markets. Voter turnout is lower among the poor than among affluent U.S. citizens.		Skilled-labor jobs are decreasing as service jobs increase in the occupational structure.
17. Education	Community income level is associated with per pupil school expenditure. High-income people are more satisfied with public schools than are low-income people.	Educational level is strongly associated with occupational success.	
18. Health and Medicine	High income is associated with reduced risk from almost every disease. Low income is associated with a relatively low level of health care services.		Adults in the labor force are less likely to apply the "sick role" to themselves or their children.
19. The Sociology of Sexuality		Sexual attitudes vary by educational level.	
20. Population	The higher the income level, the fewer children in the family.	The higher the educational level, the fewer children in the family. College graduation is associated with relatively more long-distance moves.	Business executives have relatively high residential mobility, whereas doctors and lawyers are relatively immobile.
21. Technology, Science, and Environment	Income level is associated with the ability to purchase technology for personal use (e.g., PCs).	Educational level influences the ability to use, profit from, and control technology.	Occupational position influences opposition to some technological changes (e.g., college professors oppose TV courses).

way of organizing data you will read about in the pages ahead. Now find Chapter 11, titled "Social Class and Stratification"; that is where the topic will be examined in specific detail (which is why the cells are blanked out here). For present purposes, social inequality is to be applied as an exemplar of social structure. Social inequality has existed in every known society, and the patterns of unequal distribution are well-studied structures. Well studied indeed—a computerized literature search performed by the authors found more than 2,300 books on social inequality published in the previous fifteen years. With very few exceptions, every issue of the major sociology journals publishes an article examining social class, social mobility, or some closely related topic.

The immediate purpose is not to *explain* the structure of social inequality to you; that will await the more direct study of forthcoming chapters. Table 1:1 is meant to *show* you the effects of structured social inequality and thus to show you yourself. For the moment, suspend curiosity about just how social classes are put together. Whatever the causes of that process, it clearly has human effects. Unequal levels of income, education, and occupation are directly tied to the social structure of classes. That is why these three measures of social inequality head the columns of the table. In the cells are the jewels of data.

Understanding the Table

For a first impression, observe how full the cells are. Most of them contain some concrete, soon-to-be-read evidence of a link between "social structure and human behavior" (again, the definition of sociology). This means you, but not in every case. After careful clinical study, a psychologist might predict the behavior of a particular individual. But these are statements typifying the behavior of hundreds, thousands, even millions of individuals. Such **generalizations** sift out the human tendencies only apparent at the level of social structure.

generalizations—the statements typifying the behavior of large numbers of people in a social structure.

Think of social structure as the tide. Imagine the multitude of people immersed in society; some swim against this current, but it still exerts its pull on everyone. Look at how many parts of your "Individual Life" feel the undertow of "Structured Social Inequality"! Certainly most of the "good things in life" are covered. Your life expectancy (Chapter 20), your likelihood of robust health (Chapter 18), even your choice of a mate (Chapter 14) or of a close friend (Chapter 4)—all vary by social class. Perhaps the tidal image is too weak. Given the raw volume of human experience being driven before it, social inequality is more like a tidal wave.

Expanding the Table

Remember that Table 1:1 represents the findings regarding only a *single* part of social structure—structured inequality—reported in a *single* book (this one). The hierarchy atop Figure 1:1 is packed with many such structures that have individual-level effects, as well as patterned relationships to each other. This table, then, displays only one variety of sociological treasure.

As extensive as the find already is, the treasure hunt proceeds. It is our intent to convey to you the nature of that process, which is sociological investigation itself. It is premature to attempt this in detail before acquainting you with "Sociological Research Methods" in Chapter 3. Nonetheless, we now offer a nontechnical description of a research project at the cutting-edge of our discipline—and your experience.

Recent president of the American Sociological Association (the ASA) Melvin Kohn commenced his research project in 1963 with a direct, real-world question: Why does social class matter for parents' relationships with their children? It is apparent from the Chapter 8 row in Table 1:1 that this research yielded numerous findings about social class and socialization. As is often the case in scientific investigation, Kohn's answers led to other, better questions. In particular, Kohn and his collaborators discovered that "occupation" was itself a complex social structure containing several components; moreover, the occupational effects did not restrict themselves to child-rearing practices. What began as a study of socialization values evolved into a full-blown exploration of the territory connecting social structure and personality.

Again, this is not the place for technical discussion, so we shall summarize the essence of Kohn's research team's findings. First, refer to Figure 1:3. When someone accuses sociology of being all "common sense," show them this figure. This intricate model has been a source of uncommon

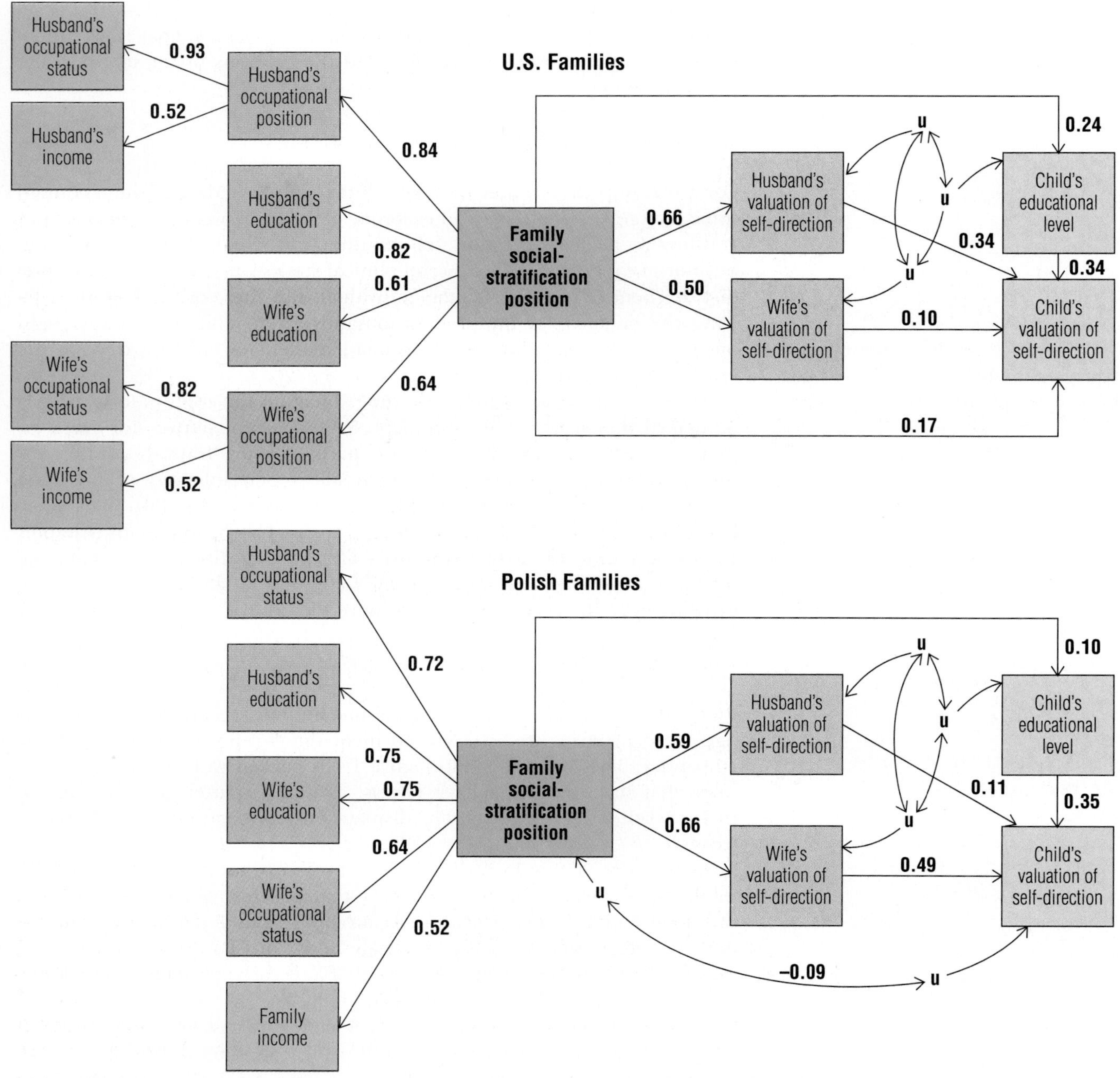

FIGURE 1:3 THE KOHN MODEL OF SOCIAL STRUCTURE AND PERSONALITY

Ex-president of the American Sociological Association Melvin L. Kohn and his colleagues have developed a model of how occupational structures affect our inner selves; the model pictured here is based on data gathered in both the United States and Poland.

wisdom. The model begins with measures very much like those employed in Table 1:1; income, education, and occupation fix the position of individuals in the system of social inequality (left-hand boxes). Then, the analysis takes apart the structure of occupation into its actual components, notably occupational "self-direction." The latter is really personal autonomy on the job; the more involved the job, the more it demands independence of action and personal initiative, the higher the level of occupational self-direction.

Obviously, such jobs are more common nearer the top of what these analysts call "family social-stratification position" (green box near the middle of the model). Not so obviously, the arrows on the right signify a flood of personal effects. Persons performing more self-directed jobs are less authoritarian toward others, have a higher sense of self-esteem, suffer less stress, are less conformist in their ideas, and are more responsible to personal standards of morality (not shown in the figure, but reported in Spenner, 1988). Note that these effects extend to both sexes and that they even span societies—the bottom half of the figure is for (then) socialist Poland, and a similar model has been successfully applied to Japan.

It is worth pondering these pearls of wisdom. Kohn and his colleagues are not just poking around in personal stuff like attitudes toward sexuality (Chapter 19). This is the stuff of personality itself. In a real sense, the research superimposes a scientific model over the deep questions pondered in philosophy class: *What is the nature of being? What explains personal experience?* And, most pointedly, *Who am I?* Now look back at Spenner's listing of Kohn et al.'s findings (just above), then look deep inside. Does not the "real you" consist of an entity that combines these basic qualities? When you say the word *I,* is the mental image that of a person with a special way of treating others, a familiar level of self-assurance and a distinctive sense of duty? If so, the arrows in the figure go right to the heart of who you are. This ongoing research program is uncovering the links between the "out there" of social structure and the "in here" of self.

SOCIAL ORDER

Where Does Society Come From?

The Riddle of Social Life

No one ever built a society. The kings of antiquity rose to power within powerful societies predating their rise, or by conquering smaller societies already built. Even the framers of the Constitution did not build the United States. They designed a brilliant blueprint to guide the further construction of a set of colonies well over a century old. One of the things that makes a society a society is that it remains standing no matter *who* dies.

So, "Where Does Society Come From?" It is a real riddle. Not only did no one person build America, but no one person—or even one hundred persons—carries its entire blueprint in his or her head. If one did, sociologists could reproduce the entire edifice of society merely by studying individual personalities (the base of the top hierarchy in Figure 1:1). Rather, the mysteries of social structure operating over individual heads must be studied on their own terms, which is what sociologists do. All of which makes the riddle even more puzzling. Only human beings can make societies, so how can no human (yet) know just how a given society got made?

The Assumption of Order

The mystery goes even deeper. Not only do we take the monolith of society for granted, but we expect it to operate in predictable fashion in our personal lives. However they get built, social structures are supposed to keep things . . . orderly. Buses are supposed to run on time. Professors are supposed to know how to lecture. Arsenic is not supposed to be in the

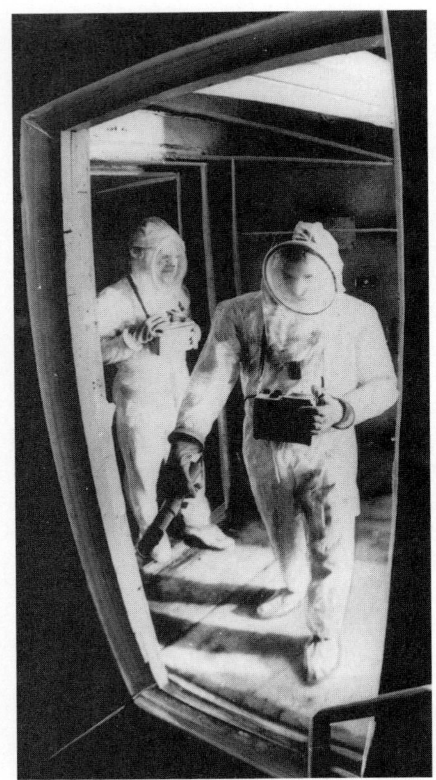

Disasters such as the nuclear accident at Chernobyl in the then-USSR (the photo shows 1986 cleanup efforts) are especially distressing because they explode "The Assumption of Order" about a given society.

cafeteria's soup. Some mysterious agent of society is supposed to take care of these things. Although the topic is to be more extensively explored under the heading "Social Disorder" (Chapter 2), the clearest manifestation of "The Assumption of Order" arises when Things Go Wrong.

While waiting peacefully at a stoplight, your car is rear-ended by a truck. The shock you feel is then compounded by the discovery that the driver has no insurance to pay your damages, who then drunkenly explains that the brakes failed. As the truck wobbles off, you wonder: Don't commercial vehicles have to be inspected and insured? Shouldn't the state police spot an erratically driven tractor trailer? *Somebody* must be responsible. In a recent summer, one of the authors went fishing with friends in a small boat in Delaware bay. The engine died, and the fishing party started to drift out into the vastness of the bay. Because the (dead) motor battery powered the radio, there was no way to transmit a distress call. After an hour or so, the current had pulled the boat all the way out into the shipping channel dominated by gigantic, threatening oil tankers. Many wild thoughts came to mind: Isn't the Coast Guard watching? Don't the other boaters notice? Aren't there helicopter patrols?

Studies of real disasters find some disastrous emotional damage. In 1972, the Buffalo Creek flood in West Virginia killed 125 people after an improperly inspected dam gave way. Mental health researchers found persistent psychiatric symptoms and, oddly enough, rage among the survivors (Erikson, 1976). The sad aftermath of Hurricane Andrew, which devastated Florida in 1992, was tainted with bitter accusations about improper construction amid the grief and shock. A common theme runs through the reactions to personal and natural disasters: The social system is *supposed to work*. In all of these cases, the assumption of order is revealed to be an illusion. This loss of control leaves scars, but most people revert to their reassuring routines. Somehow, the predictability programming takes hold again. How?

Theories versus Theorists

theory—a proposition about the relationship between two or more concepts.

concept—an abstract category for classifying aspects of reality.

It is time to stop posing provocative questions. Sociology does offer answers to the riddle of social order. Notice the plural—there are three major forms of sociological theory. A **theory** is a proposition about the relationship between two or more concepts; a **concept** is an abstract category for classifying aspects of reality. So: $E = mc^2$ is a theoretical statement relating energy, mass, and the speed of light—concepts all—in a mathematical way. The relationship between social structure and human behavior (the definition of sociology, yet again) can be stated in various ways. Each of the three sociological approaches develops theoretical propositions, but there are differences in the selection of key concepts and in the direction of the causal arrows between them.

paradigm—an intellectual model for selecting crucial concepts and forms of evidence.

When the authors were in your shoes, we each used an introductory textbook whose opening chapter presented biographical vignettes on the "Founders of Sociology." In comparing our old versions to some contemporary texts, we were shocked to see the *very same photographs* of these early theorists. This text's approach differs in two respects. First, we intend to spotlight the significance of sociology for contemporary lives. Thus the pictures of living people in Box 1:2 replace pictures of dead theorists. The fact that our discipline has progressed past the point of ancestor worship prefaces a second presentational change. Each of the three theoretical approaches is a **paradigm**—an intellectual model for selecting crucial concepts and forms of evidence. This is a fancy way of saying that each theory is a research guide. In order to grasp the cutting-edge of sociological data, it is necessary to inspect the theoretical template which is its guide.

Functionalism

Why Is There Social Order?

functionalism—a major theoretical approach in sociology that focuses on how social parts contribute to society as a system.

Society consists of an unimaginable number of bits and pieces. Think of the orderly arrangement of everyday life built from birthday parties, mealtimes, executions, prom dates, sociology midterms . . . just a listing of the familiar parts of society could fill this book. The fundamental functionalist assumption is that they are, in fact, "parts." Society is a *system,* and must be understood by how its myriad parts make up a larger whole.

Functionalists take the question entitling this section and stand it on its head. Their approach begins by *assuming* social order, then analyzing how society's working parts contribute to it. Why is the ideal family in the contemporary United States a nuclear unit? According to functionalists, a modern economy demands a mobile labor force, and small, easily moved families help that economy to smoothly fill its labor demands. Why are you expected by parents—and even by law—to attend school until you are at least sixteen years old? A proposed reason is that United States society needs literate personnel to fill its many white-collar occupations. These simple instances show how the diverse pieces serve positive functions for other system pieces, thus fitting together into an orderly whole. Despite its assumption of underlying order, functionalism does recognize the existence of pernicious parts. The harm that they cause is termed a dysfunction to distinguish it from the positive functions performed by system parts. A frontier society instilling violent, macho traits in its citizens will more quickly conquer the natives, but will also suffer the dysfunctions of senseless beatings and killings among its own citizens. A capitalist society, which designs dog-eat-dog competition into its economic institution, gains in efficient production, but loses in stress diseases (e.g., ulcers) and corner-cutting,

dysfunction—a negative consequence of a social part for the system of society.

positive function—the positive consequences of social parts for the system of society.

This is the facade of a building in Alamo village in central Texas. Consider it as an analogy for functionalism in its presentation of the orderly "front" of society and its commemoration of an historical event that helped to establish U.S. society in the Southwest.

white-collar crimes. If the social structure is to be likened to a blueprint, functionalists perform what engineers call a stress analysis: The various components are analyzed in terms of how they support and how they burden the overall design of society.

A Theorist

Despite our desire to spotlight theories rather than theorists, some of the latter are absolutely indispensable to an understanding of the former. An indispensable founder of the field was Emile Durkheim (1858–1917). He was indeed an active founder, forcefully defining the subject matter of this discipline named "sociology" by his predecessor August Comte.

social facts—Emile Durkheim's term for the supra-individual phenomena that are the subject matter of sociology.

Durkheim defined sociology as the study of **social facts**, which are to be distinguished from the kinds of facts studied by other kinds of scientists on two counts: (1) They are external to individuals, and (2) they exercise coercive control over individuals. Whatever your personal ideas about it, your college is not just some private fantasy. It is a real thing "out there" whose external existence is sometimes expressed by coercing individuals to study or even to leave school. Moreover, the school imposes itself into the heads of individual students, professors, and janitors, thus creating common conceptions about it.

conscience collective—Emile Durkheim's term for a common set of ideas and moral sentiments shared by individuals.

Do you recognize this reasoning? Our assertions (around Figure 1:1) that social structures are distinct parts of reality that create a distinctive personal programming (around Box 1:1) were brilliantly framed by Durkheim. He framed them around truly grand questions, such as: What is human nature? According to Durkheim, we each have a split personality. Inside us all is the purely personal self of physical sensations, random emotions, and idiosyncrasies; we also contain the **conscience collective**, a common set of ideas and moral sentiments shared by individuals. You are *homo duplex,* a two-tiered self with society as your soul (Knapp, 1994). Given the need to explain the source of the social soul leads back to another grand question of Durkheimian thought: "Why Is There Social Order?"

In a real sense, Durkheim's entire body of work informs this question. We shall therefore selectively present his ideas, which most clearly connect to contemporary functionalism. One of Durkheim's more provocative papers was titled "Rules for Distinguishing between the Normal and the Pathological" (1895/1964). The medical analogy is this: Like viral antibodies strengthening a human immune system, the disease of crime can improve the health of a social system. It is not a pro-crime argument. Despite its pernicious effects on victims and the social order, crime does perform a public service by providing villains that unite the community in its outrage. Think of the virtual public obsession in the news and even in popular entertainment with the bloodiest of serial killers—we all feel pangs in our "conscience collective." Additionally, crime provides employment. Without criminals, one of our larger industries would collapse with the loss of jobs of police, bail bondspersons, and prison construction workers. Here is the point: Even viciously dysfunctional acts can serve positive functions within the social system.

social integration—the forces binding society together.

The point is undeniable, and undeniably surprising. It reveals with a flash of insight a dark corner of the social order. Durkheim also illuminates the broader blueprint of society in his examination of **social integration**. He tried to identify and classify the actual forces binding societies together. In many respects, these forces are more visible when societies are falling apart, so they will be addressed in Chapter 2. For now, just consider another of Durkheim's elegant phrases: the "noncontractual bases of contract." In his analyses of the massive changes sweeping across human societies, Durkheim considered the deceptively simple device of the legal contract. Two individuals reach an agreement, then sign on the dotted line. In a famous discussion of "trust," of all things, Durkheim uncovered the impressive social machinery operating around their signatures. There are civil courts upholding a contract's validity, there are legislative dictates about what makes a valid signature, there is a reputation for being trustworthy that brings further business . . . if this machinery switches off, contracts disappear. Durkheim made visible such previously invisible functions of orderly social systems in his well-titled *The Division of Labor in Society* (1893/1933).

The Functionalist Paradigm

Real sociological theories are not just words; they are scientific charters stating how to sift social life for evidence of the theory. Durkheim wrote perhaps the most famous such charter in all of social science in his 1897 volume *Suicide* (1966).

Remember, Durkheim was trying to establish the proper subject matter of sociology at a time when intellectuals were obsessed with the powers of the enlightened individual. Durkheim went right to the most individualistic but unenlightened act of all—suicide. If something as personal as the voluntary act of self-destruction could be related to the social order, the place of sociology would be indisputable.

rate—the number of occurrences of a phenomenon for a constant base of population.

What Durkheim discovered is still startling. While no one person's suicide was (or is) perfectly predictable, the relative risk of suicide across different categories of persons was (and is). In his analysis of the rate of suicide (i.e., the number for a constant base of population), Durkheim consistently found Protestants, men, and the unmarried to be more suicidal than Catholics, women, and married persons. Why? The common factor is the level of social integration. Protestant denominations tend to encourage individualism, whereas Catholicism is more group-centered in its church hierarchy and communal rituals; women are more enmeshed in networks of family and friendship relations than are men; and married persons of both sexes are forced into more interaction by their very household arrangements. Durkheim further found exceptionally high suicide rates in the elite officer corps of the French military, much higher than among common soldiers. The explanation offered here by Durkheim concerned too much social integration. The elite officers identified so completely with the tight bonds of the military group that their very selves became disposable. Like a traditional Indian wife throwing herself on the funeral pyre of her husband, or a Japanese Kamikaze pilot diving to his death in World War II, these are cases of excessive social integration. To put it in Durkheim's terms as *homo duplex,* if the social self is too weak, there is risk of egoistic suicide because of too little interpersonal involvement; too much such involvement overdevelops the social integration of the self, and altruistic suicide rates rise.

egoistic suicide—caused by too little social integration.

altruistic suicide—caused by excessive social integration.

Leafing through the pages of *Suicide,* one sees actual tables comparing social categories of individuals. This type of statistical analysis has become a model for the social sciences for the very reason Durkheim used it: It reveals social patterns invisible at the individual level. *Suicide* was an empirical demonstration, a richly productive blend of sociological theory and data that still enriches our understanding of suicide. It also provided a glimpse of the functions of social patterns being actively explored by contemporary researchers.

Conflict Theory

Why Is There Social Order?

conflict theory—a major theoretical approach in sociology that focuses on the conflict among the social structures in a society.

Please notice the recurring format for presenting each major form of sociological theory. The above question certainly bears repeating here because the answer offered by conflict theory could not be more different. Functionalism assumes social order, then pursues its paradigm by uncovering the functions served by system parts. Conflict theory rejects the very idea of society as "system," then pursues its paradigm by showing social structures at each other's throats. The fundamental fact of social life is conflict.

A Theorist

To give content to that broad proposition, we turn immediately to the central figure in conflict theory and, arguably, real-world conflict in the twentieth century. Karl Marx (1818–1883) and his collaborator Friedrich Engels (1820–1895) produced a corpus of work that fills fifty fat books (see Knapp, 1994). "A Theorist" indeed. In these volumes is nothing less than an explanation of human history spanning prehistoric times through humanity's future. Marx's brilliance is apparent in the fact that such an enormous mass of scholarship can be stated in the form of a crisp, dazzling insight: *Social classes run human affairs.* This is simultaneously a theory of social change to be addressed in Chapter 2 and a theory of social order to be appreciated here.

means of production—Karl Marx's term for the economic structure of society.

class—a set of individuals sharing a common relationship to the means of production.

ruling class—the class that controls the means of production of a given society.

superstructure—the various forms of social life built upon the means of production.

ideology—a set of ideas justifying the interests of a class.

To understand a society, go directly to its **means of production**, Marx's term for the economic structure. The main productive mode may be cattle (pastoral society), farmland (agrarian society), or factories (industrial society). Built upon this resource base is a system of social relations between **classes**, each of which consists of a set of individuals who share a common relationship to the means of production. Serfs in the agrarian society of European feudalism, for instance, "share[d] a common relationship" in that they all worked farmland owned by someone else; the "someone else" was the **ruling class** of landowners who got to rule by virtue of owning the productive mode—land. In Marx's own words,

> The sum total of these relations of production constitutes the economic structure of society, the real foundation, on which rises a legal and political **superstructure** and to which correspond definite forms of social consciousness. *The mode of production of material life conditions the social, political and intellectual life process in general* (1859/1978, p. 4; emphasis added).

Let this idea sink in. Marx is saying that the relations of production emanate a kind of force field controlling the rest of society. Law, religion, popular entertainment . . . all are manipulated by productive relations and, in particular, by those who operate the control panel—the ruling class.

So: social order is built from the unequal relations between social classes. The ruling class funnels most of society's goodies to itself (see Table 1:1) and sets up social structures to sell the idea. The idea itself is often expressed as an **ideology**, which justifies the vested interests of the ruling class and cools out potential sources of social disorder (see Chapters 11 and 15).

Now consider the back of the facade at the Alamo building in the previous photo as an analogy for conflict theory. The various parts are haphazardly cobbled together and the mutual stresses are artificially supported to keep the structure from crashing down; in addition, the building represents a monument to violent conflict.

The Conflict Theory Paradigm

Return to the image of social structure as a blueprint. In place of the clean, logical drawings of functionalism, conflict theory substitutes a monstrosity: The rooms are of ominously unequal size, and the whole structure can readily collapse. Many neo-Marxists argue that functionalism itself is an ideology, a pseudoscientific attempt to show that the status quo all makes sense by blurring the lines of inequality.

Conflict theory researchers seek hard data about factual inequalities. Not only have these investigators filled many of the cells of Table 1:1, they have also produced evidence of the conflictual relations among groups and organizations, including sweeping patterns of war and revolution (Buraway, 1990). In short, this paradigm's project is the documentation of conflict as a principle running up the many levels of the human social order.

Symbolic Interactionism

Why Is There Social Order?

symbolic interactionism—a major theoretical approach in sociology that focuses on the meanings that arise from the interactions among individuals in a society.

The answer offered by this variant of sociological theory is straightforward: There is no such thing as social order. Such a seemingly outrageous statement follows from a few simple premises. First, there is no social structure without people. If the roughly 250 million persons constituting U.S. society disappear, what happens to the orderly relations supporting teams and corporations and government agencies? They are instantly gone. So, such orderly structures are maintained *only* by the ongoing efforts of individuals. Return to the blueprint. Instead of focusing on the framework of society as functionalists or conflict theorists do, look closer at the construction components. If every brick, strut, and rivet is likened to an individual, their collective strain is all that keeps the structure standing.

Social order, then, is not a free-standing, "out there" thing. It is a bottom-up phenomenon that only continues to exist thanks to you, and us, and all of our fellow building materials. This radical shift in perspective also extends to the insides of individuals. Why do we carry the weight of society? Symbolic interactionists reject the functionalist view that people are programmed to serve the social system, as well as the view of conflict theory that people mechanically respond to the commands of class position. The orderliness in the behavior of any individual must be viewed as *self*-programming.

Take marriage as an example. Does anyone marry just to add another family building block to society? Does anyone marry just for the money? The answer to either question can be yes, but that is just the point: It is up to the individual. In the privacy of their own hearts, people have their own reasons. Information about "family values" received from society's mainframe is adapted for personal use; "marrying up" to a higher social class can be a positive or negative factor in one's own spouse-choice program. The (symbolic) meaning of the marriage is interpreted by the self based on the relationship with the prospective spouse-to-be (interaction). Such mixed, personally customized motives are the stuff of real marriages. Contemporary divorce statistics (see Chapter 14) also dramatize the point that individuals make—and unmake—social structures.

A Theorist

The symbolic interactionist approach is often applauded for "putting people back into" sociological theory. It certainly allows people to see their personal lives as figuring into the abstract, large-scale structures of society. The first sociologist to draw the picture this way was an artist indeed: Max Weber (1864–1920). Weber himself was the creator of an "abstract, large-scale" theory of society (to be displayed in Chapter 2), but he recognized that something was missing. The something was—and is—the *meaning* of the structures to the humans within them. Weber therefore proposed the principle of **verstehen**, the attempt to understand the intentions of social actors on their own terms. In addition to finding laws of social action, sociologists should analyze the subjective side of human acts.

verstehen—Max Weber's term for the attempt to understand the intentions of social actors on their own terms.

This is a tall order, even for an intellectual giant like Weber. With today's scientific techniques of survey analysis it is still very difficult to properly poll the members of a gang or a cult and find their true, hidden motives. Without a time machine, it is impossible to survey at all across the vast gulfs of history. Weber instead developed the **ideal type**, a description of a given social phenomenon ". . . in its conceptual purity" (Weber, 1949, p. 90) in order to reveal its essential features. His actual words are used to emphasize that Weber had in mind a kind of thought-experiment rather than some survey-based statistical average. What is a gang? An ideal-type that describes its features in pure form may not perfectly represent any real-world street group, but yet may capture the essence of gang activity. It also allows verstehen. The ideal-type can picture the gang in the general terms of its meaning for gang members; words such as loyalty, friendship, and respect would be part of this human picture. It is a different picture indeed than that drawn by functionalism or conflict theory. How would they view gangs?

ideal type—Max Weber's term for the description of a given social phenomenon in its conceptual purity in order to reveal its essential features.

The Symbolic Interactionist Paradigm

In technical terms, symbolic interactionist approaches to explanation focus at a lower **level of analysis** than do the other sociological theories; in other words, the explaining tends toward the inner rather than the outer boxes of the Social Systems hierarchy in Figure 1:1. Getting theory closer to peo-

level of analysis—the higher the level, the larger the social structure under study.

This individual behind the facade of the Alamo village building reflects the symbolic interactionist view that people make up society. Notice that in the two previous photos representing functionalism and conflict theory, no individuals are visible.

ple, though, requires getting researchers closer to people. This paradigm therefore encompasses a broad, even wild, variety of investigative techniques for penetrating face-to-face worlds. These range from ethnomethodology, which studies everyday reasoning processes (Chapter 4) to labeling theory, which specializes in the explanation of deviant behavior (Chapter 9).

What links these diverse research projects is the attempt to interpret the *meaning* of individual behavior in everyday interaction. Examples include studies of violent Satanists, of saintly sect members eagerly awaiting the end of the world, and the many varieties of human action in between. Sometimes the symbolic interactionist has entered a strange and dangerous world, and sometimes the researcher has sought to illuminate the familiar by finding new patterns of personal meaning. The most famous contemporary practitioner of this paradigm was Erving Goffman (1922–1980), who examined maximum security prisons, mental asylums, and the more prosaic social setting pictured in these passages from "The Lecturer" (Goffman, 1981):

THE INTRODUCTION

The introduction, as is said, will attempt to put into perspective what is about to be discussed. The speaker lets us know what else he might have chosen to talk about but hasn't, and what reservations he places on what he is about to say . . . he is to be seen as having an ordinary side—modest, unassuming, down-to-earth . . . (p. 175).

STORIES

There are moments in a lecture when the speaker seems most alive to the ambiance of the occasion and is particularly ready with wit . . . Yet these inspired moments will often be ones to most suspect. For during them the speaker is quite likely to be delivering something he memorized some time ago . . . The little narratives we allow ourselves to interject in a current talk we are likely to have interjected in other talks, too . . . (p. 178).

> **THE AUDIENCE**
>
> An audience sensed by the speaker to be "unresponsive," an audience that does not pick up on the talker's little gems and doesn't back-channel a chuckle or offer some other sign of appreciation, will tend to freeze him to his script. . . . If an audience is to be warm, it may have to be "warmed up," a process that is consciously engineered in variety programs, but ordinarily given little thought in lecturing . . . (p. 180).
>
> **DISTRACTIONS**
>
> One source [of distraction] we owe to the fact that lecturers come equipped with bodies, and bodies can easily introduce visual and audio effects . . . [which] may be distracting. A speaker must breathe, fidget a little, scratch occasionally, and may feel cause to cough, brush back his hair, straighten her skirt, sniffle, take a drink of water, finger her pearls, clean his glasses, burp, shift from one foot to another, sway, manneristically button and unbutton a jacket, turn the pages and square them off, and so forth—not to mention tripping over the carpet or appearing not to be entirely zipped up (p. 183).
>
> **IN CLOSING . . .**
>
> Closing comments have a similar flavor, this time bringing the speaker back down from his horse . . . and generally bringing him back to the audience as merely another member of it, a person just like ourselves (p. 175).

This account obviously crackles with insights. It may not characterize all lecturers or lecturees, but we certainly recognize enough of ourselves to get more self-conscious (a very Goffmanesque term). In any case, "The Lecturer" illustrates the symbolic interactionist view of social order as locally constructed within face-to-face interactions with one's familiars.

Integrating the Theories

The three forms of sociological theory introduced here are not just alternative approaches—they are active competitors. Proponents of the various positions have critiqued, rebutted, quibbled, conceded . . . in short, they have debated the essential forces of social order in much the same way as physicists still debate the essential forces of matter (see Chapter 2). The flow of argument has driven the theories into the extreme positions pictured in Figure 1:4. The triangle not only indicates the respective distances between the positions, but also presents the useful image of the "vantage point."

Picture any complex object at the center of a triangle. Now imagine that you are viewing it from one position *only;* this is your vantage point, and all other angles of vision are closed off. Looking at a car engine or a sculpture or a hologram from a fixed spot certainly allows you to see it, but you only see it *selectively.* Certain aspects of the object are invisible from your perspective; other aspects are visible only from that angle. It is our opinion that sociological theory is in such a predicament (Alexander, 1988). We shall therefore enrich the theoretical discussion in the chapters to follow with a special "Integrating the Theories" section. The idea, simply, is to

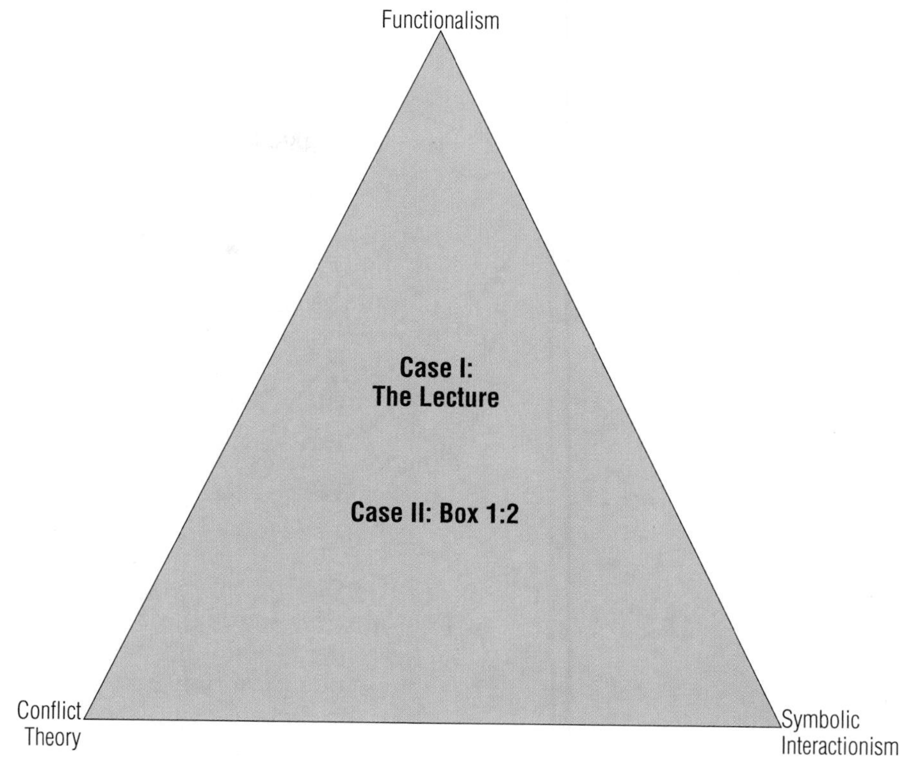

FIGURE 1:4 THE TRIANGLE OF SOCIOLOGICAL THEORY
The major theoretical perspectives viewed as vantage points offering complementary insights on sociological topics.

show you the sociological phenomenon to be placed at the center of Figure 1:4 from each of the three different theoretical vantage points. This is quite like the way in which triangulation is used in surveying: It fixes the true position of an object only after assessing it from several different angles.

Case I: The Lecture

As an experienced college student, you know what a lecture is. By a conservative estimate, your authors have delivered some 5,000 of them. Despite such vast familiarity, a sociological approach can deliver an X-ray-like vision of what we have seen all along.

A lecture is certainly an orderly affair. The professor whose antics opened this chapter got the students' attention by violating this social order. Now mentally place the college lecture at the triangle's center in Figure 1:4, and start at the symbolic interactionism corner. We confess that the Goffman excerpts from "The Lecture" have taught us about our own teaching. From this vantage point, a lecture is an immediate social situation in which nuances of behavior convey meaning between speaker and audience.

Ascend to the functionalism position, and the same lecture looks very different. For one thing, the perspective expands beyond the lecture hall. According to the leading functionalist theorist of his generation, Talcott Parsons (1902–1979), social order of any kind is only possible because of "norms" (Coleman, 1990), rules of proper conduct instilled in individuals (see Chapter 7). How do these get instilled? There are many social mechanisms to "program" you with the right norms: parents, churches, the mass media . . . even lectures. After all, the lecture does have content that is supposed to go into your notes and into your head. Besides, sitting through lectures is training in social skills that have functions in club meetings, offices, and boardrooms throughout the society.

From the conflict theory position, new features of college lectures become obvious. First, who gets them? The availability of a college class depends on one's social class. Second, what are college classes used for? Conflict theorists reject the functionalist idea that lectures change the inside of individuals' heads to improve their contributions to the social order. Instead, they identify the phenomenon as "educational credential stratification" (Collins, 1988, pp. 174–78), in which the favored few use their diplomas as weapons in the conflict for jobs. Certainly the college-degreed who sit through the required number of lectures do get more of "the good things in life" (see Table 1:1).

Ultimately, one of these theoretical positions may have more "truth value" than the others. At the present stage of development of sociological theory, however, each vantage point yields insights that bring us cumulatively closer to the truth.

Case II: Box 1:2

As a final illustration, put the autobiographical vignettes from the College Experience Box inside the triangle of sociological theory. Following the same sequence to integrate the theories, begin at the lower-right corner. From the vantage point of symbolic interactionism, these students and ex-students have engaged in acts of self-revelation in their essays. Although they were coached by the authors to be completely honest, you may react to these sketches of the personal significance of sociology as real or self-serving—that is your interpretation of their meaning. Functionalism again looks past the reader–writer interaction in the box itself. The content of the essays contains evidence of the practical utility of sociology for lives of service to business, family, and government. In this way, sociology makes its own contribution to social order. Since it generally suspects such order as being constructed by ulterior motives, conflict theory would look at the motivations behind this book. Box 1:2 is a device for capturing student interest, a "feature." If it is successful, this book will sell and make money for the authors and Harcourt Brace & Company.

The grains of truth to be gathered from each vantage point form the most compelling argument for their integration. Each theory reveals distinct patterns linking self and social structure (which is the last time we shall paraphrase the definition of sociology). Each theory is thus inspired by "The *sociological imagination* [which] enables us to grasp history and biography and the relations between the two within society" (Mills, 1959, p. 7; emphasis added).

SUMMARY

1. The field of sociology is founded on the idea of social structure and its relationship with human behavior. Social structure consists of the many and varied forms of interrelationships that make people into a society and instill the social programming by which individuals run their lives.
2. The social world can be understood as a hierarchy with the individual at the bottom. At the lowest level of interaction among individuals are patterns of interpersonal relationships known as social

networks (microstructure). Above these are the groups and formal organizations encompassed by society (macrostructure), and above all are the patterns of relationship among many societies (megastructure).

3. Empirical examination of the real social world through the scientific discipline of sociology has yielded rich, vast, and surprising insights about social structure and human behavior.
4. Human beings assume that society is orderly and expect it to operate in a predictable fashion. Three major forms of sociological theory attempt to explain why there is social order, and how social order works. Functionalist theory views society as a system whose parts fit together into an orderly whole. Because some parts perform positive functions whereas others—such as violence and stress—are dysfunctional, functionalists analyze the various components in terms of how they support and burden the overall design of society. Emile Durkheim, one of the founders of the field of sociology, held that even dysfunctional acts can serve positive functions within the social system.
5. Karl Marx, the central figure in conflict theory, explains social order in terms of social classes. The structure of society is built upon the unequal social relations between those who control the means of production and those who do not. The ruling class funnels most wealth and advantages to itself and sets up social structures to justify its vested interests and appease potential sources of social disorder.
6. Symbolic interactionism theory holds that social order is maintained *only* by the ongoing efforts of individuals. The first symbolic interactionist, Max Weber, proposed the principle of *verstehen,* the attempt to understand the intentions of social actors on their own terms. Symbolic interactionist research attempts to explain society by interpreting the meaning of individual behavior in everyday interaction.
7. These three forms of sociological theory are active competitors, but they also can be viewed as three different vantage points from which the same sociological phenomenon can be examined. While one of these theoretical positions may hold more "truth value" than the others, each vantage point yields insights that bring us somewhat closer to the truth.

Chapter 2

Personal Perspective

My name is Janine F. I'm a recent law school graduate serving as a civilian attorney for the New York City Police Department. One of my duties is to advise high-ranking officers at the scene of demonstrations and large public events. In July of 1992, I was assigned to advise Deputy Chief A. at the Democratic National Convention. The convention was a pleasant assignment—hot summer nights, the city scrubbed to within an inch of its life, and hundreds of equally well-scrubbed new graduates from the Police Academy on duty.

I had been busy all week—dispensing advice on how best to keep order while allowing the demonstrators to exercise their First Amendment rights, as many groups had been doing peacefully throughout the week. Since I'm not a police officer, and am usually the only unarmed member of the department present not wearing a bullet-proof vest and a riot helmet, I generally dispense my advice from the safety of the sidelines. Even though most demonstrations are orderly, there's always the possibility that a crowd will turn ugly. When a demonstration does turn ugly, it happens in a flash and often without warning. It's weird, but a peaceful march can turn into a riot and sometimes you don't even know why. Maybe someone's foot gets stepped on or something.

On the last night of the convention, Chief A. was notified that a hundred or so representatives of an infamous group of East Village anarchists were marching toward Madison Square Garden where they intended to hold a rally. Chief A.'s detail was to meet the marchers and shepherd them into a designated area where they could rally to their hearts' content.

So the marchers arrive at the Garden, and it becomes apparent that they don't want to be shepherded anywhere. They stop at an intersection and confront the police. Chief A. sends Captain P. to "negotiate" with them, which basically means that Captain P. is standing

Social Disorder: *The Unmaking and Remaking of Society*

chest to chest with the head anarchist. I sense that the situation is getting tense, and as I'm preparing to back off behind the lines of police, Chief A. orders me to "Stay with Captain P., close enough so that you can hear what he's saying." This is a very unorthodox position for a civilian attorney to be in, yet what could I do but take up a position at Captain P.'s shoulder?

"Negotiations" are going poorly. The marchers want to demonstrate in the roadway, not behind the barriers as Captain P. has directed. The group surges forward, the police attempt to restrain them, and suddenly I'm caught in the middle. The demonstrators rush into the roadway. Captain P. issues a standard order to his officers: "Form a line and flank them." The group of mostly rookie cops freezes. Literally. Like rabbits caught in headlights. They're scared, I'm scared, the demonstrators are running full out, and in the space of a second, the situation is out of control. Captain realizes what's wrong, and starts bellowing at the cops, "MOVE, MOVE, MOVE!!!" The sheer force of his voice gets the rookies moving. They run, overtaking the demonstrators. Captain P. runs, and I run after him because, God help me, I'm under orders to stay with the captain. The demonstrators are young and in sneakers. Captain P. is middle-aged and portly. I'm wearing pumps with two-inch heels and a Police Department windbreaker that comes down to my knees, and I haven't actually run anywhere in years. Still, somehow, we're keeping up. Then the anarchists turn and run toward us. Still facing them, I retreat, and my back hits something. I look behind me and see that I have been backed into the police barriers. I'm trapped, and for the first time, truly terrified.

At that moment, the cops tackle a demonstrator who was about to throw an M-80 (the equivalent of a quarter stick of dynamite). This distracts the rest of the demonstrators, and gives the cops the opportunity to surround them and restore order. I climb over the barriers. The demonstration has been contained, and I'm back on the sidelines where I belong.

Social Disorder: *The Unmaking and Remaking of Society*

In 1958, Nigerian writer Chinua Achebe took the title of his novel *Things Fall Apart* from "The Second Coming," a poem by William Butler Yeats:

Turning and turning in the widening gyre
The falcon cannot hear the falconer;
Things fall apart; the centre cannot hold;
Mere anarchy is loosed upon the world . . .

Achebe's story depicts life in a Nigerian village during the nineteenth-century British colonization of that society. For the European leaders of the time, colonialism meant imposing order on simple-minded savages living unholy, unruly lives in deepest, darkest Africa. For the Africans, however, whose point of view Achebe represents, it was an assault on the social institutions of a rich, complex traditional society causing those institutions to crumble.

The "Personal Perspective" and *Things Fall Apart* show that the counterpoint to social order is social disorder. As will be seen throughout this chapter, "things fall apart" in otherwise orderly societies all over the world, and they have throughout history. While the phenomenon might seem cruelly irrational to those caught where "the centre cannot hold" and "[m]ere anarchy is loosed upon the world," it is not beyond understanding. The key to such understanding is viewing social disorder as a *process*.

The "St. Bartholomew's Day Massacre" was a mass murder of French Huguenots by Roman Catholic nobles in the sixteenth century. The slaughter occurred on a traditional religious holiday and was triggered by a symbol of social order—at the tolling of a church bell.

Life and death must be understood together; the biological definition of each is the absence of the other. Similarly, the physical process by which elementary particles bind into matter is explained by direct contrast to the chaotic state out of which they form. Social life has this dual quality. We recognize social order when it gives way to social disorder, and vice versa. There are times, like the one described in the "Personal Perspective," when it happens rapidly right before our eyes. The shift is usually not so explosive. More commonly, a social order changes in subtle, nearly imperceptible ways that leave its inhabitants mystified by their new state. Sociologists seek to solve the mystery of how a society gets *unmade* into disorder, and *remade* into a new social order. These extraordinary changes in the state of society are explained by sociological theory.

Before we present the classical sociological theories of social change, consider for a moment the social setting in which they were invented. The "classical theorists"—Emile Durkheim, Karl Marx, and Max Weber—were formulating their ideas during the very disorderly nineteenth century. The traditional, agrarian, monarchical European society, which had conquered and colonized Nigeria, the remainder of Africa, and all of the Americas, had unceremoniously fallen apart. A series of violent revolutions were the bloody birth spasms of the new, industrial nation–state social order. The early sociological theorists were striving to understand this "Great Transformation" happening all around them (Knapp, 1994).

But it is important to emphasize the pervasiveness of social disorder across both time and place. Perhaps it is part of the very process by which social order is maintained, but there is a persistent, rosy myth of "the good old days." Certainly, there were "bad old days" aplenty in New York City (site of the "Personal Perspective") during the very historical period in which Durkheim, Marx, and Weber were theorizing in Europe. Lower Manhattan was a place of opium dens roamed by thousands of abandoned children and patrolled by deadly gangs who fought battles with knives, pistols, and sometimes even cannons (Sante, 1991). Disorderly behavior is well-documented everywhere and everywhen from Greece in fifth century B.C. (Orrs, 1987) to the former Soviet Union today (see Chapter 16). Despite their point of origin, these sociological theories are "classical" precisely because they apply to the unraveling of social order in all of these different times and places, including the crack neighborhood across town.

DURKHEIM: STRUCTURAL DIFFERENTIATION

For reasons that border on the obvious, explanations of social change must begin with a history of events. A proper "theory" is a *simplifying device,* making sense out of the enormous diversity and complexity of altered social structures. Further, a theory of social change is also a theory of social disorder. Explaining why the old society unraveled can explain both a descent into chaos and how the threads then wove together to form a new social order.

The Theory

structural differentiation—Emile Durkheim's theory tracing the increasing complexity and specialization of social structures.

For Emile Durkheim, the most important aspect of the development of societies throughout history has been a process called **structural differentiation**. Durkheim first proposed this ambitious set of ideas in *The Division of Labor in Society* (1893/1964), his Ph.D. dissertation. According to the theory, the story of human history begins in simple tribal societies in which all major institutional functions—political, religious, economic, and educational—are performed *within* the family. To illustrate Durkheim's vision of social change, picture a tribe of hunters and gatherers. The "economy" might be family males hunting small game and family females gathering roots and berries. Parents "educate" by passing on the skills of survival to their children around the campfire. Perhaps an uncle is the healer, an aunt the high priestess. The political leadership of the tribal group is assumed by the eldest member of the clan. Note, in the left-hand box of Figure 2:1, that the "family tree" is the social structure within which all of these functions are embedded.

As society evolves from the tribal state, these institutional functions begin to develop their own social structures separate from the family. Whereas political power in medieval European society, for instance, remained concentrated in the hereditary lines of a small number of ruling families, it had been removed from the vast majority of homes; each family no longer had its own "king." Religious functions had been taken over by a powerful church that was also now separate from the family (each family no longer had its own "priestess"), as well as from the political institution (hence, "the separation of church and state" as illustrated in the middle box of Figure 2:1). In many of today's societies, all these social institutions have become entirely differentiated from the family and from each other. Governmental institutions carry out political functions, schools educate, religious organizations tend to spiritual needs, and corporations form the backbone of society's economic structure (hence, the five separate structures within Figure 2:1's right-hand box). The separate buildings in which they are housed suggest separate social organizations for each function.

The process of structural differentiation proceeds, says Durkheim, with the development of more and more separate institutional zones, and more and more specialization within each zone. This breaking apart and breaking down of social structures is implied in his phrase *the division of labor.* A woman giving birth in a tribal family is tended by her sisters; a feudal

FIGURE 2:1 STRUCTURAL DIFFERENTIATION—DURKHEIM'S CENTRAL PROCESS OF SOCIAL CHANGE

Three stages of the evolution of human societies are shown in terms of an increasingly complex division of labor.

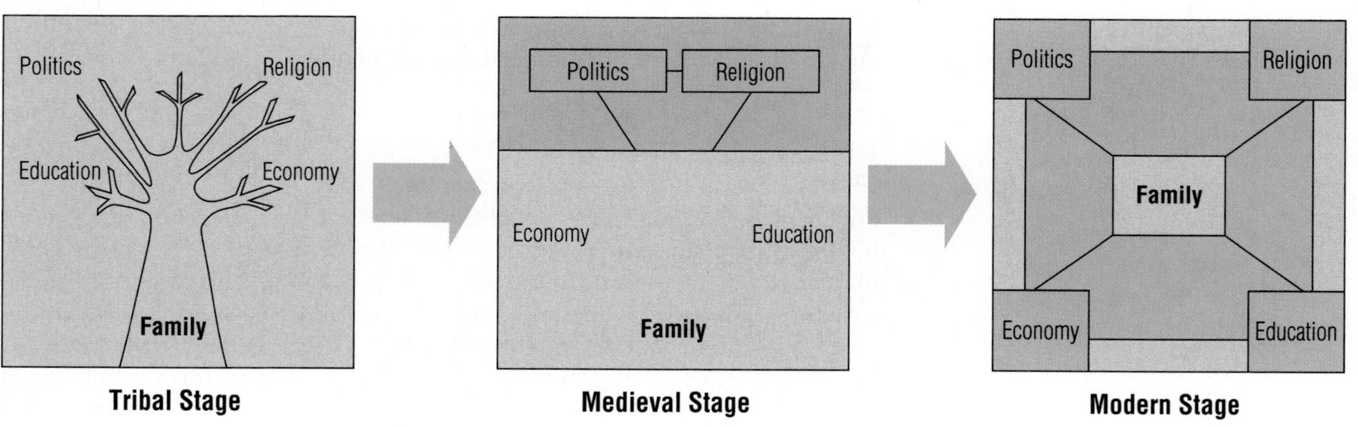

Contrast this scene from a tribal society with a typical scene from your own life. According to Emile Durkheim, the basic structure of society itself has been transformed, and this process underlies all of the superficial differences.

peasant family sends for the midwife from a nearby village. Your grandmother was probably assisted in labor by a general practitioner who also attended patients suffering from measles or broken bones; your mother most likely called on an obstetrician—a doctor who specializes only on the reproductive systems of female patients—when you were born. One very recent instance of ongoing structural differentiation involves child care. Thirty years ago, it was not unheard of for mothers of preschool children to work outside the home, but babysitting arrangements were usually allocated to grandparents or other relatives. As increasing numbers of women have entered the job market and babysitting relatives have become harder to find, daytime child care is less the province of the family and more the province of neighborhood play groups, nursery schools, and, more recently, large, institutionalized day-care centers. And within these institutions, specialization can be seen: Some programs cater to four-year-old gymnasts; some to budding computer geniuses; most segregate the children by age, including having a separate facility for infants; and a few centers are devoted exclusively to the short-term care of sick children. Most of this "structure" has "differentiated" during your lifetime.

The process of structural differentiation does more than merely redefine who does what in a society. For one thing, the process is accompanied by an increasing social *efficiency*. The general move from being a "jack-of-all-trades" to being a specialist has resulted in a society of narrow—but competent—experts. At the same time, *interdependence* increases, since all specialists need one another in order to function. Anyone who has ever had a major home repair done knows how difficult it is to coordinate the builders, plumbers, electricians, and roofers, none of whom can carry out their particular function without the skills and cooperation of all the others. On a personal level, the case of a single 13-year-old, pregnant, crack addict might require the attention of an obstetrical facility, a child welfare

Consider the separate, specialized tasks performed to produce a modern newspaper. Clockwise from the upper left are shots of an editor, a reporter, a researcher, and a printer—and there are dozens of other interdependent specialists. Contrast these operations with the *Pennsylvania Gazette,* a colonial newspaper Benjamin Franklin produced out of his own shop.

agency, a drug rehabilitation program, law enforcement authorities, a psychologist, and the local public school district—each of whom treats only one aspect of the child's plight. Similar trends are observable in pro sports and, in fact, throughout society. Efficiency and interdependence proceed together as social structure differentiates.

Social Solidarity

For a moment, step back to consider Durkheim's grand theory. It surely qualifies as grand: All of human history is related to a central process operating beneath the surface of current events such as wars, religious heresies, factory closings . . . Structural differentiation is what fundamentally changes societies, including contemporary U.S. society. This process underlying social change runs deep and transforms the very forces holding social structures together.

mechanical solidarity—**the human attraction generated by common moral sentiments, typical of tribal societies.**

In Durkheim's terminology, tribal societies are (some still exist) bound by **mechanical solidarity**, the human attraction generated by the common moral sentiments of tribal members. Because there is so little specialization, persons of the same age and sex tend to share very similar experiences (after all, these are societies of "generalists"). Similarity of experience tends to produce similar thoughts and feelings, so, by the "birds of a feather flock together" principle you will learn of in Chapter 4, social solidarity is readily achieved. It cannot be so readily achieved in more structurally differentiated societies because they are, by definition, filled with specialists with few experiences in common. **Organic solidarity** binds these dissimilar souls together by their functional dependence upon one another. Whether they like each other or not, pro football players depend on all of the other specialists to get the job done. Whatever they have in common (probably not much), professor, dean, clerk, security guard . . . all must perform their distinctive functions, or a college closes down. Simply put, specialists *need* each other.

organic solidarity—social integration based on functional dependence of specialists, typical of modern societies.

The Rise of Anomie

As was explained in Chapter 1, all of Durkheim's work can be viewed as an exploration of social integration, the various forces binding individuals into orderly social life. He did not think all such forces are equally binding; in particular, the organic solidarity characterizing modern societies is prone to unravel. Durkheim traced the rise in modern life of a phenomenon known as **anomie**. This concept is related to the idea of *homo duplex,* the individual and the social self inside each person. If the social self is weakened, obviously the rules start to slip. From the Greek—*a–* [without], *–nomos* [law]—it means people stop following the laws, and, in fact, all of the rules of the social order. This weakening of moral regulation might be seen as liberating the individual self and, to be blunt, allowing for uninhibited weekends. Instead, Durkheim argues that anomie ". . . is the cause . . . of the incessant recurrent conflicts, and the multifarious disorders" (1893/1964, p. 2). Anomie is a true "social disease," destructive of self as well as society.

anomie—the weakening of moral regulation of the self associated with personal and social disorder.

This dim view of the phenomenon is anchored in Durkheim's theory of suicide. In his classic analysis of nineteenth-century suicide rates (introduced in Chapter 1), Durkheim observed that urban, mobile, economically prosperous segments of the European population—the very vanguard of modern society—had *higher* rates of suicide than did economically stable

Durkheim never saw Las Vegas, but his theoretical ideas would see this contemporary scene as at high risk of *anomie.*

BOX 2:1 SOCIOLOGICAL IMAGINATION IN FICTION

Anomie in *The Clay*

It is two centuries in Earth's future, and one of the startling social changes is that giant, multileveled cities have been built above the surface of the land to house the billions upon billions of humans. There is a region beneath each pillared city—"the Clay"—inhabited by people in an ultimate state of social disorder. They have been abandoned there by the civilization above with all their social structures torn away, thus exposing "the Clayborn" to the state of anomie. This selection spotlights the experiences of an individual in that extreme state.

The first thing to see was darkness. Darkness colored the Clay like a dye. It melted forms and recast them with a deadly animation. It lay within and without; was both alive and yet the deadest thing of all. It breathed, and yet it stifled.

For many it was all they knew. All they would ever know.

The darkness seemed intense and absolute. It was a cloth, smothering the vast, primeval landscape. Yet there was a light of a kind.

Above the shadowed plain the ceiling ran to all horizons, perched on huge columns of silver that glowed softly, faintly, like something living. Dim studs of light crisscrossed the artificial sky; neutered, ordered stars, following the tracks of broad conduits and cables, for the ceiling was a floor, and overhead was the vastness of the City; another world, sealed off from the fetid darkness underneath.

The Clay. It was a place inimical to life. And yet life thrived there in the dark; hideous, malformed shapes spawning in obscene profusion. The dark plain crawled with vulgar life.

Kim woke from a bad dream, a tight band of fear about his chest. Instinct made him freeze, then turn slowly, stealthily, toward the sound, lifting the oilcloth he lay under. He had the scent at once—the thing that had warned him on waking. Strangers . . . strangers at the heart of the camp.

He moved to the lip of the brickwork he had been lying behind and peered over the top. What he saw made him bristle with fear. Two of his tribe lay on the ground nearby, their skulls smashed open, the brains taken. Farther away three men—strangers, intruders—crouched over another body. They were carving flesh from arm and thigh and softly laughing as they ate. Kim's mouth watered, but the fear he felt was far stronger. . . .

He whimpered, then glancing furtively about him, began to wrap the treasures as he'd found them. Only when they were safely stored did he stop, his jaw aching from fear, his muscles trembling violently. Then, like some mad thing, he rushed about the settlement on all fours, growling furiously, partly to keep up his faded courage, partly to keep away the prowlers on the hillside below.

(continued on next page)

rural dwellers. The experiences of the former, he argued, would tend to loosen the moral bonds of the social self, unleashing individual appetites but undermining the sense of life's meaning. For a current illustration, consider the linked facts that (a) Nevada has the highest suicide rate of all the United States (U.S. Bureau of the Census, 1992), (b) Nevada's population is concentrated in Las Vegas, and (c) that city has one of the nation's highest metropolitan growth rates, as well as an industry that could be described as ". . . unleashing individual appetites but undermining the sense of life's meaning." Chapter 9 presents a contemporary theory of deviance and, in particular, modern crime built around the idea of anomie. The immediate point is twofold: Anomie produces personal and social disorder, and it arises from the broader pattern of social change that is structural differ-

BOX 2:1 SOCIOLOGICAL IMAGINATION IN FICTION ***continued***

It was then that he found the knife. It had fallen on its edge, the handle jutting up at an angle where one of the strangers had dropped it. The handle was cold and smooth and did not give to Kim's sharp teeth when he tested it. Not wood, nor flint, but something far better than those. Something *made* . . . Baxi [his tribe's chief] glared at Kim, then saw the knife. His eyes widened, filled with fear and a greedy desire for the weapon. There was a fierce, almost sexual urgency in his broad, squat face as he hopped from foot to foot, making small noises, as if in pain.

Kim knew he would kill to have the knife.

"Lagasek!" Baxi barked angrily, edging closer. "Pandra vyth gwres?" His hands made small grasping movements.

Lagasek. It was the name they had given him. Starer.

Kim stood, then raised the knife high over his head. There was a gasp from the other members of the hunting party as they saw the weapon, then an excited chattering. Kim saw Baxi crouch, his muscles tensing, as if he suspected treachery.

Slowly, careful not to alarm Baxi, Kim lowered the blade and placed it on the ground between them. Then he crouched, making himself smaller than he was, and made a gesture with his hands, the palms open, denoting a gift.

Baxi stared at him a moment longer, the hairs bristling on his arms and at the back of his neck. Then he, too, crouched, a broad, toothless grin settling on his face. The chief was pleased. He reached out, taking Kim's gift gingerly by the handle, respecting the obvious sharpness of the blade.

Baxi lifted the weapon and held it high above his head. He glanced briefly at Kim, smiling broadly, generous now, then turned, looking back at his hunters, thrusting the knife time and again into the air, tilting his head back with each thrust and baying at the ceiling high above.

All about him in the almost-dark the hunters bayed and yelled. And from the hillsides and the valley below other groups took up the unearthly sound and echoed it back. . . .

He felt misplaced. Torn from the light and cast down into darkness. But if misplaced, what then? How could he change things?

Run away, a small voice inside him called out. *Run far away. To a place where the darkness ends.*

Better to stay here a thousand years. . . .

A cold shiver passed through him, ice beneath the firelight on his face and chest and limbs. No, not that. Death was preferable to that.

Critical Thinking Questions

1. Above "the Clay" where these humans dwell in a state of anomie rises a gigantic, futuristic City. According to Durkheim's theory of structural differentiation, what should life be like in this society of the future?
2. How would a symbolic interactionist interpret this sequence of events in "the Clay?"

Source: David Wingrove, *Chung Kuo: The Middle Kingdom* (1990). New York: Dell Publishing, pp. 189–90, 192–94, 206–07.

entiation. Durkheim extends this theory into the human future, and Box 2:1 imagines an extreme case of anomie haunting that future.

MARX: CLASS CONFLICT

For Karl Marx, the force driving human history is class conflict. As explained in the introduction to conflict theory in Chapter 1, the basic proposition is that any social order is built from the conquest of a given society by a ruling class. Marx's grand idea also extends to the periodic disorders that burst through a social order, as well as to the cataclysmic bursts of social change that transform a social order into something else entirely.

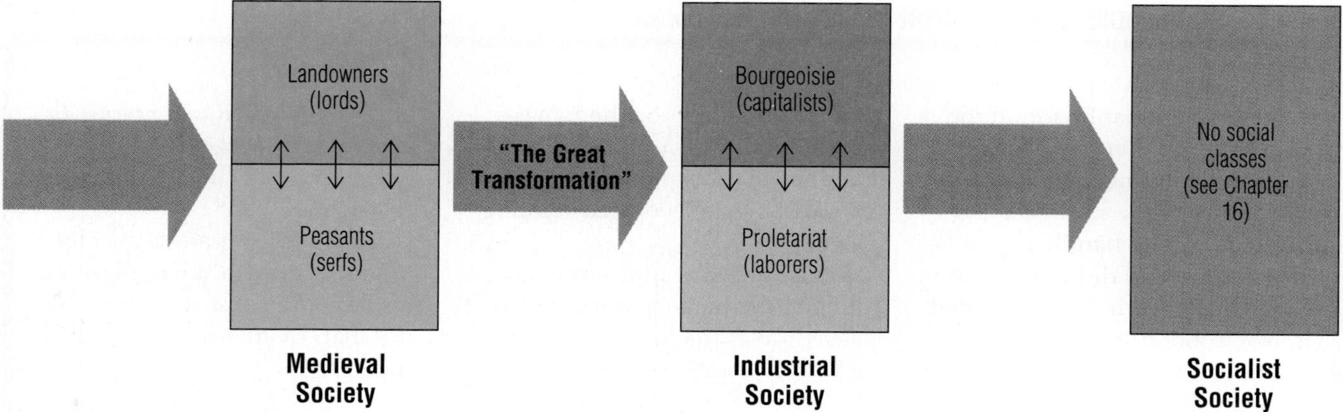

FIGURE 2:2 MARX ON CLASS CONFLICT AND SOCIAL CHANGE
According to Marx's theory, class conflict (indicated by small arrows) in medieval society gives rise to social revolution (large arrows), thus creating the industrial social order. Class conflict in the latter finally gives rise to the classless, socialist social order. The large arrow at left signifies that the theory includes class relations before this period of "The Great Transformation."

The coming explanation of this "grand idea" is illustrated in simplified form in Figure 2:2.

History As Class Struggle

The following excerpt from *The Communist Manifesto* (1848/1959, with F. Engels) was written at a time when revolution was sweeping across Europe:

> The history of all hitherto existing society is the history of class struggles. Freeman and slave, patrician and plebian, lord and serf, guildmaster and journeyman, in a word, oppressor and oppressed, stood in constant opposition to one another, carried on an uninterrupted, now hidden, now open fight, a fight that each time ended, either in a revolutionary re-constitution of society at large, or in the common ruin of the contending classes.

bourgeoisie—the capitalist class in industrial society who derive their incomes through ownership of profit-making enterprises.

proletariat—the laborer class in industrial society who derive their incomes from wages paid by the bourgeoisie.

The new industrial order did not abolish the class systems Marx observed in medieval Europe and in earlier ages; it merely changed their form. More and more, the new society was dividing into two main classes: the **bourgeoisie**, capitalists whose income is the profits stemming from ownership of industrial or commercial enterprises, and the **proletariat**, laborers who work for wages paid by the bourgeoisie. Modern industrial capitalism, Marx wrote, "has but established . . . new conditions of oppression, new forms of struggle in place of the old ones."

Evidence supporting Marx's grand view of history is ample. One need only travel back in time through the European societies to survey the litter of class division and disorder. In ancient Rome, in the shadows of magnificent temples and imperial palaces, thousands lived in squalid urban slums. The emperors provided free or low-cost grain and bloody gladiatorial contests to distract the populace—the famous formula of "Bread and Circuses" used by the Caesars to pacify the masses. The Middle Ages ("Medieval Society" in Figure 2:2) were marked by many bloody revolts. Pushed beyond endurance by the backbreaking labor and deprivation forced upon them by oppressive nobles, serfs slipped the bonds of social order and fought back, murdering the lords and burning their manor houses. Aggravating factors such as plague or heavy taxation could transform isolated outbreaks of disorder into massive uprisings. This occurred in France in 1358, when the economic pressures of the Hundred Years' War

Throughout this century, decisions by capitalists (Karl Marx's *bourgeoisie*) to automate or relocate mining operations have sparked open conflict with mine workers (*proletariat*).

sparked widespread violence and mayhem by the lower classes, followed by merciless repression by their noble enemies in this class conflict.

Class Consciousness

class consciousness—an awareness among the members of a given class of their common interests in the class struggle.

An essential ingredient in the conversion of hidden class conflict into open revolution is class consciousness. This is a dawning awareness among the members of a given class of their common interests against class enemies.

Chapter 1 (and chapters to come) discusses the devices Marx says are used by the ruling class to convince non-ruling classes to identify with the existing, exploitive social order. When these devices break down, society breaks down as classes contend with each other. It was the development of true class consciousness that helped turn a 1789 economic crisis into the French Revolution. In the century prior to the crisis, Europe had been swept by a philosophical movement called the Enlightenment, which had its birth in France. The "Philosophes" of the Enlightenment questioned the religious assumptions underlying the traditional social order of medieval European society. The rising vehemence of these criticisms fed on popular discontent. Attempts by "enlightened" monarchs such as Catherine the Great of Russia and Emperor Joseph of Austria (brother of Marie Antoinette) to reform society from the top were too little, too late. The result was what can be described as a revolutionary wave that began in France and swept on currents of class consciousness throughout all Europe.

Disorder and Change

Perhaps the most important thing to remember about his grand theory of history is that Marx saw class conflict—even violent class conflict—as a productive process. For Marx, revolution was the engine of social change, with each outbreak moving society closer to the socialist Utopia that he predicted as the culmination of history (the right-hand box of Figure 2:2).

Marx's view of history has never ceased to be a matter of dispute among historians, and the success of his predictions has been mixed; for instance, he was certain that industrialization would bring about socialist revolution in nineteenth-century England. Even so, his theory of class relations reveals much about the twentieth century. The "opening" of Japan by the arrival of American Commodore Matthew Perry in 1853 introduced capitalistic trade relations into what was an extraordinarily traditional social order. In less than a century, industrialization utterly transformed Japan into a capitalist society whose great productive capacity allowed it to make war on twentieth-century England and the United States. As we shall see in Chapter 6, the face-off of the bourgeoisie and proletariat classes is a recurrent theme in the tide of industrial modernization presently engulfing the world.

alienation—people losing control of the social order created by their labor, resulting in personal dissatisfaction and social disorder.

Perhaps his clearest connection between social disorder and social change is drawn in Marx's concept of alienation. In his view, human beings actively make social orders by their labor. Under conditions of class conflict, however, the fruits of that labor are controlled by the ruling class. This pirating away of "the good things in life" (refer to Table 1:1) means that most people are like "aliens" in the very social order their sweat creates. The subjective sense of alienation results in a dissatisfied and sometimes very disorderly industrial proletariat (to be discussed in Chapter 16). As awareness of the reality of their situation dawns on these workers of the world—the very meaning of "class consciousness"—Marx foresees disorder that will produce the final, decisive act of social change: the socialist revolution.

WEBER: RATIONALIZATION

In Chapter 1, we promised to present Max Weber's "abstract, large-scale" vision of social change marching above his more individualistic principle of *verstehen*. As that promise is fulfilled, be aware that this brilliant work emerged from the long shadow cast by Marx's theory. Weber wrote in the generation succeeding Marx, and at many points the former actively addresses the vision of the latter (Knapp, 1994).

The Protestant Ethic and the Spirit of Capitalism

This heading is also the title of one of the most famous books in the history of social science. Remember, in addition to wrestling with each other's ideas, the classic theorists were grappling with the grandest question of all: What caused this modern society then revolutionizing Europe? Weber's answer to the question of "The Great Transformation" was *The Protestant Ethic and the Spirit of Capitalism* (1904–5/1958).

The very title implies tension with Marx. Although he conceded the significance of social classes, Weber did not think that modern, large-scale industrial capitalism arose entirely out of economic conditions. One of his key ingredients in the recipe for "The Great Transformation" was, of all things, religion, and in particular the more extreme versions of Protestantism arising from the Reformation. Weber wondered why this new form of society had never before appeared in human history. Ancient China, Rome, and Egypt had politically stable social orders with complex class

FIGURE 2:3 WEBER'S MULTI-FACTOR THEORY OF SOCIAL CHANGE LEADING TO THE RISE OF MODERN SOCIETY
Weber viewed the "Protestant Ethic" as operating *in conjunction with* economic and political factors to give rise to modern society distinguished by rationalistic thinking and bureaucratic organizations.

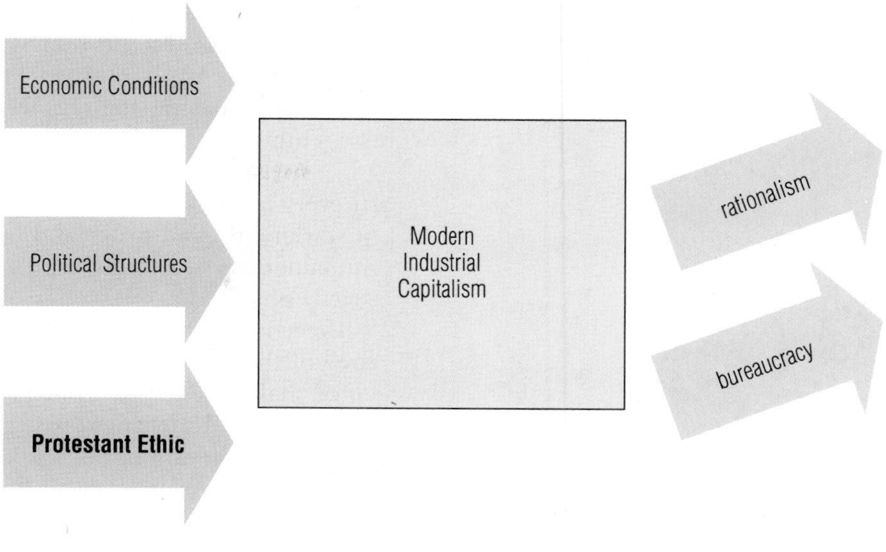

systems, but these empires dissolved into social disorder instead of changing into this dynamic new social order. Why?

Part of the answer for Weber lurks in his famous phrase "the disenchantment of the world." The major world religions root out the spirits, demons, and enchanted forces infusing the world of pre-industrial societies. The Protestant Reformation did so with a vengeance, sweeping away even the magical elements of traditional Catholicism. Weber saw resultant social changes sweeping well beyond church doors. In a "disenchanted" world, systematic, sensible, orderly behavior is possible. It is not possible when spirits inhabit every tree in the path of a lumber company, or when a factory is viewed as a house of demons. The radical Protestants created a radical transformation of reality, which cleared the path for "The Great Transformation" itself.

There were additional doctrinal elements in those denominations motivating the new social order, and certain economic and political preconditions had to be there for Protestantism to motivate, but the key point here is Weber's **multi-factor theory** (see Figure 2:3). In contrast to Marx's concentration on class conflict, Weber saw multiple sources of social change.

multi-factor theory—an explanatory approach identifying multiple sources of social change.

Rationalism and Bureaucracy

Weber's differences with Marx did not end with the origins of "The Great Transformation." He also saw different forces at the heart of the transformation as it occurred. Instead of disorderly class disputes, Weber viewed the rise of that most orderly of organizations—bureaucracy. As is explained in Chapter 5, Weber defined and clarified the nature of this distinctive new form of social organization. He had to. Wherever Weber looked at a modernizing society, he saw bureaucracies rising at its center.

As the previous section suggested, a disenchanted world clears the way for rationality. Formally, **rationalism** is the systematic application of standardized means to predetermined ends; informally, it is finding the "one best way" to perform some social task, then routinely doing so. Sound familiar? It is a form of thinking so distinctive of modern thought as to seem like a human instinct. There is nothing instinctive about rationalism.

rationalism—the systematic application of standardized means to predetermined ends.

Weber's theory finds it in the early capitalist enterprises launched by Protestant entrepreneurs. To see how it made these organizations much more efficient than the haphazard work routines of eighteenth-century artisans, consider these strictly standardized work rules of a typical nineteenth-century enterprise:

> In every large works, and in the co-ordination of any large number of workmen, good order and harmony must be looked upon as the fundamentals of success, and therefore the following rules shall be strictly observed.
>
> Every man employed in the concern named below shall receive a copy of these rules, so that no one can plead ignorance. Its acceptance shall be deemed to mean consent to submit to its regulations.
>
> The normal working day begins at all seasons at 6 a.m. precisely and ends, after the usual break of half and hour for breakfast, an hour for dinner and half an hour for tea, at 7 p.m., and it shall be strictly observed.
>
> Five minutes before the beginning of the stated hours of work until their actual commencement, a bell shall ring and indicate that every worker employed in the concern has to proceed to his place of work, in order to start as soon as the bell stops.
>
> The doorkeeper shall lock the door punctually at 6 a.m., 8:30 a.m., 1 p.m. and 4:30 p.m.
>
> Workers arriving 2 minutes late shall lose half an hour's wages; whoever is more than 2 minutes late may not start work until after the next break, or at least shall lose his wages until then. Any disputes about the correct time shall be settled by the clock mounted above the gatekeeper's lodge (Pollard and Holmes, 1968).

As a sociological footnote, also consider the exclusive use of male references in this passage. Some have argued that rationalism highlighted the crude inefficiency of excluding half the human race from industrial enterprises, thus clearing the way for women's large-scale entry into the workforce.

Once out of its bottle in industrial enterprises, the genie of rationalism assumed its dynamic form—rationalization. It progressively touches more and more regions of modern life, transforming traditional political, religious, and educational groups into large-scale, bureaucratic organizations. Rationalization and bureaucratization are mutually reinforcing, chicken-and-egg historical processes. "One best way" thinking is currently spreading through Third World development bureaucracies, and it certainly enters your mind as you study for midterms—a rationalized policy of the school bureaucracy.

In a sense, Weber's theory of social change differs from the other two in that it prophesies the long-term *decline* of social disorder. It is not an entirely rosy prophecy. Weber foresaw the gradual locking away of human individuality into the "iron cage" of bureaucratic rationality (Weber, 1922/1968).

SOCIAL PROBLEMS

This is not a social problems textbook. The task at hand is to acquaint you with the central ideas and fundamental findings of the field of sociology. In our earnest attempts to do so, we kept bumping into a hard fact—many

Max Weber's idea of *rationalism* is evident in a modern book store. Note how many of the titles offer "one best way" formulas for routinizing even the most intimate parts of your personal life.

of the field's "central ideas" and "fundamental findings" involve the dark side of human life. This is why a separate chapter is devoted to addressing the breakdown of social order.

Consider the first half of this chapter as a broad discourse on why "things fall apart" in societies. It is now time to get down to cases. People rarely react to anything as vague and abstract as social disorder. More typically, there is concern about some concrete issue. Both the concern and the concrete issue bear careful sociological scrutiny.

The Objective and Subjective Dimensions

The Duality of Social Problems

One of the basic tools of human understanding is analysis: breaking reality down into its primary parts to see how it is put together. Over a century of study, it has become clear to sociologists that social problems consist of two primary parts:

objective dimension—the concrete, measurable human harm associated with a societal phenomenon.

subjective dimension—the general level of concern about that phenomenon registered in public opinion.

1. The objective dimension—the concrete, measurable human harm associated with a societal phenomenon.
2. The subjective dimension—the general level of concern about that phenomenon registered in public opinion.

Since there has already been plenty of abstract theoretical discussion, we shall show you the uses of this analytical framework in three case studies.

Case I: Halloween Sadism. At the risk of dating ourselves, the authors remember Halloween being very different than it is today. Hordes of greedy children filled bag after bag with treats by innocently knocking on the doors of stranger after stranger without any adult escort. We know how different your experience has been. In our current neighborhoods, one expects perhaps a dozen visitations by well-known kids whose parents watch warily from the street dressed in their own disguises. What happened?

The "razor blade in the apple" happened. Fears of razor blades, poisons, drugs, and other such "tricks" being implanted in "treats" by nasty adults have fundamentally changed this children's "holiday."

Best and Horiuchi (1985) went looking for the substance behind this scare. They systematically examined the coverage in four national newspapers (including *The New York Times*) over a twenty-five-year period. The objective evidence of concrete harm was skimpy indeed. They found a grand total of 76 reported incidents, only 20 of which involved injuries and only two deaths; that is *less* than one injury per year, and less than one death per decade (both deaths were later blamed on family members). In terms of real danger, the chances of death or injury to children are much greater from being hit by a car or, arguably, from radiation damage caused by having candy bars X-rayed at a local hospital.

In terms of our analytical dimensions of social problems, this is a case of a molehill being made into a mountain: Subjective concern is far greater than the concrete evidence of real harm.

Case II: Occupational Deaths. When is the last time you worried about someone being killed by their job? We know the answer to this very rhetorical question because public opinion polls rarely register any concern at all about deaths due to occupational accidents (e.g., a painter falling from a ladder) or disease (e.g., black lung disease among coal miners). To preview an objective statistic from Chapter 16, even the most conservative estimates indicate that, on the average, you are more than *twice* as likely to be killed by occupation than by murder. Yet which of these issues generates more concern? Another rhetorical question.

To return to our analytical dimensions, this is a case of a real mountain being a perceived molehill: Subjective concern is far less than the concrete evidence of harm.

Case III: Missing Children. Perhaps the most compelling demonstration of the duality of social problems occurs when a subjective problem appears from an objective problem that had been there all along.

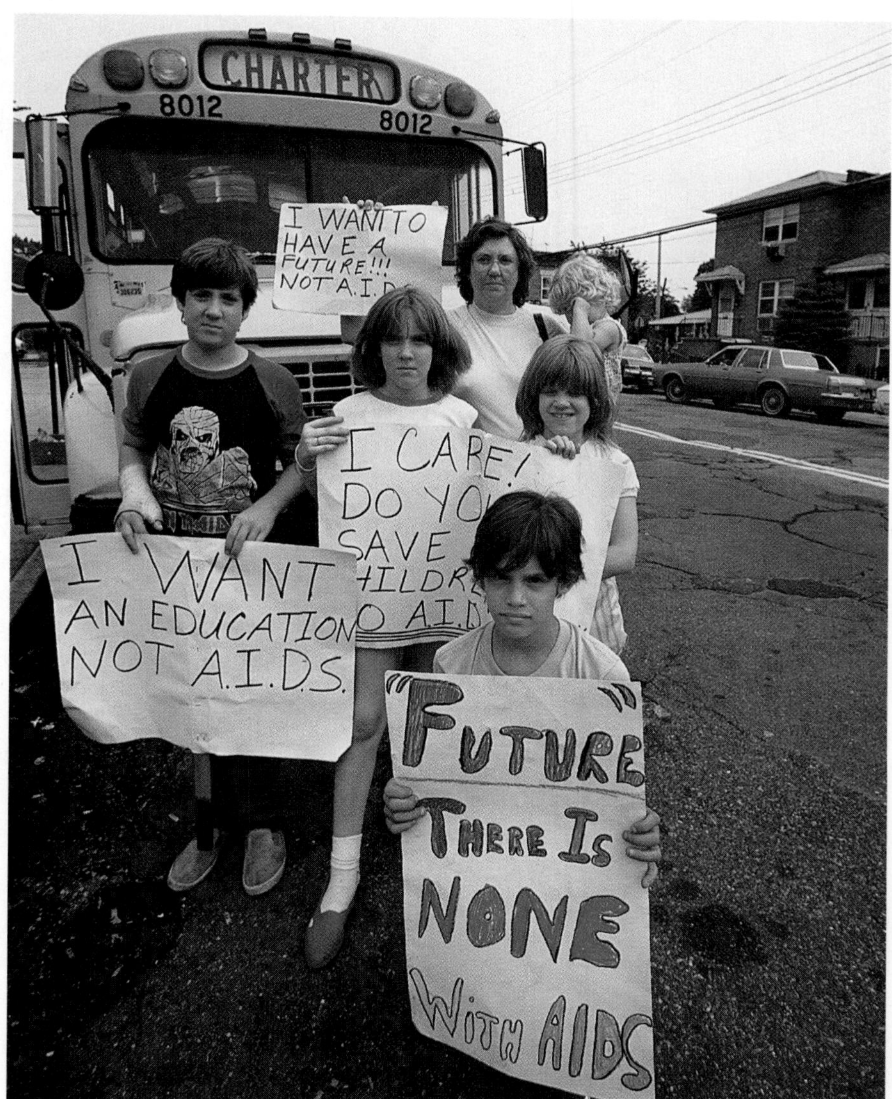

Fear of AIDS-transmission can build into subjective hysteria despite objective evidence of very low risk in most social settings.

Here we spotlight a case that flared into public consciousness in the early 1980s. Following several well-publicized incidents of missing children later found murdered (notably, Adam Walsh in 1981 and a series of Atlanta school children between 1979 and 1981), there was a national sensation. The issue was aired on "60 Minutes," "20/20" and "Good Morning, America," and there were so many articles written on the subject that the *Reader's Guide to Periodical Literature* had to establish a separate "Missing Children" heading. Soon thereafter the faces of children who were missing began to appear on milk cartons, and $10 million per year were allocated under the federal Missing Children's Assistance Act.

Sociological studies of the missing children issue (Best, 1987; Gentry, 1988) suggest that the fear and loathing about strangers abducting kids has been a gross exaggeration of the facts. The overwhelming statistical majority of children reported "missing" are recovered within one day; the overwhelming statistical majority of suspected kidnappings turn out to be runaways or kids snatched by noncustodial parents. Abductions by malevolent strangers do happen, of course, but law enforcement statistics indicate that there are between 100 and 200 per year. This is certainly not a number to be trivialized, but it does not suggest a rising epidemic of kidnapping.

What is especially interesting about this case is the *sudden appearance* of an apparent mountain from what had been a statistical molehill all along. As with the other cases, the objective and subjective sides of social problems must be seen as separate sociological dimensions.

The Objective Dimension

Causes of Social Problems. The theories of social disorder in the first half of this chapter testify to sociology's attention to the real forces that tear real societies apart. The repetition is to highlight the tie-in between the classical concerns of the field and the objective dimension. Wars, bread riots, suicides . . . all are the stuff of both human suffering and sociological explanation. Their connection can be clarified by introducing one of this book's special features. In the chapters to come, a box titled "Gender and Social Change" exposes the sociological significance of changes in gender roles. Box 2:2 describes the mighty efforts of one woman to *create* social change regarding the social problems of homelessness. We call your attention to three things. First, Sister Mary is trying to forge social order out of the social disorder that consumes personal lives on the street; this shows order and disorder as sides of the same sociological coin. Second, though it still might seem jarring to traditional stereotypes to see a woman (and a

BOX 2:2 GENDER AND SOCIAL CHANGE

CREATING ORDER FROM DISORDER

Sister Mary Scullion—in blue-and-white cotton slacks, a white short-sleeved shirt and Birkenstock sandals—seems oblivious to the heat, the humidity, the fumes, the needle, the vibrations and the drivers behind her who honk impatiently every time the car—nicknamed "The Bomb"—stalls, which it does four times.

Sister Mary, a youthful 39, drives—and talks—on.

About the homeless, and her commitment to them. She reveals that on this day in September 20 years ago, she entered the Sisters of Mercy, an Irish Catholic order founded in 1831 by Catherine McAuley, a nurse, teacher and welfare worker.

In her work with the homeless, Sister Mary is all of those. She also knows Center City the way few others do—every corner, every steam vent and alley, and just about every homeless person on or in one. . . .

In the 16 years that she has worked with the homeless, Sister Mary has seen some of them come to horrible ends. They have frozen to death and died of heatstroke. They've been run over by cars, hit by buses, set on fire and beaten with two-by-fours by skinheads.

She has also seen—with her leadership—the virtual disappearance of "bag ladies" from the streets of Center City. She has set up a half-dozen residences around the city for homeless men and women. And she has seen miracles happen. . . .

The woman's hands were balled up with arthritis and she suffered from Tourette's syndrome, a bizarre neurological disorder that made her quack and, without provocation, shout out a blur of obscenities.

Her name was Sylvia, but people called her "the duck lady."

When Sister Mary met her, Sylvia was in her 60s or 70s. She lived on a corner near Wanamakers [department store].

For two years, Sister Mary and a caseworker talked with Sylvia, listened to her, laughed with her and tried to persuade her to come in for a physical exam. The answer was always, "Not today."

(continued on next page)

nun, at that) on the front lines of this street struggle, Sister Mary is by no means a pioneer. Exactly one century before the present book was published, Jane Addams published *Hull House Maps and Papers* (1895), a sociological study of impoverished immigrants on the West Side of Chicago. Addams practiced what she preached, having founded Hull House to provide social services to the poor. She, too, was a crusader for social order amid widespread disorder. Finally, Box 2:2 is a report from the gritty, all-too-real world. Whatever their current public image, actual people are struggling with grinding poverty *right now.* Their social lives belong in the objective dimension.

Sociology's power to reveal the objective roots of human problems is magnified by the "Integrating the Theories" approach. From the functionalist side (actually, the top of Figure 1:4), many of Sister Mary's clients can be viewed as living evidence of the human damage wrought by anomie; her efforts to socially reintegrate the homeless would arguably serve positive functions for a society to which they could then contribute. We say arguably because her efforts are surrounded by real arguments. Clearly, the community groups opposing Sister Mary's programs represent clashing class interests. From the symbolic interactionist vantage point, what is most visible are the face-to-face contacts between flesh-and-blood individuals, some of whom share the meaning of Sister Mary's personal mission and some

BOX 2:2 GENDER AND SOCIAL CHANGE ***continued***

Then one day, inexplicably, she agreed. She came into Mercy Hospice and was put on medication, and a few years later, she was able to move into a room of her own in Center City. . . .

Over in Francisville and Spring Garden, there's no talk of Sister Mary being a saint. And any reference to Mother Teresa—at least as far as Mary Scullion is concerned—is sarcastic.

No. Over here, where Sister Mary has been battling for two years to open a permanent residence for 48 men and women at 1515 Fairmount Ave., the nun others want to canonize is derisively referred to as an "urban terrorist" and an "urban thug." . . .

. . . opponents contend that the neighborhood is saturated with homeless shelters, drug and alcohol rehabs, residences for troubled children, halfway houses for ex-cons, personal care and boarding homes, and group homes for the mentally ill and mentally retarded.

"This is America, the land of opportunity," [Sister Mary] says, "and those who choose the right thing should be encouraged, not have barriers put up. I think it's so unfair that they would characterize the men and women that would be living here as bringing down the quality of life in the neighborhood simply because they are disabled or have been homeless.

"We're an *antidote* to the crime and drugs the neighborhood has been fighting," she says. "And last time I checked, it was not a crime to be homeless."

She talks about combating residents' fears with love. But she can't resist. "Do you have to be perfect to live in this neighborhood?" she asks. "Just because they're rich. . . ."

Critical Thinking Questions

1. From the vantage point of symbolic interactionist theory, how does Sister Mary's "gender" help and/or hurt her attempts to effect positive "social change"?
2. Contrast functionalist and conflict theory answers to this question: Where did all of the desperately poor people ministered to by Sister Mary come from?

Source: Ginny Wiegand, "Woman of the Streets." In *The Philadelphia Inquirer Magazine* (Nov. 22, 1992), pp. 12–29.

of whom assuredly do not. Certainly the combination of three theoretical vantage points deepens our insights into this personal crusade against homelessness. The point we especially want to ram home, though, concerns causality. Each theory reveals a separate side of the objective sources of human suffering.

The Sociology of Science. Sociologists have long been interested in the social side of science. As will be explained in Chapter 21, science is something that only exists under certain societal conditions. All three of our classical theorists (Durkheim, Marx, and Weber) commented on science as part of the distinctively modern society they were attempting to explain. More recent sociologists of science have found that the process of discovery is influenced by interpersonal patterns of relationship among working scientists (see Crane, 1972; Star, 1988). It is exciting to realize that the unlocking of the stacked puzzle boxes pictured in Figure 1:1 has *all* been sociological. Every scientific discipline discovering part of nature has its own system of training, academic conventions, and awards; in short, every science is a social structure and therefore a sociological subject. Exciting as it is, this idea leads to the top hierarchy and to a confrontation with another paradox: Sociology is itself sociological.

This is not an attempt to be cute or profound. It is a practical paradox that sociologists are people in social structures who study, well, people in social structures. Can we be scientific about ourselves? A basic principle of science is **objectivity**, the existence of a thing outside the mind of the observer; the thing must be an "object" separable from the "subject" studying it. The difficulty is that even when sociologists study *other* people, the former often care very deeply what they discover about the latter. In their heart of hearts, Marxists want to find evidence of class conflict in a labor union, just as functionalists want to find a positive social function.

objectivity—the real qualities of a thing outside the mind of the researcher observing it.

Max Weber (1949) posed this as the problem of a **value-free** social *science.* What he meant was the development of "ethically neutral" procedures, which would allow sociologists to see social reality objectively, untainted by the rose-colored glasses of their own values. Weber thought complete value freedom to be an unattainable ideal for any science. Inevitably, values creep in from the start even in the choice of what to investigate. A paleontologist may choose to study dinosaurs because of a fascination with them, just as a sociologist who studies anomie may be dedicated to reducing suicide. Some believe that such intrusions of personal emotion make a scientific sociology impossible. Many, however, believe that the paradox can be resolved by drawing a parallel to other life sciences. Take the case of a medical researcher whose mother died of cancer. The central mission of that person's life is the elimination of the dis-valued disease. Despite trembling with desire for the drug under test to be effective, the researcher can (indeed, must) follow the accepted scientific procedures for establishing its clinical effectiveness. Wishful thinking must give way to the scientific method to arrive at the objective truth about the "cure." The analogous methods used by sociologists to study society are described in Chapter 3.

value-free—Weber's term for the "ethically neutral" procedures of sociology that would, ideally, allow an objective view of social reality untainted by personal values.

Chapter 3 also explains that the scientific method is inherently skeptical. Research findings are not accepted in an open-and-shut case, but rather must stand trial in the cross-examination performed by other scientists. This means that in the scientific procedures of sociology, criticism is built-in. Recall from Chapter 1 that the "Integrating the Theories" discussions have been devised because of the intensive mutual debate among the three major schools of sociological theory. Functionalism, conflict theory, and symbolic interactionism differ so drastically in their vantage point on the

Margaret Mead, one of the most famous social scientists of this century, is shown conducting one of her studies of South Pacific island tribes. The scene suggests the difficulties of scientific objectivity due to involvement with one's human "subjects."

same social phenomena that they often attack each others' interpretations. The present point: In both their methods and their theory, working sociologists rely heavily on critical thinking skills. We intend to strengthen those skills, so near to the heart of our discipline, by presenting you with *Critical Thinking Questions* already introduced within the boxes in this chapter. These are meant to develop your sense that sociology is a "discipline"; that is, a special way of looking at the social world with insights sharpened by hard questions.

The Subjective Dimension

To sum up: Sociology employs theories and methods to study the objective dimension of social problems. However, as the Halloween, occupational deaths, and missing children cases illustrate, public opinion is no objective mirror of social problems. What explains the popular images that do appear in the subjective dimension?

It is not our intent to set sociologists up as all-knowing experts who would tell the public what issues they should be upset about. Instead, we have applied our own sociological theory to make sense of the subjective side of social problems—and social life in general (Jones, McFalls, and Gallagher, 1989). Figure 2:4 represents the explanation to come as a schematic diagram.

Visibility. Though everyone suffers, no one directly senses very much of the collective suffering of a whole society. Only very rarely will you be an eyewitness to a poisoning, a fatal accident, or a kidnapping, let alone the whole range of human misery. Your main sources of information about social problems—or anything else—are communication channels built into social structure. Social information channels work like permeable membranes, passing through some reports while screening out others.

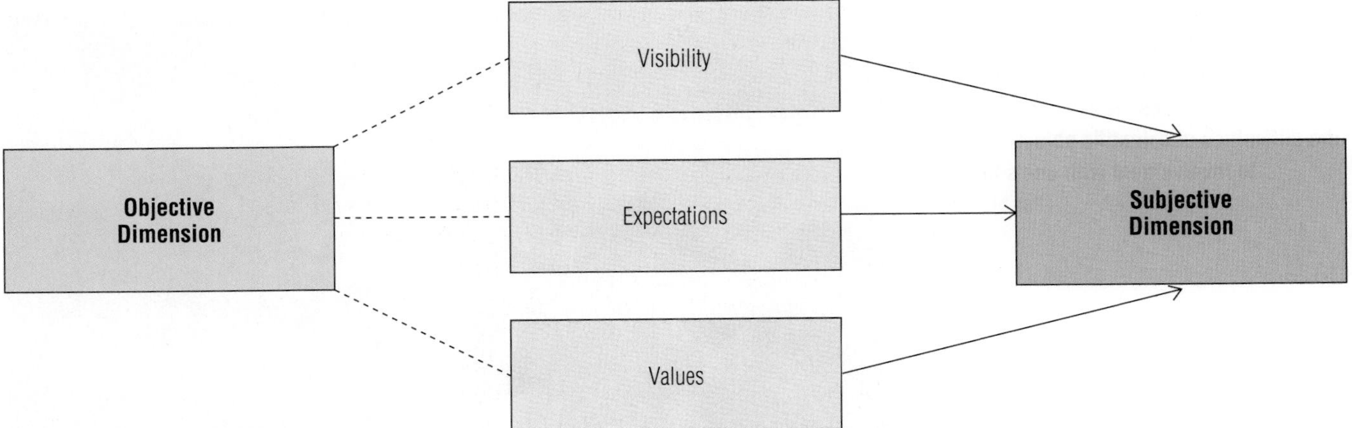

FIGURE 2:4 A SCHEMATIC DIAGRAM OF THE DUALITY OF SOCIOLOGICAL PHENOMENA
The objective facts about social problems (or social life) are not sensed directly, but rather are processed through visibility, expectations, and values to form public opinion in the subjective dimension.

One of the elements of this social filtering process is the *intrinsic drama* associated with a given social problem. Some forms of objective damage are natural attention-getters; the more dramatic the damage, the more likely it is to pass through the "membrane" and register in our heads. Consider airplane crashes. A jet spinning down in flames and killing hundreds of people on impact is a spectacularly tragic event. Even though automobile accidents kill over twenty times as many people as airplane crashes (U.S. Bureau of the Census, 1992), which worries you more? Urban slums containing block after block of squalid housing lead many to view poverty as a problem of the cities. These dramatic concentrations of human misery attract attention when, in fact, the poverty rate is higher in rural than in urban areas (O'Hare, 1988). Whatever the actual number of sufferers, it is the dramatic level of an issue that keys our subjective response.

Word of mouth may still be a significant channel of opinion concerning social problems, but *media exposure* makes a given problem visible to millions of people instantly and simultaneously. The glare of publicity does not shine similarly on all objective harms. Rather than simply holding up a mirror to society, media professionals screen, select, and edit events on the basis of their "newsworthiness" (Lester, 1980). Tales of children being maimed or snatched by strangers will get air time whereas reports of black lung deaths among coalminers usually will not. And air time does make a subjective difference. In 1970, pollution shot to the top of the public opinion polls about social problems, even ahead of the Vietnam War. Why? It was not an objective worsening of the problem; in fact, the actual amounts of air and water pollution in the United States had been declining (Barber, 1975). What had not been declining was media exposure—there were a dozen TV specials on pollution aired in the spring of 1970 alone! Finally, consider the phenomenon we call "*Sixty Minutes* syndrome," in which previously ignored problems literally leap into the public mind overnight. The point is both crucial and simple: The media-heightened drama of selected social problems may have little to do with objective significance, but much to do with subjective concern.

Expectations. If you enrolled in a sociology course expecting a grade of C, and then got a C, you might feel quietly satisfied. If you anticipated an A, however, and then received a C, you might be loudly angry. The actual grade in each case is exactly the same. The crucial difference lies in your subjective state, in the wild swing of emotions regarding an identical objective situation.

The difference between satisfaction and dissatisfaction, then, often depends on what you expect. This truth can be applied to cases at the societal level. Take, for example, the timing of revolutions, which are more likely to occur when social conditions are *improving:*

> The most perilous moment for a bad government is when it seeks to mend its ways. Patiently endured so long as it seemed beyond redress, a grievance comes to appear intolerable once the possibility of removing it crosses men's minds. For the mere fact that certain abuses have been remedied draws attention to the others and they now appear more galling (Tocqueville, 1852/1955, p. 178).

As sociological observer Tocqueville noted over a century ago, an improvement in one's lifestyle makes it clear that positive change is possible, and therefore can be expected of society. With the objective standard of living rising but expectations rising even faster, things can get better but *feel* worse. The subjective dissatisfaction may even build to the point where large numbers of people view society itself as the social problem, and revolution as the solution (Brinton, 1960).

Less sweeping views of social problems are triggered by the same subjective mechanism. A case in point is the spectacular success of American medicine in combating some forms of infectious disease. The virtual elimination of polio, for example, has saved the lives of thousands, thereby convincing millions to expect miracles of medical science. Given our apparent capacity to wipe out disease, continuing killers such as cancer and AIDS

Terrorism: the very term suggests an act designed to violate the values and expectations of civil society. Terrorists such as the airplane hijackers shown here also seek out high visibility acts for maximum impact on the subjective dimension.

As shown in Marc Chagall's "War on the Palaces," social disorder, like social order, is ultimately in the hands of "we, the people."

seem like an outrage; an objective cure makes uncured illnesses seem, in Tocqueville's phrase, "more galling." Mounting subjective concern is reflected in budgets for medical research, which have grown along with public expectations.

Whatever the social problem, the general point is that expectations have the power to swing the subjective mood of the public independently of—indeed, even *against*—the objective situation.

Values. We are at a bit of a disadvantage here because the key concept of values will not be fully addressed until Chapter 7. For present purposes, we shall use the term in the nontechnical sense of the earlier discussion on "value freedom." Values can be viewed as emotionally charged likes and dislikes widely shared in a culture. Values vary between cultures (as Chapter 7 explains, we in the United States value individualism more than do citizens of most other societies) and also between groups in the same society (e.g., some religions are more individualistic than others).

Values may minimize the objective harm associated with a societal phenomenon. Automobile accidents currently kill approximately 45,000 Americans a year (U.S. Bureau of the Census, 1992). That is more deaths than homicide, more deaths than suicide and, in fact, is close to the American combat death toll in Vietnam over the entire sixteen years of the war! Despite the exclamation point, the numbers just do not register emotionally. Curiously, even with the staggering objective statistics on deaths, disabling injuries, and billions in economic costs, most people have little subjective concern about car crashes compared to other social problems. The reason is values. The automobile is more than a device of convenience. One's car symbolizes status, personal independence, even sexual maturity. The automobile is so firmly embedded at the heart of the American value system that most of its harms are ignored or passively accepted. Public reaction is not keyed in directly to objective damage; *first* the societal phenomenon itself is ranked in relation to the value system, and *then* the significance of the statistics is weighed. Values can reduce an objective mountain to a subjective molehill.

This social problems mechanism also works in reverse: *Values may magnify the objective harm associated with a societal phenomenon.* Return to the Halloween sadism and missing children cases introduced earlier. These problems are not figments of our collective imagination; there are real, if modest, numbers of victims. But the victims are children, in everyday language "innocent children." These acts are so "heinous" precisely because they deliberately strike at one of our most deeply cherished, highly valued social types—kids. The extraordinarily high value placed on the lives of children makes sadists and snatchers seem subjectively serious, even though many times more deaths and injuries are caused each year by bicycles (U.S. Bureau of the Census, 1992). Values can raise an objective molehill to the status of a subjective mountain.

Like the proverbial tree falling in the woods, social suffering may or may not be heard. The crucial point is that the objective falling and the subjective hearing are separate processes, and that the crash we hear (or do not hear) can be explained. The three subjective factors—visibility, expectations, and values—are major sociological forces screening the sounds that enter the public mind.

The Duality of Social Life

> Professors lay out a world of uniformities—of rules, of seamless connection—and many treat change, disorder, or even improvisation as exceptional. Students, meanwhile, live in a world where disorder is around every corner and improvisation the only means of survival . . . Social science should seek principles of social process which account for chaos and normality together (Harrison C. White, *Identity and Control,* 1992, pp. 3–4).

It is time to stop talking about sociology and begin to introduce its real subject matter. Before making that leap, though, we would like you to ponder two general points.

First, does the Harrison White quote ring true? If so, it nicely captures our rationale for the joint presentation of Social Order (Chapter 1) and Social Disorder (Chapter 2). These two processes are interlinked from the level of global social structures down to the social lives of students. The order–disorder linkage is one key duality of social life.

FIGURE 2:5 GLOBAL SOCIAL DISORDER

At the time this book went to press, violent social disorders (i.e., armed conflicts) wracked the many areas marked on the map. Since that time, social order has returned to some areas, and new social disorders have broken out elsewhere in the world.

To preface another aspect that will be a chapter-by-chapter feature, consider this: We are about to tell you an enormous amount you did not know about life in your own society. To put it more diplomatically, these chapters will reveal to you the contents of sociology's puzzle boxes (from Figure 1:1). How could you be subjectively ignorant of so much about your own objective social life? In a way this is a paraphrase of the riddles posed in Chapters 1 and 2. The framework that has just been introduced can be used to solve the riddle of how a society may be mysterious to its own inhabitants.

It is not our purpose to show off by using sociology to shatter social "myths" believed in by silly nonsociologists. As the previous section suggests, what is in people's heads about social problems gets there via known sociological processes. The same is true of general knowledge about "social structure and human behavior" (i.e., sociological knowledge). Rather than show off, we shall simply apply the visibility–expectations–values framework in "The Subjective Dimension" sections of chapters to come.

SUMMARY

1. The counterpoint to social order is social disorder. Social order may give way to social disorder rapidly and explosively, or change may occur in subtle, nearly imperceptible ways.
2. The "classical theorists"—Emile Durkheim, Karl Marx, and Max Weber—formulated their ideas during the turbulent nineteenth century, as they sought to understand and explain the violent disorder that accompanied the "Great Transformation" from the pre-industrial world to the new, industrial nation–state social order.

3. According to Durkheim's theory of structural differentiation, the development of societies through history is marked by the separation of institutional structures from one another. This separation is accompanied by increasing specialization within each sphere, and the interdependence of specialists.
4. Disorder occurs as a result of anomie, a loosening of the moral bonds of the social self arising in part from the broader pattern of social change that is structural differentiation.
5. For Marx, social disorder is the product of class conflict, and it is a productive process. Rising class consciousness among non-ruling classes may lead to open revolution, which Marx sees as the engine of social change, moving society closer to the socialist Utopia he predicted as the culmination of history.
6. A clear connection between social disorder and social change is provided by Marx's concept of alienation. The expropriation by the ruling class of the fruits of labor makes workers like "aliens" in the very social order their work creates. Their resulting dissatisfaction may lead to disorder, and thence to social change.
7. In contrast to Marx's concentration on class conflict, Weber sees multiple sources of social change. Rationalism—the systematic application of standardized means to predetermined ends—progresses as society modernizes, reaching into more and more regions of life and transforming traditional political, religious, and educational groups into large-scale bureaucratic organizations.
8. Weber's theory of social change through rationalization and bureaucratization prophesies a long-term decline of social disorder, but warns of the gradual locking away of human individuality into the "iron cage" of bureaucratic rationality.
9. Social disorder manifests itself in the emergence of social problems. Every social problem has two primary parts: (a) The objective dimension is the concrete, measurable human harm associated with a societal phenomenon. (b) The subjective dimension is the general level of concern about that phenomenon registered in public opinion. Subjective response to the objective harm caused by a particular social problem may be influenced by the visibility, expectations, and values associated with that problem. Sociology employs theories and methods to study the objective dimension of social problems but also seeks to make sense of the subjective side.

Chapter 3

Personal Perspective

The young instructor's palms were sweating. She was excited by the chance to teach her first course, an introduction to sociology in the night session of an urban college. Mixed with the sense of excitement was a growing uneasiness about the students. They were a study in social diversity. There were recent high school graduates and retirees, African Americans and Africans from Africa, male and female police (in uniform), and male and female clergy (also in uniform). As a group they were older and apparently more mature than the inexperienced instructor about to lecture them on the realities of life in society.

But she was ready. On her back was a new professorial tweed jacket—complete with patches on the elbows. In her fingers were freshly written lecture notes packed with some of the most intriguing findings of modern sociology. The major points of the lecture were recent, interesting, and carefully chosen to show that scientific sociology proves it unwise to trust "the conventional wisdom." Frankly, she expected to dazzle the crowd.

"Welcome to the house of sociology. Let me lead you through some of its rooms," was her opening remark. The instructor then proceeded to reveal startling findings in several branches of the discipline. Suicide is *not* most likely at Christmas time; almost every citizen ("including those in this crowd") has committed a criminal act; females have higher morbidity rates but lower mortality rates than men ("Women get sick; men die"). . . . In the middle of this rousing recitation of sociological data, a uniformed student in the front row raised a hand. Though a bit miffed at an interruption right before a big punchline, the instructor called on him.

"How do you know all of this stuff?" asked the student.

"What do you mean?" The instructor was dumbfounded.

"Is this all just some sociologist's opinion? I've been working the streets for fifteen years, and I don't agree with what you just said about crime. Why should I believe it?"

After gathering her thoughts, the instructor previewed an upcoming lecture: "These are the findings of scientific studies. Hundreds, thousands, sometimes tens of thousands of cases have been analyzed to reach such conclusions. The results are then published in professional journals so that other sociologists may check the generalizations . . ."

"Oh," interjected the student, "you mean statistics. But you can prove anything you want with statistics!"

The instructor—angry now—said: "You can prove anything you want *without* statistics, too! At least with data what is 'proved' is more than just your opinion—or mine."

replication—the duplication of a research procedure to verify the results.

Sociological Research Methods

THIS classroom experience teaches a real-world lesson: There is a difference between sociology and revelation. Our discipline's findings are not accepted by the public as absolute truth; nor are they so accepted by practicing sociologists. One of the guiding principles of any scientific discipline is self-criticism. The burden of proof is on the investigator to draw a conclusion by assembling evidence according to accepted rules of research procedure. As judged by these rules, there is good science and bad science. Some published results have been shown to be flat out wrong—by other scientists. Computations are checked, procedures are examined, deductions and inferences are tested by the rules of logic; if the study passes muster, it may be repeated—**replicated**—to see if the conclusions hold up. "Critical Thinking" (introduced in Chapter 2) is thus a basic part of sociological research methods.

STRATEGIES OF INQUIRY

Is sociology a science? The answer is yes. Let us now elaborate that answer by considering its relevance to skeptics, to the public, and to other scientists.

Every academic discipline faces the "So what?" test. Try it with a classmate. Find out the person's major, then demand a list of important things learned in major courses that are not common knowledge. Be a smart aleck about it. If a physics major expounds on the mechanics of spin rotation and aerodynamic flow, counter with, "Any Little League pitcher knows how to throw a curve ball!" If a psychology major explains the effects of visual persistence on perception, say, "Everybody knows how moving pictures work." If an astronomy major mentions a fact of which you are totally ignorant—say, the location of the Crab Nebula—just trivialize it with the ultimate rebuttal: "So what?"

Sociology seems especially subjected to this skeptical attitude. Most people, after all, live in social groupings that they can experience without special instruments or elaborate theories. Most people, moreover, must develop an understanding of their social surroundings and some skill at applying this understanding. This is what is meant by "common sense." Although it is fashionable to do so in sociology texts, we do not dismiss common sense. It can be a helpful, insightful guide to social life—as far as it goes. But common sense is often inconsistent; take the contradictory dating tips "Birds of a feather flock together" versus "Opposites attract" (see Chapters 4 and 14). Its "sense," moreover, is often not that "common." The practical guidelines for everyday experience differ drastically for lawyers, homemakers, and astronauts because their everyday experiences are so different. Consider the stereotype of "the absent-minded professor." You probably have at least one preoccupied teacher whose head is in the intellectual clouds even when the real clouds are raining on that head. Such a professor lacks the hyper-alert street smarts needed by a cop or a cab driver. In the academic world of "publish or perish," however, intellectual preoccupation can be a survival skill. Here is the point: *Sociological research derives general propositions about social behavior.* Unlike common sense, sociology contains built-in tests of whether its propositions are true across a broad range of human experience. Sociology's main answer to a demanding critic is to invite the criticism in. As is the case with any scientific discipline, the sociological methods to be discussed put the burden of proof on the researcher. Despite this burden, researchers prove things all the time that would impress your most skeptical classmate.

The second aspect of the sociology-as-science issue concerns its place in the public mind. As you read through this chapter, reflect on how many of the terms are already familiar. Surveys (or "polls") may be *the* most widely used form of applied research on humans. "Sampling" is done for TV ratings, "demographic breakdowns" are the subject of marketing research studies, "focus groups" are probed by political pollsters, "databases" are analyzed by the U.S. Census Bureau, and business personnel departments and religious organizations do "direct mailing" to their members. Many of these techniques have been developed by and, frankly, stolen from sociological researchers. This widespread plagiarism reflects the credibility such techniques have gained in a society worshipful of science.

This is not the place for deep philosophical ramblings about whether sociology is a "true" science. Before we show you the tools of sociological research, though, two parallels to the natural sciences would be instructive. First, sociology is a young discipline somewhat less than two centuries old. By the 1800s, when sociology was being born, biologists had been working for five centuries on the direct question of where infectious disease comes from (Knapp, 1994). The thickness of this text suggests that sociology has been busily maturing as a young discipline. Second, every science has its instruments, and all are imperfect. Every space telescope, computerized centrifuge, or supercollider has its glitches and blind spots, often called "measurement errors." The same is true for sociological tools. This means

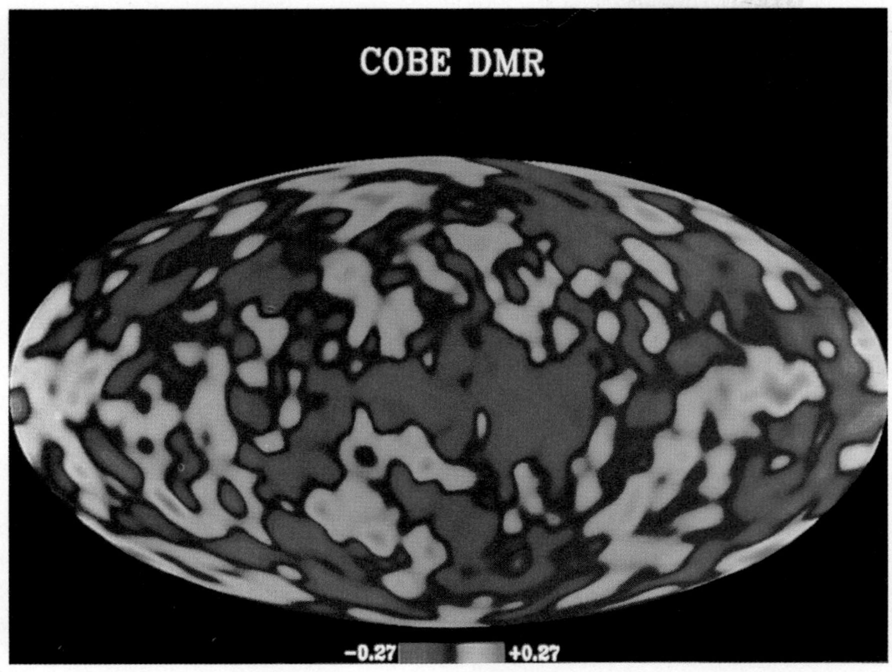

In this microwave map of our Milky Way Galaxy using the latest "hard" science instruments, notice the estimate of "measurement error" underneath the image.

that the task of the investigator is not simply to turn those tools on the face of the cosmos—or society—and observe the truth. Real scientific research is a practical matter of finding the best tool for the job and then using it properly.

Experimentation

experimentation—a research strategy that creates an artificial situation in order to simplify reality and highlight variables of interest.

In the course of writing this book, the authors often discussed what is in the minds of college students. If we really knew, this could be the perfect text: challenging without being boring, entertaining without insulting the intelligence, linking the best sociological ideas to examples straight from your life. One of the problems with student mind-reading is the personal variability of students. "Every person is unique" is a cliché that makes sociologists suspicious, but there are known attitudinal differences among students varying by age, gender, race, income, hometown, religion, major, SAT score, and residential status. Each of these nine variables (and there are dozens more), exerts its influence on personal opinion, and *all operate simultaneously on each student.* Consequently, untangling some "pure" student opinion from the thicket of group differences is indeed a tall order.

This sort of research problem is not unique to sociology. Physicists studying the mechanics of spin rotation must also consider mass and air resistance. Psychologists studying visual persistence must first account for image speed and light intensity. And astronomers mapping galaxies must deal with relative acceleration and radioactive decay. It seems as though reality itself deliberately tangles interesting variables in knots of complicating factors. One way to untie these knots is to build a system that simplifies reality.

In our search for true student opinion about this book, the authors might find two private, liberal arts colleges known to enroll mainly traditional-age resident students of upper-middle-class suburban backgrounds. To students in College A, we could submit a version of Chapter 3 without Box 3:1; to college B students would go the present version complete with Box 3:1. Because the students in these comparison colleges are much more similar to each other than to college students in general, variations in opinion due to many of the above-mentioned variables would be screened out. This would permit us to more directly assess the impact of Box 3:1 on readers' minds. What suspicions occur to you concerning this research procedure?

While you harbor these suspicions, be aware that a formalized version of this approach is the backbone of the natural sciences. It is known as the "classical" experimental design, and is represented as follows:

		Time 1		Time 2
EXPERIMENTAL GROUP	*R*	Y_1	*X*	Y_2
CONTROL GROUP	*R*	Y_1		Y_2

causality—a situation in which a change in one variable (the independent variable) produces a change in another variable (the dependent variable).

The goal of the sciences, simply put, is to figure out causality. This much-abused term defines a situation in which a change in one variable (call it *X*, the *independent variable*) produces a change in another variable (here known as *Y*, the *dependent variable*). The logical structure sketched above is designed to be a sieve, screening complicating factors out of the experimental soup so that only the key causal process remains at the bottom of the bowl.

Imagine that a health research team received a grant to investigate the cancer-causing properties of caramel candy in a study using rats. The first

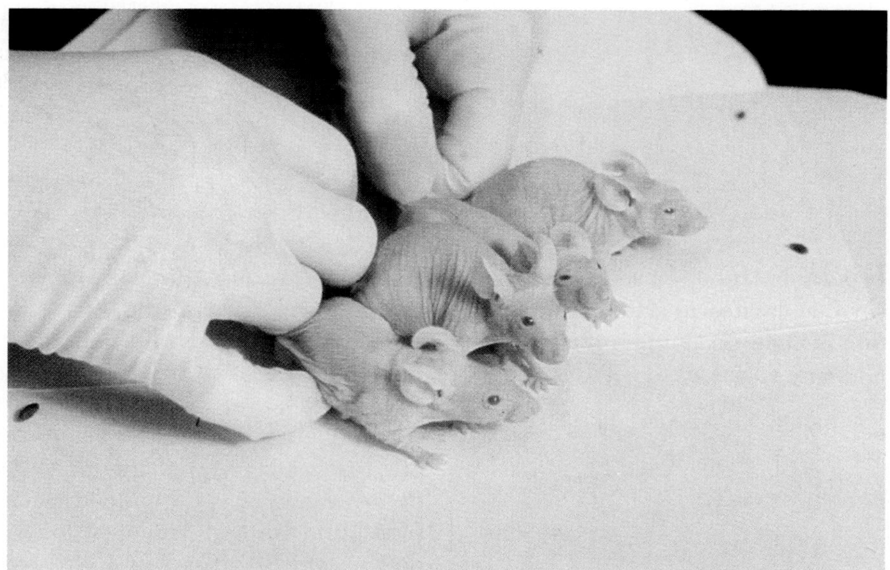

In contrast to this scene of an experimenter handling laboratory rats, sociological researchers must cope with the fact that human subjects are much more difficult to "handle."

experimental group—subjects in an experiment exposed to the experimental stimulus of the independent variable.

control group—subjects in an experiment not exposed to the experimental stimulus of the independent variable.

randomization—the method by which subjects are assigned to either the experimental or control group according to the rules of chance.

step in the classical experimental procedure is to equally divide the rats into the **experimental group**—those to be deliberately exposed to the experimental "stimulus"—and the **control group**—those to be deliberately not exposed. This division is accomplished through **randomization**, where the choice of group is dictated through the rules of chance (such as a coin flip; see *R* in the diagram). This minimizes the likelihood of more cancer-prone rats ending up in either group. The rationale for this procedure was termed the "method of difference" by philosopher of science John Stuart Mill (1891). The experimental ideal is for the two groups to be identical, with the only "difference" being to which group the experimental subjects were assigned. All the other real-world factors tied up with caramel eating and cancerous tumors are thereby cleared away. At Time 1, there is a measurement of the dependent variable, in this case the number of tumors (Y_1); they are counted again at Time 2 (Y_2) after the one group has been exposed to the sticky experimental stimulus (caramel, X). If the rate of tumor increase in the experimental group significantly exceeds that found in the control group, this is indeed evidence that caramel causes cancer, and it may be time to call the Surgeon General's office.

One reason for presenting the familiar example of rat research is that it dramatizes the extreme level of control available to some experimenters. By contrast, the causal processes of interest to sociologists are entangled in the extraordinary thicket known as society, which is inhabited by creatures more difficult to handle than rats. Procedures designed to trim that thicket may not suit the interests of stubborn human beings. One of the authors (B.J.J.) recently worked on a grant to evaluate the effects of a drug use prevention program experimentally implemented in five public school districts. The key research question was simple: Does exposure to this program reduce drug use by students? Getting all involved parties to agree to a workable research design was anything but simple. In the first place, parents in some school districts objected to direct measures of their children's actual drug use (Y_1 and Y_2 in the diagram), for fear of "putting ideas in kids' heads." In convincing the objectors that such measures are necessary to prove that the program works, the research team encountered another objection by the school districts: What if the program *does* work, and some of their students have been deprived of it because they were randomly assigned to the control group? The apparent desirability of the program led to lobbying to scrap the classical experimental design that would have provided the best proof of its real desirability. For an even more vivid example, an experiment to determine that the anti-AIDS drug AZT is safe and effective for children had to be redesigned in mid-course. The involved parties simply could not bear to administer a "placebo" (an alternative or fake drug for the control group) to children who might be sacrificed to reveal the efficacy of AZT.

subject—a participant in an experiment.

The key issue raised by both these studies is researcher versus subject (i.e., experimental participants) control. The classical experimental design maximizes control by the researcher, whereas the subjects here are attempting to wrestle away the choice of which group they will "select." Such *selection* can contaminate the experiment because the subjects volunteering themselves into one group can be very *different* from those in the other group *before* X is introduced. Imagine an experiment to determine the effect of eating ice cream on mood. If such a study were advertised on your campus, which students would flock to the free ice-cream booth (X)? Which students would avoid X, thus making themselves eligible for the control group? This self-sorting process would be driven by personal preference rather than R (randomization). A perfectly plausible result is that both groups would have similar average mood levels at Y_1, but that the ice-cream lovers in the experimental group would experience a major mood improvement by Y_2 as a result of satisfying their craving; those in the control group, meanwhile, would likely have unchanged moods. Does this mean that eating ice cream causes positive mood swings in human beings? No. It means that the dice were unfairly loaded by turning the choice of participation over to the experimental subjects, thus building in a bias toward the effects of X. This example is less trivial than it might seem. Consider how many experimenters advertise for paid volunteers on your campus; students needing the money are more likely to sign up. Similarly, which prisoners volunteer for experimental rehabilitation projects? Motives will differ—some prisoners could be sincerely motivated to change, some cynically attempting to impress the parole board. Here is the point: The greed, sincerity, or cynicism accompanying volunteers into the experimental group means they are different from control group members. This entangles such personal differences with the effects of the experimental "stimulus," thus obscuring cause and effect.

The general problem is that the social experimenter may lack sufficient control to carry out a pure form of the classical experiment. There are times and places, though, in which the experimenter does achieve substantial control over human subjects. One such case is spotlighted in Box 3:1, which describes how Philip Zimbardo and his colleagues examined the sources of prison oppression. After a selective screening at the school for "niceness," two dozen students were assigned by the random process of a coin flip to be either "prisoners" or "guards" in the mock prison set up in a dormitory over a mid-semester vacation. As the events described in Box 3:1 make clear, it was no vacation for the subjects. Freed of the maddening complications of studying real-world prison brutality, Zimbardo's artificial world seems to offer a direct look at the situation of confinement and its human consequences. But project yourself into this experimental world. Would you ever really forget that you were a college student convict—not a real "con"? If assigned to be a guard, could you ever lose sight of the fact that there were researchers around?

reactivity—artificial alterations in behavior created by an awareness of being studied.

These questions concern the problem of reactivity, the artificial alterations in behavior created by an awareness of being studied. This general

BOX 3:1 COLLEGE EXPERIENCE

A Prison Experiment

In an attempt to understand just what it means psychologically to be a prisoner or a prison guard, Craig Haney, Curt Banks, Dave Jaffe and I [Philip Zimbardo] created our own prison. We carefully screened over 70 volunteers who answered an ad in a Palo Alto city newspaper and ended up with about two dozen young men who were selected to be part of this study. They were mature, emotionally stable, normal, intelligent college students from middle-class homes throughout the United States and Canada. They appeared to represent the cream of the crop of this generation. None had any criminal record and all were relatively homogeneous on many dimensions initially.

Half were arbitrarily designated as prisoners by a flip of a coin, the others as guards. These were the roles they were to play in our simulated prison. The guards were made aware of the potential seriousness and danger of the situation and their own vulnerability. They made up their own formal rules for maintaining law, order and respect, and were generally free to improvise new ones during their eight-hour, three-man shifts. The prisoners were unexpectedly picked up at their homes by a city policeman in a squad car, searched, handcuffed, fingerprinted, booked at the Palo Alto station house and taken blindfolded to our jail. There they were stripped, deloused, put into a uniform, given a number and put into a cell with two other prisoners where they expected to live for the next two weeks.

We observed and recorded and video-taped the events that occurred in the prison, and we interviewed and tested the prisoners and guards at various points throughout the study. . . .

At the end of only six days we had to close down our mock prison because what we saw was frightening. It was no longer apparent to most of the subjects (or to us) where reality ended and their roles began. The majority had indeed become prisoners or guards, no longer able to clearly differentiate between role playing and self. There were dramatic changes in virtually every aspect of their behavior, thinking and feeling. In less than a week the experience of imprisonment undid (temporarily) a life-time of learning; human values were suspended, self-concepts were challenged and the ugliest, most base, pathological side of human nature surfaced. We were horrified because we saw some boys (guards) treat others as if they were despicable animals, taking pleasure in cruelty, while other boys (prisoners) became servile, dehumanized robots who thought only of escape, of their own individual survival and of their mounting hatred for the guards.

We had to release three prisoners in the first four days because they had such acute situational traumatic reactions as hysterical crying, confusion in thinking and severe depression. Others begged to be paroled, and all but three were willing to forfeit all the money they had earned if they could be paroled. By then (the fifth day) they had been so programmed to think of themselves as prisoners that when their request for parole was denied, they returned docilely to their cells. Now, had they been thinking as college

source of experimental contamination was tipped off by the well-known "Hawthorne effect," so called because of its discovery in the work of industrial sociologists at Western Electric's Hawthorne plant in Chicago (Roethlisberger and Dickson, 1939). They introduced various experimental changes in the work environment (such as changing lighting intensity), *all* of which seemed to cause increases in worker productivity; it soon became apparent that the real causal factor was the Hawthorne workers' accommodating desire to do what they thought was expected of them in the fishbowl of the experiment. As social creatures, people naturally tend to react to observation. Like any tool, the experimental strategy has built-in

BOX 3:1 COLLEGE EXPERIENCE *continued*

students acting in an oppressive experiment, they would have quit. . . . However, the reality was not quitting an experiment but "being paroled by the parole board from the Stanford County Jail." By the last days, the earlier solidarity among the prisoners systematically broken by the guards dissolved into "each man for himself." Finally, when one of their fellows was put in solitary confinement (a small closet) for refusing to eat, the prisoners were given a choice by one of the guards: give up their blankets and the incorrigible prisoner would be let out, or keep their blankets and he would be kept in all night. They voted to keep their blankets and to abandon their brother.

About a third of the guards became tyrannical in their arbitrary use of power, in enjoying their control over other people. They were corrupted by the power of their roles and became quite inventive in their techniques of breaking the spirit of the prisoners and making them feel they were worthless. Some of the guards merely did their jobs as tough but fair correctional officers, and several were good guards from the prisoners' point of views since they did them small favors and were friendly. However, no good guard ever interfered with a command by any of the bad guards; they never intervened on the side of the prisoners, they never told the others to ease off because it was only an experiment, and they never even came to me as prison superintendent or experimenter in charge to complain. In part, they were good because the others were bad; they needed the others to help establish their own egos in a positive light. In a sense, the good guards perpetuated the prison more than the other guards because their own needs to be liked prevented them from disobeying or violating the implicit guards' code. At the same time, the act of befriending the prisoners created a social reality which made the prisoners less likely to rebel.

By the end of the week the experiment had become a reality, as if it were a Pirandello play directed by Kafka that just keeps going after the audience has left. The consultant for our prison, Carlo Prescott, an ex-convict with 16 years of imprisonment in California's jails, would get so depressed and furious each time he visited our prison, because of its psychological similarity to his experiences, that he would have to leave. A Catholic priest who was a former prison chaplain in Washington, D.C., talked to our prisoners after four days and said they were just like the other first-timers he had seen.

But in the end, I called off the experiment not because of the horror I saw out there in the prison yard, but because of the horror of realizing that I could have easily traded places with the most brutal guard or become the weakest prisoner full of hatred at being so powerless that I could not eat, sleep or go to the toilet without permission of the authorities.

Critical Thinking Questions

1. What biases could have been introduced into Zimbardo's findings due to the exclusive use of male subjects in this experiment?
2. If this experimental setting were made less "artificial" by, for example, using real ex-prisoners rather than college students as subjects, what changes might have occurred?

Source: Philip G. Zimbardo, "Pathology of Imprisonment." In *Society*, Vol. 9, pp. 4–6.

strengths and weaknesses. Adjusting the dials to increase the experimenter's control over subjects creates a powerful device for peeling away the complications of social reality. However, it also turns up the pressure on subjects to behave according to the promptings of the device watching them.

There is another design flaw that often accompanies experimental control: the "captive population" effect. The locked doors in Philip Zimbardo's study are not all that unusual. In reviewing the experimental literature to write this section, the authors had an embarrassment of riches. Literally hundreds of experiments have been performed on college students, many

The correctional facility at Camp Hill, Pennsylvania, was in flames during a prison riot in 1992. The Zimbardo experiment described in Box 3:1 was designed to isolate the source of prison brutality.

of them the freshmen or sophomores who are the prime audience for this book. Why? *Because you are there.* Like prisoners, hospital patients, and drug addicts, you are a member of an institution commandeered by practicing social scientists and subject to the experimental mazes they construct. Not all segments of the U.S. population are so susceptible to experimental control. Turn the question this way: Do undergraduates differ from other people? The marketing ads in your student newspaper certainly suggest that this is so. The ads are mostly pitched at literate 18–22-year-olds with some disposable income. If your demographic segment is unique enough for specialized marketing campaigns, it probably has unique responses to experimental stimuli. One of the criticisms aimed at Philip Zimbardo's study, in fact, is that his hand-selected "cream of the crop" college students could hardly be *less* similar to the profile of a prison population. At issue is generalizability, the degree to which the conclusions of the research can be extended to people outside the study. The more diverse and representative experimental subjects are, the more generalizable the research results. Unfortunately, cross-sections of different types of people are notoriously difficult to round up for experimental manipulation.

generalizability—**the degree to which conclusions can be extended to the population outside of study participants.**

Participant Observation

The strength of experimentation is also its weakness. An artificial world created to magnify one causal process may be so artificial that it loses its relevance to the real world. There is a simple solution: Go out into the world and look. Instead of the experimental approach outlined by the authors at the beginning of the last section, we could seek the opinion of students about this text by going "undercover." Disguised as a paunchy, overage student, one author could enroll in a class in which these chapters were required reading. The author could then tag along to lunches, and maybe even organize a study group for discussing the text. Think of the advantages! No laboratories, no subject screenings, no formal measurements . . .

Instead, there is the thrill of discovering "on-the-street" opinions of real people in their natural, student setting. Although you might be impressed by such an exotic effort to see what is really on students' minds, is this a perfect form of mind-reading?

participant observation—the researcher participates in the group process in order to observe its natural functioning.

Some of the most insightful studies in modern sociology have been performed through **participant observation**, in which the investigator participates in the group process in order to observe its natural functioning. Consider the seemingly simple term "investigator." One very complex issue concerns that person's identity, and the extent to which it will be revealed to the people under study. It is useful to analyze this decision on a scale of "Observer Visibility":

FIGURE 3:1 OBSERVER VISIBILITY

– ├────────────────┤ +

full disguise — full disclosure

At the high end of the scale (+) is "full disclosure," in which the true identity and purposes of the research are fully revealed to those under observation. This is highly desirable from an ethical standpoint because the researchees have no false pretenses when they confide in the researcher ("full disclosure" is actually a legal term). However, such a completely open approach may result in doors completely closing in one's face. Some of the most fascinating populations for study are very uneasy about public awareness. This is obviously true for youth gangs, organized crime operations, and crack-addict networks, all of whom should be studied for theoretical and practical reasons, and all of whom would run—or worse—from full disclosure. Even if one does get inside the subjects' social world, extremely high Observer Visibility can be problematical. Rather than behaving normally in their natural setting, people acutely aware of being watched may sanitize their behavior to get a sympathetic treatment by the observer, thereby producing the kind of reactivity found in the most artificial of experiments.

The extreme other end of the Observer Visibility scale has the researcher literally undercover. The more complete the investigator's disguise, the

A police bust at a neighborhood crack house involves sociological phenomena that can be neither duplicated in an experiment nor reported in a survey.

This painting by Jacob Lawrence depicts the mass migration of African Americans from the rural south to northern cities, including the site of *All Our Kin* in Box 3:2.

BOX 3:2 GENDER AND SOCIAL CHANGE

Participant Observation among the Poor

In the spring of 1968 I began this study of urban poverty and the "domestic strategies" of urban-born black Americans whose parents had migrated from the South to The Flats. Having just completed a study of patterns of black migration to Northern cities, I chose to concentrate on family life among second-generation urban dwellers, many of whom were raised on public welfare (AFDC). I was interested to find out how such families cooperated to produce an adaptive strategy to cope with poverty and racism.

In this study I found extensive networks of kin and friends supporting, reinforcing each other—devising schemes for self-help, strategies for survival in a community of severe economic deprivation. My purpose in this book is to illustrate the collective adaptations to poverty of men, women, and children within the social–cultural network of the urban black family. I became poignantly aware of the alliances of individuals trading and exchanging goods, resources, and the care of children, the intensity of their acts of domestic cooperation, and the exchange of goods and services among these persons, both kin and non-kin. Their social and economic lives were so entwined that not to repay on an exchange meant that someone else's child would not eat. People would tell me, "You have to have help from everybody and anybody," and "the poorer you are, the more likely you are to pay back."

I spent almost three years in The Flats attempting to understand the complexities of their exchange system. I tried to learn how participants in domestic exchanges were defined by one another, what performances and behavior they expected of one another, who was eligible to become a part of the cooperative networks, how they were recruited, and what kept participants actively involved in the series of exchanges. I naturally became involved in these exchanges. If someone asked a favor of me, later I asked a favor of him. If I gave a scarf, a skirt, or a cooking utensil to a woman who admired it, later on when she had something I liked she would usually give it to me. Little by little as I learned the rules of giving and reciprocity, I tried them out.

Eventually the children of those I was closest to would stay lesser the problems of access and reactivity. But there are problems on the left side of the scale that are remarkably similar to those fictionalized in spy and police melodramas. First, there are the sticky ethical (and even legal) issues attached to deception. These may render information inadmissible in court and/or sociology journals. A second and related issue is the emotional strain of staying "in character" for the extended period of time (it can be years) necessary for subjects to drop their emotional guard and reveal themselves fully (Shaffir, Stebbins, and Turowetz, 1980). Aside from the possible dangers of being unmasked by a group on the wrong side of the law, no one wants to face accusations of betraying trust—especially if they are true.

Because of the dangers at the extremes, most observers adopt a research stance nearer to the middle of the scale. Full disguise of the investigator's identity is often impossible anyway (e.g., Carol Stack in Box 3:2 is white whereas the subjects she studied are African Americans). One way to minimize the disruptions to the group of having a social scientist in their midst is to gain "progressive entree" (Johnson, 1975). By increasing one's presence in stages—attending some group functions, then a few more, eventually becoming a steady member—the participant–observer comes to be

BOX 3:2 GENDER AND SOCIAL CHANGE *continued*

overnight or several days at my apartment, and my son stayed at their homes. I found that among kin and friends in The Flats, temporary child-exchange is a symbol of mutual trust. It provides a means of acquiring self-esteem. People began accepting my trust and respect when I trusted my son with them.

By such informal circulation of children in The Flats, the poor facilitated the distribution and exchange of the limited resources available to them. Some of my colleagues strongly advised me to enter the black community through the older black establishment; they cited various reasons: contacts were available; the research setting, they argued, was physically dangerous to a white person and I might need sponsorship and protection that such contacts could provide; and tradition dictated such a procedure. I decided instead to find my own means of entree. I decided to circumvent the obvious centers of influence—the pastors, the politicians—and try to reach families without resorting to middlemen. Through my own efforts and good luck I came to know a young woman who had grown up on welfare in The Flats and had since come to my university. She agreed to introduce me to families she had known as she was growing up there. She would introduce me to two unrelated families and from then on I would be on my own.

During the following months Ruby and I began to spend a great deal of time together and with our children. Ruby's attitudes toward men, kin, friends, and children shook many of my views, and I am still in the process of reshaping them today. For her part Ruby would get mad, amazed, and amused at some of the views I held. Whenever I expressed hesitation or uneasiness about my own ability to make it alone, with my child, Ruby would be very angry, providing me with numerous examples of women around The Flats who were doing so. Ruby was probing, observing, and interpreting my perceptions just as I was doing with hers. At times over the three years of our friendship, we would find many ways to test our perceptions of one another. . . .

Critical Thinking Questions

1. What changes in Observer Visibility and Observer Participation would occur if Carol Stack were Carl Stack (i.e., if the researcher had been a male)?
2. What are the scientific pluses and minuses of simply interviewing a cross-section of poor people from many areas, compared with using participant observation as in *All Our Kin*?

Source: Carol B. Stack, *All Our Kin* (1975). New York: Harper & Row, pp. 27–29, xi, 14–16.

a familiar part of the social world, thus reducing reactivity. Another technique to preserve as much as possible of the group's natural behavior is known as "defocusing"; that is, "describing a research project in general terms without detailing highly specific goals or procedures" (Phillips, 1985, p. 306). An example of this compromise between disguise and disclosure would be the author–student in our "text study" announcing that he is attending study sessions to "gain insights into how college students actually learn the material." This is a deliberately ambiguous statement, which discloses to students the general area of interest, but disguises the precise point of inquiry (i.e., their personal reactions to the written chapters). People have a hypnotic, almost perverse fascination with a topic once they know it to be the investigator's area of special attention. Hard experience has taught that a more explicit statement to students would render them especially self-conscious and misleading—in short, reactive—about the very subject under scrutiny.

However well-planned the investigation, it is important to remember that what is being investigated is an autonomous human world that does not willingly yield all social control to the investigator. In a study of "pick-up behavior" at singles bars, Natalie Allon told male and female patrons that she was interviewing them for research purposes. "Some said that doing research was a most clever introductory greeting, and they were going to try such a line . . ." (Allon, 1979, pp. 68–69). While she tried to achieve full disclosure, Allon's nonexperimental subjects imposed their own meanings on the situation, forcing her to a compromise position on the Observer Visibility scale.

Social observation is not a passive act. The researcher who hangs around, asks questions, and probes people's feelings is a part of the action being studied. The degree to which the researcher intervenes in the subjects' social world is again best viewed as a strategic continuum:

FIGURE 3:2 OBSERVER PARTICIPATION

Part of the attraction of participant observation is the richness of insight to be gained from being "on the inside," at the center of group activity. A central principle of science, moreover, is for the investigator to control events to better understand their meaning. These are both reasons an observer might seek group "leadership," thus steering its course toward the topic of special interest. The dangers of this course are apparent in the author-as-student example. If one of us becomes the director of a student study group and focuses discussion on this text, it changes the slower, less direct—but more natural—social process by which opinions normally form. If an author instead poses as a quiet, minimally participating "marginal" member of the group, the text opinions may evolve naturally but not be shared with "marginal" members. Moreover, even the most peripheral member exerts some group effects. In a classic study, a team of researchers joined a "Doomsday cult" and deliberately remained on the cult's quiet fringe of members. The team concluded that their silent, seemingly supportive presence solidified the group's belief that the world was about to end (Festinger, Riecken, and Schachter, 1956).

Aside from undue researcher influence upon the group under study, there is the issue of the group influencing the *researcher*. Participant–observers are people, not recording machines. They may come to sympathize and identify with group members ("going native"), or they may despise subjects with whom they are intensely involved. Either way, powerful personal emotions can involve the investigator. This is why some proponents of participant observation say that a truly "objective" reporting of events is impossible (Denzin, 1989). Investigators generally try to avoid the excesses of the technique by steering a middle course on the Observer Participation scale. "Moderate involvement" is some defense against emotional entanglements, and it seeks a balance between controlling events and missing the boat.

Box 3:2 puts the strengths and weaknesses of the participant observation research strategy on clear display. Let us first locate Carol Stack's study in relation to the crossed scales of Observer Visibility and Participation, which is a useful exercise for any such study.

FIGURE 3:3 OBSERVER VISIBILITY BY OBSERVER PARTICIPATION

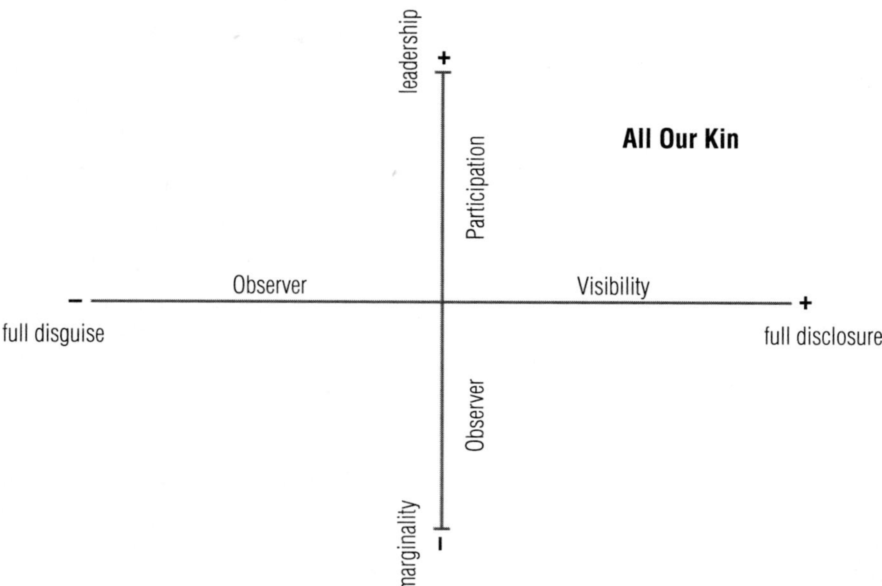

Carol Stack's race and university background automatically place her on the high side of Visibility, although she describes a process of gradual acceptance that undoubtedly reduced the reactivity of her less-educated African American informants. This process was activated in part by Stack's immersion in the chores and social life of the "Flats" families. This active Observer Participation was stepped up by her purchase of a car, unusual enough in this impoverished community that she became the designated driver for sick children or food to be shared. The precise position of *All Our Kin* in the upper-right quadrant of the diagram was strongly steered by Carol Stack's gender. If the investigator were not a woman—and, in particular, a single woman with a child—it is doubtful that she could have achieved "progressive entree," and a near certainty that she would have been denied such intimate participation in these maternally centered families. During the "War on Poverty" of the sixties, this study offered a glimpse of the "feminization of poverty," one of the major social changes affecting slum communities today.

It is quite obvious in the passages quoted in Box 3:2 that Carol Stack's participation deeply touched her, and doubtless also affected the feelings and attitudes of the people she touched. This is not the account of a recording machine. But assuming that Carol Stack sufficiently distanced herself from her emotional entanglements to give us an objective account, just how *typical* are Ruby and her associates? This is one set of kinfolk in one slum neighborhood in one Midwestern city. There are no data to determine how typical these families are even for the African American poor in "The Flats," let alone for Chicanos in Seattle or whites in Appalachia. The problem is generalizability, and it is a general one for participant observation studies because of the time and energy that must be expended to get inside even a small social world. But there can be revelations. Carol Stack discovered a form of social organization—the "kin-based exchange network"—that had been missed by poverty scholars using other research methods.

Survey Research

respondent—a participant in a survey.

You have been a participant (known as a **respondent**) in a survey. We can say this with near certainty not only because of the wide use of this sociological strategy by every branch of society, but also because you are a college student. To get into college, you had to take the Scholastic Aptitude Test (SAT); to determine your residency status you had to return forms to the college checking "on-campus housing" or "commuter"; your tuition is in part the result of educational funding decisions based on the massive survey known as the U.S. Census. These personal examples may be multiplied by what you find in your campus mailbox today.

By comparison to the other two major strategies discussed, survey research depends more heavily on *asking people questions*. In both experimentation and participant observation, the researcher is there to see what goes on. Surveys make people reporters about their own knowledge, attitudes, and behavior. The authors used this approach on students reading early drafts of these text chapters. Instead of experimentally comparing student reactions or spying on study sessions, we passed out forms at the end of courses asking students to tell us, in their own words, the "positive aspects" and the "negative aspects" of the chapters they reviewed. Most—but not all—of the students returned this simple survey. Some—but not all—signed their comments. Before examining the technical issues involved, how far would you trust these student responses?

Sampling

It has been said before: Survey research is the most common form of applied investigation of human beings. It is also the strategy of choice for many sociological scholars. The rise of survey research among both practitioners and professionals has not occurred because it is an error-free approach, but rather because surveys are strong where other strategies are weak. Consider the issue of generalizability, now familiar because it has been discussed as a common weakness of both experiments and participant observation studies. Survey techniques have developed in close conjunction with the techniques of scientific sampling, whereby the respondents are chosen by formula rather than by convenience. Generally, a **sample** is a set of units systematically selected from the larger population about which the researcher wishes to generalize. Let's face it, researchers really don't care about the opinions of the people in the study; their real concern is about the much larger body of persons those in the study *represent*. The real issue, then, is whether the sample is a mini-version of the population in all its human diversity. What techniques can be depended on to build a small-scale "replica" of the population?

sample—a set of people systematically selected from the larger population about which the researcher wishes to generalize.

bias—a distortion introduced into a study by improper sampling or measurement procedures.

How about the mall surveys conducted by the marketing research firms stationed there? Do they truly represent national consumer tastes about a product? No. Think about the distortion—technically known as **bias**—in this reflection of society. First, such surveys are automatically restricted to mall-goers, and mall-goers are not a representative cross-section of the general population. Homemakers, the elderly, and, especially, teenagers frequent malls all out of proportion to their statistical representation in society (and this disproportion is even more extreme at certain hours of the day). Moreover, these already atypical mall-goers are not equally likely to be surveyed. Just among teenagers, those willing to submit to a public interview are the outgoing, verbal types not afraid of looking uncool to their friends; insecure teenagers therefore have their opinions underrepresented. Now consider the built-in distortion of the sex polls conducted by popular magazines. Sampling bias is evident in their wildly contradictory findings about the intimate behavior of the same American population. One *Cosmopolitan* study (over 100,000 respondents) found that 54 percent of wives in the United States have been sexually unfaithful; a *Ladies Home Journal* survey (over 83,000 respondents) taken the same year found only 21 percent to have strayed sexually, and 85 percent to be basically satisfied with their married sex lives! To break down the bias, begin with the distribution of these surveys. Generally, they are included as tear-out forms in the magazines themselves. Are the readers of *Cosmo* or *LHJ*—the only people with a chance to participate—a true cross-section of the American population? The magazines' marketing departments can tell you that they are disproportionally female, middle- to upper-class and have distinctive political and consumer profiles (as reflected in the advertising). Again, the typical respondent is probably not even a typical magazine reader. Those who take the trouble to rip out the form are undoubtedly *different* from the many who flip past it, especially in their attitudes toward the topic being surveyed. The huge numbers of respondents in these polls just magnify the distortion, thus creating a fun-house mirror image of the population.

The "singles" bar is a prototypical setting for marital infidelity. Generalizing about such intimate matters beyond such settings requires the techniques of scientific survey sampling.

random sample—a procedure in which all population units have an equal probability of being selected.

These two cases of how *not* to do it set up the scientific solution to the sampling problem: Depend on the laws of chance. This simple principle sometimes requires heroic measures, but it has enormous power. Physicists count seemingly infinite stars by carefully selecting portions of the skyfield. On a less cosmic scale, TV ratings companies generalize about the viewing habits of a whole nation of roughly 250 million people from a sample consisting of only about 4,000 families! Most national surveys—including presidential polls—sample approximately 1,000 people (look under the poll results' tables in any news magazine). The main technique for constituting these tiny, well-made mirrors of gigantic populations is the **random sample**, in which all population units have an equal probability of selection. To show how this technique works, say you have been assigned the task of randomly selecting ten of your sociology classmates to evaluate the professor's teaching. Follow these straightforward steps:

1. *Get a list of the population.* For this task, you could compile the list yourself by passing around a sheet of paper. Once you have all of the names in the class population, scramble them by arranging the names in alphabetical order; this will prevent the "clumping" of smarter or friendlier or more critical students next to one another on the list. Once alphabetized, simply assign numbers 00 through 99 to the names (we'll assume a class size of 100; note that 00–99 = 100 units).
2. *Get a randomizing device.* This sounds technical, but all it really means is a way of giving each unit an equal chance of being chosen. Assuming that they are of identical size and are thoroughly mixed, putting the 100 student numbers on bingo balls in a canister or on slips of paper in a hat would do the trick. A less cumbersome technique is to use a "random numbers table," a portion of which we reproduce here.

24	72	03	85	49	24
51	82	86	43	73	84
78	44	63	13	58	25
77	80	26	89	87	44
33	62	62	19	29	03

Source: M.G. Kendall and B.B. Smith, *Tables of Random Sampling Numbers.* Copyright 1939 by Cambridge University Press. Reprinted by permission.

3. *Draw the sample.* Now, by definition this computer-generated table (many pages of which can be found in any statistics book) lists randomly mixed numbers no matter where you begin and in any direction you move. Play pin-the-tail-on-the-donkey with your index finger; say it lands on 86 in the third column. You may now select your ten classmates by proceeding down the columns: 86, 63, 26, 62 (to next column), 85, 43, 13, 89, 19 (to next column), 49. The names corresponding to these numbers constitute your random sample.

The advantages of this form of sampling over looser methods are both obvious and subtle. It should be obvious that the random technique is more likely to get a cross-section of student opinion about the teacher than would a direct "Who wants to evaluate our professor?" appeal. The latter would likely oversample disgruntled students and brown-nosers. Short of polling everyone, though, no sampling process can guarantee a perfect, no-bias replica of the population. The less obvious advantage of random techniques is the ability to *estimate the chance of sampling error.* All forms of

THE NATIONAL OPINION RESEARCH CENTER'S (NORC) GENERAL SOCIAL SURVEY (GSS)

What is the NORC General Social Survey?

The General Social Survey data come from personal interviews administered to NORC national samples using a standard questionnaire with identical questions appearing in every survey or according to a rotation pattern.

It contains items of general interest to social scientists and to social indicator researchers. The survey is also part of a data diffusion project. Social scientists, students—or anyone else—may obtain copies of the data at cost immediately upon completion of field work and data preparation.

What are the purposes?

There are two basic purposes: one is to measure trends (and constants) in social characteristics and opinions, the other is to make fresh, interesting, high-quality data available to social scientists and students who may not be affiliated with large research centers.

What time periods are covered?

The first General Social Survey was conducted in March of 1972. . . . Since some of the baseline items are repeated from surveys going back to the late 1930's, selected trend comparisons can be made for the entire post-World War II period. . . .

What is the sample?

The sample is a national cross-section of adults, 18 years of age and older. [The current sampling plan is a "multi-stage probability" design, meaning that randomizing techniques are applied to pick smaller and smaller social units. The first "stage" is the Standard Metropolitan Statistical Areas (SMSAs) devised by the U.S. Census Bureau. Within the SMSAs selected, there is a random selection of some block groups (BG; about ten blocks each), and then random selection of actual blocks at this third "stage." Interviews are conducted with a quota (i.e., a preset number) of individuals based on age, gender, and employment status only from the selected blocks. . . .]

How can I obtain the data?

Distribution of the data sets is handled by the Roper Center, University of Connecticut, Box 440, Storrs, CT 06268 (AC 203-4864882/4440). Users do *not* have to belong to the Roper Center. Inter-University Consortium for Political and Social Research members can obtain the data through that institution at no cost.

Source: "The NORC General Social Survey: Questions and Answers." Revised and updated, July 1987. Author's paraphrased insert indicated by brackets.

probability sampling—a procedure in which the chance of a unit's selection is known in advance, and therefore the chance of sampling error can be estimated.

sampling frame—the list of population units from which a sample is drawn.

probability sampling—in which the probability of a given unit's selection is known in advance—have this advantage. For both your random sample and the much more elaborate multi-stage sample described in the GSS insert, the amount of sampling error is a known quantity. Presidential polls generally report not only the percentage of support for each candidate, but also the percentage level of error. This is quite like physicists giving the number of stars in the Milky Way galaxy within a certain plus/minus range.

So much care goes into the sample selection process that investigators often neglect a more basic question: Selection from what? The sampling frame is the list of population units from which a sample is drawn. If the list has deletions and distortions, they will reappear in even the most perfect selection process. Consider the simple instruction to pass around a sheet on which to write the names of your classmates. Did you stop to think about absences? A class list from the registrar would probably be an improvement, but it might exclude late sign-ups or students who have not paid their tuition bills. Application of the random numbers table *cannot* represent members of the student population not appearing on the list. An oft-used sampling frame in applied research is the phone book. Pick up your local edition and think about who is missing. Two obvious exclusions are people who lack a telephone and people who have unlisted numbers. The trouble is that such exclusions can be connected with other human

Probability sampling permits an estimate of sampling error, shown as "Margin of Error: 2 Points" in a national survey of President Clinton's "approval rating."

BOX 3:3 A BRIEFING ON THE CENSUS

Although it is not one of our regular boxed features, this selection has been chosen to introduce you to the methodological issues underlying the many 1990 U.S. Census figures cited in chapters to come.

After many years of planning and preparation, the census is here: for the twenty-first consecutive time, the nation is conducting its decennial enumeration. The Census Bureau has its first female director, market researcher Barbara Bryant. The post office is to deliver questionnaires to about 88 million housing units in March and census officials hope that people will complete them and mail them back for Census Day, April 1. Sociologists past and present have contributed to the development of the census and sociologists are heavy users of census data, in research and teaching. . . .

In most ways the new census is like the 1980 version. Every household will be asked six questions about its housing and seven basic sociodemographic questions, including the age, race, and sex of each resident. . . .

One-sixth of all households will receive a "long form" which includes 26 sociodemographic and 18 housing questions in addition to the 13 basic questions. Items dropped from the 1980 questionnaire are: activity five years ago, disability in using public transportation, carpooling, weeks looking for work, and marital history. New questions include: military service, pension income, time of departure to work, and two items on disabilities.

The basic data collection procedure will be the same as in the 1980 "Mailout-mailback" for 83 percent of the nation's 106 million housing units. In rural areas, census enumerators rather than postal carriers will deliver the forms and ask people to mail them back; 11 million households will be contacted this way. In very sparsely populated areas, representing seven million housing units, enumerators will conduct face-to-face interviews. Later, the Census Bureau will send enumerators to addresses from which no questionnaires were received. There has been a large-scale outreach program including advertising and community work to contact leaders and members of minority groups, attempting to elicit their cooperation.

The 1990 Census also incorporates some major changes. Homeless persons will be counted in new ways. Persons in shelters for homeless persons and abused women will be counted on March 20, from 6 p.m. to midnight and persons on the streets will be counted from 2 a.m. to 4 a.m. on March 21. . . .

factors known to influence survey responses. Studies have established that people without phones tend to be poor and people with unlisted numbers tend to be rich. Consequently, a random sample of your phone book would automatically undersample both ends of the income distribution. As the accompanying Box 3:3 illustrates, even the most expensive piece of social research on Earth—the U.S. Census—has population gaps. The trick is for the investigator to be aware of these gaps and try to fill them.

Asking People Questions

From everyday life, you already know it is a tricky business accepting what people say. Human beings lie, exaggerate, bend, fold, spindle, and mutilate the truth. This does not mean that verbal information is useless. After all, you do know all of these distortions can occur, and, as an applied student of human behavior, you can take counter-measures. You carefully phrase questions; you match up different bits of a conversation to make sure they are consistent; you weigh what was said to you versus what was said to others; you use all of these techniques more heavily on sensitive personal issues than you do on matters of simple information. Survey research has taken these skills from the art of conversation and tried to build them into a science of asking people questions.

BOX 3:3 A BRIEFING ON THE CENSUS *continued*

As in the past, several internal research projects are embedded in the census for such purposes as evaluation, measuring public awareness of the census and testing techniques that might be used in the future, such as new forms to the questionnaire. The research program includes a set of ethnographic microstudies in low-income areas. Anthropologists and sociologists have been hired to conduct these studies, which will include mini-censuses, in an attempt to learn more about why the census fails to get a full count of certain categories of persons such as poor, adult, African-American males. Results of the local mini-censuses will be compared with those of the regular census.

Despite these developments, there have been plenty of problems in the gestation of the 1990 Census. Along with a contretemps over the working of the race question, there was also a dispute over whether military personnel abroad and their dependents would be counted for the purpose of the reapportionment of congressional seats. . . .

The biggest controversy, of course, is the undercount and whether to adjust census counts statistically. The undercount signifies that proportion of the population that remains uncounted in the census. Actually, the census regularly produces a differential undercount since African-Americans are missed at a higher rate than whites. Recent research has shown that Hispanic persons are also missed at higher rates. Although each census has a smaller net undercount than its predecessor, the differential persists. Demographic analysis of the 1980 Census showed undercounts of 1.4 percent overall; 5.9 percent for blacks; and 0.7 percent for "white and other races."

The undercount began to be politically important when census numbers became useful in voting rights cases and in the allocation of federal dollars. Two turning points were the 1962 Supreme Court decision, *Baker v. Carr*, that established the one person, one vote principle and the 1965 passage of the Voting Rights Act. Legal disputes over forms of discrimination in legislative districts must invariably rely upon census data as evidence. Census numbers are also important to big city mayors, who contend that their cities get shortchanged by many federal grant programs that distribute funds by means of population-based formulas. Mayors complain that their cities suffer disproportionately because they house larger numbers of those poor minority groups that are most likely to be undercounted.

Source: Harvey M. Choldin, "A Briefing on the Census," In *Footnotes* (March 1990), p. 4.

items—the questions asked in survey research.

response rate—the percentage of the sample actually responding to the survey.

The initial problem is getting people to answer the questions at all. However the questions—known as **items**—are administered, they are useless words on paper unless the respondents respond. This is not as obvious as it sounds. How many "junk mail" surveys have you dumped into the "circular file"? How many prerecorded marketing polls have you hung up on? The percentage of the sample actually responding to the survey—known as the **response rate**—can be as important as the sample itself. To cite one famous case, a 1936 *Literary Digest* poll of U.S. voters predicted that Alf Landon would win when, in fact, Franklin Delano Roosevelt was easily re-elected president. A survey analyst has recently shown that if all those contacted in the sample had responded, FDR would indeed have been chosen as the winner (Squire, 1988). Imagine that only three of the ten students picked for your sample agree to evaluate the teacher. While your first reaction might be to shrug and randomly choose seven more classmates, think about this: *Those who agree to be polled are probably different from those who refuse.* Maybe only students getting A's are willing to register a positive opinion, or maybe only seniors or non-majors are willing to risk teacher retaliation. Whatever the bias, picking seven more students will only magnify it. Surveys with severe response-rate problems of this kind suffer the same kinds of distortions as do experiments in which interested subjects voluntarily "select" their participation (like the ice-cream study mentioned earlier).

The bottom line is that improving response rate improves generalizability. With their eyes on that bottom line, contemporary survey researchers have developed a bag of tricks for enticing respondents to respond (Fox, Crask, and Kim, 1988). Among the more effective techniques are "pre-notification" (telling them they will be surveyed) and "follow-ups" (please respond prompts) of the potential respondents. Interestingly, surveys sponsored by universities receive greater returns than do those sponsored by other kinds of institutions. Some surveys pay people or give prizes for participation (coupons, stickers, etc.). Although these "bribes" do elicit more responses, the value of the prize does not matter; perhaps getting a present just makes people feel the survey is important enough to warrant their personal attention. Even the color of the polling paper appears to influence the rate of return! These survey techniques may appear to be haphazard gimmicks, but they have a unifying feature: They establish the importance of the study to the respondent. Studies that seem to have personal and/or social significance (like the General Social Survey or a well-managed teaching evaluation) energize cooperative respondents. And the higher the response rate, the better the chance of generalizing the truth about the larger population.

mail questionnaire—the survey format in which the items and available responses are prewritten for respondents who must answer and return the instrument by mail.

face-to-face interview—the survey format in which the items are presented to respondents in a personal conversation.

telephone interview—the survey format in which the items are presented to respondents over the telephone.

One of the key questions in any survey is *how* to ask the questions. The three major forms of survey administration are the **mail questionnaire**, in which the items and available responses are prewritten for respondents who must answer and return the instruments themselves; the **face-to-face interview**, in which the survey items are presented to respondents in a personal conversation; and the **telephone interview**, which solicits responses over the phone. The strengths and weaknesses of these alternative formats are most apparent in a concrete case study.

Instead of the small-scale class assignment of picking ten classmates to evaluate your sociology teacher, let us assume that you have been awarded a consulting contract to evaluate the teaching of all the professors at the college. One of your options is to mail out the "Student Instructional Report" (SIR) questionnaire to a random sample of students. In the segment of the real form displayed in Figure 3:4, note the familiar question

STUDENT INSTRUCTIONAL REPORT

SIR Report Number

This questionnaire gives you an opportunity to express anonymously your views of this course and the way it has been taught. Indicate the response closest to your view by filling in the appropriate circle. Use a soft lead pencil (No. 2) for all responses to the questionnaire. Do not use a pen (ink, ball-point, or felt-tip).

SECTION I. Items 1-20. Fill in one response number for each question.

NA (0) = Not Applicable or don't know. The statement does not apply to this course or instructor, or you simply are not able to give a knowledgeable response.

SA (4) = Strongly Agree. You strongly agree with the statement as it applies to this course or instructor.

A (3) = Agree. You agree more than you disagree with the statement as it applies to this course or instructor.

D (2) = Disagree. You disagree more than you agree with the statement as it applies to this course or instructor.

SD (1) = Strongly Disagree. You strongly disagree with the statement as it applies to this course or instructor.

	NA	SA	A	D	SD
1. The instructor's objectives for the course have been made clear	⓪	④	③	②	①
2. There was considerable agreement between the announced objectives of the course and what was actually taught	⓪	④	③	②	①
3. The instructor used class time well	⓪	④	③	②	①
4. The instructor was readily available for consultation with students	⓪	④	③	②	①
5. The instructor seemed to know when students didn't understand the material	⓪	④	③	②	①
6. Lectures were too repetitive of what was in the textbook(s)	⓪	④	③	②	①
7. The instructor encouraged students to think for themselves	⓪	④	③	②	①
8. The instructor seemed genuinely concerned with students' progress and was actively helpful	⓪	④	③	②	①
9. The instructor made helpful comments on papers or exams	⓪	④	③	②	①
10. The instructor raised challenging questions or problems for discussion	⓪	④	③	②	①
11. In this class I felt free to ask questions or express my opinions	⓪	④	③	②	①
12. The instructor was well prepared for each class	⓪	④	③	②	①
13. The instructor told students how they would be evaluated in the course	⓪	④	③	②	①
14. The instructor summarized or emphasized major points in lectures or discussions	⓪	④	③	②	①
15. My interest in the subject area has been stimulated by this course	⓪	④	③	②	①
16. The scope of the course has been too limited; not enough material has been covered	⓪	④	③	②	①
17. Examinations reflected the important aspects of the course	⓪	④	③	②	①
18. I have been putting a good deal of effort into this course	⓪	④	③	②	①
19. The instructor was open to other viewpoints	⓪	④	③	②	①
20. In my opinion, the instructor has accomplished (is accomplishing) his or her objectives for the course	⓪	④	③	②	①

SECTION II. Items 21-31. Fill in one response number for each question.

21. For my preparation and ability, the level of difficulty of this course was:
① Very elementary
② Somewhat elementary
③ About right
④ Somewhat difficult
⑤ Very difficult

22. The work load for this course in relation to other courses of equal credit was:
① Much lighter
② Lighter
③ About the same
④ Heavier
⑤ Much heavier

23. For me, the pace at which the instructor covered the material during the term was:
① Very slow
② Somewhat slow
③ Just about right
④ Somewhat fast
⑤ Very fast

24. The instructor used examples or illustrations to help clarify the material:
④ Frequently
③ Occasionally
② Seldom
① Never

Questionnaire continued on the other side.

I.N. 401642

FIGURE 3:4 A STUDENT INSTRUCTIONAL REPORT
Part of a real survey instrument asking students questions about teachers.

closed-ended item—a survey question in which available answer choices are provided to the respondent in precoded form.

format with blacken-the-bubble answers; this is one type of **closed-ended item** in which available answers are provided and precoded for computer input. One clear benefit of administering the survey in this way is cost. The copyrighted SIR forms can be purchased from the Educational Testing Service (ETS) for only a few dollars apiece, so you can afford to contact a relatively large sample. But another kind of cost concerns the response rate. In general, a blind-mailed, general-purpose questionnaire will be completed and mailed by less than one-quarter of the contacted sample; to be blunt about it, something must be strange (i.e., unrepresentative) about such a motivated minority. Since students have a personal stake in the quality of instruction at their school—and since you will follow the tips above for establishing the importance of the survey to the respondent—a return rate in excess of 50 percent is feasible in your project. The "response setting" in which students will register their opinions also encourages honest opinions. Respondents get to fill out the SIR in the familiar privacy of their own rooms and to send it back in the enclosed, self-addressed (to you) envelope that does not identify them by name.

Face-to-face interviews are very expensive, running up to $60 for the administration of a half-hour survey (you would probably subcontract the interviewing to a specialized firm). These dollars could be costly in terms of generalizability because they mean a smaller sample size (compare the cost per respondent to the SIR questionnaire). However, the principle of scientific sampling is that a small, well-made sample beats a large, biased one. When it comes to response rate, face-to-face interviewing excels. If personally contacted, told of the general purpose of the study, and met at their convenience, some 90 percent of a sample will typically agree to be face-to-face respondents. Sitting in the respondent's chair across the desk from an interviewer reading prepared questions and recording answers differs drastically from blackening bubbles on a questionnaire at one's home desk. This is a live social situation. It is well established that the interpersonal characteristics of the interviewer and interviewee can affect responses. The differences observed every day in the way a male–male versus a male–female pair interact cannot be erased from the interviewing situation, and these differences tend to be magnified when the topic of the survey relates to such social relations; expressed racial attitudes, for example, show a marked

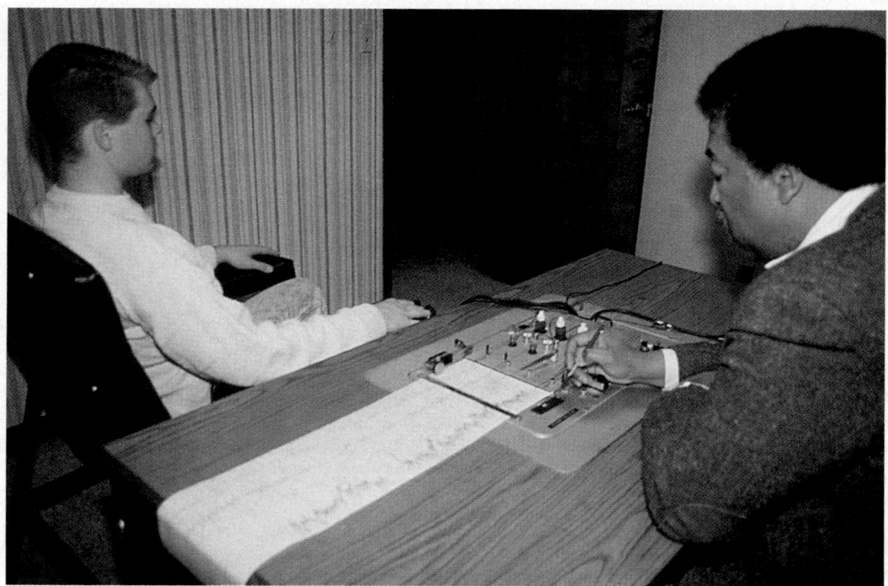

The interpersonal characteristics of interviewer and interviewee (such as age, gender, and race) can affect responses in a face-to-face interview. Although they cannot detect such distortions by using polygraph equipment, as shown here, survey researchers have developed techniques for improving the quantity and quality of responses.

shift depending on whether the interviewer is African American or white (Anderson, Silver, and Abramson, 1988). Moreover, familiarity with the interviewer seems to lead to underreporting of respondents' deviant behaviors such as drug use (Mensch and Kandel, 1988).

So why go to all of the trouble and expense of surveying face to face? For the same reasons that you prefer to conduct important conversations in person: It reduces misunderstandings. No matter how carefully they are prepared, some questions will be unclear to some respondents. Interviewers can clarify what is being asked, an impossibility on a mail questionnaire with a closed-ended format. Interviewers can also seek greater depth in an answer by asking follow-up or "probe" questions. Open-ended items allowing respondents to phrase their own answers are often used in face-to-face surveys to capitalize on this strength of the trained interviewer. As an example, imagine Item 20 from the SIR form (Figure 3:4) as a question followed only by blank lines to be filled in by the respondent's own words. If the respondent were to reply, "I thought the teacher did a pretty good job," the interviewer could probe for the specifics behind such a vague statement. Since they are by definition face to face, interviewers can verify the respondent's personal characteristics (such as race and age) and read nonverbal signs of confusion, evasiveness, or boredom.

open-ended item—**a survey question that allows a respondent to phrase his or her own answers.**

In sociological surveys as in real life there is an alternative to face-to-face conversation: the phone. Telephone interviewing is in many respects a compromise between the weaknesses of the other two techniques, a fact that explains its rising popularity. The interviewer's personal characteristics (even sex) are much less apparent over the phone, thus reducing interviewer bias. The telephone is less personal than eye contact, so respondents may be less motivated to cover up embarrassing behaviors or opinions. Of course both of these problems are nonexistent in a mail questionnaire, but the tradeoff is in question comprehension and response rate. Although the studies show the percentage responding to telephone surveys approaches that of face-to-face interviews (Herzog and Rodgers, 1988), that is the compliance rate *once the respondent has been contacted.* As with getting a date, the trick is to first get the "target person" on the line. Busy signals, no answers, and call-backs drive up the cost of telephone interviews (now about $25 per half-hour survey) and drive down the real response rate. An ingenious innovation to deal with some sampling frame exclusions of the phone book is random-digit dialing (RDD). This technique obtains the area codes and local exchange (the first three digits of a phone number) from the telephone company, then uses a random-number process to select the last four digits instead of looking up the actual numbers. If you think about it a moment, it should be clear that RDD will automatically select some unlisted numbers and some respondents who have recently changed phone numbers (without the necessity of call-backs after consulting telephone company information). Despite such technical breakthroughs—or maybe because of them—survey experts say that response rates are dropping due to the "phone fatigue" generated by the overuse of the technique.

Whatever the format for posing its questions, the raw material for any survey is a stack of answers given by respondents. Should we believe them? The answer is yes, but . . . It is the same "but" that we alluded to concerning personal conversations, with this key difference: Sociological methods have been developed for dealing with such doubts. One major misgiving concerns validity, the degree to which the procedure measures what it is supposed to measure. This sounds like circular reasoning, but it is by no means obvious that a set of items designed to tap some human dimension will actually reach it. Look over the teacher evaluation questions in Figure

validity—**the degree to which a measurement procedure measures what it is supposed to measure.**

reliability—the degree to which a measurement procedure yields consistent results.

3:4. Will they elicit real student opinions about professor performance? Critics have wondered whether SIR really measures likability, looks, or even a student's projected grade. To confront such legitimate doubts, investigators use a variety of testing methods. One such method is "known group" validation. If SIR forms are distributed to the students of known excellent professors (recipients of teaching awards, let's say) and known sub-par professors (e.g., those having been censured by deans for many student complaints), and the teaching scores of the former surpass the latter, that is evidence of SIR validity. A related source of doubt concerns reliability, the degree to which a measurement procedure yields consistent results. Do student assessments of a professor remain the same over time, or are the measurements so up and down that one cannot "rely" on them to make real-world decisions (like giving teachers raises)? ETS, the parent company of SIR, addressed such concerns with an innovative study design. They surveyed about 500 recent alumni of one college, and compared their ratings of teachers' effectiveness to those of current students. This test checked reliability by determining whether ex-student opinions persist over time, and checked validity by polling persons no longer under grade pressure who could view professors through the hindsight of life experience. SIR checked out on both counts, with ". . . considerable agreement between alumni and student ratings of the same teachers" (Centra, 1973, p. 5). Student surveys are not the only criteria of teaching performance, but such measurement studies do build the case that SIR is measuring something real and consistent.

Checks on sociological measurement are simply good scientific practice, although not all of them are simple. Sociological surveys are haunted by "social desirability bias," the desire of some respondents to please or impress the investigator, which leads to distorted answers. Survey analysts have been acutely aware of this bias for decades (Crowne and Marlowe, 1964), so they *measure* it. Questions such as the following are routinely included among the survey items.

> I am always a good listener.
> I never deliberately hurt someone's feelings.
> I am always courteous.

Given the fact that even a community of saints could not circle "true" for all of these items, human respondents who do so should have their responses ignored or adjusted. This is the sort of sensible methodology sociologists apply so that survey results may be treated as scientific data. The nature of that treatment will be illustrated with the special case of the General Social Survey.

SOLVING SOCIOLOGICAL PUZZLES

Sociological research is *important;* many departments of our society's government have staff sociologists, and some foreign governments have even outlawed the discipline because of its powerful implications. Sociological research is *valuable.* In Chapter 2 we discussed the special meaning of value freedom as it concerns flesh-and-blood investigators, and in Chapter 1 the flesh-and-blood individuals whose lives can be touched by the value of sociological research. Here, we wish to convey one more aspect of our discipline at work: Sociological research is *exciting.* The authors have all been hooked by the thrill of discovery, by finding a glittering truth about human behavior in a dull pile of data. Now, it is your turn.

TABLE 3:1 The Frequency Distribution of Happiness

HAPPY	*Taken all together, how would you say things are these days—would you say that you are very happy, pretty happy, or not too happy?*			
Value Label	**Value**	**Frequency**	**Percent**	**Valid Percent**[a]
Very happy	1	438	28.6	28.6
Pretty happy	2	918	59.8	60.0
Not too happy	3	174	11.3	11.4
	.	4	.3	missing
	Total	1,534	100.0	100.0

Mean: 1.827 Median: 2.000 Valid Cases: 1,530 Missing Cases: 4

[a]The slight differences between Percent and Valid Percent are due to the missing cases of respondents reporting no information on this item.

Source: The NORC 1985 General Social Survey.

The Flow of Sociological Analysis

The temptation in a section like this is to load the sociological dice. It would be easy to select a successful piece of research with an impressive result, thus suggesting that all one need do is toss sociology into the real world for "important," "valuable," and "exciting" knowledge to appear. This is seriously misleading. Sociological reality is anything but simple, with an alarming number of social factors complicating the subject of study. So instead of cheating by dusting off one of our already-published studies, the authors have decided to show you an actual work-in-progress.

variable—a measured concept whose values can vary.

frequency distribution—a display of the numbers and percentages of respondents for each value of a variable.

Table 3:1 shows the individual responses for one measured concept—known as a **variable**—from the General Social Survey (GSS). The GSS is probably the most widely used dataset in sociology, and we shall regularly rely on it for evidence in the chapters to follow (the GSS was introduced to you on p. 79). Table 3:1 is in the form of a **frequency distribution**, which displays the raw numbers and percentages of respondents at each level of personal happiness. Be advised that this seemingly naïve question has been carefully tested for validity and reliability, and that it really seems to measure the elusive thing called happiness (Fordyce, 1988). Table 3:1 tells us this: about six out of every ten American adults (60.0 percent) are "pretty happy," nearly three out of ten (28.6 percent) are "very happy," and just over one in ten (11.4 percent) are "not too happy." This is an interesting peek into people's souls, but the really interesting question is: *Why?*

Previous sociological investigations probing individual happiness have found it to be rooted in relationships. Patterns of personal relations have been linked to both depression levels (Mirowsky and Ross, 1989) and levels of personal stress (House, Umberso, and Landis, 1988). Such intriguing—but vague—findings have enticed us to further exploration. We have been exploring the 1985 General Social Survey, the most extensive U.S. study to date of personal networks (the sociological term for interpersonal relationships, which are the focus of Chapter 4). A very basic measure is the raw number of network members, which was compiled through the survey item shown at the top of Table 3:2. Please notice the phrases underlined and capitalized for emphasis by the interviewers hired to administer the face-to-face GSS. Also notice the profile of U.S. citizens' networks revealed in Table 3:2; beneath the frequency distribution it explains that

TABLE 3:2 The Frequency Distribution of Network Size

NETSIZE	*From time to time, most people discuss important matters with other people. Looking back over the last six months, who are the people with whom you discussed matters important to you? Just tell me their first names or initials.* *IF LESS THAN 5 NAMES MENTIONED, PROBE, Anyone else?*		
Value	**Frequency**	**Percent**	**Valid Percent**[a]
.00	136	8.9	8.9
1.00	228	14.9	14.9
2.00	235	15.3	15.3
3.00	321	20.9	21.0
4.00	233	15.2	15.2
5.00	294	19.2	19.2
6.00	84	5.5	5.5
.	3	.2	missing
Total	1,534	100.0	100.0

Mean: 2.983 Median: 3.000 Valid Cases: 1,531 Missing Cases: 3

[a]Below the frequency distribution itself, the computer output here includes the values of two widely used statistical measures. The Mean is simply the arithmetic average: that is, the value generated by adding up the network sizes of all respondents, then dividing by the number of respondents (1,531 since 3 are missing from the total of 1,534). The Median is the category that contains the "middle" respondent: that is, the respondent whose score on the variable divides the distribution in half. Note that counting repondents with no network members, plus those with one and vo network members (136 + 228 + 235) yields a subtotal of 599 respondents. To reac the midpoint of this distribution (1,531 ÷ 2 = 766), one must count into the third category of NETSIZE; therefore, Median = 3.

Note also that the values of the mean and median differ slightly. In general, the mean is the preferred measure of CENTRAL TENDENCY; that is, the "typical" case in a distribution. The exception to this rule is in distributions with a few extremely high or low scores, like a survey of student family incomes that includes a stray billionaire. In such a situation the median would give a truer picture of a typical student income.

Source: The NORC 1985 General Social Survey.

the "typical" respondent reports about three network members with whom they "discuss important matters." As with the frequency distribution of happiness, there is fascination in peeking into the intimate worlds of other people, but the *really* fascinating question is . . .

bivariate relationship—a statistical association between two variables.

crosstabulation—a table that "crosses" the frequencies of different variables to look for statistical relationships.

Does network size affect personal happiness? Posed in this manner, the question concerns a **bivariate relationship** (i.e., a statistical connection between two variables) by contrast to the univariate (i.e., one variable) distributions displayed in Tables 3:1 and 3:2. A standard sociological tool for answering such questions is a **crosstabulation**, literally a "table" that "crosses" the frequencies of different variables. Table 3:3 is an example reproduced from actual computer output of the CROSSTABULATION command using the Statistical Package for the Social Sciences (SPSSx), a software package you

TABLE 3:3 Crosstabulation of Happiness by Network Size

NETSIZE	HAPPY		
Count ROW PCT	Very happy	Pretty happy	Not too happy
Low	152 **25.5**	366 **61.5**	77 **12.9**
High	284 **30.5**	551 **59.1**	97 **10.4**

$n = 1{,}527$

Main point: Despite some small differences in row percentages (boldfaced numbers), there is no statistically significant relationship between Happiness and Network Size.

Source: The NORC 1985 General Social Survey.

will probably get to know if you decide to major in sociology. For easier interpretability, we have collapsed the full network size variable shown in Table 3:2 from seven categories (0–6 persons) to two: "low" (0–2 persons) and "high" (3–6 persons). Before seeking the solution of the puzzle inside the crosstabulation, look at the information surrounding it. In the lower right-hand corner of the output you see 1,527, which is the total number of respondents whose characteristics are crosstabulated (the total GSS sample size was 1,534 in 1985, but this can be smaller because of missing responses on some variables). In the upper-left area of the output is a key to the numbers inside each "cell," or square, making up the crosstabulation. COUNT refers to the simple frequency of cases per cell—there are 152 respondents who are both "very happy" and "low" on network size (upper-left cell). ROW PCT is the percentage of all cases in the row (i.e., the cells going across) that are in a given cell; the second number in the upper-left cell means that 25.5 percent of the 595 cases in the entire top row are in the low size/high happiness cell. In the tables to come, the ROW PCT will be shown in boldfaced type to highlight it for comparison purposes.

One of the true joys of sociological research is looking inside a crosstabulation like this one and seeing a question answered. What to you may now seem like a mass of confusing numbers is actually a device for revealing the patterns in the data. Using it is often called "the art of table-reading," and it takes as much practice as any art. For your first lesson, compare the ROW PCT in the top and bottom cells of the first column. What you see is 5 percent more "very happy" respondents in the larger than in the smaller networks (30.5 percent for "high," 25.5 percent for "low"). Repeat the same cell comparison for the second and third columns. There are differences there in happiness by network size, but they are slight (under 2 percent). Remember, too, that Table 3:3 is only a sample image of the U.S. population, not a view of the whole thing. The differences in column one could be the result of only a handful of unusually happy social butterflies landing in the sample. To formally consider such possibilities, social scientists apply **inferential statistics** to sample data. Although their computation is beyond the scope of this text, you should know that these formulas calculate the likelihood that patterns shown in the table could appear by chance (i.e., bad luck in good sampling). Even in scientific samples, biases can occasionally creep in and make a bivariate relationship appear in a sample table when there is no real relationship in the population. To compensate

inferential statistics—the formulas used to draw a generalization about a population on the basis of sample values.

TABLE 3:4 Crosstabulation of Happiness by Network Size for Females

NETSIZE	HAPPY		
Count ROW PCT	Very happy	Pretty happy	Not too happy
Low	81 **25.0**	208 **64.2**	35 **10.8**
High	156 **30.2**	299 **57.9**	61 **11.8**

$n = 840$

Main point: Despite some small differences in row percentages (boldfaced numbers), there is no statistically significant relationship between Happiness and Network Size for females.

Source: The NORC 1985 General Social Survey.

statistically significant—a conclusion (on the basis of an inferential statistic) that a relationship exists in the population beyond a reasonable doubt.

multivariate analysis—an examination of statistical relationships among more than two variables.

for this possibility, inferential statistics are used that impose stringent rules about when one should "infer" that the sample image is real. If the sample values pass the test of one of these formulas, the bivariate relationship is said to be **statistically significant**. One can then conclude the relationship really exists in the population beyond a reasonable doubt (usually, the "reasonable doubt" is one chance in twenty that the investigator is wrong). When these rules of inference are applied to Table 3:3, they lead to this conclusion: There is no statistically significant relationship between network size and happiness.

But it is not yet time to abandon our overriding question. One of the truisms of sociological investigation is that bivariate relationships rarely appear in pure form. Like any precious substance, they must be separated from various impurities before we can see their distinctive qualities. The purification process sociologists use is known as **multivariate analysis**, which views the bivariate relationship of interest against the real-life background of other (hence, "multi-") variables. Let us now consider the network size/happiness relation separately for each sex. Table 3:4 takes the 840

TABLE 3:5 Crosstabulation of Happiness by Network Size for Males

NETSIZE	HAPPY		
Count ROW PCT	Very happy	Pretty happy	Not too happy
Low	71 **26.2**	158 **58.3**	42 **15.5**
High	128 **30.8**	252 **60.6**	36 **8.7**

$n = 687$

Main point: As is suggested by the row percentage differences in the "Very Happy" and, especially, "Not too happy" columns, there is a statistically significant relationship between Happiness and Network Size for males.

Source: The NORC 1985 General Social Survey.

females from Table 3:3 and re-examines the network size/happiness question for them alone. Reading the table by row percentage differences reveals similarities to Table 3:3 in columns one and three: Respondents with larger networks are overrepresented in the "very happy" column (30.2 percent for "high" vs. 25.0 percent for "low" network size) and differ from smaller networks by only a percent among "not too happy" respondents (11.8 percent versus 10.8 percent). The difference in the "pretty happy" column is over 4 percent, but inferential statistics (and even common sense) find the relationship to be insignificant. Not so for the males in Table 3:5. The familiar overdistribution of "high" network size respondents appears in column one (30.8 percent versus 26.2 percent), but this is matched by an even larger percentage shift in the opposite direction among "not too happy" respondents (15.5 percent for "low," 8.7 percent for "high" networks). In everyday language, this means males with more network members tend to be "very happy," and males with fewer network members tend to be "not too happy." The rules of inferential statistics find the network size/happiness relationship to be real for males, but not for females in the U.S. population.

positive relationship—a statistical association in which a higher level of one variable is associated with a higher level of another variable.

negative relationship—a statistical association in which a higher level of one variable is associated with a lower level of another variable.

There are two immediate lessons to draw from this illustration of sociological data analysis. One simply involves terminology. The finding in Table 3:5 illustrates a **positive relationship**, where the two variables "move together"—larger networks are associated with more happiness, smaller networks with less happiness. The opposite type of effect is called, logically enough, a **negative relationship** (a.k.a. an "inverse relationship"). Chapter 18 presents a clear example in which two variables "move in opposite directions"—lower-income segments in the United States have more illness symptoms, and upper-income segments have fewer symptoms; this defines a negative relationship between illness and income. There is a third alternative, namely *no relationship at all.* It can be very important to show that a bivariate relationship does *not* exist. Emile Durkheim did the study of suicide a great service by showing that climactic factors per se were unrelated to suicide rates, thus clearing the way to find real social "risk factors" (see Chapters 1 and 2). The second lesson to be drawn from this series of tables is the series itself. It represents the progression of the research process we have titled "The Flow of Sociological Analysis." Real research usually moves by a series of statistical steps into the complex zone of multivariate relations. It is worth braving that complexity for the payoff of discovery. Bivariate relationships can undergo dramatic transformations, as in this case where an apparent nonrelationship resolved itself into one nonrelationship (for females) and one clear relationship (for males) that only materialized after the sexes were separated.

Research Methods and Theory

While receiving training in research methods, one author (B.J.J.) was told a tragic tale by a graduate school professor. The story concerned a large-scale, grant-supported survey involving hundreds of variables. This study generated tens of thousands of the type of tables shown here, literally filling a room with computer paper. The only real result of all this effort was a single statistically significant finding for which the investigators had no sociological explanation. The professor called this "dust bin empiricism," in which statistics are thoughtlessly applied in the hope of finding a sparkling insight amid the pile of meaningless data. The moral of the story is that worthwhile sociological research requires intellectual guidance.

The type of statistical analysis illustrated by the tables in this section is spreading in modern sociology. Part of the reason is the technical advancement and dissemination of computer technology. A student today operating a laptop has more analytical power than did the technician operating UNIVAC, a first-generation digital computer (circa 1951).

hypotheses—the predictions drawn from theory that can be empirically tested.

A generation ago, the enormously influential sociologist Robert K. Merton (see especially Chapter 9) wrote an essay titled "The Bearing of Sociological Theory on Empirical Research" (1968). His central point was—and is—that lab-coated, computer-wise researchers cannot proceed without theory. To begin with, the general statements of theory lead to specific predictions—called **hypotheses**—about how reality should behave. Without such simplifying devices indicating to sociologists what to test, they would have to proceed blindly into the complexities of the social world hoping for dumb luck. Sociological theory also illuminates the meaning of a finding once it is found.

Although we are as interested in happiness and personal relationships as anyone else, it has not been simple curiosity driving the analysis excerpted above. The theoretical guidance comes from the "identity accumulation hypothesis," a prediction derived from the symbolic interactionist idea that the self is developed through personal relations (Thoits, 1983). A direct deduction from this theory is that more network contacts should provide one with a more fulfilling sense of life's meaning, whereas social isolates should tend to be unfulfilled and unhappy. The decision to analyze the network size–happiness relationship separately for each sex likewise does not come out of the blue, but from previous research suggesting male–female differences in network adjustment. This is not a jewel of data that we stumbled upon in the dark; the sociological literature has been our guide.

In the very same 1968 volume, Merton published the follow-up essay titled "The Bearing of Empirical Research on Sociological Theory." The point of this title switch is that data also shape theory. Just as unexplained measurements prodded Einstein to develop the theory of relativity in physics, findings from the field rework the human laws of sociology. In Chapter 4 we present the theoretical idea of "role strain," a personal difficulty that can result from too many social demands pulling an individual in different directions. The tables in this chapter have very powerful implications for role theory. According to Table 3:3, people with larger networks do not generally suffer enough role strain to affect their overall levels of happiness. For males, moreover, larger networks are linked to *higher* happiness levels despite the seemingly greater danger of role strain (Table 3:5). Our findings have been guided by theory, and now may prod further theoretical refinements. This is precisely the sort of intellectual reciprocity Merton defined as the sociological ideal in his famous essays.

The Multi-Method Approach

As each method of sociological research has been introduced in this chapter, we have taken special care to point out limitations as well as strengths. The straightforward advice has been to suit the tool to the topic. If the research demands on-the-street insights into a deviant world not easily accessed by surveys or experiments, use participant observation. If large-scale generalizations need be drawn regarding public opinion toward educational reform, this plays to the strengths of surveys. For teasing out complex causal processes over which the investigator has direct control, experimentation is the tool of choice. Many sociologists wise to the ways of research methods take such advice a step further: Turn *several* instruments upon the social world. This is known as the **multi-method approach** (Brewer and Hunter, 1989).

multi-method approach—the use of several research techniques in the same research project.

secondary analysis—the re-use of datasets already compiled by public or private organizations.

It is increasingly common for research projects to begin with an analysis of existing datasets already compiled by public or private organizations. This is known as **secondary analysis** of data. The advantage of beginning with the census, school district records, or the GSS is that these data have been previously gathered by someone else. Consequently, the secondary analyst need not expend resources or further intrude upon the respondents. The disadvantage, of course, is that the data have been previously gathered by someone else. Consequently, the precise research question might not be answerable by secondary analysis alone. This is where the multi-method approach comes in.

focus group—an open-ended discussion among several respondents guided by the interviewer.

The drug and alcohol prevention project discussed under "Experimentation" began with school district data on students' standardized test scores and attendance records, then supplemented the secondary analysis with (a) additional sample surveys of student drug use; (b) elements of experimental design, including treatment and control groups; and (c) **focus groups** (guided, open-ended interviews) involving selected faculty and student peers. *Men and Women of the Corporation* is a widely praised and publicized book based on a true arsenal of research techniques. Sociologist Rosabeth Moss Kanter used ten different methods in her design (1977), including a mail questionnaire, a focus group, several types of face-to-face interviewing, participant observation in meetings, and secondary analysis. While at first glance this might seem to be a sloppy, everything-but-the-kitchen-sink research design, Kanter made a true discovery. Rather than finding simple, closed-minded prejudice against women executives, her research revealed subtle social processes in corporations that are not discriminatory in intent, but which nevertheless exclude women. No one research method showed this as clearly as did all the methods taken in combination.

The point is really a simple one: Given their respective limitations, there is a greater-than-the-sum-of-its-parts benefit to using several sociological tools. The multi-method approach in sociology just offers more pieces of the puzzle of the social world.

FIGURE 3:5 THE GLOBAL SPREAD OF SCIENCE

The scientific method, broadly defined as the interplay between theory and data described in this section, is represented on the map by the percentage of each society's GNP spent on science. Note three things: (1) The scientific method is widespread across the globe; (2) it nevertheless varies according to distinctive sociological traits within societies; and (3) the level of spending roughly corresponds to the level of sociological research performed worldwide.

Source: Peters Atlas of the World, (1990). New York: Harper & Row, Publishers, p. 123.

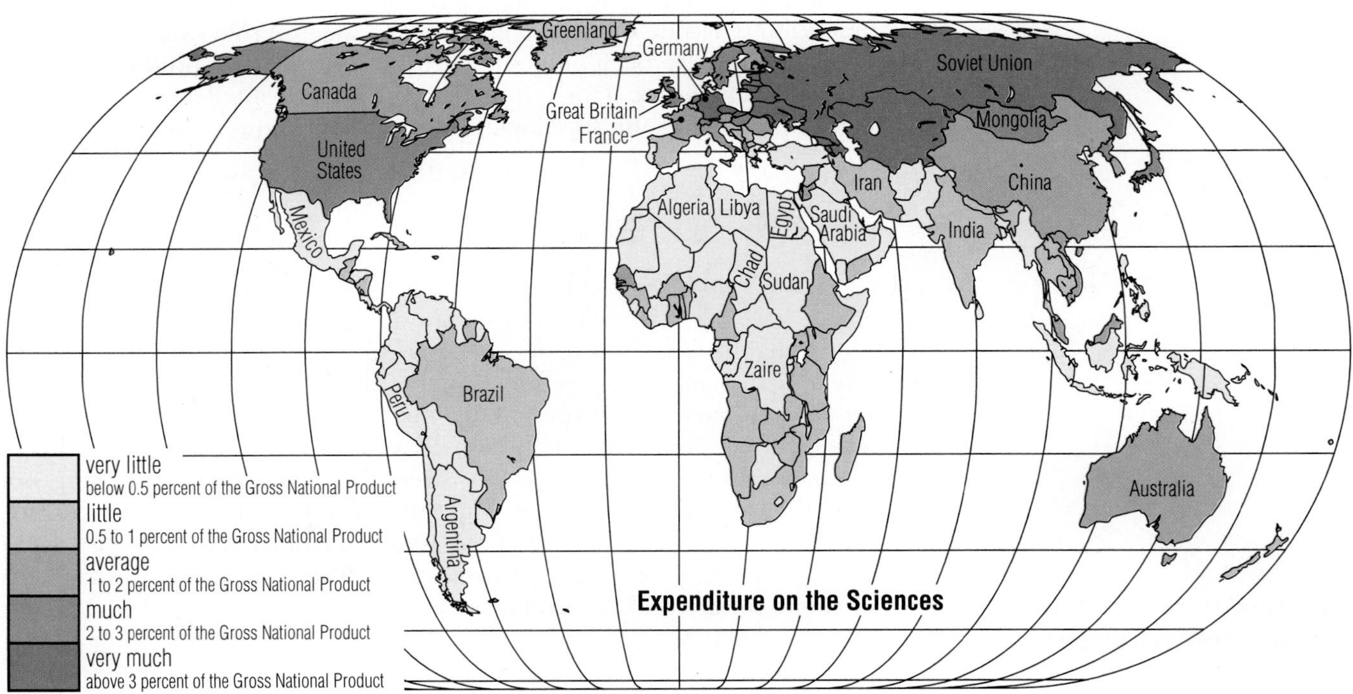

SUMMARY

1. Sociology is a science that derives general propositions about social behavior. Unlike common sense, it contains built-in tests as to whether or not its propositions are true across a broad range of human experience.
2. Like every science, sociology has research instruments, all of which are imperfect. This means the task of the investigator is to find the best tool for the job at hand and then apply it properly.
3. In the natural sciences, experimentation is used to determine causality. However, the causal processes of interest to sociologists are entangled in the thicket of society, and the social experimenter may lack sufficient control over human subjects to carry out a pure form of the classical experiment.
4. Reactivity and the "captive-population" effect are experimental design flaws that may impair the investigator's control and reduce the generalizability of the conclusions of a study.
5. In participant observation, the investigator participates in the group process in order to observe its natural functioning. One issue involved in using this method concerns the extent to which the identity of the investigator will be revealed to the people under study; "full disclosure" may cause the persons being observed to change their behavior, while "full disguise" can be difficult, dangerous, and ethically questionable. Problems are also associated with the degree of researcher participation in the group.
6. Despite these drawbacks and a problem of limited generalizability, participant observation can yield revelations that would be missed by other research methods.
7. Survey research is the most common form of applied investigation of human beings, and the strategy of choice for many sociologists. Scientific sampling, which constructs a small-scale model of the population, increases the generalizability of a study while decreasing the sampling bias that distorts the conclusions of nonscientific surveys. Improving response rate also improves generalizability and may depend on the questioning format used.
8. Sociological methods have been developed to ensure that a questioning procedure measures what it is supposed to measure, and to measure and adjust for "social desirability bias" on the part of respondents. Once data are collected, they can be analyzed for significant relationships among variables by applying inferential statistics.
9. Worthwhile sociological research requires intellectual guidance. General statements of theory lead to specific predictions, called hypotheses, indicating to sociologists what to test. Data also shape theory, as findings from the field rework the human laws of sociology.
10. The sociologist decides which research tool is best suited to uncover these findings, or may combine several tools in a multi-method approach.

Skydivers form the Olympic rings 8,000 feet over Seoul during the 1988 Summer Games. This is an apt photo for this part opener, for the skydiver network symbolizes a microstructure (Chapter 4), Korea represents a macrostructure (Chapter 5), and the Olympic Games is a megastructure (Chapter 6) linking the societies of the world together.

PART TWO

SOCIAL STRUCTURE

When people ask you what sociology is, you might tell them that it is "the study of the relationship between social structure and human behavior." The natural follow-up question is, "What is social structure?"

Part Two provides the answer in three broadening levels. "Microstructure" (Chapter 4) presents the world of interpersonal relationships called social networks, as well as the familiar personal territory of statuses and roles. "Macrostructure" (Chapter 5) steps up to the world of groups, from the lowliest club to the dizzying heights of society. "Megastructure" (Chapter 6) examines the world *itself* as a social structure linking whole societies.

Chapter 4

Personal Perspective

THE sunset was dazzling. From the porch of my seashore apartment, I gazed over the expanse of the bay while the sun submerged. The scene was so hypnotic that I was startled by a motion inches from my face. A ferocious-looking spider had pounced upon a fly delivered to its web by the evening breeze. Having no desire for my nose to be the site of the battle, I stepped back from the railing to behold a masterpiece. The entire front of the porch was curtained by a web of stunning complexity. Hundreds of intricately connected strands fanned out from the spider, who lurked at the web's center. The most vivid part of the memory is the fact that I had nearly missed seeing what was right before my eyes.

Microstructure: *The Social World of the Self*

IN a very real sense, every human being is like the spider in this professor's parable. Attached to each of us are the strands of personal relationships that anchor our everyday lives. The strands, moreover, are not arranged randomly. Like the cross-connecting of a web, our relations link up with other relations—friends of friends, for example—to form complex social patterns. The web brings the spider nature's bounty in the form of food; similarly, sociological research shows that the web of human relationships brings you the good things in life. But as a wasp in the web can bring the spider pain, so too is human suffering often transmitted along the strands of relationships. While the relevance of the "web" remains to be proven to each reader, the key point here is that *the pattern of social relationships is real.* When viewed from the proper perspective—the sociological perspective—this pattern snaps into focus as a tangible, tantalizing mystery to be unraveled.

Consider an odd question: Where did this book come from? If asked to reflect upon what caused this textbook to end up in your hands, a student's mental model might look something like this—

> An individual with a personal interest in sociology receives training in that field at a professional school, and then proceeds to do further research. Thanks to this personal application, said individual is motivated to write down the stuff from his/her head in manuscript form. The manuscript is turned over to a company that pays the author, then prints, markets, and distributes the book. You go to the bookstore and buy the book, and now here you are reading it.

Granted this is a shorthand version, but it is very typical. It is also incorrect. Here is the real story—

> One of this book's co-authors needed money. Thanks to the success of another book the authors had recently written, a developmental editor from Harcourt Brace College Publishers telephoned this author to express interest in their teaming up on a new sociology text. Flattered and still needy, this author called the other two and told them of the offer. They at first rejected the idea, one claiming that he was burned out, and the other that he had too many childrearing responsibilities. The enthusiastic author convinced the others to at least meet with the editor and get a "free lunch." The editor was smart, ambitious, and knowledgeable about sociology. They liked her. She liked them. Since her folks lived near their area, she proposed to return in a few weeks with a contract offer. At the next meeting, the editor soothed the

Like this spider, individual human beings are lodged at the center of a web of relationships—the social network—that affects their everyday experience.

> reluctant authors by offering to delay their writing responsibilities, and enticed the enthusiastic author with a generous advance. A contract was signed, and they all drank a toast together. Over a period of years, the authors wrote this book. Amid hundreds of phone calls, chapters were submitted to their editor, read and criticized by other professors, and revised. Through it all, the authors met over the progress of the work, sometimes applauding it, sometimes arguing over it. Finally, the completed manuscript was published and shipped to college bookstores.
>
> At the first meeting of your sociology class, the professor distributed a syllabus that included this text. Accepting the offer of a friend to walk with you to the bookstore, you went and bought it. After some prodding by the teacher—and because your roommate finally went to the library—here you are reading this.

This second version of events is not just more long-winded than the first. Most significantly, what winds through the second story is the sticky substance of social relations. Every move made by authors and students alike follows a path marked by telephone conversations and face-to-face interactions. The first story depicts a very personality-centered series of events. Prompted by the individualistic values prominent in U.S. culture (see Chapter 7), we tend to view human behavior as the product of self-contained individuals. To extend the earlier analogy, our culture looks at people as wolf spiders, aggressive individual predators making their own way free of any restraining "web." While your personality and private motivations obviously do make a difference, ignoring the living social structures within which people behave leads to serious misunderstandings about their behavior. For a final example, consider how you ended up in this sociology class. Although you undoubtedly had personal ideas and opinions about sociology before choosing the class, (a) those ideas and opinions were likely

Look at the familiar experience of college registration through the relatively unfamiliar concept of the social network: How many conversations with friends, professors, and even students in the line affect the courses for which you actually register?

influenced by prior conversations with friends, (b) you probably consulted the student "grapevine" about what this professor is like, and (c) you may have had a face-to-face contact with a faculty advisor to authorize your entry into this class. You and the authors are caught in the web called *society.* The task of Chapter 4 is to reveal the delicate, nearly invisible filaments of this human web, both in how individuals create it and in how it then constrains their lives.

PERSONAL NETWORKS

Social Structure from the Bottom Up

As Chapter 1 explained, social structure is a puzzle-boxlike phenomenon. It can be analyzed in terms of the interrelationships of whole societies (megastructure), through the linkages of groups and formal organizations (macrostructure), and also through the patterns of social relations among individuals (microstructure). The levels of social structure enfold each other as in the world of the spider, which can be viewed within the whole ecology of organisms, or within the food chain of the garden, or within its own web. In this chapter, we begin by highlighting the patterns of interpersonal relations. Once these basic elements of microstructure have been outlined, it will be possible to see how they—and you—are threaded into the grander design of human society.

Merely remarking that our mainstream American values tend to be individualistic does not make the cultural programming disappear. After a lifetime of immersion in this culture, it is difficult for any of us to shake the idea that persons are self-contained systems and that society just sort of happens when they make common choices. This seems like "common sense," the wisdom of which will now be put to the test. Consider the very personal matter of friendship. How do you pick your friends? Common sense offers two alternative answers: "Birds of a feather flock together," meaning

TABLE 4:1 Educational levels of 1985 GSS respondents and their "closest friend"

RESPONDENT'S EDUCATIONAL LEVEL	CLOSEST FRIEND'S EDUCATIONAL LEVEL	
Count ROW PCT	High school grad or less	At least some college
High school grad or less	371 **70.5**	155 **29.5**
At least some college	124 **30.2**	286 **69.8**
		$n = 936$

Main Point: Note that respondents have "closest friend" within the same educational level as themselves in about 7 out of every 10 cases.

Source: General Social Surveys, 1972–1985 by James A. Davis and Tom W. Smith. National Opinion Research Center, 1985. The variables shown here are slightly altered versions of items from the 1985 GSS asking respondents for the highest school grade completed by themselves and by the first friend named as someone "with whom you discussed matters important to you."

that you select people like yourself as friends; and "opposites attract," meaning that dissimilar personalities entice you as friends. Please note that these commonsensical clichés are logically contradictory, a natural hazard of relying on street knowledge rather than the real thing.

The real thing is sociological research. Empirical evidence gives a definitive answer: Birds of a feather do indeed flock together. One analysis of the Detroit Area Study that interviewed 985 men in that metropolitan region even estimated the statistical likelihoods for friendship selection: Men choose friends from their own occupational level, ethnic group, and age category about twice as often as would be expected by chance alone (Jackson, 1977). A recent study of people like you found "much of the social behavior of [college] students is concerned with sorting through the many social contacts on campus to find close friends that are similar to themselves in racial group, ethnic group, gender and academic performance" (Antrobus, Dobbelaer, and Salzinger, 1988, pp. 243–44). The general point is driven home by Table 4:1, which shows U.S. adults "flocking together" by educational level. Indeed, this detail of the 1985 General Social Survey—the only in-depth national study of personal networks—indicates respondents name a "closest friend" at the same educational level as themselves seven out of every ten times (note the row percentages in the upper-left and lower-right cells). These data make many people squirm. A friend is supposed to be "one joined to another in mutual benevolence and intimacy," the classic definition by eighteenth-century literary figure Dr. Samuel Johnson. Can we really be so small-minded as to select soulmates who are like us right down to the last personal trait?

Well, yes. There is more to the process, though, than small-mindedness or self-love. Personal traits such as education, occupation, and race are more than personal traits—they are also elements of the wider structure of society. To the extent that structures such as schools sort and select similar individuals, they alter the immediate social environments from which individuals pick friends. You therefore become likely to have mostly single, female friends of above-average intelligence because that is who you are, that is who is in most of your classes, and (because of similar past experiences) that is who will have "something in common" with you. This nei-

Edward Hopper's painting *Automat* evokes a sense of social isolation, of dropping through the gaps of the "egocentric network."

ther says that all of your friends are identical, nor that they all agree with you on every particular of life. It *is* to say that the differences found among friends tend to be rare spice in an otherwise familiar stew.

The sociological generalizations to be gleaned from all of this rummaging in your personal life are threefold. First, personal relationships do not form randomly. The links among individuals—especially for friendship—follow a pattern of personal similarity. Second, the forces that throw similar persons together operate through institutions and large-scale organizations like colleges (Feld, 1982); these macrostructures work "over the heads" of the individuals making choices. The process of activating relationships is best understood as a **choice/constraint model**, in that people make social choices within the constraints imposed by the larger social structure. The third and most intriguing conclusion concerns the surprise you may have felt at the findings of friendship research. Apparently, people can weave such intricate patterns of association *without being aware of the underlying structure of their behavior.* Like the spider upon its web, we are so busy tending each strand that we rarely survey the overall pattern.

choice/constraint model—people making social choices within the constraints imposed by larger social structures.

The Network Concept

It is time to stop speaking of spiders and their webs. While analogies are a useful way to introduce new and unfamiliar ideas (like your physics professor likening the Earth's rotation to that of a basketball), such comparisons must now give way to more precise scientific terminology. The **social networks** we have begun to describe are technically defined as the patterns of ties among the units of a social system (Wellman and Berkowitz, 1988). The "units" might be individuals (as in the discussion above), but also might be two fraternities considering a joint party or even two nations deliberating over trade relations. Our focus thus far has been on "egocentric" networks, in which the "tie" is some form of personal relation such

social network—the pattern of ties among the units of a social system.

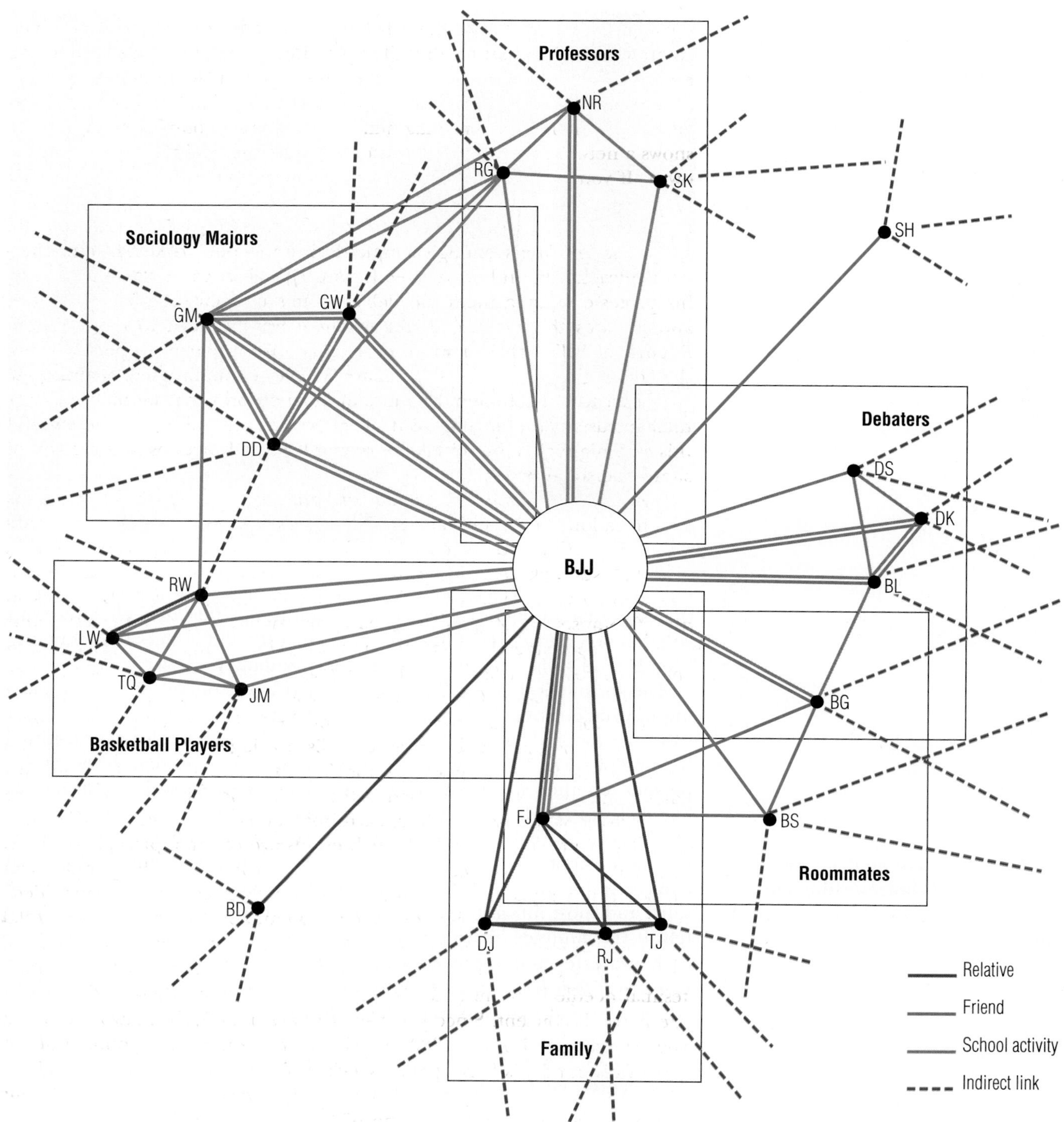

FIGURE 4:1 A COLLEGE STUDENT'S PERSONAL NETWORK
A sketch of one author's (BJJ, large center circle) social network during college. The various types of lines represent network ties to the individuals represented as initialed dots.

that the ego—me or you—is viewed at the center of a netlike structure. Figure 4:1 provides a concrete illustration of this unfamiliar (but necessary) terminology. It depicts the egocentric network of a real person back when he was in college.

Unraveling the network outward from BJJ, notice that solid lines connect him to each of the individuals throughout the inner region of the network; the solid lines signify an active, direct personal relationship between BJJ and that person. The dashed lines represent indirect links to others through BJJ's active social ties—friends of friends, for the most part. The colors of the ties indicate the different kinds of relationships among the network strands (see the code to the lower right of the figure).

Before dissecting the nature of those strands, pay attention to two overall aspects of the network diagram. The first is its complexity. Figure 4:1 shows a network fairly typical for a college student (feel free to sketch your own). If you picture each tie to be a real string pulling BJJ with its social tension, how much of his day can be exempt from these tugs? Moreover, the intricate cross-pressures often require careful choices to keep the "units" happy. The seemingly simple decision to play basketball one afternoon pleases RW and some friends, but BJJ's absence in class is noted by his professors, unbalances the debate teams in their scheduled practice, and irritates the roommates for whom it was his turn to cook dinner. Reports of BJJ's behavior will then circulate from person to person along the connecting lines. Sound familiar? We are so conditioned to anticipate and react to the complex dynamics of our networks that we may overlook their intrusions on our lives. But the structures are there nonetheless, and this case highlights the mistake of seeing BJJ's daily actions as the result of simple personal preferences.

Despite its apparent complexity, on another level Figure 4:1 is a gross simplification. In the first place, BJJ had many more direct social contacts than are represented by the solid lines in this diagram; so, very probably, do you. Network research estimates that the typical college student is "acquainted with" (i.e., knows by name) over 5,000 individuals (Freeman and Thompson, 1986). As complex as the figure appears, it really shows only the "core" members of BJJ's network. The fading off of the figure at the edges so that it may fit onto the page precludes any view of the true scale of this network. To suggest to you just how far-flung an interpersonal structure can be, consider for a moment the "small world" phenomenon.

Everyone has had the experience of discovering common contacts in the unlikeliest of circumstances. BJJ finds that his karate teacher also fixes JM's car radio; two scientists stationed at the South Pole discover that they have dated the same lab assistant; you learn from a new roommate that you share a second-cousin twice-removed. Such events are commonplace, and yet, in terms of random chance, they virtually cannot happen! The paradox can be posed in simplistic statistical probabilities: Your chance of being "tied" to any other U.S. citizen is about one in 250 million (the approximate total population). Since the same numbers apply to your roommate's ties, the likelihood that any two such longshots will match seems to be an infinitesimal needle in an infinite haystack. The solution to the paradox lies in the network concept. Since you have (on average) 5,000 network ties and your roommate also has 5,000, the chance that one of your bundle ties to one of his bundle is fairly good, especially since each of the ties has a bundle of its own. Current research suggests it is very likely that one of your acquaintances actually knows one of BJJ's acquaintances, so that you are now socially tied to the authors (Kochen, 1989). Networks explain the cliché "Isn't it a small world?" by showing how our personal relations string us together into the giant mesh of society.

But strings are just another analogy. Obviously, the thousands of social relations tying you to others in this society—and perhaps in other societies—are not all the same. Sociologists have devised a tool kit of terms for dissecting the differences in network ties and the differences these can make to you. One of the most powerful tools for sorting out the tangle of the network is classification of the *form* of interpersonal ties. Just like regular people, sociologists distinguish the following types of relationships:

Kin

Relatives really are different. Ties reinforced by blood or marriage are generally viewed as lasting and involuntary. Although one is free never to call obnoxious Aunt Oprah, the relation is perceived as still there, but inactive. Network research typically shows relatives to be ready sources of emotional and economic support; hence, the pop term "support network."

Friend

Friendship is distinguished by its voluntary nature. The fact that we are attracted to social clones does not rule out the influence of friends upon us. Indeed, a major reason for friends being such birds of a feather is the interpersonal effects exerted after they flock together (see the "Personal Networks" section). While it would be an exaggeration to say that we "use" our friends, friendship is a key to the accomplishment of instrumental tasks such as job-hunting, finding a doctor, or choosing a professor; hence, the pop term "networking."

Neighbor

Good neighbors are friendly but not friends, so the saying goes. A contemporary study of Toronto residents finds neighbors to constitute about one-fifth of their network ties, but "Neighbors are rarely intimate; their relationships are based upon quick physical access for companionship and small amounts of aid" (Wellman, Carrington, and Hall, 1989, p. 142).

multiplex—a social tie with more than one relationship type.

There are many other classifications of relationship types such as teammate, coworker, and classmate. While these distinctions do clarify our social obligations, each network tie cannot be neatly dropped into one category. Notice how many of BJJ's relations are **multiplex**, that is, bound to him by more than one relationship type (connected by more than one line in Figure 4:1). BJJ's recent research on the 1985 General Social Survey indicates that about six out of ten network ties in the national sample are multiplex. How do such ties differ from single-stranded, "uniplex" social bonds? The literature suggests that the difference is analogous to that between a thread and a many-stranded rope: The multiplex rope can exert a heavier social pull (Jones, 1979). BJJ was the roommate of BG, but also his friend and debate teammate; BG's expectations and opinions naturally mattered more to BJJ than did those of DS, who shared only one strand with BJJ. Which one of your friends affects you most? Network theory predicts that, in general, it will be the person tied to you in multiplex ways.

density—the degree of interconnection among network members.

Despite their complex combinations, such distinctions in the form of network ties involve familiar, everyday social categories. A less commonsensical concept used by network researchers is **density**, defined as the degree of interconnection among an individual's network members. Imagine two students, Jack and Jill, each with three friends in their core networks. Jack's friends are all also friends of each other independently of Jack; Jill, on the other hand, has stayed close with one high school friend, made one friend on campus, and one at work—but none of her friends knows the others. The form of Jack's network is dense, whereas Jill has a loosely connected network. BJJ's network (in Figure 4:1) shows an intermediate situation in which some of the individuals are tied to each other and some are not. Research shows that the level of network density is more than a game of connect the dots. In a classic early study, Elizabeth Bott (1971) found density to be related to marital role segregation; that is, the

Two scientists recently assigned to the remoteness of Antarctica discover that they have a common friend. This is a tale typical of the "small world" phenomenon of far-flung networks.

degree to which husbands confined themselves to being breadwinners and the wives to being housekeepers. When both spouses were immersed in densely knit networks—males with their old high school gang and women with only female kin—they were both likely to behave like traditional stereotypes. When socializing was done in less densely connected, gender-exclusive networks, wives were more likely to work and husbands to help with the kids. What is most intriguing about the density concept is its focus on pure social structure. Everyday social relations are not simply a series of one-to-one interactions with individual network units. If the units themselves are connected, each tie carries more weight in both social support for your behavior, and social control over it (Wellman and Berkowitz, 1988).

This is not to suggest that what is inside each relationship is irrelevant. Indeed, the other major tool for sorting network ties concerns their *content.* Again, network analysts begin with some familiar distinctions about the intimate spaces within our ties. One of the most basic distinctions is the emotional closeness attributed to a social relation. Not all of the solid lines in Figure 4:1 are identical. BJJ felt that BS and RW were his "best friends" during college, just as BD had been during high school. This sort of qualitative difference in the importance attached to a tie is distinguished by sociologists and regular people alike from quantitative differences in interaction frequency. Ties vary enormously in how often they are "activated" by personal communication. BJJ only contacted TQ before basketball games but was supposed to call Mom and Dad at least weekly. Despite

closeness—**the degree of emotional intimacy in a network tie.**

interaction frequency—**how often a network tie is activated by personal communication.**

No doubt you have already experienced the strain of maintaining even the closest high school friendships. Longer-duration network ties have a distinctive social content, but frequent interaction is difficult to maintain due to life changes.

promises of undying loyalty, the frequency of face-to-face contact is strongly conditioned by residential distance; dorm acquaintances may be seen daily, whereas hometown friends are only visited a few times a year. The **duration** of network relations is another aspect of their content. More durable ties carry an interpersonal history that affects the day-to-day process of interaction. More recently made social contacts are still in the process of formation. This is why one spends more time reminiscing with long-duration contacts (old friends telling each other favorite high school stories) and more time comparing opinions on the present (What did you think of last night's concert?) with newer social contacts.

duration—the time span over which a network tie has endured.

These aspects of relationship content combine in complex ways to create the customized quality, the distinctive "feel" of each social tie. Relations with one's immediate family members are durable by definition because they begin at birth (kin are also high-density relations because the branches of the family tree have built-in connections to each other). Despite all of the publicity concerning the decline of the U.S. family, a recent national survey found over 70 percent of adults to feel "close" to parents and siblings, and well over half of all adults to see their parent and siblings face to face at least once a month (Hugick, 1989). Non-kin relations contain a more variable mix of contents. Consider this intriguing conclusion from the study of Detroit men cited above: "Longer-lasting friendships were more intimate [i.e., close]; intimate friends were seen more often but friends who were known longer were seen less often" (Jackson, Fischer, and Jones, 1977, p. 47). This pattern probably reflects the quality of your present friendships. Of course you make more of an effort to hang out with closer friends, so that intimates have higher interaction frequency. The older the friendship, though, the greater the likelihood of the friends "growing apart" across their life span. You may still feel very close to your best high school friend, but your moves to different colleges make weekends together just too impractical.

Such examples show that the classification of network ties by form and content can reveal underlying structures in the social life of BJJ, you, or anyone else. However impressive these network structures are, there is still a perfectly legitimate intellectual question: So what? If network research is to be more than an excavation of hidden social structures, it should be able to prove that relationship patterns *make a difference* to the persons enmeshed in them. That is the task of the following section.

Personal Networks: Interpersonal Effects

Networks are anything but passive structures. While there is personal choice involved in which relative to visit or which student to admit into one's circle of friends, that choice must also come from the other side of the tie. Sometimes he says no to a date, or she rejects your overtures of friendship, or they dump you from the party. Even when one is accepted by others, each relationship necessarily contains some measure of "social obligation." This innocent-sounding term holds profound implications for personal behavior. A major theme of this section will be the many influences flowing along network strands into each individual life.

Before we attempt to summarize these influences, let us reconsider the social reality of friendship similarity. A classic examination of this phenomenon is Denise Kandel's (1978) study of marijuana use among adolescents. Her study dug deeper into the established finding that having a friend who is an illegal drug user predicts one's own drug use *better than does any other personal trait.* But, did users select pot-smoking friends, or did such friends influence adolescents to become users? Kandel's research revealed both processes at work; in fact, the "social selection" process was about equal in strength to the "social influence" process in explaining why pot smokers hang with smokers and nonsmokers with nonsmokers. As the choice/constraint model implies, we choose our associates, and that association then constrains our behavior. The catalog of effects presented next shows the pervasive individual influences of network ties, both for good and ill.

Life

It might strike you as overly dramatic to call networks a matter of life and death. It is, nevertheless, true. Some of the most powerful evidence of network effects concerns personal mortality (i.e., death rates). For years researchers have known that unmarried persons have a greater chance of dying prematurely than do married persons. Moreover, the death of a spouse increases one's own death risk—at any age—and remarriage restores a lowered mortality risk (Helsing, Szklo, and Comstock, 1981). Such data suggest the general relevance of social contacts to life expectancy, a suggestion that has been confirmed by a famous mortality study. A sample of nearly 5,000 residents of Alameda County, California, were assessed on a battery of health risk factors in 1965, and then followed up nine years later to analyze mortality patterns. The analysis showed that individuals who had scored low on the "Social Network Index" (i.e., those with fewer contacts with relatives and friends) were about *twice* as likely to have died during this period than individuals high in network contacts who were otherwise similar in terms of medical risks (Berkman and Syme, 1979). These startling results have been replicated in several different regions of the United States and in Sweden (House, Umberson, and Landis, 1988).

Network patterns wind through morbidity (i.e., illness) rates as well as mortality rates. By comparison to the less socially involved, persons integrated into cohesive networks are less likely to suffer heart attacks, pregnancy complications, joint swelling, postsurgical pain; in fact, virtually every form of illness that has been studied (Caplan, 1981). Flying in the face of both common sense and purely biological models of disease are data indicating that *more* social contacts are associated with *less* incidence of infectious disease, despite the apparent hazards of kissing, handshaking, and talking in network members' faces. Box 4:1 presents the authors' own research on college students' "everyday illness" symptoms associated with infections such as colds and the flu. Such data show that personal networks reach down under your skin.

Liberty

Please notice that the headings organizing this section are the "inalienable rights" proclaimed in the Declaration of Independence. This is meant to suggest that networks affect the most basic elements of individual existence in our society. Although the framers of the Constitution did not have access to the sociological literature on networks, they did include "freedom of association" in the Bill of Rights. In a sense, then, the right to build and participate in one's own network is a fundamental form of liberty.

Another form of liberty is economic freedom. The notion that the streets of this society are paved with gold that the individual is free to scoop up with sweat and smarts has drawn tens of millions of immigrants to the United States. This version of the "American Dream" is simplistic in its vision of the individual working alone in a wide-open "free market." Even the immigrants propelled by this dream to a new society did not make the move alone. Demographers have painstakingly recorded a process they call "chain migration," whereby people in their country of origin first contact a network member who has already moved to the United States, then use their contact's contacts to find lodging and jobs upon arrival, and finally send for their own relatives and friends to add further links to the chain (see Chapter 20).

Recent arrivals from Asia are shown at a Thanksgiving dinner in the United States. The path of assimilation into U.S. society often follows the network links of "chain migration."

BOX 4:1 COLLEGE EXPERIENCE

Do Your Relatives Make You Sick?

In a recent semester, the authors conducted a research project involving a probability sample of 297 undergraduate students at Villanova University, the institution where all three now teach. Motivating their research was the growing evidence summarized in this section that network patterns affect personal health patterns. As intriguing as these studies are, many of them have focused on mortality or very serious forms of morbidity such as heart disease. The authors decided to extend the examination of the network–health connection by studying "everyday illnesses"; that is, the types of physical problems that would typically cause you to miss class or work. Following is the scale we used to measure the frequency of such conditions among college students:

> In this section, we would like you to indicate whether you were sick or had any injuries at any time during the past two months. Please do not include any continuing health problems you may have all of the time. We are interested only in occasional illness or injuries. We would like you to indicate how often over the past two months you have experienced the conditions listed below by writing the appropriate number from the following scale in the space to the right of each symptom—

Scale:
1) several times a week over the past two months.
2) once a week over the past two months.
3) at least twice over the past two months.
4) once in the past two months.
5) not at all in the past two months.

Example: A person who had a "rash" once in the previous two months would put a "4" in the space. (_4_)

Your Responses:

headache	(___)
stuffy nose	(___)
abdominal pain	(___)
cough	(___)
vomiting	(___)
chills or fever	(___)
sore throat	(___)
indigestion	(___)
muscular aches and pains	(___)
diarrhea	(___)

The same survey instrument also included a question on the number of "close relatives"; that is, the number of kin student respondents "see or have a conversation with at least several times a month."

This mail questionnaire study contained a surprise. Among undergraduate males, the network–health relationship was as predicted by the literature: Those in contact with more relatives suffered fewer symptoms over the previous two months than did their less kin-oriented male classmates. Not so for the opposite gender. Among undergraduate females, *more* kin contact was associated with *more* illness. The authors are working on an explanation of this unexpected finding, but two conclusions can now be drawn. First, the influence of networks clearly does extend to the types of symptoms you might suffer from today. Second, the nature of that influence is complex enough to call for further sociological investigation.

Critical Thinking Questions

1. *Why* do male and female college student networks have these contrasting effects? Use one of the major theoretical perspectives—functionalism, conflict theory, or symbolic interactionism—to answer this question.
2. Why might the findings be misleading or "biased"? (Hint: Scrutinize the sample and the use of a mail questionnaire based on your knowledge of sociological research methods from Chapter 3.)

People born in the United States are conditioned from an early age to believe in the "ladder of success" to be climbed by personal effort (see Chapter 11). While it is a truism that economic success is influenced by individual striving, recent research has exposed the intricate involvement of networks in our movements up (and down) the ladder's rungs. One of the seminal studies of the process popularly called "networking" is Mark Granovetter's well-known work "The Strength of Weak Ties." This unusual title is based on a conceptual distinction made by Granovetter between "strong" ties—those high in interaction frequency, closeness, and duration—and "weak" ties, which are low on such measures of relationship content (1973, p. 1361). His findings on the flow of information about jobs are a shock to both individualistic images of achievement and to common sense about "who you know." Granovetter marshals an impressive range of evidence showing that *weak* ties are more likely to be the source for information actually leading to a job. Would this have been your guess? Most people suppose that one's intimate, everyday associates have the greatest motivation and opportunity to pass along job tips. Granovetter supposes the opposite:

> Those to whom we are weakly tied are more likely to move in circles different from our own and will thus have access to information different from that which we receive (1973, p. 1367).

By serving as "bridges" to social contacts far beyond the "core network," weak ties tap into rich stores of information not already circulating among one's intimates.

A growing network literature has echoed Granovetter's challenge to the individualistic model of economic liberty. Labor market studies consistently show that the largest single source of job information is the personal network. Surveys of recent graduates indicate that about four out of ten students from the authors' university found their first job in this way rather than through placement services or newspaper ads. Granovetter's findings for upper-white-collar occupations have been extended to other rungs of the economic ladder (again, see Chapter 11). Let us consider some personal applications of these network research findings. Two of the authors got their present university jobs on a tip from a weak tie (ex-professors they saw only once in a while); the third author learned of a job vacancy through his strong tie to one of the (already hired) authors. For yourself, reflect on network tips about jobs you have already had. After graduation or during any spell of unemployment in your life, always work your network—especially weaker ties—for occupational information. This good practical advice will also serve as a reminder of what you first read here: We do not seek our economic fortunes alone.

No relationship is a free lunch. Despite their many benefits, every network tie carries its costs in energy and effort. This is why we place limits on the number of contacts we maintain, and why we sometimes hide from the burdens of intimacy. Do you have a younger brother or sister? If so, at some time you must have said, "Dad, do I *have* to bring _______ along?" For some people, network obligations become burdensome indeed. Because of the personal burnout that accompanies round-the-clock care for a mentally infirm loved one, the Alzheimer's Disease and Related Disorders Association has organized support groups for the millions of caretakers who are virtual "prisoners of love." These few examples reveal the double-sided nature of personal networks: They are links to liberty, but also ties that bind.

Pursuit of Happiness

In addition to health and freedom, people pursue the elusive psychological state known as happiness. Much folk wisdom in song and literature comes to the conclusion that one simply cannot explain happiness. Although there is a mysterious aspect to miserable rock stars and cheerful cancer patients, happiness is not a random event. The social science literature has shown, for example, that upper-income people tend to be happier than lower-income people, and that rural dwellers tend to be happier than urban dwellers (Fernandez and Kulik, 1981). These findings suggest underlying social patterns that have their individual exceptions, but are nevertheless rules of happiness.

social support—emotional and practical help provided by network members.

Personal networks are entangled in these social patterns on several levels. A network term that has been borrowed by social workers, psychiatrists, and talk-show hosts is **social support**. In its technical and nontechnical meanings, it denotes the compassion, advice, and pep-talks that flow from one's network members. Social support is powerful stuff. Not only does it feel good, but studies have shown that social support is associated with lower depression and anxiety (Mirowsky and Ross, 1989), as well as with higher well-being and morale (Ward, Sherman, and LaGory, 1984). How do network members support the pursuit of personal happiness? Research has revealed the special significance of having a confidant to whom one can express deepest personal concerns. In addition to this expressive function, one's social support team can provide real-world guidance such as advice and information that is a practical contribution to personal happiness (Lin, Dean, and Ensel, 1986). Individuals with such supports seem to have a "social buffer" against life's inevitable rough spots. If you are having trouble in school, for example, your social supporters can both offer reassurance that you will do better and refer you to a tutor for academic help.

Network ties bring burdens as well as benefits. Victims of Alzheimer's disease may unwittingly victimize spouses or other family members who must provide care around the clock in the simple routines of daily life.

Social support is not a one-way street. Network members may lighten your burdens but, as suggested above, you have to carry your load, too. Evidence is mounting that the support of others can be costly in terms of emotional resources, and possibly even damaging to health (House, Umberson, and Landis, 1988). The shared misfortunes that travel along network strands are both common and far-reaching. The General Social Survey asked its respondents how many "traumatic events"—deaths, divorces, unemployments, hospitalizations/disabilities—had happened to their relatives during the past five years; over 70 percent of this national sample had at least one such event shaking the kin network, and many had suffered two or more. Network strands can bring grief from afar. Research conducted on Armenian teenagers residing in the United States during the first week after a devastating earthquake struck Soviet Armenia in December 1988 uncovered their feelings of guilt, remorse, and rage over an event that occurred across the world (Yakoubian, 1989). Given the phenomenon of "chain migration" discussed earlier, some of these teenagers undoubtedly had direct network ties to Armenians who had perished in the quake.

Whether the example is exotic or everyday, it is clear that networks are a key to our emotional states. Looking at the level of happiness as a purely personal trait is like looking at the mercury in a thermometer as rising and falling on its own.

STATUSES AND ROLES

Who are you? Some people shy away from philosophy because they view it as an abstract discipline that has little to do with the real world. Although philosophical debates can be tiresome, their subject matter is often the basic questions we all ponder in our meditative moments. In such moments philosophy bumps smack into sociology.

Consider this basic question that could be borrowed from any introductory philosophy class: *What is the self?* As you ponder who you really are, the natural course is to cast aside those parts of life that are not really "you." Others may apply the convenient label "college student" even though you feel schoolwork to be a set of occasionally onerous duties outside your real self. Are you a "daughter"? Despite your love of your parents, daughterhood probably feels like an unusually close form of network attachment *to* the real you rather than *being* you. Maybe you are an aspiring rock star playing in a bar band. Are the weekend gigs the real you, or just an interesting hobby? If you make it in music, there will be contractual dates, transportation schedules, loneliness, all the rigors of "the road" that make rock stars sing of getting away to "be myself."

College student, daughter, rock star—these are examples of the bits of society that become part of our inner lives. As we discard such seemingly nonessential bits in search of the true self, what is left? While it is an extreme position to say that the real you is *only* these parts, philosophers and sociologists would agree on this truth: The parts one plays in social life become entangled with personal identity.

Society As Theatre

Speaking of parts to be played, let us spotlight the example of a theatrical production. The production company has a certain number of positions to be filled—lead roles, supporting players, set designers, ticket-takers, and so forth. Individuals apply for these positions (many by auditioning for parts) and are hired. If they fail or die, someone else is hired for each vacated position because "the show must go on." Theater people in general—and especially lead actors—are known to immerse themselves deeply in their roles. They sometimes take the role so much to heart that there are emotional difficulties getting into and out of character.

dramaturgical school—those analyzing social life as a theatrical production.

Now think of society as the most stupendous theatrical production of all. That is the analogy drawn by the **dramaturgical school** of sociology (see Goffman, 1959), which has developed a language for talking about the parts we play. Take the position of quarterback on a football team. It is a social slot for which various individuals may audition (i.e., try out), and which must be filled by someone else if an injury occurs. Your professors fill just such a slot for which they undoubtedly had to audition; sad to say, if one drops dead, another individual will appear as your lecturer. The same is true for filling your position, since you are one of a limited number of (replaceable) students at the school. No matter how superbly an individual performs, these slots all have an existence of their own over and above the occupant of the moment. In sociological terminology each slot is a **status**, a structural position in a social system. An actor who wins a part must then perform; similarly, occupying a status means an individual is supposed to *do* something. The dynamic aspect of the slots we fill is known as the **role**, a pattern of behavior appropriate for a given status (Linton, 1937).

status—a structural position in a social system.

role—a pattern of behavior appropriate for a given status.

role expectations—the specific behaviors a status occupant is supposed to exhibit.

The drama analogy is particularly illuminating of the relationship between self and role. There are days when you just do not want to live up to the demands of your present status. The specific **role expectations** of college student—paying attention in lecture, doing the reading, performing on tests—can become burdensome. In a weak moment, you may decide to cut class. Such a violation of role expectations does not deny the existence or importance of statuses; on the contrary, the decision is often accompanied by guilt, self-consciousness (especially if you bump into your professor), or some other emotion that reflects personal identification with one's official position as a student. Everyone in the play called "society" has similar experiences—even professors. At this very moment, I am wrestling with the urge to watch TV despite the role expectation that I finish writing this page. As soon as I arrive home after a hard day of lecturing, I immediately shed my professorial tweeds (complete with patches on the elbows) and get into old clothes. This is the process known as getting "offstage," away from the demands of one's official role just as an actor sheds a costume.

As in acting, there are virtuosos of societal roles. Some people perform their role expectations so expertly that the status seems to dissolve from the very force of their personality; what they do then seems personal rather than social. Biographical accounts of the great figures in history, however, show them to have been acutely aware of duty, honor, service—all great ideals that sociologists unromantically call role expectations. Moreover, the roles persist after the great perish; there was still a presidency after George Washington, and another emperor followed Caesar. Although such cases highlight the universality of role-playing, they also show that people are not status robots. A generation ago Dennis Wrong (1961) wrote a famous article cautioning sociologists against the image of an "oversocialized" person mechanically carrying out role programming. There is a creative aspect to the playing of roles in which the self expresses its individuality. While all of your classmates occupy the student status, there are many different styles of role performance. Some students are enthusiastic, some fashionably bored; some attend all lectures but skip the readings, some do the reverse; some students pester professors, some avoid eye contact with professors. Quite like actors, we all play our roles a bit differently. Unlike actors, we often have our parts thrust upon us by society. An amateur sociologist named Shakespeare summed up the point fairly well: All the world is a stage, and all the men and women merely players.

Building Social Structures

status set—the multiple social positions occupied by an individual.

The idea that social structure is inside each of us is intriguing, but it is really only a teaser to appreciating the grand design of society. That design looms outside of any individual consciousness. The concepts of status/role are often referred to as the "building blocks of society." Discovering how the blocks are assembled to make up a society is a main mission of sociology. This much is already clear: Most individuals sit within several linked "building blocks." Figure 4:2 shows a college student's **status set**, which is composed of the multiple social positions occupied by an individual. Now for some simple logic: If you fill several social slots, and if each slot has different role expectations, then you must be several different people in the course of a typical day. Imagine yourself in class with the student role in place: You are quiet, diligently take notes, and raise your hand before

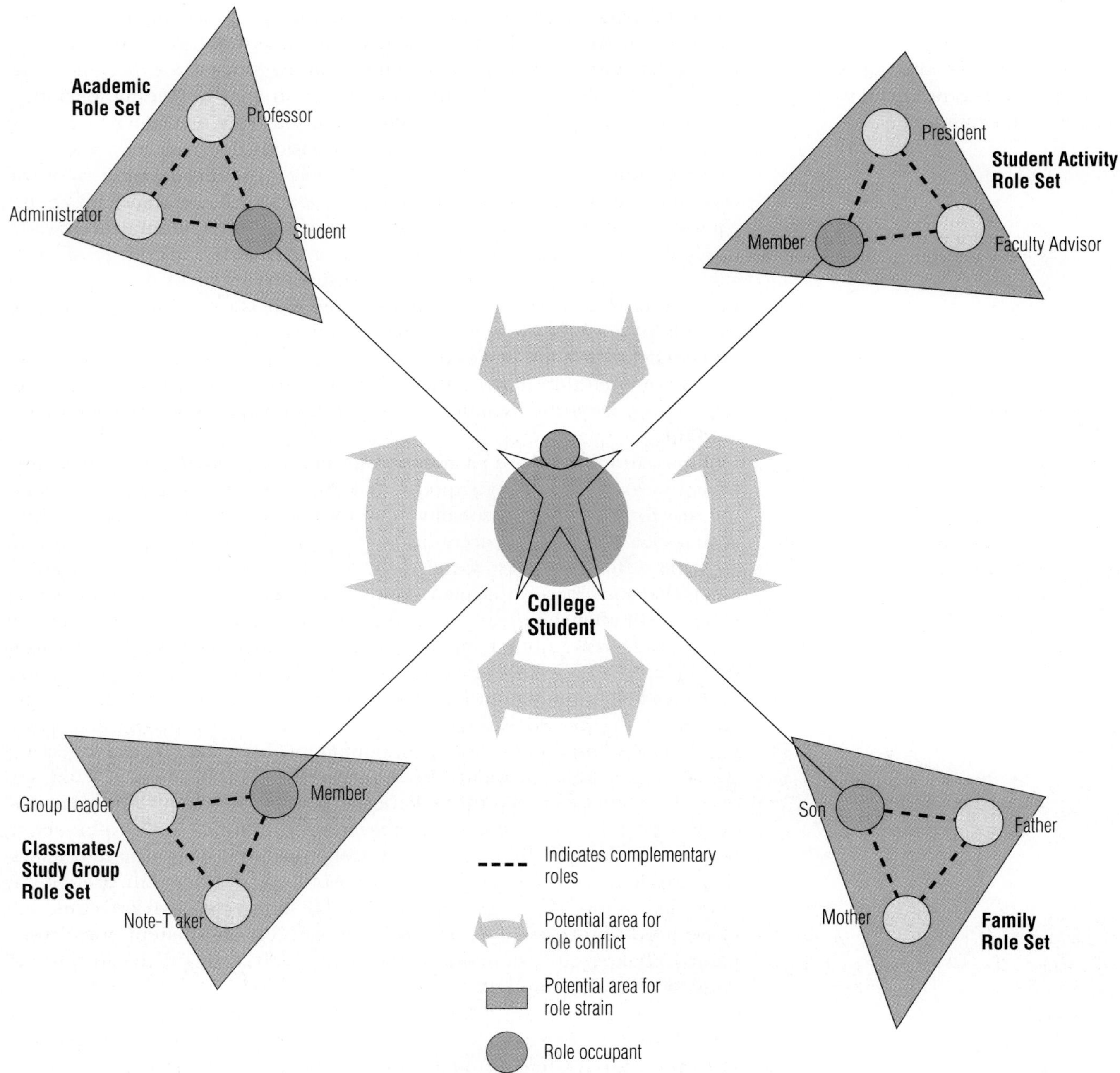

FIGURE 4:2 A COLLEGE STUDENT'S STATUS SET
A sketch of the several statuses occupied by a typical college student.

speaking. The instant the bell rings, your personality is transformed. As you walk out with classmates, you loosen up your demeanor, put the notebook under your arm, and openly discuss varied topics from the teacher's tie to Saturday night's party. Soon, when you arrive home and slip into the son/daughter status, you change again. There are certain topics you just do not discuss with Mom, who has an element of authority absent from your relations with classmates. In a real sense, each of us is a social chameleon changing the spots of our selves to match the changing background of the status set.

Unless someone like a sociologist is impolite enough to point out such shiftiness, the transformation from one personality type to the next usually proceeds so smoothly that one is not even aware of it. There are times,

role conflict—the inconsistency of demands across the positions of an individual's status set.

master status—the individual's role that is given the greatest societal significance.

role set—a pattern of complementary roles linked to a single status.

though, when these smooth shifts are interrupted by complications built into social structure. Students facing examinations, working parents, and rising young executives all face a common problem: role conflict, the inconsistency of demands across the positions of an individual's status set (i.e., *between* the triangular zones in Figure 4:2). In the week before finals, it is commonplace for college students to shortchange friends and family to service the all-consuming need to study. If your parents get angry because you forget to call home during this period, your resulting frustration is caused by role conflict. Similarly, a working parent may feel pulled apart by conflicting status demands when the baby gets sick on the day of the big business presentation. The upwardly mobile young "organization man" (a phrase coined by sociologist William H. Whyte) expected by a watchful boss to work seventy hours a week may thereby wreck his marriage. In all of these cases the irony is that individuals suffer *despite doing exactly what they are supposed to do* in one of their statuses. The problem is that the other roles in the status set cannot be properly performed because one of the individual's performances demands so much.

Role conflict is a true "social disease," a malady caught from a person's position in the social structure. One natural defense against this disease comes from the fact that not all of the individual's statuses are created equal. Most people have a master status, the position given the greatest societal significance that most affects personal identity. The high value of the work ethic in U.S. society leads many people to think of occupation as their primary status. Listen to old friends meeting at parties—especially at high school reunions. The ritual question, "How are you doing?" is usually answered, "Great! I'm a bond trader" or, "Not so well. Our firm just closed down." These assertions are offered as statements of personal identity, but they also clarify how the assumption of a master status can serve as a decision-making tool. At exam time, most of your friends and family will understand that, as a college student, you must shirk your other statuses. The woman with the part-time job who defines herself as a "mother first" knows her priorities when the baby runs a temperature. Interestingly, recent studies show that more and more working women in the United States are defining career as their master status. This trend does simplify some decisions such as the timing of and desired number of children, but it does not eliminate role conflict because family roles are so much more demanding of working women than they are of working men (Staines and Peck, 1983).

Despite the symptoms that do arise from playing multiple roles in society, it is the rare person who seeks to wear only a single hat. People who say their lives are "empty" generally try to add slots to the status set. In an intriguing community study, Peggy Thoits (1983) found that individuals with larger status sets typically experience *lower* levels of psychological distress than do individuals occupying few social slots. Wearing many hats can be stressful, but it appears to have its human compensations as well.

Return now to the general point: Statuses and roles are not merely the costumes worn by the inner self, they are also elements of social structure. Perhaps the most concrete demonstration of how these elements fit together is the role set, defined as a pattern of complementary roles linked to a single status (Merton, 1968). Role performance is almost never a one-person show. Most of the time, roles are played in tandem with others within the role set. Your quiet attention and pen poised to take notes are role expectations that only make sense in relation to a lecturer; the professor's dutiful preparation of notes and rehearsal of the lecture only make

A jury trial is a *role set.* Identify the various roles being played in this dramatic setting, and consider how they complement one another.

role strain—inconsistent expectations within the role set.

sense if there is to be an attentive audience of students. Please note how the two roles complement each other, forming a sort of role duet.

This is a nice illustration of how roles are structured in sets, but the fit is not always so snug. **Role strain** arises from inconsistent expectations within the role set (i.e., *within* one of the triangular zones in Figure 4:2). To expand on the college example, another member of the set is the educational administrator, whose role expectations involve overseeing academic operations so that professors and students can perform their roles. A current issue on many campuses is "grade inflation," the upward shift in grades over those typical of a generation ago. Why is this happening? A number of studies attribute rising grade-point averages to insistent expectations from students that they receive higher grades, which some trace to the Vietnam era when flunking out could mean getting drafted (Quann, 1982). Throughout this period, college administrators have been urging professors to "hold the line" and to "maintain standards." The contradictory expectations of students and administrators make professors the victims of role strain. Other examples abound. The secretary required by the boss to type a report on the very day that the office accountant expects the timesheets is experiencing role strain. If Mom wants you to be a great athlete but Dad abhors the violence of football, you feel role strain within the family. In all of these cases, individuals are trying to respond to the tugs they feel inside the role set. Because the structure of the role set is poorly linked, however, the individuals feel the strains as an internal tug-of-war pulling them apart when they try to do what they are supposed to do.

Although its insights and research findings are becoming ever more visible in popular culture, sociology is a discipline with a slippery meaning in the public mind. Astronomers study stars, political scientists study voting, economists study supply and demand . . . but sociology is not so easily defined by the stuff it studies. The patterns linking people into social structures are less obvious, and yet they encompass astronomers' associations, political organizations, and the nature of economic markets. It is one purpose of this book to reveal those patterns from the inside out, from personal experiences with social structure all the way up to the "global village" of human society. Your and my daily efforts to manage our roles prove that we have felt the stuff of social structure firsthand. The fact that sociologists are studying something very real only leads to another fascinating question: *What organizes social structure?*

THEORETICAL PERSPECTIVES ON MICROSTRUCTURE

To pose this question properly, a bit of summary is in order. The chapter began by showing that informal personal relations form elaborate, far-reaching social networks. The next section showed the patterns of statuses within which people play out their daily roles. Now compare Figure 4:1 and Figure 4:2. In both diagrams the individual is depicted at the center of a complex social structure reaching outward into society. Compounding the complexity is the fact that in real life the figures are not separate: The same individual sits at the center of both network and status structures, so picture them superimposed. Much sociological research supports this visual image. One of the strongest influences on network formation radiates from the roles one plays. As noted in the studies on friendship networks, people with the same job are much more likely to be friends than are people who do not share an occupational role. Your family status automatically links you to the entire kin network of the "family tree." Some sociological researchers argue that any separation of the two figures is artificial. They view a role as actually being a pattern of social contacts (White, 1988). A typical person playing the CEO role will have an "inner circle" of corporate advisors, an executive secretary to make appointments, and a regular Wednesday golf game with business contacts. In fact, any of the role sets shown in Figure 4:2 can be viewed as a very partial piece of that college student's network diagram.

So: Networks and roles interweave to create microstructures much more intricate than any spider web. And, like a spider, the individual at the center of each microstructure is more a tender than a designer. BJJ in Figure 4:1 does decide whom to call on a given day, but note how much of the network is self-sustaining contacts independent of BJJ (all of the cross-connections); the college student in Figure 4:2 does pick and choose classmate contacts, but the structures of the academic and family role sets are pretty well established. The same is true for any individual. Even the president of the United States—arguably the most powerful person on Earth—steps into a slot with social structures such as the State Department and the Secret Service already in place.

Here is the paradox: A society is seemingly made up only of individuals, and yet no single individual is responsible for the surrounding social order. There is no Secretary of Social Structure who patterns social life, and yet it gets patterned. Each of the three major theoretical perspectives in sociology has sought to solve this paradox. We will now consider in turn the organizing principles of social structure discovered by each perspective. As has been the case throughout this book, the separate theoretical pieces will then be snapped together to see what complementary insights they can yield about the puzzle of microstructure.

Functionalism

In certain respects the paradox of social structure falls most naturally into the realm of functionalist theory. Remember the central tenet of this perspective: The parts of a society are to be explained by the functions they serve in the overall social system. In general, then, microstructures make sense in terms of what they do for macrostructures (Turner, 1985). The far-reaching networks revealed in the "small world" research not only bring information to individuals from afar, they also bind diverse social segments together into the unified whole called society. By playing their roles, individuals perform essential social tasks that blend together in society's grand play. Despite its emphasis on the benefits of existing structures, functionalism does analyze negative functions as well. Such "dysfunctions" are like the costs of doing business for a given set of social arrangements. In this sense, functionalism performs a kind of cost–benefit analysis on existing microstructures.

Consider the accounting ledger for youth networks. Both the conventional wisdom and sociological studies document the operation of what is commonly termed "peer group pressure" on young people. Network members can push you to use drugs and dare you to break the law. These dysfunctional pressures, though, are balanced by the positive functions of peer group pressure. Much sociological research has shown the networks of "good kids" to be populated primarily by other "good kids." For example, two recent studies of college students have found clear associations between the grade-point averages of respondents and the grade-point averages of their college friends (Antrobus, Dobbelaer, and Salzinger, 1988; Colbert, Lachenmeyer, and Good, 1988). Such evidence suggests that the everyday editorializing against peer group pressure is too one-sided. In a functionalist analysis, youth networks' social benefits generally outweigh their costs, and that is why most young people are enmeshed in one.

The general functionalist solution to the paradox of social structure is not entirely satisfying. Viewing your network as appearing because it somehow serves society overlooks one key detail: you. Another approach to explaining social structure begins with one-to-one relationships and the logic that drives them. It is called **exchange theory**, and it is often associated with the functionalist perspective (Collins, 1988). In essence, exchange theorists view social relations as transactions within which resources are given and taken. The resources include not only material goods and services, but also love, hate, and the whole repertoire of human emotions. Lovers give emotional fulfillment, and receive it in return—as the Beatles put it, "The love you take is equal to the love you make." Enemies exchange their hate in the give-and-take of fighting. Well-known exchange theorist Peter Blau recounts the case of a government agency in which agents were assigned to investigate a firm by their supervisor, but

exchange theory—an approach to social structure that views social relations as transactions within which resources are given and taken.

were forbidden to discuss the investigation with their colleagues. Despite this prohibition, a regular pattern of consultations existed between expert and inexperienced agents. Blau explained this forbidden microstructural pattern as a straightforward exchange:

> The questioning agent is enabled to perform better than he could otherwise have done, without exposing his difficulties to the supervisor. By asking for advice, he implicitly pays his respect to the superior proficiency of his colleague. This acknowledgement of inferiority is the cost of receiving assistance (Blau, 1963, pp. 126–28).

The groupie trades sex for a touch of fame; the brown-nosing student trades flattery for better grades; you trade a sympathetic ear to your classmate's boring romantic misadventures for a ride home.

As these examples demonstrate, the exchange approach can be flexibly applied to an enormous variety of human relationships. The theory has two especially attractive features. First, it supplements the traditional functional approach by suggesting *how* microstructures get built up to perform their societal services. The central mechanism is people maintaining relationships that pay off, and avoiding relationships that are too costly. Second, exchange processes highlight the involvement of *individuals* in building their own microstructures. Early exchange theorist George Homans called this "bringing men back in," but it also brings theoretical problems. For one thing, exchange theory applies a thoroughly economic model to personal relationships. Do you really calculate a profit-versus-loss statement in deciding whether to visit home this weekend? There is certainly a utilitarian element in many relationships, but is it the key element? Workers keep jobs they hate, couples stay in bad marriages, and offspring care for infirm parents who cannot even remember their children's names. These microstructural cases just do not "pay." The fact is most people are not ruthless enough to calculate the selfish value of each personal contact. Most people also lack the mathematical ability. Because the feelings of other network members about a given relationship affect the value of that relationship (What would Dad think if you stopped talking to your sister?), the calculations can become complex indeed. Interwoven into the microstructures of Figures 4:1 and 4:2 are matters such as social obligation and personal meaning, which are hard to factor into functional equations, but which are still powerful human forces.

Conflict Theory

Conflict theorists derive different answers than do functionalists to the mystery of microstructure largely because they ask different questions. Instead of proceeding from the assumption that social structures are "functional" for societies or the individuals within them, the conflict approach is to project such structures against a background of antagonism. Who benefits from this social arrangement? Who loses? What are they fighting over? The cost–benefit approach of functional analysis gives way to a win–loss statement for the various segments of society.

A practical demonstration of the conflict approach at a very fundamental level is Georg Simmel's analysis of two-person (dyad) and three-person (triad) microstructures. Any dyad, according to Simmel, is characterized by a "peculiar closeness" and a "greater individualization" of the parties than is possible in any other form of relationship (Simmel, 1950, pp. 134, 137). Why?

> The essential point is that within a dyad, there can be no majority which could outvote the individual. This majority, however, is made possible by the mere addition of a third member (1950, p. 137).

Consequently, triads (and larger structures) are inherently more unstable and conflict-ridden than dyads *regardless of the individuals involved.* According to Simmel's theoretical statement, the "romantic triangle" should be more subject to relationship problems even in cultures where it is an acceptable sexual arrangement; there is evidence that such frictions were common in Mormon families with "plural wives" during the past century (Kephart, 1976). Within our culture, observe a children's play group. The balanced interaction of a playing pair is often disturbed when a third child arrives and an argument ensues over who is whose "best friend" (see BJJ's daughter's depiction of this experience in the drawing on p. 127). It is commonplace in adolescence for hard feelings to ensue when one person in a same-sex pair of close friends starts to date the opposite sex. The conflict in these triads often appears as a "coalition" of two against one. Such a conflictual structure is impossible in any dyad. What is central for Simmel is that arguments will occur not because of personal pettiness, but because of the social pattern. Social conflict is simply built into the structures of association surrounding most people.

The centerpiece for most conflict theory is Karl Marx's vision of the modern class system. Although Marx was most concerned with the broad historical outlines of this system, his vision has several implications for microstructures in the contemporary United States. In the first place, consider the sociological truism that occupational role is generally considered an adult's "master status" (as defined earlier, the most significant in the individual's status set). This is consistent with the whole thrust of Marx's writings on the key place of labor in human life. The economic interests

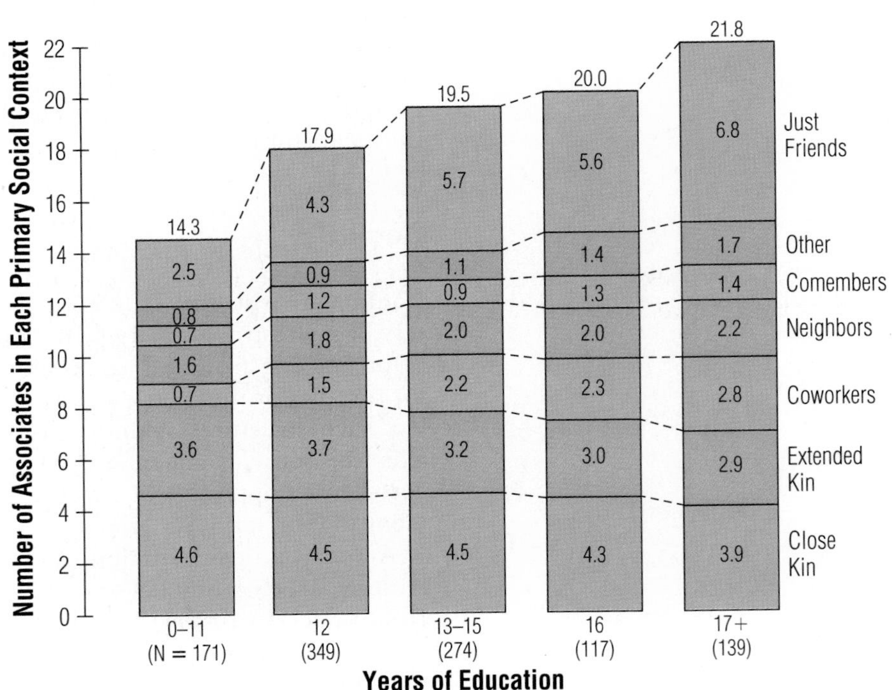

FIGURE 4:3 PERSONAL NETWORKS AND SOCIAL CLASS
Network size and composition varies with years of education—a key measure of social class.

of the capitalist class are best served by hired managerial workers for whom the job becomes an obsession—"workaholics." For factory workers and other members of the proletariat, jobs become so monotonous and controlled that work dissatisfaction becomes life dissatisfaction. Evidence on job satisfaction and alienation is spotlighted elsewhere in this book. Its immediate relevance concerns the content of occupational roles, and how these can pervade one's life for good or ill—depending on one's class position.

The conflict conception of class structure has implications for network content as well. If everyday life is truly ruled by the economic order, then the shapes of personal networks should follow the contours of the class system. They do. The results of a network survey of 1,050 adults from over fifty northern California communities are displayed in Figure 4:3. Notice that each higher level of education has a higher stack of network members. More-educated individuals are especially likely to have greater numbers of friends (an average of 6.8 for those with 17+ years of schooling compared to 2.5 friends for those with less than a high school degree). Less-educated individuals have slightly more kin in their smaller networks and, as a result, a much higher percentage of their contacts are with relatives. Analyses using other measures of social class and more recent national results from the General Social Survey have confirmed these findings (Davis and Smith, 1985; Fischer, 1982). The general conflict model—the higher one's social class, the greater one's "life chances"—likewise seems to be confirmed. Friendship, after all, is one of "the good things in life" and is more abundant at higher rungs of the class ladder. Since friends are key sources of information about economic opportunity (see Chapter 11), moreover, these microstructural differences provide a clue to how the rich get richer and the poor get poorer.

Symbolic Interactionism

To the nonsociologist, there is something odd about analyzing intimate personal relations through the abstract lens of social theory. It seems like the scientific study of touch. Anatomical descriptions of nerve routes and electronic impulses just do not capture the feel of a caress. What is missing is the sense of the experience from the *inside.* In a broad sense, symbolic interactionism answers this need within sociological theory. It is critical of elaborate systems that speak of society as though it were a free-standing thing. Symbolic interactionists call the fallacy of treating an abstraction as real **reification**, and they argue that without individual human beings there is no "society" at all. The proper approach, then, is to begin by stepping inside the world of face-to-face relationships rather than looking directly at the larger social structures built up from them.

reification—the fallacy of treating an abstraction as real.

In the classic theoretical statement *Symbolic Interactionism* (1969), Herbert Blumer laid out the central principles of this approach:

1. Human beings act toward things on the basis of the meaning which these things have for them.
2. The meaning of a thing for a person grows out of the ways in which other persons act toward the person with regard to the thing.
3. The use of meanings by the actor occurs through *a process of interpretation* (author's italics; 1969, pp. 2–5).

BOX 4:2 SOCIOLOGICAL IMAGINATION IN FICTION

Social Interaction and Survival

This is a scene from the science fiction novel *Dune* in which refugees from a conquered royal house encounter desert warriors whose law of tribal survival requires them to drain the precious water from the bodies of strangers. The exotic setting allows us to view at arm's length the dynamics of social interaction taken for granted in our more familiar world.

"Get their water," the man calling out of the night had said. And Paul fought down his fear, glanced at his mother. His trained eyes saw her readiness for battle, the waiting whipsnap of her muscles.

"It would be regrettable should we have to destroy you out of hand," the voice above them said.

That's the one who spoke to us first, Jessica thought. *There are at least two of them to our right and one on our left.*

"Cignoro brobosa sukares hin mange la pchagavas doi me kamavas na beslas lele pal hrobas!"

It was the man to their right calling out across the basin.

To Paul, the words were gibberish, but out of her Bene Gesserit training, Jessica recognized the speech. It was Chakobsa, one of the ancient hunting languages, and the man above them was saying that perhaps these were the strangers they sought. . . .

Scrambling sounds came from the rocks above and to both sides dark motions in the moonlight. Many figures flowed through the shadows.

A whole troop! Paul thought with a sudden pang.

A tall man in a mottled burnoose stepped in front of Jessica. His mouth baffle was thrown aside for clear speech, revealing a heavy beard in the sidelight of the moon, but face and eyes were hidden in the overhang of his hood.

"What have we here—jinn or human?" he asked.

As Jessica heard the true-banter in his voice she allowed herself a faint hope. This was the voice of command, the voice that had first shocked them with its intrusion from the night.

"Human, I warrant," the man said.

Jessica sensed rather than saw the knife hidden in a fold of the man's robe. She permitted herself one bitter regret that she and Paul had no shields.

"Do you also speak?" the man asked.

Jessica put all the royal arrogance at her command into her manner and voice. Reply was urgent, but she had not heard enough of this man to be certain she had a register on his culture and weaknesses.

These principles undermine generalizations about how any one "professor" or "college student" will act. No individual, symbolic interactionists argue, is an unconscious robot of social structure. Real people decide the meaning of things for themselves, and then act. In the story in Box 4:2, both sides are carefully sizing each other up—that is, deriving the "meaning" of Principle 1—in order to choose a course of action. Notice also that each individual in the confrontation takes cues from his/her associates in deriving that meaning; as per Principle 2, Paul is alert to the cues of his mother Jessica, and Stilgar is prompted by the tribal voice from the dark. Finally, Principle 3 is highlighted in the italicized passages that represent the inner voices of the characters. These show the process by which each actor interprets events for herself/himself. A key point of reference for symbolic interactionists is the inner conversation between the "I"—the active, personal

BOX 4:2 SOCIOLOGICAL IMAGINATION IN FICTION *continued*

"Who comes on us like criminals out of the night?" she demanded.

The burnoose-hooded head showed tension in a sudden twist, then slow relaxation that revealed much. The man had good control.

Paul shifted away from his mother to separate them as targets and give each of them a clearer area of action. . . .

"A likely cub," the man said, "If you're fugitives from the Harkonnens, it may be you're welcome among us. What is it, boy?"

The possibilities flashed through Paul's mind: *A trick? A fact?* Immediate decision was needed.

"Why should you welcome fugitives?" he demanded.

"A child who thinks and speaks like a man," the tall man said. "Well, now, to answer your question, my young wali, I am one who does not pay the fai, the water tribute, to the Harkonnens. That is why I might welcome a fugitive."

He knows who we are, Paul thought. *There's concealment in his voice.*

"I am Stilgar, the Fremen," the tall man said. "Does that speed your tongue, boy?"

It is the same voice, Paul thought. And he remembered the Council with this man seeking the body of a friend slain by the Harkonnens.

"I know you, Stilgar," Paul said. "I was with my father in Council when you came for the water of your friend. You took away with you my father's man, Duncan Idaho—an exchange of friends."

"And Idaho abandoned us to return to his Duke," Stilgar said.

Jessica heard the shading of disgust in his voice, held herself prepared for attack.

The voice from the rocks above them called: "We waste time here, Stil."

"This is the Duke's son," Stilgar barked. "He's certainly the one Liet told us to seek."

"But . . . a child, Stil."

"The Duke was a man and this lad used a thumper," Stilgar said. "That was a brave crossing he made in the path of shai-hulud."

And Jessica heard him excluding her from his thoughts. Had he already passed sentence?

"We haven't time for the test," the voice above them protested.

"Yet he could be the Lisan al-Gaib," Stilgar said.

He's looking for an omen! Jessica thought.

"But the woman," the voice above them said.

Jessica readied herself anew. There had been death in that voice.

"Yes, the woman," Stilgar said. "And her water."

Critical Thinking Questions

1. The desert tribe's general practice of draining the water from outsiders found in its terrain seems downright evil. How would you reanalyze this practice using functionalist theory?
2. Using the same passage, how would you contrast conflict theory with your functionalist interpretation?

Source: Frank Herbert, *Dune* (1975). New York: Ace Books, pp. 286–88.

self—and the "me"—the social self of roles and network positions. One of the reasons you can never be quite sure how any one person will act is because the "I" is always interpreting the "me" within the individual.

Now to apply these principles to more familiar earthly interactions. To the symbolic interactionist, Figures 4:1 and 4:2 have a false solidity. Instead of drawing these abstract patterns and then trying to explain their functions or conflicts, the focus should be on the interpersonal principles by which each relationship line is maintained. Without these face-to-face dynamics, the seemingly hard structure in the figures simply disappears.

ethnomethodology—the study of commonsense practical reasoning.

One branch of symbolic interactionism takes a microscope to everyday interaction: **ethnomethodology**, which is defined as the study of commonsense practical reasoning (Collins, 1988, p. 274). Harold Garfinkel, the founder of ethnomethodology, has his students engage in conversations where they ask for a full explanation of everything that comes up. Here is one student's account:

> On Friday night my husband and I were watching television. My husband remarked that he was tired. I asked, "How are you tired? Physically, mentally, or just bored?"
> (S) I don't know, I guess physically, mainly.
> (E) You mean that your muscles ache or your bones?
> (S) I guess so. Don't be so technical.
>
> *(After more watching)*
>
> (S) All these old movies have the same kind of iron bedstead in them.
> (E) What do you mean? Do you mean all old movies, or some of them, or just the ones you've seen?
> (S) What's the matter with you? You know what I mean.
> (E) I wish you would be more specific.
> (S) You know what I mean! Drop dead!
> (Garfinkel, 1967, p. 43)

Try a version of it yourself. When the next person asks, "How are you?" actually tell them: "I have uncomfortable shoes on, my bowels are acting up after a greasy lunch, I'm late for my next class, and now I have to run into you." It is taken for granted that you will not really answer this ritual question, just as it is taken for granted that a spouse's statements will not be cross-examined. By using such unconventional procedures, the ethnomethodologists uncover an intricate framework of assumptions and expectations entangling every human relationship. The "common sense" we apply in daily interaction is indeed common, but it is not simple.

Integrating the Theories

The boundary between self and society is a mysterious one, but it is not unknown. It is a zone occupied by the networks and statuses to which we have applied the general term *microstructure.* Now visualize structures like those in Figures 4:1 and 4:2 as occupying an area that cannot be directly entered but can be surveyed from a distance. The surveying teams at the perimeter are functionalists, conflict theorists, and symbolic interactionists. Each team has glimpsed organizing principles of microstructure from its own angle of vision. This section will attempt to pool the theoretical maps in order to develop a more complete picture of this sociological terrain.

Since it is a real-life microstructure, we offer our authors' team as a case study of theoretical integration. A functionalist would begin with the fact that authors produce textbooks, textbooks inform students about the workings of social structures, and people so informed are presumably better able to perform roles and manage others for the good of the society. While these are certainly noble goals, we did not form our team with such grandiose societal functions in mind. This is where exchange theory comes in. Our contract with the publisher stipulates that we trade words for money, but this is not the whole story either. The way we told the story in the chapter introduction shows that there are nonmonetary benefits being traded in this little interpersonal market—mutual respect, reviewers' praise,

This is a child's view of social conflict in a triad (art by Megan Jones).

and ego-stroking all around. Despite these happy feelings, there is a serpent in Eden. Like every other set of authors we know, there have been conflicts interwoven with the mutually beneficial exchanges. Why?

To a conflict theorist, such oppositions are an inevitable part of any microstructure. We have experienced two main types of conflict in the social process of producing this book. In our formal roles as authors, our job is to create what we think of as the ultimate lecture on each sociological topic. Although the book becomes "our baby" to the authors (and, in fact, takes a lot more time to make than a baby), to the publisher it is a "product" to be marketed along with the products of numerous other authors. While both sides understand these role differences (they are in the contract), tensions do arise between the authors and the company that are typical of any "business" relationship. Karl Marx would trace these conflicts to the "cash nexus" connecting the workers (us) to the capitalists (the publisher) in an unequal relation dominated by economic concerns. An interesting development within conflict theory is the insight that conflict can actually have useful social functions (Coser, 1956). One such "positive function of conflict" is a growing closeness as the members of an embattled group unite against a common opponent. This is a nice example of the theories complementing one another that we actually experienced. Differences of opinion that the co-authors had with the company tightened the bonds of the authors to each other, and actually improved the book—thus improving relations with the publisher.

The other main type of conflict on this project has been among the authors themselves. After each of us completed a first draft of a chapter, we would give a copy to the co-authors for criticisms and corrections before submitting it to the publisher. In some of our meetings for discussing chapter revisions, bruised egos gave way to open argument. More often than not, these disagreements assumed the form of the "coalition" in Simmel's classic triad, with the two critics ganging up on the pouting author of the finished chapter. As the conflict theorists would have it, such tensions came to be an accepted and intrinsic part of the co-author microstructure.

Symbolic interactionist theory draws different insights from the same social facts. Instead of this pat summary of functions and conflicts, emphasis should be placed upon the shifting meaning of the project based on the interactions of the co-authors. One's personal interpretation of the project *did* vary over time as a result of current relations with the publisher, or even the most recent phone conversation with a co-author. Perhaps the most intriguing insight to be drawn from the symbolic interactionist perspective concerns the "social construction of reality" (Berger and Luckmann, 1967). The idea is that human beings do not simply inhabit preexisting social structures, they create them. Our authors' team with all of its understandings and misunderstandings *was not there until we made it.* This microstructure will continue only so long as we cooperate in its social creation.

SUMMARY

1. The individualistic values of U.S. culture tend to make us see ourselves as self-contained individuals. However, every human being is connected to others in relationships that form complex social patterns called social networks.
2. The form and content of a person's social network affect many aspects of that person's life, including choice of friends, marital roles, health, habits, and even mortality.
3. At a micro level, societies can be viewed as constructed from the basic building blocks known as statuses and roles. From this perspective, the individual is thought of as less important than the structure. Nevertheless, individual identity can be seen as made up of the roles people play in the structure.
4. The conflicts and strains associated with the multiple roles people perform are often felt as an internal tug-of-war pulling them apart when they try to do what they are supposed to do.
5. In real life, the same individual sits at the center of both networks and status structures, and some sociological researchers argue that any separation of the two is artificial. Networks and roles interweave to create intricate microstructures, thus presenting a paradox: A society is seemingly made up only of individuals, yet no one of those individuals is responsible for the surrounding social order.
6. Each of the three major theoretical perspectives in sociology has sought to solve this paradox. For functionalists, microstructures make sense in terms of what they do for macrostructures. By playing their roles, individuals perform essential social tasks that blend together in society's grand play. Exchange theory, often associated with the functionalist perspective, views social relations as transactions within which resources are given and taken. Microstructures get built up to perform social services as individuals maintain relationships that benefit them and avoid relationships that are too costly.
7. Conflict theorists seek to solve the mystery of microstructure by projecting social structures against a field of antagonism. According to this perspective, social conflict is built into the structures of association surrounding most people. The conflict conception of class structure, for instance, is reflected in the shapes of the social networks of individuals and the economic opportunities—or lack of them—offered through personal ties.

8. Symbolic interactionists argue that without individual human beings, there is no "society" at all. Without the face-to-face, interpersonal dynamics by which relationships are maintained, any larger social structure disappears. Social structure is built upon the complicated framework of assumptions and expectations entangling every human relationship.

Chapter 5

Personal Perspective

My hobby is weightlifting. Normally I wouldn't bore you with a tiresome tale of men and women grunting in their spare time. Recently, though, I had an enlightening experience of sociology intruding upon my hobby. The reverse may now enlighten you.

Most of the time, this "leisure" activity is spent sweating with two or three overweight friends in a garage gym. There is no glamour but plenty of noise. As each lifter lifts, all of the others shout encouragement while watching closely in case she or he needs assistance. The lifts we perform would be dangerous as a solitary activity. Only persons one truly trusts are recruited as "spotters," and those who perform this risky service tend to be recruited as friends. This is where the sociology sneaks in: All of our everyday workouts are enmeshed in social network relations familiar from Chapter 4.

At the prompting of an ex-student, I decided to enter a local lifting contest along with the other members of our peculiar microstructure. To be eligible for cheap plastic trophies, we registered as a team. It changed everything. Now, we were a known entity with an official members list and a collective insignia—on T-shirts never worn at the garage gym. People recognized us by team name and credited points to this new thing. In effect, we had entered a whole new level of social structure that even *felt* different. Just before a personal record attempt, I had a revelation: What had been a set of loosely connected relationships was now transformed into a group.

I missed the lift, but the insight stuck with me. Mulling it over, I started to see whole new patterns of social organization. There were the other teams, whose mutual relations were structured around competition and, in some cases, open rivalry. The meet officials were a separate group (marked by special jackets) with authority over the competitors. Over their heads, I discovered, loomed a national organization with an official membership list (we had each paid $20 for a card) and executive officers. I even sought out the minutes of this organization and found it to be locked in involved interactions with other national associations. All of this from friends straining together in the garage. . .

BJJ

Macrostructure: *The Social World of Groups*

THERE is a twofold moral of this little tale. First, social structure is a multilayered phenomenon. Overlaying the personal patterns of networks and roles is the world of groups that we are about to enter. It is a vast area, encompassing everything from a sports team to a whole society. The second moral is a warning about sociology. Beware: It has the power to change the way you see every aspect of your life—even sweaty hobbies.

"GROUP"

The quotation marks around the heading "Group" suggest that the term has been the source of some confusion. It has. One reason for precise definition here is the haze brought by everyday usage. People use the term all the time, feeling they know the meaning from their experiences as group members. As any sexologist will verify, scientific understanding requires more than just experience.

Take the everyday term "age group." Despite your being included in one, you have not even *met* the overwhelming majority of persons your age. This makes an age group a very different thing from a rock group composed of

Jumping rope is a commonplace activity that can be performed in networks of neighborhood acquaintances. The case shown, however, is double-dutch team competition—i.e., "group" vs. "group."

social category—an aggregate of individuals who share a common trait.

group—a set of persons with 1) social boundaries, 2) internal structure, and 3) common expectations.

familiar people your own age. The former is a **social category**, an aggregate of individuals who share a common trait. Females, Asians, Catholics . . . all are such aggregates, often loosely referred to as "groups." Sociologists sometimes contribute to the confusion by analyzing, say, college graduates versus high school graduates as though these were true groups rather than just piles of people sharing traits.

To banish the clouds of confusion, we propose three defining properties of **groups**:

1. social boundaries
2. internal structure
3. common expectations

The first property concerns membership. In a true group—like a family or a chess club—there is a clear division between members and non-members. As in the powerlifting case, the in-group may even be distinguished from the out-group by an official list. Social networks do not have this closed quality. They are open, outreaching patterns of relationship, whereas groups are encased in a kind of social cell membrane. Compare the density of the interaction pattern within the group boundaries of Figure 5:1 to

FIGURE 5:1 GROUPS AS BOUNDED SETS OF RELATIONSHIPS

The dots represent individuals, and the lines are relationship ties linking them. Note that in the encircled areas—"groups"—all people are linked to each other within the boundary.

Source: Special thanks for the inspiration for this figure (and this section) to Charles S. Palazzolo, *Small Groups*, New York: D. Van Nostrand Co. (1981).

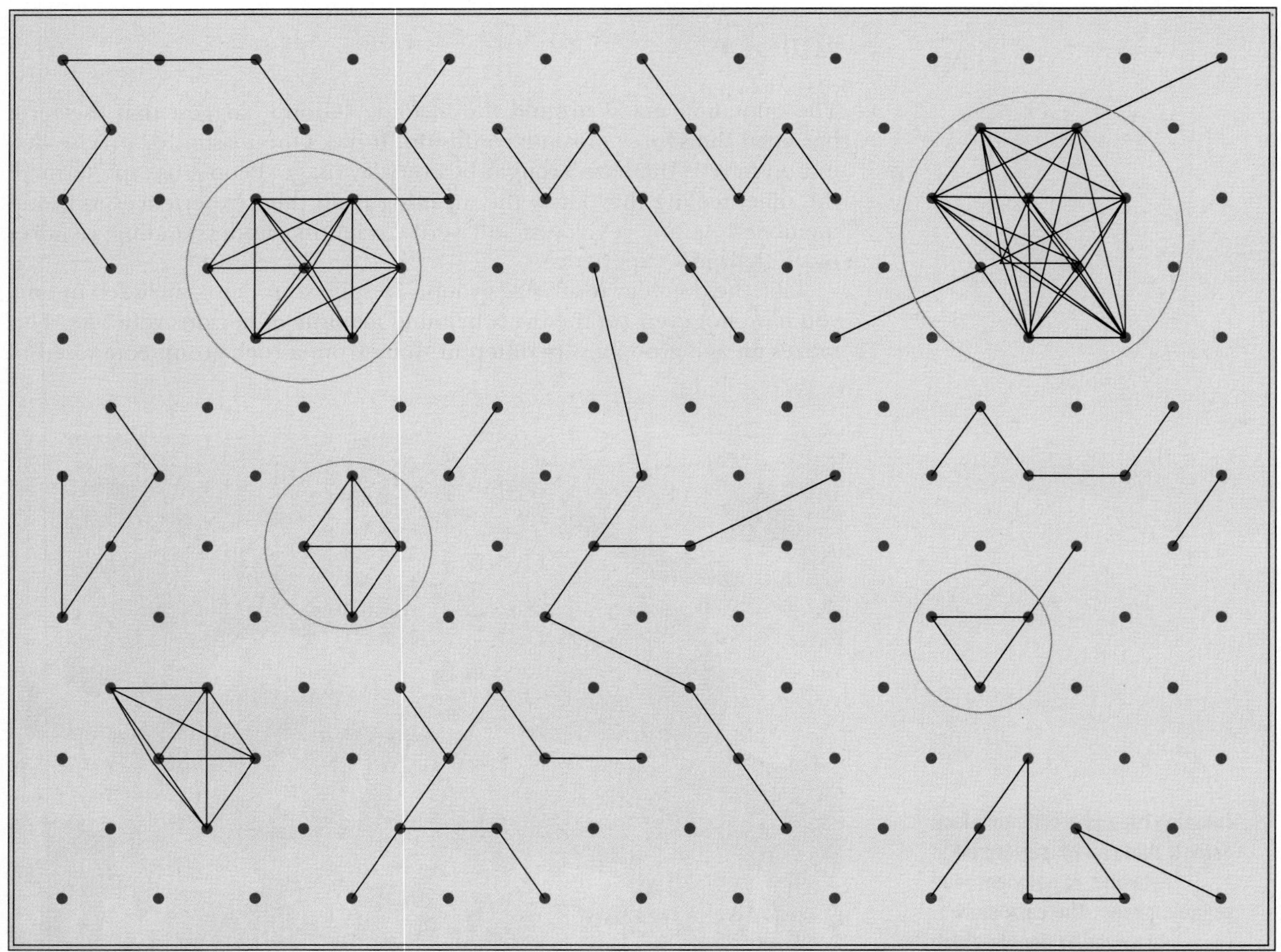

the looser network relations all around them (Palazzolo, 1981). This busy intersection of lines indicates an internal structure of varying complexity. The military hierarchy of rigid, ranked roles is obvious in the U.S. Marine Corps, but even the most humble of groups has some such structure. If you have a regular band of fans who attend college games together, typically one member gets the tickets, one drives the car, one tells the jokes . . . this is a basic group structure. The primitive roles revealed in the last example are related to defining property 3: common expectations. Compared to networks, which may be composed of very diverse relations (compare your relationship with your hometown best friend and your college best friend), groups have a more standardized set of norms. Imagine what would happen if you decided not to attend the big playoff game because of the upcoming sociology midterm. Inevitably, group members would start disapproving, nagging, joking about your studiousness . . . all part of their structured roles as group co-members with common expectations. Got it? To confirm comprehension of the concept, consider this question: *Is your introductory sociology class a "group"?*

Sociology has been preoccupied with this form of social organization. Until recently, many defined the discipline as "the study of groups." Much wisdom has been gained by the direct study of cops and criminals, hippies and hoboes, even saints and sinners. But we now know that the social structure of society has several distinct levels. It is clear that social networks form human linkages that do not fall together within groups. As we shall presently see, groups themselves form multileveled patterns: Introductory sociology class is a group inside the pattern of groups making up a college, inside the institution of education, inside the pattern of institutions that make up U.S. society. We have termed the latter levels *macrostructure* to distinguish them from the smaller-scale *microstructures* discussed in Chapter 4. Looming above the level of groups are the *megastructures* formed from the relations of whole societies (Chapter 6).

TYPES OF GROUPS

Even after all of this definitional fussing to clarify our subject matter, the classification of group types is still a daunting task. To cut the job down to size, we turn to the familiar landscape of personal experience. In your mind's eye, review the actual landscape near school. Picture the main street of the city or the college town. Mixed among the restaurants and retail shops offering you goods and services are the offices of groups who want *you.* Churches, health clubs, military recruitment centers, martial arts studios . . . all locate near the college so that students will be enticed to become members. Because of the commercial atmosphere, it is tempting to view the smorgasbord of groups as just another sort of merchandise you may purchase for your pleasure. This image is both true and false. The truth of it is that group participation can indeed be among the deepest and most human of pleasures. The falsehood in the consumer analogy is that your membership card is not just another possession like a coat or a CD. The group you selfishly select can come to possess your very self.

Reference Groups

To be sure, not all group memberships are meaningful. Everyone has had that cringing, I-can't-wait-to-get-out-of-here sensation at a first group meeting. Just as surely, everyone has had that stimulating, I-want-in feeling when exposed to certain other groups. Such personal signals help us to select the few schools we do swim with from the multitude of groups in the sea of society.

reference group—a group whose standards one applies to the self.

To move from marine to sociological classification, we shall define a **reference group** as a group whose standards one applies to the self. The term "group" is repeated as a reminder that this is not some loose association of relationships, but it must have the three properties defining that form of social structure. One property, remember, is "common expectations," which appear here in a new dimension. For one's chosen few reference groups, those outside expectations are taken inside the personality—that is, internalized (see Chapter 8)—to become standards for judging the self. This is the source of their power to possess us.

It is hard for residents of "The Land of the Free" to swallow the idea that groups they freely choose can swallow them. Instead of an argument, we offer evidence. Much of the empirical work establishing the power of reference groups was performed on college students. Herbert Hyman (1942) is credited with the first use of the term, and he derived it from money, looks, brains, and many other clique qualities students used for "reference" to their personal status. The implicit idea that students adapt their selves to meet such standards was explicitly tested by Theodore Newcomb (1950) in a classic series of studies at Bennington College. Newcomb's research team administered a political attitudes scale to a class entering Bennington, then readministered it each year until their graduation. As the women generally had come from upper-class communities in New England, it is not surprising that their entering attitudes were very conservative. By pointed contrast, the faculty and administration at Bennington were politically liberal. The data on the students showed a significant shift toward liberalism by their senior year, but it was not uniform. Those women who were more involved with campus social life and extracurricular activities—those who chose Bennington reference groups—changed the most. The least political change registered among those women who retained the strongest social ties with their families and/or boyfriends in their home communities; that is, they retained their pre–Bennington reference groups.

Does your college or university have a dress code? Although this one may seem to have one, the uniformity is produced by reference group standards rather than by college policy.

Do not read this as a perplexing commentary on the fickleness of human beings. In fact, otherwise odd switches in behavior make sense once one sees reference groups as the switching mechanisms. How many times have you watched a person transform their clothes, speech, and even opinions in the hope of gaining group acceptance? This commonplace of social life suggests a refinement in the concept. We often observe personal transformations *before* the individual is admitted into the desired social circle. By definition, an **anticipatory reference group** means that the group's standards are internalized prior to personal membership. Pioneering research during World War II reported in *The American Soldier* showed that inexperienced recruits imitated the social style of the veteran groups they hoped to join in battle (Merton, 1968; Stouffer et al., 1949). This phenomenon is well observed when people are about to enter the job market and are anxious about acceptance. One author started graduate school along with 10 other teaching assistants, each of whom had to face a classroom full of undergraduates for the first time. BJJ now understands why four of the assistants started smoking pipes, and six of them bought tweed jackets like those favored by the experienced professors.

anticipatory reference group—a group whose standards are internalized in advance of personal membership.

Such clear switches may appear at critical life transitions, but the more common situation is **multiple reference group** memberships. Most of us belong to several reference groups, and this means several different sets of expectations being applied to the self at any one time. Multiple memberships help to explain why virtually no one *completely* fulfills a group's expectations—there are other ties that bind. Some have proposed that personal identity itself is built from the complex interplay of several reference groups around a "self." In any case, it is a stereotypical blunder to see society as a mass of individuals each neatly tucked into a single social boundary. There are patterns within us reflecting multiple reference groups, and larger patterns linking those groups beyond the boundaries of personality.

multiple reference groups—an individual's membership in several reference groups at one time.

For some proof, refer to Table 5:1, which shows numbers of group memberships in the 1990 GSS sample. These are only *official* memberships in clubs and associations (over and above unofficial participation in informal family, friendship, and co-worker groups). Notice both that many

TABLE 5:1 Number of Group Memberships Crosstabulated by Education Level

NUMBER OF MEMBERSHIPS	LEVEL OF EDUCATION			
Count ROW PCT	Less than High School	High School	College	
No memberships	101 **33.2**	168 **55.3**	35 **11.5**	**304**
One membership	52 **22.9**	131 **57.7**	44 **19.4**	**227**
Two to eleven memberships	39 **10.6**	178 **48.5**	150 **40.9**	**367**
				$n = 898$

Main Point: Many respondents have more than one "official" group membership, and more highly educated respondents tend to have more such memberships.

Source: The NORC General Social Survey, 1990.

respondents have more than one such membership—367 of 898 respondents are in the bottom row—and that more education is associated with more memberships. The latter relationship is apparent in comparing row percentages; while about half of each membership row consists of high school grads (e.g., 55.3 percent of top row), the percent of ex-college students increases as memberships increase (in the right-hand column, 11.5 percent for no memberships, 19.4 percent for one membership, 40.9 percent for two to eleven memberships). Confirm for yourself that the reverse occurs among less-than-high-school respondents.

Primary versus Secondary Groups

The approach of this book is to enter sociological subjects from below, stepping through the door of individual experience, then working our way up to higher levels of social organization. The reference group concept is such a door. But now that we are inside the edifice of groups, it will be helpful to inspect the floor plan before climbing to the top. Figure 5:2 provides an overview of where we are going by displaying the linked institutional sectors that, according to sociological theory, are the fundamental elements of society. Note that each institutional sector has been filled with some suggestive group numbers. Only suggestive because, huge as they appear, these counts represent the tip of the iceberg of groups in the United States. Take, for example, the 83,237 governmental units listed within the Political Institution. Just one of them is the federal government itself, whose various branches, agencies, and offices surely run into hundreds of thousands of constituent groups. Or take your single school from among the 148,600 inside the Educational Institution box. Can you even name all of the academic departments, administrative offices, and student activity groups? And how about the unofficial reference groups of friends that form among students? The point is clear: The more than 68 million units pictured in Figure 5:2 vastly *undercount* the groups it is our sociological task to classify.

primary group—a group characterized by intimate, multiplex, expressive relations.

Zoology has a parallel problem. That discipline uses a set of logical principles to create order from the mass of living creatures. Our discipline uses a set of *socio*-logical principles to create order from the mass of human groups. One of the most basic principles distinguishes **primary groups** from

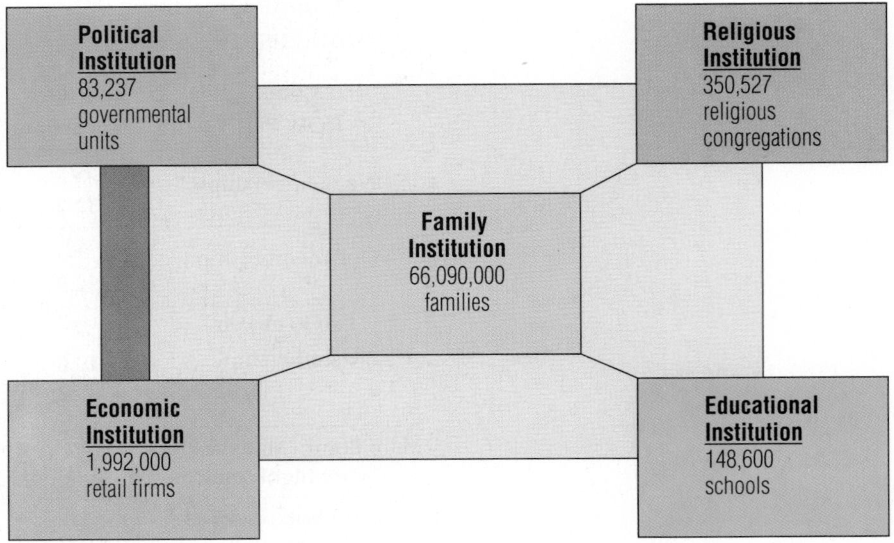

FIGURE 5:2 THE MACROSTRUCTURE OF GROUPS IN THE UNITED STATES
Source: U.S. Bureau of the Census, *Statistical Abstract of the United States: 1991.* Washington, D.C.

A parade is actually a pageant of many groups in which each attempts to display its distinctiveness.

secondary group—a group characterized by impersonal, uniplex, instrumental relations.

secondary groups (Cooley, 1908). To preface this distinction, return to Figure 5:2. While they all fulfill our technical definition, isn't it odd to see your family counted just like the more official "groups" in the other institutional boxes? There seems to be something fundamentally different about the insides of a family and an office. Precisely. To clarify the difference, we offer the scale in Figure 5:3 instead of a simplistic, one-sentence definition.

FIGURE 5:3 THE PRIMARY–SECONDARY GROUP SCALE

Primary	**Secondary**
intimate multiplex expressive	impersonal uniplex instrumental

Contrast the emotionally close and open—in a word, "warm"—relations of a model family with the distant and standoffish—in a word, "cool"—relations of a corporate headquarters. These are the opposite ends of the *intimate* versus *impersonal* dimension of Figure 5:3. The second dimension reapplies the concept of *multiplexity* first applied to network bonds in Chapter 4. In the present context, it means the kind of many-faceted relationship that leads to confusion in surveys when people try to describe their bond to a family member. A sibling may also be a classmate, a friend, a neighbor . . . in short, someone whose interpersonal tie consists of many strands. By contrast, the interpersonal tie to a tax accountant tends to be *uniplex,* with a severely limited range of shared activities and emotions. It's "all business." The latter example well illustrates the right-hand pole of the final dimension as well. *Instrumental* relations are instruments; that is, tools for achieving some specific goal. You go to a tax accountant to get your taxes done. *Expressive* relations are sought out because they are satisfying in themselves; that is, fun. Teenagers hang out at their chosen spot at the mall because they enjoy each other's company. This can perplex adults who ask, "What do you *do* there?", thus seeking instrumental goals in an expressively oriented group.

That last word is an important reminder. Although we have been dissecting different dimensions of social relations, they are here to be viewed as packed into real groups rather than as loose network ties. The word *real* modifying groups is also important. The dimensions in Figure 5:3 have been distinguished as "ideal types," Max Weber's term for picturing a social

This drug treatment facility for young adults has some "ideal–typical" features of both primary and secondary groups. Note the home-like setting (beds at top), as well as the goal-oriented seriousness of the group therapy session.

reality in pure form to clarify its essential nature (see Chapter 1). No real family should actually be situated at the extreme left end of Figure 5:3's scale. It has doubtless occurred to you that your bonds to some relatives are very cool, distant, and goal-directed ("Let's just get this dinner over with . . ."). Even the closest real primary relationships have some secondary aspects. Have you ever spent expressive quality time with Mom just to warm her up to the instrumental goal of letting you borrow the car? How about coolly putting Dad off when he asks about your love life, thus nudging the family toward the impersonal, uniplex end? The same dose of reality must be taken for secondary groups. The chilly, clinical atmosphere of office efficiency often warms up in groups of co-workers who come to share intimate secrets, engage in multiplex activities, and expressively seek out each other's company off the job.

The point is not that the primary–secondary distinction is a false one. Indeed, placing a group along the Figure 5:3 scale yields penetrating insights into its nature. The point is that real groups rarely—or never—are to be found at the extremes. Consider the final case of support groups: voluntary self-help meetings that are estimated to include some 15 million U.S. citizens. The sometimes painfully open intimacy of, for example, an Alcoholics Anonymous (AA) meeting is balanced by the restricted, uniplex sessions (once a week in a controlled format) and the instrumental purpose of the group (to beat the addiction). Knowing that a typical AA group belongs near the middle of the primary–secondary continuum furnishes an intellectual X-ray into this type of social structure. The concepts in Figure 5:3 provide us with an additional intellectual service. Aside from classifying subtypes of small groups, they are a stepping-off point into the higher levels of social organization that encompass families and offices. Charles Cooley concentrated on the definitive sociological features of primary groups (he coined the term), but he never actually used the term *secondary group*. Nevertheless, the implications lurking in the distinctions Cooley drew are like stairs to the next floor of macrostructural complexity—organizations.

ORGANIZATIONS

mesostructures—social relations that link higher to lower levels of social structure.

Over recent decades, organizations have been among the highest-profile areas of sociological study. Leading theorists in the discipline point to organizations as critical mesostructures, meaning social relations that link lower to higher levels of social structure ("stairs" in our analogy; see Collins, 1988). As you are about to see, researchers inside the discipline have spotlighted some fascinating features of organizational behavior. Perhaps most telling of all, practitioners *outside* the discipline have been eagerly stealing sociological concepts for their real-world practices. Whole applied fields such as organizational development, total quality management (TQM), and information systems analysis have been applying the sociology of organizations.

Weber on Bureaucracy

bureaucracy—according to Max Weber, the distinctively modern group form characterized by specialization, hierarchy, regulations, impersonality, and technical qualifications.

This current flurry of activity has its roots in the formulation of Max Weber, which, according to the *Encyclopaedia Britannica,* "set the foundations for all subsequent work on the subject" (1991, p. 642). The concept is bureaucracy, and even as these words are written, the authors mentally picture textbooks snapping shut. As the *Britannica* so genteelly puts it, this stems from "the pejorative associations of popular usage" (1991, p. 642). Since bureaucracies are omnipresent features of modern life, we all have a background of unsatisfying experiences with red tape, waiting rooms, and snotty bureaucrats. The collective memory is of a dull, unpleasant subject. Nevertheless, Weber's whole theoretical framework places bureaucracy squarely at the center of what makes a modern society a modern society (Knapp, 1994). Presumably, Eskimo igloo-dwellers also find igloos boring, however central they are to Eskimo existence.

This raises a further point that should keep you from closing this book: Familiarity may breed contempt even for what is unfamiliar to most of humanity. However commonplace bureaucracy is to you, it is a unique organizational form. In the vast garden of groups filling human history, bureaucracy is an exotic plant. According to Weber, this orchid of organizations springs up in the cultural soil of rationalization (see Chapter 2), which then spreads bureaucracy weedlike within and across societies. The process of bureaucratization is rampant in our own society and, according to Weber's theoretical predictions, is going to flourish wherever humanity forms groups.

So what is distinctive about bureaucratic organizations? Again the answer is a complex one, and again we resort to visual aids. Figure 5:4 represents the five major elements of bureaucracy as high–low scales. Remember, these elements were distilled by the theorist of the ideal type; Weber intends each scale to be a pure characteristic along which actual organizations can be placed nearer the high (bureaucratic) or low (non-bureaucratic) extreme.

This is an important observation to make when approaching the first element in the figure. It is a basic principle of social life that groups breed specialization. The "internal structure" we referred to around Figure 5:1 as a defining property of groups means that tasks are broken down and separately assigned to group members—one drives to the stadium, one buys game tickets, and so on. This very basic specialization from the left-hand side of the scale is magnified as one moves toward the bureaucratic side. In Weber's own words: "The regular activities required for the organization are distributed in a fixed way as official duties" (1947, p. 196). The specialized task to be performed by a bureaucrat is formally assigned as the occupational role, and ideally etched in stone as a job description (courts have ruled in favor of secretaries testing vague job descriptions because no official reason could be found as to why they had to fetch coffee). Additionally, the raw amount of specialization skyrockets in full-scale bureaucracies. Your professors probably lecture on only a few very specialized

FIGURE 5:4 THE ELEMENTS OF BUREAUCRACY

Non-Bureaucracy		Bureaucracy
Low	Specialization	High
Low	Hierarchy	High
Low	Regulations	High
Low	Impersonality	High
Low	Technical Qualifications	High

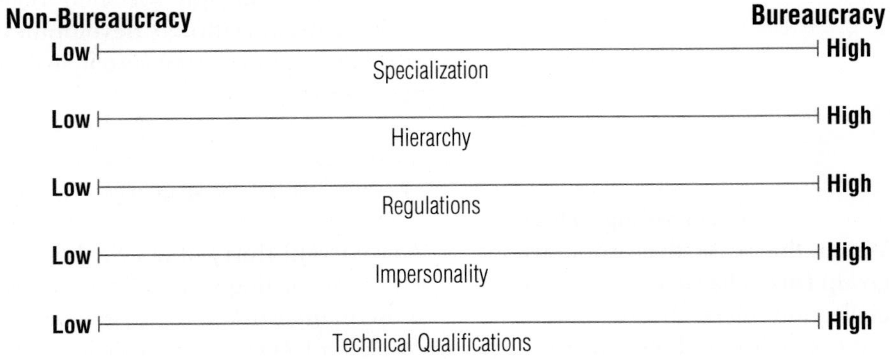

topics. Or think of the inevitable comment, "Imagine doing that one job all day!" uttered as the bridge toll-collector takes your change. That person is just one functionary in a local governmental bureaucracy that may include hundreds of specialized slots. All groups specialize, but bureaucracies break tasks down more finely and assign them more formally than do other kinds of human groups.

The second scale is also puzzling at first glance. Having read any part of this book, you are already aware of many group hierarchies. Elaborate leader-to-follower structures are everywhere in human history and (as Chapter 11 will relate) can even be found in ant colonies. Weber's distinction, again, is a matter of comparative degree. Compared to non-bureaucracies, bureaucracies structure the lines of authority *more* explicitly: "The organization of offices follows the principle of hierarchy; that is, each lower office is under the control and supervision of a higher one" (Weber, 1947, p. 331). Such explicit hierarchies can pile this, office upon office, to Olympian heights. According to Peter M. Blau and Marshall W. Meyer (whose distillation of Weber's concept is employed here), the General Electric Company circa 1890 had *twenty separate levels* between the president at the top and the workers at the bottom of the bureaucratic pyramid (1987). Note, by the way, the pyramidal shape is typical of the organizational charts hanging on the walls of most bureaucracies. The passionate attention to the details of the "lines of authority" making up these charts is exceeded only by the passionate reaction when one steps out of line. One of the authors was fired from a college summer job for committing a cardinal sin of bureaucratic life: violating the hierarchical "chain of command" by complaining to a supervisor (two authority levels up) instead of to a foreman (his immediate supervisor). This degree of hierarchical rigidity is a world away from the simple authority structure of your family hierarchy.

Perhaps Weber's formulation has now distanced you enough from everyday group experience to see familiar bureaucracies in a new light. Turn that illumination on your college and, in particular, its regulations. According to the laws of bureaucratic behavior, the school runs ". . . by a consistent system of abstract rules . . . [and] . . . the application of these rules to particular cases" (Weber, 1947, p. 330). Although a popular cliché has it that colleges are asylums of free thought, every official move a student (or professor) makes is covered by an "abstract rule." Admission, orientation, course registration, application for a major, even graduation all involve carefully crafted regulations. How much of your time is spent getting signatures and/or rubber stamps on the proper, carbon-copied forms? Another thing you have learned from this book is that every type of human association creates norms. Even head-over-heels new lovers invent rules for their lives as a couple. The difference to the right of the "regulations" scale of Figure 5:4 is in quantity and quality.

Evidence of the robust rule-making characteristic of bureaucracy can be found in Box 5:1, as well as in your everyday experience. Literally everyone has been stalled by seemingly silly regulations treated with utmost seriousness by some very unsilly bureaucrats. In his classic essay "Bureaucratic Structure and Personality," Robert K. Merton termed this phenomenon **bureaucratic ritualism**. It is a sort of regulation worship, a ". . . transference of the sentiments from the *aims* of the organization onto the particular details of behavior required by the rules" (1968, p. 253). Imagine an admissions clerk at an emergency room fussing with the insurance forms of a bleeding patient even though the "aim" of the hospital is to stop the bleeding (perhaps you don't have to imagine such an experience!). The

bureaucratic ritualism—bureaucratic regulations being treated as more important than bureaucratic goals.

BOX 5:1 COLLEGE EXPERIENCE

Red Tape and the Pregnant Parents

Ms. P has been the senior member of the sociology department's research staff for 11 years, working part-time. Her husband, Mr. P, works full time for the university's theater department. For 11 years the P's happily commuted to work together in the car they share, reporting to offices in the same building, using the same parking lot. Not until this past July did things become complicated. Mr. and Ms. P were awaiting the arrival of their third child when the sociology department was moved to a new building on the other side of campus. The P's had to choose which parking lot they wished to use because each permit cost $100 and was valid for only one lot. The choice was easy: Because Ms. P would only be working for a month and a half more, it made sense to renew the year-long permit for the lot by Mr. P's building.

At first this was not a problem. On mornings when Ms. P worked, Mr. P would drop her off at the new building and then park the car by his office. In the afternoon Ms. P, who left work two hours before her husband, would make her way to the car on foot—a reasonable arrangement, as her girth was still manageable enough to allow her to make the trip with hardly a wheeze.

But in August the system began to fall apart. Mr. P was scheduled for two weeks' vacation and would not be available to drive Ms. P to work. Ms. P, now in her ninth month of pregnancy, had begun to assume the dimensions of a small tank and was further afflicted by ligament spasms in her legs that struck without warning as she walked. Needless to say, the prospect of walking to and from the parking lot had lost its appeal.

The solution seemed simple enough: Ms. P would get a temporary permit to park in the lot by her new office. Since the baby was due in three weeks and she worked only three days a week, there would be no more than nine days for which she would actually need the permit. Further, it was summer, which meant that fully three-quarters of the parking lot was empty every day.

No problem, right? Wrong. Ms. P telephoned the university's department of public safety and made her request. Much to her surprise, the officer who answered the phone did not immediately say, "Sure. Come on over and we'll give you the permit." Instead, she said she'd have to talk to her supervisor and call back. Half an hour later, the answer came: No. All the spaces in the parking lot had been "sold." If one day all the permit holders should show up and find themselves one space short because Ms. P was parked there, there would be hell to pay.

"But the lot is almost empty."

"I'm sorry. That's the directive from the head of the department. No exceptions."

"Well, what about a permit just for the three days I have to park until my husband comes back from vacation?"

"Sorry. Mr. H says no exceptions."

maddening tangle of red tape that must be untangled to pay the hospital bill is further evidence of the extreme—even pathological—emphasis on the rules of the bureaucratic game.

The scaled elements pictured in Figure 5:4 have been separated for purposes of analysis, but they are joined (at the right) in any real bureaucracy. It is useful to illustrate this point by fleshing out features of the "bureaucratic personality" aside from a passion for rules. "The ideal official conducts his office . . . [in] a spirit of formalistic impersonality . . . without passion . . . or enthusiasm" (1947, p. 340). In other words, the bureaucrat is *supposed* to be a cold fish. This detached aloofness is designed to promote a fair application of the rules. If the registrar does not treat you as a number but as a real person deeply yearning to get into this sociology section,

BOX 5:1 COLLEGE EXPERIENCE *continued*

A short time later, Ms. P talked to a friend, who suggested she call a Mr. M, who was chairman of the parking board. Mr. M seemed very anxious to do battle with Mr. H. "Just go to the public safety office and fill out an appeal," he told Ms. P, "and I'll pick it up in the morning." That afternoon, Ms. P drove to the public safety office, where she told her sad tale once more. The officers seemed sympathetic.

"Are you on the list for the new building?"

"Well, I work there."

"It looks like you're not on the list. You'll have to get an authorization from Dean E saying you work in the new building."

"But I've worked for the sociology department for over 10 years."

"I'm sorry. You'll have to get an authorization. Mr. H says no exceptions."

Ms. P headed back to the new building to Dean E's office, where she told her story yet again to the receptionist and then repeated it to Dean E's secretary. Dean E wasn't in, so Ms. P was referred to Dr. D, the assistant dean. Much to Ms. P's relief, Dr. D was a woman, and the first person in authority Ms. P had encountered who actually seemed to know what it was like to be nine months pregnant. She immediately called Mr. H directly, spoke for a few moments, and told Ms. P her permit was waiting for her at the public safety office.

It was by now the end of the day, and Ms. P was exhausted as she once more hauled her considerable bulk to the parking department. This time the friendly officers were ready for her. They handed her a permit good for one year's worth of parking at the new building.

"All you have to do," they said, "is turn in your husband's permit for the other lot."

Ms. P's weary mouth dropped open. "I don't need this permit. I just need a temporary permit."

A man she did not know entered the room.

"I'm sorry," he said, "that's the rule. No exceptions."

"But Mr. H said—"

"I *am* Mr. H."

For a moment Ms. P considered giving birth right then and there. It might exact some small measure of revenge on the public safety people, and spoil their carpet as well. But the baby wouldn't cooperate, so instead she trudged out to her car, got the permit and turned it in.

"This permit expires in two weeks," said the officer. "You'll have to turn in the new one as well."

"It's at home."

"Bring it in tomorrow."

The following morning Mr. P returned to work. He brought in the other permit. He filled out a form. For the next week Mr. and Ms. P parked in the nearly empty new lot with their new permit, after which Ms. P was delivered of a healthy baby, and Mr. P returned to the office of public safety to get his old parking permit back.

LFP (Ms. P)

Critical Thinking Questions

1. How do the events in this story illustrate each of the five elements of bureaucracy displayed in Figure 5:4? Discuss.
2. Silly as they might seem, what bureaucratic purposes are served by the regulations Ms. P kept bumping into?

some other student will be unfairly excluded just because she liked your smile. The bureaucrat must be passionless toward clients or the passion for general rules will be unfulfilled.

How does any bureaucracy get human beings to act like rules robots? According to Weber, it is by establishing a clear path for advancement: "It constitutes a career. There is a system of 'promotions' according to seniority or to achievement, or both" (1947, p. 334). In a non-bureaucratic setting such as a medieval court, one's fortunes would depend on the personal whims of the ruler. In the federal government bureaucracy, by contrast, the standards for rising in the civil service are clearly written matters of public record. Such technical qualifications allow the dutiful bureaucrat to foresee an upward climb within the organization, thus building personal

At the admissions desk of a hospital emergency room, the clerk's job is not to heal, but to make sure that the regulations are fulfilled and that all the paperwork is done.

commitment and loyalty. Once one feels at home with one's future in a company, it is natural to accept the house rules on matters of policy, dress, and demeanor.

It is important to again emphasize the totality of these bureaucratic elements. The vast array of human groups can *all* be ordered somewhere along these scales. The increasingly common few that score near the right-

Does looking at George Tooker's *Government Bureau* conjure up your own experiences with "faceless," impersonal bureaucrats?

hand pole for all five elements are bureaucracies, a totality that produces a whole greater than the sum of its social parts: "The fully developed bureaucratic mechanism compares with other organizations exactly as does the machine with non-mechanical modes of production" (Gerth and Mills, 1946, p. 214). The machine of human organizations—it is a riveting image of bureaucracy. The superior efficiency generated by this type of group explains its runaway, worldwide expansion; in Weber's terms, it is the engine driving the future of humanity.

The Myth in the Machine: Real-World Bureaucracies

Given your own everyday experiences in and around bureaucratic organizations, the previous section had to make you squirm. In a real world of surly clerks, paperwork glitches, and bumbling bosses, it is hard to swallow the idea of bureaucracy as the ultimate efficiency engine. To some degree, this is because Weber was sketching an ideal–typical picture that could never be brought fully to life by fallible humans. Much contemporary research reveals the reality of bureaucratic behavior to be a complex interplay between official structures and living, breathing people.

Bureaucracy's "Other Face": A Network Analysis

Return now to the familiar bureaucracy of your college. Somewhere in the administration building there undoubtedly is an organizational chart hanging on some bureaucrat's wall. It shows specialized positions stacked in neat hierarchies of authority; in short, it is a simplified version of Weber's sketch of bureaucracy. The bold, clear lines connecting school statuses depict the official, formal structure, *which you know is a cartoon version of college social life.* Every campus has its rebel professors who refuse to interact with students according to college policy; every campus has its own "office politics" cliques jockeying for a better position than that displayed on the chart; and every campus has a rich, nasty, scandalous world of student relationships that do not even appear on the official version. This is the informal "other face" of formal organization. Every bureaucracy has one, and no bureaucrat should ever forget it.

The way to bring this bureaucratic fact into focus is with a network analysis. In your mind's eye, picture the simple lines of the organizational chart being overlaid by an intricate web of informal links of administrator to administrator, professor to professor, student to student, and every combination thereof. You now have a much more complex—and accurate—image of the school social structure.

To animate that image, consider some classic conclusions from the insides of actual bureaucracies. In 1924, the Western Electric Company commenced a series of studies so important that they later served as the foundation of the "human relations" school of management, and also influenced sociological research methodology (see the "Hawthorne effect" in Chapter 3). At the Hawthorne plant near Chicago, company officials launched an investigation of aspects of the work environment; for example, lighting, pay incentives, and wall colors that could affect worker productivity. Their data so perplexed them that Elton Mayo of Harvard Business School was called in to head a research team including industrial psychologist F.J. Roethlisberger and Western Electric manager W.J. Dickson (Ford, 1988). Researchers found an overgrown forest of social relations around the trees of bureaucratic roles. This network of relationships, moreover, acted back upon the bureaucracy from which it had sprung. Observations in the "Bank Wiring Room" revealed network bonds that were the basis for helping workers who lagged behind in output, as well as actively punishing workers who overproduced. Both of these actions of the informal social structure violated official Western Electric policy, and both affected bureaucratic efficiency (Roethlisberger and Dickson, 1946).

A fascinating advancement of these seminal studies was performed by Rosabeth Moss Kanter, whose findings have been so widely applied that she (like Roethlisberger) took her sociological approach to the Harvard Business School. As its title implies, *Men and Women of the Corporation* (1977) was a study of an industrial supply company (called Indsco) in which men are dominant employees and women are numerical tokens. It is not an account of open discrimination, of official bureaucratic policy locking women out of managerial positions. Rather, Kanter uncovered a muscular and complex informal structure flexing on the skeleton of the formal structure. Female sales agents are outsiders to social circles sharing gossip, drinking, and even dirty jokes. Although it sounds as though the Indsco women might be secretly glad to be excluded from such "old-boy" network activities, there is a career cost. "Peer acceptance" is part of the performance evaluation procedure, a key to raises and promotions; such acceptance is easy to come by if one is already "one of the boys." Rising executive stars, moreover, typically have a "sponsor"—a supportive corporate chief well connected among the Indsco hierarchy. Because most chiefs are male, they more naturally take under their wings young, hard-driving male executives such as they once were. Kanter's finely detailed analysis of the Indsco social structure is remarkably free of evidence of blatant sexism. What develops instead is a picture of the everyday social process of "getting along" determining who "gets ahead."

The literature on informal bureaucratic networks teaches two crucial lessons. First, they are *always* present. Even the coldest, most mechanical top-down organization will sprout love affairs, hatreds, friendships, and rivalries. These networks of unofficial relations cannot be weeded out. Perhaps the most formal bureaucracies of all—military organizations—recognize this reality and attempt to use it. Official training and staffing policy is designed to build *esprit de corps,* combat-ready team morale built from flesh-and-blood personal bonds. The latter example suggests lesson number two: Informal networks inevitably influence formal bureaucratic functioning. Sociological studies in World War II found that the most effective fighting units of the German army were characterized by close-knit interpersonal ties (Janowitz and Shils, 1948). Worker cliques controlled bank wiring output at the Western Electric plant, and sex-typed networks fixed the corporate race at Indsco. Its "Other Face" affects the workings of bureaucracy.

Primary relations arise within all secondary organizations and entangle every bureaucratic element. Be aware of this in your next sociology class. Chances are that you share at least one network bond with a classmate (Did she or he meet you there?), and that changes in-class behavior. Classroom studies suggest that students adopt the posture of "civil attention"—coolly listening to the lecture without being very responsive—in order not to appear too eager to please the professor (Karp and Yoels, 1976). The subterranean social world of informal student networks thus intrudes upon the formal classroom setting. One reason more students are not brown-nosers and many professors think students are sedated is the school bureaucracy's "Other Face."

The Limits of Bureaucratic Rationality

According to Weber, rationality is the fuel that drives the machine of human organizations. A bureaucracy is a designed group built to systematically achieve some planned purpose. If a new department or procedure is shown to be more efficient, old components are removed and the new components installed. Bureaucrats are supposed to operate "without passion or enthusiasm" (Weber again) so that they can busily gather information and impartially apply abstract rules to their decision making. Inspiration and charisma are admirable, but irrational. The passionate bureaucrat is a "cog" who can overheat and disrupt the organizational machine; rational, roboticized behavior is the "ideal type."

Sociological research has rejected the reality of the bureaucrat as an omniscient thinking machine. Herbert Simon (1976) developed a model of real bureaucratic behavior that earned him the Nobel prize. He begins with a fundamental fact of modern life: information overload. Imagine yourself in the position of the college president. Can you possibly read and analyze every report, statistic, article, and policy statement relevant to even a single decision? Imagine the seemingly simple choice of whether or not to increase the size of the student body. Your choice would affect faculty employment, local housing, parking spaces . . . the list goes on forever. Even with the information-processing resources of the college administration at your command, no president could gather and rationally weigh *all* of the relevant factors. Bureaucrats instead come to depend on **bounded rationality**—a simplified model of the problem that includes only key pieces of the puzzle. Much information must be excluded because of the limitations of the meat computer that is the bureaucrat's brain.

bounded rationality—a simplified model of a decision-making problem based on selected sources of information.

Such mental models often begin with the straightforward step of looking within the bureaucracy. Existing procedures and policy statements (most colleges have a "mission statement" expressing its basic aims) are a starting point, but their criteria of rationality may be unclear; besides, there must be new factors at work or the policy change would not even be on the table. To gather data about these novel features of the problem, you, as president, would undoubtedly create some *ad hoc* college committees to explore the options. In addition to these temporary data processing social structures, you might consult specially trusted colleagues (other college presidents?) to help eliminate bad choices. Such network simplifying devices make the issue mentally manageable. The result: a decision that **satisfices**; that is, is satisfactory and sufficient, rather than a perfect choice based on complete rationality.

satisfice—making a decision that is satisfactory and sufficient, rather than a perfect decision based on complete rationality.

Contemporary research has supported the case for Simon's bounded rationality model. Albrecht and Ropp (1984) have found that bureaucrats more freely discuss new, innovative ideas when they share several levels of social contact; in our terminology, "multiplex" network ties. It seems that interactions restricted to the official hierarchy give rise to uncertainty about how proposed changes might be received up the chain of command. Interactions including non-bureaucratic social or personal matters reassure such anxieties, opening up the boundaries of rationality to consider innovations. Milgrom and Roberts (1988) have built a formal model of organizations in which they assume that: (1) bureaucrats possess the best information concerning their own specialized functions (e.g., the registrar is the best-informed person about student enrollments); (2) bureaucrats manipulate the information they provide the organization to benefit themselves (e.g., registration numbers might be artificially inflated by including dropouts if the registrar is against an enrollment increase); consequently (3) fully rational bureaucratic decision making is an unreal assumption. Although you are certainly no bureaucracy, consider your college choice in terms of the Simon model (Robbins, 1989). Did you fully process all of the information about some 2,000 U.S. colleges before applying, then scrutinize the hundreds of differences between the colleges that accepted you? No. You compared a few key aspects of each institution, polled friends and parents for what they thought . . . you used bounded rationality.

As suggested above, a major reservation about Weber's idea of bureaucracy as a rationality engine arises from the mechanical breakdowns we have all witnessed. Some of the wrecks have been quite spectacular. Take the nuclear accidents at Three Mile Island (TMI, 1979) or Chernobyl (1986), and the chemical factory explosion in Bhopal, India (1984), that killed thousands. To be fair to Weber, the aforementioned all involved complex technological processes unknown in his day. All three incidents, however, occurred in the care of bureaucratic organizations, and all were attributed to "human error."

normal accidents—breakdowns that are an inherent property of certain kinds of tightly coupled, complex organizations.

Leading organizational theorist Charles Perrow has coined the term **normal accidents** to apply to such cases: ". . . it is normal in the sense that it is an *inherent property of the system* to occasionally experience this [accident]" (emphasis added; Perrow, 1984). He even subtitled a chapter in his book "Why We Have Not Had More TMIs—But Will Soon." Two years following its publication, the Chernobyl disaster unleashed more radiation than the Hiroshima and Nagasaki atomic bombs. Behind this chilling prediction lies Perrow's typology of organizational types pictured in Figure 5:5. The "Interactions" dimension across the top distinguishes "linear"—relatively simple

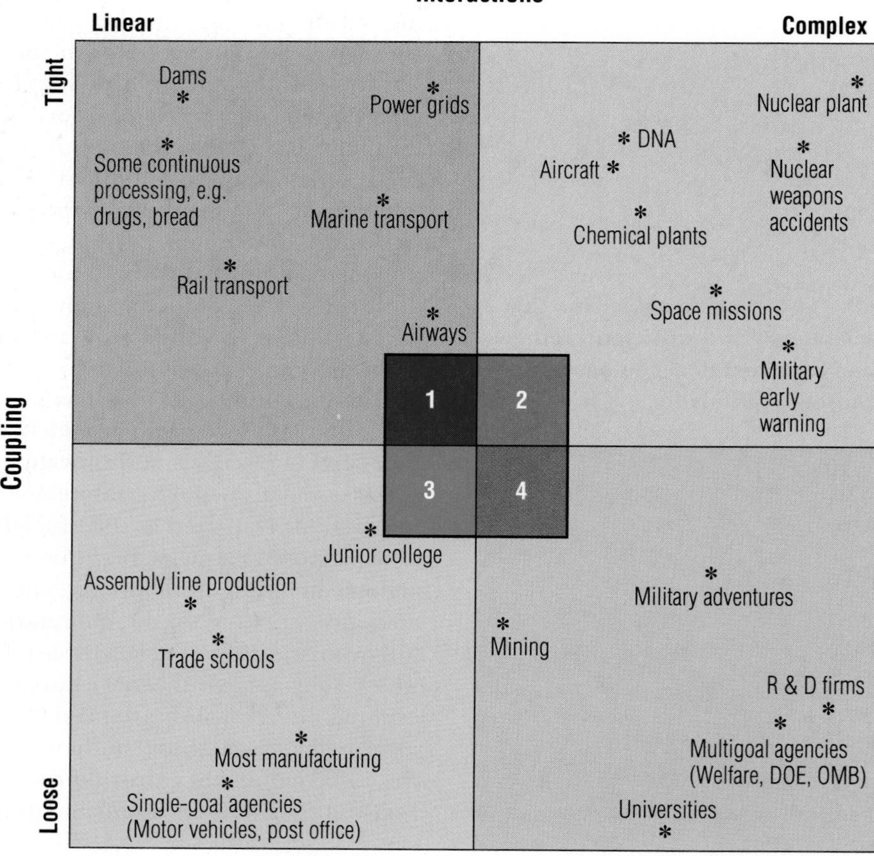

FIGURE 5:5 A TYPOLOGY OF ORGANIZATIONAL TYPES
According to Perrow's organizational typology, it is "normal" for the bureaucratic systems in the upper-right quadrant to have "accidents."
Source: Charles Perrow, *Normal Accidents* (1984). New York: Basic Books, Inc.

Even with the latest high-tech equipment, air traffic controllers must cope with the hazards of a complex, tightly coupled system.

and sequential systems—from "complex"—relatively intricate and interrelated systems. To illustrate, a jet engine is linear: air enters its combustion chamber, is ignited by fuel, and generates thrust. Your car's internal combustion engine, by contrast, is very complex; there are many interconnected functions and subsystems such that if one thing goes wrong (leaked transmission fluid, for instance) the spreading gunk can cause malfunctions in the drive train as well as in the air-conditioning, engine-cooling, and windshield-washing components. Note that "power grids" are near the middle of the interactions continuum. Nevertheless, the infamous 1967 New York City blackout has been traced to the interaction of two separate system components, which led to a by-the-book bureaucratic procedure that eventually shut down the power. Note further that nuclear plant operations, chemical plants, and space missions are, ominously, near the right-hand limit of complexity.

The "Coupling" dimension on the left side of Figure 5:5 is well illustrated by the case of marine transport. When a large ship enters a river channel, it begins a "tight" coupling process: First, because it is very time-dependent; there are tides to consider, and other ships entering the channel right behind. Second, this is an invariant sequence; the second bend in the river cannot be negotiated until the first is passed, and so on into port. A secretarial trade school (lower-left quadrant), on the other hand, can teach typing before shorthand or vice versa because timing is not crucial. In general, tightly coupled systems have little slack. They are exacting, nerve-wracking, and perilous processes, as the historic string of marine disasters like the Exxon *Valdez* oil spill of 1989 illustrate.

Now inspect the upper-right-hand quadrant of the figure containing complex, tightly coupled organizations. For still other scary predictions-come-true, Perrow placed "space missions" in this high-risk cell years before the 1986 *Challenger* space shuttle catastrophe. Although it only approximates his "military early warning" case, analysis of the Patriot missile battery that misfired and struck a U.S. barracks in Saudi Arabia during the Persian Gulf War indicates a breakdown of a complex, tightly coupled system. The "DNA" case has not yielded a disaster—yet—but its nonfictional hazards are feared by many critics of genetic engineering, and its potential dangers due to Perrow's dimensions are suggested in Box 5:2.

What is sociologically striking about all of these cases is the inadequacy of the "human error" explanation. The high-risk quadrant contains some

BOX 5:2 SOCIOLOGICAL IMAGINATION IN FICTION

A "Nomal Accident" in Jurassic Park

This story is set in the near future in which a group of investors have set up a Disneyland-like amusement island—Jurassic Park—stocked with genetically engineered dinosaurs. The park is a tightly coupled, complex organization like those in the upper-right quadrant of Figure 5:5 (see DNA). Despite the rational precautions, a "normal accident" happens. . . .

". . . Hammond's project," Malcolm said, "is another apparently simple system—animals within a zoo environment—that will eventually show unpredictable behavior."

"You know this because of . . ."

"Theory," Malcolm said.

"But hadn't you better see the island, to see what he's actually done?"

"No. That is quite unnecessary. The details don't matter. Theory tells me that the island will quickly proceed to behave in unpredictable fashion."

"And you're confident of your theory."

"Oh, yes," Malcolm said. "Totally confident." He sat back in the chair. "There is a problem with that island. It is an accident waiting to happen. . . ."

". . . I gave all this information to Hammond long before he broke ground on this place. You're going to engineer a bunch of prehistoric animals and set them on an island? Fine. A lovely dream. Charming. But it won't go as planned. It is inherently unpredictable, just as the weather is."

"You told him this?" Gennaro said.

"Yes. I also told him where the deviations would occur. Obviously the fitness of the animals to the environment was one area. This stegosaur is a hundred million years old. It isn't adapted to our world. The air is different, the solar radiation is different, the land is different, the insects are different, the sounds are different, the vegetation is different. Everything is different. The oxygen content is decreased. This poor animal's like a human being at ten thousand feet altitude. Listen to him wheezing."

"And the other areas?"

"Broadly speaking the ability of the park to control the spread of life-forms. Because the history of evolution is that life escapes all barriers. Life breaks free. Life expands to new territories. Painfully, perhaps even danger-of the most sophisticated bureaucratic structures and some of the sharpest, most highly trained minds on Earth. Despite the apparent excess of rationality, smoking ruins are more likely in this zone than in much simpler organizations. A ticking time bomb is built into the very structure of these bureaucracies. It is almost as though the outer limits of bureaucratic rationality have been passed, with sometimes disastrous results.

MACROSTRUCTURE

Remember where we are. The guiding analogy of this chapter places us high within the edifice of groups. Each of the topic headings ascends another level inside the towering social structure called "society." At the last stairwell, we surveyed groups of such scale that they contain myriad smaller structures (reference groups and network relations in your college, for example) while displaying properties distinctive of bureaucratic organizations. In this section we reach the floor showing the linkages *between* elevated entities such as General Motors, the United Autoworkers Union, and the Federal Trade Commission. It is a vantage point from which one can spot the patterns forming the apex of macrostructure—society itself.

BOX 5:2 SOCIOLOGICAL IMAGINATION IN FICTION *continued*

ously. But life finds a way." Malcolm shook his head. "I don't mean to be philosophical, but there it is."

Gennaro looked over. Ellie and Grant were across the field, waving their arms and shouting.

. . . Outside, the tyrannosaur rolled its head and took an awkward step forward. The claws of its feet had caught in the grid of the flattened fence. Lex saw the animal finally, and became silent, still. She watched with wide eyes.

Radio crackle. "Tim."

"Yes, Dr. Grant."

"Stay in the car. Stay down. Be quiet. Don't move, and don't make noise."

"Okay."

"You should be all right. I don't think it can open the car."

"Okay."

"Just stay quiet, so you don't arouse its attention any more than necessary."

"Okay." Tim clicked the radio off. "You hear that, Lex?"

His sister nodded, silently. She never took her eyes off the dinosaur. The tyrannosaur roared. In the glare of lightning, they saw it pull free of the fence and take a bounding step forward . . .

Now it was standing between the two cars. Tim couldn't see Dr. Grant's car any more, because the huge body blocked his view. The rain ran in rivulets down the pebbled skin of the muscular hind legs. He couldn't see the animal's head, which was high above the roofline.

The tyrannosaur moved around the side of their car. It went to the very spot where Tim had gotten out of the car. Where Ed Regis had gotten out of the car. The animal paused there. The big head ducked down, toward the mud.

Tim looked back at Dr. Grant and Dr. Malcolm in the rear car. Their faces were tense as they stared forward through the windshield.

The huge head raised back up, jaws open, and then stopped by the side windows. In the glare of the lightning, they saw the beady, expressionless reptile eye moving in the socket.

It was looking in the car.

Critical Thinking Questions

1. Where would you place *Jurassic Park* in Figure 5:5? Explain why.
2. What are the "primary" and "secondary" interactions in this selection? (Hint: see Figure 5:3.)

Source: Michael Crichton, *Jurassic Park* (1991). NY: Ballantine Books, pp. 75–6, 159, 185–86.

Interorganizational Relations: Networks Again

Informal Relations

As usual, it is useful to step into the structural level through the door of personal experience. Recall that Chapter 4 opened with an account of how network ties pulled the authors' strings to sign the contract for this book. Now imagine that you are a book editor within the publishing bureaucracy known as Harcourt Brace & Co. Your job requires that you comb through the thousands of would-be professor–authors to sign some precious few to contracts. The stakes are high. If you pick a loser who misses the writing deadline or writes a rotten book, you may lose your bureaucratic position. According to a study of the publishing industry by an organizational sociologist (Powell, 1985), editors rely on *inter*organizational, informal contacts. Aspiring editors build up a small social circle of professors to recommend potential authors and to critically review manuscripts. Perhaps tipped off by other Harcourt Brace employees (*intra*organizational informal ties like those discussed in "Bureaucracy's 'Other Face'"), editors like you cultivate helpful informal relations with employees of other bureaucracies.

Research has revealed extensive informal networks connecting organization to organization to organization (Hall, 1987). Old school chums in the same industry stay in touch in case they want to change jobs. Members of a church discover that their separate charity organizations can pool resources. Representatives of different governmental agencies "do lunch" over business, then form a friendship. Just as the official organizational chart cannot impede informal relations among bureaucrats, the walls of the organization are a permeable membrane through which social bonds pass.

Interlocking Directorates

In addition to primary relations tying separate bureaucracies together, there are organizational linkages of a more official, secondary character. One such bond is the **interlocking directorate**, in which a member of the executive board of one organization also sits on the board of another organization. This one person creates a semi-official relationship between the two bureaucracies, and the further ties that "interlock" these "directors" form impressive social structures. We would bet that *all* members of your college board of trustees: (1) serve on some other board, (2) sit on another board with at least one other trustee, and (3) that your college administration uses this interlocking directorate to solicit resources for the school.

interlocking directorate—members of the executive board of one organization also sitting on the board of other organizations.

Figure 5:6 illustrates the structure—and functions—of an interlocking directorate for a major corporation. Both because of limited resources and federal merger (anti-trust) restrictions, the Firestone Tire and Rubber Company could not acquire the Cleveland Trust Bank, the airlines, or their subsidiary companies (indicated by solid vertical lines). Though direct control is precluded (curved arrow lines mean market constraint), Firestone's board of directors has a member on Western's board and a member on the bank's board, which is also attended by directors of both other airlines (dotted lines indicate interlocks). The growing literature on this form of interorganizational network suggests that financial institutions exert the most control through interlocking directorates (Mintz and Schwartz, 1981). According to a study of the 797 largest American business firms, only 62 had no interlocks with the other giant firms (Pennings, 1980). Director interlocks are not restricted to the corporate economy. Nonprofit organizations—such as the YMCA, the United Way, and, as we suggested, your college—depend heavily on these interorganizational ties.

FIGURE 5:6 AN INTERLOCKING DIRECTORATE

Arrows represent market constraint, solid lines represent ownership, and dashed lines represent interlocks.

Source: Ronald S. Burt, Kenneth P. Christman, and Harold C. Kilburn, Jr. (1980). "Testing a Structural Theory of Corporate Cooptation: Interorganizational Directorate Ties as a Strategy for Avoiding Market Constraints on Profits," *American Sociological Review,* 45 (Oct.): 827.

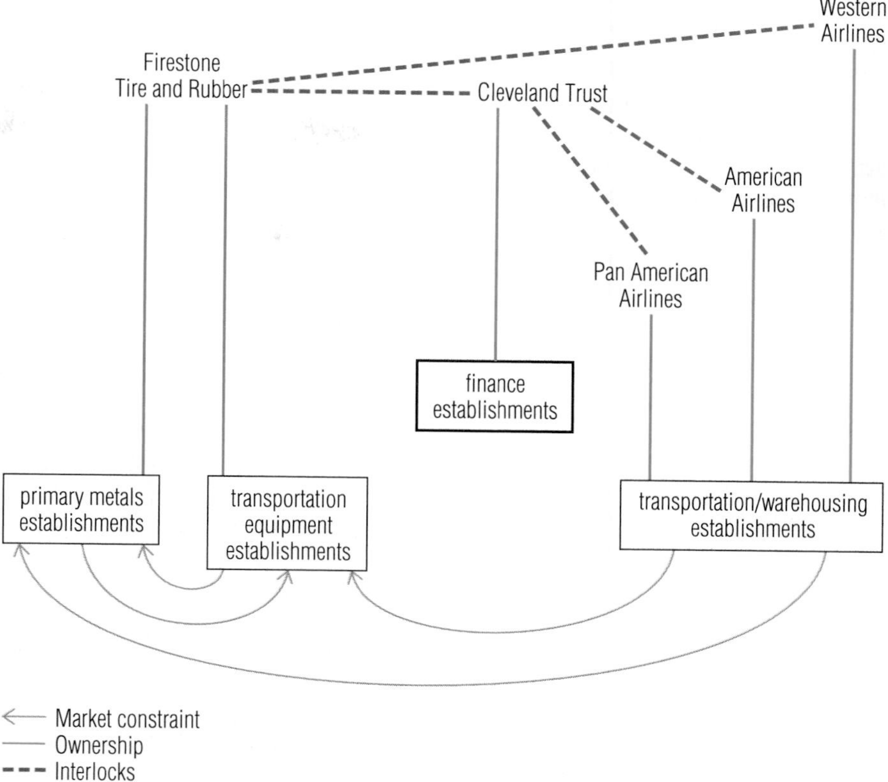

Formal Relations

Some ties between organizations are every bit as formalized as those within bureaucratic offices. Every corporation is enmeshed in a maze of contracts with producers, suppliers, consumers, consultants, security firms, and so on. A contract is the prototype for a secondary relation, a very official piece of paper stating the nature of the bond between these companies. To step over into the realm of public organizations, consider the formal network structure that *defines* the federal government of the United States.

Remember the basic lessons of grade school civics class outlining the "separation of powers" laid down in the Constitution. The executive, judicial, and legislative *branches* (a very suggestive network term) of government have formally stated, virtually sacred relationships to one another. Moreover, the bureaucratic units within each branch are integrated rather than independent. A decision passes from the Defense Department to the White House; an appealed decision passes from a district court to the Supreme Court; a law overrides presidential veto to pass in Congress—the lines of each such passage *are* etched in stone. In a real sense, the U.S. government itself consists of formal interorganizational relations.

To tie up all of the network threads enmeshing organizations, we present the final diagram of this chapter (we promise). Figure 5:7 depicts the results of a study of programs serving problem youth. Although police are at the center as employees of the organization that apprehends delinquents, much "police work" involves coordinating relations with other agencies. Some of these relations are highly formalized (bold lines), such as the procedures by which delinquents are turned over to the Probation and Parole Department; some are less formal (dotted lines), such as conferences with the Mental Health Clinic over problem cases; informal relations (thin lines) also arise from contacts with community counselors at the

FIGURE 5:7 INTERORGANIZATIONAL RELATIONS ILLUSTRATED

Network linkages revealed in a study of programs serving problem youth. The police organization at the center has active relations at various levels of formalization with organizations in various institutional zones.

Source: Richard H. Hall, *Organizations: Structures, Processes and Outcomes* (1987). Englewood Cliffs, NJ: Prentice-Hall, Inc., p. 237.

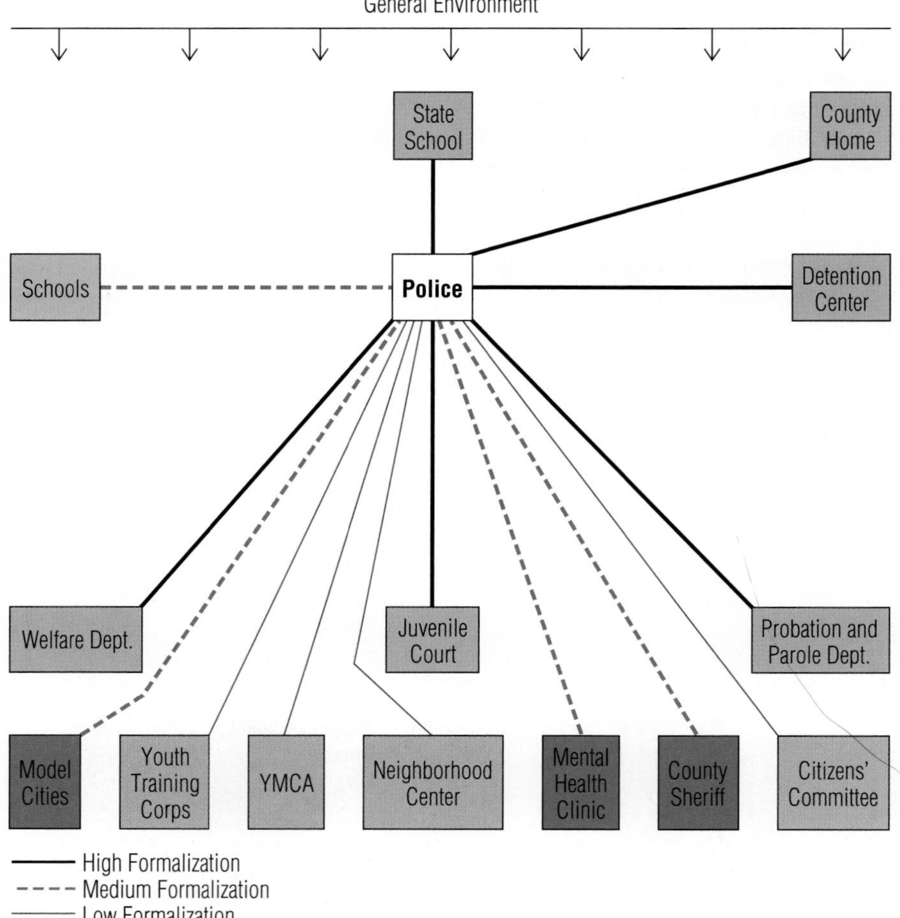

YMCA and Neighborhood Centers. Two conclusions are apparent. First, this is visual evidence of the complexity of the networks that entangle real organizational behavior. Second, the various strands reach into other institutional zones such as education (Schools) and the family (County Home), which brings us to the door of the next topic.

INSTITUTIONS

institutions—large-scale social structures that address basic societal needs.

We are now at the top floor. From this height, the broad contours of society are clearly visible. They are formed by **institutions**, large-scale social structures that address basic societal needs. This is not the everyday meaning of the word. You might refer to your own college as an institution, though technically it is a mere organization. Sociologists have defined institutions to distinguish such massive macrostructural elements from the organizational level we have left below.

There is broad consensus within the discipline about a society's "basic needs." The large-scale social structures that address these needs are illustrated in Figure 5:2. To survive, *every* society must (1) produce and distribute material resources (Economic Institution); (2) produce a new generation of that society's inhabitants (Family Institution); (3) instill the culture in the new generation (Educational Institution); (4) organize decision making and maintain social order (Political Institution); and, finally,

POLITICAL INSTITUTION

RELIGIOUS INSTITUTION

FAMILY INSTITUTION

ECONOMIC INSTITUTION

EDUCATIONAL INSTITUTION

The pictures in this mural represent the separate institutions of the macrostructure of ancient Egypt.

(5) provide a framework of personal meaning for its members (Religious Institution).

Please compare the layout of Figure 5:2 to our table of contents for Part V. Note first that "Political Economy" is a single chapter. As will be explained in Chapter 16, the classic sociological theorists have emphasized the interconnection between these two institutions (note the broad connecting line in the figure), and the dominance they exert together over the other three. Also observe the absence of some major structural spheres from Figure 5:2. Health care and science structures are dealt with in Chapters 18 and 21, respectively, because of their dynamism as sources of "Social Change" (Part VI in the table of contents).

Why are we explaining all of this? Because, frankly, Figure 5:2 looks too simple to carry the grand title "macrostructure." Nevertheless, this simplistic sketch shows the current state of our knowledge. Beyond its agreement about basic societal needs, sociology has not yet developed an explanatory theory of social institutions (Coleman, 1990). The institutions themselves are well documented and described—as we said, they are visible at this top floor of society. What is missing is how we got up here. It is quite like real skyscrapers, which, by tradition, have no thirteenth floor. Similarly, there is a missing story here about how organizations lead upward into the heights of society. To seek an answer, we must go back to the busy drawing board of sociological theory.

THEORETICAL PERSPECTIVES ON MACROSTRUCTURE

The span of human groups is vast indeed. Think of the dizzying distance between the ground floor of reference groups and the summit of social institutions. In all of its grandeur, society itself is, in fact, a group—it fulfills all of the criteria of our definition while also enclosing all of the other group types. In the following chapter, the macrostructures that are societies will themselves be incorporated into the wider patterns of globalization. For now, the sociological spotlight is turned onto the forces that power group structures *inside* the skyscraper of a society.

Functionalism

Functionalists are not sure just how the skyscraper got built, but they know society is still standing. The presumption is that the structure of groups is a self-supporting system. Much of the theoretical work blueprinting that idea has been done up at the organizational level.

isomorphism—the structural similarity of organizations.

organizational environment—the larger social setting of an organization, including other organizations.

Begin with the observable fact of the similarity of organizations. Recall your visits to strikingly familiar colleges, or your conversations with friends attending elsewhere suffering academic pressures like yours. The structural similarity, or **isomorphism**, of schools can also be observed among department stores, professional football teams, and government offices (Di Maggio and Powell, 1983). Why does this happen? A major force creating sameness is the **organizational environment**. Big and powerful as they are, bureaucracies live in larger social settings. Governmental regulations exert controls over the structure of universities, which is why you see affirmative action and financial aid offices on nearly every campus. Corporations must respond to shifts in the consumer environment, so GM, Ford, and Chrysler all have big marketing departments. One of the most influential sociological approaches refers to the "population ecology" of organizations (Hannan and Freeman, 1977). This model draws a parallel to the environmental niches occupied by biological organisms. Just as unfit animals perish from their place in the ecology, bureaucracies that fail to fit the functional requirements of the organizational field become fossils. The implication is that surviving organizations serve society's larger needs.

Functionalist theories have also illuminated the insides of bureaucracies. One of the most famous studies of corporate life was William H. Whyte's

The Organization Man published in 1957. The phrase has passed into common speech to refer to a workaholic whose life is consumed by devotion to the organization. No doubt you have met such people. They are living evidence of the power of organizations to capture the souls of career bureaucrats, a phenomenon noted by Max Weber. Such zeal can drive impressive social contributions, but there are dysfunctions as well. Unbounded loyalty to good old _______ College can retard necessary changes in a bureaucratic structure that seems sacred to its employees (Blau and Meyer, 1987). Whyte's "organization man" also referred to a person who had replaced a love of family and community with a fanaticism for the firm.

Conflict Theory

How does the "organization man" get to be such a slave? Moreover, why were "organization women" not addressed in Whyte's famous study? These questions pose riddles of social organization in the typically provocative terms of conflict theory.

compliance theory—explanation of the mechanisms by which organizations gain the compliance of their members.

According to Amitai Etzioni (1975), the answer to the first question lies in the three mechanisms of **compliance theory**. First, organizations use coercion to get members to comply. Prisons and military branches rely heavily on coercive techniques, but even universities and corporations may force folks to toe the line or get fired. The second mechanism is from the heart of the conflict approach: greed. By dangling material rewards in front of bureaucrats and rewarding them for service, bureaucracies build loyalty through bribery. Finally, organizations do not have to depend entirely upon their own brainwashing machines. The third mechanism is social selection. Think of the typical corporate job interview. The sharply suited applicant tries to convince the firm that he is *already* an "organization man" committed to the firm thanks to the first-rate MBA training (brainwashing) he received at good old _______ University.

Conflict theory thus sees the same slavish bureaucrats in an entirely new light stressing mind control. This theoretical illumination also reveals a different view of bureaucratic structure. Instead of a rational system made to service the social environment, there is a battle-scarred framework built of war, truce, and alliance. At a time when functionalist theories were ascendant in sociology, Melville Dalton caused a minor sensation with his conflict-riddled view of *Men Who Manage* (1957). He worked as a participant–observer in six business firms and documented seemingly ceaseless struggles between management cliques. At about the same time, Michael Crozier (1962) observed the wrestling for control of two French government agencies among different occupational groups. Such seminal studies show "office politics" to be an inescapable fact of organizational life. The overwhelmingly male subjects of these studies (and Whyte's, too) also suggest a gender conflict hidden under the management wars.

Conflict theory throws a similarly harsh light on interorganizational relations. Why do labor unions and political parties exist at all? These are "conflict organizations" made to battle other organizations. Why do corporations cease to exist? Rather than the bloodless view of "population ecology," which says that the most functional organizations survive, conflict theorists point to the trail of blood. When "unfit" companies fail, people suffer. Moreover, their failure did not just happen; other corporations killed them. Who fell when Honda and Apple rose?

Observing the stock exchanges in South Africa and Indonesia (at right), functionalists would point to the structural similarities (i.e., "isomorphism") due to common organizational environments; conflict theorists to the apparent dog-eat-dog competition; and symbolic interactionists to the interpersonal ties between buyers and sellers.

Symbolic Interactionism

As is their habit, symbolic interactionists attempt to deflate grand structural claims about organizations. Instead of focusing on functional requirements or compliance mechanisms, the theoretical lens zooms down to the people manning the desks. How do individuals in bureaucracies behave, and what meaning does this behavior have for them?

The maestro in this interpersonal zone is Erving Goffman. His theoretical instrument dissects face-to-face interactions and the motives behind them. In his best-known work *The Presentation of Self in Everyday Life* (1959), he unmasks us in our attempts to manage the impressions we create. Instead of viewing the job applicant discussed earlier as an automaton trained for corporate compliance, Goffman's method is to view the interview as a performance (remember, Goffman is a founder of the "dramaturgical" school; see Chapter 4). The dark, pin-striped suit and severe haircut are a costume meant to look businesslike; one secretly wipes sweaty palms to conceal nervousness about impressing the interviewer, who is also trying to impress the interviewee with a suave, upper-management demeanor. Many a corporate climber has made vice-president by carefully presenting the appropriate self in the conference room, at the cocktail party, and around the water cooler. This could be risky, but visit your professor's office using Goffman's approach. Notice the props on the walls

(diplomas, teaching awards, etc.) that authenticate the professor's expertise. Catch yourself in the act of pretending to be a model student.

Bureaucracies are big, intimidating social structures that control much of our lives. Symbolic interactionists delve into the selves operating all of this heavy societal machinery. It is an inside-out approach to organizational behavior, an attempt to find primary human motives in secondary settings.

Integrating the Theories

Your authors' university is currently "downsizing"; that is, reducing the size of its student enrollment and, therefore, the number of full-time faculty. As we have repeatedly argued, sociology has the power to explain common issues influencing individual lives. Here is a case where we have seen the power of social theory firsthand.

A recent national poll of college administrators found that nearly half are planning faculty cuts. As in private industry during a recessionary period, such layoffs are generally justified by the goal of making the university "leaner and meaner." This is a functionalist argument. In effect, a school claims that cost-cutting will improve its ability to perform essential educational functions while surviving in a harsh, competitive environment. Such streamlining certainly has brought fiscal stability to some colleges, but conflict theory raises a related question: Who gets "streamlined"? Staff cuts can elicit the most vicious fights ever observed in the hallowed halls of academe. Departments openly compete to escape the axe; faculty senates may call for the head of the president, or even slashes in the football budget. Much of this dirty in-fighting is done at the interpersonal level. A symbolic interactionist could have a field day at our university tracking the corridor conversations, animated phone calls, and angry colleagues avoiding eye contact.

A particularly nice illustration of the complementarity of sociological theories can be observed at the departmental level. Open conflict over jobs often creates a sense of unity among colleagues teaching the same discipline. This is what Lewis Coser has termed *The Functions of Social Conflict* (1956). Sociology professors draw together into a more functional political organization *because* of the hostile environment; the sense of interpersonal unity within the department improves as well. This integrative understanding does not apply only to *our* situation. The poll just cited also says that college administrators are planning tuition raises and student service cuts . . .

SUMMARY

1. Social structure is a multilayered phenomenon in which groups overlay the personal patterns of networks and roles. There are three defining properties of groups: social boundaries, which make a clear division between members and non-members; internal structure; and common expectations.
2. The expectations of one's reference groups are internalized to become standards for judging the self. However, because most of us belong to several reference groups, virtually no one completely fulfills the expectations of any one group. Some sociologists have proposed that personal identity itself is built from the complex interplay of several reference groups around a "self."
3. Above small groups in terms of macrostructural complexity are organizations. Leading sociological theorists point to organizations as critical mesostructures, meaning social relations that link lower levels of social structure to higher levels.
4. Central to the sociology of organizations is Max Weber's concept of bureaucracy. Bureaucracy comes about as a result of cultural rationalization and then spreads within and across societies. Bureaucratic organizations are characterized by their high degree of specialization, hierarchy, regulations, impersonality, and technical qualifications. The superior efficiency generated by this type of group explains its runaway, worldwide expansion. In Weber's terms, it is the engine driving the future of humanity, but it is a flawed engine, subject to sometimes spectacular breakdowns.
5. Ascending another level within social structure takes us above bureaucratic organizations to the linkages among such entities. Research has revealed extensive informal networks connecting organizations, as well as more official linkages such as the interlocking directorate.
6. From the top of society can be seen the broad contours formed by institutions—the large-scale social structures that address basic societal needs. These include the economic, family, educational, political, and religious institutions.

MADD®

A Study of Social Structure

Mothers Against Drunk Driving (MADD) is a part of your social landscape that did not even exist until the 1980s. Today, MADD wields significant influence over public opinion and policy about drunken driving. MADD is but one sociological example of the trend called globalization. Think about this example in personal terms. We are aware from statistics that you may have known someone killed or injured by a drunken driver. Whether it was a relative, friend, or friend of a friend, this trauma touched you through your social network (microstructure) and may have moved you to join a MADD chapter (macrostructure). An understanding of the sociological forces allows not only a prediction that organizations such as MADD will expand throughout the world (megastructure), but also an understanding of how individual lives are transformed. The acetate overlays in this section walk you through this process. Turn the page and look first at the microstructure (paper layer). After completing this exercise, use the micro/macro/mega structural framework to analyze other social issues.

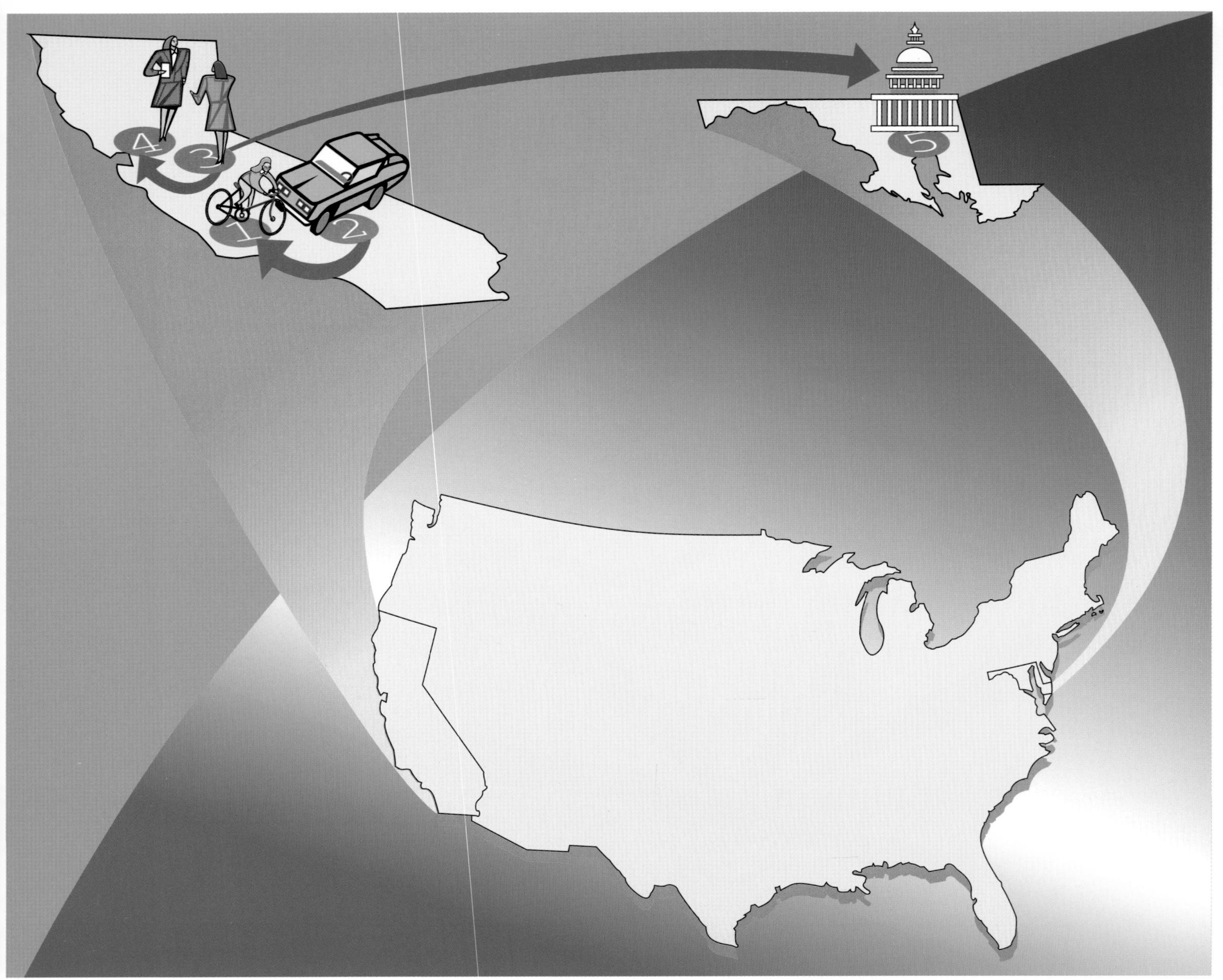

Microstructure

Individual Relations

The microstructure linking individuals is a familiar level of social structure made of networks of personal contacts and roles played by individuals. The microstructure of MADD can explain MADD's success relative to organizations such as RID (Remove Intoxicated Drivers), which had been founded in 1978 but did not become connected to such an influential social network.

The story of MADD began on May 3, 1980, when 13-year-old pedestrian Cari Lightner ① was killed by Clarence Busch ②, a man with two previous drunken driving convictions. He had been released from jail just two days earlier, after another hit-and-run drunken driving charge. Outraged, Cari's mother, Candy Lightner ③, and her friends formed MADD in the summer of 1980. They contacted Jean Moorehead, a representative of the California State Legislature ④, to spearhead passage of a new drunken driving bill. In Washington, D.C. ⑤, Lightner gathered 100 people to picket the White House and addressed the president of the United States at two press conferences. She received enough news coverage to motivate the governor of California to establish a task force on alcohol, drugs, and traffic safety. By 1982, the president had set up the National Commission on Drunk Driving and appointed Lightner as a member (Weed, 1987, p. 262).

- How might groups such as RID gain power? Add the macrostructure layer for a clue.

7. According to functionalists, the structure of groups is a self-supporting system. Those bureaucracies that fail to fit the functional requirements of the organizational environment become extinct; those that survive serve society's larger needs.
8. Conflict theorists do not see such a rational system made to service the social environment; rather, they see a battle-scarred framework built of war, truce, and alliance. Conflict is the force behind organizational relations from the level of individual bureaucrats to that of corporations battling other corporations.
9. Symbolic interactionists attempt to deflate grand structural claims about organizations by focusing on the behavior of individuals in bureaucracies in an effort to find primary human motives in secondary settings.

Chapter 6

Personal Perspective

We were on our way back from Bonampak, the famous cathedral of the ancient Mayas in the rain forest of southeastern Mexico. It was four o'clock in the humid afternoon and we had eight miles to go back to our campsite. There was no concrete pavement—far from it. Instead, we faced a two-feet-wide path pressed on both sides by a thorny thicket. From the wall of hostile greenery we could hear the sounds of strange birds and animals and, very distinctly, the hissing of snakes. Dark was falling, and the responsibility settled on me as leader of the pack to find the way back. Rain started to fall.

As we set out for our temporary home, thunder and lightning crackled above the surrounding forest. As leader I had to push our way along the path, so I used a long stick to guide my steps. The trek was hard, scary work, and we soon realized how thirsty we were. Our drinks had long since been drained, and the sweaty, swampy smells made us thirstier than ever. Suddenly, a bolt of lightning lit up an object in a clearing about a mile ahead. We made for it somewhat desperately, more than once hearing angry snakes hiss their way out of our path. Just as we arrived at the spot, another lightning bolt flashed on cue illuminating a sign with these words:

Toma Coca Cola

In the middle of the Mexican wilderness, we had found an advertisement encouraging us to "Enjoy Coca Cola." There was, unfortunately, no coke dispenser in sight.

SRP

Megastructure: *The Social Structure of Globalization*

THE incident described in the "Personal Perspective" has close relatives in the two previous chapters. In the "Microstructure" chapter we reminded you about the "small world" phenomenon in which the unlikeliest of strangers have common social contacts. The reason? Microstructures of social networks weave wide-ranging patterns linking millions of individuals. The "Macrostructure" chapter observed the striking similarity (called "isomorphism") between bureaucracies, whether they are colleges, churches, or professional athletic organizations. Part of the reason is the pattern we have called "interorganizational relations": Bureaucrats have networks of ties with other bureaucrats in a common organizational environment. Here is the point: At both levels of social structure, seemingly amazing coincidences are readily understood from the sociological perspective. Once one sees the social linkages connecting persons and organizations, the insight is like a light bulb appearing above a cartoon character's head.

In this chapter, we step up to the highest available level of social structure: patterns of relations encompassing whole societies. Again we begin with a mystery of similarity. As the Personal Perspective suggests, the planet Earth and all of its occupants are being transformed by a process so fundamental and powerful it is difficult to name. For the moment we shall name it "modernization." It is a maturation of the very process that Durkheim, Marx, and Weber attempted to explain in their own dynamic century (see Chapter 2). No longer confined to the bottle of Western civilization, it has now emerged like a genie to be truly global in scope.

Kayapo tribal members in traditional costumes with state-of-the-art video cameras are filming the destruction of the Brazilian rain forest by the engines of "modernization."

Travelers often note how similar big cities are on every continent ("It's just like New York!"), or how all airports look alike. The process, though, proceeds unevenly. State-of-the-art hydroelectric dams pool up rivers in which stone-age tribes spear their catch; dazzling skyscrapers jut above thatched huts. But every part of the world has now felt some touch of modernization, even if it is only blown-in air pollution or the odd soda sign.

Non-sociologists have sensed this process for a long time. Many phrases in popular speech refer to it, such as "the global village," "the human community," or even the somewhat unfashionable idea of "progress." These are weak, vague references. Sociology has developed concepts that are much more powerfully explanatory of what is happening to us all. As at the microstructural and macrostructural levels, these concepts reveal social structures that are interlinked, but this time the links connect whole societies. Before we unravel some of those connections, it will be instructive simply to describe the process sociologists are attempting to explain.

MODERNIZATION

Conveniently enough, a major sociological study has recently summed up the linked trends within the modernization process:

> The big trends that have been running in the United States since its first settlement by Europeans, and in the rest of the world for varying lengths of time, go under the general name of *modernization*. They include a continuous increase of population, and more than proportionate increases in mechanical energy, goods and services, information and images, together with urbanization, militarization, the erosion of local cultures, and the disturbance of ecological balances. *These major trends, in turn, include thousands of smaller trends.* The increase of services, for example, includes the spectacular growth of education, health care, government, transportation, marketing, communication, and entertainment services and of the organizations that provide them (emphasis added; Caplow, 1991, p. 18).

Think of how many diverse threads of social change run through this same, developing tapestry. Caplow's concluding phrase ". . . and of the organizations that provide them" echoes Chapters 2 and 5, which describe the worldwide rise of large-scale bureaucratic organizations. The mass media's effect on socialization (see Chapter 8) and, in fact, the media exposure of social issues discussed throughout this book are rising forces in the world due to the global dissemination of TVs and other devices of modernization.

One such device, the telephone, is used by experts as an overall index of how "modernized" a given society is. Not only is the number of telephones strongly statistically related to other modernization measures such as per capita income and food consumption; the phone is also a powerful symbol of the fact that any person with the device can be socially linked to any other person with the device throughout the world. Table 6:1 shows the ranks of some 30 societies in terms of telephones per capita (i.e., the number of phones per person in the society). Notice that the United States leads the list, and that the 10 top-ranked societies are much more "modern" in many different senses of the word than are the bottom 10. Speaking of the bottom, *most* societies on Earth are not on the list, and many are now striving mightily to modernize.

TABLE 6:1 Modernization Rank of Societies Based on Telephones Per Capita

RANK	SOCIETY
1	United States
2	Canada
3	West Germany
4	Netherlands
5	France
6	Japan
7	Australia
8	Great Britain
9	Austria
10	Belgium
11	Italy
12	Spain
13	Greece
14	Czechoslovakia
15	East Germany
16	Bulgaria
17	Portugal
18	Hungary
19	South Africa
20	Poland
21	USSR
22	Argentina
23	Mexico
24	Venezuela
25	Brazil
26	Colombia
27	Chile
28	Cuba
29	Algeria
30	Egypt

Source: Based on *Telephones of the World,* published intermittently by American Telephone and Telegraph Company, 1912 to 1989. Data for 1985 were not available for Sweden and Switzerland, ranked second and fourth, respectively, in 1965. The USSR in 1985 was considered a single society.

Big Trends

To show the complexity of the modernization process, we have been employing verbal images suggesting its many different facets. But some facets are more fundamental than others, and they prompt an entirely new image—a steamroller. Many-sided though it may be, modernization is an inexorable generator of several central kinds of social change.

A steamroller first suggests the machines associated with the Industrial Revolution. Machines were a source of awe because of their ability to multiply human powers of production. Indeed, this is a major reason many societies are trying to jump-start the modernization engine to enhance their own standards of living. There is still every reason for awe in the growing capacity of modernized institutions to make, well, everything. Table 6:2 presents the total dollar value of food and all other commodities produced

TABLE 6:2 Total World Production (in 1980 Dollars)

YEAR	IN BILLIONS OF DOLLARS
1800	$ 230
1900	970
1950	2,630
1980	11,720

Source: Theodore Caplow, *American Social Trends* (1991), Dallas, TX: Harcourt Brace Jovanovich, Table 3–2, p. 21.

over the past two centuries. Note that production increased nearly 450 percent between 1950 and 1980; note as well how fast the pace has picked up, as that 30-year increase is more of a relative gain than occurred in the entire nineteenth century (1800–1900). Clearly, the acceleration of the modernization process is reflected in skyrocketing production.

The point of production is human consumption, which brings us to another "big trend." As will be detailed in Chapter 20 and discussed later in this chapter with respect to worldwide urbanization, the human population has exploded. More precisely, it *is* exploding. The growth in production has nevertheless kept pace; *per capita* world commodity production more than doubled over the 1950–1980 period (Caplow, 1991). This conjunction of two trends is, in part, the result of increased energy production—a third "big trend"—driving production above population growth. The total amount of electricity generated worldwide has doubled since 1970, and the amount of petroleum consumed in the 1960–1970 decade exceeded the total of all previous human consumption!

Bad Trends

The steamroller is not only an image of awesome power, it also suggests destruction. Modernization proceeds by clearing a path that leaves human

Dean Cornwell's *Forward* does not depict our textual image of a steamroller, but it does suggest the dynamic power driving the modernization process.

and natural damage in its wake. These two forms of damage are inseparable. The growth in the human population damages nature by simply requiring more natural resources, including living space. More people thus means habitat destruction and the extinction of species. The increase in commodities per capita also means more intensive pressure on the environment imposed by each person, as indicated by the pollution-generating, resource-guzzling energy growth (the third "big trend"). Damage to the natural environment may lead to massive human damage. Some expert forecasts of ecological catastrophe have pointed directly to the growth demands of modernization as the culprit (e.g., Meadows et al., 1972).

Modernization also expands the capacity to wage war. This is easy to prove by the numbers of corpses. War deaths in the twentieth century are more than *10 times* greater than total fatalities in the eighteenth and nineteenth centuries *combined.* The horrific example of oil fires in Kuwait burning long after the Persian Gulf War dramatizes the interconnection between human and natural damage in modern warfare.

Smaller Trends

Many of the changes associated with modernization are more subtle than the image of a runaway steamroller. Nevertheless, they clearly follow its clanking path.

One of the "smaller trends" mentioned by Caplow in his overview quote is the growth in services such as education, health care, and entertainment. The more advanced modernization is within a society, the greater the proportion of its workforce who are in service rather than in manufacturing jobs. Despite our huge industrial production, most U.S. citizens do things for other people rather than making things (see Chapter 16). One consequence of all of these human services is, quite simply, a better life: "The great majority of people throughout the world today are healthier, better fed, longer-lived, and better protected against pain and suffering than their grandparents" (Caplow, 1991, p. 25). This, again, is a reason so many Third World societies are straining to become First World societies.

The expansion in services includes communications, which brings us back to telephones and televisions. The network of transcontinental cable lines obviously means a massive worldwide expansion in person-to-person contact. There is more to this trend than mere conversation. Until very recently, the vast majority of human beings only had personal access to other members of their own culture. There was the occasional trader or explorer, but most people were born, lived, and died without even a glimpse of the cross-cultural variety discussed in Chapter 7. No more. Global communication hook-ups expose virtually everyone in the world to the set of messages transmitted by the more modernized societies. Most of humanity can now watch the Superbowl or the Olympic Games along with the inevitable jeans and beer commercials. Very subtly but very powerfully, this leads to a kind of cultural homogenization. Cultures that used to be self-contained start imitating "modern lifestyles." The Chinese buy jeans instead of their native garb; the Japanese have big-league baseball complete with hot dogs. In a million little ways, traditional cultures give way to the modern.

So, modernization is a many-sided process sweeping through human societies. Since we are in the vanguard of the process, it is difficult for citizens of the United States to see its distinctiveness. Box 6:1 puts the momentum of modernization in the form of a tale told to someone who is out of our culture and, in fact, out of our species.

BOX 6:1 SOCIOLOGICAL IMAGINATION IN FICTION

Modernization Explained to a Non-Human

What follows is a story told by a human being to Ishmael, a mutant ape aghast at the expansion of this new form of human civilization. The story expresses the unspoken assumptions and goals of the process from the point of view of one riding the cultural steamroller of modernization.

"The world was made for man, but it took him a long, long time to figure that out. For nearly three million years he lived as though the world had been made for jellyfish. That is, he lived as though he were just like any other creature, as though he were a lion or a wombat."

"What exactly does it mean to live like a lion or a wombat?"

"It means . . . to live at the mercy of the world. It means to live without having any control over your environment."

"I see. Go on."

"Okay. In this condition, man could not be truly man. He couldn't develop a truly human way of life—a way of life that was distinctively human. So, during the early part of his life—actually the greater part of his life—man just foozled along getting nowhere and doing nothing. . . .

"To get beyond that point, he had to settle down, had to have a permanent base from which he could begin to master his environment.

"Okay. Why not? I mean, well, what was stopping him from doing that? What was stopping him was the fact that if he settled down in one place for more than a few weeks, he'd starve. As a hunter-gatherer, he would simply clean the place out—there would be nothing left to hunt and gather. In order to achieve settlement, man had to learn one fundamental manipulation. He had to learn how to manipulate his environment so that this food-exhaustion didn't occur. He had to manipulate it so that it produced *more human food*. In other words, he had to become an agriculturalist.

"This was the turning point. The world had been made for man, but he was unable to take possession of it until this problem was cracked. And he finally cracked it about ten thousand years ago, back there in the Fertile Crescent. This was a very big moment—the biggest in human history up to this point.

". . . The limitations of the hunting-gathering life had kept man in check for three million years. With agriculture, those limitations vanished, and his rise was meteoric.

"Settlement gave rise to division of labor.

"Division of labor gave rise to technology. With the rise of

This monoculture involves single-crop cultivation on a Nebraska wheat farm. Notice that the application of modern farming techniques has drastically reduced other plant and animal species while increasing wheat production.

BOX 6:1 SOCIOLOGICAL IMAGINATION IN FICTION *continued*

technology came trade and commerce.

"With trade and commerce came mathematics and literacy and science, and all the rest. The whole thing was under way at last, and the rest, as they say, is history. . . .

"Okay. Man's destiny was to conquer and rule the world, and this is what he's done—almost. He hasn't quite made it, and it looks as though this may be his undoing. The problem is that man's conquest of the world has itself devastated the world. And in spite of all the mastery we've attained, we don't have enough mastery to *stop* devastating the world—or to repair the devastation we've already wrought.

"We've poured our poisons into the world as though it were a bottomless pit—and we *go on* pouring our poisons into the world. We've gobbled up irreplaceable resources as though they could never run out—and we *go on* gobbling them up. It's hard to imagine how the world could survive another century of this abuse, but nobody's really doing anything about it. It's a problem our children will have to solve, or their children.

"Only one thing can save us. We have to *increase* our mastery of the world. All this damage has come about through our conquest of the world, but we have to *go on* conquering it until our rule is *absolute*. Then, when we're in *complete* control, everything will be fine. We'll have fusion power. No pollution. We'll turn the rain on and off. We'll grow a bushel of wheat in a square centimeter. We'll turn the oceans into farms. We'll control the weather—no more hurricanes, no more tornadoes, no more droughts, no more untimely frosts. We'll make the clouds release their water over the land instead of dumping it uselessly into the oceans. All the life processes of this planet will be where they belong—where the gods meant them to be—in our hands. And we'll manipulate them the way a programmer manipulates a computer.

"And that's where it stands right now. We have to carry the conquest forward. And carrying it forward is either going to destroy the world or turn it into a paradise—into the paradise it was meant to be under human rule.

"And if we manage to do this—if we finally manage to make ourselves the absolute rulers of the world—then nothing can stop us. Then we move into the *Star Trek* era.

"Man moves out into space to conquer and rule the entire universe. And that may be the ultimate destiny of man: to conquer and rule the entire universe. . . ."

Critical Thinking Questions

1. Throughout this human being's speech, the term "man" is used generically to refer to humanity, thus slighting the female half of the race. What are the conflict theory implications for the modernizing civilization?
2. How are Theodore Caplow's "big trends" and "smaller trends" woven together into this account?

Source: Daniel Quinn, *Ishmael* (1992). New York: Bantam Books, pp. 70–71, 82–83.

MODERNIZATION THEORIES

On the Nature of International Networks

The preceding pages are a sociological portrait of what has been and what might be in the global future of humanity. However illuminating or disturbing, it is still just a description. The turbulence of human history teaches caution about simple projections of today into tomorrow unless the underlying causes of events are understood.

The present section is devoted to three major theories of modernization, which we shall overview with two major points. First, each theory depicts a worldwide *megastructure*. Implicitly or explicitly, they all open up the final box in the hierarchy of social systems (see Figure 1:1). The shared assumption is that a society can no longer be viewed as a self-contained, hermetically sealed container of human behavior. Structures *between* societies

FIGURE 6:1 MILLION-PLUS CITIES AND WORLD POPULATION

In addition to the rapid rise in world population represented by the expanding size of the circles, please note the increasing proportion of humanity residing in cities—especially million-plus cities.

Source: J. Palen (1992), *The Urban World.* New York: McGraw-Hill.

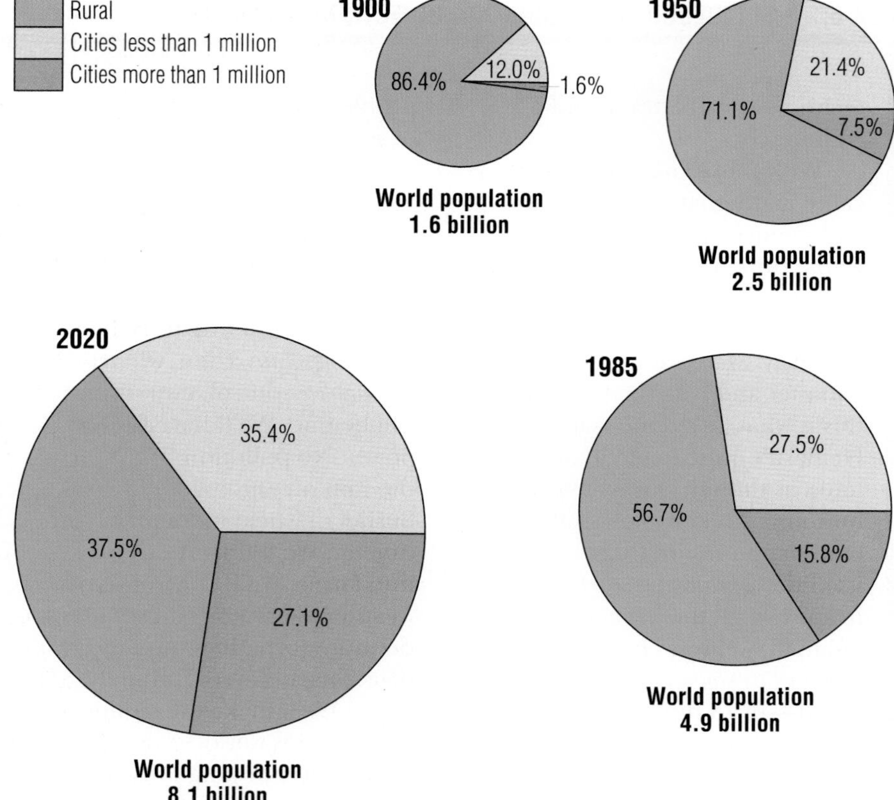

control what is *inside* societies. The theoretical argument is over the nature of that large-scale network linking nations, and how it relates to their modernization. The second point transcends argument for argument's sake. These theories are not armchair accounts, but rather are immersed in real-*world* events. Massive cargoes of armaments, commodities, people, and money are now moving around the world based on a theory of modernization.

Development Theory

As we have seen, sociology has been grappling throughout its own history with the question of why some societies are "modern" whereas others are not. Durkheim, Marx, and Weber all anchored their theories of social change in "The Great Transformation," which had already transformed some European societies in their day. A unique set of post-World War II events brought such questions to current headlines. The societies in which the classical sociologists had hatched their theories of change lay devastated after 1945. The Marshall Plan (named after then U.S. Secretary of State, George C. Marshall) was a massive program of direct aid and loans aimed at the reconstruction of the European economic base. It worked. The rapidly rebuilt industrial structures powered a surge in these nations' Gross National Product (GNP), which then encouraged further foreign investment. In a historical flash, these societies rose from the smoldering ashes of the war to return to the path of modernization.

Outside of Europe and North America lay an ever-expanding set of sovereign nations, many recently released from European colonialism. The Marshall Plan seemed to be an object lesson that, with the proper help and motivation, nations could be released quickly from famine, poverty, disease, and other attendant miseries of traditional society. In the language of the time, these "underdeveloped" areas (now called the Third World) could soon join the ranks of "developed" nations (now, the First World)—hence, "Development Theory." This outcome was earnestly desired by the United States and its allies, and not just for humanitarian reasons. The fear was that very poor societies would be open to the political seduction of communism headquartered in the (then) USSR and China.

The spectacular success of the Marshall Plan combined with the geopolitical situation to create a broad consensus about social development among social scientists, politicians, and the general public. Among the former, sociologist Talcott Parsons furnished the most comprehensive theory (1951). Essentially, it was an evolutionary framework: Simple, underdeveloped societies evolve into complex, developed societies (1971). Much more is involved than building factories in the bush. To truly develop, the new productive structures must be surrounded by political stability, an autonomous legal system, widespread education—in short, the set of "structurally differentiated" institutions first outlined by Durkheim (see Chapter 2). Most crucially for Parsons, the new order must be staffed by people with the proper value system emphasizing achievement and individualism. Thousands of surveys were conducted in many countries measuring a host of attitudes related to development (Inkeles and Smith, 1974). Typically, these analyses have shown a consistent value pattern, with the United States a bit more "modern" than the other developed nations. Table 6:3 illustrates a comparative measure on the core value of the "work ethic" (hours worked per week).

So: If, (a) public and private capital were transferred to the undeveloped world along the lines of the Marshall Plan and (b) developed countries would teach them modern values through training programs and education, then (c) impoverished societies would achieve "self-sustaining growth" (Rostow, 1960) and become modern like us. Box 6:2 encapsulates the idea

TABLE 6:3 Hours Worked Per Week in Selected Developed Societies[a]

Count **ROW PCT**	**HOURS WORKED PER WEEK**		
Societies	Low (less than 36 hours)	Medium (36–40 hours)	High (more than 40 hours)
Australia	169 **24.0**	334 **47.4**	202 **28.6**
Germany	195 **14.3**	679 **49.9**	486 **35.8**
Great Britain	219 **28.0**	336 **43.0**	227 **29.0**
United States	198 **12.3**	341 **47.2**	323 **40.5**

[a]Main Point: Although the United States and Germany exhibit higher levels of work (see especially the row percentages for High across the four countries), this table illustrates the common "work ethic" pattern of developed societies.

Source: International Social Survey Program (ISSP). Social Network and Support Systems, 1986 computer files. Köln: Zentralarchiv Für Empirische Sozialforschung, 1988 producer. Ann Arbor, MI: Inter-university Consortium for Political and Social Research, 1989 distributor.

BOX 6:2 GENDER AND SOCIAL CHANGE

Caste, Modernization and "Purity"

Caste is undoubtedly an all-India phenomenon in the sense that there are everywhere hereditary, *endogamous* groups which form a hierarchy, and that each of these groups has a traditional association with one or two occupations. Everywhere there are Brahmins, Untouchables, and peasant, artisan, trading, and service castes. Relations between castes are invariably expressed in terms of pollution and purity. . . .

During the nineteenth century the British slowly laid the foundations of a modern state by surveying land, settling the revenue, creating a modern bureaucracy, army, and police, instituting law courts, codifying the law, developing communications—railways, post and telegraph, roads and canals—establishing schools and colleges, and so on. The British also brought with them the printing press, and the profound and many-sided changes this brought about in Indian life and thought deserve a volume in itself. One obvious result was that books and journals, along with schools, made possible the transmission of modern as well as traditional knowledge to large numbers of Indians—knowledge which could no longer be the privilege of a few, hereditary groups. . . .

Christian missionaries played a notable part in humanitarian activity, especially in providing education and medical aid to sections of Indian society most in need of them—Harijans, women, orphans, lepers, and tribal folk. Equally important were their criticisms of such Hindu institutions as caste, Untouchability, the low position of women, child marriage, and *polygyny*.

In the old days, women were extremely particular about pollution, and the kitchen was the heart of the pollution system. The modern educated housewife, on the other hand, is much less particular about pollution and more conscious of hygiene and nutrition. Many observe rules of pollution only when they are living with their parents or in-laws. They become lax about the rules when they form separate households; a punctilious observance of pollution rules is not easy when there is only one adult woman in the house, unlike in a traditional joint family. Even in the latter, pollution rules are observed more strictly when

caste system—a hierarchical arrangement of social strata in which an individual's status is fixed at birth.

with its view of women in the developing society of India. Traditionally, that society's **caste system** divided its population into a hierarchical arrangement of social strata within which the individual was born, married, and assigned an occupation. Social mobility like that in the developed nations was virtually nonexistent, and women were assigned demeaning duties such as "ritual purification" of objects defiled by contact with the lower castes. Obviously, this is no way to run a "modern" society. Proponents of development theory read accounts like Box 6:2 as the dismantling of a traditional value system so it can be revved up into a modern one. From this vantage point, England's subjugation of India can be viewed as a developed society priming the engine of social change by introducing factories, schools, and less sexist family role models.

Return now to our two overviews of this section. Clearly, development theory depicts a particular kind of megastructure. The key linkages between societies are those between the "haves" and the "have nots." If developed societies were to fill those network links with armaments for social order—capital for growth and values for motivation—the "have nots" would transform themselves into "haves." The second overview is closely related. U.S. foreign policy essentially bought development theory, choosing allies and

BOX 6:2 GENDER AND SOCIAL CHANGE *continued*

there are old women who are widows and whose lives are centered in the kitchen and in the domestic altar. . . .

Traditionally, a young Brahmin girl worked in and around the kitchen with her mother until her marriage was consummated and she joined her affines [in-laws]. All that was required of her was knowledge of cooking and other domestic chores, the rituals that girls were expected to perform, knowledge of caste and pollution rules, and respect for and obedience to her parents-in-law and husband, and other elders in the household. Education changed the outlook of girls, and gave them new ideas and aspirations. It certainly made them less particular about pollution rules and ritual. . . .

The education of women has produced a situation in which young girls do not have the time to learn rituals from their mothers or grandmothers, and the small households in big cities frequently lack the old women who have the know-how and the leisure. The educated wife has less of the traditional culture to pass on to her children, even should she want to. Still more significant is the fact that elite households have become articulators of the values of a highly competitive educational and employment system. Getting children admitted to good schools, supervising their curricular and extracurricular activities, and worrying about their future careers absorb the energies of parents.

Critical Thinking Questions

1. The second paragraph of this selection describes the British as laying "the foundations of a modern state" in India. Keeping in mind the parallel to the destruction of traditional Nigeria described at the start of Chapter 2, how would you analyze the positive functions *and* dysfunctions of such "modernizing colonialism"?
2. Find the two italicized terms (our emphasis added) in the selection, and find their meanings in Chapter 14. As these aspects of India's family system have changed, what change would a symbolic interactionist expect to find in dating and marriage practices?

Source: M.N. Srinivas, *Social Change in Modern India* (1971). Berkeley: University of California Press, pp. 46, 49–50, 124, 127–28.

shipping aid to promote anti-Communist Third World regimes. "Self-sustaining growth" would stimulate both democracy and the betterment of humanity. That, at least, was development theory.

Dependency Theory

Development *did not happen*—or, at least, not according to the dictates of development theory.

Modernization as we have described it is a powerful global process, but most of the power is still generated by the societies that were already "developed" after World War II. A few Third World nations have modernized rapidly, but vast regions of Africa, Asia, and South America remain fundamentally the same—or worse off. Certainly, "self-sustaining growth" did not happen the way it was supposed to. This partly explains the rise of alternative theories of the global megastructure in recent decades (note that the development theory citations are rather dated).

Dependency theorists paint an alternative picture of the global megastructure. Generally, they portray development theory as a functionalist alibi for the First World to clean out the Third World. How can this be so

These Iranian children are wearing Western-style school uniforms. During the regime of the Shah Pahlavi (1941–1979), the spread of institutions and attitudes emulating the developed world accompanied the modernization effort. Subsequently, Iran has suppressed Western influence.

with the huge amounts of resources that have been devoted to the Third World? The answer, in a nutshell, is greed. The British did not colonize India to spread the benefits of modern civilization; they plundered that society until the Indians kicked them out in 1947. (Reread Box 6:2 from this conflict theory vantage point.) Not only England, but all of the early developed societies engaged in the open exploitation of colonialism (including the United States taking slaves from Africa). After the colonial era, the exploitation was less open and further disguised by development theory.

So, why did foreign investment in the post-colonial Third World *not* lead to lots of growing, mini-USAs? In answer, dependency theory extends Marxist conflict theory beyond national boundaries. Capital investment does not

TABLE 6:4 Multinational Industrial Companies

RANK	COMPANY	1991 SALES (IN BILLIONS OF $)
1	General Motors	$123.78
2	Royal Dutch–Shell Group	103.83
3	Exxon	103.24
4	Ford Motor	88.96
5	Toyota Motor	78.06
6	IBM	65.39
7	IRI	64.10
8	General Electric	60.24
9	British Petroleum	58.36
10	Daimler–Benz	57.32

Source: Fortune magazine, July 27, 1992.

fall uniformly upon a society like a kind of development seeding; rather, it tends to land in the financial gardens of the local ruling class. Not only do the First World rich get richer, but the Third World rich now have more resources to resist modernizing changes like land reform (see Baran, 1957; Frank, 1972).

multinational corporations—large firms operating beyond the macrostructure of a single society.

Moreover, the First World rich are not a bunch of unorganized jet-setters. A new sociological power has risen in the world: **multinational corporations**. In our terms, they are bureaucracies that have burst through the macrostructural boundaries of societies to create their own for-profit megastructures. They are profitable indeed. Table 6:4 lists only the top 10 such organizations, the *poorest* of which has annual sales exceeding the GNPs of Pakistan and Bangladesh *combined.* Capital rich though these obviously are, dependency theorists claim that these corporate giants transfer little working capital to poor countries. Instead, they use their enormous influence to drain capital from the domestic markets of the Third World, thus diverting local investment that could lead to development (Bierstaker, 1981; Muller, 1974). Much of the profit from such ventures is shipped back to the First World nations where the multinationals are based.

The emergence of the global economy has released capital to flow where labor costs are lowest, as in this carpet-weaving factory employing Nepalese children.

Even massive public and private loans have not paid off. Because of slower-than-predicted development, the Third World has run up an equally massive debt owed to the First World; interest paid on this outstanding debt shortchanges investment in further development. Why did development not happen? The answer of dependency theorists is now clear. Under the thumb of gargantuan multinational firms, less-developed societies are in hock up to their eyeballs, and controlled by local elites who receive most of the financial aid. Therefore *dependency* has been substituted for development.

World System Theory

In some respects, both the development and dependency theorists have been right. Societies such as South Korea, Taiwan, Malaysia, and, most spectacularly, postwar Japan have followed the garden path of rapid development. Dependency theorists select their cases from Africa and Latin America where, they argue, *under*development is the rule. To step back from the concepts for a moment, here are the facts: (1) Modernization is a global process marked by the overall trends previously described, (2) some societies are on the fast track of modernization, and (3) some societies have fallen by the wayside.

Immanuel Wallerstein proposed world system theory to reconcile these puzzling facts. The most fundamental shift is in scale—the *world* is now the key social structure. Instead of digging up religious values blocking development in India, instead of finding credit practices that make Mexico dependent upon Canada, *look at the positions of all these societies in the same global system.* In our terms, Wallerstein sees the macrostructure of a whole society in the background. In the foreground are the relations linking societies. The term "relations" is another key. Also in our terms, the "world system" is to be viewed as a single massive international network. Wallerstein uses the analogy of "coral reefs of human relations" (1974, p. 3). Coral reefs are the largest living things on Earth, composed of innumerable organisms. Much of what goes on inside any single small organism or even a big section of the colony depends on the pattern of the reef as a whole. By analogy, Wallerstein says we should look at the entire structure of the "reef" of world relations being built up over historical time.

core—the set of technologically advanced, developed countries with a dominant position within the world system.

periphery—the set of less-developed countries providing labor and raw materials to the core within the world system.

semiperiphery—the set of countries intermediate between the core and periphery within the world system.

The world system is divided into three major types of societies based on their position in the global social structure. **Core** countries possess the lion's share of the world's capital and technology, and they thus exert lion-like control over the terms of world trade and financial transactions; currently, core nations are in Western Europe, the United States, and Japan. Countries in the **periphery** produce mainly labor-intensive raw materials and commodities on terms favorable to the core; the periphery encompasses most of the contemporary Third World. The final major class of countries is the **semiperiphery**, in an intermediate position between core and periphery; these include societies that may one day move into the core such as Singapore, Israel, and Portugal (Chase-Dunn, 1991).

This is a powerful set of ideas. The theory offers a solution to the "puzzling facts" posed here. The global process of modernization is being driven by core countries because, simply, it has to be. It is a zero-sum game: Rapid development must occur at the expense of societies being looted of their labor and raw materials. For there to be a growing core, there must be a waning periphery. Even the nations of the semiperiphery like Malaysia and Singapore power their own development by using nearby countries in the periphery.

Powerful though it is, this set of ideas has been subjected to sociological critique. Some argue that world system theory underestimates the development role of domestic institutions, notably the state (Pattnayak, 1992). While we await further evidence, this approach has already performed an invaluable intellectual service. Quite literally, it changes our view of the world to a world view. International relations can be understood as network relations operating at the level of megastructure (Smith and White, 1992).

URBANIZATION

All of the modernization theories picture an international network structure at the very heart of the process. Now picture such a megastructure as a giant assembly of Popsicle sticks reaching across and within human societies. On the sticks is a sweet, rich substance. As you can readily imagine, such a structure would naturally attract teeming piles of ants. It is an unflattering but apt analogy. The structure and process of modernization is associated with the swarming of humans in insectoid millions. Urbanization, indeed, is one of the "big trends" by which modernization is defined (Caplow, 1991).

The Rise of Cities

Human beings evolved as a species about 3 million years ago. During most of that time, urban places did not exist. The first city appeared just within the past 8,000 years—or at 11:57 p.m., if all of human history were viewed as a single day. This recent human invention also caught on rather slowly over the next "minutes" of history. Ninety-seven percent of the world's population still lived in rural places 200 years ago, and 86 percent lived out of cities at the dawn of the twentieth century. During this century, however, there has been truly explosive growth in the proportion of the world population living in urban places. Indeed, the world is about to pass a demographic milestone—shortly after the year 2000, more people will live in urban areas than in rural areas.

Urbanization has proceeded at different rates in various parts of the world. In 1990, 73 percent of the people in the more developed societies resided in urban areas, as did 34 percent of those in the less-developed societies (see Table 6:5). No society had ever been predominantly urban until the late nineteenth century. At that time, England became the first to have at least half of its population residing in cities. The United States passed the milestone in 1920. By 1992, nearly half of all nations were predominantly urban. Presently, the world's most urban nations are Singapore (100 percent) and Macao (97 percent) in Asia and Belgium (95 percent) in Europe; the least urban are the African nations of Burundi (5 percent) and Rwanda (7 percent; PRB, 1992).

The cities of antiquity had relatively small populations by today's standards. At their peaks, ancient Athens and Rome had perhaps 80,000 and

Mexico City is projected to have more than 30 million people by the year 2000.

TABLE 6:5 Percent of Population That Is Urban: 1970–2015

CATEGORY	YEAR				
	1970	1990	2000	2005	2015
World	37	43	48	50	56
More-developed regions	67	73	76	77	81
Less-developed regions	25	34	40	44	50

Source: UN Population Division Department of Economic and Social Development, *World Urbanization Prospects 1992: Estimates and Projections of Urban and Rural Populations, Including Urban Agglomerations,* 1993.

500,000 inhabitants, respectively. London became the first city with 1 million or more residents sometime around the year 1800. But as urbanization has progressed over the past centuries, the number of million-plus cities has grown like, well, ant colonies. By 1990 there were about 300 of them, pretty evenly divided between the more-developed and less-developed nations. The urban colonization also has given rise to truly gigantic cities. By the turn of this century, there will be more than 50 such megacities having 5 million inhabitants or more. Twenty-one of these places will actually have 10 million inhabitants by the year 2000, making them all more populous than current-day New York City!

megacities—cities with at least 5 million inhabitants.

Most of these current and projected megacities are located in Third World nations. Contrast this with the situation as recently as 1950, when the only Third World city with more than 5 million people was Shanghai. You may never have heard of Surabaja, Lanchow, Jos, or Curitiba—unless you are well acquainted with the geography of Indonesia, China, Nigeria, or Brazil. But you will be hearing their names frequently in the future, for these are among the more than 50 cities whose populations will have burst through the 5 million mark by the year 2000.

Causes of Urbanization

Why do cities grow, and, in particular, why are so many of them growing so rapidly *now*? The question is obviously a complex one with several answers and some society-to-society variations. In fact, several of the answers can be gathered from elsewhere in this book: (1) A steep drop in the death rate due to medical advances has resulted in population growth and a surplus rural labor pool (see Chapter 20); (2) the spread of scientific management of agriculture has also reduced the need for rural laborers (see Chapter 21); (3) the development of transportation and communication systems has eased the rural-to-urban migration process (see Chapter 21); and (4) the expansion of the manufacturing and, later, the service sector of urban economies has attracted surplus rural labor (see Chapter 16). Now read back over these four factors, noting that every single one of them is closely related to the modernization process itself (Palen, 1992). Again, urbanization and modernization are linked trends.

On a personal level, urban areas attract and retain people simply because they offer more of several kinds of opportunity than do rural areas. Greater economic opportunities arise in part because factory work is more diversified than farm work, and service sector (office) work is even more diversified than factory work. Consequently, there are many thousands of occupations in urban areas compared to only a few dozen in rural ones. Additionally, as we have seen, the modernization of agriculture has eroded the rural job base. Urban areas are particularly attractive to educated young people for whom social mobility is a real possibility (Weeks, 1992).

You probably have no trouble understanding the reasons why most U.S. college students begin their careers in urban areas. But do you know why Third World young people are drawn to the squalid "squatter settlement" cities described next? Their motivation is pretty much the same as yours. Despite the horrid conditions in many Third World slums, these places still afford better access to jobs, education, health care, and diets than are available in their rural communities (Linden, 1993).

Consequences of Urbanization

The social impact of cities has been immense and pervasive. Even though such places have existed for only 8,000 years and have been widespread for a much briefer time, their era comprises the entirety of the period known as "civilization." In the words of one urban sociologist:

> The saga of wars, architecture, and art—almost the whole of what we know of human triumphs and tragedies—is encompassed within that period. The story of human social and cultural development—and regression—is in major part the tale of the cities that have been built and of the lives that have been lived within them. The very terms "civilization" and "civilized" come from the Latin *civis,* which means a person living in a city (Palen, 1992, p. 3).

gemeinschaft—("community") a place of personalized relationships based on mutual acquaintanceship.

gesellschaft—("society") a place of impersonality based on a lack of mutual acquaintanceship.

In short, cities have been the true "cradle of civilization." They clearly have been the headquarters for the worldwide modernization campaign.

The quoted passage uses the terms "tragedies," "wars," and "regression" in reference to cities. Indeed, it is a truism that urban life has a dark side. Near the end of the classical century of sociological theory, Ferdinand Tönnies (1887) drew a distinction between traditional and modern human living places. A **gemeinschaft** typifies rural village life. The term roughly translates from the German as "community," with its overtones of a warm, secure place where people know one another. Tönnies saw such places giving way to the modern, industrial city, known as a **gesellschaft**. It translates as "society," a place of impersonality and interpersonal distance where the

George Tooker's *The Subway* elicits a sense of threat and alienation in a *gesellschaft* setting; Marc Chagall's *I and the Village* depicts a self enfolded by the warm security of *gemeinschaft.*

major proportion of a vast population are unacquainted with each other. Tönnies' sociological distinction explains the sense of threat small-town people feel when they enter a big city bustling with strangers.

Echoing concerns of the classical theorists about this distinctively modern residential pattern, American sociologist Louis Wirth wrote a famous essay, "Urbanism as a Way of Life," in 1938. Surveying firsthand the excesses of wide-open Chicago, Wirth argued that city life undermines the social bonds that hold together other forms of human community; the result is individual isolation and the darker forms of deviance unleashed by the loosened bonds of social control. Both pre-Untouchables Chicago and today's big-city crack zones fit Wirth's theoretical picture. But contemporary social network research suggests that the interpersonal effects of urbanism are not necessarily negative. In fact, several studies in North America report that city dwellers have *more* friends than do residents of small towns; since "birds of a feather flock together" (see Chapter 4), there are just more birds in a city to make up a familiar friendship flock. Such studies show no consistent rural–urban differences in involvement with kin, either (Fischer, 1984). As powerful as the "Consequences of Urbanization" clearly are, they are also complex enough to bear continued sociological scrutiny.

Squatter Settlements

squatter settlements—areas surrounding cities populated by masses of migrants lacking access to city services.

The forces of urbanization bear special scrutiny in the Third World, where their power is unprecedented in human history. The urban population there has increased better than *five times* since 1950. This staggering pace of urbanization has created **squatter settlements** on the outskirts of new cities in which every available scrap of space is already taken. Consequently, great masses of desperate people live in horrid, subsistence-level conditions in sprawling shantytowns. They squat illegally wherever they can find space, often on unoccupied land in an expanding doughnut surrounding the real city. They build their shelters from cardboard, packing crates, and other scrap material. Settlements of shacks spring up on empty lots almost overnight. Many lack electricity, running water, sewer systems, and garbage collection. People often live 40 to a shack, 10 to a room, and sleep in shifts. Water is contaminated by raw sewage and garbage. Obviously, major public health problems are common.

Squatters make up more than 25 percent of the residents of most large cities in developing nations. However, in some cities, such as Kinshasa (Zaire), Colombo (Sri Lanka), and Cartegena (Colombia), squatters constitute 50 to 70 percent of the inhabitants.

MEGASTRUCTURE AND SOCIAL PROBLEMS

The Objective Dimension

The title and the content of this chapter carry the same message: Societies are open systems. The internal order of a macrostructure is deeply touched by its megastructural relations with other societies. The same is true for internal *disorder*. Social problems should no longer be viewed as homegrown social diseases; they are communicable across borders.

To prove the point, we present Exhibit A in the form of Figure 6:2. The "human suffering index" was compiled as an objective measure of misery across the globe. As you might expect, the international differences are gigantic. Now look at the criteria that make up the index. Do you

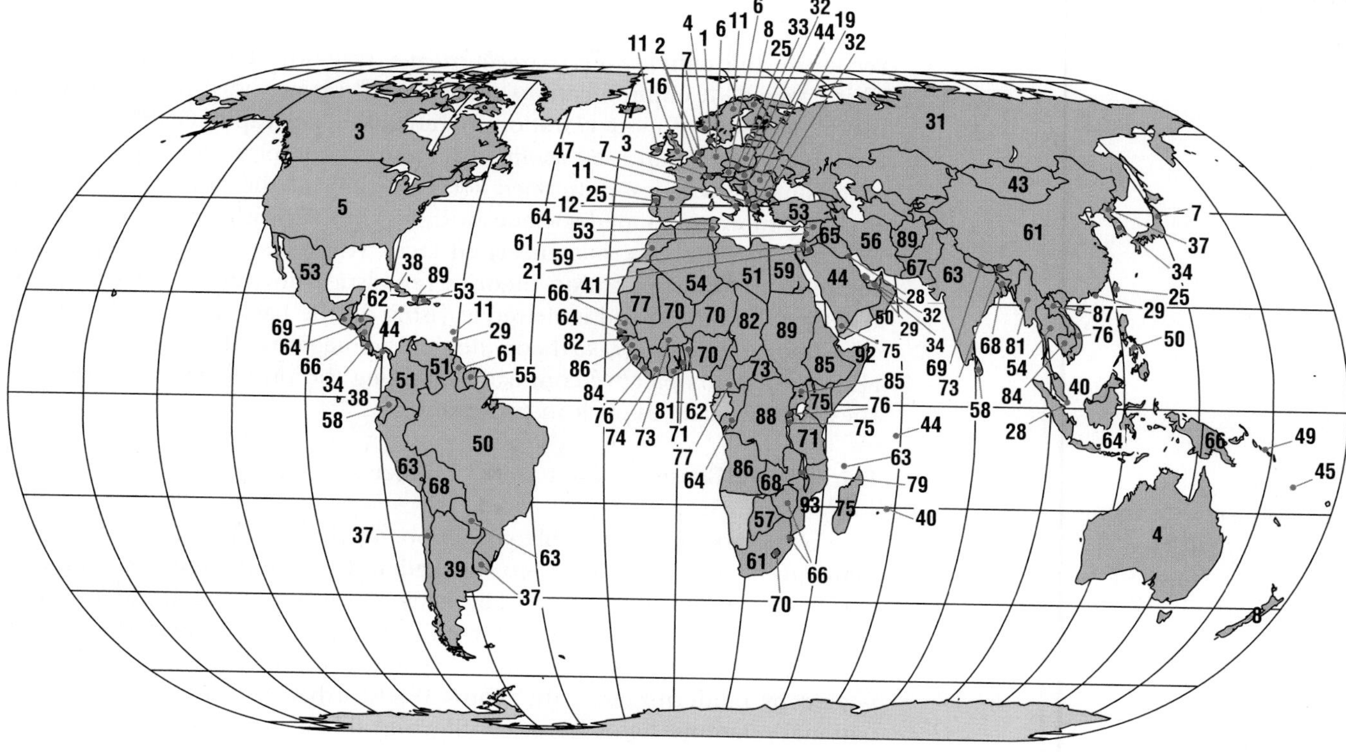

FIGURE 6:2 THE MEASURE OF MISERY ACROSS THE GLOBE

Source(s): Ray White and Ron Cortes, *The Philadelphia Inquirer*, May 31, 1992, p. E3, and the Population Crisis Committee.

How the scores for the index were computed

To evaluate the quality of life around the world, 141 countries were rated on a scale of 0 to 10 on the following criteria:

Life expectancy: Life expectancy of at least 76 years rates a 0; 53 years or less rates a 10.

Food availability: A per capita daily calorie supply at least 126 percent what is required to sustain health rates a 0; less than 80 percent rates a 10.

Access to clean water: If 92 percent of people have reasonable access to safe drinking water the rating is 0; if less than 10 percent do, the rating is 10.

Infant immunization: If 95 percent of 1-year-olds are immunized against diphtheria, whooping cough, tetanus, measles, polio (and in some cases tuberculosis), the rating is 0; less than 45 percent rates a 10.

Secondary school enrollment: If 95 percent of youths attend secondary school, the rating is 0; if less than 50 percent do, it rates a 10.

Per capita GNP: If over $15,000, the rating is 0; if under $250, the rating is 10.

Communications technology: If there are 900 or more telephones per 1,000 people, the rating is 0; if there are fewer than 20, it rates a 10.

Political freedom: Ratings based on fairness of electoral laws, actual power vested in elected officials, the right to form parties, right of self-determination, and freedom of expression.

Civil rights: Ratings based on freedom of assembly, equality under the law, equality of opportunity, protection from political terror, and personal social freedoms.

The higher the score, the worse the conditions. The worst possible total score would be 100.

A ranking of living conditions shows the spread of suffering across the globe.

"Three-quarters of the world's people live in countries where human suffering is the rule, rather than the exception," says Sharon L. Camp, senior vice president of the Population Crisis Committee.

Camp is editor of the International Human Suffering Index, produced by the committee two weeks before [the] opening of the Earth Summit in Rio de Janeiro.

For the index, researchers evaluated 10 indicators of well-being in 141 countries with more than one million citizens. The rating scale was 0 to 10, with 10 reflecting the highest level of suffering.

The ratings came from data —often provided by official government sources—that researchers acknowledge are somewhat artificial but that they believe most readily measure actual living conditions.

To measure the availability of food, for example, a country's food supply, expressed as a total number of calories, was divided by the country's population. Researchers compared that answer to how many calories the average person would need to sustain normal activity and health. Countries where the average daily calorie supply was 126 percent or more of what is required received a 0; countries where the calorie supply was 80 percent or less received a 10.

To rate political freedom and civil rights, researchers relied on analyses by Freedom House, a nonprofit New York organzation that studies human rights issues. For example, the United States was given a 1 for civil rights—its less-than-perfect score reflecting an assessment that not all citizens have equal rights.

The study lists 83 countries with 73 percent of the world's population as places where human suffering is either high or extreme. At the top of the scale is Mozambique, a one-party socialist state where the average citizen has an income of $80 a year, faces annual inflation of more than 80 percent, and gets 76 percent of the food needed to sustain healthy life.

141 countries, ranked by scores in suffering index

93 Mozambique
92 Somalia
89 Afghanistan, Haiti, Sudan
88 Zaire
87 Laos
86 Guinea, Angola
85 Ethiopia, Uganda
84 Cambodia, Sierra Leone
82 Chad, Guinea-Bissau
81 Ghana, Burma
79 Malawi
77 Cameroon, Mauritania
76 Rwanda, Vietnam, Liberia
75 Burundi, Kenya, Madagascar, Yemen
74 Ivory Coast
73 Bhutan, Burkina Faso, Central African Republic
71 Tanzania, Togo
70 Lesotho, Mali, Niger, Nigeria
69 Guatemala, Nepal
68 Bangladesh, Bolivia, Zambia
67 Pakistan
66 Nicaragua, Papua-New Guinea, Senegal Swaziland, Zimbabwe
65 Iraq
64 Gambia, Congo, El Salvador, Indonesia, Syria
63 Comoros, India, Paraguay, Peru
62 Benin, Honduras
61 Lebanon, China, Guyana, South Africa
59 Egypt, Morocco
58 Ecuador, Sri Lanka
57 Botswana
56 Iran
55 Suriname
54 Algeria, Thailand
53 Dominican Republic, Mexico, Tunisia, Turkey
51 Libya, Colombia, Venezuela
50 Brazil, Oman, Philippines
49 Solomon Islands
47 Albania
45 Vanuatu
44 Jamaica, Romania, Saudi Arabia, Seychelles, Yugoslavia (former)
43 Mongolia
41 Jordan
40 Malaysia, Mauritius
39 Argentina
38 Cuba, Panama
37 Chile, Uruguay, North Korea
34 Costa Rica, South Korea, United Arab Emirates
33 Poland
32 Bulgaria, Hungary, Qatar
31 Soviet Union (former)
29 Bahrain, Hong Kong, Trinidad and Tobago
28 Kuwait, Singapore
25 Czechoslovakia, Portugal, Taiwan
21 Israel
19 Greece
16 United Kingdom
12 Italy
11 Barbados, Ireland, Spain, Sweden
8 Finland, New Zealand
7 France, Iceland, Japan, Luxembourg
6 Austria, Germany
5 United States
4 Australia, Norway
3 Canada, Switzerland
2 Belgium, Netherlands
1 Denmark

recognize the pattern? *Every single criterion* splits the First World from the Third World. "Communications technology," in fact, was used as the best overall measure of modernization in Table 6:1; "per capita GNP" and "food availability" are often used as direct measures of level of development. Not surprisingly, then, less-developed societies rank at the bottom (most misery) and more-developed societies with less human suffering (least misery) top the list. These are not unrelated facts. The mass of sociological scholarship in the modernization theories reveals a truly international process. Whether the First World is viewed as rising on the back of the Third World or as boosting them up, *no* theory denies the megastructural nature of modernization. The objective connections among the problems of various societies will be made explicit in two examples.

Third World Causes of First World Problems

In reading about the horrible conditions in the Third World's mammoth shantytowns, you may have been shocked and/or sympathetic, but you may also have felt detached from it all, living as you do in the affluent United States. But you are not detached from it. You have *already* been affected by the conditions in these places, and it looks like the effect will increase. Fueled by modernization, the Third World urban explosion harms international relations, helps foster conflict and terrorism, and fans frustrations exploitable by groups willing to trade peace and development for their own political objectives.

Teeming squatter settlements are natural spawning grounds of alienation and frustration, particularly among young people who are disproportionally unemployed. They increasingly resent their own intolerable living conditions, which contrast sharply with the highly visible wealth of the cities' elite. As discussed in Chapter 2, revolutions and other forms of social disorder are more likely to occur when conditions are improving than when things are stagnant. This is because rising aspirations often exceed the society's rate of actual progress. The gap between rising aspirations and real progress is sociological dynamite. It is in Third World cities that modernization is proceeding slowly, and it is there that unrest is building.

Unrest in the Third World's cities has already had serious international impacts, some of which have been felt in the United States. Consider, for instance, the upheaval in Iran, which occurred in the late 1970s, with its American hostages, its negative effect on the availability and cost of oil, and a variety of later political consequences. Analyses of the causes of that serious international problem pointed not only to the Shah's spendthrift and corrupt government, but also to the country's massive urban growth driven by unusually rapid modernization. George Lencgowski, in his analysis appearing in *Foreign Affairs,* noted that Iran's rural to urban migration produced "a new city proletariat, clustering in shantytown slums, increasing by leaps and bounds and providing typical 'cannon fodder' for any skilled agitator with a demagogic appeal" (cited in Green, 1981).

There is growing international concern that megacities and their shantytowns are becoming incubators for future plagues. An epidemic of hepatitis recently raged for more than a year in Karachi, Pakistan. Cholera spread through many Latin American cities in 1992, killing 4,000 people and hospitalizing more than 400,000 in a few months. Giant, growing, filthy cities are natural breeding grounds for novel, antibiotic-resistant strains of germs. According to Harvard public-health expert Jonathan Mann, "We only have a truce with infectious disease, and if a city's infrastructure gets overloaded, the balance can tip back to microbes at any time" (*Time,* Jan. 11, 1993,

A family ekes out an existence in a Third World shantytown. Sociologists link the conditions in these expanding squatter settlements to social problems in the First World.

p. 35). As we have tragically learned from the AIDS epidemic in U.S. cities, microbes do not recognize human boundaries.

First World Causes of Third World Problems

According to some sociological theories, the First World's reckless driving of the modernization steamroller has caused human wreckage in the Third World. But the intent here is to provide a specific instance in which objective damage in the latter can be clearly traced to the former. Unfortunately, news headlines while this section was written did provide a perfect case—the society ranked next to last in Figure 6:2's "misery index."

A SOMALIA SAMPLER

> **"Somalia is dying not from a lack of food or medicine but from an absence of order."**
>
> . . . it is hard to turn away from the agony of Somalia. On any scale, the suffering is staggering. Hundreds of innocents are dying every day of entirely preventable causes: starvation and disease.
>
> Somalia's problem, however, is not lack of food. A huge international aid effort, although delayed, is in place. Now the rains have come and thousands are dying of hepatitis, measles, dysentery and tuberculosis. These are preventable killers, but relief workers say they are reluctant to ask for sophisticated medicines for the same reason they are wary of food shipments: when they get anything of value, they become the target of armed thugs.
>
> Somalia is dying not from a lack of food or medicine but of order.
>
> Charles Krauthammer, *The Philadelphia Inquirer,* Oct. 13, 1992

> **"Superpowers fed Somalia's chaos"**
>
> Superpower strategists once grandly dubbed a broad swath of troubled Asian and African nations "the arc of crisis," and anchored it with poor, remote Somalia.
>
> Now the arc has come full circle, outsiders are shipping in grain instead of guns, and some observers are blaming the superpowers for causing a human catastrophe.
>
> The U.S. troops moving into Somalia will find many American weapons among those littering the devastated landscape. In 21 years as dictator, Mohamed Siad Barre was given thousands of tons of rifles, artillery and other arms—first Soviet, then U.S.—as the Cold War giants jockeyed for advantage.
>
> As he amassed his arsenal, Siad Barre destroyed much of the inner workings of Somali society—political parties, professional groups, the National Assembly, a free press. He even forbade wedding parties unless they were government-supervised.
>
> The Somalia that finally overthrew its tyrant in January 1991 was less a nation than a collection of clan-based armed bands. And the bands next turned on one another.
>
> "The savagery of the fighting points up the absence of civilian institutions to mediate the conflict—an absence that is the legacy of 21 years of dictatorship under Mohamed Siad Barre," writes Rakiya Omaar, a Somali who until recently headed the Africa Watch human rights organization.
>
> Charles J. Hanley, Associated Press, Dec. 9, 1992

> **"Dealing with Anti-Countries"**
> For nearly two years, while as many as half a million Somalis starved to death, the international community sought consent for famine relief from the leaders of warring clans, as though they represented their people's interests. In fact, these Mad Max characters have been conducting an experiment in anarchy. They have proved that there is an even worse fate for a nation than the most dictatorial regime imaginable, and that is the absence of any regime at all.
> The implosion of civil authority in Somalia has created a black hole that sucks in help from the outside and crushes it before it can do much good. Convoy drivers hijack their own cargoes. Relief workers, many of them volunteers and all of them unarmed, have been subjected to death threats, shakedowns, looting and kidnapping.
>
> Strobe Talbott, *Time,* Dec. 14, 1992

The sampler of quotes from articles and editorials about Somalia presented here highlights three disturbing facts. First, that society has suffered much more than a shortage of food. The biblical "Four Horsemen of the Apocalypse"—famine, strife, war, and pestilence—have all been rampant. Second, the cause was not the breakdown of a single law or institution. The entire macrostructure of Somali society collapsed. Finally, the former USSR and the United States were clearly accomplices in this criminal situation. Both indirectly by destabilizing the political system and directly by showering guns on the region, the "Superpowers" shoved Somalia into a state of utter social disorder.

The Subjective Dimension

Such worldwide patterns of social problems are now becoming apparent, but they still are seen very selectively. In the United States, our attention to international issues tends to be episodic. In the 1970s, there was a flare of public concern about illegal immigrants; in the 1980s, this spotlight shifted onto the flight of American industry into the Third World. At base, these issues had the same subjective source: the great *value* placed on jobs in the United States, and the potential threat from wage-hungry, populous societies.

The *visibility* of megastructural problems likewise is very selective. Media exposure tends to overexpose famines—concentrated, large-scale starvations like Somalia—even though the slow, scattered starvation of chronic undernutrition is much more deadly. In large part, the weak subjective response to objective problems around the globe stems from weak *expectations.* The general sense is that little we do here truly affects the human condition there. Consider this entire chapter a sociological treatise on why that expectation is in error.

At the heart of the "sociological treatise," of course, is the idea of *megastructure*—concrete relations linking society to society to society . . . This idea shows the social structure underneath the process of globalization. To serve as a subjective reminder of the reality of megastructure, we shall mark our objective discussions of that reality in the chapters to come with the suggestive icon in the left margin.

SUMMARY

1. The Earth and all its occupants are being transformed by a fundamental and powerful process called modernization. Modernization is an inexorable generator of several central kinds of social change. Skyrocketing production of food, energy, and other commodities has kept pace with an exploding world population while damaging the environment and expanding the capacity to wage war.
2. Smaller trends associated with modernization include the growth in services such as education, health care, and entertainment. A kind of cultural homogenization has come about as the result of the global spread of communications.
3. Several theories attempt to explain modernization in terms of how structures *among* societies control what is *inside* societies. Development theory was inspired by the success of the Marshall Plan after World War II. It holds that "underdeveloped" areas, with the proper help and motivation, can be quickly released from the miseries of traditional society to join the ranks of "developed" nations. Essential to this change is the dismantling of a traditional value system in order to replace it with a modern one. Proponents of development theory typically hold the most "modern" value pattern to be that of the United States, whose foreign policy was long based upon the promotion of self-sustaining growth in anti-Communist Third World regimes.
4. Dependency theorists portray development theory as a functionalist alibi for the First World to plunder and exploit the Third World. Rather than seeding development in the Third World, foreign capital investment goes into the pockets of the local ruling class, who resist modernizing changes such as land reform. Multinational corporations drain capital from the domestic markets of the Third World, thus diverting local investment that could lead to development and shipping profits back to First World nations.
5. World system theory sees the global process of modernization as driven by "core" countries, whose rapid development must occur at the expense of societies of a waning "periphery" as they are looted of their labor and raw materials.
6. Despite their differences, the mass of sociological scholarship in the modernization theories reveals a truly international process. Problems in Third World areas related to the advance of modernization are felt in the First World in such forms as terrorism, spreading disease, and the threat of deteriorating international relations.
7. By the same token, the First World's reckless driving of the modernization steamroller has brought about human wreckage in the Third World.
8. Our selective view of such problems, based on values, visibility, and expectations, tends to make us overlook worldwide patterns and to believe, erroneously, that little we do here truly affects the human condition elsewhere.

College students riot in France during 1994.

PART THREE

PROCESSES OF SOCIAL CONTROL

Why are you reading this? Sociology is the product of a particular "Culture" (Chapter 7), the many varieties of which mark the many varieties of human being. More to the point, this culture applies social controls to get you to do course readings; some of these controls are inside, planted there by the process of "Socialization" (Chapter 8).

Not everybody does the assigned reading. Why not? Chapter 9 furnishes sociological insights into this and other forms of "Deviance." Finally, Chapter 10 analyzes the "collective behavior and social movements" that can burst through the orderly routines of the social world and shake it to the core.

Chapter 7

Personal Perspective

IT was my first week on the job as the new foreign student advisor at a major California university. What a start! On Monday, a student from Taiwan came into my office visibly shaken. His English skills were not too keen to begin with and whatever had made him upset had stifled the little English he could speak. He had only arrived at the university a few days before, so I assumed he was going through a bout of homesickness, but it turned out to be more serious. After a good deal of concentration on both of our parts, I came to understand that he had been stopped by the police for driving a stolen car. When I obtained more information from the local authorities, I found that the student had *purchased* the car. There was a sign posted somewhere on campus that a 1984 Honda Civic with 20,000 miles was for sale for $1,500. The student made a phone call, the seller brought the car to the student's apartment and the student cashed his traveler's checks to pay for the car. No title was exchanged since he knew nothing about titles. When the student was finally stopped by the police, he had no title, no license, and no insurance. The cops were not pleased. The student was frightened and confused. What a lousy welcome to the United States.

SM

Culture

culture—the socially standardized ways of thinking, feeling, and acting that a person acquires as a member of a particular society.

society—a large number of people who live in the same territory and are relatively independent of others outside their area.

symbols—the mechanisms necessary for the storage and transmission of the large quantities of information that constitute culture.

FOREIGN college students have problems beyond the usual challenges of course work. They have the added burden of living in another society whose culture is mysterious and misleading. What is **culture**? The popular meaning of the word refers to being sophisticated in the worlds of music, art, literature and the theater. Another use of the word differentiates between the serious creations of an elite group ("high culture") and those which appeal to the masses ("popular culture") (Shrum, 1991). The pure sociological meaning of the term refers to socially standardized ways of thinking, feeling, and acting, which a person acquires as a member of a particular society.

Culture is what makes human beings unique. In fact, all social structures depend on culture for their existence. This includes objects and ideas within a society from religious rituals to jazz music to baseball. Culture is a symbolic-expressive aspect of human behavior. This delineation of subject matter may cast a large net but humanity's invented part of the environment is indeed a large sea. The only other term in sociology that is broader is **society** because it includes large numbers of persons who reside in the same territory and are relatively independent of others outside their own area. Culture is fundamental to society as society is to culture; neither can exist without the other. Culture includes all the shared products of society and society consists of all the people who share a culture.

Perhaps Sanderson has defined culture as succinctly as anyone. He holds that there are four primary characteristics:

> First, culture rests on **symbols**. Symbols are essential to culture in that they are the mechanisms necessary for the storage and transmission of the large quantities of information that constitute culture. Second, culture is *learned* and does not depend upon biological inheritance for its transmission. Third, culture is a system that is *shared* by the members of a society; that is, it is representative of a society considered collectively rather than individually. . . . Finally, culture tends to be *integrated.* The various parts or components of culture tend to fit together in such a way that are consistent with one another, despite the conflicts, frictions or contradictions that are also present (Sanderson, 1988, pp. 31–32).

Understanding and defining culture is clearly necessary to an appreciation of sociological principles. But it is equally important to realize how singularly important culture is to the macrosocial development of civilization and the microsocial activities of everyday life. What would life be without culture? This chapter is being written near a window of a house. Virtually everything outside represents cultural knowledge passed down and perfected from one generation to another. Some of the more visible examples include a basketball court, conservation-oriented landscaping, a solar heating system, and the mind-boggling technology saturating the neighbor's car. Can you imagine if our learned knowledge to modify the natural environment were not transmitted from one generation to the next? Then imagine being dressed in a loincloth and living in a cave because that is what starting over would be like.

ELEMENTS OF CULTURE

value—a socially shared standard about what is good, desirable, and right in a particular culture.

Culture is the "big picture" of human social organization. It is an oceanful of feelings, thoughts, expectations, behaviors, traditions, customs, communications, technologies, lifestyles, conflicts, gestures, and . . . the list goes on. It is an ocean fed by many large rivers that ebb, flow, and change course over time. The most fundamental element of culture is a **value**—a socially shared standard about what is good, desirable, and right; or bad, undesirable, and improper—in a particular culture (Thompson, 1986).

Examples abound in U.S. society. We are a people who have been regularly characterized as elevating a number of values. These include an *activistic* view of the world—not being socialized to passively accept things as they are. From this may flow our low tolerance of frustration and the positive encouragement of progress. Compare people from India with Americans when it comes to responses to Mother Nature. Indians are regularly hit by devastating cyclones that drive them to safe ground. Then they resignedly march home and simply rebuild. Hurricane Andrew, on the other hand, devastated southern Florida in 1992. The response was volatile citizen outrage over shoddy construction and government delays in aid.

We are also known as a people who place an emphasis on *materialism* and value the "good life"—one driven by wealth and a high standard of living. We are seen as having an *open* view of the world insofar as we are adaptive to change, flux, and movement. And we are *future-oriented* as opposed to more traditional societies, which worship the past.

These values were noted by Robin Williams (1970). Williams also painted a picture of American culture laced with values promoting individualism, achievement and success, the work ethic, equality, freedom, and the democratic right of political participation. No one is saying that these values are respected by all Americans. Once again, they are standards of the desirable. Are some values more deeply ingrained than others? That is a difficult question to answer, but, in 1985, Robert Bellah and his colleagues made a persuasive case that one value—the commitment to individualism—has become a "habit" of the American heart. Other American "habits" include the importance of success, freedom, and justice, values that have been heralded in America for hundreds of years. But the lofty place of individualism in our society gives the Bellah group pause. They fear that individualism has grown cancerous and may be threatening the very survival of freedom itself.

norms—those established standards of behavior which reflect societal values.

folkways—the norms governing everyday behavior whose violation causes little concern.

Whether your position is that individualism is a good thing or a runaway train, it is clear that it permeates our daily activities through norms. **Norms** are established standards of behavior that reflect the values supported by a society. Norms run the gamut from being quiet in church to "Thou shalt not covet thy neighbor's wife." The value of individualism is alive and well on every U.S. campus. One of its forms is academic integrity that translates into the norm, "Study hard and do your own work." Not abiding the norm against cheating takes many forms, some serious and some not so serious. Less serious violations are **folkways**—norms governing everyday behavior whose violation causes little concern. Folkways are followed because they represent proper etiquette, manners, and generally acceptable ways that people behave in certain situations. Your professor, for instance, may violate a folkway by wearing a wetsuit or smoking cigars while lecturing. Folkways are also violated when somebody steps into an elevator and stands next to the only person on board. Let's get back to the academic integrity example. A folkway type of norm violation would be attending class in a hung-over haze and simply photocopying a classmate's notes. Do it regularly and you are not likely to garnish the respect of your friends and, over time, may become known as a lazy loser.

mores—the norms that are sanctioned strongly.

Lazy losers violate folkways. Outright cheaters violate more serious norms known as **mores**. Mores (pronounced more-ays) are the most strongly sanctioned norms. They are *taboos* that people consider central to a society's sense of morality. Cheat on an exam or plagiarize a term paper and the consequences can be severe (if you are caught). Some professors assume you know that. Others (like one of your authors) verbally wave this norm before passing out a test. It can sound like this:

> I shouldn't have to remind you of the "cheating rule" but I will anyway. If you cheat on this exam the consequences are many and nasty. You will flunk the exam. You will flunk the course. You may very well flunk college, and don't be surprised if you flunk life as well.

Despite such warnings, cheating is not unusual on campuses. In fact, America's growing preoccupation with individualism may have produced a

One taboo that is shared around the world is a prohibition of cheating. On college campuses, special committees deal with things like plagiarism. The problems are usually handled in quiet ways. That was not the case at the Naval Academy where an organized cheating incident resulted in national publicity, disgrace, shame and expulsion. Midshipmen especially are expected to be "honorable."

BOX 7:1 COLLEGE EXPERIENCE

American Youth: Is Selfishness Up?

The United States is known to be a culture in which individualism is a highly prized value. That is not necessarily something altogether good. It may actually promote selfishness and cheating in order to "get ahead." The report below summarizes the findings of a recent study of cheating among American youth, with a focus on college students.

When Michael Josephson frets about the hole in the ozone, he isn't worrying about sunbathing penguins in Antarctica.

Josephson's concerns are a lot closer to home—right in the United States, where he says he has mapped "a hole in the moral ozone" that has blinded a generation of American youth to the age-old virtues of honesty, trustworthiness and personal responsibility.

In a two-year study released earlier this month, Josephson, the independently wealthy founder of the Josephson Institute for Ethics in Marina del Rey, Calif., reported that large numbers of American youth admit to stealing, lying and cheating at school, work and home.

Josephson billed the study as "the most comprehensive survey of American ethical attitudes and behaviors ever undertaken."

"We're setting up a kind of backward society where cheaters do prosper and honesty is not always the best policy," he said.

For example, the study found that 33 percent of high school students and 16 percent of college students admitted shoplifting in the previous 12 months. The survey found that 11 percent of high school students and 4 percent of college students admitted stealing at least four to five times within the previous year.

Thievery also begins at home, according to the survey: 33 percent of high school students and 11 percent of college students say they have stolen something from parents or relatives at least once.

Other findings:

- One in eight college students admits to fraud, such as lying to an insurance company, lying on financial aid forms or borrowing money with no intention of paying it back.
- About one-third of high school and college students say they are willing to lie to get a job. And about one in

generation of young adults who are especially selfish and willing to violate values and break norms. Box 7:1 addresses this question among young people in general and students in particular.

sanction—a reward or punishment for adhering to or violating norms.

law—a formal sanction.

Norms vary in terms of how absolute they are. One measure of this variation is the degree of reward or punishment for adhering to or violating norms. This is a barometer of their degree of **sanction**. Sanctions can range from a look of disgust at a drunk vomiting in public to a formal legal code known as a **law**. Laws are proscriptive in that they state what behavior is forbidden, such as taking another's life, rape, and income tax evasion. In the case of cheating in college, sanctions are relatively mild for the student who writes two papers with identical themes and overtly illegal for the persons who sell term papers as an organized business. Laws and sanctions are discussed further in Chapter 9 ("Deviance").

One of the other fundamental elements of culture is the distinction between material and non-material culture (Ogbrun, 1922). Earlier we stated that the concept of culture is so broad that it includes everything from thoughts to technologies but dividing the topic into two major forms allows us to study culture in a more manageable way. One of these cate-

BOX 7:1 COLLEGE EXPERIENCE *continued*

six admit they already have at least once. Moreover, about one in five college students say they would falsify a report to keep their job, while a similar number say they probably would cheat if it helped them compete on the job.

- A majority of high schoolers—61 percent—and 32 percent of college students admit to cheating on an exam at least once.
- Large majorities of both high school and college students—77 percent and 78 percent—listed "getting a job you enjoy" as their most important goal. Yet 71 percent of college students also say that their second most important goal was teaching "firm ethical values" to their children.

Ironically, the study found that many students also lied when answering survey questions. When asked by surveyors, about 40 percent of high school students and 30 percent of college students admitted they "were not completely honest" on at least one or two questions. Consequently, the study asserts, it is "highly likely" that the survey understates "perhaps substantially" the frequency of dishonest behavior.

The findings are based on a 100-question survey of 3,243 high school students and 3,630 college students from all regions of the country. Students from religious, private and public schools participated, and most had middle- and upper-middle-income backgrounds. The margin of error is plus or minus 2 percentage points. The report expands an initial study released by the institute two years ago. While that study painted a similarly bleak picture of youthful morals, it relied on data gleaned from a wide variety of sources. This time, Josephson said, the institute gathered its own data to produce a "benchmark" study of the nation's mores. A similar survey of adults will be released later.

Josephson is especially appalled by students who say they would be willing to cheat or lie to get ahead on the job.

"Everybody's going to be hiring these people," he said. "The willingness to do something (unethical) is a very important question because young people may not have had a chance to do it yet."

Critical Thinking Questions

1. The data above clearly indicate that cheating is common; but is there any reason to believe that it has increased in recent years?
2. What kind of background experiences would make a student especially likely to cheat and lie?

Source: Garry Abrams, *Los Angeles Times*, November 26, 1992. By permission of publisher, p. 12.

material culture—the total tangible items in society.

non-material culture—the ideas, beliefs, attitudes, and values of a society.

gories, **material culture**, includes all of the tangible products in society from Corvettes to books to trash disposal. These basic raw materials and social forms related to human survival and adaptation comprise the material infrastructure of our society. All of these components of material culture have our handprint since they were fashioned by people. **Non-material culture** embodies the intangible creations of human society: all of our ideas, beliefs, attitudes, and values. This ideological superstructure of a society involves the patterned ways in which people think, evaluate, conceptualize, and feel. Religion, folkways, laws, and economic systems such as capitalism and socialism are all examples.

Generally, material and non-material culture are in harmony. When in "sync," they produce a state of cultural integration. But, as we shall see later in this chapter, that is not always the case because social change inevitably appears in almost any part of our culture. When this happens, it is the non-material culture that is most resistant to change. We are much more open to new technologies that make our lives easier than to new ideas that challenge our way of viewing the world. Consequently, we see more foreign *cars* in the United States than foreign *ideas*.

Social change is often first noticed among college students. These three photos are from campus life from the '50s, '70s and '90s. They look very similar but ideology differed radically. The '60s and '70s were not just known for bell-bottomed pants. They were also a hotbed of political activism. The '50s and '90s are similarly serene. There is one noticeable difference—'90s campuses are much more multicultural.

U.S. CULTURE

Earlier we described American culture with words such as *individualistic, achievement-oriented,* and *democratic.* Although some argue that individualism is the center of all American values (Bellah et al., 1985), there is an interesting pile of different values woven through the American social fabric. Words that designate some of the "core objects" in American culture are *freedom, responsibility, independence, choice, security, limits, authority, happiness, duty,* and the *future* (Hewitt, 1989).

No discussion of American values would be complete without special mention of social mobility, whether it be actual, potential, or imagined. After all, this is the country known as "the land of golden opportunity," a feature that has attracted millions of emigrants from around the world and kept most native borns right where they are. This mobility is not merely an observable social fact; it is a part of the American lifestyle that has had and continues to have a formative influence on American culture.

It is interesting to note how many core American values hang together and play off of each other. Individualism sparks an achievement orientation, which in turn can pay off in the form of upward social mobility (see Chapter 11). Yet how could achievement and mobility be experienced without hard work? They couldn't. So what? The "so what" is that many Americans work hard so that they can enjoy the paradoxical luxury of leisure. Sound weird? At first glance, perhaps, but not when you look at some of the typical routines of American living.

Take the weekend, for example. It has become such a traditional break from the routine of work that some believe we couldn't survive without it.

> It's the time we think of as our own. On the weekend we dress differently, we "go away," we build weekend retreats, we sleep in, we go out, we linger over the Sunday paper. We become different people. Yet why, when asked, "What did you do on the weekend?" do we often answer "The usual" (Rybczynski, 1991, p. I)?

That's an interesting question because it shows that many Americans have the work ethic so deeply ingrained in their psyches that they turn their leisure times into little organized rituals. This can be especially visible during the traditional two-week vacation period. It's supposed to be a vacation, right? Yes is the logical answer, but when you look at how some people behave during their vacations you wonder where the logic is. They are so determined to have a good time that they work themselves into a frenzy to make sure tons of activities are *planned* out. They might as well have stayed at the office where they would have been less strung out.

We may be stretching the truth a bit about how Americans work at leisure but sometimes a little overkill helps to make a point. Speaking of points, let's take a quick look at the role of another value in our society—the importance of self-fulfillment (creativity). *New Rules* by Daniel Yankelovich (1981) reports that although most Americans have traditionally been a thrifty and productive people, enjoying and helping to create an abundant and expanding economy, things have undergone a strong reversal since the 1960s. In a "world turned upside down," Yankelovich shows the turbulent effect that these sharply changed circumstances have had—not only on individual Americans but on America itself. *New Rules* tells about how 80 percent of Americans are now committed to the search

FIGURE 7:1 THE VALUE OF CREATIVITY AS PART OF THE AMERICAN LIFESTYLE
United States culture places strong emphasis on individualism and creativity.
Source: Daniel Yankelovich, *New Rules: Searching for Self-fulfillment in a World Turned Upside-Down.* NY: Random House, 1981, pp. 82–84. By permission of the publisher.

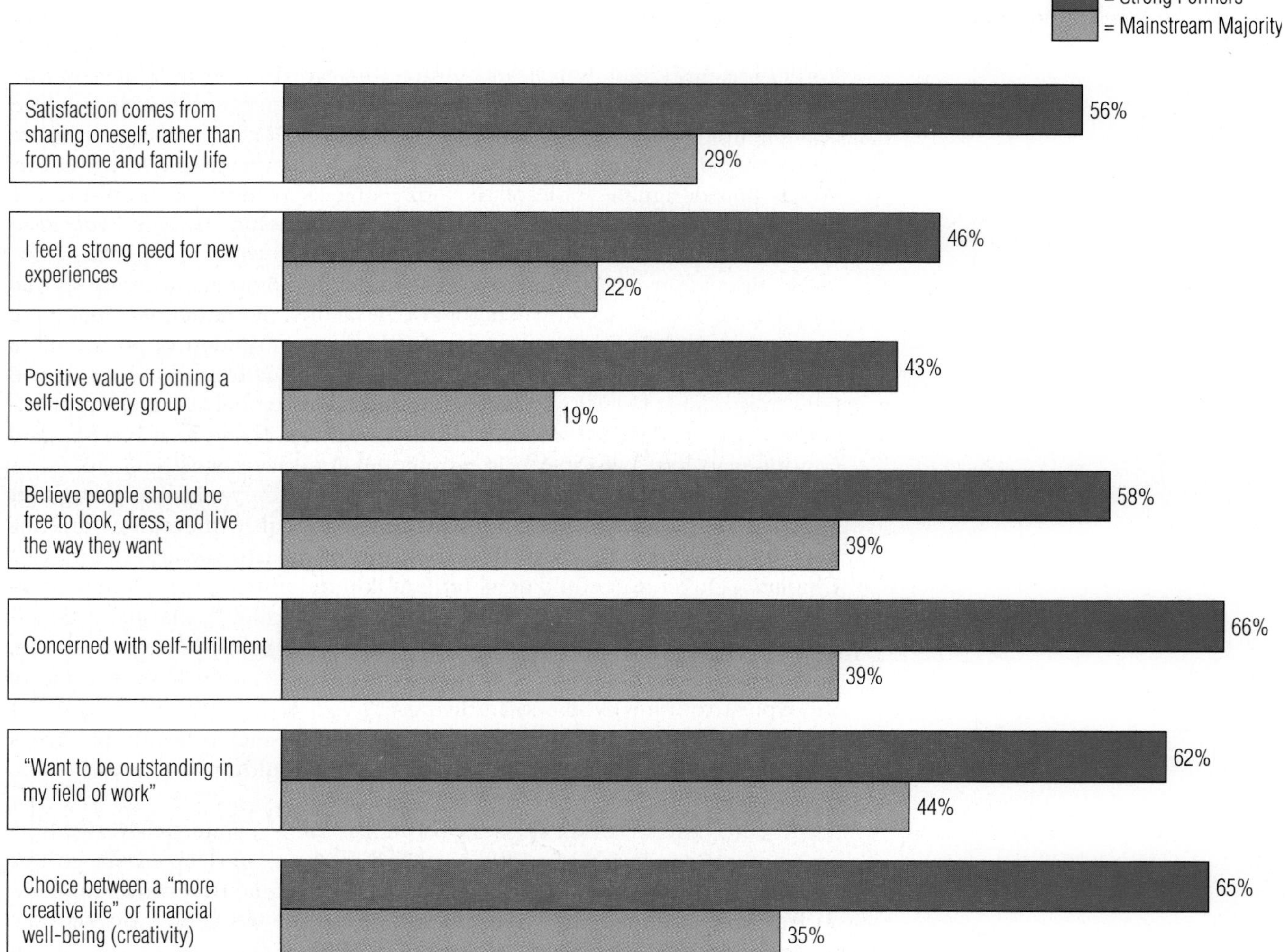

for self-fulfillment at the expense of the older, altruistic ethic of earlier years. Figure 7:1 is from the Yankelovich study, which separates American personality types into those more driven by the need for self-fulfillment ("strong formers") than others ("mainstream majority").

The need for new experiences and being outstanding and creative are big items on Yankelovich's "American Value Hit List." But they are only a list. And obviously not a list found in equal doses in all Americans. There are some, of course, who reject these values as well as some of our nation's most fundamental institutionalized norms. Live life in a slum and concepts like mobility and self-fulfillment seem ludicrous.

We live in a large, diverse society and, in this setting, the incubation of general values is no simple matter. It doesn't matter what the value is: It could take a form as homely as Benjamin Franklin's how-to-get-rich maxims or Lincoln's sublime second Inaugural Address or Martin Luther King's feisty vision of an American dream.

U.S. SUBCULTURES

subculture—a group that stands apart from the larger society by supporting different values, language, religion, traditions, and the like.

The points about intracultural variation and people's values running the gamut from A to Z relate to a formal concept in sociology known as **subculture**. Subcultures are smaller cultures existing within the framework of the larger culture. Many of us belong to groups of this type, groups that share to varying degrees the norms, values, and patterns of behavior of the dominant society but also maintain their own personal and distinctive beliefs and lifestyles. Some sociologists believe that *all* of us belong to *numerous* subcultures but we believe that is stretching the concept to the point where every occupation or club is seen as distinct enough to merit the label. To us the concept of subculture loses its meaning if it is used in such a general way. So we restrict our definition to the more extreme and unusual. Still examples abound, especially in places like college campuses. In the 1960s, all kinds of subcultural trends permeated student life, from dedication to acid rock to experimenting with "alternative life styles" to transcendental meditation to LSD trips. The sixties' students now have their own kids in college and subcultural forces continue. Except that they are a whole lot different in the 1990s. Fraternity and sorority rituals of the 1950s are back and well. And a burgeoning number of students are swallowing a piece of subculture their parents experienced—the LSD microdot.

New York City is a place traditionally rich with subcultures including seedy 42nd Street, the nightclubs that specifically cater to drag queens, and bars where "dwarf tossing" is a big hit. The Big Apple may be a hotbed of subcultures but it by no means has a monopoly on them. They are spread all over the United States and include rock groups, vagrants, witches, criminals, Little Italys, Chinatowns, gypsies, Skinheads, and Deadheads, as well as people whose hobbies include collecting and trading tacky things like little vials of Elvis's sweat.

Religious communities are some of the more interesting examples of subcultures. The Old Order Amish in Pennsylvania live a life that rejects virtually all the components of modern civilization: television, automobiles, electric lights, higher education, movies, politics, jewelry, pictures, life insurance, and musical instruments, to name a few (Kephart, 1982). Members of the Oneida Community in New York state were known for their practice of "complex marriage" with "advanced" sex practices. And the Hutterites in South Dakota follow a way of life that includes pacifism, economic communism, and nonassimilation into U.S. society.

The Amish, who reject many of the conveniences of modern technology, plod along in horse-drawn buggies in the midst of U.S. commercialism. They are a tightly knit, God-fearing people who are dedicated to the principle of hard work. Crime is almost non-existent among the Amish. In fact, until the 1990s there had not been a single case of homicide in more than a century.

When you think about some of the exotic religious communities you may wonder what there is that connects them to American culture at all. Geographical location? In cases like the Oneida that may be all there is. However, the most extreme example of a subculture is a subtype known as a **counterculture**. A counterculture is not simply unusual; it is a subculture that actively challenges the norms and values of mainstream society. Essentially it was a counterculture that forged the demise of Socialist Poland and turned it into a democracy. And it was a counterculture in the 1960s called the New Left that wanted to remove the capitalism in the United States even if it meant blowing up banks and corporate buildings. The New Left attracted millions of young Americans who were not only turned on by the antimaterialism idea but also by other anti-American values centering on drug use, sexual freedom, and the immorality of war. It is not unusual for countercultures to attract the young. Face it. They have the least investment in culture as it is and are much more open to change and experimental lifestyles than their elders (Gallagher, 1974).

counterculture—a subculture that actively challenges the norms and values of mainstream society.

The length of the list of American countercultures varies. Some reserve the term for highly visible organized terrorist-type groups such as the Ku Klux Klan. Others feel that many young urban African Americans constitute a counterculture. They are so alienated from the American mainstream that, organized or not, even African-American leaders and celebrities can't get through to them because their world is so defined by drugs, violence, and hopelessness about the future.

BOX 7:2 GENDER AND SOCIAL CHANGE *continued*

leaving an aperture only about the width of her thumb to allow her to pass urine and menstrual blood.

There was no anesthesia. She was not allowed to cry, and was told to bite on a stick of wood to help her bear the pain. For weeks, her legs were tied together, held motionless, while her wound healed.

In this way she was made ready for the world. No clitoris, no desire. No opening, no risk of shame visited on her family. No dishonor to the clan.

Theoretically, when she was ready for the ceremony of an arranged marriage, she would be reopened—though, of course, without ever attaining a full capacity for sexual pleasure.

In the last decade, female circumcision has been the target of a worldwide feminist and humanist campaign. This year, that campaign was energized by the publication of Alice Walker's bestselling novel on the subject, *Possessing the Secret of Joy.*

Opponents describe the practice as barbarism—tragically misguided tradition at best, unconscionable child abuse at worst. Increasingly, it is becoming a public health problem in Western countries, as refugees from African famine and civil wars find their way into clinics and emergency rooms that are ill-prepared to deal with the arcane medical problems that these refugees present, including chronic infections caused by the crude surgery.

But there are also those on the other side of the issue, who argue no less fervently that condemnation of female circumcision is a form of cultural chauvinism; that the practice is so rooted in tribal custom as to be a part of a cultural identity; that by making women less dependent on men for their sexual happiness, circumcision is actually an empowerment of women.

"There are traditional practices which are intolerable," says Berhane Ras Work, an Ethiopian who heads the Inter-African Committee on Practices Affecting the Health of Women and Children. She is speaking on a videotaped documentary produced to build resistance to female circumcision, tribal marks, nutritional taboos and early marriages. "There are traditional practices toward which nobody should be indifferent," Work says. "Female circumcision has no reason to persist—because of the danger . . . because of the torture which children, innocent children, have to go through."

"Everybody should stand up in solidarity, men and women, to abolish these practices in order to save our children from this unnecessary and gruesome suffering."

There is another side, one expressed by intellectuals who claim that Western critics of female circumcision are guilty of cultural condescension. Even as these intellectuals recognize the dangers and the seeming senselessness of the practice, they respect the roots of the tradition, and resent highhanded condemnations delivered from afar. Clitoridectomies, they point out, were performed by American physicians in the 1800s and up until at least the 1930s as a cure for "hysteria."

Westerners "always talk to African women like the Westerners are the ones taking the lead," Yahne Sangarey, an international activist from Liberia, says about groups that oppose circumcision. "They have never come to us on an equal basis. There are certain issues we don't need white American women up front for. Let them leave us alone."

Critical Thinking Questions

1. What is the difference between an ethnocentric and culturally relativistic view of circumcision, from the perspective of U.S. culture?
2. How would a functionalist and a conflict theorist explain the origin of female circumcision?

Source: Mary Ann French, "A Practice Some Call Mutilation," *The Philadelphia Inquirer*, January 17, 1993. By permission of publisher, pp. C1, C3.

Box 7:2 is a more detailed description of a practice performed on millions in Africa, the Mideast, and Southeast Asia—female circumcision. By U.S. standards, it is alien to even our most vivid imagination. We offer it here as a case example of an accepted practice that others call outright mutilation.

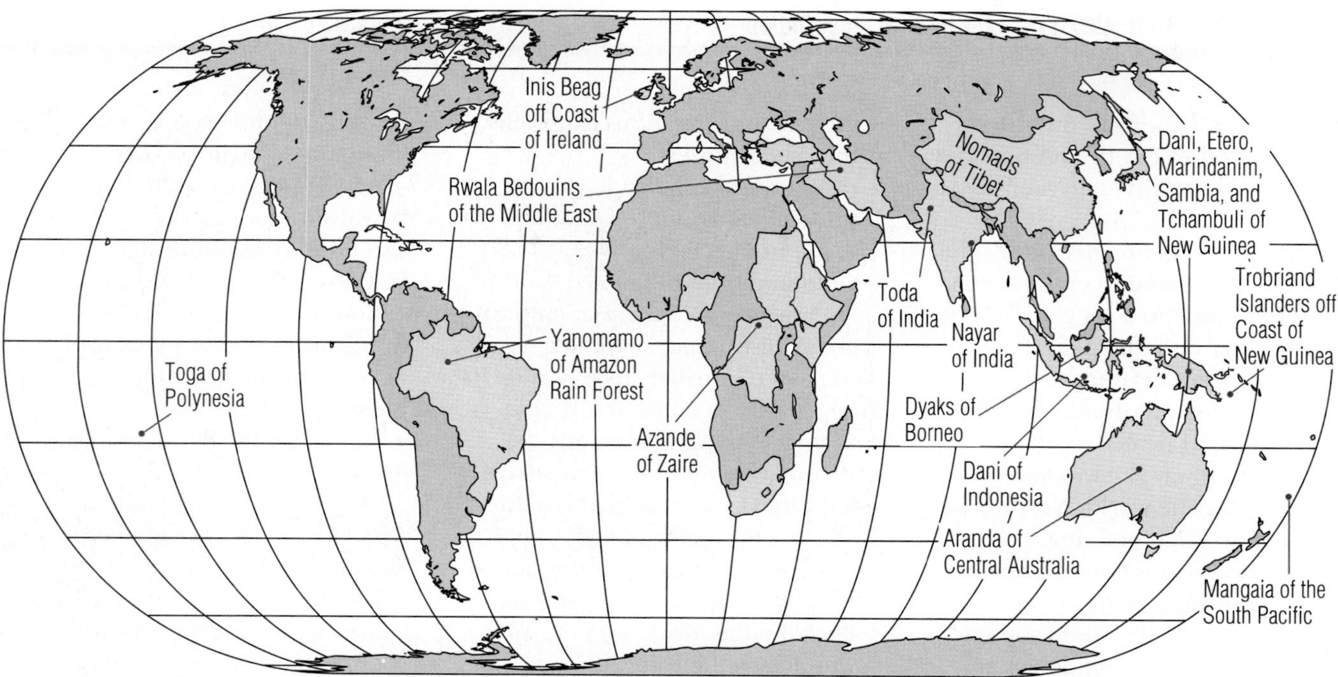

FIGURE 7:2 SOME CULTURES OF THE WORLD
Shown here are the locations of some of the cultural groups discussed in this chapter.

The Family

The family, the basic social unit, is an institution brimming with examples of how culture can affect social structure. In this regard, the work of George Murdock (1957) is especially relevant. His "Human Area Relations Files" are a painstaking categorization of not only different forms of family life but also other cross-cultural variants such as social stratification and politics. Here we look at some of the "kinship terms" researchers like Murdock use to describe different types of familial structures around the world.

Number of Partners

monogamy—a marriage consisting of one spouse of each gender.

polygamy—a marriage involving more than two parties.

polygyny—one man married to two or more women.

polyandry—one woman married to two or more men.

In the United States and many other countries, **monogamy** is the norm. This is a marriage of one spouse of each gender. Actually, with our high divorce rate, perhaps the term *serial monogamy*—one at a time—is more accurate. **Polygamy** is marriage involving more than two partners. One form of polygamy is **polygyny**, where one man has two or more wives. That is not uncommon in some parts of the Middle East and Africa. One special form of polygyny occurs in India when a man is granted "access" to his wife's sisters. Another form of polygamy is **polyandry**. This is a rare form of marriage where one woman marries two or more men. Examples (few and far between) include the Toga of Polynesia, the Nomads of Tibet, and (once again) India, where a Toda woman becomes wife to all her husband's brothers.

Murdock notes that while monogamy and polygamy are general patterns found in cultures around the world, there are many variations. One such variation is the case of limited polygyny in which unions of one man with two or more wives are culturally favored but relatively infrequent. Actually, polygyny is reported to be the most favored form of marriage around the world, but monogamy is the most widely practiced. The reason? Anthropologists point to numbers—as in not enough women. Others regard the favoring of polygyny as sexism in its most primitive form.

The family takes many forms around the world but, in the United States, the only legal form is monogamy. Not everybody conforms to the norms. Jonathon Swapp (left), and his brother Addom Swapp are shown here entering Third District Court in Salt Lake City for a preliminary hearing on murder charges. They had been part of a radical group that dynamited a Mormon church in 1988 because of a dispute over its leadership. They held off the FBI, ATF, and other agencies for longer than a week while bunkered in a house with all of their wives. A shootout ensued.

Choice of Spouses

endogamy—choosing a spouse from within a particular group.

exogamy—a custom requiring that marriage partners be chosen from outside a defined group.

Cross-culturally, two major patterns of mate selection emerge. **Endogamy** is a custom that requires people to choose spouses from within their own group. The group could be a community, tribe, social class, nationality, religion, or some other collection. In India, for instance, marriage is limited to members of the same caste. In the United States, endogamous patterns exist among African Americans and Jews, although it is not a fixed rule. **Exogamy** is the opposite; it is a custom that requires that partners be chosen from outside a defined group. While this usually takes the form of prohibiting marriage between members of the same family lineage, it also occurs in more exotic ways. The Aranda of Australia, for example, divide themselves into two groups and only permit marriages between them.

Residence

This part of family life may be the most complicated of all—where to live. Here is a quick list of some of the more common patterns:

matrilocal—near or in the wife's family's home
patrilocal—near or with the husband's family
neolocal—husband and wife establish their own residence

Cross-culturally there are some strange exceptions to these patterns. The Trobriand Islanders off the coast of New Guinea follow an avunculocal pattern. It does not have to do with the couple's residence per se. It is their sons who are required to leave home at age 12 and move in with the mother's oldest brother who functions as a type of "sociological father." And one last example, the Nayar of India. Until the late 1940s they basically had no marriage system at all. There was plenty of sex, however. It was random and frequent and took place in a *tarvade* (what some would call a whore house). The kids stayed with the mother, the only known biological parent. Murdock dubbed this lifestyle *duolocal*.

Descent

How is ancestry traced? Along what lines is inheritance of property established? In U.S. society descent follows the family tree of our mothers and fathers, a custom known as *bilineal*. The relatives of both parents are considered kin, and property is passed down to children of both genders.

Other societies center around *patrilineal* descent systems in which the male bloodline is the center of self-identification and inheritance. Here the lineage of grandfather, father, and son form the dominant set of blood ties, although women can maintain relations with their own family. Females, however, are expected to defer to the husband and his family.

There are also *matrilineal* systems in places like West Africa. Membership is traced through the female line, from mother to her offspring. Children take the mother's family name and inherit property through an XX route, particularly from the mother's brothers.

Authority and Dominance

patriarchy—the societies in which men have the greatest power and make most of the family decisions.

matriarchal—a society in which women assume the dominant positions of power and authority.

Regardless of the specific patterns of marriage followed in cultures around the world, there is always an underlying dimension by which certain groups of people are socially dominant or relatively powerless. Given that patrilocality, polygyny, and patrilineal descent predominate cross-culturally, it follows that these customs are based on male dominance. **Patriarchy** is the formal name for these setups. These are societies where men have the greatest power, including making most of the family decisions. Are there **matriarchal** societies where women are the dominant authority figures? They are so rare you could count them on one hand. They include the Tchambuli of New Guinea, which are discussed in the "Personal Perspective" of Chapter 13. Matriarchal systems occur in places where there is a surplus of men, and women have their individual sources of power. Maybe Iraq, with such anti-female practices as "honor death" (See Table 7:1), will develop this way in the next century.

In places like the United States and other industrialized societies, there has been a visible shift in power within the family over recent decades. Traditionally these societies have been organized around distinct patriarchal arrangements. As you know, that is changing, largely as a function of the Women's Movement. If we reach a point where authority in family systems is truly shared by both sexes, the term **egalitarian** will be the correct label.

egalitarian—family authority and decision making is shared by both genders.

The family is a fertile example of how cultures vary around the world. The patterns described here are merely a part of that variation. Much has also been researched on how other family forces vary cross-culturally, including parenthood (Tripp-Reimer and Wilson, 1991) and forms of childrearing (Tobin, Wu, and Davidson, 1989). Is there *anything universal* about the family? Murdock's (1949) analysis of 250 societies led him to conclude that *some* form of *nuclear* family is found in every society. But even that is questioned in some sociological circles.

Homosexuality

Cultural variation is also evident in homosexual behavior. No exclusively homosexual society has been found, but a few societies have been identified that prefer homosexual to heterosexual behavior, including two New Guinea tribes: the Marindanim and the Etero. The former kidnap children from other groups to compensate for their low fertility, and the latter attach taboos against heterosexual intercourse to 295 days a year (Herdt, 1981; Kelly, 1977; Van Baal, 1966). At the other extreme, a substantial minority (37 percent of Ford and Beach's sample, for instance) of societies forbid and condemn homosexual behavior, including China, where authorities refuse to admit that it even exists (Burton, 1988; Ruan and Tsai, 1988). Those convicted of homosexuality face three years in prison in parts of Russia (Lemonick, 1989), life imprisonment in Ireland though the law is now rarely invoked (Majendie, 1990), and the death penalty among the Rwala Bedouins (Ford and Beach, 1978). However, most societies fall in between these extremes of preference and condemnation, and approve or at least accept homosexual behavior (Gray and Wolfe, 1988). Homosexual behavior takes three major forms in these societies.

One rare form is *transvestism,* in which some men adopt a gender role that might be labeled "not men" or feminine (Callender and Kochems, 1986). They assume feminine dress and/or occupations and spurn the masculine gender role. Some societies expect such "not men" to behave homosexually, whereas others permit but do not necessarily mandate it (Whitehead, 1981).

The second major form of socially approved homosexuality is *pederasty,* which is probably the most common of the three. Pederasty is sexual relations between two males, especially when one is a minor. Some primitive societies simply allow pederasty but others insist that males behave homosexually for at least a portion of their life cycle, usually adolescence. There are two cultural patterns associated with pederasty, one typified by the Azande of Africa and the other by Melanesian groups.

In the Azande patterns boys play the role of wife during adolescence. Gray and Wolfe (1988) describe the situation this way:

> In Azande society, there was a shortage of unmarried women because men could have more than one wife. As a result, some males turned to . . . homosexual behavior for sexual release. This pattern was institutionalized in organized military companies in which older men married boys aged 12 to 20. The husband paid bride-wealth to the boy's parents and was expected to behave as a dutiful son-in-law. The Azande had strict rules against adultery, and if a boy slept with another man his husband could press charges for adultery. The boy performed all the household and caretaking duties appropriate to the feminine gender role. The couple slept together at night and engaged in sex. . . . When the boy–wife matured, he became a warrior and left his husband, perhaps to marry a woman. If he could not find an eligible woman or could not afford the bride price, he might marry a young boy (Gray and Wolfe, 1988, pp. 664–65).

The bottom line is that homosexual behavior among the Azande is performed by males who have a heterosexual erotic preference. These males are not viewed by society as morally or biologically deviant, neither are they or their older husbands thought to have a feminine identity owing to their homosexual behavior. Given the shortage of women, homosexual behavior is simply considered an expedient substitute for heterosexual behavior.

The Melanesian pattern of pederasty is found in societies that prescribe regular homosexual activity for all males at certain developmental stages (Gilmore, 1990; Herdt, 1981, 1982, 1984, 1986). The practice is usually based on the belief that a boy will not develop into a man naturally (and be capable of heterosexual intercourse) unless he is masculinized by consuming semen. Money (1988) describes one such society in the following passage:

> The Sambia people of the eastern highlands of New Guinea are among those for whom traditional folk wisdom provided a rationale for the policy of prepubertal homosexuality. According to this wisdom, a prepubertal boy must leave the society of his mother and sisters and enter the secret society of men, in order to achieve the fierce manhood of a headhunter. Whereas in infancy he must have been fed woman's milk in order to grow, in the secret society of men he must be fed men's milk, that is, the semen of mature youths and unmarried men, in order to become pubertal and grow mature himself. It is the duty of the young bachelors to feed him their semen. They are obliged to practice institutionalized pedophilia. For them to give their semen to another who could already ejaculate his own is forbidden, for it robs a prepubertal boy of the substance he requires to become an adult. When a bachelor reaches the marrying age, his family negotiates the procurement of a wife and arranges the marriage. He then embarks on the heterosexual phase of his career. He could not, however, have become a complete man on the basis of heterosexual experience alone. Full manhood necessitates a prior phase of exclusively homosexual experience. Thus homosexuality is universalized and is a defining characteristic of head-hunting, macho manhood (Money, 1988, p. 10).

The last major form homosexual behavior takes is *homophilia.* In this situation, erotic lust (and sometimes love) is attached to those of the same gender, and there are usually no gender role changes (Money, 1988). Unlike pederasty, homophilia involves males of all ages and does not necessarily involve man–boy relationships. This form of behavior is not found very frequently in historical or primitive societies, but seems to be a product of modern industrial societies. The gay subculture in the United States and in other societies consists mainly of men (and women) who are homophilic.

It is rare for more than one type of approved or condoned homosexuality to be present in a given society. Where one is present, the other two are usually ridiculed or despised, not just by the society as a whole, but by the practitioners of the condoned forms.

This discussion of homosexuality has centered on males for many reasons, including the aforementioned paucity of cross-cultural information on the sexual behavior and attitudes of women (Gay, 1986; Sankar, 1986). Lesbianism does exist in many societies, usually in the homophilic form. Nevertheless, lesbianism is not as widely reported as its male counterpart. While a handful of societies that openly approve of lesbian behavior have been identified, most societies either overlook the behavior, especially if it has a low profile, or strongly disapprove of it. Among the latter societies are the Azande who believe that once women engage in lesbian activity they then control their own sexual gratification to the detriment of heterosexual men. Moreover, the Azande believe that sex between two wives in a polygynous household could cause the husband's death supernaturally (Gray and Wolfe, 1988). Incidentally, clandestine lesbianism is thought to be relatively common in polygynous societies where wives reside together in harems.

We would not be surprised if some of the things you read about in this section on world cultures shocked and mystified you. Things like female circumcision, cannibalism, and simultaneously worshipping and eating dogs are not part of the U.S. cultural agenda. Why are these things shocking? How did these practices arise in the first place? We provide some answers to these questions in the "Subjective" section later in this chapter. There you will see how cross-culturally exotic behavior can be sensibly explained through sociological analysis. Figure 7:2 provides a map showing some of the many cultural groups mentioned throughout this chapter.

Ethnocentrism and Cultural Relativism

For now let this discussion on world cultures serve to erect some basic principles. One idea is to recognize the high degree of variance in human behavior around the world. Some of the examples we use may have been jarring but we want to guarantee your attention. There are plenty of people who would read about these things and not appreciate the complexities of the human condition. Rather, they would make judgments of others' cultures based on their own standards. The outcome is a negative one. Other people are not only seen as different but also as backward, ignorant, immoral, and the like. This type of thinking, known as **ethnocentrism**, is a rigidity in the acceptance of the culturally alike and in the rejection of the culturally unalike. For obvious reasons, it is more common among less-educated people who have a smaller view of the world, a view known as "culture bound." (See Figure 7:4, which outlines some of the components of ethnocentric thinking.)

ethnocentrism—a cognitive rigidity in the acceptance of the culturally alike, and in the rejection of the culturally unalike.

Ethnocentrism is the feeling that one's own culture is the best in all respects and others exist in various degrees of inferiority. In its extreme form, some call it *xenophobia.* It is not unusual for people to believe their way of life is the best. It could be in comparison to other nations. It could be between New Yorkers and Texans. It takes numerous forms, most of which spell bigotry.

Ethnocentrism is difficult to overcome. Social scientists are not immune to it. Read the quote about the culture-shock experience of one well-trained anthropological fieldworker and you will see what we mean.

> I looked up and gasped when I saw a dozen burly, naked, filthy, hideous men staring at us down the shafts of their drawn arrows! Immense wads of green tobacco were stuck between their lower teeth and lips making them look even more hideous, and strands of dark-green slime dripped or hung from their noses.
>
> . . . My next discovery was that there were a dozen or so vicious, underfed dogs snapping at my legs, circling me as if I were going to be their next meal. I just stood there holding my notebook, helpless and pathetic. Then the stench of the decaying vegetation and filth struck me and I almost got sick. I was horrified. What sort of welcome was this for the person who came here to live with you and learn your way of life, to become friends with you? . . .
>
> . . . I pondered the wisdom of having decided to spend a year and a half with this tribe before I had even seen what they were like. I am not ashamed to admit, either, that had there been a diplomatic way out, I would have ended my fieldwork then and there (Chagnon, 1977, p. 5).

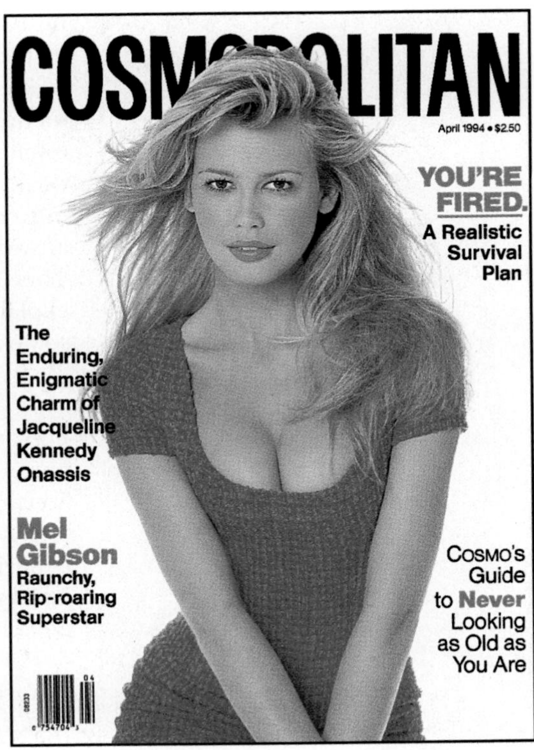

The United States and the Islamic world are polar opposites when it comes to the appearance of women in society. In the Islamic setting, a woman's appearance is limited to dark clothes and a pair of eyes. In the United States, the physical aspects of femininity are flaunted.

The critique of ethnocentrism is often associated with an opposite intellectual position known as cultural relativism. This point of view holds that there is no universal standard that an outsider can use to evaluate cultures. Each culture must be seen in its own terms. This is the open-minded view that not only smacks of intellectual sophistication but also has some practical applications. It has been reported, for instance, that managers on intercultural work assignments are more effective with a healthy dose of cultural relativism. Their job performance is enhanced by applying their understanding of the culturally based differences in values among the firm's employees (Hofstede, 1984).

cultural relativism—**an open-minded way of thinking, which holds that there is no universal standard by which to evaluate cultures.**

We hope to instill a sense of cultural relativism in you as you move through the pages of this book. We refer again to the "Subjective" section of this and many other chapters for objective information about so many of our misperceptions regarding other nations, races, ethnic groups, social classes, sexual orientations, lifestyles, religions, educational systems, economies, families . . . . There is a negative flip side to cultural relativism, however. If it is applied universally, it can lead to some highly flawed conclusions. Hitler's mass extermination, Pol Pot's rape of Cambodia, and human rights violations around the world do not have *any* redeeming value a la cultural relativism. They are simply wrong. You don't need a sociology course to know that.

CULTURAL STABILITY AND CHANGE

Cultural Constants and Universals

Let's shift gears. Much of the discussion so far has centered on the countless differences among cultures of the world. It is equally important to note that all cultures also exhibit some identical traits. We call these cultural con-

cultural constants—the elementary social structures found in every society.

stants. Actually they are more important than the differences because without the presence of certain elementary social structures, a society would cease to exist. (See Figure 5:2, which lists the macrostructure of groups in the United States.) Those groups are the five institutions that constitute the "floor plan" of our society. They are also the fundamental elements of *every* culture. Think of it. Have you ever heard of a culture without some form of politics, economy, religion, family, and education? The answer is a profound NO because each of these institutions *must* be present to maintain a cultural pulse. View them as the major organ systems of the human body. If one fails, death is imminent.

These five institutions are cultural constants. Each is organized about the satisfaction of a particular vital need. Politics distributes power in an orderly fashion. The economy provides for material needs. Religion serves as a social cement bonding those with common beliefs. The family acts to procreate and socialize. And educational institutions function to pass on accumulated knowledge to members of new generations. Despite their universality, the form of these institutional functions will vary from culture to culture. Politics may be the sole inherited right of a chieftain until his death or it may take the complicated U.S. style with different levels of government, offices, terms, and electoral procedures. In preliterate cultures, religion may be simple sorcery. In other cultures it is a complicated set of coexisting and contradictory theologies with all manner of rituals. You already know how many diverse rules and forms can shape the family. But the family doesn't hold a candle to the complexity of some economies. In the United States, for instance, there are some 29,000 different types of occupations. Less-developed cultures may simply divide labor by gender. Finally, take a look around campus and count its components: an administration, professors, students, research assistants, dorms, classrooms, curricula . . . The same basic educational function exists cross-culturally but, in a place like Borneo, the young learn from elders by simple word of mouth.

cultural universals—the specific practices found in every culture.

That's the big picture of cultural constants. The more detailed view, often referred to as **cultural universals**, is of more specific practices found in every culture. Murdock (1945) compiled an elaborate list of cultural universals including the following: music, incest taboos, toolmaking, weather-making efforts, calendars, dream interpretation, folklore, sexual restrictions, funeral ceremonies, games, courtship, dancing, bodily adornment, numerals, gift giving, cooperative labor, cooking, food taboos, and language. Note that each of these are general traits; their specific form differs from culture to culture. Note also how each of these "universals" fits into one of the five institutional "constants." Sexual restrictions with family. Cooperative labor with economy . . . *And language with everything.*

Language

The Importance of Language

The all-encompassing nature of language deserves special attention. All forms of human communication are distinctive in that they are based on symbols. Individual symbols provide the building blocks for that distinctive accomplishment of all human cultures, *language.* It is not understood exactly when and how language first arose. Some linguists see it as a relatively recent development, perhaps no more than 100,000 years old,

Cross-cultural variations and cross-cultural constants are expressed in just about every activity imaginable. Sports are a part of every culture's pulse but the form varies immensely around the world. Here in the United States baseball is a big "hit," drawing millions of fans. But did you know that, in Afghanistan, big crowds attend the national sport of *buz kashi*? It is a wild version of polo that uses a headless calf for a ball. Knives and chains were finally outlawed but sudden death on the playing field is not unusual.

whereas others believe that it may have originated as long as a million years ago.

Ordinarily, language is taken for granted as simply a way of expressing feelings, and communicating ideas and messages. But such a commonsense view overlooks the fact that the evolution of language was of crucial significance for the emergence of culture. Despite the limited success of recent attempts to teach apes the rudiments of language, it appears that symbolization (and hence language) is uniquely human. Apes may learn the use of some symbols but humans have been the only group to have invented symbols.

Language is the nexus of culture; it is not only a cultural universal but it also permeates all of the cultural constants in every society's floor plan. It is true that some cultural skills, such as hunting and music, can be learned through imitation without the use of language. However, some of the complexities in areas such as education and religion could never be transmitted across generations without the spoken word.

> Language is a guide to "social reality." Though language is not ordinarily thought of as of essential interest to the students of social science, it powerfully conditions all our thinking about social problems and processes. Human beings do not live in the objective world alone . . . but are very much at the mercy of the particular language which has become the medium of expression for their society (Sapir, 1958, p. 162).

Sapir–Whorf Hypothesis

Two American linguists, Edward Sapir and Benjamin Whorf (Sapir, 1929, 1949; Whorf, 1956) believe that language is more than an aid to thought; it pervades the content and style of thought itself. Language actually constructs reality by determining which things we carve out of the flux of life experiences. Language is culturally determined and leads people of different cultures to interpret reality in different ways by focusing their attention on particular phenomena. Stated directly, the Sapir–Whorf hypothesis holds that language does not just *describe* reality but also *shapes* it. Numbers, mathematics, and computers are a few categories that widely separate industrialized societies from less-advanced social systems. Consider our everyday lingo that includes words like *million, billion, thousand, software,* and *bytes.* Other cultures are a radical departure from our complex system of numbers and interfacing computers. In South America, for example, the Yanomamo have only three numbers in their language; in English they would be *one, two,* and *more than two.*

The Sapir–Whorf hypothesis is a huge idea. Known also as the *linguistic-relativity hypothesis,* it holds that, since different cultures use different language systems, a Chinese, an American, and a Colombian live in different worlds, not just the same world with different labels attached (Sapir, 1949, p. 162). Huge ideas trigger big responses. That is certainly the case here as evidenced by the interesting debates among sociologists as to the way that language and culture really connect. Some believe that the relationship between a culture's language and view of the world is simply cause and effect. Others believe that it is a two-way street—cultural reality shapes language as well as the reverse. There is much to suggest that this last position is the most accurate. Regardless of the degree to which a culture's language and interpretations of reality can affect each other, one thing is clear: *Cultures are uniquely human, transmitted over time, and strangely different due to the significant role of language.*

Language and Everyday Life

Step back from the big picture of culture for a moment and look at the interesting ways language intersects with the everyday lives of individuals. We experience only that for which we have symbols. Example 1: Research on the eye has shown that humans have the physiological capacity to experience about 6 million hues of color. Yet we usually perceive only about a dozen because these are the ones for which we have common words. Example 2: When winter arrives and little white flakes fall from the sky, we call it one word—snow. Not the Eskimos. They have dissected falling snow into 13 different forms, each with its own separate name. Example 3: Naming a newborn is a big deal in our society. It is not just the concerted result of family tradition and parental bickering. There is an unspoken cultural pattern at work as well. Girls tend to be given novel names, which are fashionable and attractive; whereas boys' names are more often chosen from the existing stock of long-standing names in society (Lieberson and Bell, 1992). All of this suggests that boys are taken more seriously as it were. This "seriousness" is one of the issues highly intertwined with differences in U.S. gender roles presented in Chapter 13.

Examples 4 and 5 take us back to the world of college students. Example 4: College is known for its slang, or "inside language" that lies below more formal verbal expression (Eschholz and Rosa, 1984). The use of such names as *dirt farming* for "History of American Democracy," *God* for "Christian Theology," and *nuts, sluts, and weirdos* for "Abnormal Psychology" are noteworthy departures from clipped forms such as *soc, psych, poli sci,* and *bio* that college students have traditionally used. Table 7:2 contains a list of rhyming pair formations found only in the subcultural language of America's hilarious students.

The American college scene is a linguist's treasure chest of example, exotics, and eccentrics. To many, it's a big laugh. That's okay. College should be a rewarding time ("The best years of your life").

If you are not part of the mainstream of American culture, life in the United States can be a maze of confusion and despair. Language is a big

TABLE 7:2 Language And Culture: The Case Of College Student Slang

Priests and beasts	Introduction to the Study of Western Religion
Trees and bees	Dendrology
Socks and jocks	General Physical Education
Slums and bums	Urban Local Government
Gabs and blabs	Foundations of Oral Communication
Stars and Mars	The Solar System
Trees and leaves	Dendrology
Hicks and sticks	Rural Local Government
Stones and bones	(Anthropology) World Pre-History
Places and spaces	World Geography
Cuts and guts	Principles of Biology
Flicks and tricks	Development of the Motion Picture
Weeds and seeds	Introduction to Plant Biology
Trains and planes	Transportation and Public Utilities
Maps and naps	Introduction to Physical Geography
Spaces and races	Introduction to Human Geography
Rocks for jocks	Introductory Geology
Drugs for thugs	The Psychology of the Drug Culture
Choke and croak	First Aid and Safety Education
Cut 'em and gut 'em	Mammalian Anatomy and Physiology
Bag 'em and tag 'em	Field Zoology
Seed and breed	Advanced Livestock Production

Source: Paul A. Eschholz and Alfred F. Rosa, "Student Slang for College Courses," in James P. Spradley and David W. McCardy, *Conformity and Conflict; Readings in Cultural Anthropology (1984).* Boston: Little, Brown and Company, pp. 71 and 72. By permission of the publisher.

part of the despair of foreign students, as it was in the case of the Taiwanese student who was suckered into buying a stolen car. Unfortunately, there are worse scenarios, all of which are driven by unfamiliarity with the meaning of a culture's language. We will leave you with one, a deadly one.

Example 5: On Halloween of 1991, all of Japan's TV networks took time during their national news program to offer a lesson in English. In tones of amazement and terror, the news anchors explained how the word *freeze* can be used to mean "Don't move or I'll shoot!" A failure to understand that American usage led to an intercultural tragedy when a Japanese exchange student living in Baton Rouge, Louisiana, was shot to death by a neighbor. He had been going to a party when he walked to a neighbor's house by mistake. The neighbor heard someone in his yard and shouted, "Freeze!" The student, after two months in America, did not understand the command and kept walking. The neighbor opened fire with a .44 magnum.

For the American news media, it was just another accidental killing. In Japan, the case confirmed all the worst impressions the Japanese people hold in their intense love–hate relationship with the colossus across the Pacific. It was an accident. It was a homicide. But it wasn't an intended murder. It was a killing compounded by the presence of a stranger in a land of strange talk.

Cultural Change

culture shock—a feeling of disorientation engendered by moving from one culture to another.

In a way, the Japanese student suffered the ultimate by temporarily switching cultures. Rapid exposure to a new culture can produce feelings of disorientation, frustration, and helplessness, which sociologists call **culture shock**. The foreign student is an extreme example. On another level—an imaginative one—Box 7:3 details a day in the life of a modern American woman adjusting to the backwardness of Iran. It is not a pleasant story.

Culture shock can be induced when you encounter people who do not share your values or lifestyle. It is not called "shock" because it induces violence as in our example. It can simply be a slight stun. Even a vacation can provide it. Go to the Bahamas. Get on the bus to "downtown" Nassau. Driving on the left side of the road is the first thing to get your attention. Noticing that people pay the fare if they feel like it won't escape you either. But as you drive by houses that are shorter than their owners, you know you are on a unique ride. An encounter with any of the practices around the world listed in Table 7:1 may also increase your heartbeat.

The traditional sociological meaning of cultural change is not one of shock but of broad patterns of change over long periods of time that don't necessarily produce a jolt. Cultures are constantly changing because societies must adapt to new social, religious, economic, and political demands. The changes may emanate from within the society itself or may be a reaction to changing world conditions. They could be slow or fast and may be readily accepted or energetically resisted. Because human behavior is shaped so much by culture, study of the impact of *changing* cultures on individuals has become the focus of the life work of many sociologists and anthropologists (Segall et al., 1990).

Inferences about Past Cultures

Since culture tends to be inherently conservative, especially the nonmaterial components, cultural change is typically slow. This is evident in

BOX 7:3 SOCIOLOGICAL IMAGINATION IN FICTION

Life in Tehran

The following is an excerpt from the book *Not Without My Daughter.* It is a fictional presentation of a horror story. An American woman and Iranian man marry and assume a happy life in the United States. Until they go on a "vacation" to Tehran. There the husband assumes the behavior that Iranian men often display toward women. He has their daughter carted off to life in a fanatical religious hell-hole and turns their marital life into an existence of violence and submission. Appropriately, his first name is Moody. It's a kidnapping of the body and spirit. And it's a regression to the dark ages of women's rights—social change in reverse.

Mammal loomed in my mind as a major cause of all my troubles. He was the one who had invited us to Iran in the first place. I could see his smirking face, back in Detroit, assuring me that his family would never allow Moody to keep me in Iran against my will.

I stood up. Looking down at Moody, I blurted out, "He's a liar. He's just a plain liar!"

Moody jumped to his feet, his face contorting into a demoniac rage. "You are calling Mammal a liar?" he shouted.

"Yes! I'm calling him a liar," I screamed. "And you are too. You both are always saying things—"

My outburst was cut short by the strength of Moody's clenched fist, catching me full on the right side of my head. I staggered toward one side, too stunned to feel the pain for a moment. I was conscious of Mammal and Nasserine entering the room to investigate the commotion, and of Mahtob's terrified shrieks and Moody's angry curses. The hall reeled in front of my eyes.

I stumbled for the sanctuary of the bedroom, hoping to lock myself in until Moody's fury abated. Mahtob followed me, screaming.

I reached the bedroom door with Mahtob at my heels, but Moody was right behind. Mahtob tried to wedge herself between the two of us, but Moody pushed her aside roughly. Her tiny body slammed against a wall and she cried out in pain. As I turned toward her, Moody slammed me down onto the bed.

"Help me !" I screamed. "Mammal, help me."

Moody clutched my hair in his left hand. With his free fist he pounded me again and again on the side of my head.

Mahtob raced to help, and again he pushed her aside.

I struggled against his hold, but he was too powerful for me. He slapped me across the cheek with his open palm. "I'm going to kill you," he raged.

I kicked at him, freed myself partially from his grip, and tried to scramble away, but he kicked me in the back so viciously that paralyzing pains shot up and down my spine.

With Mahtob sobbing in the corner and me at his mercy, he became more methodical, punching me in the arm, pulling at my hair, slapping me in the face, cursing all the time. Repeatedly, he screamed, "I'm going to kill you! I'm going to kill you!"

"Help me!" I yelled out several times. "Please, somebody help me."

But neither Mammal nor Nasserine attempted to intervene. Nor did Reza or Essey, who surely heard it all.

the work of archeologists who examine the big picture of change from the beginning of recorded time. They use such terms as "Stone Age," "Bronze Age," and "Iron Age" to denote levels in the sequential development of culture. There are some interesting inferences these people can make about the cultural base of a society that perished thousands of years ago. Dating of material artifacts through the use of Carbon-14 and Potassium-argon (K–40) analyses allow rough estimations of age. Items found in unearthed

BOX 7:3 SOCIOLOGICAL IMAGINATION IN FICTION ***continued***

How many minutes passed as he continued to pound away at me, I do not know. I waited for unconsciousness, for the death that he promised.

Gradually, the force of his blows lessened. He paused to catch his breath, but he still held me firmly on the bed. Off to the side, Mahtob sobbed hysterically.

"*Daheejon*," a quiet voice said from the doorway. "*Daheejon*." It was Mammal. Finally.

Moody cocked his head, seeming to hear the Mil-gramquiet voice of returning sanity. "*Daheejon*," Mammal repeated. Gently, he pulled Moody off me and led him out into the hall.

Mahtob ran to me and buried her head in my lap. We shared our pain, not merely the physical bruises, but the deeper ache that lurked inside. We cried and gasped for breath, but neither of us was able to speak for many minutes.

My body felt like one huge bruise. Moody's blows had raised two welts on my head so large that I worried about serious damage. My arms and back ached. One leg hurt so badly that I knew I would be limping for days. I wondered what my face looked like.

After a few minutes Nasserine tiptoed into the room, the picture of a submissive Iranian woman, her left hand clutching the *chador* about her head. Mahtob and I were still sobbing. Nasserine sat down on the bed and slipped her arm around my shoulders. "Do not worry about it," she said. "It is okay."

"It's okay?" I said incredulously. "It's okay for him to hit me like this? And it's okay for him to say he's going to kill me?"

"He is not going to kill you," Nasserine said.

"He says he is. Why didn't you help me? Why didn't you do something?"

Nasserine tried to comfort me as best she could, to help me learn to play by the rules of this horrid land. "We cannot interfere," she explained. "We cannot go against *Daheejon*."

Mahtob took in the words carefully, and as I saw her tearful young eyes trying to comprehend, a new chill ran up my screaming spine, caused by a fresh, horrible thought. What if Moody really did kill me? What would become of Mahtob then? Would he kill her too? Or was she young and pliant enough that she would grow to accept this madness as the norm? Would she become a woman like Nasserine, or Essey, cloaking her beauty, her spirit, her soul, in the *chador*? Would Moody marry her off to a cousin who would beat her and impregnate her with vacant-eyed, deformed babies?

"We cannot go against *Daheejon*," Nasserine repeated, "but it is okay. All men are like this."

"No," I replied sharply. "All men are not like this."

"Yes," she assured me solemnly. "Mammal does the same thing to me. Reza does the same thing to Essey. All men are like this."

My God! I thought. What's next?

Critical Thinking Questions

1. Why are there such vast differences in the place of women in society between Western cultures and countries like Iran?
2. What would be necessary to unravel the cultural threads responsible for the lowly status of women in some Eastern societies?

Source: Betty Mahmoody and William Hoffer, *Not Without My Daughter* (1988). New York: St. Martin's Press, pp. 99–101. By permission of the publisher.

caskets present an idea of that people's view of an afterlife; they include what they think the dead person will need. Double graves, in which one corpse is unadorned and the other is relatively adorned, indicate slavery. Perhaps the trickiest task is in interpreting the *symbolic* meaning of an artifact. An arrow slotted to shoot with a flat head directed perpendicular to the Earth indicates it was designed to penetrate the vertical ribs of a walking animal. Thus a *hunting* society. An arrow designed with a horizontal

The cave-dwelling Tasaday Tribe of the Philippines form one, but not the only, group of preliterate people in the 20th century. The Tasaday are a sharp contrast to the Yanomamo, for whom warfare is a regular part of life. The Tasaday are one of the most peace-loving groups in the world. Until 1970, they had no contact with modern society.

position of head to Earth more likely means a *warring* society. The reason? That is the type of weapon designed to penetrate the horizontal rib construction of humans.

Another approach to understanding the make-up and degree of sophistication of a past culture utilizes the broad categories of "preliterate" and "civilized." These ideas were touched upon in Chapter 2. The main difference between the two is that a preliterate society is largely oriented toward survival needs, whereas a civilized society has moved beyond survival into the intellectual realm of questioning the meaning of life (self-reflection). Examples abound. Preliterate cultures have art but civilized cultures have an appreciation of the meaning of art (aesthetics). Similar distinctions separate the two: religion versus theology, agricultural techniques versus science, tools versus technology, legends versus literature, language versus a writing system, custom versus laws, and a simple view of the world versus a developed philosophy.

Changes in U.S. Culture

The Yankelovich data presented earlier in this chapter demonstrate that some of our fundamental cultural values have very much changed in recent decades. This is particularly evident in the growing preoccupation with self-fulfillment and the declining importance placed on family life (see Chapter 14 on the family). Your authors have been tracking changes in the cultural fabric of the United States as well. Among college students in the 1970s, for instance, there was a monstrous shift from their parents' conservative views toward religion, politics, the role of women, and sexual freedom (Gallagher, 1974, 1979). Then, in the late 1980s and early 1990s, we uncovered a move back toward conservatism. This is particularly visible with students' desires to get a job that pays well, although it may not necessarily be what "turns them on" (McFalls, Gallagher, and Jones, 1993).

Consider the changes in material culture experienced by people born before 1945. These people predated television, penicillin, polio inoculation, microwavable foods, contact lenses, and the "Pill." They also were born before radar, credit cards, split atoms, laser beams, ballpoint pens, pantyhose, dishwashers, clothes dryers, electric blankets, air conditioners, and the first walk on the moon. Non-material changes saw a great upheaval in values as well. People born before 1945 got married *first* and then lived together. House-husbands, gay rights, computer dating, dual careers, commuter marriages, day-care centers, nursing homes, and group therapy were unheard of. Language changes have been humorously different. In 1940, "Made in Japan" meant junk and the term "making out" referred to how well you did on an exam. *Grass* was mowed, *coke* was a cold drink, and *pot* was something you cooked in. *Rock music* was Grandma's lullaby, and *aids* were helpers in the principal's office.

You don't have to go back that far in recent history to see how rapidly our culture changes. Look at some of the things that have happened just since John F. Kennedy's time as president. The Peace Corps was created. The Supreme Court banned prayer in public school. There were "wars" declared on poverty and drugs. Heart transplants were developed, and television became an unintended influence on adult's values and children's developing personalities.

Patterns of Change

The role of cultural change in U.S. society has been awesome. Many may not like America's politics or military prowess, but millions the world over surely love its way of life. Whether it be food, music, or clothes, culture American-style can be found in some of the unlikeliest places. Indeed, sometimes the ways of foreigners become even more American than the ways of those in the states. This is an example of one of the observed patterns of cultural change: **diffusion**. Diffusion is the spread of cultural elements from one culture to another—Japanese technology to America, French cuisine to Indochina, Judaism to Russia.

diffusion—the spread of cultural elements from one culture to another.

Diffusion occurs in different ways including method of transmission and the willingness of people to acquire something new. If it is a new form of government imposed by a foreign power through military conquest, change occurs as conflict theory would predict. A new order is imposed through the force of a more powerful *outside* group. If changes occur violently *within* a given culture, force still drives the engine of cultural change except that the form is now called "revolution."

Diffusion through trade, missionary work, the influence of the mass media, and other types of peaceful interactional contacts comprise a qualitatively different mode of change. Here a culture's base is altered by the more passive internalization of another people's practices. This process is consistent with structural-functionalist theory and its premise of change benefiting all.

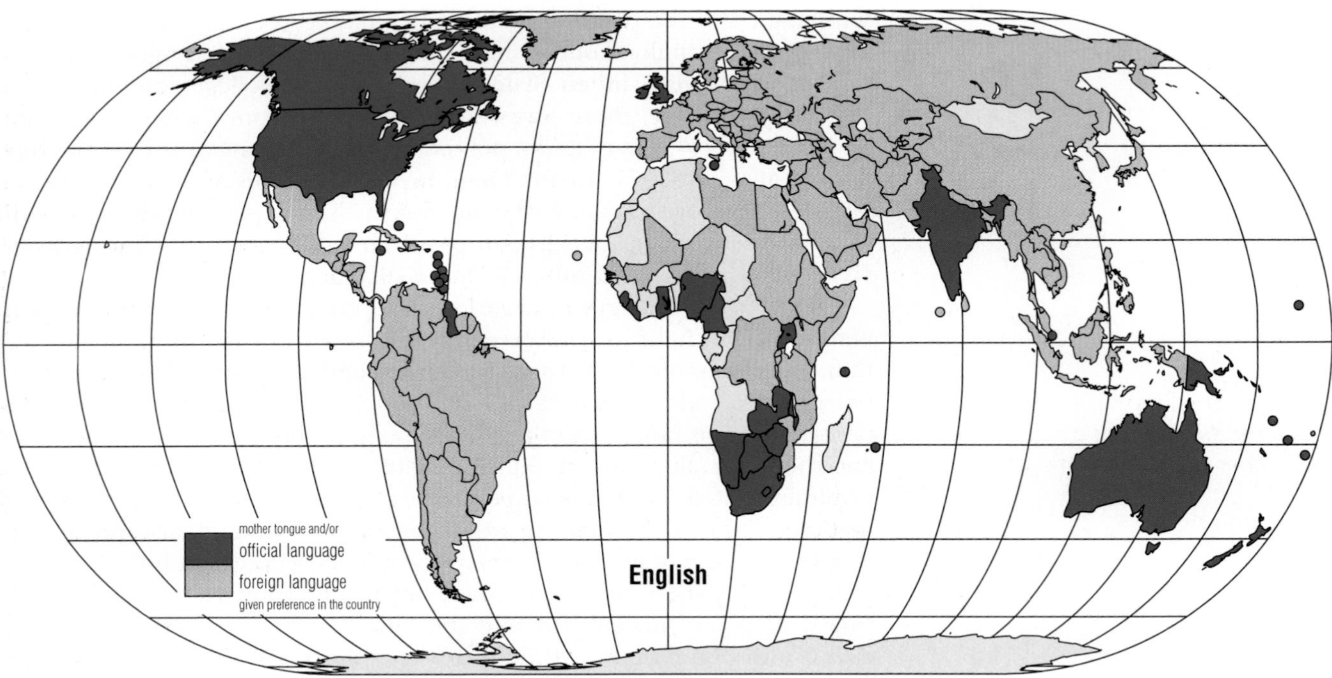

FIGURE 7:3 ENGLISH AS THE MOTHER TONGUE

English is the official language in several world regions, and has become the preferred second language in most of the world.

Source: Peters Atlas of the World (1990). New York: Harper & Row, p. 115.

acculturation—**the process of taking norms and values from one culture and incorporating them into another culture.**

Regardless of the form of cultural diffusion, the result is the same. One people exports norms and values from their culture. Another people incorporates these through intercultural contact, borrowing, or imitating. This process of taking and incorporating is also referred to as **acculturation**. Figure 7:3 demonstrates how the English language has diffused throughout the world.

Aside from cultural diffusion, there is another pattern of change that is unrelated to contact between cultures. It originates within a culture by creation of the new, a process known as *innovation*. One form of innovation is *discovery*, where new knowledge about existing realities occurs. This takes place when new regions of the brain are mapped, the mysteries of genetics are unraveled, or some previously unresearched fact of society is uncovered, such as the influence of social networks.

Another form of innovation is *invention*. Existing knowledge and cultural items are combined to produce something that did not exist before. The jet engine, pacemakers, and computers are only three of numerous past inventions; U.S. government offices are presently filled with "patent pending" ideas.

Can you imagine future inventions? One list comes to mind: robots that do marriage counseling; boats so electronically laden they do all the fishing, with people lazily going along for the ride; shopping completed with home computer selection and delivery functions; and a "nutso" computer program of brilliance, dictionary, encyclopedia, literary genius, and a flair for the macabre to automatically produce a Stephen King novel by the year 2000.

Cultural Lag and Lead

Changes in a culture take many forms that are often far from harmonious. Outside influences are not the necessary grit of disharmony. They often come from within. This was noted long ago by William F. Ogburn (1922), who examined the ways in which changes occur within a society and the social disequilibrium that can result. It was Ogburn who first divided cultural elements into material and non-material forms, an idea that allowed a sociological X-ray of the processes of intracultural change.

A central component of Ogburn's model is that change usually originates in material culture (inventions, new technology). This in turn requires a change in non-material culture (beliefs, values, norms). New technologies, such as computerization of the office, require retraining people as well as revamping some of their general attitudes toward the world of work. Those experiences are often not smooth processes because people's values (and habits) can be deeply entrenched and highly resistant to change. In a nutshell, they want to cling to the familiar and the known.

culture lag—the period of social maladjustment during which non-material culture is adapting to changes in material culture.

Ogburn used the term **culture lag** to refer to the period of maladjustment during which the non-material is still adapting to new material circumstances. In some instances, this can be a big chunk of history as in the case of Copernicus. His accurate contention that the sun (and not the Earth) is the center of the solar system was unaccepted for a long time. The same is also true for the discoveries of Einstein, Freud, and Darwin.

Culture lag has implications for changes that otherwise might be overlooked. Can you think of any logical connection between the invention of self-starters on cars and the place of women in society? Here it comes. In the earlier part of this century, cars could be started only with a powerful turn of a hand-held crank. Women were dependent on the men to do the cranking. Thus women traveled when men were agreeable to it. Then along came the ignition key and off went the women. They had a whole new sense of freedom. We are not saying that this was the big "key" to the origin of the Women's Movement. We *are* saying that a small invention did impact on relations between the sexes.

Later in this century the widespread use of cars also impacted on another value system—premarital sex. When teenagers gained access to the family car, the back seat provided a new land of opportunity for sexual endeavors, and prompted a new code of sexual values in the process. This process was a lengthy period of adjustment many parents were determined not to make.

All of these examples are similar insofar as there was a sense of social strain during the period of adjustment to the new material artifact. Culture lag theory is typically explained in terms of "material change affects non-material change wreaking havoc in the process." There is more to it than that. Other types of cultural changes follow the exact opposite pattern. Ogburn called this phenomenon a **culture lead**. It is where a change occurs in people's thinking and perceived needs, which in turn cry out for a material breakthrough. Here the agony of the "waiting phase" can be especially deep. It's not so serious if it's an instance where people crave a new luxury item such as robotic food shopping. But it is grave in places like the world of medicine. Medical research presently labors under the inability to meet people's specific cries for cures for cancer and AIDS as well as their general hope for extending the average human life span.

culture lead—a social strain generated by a change in non-material culture that calls for a new material breakthrough.

Some changes that touch the sensitivities of the U.S. population don't really fit either the "lag" or "lead" format. What, for instance, does a new law represent? Is it an invention, a part of material culture? Or is it a new formal norm, a component of non-material culture? It certainly isn't a neat fit with a strict interpretation of Ogburn's model but a solid case can be made that laws are part of non-material culture because they are formalized norms. However, they often require a change in people's thinking. One non-material shift can therefore engender another one. There is no formal term for this in sociology but, if Ogburn were alive today, he might feel comfortable calling it a *cultural lead–lead.*

Examples of lead–lead abound at this writing. Here's a long-standing case. Legalization of abortion has been met with massive social protest, including violent confrontations between groups on both sides of the issue (see Chapter 10 on collective behavior). More recently, President Clinton's pledge to revise the ban on gays in the military is another lead–lead form of cultural change. It incited a massive protest both within the armed services and in a big chunk of the population at large. As you know, the outcome was the "don't ask, don't tell" rule. The sociological point? Many forms *(lags)* of cultural change originate from science and technology. Others *(leads)* are responses to people's needs for material invention. And others *(lead–lead)* are flamed by changing value systems per se. All three forms are more than capable of causing social disequilibrium during the "catch-up" phase.

HUMAN NATURE

Is Culture Uniquely Human?

The high degree of variance in human behavior around the world implies that much of the significance of culture is its adaptive capacity. Culture created a means for humans to adjust to the conditions of their existence. This mode of adaptation is vastly superior to biological adaptation available at lower phylogenetic levels. As societies evolved to greater levels of complexity, and as conditions came about for the emergence of symbolic systems, culture itself developed as an evolutionary product.

The discovery that some nonhuman primates display rudimentary forms of tool use has led scientists to question the long-standing belief that culture is distinctly human. Chimpanzees, for example, use blades of grass as crude devices for extracting termites from their holes. The chimps actually shape the tools before using them. Japanese macaque monkeys have been observed washing sweet potatoes and wheat before eating them. Other members of the group learn these practices through observation. Baboons have employed stones as weapons, and chimps can hurl objects at targets (Sanderson, 1988).

These elementary uses of tools may be regarded as rudimentary forms of culture. They vary from group to group of the same species and thus appear to be learned behaviors that are not the result of biological inheritance. However, while nonhuman primates have a few crude elements of culture, the distinction between humans and other primates is easy to draw. The quantitative difference is so great that it can be argued that culture is uniquely human, at least for all practical purposes (Sanderson, 1988). No researcher has found any group of chimpanzees who worshipped gods, exchanged goods as bride payments, or created likenesses of themselves in clay, paint, or wood, to name a few from the long list of cultural universals.

The Biological Basis of Human Culture

The premise that culture is uniquely human leads to the related but more difficult question: How much of human culture is biologically determined, and how much is learned from life experiences?

Human Nature

In commonsense explanations of behavior, the term *human nature* is regularly mentioned. "It is just human nature to be selfish . . . or jealous . . . or friendly . . . or aggressive." This catchall phrase has been offered to explain everything from a mother's love for her child ("maternal instinct") to adolescent males fist-fighting. As we will see in Chapter 13 on gender, many of the behaviors (aggression, competitiveness, etc.) displayed by men are regarded as "natural." Similarly, we attribute many qualities associated with women (tenderness, nurturing, etc.) to biological factors. The question of whether human behavior in general, as well as gender-specific acts, are the result of nature or nurture is one of the oldest and most controversial questions in the social sciences.

During the early decades of this century, some answers to this question used the term *instincts*—biologically inherited predispositions that impel members of a species to react to a given stimulus in a specific way. McDougall (1908), in his ground-breaking social psychological textbook, argued that instincts are the basis of human behavior. These included curiosity, self-assertion, submission, food-seeking, mating, acquisitiveness, fright, repulsion, and parental feeling. Later theorists both added to and subtracted from McDougall's list. Some have claimed, for instance, that aggression can be unlearned (Lorenz, 1966).

It is clear that many aspects of "human nature" vary tremendously from one society to another; one society might value aggressiveness, whereas another values nonviolence. Quakers typically believe in and practice nonviolence. In contrast, some societies regard fighting as a pervasive way of life. The Yanomamo Indians—a group of about 15,000 people living in the Amazon rain forest—constantly fight among themselves. According to data gathered over the past three decades, 44 percent of the Yanomamo men over age 25 have killed someone (Chagnon, 1977; Rensberger, 1988). When we compare the peaceful ways of the Quaker community and the violent behavior of the Yanomamo, claims of a universally aggressive "human nature" clearly seem out of line.

The pervasive violence among the Yanomamo extends to all aspects of their lives; it is not just their treatment of enemies. Males are quite violent with their own families as well. Yanomamo husbands often punish their wives brutally. As a "minor" discipline, husbands pull at the small sticks that the women wear through pierced earlobes. As more severe punishment, husbands jab their wives with a machete or burn them with glowing firewood. The Yanomamo wife *expects* this treatment as a routine part of married life. One anthropologist who lives with the Yanomamo overheard two women talking about scars their husbands had given them. One commented that her husband must care a great deal for her since he had beaten her on the head so many times (Harris, 1974).

The Yanomamo socialize their children—particularly the males—into violence as a normal part of everyday life. When small boys display aggressive behavior, they are rewarded and encouraged by their fathers. Understandably, the Yanomamo have been called "The Fierce People" (Chagnon, 1977). As the contrast between the Quakers and the Yanomamo demonstrates, the contention of the human nature theory that there are universal, inborn human characteristics is extremely dubious.

Instinct theory poses many difficulties. First it involves circular reasoning (e.g., birds fly because they have a "flying instinct"). Second, human behaviors frequently attributed to instincts are rarely found in the entire species. Mothers who abandon their newborns in trash dumpsters clearly contradict the instinct theory.

Biological Drives: Cultural Learning

Failing to discover a core set of instincts responsible for much of human behavior does not necessarily mean that humans are free of biological constraints. Many social scientists hold the view that human beings have biological drives, such as hunger, thirst, and sex, which are strongly influenced by "tensions" within the body. The fact that such drives can be satisfied in a variety of ways suggests that cultural learning plays an important role in human behavior as well. As suggested by some of the entries in Table 7:1, the human sex drive can be satisfied in a multitude of ways. Humans alleviate sex drives with opposite-gender partners, with same-gender partners, with inanimate objects, with animals, and through masturbation. The Inis Beag group suggests that the sex drive can also be largely ignored. This demonstrates not only the malleability of the human sex drive but also illustrates that important cultural values—particularly religious values—strongly affect the specific ways in which libido is fulfilled in each society.

Sociobiology: Biology and Culture

Contemporary biologists who research human behavior are typically referred to as "sociobiologists." To date, they have studied a number of forms of basic social interaction, including courtship, mating, childbearing, aggression, dominance, submission, altruism, and homosexuality (Wilson, 1975). They reason that, since these behaviors occur in virtually every human society, they must have some biological base.

A fundamental premise of sociobiology is that human behavior reflects genetically inherited traits. Sociobiologists argue that human characteristics are the product of the Darwinian concepts of natural selection and evolution. **Natural selection** is the theory that the fittest of any species survive and consequently spread their traits throughout the population over time.

natural selection—the Darwinian concept based on the idea of the survival of the fittest.

Pioneer sociobiologist Edward O. Wilson (1979) noted that, whereas we do not inherit an *instinct* that directs us to engage in specific types and quantities of aggression, our capacity and tendency to engage in violent behavior is *hereditary*. Wilson argued further that "it is entirely possible for all known components of the mind, including will, to have a neurophysiological basis subject to genetic evolution by natural selection" (Wilson, 1979, p. 13). Although humans are highly adaptable, learning and adaptability have evolved through natural selection. According to sociobiologists, the flexibility that distinguishes us from other animals is itself part of our genetic makeup.

Some controversy surrounds sociobiology, especially when its findings are applied to very complex social issues. One such issue is the origin of behavioral differences between human males and females, which will be discussed later. The human capacity to feel love is another ideal topic to illustrate the sociobiological approach. The basic notion is that the great majority of men and women are born with a genetic capacity and need for forming lasting emotional attachments (Mellen, 1981). Sociobiologists explain human love in the following way. When early humans survived by hunting and gathering food, they covered a vast geographical area. Hunting required much speed and mobility. During the times when women were pregnant and/or caring for young children, they had to be relatively sedentary and needed assistance. If the women and their children were to survive under these conditions, men, who were not physically restricted, had to return to them with sustenance. Sociobiologists reason that a selfish male might not provide for the woman and children, but a man born with a tendency to feel attachment to the woman who bore his child (love) would show responsibility. Thus the child carrying his genes would be more likely to survive (Mellen, 1981). Many features of this sociobiological explanation are untestable. No one has isolated a gene that endows people with the capacity to love. Additionally, very little is known about the lives of prehistoric humans, so much of the above scenario is simply conjecture.

One student of primate behavior reaches the following conclusion on the nature–nurture issue:

> I would be the first to agree that the full understanding of the behavior patterns of any species must include biology. But the more that learning is involved, the less there will be of any simple relation between basic biology and behavior. The laws of genetics are not the laws of learning. As a result of intelligence and speech, human beings provide the extreme example of highly varied behavior that is learned and executed by the same fundamental biology. Biology determines the basic need for food, but not the innumerable ways in which this need may be met (Washburn, 1978, p. 75).

An Integrated View of Human Evolution

A balanced view of the nature–nurture issue has been offered by Boyd and Richerson (1985), who, while acknowledging that humans are cultural organisms, explain human evolution from a Darwinian perspective. In their view, human evolution involves—through both genetic and cultural transmission—two processes that are clearly different but that share some parallels.

Cultural transmission, a distinctly human process involving intergenerational learning, differs from biological transmission. Through cultural transmission, children are affected by persons other than their biological parents. Biological transmission, on the other hand, only involves genetic parents as sources of influence (Segall, Dasen, Berry, and Poortinga, 1990).

Genetic and cultural evolution are also analogous. Both proceed through interaction with the environment; both include changes that either become established or lost depending on how well they fit the environment in which they emerged. Campbell (1975) and Skinner (1974) suggest that neither cultural evolution nor biological evolution is predetermined; they proceed through random variation and environmental selection. Thus some argue that the nature versus nurture controversy is an inappropriate conceptualization of the relationship between biological and cultural factors. While both may involve some different processes, they are parallel processes rather than competing processes.

Sizing up the Sexes: Biological Tidbits

In Chapter 13 on gender, you will read much about how the environment fosters between-gender differences. Here we present a few snippets from the biological side. Biology has a funny way of confounding expectations. In this era charged with challenges of sexism, the evidence for innate

One often refreshing view of culture is the beautiful terrain that transcends many cultural contrasts. The rocky island of Irishmaan, one of Ireland's Aran Isles, is not far from Inis Beag, the island whose very repressive sexual norms are discussed by sociologists. Irishmaan is a subculture of Ireland where everything is tranquil and people work only when the rain stops. Northern Ireland, with its tightly packed rowhouses and religious civil war, is a violent and stressful contrast.

gender differences is ironically mounting. For instance, medical researchers document that heart disease strikes men at a younger age than it does women. They also report that women have a more moderate physiological response to stress.

Neurological differences between the genders, both in the brain's structure and in its functioning, are interesting. Here are a few examples. More women focus their language skills in the frontal lobe of the brain, whereas more men focus language skills in the parietal lobe. The corpus callosum is a thick bundle of nerves connecting the brain's right and left hemispheres and is often wider in the brains of women. Some believe this allows for greater "cross talk" between hemispheres, possibly the basis for "woman's intuition." The hypothalamus is associated with sexual behavior. A group of neurons in the anterior hypothalamus is noted to be larger in heterosexual men than in women or homosexual men.

By the way, male homosexuality is a really hot issue in the nature–nurture debate. It was not that long ago that psychiatrists were convinced that being gay stemmed from life experiences, especially the ever-popular idea that "Your parents did it to you." No more. Your authors found otherwise. An overwhelming number of "shrinks" now believe that men are gay because they were born that way (Vreeland, Gallagher, and McFalls, 1994).

The nature–nurture analysis of gender differences is so complicated it may even beat out design of workable heart transplant procedures in terms of degree of complexity. The hearts have been done. The gender issue is just beginning to be unraveled. Here we kicked around some evidence that nature may be more important than nurture after all. But it is just a teaser for Chapter 13. After you finish reviewing evidence to the contrary, you will realize that no one really knows whether genetics (nature) or culture (nurture) is more prominent. It is still a budding field of research, and that is the time when nothing is ever equal.

SUBJECTIVE DIMENSIONS OF CROSS-CULTURAL PHENOMENA

Earlier we listed a host of cross-cultural phenomena around the world, phenomena which the average American may call weird, macabre, or perhaps downright unbelievable. Tales of people who sit on the top of trains, rarely have sex, typically have sex, stretch their earlobes, or believe men can become pregnant evoke reactions like, "Are you kidding?" "Really?" "Why?" We are going to make a stab at answering these questions about how such practices may have originated as well as some explanation about your own feelings.

If you recoil at hearing the bits and pieces of information about what occurs with unquestioned frequency in other societies, remember that there may be a very straightforward reason for your shock—you have never heard of it before. Things like sexless marriages in Inis Beag don't make the front page of *The New York Times.* In fact, they are rarely reported in any popular medium. They are instead hidden in the deep recesses of anthropological journals and only sociologists and the like get to know about them. That's why we have such lively dinner conversations.

Return to our three-variable subjective model detailed in Chapter 2. The *visibility* component of the model is a neat fit with our view that people may be astounded at the behavior of another group. Astounded because it is new, different, and, in this case, something that has remained largely invisible in the public mind. Add to that the intrinsic drama of special forms of sex and murder and the shock intensifies. If these things were the regular stuff of high school social studies classes, they would seem less macabre and more like a twisted mirror image of our own cultural rails.

There is another reason why other people's behavior may have stunned you—it violated your *expectations* of how life normally proceeds. That is one way in which the "expectations component" of the subjective model applies. However, it also has an added value in the case of culture. It can help explain the existence of certain cultural practices.

Here Abraham Maslow's (1943) theory of "human needs" may shed some useful light. People at different levels of so-called development are concerned with different things because their worlds are so different. Thus their expectations may vary radically. An underdeveloped society, for example, is oriented toward lower-level needs such as food and basic survival.

Maslow posits a psychological theory of differences between individual personalities. As far as we know, it has never been applied to culture, but it seems to work. Maslow holds that people look for life in parts. First, satisfy the requirements for basic living. Then, if you're lucky enough, go on to new avenues of experience, the mightiest of which is "self-actualization"—realizing one's potential to the fullest, like being a great student.

Return to Figure 7:1. It brims with the U.S. preoccupation with creativity. Why the United States? Because it is a luxury that underdeveloped societies simply cannot afford. Some of the values and behaviors found in different cultures are a simple reflection of what people are allowed to expect. Thus creativity is an irrelevant value to the starving society of Somalia. Consistently well-fed Americans don't lead lives directed by plans for the next meal.

Other cultural practices do not connect very well with the idea that they originate from expectations associated with level of development. But they do connect with *values*, the third component of the subjective model. There is no way to comprehend cross-cultural variations in behavior without recognizing the complex web of values around them. Historical accident, geographic location, and religion are a few of the formative influences. These forces will never be neatly measured in some kind of equation as we find in math and accounting. They simply *are*. If that doesn't satisfy you, then keep asking. But be prepared to eventually end up with questions as befuddling as the origin of life and the existence of God.

Expectations and values affect behavior around the globe. How can you tell whether a certain behavior is a complicated artifact (value) of a particular society or more related to degree of development (expectation)? It's tough. You have to use your own judgment in estimating where a particular behavior connects. Try these two societal case examples for starters.

Case 1. In Saudi Arabia, a man with many wives raises no protest from his neighbors, let alone an eyebrow.

Case 2. In Colombia, responsible and religious women find secure employment in drug cartels. They are paid to plot, grow, and harvest the coca plant.

FIGURE 7:4 SUBJECTIVE AND OBJECTIVE DIMENSIONS: CULTURAL PHENOMENA AROUND THE WORLD
Ethnocentrism partially stems from variations in visibility, expectations, and values between members of different cultures.

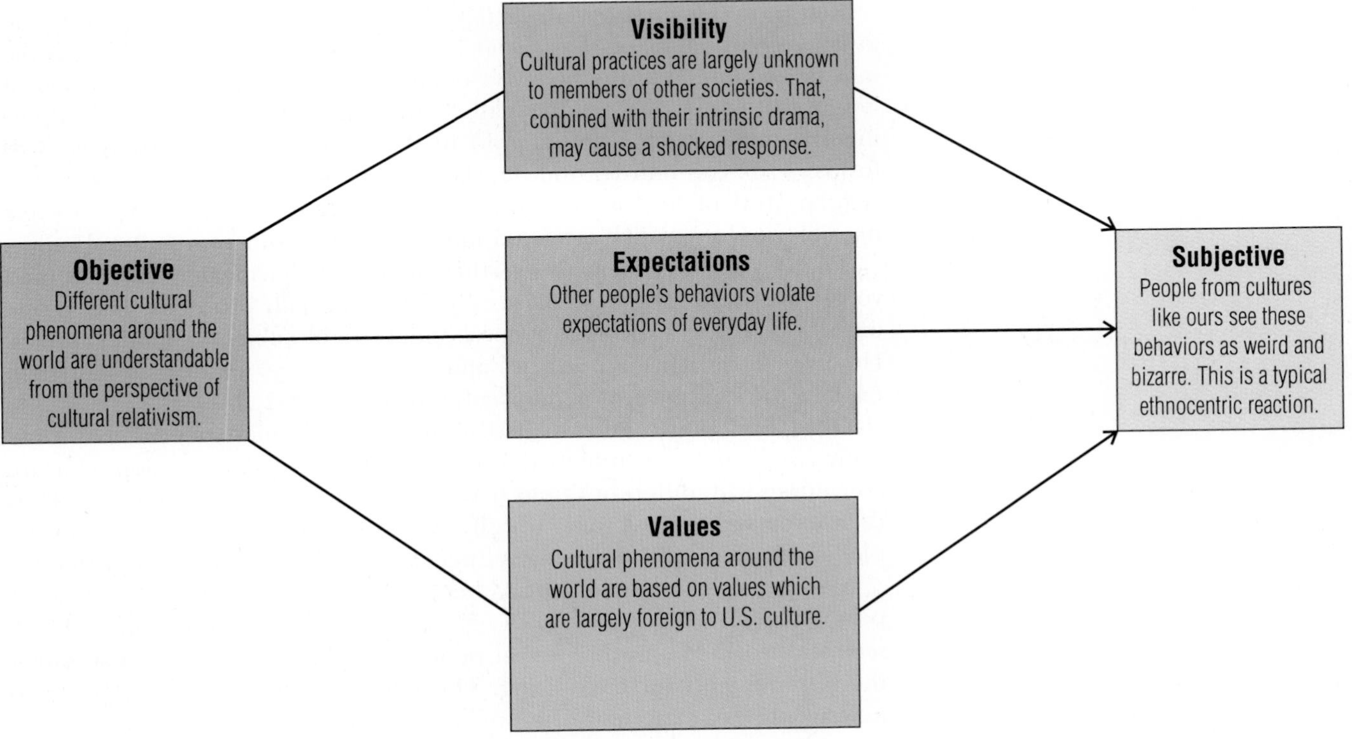

Get the point? The Saudi Arabian example is a complex function of values evolved through historical–religious interaction. The Colombian example, as we believe you have guessed, is a direct connection between behavior (drudgery work for drug lords) and economic need (avoiding poverty). Point made? We hope so, but we want to add a postscript without belaboring the point. The postscript? Pay particular attention to the subjective section in each chapter. It will not just increase your input at cocktail party chatters. More important, it will give you a broader intellectual grasp of the connection between sociological issues of our time and people's perceptions of them. Figure 7:4, for instance, outlines how ethnocentrism stems from variations in visibility, expectations, and values.

SOCIAL NETWORKS: CROSS-CULTURAL PATTERNS

In Chapter 4 (microstructure) we compared the complexities of a spider's web to the social patterns of human interaction. Like the cross-connections in that web, our relations link up with other relations—friends of friends, friends of relatives—to form the intricate social networks of our everyday lives. As one analyst of social networks puts it:

> Within a network, the effects of interpersonal processes depend both on the features of interpersonal relationships and on where these relationships fit into the structure as a whole. For example, the closer two friends are to one another, the more likely they are to agree on intimate matters (Erickson, 1988, p. 100).

TABLE 7:3 Cross-Cultural Differences in Friendship

Percent who would turn to closest friend first for help with:	NATION						
	Australia	Germany	Great Britain	United States[a]	Austria	Hungary	Italy
Household tasks	4.9	6.6	2.8	8.7	4.9	7.2	4.6
Illness	5.2	5.4	2.9	8.7	3.6	2.2	2.6
Borrow money	2.3	1.9	1.5	4.1	2.3	3.4	4.6
Problem with money	24.6	26.1	18.7	27.3	17.9	12.4	25.9
Feeling depressed	20.0	14.8	14.5	25.6	13.9	18.0	29.3
Advice about life change	8.9	7.7	4.3	10.8	6.1	3.4	7.6

[a]Main Point: Americans with personal problems are more likely to go to friends for advice than are people from Europe and Australia.

Source: International Social Survey Program: Social Networks and Support Systems, 1986 computer file. Köln Zentralarchiv Für Empirische Sozialforschung, 1988 producer. Inter-University Consortium for Political and Social Research, 1989 distributor.

Here we offer a glance at a specific aspect of friendship: How often would the average person turn to their closest friend if he or she needed help? That is one question; the other: Is this kind of decision affected by a person's culture? By way of preview, it is. Take a look at Table 7:3. It is a cross-national test of the hypothesis that networks and culture interconnect. Overall, the data don't show troubled people rushing to close friends for help. This is especially visible in Austria. What the data do show, however, is that non-Americans are more likely to seek a friend's help with psychological problems like depression and less so if they need to borrow money. More important, they show that Americans lean on their friends more often than those in the other six countries examined. This is especially apparent when there is a problem involving health, household tasks, and dealing with a big life change. Americans are also more likely to turn to a friend for help with money problems and feelings of depression. (They go hand-in-hand, don't they?) Money and depression drive Italians and our friends from Down Under to seek out their friends with similar frequency. That manifests a degree of cross-cultural similarity. The remainder of the table is filled with differences between nations, differences that demonstrate that the *intensity* of the tiny lives of social networks clearly connects with the big pulse of cultural forces.

SUMMARY

1. Although culture has many meanings, the pure sociological meaning of the term refers to socially standardized ways of thinking, feeling, and acting that a person acquires as a member of a society.
2. Culture permeates our everyday lives and rears its head in many ways. One of countless examples is the value system of a society. In the United States, for instance, emphasis is placed on materialism, individualism, and a future orientation. Besides values, other elements of culture are norms, folkways, and mores.
3. Subcultures are smaller cultures within the large culture. Subcultures share the cultural elements of society, but also have their own distinctive beliefs and lifestyle. The most extreme type of subculture is a counterculture, a group that actively challenges the norms and values of mainstream society.
4. There is a lengthy list of unique differences in cultures around the world. This is evident in the organization of the family, degree of technological sophistication, laws, religion, and the way that a person's sexual orientation is viewed. Beneath these differences are cultural constants, the five institutions that constitute the basis of every culture, and cultural universals, which are specific practices found everywhere on Earth. Some sociologists feel that language is the most all-encompassing component of human culture because it actually shapes reality.
5. Cultures change over time but not in what is necessarily a smooth process. Change can emanate from the diffusion of cultural elements from one culture to another or from innovations within a society itself.
6. Ogburn's model of internal changes notes that change usually originates in material culture, which, in turn, requires a change in non-material culture. The period of adjustment—culture lag—may

cause social chaos. So also may a culture lead, in which a change in people's thinking calls for a new material breakthrough.

7. Culture is uniquely human. It provides a way for people around the world to adjust to the conditions of their existence. It is not known, however, how much of culture is biologically based in human nature. This question is the center of debate in the well-known nature–nurture controversy.

Chapter 8

Personal Perspective

A Japanese student, Motoko, like many before her, sits in the front row of my Introductory Sociology class. American students seem to believe that the front row is off-limits. She writes down in pencil everything that I say. She is very quiet, never asks a question during the class, but after each class, she approaches me to ask for clarification of words or phrases she did not understand. As I glance down at her pages, I notice that above every English word is its Japanese translation. I have since learned that each night Japanese students translate all of their notes into Japanese, then back into English! What an arduous task. I think: Would American students be so persevering? I have also discovered through working with quite a few Japanese students that, although many speak English very poorly, they invariably do extremely well on written exams. As a group, my Japanese students could not have below a B+ average, I muse. Motoko tells me that it is expected that she will earn excellent grades; anything less would be unacceptable to her family. She also tells me that, "In my country, students do not ask questions of the teachers. Students are not encouraged to speak in class at all." No Japanese student has ever offered a comment in class; even when I have specifically asked for a response, they are quite reluctant to participate. Certainly, many American students do not speak in class either—but others are quite ready and willing to offer their own opinions, ask questions, and disagree with an idea that the professor is presenting.

For a time, I was academic advisor to many Japanese students. I could depend upon them to have planned and neatly written out their own schedule of courses for the next semester before they came to my office. American students often had not even looked at the schedule of classes for the following semester. Japanese students want to take the maximum number of credits allowable each semester—including many science and math courses in which they do very well. Many American students want to take the fewest credits possible to retain their full-time status and avoid math and science courses until the last moment.

When a Japanese student comes to my office or speaks to me after class, he or she makes a slight bow, before and after our conversation. I had believed bowing was a long-gone part of Japanese history—not so, apparently. Japanese students do not look at me directly when they address me, I have noticed, another living tradition. American students, on the other hand, want to call me by my first name, will often touch me while talking to me, and ask personal questions. Japanese students speak to me only in a very formal way and ask only about academic matters.

When I ask Motoko what she will do when she finishes her schooling in the United States, she answers, as do all Japanese students whom I have asked, "I will go back to my country and work there." I inquire, "Would you want to stay in this country?" "Well, maybe but only for a few years; then I will go back to Japan. It is expected that I will return," she tells me. "Would you consider marrying an American man?" I pursue. Her answer is very quick and clear, "No, that would present many difficulties. Mixed marriages are not well looked upon in Japan. An American husband would not be acceptable."

C.C.

Socialization

socialization—a basic social process through which an individual becomes integrated into a social group by learning the group's culture as well as his or her role in that group.

enculturation—another term for socialization.

secondary socialization—the socialization that occurs during adulthood.

THIS incident demonstrates two important aspects of **socialization**. First, socialization is a process through which individuals become members of the human community and find appropriate places within that community. Second, socialization is a process whereby a society reproduces itself in a new generation. Socialization is a basic social process through which an individual becomes integrated into a social group by learning the group's culture as well as his or her role in that group. This is a life-long process sometimes referred to as **enculturation**. But the critical phase occurs during childhood as the person internalizes the values, attitudes, and roles that shape his or her personality. Through socialization, the special values and traditions of past years are perpetuated. Socialization helps to give a society continuity. Thus, the Japan of yesterday is imprinted in my Japanese students today, as they study in the United States, to help prepare them for positions to which they will return in their country.

In exploring the process of socialization, we first consider the ways in which nature (heredity) and nurture (environment) interact to create individuals who are like all other human beings and yet are also distinctive and capable of unique contributions to their society. Second, we will look at several different theories of the specific mechanisms of the socialization process itself. Also, several dimensions of socialization—development of a self-image, an identity, and cognitive and moral development—will be explored. Third, we will assess the contributions of several agents of socialization—the family, the school, the mass media, and the peer group. We will then examine the process of **secondary socialization**—socialization that occurs during adulthood, such as the effect of entering a new occupation. Finally, we will look at the impact of transitions into young and middle adulthood, and old age on the socialization process.

NATURE AND NURTURE: HEREDITY AND ENVIRONMENT

Are the individual's character and personality determined by inherited, genetic makeup (nature) or by the social environment—family members, size of family, religion, ethnicity, parents' education, and so on—in which one is raised? Scientists have debated this issue for many years. At one end of the spectrum are those who believe that the infant is a *blank slate* at birth and is completely shaped by life experiences. The early-American psychologist John Watson states this view strongly:

> Give me a dozen healthy infants, well-formed, and my own specific world to bring them up in and I guarantee to take any one at random and train him to be any type of specialist I might select—doctor,

Everyone is familiar with the twisted meaning of the swastika. However, another twist to the picture is how effectively socialization can promote just about anything. The children shown in this photo were being oriented toward some of the fundamental principles of the Third Reich including hatred of other groups of people and an unquestioned belief in the superiority of their own kind.

> lawyer, artist, merchant, chief, yes, even a beggarman and thief, regardless of his talents, penchants, tendencies and abilities, vocations, and the race of his ancestors (Watson, 1925/1970, p. 104).

What might happen if John Watson's theory were to be put into action? B.F. Skinner suggests an eerie realm of possibilities in Box 8:1 containing an excerpt from his 1948 book *Walden Two.*

At the opposite pole are those who argue that personality and behavior are fixed by heredity, and experience cannot alter genetic destiny. This view has been invoked to account for observed differences in abilities between genders and racial and ethnic groups, and to explain criminal and deviant behavior (Jensen, 1969). While this controversy continues to rage, behavioral scientists now recognize that both elements are crucial in the development of human beings. An infant is affected especially by extremes of parenting—severe physical, emotional, sexual abuse of a child certainly alter a child's personality—yet that effect will vary from child to child, depending, in part, upon genetic makeup (Thomas and Chess, 1980).

BOX 8:1 SOCIOLOGICAL IMAGINATION IN FICTION

The Case of *Walden Two*

A young woman in a white uniform met us in a small waiting room near the entrance. Frazier addressed her as Mrs. Nash.

"I hope Mr. Frazier has warned you," she said with a smile, "that we're going to be rather impolite and give you only a glimpse of our babies. We try to protect them from infection during the first year. It's especially important when they are cared for as a group."

"What about the parents?" said Castle at once. "Don't parents see their babies?"

"Oh, yes, so long as they are in good health. Some parents work in the nursery. Others come around every day or so, for at least a few minutes. They take the baby out for some sunshine, or play with it in a play room." Mrs. Nash smiled at Frazier. "That's the way we build up the baby's resistance," she added.

She opened a door and allowed us to look into a small room, three walls of which were lined with cubicles, each with a large glass window. Behind the windows we could see babies of various ages. None of them wore more than a diaper, and there were no bedclothes. In one cubicle a small red newborn was asleep on its stomach. Some of the older babies were awake and playing with toys. Near the door a baby on all fours pressed its nose against the glass and smiled at us.

"Which is yours?" asked Frazier.

"Over there asleep," said Mrs. Nash, pointing to a far corner. "Almost ready to graduate, too. He'll be a year old next month." She drew the door gently shut before we had satisfied our curiosity. . . .

"Why don't you put clothes on them?" said Barbara. "Clothing and blankets are really a great nuisance," said Mrs. Nash. "They keep the baby exercising, they force it into uncomfortable postures—"

"When a baby graduates from our Lower Nursery," Frazier broke in, "it knows nothing of frustration, anxiety, or fear. It never cries except when sick, which is very seldom, and it has a lively interest in everything."

"But is it prepared for life?" said Castle. "Surely you can't continue to protect it from frustration or frightening situations forever."

"Of course not. But it can be prepared for them. We can build a tolerance for frustration by introducing obstacles gradually as the baby grows strong enough to handle them. Our babies are especially resistant. It's true that a constant annoyance may develop a tolerance, but the commoner result is that the baby is worn down or enervated. We introduce annoyances slowly, according to the ability of the baby to take them. It's very much like inoculation."

"Another thing," said Castle. "What about mother love?"

Frazier and Mrs. Nash looked at each other and laughed.

"Are you speaking of mother love as an essence, Mr. Castle?" said Frazier.

"I am not!" said Castle, bristling. "I'm speaking of a concrete thing. I mean the love which the mother gives her baby—the affection—well, to be really concrete, the kisses, the fondling, and so on, I suppose you'd say. . . ."

Frazier said quietly, "We supply it in liberal doses. But we don't limit it to mothers. We go in for father love, too—for everybody's love—community love, if you wish. Our children are treated with affection by everyone—and thoughtful affection too, which isn't marred by fits of temper due to overwork or careless handling due to ignorance. . . ."

In a moment five or six children came running into the playrooms and were soon using the lavatory and dressing themselves. Mrs. Nash explained that they were being taken on a picnic.

"What about the children who don't go?" said Castle. "What do you do about the green-eyed monster?"

Mrs. Nash was puzzled.

"Jealousy, envy," Castle elaborated. "Don't the children who stay home ever feel unhappy about it?"

"I don't understand," said Mrs. Nash.

"And I hope you won't try," said Frazier, with a smile. "We all know that emotions are useless and bad for our peace of mind and our blood pressure," he went on. "But how arrange things otherwise?

"We arrange them otherwise here," said Frazier. He was showing a mildness of manner which I was coming to recognize as a sign of confidence.

"But emotions are—fun!" said Barbara. "Life wouldn't be worth

BOX 8:1 SOCIOLOGICAL IMAGINATION IN FICTION *continued*

living without them."

"Some of them, yes," said Frazier. "The productive and strengthening emotions—joy and love. But sorrow and hate—and the high-voltage excitements of anger, fear and rage—are out of proportion with the needs of modern life, and they're wasteful and dangerous. Mr. Castle has mentioned jealousy—a minor form of anger, I think we may call it. Naturally we avoid it. It has served its purpose in the evolution of man; we've no further use for it. If we allowed it to persist, it would only sap the life out of us. In a cooperative society there's no jealousy because there's no need for jealousy."

"That implies that you all get everything you want," said Castle. "But what about social possessions? Last night you mentioned the young man who chose a particular girl or profession. There's still a chance for jealousy there, isn't there?"

"It doesn't imply that we get everything we want," said Frazier. "Of course we don't. But jealousy wouldn't help. We undertook to build a tolerance for annoying experiences. The sunshine of midday is extremely painful if you come from a dark room, but take it in easy stages and you can avoid pain altogether. . . ."

"How do you build up a tolerance to an annoying situation?" I said.

"Oh, for example, by having the children 'take' a more and more painful shock, or drink cocoa with less and less sugar in it until a bitter concoction can be savored without a bitter face."

"But jealousy or envy—you can't administer them in graded doses," I said.

"And why not? Remember, we control the social environment, too, at this age. That's why we get our ethical training in early. Take this case. A group of children arrive home after a long walk tired and hungry. They're expecting supper; they find, instead, that it's time for a lesson in self-control: they must stand for five minutes in front of steaming bowls of soup.

"The assignment is accepted like a problem in arithmetic. Any groaning or complaining is a wrong answer. Instead, the children begin at once to work upon themselves to avoid any unhappiness during the delay. One of them may make a joke of it. We encourage a sense of humor as a good way of not taking an annoyance seriously. The joke won't be much, according to adult standards—perhaps the child will simply pretend to empty the bowl of soup into his upturned mouth. Another may start a song with many verses. The rest join in at once, for they've learned that it's a good way to make time pass.

"But there's a world of difference in the way we use these annoyances," he continued. "For one thing, we don't punish. We never administer an unpleasantness in the hope of repressing or eliminating undesirable behavior. But there's another difference. In most cultures the child meets up with annoyances and reverses of uncontrolled magnitude. Some are imposed in the name of discipline by persons in authority. Some, like hazings, are condoned though not authorized. Others are merely accidental. No one cares to, or is able to, prevent them.

"In Walden Two we have a different objective. We make every man a brave man. They all come over the barriers. Some require more preparation than others, but they all come over. The traditional use of adversity is to select the strong. We control adversity to build strength. . . ."

The control of the physical and social environment, of which Frazier had made so much, was progressively relaxed—or, to be more exact, the control was transferred from the authorities to the child himself and to the other members of this group. After spending most of the first year in an air-conditioned cubicle, and the second and third mainly in an air-conditioned room with a minimum of clothing and bedding, the three- or four-year-old was introduced to regular clothes and given the care of a small standard cot in a dormitory. The beds of the five- and six-year-olds were grouped by threes and fours in a series of alcoves furnished like rooms and treated as such by the children. Groups of three or four seven-year-olds occupied small rooms together, and this practice was continued, with frequent change of roommates, until the children were about thirteen, at which time they took temporary rooms in the adult building, usually in pairs. At marriage, or whenever the individual chose, he could participate in building a larger room for himself or refurnishing an old room which might be available.

Critical Thinking Questions

1. What kinds of factors does Skinner overlook in constructing the "controlled" environment in *Walden Two*?
2. How might Skinner's plan to create a "perfect society" backfire?

Source: B.F. Skinner, adapted from *Walden Two* (1948). New York: Macmillan, pp. 96–119. By Permission of the publisher.

Genes establish a blueprint for human potential. At conception each child is provided a timetable for development; each progresses from crawling to walking, from babble to speaking single words. Few, if any, children talk before 9 months (Chomsky, 1957); by 24 months, all are talking. Similar timetables exist for physical skills, for cognitive development (Piaget and Inhelder, 1969), even for social (Erikson, 1963) and moral development (Kohlberg, 1976).

Emotional development also appears to follow a biological timetable (Goleman, 1984). Newborns exhibit intense feelings, but their range of feeling is limited to pleasure and surprise, distress and disgust. Joy appears at 6 to 8 weeks; anger between 3 and 4 months; fear and sadness between 8 and 9 months. Feelings of shame develop around 18 months; pride at about 2 years, and guilt between the ages of 3 and 4. According to researchers, these psychological changes are linked to maturation of the central nervous system. Thus nerve connections that allow an older child to experience doubt and envy are not yet functioning in the infant and toddler (Kagan, 1984). This is a biological fact that has clear implications for the socialization process. Thus, the social emotions (insecurity, humiliation, confidence, envy, etc.) are not shown until age 5 or 6. Biological outlines are not etched in stone, however. An abused infant, as young as 3 months, typically shows premature expressions of fear and sadness (Gaensbaver and Hiatt, 1984).

Some physical traits are genetically fixed—male/female; blond/brunette; blue-eyed, light-skinned/dark-skinned. In many areas, though, genes establish a range of potentials; realization of that potential depends on a child's environment and experience. Height is hereditary, for example. Tall parents generally have tall children, but how tall a specific individual grows depends on nutrition and overall health. If a boy with "tall genes" grows up in a low-income rural village where protein is scarce, or is sickly as a child, he might only be 5 feet 7 inches tall as an adult. If he grows up in a middle-class suburb where he is healthy and well fed, he might grow to be 6 feet 2 inches tall. Consequently, children of immigrants often grow much taller than their parents (Temerlin, 1975).

This principle applies to other traits as well. A stimulating learning environment can stretch genetic potential to its limits. This is apparent in chimpanzees who have been taught to use sign language and have been socialized to interact as members of human families (Temerlin, 1975). Nonetheless, a rich environment cannot alter genetic structure; chimps lack the biological capacity to formulate complex sentences, or to teach sign language to other chimps.

Human personality development presents a more complex interaction of genetics and environment. Personality may be defined as characteristic modes of thinking, feeling, and acting, which individuals develop as a consequence of experience. Infants, who have little experience, do not have personalities in this sense. Research shows, however, that infants do enter the world with genetically distinctive temperaments. From the first days of life, infants differ in their level of activity, their reactions to new experiences (approach versus withdrawal), their adaptability, the intensity of their reactions, their need for physical contact (cuddlers/noncuddlers), their general mood (happy/friendly–unhappy/unfriendly), and other traits (Goleman, 1986). Alexander Thomas and Stella Chess (1977, 1980) followed 140 children from birth to adolescence and discovered three patterns of temperamental qualities. "Easy babies" are calm, playful, and adaptable. They approach new experiences enthusiastically. "Difficult babies" are agitated, fearful, and easily distressed. They display high levels of activity, but

Although there is no "typical" experience for any American kid growing up, very different experiences separate families by race and class. Unfortunately, the stereotypes shown here are frequently accurate. African-American children living in poverty play basketball on an inner-city playground. The more privileged white youngster is treated to lessons in the famous "Anglo" game of golf with parental supervision.

brief attention spans. "Slow-to-warm-up babies" are between these two patterns; they show less-intense emotions and tend to withdraw from novel experiences. These differences among children are *present from birth* and tend to continue over time, thus suggesting that temperament is innate (nature).

Inborn traits are important in the socialization process because different temperaments often evoke different responses from other people. For example, a baby who smiles easily and likes to be picked up by anyone will receive more attention than an unresponsive baby who does not smile very much or one who cries when a stranger approaches. Mothers themselves report that they avoid contact with their difficult babies and view themselves as inadequate in mothering skills (Maccoby, Snow, and Jacklin, 1984).

In similar ways, inherited physical characteristics evoke particular responses from others and can cause children to pursue or avoid certain activities. Children who meet society's standards of "good-looking" tend to have different experiences than those who do not. When adults and children are shown pictures of attractive and not-so-attractive children, they describe the former as smarter, nicer, and friendlier than the latter (Langlois and Stephan, 1977). These expectations can become self-fulfilling prophecies because people respond positively to a good-looking child. These positive responses, in turn, enhance the child's self-esteem and promote further social interaction. This confirms the belief that good-looking children are nicer and smarter than their less-attractive peers. In adolescence, early-maturing boys are more likely to excel in athletics, to be popular with their peers, and to be viewed as social leaders than are late-maturing boys (Jones, 1965). Peers describe these children as poised, relaxed, good-natured. These personality traits are, at least in part, a consequence of social responses to their physical characteristics; that is, the meanings of these physical traits are socially constructed. Thus, it appears that genetics provide the raw material for development, but that raw material is shaped by experiences sought out by children on their own and evoked as responses from the family and from society as a whole.

HUMAN NEED FOR SOCIALIZATION

The intrinsic nature of humans requires socialization. At birth, the human infant is helpless; other animals have instincts—built-in responses—that help them survive. They have genetic codes for finding food, avoiding danger, and for reacting to certain environmental events. Human infants lack such innate equipment and, if abandoned, would perish. They are, however, born with a tremendous capacity to learn from their environment and experience.

For obvious ethical reasons, researchers do not carry out experiments involving the social isolation of human infants. Thus, much of what is known about social isolation is drawn from rare cases, such as Anna, described later. Even then, social scientists typically enter the picture at the end of a horrible ordeal and must piece together events over a period of years. Researchers have, however, studied the effects of social isolation on some animals.

One classic piece of research was conducted with nonhuman primates by psychologists Harry and Margaret Harlow (1962). The Harlows placed rhesus monkeys (whose behavior is surprisingly similar to that of humans in certain areas) into various conditions of social isolation to observe the effects. Baby monkeys were separated from their mothers and from all contact with other monkeys for six months. Although adequate nutrition, warmth, and light were provided, serious disturbances in the monkeys' social development occurred. When these monkeys were later introduced to other monkeys, they refused to interact, refused to mate, and had to be forcibly mated. When these deprived mother monkeys gave birth, they refused to care for their own offspring.

In a related study, the Harlows placed infant rhesus monkeys into cages containing an artificial mother constructed of wire mesh with a wooden head, and a nipple feeding tube where the breast would normally be. These monkeys survived physically, but they, also, were unable to interact with other monkeys. Interestingly, when the artificial mother was covered with soft terry cloth, the baby monkeys clung to it and gained emotional benefit from its presence. These monkeys demonstrated less developmental disturbance. In situations where infant monkeys were presented with both a wire model that gave food and a terry cloth model that did not give food, the babies went to the wire model for feeding, but spent the majority of their time cuddling with the soft cloth mother. Thus the Harlows concluded that normal emotional development requires consistent physical contact with a warm caregiver.

The Harlows also made two other discoveries. First, even monkeys deprived of mother–infant contact did not suffer adversely when they were surrounded by other infant monkeys. Thus, it seems to be lack of all social experience, rather than the specific absence of a maternal figure, that produces debilitating consequences. Second, the Harlows found that infant monkeys socially isolated for shorter periods (three months) eventually regained normal emotional patterns after rejoining other monkeys. Thus they concluded that the effects of short-term isolation can be overcome. Longer-term isolation, on the other hand, appears to cause irreversible emotional and behavioral damage.

Due to extreme neglect, some human babies have been almost completely alone during their early years. These cases provide clues about the dynamics and importance of socialization for humans. The best-known case is that of Anna (Davis, 1947), the illegitimate and unwanted child. Because she was unable to place the girl in a foster home or institution, Anna's mother confined her to a dark attic room for five years. During that time, she gave her enough milk to keep Anna alive, but rarely bathed her, never talked to her, held her, or played with her.

Anna became completely withdrawn and apathetic. When social workers found her she did not talk or walk. They thought she was mentally retarded, and/or deaf. She did not know how to dress or feed herself or even how to chew. She never laughed or cried. In the hospital where she was placed, she only stared at the ceiling from her bed. If a person approached, she froze in terror or exploded into a terrible temper tantrum.

At age 6 she was placed in a foster home, and, with great care and attention, she began very slowly to walk, talk, run, and play with other children. She began to learn to wash and dress herself. She was not able to overcome completely the five years of early neglect, and died of a blood disorder at age 10 (Davis, 1947).

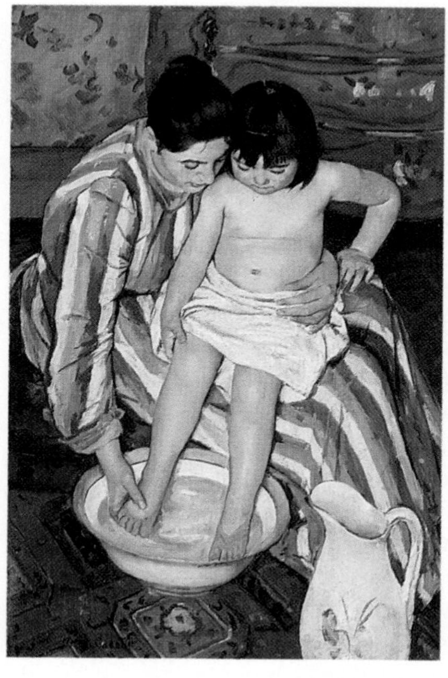

Mary Cassatt's painting, *The Bath* (1883), is a tranquil portrayal of a process that knows no cultural bounds—care, love, and affection mothers naturally feel for their children. The painting also demonstrates how civilized practices are passed from one generation to another.

Another case of severe childhood isolation involves a 13-year-old girl in California who was confined in a small room from age 2 (Pines, 1981). When she was discovered, her condition was similar to Anna's. She was emaciated, weighing only 59 pounds, and had the mental development of a 1-year-old. Genie, as she came to be known, was given intensive treatment by specialists and is still alive. Yet, even after years of care, her speech is very limited. She uses only "telegraphed" speech—three words instead of a complete sentence—and she cannot walk correctly or run at all. This evidence demonstrates the importance of social interaction for the proper unfolding of the genetic blueprint. Human beings are resilient, sometimes able to recover from devastating experiences of prolonged isolation. Consistent with the Harlows' research, though, there may be a critical point beyond which social isolation results in irreparable damage to social, language, and motor skills. Precisely what this point is, however, remains unclear from the small number of cases that have been studied (Pines, 1981).

Other studies of less extreme cases of neglect also illustrate the importance of socialization. Rene Spitz (1951) studied babies who had been placed in an orphanage. These children received adequate physical care—good food, regular bathing, diaper changes, clothing changes, clean sheets—but little personal attention from a consistent caregiver. They rarely smiled or cried and made little effort to speak. Psychological testing at age 1 revealed most to be mentally deficient. They were emotionally withdrawn, and some suffered physical deterioration and died. Other studies of social and physical attachment (Bowlby, 1979) report similar findings; adequate meeting of physical needs alone is not sufficient for normal development. Children need dependable social interaction with a consistent loving caregiver as much as they need food (Spitz, 1951).

Bowlby's observations of children who experienced maternal deprivation make it clear that severe deprivation can have very grave consequences, particularly if they occur between 6 months and 3 to 4 years of age. Bowlby noted three forms of maternal deprivation:

1. Lack of any opportunity for forming an attachment to a mother figure during the first three years.
2. Deprivation for a limited period—at least three months and probably more than six—during the first three or four years.
3. Changes from one mother figure to another during the same period (Bowlby, 1965, p. 54).

Bowlby reported that these types of experiences are especially risky for normal personality formation and are likely to produce an "affectionless" child who shows little interest in other people, let alone develops loving bonds.

The impact of socialization is not felt just by children, but also by their parents and others involved in the socialization process. Few parents emerge from the socialization process without noticing some change in their own attitudes, character, or behavior. Children socialize their parents as well as the reverse. Socialization is best viewed as a dynamic and reciprocal process (Berger and Berger, 1979).

THEORIES OF SOCIALIZATION

What are the components of the process of socialization? Many different explanations have been offered. Overall the various theories are complementary rather than mutually exclusive, each emphasizing different dimensions of the process. Together they can present a fairly complete picture. We begin by discussing the work of three very influential thinkers—Charles Horton Cooley, George Herbert Mead, and Sigmund Freud. Then we examine the work of Erik Erikson, Jean Piaget, and Lawrence Kohlberg, each of whom focuses on a specific aspect of the socialization process.

Charles H. Cooley: The Looking-Glass Self

The term *self* indicates the idea that each person possesses a unique and distinct identity. The self involves a set of images, traits, and attitudes that we use to define or characterize ourselves. The self is not an innate entity; an infant is not born with a sense of self. Instead we actively create our self-image over time through interactions with others.

Charles Horton Cooley (1864–1929) was one of the first theorists to consider the social origins of the self. Based on observations of his own children, Cooley developed the concept of the "looking-glass self"—the sense of self reflected in other people's attitudes and behaviors toward us. According to Cooley (1956), the looking-glass self has three parts: (1) what we imagine others see in us, (2) how we imagine their judgment of what they see, and (3) our reactions to those judgments. Based on other people's comments and actions, a 5-year-old girl thinks her parents see her as someone who runs and swings and plays school with her dolls. She imagines that they are proud that she is strong and interested in school. She may feel pleased with this image or worried that her parents see her as more competent than she actually is. Thus the looking-glass self is *not* a direct reflection (mechanical reproduction) of what others see in us. It is a complex mixture of observation, imagination, and subjective interpretation. The looking-glass self is also a social construction, which incorporates the influence of social class, values, ethnicity, and a host of other psychosocial forces.

George Herbert Mead: Role Taking

Pursuing Cooley's ideas further, George Herbert Mead (1863–1931) traced the development of a sense of self to early social interaction (Turner, 1981). Mead suggests that from earliest infancy, babies recognize that they are dependent on others to help satisfy their needs and that their own actions can influence the way that others behave toward them. They learn, perhaps, that crying brings a bottle and smiling brings a warm embrace. Over time, they learn many different ways of evoking desired responses in others; children acquire a repertoire of symbolic gestures and, later, words that others understand. Through symbolic interaction, children learn to anticipate what others expect and to evaluate and adjust their own behaviors accordingly.

Mead suggests that the self is composed of two parts: the "I," the active spontaneous, idiosyncratic self; and the "me," the social self, composed of internalized social expectations. The subjective "I" is created by individual distinctiveness. The objective "me" is the result of socialization. Without the "me," orderly social interaction could not occur. Without the "I," social interaction would be repetitive and monotonous. With these two complementary parts, we can reflect on our experience and behavior and acquire a sense of inner continuity and identity.

Mead did not answer the question of how we gain an "I," but modern-day sociologist Norbert Wiley (1979) suggests that, initially, infants have no sense of "I"; they view themselves as part of the mother as they are bathed, fed, and changed. Eventually, the baby and the parent exchange smiles, and the baby begins to experience a "we" relationship; through this interaction the baby acquires an awareness of being a subjective "I." The baby realizes that the parent is reacting to that "I." The sense of "I" allows the child to hold internal conversations with the "me" and thereby enhances the socialization process.

We emphasize throughout this chapter how socialization is a lifelong process, from womb to tomb. Sometimes it seems to race ahead of itself. Here is a couple of 5-year-olds all dressed for adult roles. Do they really have a long way to go? Add 20 years to their age and you will not see much of anything new except older faces on taller people.

Mead holds that the child develops a "me" through playing at being others and through participating in games. Children spend hours in fantasy taking on the roles of important others in their social world. Mead called these "significant others" (Sullivan, 1953). The young girl whose mother is a teacher seats her dolls and stuffed animals in rows to give them the day's lesson. In this play, children develop the ability to view themselves from another person's perspective.

As children gain social competence, they can move from playing a single role to games involving interaction of many roles. Games are critical in the emergence of the self because they require children to understand how different roles are coordinated. To play baseball, for example, the base runner must anticipate what various other players will do when the ball is hit. Without an understanding of the different actions and responses of others, the child cannot play roles effectively.

The "self" finally emerges when the child begins to feel a part of the society and internalize the attitudes and beliefs of others within the personality. Mead referred to this internalized impression of societal expectations as the "generalized other."

Since Mead's early work on the social origins of the self, others have refined his ideas. Robert Leahy (1983), for example, sees Mead's theory as a vision of the child moving from a primitive state of isolation to a mature state of socialization; that is, sharing the views of others toward the self. As the child moves beyond childhood to adolescence, Leahy believes, reality becomes more complex (Leahy and Shirk, 1985). Concern with how others regard the self peaks in early adolescence. In later adolescence, they begin to move from other-directed reasoning to more self-directed reasoning and begin to create an image of themselves that is relatively independent of others' views.

Sigmund Freud: Elements of Personality

No work has influenced thought about socialization more than that of Sigmund Freud (1856–1939). Freud lived in Vienna at a time when most Europeans viewed human behavior as an imprinted reflection of biological forces. Freud's importance today, of course, is based on his revolutionary description and analysis of human personality. Some of Freud's findings have a direct bearing on the process of socialization.

Freud believed that biological factors play a crucial role in human personality, but he did not conclude that human behavior reflects biological instinct alone. By the term *instinct* Freud meant very general human needs in the form of basic urges or drives. Freud postulated that there are two basic human drives: First, a drive to bond with others, which he called *Eros*, or the life instinct; second, he asserted that people also have a death instinct—an aggressive drive—or *Thanatos*. Freud hypothesized that these two opposing forces generate tension in the person and constitute the foundation of human life.

Freud's Model of Personality

Freud incorporated both basic biological needs and societal influences into a model of personality. The model has three components: id, ego, and superego. The *id* (Latin for "it") is a reservoir of the human being's basic needs, which are largely unconscious and always seek gratification. Rooted in the biological organism, the id is present at birth, meaning that the human infant is a bundle of needs—for attention, for physical contact, for food, and so forth. Freud suggested that there are four basic needs present at birth: hunger, sleep, sex, and aggression. Unlimited personal physical satisfaction is not acceptable in society, so id desires inevitably meet with resistance. Over time, the child learns that personal needs will not be fulfilled immediately, so the world must be approached more realistically. This is accomplished by the *ego* (Latin for "I"), the second part of the personality, which gradually differentiates from the id. The ego represents the conscious part of the self. The ego attempts to balance the innate pleasure-seeking drives of the id with the demands of society. For example, through the ego's functioning, the person realizes that sexual needs are best fulfilled with one person in a long-term, committed relationship, rather than by having casual sex with a different person each night. The ego is in contact with reality and tries to satisfy id needs in a socially acceptable manner. Ego functions eventually include language, thought, reason, and judgment.

Finally, the *superego* ("beyond the self") differentiates from the ego. The superego is the conscience, our internalized set of values and norms, which includes an understanding of why we cannot have everything we want. The superego is initially an acknowledgment of one's parents' demands, but gradually enlarges its scope as the child recognizes that parental standards

The Banjo Lesson, **a late 1800s painting by Henry Ossawa Turner, is a picture of love, respect, and intergenerational transmission of cultural tradition. In many ways, things have not changed much during the last hundred years. Children still rely on adult role models for guidance. And the interaction between children and adults takes many forms. In some families grandparents play a very important role.**

reflect the moral demands of the society as a whole. According to Freud, the superego can become quite powerful, often repressive of basic id impulses. The ego's task is to mediate between the id and superego—to satisfy id drives in ways acceptable to the superego, so that the person does not experience excessive guilt or remorse.

In order to become a well-socialized child, the toddler must curb various id drives for pleasures. This first occurs by giving up sucking on the bottle or breast and being weaned to a cup (oral stage). Second, the child learns, through the process of toilet training, to control the anal sphincter muscles and give up freedom to defecate at any time (anal stage). Freud argued that the particular way in which these conflicts between the individual's id and society's "rules of the game" are resolved shapes the personality. A final critical development of the superego occurs at about age 5, when the child experiences extreme love for the opposite-gender parent, along with jealousy of the same-gender parent (phallic stage). Freud called this psychological phenomenon the Oedipus Conflict (Complex). Eventually, the child recognizes that he or she cannot have sole possession of the opposite-gender parent and learns to view the parents' relationship to each other in a more realistic way. The Oedipal wishes are then repressed. This adds a powerful component to the superego. As a result, the child learns to identify with the same-gender parent, thus taking on gender role identity and adopting that parent's attitudes and moral values.

If the ego successfully manages the opposing forces of the id and the superego, the personality is "well-adjusted." If the conflict between the two is not resolved successfully, psychiatric symptoms often result. Freud believed that early childhood (birth through age 5–6) is the critical period for personality development; unresolved conflicts experienced during this stage continue to exist as unconscious sources of emotional difficulties. Freud also argued that little change in basic personality structure occurs after age 6.

Freud termed society's controlling influence on the drives of the individual *repression.* In his view, some repression is necessary and inevitable because individual urges cannot be satisfied on demand without some compromise. This compromise is accomplished through redirecting these desires into socially approved forms, a process Freud calls *sublimation,* the transformation of fundamentally selfish drives into more socially acceptable objectives. As examples, sex drives can be channeled into marriage, and aggressive urges are often redirected into competitive sports.

Certainly, Freud's view of socialization is radically different from that of Mead and Cooley because Freud focuses so heavily on the power of biological drives. Freud viewed socialization as a continuous battle between the demands of society and the individual's biological needs. Ultimately, society must win out, otherwise civilization would disintegrate into egocentric chaos created by pleasure-seeking robots. To Freud, art, philosophy, architecture, literature, science, and all great achievements of humanity are the result of redirecting the instinctual urges of the id.

Erik Erikson's Eight Stages

Erik Erikson greatly extended Freud's theory beyond childhood into adolescence and adulthood and examined the influence of cultural factors on socialization. Freud focused primarily on the id drives—their satisfaction, repression, and redirection. Erikson, however, looks at the ego as it develops *alongside* the id.

Each of his eight stages is represented as a set of alternative ego attitudes. If one's experiences during the stage go well, a maturing person finds a positive solution to the crisis. If one is unable to adjust comfortably to the society's demands at that stage, more negative feelings toward the self may result. Erikson's stages are briefly outlined below:

I. *Trust versus Mistrust* (birth to 18 months)
If the baby's physical needs are consistently met, the baby learns to trust that someone will be there. The young child begins to allow the parent out of its sight without undue anxiety or rage.

II. *Autonomy versus Shame and Doubt* (2 to 3 years)
In this period children face the crisis of having to control their actions. Small children begin to suppress aggressive impulses, but they need to be protected from feelings of shame and humiliation when they do lose control. This stage is crucial for balancing cooperation with self-esteem and pride.

III. *Initiative versus Guilt* (3 to 5 years)
At the age of 3 to 5, along with feelings of love toward the opposite-gender parent, children begin to play imaginary games and try out new roles. While they learn to inhibit some fantasies, children begin to sense that some of their behaviors are quite permissible.

IV. *Industry versus Inferiority* (6 to 12 years)
School-age children learn to gain recognition for their accomplishments: good grades, athletic events, and other activities. The danger at this stage lies in a sense of inadequacy and inferiority that can result from even a small failure. The child needs a supportive family to help overcome setbacks.

V. *Ego-Identity versus Role Confusion* (age 12 onward)
Erikson's most famous insights pertain to the identity crises. Faced with rapid physical growth and new and mysterious sexual maturity, young people struggle to combine present ideas about themselves with a prospective future adult role to form a comfortable identity. The inability to settle on a compatible identity results in the playing of various roles to please others.

VI. *Adult Stages: Intimacy versus Isolation* (young adulthood)
Unresolved identity struggles manifest themselves in the problem of developing an intimate relationship with another person. The person who has yet to form an identity is often unable to commit to another person.

VII. *Generativity versus Stagnation* (middle-age)
This stage involves one's career, activities, and children. Is the person able to give to the next generation, or has the person remained mired in the search for self, feeling bored or resigned and thus unable to give significantly to others, to children, or to colleagues?

VIII. *Integrity versus Despair* (old age)
As one approaches old age and death, the meaning and order of the life cycle can be accepted, and the person can feel some comfort in the choices made. The person may, however, experience despair that he or she never made choices based on personally defined goals.

Erikson's stages suggest that the socialization process never ends, each period offering new challenges to be faced and new roles to be learned. A person's "self" is never fixed permanently, as Freud suggests, neither is it as biologically based as Freud implies.

Jean Piaget: Cognitive Development

During his long life, Jean Piaget (1896–1980) became one of the most influential psychologists of the century. Much of his effort was devoted to the study of human *cognition*—the process of thinking and understanding. Early in his career, Piaget became fascinated by the diversity of thought and behavior of his own three children; he wondered both *what* they knew and *how* they understood the world. He gradually concluded that a child's particular conception of the world is related to developmental age and identified four stages of cognitive development, which involve elements of both biological maturation and social experience.

Sensorimotor Stage

The first stage of development in Piaget's model is the sensorimotor stage, in which the world is experienced almost exclusively through sensory contact. In this stage (about the first two years of life), the infant explores by touching, looking, sucking, and listening. By about 4 months of age, this exploration leads children to distinguish their own bodies from the larger environment. As they near the end of this stage, children recognize *object permanence,* the knowledge that objects or people continue to exist even when they are no longer directly visible.

Children become more skilled at imitating the actions and sounds of others during this period, but they do not have the capacity to comprehend or use symbols. Thus, during the sensorimotor stage, children do not *think;* they know the world only in terms of their direct physical contacts.

Preoperational Stage

During the preoperational stage, language and other symbols are first used. This stage begins at about age 2 and lasts until about age 7. Because they can now use symbols, children engage the world mentally. They begin to distinguish between their own fantasied ideas and objective reality. They no longer necessarily believe their nighttime dreams are true, and can recognize the element of fantasy in fairytales (Kohlberg and Gilligan, 1971; Skolnick, 1986).

At this time, a child has no conception of capacity such as size, weight, and volume. To illustrate this Piaget performed a simple experiment. He placed two identical glasses filled with equal amounts of water on a table and asked children age 5 and 6 if the amount of water in each glass was the same. They acknowledged that it was. The children then watched Piaget pour the contents of one of the glasses into a much taller, narrow glass, thus raising the water level. He asked again if each glass held the same amount of water. The typical 5- and 6-year-old now claimed that the taller glass held more water. Children over age 7, however, who typically have some ability to think abstractly, comprehended that the amount of water remains the same.

During the preoperational stage, children have a very egocentric view of the world (Damon, 1983). For example, young children place their hands in front of their faces and exclaim, "You can't see me." They assume that if they can't see you, you must be unable to see them. Preoperational children experience the world only from their own perspective and are unable to realize that others see it differently. They cannot yet take the role of others. As a consequence, children under age 7 are not skilled in playing games that involve conceptualizing the actions of other players.

Concrete Operational Stage

At the third stage, the concrete operational stage, human cognitive development is characterized by the use of logic to understand events and objects. During this stage (from about age 7 to age 11), children make great progress in their ability to comprehend and act upon their environment. They begin to connect events in terms of cause and effect. During this stage, children's thinking remains focused on *concrete* objects or events. A child may know that hitting another child without provocation will bring punishment, but cannot imagine situations where hitting another child might be acceptable or understand why parents punish children. During this stage, children begin to transcend their egocentrism and become capable of putting themselves into the roles of others. This ability is very important for playing games, for getting along with others in school, and for participating in structured activities such as Girl Scouts and Little League.

Formal Operations Stage

The fourth stage, formal operations, is the period of cognitive development characterized by abstract thought and the ability to imagine alternatives to situations. Beginning at about age 12, children can think of themselves and the world in abstract terms. The child can now conceptualize and evaluate hypothetical alternatives. Children entering this stage often enjoy highly fantastic literature, such as science-fiction (Skolnick, 1986). This new capacity allows children to comprehend metaphors. Hearing an adage such as "a penny for your thoughts" suggests sharing, not saving. Research indicates that a substantial proportion (30 percent) of 30-year-olds have not reached the formal operations stage (Kohlberg and Gilligan, 1971). This again demonstrates the importance of social experience in the development of personality. Regardless of inborn capacity, children who are not exposed to creative and imaginative thinking are unlikely to develop this capacity on their own.

Unlike Freud, who viewed humans as torn by the conflict between individual biology and society, Piaget believed that, through the active creative capacity of their minds, people have considerable ability to shape their own social worlds. This idea is supported by the research of others (Corsaro and Rizzo, 1988).

Some have questioned whether Piaget's model applies to human beings in all cultures. Living within a traditional society that changes very little, for example, might limit a person's ability to imagine cultures that are radically different. In addition, Carol Gilligan (1982) suggests that science has not yet adequately examined how being male or female affects the process of cognitive development, though Maccoby, Shar and Jacklin (1984) have begun to examine some of Piaget's assumptions about gender differences.

Lawrence Kohlberg: Moral Development

Piaget suggested that children's ideas of right and wrong also develop in stages. His studies revealed that a child's conception of morality changes from the early belief that moral rules are absolute to the more mature understanding that they are the result of mutual agreement and compromise. Lawrence Kohlberg (1976) has elaborated Piaget's insights into a theory that children establish their own moral values as they grow up.

Kohlberg's research in the United States, Great Britain, Taiwan, Turkey, and Mexico has convinced him that children are taught very similar moral values in every culture. He has found that different societies hold different beliefs about specific wrongs (eating pork, smoking opium) but they believe in the same larger moral principles of empathy (concern for others) and justice (concern for equality and reciprocity). According to Kohlberg, people differ in their moral judgments primarily because they have attained different levels of maturity.

Children in different parts of the world were asked to respond to the following story.

> A man's wife was dying of cancer and there was only one drug that might save her. The pharmacist who had discovered the drug was charging ten times its cost to him or $2000 for a small dose. The sick woman's husband tried to borrow the money, but he could raise only about $1000. He told the pharmacist that his wife was dying and asked him to sell it cheaper or let him pay later. The druggist refused. In desperation, the man broke into the drugstore and stole the drug for his wife. Should he have done that (Kohlberg, 1976, p. 183)?

Kohlberg was not concerned with whether the children thought the man should have stolen the drug; he was interested in their reasons for thinking so. On the basis of these responses, he identified three levels of moral development, each representing a more complex way of resolving moral dilemmas. Children move through these levels as they gain cognitive abilities, such as the ability to take on the role of others and the ability to think abstractly.

Young children, Kohlberg found, tend to demonstrate what he calls a *pre-conventional morality*. They behave correctly only because they fear punishment for a particular behavior or wish to be rewarded for another behavior; there is no internal reason for behaving in a certain way. They define right and wrong in terms of consequences of an act, rather than its intention.

Children generally progress to the next level—*conventional morality*—during adolescence, as they gain the ability to see the world from other viewpoints. They adopt a "good boy" morality based on identifying with an authority figure (parents or teachers) who defines right and wrong to them. People at the conventional level show a high degree of regard for "rules," although they can give no personal reason for following the rule. In the example about the man whose wife was dying, a person at a conventional level of morality would reason that it is wrong to steal the drug, simply because stealing is illegal in any situation.

Later, the individual begins to think abstractly and evaluate alternatives and may enter what Kohlberg terms *post-conventional morality*. At this level the person recognizes the possibility of conflicting values and tries to make a reasoned, personal decision among them. The individual becomes a philosopher and makes informed choices among legitimate sets of moral principles such as the Golden Rule versus "the greatest good for the greatest number." At a post-conventional stage, a person may believe, for example, that the value of saving a human life supersedes that of obeying societal laws. Thus, stealing the drug is the moral behavior, from this perspective.

In everyday life, a person rarely faces complex moral dilemmas that cannot be resolved using conventional definitions of justice and respect for human life. One exception was the My Lai massacre during the Vietnam

War in which hundreds of Vietnamese women and children were murdered by American soldiers. Kohlberg interviewed the one soldier who had refused to shoot civilians and concluded that his reasons demonstrated the personal moral convictions of post-conventional thinking. The other soldiers, however, had reached only the conventional level of moral judgment; they reasoned that they *must* obey the command to shoot, even if the targets were unarmed civilians.

Kohlberg's theory of moral development has been criticized for failing to show a connection between moral judgment and action. Certainly some of the U.S. soldiers firmly believed that they were committing an immoral act in shooting unarmed civilians. They may have obeyed orders, not because they thought it was right, but because they were afraid to disobey, or because they were angry about their unit's heavy casualties, or because they feared the Vietnamese army. The ability to *know* what is *morally right*, then, does not necessarily deter people from taking *immoral actions*.

Kohlberg's research has also been criticized because it has studied only males. When psychologist Carol Gilligan (1982) presented the same moral dilemma to children of both genders (who were the same age, had the same intelligence, education, and social class background), she found that boys and girls viewed the problem quite differently. An 11-year-old boy responded just as many of Kohlberg's post-conventional subjects did. He said that the man should steal the drug because "a human life is worth more than money." He saw the dilemma as a conflict between two values—property and life—and chose what he considered the more important value.

An 11-year-old girl saw the moral conflict differently. She replied that the man should not steal the drug, but should save his wife's life by borrowing the money. The girl's concern was not with the law or right to property, but with the relationship between the man and his wife.

> If he stole the drug, he might save his wife then, but . . . he might have to go to jail and then his wife might get sicker again, and he couldn't get more of the drug, and it might not be good. So, they should really just talk it out and find some other way to make the money (Gilligan, 1982, p. 79).

Perhaps gender is the best example of the relationship between socialization and social change. Women now aspire to virtually every activity previously viewed as "for men only." The changes have been especially visible in the world of work but they have also touched the very expression of masculinity itself. Boxers, for example, are no longer Muhammed Ali types.

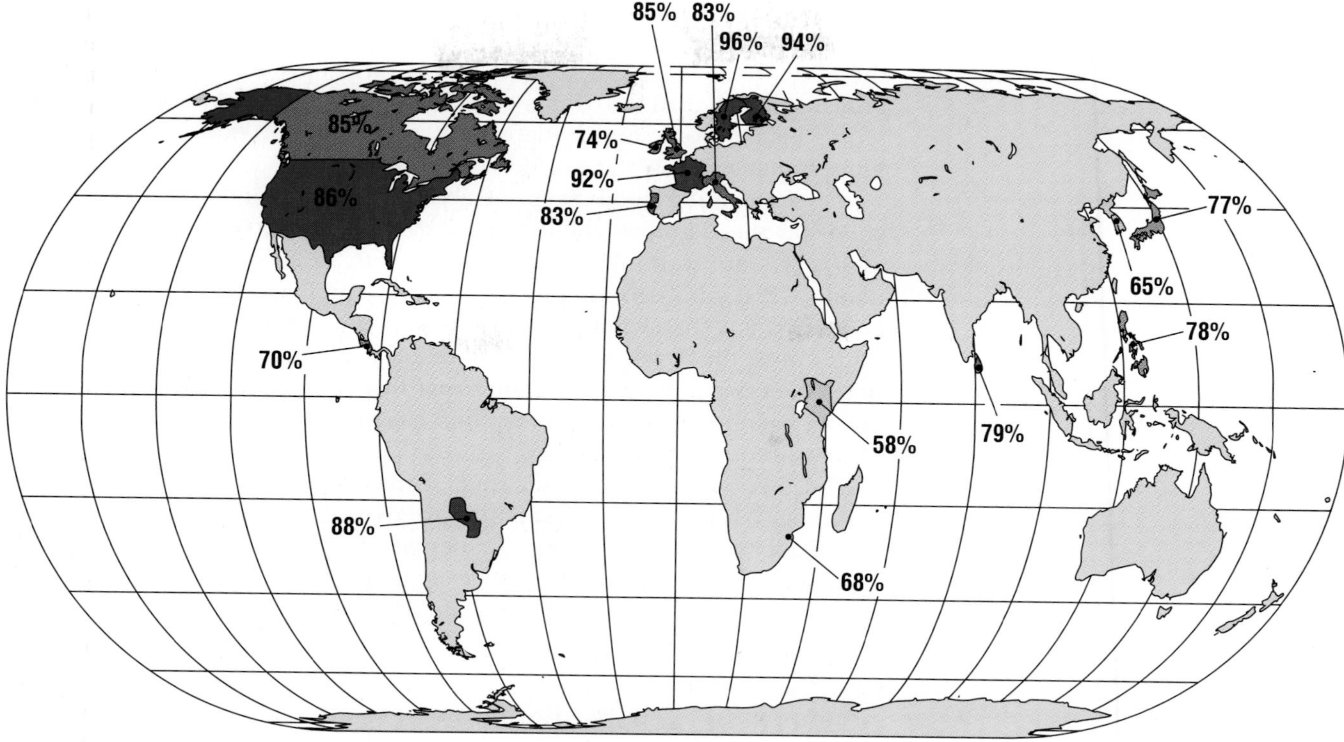

FIGURE 8:1 CROSS-CULTURAL DIFFERENCES IN SOCIALIZATION BY GENDER

The Human Development Index (HDI) measures the opportunities provided to people to lead a full life as they grow up. As this map shows, males receive more opportunities than do females; this difference is culturally consistent, though the percentages vary.

Country	Women's HDI as a Share of Men's (percent)
Sweden	96
Finland	94
France	92
Paraguay	88
USA	86
Canada	85
United Kingdon	85
Italy	83
Portugal	83
Sri Lanka	79
Philippines	78
Japan	77
Ireland	74
Costa Rica	70
Swaziland	68
Korea	65
Kenya	58

Source: United Nation Development Programme. *Human Development Report 1992* (New York: Oxford University Press, 1992).

Gilligan argues that boys and girls have different views because they grow up in different social worlds. Both recognize the need for agreement, but see it as mediated in different ways: he, impersonally through systems of logic and law; and she, personally through communication in relationships. Females are more likely to see the world as a network of *relationships* in which they are involved, whereas males experience the world as a *rational hierarchy* with people in differing positions. Men are more likely, she says, to rely on impersonal rules to reach agreement, whereas women tend to rely on communication in personal relationships. One thing is certain about differences in socialization by gender—boys typically receive more opportunities and attention than girls. As Figure 8:1 demonstrates, the amount of the difference varies by culture.

Integrating the Theories

A review of all of the theories of socialization discussed here can offer a comprehensive picture of the complex process that contributes to the socialization of a child. First, Sigmund Freud gives us the biological underpinnings of personality. The child begins as instinctual needs that must be fulfilled if one is to survive. At a different stage, another drive assumes center stage: hunger and sleep, then aggression/control, then sexuality. Erikson and Piaget add in the important ego development that occurs as the child copes with the demands of the id. Erikson focuses on the personality traits of the ego, whereas Piaget examines the cognitive functions of the developing ego.

As these ego dimensions are being assembled, a superego begins to differentiate from the ego. Lawrence Kohlberg fills in this section of the portrait with his examination of moral development. Parallels can be drawn between Piaget's preoperational morality, in which a child behaves solely on the basis of expected consequences of an action for that child, with no thought of the effect of that action on anyone else. During this same growth period, Erikson draws our attention to the development of the senses of autonomy and initiative, by which a child explores and asserts himself or herself in the world.

It is not until Piaget's stage of abstract thinking (adolescence), that a child has the cognitive ability to step back and observe himself or herself as a "self," and to think hypothetically—both so necessary to the development of Erikson's ego identity. Similarly, a child cannot understand principles in a way that would allow the construction of a set of personal moral values until this level of abstract thinking is attained. Importantly, by this time, the crises involved in Freud's first three stages of development have, ideally, been resolved, so that the child has freed the psychic energy needed to devote to ego and superego growth.

The theories taken together suggest that development does not unfold naturally. Without interaction with parents and significant others, neither personality traits, cognitive ego functions, nor moral principles will simply "appear." They require nurturance, and the four areas of development must work together for proper socialization to occur.

AGENTS OF SOCIALIZATION

We are affected, at least in a small way, by every social experience. In modern industrial societies, several agents of socialization have particular importance—the family, the school, the peer group, and the mass media.

The Family

Clearly, the family is the most important agent of socialization. Infants, as noted earlier, are completely dependent on others to meet their needs, and this responsibility almost always lies with the immediate family. However, the family no longer plays the all-pervasive role in socialization that it once did. Schools, day care, and nursery schools have taken over many of its functions. Children used to begin school at age 6; now most go to kindergarten or nursery school at age 4 or 5. Many go to day-care centers as infants or toddlers. The long-term effects of these extrafamily agencies on socialization have yet to be fully studied. Additionally, television serves as a baby-sitter within the home, suggesting the mass media effects we discuss later.

The family is the agent of intentional as well as unintentional socialization. A mother who insists that a preschooler return a toy to its owner may plan to teach her child about getting along with other children, but she is also, less intentionally, urging that child to respect the private ownership of property. In another society that places less value on private property, a mother might be more worried about a child who clings to his or her possessions and refuses to give them to others. Parents may intend to teach a child that race or religion do not matter, but their activities, the clubs they join, and the neighborhood in which they reside may convey very different messages. The family introduces the child to intimate personal relationships and gives the first experience of being a distinct individual. The family is the child's first reference group, the first group whose standards the

Some families stay together and others are torn apart. Family division has many roots, from violence to drugs to infidelity. Recently, the United States has witnessed a new issue: single mothers who give up their children for adoption and change their minds later. This can be a horrifying experience, especially for the child who may have already "bonded" with the adoptive parents. Here is an image from one such famous case—Baby Jessica being handed over to her biological mother's lawyers. To some it exemplified a tragic interaction between child-rearing and the law.

child applies to the self (see Chapter 5). The family also introduces the child to group living—learning to share household resources, space, objects, and parental attention.

Fathers and mothers have different styles of parenting and thus provide varied experiences to their children. With small children, fathers typically engage in physical play and initiate unfamiliar games. Mothers tend toward spoken interaction and more familiar games such as peek-a-boo. Patterns of socialization in the home also reflect the parents' relationship with one another; whether interaction in the family is relaxed and good-humored, or tense and guarded; whether the interaction emphasizes or minimizes distance between males and females; and whether the family spirit is cooperative or competitive (Elkin and Handel, 1984).

The birth of siblings adds new dimensions to family life. Through interaction with siblings, children gain experience in cooperation and conflict; negotiation and bargaining; inequalities based on age, size, and experience; and the limits of other people's tolerance. In addition, a mother's response depends not only on the child's innate disposition but on that child's position in the family. For example, mothers are known to spend twice as much time with first-born as with later-born children (White, Kaban, and Attanucci, 1979).

Many researchers agree that birth order has a significant effect on socialization. First-born children tend to be more strictly disciplined than later-born children; they also tend to be more a focus of parental attention. The birth of a sibling often arouses competitive responses in the first child. Consequently, firstborns are often more conscientious, achieve more scholastically, and go to school longer than later-borns (Forer, 1976). Firstborns are also more likely to achieve success: more likely to become presidents, members of Congress, or astronauts, and to appear on the cover of *Time* magazine (Goleman, 1985).

Laterborns, on the other hand, must learn to work with other siblings, so they often become skilled at diplomacy and negotiation (Jiao, Ji, and Jing, 1986). Parental discipline is usually less rigid with laterborns, a phenomenon that encourages more flexible relationships with other people (Snow et al., 1981). The eldest child's "pioneering" function often continues over the life span, providing younger siblings with a role model in coping with marriage, divorce, children, bereavement, and retirement (Sobel, 1980). Because of today's high rate of divorce and remarriage, many children form more enduring bonds with their brothers and sisters than they do with their parents (Cicirelli, 1980).

Language

At the core of socialization is language—the system of symbols and meanings that people of a culture use to communicate. Based on detailed studies, Basil Bernstein has uncovered significant differences in the content and structure of language used in middle-class and working-class families. Bernstein (1971, 1981) concludes that in Great Britain and the United States there are two distinct "speech codes"; that is, two different sets of rules about how words are selected and linked together. One Bernstein calls a *restricted speech code*; this is based on the assumption that the people talking share the same knowledge, assign the same meanings, and hold the same worldviews. People who use this type of communication leave much unsaid. They use a "linguistic short-hand." Bernstein finds that working-class parents often use a restricted speech code.

Many middle-class parents, however, use what Bernstein calls an *elaborated speech code.* This is used to convey ideas different from those of people around them. This, Bernstein says, is the speech used for persuasion, distinctions, and explanations, rather than everyday practical conversation. Elaborated speech is, of course, more complex and precise than restricted speech. Bernstein suggests that a child exposed to an elaborated speech code will actually develop differently intellectually and socially than a child who hears only a restricted speech code. Because a restricted code is based on the assumption of *shared* knowledge and understanding, it does not encourage children to develop a sense of themselves as separate individuals with their own ideas. Children who acquire an elaborated code are encouraged to be more independent, self-sufficient, and autonomous in their thinking.

Bernstein sees speech codes as closely related to the social structure within a family. Middle-class families are more likely to have an open role system in which each family member's role is cooperatively determined to some extent. In this kind of family, children can choose from among a range of roles (baby, mother's helper, teaser, serious student, etc.) depending on their changing wishes. Since individual qualities and personal choices are frequently discussed among family members, an elaborated speech code is essential to maintain autonomy. In sharp contrast is the family with a closed role system, often found in working-class families where roles are assigned to children without discussion. Children are simply expected to accept their positions. In these settings, a restricted speech code is sufficient, and perpetuates the family social structure.

Bernstein further suggests that speech codes and family social structure are related to a third important factor: the type of control used by parents to socialize children. According to Bernstein, many working-class families rely on what he calls *position-oriented control*, in which a person's position within the family is the determinant of appropriate behavior. Thus, a working-class mother might insist that her teenage daughter baby-sit her little brother simply because she is the eldest girl in the family. In position-oriented control, orders are issued without explanation. Here, again, restricted speech code is the norm. The middle-class family, on the other hand, is more likely to use what Bernstein calls *person-oriented control*. Here, rules are modified to fit both the situation and the particular child. A middle-class mother might ask her teenage daughter, "Would you be willing to baby-sit tonight since no one else is going to be home and you're very good with your little brother?" The daughter is given the opportunity to participate in the decision and is offered reasons for the request. An elaborated speech code is necessary for these kinds of interactions. These experiences encourage the daughter to be more open-minded and analytical in her thinking, thereby helping her prepare for higher status roles in later life. Restricted speech codes and position-oriented control in working-class families, however, may limit a child's potential to attain higher status careers.

Social Class and Family

Melvin Kohn's (1977) landmark study of the relationship between social class and child-rearing involved intensive interviews over a 20-year period with thousands of working-class and middle-class parents in the United States. He and his associates found consistent differences by social class in the values people hold. Those, in turn, are passed on to their children (Kohn, 1959; Kohn and Schooler, 1983). People in higher social classes are more likely to value self-direction, whereas working-class people tend to value conformity to external authority. Working-class parents stress manners, neatness, being a good student, honesty, and obedience. Middle-class parents, on the other hand, emphasize consideration, interest in how and why things happen, responsibility, and self-direction. In other words, working-class standards stress obedience to prescribed rules, whereas middle-class values emphasize development of one's own internal standards. Note how closely differences in class values parallel Bernstein's differences in speech codes.

Working-class and middle-class parents' behavior is also greatly influenced by their different ideas about how children should act. Working-class parents value conformity to established rules, so they tend to focus on the immediate *consequences* of a child's actions. If a child breaks a rule, he or she is likely to be punished even if the child did not intend to do anything wrong. Middle-class parents, in contrast, tend to be more concerned with the *motives* behind the child's behavior, rather than the act itself. Middle-class parents are more likely to explain why a certain behavior is or is not acceptable, whereas working-class parents are likely to punish the child without any discussion, and they are also more likely to use *physical* punishment than are middle-class parents, who are noted to use *psychological* forms of punishment such as appealing to the child's guilt and social isolation ("Go to your room!").

Do these values stressed in the home actually influence the traits that children develop? Jeylan Mortimer and his colleagues (1986) tested Kohn's finding that parents who value self-direction tend to be more supportive and encouraging toward their children than those who value conformity.

In his research on father–son relationships, Mortimer found that a father's encouragement and support fosters self-confidence, and a tendency to become highly involved in one's work. These are traits that often underlie achievement and the pursuit of high-status careers. (For more on the personal effects of work structures, see Chapter 1.)

TABLE 8:1 Trait Most Desired in Child Crosstabulated with Highest Year of School Completed[a]

Count COL PCT	YEARS		ROW TOTAL
DESIRED TRAIT	1–12 Years Education	1–8 Years College	
Honesty	279 **32.1**	164 **29.3**	443
Good judgment	141 **16.2**	124 **22.2**	265
Obedient	169 **19.4**	54 **9.7**	223
Responsible	63 **7.2**	59 **10.6**	122
Considerate	55 **6.3**	61 **10.9**	116
Interested in a variety of things	23 **2.6**	31 **5.5**	54
Tries hard to succeed	35 **4.0**	18 **3.2**	53
Good manners	31 **3.6**	8 **1.4**	39
Self-control	14 **1.6**	12 **2.1**	26
Amicable	19 **2.2**	20 **3.6**	39
Good student	22 **2.5**	5 **0.9**	27
Clean	11 **1.3**	2 **0.4**	13
Displays gender-appropriate behavior	8 **0.9**	1 **0.2**	9
COLUMN TOTAL PCT	870 **60.9**	559 **39.1**	1,429 **100.0**

[a]Main Point: People with higher levels of education are more concerned with the intrinsic development of their children (good judgment, considerate) and less concerned with extrinsic behavior (obedient, clean).

Source: 1984 General Social Survey.

Table 8:1 shows the relationship between the parents' educational level and the personality traits most valued in their children. The table suggests that parents with low educational attainment valued traits indicating obedience and adherence to rules (being a good student, being clean, being obedient, having good manners) much more highly than did parents with at least some college education (1–8 years). College-educated parents valued the child's *interest*, responsibility, consideration, and being friendly (amicable) with others most strongly.

School

Formal schooling introduces unfamiliar people, new social settings, challenging tasks, and unique new social experiences into the socialization process. As children encounter social diversity, they become more aware of their own social identities and respond to others accordingly. One study of kindergarten children, for example, demonstrated that whites and African Americans tended to form same-race play groups (Finkelstein and Haskins, 1983; see also Chapter 12). Similarly, boys and girls tend to form same-gender play groups (Lever, 1978).

hidden curriculum—the knowledge gained by students as a consequence of going to school, though it is not intentionally taught.

While the most recognized task of schools is to teach children a wide range of basic skills and knowledge, what is often most significant in school is the **hidden curriculum**, which imbues children with cultural values and traditions. School activities, such as exams and sports events, encourage competitiveness in children. Schools also further socialize children into appropriate sex-role behaviors.

Another schooling experience is being evaluated in tasks such as reading, writing, arithmetic, and athletic performance according to the standard of the school, rather than on the basis of a mother's or father's response to the child's performance. Such impersonal evaluation may greatly affect the children's perceptions of themselves and their abilities. Perhaps the most important point is that school is the child's first encounter with impersonal rules.

In some societies, socialization has become institutionalized, as in this picture of "tots on pots" in Russia. These preschoolers are communally toilet trained at the day care center of a wood-finishing plant in the Buryat region. The children have their own numbered pots.

Peer Group: A Network Interpretation

By the time they begin schooling, children have already discovered a unique setting for social activity in the *peer group*—people in consistent, predictable interaction who share common interests, social position, and age. Peer groups provide children with their first experience of egalitarian relationships (Erikson, 1963). Because adults are always older, stronger, bigger, and wiser than children, adult–child relationships are always asymmetrical. Children are subordinate to adults at least at home and at school. Peers, however, are social equals by definition.

Children naturally develop close relationships of their own choosing. Friendships give them insight into others' feelings and help develop mutual understanding. In early childhood, friendships are usually based on proximity (same neighborhood); in middle childhood, on shared interests and activities; and in adolescence, on shared secrets and mutual trust (Corsaro, 1985). In peer groups children also learn that social interaction can be difficult and complex and that friendship is not automatic. Peers also initiate one another on subjects adults consider sensitive or even taboo, such as sex. Adolescents get most of their information about and experience with sex from age-mates. Parents report shock at the amount of accurate information their 10- to 12-year-old children possess about sexual intercourse, different sexual positions, and birth control apparatus. Parents exclaim, "Where did you learn all this?" The child snickers, blushes, remains silent, or replies "at school," meaning from peers.

The peer group is especially important during adolescence when children begin to assume an identity of their own and move in an adult direction. A sense of belonging within a peer group can alleviate some of the anxiety generated by the process of separating from the family. During this period, also, peer groups often pressure their members toward conformity with their special standards, such as wearing a particular type of clothing; for example, boys wearing an earring, or girls wearing Doc Marten boots.

According to some researchers, the conflict between parents and their children during adolescence may be more apparent than real. While the peer group may guide short-term concerns such as style of dress and musical taste, parents continue to affect the long-term career aspirations of their

This scene shows how socialization may have gone awry. Teenagers, truancy, marijuana, sex, and tattoos are a mixture for many parents's nightmares. Some see it as a "stage"; others see it as a training ground for decadence. Whatever your point of view, it clearly is an example of peer group socialization.

children. One study found that parents exerted greater influence than even best friends on young people's educational plans (Davies and Kandel, 1981).

A neighborhood or school is a social network of many peer groups whose members often cast their own group in positive terms while portraying others negatively. A diversity of peer groups can be central to the socialization process because people often attempt to conform to their own groups by forming an identity in opposition to others. Sociologists call this a **negative reference group**. In other cases, people are strongly affected by peer groups they would like to join. For example, when entering a new school, a young woman might wish to excel at gymnastics so she may try to become part of the gymnastics social crowd. She is likely to adopt the hangouts, behaviors, dress styles, language, and social activities of this group in the hope of eventual acceptance. This represents what sociologists call **anticipatory socialization**, the process of learning directed toward gaining a desired membership in a peer group. (Hence the "anticipatory reference groups" discussed in Chapter 5.) Later, sororities and fraternities, and, after graduation, the desire for certain jobs are likely to provoke further anticipatory socialization.

negative reference group—a group by which an individual is heavily influenced, primarily because the individual does *not* want to become a member of this group.

anticipatory socialization—a process of learning directed toward gaining membership in a group a person would like to join.

"Peer group" is a sociological term that has been adopted into popular speech. Although we have utilized the terminology here, be aware that not all early peer relations occur in a neatly bounded group setting. Many such social relations are haphazard, experimental, first attempts at interpersonal bonding that may or may not fall together into a concrete "club" or "clique." Adolescent and teenage years are when individuals first flex the social skills muscles they will use to maintain networks throughout their lives. In a real sense, the network sections throughout this book reflect the formative social experiences in early "peer groups."

Mass Media

The mass media are impersonal communications directed to a vast audience. Children are exposed to a wide variety of mass media—television, radio, movies, videos, records, comics, magazines, and newspapers portraying events all over the world. While all are significant agents of socialization, the most influential is probably television. Certainly no other medium consumes more of children's time than television; at 9 months many infants watch television for 1.5 hours without comprehension (Singer, 1983). By age 3 or 4, they average 4 hours per day (NIMH, 1989). In middle childhood and adolescence they average 20–25 hours a week; and some children spend 40 hours each week in front of the TV (Hodge and Tripp, 1986). Thus children in the United States spend more time watching television programs than they do in school or in direct communication with their parents (Winn, 1985).

Parents, teachers, and many others are concerned about the ways in which television is socializing children. They are displeased with the violent and sexual content of many shows, and worry about the intensity of children's emotional involvement in programs (NIMH, 1982). They fear that television keeps children away from more active, constructive behavior, such as reading or outdoor physical play. The underlying fear seems to be that television is an extraordinarily powerful medium, and that children possess neither the cognitive ability nor the emotional maturity to protect themselves from it.

A close examination of research on the impact of television on children offers mixed findings. On the positive side, watching programs (such as

"Mister Rogers' Neighborhood"), that emphasize sharing, cooperation, and self-discipline encourages social interaction skills in children (Cater and Strickland, 1975). For children who live in an intellectually, culturally depleted environment, shows such as "Sesame Street" offer stimulation and instruction. On the negative side, many studies have demonstrated that consistent viewing of violence on television is associated with aggressive behavior. One long-term study of teenagers, for instance, found that preference for violence in television programs was a more accurate predictor of aggressive behavior than socioeconomic background, family relationships, or any other single factor (Cater and Strickland, 1975). Some researchers feel confident that television viewing affects behavior, especially heavy television viewing in the preschool years, which puts a child at risk for problem behavior in elementary school.

Until very recently, television has portrayed men and women in accordance with cultural stereotypes, showing males in powerful roles and females as mothers or subordinates. This is beginning to change with the proliferation of TV female attorneys, journalists, designers, and the like (Ang, 1985; Cantor and Pingree, 1983). Similarly, television shows have long portrayed affluent people in favorable terms while suggesting that less-affluent Archie Bunkers are ignorant and misinformed (Gans, 1980). In addition, although racial and ethnic minorities tend to watch more television than whites, until relatively recently, these minorities have been all but absent from programming. This situation has improved over the 1980s and into the 1990s, however, as advertisers have recognized the marketing advantages of appealing to African Americans, Hispanics, and Asians.

It is also important to note that television affects us through what is *not* portrayed on programs, such as the lives of the have-nots and the large homosexual minority in the United States. In this way, television sends the message that these groups are relatively unimportant.

THE SUBJECTIVE DIMENSION

Although the focus in this chapter is on the process by which personalities are formed, the subjective factors discussed everywhere in this book cannot be separated from that process. Indeed, their operation should be understood as a *result* of socialization since people's subjective impressions of the world are largely formed through the different agents of socialization discussed previously. That is a very large principle of human behavior. Let's look at it more microscopically by using examples massaged by the three determinants of the subjective dimension.

Socialization occurs in many forms but one agent with the greatest degree of *visibility* is television. Television doesn't just affect the short-term content of our heads; it injects long-standing patterns by which we process information. A person who has watched 1,000 hours of dismemberments will tend to be desensitized to violent crime. Years of "Dynasty" and "Lifestyles of the Rich and Famous" alter personal judgments of economic success and failure. Figure 8:2 demonstrates how television affects subjective attitudes toward sex.

Religion provides a classic example of how some subjective dimensions of personality affect our *values* and *expectations* of things to come. If there is *one most powerful factor* that imparts a person's religious view of the world, it probably is the family. Although the church may be the most visible agent of religious socialization, who decides which religion to choose in the first place? It's your parents. The connection is overwhelming. While it is true that these patterns may lose their effect on people as they grow older and

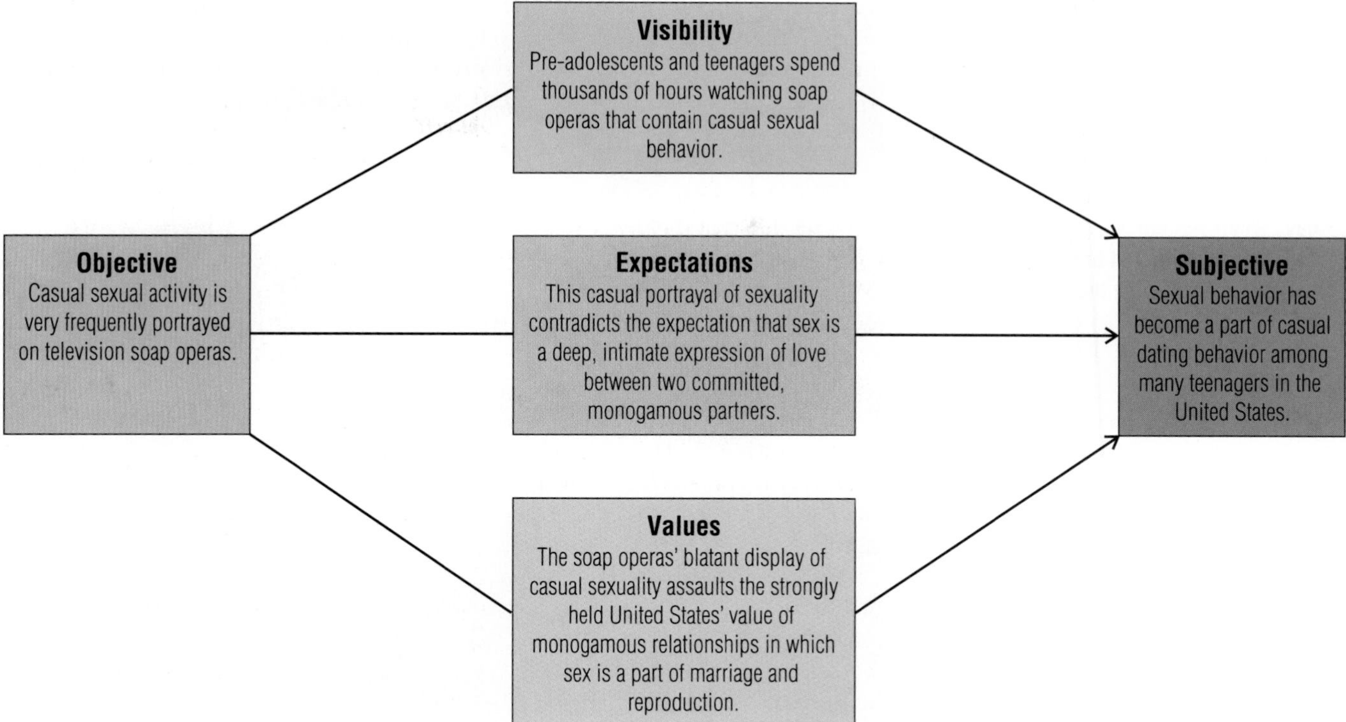

FIGURE 8:2 SUBJECTIVE AND OBJECTIVE DIMENSIONS: THE CASE OF SOCIALIZATION

Sex is portrayed as a casual activity by the media, especially television. How has this subjective dimension affected sexual behavior among teenagers?

perhaps become less religious altogether, the value "software" cannot help but have some lasting effect.

SECONDARY SOCIALIZATION

To this point we have examined socialization in the early stages of life, what might be termed *primary socialization.* As indicated by Erikson, the processes of acquiring the norms and values of one's society, learning a social role in one's community, and developing an individual identity do not stop at age 18. Starting a career, living on one's own, marrying, becoming a parent, changing jobs, changing neighborhoods, and changing spouses all involve new challenges. Here we explore additional processes of socialization that come into prominence as children enter the adult world.

Resocialization

resocialization—the learning and internalization of a new set of norms, values, and skills.

total institutions—organizations that exercise nearly complete control over the lives of their members.

Some life transitions continue to build on existing norms, roles, and values (Bachman, 1978), whereas others require **resocialization**, the learning and internalization of a new set of norms, values, and skills. Resocialization occurs most clearly in extreme institutional settings such as a military boot camp, a prison, a mental hospital, or a convent. Erving Goffman (1961) has termed them **total institutions** because of the monolithic control they exert over the life of the inmate to be resocialized. Certain professions, such as medicine, nursing, law, and police work, while their confinement is not nearly as total, depend on training programs that partially strip the individual of the self-image, identity roles, and values acquired in earlier socialization—a process termed *desocialization*—then replaces these with a new identity, worldview, and roles.

Notice anything here? By the 1990s the female recruit in line with the male sailors was old news. But, for a long period of time, this scene was unfathomable. Now the military, among many other fields once dominated by men, is an option for both genders. The days when women were socialized only towards marriage and home-making are in the history books.

Resocialization into a profession has been described as a six-stage process (Light, 1980). During the first stage, recruits are made to feel very differently from what they previously felt. Psychiatric residents, for example, who had learned to view themselves as competent young doctors are told that they will go slightly "crazy" during their residency. The second stage involves a discrediting process. Veteran cops tell rookies to forget everything they learned in the police academy because it will be useless on the streets. Often, a third stage of confusion and conflict about one's choice of career follows: Nursing students complain that school is not what they had hoped (Simpson, 1979); rookie cops find that their ideas of absolute right and wrong are undermined. In the fourth stage, the initiate experiences despair. Some consider dropping out of the profession, some do leave, while others muddle through—they cease trying to understand what is happening to them and just do as they are told. During the fifth stage, the recruits who remained begin to see themselves as what they had aspired to become. Nursing students, for example, begin to identify with their teachers instead of with ward personnel. The sixth stage involves reaffirmations as initiates internalize the worldview of the career and adopt its values and norms as their own. They can now look back on their initiation with some humor.

Current interest in the issue of resocialization reflects changing ideas about the nature of socialization. Earlier, many behavioral scientists, such as Freud, believed that childhood experiences almost completely shaped the personality. Adult socialization was simply a refinement of this roughly polished stone. Today, many sociologists believe that adult experiences (working, becoming a parent, divorce, becoming middle-aged, etc.) have as much significance for adult behavior patterns and attitudes as do childhood experiences.

Occupational Socialization

Occupational socialization is the process of aligning the norms, values, and beliefs of a new worker with those of the organization or occupation. At best, schools prepare people in only a very general way for actual positions in the workplace. All occupations require some on-the-job training, whether through formal classes or informal initiation. Socialization into a job requires "learning the ropes": the values and ethics of the occupation, the unofficial rules, and the way people on different rungs of the hierarchy are expected to relate to clients and colleagues.

Workplaces vary in the degree to which they socialize their workers to new roles. At one extreme, socialization in IBM, in leading accounting firms, or in the State Department touches many subtle and personal dimensions of the individual. Management training may be very extensive. Employees are expected to personify the organizational image every minute of the day. Other companies require much less, expecting only that employees perform their assigned tasks competently.

Edgar Schein (1978) of the Sloan School of Management at Massachusetts Institute of Technology has concluded that socialization to one's first major job involves four tasks.

The first task is to come to terms with the organization. New employees quickly discover that others in the organization impede what they plan to accomplish. New employees find that co-workers do not seem as bright, competent, and productive as they had expected. The newcomer must learn to accept the weaknesses inevitable in a human organization. The skills of selling, compromising, and politicking must be developed.

The second task is to learn to cope with resistance to change in the organization. New employees frequently complain that their recommendations, which seem technically sound to them, are not implemented. The degree to which the new employee learns to adapt to such resistance to change has consequences for future career paths.

The third task for the novice is resolving ambiguities inherent in the job. Novices find that some aspects of their work are very vaguely defined, and that it is difficult to obtain the feedback needed to judge their own performances. Carving out the specific territory of one's own job is a crucial experience in adjusting to a new workplace.

The fourth task Schein lists is learning how to move upward in the organization. New employees must develop a relationship with their superior, balancing between being too dependent and becoming too independent. Also, they must ascertain and comprehend the reward system. This involves identifying what behavior is expected, what behavior is actually rewarded, and the degree to which one can believe official statements of policy.

Ongoing Transitions: Early Adulthood through Middle-Age

Daniel Levinson (1978) pioneered the systematic investigation of the adult life cycle, focusing on the shift from early adulthood to middle age. Although Levinson studied a small group of only men, his work was crucial in *redirecting attention* to a critical phase of adulthood as well as redefining our conception of this time of life. In the young man's transition into early adulthood he becomes a novice adult with his own home base. He begins to make choices about marriage, occupation, and residence, which shape his place in the world. By the later thirties, settling down and firmly anchoring oneself in society, and advancing in one's chosen field (or moving to a different new field) become paramount.

According to Levinson, the mid-life transition usually occurs between age 40 and 45. At this time, men confront the signs and limitations of aging. For 70 to 80 percent of the men in his study, the mid-life crisis was emotionally anguishing. Men questioned themselves: "What have I done with my life? What do I really get from and give to my wife, children, friends, work, community, and self? What is it I truly want for myself and others?" (Levinson, 1978, p. 60). For a number of these men, the realization that their youthful dreams might never be realized was truly agonizing.

The men who navigated this mid-life transition successfully found middle adulthood (over age 45) to be the most productive period of their lives. They became more secure in themselves and more comfortable with their attachments to friends and family. They came to joyfully accept responsibility for passing on knowledge and experience to the younger generation.

Levinson suggests that another transition begins at about age 60. As men approach old age, they must deal with the fact that their generation may no longer be dominant. Their task is to reframe their vitality in new forms appropriate to late adulthood and old age.

Other research confirms some of Levinson's findings while qualifying other points. The Grant study of adult development followed 270 Harvard freshmen males from college into adulthood. George Vaillant (1977) interviewed 94 of these men at their 25th college reunion where they were in their mid-forties and then again when they were in their mid-fifties. (Of course this study focuses only on one cohort of very similar men and is thus not representative of all adult men.) Like Levinson, Vaillant found early adulthood to be focused on launching a career and creating a family, whereas mid-life presented men with much psychological turmoil. Vaillant describes mid-life as a second adolescence: "Men leave the compulsive, unreflective, busy-work of their occupational apprenticeships and once more explore the world within" (p. 220). Unlike Levinson, however, Vaillant found that the age at which men began questioning their life's work and choices varied by as much as a decade. Some became introspective at age 30; whereas at age 45, others were still resolving issues of identity and establishing relationships. Vaillant contends that self-questioning can occur at any point in the life span and is related more to events (divorce, failure to get a promotion, and others) than to age.

Adult socialization poses a somewhat different set of issues for women, though research on female socialization lags behind the research on males. For a discussion of these important factors, see Box 8:2.

BOX 8:2 GENDER AND SOCIAL CHANGE

Adult Socialization in Women

A major in-depth study of a cohort of women has yet to appear. The available evidence suggests that the "ages and stages" approach may not be as appropriate for women as for men due primarily to the timing of childbearing, which has an important impact on women's career decisions (Rosenfeld and Stark, 1987). A woman who bears children during her twenties may not embark on a career full time until her late thirties to early forties, 10 to 15 years later than men. Another woman (and this seems to be the direction taken by larger and larger numbers of women) may concentrate on her career during her twenties and delay having children until her thirties. Increasingly in today's society, a woman's age tells very little about her marital, parental, or occupational status. However, the number and ages of her children continue to be the best predictors of her occupational participation and advancement (Hanson, 1983).

On the whole, it is presently unclear how the recent influx of women into full-time careers and the tendency for younger women to combine job and family roles will change the female life course in adulthood. Even if women do not pass through specific stages in as predictable a way as men do, they seem to experience similar types of changes in adulthood. According to a longitudinal study of 132 graduates of Mills College, a women's college in California, women became more committed to duties and more self-disciplined in their twenties; more confident, assertive, and achievement-oriented in their thirties; and more generative and involved in activities outside the family in their forties (Helson, Mitchell, and Moore, 1984).

Critical Thinking Questions

1. Why has research on women's age cohorts lagged so far behind research on men's age cohorts?
2. In what specific ways might women's stages of adult socialization differ from those Levinson found among men?

Aging/Old Age/Dying

Old age includes the later years of adulthood and the final stage of life itself, beginning in about the mid-sixties. Different societies attach quite varied meanings to this period of life. In pre-industrial societies, old age typically brings a person much social influence and respect because the elderly control land and wealth, and are seen as embodying a lifetime of wisdom. In these societies, the elderly affect important decisions for younger family members (Hareven, 1982; Sheehan, 1976).

In modern industrial societies, however, younger people usually work away from their family, thus diminishing the influence of the elderly. In a rapidly changing society, the knowledge of matured people is often viewed as dated, marginal, or obsolete, and their experience is seen as irrelevant to the social trends of the more youthful.

Youth orientation in the United States may very well diminish as the proportion of matured Americans continues to increase. The percentage of Americans over age 65 has almost tripled since the beginning of the twentieth century, and today more Americans are 65+ than are in their teens. Longevity is also increasing. The U.S. Census Bureau predicts that in the next century the fastest-growing segment of the U.S. population will be those over age 85. It is also projected that there will be almost six times as many people over that age a century from now as there are today.

Socialization in old age today differs significantly from socialization earlier in life. For the young, advancing age means learning new roles with new obligations. Old age, however, involves the opposite process: One must leave roles that have long been a source of social identity and meaningful activity. Retirement is the most obvious illustration. Although retirement may involve restful activity, travel, and leisure after years of work, it often means the loss of familiar routines. Like any life transition, retirement demands that a person learn unfamiliar modes of living while simultaneously unlearning comfortable patterns of earlier periods of life. A nearly equal transition is required of the nonworking wife or husband who must change routines to accommodate a spouse who now spends more hours in the home. Also, socialization in old age cannot be separated from the ultimate acknowledgment of impending death.

As a result of her study of many dying people, Elisabeth Kübler-Ross (1969) described death as an orderly transition involving five distinct stages. Because U.S. culture tends to ignore the reality of death as part of the life cycle, people's initial response to the prospect of their own death is *denial*, which involves avoidance of anything that reminds one of the inevitability of death. The second stage is *anger*—the person begins to acknowledge impending death but views it as an offense committed unfairly specifically against him or her. In the third stage, *bargaining* replaces anger, as the person tries to negotiate with God for more time. In this stage, the person tries to maintain the sense, appropriate to earlier stages of life, that he or she *controls* their own destiny and that, with sufficient effort, anything can be accomplished. The fourth stage is *depression*, during which one becomes resigned and mourns his or her own anticipated death. After this grieving period comes the final stage of *acceptance* characterized by attempts to use the remaining time constructively.

As the proportion of Americans in old age changes, attitudes toward death will no doubt also change. Today, death is more widely discussed than it was earlier in this century, and people are beginning to view death as preferable to months or years of suffering or numb vegetation on life support systems in hospitals or nursing homes. Married couples are also more likely to plan for their deaths. This may alleviate some of the disorientation that usually accompanies the death of a spouse, which is a greater problem for women, who usually outlive their husbands.

This examination of the life course presents two general conclusions. First, although the biological processes of growth and aging underlie the process of life, the essential characteristics of each stage are also socially constructed. For this reason, any stage of life may be experienced very differently within various cultures. Second, each period of the life cycle presents specific problems and transitions that necessitate learning new roles and, often, unlearning what has been familiar.

Two additional points should be noted. Although in every society, social experiences are organized according to age, this in no way diminishes the effect of other factors such as race, ethnicity, sex, and socioeconomic status. Thus the overall patterns described are subject to modification according to sociodemographic groupings.

Finally, the social experience accumulated over the life course also depends on the particular point in the history of a society when a life begins. The lives of people born within a particular cohort (a category of people born at about the same period) are likely to be shaped by the same major historical events (Riley, Foner, and Waring, 1988). Americans born early in this century, for example, are a cohort influenced by two world wars and an economic depression unknown to many of their children.

Each individual's generational experience, amassed over a lifetime, represents the culmination of the socialization process, which has been examined in this chapter. Each person is faced with the awe-inspiring, inevitable, and incredible prospect of linking one's own specific genetic traits with the particular matrix of family, school, and peer group relationships, as well as encountering maturational crises to create a distinct individual. The socialization process is continuous and unending. At each age, the person is complete and stable, yet, at the same time, unfinished and changing. Although the results of much research has been presented, much remains unknown and still to be discovered in studies conducted by members of your generation.

SUMMARY

1. Socialization is the reproduction of society in a new generation. It is a process through which individuals become members of the human community and that is life-long in duration—from womb to tomb.
2. The critical phase of socialization occurs in childhood when much of the personality is formed. Some behavioral scientists believe that the infant is a blank slate at birth and is completely shaped by life experiences. Others argue that personality is fixed by heredity and cannot be altered by experience. These polar schools of thought represent the extremes of the nature–nurture controversy. What is not controversial is that the intrinsically helpless nature of the human infant requires socialization.
3. There are many different theories about the components of the socialization process. Charles H. Cooley developed the concept of the "looking-glass self"—the sense of self developed by other people's attitudes and behaviors toward the individual. George Herbert Mead traced the development of a sense of self to early social interaction, which produces individual distinctiveness (the "I") and a social self (the "me").
4. Sigmund Freud's model of socialization rests on the idea that the human personality is the end result of a process of moving through a series of psychosexual stages. The specific experiences at each stage cumulatively contribute to the final personality. Erik Erikson extended Freud's theory beyond childhood into adulthood and examined the influence of cultural factors on socialization as well.
5. Jean Piaget's theory of personality development holds that a child's view of the world is related to developmental age and stages of cognitive development, which contain elements of both biological maturation and social experience. This is consistent with Lawrence Kohlberg's model of moral development, which is more elaborate than Piaget's and asserts that children establish their own moral values as they grow up.
6. Socialization is a huge topic. It is also a complicated issue and not simply something that occurs between parents and children. There are many other influential agents of socialization, including peer groups, social class setting, language, schools, and the mass media.
7. There are also instances of resocialization when new norms, values, and skills replace old ones. Resocialization occurs most visibly in extreme institutional settings such as a convent or a prison. It also frequently occurs in an occupational setting where a new recruit is socialized into unfamiliar roles.

Chapter 9

Personal Perspective

I am not a philosopher but I have often wondered about the meaning of life as well as other big questions such as "What is right?" and "What is wrong?"

By the time you reach college, you know that life is complicated. However, perhaps no aspect of life is more complex than knowing what is normal behavior and what is deviant behavior. The difference between normal and deviant behavior is, to use a cliché, "in the eye of the beholder." It is socially constructed. This is dramatically evident when you look around the world and see that the same behavior may be viewed as deviant in one cultural area and applauded in another.

Take the case of suicide. In 1983, near Los Angeles, a Japanese woman walked into the Pacific Ocean with her two infant children in an attempt to drown them all. She lived. The children died. Under United States law, she was charged with homicide and convicted. Had she tried the same thing on the Oriental side of the Pacific, there would have been sympathy for and acceptance of her act. Having been deserted by her husband and unable to provide for her children, she did what would have been accepted in Japanese culture as an act of personal honor.

BJG

Deviance

DEVIANCE includes an incredible variety of behavior. As one author puts it,

> The subject . . . is knavery, skullduggery, cheating, unfairness, crime, sneakiness, malingering, cutting corners, immorality, dishonesty, betrayal, graft, corruption, wickedness, and sin. . . . It may be a matter of cheating on one's income tax or cheating on one's wife, of disrespect to the flag or failing to take one's turn in carrying out the trash (Cohen, 1966, p. 1).

In other words, deviance, in one form or another, is everywhere.

An experiment by Stanley Milgram (1975) at Yale University made it clear that undesirable behavior abounds in our society. In that classic study, Milgram wanted to see whether or not people would comply with an experimenter's order to administer painful electric shocks to others. Milgram's subjects were told that they would be participating in a learning experiment in which one subject was randomly selected as the "learner" and the other as the "teacher." Actually the choices were rigged so that the real subject would always be the teacher. A confederate of the experimenter served as the learner.

The learner was then strapped to an electrical apparatus, and the teacher controlled a "shock generator" in a separate room. Every time the learner gave an incorrect response on a memory test involving paired

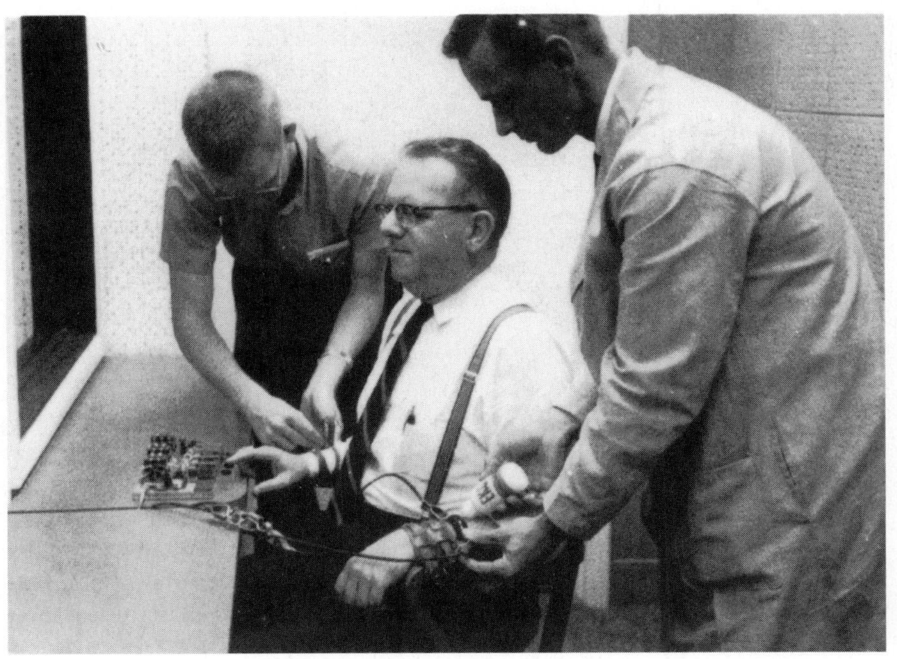

Stanley Milgram's famous experiment on obedience to authority was a creative way of testing just how much people are willing to conform to an authoritative figure. In this scene, the "learner" is strapped into a chair and electrodes are attached to his wrist. Although no electricity was actually administered, the "teacher" thought that painful electric shocks were the price for a wrong answer.

words, the teacher was told by the experimenter to administer an electric shock. Although no shocks were really inflicted, the teachers *thought* they were. When the learner gave deliberately incorrect responses, the experimenter (decked out in an official, authoritative white coat) told the teacher to administer increasingly higher, more painful doses of electricity. Milgram first ran the experiment with students at Yale. He was surprised to see that *every* member of this "independent-minded" group of select students followed the experimenter's order to administer shocks up to the maximum voltage. Milgram then ran the experiment with nonstudent volunteers from the New Haven community. This time the teachers also had to deal with verbal protests from the learners.

How many so-called law-abiding citizens were willing to turn up the juice to the point where the learner would scream in agony and eventually pass out? Psychiatrists had predicted that only a "pathological fringe" of less than 2 percent would administer shocks up to the maximum level. The results, however, were astonishing. *Almost two-thirds of the subjects carried out the experimenter's command to the maximum!*

One version of the experiment tested to see whether or not obedience to authority would vary when the teacher was brought into increasingly close physical proximity with the learner. As predicted, the teacher was more likely to end the experiment when the learner was *visibly* writhing in pain in another room. Then Milgram put the teacher and learner in the same room and instructed the teacher to administer shock by pushing the learner's hand down onto a "shock plate." Even in this extreme version of the experiment, with the learner screaming about a heart attack, an astonishing 30 percent of the subjects went all the way to the maximum shock level of 450 volts.

This laboratory experiment is rich with real-world implications for the sociology of deviance. One telling point is the raw number of everyday citizens who seem willing to inflict pain at a level that might be considered torture in another social setting. In a real sense, the subjects' behavior is both conformity *and* deviance simultaneously. Milgram drew parallels to Nazi Germany ("I didn't want to throw the switch; I was just following orders"). And consider contemporary parallels among violent gang members and orange-headed punkers deviating from society's mainstream while they are actually conforming to their own codes. Some of Milgram's subjects suffered remorse, guilt, and even clinical depression for having committed acts that were justifiable at the time. Have any of us not felt misgivings over a difficult decision that only seemed like deviance after the fact? Deviant behavior is not simply immorality and it is not just macabre behavior limited to the pages of a Stephen King horror novel. It is a complex set of issues worthy of close sociological scrutiny.

DEVIANCE AND SOCIAL CONTROL

deviant behavior—any behavior that fails to conform to the norms or rules of the group.

deviant person—someone who regularly violates society's most valued norms, particularly those norms established by socially elite groups.

What is the definition of normal and deviant behavior? *Normal behavior* is behavior that abides by the norms or rules of the group in which it occurs. **Deviant behavior** is any behavior that fails to conform to the norms or rules of the group (Durkheim, 1893/1964). It includes minor violations of norms, such as showing up late for an appointment, as well as totally reprehensible behavior, such as rape and murder (Pontell, 1993).

Because all of us violate norms to some degree at one time or another, it is important to distinguish between *deviance* and *deviants.* Deviance is the act of breaking a rule. A **deviant person**, on the other hand, is someone who *regularly* violates society's most valued norms, particularly norms established by socially elite groups. As a result, the deviant person tends to become a disvalued member of society, is met with hostility, and is typically punished by official institutions (Goffman, 1963). Such is the case with arsonists, rapists, child molesters, and other practitioners of the most high profile type of deviance—crime—the violation of those key norms formally legislated into criminal law.

Deviance is produced by society, not by individuals' behaviors. For one thing, people only become known as deviant if others define them that way. A second aspect of the social construction of deviance is the fact that it is often defined by the socially powerful. Demolishing a building to make way for a new casino in Atlantic City is acceptable because it is in line with corporate growth. But if members of an activist group block the demolition workers to protest the moral decline associated with gambling, they are likely to be arrested.

A third reason why we say deviance is produced by society is a fact mentioned earlier: *Deviance is relative.* No act is inherently deviant. An act only becomes deviant when it is socially defined as such. The definitions vary widely by *time, place,* and *group.* Take the case of time of day. A few drinks at the cocktail hour is okay but at 9 in the morning it is viewed as deviant and indicative of a drinking problem. Take the case of changes over historical time. At one time gay people were widely viewed as deviant, perverted, and maladjusted. Then, in 1973, the American Psychiatric Association stated that there is no evidence that homosexuality indicates a psychological problem. As a consequence, some people became more accepting of gays. Today, however, we witness a backlash movement in the form of widespread violence against gays ("gay-bashing"). It even occurs on college campuses. As gay students have become more visible and vocal, many schools report a rash of anti-gay graffiti, anonymous hate mail, and unprovoked attacks. In the United States as a whole, a new surge of negative attitudes toward homosexuals results from the anti-AIDS backlash of the 1980s, and the 1990s issue as to whether or not gays should be allowed in the military.

In the past, people considered deviant such things as long hair on men, believing that the Earth is round, divorce, childlessness, women working, taking a bath, contraception, rock and roll music, cursing at animals, coed dorms, and living alone. Some of these actions were punishable by law. Today they are perfectly acceptable. There are, however, some very strange laws still "on the books." In Minnesota, for instance, it is prohibited to hang male and female undergarments on the same clothesline. And women in Oxford, Ohio, are forbidden to undress in front of a man's picture.

Take the case of place, as we did in the "Personal Perspective" example of the Oriental woman who attempted suicide in the wrong country. Prostitution is a further example of the relativity of deviance by place. It is illegal in the United States except in Reno County, Nevada. That is an *intracultural* example of the relativity of deviance.

And finally, take the case of group. The differences in the structure of societies around the world (democratic, religiously righteous, etc.) can have a tremendous impact on attitudes toward the "acceptable." An American author advocating more political democracy in the United States is applauded. Another author with similar ideas in a different country is suppressed, such as Soviet writers who, in the past, were sent to mental hospitals. That is a *cross-cultural* example of the relativity of deviance. Sex presents a further cross-cultural example of how different groups view the same behavior in different ways. Look at the difference in attitudes toward sex between residents of Inis Beag and Mangaia. In Inis Beag, a small island off the coast of Ireland, sex is rarely discussed or practiced (Goode, 1978). Premarital or adulterous sex is unknown, and only marital man-on-top intercourse is allowed. Affection and foreplay between spouses is rare. So also is intercourse, which takes place in long undergarments that unbutton at the appropriate places. In this sexually repressed society, nudity is abhorred. Female sexual pleasure is not valued either, and female orgasm is unknown. So are many other sexual practices such as French kissing and oral sex. Thousands of miles away, in the South Pacific, is the small island community of Mangaia. There sex is a central concern; premarital and extramarital intercourse occur regularly and are considered normal (Goode, 1978). Men are rated on their ability to sustain vigorous intercourse for long periods of time without ejaculating. The average person has intercourse three times a night, seven nights a week.

International studies provide a rich and varied list of examples of the relativity of deviance. Take a look at Table 9:1, which documents the wide

TABLE 9:1 Number of Societies Punishing Specific Types of Sexual Behavior

NUMBER OF SOCIETIES MEASURED	PERCENTAGE PUNISHING	TYPE OF BEHAVIOR AND PERSON PUNISHED
54	100	Incest
82	100	Abduction of married woman
84	99	Rape of married woman
55	95	Rape of unmarried woman
43	95	Sexual relations during postpartum period
15	93	Bestiality by adult
73	92	Sexual relations during menstruation
		Adultery:
88	89	Paramour punished
93	87	Wife punished
22	86	Sexual relations during lactation period
57	86	Infidelity of fiancée
52	85	Seduction of another man's fiancée
		Illegitimate impregnation:
74	85	Woman punished
62	84	Man punished
30	77	Seduction of prenubile girl (man punished)
44	68	Male homosexuality
49	67	Sexual relations during pregnancy
16	44	Masturbation
		Premarital relations:
97	44	Woman punished
93	41	Man punished
12	33	Female homosexuality
67	10	Sexual relations with own betrothed

Source: Julia S. Brown, "A Comparative Study of Deviations from Sexual Mores" (April 1952). In *American Sociological Review*, Volume 167, p.138. By permission of the publisher.

variation in the degree of condemnation of different forms of sexual behavior around the world. The study was conducted in 1942 among 110 preliterate societies in six different parts of the world. Known as the Human Relations Area File, Inc., it is still one of the most comprehensive cross-cultural sources on Earth. It provides some interesting historical data on sexual practices that may seem bizarre to a college student in the 1990s. Some of the punishments for these sex acts are equally strange from the overall perspective of contemporary U.S. culture. They include duel, temporary exile, humiliation at one's wedding, facial mutilation, public raping, and enforced suicide. Other international examples of extreme views toward human sexuality exist today. For instance, in Arab societies, homosexuality is strictly prohibited. In fact, Islamic law regards male homosexuality as a heinous crime.

social control—a set of methods designed to ensure that people abide by the norms and rules of the empowered group.

If a society is to operate smoothly, there must be an effective means of **social control**—a set of methods designed to ensure that people abide by the norms and rules of the group. Without social control, life would be chaotic at best since there would be no way of keeping people's behavior within tolerable limits. Social control occurs at all levels of society—within the family, among peer groups, and through state and federal laws. It is a way of preventing deviance as well as a system of punishing those who do deviate.

There are a few different forms of social control processes. One is the risk the deviant runs in the form of punishment, be it a traffic ticket, a jail term, a death sentence, or more informal punishments such as hatred or ostracism. That is an *external* form of social control. (See Box 9:1 for an account of a fictionalized form of several of these punishments: hatred, ostracism, and capital punishment—the ultimate type of external control—all operating at once.) A mechanism of *internal* social control is the process of socialization discussed in Chapter 8. As the human personality develops, it internalizes norms of society, and usually a conscience is formed. The conscience then acts as an internal form of control by inflicting a sense of apprehension or guilt for violating the moral code. Thus people become their own agents of social control and conform to social norms habitually.

sanctions—the rewards for conformity or punishments for nonconformity.

stigma—a mark of social disgrace inflicted upon a deviant person.

On the other hand, there are always those whose socialization is incomplete—people who do not conform to an internalized moral code. They are especially likely to run the risk of external punishment, or **sanctions**. While positive sanctions are rewards for conformity (such as an award or diploma), negative sanctions are punishment for nonconformity. Sanctions can be *formal* such as being dismissed from school, being fired from a job, or receiving a jail sentence. Or they may be *informal* as when a person's reputation is damaged. When this occurs, a **stigma** is attached to the individual. Stigma is a mark of social disgrace inflicted upon a deviant person. As Goffman states, "The term stigma refers to an attribute that is deeply discrediting and reduces the person . . . from a whole and usual person to a tainted, discounted one" (Goffman, 1963, p. 3).

As shown in this scene celebrating Gay Awareness Day, some people become their own agents of social control. Many gays lead secret lives and others are exposed by other gays, a phenomenon known as "Outing." This couple obviously has no problem making their sexual orientation visible.

As the definition of deviance is relative and subjective, so is the distribution of stigma. It is regularly applied to people who flagrantly violate important norms, as in the case of an arsonist. Unfortunately, it is also applied to people who are not responsible for their own actions and are frequently misunderstood, such as the mentally ill. Minority groups are also stigmatized because they have some trait other people cannot accept. Witness the plight of the deformed, AIDS victims, short people, obese people, African Americans, and Hispanic Americans, all of whose lives are limited by some degree of stigma.

BOX 9:1 SOCIOLOGICAL IMAGINATION IN FICTION

Steve Allen's "Public Hating"

The following excerpts are from a short story about how a deviant is punished in an imaginary world of hi-tech. The person, a professor accused of treason, is brought to a stadium where a large group of people have gathered to "will" public humiliation and physical punishment upon him.

Laughing and shoving restlessly, damp-palmed with excitement, they came shuffling into the great concrete bowl, some stopping to go to the restrooms, some buying popcorn, some taking free pamphlets from the uniformed attendants.

Everything was free this particular day. No tickets had been sold for the event. The public proclamations had simply been made in the newspapers and on TV, and over 65,000 people had responded.

"We have all followed with great interest," the Premier had said, looking calm and handsome in a gray double-breasted suit, "the course of the trial of Professor Ketteridge." Early this afternoon the jury returned a verdict of guilty. This verdict having been confirmed within the hour by the Supreme Court, in the interests of time-saving, the White House has decided to make the usual prompt official announcement. There will be a public hating tomorrow. The time: 2:30 P.M. The place: Yankee Stadium in New York City. Your assistance is earnestly requested.

"All right," said the speaker. "Good afternoon, ladies and gentlemen. On behalf of the President of the United States, I welcome you to another Public Hating. This particular affair," he said, "as you know is directed against the man who was yesterday judged guilty in United States District Court here in New York City—Professor Arthur Ketteridge."

The first speaker rose. "All right," he said. "You know we all have a job to do. And you know why we have to do it."

"Yes!" screamed thousands of voices.

Dr. Weltmer stepped forward, shook hands with the speaker, and adjusted the microphone. "Thank you," he said. "Now, we won't waste any more time here since what we are about to do will take every bit of our energy and concentration if it is to be successfuly accomplished. I ask you all," he said, "to direct your unwavering attention toward the

SUBJECTIVE ASPECTS OF DEVIANCE

Although some see deviance as definable in ways that are both obvious and objective, many sociologists today believe that such an absolutist point of view is too simpleminded. We agree. Deviance is more complicated than that. It has both objective *and* subjective dimensions. Some experts in the field ". . . prefer to think of it as existing solely and exclusively as a *consequence of social definitions and judgments*" (Goode, 1978, p. 23). In other words, the nature of deviance is outside of the act itself. Aside from the processes involved in subjectively defining an act as deviant, there is a second component of subjective aspects of deviance. This is the distinction between the objective reality of an act and the way it is subjectively perceived by the public.

Later in this chapter you will be shown how seriously Americans perceive crime as a major social problem. Sometimes, however, the seriousness is—literally—misplaced. For example, there is a widespread perception of New

BOX 9:1 SOCIOLOGICAL IMAGINATION IN FICTION *continued*

man seated in the chair to my left here, a man who in my opinion is the most despicable criminal of our time—Professor Arthur Ketteridge!"

The mob shrieked.

"On the souls of your mothers," Weltmer was saying, "on the future of your children, out of your love for your country, I demand of you that you unleash your power to despise. I want you to become ferocious. I want you to become as the beasts of the jungle, as furious as they in the defense of their homes. Do you hate this man?"

"Yes!" roared the crowd.

"Fiend!" cried Weltmer, "Enemy of the people—Do you hear, Ketteridge?"

Traub watched in dry-mouthed fascination as the slumped figure in the chair straightened up convulsively and jerked at his collar. At this first indication that their power was reaching home, the crowd roared to a new peak of excitement.

At that moment Traub was at last convinced of the enormity of Ketteridge's crime, and Weltmer said, "All right, that's it. Now let's get down to brass tacks. Let's concentrate on his right arm. Hate it, do you hear. Burn the flesh from the bone! You can do it! Come on! Burn him alive!"

Traub stared unblinking through the binoculars at Ketteridge's right arm as the prisoner leaped to his feet and ripped off his jacket, howling. With his left hand he gripped his right forearm and then Traub saw the flesh turning dark. First a deep red and then a livid purple. The fingers contracted and Ketteridge whirled on his small platform like a dervish, slapping his arm against his side.

"That's it," Weltmer called. "You're doing it. You're doing it. Mind over matter! That's it. Burn this offending flesh. Be as the avenging angels of the Lord. Smite this devil! That's it!"

The flesh was turning darker now, across the shoulders, as Ketteridge tore his shirt off. Screaming, he broke away from his chair and leaped off the platform, landing on his knees on the grass.

"Oh, the power is wonderful," cried Weltmer. "You've got him. Now let's really turn it on. Come on!"

Ketteridge writhed on the grass and then rose and began running back and forth, directionless, like a bug on a griddle.

Critical Thinking Questions

1. How does the story about Professor Ketteridge connect with the functionalist theory contention that deviance can have positive outcomes?
2. How would a conflict theorist interpret the same story?

Source: Adapted from Steve Allen, "The Public Hating" (1975). In Martin Henry Greenberg, John W. Milstead, Joseph D. Olander, and Patricia Warrick (editors), *Social Problems through Science Fiction.* New York: St. Martin's Press, pp. 323–28. By permission of the publisher.

York City as the hotbed of criminal misbehavior. However, statistics compiled by the FBI (1987) show something else. Although New York City does have a high crime rate, it turns out objectively that some of the rapidly growing cities in the Southwest have the highest crime rates. Why the big difference between subjective perceptions and objective facts? Because of the high degree of *visibility* attached to the Big Apple by way of the media covering stories that have a lot of intrinsic drama. New York is loaded with exotic people and groups. As you may recall, Chapter 7 on culture discusses some interesting examples.

Mental disorder provides another example of the contrasting objective and subjective dimensions of deviance. When people read dramatic accounts of gruesome behavior by such obviously disturbed people as Charles Manson or Jeffrey Dahmer, they get the subjective misimpression that all "crazy" people rant, rave, murder, and rape. In reality, mentally disordered people are not typically dangerous or assaultive (Gallagher, 1995). They usually lead lonely, miserable lives and pose no physical threat to anyone.

The subjective controversy surrounding marijuana has had a long and complicated history. There were times when it was as acceptable as any other kind of smoking. The 1960s saw it connected with the youth countercultural movement. But the 1930s were especially interesting because a moral crusade against marijuana centered on the idea that a puff of pot was a tragic assassin of youth.

Other "at odds" examples are more hidden and have some surprising twists. Corruption is one. Honesty is widely valued by the U.S. public. Yet what really happens to honest, concerned people is more often punishment than praise. Such is the case with "whistle-blowers," people who have a strong conviction that evil is no match for good. When they see corruption and dishonesty in the workplace, they report it. Their reward is often stigmatization as a "squealer" and, in some cases, the loss of job, career, and bank account. This gap between the subjective and objective dimensions centers on *expectations* and *values.* We highly prize honesty in our society and expect that honest behavior is rewarded behavior. The whistle-blower's reward, however, is often punishment.

Another hidden example of contrasting objective and subjective aspects of deviance may reside in the very fabric of our society—our children. Kids are widely perceived as innocent, only becoming deceptive after a long dose of a deviant lifestyle. Perhaps not. One experiment reports that children as young as 3 years old can mask their feelings intentionally while attempting to deceive an adult. This indicates that humans adopt deceptive strategies early in life (Lewis, Stranger, and Sullivan, 1989).

We do not want to give you the impression that subjective and objective dimensions are usually wildly at odds with each other. The opposite is often the case. For instance, the way people in the United States perceive crime and what crime really does are closely matched. Crime is a real and present danger in everyday life. The public sees it as just that, particularly certain types of crime with objectively damaging consequences (see Table 9:2). Figure 9:1 outlines the processes by which crime is subjectively perceived by the American public as one of the most serious social problems.

It is inaccurate to assume that the fear of crime is identical across groups. Victims of crime, for instance, are especially likely to fear it (Skogan, 1987).

TABLE 9:2 American Views on the Severity of Various Offenses

SEVERITY SCORE AND OFFENSE[a] (0 TO 100)	
72.1—Planting a bomb in a public building. The bomb explodes and 20 people are killed.	14.1—A doctor cheats on claims he makes to a federal insurance plan for patient services.
52.8—A man rapes a woman. As a result of physical injuries she dies.	11.2—A company pays a bribe to a legislator to vote for a law favoring the company.
26.3—An armed person skyjacks an airplane and demands to be flown to another country.	7.4—Illegally receiving monthly welfare checks.
22.9—A parent beats his young child with his fists. The child requires hospitalization.	4.5—Cheating on federal income tax returns.
	1.4—Smoking marijuana.
19.5—Killing a person by recklessly driving an automobile.	0.8—Being drunk in public.

[a]Main Point: In the severity scale, 0 is the least severe and 100 is the most severe score.

Source: Center for Studies in Criminology and Criminal Law. University of Pennsylvania, Philadelphia. *The Seriousness of Crime: Results of a National Survey,* as reported in U.S. Department of Justice, Report to the Nation on Crime and Justice (Washington, DC: U.S. Government Printing Office, October 1983), pp. 4–5.

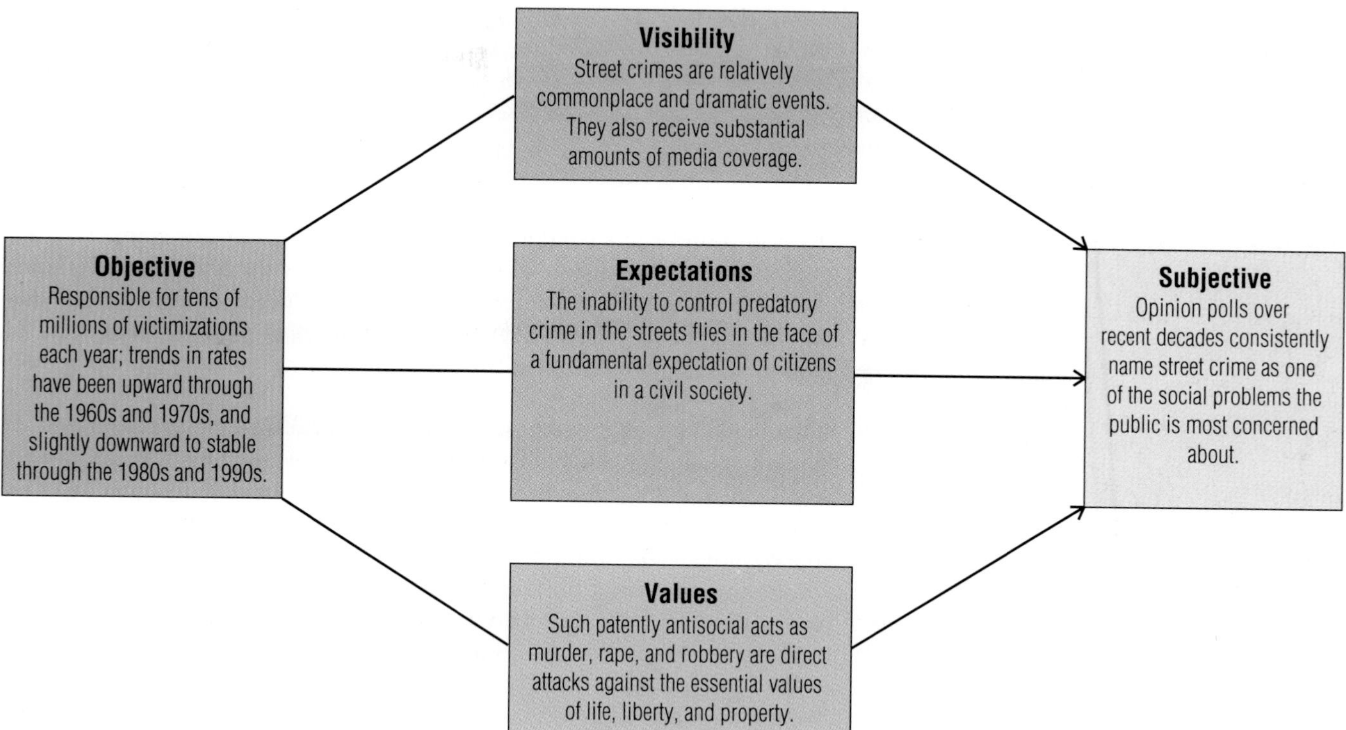

FIGURE 9:1 SUBJECTIVE AND OBJECTIVE DIMENSIONS: THE CASE OF STREET CRIME
Street crime is an example of a social problem that causes a great amount of objective damage and consistently is subjectively perceived as a major social problem.

The fear may vary from group to group, but one feeling appears to be growing—the disgust that Americans have toward crime. Events such as the widely publicized 1989 "wilding" attack on a Central Park jogger may have fueled this feeling. And people like Jeffrey Dahmer can move the public to even higher levels of revulsion. In 1989, the "Subway Samaritan" became a new hero for New York City. He killed a mugger on a subway, then disappeared into the night. The media reported that he had wide support because he symbolized the city's frustration with crime.

Another instance where the public perception of deviance matches its objective dimensions centers on the issue of drugs. The economic costs of drugs are staggering—more than $100 billion a year in reduced productivity, lost work, and medical bills. Additionally, there is a dangerous connection between drugs and crime, unemployment, marital breakup, poverty, accidental deaths, and "crack wars," to name a few horrors. Public opinion polls have regularly shown that U.S. citizens see drugs as one of the most important issues facing the nation in the 1990s. In this case, objective facts and subjective perceptions match closely.

THEORETICAL PERSPECTIVES ON DEVIANCE

Deviant behavior has long been a topic of interest to sociologists. The four sociological views presented next all have one theme in common: the notion that deviance is a reflection of the social system in which it occurs.

Functionalist Theory

structural strain—the distress in people's lives that can cause them to deviate.

Functionalist theory views deviance as the result of pressures put on people by society itself. These pressures may be applied to entire groups of people because of **structural strain**—the distress in people's lives, which can cause them to deviate (Pontell, 1993). Ghetto-dwellers, for instance, may turn to crime to alleviate the stress of poverty. Functionalists view deviance as a normal part of life that has useful functions, such as defining the limits of proper behavior. Stiff punishments for drunken drivers, for example, warn others to keep the car and the bottle separate. Positive functions (in the form of warnings to others) are also provided; for example, the dismissal of a salesman for padding his expense report, or the penalties imposed on a college student for cheating on an exam.

One of the unique propositions of functionalist theory is that deviance has useful functions in society, provided that deviance is kept within certain limits. Durkheim (1895/1964) identified four positive functions of deviance.

1. *Deviance can promote social unity.* By reacting against deviance, members of society share a sense of collective outrage. This was manifested in the "Public Hating" story in Box 9:1. In that instance, a sense of social cohesion was promoted by reminding people of their shared norms and values. This can also occur in a small group, as when strangers on a bus react to a loud drunk by complaining to each other. In a larger societal setting, solidarity may be increased by a public reaction of outrage toward a gruesome homicide or, in the case of Professor Ketteridge, to an act of treason. There are also instances where a society *needs* deviance and may even *create* it in order to maintain stability. An excellent historical example of this centers on witchcraft in Salem, Massachusetts. In 1692, a hysterical preoccupation with witches resulted in jailings and executions. It was largely an attempt to sustain the Puritan values of strict devotion to God in a situation of growing uncertainty. Many innocent people were labeled as witches and executed, but the common furor over the devil acted to sustain the failing moral order (Erikson, 1966).
2. *Deviance can reaffirm cultural norms.* Earlier it was noted that deviance can outline the boundaries of acceptable behavior. People who break the rules remind us what the boundaries of the rules are. They may even help to establish new rules. In 1987, for instance, Ivan Boeski's use of inside trader information led to the establishment of more refined ground rules for stockbroker behavior.
3. *Deviance can act as a safety valve.* Discontented people can strike out against the social order of things without necessarily harming anyone. For example, prostitution can be useful because it alleviates people's varied sexual needs without necessarily disrupting the structure of the family.
4. *Deviance can identify problems.* Deviance can "red flag" social problems that might otherwise go less noticed. The widespread "crack craze" in the United States, for instance, may be more than just a drug problem. The very fact that it is so noticeably concentrated among the urban underprivileged points to a host of boiling inner-city stresses.

You should not get the impression that functionalists believe deviance is a great thing. It has some obvious *dysfunctions* as well. It can destroy lives, undermine trust in institutions, and lead to a confusion of norms and values. Even people who are driven, hard-working individuals—prized "conformists"—may find themselves suffering for their endeavors. Such is the case with the Type A personality, an individual often plagued by ulcers and heart disease because of a workaholic lifestyle.

Emile Durkheim (1895/1964, 1897/1951) is credited with the idea that punishing deviance outlines the boundaries of acceptable behavior and urges people to reaffirm their commitment to the moral order of society. This promotes a sense of belonging and unity necessary for the survival of any group. Without the reinforcement of social norms, society and the individuals within it may fall into a state of confusion, a condition that Durkheim called *anomie*. Anomie occurs when social norms are ambiguous, conflicting, or altogether absent as in the case of *normlessness* (Mestrovic and Brown, 1985).

According to Durkheim, society needs crime to survive because without crime there would be no rituals of punishment and without punishment rituals there would be no constant reminder of society's norms. Without crimes and punishments, the bonds of society would evaporate. Before Durkheim's explanation, deviant behavior was generally considered to exist only within the person or the act itself. Durkheim's insights allow us to see deviance in its whole societal context and to develop a view of deviant behavior that goes beyond biology, psychology, or theology.

Robert K. Merton (1968) has developed Durkheim's concept of anomie further and specifically applied it to deviant behavior. According to Merton, anomie results from the confusion and frustration people feel when what they have been socially conditioned to desire cannot be obtained by socially acceptable means. Anomie is generated by the imbalance between socially approved *goals* and the opportunity to use socially approved *means* to achieve them. Merton's classic example of this dilemma is the great value placed on material success ("making it") as a cultural goal in our society. People in the United States are also socialized to believe that only certain means of making money are legitimate—go to college, study hard, get a good job, and work hard.

Obviously, not everyone can be rich. People born into low-income families are less likely to have the opportunity for higher education. Even those

The entrance of the Japanese into World War II witnessed behavior based on the belief of "death for the cause." Here a kamikaze pilot flies his plane into an Allied ship. Although the pilot knew that he was going to die, the ends justified the means. Robert Merton calls people like this "innovators." In this case, the word may be an understatement.

FIGURE 9:2 MERTON'S TYPOLOGY OF MODES OF INDIVIDUAL ADAPTATION
Merton noted that + indicates acceptance, – indicates replacement, and ± indicates replacement with new goals and means. People therefore conform or deviate according to whether they accept, reject, or replace culturally approved goals and/or means.

FIGURE 9:2 Merton's Typology of Modes of Individual Adaptation

MODES OF ADAPTATION	CULTURE GOALS	INSTITUTION-ALIZED MEANS	PRESCRIBED GOAL: SEXUAL SATISFACTION PRESCRIBED MEANS: MARRIAGE
I. Conformity	+	+	Person who achieves sexual satisfaction through intercourse in marriage.
II. Innovation	+	–	A sadomasochist.
III. Ritualism	–	+	Person with inhibited sexual desire (ISD) who goes through the motions because of duty.
IV. Retreatism	–	–	A celibate person.
V. Rebellion	±	±	Members of the Father Divine Movement who outlaw sexuality and marriage and replace it with loyalty to an asexual religious group.

with a college degree are not guaranteed wealth. Other factors, such as personality traits and specific opportunities in high-paying lines of work, are also involved. What happens to people who do not have access to the socially acceptable means of achieving success? According to Merton, there are five logically possible reactions to the social pattern of goals and means. These are displayed in Figure 9:2, along with an example of how they can be applied to other areas of life such as sexuality and marriage.

conformist—a person who accepts both cultural goals and socially accepted means of achieving those goals.

innovator—one who accepts cultural goals, but pursues them in socially unacceptable ways.

ritualists—the people who have given up on pursuing cultural goals but still go through the motions of achieving the goal.

1. *Conformity.* A **conformist** is the opposite of a deviant. Conformists accept both cultural goals and approved means. In the Merton example of desire for wealth, these are people who want to become affluent through the approved means of working hard. Examples include suburban middle-class families and hard-working low-income people. Note that one does not have to actually *be* successful to conform but only to *approve* of financial success and hard work. Sexual fulfillment is another approved goal. Some achieve it through the legitimate path of marriage. Others achieve it in deviant ways such as swingers' clubs.
2. *Innovation.* An **innovator** accepts cultural goals, but pursues them in socially unacceptable ways. This is reportedly the most common form of deviance. It occurs when a person acquires money by holding up a bank or when a student plagiarizes a term paper for a good grade. It can occur in high echelons of society, as when stockbrokers engage in insider trading or the treasurer of a teacher's union embezzles union funds and gambles them away in Atlantic City.
3. *Ritualism.* Some people, called **ritualists**, have given up on becoming rich (or obtaining some other cultural goal), yet they are compul-

sively committed to institutionalized means. Such is the case of the disgruntled office worker who mindlessly adheres to every bureaucratic rule with little awareness of the purpose of the rules. Other examples are the workaholic who works for the sake of keeping busy rather than for the sake of success and the student who compulsively studies beyond the point of necessity.

4. *Retreatism.* People who have relinquished culturally prescribed goals and whose behavior does not conform to acceptable norms are called **retreatists**. Included in this group are psychotics, drug addicts, skid-row alcoholics, and vagrants. Also included are more positive examples such as MBAs who drop out of the business world and pursue the relatively modest lifestyle of a sociology professor. Two of the authors of this book fall into that category.
5. *Rebellion.* **Rebels** go one step farther than retreatists. They reject cultural goals and institutionalized means and then replace them with disapproved ones. These are the people who drop out of mainstream society and seek a whole new social order as in the case of a revolutionary group. In the contemporary United States, examples include "white power" groups like the Skinheads and registered members of the Communist party.

retreatists—the people who reject cultural goals and socially accepted ways of achieving goals.

rebels—the people who reject cultural goals and means and replace them with their own personal forms.

Although Merton's theory of deviance remains quite popular, it has also received some criticism. Those who question its relevance to the everyday world wonder how comprehensive the modes of adaptation are, specifically how much deviance falls into Merton's neat categories. It has additionally been criticized for failing to explain individual differences. Why, for instance, does one person become an innovator while another person from

Rebellion often takes bloody forms. In 1993, David Koresh, self-proclaimed "God" and leader of a religious cult known as the Branch Davidians, engaged in a confrontation with federal agents at his compound near Waco, Texas. The first day resulted in the loss of some 20 lives —including those of federal agents and Koresh's followers. Koresh and his followers remained secluded for several weeks in the name of the greater glory of God until the showdown ended in the fiery Armageddon he had predicted.

an equally disadvantaged life retreats entirely? Despite these criticisms, one test of the relevance of Merton's theory to juvenile delinquency concluded that it held up quite well (Farnworth and Leiber, 1989). Merton's paradigm appears to be one of the more durable and flexible theories of deviance in contemporary sociology.

Conflict Theory

alienation—a sense of estrangement from self and others in society.

This perspective on deviance originated with the nineteenth-century writings of Karl Marx, who held that what is seen as deviant is a reflection of the interests of the socially powerful. In capitalistic society a rich and influential ruling class exploits the masses. Capitalistic oppression forces so much misery on the working and impoverished classes that their lives are shattered. Marx called this misery **alienation**, a sense of estrangement from self and others imposed by the rich and fortunate ("owners of the means of production") on those enslaved in factory jobs ("proletariat") as well as the real down and out ("lumpenproletariat"). The bottom line is that the misery of the socially powerless is so great that it triggers a host of different reactions—such as crime, mental disorder, and drug abuse—reactions defined by the ruling class as deviant. The capitalists control society, including the means of defining deviance. As a result, the impoverished are alienated and exploited in a number of ways. One such way is the very fact that the lower socioeconomic classes are more likely to be defined as deviant.

According to conflict theorists, the reason why certain behavior is seen as deviant is that members of the ruling elite define deviance in a way that suits their own interests. The *overt* reason behind laws may be to maintain order but the *hidden* reason is to maintain inequality so that those with social power can continue to enjoy it over time. By continuing to control the means of production, the powerful groups can also maintain control over the workers and force them to produce more. At the same time, the ruling elite creates a "crisis of legitimacy"—the impression that the established system serves the needs of everyone within it, and therefore order must be maintained (Pontell, 1993).

This view of deviance centers on the conflict between the powerful and the oppressed, whether it be "haves" against "have-nots" or one race against another. Examples of economic and social inequality in deviance abound. At the end of the Civil War, John D. Rockefeller, Sr., Andrew Carnegie, J.P. Morgan, and other "robber barons" accumulated massive fortunes through illegal means. They used violence to crush strikes and drive settlers off their land, and fixed the prices of steel and oil to eliminate competition. During the Vietnam War, protest groups claimed that those in charge of the profitable war machine were the real criminals, yet their political power insulated them from others' control. And today in our inner cities there is a regular violation of human rights by slum landlords who own inadequate housing and rent it at jacked-up prices.

Perhaps there is no more blatant example of inequality than the ways in which the poor and rich are punished for a criminal act. If the impoverished commit crimes against people and property, they are likely to receive a prison sentence. This is especially true for African Americans and Hispanics who receive longer sentences than whites convicted of the same crimes. Additionally, crimes against minorities are seen as less important and consequently are more likely to be "downgraded" from serious offenses to minor offenses (Gibbons, 1985). Crimes by the rich, such as fraud, deception, embezzlement, and environmental pollution are more likely to be treated lightly or ignored (Etzioni, 1985). As mentioned earlier, if someone "blows the whistle" on a corporate executive, the "whistle-blower" may be the one who is punished.

A contemporary conflict approach to deviance has been voiced by Richard Quinney (1974, 1980). He emphasizes the role of power in society and holds that those who have power control the lives of those who do not. For instance, legislators and law enforcement officials embed crime within their own politically defined context of acceptable human conduct. "Law," says Quinney, "is the tool of the ruling class" (1974, p. 8). Without the unequal opportunites provided by capitalism, the socially powerful would not be able to commit *crimes of domination* (such as environmental pollution and price-fixing), and the socially powerless would not be driven to *predatory crime* (such as prostitution and drug dealing) to make a living.

Conflict theory provides us with a useful sensitivity toward the political forces at work in the process of defining deviance (Davis and Stasz, 1990). Yet it still has its shortcomings. It assumes that class struggle is the driving force behind the creation of official limits of deviant behavior as well as laws imposed on those who violate the legal code. But what does class struggle have to do with the formulation of personal-violence laws, such as those designed to control murder, incest, rape, and child molesting? Clearly these are not laws designed to protect just the interests of the *powerful* but to protect the interests of *people in general* (Liska, 1987).

Another criticism of the Marxist approach to deviance lies in the terminology itself. Who, for instance, is specifically included by such terms as "ruling elite," "socially oppressed," and "powerful interest groups"? More specificity is required to empirically test various aspects of the theory's central proposition—that deviance is mainly a conflict between the interests of the powerful and those of the weak.

One final point. Maybe it is simple tunnel vision to believe that functionalist theory and conflict are opposites of each other. Perhaps, as Reiman (1984) states, criminal deviance can be functional by providing a convenient ideology to justify existing social inequities. In other words, if the socioeconomically deprived are deviant, then they do not deserve a better lot in life.

Symbolic Interactionism

Symbolic interactionism rests on the propositions of the classic sociological theories of personality developed by Charles Cooley and George Herbert Mead (see Chapter 8). Both believed that one's personality is largely a reflection of how an individual interprets other people's reactions to himself or herself.

More recently, symbolic interactionism has been applied to specific forms of deviance in the form of *labeling theory* (Pontell, 1993). The labeling theory of deviance proposes that people come to see themselves as deviants in the process of being caught in a deviant act. If a person acts bizarre, that individual may receive psychiatric treatment and acquire the identity of "mentally ill." If a person breaks a law and is arrested and jailed, this may label that individual "delinquent." The experience of being monitored by parole officers cuts one's ties with "straight" society and reinforces a criminal identity (Collins, 1988, p. 270).

Scheff (1966) and Szasz (1961) are pioneers in utilizing labeling theory to unravel some of the complexities of mental disorder. They hold that if the reactions of others to a person are generally negative, and if the person

primary deviance—the original deviant act.

secondary deviance—the deviant acts that result from a person being labeled a deviant.

perceives and accepts this negative evaluation, that individual will suffer a high degree of anxiety and eventually develop a disorder. Labeling theorists consider abnormal behavior to be a process by which an individual moves from **primary deviance** to **secondary deviance**, a distinction made by Lemert (1951). Primary deviance is the original deviant act, which may have a wide variety of causes. Secondary deviance results from being labeled a deviant. In other words, a primary deviant act is followed by negative social sanctions. Then the deviant person reacts to others' stigmatization and penalties, not by stopping the deviance, but by accepting the deviant status within his or her personal identity over time.

It is one's self-concept that underlies mental illness, and one's self-concept depends on the attitudes of others. It is the socially generated *negative self-image* that creates feelings of inadequacy and forms the core of a later problem. For example, children are likely to become disordered if they are taught to seek perfection in themselves, because they will feel compelled to spend their lives trying to achieve the unattainable and to win the approval of everyone. This is evident in the case of an unusually good-looking 17-year-old female, an accomplished dancer and sculptress, with an IQ of 178. She considered herself ugly, untalented, and stupid. The origin of this distorted self-concept was her mother, who always complained that her daughter was a failure in school because she received a 98 in a subject rather than a 100 (Gallagher, 1995).

The role of labeling in mental disorder received national attention in 1973 when David Rosenhan, a psychiatrist, studied admissions procedures at mental hospitals around the country. Specifically, Rosenhan wanted to see what would happen if perfectly normal people applied for admission, so he arranged for some of his associates to present themselves at 12 different hospitals. They were instructed to complain of hearing a voice saying a word such as "hollow," "empty," or "thud." All of the pseudopatients were diagnosed as severely disordered and were admitted. The most alarming outcome, however, occurred when they acted normally after they were admitted and no longer claimed to hear voices. No single staff member of any hospital realized they did not belong there! The only people who caught on to the experiment were the real patients. The pseudopatients were held for an average of 19 days. During that time, all of their behavior was interpreted on the basis of their respective diagnoses. One woman, for instance, became so frustrated with the situation that she began making handwritten notes about her experiences. She was further diagnosed as having "compulsive handwriting."

After publishing his exposé, Rosenhan warned another mental hospital that he would be sending a pseudopatient there between January and March. Of the 193 patients admitted during that period, 43 were designated as pseudopatients by the staff. Rosenhan had not actually sent any fake patients! Such imprecision in the diagnosis of mental disorder is a major obstacle to gaining accurate knowledge on how to effectively handle this common form of deviance. As Rosenhan notes:

> We seem unable to acknowledge that we simply don't know. The needs of diagnosis and remediation of behavioral and emotional problems are enormous. But rather than acknowledge that we are just embarking on understanding, we continue to label patients—as if in those words we had captured the essence of understanding. The facts of the matter are that we have known for a long time that diagnoses are not useful or reliable . . . (Rosenhan, 1973, p. 257).

Because of studies like Rosenhan's, labeling theorists believe that mental illness cannot be defined objectively because it really is *social* misbehavior. The truth of the matter is that there is empirical evidence to support some of the claims made by labeling theorists. Those claims that have received support, however, are not directly related to the theory's central proposition that mental illness is simply the acting out of behavioral expectations associated with a particular label. Instead, peripheral issues have been tested, and evidence has been compiled demonstrating that there is indeed an important social aspect to mental illness. Some of the typical ways in which significant others react to abnormal behavior can increase the chances of a person becoming more disordered and remaining ill for a longer period of time. These social reactions can adversely affect the troubled person before, during, and after psychiatric treatment.

One weakness of the labeling theory of deviant behavior in general, and mental disorder in particular, is that it assumes that negative evaluations by others are automatically accepted by an individual. Certainly some people ignore others' criticisms and live mentally healthy lives. What is peculiar to those who accept the label? Is there an inherited weakness or an unconscious problem that leads some to respond poorly to others' evaluations? Clearly, these questions remain to be answered.

Social Networks Perspective

The prior discussion of societal functions and class conflicts is at the macrosociological level involving broad, abstract social forces. These forces are perfectly real, but are hard to relate to everyday questions like: Why did Rotten Ralph from the wrong side of the tracks become a pillar of society? or, Why did Charming Chauncey whose family built the tracks wind up in prison? Some answers to these questions are offered by the analysis of social networks.

A classic attempt to conceptualize deviant behavior in network terms is Edwin Sutherland's (1940) theory of *differential association.* When we look at the entire pattern of social contacts—what we now call the social network—individual predispositions to deviate are revealed. If Rotten Ralph spends most of his time with law-abiding, nose-to-the-grindstone friends and avoids contact with neighborhood pimps and drug dealers, he will probably go straight. If Charming Chauncey falls in with the wrong crowd, on the other hand, they may lead him into a life of crime despite his distinguished family. These "different associates" exert their effects both by interpersonal influence ("Come on, Chauncey, we all did it!"), and by teaching the techniques of proper rule breaking. As Donald R. Cressey (1971) has shown in applying Sutherland's theory to embezzlement, deviance may involve the mastery of sophisticated skills one can only get from other deviants.

A closely related conceptual scheme is the *deviant subculture.* Remember the fact established in Chapter 7 that culture is not uniform throughout a society. There are "core values" in the mainstream of social life, but there are also islands of individuals who share different values. In some cases, paradoxically, these individuals may define deviance from mainstream norms as *normative* behavior for themselves. Since the 1920s, delinquent gangs have been analyzed according to the subculture model. The working assumption that kids in slum neighborhoods are trapped into joining a gang, which then trains them in a "code" of antisocial violence and drug

The bombing of New York City's World Trade Center in 1993 will go down in history as one of the most outrageous acts of international terrorism ever witnessed. The terrorists were a half dozen Fundamentalist Muslims. Each terrorist was sentenced to more than 200 years and each was defiant to the end, even during the sentencing. Sociologists call these people "rebels." The legal system uses terms like "murderers."

use, still has currency. Punks, Skinheads, revivalists, religious cults . . . all can be productively analyzed as subcultures defining deviance in a positive way, and sustaining this view through regular network relations (Fine and Kleinman, 1979).

Recent developments in network research have filled in some of the gaps in explaining deviance and conformity. Not only is social isolation—the lack of a social network—a risk factor in the development of some forms of mental illness, but also the behavior of relatives and friends once symptoms develop affect the diagnosis and treatment of the disorder (Gallagher, 1995). The involvement of networks in patterns of drug use is well known. In *Becoming a Marijuana User* (1953), Howard Becker noted that both the acquisition of the drug and the interpretation of its physical effects as a "high" are face-to-face social processes. Cross-cultural studies have established that peer influences are the strongest predictors of marijuana use in other countries as well as in the United States (Kandel and Adler, 1982). In addition, involvement with family members can both help and hurt alcoholism treatment, the direction of the effect apparently depending on the actual content of family network relations (Hahn and King, 1982).

International terrorism also fits the specifications of social network theory. There is something especially repulsive about people who feel comfortable obliterating a planeload of human lives with a bomb. Yet note how common such acts have become in recent years (Davis and Stasz, 1990). Terrorists have their own deviant subculture—a hotbed of murderous ideas based on the common value of death for the cause. The cause may be sociopathological from the point of view of the rest of the world, but terrorists cling to it with the frenzy of each other's fervor.

Integrating the Theories

The four theories of deviance presented here may make sense but some would say that sense is limited. One limitation is that the theories do not account for people who are truly abnormal and do not fit any sociological explanation. Psychologists would point to the person who inflicts misery on others but who came from a "mainstream" background and did not affiliate with a social network of deviants. Such is the case with "black sheep" from middle-class families. Their brothers and sisters were rule abiding, yet the "black sheep" murdered and/or raped because it was a thrill they sought without any pangs of guilt. What makes such a person tick? It could be a conscience defect stemming from the dynamics of early childhood. Or, as biologists would point out, it could be a tendency for antisocial behavior that stems from a person's constitutional makeup.

The four sociological theories of deviance are neither completely at odds, nor are they mutually exclusive. They can, however, be viewed as an opportunity to apply *critical thinking*. As functionalist theory would predict, people who are denied access to opportunities may turn to deviant means of achieving those goals. As conflict theory would predict, people without opportunities are often so because of the relatively superior power of the privileged. As symbolic interactionism would predict, these same people are especially likely to continue being deviant because they are labeled as such. And, as the social networks perspective would predict, the deviant process is often culturally transmitted within a web of social relationships, which is consistent with all of these scenarios.

Sociological theories of deviance have different degrees of relevance when applied to particular forms of deviance. Crime, for instance, fits all four of the theories well since some of the more common forms of crime, such as robbery and other types of "street crime," are committed typically by socially powerless individuals who associated with people for whom crime was the norm. However, crimes committed by people who do not come from underprivileged backgrounds do not fit the theories as neatly. This is evident in the coming section, "Suite Crime."

Mental disorder, another common form of deviance, has many different causes. Some of the more extreme forms, such as schizophrenia, are often genetic in origin. But other forms, such as antisocial behavior, occur more frequently in the very group predicted by most of the theories—the lower class. A third form of deviance, drug abuse, connects well with the functionalist contention that deviance occurs most frequently among those who are frustrated by the gap between their aspirations and their achievements. But perhaps drug abuse is even more fully explained by the simple fact that it typically occurs among *networks* of people who enjoy the euphoria of drugs for a variety of reasons.

Deviant behaviors, like theories of deviance, often overlap. In a study of the mental health makeup of a criminal population, two of this text's authors found that the typical criminal was not only a lawbreaker but also a person who abused drugs *and* suffered from some type of mental disorder (Jones, Gallagher, Kelley, and Arvanites, 1992). Many of the criminals came from impoverished backgrounds filled with stress (consistent with functionalist and conflict theory) *and* developed a dependency on drugs through interacting with drug-dependent people (consistent with the social networks perspective).

COMMON FORMS OF DEVIANCE

Next we describe some of the current facts about crime, mental disorder, and drug abuse. The chosen facts not only deal with terminology but also with issues such as rates of crime, types of crime, the shattered lives of the mentally disordered both in and out of the hospital, as well as the great costs associated with drug abuse in the United States today.

Crime

Sociological theories of deviance are especially relevant to crime (Barlow, 1993). They can account for why criminal behavior is more common among some groups than others. But they cannot presently account for all individual criminals. John Martini, for instance, is an interesting exception. Born in Yonkers, New York, in 1930, he came from a stable background; was known as a warm, caring family man; and led 33 crime-free years. Then something happened. Beginning with the theft of a truckload of women's underwear, Martini adopted a criminal lifestyle that included eight alleged murders by the time he was 58. He fits none of the theories. People like Martini make it seem natural to think of crime as self-evident evil, a kind of intrinsic defect of human nature. However, cross-cultural studies of crime make it clear that the criminal form of deviance is typically patterned by social forces. Consider a crime as basic as murder. All societies have rules against killing, but the rules are very different cross-culturally. We permit police officers discharging their duty to kill criminals under certain circumstances. However, in some societies, not only would a killing by a stranger be a crime, but cultural norms would actually require family members to kill the killer. At this writing, a Sudanese court is asking the families of seven victims of a terrorist gang's bomb to decide whether the first Palestinians convicted should live or die.

Too exotic? Rather than qualitative differences in the definition of crimes, let us consider quantitative differences in individual evildoers among societies like ours. According to a study by the World Health Organization, the homicide rate (i.e., number of victims per 100,000 people) in the United States was nearly 8 times as high as that in England and West Germany, and more than 10 times the rate in Norway and The Netherlands. Despite an undeclared civil war, one's chance of being murdered in Northern Ireland is 39 percent less than in the United States. These are all further examples of differences in deviant behavior by place.

It is difficult to believe that the United States is one of the most murderous societies on Earth because we somehow have gathered the most evil individuals into our society. Similarly, Canada's population cannot have so much less risk of violent killing simply because more peaceful people have decided to settle north of our border. As one surveys the staggering cross-cultural variety in the types and amounts of crime, a sociological truth becomes increasingly clear—*patterns of criminal behavior grow out of the structure of society rather than from the psyches of individuals.*

Counting Crime

One vantage point on the significance of the crime problem is the simple numbers of individuals who have perpetrated illegal acts. If we look at the number of prisoners in state and federal prisons, some remarkable figures emerge (Conklin, 1992). According to the Bureau of Justice Statistics, the nation's prison population included a record of 673,565 men and women in 1992. As early as 1947, a survey in the New York City metropolitan area revealed that nearly everyone sometimes breaks the law. In Wallerstein and Wyle's classic study (1947), 1,681 out of the 1,698 individuals polled—that is 99 percent—checked off at least one offense sufficiently serious to draw a maximum jail sentence of not less than one year under the New York penal code. Three decades of studies in a variety of communities, states, and regions confirm the basic finding that almost everyone contributes to the social problem of crime by breaking the law.

While it does undermine popular misconceptions about the nature of the criminal, the statistical fact that so many "ordinary" citizens do commit crimes oversimplifies the objective picture of the problem (Barlow, 1993). In the first place, *prevalence* statistics suggesting that nearly everyone breaks the law must be distinguished from measures of *incidence*, which count the frequency of lawbreaking. The fact is that many studies report that the majority of serious offenses are committed by a relatively small minority of **chronic offenders**.

chronic offenders—the people who regularly violate the law.

But a two-group characterization of criminal incidence as bad men versus most-of-the-time good men is likewise too simplistic. One complication is the extent to which criminality exclusively involves men. The results of the National Youth Study (Elliott and Ageton, 1980) shake "sugar and spice" stereotypes of the female noncriminal. But while the prevalence patterns show that many women break the law, the gender gap in incidence looms large for more serious offenses (e.g., the ratio of men to women admitting to larceny over $50 is 11 to 1). Box 9:2 provides some recent statistics on the increasing numbers of women ending up in jail, a phenomenon that has been fueled by the drug epidemic of the 1980s and 1990s.

Another key to the pattern of criminal incidence is age. While there are no national surveys enumerating illegal acts across the entire life course, the National Youth Study uncovers important trends up to age 17. Simply stated, juveniles report committing a lot of crime, much of it while they are quite young. Remarkably, the incidence of some serious violent and property offenses actually peaks among 13- to 15-year-olds (Ageton and Elliott, 1979).

Self-report studies of the frequency of crime have uncovered other aggregate differences between groups of people. African American adolescents, for instance, report more violent offenses and more offenses

BOX 9:2 GENDER AND SOCIAL CHANGE

More Women Landing in Jail

The composition of the prison population typically undergoes many changes over time. It is more common, for instance, for lower-class males to be imprisoned. Now there has been a significant increase in the numbers of female inmates.

There are many forms of negative sanctions for deviance but clearly one stands out as the ultimate—capital punishment. Execution is a hotly debated topic in the United States, but in other parts of the world it is taken for granted and carried out routinely. Magdalena Abakonowicz's sculpture *The Funeral Infantes* suggests the facelessness and anonymity of prison lines and firing squad victims.

When Bucks County's new jail opened in 1985, Warden Art Wallenstein believed that the 26-cell women's unit would be sufficient for 20 years. It had been carefully planned to accommodate more than a 100 percent increase in female inmates.

Four years later, it is overcrowded. The number of female prisoners has exploded from 12 a day in the old prison in 1985 to 63 on a recent day, an increase of more than 400 percent.

Last month, with some women sleeping on mattresses on the floor and 22 living in classrooms, Wallenstein took what he called "extraordinary" action. He moved the female inmates to a much larger, previously male unit of the prison and transferred men into the former women's unit.

What's happening in Bucks County is happening throughout the Philadelphia region. Local jails are overflowing with female prisoners.

The dramatic increases, according to authorities, are mostly due to women committing more drug-related crimes and to recently enacted mandatory jail sentences for those offenses. In addition, some officials and penal experts say that judges, heeding society's

involving cars than white teenagers (Empey, 1982). In addition, the National Youth Study reports a higher incidence of serious crimes against persons and property among lower-class people, although this is the subject of some debate (Tittle, Villemez, and Smith, 1978). The between-race differences in crime rates is likely explained by the fact that African Americans are more likely to come from a lower economic class and therefore subject to the additional frustrations imposed upon the impoverished. Here is another case of variation in deviance between groups.

A second major strategy for measuring crime is counting the number of times individuals are touched by the crime problem. Here again, estimates are derived by both scientific surveys and official statistics.

BOX 9:2 GENDER AND SOCIAL CHANGE *continued*

call for harsher punishment for criminals, are treating women the same as men, abandoning their traditional leniency for women who are mothers and heads of households.

Nationwide, the percentage increase in female prisoners has outpaced that of male inmates in each year since 1981, according to the Bureau of Justice Statistics, an arm of the U.S. Justice Department.

A recent report from the bureau said there were 32,691 female inmates in American jails in 1988, compared with 29,064 in 1987, an increase of 12.5 percent. The male inmate population grew from 555,371 in 1987 to 594,711 in 1988, an increase of 7.1 percent, the bureau said.

In some counties in the Philadelphia region, the increase has been more dramatic: Philadelphia prisons had about 180 female inmates in 1985. Now there are about 300. Camden County's jail averaged between 23 and 25 female inmates in 1985. This year the daily average was 100 to 110. In Chester County, the female population has doubled from an average of between 10 and 12 a day in 1985 to 20 to 25 now. Montgomery County's jail averaged between 22 and 25 female inmates daily in 1985. The average is now 80 a day.

"County jails by and large are not prepared to deal with women, just by virtue of the numbers," said Karen Spinner, director of public education and policy for the New Jersey Association on Correction.

"Women's units are overcrowded more than male units. They are packed in like sardines and they don't get their fair share of services."

As Spinner sees it, "Crime is an equal opportunity employer. In the past there was a perhaps chauvinist attitude that women didn't get jail time where a man might. But society is less tolerant of all kinds of crimes now. We have a tendency to throw the book at criminals. And women are caught up in that phenomenon."

Women are also caught up in what were once considered "male" crimes.

"They are being charged with selling drugs, aggravated assault and even armed robberies, which we never had before, and also drunken driving," said Frame of Chester County.

"Before," said Roth, Montgomery County's warden, "we used to get women for disorderly conduct and once in a blue moon a few prostitutes and some minor violators. We don't have that anymore. They are coming in on serious charges; burglary, selling drugs, and we have quite a few more females this year on murder charges."

Critical Thinking Questions

1. What factors—other than drug abuse—may contribute to the increasing numbers of women in prison?
2. Is there a relationship between the reported increase in the numbers of female criminals and the Women's Movement? If so, describe. If not, why not?

Source: Lacy McCrary, "More Women Landing in Jail" (1989). In *The Philadelphia Inquirer*, December 17, p. 15. By permission of the publisher.

Let us open the discussion with the latter, since these records include one of the best-known enumerations of any American social problem: the Federal Bureau of Investigation's Uniform Crime Reports. This source usually yields annual headlines about national increases or decreases in the crime rate. Most media attention is focused on only the eight crimes that constitute the so-called Index Offenses listed in Figure 9:3. Aggregate numbers of these offenses are taken mainly from citizens' reports of victimization to local law enforcement agencies, who in turn pass the totals to the FBI. In the latest year for which the national statistics are available (Federal Bureau of Investigation, 1987), about 243,400,000 offenses were known to police. That is enough reported crimes to roughly equal the total

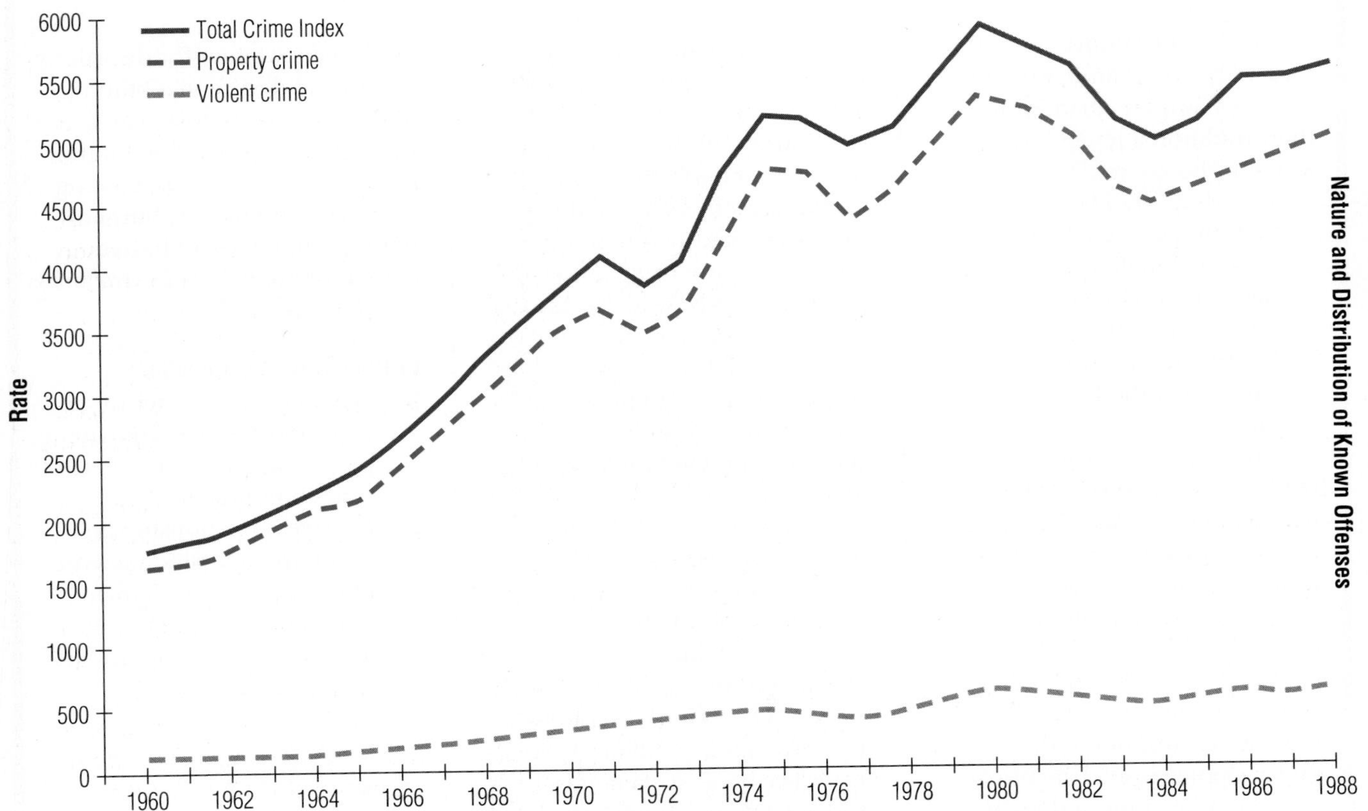

FIGURE 9:3 ESTIMATED RATE (PER 100,000 INHABITANTS) OF OFFENSES KNOWN TO POLICE, BY TYPE OF OFFENSE, UNITED STATES, 1960–1988

Crime has increased enormously over the past three decades, making everyday life a much riskier proposition.

Source: U.S. Department of Justice, Federal Bureau of Investigation, *Crime in the United States,* (Washington, D.C.: U.S. Government Printing Office). Figure constructed by SOURCEBOOK staff.

number of people in the United States. Clearly, the phrase "repeat offender" has merit.

Figure 9:3 displays FBI Index crime rates over the past three decades, and the long-term trend is clear—life has been getting riskier. A typical person's chances of becoming an official statistical victim are much greater now than they were in 1960.

The risk of becoming a victim of violence varies enormously depending on where you live (Barlow, 1993). In fact, if you were to move from a large metropolitan area to a smaller one, and then subsequently to a rural small town, your likelihood of becoming a victim would be cut by about half with each move. This dimension of the crime problem is emphasized because it uncovers the broad social factors looming above individual criminals and their victims. Just as cultural differences across societies materially alter the nature of crime and the identity of criminals, so do community differences within American society also determine a person's chances of being robbed, raped, or murdered; and, college campuses are far from safe. They are rife with violent crime, including murder and rape. See Box 9:3 for one horrifying example.

Finally, consider a couple concrete—and chilling—illustrations of the levels of risk of becoming a victim of a violent attack. Roughly 6 percent of white males in the 12 to 15 age group are victims of violence in a typical year, and there is a staggering 1 chance in 21 that an African American male will eventually become a homicide victim (Conklin, 1992).

Another fact about victimization is that people who are most likely to be victimized are not necessarily the ones who fear it most. Data from the General Social Survey show that, while males are more likely to be victims of

BOX 9:3 COLLEGE EXPERIENCE

Crime on Campus

The issue of crime on campus has reared its head in the 1990s. Like many other social concerns, it is uncertain whether campus crime is actually rising or simply being reported more frequently. The case described here is real and extreme—the unsolved murder of a student.

Jeanne Clery, Lehigh University Class of '89, would have graduated last June 4. Instead, her dreams and her parents' hopes for her ended forever on April 5, 1986. At 5:00 a.m. that day, the 19-year-old freshman awoke to find fellow student Joseph Henry burglarizing her dorm room. Henry raped and beat Jeanne savagely. Then he strangled her.

At the University of California at Berkeley in 1987, a gang of teens police call a "rat pack" followed three students to their dormitory. Words were exchanged, and a pack member suddenly smashed the face of a female student with a brick.

Despite the idyllic images college brochures present, violence is a fact of life on the nation's campuses. Last year colleges reported to the FBI a total of 1990 violent crimes—robbery, aggravated assault, rape and murder. This is a startling number, considering the fact that almost 90 percent of U.S. colleges do not report crime statistics. The incidence of property crime was even greater—more than 107,000 cases of burglary, larceny, arson and motor-vehicle theft at reporting schools alone. Shockingly, 78 percent of the violent crimes were committed by students, according to the Center for the Study and Prevention of Campus Violence, at Towson State University in Maryland.

WANTED BY THE FBI

INTERSTATE FLIGHT - MURDER

THEODORE ROBERT BUNDY

DESCRIPTION

Born November 24, 1946, Burlington, Vermont (not supported by birth records); Height, 5'11" to 6'; Weight, 145 to 175 pounds; Build, slender, athletic; Hair, dark brown, collar length; Eyes, blue; Complexion, pale / sallow; Race, white; Nationality, American; Occupations, bellboy, busboy, cook's helper, dishwasher, janitor, law school student, office worker, political campaign worker, psychiatric social worker, salesman, security guard; Scars and Marks, mole on neck, scar on scalp; Social Security Number used, 533-44-4655; Remarks, occasionally stammers when upset; has worn glasses, false mustache and beard as disguise in past; left-handed; can imitate British accent; reportedly physical fitness and health enthusiast.

CRIMINAL RECORD

Bundy has been convicted of aggravated kidnaping.

CAUTION

UNDY, A COLLEGE-EDUCATED PHYSICAL FITNESS ENTHUSIAST WITH A PRIOR ISTORY OF ESCAPE, IS BEING SOUGHT AS A PRISON ESCAPEE AFTER BEING CONVICTED F KIDNAPING AND WHILE AWAITING TRIAL INVOLVING A BRUTAL SEX SLAYING OF A OMAN AT A SKI RESORT. HE SHOULD BE CONSIDERED ARMED, DANGEROUS AND AN CAPE RISK.

Campus security is a huge and highly visible issue these days. Some colleges have their own security forces complete with patrol guards, surveillance systems and sophisticated, hi-tech head-quarters. This is a far cry from the 1960s and 1970s when serial killers like Ted Bundy had little trouble accessing students' living quarters.

Traditionally most colleges have kept quiet about crime. Fearing adverse publicity, they have tended to deal with offenders internally instead of referring them for prosecution.

The Clerys were a major force behind a new Pennsylvania law that requires all colleges in the state to disclose crime statistics. They also advocate federal legislation requiring such disclosure.

The failure of colleges to warn about crime has created a dangerous situation. Too often, parents and students are unaware of the hazards of life on campus. But concerned parents, students and college administrators are taking action around the country and setting examples for others to follow.

Critical Thinking Questions

1. What impact has crime had on your campus? Are there effective measures of control, or are some illegal acts ignored?
2. Assume for the moment that there has been a real rise in campus crime over recent decades. What factors might contribute to a more lawless college environment?

Source: Adapted from Marie Hodge and Jeff Blyskal, "Who Says College Campuses Are Safe?" (October, 1989). In *Readers Digest*, pp. 141–48. By permission of the publisher.

TABLE 9:3 Are You Afraid to Walk at Night in Your Neighborhood[a]

GENDER	FEAR[a]			
	Yes		No	
	Percent	Frequency	Percent	Frequency
Male	18.2	141	81.8	632
Female	56.3	580	43.7	451

[a]Main Point: Women have much more fear of becoming a victim of crime than men, even though men are more likely to be victims of crime.

Source: General Social Survey, 1972–1987.

crime, females fear it more (see Table 9:3). Public awareness and fear of crime has formally reached college campuses in Pennsylvania through the nation's first "right-to-know" measure about crime on campus (see Box 9:3). The law—called the College and University Security Information Act—requires schools to compile statistics about on-campus crime and make these available to the public. Some colleges fear that the law will cause a drop in enrollment.

Suite Crime

Suite crime is a play on the familiar phrase "street crime" and our new term for what is traditionally called "white-collar crime." The voluminous *Sourcebook of Criminal Justice Statistics* presents more than 100 pages of data on public attitudes toward various aspects of crime, yet not a single poll concentrates on the white-collar criminal. The point is not that people are unaware of the existence of white-collar criminals; E.F. Hutton, ABSCAM, and other well-publicized fraud schemes have put white collar crime before

Bhopal, India, was the scene of the famous Union Carbide "accident." The result was death by corporate mismanagement, though the immediate cause was a chemical leak. This is an example of "suite crime," a type of criminal action that may draw protest but not necessarily time in prison.

the public eye. It is just that, with rare exceptions, people seem to see no serious evil there. This lack of concern may reflect the widespread erroneous perception that few are affected badly by suite crime. Although less dramatic and obvious than a street criminal putting a gun to somebody's head and pulling the trigger, the effects of white-collar crime are no less lethal (Pontell, 1993).

Consider the Buffalo Creek disaster in which a dam of coal wastes burst, killing 125 people and leaving some 5,000 homeless in the flooded towns. The disaster was a result of the irresponsible corporate decisions of the Buffalo Mining Company (owned by the Pittston Corporation), later found culpable by the courts. Or consider the case of "Pinto Madness" in which the car was marketed despite dangers documented by Ford (the manufacturer) studies. According to an internal company memo, the total costs of installing a plastic piece that would prevent the car from exploding on rear-end impact ($11 dollars per car, $137 million total) were balanced against the corporate legal costs of the estimated l80 burn deaths a year ($200,000 per death, $49.5 million total), and a criminal decision was reached: Put profits ahead of safety.

Whether or not you would call these cases cold-blooded mass murder, there is certainly clear evidence of real injuries caused by people wearing white collars. Isolated examples? No: "Corporate crime is exceedingly violent, killing and maiming thousands of people each year" (Kramer, 1983, p. 181).

The fact that white-collar criminals cause serious economic harm is even better documented (Conklin, 1992). In one study focusing on 300 white-collar felons, the upper level of the studied group was involved in frauds averaging more than $22 million (and their prison sentences averaged less than a single year; Bequai, 1978). One exception, however, to the rule of thumb that white-collar criminals go relatively unpunished occurred in 1989 when Jim Bakker, the television evangelist, received a 45-year prison term and a $500,000 fine on nine counts of fraud. Characteristically, his attorney said he was shocked at the stiff punishment because Bakker was, after all, *only* a white-collar criminal.

To bring the point even closer to home—perhaps your own home—take the case of income tax evasion. In the aggregate, U.S. citizens now cheat their own government of $120 billion annually (or about $500 per person compared to the average larceny theft loss of $340). Lest this lead to holier-than-thou thoughts about the moral decay of the older generation, about $4 billion has been stolen from the government (and thus from other taxpayers) by students defaulting on college loans.

Other so-called victimless crimes include prostitution, an age-old, worldwide phenomenon. However, as Figure 9:4 indicates, prostitution is a cross-cultural constant although its prevalence varies significantly from society to society.

Juvenile Delinquency

A whole special category of crime (juvenile delinquency) is reserved for youth. Unfortunately, the definition of this category is unclear. Although many jurisdictions officially decree adulthood to begin at age 18, upper-age limits for the juvenile offender in some areas vary between ages 15 and 21. As little agreement as there is on what constitutes a juvenile, there is even less certainty regarding the definition of delinquency. One-third of the states do not even have a statutory definition; among those states that do, a survey of statutes has found some 25 separate acts or conditions

FIGURE 9:4 FREQUENCY OF PROSTITUTION IN THE WORLD
Prostitution exists in all parts of the world but is especially common in societies where women, in comparison to men, have a low social standing.
Source: Peters Atlas of the World. (1990). New York: Harper & Row, pp. 180–81.

defining delinquency (Eldefonso, 1978). This is another example of variation in the definition of deviance by place.

One clear distinction of delinquents from adult criminals involves so-called status offenses. These are various acts not defined as illegal if committed by adults. Juveniles can be picked up by the police for being runaways or truants (imagine how many of you would be arrested if cutting class were against the law), or even for such vague behavior as being "incorrigible," "wayward," or "stubborn." In California alone, an average of 100,000 status offenders are arrested annually (Eldefonso, 1978).

In recent years, societal pressure has been building to overhaul the juvenile justice system. Some experts have argued that the dubious benefits of "kiddie courts" in preventing future crimes are not worth the tradeoff in juveniles' constitutional rights. Due in part to well-publicized episodes of youth violence, there has been a rising public perception of both the seriousness of delinquency and the leniency of juvenile courts. This increasing subjective dimension of youthful deviance has provided political support for the growing numbers of juveniles who are being diverted into the adult criminal system (U.S. Department of Justice, 1984).

Mental Disorder

Mental disorder is not only an agonizing personal experience but also a major social problem, as evidenced by a large number of studies reporting that an alarmingly high percentage of the American population is mentally disordered (Gallagher, 1995). Although there is a wide array of estimates, the National Institute of Mental Health found that, in a typical year, approximately 20 percent of Americans have some type of mental disorder at any given time. Additionally, approximately 80 percent of the population have mild psychiatric symptoms at some point in their lives. This means that almost every person reading this book has experienced mental illness themselves or seen it firsthand somewhere in their social network.

Perhaps no other issue better exemplifies the dramatic difference between the objective and subjective dimensions of deviance than mental disorder. Because so many victims go untreated, the objective dimension of

Mental disorder is one of the most serious and widespread social problems in the United States today. Depression is one of the most common forms of mental disorder, affecting millions of people. In its extreme form, depression can reach suicidal heights.

the problem is broader than any official statistics indicate. Yet even the official statistics would shock most people because mental disorder has traditionally been denied, ignored, or explained away as something else.

The public is also largely unaware of the total economic costs of mental disorder to American society. Although the costs cannot be precisely determined, an estimate is offered by the National Foundation for Brain Research to be about $136 billion in 1991. This figure includes private fees and taxpayer dollars for government-supported institutions. The average annual cost of caring for each patient in a state mental hospital alone is more than $90,000. There are other indirect costs that could be added to the direct costs of patient care, such as a 25 percent loss of productivity to the workforce due to employee illness and inefficiency.

medicalization—people's abnormal behavior being viewed as a medical problem requiring treatment by physicians.

For a long time, psychoanalysis was the dominant perspective in psychiatric research and treatment. Psychoanalysis is a lengthy, intense "talking out" approach between a patient and therapist. It was originally developed by Sigmund Freud. Currently there is a **medicalization** of mental disorder taking place. This means abnormal behavior is becoming more frequently defined as a medical problem that should be handled by physicians only through treatments such as hospitalization and drugs. This is partly a reflection of the substantial political power the medical profession has gained through its special-interest group: the American Medical Association (AMA). Alternative professions, such as clinical psychology and psychiatric social work, have far less power. Another reason for the medicalization of mental health problems is the limited success of social approaches to mental health care, such as the community-based mental health clinics. These have failed miserably because of such problems as limited funding and poorly trained staffs.

Stress and Mental Disorder

One of the factors related to the onset of mental disorder is stress. Many people who seek treatment have experienced an unusual number of stressful events in the weeks or months prior to their breakdowns. In some instances, stress may be a direct cause of mental disorder and not simply a precipitant. Holmes and Rahe (1967) have measured the amount of stress produced by various types of events. The death of a spouse, for instance, is more stressful than being fired at work, which is more stressful than trouble with one's in-laws. Although some of the events in their list are intrinsically pleasant (such as getting married), all of the events are stressful because they require people to readjust their lives. Holmes and Rahe report that people with a high life-crisis score during a particular period of time are especially likely to become disordered. Others find that high scores on life-events scales are related to suicide attempts and heart disease as well as to psychiatric symptoms (Dean and Lin, 1977). Stress has become such an important topic today in sociology that a specific group of sociologists devote much of their research toward understanding the nuances of stress and how it affects (and is affected by) other variables such as social networks and mental health. These sociologists are known as "sociological stress researchers" (Pearlin, 1989).

Of course, not all people are affected equally by life changes. Some appear to have an emotional insulation against stress, whereas others are quite vulnerable. The vulnerable people (the genetically predisposed, the biochemically imbalanced, or those who were improperly socialized) may react dramatically to seemingly trivial events. This may be because the events uncover old, recurring problems and give them new meaning, as in the case of the rejected woman whose sister becomes happily married.

There is no doubt that stressful life events can deteriorate mental health over time. It is also evident that particular social roles, such as the stressfulness of women's family roles, can affect psychological well-being (Kandel, Davies, and Ravies, 1985). Is it also possible that specific people are vulnerable to stress, whereas others ("hardy personalities") are barely affected? A number of studies report that the reaction to stress depends on whether the person has adequate social supports, such as friends and relatives (see Chapter 4). Some believe that supportive people can act as a buffer against stressful events by providing sympathy and advice. Inadequate social supports may be why certain groups (such as single people) have high rates of mental disorder; life events could have a greater impact on them because supportive others are not available to mediate the effects of the stress.

Problems of Mass Discharge

Today we witness a mass discharge of disordered people into the community. Community mental health clinics are supposed to be treating these people, but have largely failed to do so. Many of the patients released from state hospitals have moved into inner-city areas or neighborhoods near the hospital, creating psychiatric ghettos. They live in boarding homes that house only schizophrenics, manic-depressives, the retarded, alcoholics, drug addicts, and the marginally menacing. The boarders mostly wander aimlessly around mildly sedated, or lie on their beds sorting out bewildering thoughts. They have been simply dumped into the community, still hearing voices, still hallucinating, still paranoid, and still with the unmistakable look of the deranged. Others are not fortunate enough to even

Anguish, pain, social isolation, and psychic hell are some of the terms commonly used to refer to the despair of people who are severely mentally ill. This photo was taken in a "back ward" of a state mental hospital, where people waste their lives away watching television, smoking cigarettes to the butt, and engaging in conversations with imaginary others. Scenes like this are less common today with the movement toward "deinstitutionalization." This does not mean that the mentally ill are better off; they are simply in a different place—out on the streets where things are even worse.

have a roof over their heads. They constitute part of the growing number of destitute people commonly referred to as the homeless or street people. This is a classic instance of one social policy causing another, new social problem. To date, more than 400,000 patients have been released into the squalor of boarding homes or the ranks of the homeless, a process known as **deinstitutionalization** (Torrey, 1988).

deinstitutionalization—the mass release of patients from mental hospitals into the community.

Drugs

While it is true that illegal drugs have become an increasingly common part of our everyday lives, it is also true that drug abuse has become a major public policy issue. Increasing concern over the dangers of drugs has led to growing support for mandatory drug screening through urine testing since the military began using it in 1982. And, in 1986, President Reagan declared a "war on drugs," calling for mandatory drug screening of hundreds of thousands of federal workers, the death penalty in some drug-related murder cases, and a $3.1 billion drug-abuse program. In 1987, Reagan partially reversed himself by calling for a $915 million cutback in funding for 1988. And in 1989, President Bush pushed for a new attack against drugs centered on major points of origin such as Colombia. This move has provoked South American "drug lords" into murderous attacks on government officials and their families. The problems continue through the years of the Clinton administration. They are a prime example of the worldwide interconnection of social issues. These may not be problems without positive benefits. As functionalist theory suggests, a phenonemon like a war on drugs is also a battle against a perceived loss of moral values. The international tension and murderous acts, which are part of a war on drugs, may be the necessary costs of reestablishing moral boundaries.

In the past, alcohol and tobacco were the common avenues to pleasure. Alcohol is still a common drug, reaching the bloodstreams of some 100 million people each year. But today our country faces problems with other chemical substances including heroin, cocaine, amphetamines, and barbiturates. The menu of substances expands with regularity; in 1989, law enforcement encountered a smokable form of speed called "ice." It is already rivaling crack cocaine as a health and crime problem in Hawaii and Southern California.

What is a *drug problem*? The term means different things to different people. To some, the use of drugs is itself a serious problem, but to others the *effects* of drug use constitute the problem. Those holding the latter view feel that as long as drug use does not harm society, the government should not interfere with individual choices. One common view of a drug problem is that the use of some drugs is deviant regardless of effects. This highly subjective view typically reflects the values of mainstream culture and does not always reflect the objective harm of different drugs. Heroin, for instance, is used largely by minority groups and has traditionally been repressed by society. Yet it causes fewer health problems than alcohol and cigarettes, which are more socially acceptable. Alcohol is actually the drug that takes the most expensive toll on the nation. It is a cradle-to-grave threat beginning with the fact that it is directly linked to 5,000 cases of birth defects a year and ending with its role in an estimated 200,000 deaths a year. Marijuana is another case in point. At one time it was highly unacceptable, but when its use shifted in the 1960s to middle-class college youth, attitudes toward it liberalized.

This painting by African-American artist William H. Johnson is titled *Chain Gang.* It is a human drama intertwining race and violation of the law. Johnson's art is known for its visually throbbing pictorial structure.

Economic Cost of Drugs

A number of estimates have been made on how much drugs cost society economically. In 1990, Americans' addiction to alcohol and other chemical substances drained from the economy more than $170 billion annually in reduced productivity, days lost from work, and medical bills. In 1990, the U.S. Department of Health and Human Services estimated that excessive drinking alone cost $117 billion in medical costs and lost work hours. In 1986, the National Institute on Drug Abuse estimated that on-the-job drug and alcohol abuse by workers cost U.S. automakers $175 per vehicle in lost productivity and increased injury claims. There are many other indirect costs paid to support drug-dependent persons that should be added to the total bill. These include treatment and control of drug abuse, welfare funds to support the unemployable drug abuser, and the costs of processing drug users through the criminal justice system (Davis and Stasz, 1990). The impact of drugs on the criminal justice system is especially dramatic and demonstrates the interrelationship among different forms of deviance. Because so many drug users commit crimes to support their habit, U.S. prisons are overflowing with inmates. Additionally, prisons are not only overcrowded but also are ill-equipped to rehabilitate arrested drug offenders.

Although it is difficult to measure accurately the total economic costs of drug abuse, it clearly exacts a huge financial toll on society. Regular annual reports of the International Narcotics Control Board state that drug trafficking and the abuse of illegal narcotics have become so pervasive worldwide that national economies are being disrupted and the very security of some countries threatened.

SUMMARY

1. We began this chapter by telling you that deviance is complicated. Now you know some of the reasons why. First, it occurs in people who run the gamut from everyday good citizens to grossly deranged serial killers.
2. Second, there is a great deal of disagreement about how to define it.
3. Third, deviance takes many forms—from being drunk in public to cheating on tax returns to mass murder.
4. Fourth, all we have are theories about what causes deviant behavior; there is no final consensus about the theories.
5. Although your final reaction to reading this chapter may be that deviance is an unfortunate fact of life, there is the paradoxical possibility that deviant behavior has some positive functions by promoting social unity and identifying social problems.
6. We want to leave you with the proposition that deviance is an unfortunate cost of living in a free society. If we were not guaranteed such things as freedom of expression and religion, would we have fewer people involved with pornography and cult groups like the religious fanatics who captured 1993 national headlines in Waco, Texas? Probably. Totalitarian societies may not experience the degree and diversity of deviant behavior we find in the United States, but they may exact a qualitatively different price in doing so: the price of individual liberty.

Chapter 10

Personal Perspective

IT was the fall semester of 1966 at the Madison Campus of the University of Wisconsin. We were walking to the Business School, where Dow Chemical Company was scheduled to send its recruiters that day. We had not signed up to interview with Dow Chemical, however. Dow Chemical Company manufactured napalm, which was thrown from planes to burn foliage in Vietnam. In the process, napalm also killed women, children, animals, and anything else nearby. Instead, some of us were going to demonstrate outside the building, while the rest planned a sit-in in the narrow corridors to prevent the Dow recruiters from entering. I was one of hundreds of students squeezed into the halls. We filled all of the available space. We sang "We Shall Overcome" and other rallying tunes. After about an hour, state policemen suddenly loomed in the doorway, wearing gas masks. They began pelting us with tear-gas canisters. The canisters hit the floor and spewed their noxious fumes. With barely registered shock, I raced with everyone else for the exit. People fled crying; there is no other option when tear-gas sears your eyeballs.

Later that day when I was capable of thought, I felt extraordinarily betrayed by the university; the university had never before called in an outside policing force to discipline its students. By so doing, the university had breached an unspoken agreement with us. We were a family! How could they turn on us, their own students, and give us up for slaughter by these militaristic aliens?

Apparently, many other students shared my sentiments. The heaving of tear-gas canisters at students lathered us into a rage. Rational thought evaporated, it seemed. The phrase "crowd psychology" comes to mind. By the afternoon a frenzied crowd had amassed on Bascom Hill, the oldest part of campus, which housed the liberal arts buildings. Someone set up a public address system to incite the masses—not a difficult task, at that point.

Collective Behavior and Social Movements

By launching stones and obscenities at buildings and storming the Student Union, we expressed our shared sense of betrayal. On that day, interest in the civil rights movement died. All of our energies became focused on the anti-war protest. The most immediate personification of the pro-war government became the university itself. We were at war with the university. The tear-gassing incident was concrete evidence to us that the university was conspiring with Dow Chemical and with the military, too, we believed. On that day, the campus was "radicalized."

CC

social movement—a conscious, collective, organized attempt to bring about or resist large-scale change in the social order by non-institutionalized means.

THESE phenomena, fairly common in the 1960s, seem somewhat bizarre in the retelling in the 1990s. What insights can sociologists offer to help us understand sit-ins, protests, demonstrations, and other similar behaviors? The events described in the "Personal Perspective" are examples of collective behavior—socially shared, but noninstitutionalized responses to events or ideas. These nonroutine responses differ (often radically) from the more habitual patterns of everyday life in which people follow established social norms (Rose, 1982). Collective behavior tends to involve large numbers of people who frequently do not even know each other. Thus, a clothing fashion—blue jeans with holes in the knees—a craze of Cabbage Patch Dolls™, Hula Hoops™ in the 1950s, bungee jumping in the 1980s and a rumor that the world is going to end on a specific date, are examples of collective behavior. A demonstration or other out-of-the-ordinary crowd action, such as the rioting in south-central Los Angeles following the not guilty verdict in the Rodney King police brutality case in 1992, are also cases of collective behavior.

Occasionally, collective behavior is transformed into a **social movement**, "a conscious, collective, organized attempt to bring about or resist large scale change in the social order by non-institutionalized means" (Wilson, 1973, p. 8). Sociologists who take a functionalist perspective tend to group social movements and collective behavior together. They see both as involving breaks with established social norms and as disrupting the social order. Those who favor a conflict perspective, however, argue that most social movements are only superficially related to sudden, irrational phenomena, such as fads, mass hysteria, and panics. In their view, social movements are the result of rational thought and planning. They represent intentional efforts to resist or create change by a group that lacks the power to alter the system through means other than mass protest. From the conflict perspective, then, collective behavior and social movements are quite separate and different phenomena.

TYPES OF COLLECTIVE BEHAVIOR

Spontaneous Forms of Collective Behavior

Events that are relatively spontaneous are often also short-lived, expressive, and lack clear goals. Such widespread phenomena as just described are so unpredictable that they are assumed to be irrational as well. But even the most unstructured form of collective behavior is rarely random. By examining some cases in detail, we can uncover the social processes underlying apparently spur-of-the-moment activities.

Fads are one of the more superficial forms of collective behavior. They come and go with great speed and for the most part, they do not make a permanent impression on a society's cultural base. Here are three examples. In the 1950s, a lot of people twirled with Hula Hoops. You may still find an occasional one in the forgotten corner of a garage. The 1980s witnessed the popularity of cute little "kid's things," called Cabbage Patch Dolls. In the 1990s, things got hot, heavy, and potentially deadly with bungee jumping.

Mass Hysteria

On March 23, 1954, Seattle newspapers carried the first of several stories about damage to automobile windshields in a town 80 miles to the north of the city. The windshields contained small pit marks and bubbles, a few with very small metallic particles embedded in the glass. Police suspected rowdy vandals but had no clear evidence.

On the evening of April 14, the mysterious destruction appeared in Seattle. Over the next two days, the Seattle police received nearly 250 calls reporting windshield damage to more than 3,000 cars. The most widely circulating explanation for the damage was radioactive fallout from H-Bomb tests in the North Pacific. As this theory swept Seattle, terrified residents desperately attempted to devise protective shields. By the evening of April 15, the mayor had appealed to the governor and the president for emergency help. Then, inexplicably, the mass hysteria disappeared as quickly as it had appeared. Later, experts determined that the pit marks had always been in the windshields. People simply had not noticed them before because drivers usually look *through* their windshields, not *at* them (Medalia and Larson, 1958).

At first glance this case of mass hysteria—an uncontrollable emotional outburst, often of fear, by a group of people—seems to have arisen out of nowhere. Someone in the Seattle area first noticed pits in a windshield and called others' attention to them. This led to more being noticed, until an epidemic was in motion and strange rumors were voiced, causing people to panic. Sociologists have found, however, that, as bizarre as these incidents seem, a number of determining factors can be identified.

First, Seattle is a densely populated area in which rapid, widespread communication is possible through newspapers and radio. Second, Seattle residents were then under psychological strain because of their physical proximity to hydrogen bomb test sites. They were concerned about possible harm from nuclear fallout but did not know how to protect themselves. Third, a general belief had been fostered by the local press, which, for several months before the windshield-pitting incident, had published stories about recent hydrogen bomb tests in the Pacific Ocean. One headline announced "Atomic Energy Commission Discloses Blast Amid Mounting Concern." Another warned, "Witness Says Hydrogen Test Out Of Control." A third stated "Three H-Bomb Victims Face Death." Such distressing reports helped substantiate people's fears.

Then a precipitating event occurred—the discovery of a few pitted windshields. To people already in the grip of apprehension about nuclear testing, these discoveries were interpreted as clear evidence of looming, horrible consequences of nuclear fallout. This terror resulted in mass hysteria. For other examples of this phenomenon, known as "urban legends," see Box 10:1.

Rumors

rumor—an often unreliable story that circulates quickly from person to person and is accepted as true, though its source may be unknown.

The Seattle windshield-pitting hysteria was spurred both by front-page news coverage of what was felt to be an emergency and by rapidly spread rumors among area residents. A **rumor** is an often unreliable story that circulates quickly from person to person and is accepted as fact, although its original source may be unknown. Rumors proliferate in tense and ambiguous situations and often resonate with existing anxieties and prejudices, as when stories about tainted hamburgers confirm our worst fears about fast-food restaurants.

BOX 10:1 SOCIOLOGICAL IMAGINATION IN FICTION

Urban Legends and Social Networks

The two "classic" modern urban legends summarized here are stories that have been told as true in different locales across the United States for at least a decade. They are believed by most tellers and a great many listeners. These two tales are just the "bare bones" of the stories as they are told and lack specific local details. One quality of the urban legend is its spontaneity. Each time it is told, it becomes slightly different. Here, in each story, only the major stable elements are presented.

"The Boyfriend's Death"

A teenage couple is driving to a party when they run out of gas. The boy tells the girl that he's going to get some gas, and he'll return shortly. "Lock the doors and don't open them for anyone," he warns her, "you never know what kind of a maniac might come by." Some time passes, and the girl hears a scraping on the roof of the car—"scrape, scrape, scrape." She becomes very frightened and hides in the car. An hour goes by, then two, then three. The scraping continues all night—"scrape, scrape, scrape." By now, the girl is scared to death, but she dozes off. She awakens when the sun comes up. A police officer is at the window with a horrified look on his face; his patrol car is parked nearby. He indicates to the girl that she should get out of the car, which she does. "Come with me," he says, "and don't look back!!" But she does look back and sees her boyfriend hanging by a rope from a tree branch, his shoes scraping against the roof of the car (Brunvand, 1981, pp. 5–10).

"The Poison Dress"

A young woman was invited to a dance. For the occasion she purchased an elegant dress from a local department store. During the dance, she began feeling dizzy, and her escort noticed an

Rumor-mongering is not merely a consequence of idle curiosity, although rumors about the latest sighting of Elvis in a supermarket or the rumor that the green M & M's™ make people more sexy may appear so on the surface (Brunvand, 1988; Wachs, 1988). What about the Halloween rumors of a sadist who hands out apples containing razor blades (Best, 1985)? These stories are rarely verified, yet they are widely repeated and believed partially because they reflect people's desire to find meaning in events that are perceived as beyond personal control—evil in the world, fear of death, people who prey on children, and a general feeling of powerlessness in the modern world. In a sense, rumors may be a form of group problem solving.

In Seattle, residents thought that the pittings in their windshields were caused by radioactive fallout from nuclear bomb tests. Although this interpretation was later shown to be incorrect, it did temporarily solve people's dilemma of finding some explanation for the mysterious damage. Similarly, in Chicago in 1968, rumors surfaced at the mayor's office that demonstrators at the Democratic convention planned to assassinate the presidential candidates and lace the city's water supply with LSD (Albert and Albert, 1984). These rumors, however unlikely, were people's way of understanding the protestors' threat to come to Chicago.

BOX 10:1 SOCIOLOGICAL IMAGINATION IN FICTION *continued*

unusual odor emanating from the dress. She went into the women's room, took off the dress, and examined it. There appeared to be nothing wrong with the dress, so she put it back on and returned to the dance. Throughout the evening, she continued to feel faint and the odor remained. Her escort decided to take her home and call a doctor, but the young woman died before the doctor arrived. An autopsy was performed that revealed formaldehyde in her bloodstream, which caused her blood to stop flowing. An investigation found the dress she purchased had originally been bought and was worn by a corpse, but it was returned to the store and resold to the young woman. When she wore it, the formaldehyde entered her body through her pores and killed her (Brunvand, 1984, pp. 112–14).

What is the appeal of these urban legends? Aren't we knowledgeable enough in the late twentieth century to squelch these legends each time they are told to us? Most of these tales contain at least one element that is *so* unlikely to be all but impossible. A dress that once draped a corpse is unlikely to have been returned to a store and resold to another customer, and it is unlikely to have absorbed enough formaldehyde to kill its wearer.

Moreover, many of these stories depend tremendously on coincidence: someone being in exactly the right place at exactly the right time. Yet, these legends do circulate. Jan Brunvand (1981) suggests that these tales possess certain characteristics that make it likely that we will tell and retell them.

According to Brunvand (1981) stories will become urban legends to the extent that they contain the following factors: (1) they tell a strong, interesting, dramatic story; (2) they tell a story with a meaningful moral or message; (3) they reflect contemporary fears; (4) they contain a "grain of truth" with respect to current beliefs; (5) they supply supportive detail or local color; (6) they point to a credible source; and (7) they are circulated by the mass media. These tales become perceived as true *because* they are passed on from one person to another and are told and retold, thus making them real. Informal social networks function to give credibility to these legends.

Critical Thinking Questions

1. How is people's attraction to these "urban legends" similar to people's liking for frightening horror movies?
2. What can we learn about the power of social networks from the passing on of these urban legends?

Competitiveness and secrecy encourage rumors. War and politics give rise to many rumors, as do financial dealings. The competition and secrecy that encompass important exams make college students especially receptive to rumors. In the former Soviet Union, where an authoritarian regime restricted the free flow of reliable information, people relied extensively on word-of-mouth rumors to help make sense of current events (Rosnow and Fine, 1976).

Most rumors are born, passed on, and meet their death within a relatively short period of time. After studying the transmission of rumors, psychologists Gordon Allport and Leo Postman (1947) discovered a basic pattern in them, a pattern that resembles the child's game "Whisper Down the Lane." A person hears an interesting story and repeats it—or what he or she remembers of it—to a friend. Gradually, the original story is reduced to a few essentials, a process Allport and Postman call *leveling*. As a consequence of leveling, certain details are spotlighted, and the rumor is sharpened.

As a rumor circulates, people also alter details to make the story both more coherent and more consistent with their existing attitudes or expectations. In one of Allport and Postman's experiments, for example, a story about an ambulance carrying explosives became changed through retelling

College campuses were the center of social protest and social change during the 1960s and 1970s. Who can forget this shocking photograph of a dead Kent State University student? He was one of four students killed by the National Guard during one day of on-campus protest of the U.S. invasion of Cambodia in 1970. On that day, participation in a social movement literally meant putting your life on the line.

to a story about an ambulance carrying medical supplies. The retold version more closely conformed with people's expectations. Similarly, in the summer of 1968, anti-war activists adorned rumors that the Chicago police would deal severely with demonstrators (attacking them with dogs, jailing them in sewers) because they expected such harsh treatment from the governing establishment.

Panic

panic—the relatively rapid spread of fear from one person to another.

Just as rumors are products of tension and stress, so often is panic—the relatively rapid spread of fear from one person to another. The 1954 hysteria over pitted windshields in Seattle involved some panic. Panics occur on Wall Street when buyers, fearing losses, sell off securities, creating a tremendous drop in values, which in turn leads to more selling.

Researchers have studied many incidents of panic. In 1972, for example, 35 women who worked in a university data processing center were stricken with nausea, dizziness, and fainting spells (Stahl and Lebedum, 1974). Ten had such severe symptoms that they had to be hospitalized. Rumors circulated that the symptoms were caused by an unidentified gas leaking into the data processing workrooms. Investigators closed the building and searched for the alleged gas but found nothing. No traces of toxic gases could be located in the victims' bloodstreams. Nonetheless, when the building was reopened for work the next day, more people became ill. Again, the building was shut down, and again a thorough investigation produced no physical cause for the symptoms.

Investigators did find, however, a consistent social psychological pattern among those women with the most severe symptoms. They tended to be those most dissatisfied with their jobs. The spread of severe symptoms itself also followed a social pattern. The women who became most ill did not work close to one another, as would be expected if a toxic gas was the cause.

Instead, symptoms spread along friendship networks, regardless of physical proximity or distance to one another in the workplace. Such findings are strong evidence of a panic caused by social contagion.

Crowd Behavior

Types of Crowds

Temporary collections of people who gather around a person or event and who are conscious of and influenced by one another's presence are called crowds. Crowds differ from other social groups primarily in that they are short-lived and loosely structured, and often use conventional areas or buildings for unconventional purposes (Snow, Zurcher, and Peters, 1981). The scope of a crowd is also limited to its actual members at a given time.

In his classic essay, "Collective Behavior," sociologist Herbert Blumer (1951) described four kinds of crowds. One is a *casual* crowd, which forms spontaneously when something attracts passing people's attention. When a number of people walking along a city street pause to view the effects of a wrecking ball on an old building, they form a casual crowd. The members of this kind of crowd give only temporary recognition to the object that has caught their interest and have the most minimal association with one another.

In contrast, passengers on a plane, shoppers in a store, and an audience at a concert or a sporting event compose a *conventional* crowd. Members of

Conventional crowds gather for a particular reason such as a sporting event. In the United States, people perform the "wave" at a football game. In some countries, it is not unusual for crowds of athletic contests to turn violent. Soccer games, for instance, have often turned into ugly confrontations between rival fans.

Eugene Delacroix's *Liberty Leading the People* shows a mob storming the Bastille in France in 1789. Scenes such as these were common at the time of the French Revolution. Part of Gustave LeBon's theory of the power and collective mind of mobs was rooted in that well-known civil war. This painting symbolizes both the power of collective behavior to bring about social change as well as its violent potential.

a conventional crowd gather for a specific purpose and behave according to established, predictable norms. For example, booing is expected of a crowd at a football game but is deemed quite inappropriate for a crowd at a symphony orchestra concert. Little interaction takes place in a conventional crowd. People are pursuing a common goal, but they do so individually. Exchanges among members of conventional crowds are highly routinized and impersonal.

Both casual and conventional crowds can be transformed into expressive or acting crowds. An *expressive* crowd emerges when participants are carried away by intense feelings that overwhelm customary normative controls. People at rock festivals, revival meetings, and carnivals (such as Mardi Gras in New Orleans) are examples of expressive crowds. People in these situations may behave in ways that they would consider unacceptable in other settings. Expressing their feelings becomes their primary aim. The legendary Woodstock Music and Art Fair, held in New York's Catskill Mountains in August 1969, illustrates such a crowd. A slate of rock and folk music performers drew more than 300,000 young people to the farm where the festival was held. As the day's events proceeded despite mud, rain, and unexpected numbers of cars, vans, and people, the mood became increasingly joyous and exuberant. Today the event has been memorialized perhaps more for the expression of good feeling than for the music itself.

The emotional tone of an *acting* crowd is quite different from that of an expressive crowd. An acting crowd is an excited, volatile mass of people focused on a controversial event (such as the "not guilty" verdict in the 1992 Rodney King beating trial) that provokes their anger, indignation, and urge to act. Unlike members of an expressive crowd who view release of feelings as a goal in itself, members of an acting crowd seek redress of a perceived wrong. Fueled by the belief that only action outside the norms can accomplish this end, a large acting crowd may engage in violence or threaten to do so. Then it becomes a mob. African Americans living in south-central Los Angeles felt that a great injustice had been committed when the policemen accused of beating Rodney King were acquitted of any wrongdoing. They believed that this had to be redressed; the trial outcome confirmed their notion that *only* action outside the norms would achieve this aim.

mob—a cohesive, emotionally aroused acting crowd that often engages in violent disruptive acts.

A **mob** is a cohesive, emotionally aroused acting crowd that often engages in violent or disruptive acts. The Boston Tea Party was a mob action that has become a hallowed event in the history of U.S. independence, much as the storming of the ancient Bastille prison in 1789 is glorified by the French. After years of waiting for civil rights reforms to be enacted in the 1960s, violent mob actions erupted in many urban ghettos across the United States. Rioting continued for days and prompted city officials to call in the National Guard to help restore order.

riot—a violent active crowd composed of a large number of people and developing over long periods of time.

A **riot** is another type of violent acting crowd. Riots are somewhat less spontaneous than mob actions and typically embrace larger numbers of people over longer periods of time. Racial and ethnic inequalities have been a focus of riot behavior throughout world history. In the United States, gangs of whites burned and looted African- and Asian-American communities in the 1940s and 1960s. In the late 1960s, as described later, minority ghetto residents destroyed white-owned businesses and property in a number of northern cities, including Detroit, Philadelphia, and Newark. In 1988, rioting broke out in the Howard Beach area of New York City following the beating of several African-American youths stranded in a white neighborhood.

Why do riots break out? Why do people reject the normal routines of daily life and participate in hostile crowds? One popular explanation is the "riffraff theory." It argues that only criminal types of people participate in riots and that a hard core of agitators incite violence despite the strong

Some people called this scene a "scavenger hunt," but it was actually the aftermath of a 1992 version of a U.S. mob. The acquittal of the white police who beat African-American Rodney King touched off riots throughout south-central Los Angeles.

TABLE 10:1 Crosstabulation of Educational Degree[a] by Opinions Concerning Organized Marches and Demonstrations

Question #402: Do you think organizing protest marches and demonstrations against a government action should be allowed or not allowed?

	EDUCATIONAL DEGREE		
PROTEST Count **ROW PCT**	Less than high school	High school	College
Definitely allowed	36 **15.9**	109 **48.0**	82 **36.1**
Probably allowed	42 **23.2**	95 **52.5**	44 **24.3**
Probably not allowed	39 **33.3**	61 **52.1**	17 **14.5**
Definitely not allowed	31 **34.4**	50 **55.6**	9 **10.0**

$n = 615$

[a]Main Point: Better-educated people are more likely to approve of organized marches than are poorly educated people.

Source: General Social Survey, 1985.

disapproval of area residents. The National Advisory Commission on Civil Disorders, appointed by President Johnson, disproved this theory. In the Detroit riots of 1967, for instance, it was found that nearly 40 percent of ghetto residents either participated in the mob action or were bystanders to it. This hardly represents a deviant minority of criminals. The Detroit rioters, moreover, were on average better educated, better informed, and more involved in the community than were non-rioters. Table 10:1 confirms the finding that better-educated people are more likely to *approve* of organizing marches and demonstrations than are poorly educated people. Keep in mind that Table 10:1 demonstrates that, while better-educated people are more likely to endorse demonstrations, their approval is of organized demonstrations, not necessarily riots. In the specific case of the Detroit situation, however, most of the rioters were employed, although they felt overqualified for their jobs. So, why, then, did these people become involved in violent mob actions? The following account of the Detroit riots based on the 1968 Report of the National Advisory Commission on Civil Disorders offers some insight into the causes of rioting.

Profile of the Detroit Riot

In the summer of 1967 African-American ghettos in 23 cities exploded in violence. Civil rights legislation had raised expectations, but few concrete improvements had been delivered. Many African Americans were frustrated and disillusioned. The Commission found that 70 percent of the rioters believed that they deserved better-paying jobs and viewed their problems as the result of racism and not their own lack of training, ability, or motivation. These ghetto residents suffered considerable social strain.

Because ghetto residents live in social environments riddled with social strain, ghettos are structurally conducive to mob action. Residents live in close proximity to one another, and substandard housing pushes many to spend much time outdoors, especially during the summer. The streets, then, are frequently filled with people. But even when people experience social strain in a conducive social setting, they do not necessarily resort to mob violence. This is a step intimately associated with the belief that they have suffered great injustice. In a ghetto, stores tempt residents with products they cannot buy, and police who harass and abuse residents are ever-present symbols of Anglo domination. Anger and resentment are common, everyday feelings. All it takes is a spark to detonate such a powderkeg.

That spark occurred on Saturday night, July 22, 1967, when the Detroit vice squad raided five predominantly African-American social and gambling clubs, resulting in mass arrests. These arrests became the focus for ghetto dwellers' discontent. By the time police had hauled away the last of the gamblers on Sunday morning, a crowd of 200 had amassed on the street. A single bottle hurled from the crowd crashed through the window of the last retreating police car. This act signaled a breakdown of control, spurred further aggressive acts, and mobilized people for more violent action.

By 8 A.M. the crowd had grown to 3,000. Outnumbered, the police withdrew, and for a few hours a revelous mood prevailed. By noon, however, the cops had stationed themselves on nearby streets. Several rumors spread quickly among the crowd members; one claimed that a police officer had bayoneted an African-American person a few blocks away. Police reinforcement numbers mounted and rumors accelerated; the crowd's mood shifted into rage. People began to stone police and set fire to stores. Firefighters were summoned and attempted to quell blazes, but by 4:30 P.M. they were exhausted and stunned, and fled the scene. The mayor of Detroit proclaimed a curfew and called in the National Guard.

Over the next few days, the reports of fires and lootings declined, but sniper incidents increased. The number of reports peaked at 534 by Wednesday, July 26. Panic and confusion gripped ghetto residents. Police exacerbated the terror by breaking into homes for the frailest of reasons and arresting anyone found with a weapon. These desperate efforts to impose social control served only to intensify the violence.

By the end of the week, police had arrested 7,200 people, and 34 persons had been killed (30 or more by police and soldiers, 2 by store owners, 2–3 by rioters). Of the victims, 33 were African Americans; 10 were white. Property damage was estimated at $23 million.

Researchers report that participants in the ghetto riots of the 1960s sought to benefit from, not overthrow, the social system (Allen, 1970). These collective actions were spontaneous protests against unjust conditions, and they proved to be effective (Campbell and Schuman, 1968):

> Reporters and cameramen rushed into ghettos; elected and appointed officials followed behind; sociologists and other scholars arrived shortly after. The President established a riot commission, so did the governors (Fogelson, 1970, p. 146).

Thus, the riots brought immediate, if not long-term, results that had not been produced by decades of peaceful protests (Button, 1978).

Analyzing Mob Behavior

The consensus regarding the 1960s riots is that these particular civil disorders were purposeful attempts to verbalize anger at white oppression and redress racial injustice. The destruction was not haphazard; in most cases, only white-owned ghetto stores were burned and looted. This view of mob action as relatively rational behavior has not always been accepted. Until recently, mobs were seen as hordes of unchained wild animals, motivated only by overwhelming destructive urges. Gustave LeBon (1895/1960) was a primary proponent of this psychological theory.

The Psychology of Crowds. In his book *The Psychology of Crowds* (1895/1960), LeBon argued that involvement in crowds transports individuals into a "collective mind" through which they think, act, and feel quite differently than they would if each were alone. Crowds gain a magnetic hold over people, LeBon suggested. Individuals in crowds become highly suggestible, and tides of emotion divest one person after another of the thin layer of civilization. Thus primitive instincts and antisocial urges roam the streets. Herbert Blumer later (1951) refined LeBon's thesis. His *emotional contagion* model holds that an initial exciting event causes unrest and anxiety in a group of people. This is followed by a period of milling about, "as if seeking to find or avoid something, but without knowing what it is they are trying to find or avoid" (Blumer, 1951, p. 173). As they search about, some unusual behavior or rousing rhetoric captures their attention. Rather than evaluating these actions as they normally would, they respond impulsively and model their own behavior after them, as the bottle heaved through the police car window modeled further aggressive acts in the Detroit riots. This reaction, in turn, reinforces the original actors, creating a circular reaction that continues to raise the intensity level of the crowd. Such a group, Blumer says, is primed for action by their mounting agitation.

Emergent Norms and Social Relationships. Few sociologists would disagree with the observation that emotions and behavior may spread through crowds as if they were infections. Most contemporary sociologists believe, however, that LeBon and Blumer underestimated the capacity of crowds for rational behavior. Sociologists Ralph Turner and Lewis Killian (1972), for example, question the assumption that social conformity ceases in a crowd. According to their *emergent norm theory*, people evolve new social norms as they interact in situations that lack clear guidelines for behavior, and the new situation-specific norms become the primary determinant for action.

New norms develop through a process of social experimentation. One or more persons model a course of action (shouting a slogan, throwing a bottle). Different actions often follow. The crowd quickly, almost intuitively, evaluates each "suggestion" and thereby constructs the situation and justifies behaviors that would be unacceptable in other realms. In this way, crowd norms may emerge that sanction violence and destruction, but still impose some limits on behavior. This emergence of new norms does not mean that crowd members begin to think and feel as one. Some participants go along merely to avoid criticism or ridicule by other crowd members. Crowd unanimity, Turner and Killian conclude, is an illusion created by the requirement of at least surface conformity to new norms.

Pursuing Turner and Killian's ideas, other sociologists have suggested that new social relationships (Weller and Quarantelli, 1973) and new sets of meanings (Wright, 1978) also evolve in crowds. In lynchings, a fairly common form of crowd violence in the early American West and South, the mob dispenses with conventional norms of trial by jury and execution by the state. These are replaced with norms of vigilante trial and punishment by mob consensus. Crowd participants informally designate social roles of prosecutor, witnesses, jury members, and executioners. Thus, social relationships and social constructions of meaning emerge in mobs, rendering them much more structured than they initially appear.

This picture summarizes the sociology of a number of different phenomena. The Ku Klux Klan is not just a small group of lunatics running around in white sheets. It is a highly organized movement with collectivities all across the United States. Bent on racism and violence, the Klan smacks of deviance. As this scene demonstrates, it also represents another connection between gender and social change. Notice anything different about the faces?

Mob Behavior and Rational Decision Making. One question that Turner and Killian fail to address is why new crowd norms are often so extreme. Crowds sometimes endorse behaviors (such as looting, arson, and personal assault) that would be strongly condemned under normal circumstances. Richard Berk (1974) suggests one answer. Drawing on *rational choice theory*, Berk argues that people do not give up rationality simply because they are in a crowd. They continue to weigh the costs (risk of personal injury and likelihood of arrest) and benefits (redressing social injustice) of possible courses of action. In a large crowd, which greatly outnumbers police, these risks are relatively small. On the other hand, the benefits of mob action may be great for those who have been disadvantaged for many years. These benefits may be concrete (looted merchandise) or intangible (social recognition or emotional catharsis). In any case, Berk contends, people in crowds calculate that, for the here and now, violent action is worthwhile.

Certainly not all sociologists agree that crowd action is so rational. The fact that the ghetto riots of the late 1960s did gain frustrated African Americans the attention of white America lends Berk's theory some support. Similarly, the riots in south-central Los Angeles following the not guilty verdict in the Rodney King case in 1992 gained considerable support for a retrial of the policemen involved.

SOCIAL MOVEMENTS

We have thus far examined relatively transitory forms of collective behavior. Mass hysteria arises and just as quickly dies down; crowds amass and soon disperse; even riots spurred by deep-seated social injustice tend to persist no more than several days. At other times, however, collectivities of people launch much more long-lived deliberate efforts to enact change. These are called *social movements*.

Social movements differ from other forms of collective behavior not just in their endurance, but also in their degree of organization. Social movements, such as the Women's Movement (profiled later), the Anti-Abortion/Pro-Life movements, or ACT-UP, that have existed for a long time and have become large and influential often develop hierarchical organizational structures.

This does not mean, however, that social movements are the same as institutionalized efforts to bring about or resist social change. When oil companies lobby Congress to pass tax laws in their favor, or when physicians petition the FDA to speed approval of a new drug, they are not participants in social movements. Social movements involve some non-institutionalized means of persuasion—marches and rallies, boycotts, sit-ins, and sometimes sabotage or other illegal acts (Traugott, 1978). Participants

This picture is a vivid reminder that crowds can turn in any direction without rhyme or logical reason. In 1994, college students in France celebrated in the streets because a sub-minimum wage scale had been withdrawn. The results were staggering. Renegade youths used the cover of a student march to smash cars and shops and attack police and journalists.

in social movements turn to non-institutionalized methods because they lack the social power to advance their collective interests through the governmental system (McAdam, 1982). In the 1960s (and still today in the 1990s) minorities in the United States use(d) boycotts, mass demonstrations, marches, and violent insurrections to manifest the extent of their dissatisfaction. They lack(ed) the political power to enact changes through conventional interest group strategies. This is a characteristic generally true of participants in social movements.

Types of Social Movements

Social movements center on almost any important social issue, such as environmental quality, nuclear weapons, women's rights, apartheid in South Africa, drug abuse, and religious salvation, to name only a few. Some sociologists have attempted to classify this wide range of social movements. Drawing on Cameron (1966), Aberle (1966), and Goode (1992), we can categorize social movements in terms of the direction and degree of change they seek; these may be reactionary, conservative, reformative, revolutionary, or escapist.

reactionary movement—a movement that seeks to restore society, or a large part of it, to a former condition.

A **reactionary movement** seeks to restore society, or a major part of it, to a former condition. The Moral Majority, now defunct, was a reactionary social movement whose members looked fondly to the past. They wanted to revive a time when only marital sex was acceptable, homosexuality was viewed as a sin or a disease (or both), and abortion was illegal and available only to the wealthy or the most desperate. Racist groups such as the Ku Klux Klan and the American Nazi Party seek to restore white supremacy and return to the days when African Americans were subservient to whites and when Jews were relegated only to jobs no Christian wanted (*The New Republic,* April 3, 1989). Renewed interest in such reactionary groups was demonstrated in and has been enhanced by the recent election of a former Klan leader to a seat in the Louisiana state legislature, as well as other successful appeals to racial fears in the 1988 presidential election (*McLean's,* January 3, 1989).

conservative movement—a movement that seeks to retain the status quo and resist possible change.

A **conservative movement** seeks to retain the status quo and resist possible changes. It most likely arises when there is a threat of change, and is frequently organized to combat activities of other change-oriented movements. The National Rifle Association (NRA), for example, organizes to prevent the imposition of controls on handgun ownership.

reformative movement—a movement oriented toward partial or moderate change in society.

A **reformative** (or revisionist) **movement** is oriented toward partial or moderate changes in the society. Usually its focus is on specific concrete issues such as saving whales, protecting the environment, promoting rights for homosexuals, decriminalizing marijuana, and so on.

revolutionary movement—a movement that seeks large-scale, sweeping social change.

A **revolutionary movement** seeks sweeping large-scale social change. The line between reformist and revolutionary movements may not always be clear because the same social movement may contain both reformist and revolutionary factions. Some members of the Women's Liberation Movement, for example, want society to grant equal occupational rights to women—equal pay for equal work, adequate maternity or paternity leave, protection from sexual harassment, and adequate on-the-job day-care facilities. While this represents a major change, it is essentially a reformative goal. Other feminists argue that these changes cannot occur without a significant restructuring of gender roles. These include altering the way men and women think and interact with one another; orienting men toward their softer, more emotional qualities; and men treating women as full

BOX 10:2 GENDER AND SOCIAL CHANGE

The Women's Movement

Protest by women predates the 1960s. In the early twentieth century, women joined together to demand the right to vote. Following this accomplishment, feminism entered a period called the "barren years" (Klein, 1984). Even during this dormant time, a small group of professional upper-middle-class women remained active and kept women's issues alive until later societal conditions unleashed renewed grass-roots support (Rupp and Taylor, 1987).

A contributing social factor to the contemporary Women's Movement was the 1963 publication of Betty Friedan's book, *The Feminine Mystique.* Friedan spoke to millions of American women about "the problem that has no name." Many women trained from childhood to relinquish self-reliance, careers, and personal autonomy, and to dedicate their lives to the full-time care of home and children felt dependent, isolated, and unfulfilled, Friedan argued. She identified some of the causes of this condition and brought public attention to the private grievances of women working outside of the home in dead-end, low-paying, unchallenging jobs. Thus women across the country became conscious of their shared discontentment.

Friedan's book did not stimulate this new outlook by itself, however. Several other factors launched the Women's Movement as well. One was the civil rights movement, which stimulated increased awareness of injustice and oppression in society at large. Ironically, women in the civil rights movement were often relegated to making coffee, typing newsletters, and answering telephones. Thus they began to address the contradiction of working in a freedom movement while simultaneously being subsidiary.

A social movement requires more than a shared sense of injustice, of course. Resource mobilization is also necessary. This occurred when commissions were established in each of the 50 states in 1963 to investigate the status of women. The commissions brought together large numbers of knowledgeable and politically active women, channeled discussion of their common problems, and facilitated the proposal of corrective solutions.

Organizational structure was furthered in June 1966, when a small contingent of women attending the Third National Conference of Commissions on the Status of Women met in Betty Friedan's hotel room and founded the National Organization for Women (NOW). Through its national board and 800 or more local chapters, NOW has used legal suits, lobbying, demonstrations, boycotts, and other methods to press for such goals as educational reform; nonstereotyped portrayal of women in the media; repeal of laws outlawing abortion; lesbian rights; enhanced roles for women in religion, politics, and sports; and passage of the Equal Rights Amendment (ERA).

Simultaneously, at the grass-roots level, many younger women also began organizing.

human beings, as well as taking on some traditionally women's tasks such as housework and child care. Proponents of more revolutionary changes argue that merely putting more women into traditionally male jobs would not change much at all. (For more about the Women's Movement, see Box 10:2 on "Gender and Social Change.")

escapist/retreatist movement—a movement that withdraws from what it perceives as a corrupt society.

An **escapist** or **retreatist movement** withdraws from what is perceived as a corrupt society. One example was Marcus Garvey's "Back to Africa" movement during the 1930s in which African Americans sought to escape discrimination in the United States by organizing to emigrate to Africa. Escapist movements need not withdraw from society physically; they can

BOX 10:2 GENDER AND SOCIAL CHANGE *continued*

They created egalitarian women's groups, which sought not only to increase opportunities for women, but also to change the entire structure of male—female relationships and roles. Additionally, these groups undertook a variety of local, educational, and service projects. They established women's centers, birth control counseling clinics, centers for rape victims and battered wives, day-care facilities, and feminist bookstores and publications.

By the 1970s the Women's Movement had made substantial progress in expanding career opportunities. Although inequities continued, women were entering fields once completely dominated by men. Their salaries were also rising. The entrance of many women into full-time professional jobs, however, brought with it the new dilemma of managing both career and family roles. This prompted women to pursue new objectives, including affordable day care, paid pregnancy leaves, more flexible work hours, and household duty-sharing between husband and wife (Klein, 1984).

A major obstacle has, however, slowed the work of the Women's Movement. An antifeminist movement emerged to block passage of the ERA. Leaders of this countermovement blamed feminists for social changes, such as no-fault divorce laws and legalized abortion, changes they viewed as threats to the stability of the family. To them, the ERA was the final assault on traditional roles of wife and mother. To thwart its ratification, they formed organizations such as Humanitarians Opposed to Degrading Our Girls (HOTDOG) in Utah and Women Who Want to Be Women (WWW) in Texas (Marshall, 1985). At the national level, antifeminist activist Phyllis Schlafly amassed several thousand women into a campaign called STOP-ERA. All these efforts proved successful. Strong initial support of the ERA slowed dramatically after 1973 and came to a dead stop by 1977. The final vote total was 35 states approving, 3 votes short of the number needed to pass.

Today the battle lines between the Women's Movement and the antifeminist countermovement are clearly drawn. On one side are young, well-educated, professional women who want to extend the gains of the 1960s and 1970s. The countermovement is composed largely of older, less-educated women who are full-time homemakers with strong religious beliefs (Burris, 1983; Deutchman and Prince-Embury, 1981; Mueller and Dimieri, 1982). With the ERA defeated, the antifeminists have new goals, such as rescinding both legalized abortion and affirmative action programs for women. Members of NOW and other feminist organizations are committed to devoting time, effort, and funding to continue their cause (Chavez, 1987). As both sides are strongly committed to their objectives and are able to mobilize resources on their behalf, the struggle between movement and countermovement can be expected to continue through the 1990s.

Critical Thinking Questions

1. How would conflict theory explain the development of the antifeminist countermovement?
2. Can the Women's Movement be usefully analyzed as a revolution of rising expectations? If so, how? If not, why not? What factors created a sense of relative deprivation among young, well-educated women in the 1960s?

simply isolate themselves socially and emotionally, limiting contact with outsiders to a minimum. Utopian movements, for example, seek the ideal society for a select group of true believers. There have been many attempts to create such a community, though few have lasted more than several years. One example of utopian idealism in the contemporary United States is the *commune,* in which members share common living quarters and pool their incomes (Oved, 1988; Veysey, 1988). Major problems in communes have involved effective leadership, control of sexuality, and long-term commitment to the group and to the commune (Kanter, 1972; Petranek, 1988; Zablocki, 1980).

The Soviet Union was the scene of numerous uprisings and political upheavals in its final years. This picture shows the Parliament building under attack in 1993. The bottom line of all of this discontent was the dismantling of the U.S.S.R. and the recreation of Russia's old nation states. This revolution caused sweeping social change much like its 1917 Bolshevik counterpart.

Explaining Social Movements

Why does a social movement develop? Under what conditions do people engage in collective action to bring about or resist change? Sociologists have proposed two types of answers. One theory suggests that social movements arise from conditions of social and economic deprivation. According to this view, when discontentment with the way things are reaches a boiling point, people become motivated to overturn the existing order. Most sociologists, however, contend that deprivation alone is not a sufficient explanation for the rise of a social movement. They argue that deprivation and discontentment are often widespread, yet full-fledged social movements are quite rare. They suggest, instead, that discontentment must be paired with some ability by an aggrieved group to mobilize resources on its own behalf. Without sufficient resources and the organization to employ them effectively, even the most dissatisfied group cannot get a social movement into first gear.

Social and Economic Deprivation

The most basic deprivation in life is that of its necessities—food, shelter, and clothing. This condition can be a precursor of revolution. The French Revolution, for instance, was preceded by a sharp increase in the price of bread (the highest price in 70 years) due to poor harvests in 1787 and 1788. Workers in cities and even rural dwellers confronted severe hunger and, in 1789, they turned toward rebellion.

The argument that revolutionary movements develop when people cannot fulfill their fundamental needs was central to Karl Marx's theory of social change. Marx held that the ever-increasing use of machinery and factory production would condemn workers to more and more menial tasks, thus lowering their wages and accelerating their sense of alienation and discontent. Eventually, Marx argued, workers would not tolerate further exploitation and would organize to overthrow the owning class.

Not all sociologists agree that progressive impoverishment leads to revolution. The French social observer Alexis de Tocqueville (1856) studied economic and social *decline* in the seventeenth century and found this to be followed by *advancement* in the eighteenth century. He concluded that revolutionary movements occur not when conditions are most hopeless, but after they have begun to improve slightly. After they experience some progress, de Tocqueville argued, people begin to realize that abject deprivation is *not* inevitable. They recognize that a better life is possible; their expectations soar, and the remaining deprivation seems more unjust and unbearable than ever. Sociologists call this gap between people's expectations and their actual living conditions **relative deprivation** (Gurr, 1970).

relative deprivation/rising expectations—after a long-disadvantaged group begins to experience a slight improvement in conditions, its members see that a better life is possible, their expectations soar, and the remaining deprivation feels greater than ever, even though actual conditions have improved.

Relative deprivation can be experienced in a variety of circumstances. De Tocqueville described one condition: that of **rising expectations**. Some contend that a sense of rising expectations nurtured the civil rights movement and subsequent ghetto riots in the 1960s (Abeles, 1976; Geschwender, 1964). The economic prosperity of the 1950s and the early gains of the civil rights movement led African Americans to believe that their lives would improve appreciably in the near future. The new civil rights legislation and President Lyndon Johnson's War on Poverty resulted in little concrete improvement. Dreams of a Great Society faded, particularly as the United States became increasingly concerned with Vietnam and less centered on problems at home. To raise people's expectations that a feast is at hand and deliver only crumbs is to create a socially explosive situation. It is no surprise, from this perspective, that ghetto riots and the Black Power movement appeared at this time.

Sociologist James Davies (1962, 1974) has identified another condition that engenders feelings of relative deprivation—"a rise-and-drop situation."

The environmental group Greenpeace is well known to many people in the United States and around the world. It is a highly effective reactionary type of social movement bent on preserving the earth's national resources. Greenpeace demonstrates how organization, not size, can achieve impact. Driven in the right direction, this little boat can keep a huge oil tanker at bay.

Based on analyses of events such as Dorr's Rebellion in Rhode Island in 1842, the Pullman Strike of 1894, the Russian Revolution of 1917, and the Egyptian Revolution of 1953, Davies concludes that revolutionary movements are most likely when a prolonged period of economic and social improvement is followed by a drastic reversal in people's fortunes. The initial period creates the expectation that things will steadily improve and the reversal period stimulates tremendous fear that all progress is irretrievably lost. Davies believes that the actual conditions during the reversal period are less important than the psychological state they foster. Some people may even be objectively better off than they were before the economic downturn began, but they *feel* robbed of what they expected to receive. Consequently, they become intensely frustrated, perhaps ready to initiate violent demands for what they believe is due them.

The Subjective Dimension of Collective Behavior

The following excerpts from a newspaper article ("Problems of Urban America Revert to Back Burner") about the Los Angeles riots of 1992 and their aftermath illustrate the contributions made by the subjective dimension to the initiation and continuation of an episode of collective behavior:

> Six short months ago, as widespread violence terrorized Los Angeles and threatened to spread to other cities across the country, America's attention was riveted on a long-neglected topic: the decay of once-great urban centers and the smoldering problems within them.
>
> For one fleeting moment, it was as if a window had flown wide open after being frozen shut for years. Political leaders dusted off the hoary notion of an urban agenda. The nightly news bristled with tales from the inner city. Many Americans hoped that, somehow, the stubborn problems of crime and poverty that so dehumanize urban life would be tackled with a renewed public will.

For a few weeks, *visibility* had been achieved; the public was made painfully aware of urban poverty, decay, and everyday crime so often absent from the television screen. Clearly the massive media coverage, as the article points out, generated the *expectation* among Americans that tangible funds and viable projects might truly be forthcoming. But without continued repetition, the American public's memory is quite brief; its concern is very mercurial. Expectations often go unfulfilled. The article continues:

> Yet, except for a flurry of local efforts, nothing much has happened at all. What was touted as a major post-riot urban aid bill has been transformed by Congress into an unrecognizable mishmash of tax breaks, including benefits for the affluent, that remains in political limbo. As the horror of Los Angeles' violence recedes in people's memories, public attention has turned elsewhere—to the presidential election, the economy and other concerns.
>
> And now, just half a year after a nation watched horrifying scenes from Los Angeles played over and over on their TV screens, some advocates of the cities fear the window of opportunity has slammed shut once again: "It takes more than one riot to get people's attention, particularly when people are preoccupied with other things and when there's a huge argument over whether anything will do any good," said Edwin Dorn, a researcher at the liberal Brookings Institution in Washington. . . .

This article suggests that our conception of what an "important problem" is at any given time is very much a construct of media coverage. The media devoted tremendous attention in print and on television to the riots following the not guilty verdict in the trial of four policemen for beating Rodney King. The public was outraged by that verdict, but that sense of injustice was largely generated by the graphic televising of rioting, looting, and demonstrations in south-central Los Angeles. For those few days at the end of April 1992, the people of the United States strongly championed the idea that we must work to alleviate urban economic suffering and address racial inequities. The *value* of equality and opportunity for all began to be voiced loudly. Yet, just six months later, that cherished "value" had disappeared—pushed to the back of the shelf behind the more visible concerns of the presidential election and the national economy. The newspaper article concludes:

> One sign of urban America's brief shelf life atop the national agenda was the pattern of post-riot television news coverage.
>
> In the month before the outbreak of the riots on April 29, ABC, NBC and CBS news broadcast just three feature stories exploring the problems of urban America, according to a tally by the Center for Media and Public Affairs in Washington. Following the spasms in Los Angeles, coverage expanded dramatically.
>
> In May, the number of stories about inner-city issues rocketed to 37. Then, as public attention started to fade, so did the coverage. The total slipped to 29 stories in June, 12 in July and seven in August. By September, the cycle was complete when there were just three pieces.
>
> The pattern is typical for perplexing social problems, said Daniel R. Amundson, research director for the media center. Stories about the homeless, for example, increase in the dangerous winter months and then subside as soon as the weather warms up. "I think it's the same with urban problems," he said. "The television camera just goes elsewhere [after a crisis]. It doesn't cover long-term, intractable problems very well" (*Philadelphia Inquirer*, October 27, 1992, pp. 6–8).

Do we actually have strong values, or are our values merely a product of what is shown to us each night on the television screen and thus subject to constant shifts? The article implies that values have, perhaps, become something very different from the stable, consistent phenomena that they were before the advent of television. Values today seem transient, easily shaped and reshaped by the media. Thus, for a social movement to be successful, its members must keep their sought-after values in the forefront of the flighty American mind. Those values must be concretely reinforced over and over, or, as in the case of the Los Angeles riots, they will extinguish. If they are, the change in American attitudes toward the plight of the impoverished will become more prominent. See Figure 10:1 for an analysis of this change.

Resource Mobilization

As suggested earlier, many contemporary sociologists argue that *perceived deprivation* is only one factor precipitating a social movement, and they contend that to change existing values or norms, resources must be mobilized (Snow et al., 1981). These resources include both human skills and concrete assets (Freeman, 1979). Among the primary tangible assets are money,

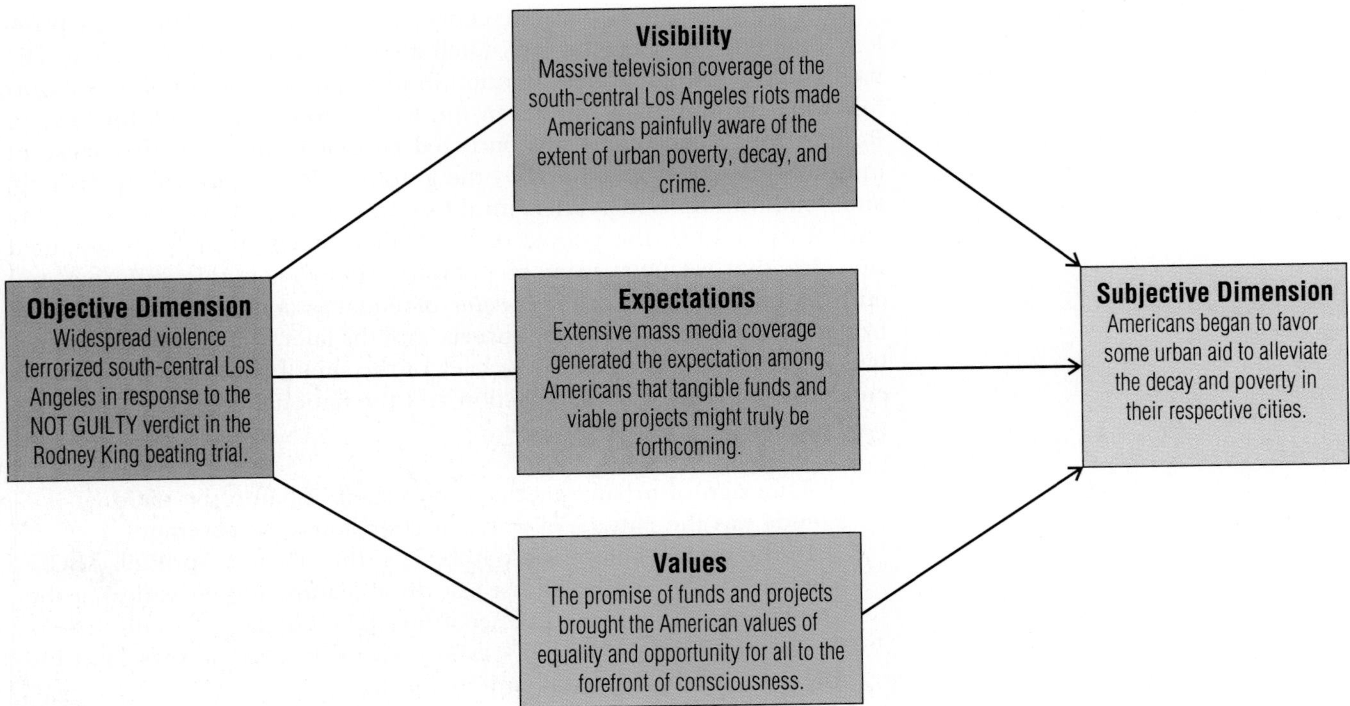

FIGURE 10:1 SUBJECTIVE AND OBJECTIVE DIMENSIONS: THE CASE OF THE LOS ANGELES RIOTS
Widespread violence in Los Angeles led a greater percentage of Americans to favor financial aid to alleviate urban decay and poverty.

channels of mass communication (as we have seen), and a physical location in which to coordinate activities. Extremely important also are *human skills,* including leadership, organizational talent, personal prestige (which can help attract other followers), and in-depth knowledge about the institutions the movement seeks to change. Large blocks of *time* and deep *commitment* (which may involve willingness to risk one's life) are also essential. In its early years, for example, the civil rights movement relied heavily on students who had quantities of time and moral support to offer. Both African-American and white students were recruited and trained for sit-ins, marches, and voter registration drives. Large-scale student involvement allowed the movement to gain a great deal of national attention at a relatively low cost. Similarly, Chinese university students were the primary participants in the 1990 demonstration for democratic reforms in Tienanmen Square in Beijing, China. These students were willing to sacrifice their lives—some were crushed by government tanks—in pursuit of their goals.

Student participation in the social movement illustrates another important point: Resources for a social movement are typically not found only within the aggrieved groups since the resources of a disadvantaged minority are often insufficient to support a social movement. Some of the resources must be contributed by sympathetic people who will not benefit directly from the changes sought by the movement. Even with outside help, resource mobilization is difficult. Success depends on several factors. One is the degree of *organizational support* for the movement (McAdam, 1982; Tilly, 1978). For example, African-American churches, colleges, and long-established structures—such as the NAACP—provided an essential organizational base for the civil rights movement of the 1950s and 1960s. In Gdansk, Poland, the Catholic Church, through its prelate Cardinal Karol Wojtyla (now Pope John Paul II), provided moral and organizational support to the shipbuilders who initiated the movement to overthrow communism in the late 1970s.

The year 1968 had the vibrations of earthquake about it. Many parts of the world were the scene of mass protest. This French student was one of millions the world over who were part of a counter-cultural youth movement.

A second factor is the *degree of opportunity* within the social environment. It was fortuitous for African Americans that the 1950s and 1960s were economically prosperous years. During strong economic times people are more receptive to improving conditions for less-privileged groups. In a study of African-American protests in U.S. cities during the 1960s, Peter Elsinger (1973) concluded that protests were more numerous in those cities where the governmental officials were open to change. Resource mobilization, therefore, depends to some extent on favorable political opportunities.

A third factor involved in successful resource mobilization is what McAdam (1982) calls *cognitive liberation*—a shared perception by members of a disadvantaged group that their unjust situation can be changed through collective action. Such a collective perception is linked to both a favorable opportunity structure and strong organizational support.

Any collective action often owes much of its success to effective leadership. Sociologists have identified several types of leaders, ranging from the "agitator" (also known as the "prophet") whose skills at expressing particular demands compel public attention to the "administrator" who operates the nuts and bolts of a social movement (Wilson, 1973). A single leader may fill several of these functions. Martin Luther King, Jr., and Betty Friedan were both influential prophets who articulated concerns of African Americans and women respectively. Both also served as administrators. King was the spokesperson for the Southern Christian Leadership Conference. Friedan was a founder of the National Organization for Women. (For more on the opportunities in the environment and the role of Friedan in the Women's Movement, see Box 10:1.) More recently, Vaclav Havel seems to have fulfilled both of these functions in the former Czechoslovakia. A well-known playwright, Havel had been quite outspoken in urging the overthrow of communism for many years. After the revolution, as the first elected president, he served an administrative role. Such versatile leaders are rare, however. More typically, a movement divides tasks among several leaders possessing different skills.

John McCarthy and Mayer Zald (1973, 1977) have suggested that many modern social movements are largely the creation of outside leadership. They contend that massive discontent among a less-privileged people is of secondary importance in launching a social movement. Skilled, trained leaders can broaden the base of even rather weak and poorly defined disaffection. Thus, grass-roots support for some social movements actually develops after the movement is under way. The movement to provide federally funded health care for the elderly, for example, was not the product of an outcry from senior citizens. Actually, the movement's principal organization, the National Council for Senior Citizens for Health Care through Social Security (NCSC), was staffed primarily by young and middle-aged professionals and was funded by the AFL-CIO. Administrative leaders staged rallies across the country and organized mass petitioning. Later, as the movement encountered opposition from the American Medical Association, the NCSC worked to recruit a large membership base among the elderly. Thus active support from the wronged group was sought only after the movement was in full swing (Rose, 1967).

This view of the emergence of social movements is very different from the more traditional idea that sees dissatisfaction among members of a deprived group as key. The social and economic deprivation model suggests that internal frustration and feelings of unfair treatment spur people to take action to seek change. The resource mobilization theory focuses on the external conditions that make organized protest possible. The two views are not mutually exclusive. Both provide significant perspectives; neither is adequate by itself. Only by considering both the impact of social disaffection and the process by which resources are mobilized can we construct a complete picture of how social movements arise, develop, and decline. In this regard, Theda Skocpol has made a notable contribution in her theory of social revolutions.

Theda Skocpol and Social Revolution

Skocpol defines social revolution as "rapid, basic transformations of a society's state and class structures . . . accompanied and in part carried through by class-based revolts from below" (Skocpol, 1979, p. 4). The simultaneous occurrence of class upheaval and sociopolitical transformation distinguishes a social revolution from a rebellion (which does not result in structural change) and from political revolution (which involves no change in social structure). Skocpol combines aspects of Marxist and resource mobilization theories in her explanation of social revolution. She argues that, although underlying class conflict is fundamental to revolution, the organizational structure and resources available to class members must also be considered.

Based on careful study of three social revolutions (the French overthrow of Louis XVI in 1789, the Russian Revolution of 1917, and the Chinese ouster of the Ching dynasty in 1911), Skocpol examines three factors often overlooked in other theories of revolution. First, revolutions are rarely begun intentionally; rather, they usually emerge from crisis situations. Second, revolutions are not products only of a nation's internal conditions. International developments (such as prolonged military clashes) contribute to the emergence of revolutions by undermining the existing political regimes. Third, states have an existence of their own and are not necessarily dependent on the interests of the dominant class.

Other studies have centered on the economic consequences of revolution. In research on the aftermath of the Cuban Revolution, led by Fidel Castro in 1959, Michael Lewis-Beck (1979) finds that, in the short run, the revolution had positive effects on the Cuban economy, as indicated by an increase in the growth of the per capita gross national product. These upturns were short-lived, however. Due to trade difficulties, scarcity of managers and materials, and administrative errors, the Cuban economy soon declined. Lewis-Beck calls this a "euphoric" pattern: Initial prosperity immediately following the revolution generates a feeling of unblemished success, but it cannot be sustained for long.

International terrorism can be loosely defined as a revolutionary movement. Its impact on global terror has been enormous. Yet even irrational acts such as car bombings and airline hijackings can be understood as part of a pattern. It is not a simple pattern involving a direct strike by the fanatics of one country against the populace of another. As Figure 10:2 demonstrates, state involvement in international terrorism involves ideological and facilitating sources as well as immediate and ultimate targets. Additionally, a small number of countries consistently fall into one of the four levels of involvement.

THEORETICAL PERSPECTIVES ON COLLECTIVE BEHAVIOR

Because some forms of collective behavior spring up suddenly and are so emotionally charged, they often seem beyond comprehension. Keep in mind the earlier specific examples of collective behavior as we examine two perspectives that help us understand why collective behavior does not just happen at any time, in any place.

Functionalist (Social Strain) Theory

According to Neil Smelser (1962), six conditions precede an episode of collective behavior: structural conduciveness, social strain, a generalized belief, precipitating events, mobilization of participants, and a breakdown of social control. These conditions occur in sequence, each creating a social environment that makes the next one possible. Smelser does not say that collective behavior will always result when a few or even all of these preconditions exist. As each one is added, however, the likelihood of alternative responses decreases, until eventually collective behavior becomes nearly inevitable.

FIGURE 10:2 PATTERNS OF INTERNATIONAL TERRORISM
International terrorism is more than a simple strike by one country against another. There are ideological and facilitating sources as well as immediate and ultimate targets.

Source: Adapted from Pattnayak, Satya R., and Arvanites, Thomas M. (1992), "Structural determinants of state involvement in international terrorism," *Current World Leaders* 35(2): 269–85. By permission of the publisher. Figures constructed by David W. Schlosser.

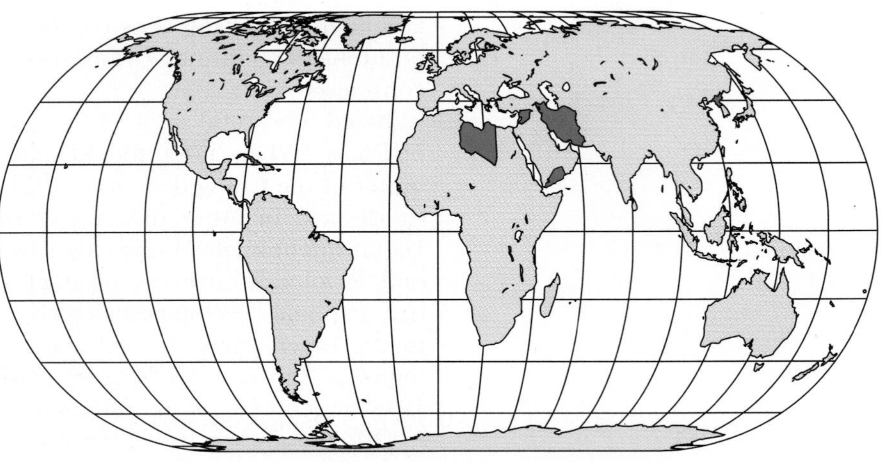

Ideological sources of terrorism are those countries that represent the main sources of terrorism.

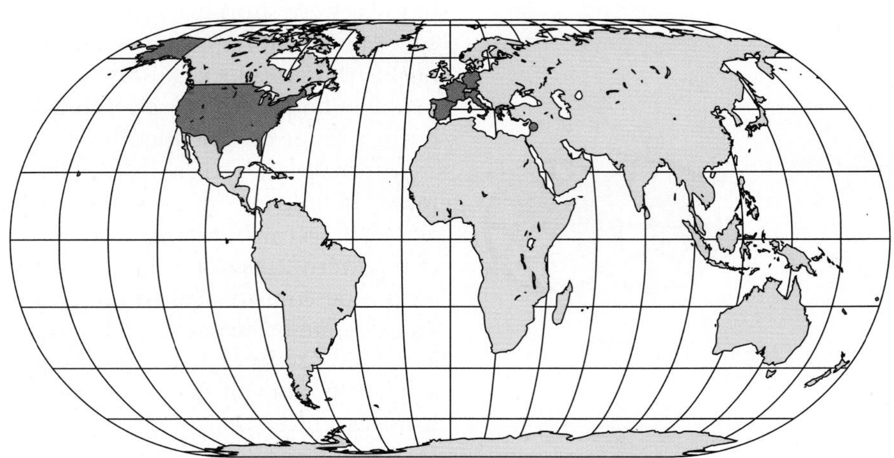

Major *immediate targets* of international terrorism represent nearly half (43.1 percent) of all international terrorist events.

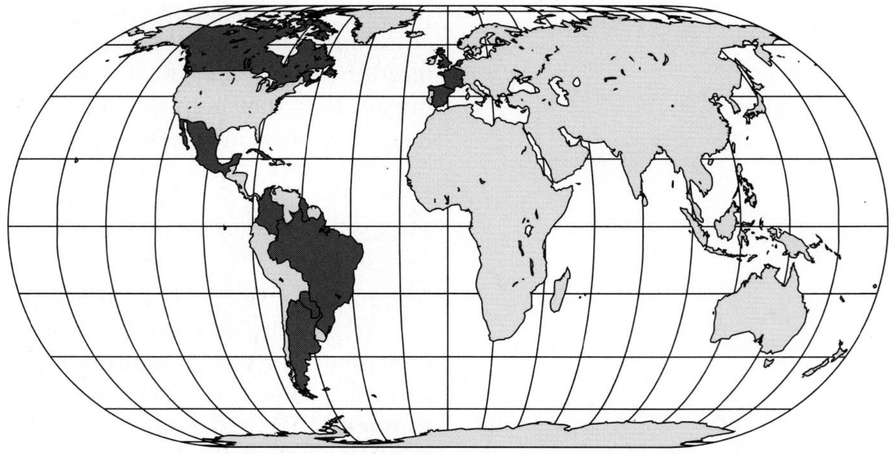

Those countries that are major *facilitating sources* of terrorism. Nearly half (46.9 percent) of the world's incidents of international terrorism include links with other nations.

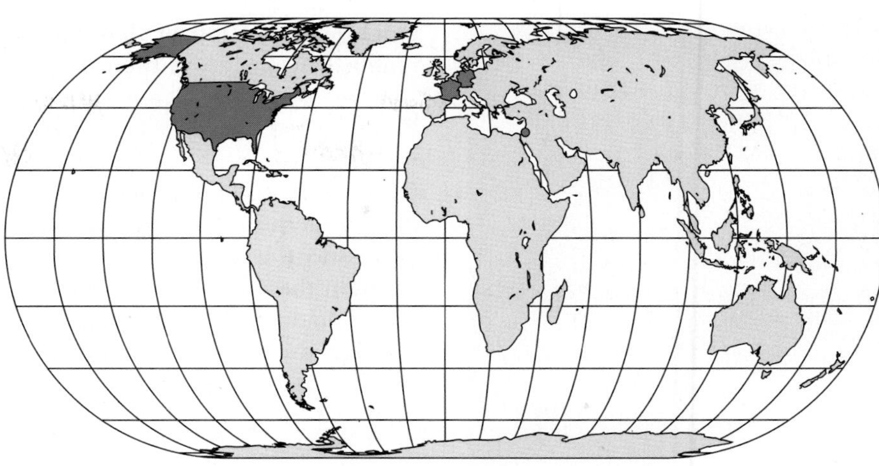

Countries that are categorized as being *ultimate targets* of international terrorist events.

Structural Conduciveness

structural conduciveness—certain aspects of a society that facilitate collective action.

By **structural conduciveness** Smelser means that certain aspects of social organization facilitate collective action. For example, in 1968, nationwide television networks aired anti-war views on newscasts. Television coverage of the Democratic National Convention served as a forum where student activists could voice their opposition to the government's policy in Vietnam. The wide-ranging coverage of the trial of the four policemen accused of beating Rodney King in 1992 in Los Angeles, as well as coverage of King's reaction to the not guilty verdict reached into homes across the entire country. Structural conduciveness is an initial precondition and does not guarantee that collective behavior will occur. It does, however, provide a receptive setting that makes possible certain forms of collective action.

Social Strain

social strain—a social setting receptive to collective action, due to sudden disruption, long-term social change, or ongoing value conflicts, which generate feelings of tension.

Social strain can arise from a diversity of sources. It can spring from sudden disruption of the existing social order, as when a disastrous flood or hurricane strikes. It can also develop from long-term social changes, such as those that led to the civil rights movement in the 1960s. Strain can also arise when the culture fails to offer adequate guidelines for responding to an event or situation. It may result from persistent value conflicts between different segments of society. This seems to have been the situation in Los Angeles in 1992. The political establishment had consistently failed to offer true aid to inner cities to remedy crime and poverty. This value clash between an unhearing government and disillusioned, economically deprived city residents proved a powerful source of social strain.

Generalized Belief

generalized belief—a widely shared explanation of strain experienced by members of a society.

A **generalized belief** develops to explain the strain that members of a society are experiencing. In 1992, residents of south-central Los Angeles constructed the generalized belief that high-ranking public officials were insensitive to the impoverished African Americans' plight and were determined to ignore even the most blatant instances of mistreatment, as in the Rodney King case. As the trial of the four policemen wore on, the belief heightened tension by defining once-vague ideas and expressing a shared reality. The stage was then prepared for a collective incident to surface.

Precipitating Events

Often an episode of collective behavior erupts when an event confirms people's generalized belief. In south-central Los Angeles the precipitating event was the not guilty verdict in the policemen's trial. In the personal incident that opens this chapter, the precipitating event was the report that police had tear gassed the student demonstrators. Rumors soon spread through the college community. In both cases the precipitating event was *perceived* as concrete evidence that the political establishment was indeed oppressive and would use any measures to stamp out opposition views.

Lynch mobs and race riots reached a peak in the late 1800s and early 1900s in the Deep South. This is African-American artist Jacob Laurence's portrayal of the violent chaos of a race riot. The painting is from his 1940–1941 series *The Migration of the Negro* (another panel is shown in Chapter 3).

Mobilization of Participants

When evidence for a cause accumulates, people begin to act on their beliefs—they mobilize. Mass hysteria breaks out, panic erupts, mobs form, or social movements organize. In 1992, this mobilization took the form of a decision by the impoverished residents of south-central Los Angeles to commit destructive acts, riot, and demonstrate, regardless of the consequences.

Breakdown of Social Control

Governing groups often attempt to deter collective behavior. In so doing, they can affect the timing, content, direction, and even specific outcomes of the collective action. The results may not be what the agents of social control intend. Sometimes their efforts backfire totally. In Los Angeles, slow and ineffectual police responses, coupled with the dispatching of the National Guard, only fueled further protest and violence. This theory focuses on the interaction of social strain with several other social factors to give rise to an episode of collective behavior. The social strain view is based on functionalist theory portraying collective behavior as a breakdown of the established social order, an event that signals disruption of the normal, harmonious working of the social system. This disruptive process is ignited by an intensely stressful event or situation that exhausts people's coping ability. If the situation persists, established norms may be ignored and collective behavior can erupt.

Conflict Theory

Not all sociologists concur with the social strain view. Those who take a power (conflict) perspective argue that there are always some groups in a society who are under considerable strain. The conflict perspective holds that a society is dominated by an elite group who prohibit others' access to prosperity. The vast majority of people thus lack wealth and privilege, and many feel enormously deprived and stressed.

The examples in modern America and throughout history abound. Just check out the table of contents of this book, and you will see a listing of some of the more blatant examples of oppression. They include clashes among social classes, races, ethnic groups, religions, and men and women. According to conflict theory, collective behavior is the expected collective *action* of people who have simply had enough of the existing order because the existing order spells deprivation.

Social Networks Perspective

What enables some groups who feel unjustly treated to act on their own behalf and challenge the existing structure, while other groups—equally disadvantaged—tend to tolerate their plight? One answer is differing effectiveness in generating social networks. In order for collective action to occur, strong formal and informal social networks must develop. Box 10:1 presents two strong informal social networks that passed along rumored stories that became widely believed. The mere fact of joining people through the telling and retelling of the tale formed a social network with a shared agenda.

More formal and complex social networks must be constructed to create a full-scale social movement. As described in Box 10:2, Charles Tilly (1978, 1991) is a leading proponent of the social networks perspective. He suggests that such complex social networks emerge through a four-stage process: (1) shared interests, (2) organization, (3) mobilization of resources, and (4) opportunity.

Shared Interests

The framework for a social network is laid when a group of people begin to recognize that they have some common concerns. In this first stage, people realize that their needs are not unique—they are shared by others. More important, people acknowledge that joining efforts with one another could result in some desired social change. Throughout 1991, many citizens of the former Soviet Union became aware that vast numbers of compatriots shared their tremendous disaffection with the existing Communist government. They began to be convinced, in part through observing the fall of communism in other nations, such as Poland, Czechoslovakia, and Yugoslavia, that they could unify to bring about democratization.

State terrorism does not draw as much publicity in the United States as revolutionary terrorism does. That is ironic, since the overwhelming majority of terrorist acts are perpetuated by a country's government against its own people. "Ethnic cleansing" in Eastern Europe and the Pol Pot regime in Cambodia are two recent examples of how state terrorism has eliminated millions of lives during the twentieth century. Pablo Picasso's *The Korean Massacres* portrays robot-like beings anonymously executing people for some revolutionary cause.

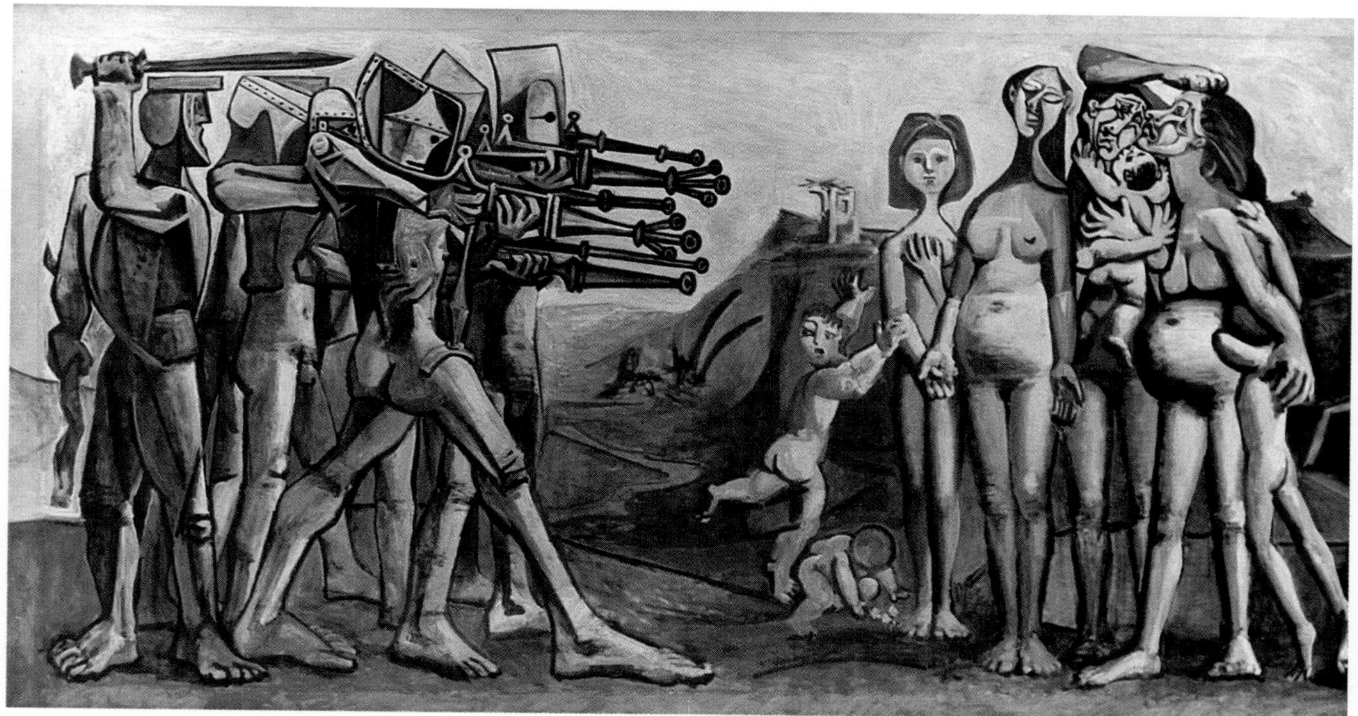

Organization

Shared interests alone cannot create a social network. During the early 1800s, slaves in the United States had shared interests, but they were unable to organize a formal social network, so collective protests against slave-owners were extremely rare at that time. A formal organization is a second step toward action. The anti-war protestors of the 1960s created strong social networks. Anti-war organizations on college campuses across the country were linked together by an effective communications network. This network encouraged thousands of students to go to Chicago where the 1968 National Democratic Convention was meeting. As described earlier, Gdansk shipbuilders in Poland were the first to forge a strong social network that became the model for developing other such groups throughout the country.

Mobilization of Resources

In the third stage of the process a social network gains control of resources needed for collective action. In mobilizing resources, Tilly argues, a social network moves from passive acceptance of the status quo to active effort to alter the existing situation. In the former Soviet Union, President Gorbachev himself (this is very rare, of course) mobilized resources through his policies of Glasnost and Perestroika. These policies provided the impetus for the Soviets to turn the corner through more contact with Western countries and through initiation of democratic reforms.

Opportunity

For the fourth phase to come to fruition, some aspect of the social network's environment changes, opening a new avenue through which to act on its own interests. The policies of Glasnost and Perestroika altered the government and the atmosphere in the Soviet Union significantly. Soviet citizens had the opportunity to experience a more democratic way of life. Widespread international exposure of these policies and their effects on the Soviet people provided a final impetus for the huge social network to undertake irreversible collective action.

Integrating the Theories

The three theories presented here shed light on different aspects of the same picture. They need not be incompatible with one another, though they clearly focus on different aspects of the emergence of an episode of collective behavior.

Social strain (functionalist) theory and conflict theory illuminate the "whole society" perspective. Social strain theory directs us to locate groups that experience tremendous misery on an everyday basis because, for them, the social system is out of harmony. They do not receive the treatment that they expect based upon their education, motivation, and/or effort.

The conflict theorists would add that there are *always* many such groups—women, people of color, the disabled, the indigent, and others. To the conflict theorist, strain is inevitable and not due to a temporary disruption. There will always be people who are disaffected and disillusioned. A particular event—such as the not guilty verdict in the Rodney King trial—can push that strain over the edge. People become unwilling to tolerate the status quo; pent-up anger spills over into riots, demonstrations, and other collective behavior.

The social networks perspective directs us to the "smaller picture," the inner workings of the collectivity of people themselves. It is the quality of the social network itself that determines whether a strained group will be able to organize itself to move beyond rioting to effect true social change. Women and African Americans have been relatively successful in negotiating that shift. That journey has lasted well over 20 years for both and is still ongoing. As implied earlier in the article on the riots following the Rodney King verdict, the corner has yet to be turned. For the moment, the inner-city impoverished have not organized effective social networks that can mobilize resources to unrelentingly keep crime and poverty in the public eye. Only by continuous visibility of the strains created by crime and poverty will Americans recognize their shared interest in changing the present situation into far-reaching reform.

SUMMARY

1. Collective behavior encompasses a wide range of activities from spontaneous forms to crowds to organized social movements. Spontaneous forms of collective behavior are short-lived, expressive, and lack clear goals, as in the cases of mass hysteria, rumors, and panic. Crowds, on the other hand, are collections of people who consciously gather around a person or event and are influenced by one another's presence. There are many types of crowds, including casual, conventional, expressive, and acting forms. Mobs and riots are the most volatile brand of an acting crowd.
2. LeBon's theory of crowd behavior centers on the notion of emotional contagion, the idea that individuals in crowds think, feel, and act through a "collective mind." Other perspectives on crowd behavior are emergent norm theory and rational choice theory.
3. Social movements are categorized in terms of the direction and degree of change they seek. Reactionary movements seek to restore society to a former condition. Conservative movements are geared toward maintaining the status quo. Reformative movements are oriented toward moderate social change, whereas revolutionary movements are designed to accomplish large-scale social overhaul.
4. One theory of social movements suggests that they arise from conditions of social and economic deprivation that cause discontentment. Other theories hold that discontentment alone is not enough; it must be paired with a group's ability to mobilize resources.
5. Functionalist theory, also known as social strain theory, contends that six conditions are necessary to produce any form of collective behavior: structural conduciveness, social strain, a generalized belief, precipitating events, mobilization of participants, and a breakdown of social control. Conflict theory argues that there are always some groups who are under considerable strain; namely, those who lack wealth and privilege. The social networks perspective, noting that not all disadvantaged groups create social movements, holds that formal and complex social networks are a driving force for full-scale action.

Norman Rockwell's *The Problem We All Live With* shows a black girl being led to school by U.S. marshalls during the early days of desegregation. Rockwell's painting is an apt part opener, for such black girls are often victims of racial, gender, and class inequalities.

PART FOUR

SOCIAL INEQUALITY

Part Four commences with a shocking fact: There is no such thing as equality—there is none in your personal life and, in fact, no social equality in any known society.

Chapter 11 examines patterns of inequality in the orderly distribution of "the good things in life" according to the structure of social classes. Chapters 12 and 13 focus on familiar "facts of life"—race and gender—and how they intertwine with patterns of social inequality.

Note, by the way, that your careful reading of Part Four can affect your position in the class's grade distribution. That is yet another aspect of . . . social inequality.

Chapter 11

Personal Perspective

THERE is no equality in your life. None.

If this seems like an extreme statement, act like a scientific sociologist and examine data from your own status set.

Is there equality in the family?

Before giving a lip-service response, really think about it. In general, the answer must be no. If you live with a mom and dad, they probably have been bossing you around for most of your life, a prime reason why many college students want to move out. Sisters? Brothers? Despite the best efforts of parents, the authors are aware of no case in the child development literature of siblings feeling that their family treatment has been uniformly equitable. Think of how many disputes in your childhood resounded with "That's not fair!"

Is there equality at work?

The question even sounds silly. Take the common college-age job of waitron (this is the politically correct dictionary term for "waitress" or "waiter," both of which imply gender inequality). Although there is little visible hierarchy at most restaurants, a manager usually does the hiring. How were you chosen for the job? Undoubtedly, by possessing more of some personal quality—punctuality, hustle, or "niceness"—than other applicants, who are therefore not your equals. The manager manages in part by firing if you are not equal (there it is again!) to the performance of your coworkers. Even the customers treat you unequally with their tips.

Is there equality at school?

After all, higher education is widely viewed as a democratic institution that equalizes group differences. Of course, the term *higher education* sounds suspicious—higher than what? Is there equality in your introductory sociology class? The professor is in charge, and therefore is not your peer (some college students still raise their hands to receive permission to go to the restroom!). Is there equality among classmates? Consider what happens when a graded

Social Class and Stratification

test is passed back. Most students cannot resist peeking at others' tests, then carefully inspecting the grade distribution to find their place in the mid-term pecking order.

This quick perusal of your status set is not intended to inflame you about personal injustice. It is to document your direct experience with a primary sociological principle: Social inequality is everywhere. It is there at the level of megastructure, in the mountain of resources differentiating First and Third World nations; it is there in the macrostructure within these societies, in their superrich and homeless, in their corporate booms and unemployment gluts; and it is assuredly there in the microstructures you experience most directly at the level of who has a better car. Inequality is there in every room, wing, and floor of the grand edifice of human society. The key blueprint for the unequal treatment of any person by another is *social structure.*

This is the reason sociologists have so busily documented the shape of social inequality. Busily indeed: As we pointed out in Chapter 1, social inequality may be *the* most massively studied subject in sociology. Before we sketch the patterns that have emerged from this mass of research, please mull over two points. First, there is a perverse fascination for the topic in a society founded on the idea of equality. Second, social inequality is not just an external, "out there" phenomenon. Individual human beings build and sustain this structure, and it in turn penetrates their very selves. As we have already seen, this is true for you.

BJJ

Social Class and Stratification

ON THE NATURE OF SOCIAL INEQUALITY

THE *Oxford English Dictionary (OED)* defines *society* as "association with one's fellow men, especially with intimacy and fellowship" (1971, p. 359). Try asking a handful of your "associates" for their definitions of the term. We bet that descriptive words such as *levels, system,* and *hierarchy* will keep popping up. Although the warm fellowship suggested by the *OED* is clearly part of social experience, it is not all there is to society.

One reason your respondents may stammer in their attempts to define society is because of its maddening complexity. Who can envision even the organizational chart of your college let alone the whole structure of the "United States of America"? One key for unlocking complex phenomena is suggested by a classical work of Emile Durkheim, who was in search of a theory that would penetrate the essential nature of religion in all human societies (for more detail, see Chapter 15). This was a tall order, given the elaborate liturgy and church structure of French Catholicism, let alone the exotic variations in world religions. Durkheim's approach was to seek out the simplest known human societies at the time—namely, Australian aboriginal tribes—and probe their religious behavior. In *The Elementary Forms of Religious Life* (1912), Durkheim analyzed religion's place in society when both were in a simpler state.

For the present problem of picturing the place of inequality in this thing called society, we shall seek simplicity even below that of the evolutionary level of human beings. Consider the ants. They are classified as "social insects" not just because ants cluster together in large groupings. Indeed, swarms of pill bugs and flies can be observed in any garden. According to Harvard sociobiologist E.O. Wilson, one thing that makes a teeming mass of ants a social system is "hierarchy": "Groups of workers specialize as castes for particular tasks, and their activities are subordinated to the needs of the whole colony" (Holldobler and Wilson, 1990, p. 355). The tasks performed by a caste are known as its "role," and colony members use elaborate visual, tactile, and chemical forms of communication that meld them into a social unit. Ants make war, enslave other insects, and even have "social mobility" from one caste to another. The level of social organization is so high that leading myrmecologists (ant experts) consider the whole colony one "superorganism" greater than the sum of its individual, crawly parts.

For the non-myrmecologist, there are instructive lessons about human social systems. First, understanding inequality is a key to understanding society; the blueprint underlying ant or human social organization can be read in the social hierarchy. Second, position in the hierarchy affects the experience of the individual. Ant castes differ in their social duties, death

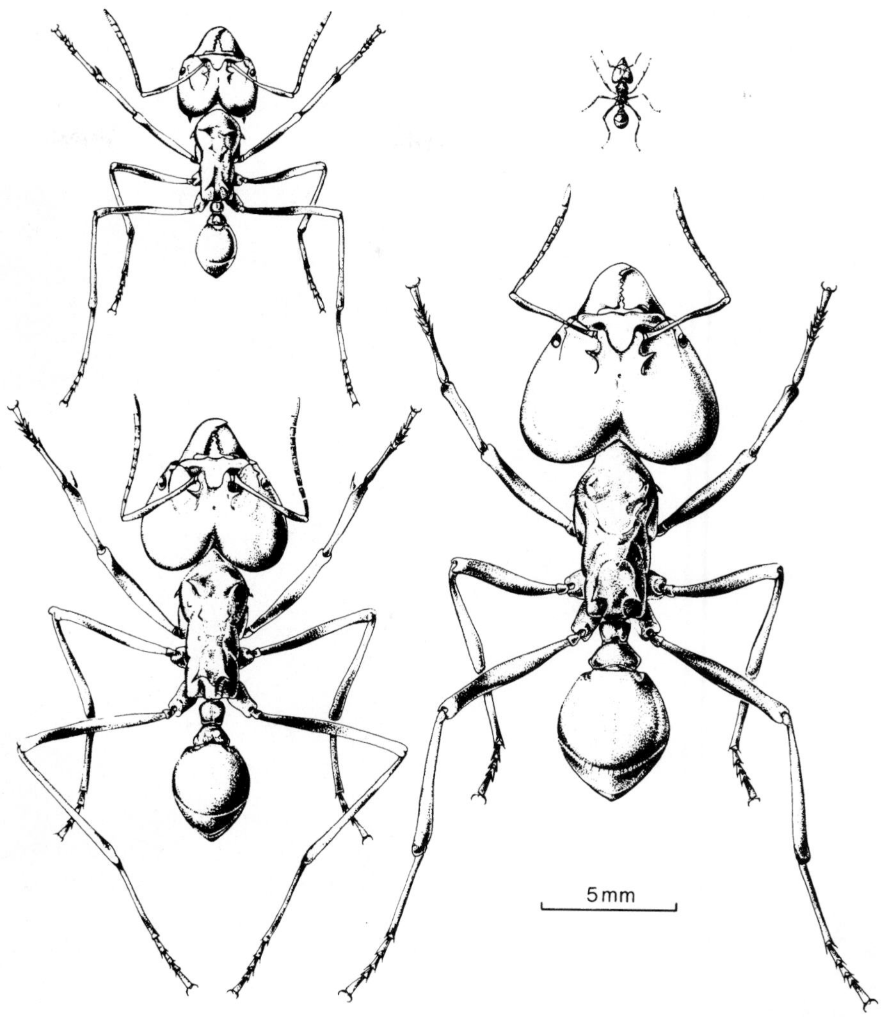

What lessons can you derive about human social order from these detailed drawings of members of a single ant society? Note the dramatic differences in physical structure of varying castes in the same species. The differences reflect a complex social hierarchy that controls the life experience of individual ants.
Source: Hulldobler and Wilson (1990).

rates, food quality, and even leisure time. It is well documented in the United States and elsewhere that the class structures of human societies allocate these and myriad other aspects of life unequally to people. A final lesson concerns the design of social organization. With a brain of microscopic size, no individual ant has the cognitive capacity to organize the up to 50 castes of varying sizes that constitute a colony. Yet somehow the activities of individuals numbering into the hundreds of millions do produce an elaborate society. This suggests the more intriguing mystery of human social order introduced in Chapter 1. Though no one person has designed the structure of social inequality in the United States, the activities of hundreds of millions of people do create it. How? The sociological theories that would answer this question are spotlighted next.

THE SYSTEM OF STRATIFICATION

Our brief excursion into myrmecology has provided illuminating images, but no direct light on the inequality in your life. Ants are *so* alien from humans that their societies must be drastically different. So they are, but ideas borrowed from diverse disciplines can yield flashes of insight into the logic of social life. The term titling this chapter, in fact, comes from geology. The sociological concept of "stratification" is loaded down with

FIGURE 11:1 THE SOCIAL STRATIFICATION SYSTEM OF THE UNITED STATES
This sequence of triangles adds progressive detail to a sociological model of a stratification system. Triangle A shows the relative ranking of social statuses (circles) from elite, highly rewarded positions at the top to the much more numerous, poorly rewarded positions at the bottom; triangle B creates three subtriangles (income, prestige, and power) representing the dimensions of Max Weber's multidimensional stratification system; and triangle C superimposes horizontal lines for levels of social reward penetrated by arrows representing mobility up and down these "strata."

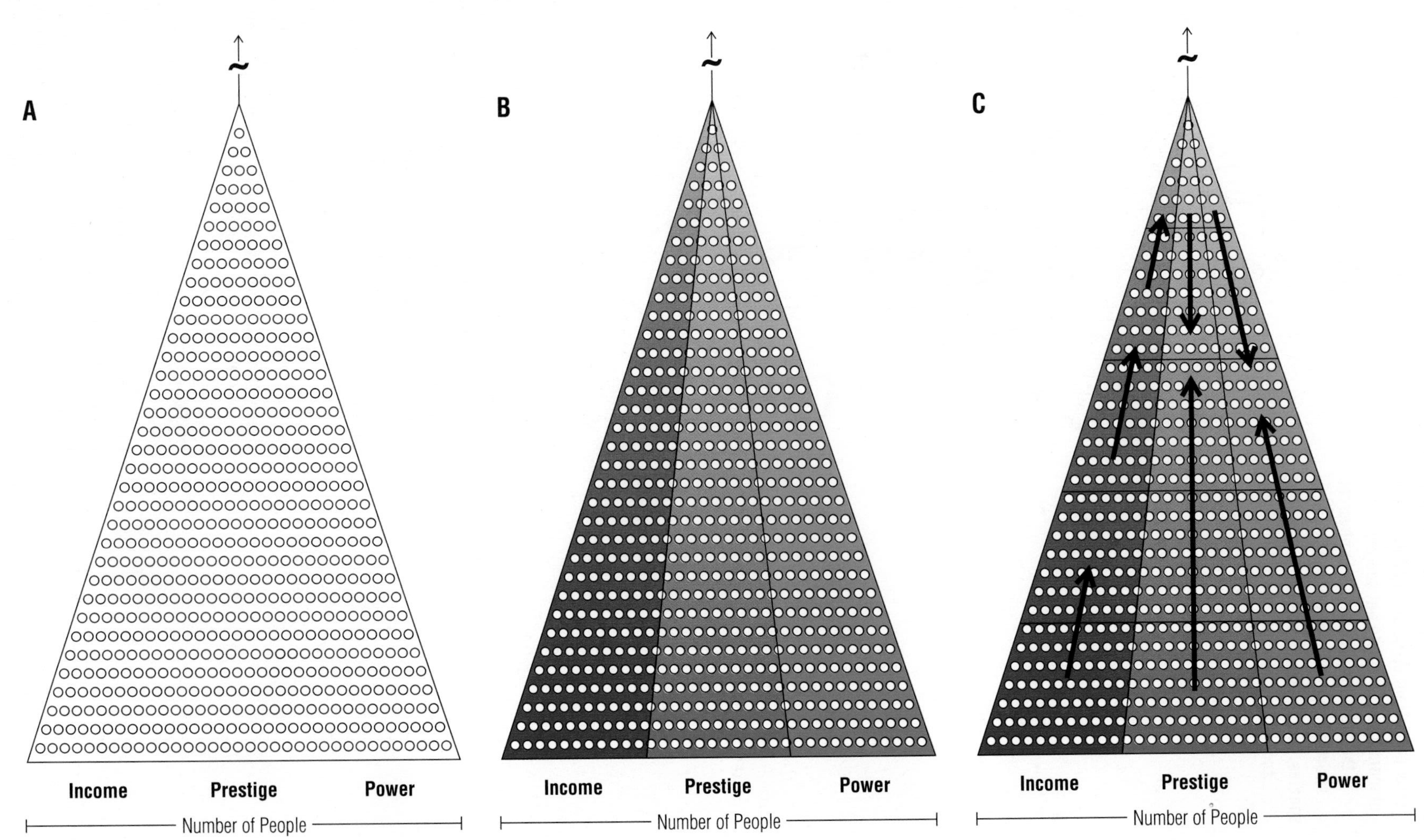

implications that human societies have levels as distinct and ordered as the layers of the Earth. Geology offers little beyond this vivid image. Core sampling and satellite topography are of no use in displaying the insides of social inequality. For that purpose, we now proceed directly with the specialized tools of sociological theory and research.

The Dimensions of Stratification

Following Durkheim, the way to understand a complex phenomenon is to build a simplified model, and then progressively add detail. Begin with triangle A of Figure 11:1. The triangle shape represents the structure of U.S. social inequality in the vertical plane—that is, an unequal, up and down ranking of rewards—and in the horizontal plane approximating the relative number of ranked positions. The term "position" is used advisedly. Notice that each triangle contains open circles representing statuses, the structured positions that make up a social system. These social slots are of course filled by people, but their individuality is secondary. Primary to the logic of inequality is the position, not the person. (Recall the discussion in Chapter 4 of what the college does with your student status if you disappear.)

multidimensional stratification system—the approach associated with Max Weber that analyzes the several distinctive, key, related dimensions of social inequality.

Now examine triangle B. The segmentation into three subtriangles shows the United States to be a **multidimensional stratification system**. The terms *income, prestige,* and *power* labeling the base of each subtriangle are derived from theoretical distinctions drawn by Max Weber (1922). The idea is that a stratification system such as the United States is built from a set of related—but distinct—social rewards. Perhaps you read this chapter expecting to learn about the many mysteries of money. Certainly income allocation is a key formula of social inequality, but it is not the whole equation. Weber's theoretical position is that the three dimensions pictured here are those essential to understanding the social structure of inequality.

Income

To see the real-world implications of Weber's theory, we must first confront a realm of truly amazing sociological phenomena. Imagine a mountain of money made of the sum \$5 trillion—(\$5,000,000,000,000)—that fills the U.S. economy. Somehow this titanic treasure chest must be individually parcelled out to the more than 250 million U.S. citizens filling the slots pictured in Figure 11:1. This is a job that dwarfs the building of the pyramids, yet it is performed every year! Now for the mysterious part: How is it done? Unlike pyramid construction, the task of dividing up the money in the United States has no straightforward blueprint. There is no master list of how much each status-occupant should receive, no control desk before which one reports to receive society's personal evaluation in dollars. Compounding the mystery is the extraordinary, robotic reliability of this money machine. Table 11:1 depicts the distribution of monies to each quintile of families in the United States; that is, families are sorted into fifths, with the best-paid 20 percent in the top row, the worst-paid quintile in the bottom row, and so on. The monies considered here are termed **income**, defined as employment pay (salaries, wages, tips, etc.) and transfer payments from the government (including welfare and Social Security).

income—all monies received as employment pay and government transfer payments.

In a system of truly equal income distribution (of which we have no real example), each quintile of families would get 20 percent of the trillions in the treasure chest. The numbers in the columns of Table 11:1 show how

TABLE 11:1 The Distribution of Income in the United States

	PERCENT DISTRIBUTION OF FAMILY INCOME[a] (BY YEAR)		
INCOME QUINTILE	1964	1974	1984
Highest fifth	41.2	41.0	42.7
Fourth fifth	24.0	24.1	24.4
Middle fifth	17.7	17.6	17.1
Second fifth	12.0	12.0	11.1
Lowest fifth	5.1	5.4	4.7

[a]Income includes earnings from employment and transfer payments (such as Social Security and welfare) but excludes wealth (such as stocks and bonds).

Sources: Adapted from United States Bureau of the Census, "Money Income of Households, Families, and Persons in the United States: 1980," *Current Population Reports*, Series P-60, No. 149. Washington, DC: U.S. Government Printing Office, March 1985.

far the United States has deviated from this ideal of equality. In 1964, the top quintile received more than double its proportionate share (41.2 versus 20.0 percent). The poorest fifth of families received only 5.1 percent of income, about one-quarter of what they would have been allocated in a system of equal distribution. Clearly, there was no equality of pay in the United States in 1964.

In the decade to follow, the Gross National Product (GNP) of the United States doubled, and the economy sustained major shifts in industrial structure (Chapter 16). Moreover, in March of 1964 (where our table begins), President Lyndon Johnson declared the "War on Poverty" to directly attack inequality of income distribution and—paraphrasing another poverty warrior, Robin Hood—to take from the rich (upper quintiles) and give to the poor (bottom quintile). The effects of these major societal changes are numerically summarized in the 1974 column, and can be verbally summarized in three words: almost nothing happened. Although the dollar amounts received by each quintile of families did increase, *in no case did their relative shares change by even 1 percentage point!* The pattern remained ironclad over 1974–1984, a period also filled with social changes—the 1981 recession, corporate mergers, Japanese acquisitions—none of which disturbed the programming of the money machine. In the chapter's concluding discussion, we shall further examine the persistence of this pattern into the 1990s.

This overview of recent historical data for the United States reveals income allocation to be a social *system*—a precise process that is also robust enough to repel forces of change. But it is not a consciously designed mechanism like a government department. In fact, a cynic would state that no such agency could manage the kind of sustained efficiency shown in Table 11:1. The system is more like a computer that, once programmed, will perform the instructions of its software with no further input from a programmer. Decoding the inequality program is a challenge sociologists accept, but we must also accept the additional complexities posed in Figure 11:1.

Prestige

In a society with credit cards so dear to our collective heart, it is difficult to accept prestige as a real thing. It is inedible, unspendable, and invisible—seemingly the stuff of personal whim. Nevertheless, Weber identifies

TABLE 11:2 Occupational Prestige Rankings

OCCUPATIONAL TITLE	PRESTIGE SCORE	OCCUPATIONAL TITLE	PRESTIGE SCORE
Physician	77.9 (top)	Garage mechanic	42.9
University professor	77.6	Mechanic, repair worker	42.8
Lawyer, trial lawyer	70.6	Shopkeeper	42.4
Head of large firm	70.4	Printer	42.3
Engineer, civil engineer	70.3	Typist, stenographer	41.6
Banker	67.0	Police	39.8
Airline pilot	66.5	Tailor	39.5
High school teacher	64.2	Foreman/forewoman	39.3
Pharmacist	64.1	Soldier	38.7
Armed forces officer	63.2	Carpenter	37.2
Clergy	59.7	Mason	34.1
Artist	57.2	Plumber	33.9
Teacher, primary teacher	57.0	Sales clerk	33.6
Journalist	54.9	Mail carrier	32.8
Accountant	54.6	Driver, truck driver	32.6
Civil servant, minor	53.6	Bus, tram driver	32.4
Nurse	53.6	Miner	31.5
Building contractor	53.4	Barber	30.4
Actor	51.5	Shoemaker, repairer	28.1
Bookkeeper	49.0	Waiter	23.2
Traveling sales representative	46.9	Farm hand	22.9
Farmer	46.8	Street vender, peddler	21.9
Electrician	44.5	Janitor	21.0
Insurance agent	44.5	Servant	17.2
Office clerk	43.3	Street sweeper	13.4 (bottom)

Source: Donald J. Treiman, *Occupational Prestige in Comparative Perspective* (1977). New York: Academic Press

prestige—"social honor," one of Weber's key dimensions of stratification systems.

it as a pillar of modern stratification systems, defining prestige as a substance of "social honor" (Gerth and Mills, 1972). Prestige does not depend on personal charm. Observe the differences in parental reactions if you announce you are bringing home a pimp and a professor for dinner; the unequal amounts of "social honor" arise *before* the family meets each guest. Note also that your parents' assessment of prestige is quite distinct from the assessment of the guests' income levels.

Weber's analysis of prestige was a seminal one, but it did not have the benefit of modern sociological methods. An enormous weight of studies has been brought to bear on the subject of occupational prestige, and they have revealed the job ranking shown in Table 11:2. This orderly arrangement of occupational respect has been documented . . .

. . . across time (in studies from 1929 to the present).

. . . across different occupations (i.e., people working near the bottom tend to rank jobs like those at the top).

. . . across societies (some 50 countries show similar rankings).

Occupational prestige ranking has been called *the* major discovery of scientific sociology (Davis, 1987). Although that may be an overstatement, it certainly qualifies for the realm of amazing stratification phenomena we

Joyce Paul's painting *Come As You Are* is a snide characterization of these elegantly arrayed partygoers. Their obvious riches are not just sources of personal pleasure, but part of a social structural system. Place this elite into the appropriate income niche in Figure 11:1, and draw inferences about their prestige and power positions as well.

have been exploring. Based on our experience with in-class surveys, we would bet that you could better guess the prestige rankings in Table 11:2 than the actual salaries of the occupations. Quite clearly, the unequal allocation of respect is as much a social system as is the computer program for cold cash.

Although one's occupation is typically the master status in modern industrial societies, Weber identified other kinds of "status groups" that affect one's rank in the prestige subtriangle. Pointedly, Weber distinguished the *nouveau riche* (e.g., a new millionaire) from the "gentleman" (i.e., inherited "old money") group. The distinction has relevance today in the social selection of country club members and in which weddings are spotlighted in the society pages of a newspaper. It is not just a matter of money, or every lottery winner would be as honored as the town founders. The "upper crust" is envied by "social climbers" because of exclusivity, a social circle drawn by the former to keep out the latter—and to keep in prestige. Weber observed that a distinctive "style of life" identifies members of a status group (Gerth and Mills, 1972). Contemporary theorist Pierre Bourdieu (1984) views the parade of countercultures in modern life—beatniks, hippies, punks, rappers—as status groups whose openly outrageous lifestyles reject the conventional standards of prestige.

For the majority in the United States, the magic wand for making income and prestige treasures appear is the one you are now waving—education. As you will see here and in Chapter 17, there is a clear increase in average income with each additional year in school completed. In some respects the conversion of education into prestige is even more direct. Whole broad categories of jobs (especially those near the top of Table 11:2) depend directly on educational credentials. Try becoming a professor without a PhD, pursuing law without a JD, or practicing medicine without an MD. Education also provides training in a broad spectrum of "respectability skills": fancy speech, knowledge of the arts, dress codes, and so on. College campuses even offer the latest countercultural groups with their own exotic prestige standards (often symbolized by musical taste). Some sociologists contend that the massive expansion in education in the post-World War II U.S. has been driven by a mad scramble for prestigious schooling credentials, and that education therefore governs the whole stratification system as well as one's own destination (Collins, 1988). It is certainly clear that education is part of the operating system of the prestige program of the United States.

Power

power—the ability to influence other people, even against their resistance.

There is a third major dimension of Figure 11:1 to be sorted out: power. Weber defined power as the ability to realize one's "own will . . . even against the resistance of others" (Gerth and Mills, 1972, p. 180). The very essence of power, therefore, is inequality. Power is unequally distributed in the occupational structure. Your professor's ability to pop a quiz despite student objections is not based on power of personality—it is built into the job. The broad category "manager" contains occupations in which bossing other people around ("managing" them) is written into the job descriptions. Similarly, people playing the role of street sweeper (at the bottom of Table 11:2) have relatively little influence over others at work whatever force of character they possess. Weber recognized that power may be collectively exercised by groups ("parties") seeking to control society's machinery, as in occupational interest groups such as the American Medical Association (AMA) or the American Association of University Professors (AAUP). Whatever its other payoffs, he also viewed power as something valued "for its own sake" (Gerth and Mills, 1972, p. 180). Hence, its pictured position as the right-hand reward dimension.

The verbal picture of Figure 11:1 is now complete: Modern stratification systems are three-dimensional, with social programs allocating pay/prestige/power in computer-like fashion. The reason it has taken brilliant theoretical insights and a massive research effort to reveal this simple figure is because the dimensional programs interact. As a consequence, a given

Consider this sampler of individuals dressed in their occupational "uniforms." Now consider the "uniformity" of social rewards known as *status consistency.* Do these occupational statuses each receive similar rankings across the stratification dimensions of Figure 11:1?

social position tends to be ranked at a remarkably similar level in each of the three triangles. Verify this for yourself: Place a few of the occupations from Table 11:2 in their relative positions within triangle B of Figure 11:1. With occasional exceptions (the pimp and professor dinner guests, for example), society's statuses receive relatively similar ratings in each inequality program (e.g.: physician—high, high, high; street sweeper—low, low, low). This phenomenon is termed **status consistency**, and it tends to blur the sociological forces at work. People come to take for granted that the three dimensions are delivered together depending on how "successful" one is. Operating over the head of this simple, commonsense assumption is a complex sociological system that controls the delivery of social rewards to the tens of thousands of statuses that make up this society of ours. For now, it is enough to note the efficiency and coordination of the inequality programs. Explanations of the operating system itself will await the section appropriately titled "Theoretical Perspectives on Social Stratification."

status consistency—the common situation of relatively similar rankings of a status in terms of the differing dimensions of inequality.

Stratification and Mobility

There is something exhilarating about discovering an elaborate realm of inequality looming above one's own little spot in the social structure. From that spot, though, consider these not-so-innocent questions: Whatever happened to the American Dream? Is the hard copy of the inequality program pictured in Figure 11:1 the American Nightmare?

Types of Inequality

The answers to these questions depend on just what is meant by "equality." The situation portrayed in Figure 11:1 is defined as **inequality of condition** because, quite simply, those above are getting more of each dimension than those below. There is no denying the reality of unequal pay, prestige, and power in our society. Now examine your own feelings about this oft-quoted (if sexist) phrase from the Declaration of Independence: Does "all men are created equal" concern *what* people get or *how* they get it? To personalize the issue further, take the system of student grade ranking. You might be willing to accept the unequal conditions of a system giving A's and F's, but probably would be outraged if some students got to see the test in advance. **Inequality of opportunity** concerns selective access to social rewards. Cheating is deplored not because cheaters get A's (hard workers get A's, too) but because the system is rigged to reward the wrong stuff. In the classroom as throughout U.S. society, the issue is equitable opportunities for advancement. "All men are created equal" is an idealization of equality of opportunity: "The American equalitarian ethic is in one sense an inequalitarian ethic, because it values the opportunity to become unequal" (Vanfossen, 1979, p. 210).

inequality of condition—the unequal allocation of social rewards.

inequality of opportunity—the unequal access to social rewards.

Mobility Research

With this distinction in mind, turn now to triangle C of Figure 11:1. The arrows across the stratification levels in this figure suggest up-and-down mobility. These arrows are aimed at the very heart of the American Dream, representing people rising—or falling—on the basis of merit. Are they real? This question has preoccupied sociology for decades. It still does: Most major sociology journals present an article on the topic of occupational mobility in *every issue*. This is a nice demonstration of values affecting the

TABLE 11:3 Occupational Mobility in the United States

RESPONDENT'S OCCUPATION	FATHER'S OCCUPATION[a]					
Count **ROW PCT**	Professional, Technical, Managerial	Clerical, Sales	Craftsmen	Operatives, Laborers, Service	Farm	
Professional, technical, managerial	153 **41.9**	38 **10.4**	79 **21.6**	61 **16.7**	34 **9.3**	365
Clerical, sales	85 **30.4**	34 **12.1**	53 **18.9**	70 **25.0**	38 **13.6**	280
Craftsmen	26 **25.5**	4 **3.9**	33 **32.4**	25 **24.5**	14 **13.7**	102
Operatives, laborers, service	50 **16.3**	17 **5.5**	56 **18.2**	123 **40.1**	61 **19.9**	307
Farm	2 **7.7**	1 **3.8**	2 **7.7**	0 **0.0**	21 **80.8**	26
	316	94	223	279	168	$n = 1,080$

[a]When respondent was age 16.

Main Point: A national sample crosstabulating respondents' current occupations (row labels on left) by their fathers' occupations when respondents were 16 (column labels across top).

Source: General Social Survey, 1990.

choice of research topic (see the section "Sociology of Science" in Chapter 2); it reveals sociologists to be creatures of a society passionately devoted to the ideal of occupational achievement. Table 11:3 is the attempt of some of those creatures to represent the realities of opportunity in the United States. It is compiled from the 1990 General Social Survey and cross-tabulates questions about the respondent's current occupation by father's occupation when the respondent was 16 years old. (See Box 11:1 for a discussion of the relative absence of women from intergenerational mobility studies.)

In Table 11:3, start with the so-called main diagonal, the cells stretching from the upper-left to the lower-right corner. These contain cases of current immobility; that is, respondents at the same broad occupational level as that of their father. The immobility diagonal contains roughly one-third of those in the GSS national sample (153 + 34 + 33 + 123 + 21 = 364 = 33.7 percent). Before jumping to the conclusion that the remaining two-thirds prove this is "The Land of Opportunity," consider three points raised by sociological experts. First, much of the occupational movement off the diagonal is not of the rags-to-riches (or riches-to-rags) variety. Nearly two-thirds (63.5 percent) of all respondents, in fact, are within one occupational level of their father's position (i.e., at the same occupational level or one up/down). Second, some amount of the remaining third of respondents are actually in transitional career stages that are termed "pseudo-mobility" (Knapp and Spector, 1991). Since it includes respondents as young as age 18, the occupational snapshot of the GSS freezes into position college students now working as clerks in firms they may eventually manage after earning MBAs. A more important third point concerns the social structure surrounding any single career history. Notice the numbers at the foot of the columns for fathers' occupations, and to the right of the rows for respondents' occupations. These are called the marginal distributions (they're in the "margins"), and they tell a story of macrostructural

BOX 11:1 GENDER AND SOCIAL CHANGE

The Status of Women in Research on Occupational Mobility

As should be obvious from the studies summarized in this section, there is something missing from sociological research on intergenerational mobility—women. We present here a glimpse of the professional literature coming to grips with this problem, and proposing solutions. It is a bit technical, but it shows real sociologists struggling to understand the real social changes in women's occupational achievement.

Given the strong concentration on occupational status, stratification researchers have found it difficult to deal with women (Acker 1973). To begin with, for the respondents' generation, many married women are outside the labor force. This is even more true for women in the parental generation (mothers). An additional impediment is that the occupational distribution of women is so different from that for men that applying existing status or class categories to women is problematic (Bielby & Baron 1986). Faced with these problems, many of the major data collection efforts in the first two generations simply excluded women from the sample altogether. Most of our comparative knowledge on the intergenerational mobility of women therefore stems from other sources than the major mobility surveys (Roos 1985). Roos shows that throughout the world the process of educational and occupational *status* attainment is similar for men and women, except that the direct effect of father's occupation on occupational status is weaker for women. However, women's occupational *class* position is quite different from that of men and is somewhat less associated with father's class position than is true of men, particularly with respect to class immobility (Portocarero 1983a, b). As compared to their fathers, women are on average more upwardly mobile than are men (i.e., they enjoy higher social status than do men from similar origins), but this conclu-

change across the generations. The "Farm" sector, for example, employed some 15 percent (168/1,080) of fathers but just over 2 percent (26/1,080) of respondents. In general, the workforce has been closing down in its lower-skilled sectors (compare the relative number of fathers to respondents in the marginals for "Craftsmen" categories), and expanding in higher-skilled occupations (do the same comparison for the "Clerical" and "Professional" marginals). This phenomenon is termed **structural mobility**, and it means that much of the movement in Table 11:3 is caused by the changing shape of the "ladder of success." True movement between the rungs—called **circulation mobility**—certainly does occur, but even this purer form of the American Dream is clouded by a fact of sociological life.

structural mobility—the shifts in occupational position that occur because of changes in the underlying occupational structure.

circulation mobility—the shifts in occupational position that occur within a given occupational structure.

Reconsider the distinction drawn between the two types of inequality. In the abstract, equal opportunity can exist even under great inequality of condition; whatever the distribution of prizes to one's parents, each generation could begin at the same starting line. In reality, the race is staggered from the start. The winners from the previous generation quite naturally share the wealth, especially since improving the lot of one's children is a traditional part of the American Dream. *Inequality of condition inevitably means some inequality of opportunity.* The neighborhood your parents can afford to reside in has a built-in level of public school quality. Their salaries

BOX 11:1 GENDER AND SOCIAL CHANGE *continued*

sion is likely to be contingent upon the exclusion of nonemployed women and upon the (male based) status measure that is used (Blishen & Carroll 1978; Boyd 1982).

One of the traditional arguments for the exclusion of women from social mobility research has been that the unit of stratification is the family, and not the individual, in conjunction with the argument that the husband's status dominates the family's life chances. This latter assumption has become more and more questionable, if it was ever applicable. In recent years, the relation between the effect of husband's and wife's status on the family's social characteristics has stirred a hot debate in Britain (Goldthorpe 1983, 1984, Erikson 1984, Heath & Britten 1984, Stanworth 1984, Goldthorpe & Payne 1986).

Although it is a commonplace that women should be included in all future stratification research, some additional remarks can be made with respect to why and how women's statuses should be considered. An unresolved issue here is the measurement of women's occupational status. The fact that women are concentrated in a smaller number of occupations than are men should be incorporated in both measurement and structural models. Apart from this, future research should take the issue of family as the unit of stratification not as a debate about definitions but as an empirical problem. This requires developing models of how the status characteristics (and social origins) of each member combine to produce status outcomes measured at the level of the family rather than at the level of the individual (Haller 1981). This agenda provides a new role for the old problem of homogamy (Ultee & Luijkx 1990). Paradoxically, such questions gain importance as more women enter the labor market and the traditional nuclear family is in decline, since in such circumstances the stratification of individuals and the stratification of families is truly different.

Critical Thinking Questions

1. To help provide gender balance in our understanding of the process, how would you design a large-scale study of women's intergenerational occupational mobility using the "Multimethod Approach" from Chapter 3?
2. What are some important distinctions between the "status attainment model" and the "structural model" as they apply to women's occupational achievement?

Source: H.B.G. Ganzeboom et al., "Comparative Intergenerational Stratification Research: Three Generations and Beyond" (1991). In *Annual Review of Sociology* 17, pp. 293–94.

can be directly exchanged for differing amounts of junior college versus state college versus Ivy League tuition. And there are only so many country club memberships through which parents can pull the strings of their social contacts. Everyone has a story of a hard-working person who overcame the handicap of poverty, but it was a handicap in the success race nevertheless. This real-world link between the two types of inequality explains why Max Weber defined *position* in the stratification system by the "life chances" people at that position share at birth. It also explains why most of the mobility in Table 11:3 is such a short step on the ladder.

Clearly, the reality of stratification and mobility is far more intricate than the simple arrows in Figure 11:1. One way to clarify the complexities is to track the mobility process against some sort of comparative baseline. Two are available: other countries, and our own past. *Is the United States more open in its opportunity structure than are other societies?* The answer is a qualified yes. Recent studies generally find the highest rates of circulation mobility in the United States and Sweden (Ganzeboom, Treiman, and Ultee, 1991). However, our (shared) lead in opportunity over the international pack is a narrow one. The conclusion of the earliest comparative mobility studies still holds: "The overall pattern of social mobility appears to be much the same in the industrial societies of various Western countries"

The hallowed halls of Harvard University are shown above the converted trailer halls of California State University at Northridge. The contrast in the "life chances" of the students at these schools is even more of a mismatch than the physical facilities. Given the differences in parental social class, these two scenes illustrate *inequality of condition* leading to *inequality of opportunity.*

(Lipset and Bendix, 1959). *Is the United States now more open in its opportunity structure than it has been in the past?* The answer is an unqualified yes. There is greater circulation mobility in our society today than there was even as recently as the 1970s (Hout, 1988). Again, comparative research provides perspective on the "Land of Opportunity" question. A contemporary study of 18 societies (including the United States) finds significantly increasing mobility chances in 16 of them (Ganzeboom et al., 1989).

The Status Attainment Model: Alone on the Ladder

Instructive as they are for evaluating the ideals of an entire society, such large-scale analyses miss something essential about the American Dream. To really penetrate that vision, our studies must also tap mobility aspirations at the personal level. Like everyone else, sociologists start out wondering what to be when they grow up. And like everyone else, we get advice from significant others shaping the Dream: "Stand on your own two feet" . . . "To get a good job, get a good education." Such formulas are whispered (and shouted) into the ear of virtually everyone, and have gained substance in the sociological model materialized in Figure 11:2.

status attainment model—an approach to occupational mobility that focuses on individual-level traits.

This is the central model of the **status attainment** approach introduced by Peter M. Blau and Otis D. Duncan in the enormously influential 1967 book *The American Occupational Structure.* It initiated a massive research effort to find the solution to the personal success formula in the United States. To illustrate through Figure 11:2, mother's occupation (within "Family Background") contributes to respondent's "Occupational Achievement" both by a direct pathway (e.g., following in Mom's footsteps), and by the indirect effect of the mother's position on the offspring's education (mothers with certain jobs can afford Ivy League tuitions, which can pay off in a Wall Street job). Instead of sifting aggregate occupational data for the size of the movement across strata, this approach focuses on the traits—and fortunes—of individuals.

Status attainment research has added rich empirical detail to the schematic in Figure 11:2. Blau and Duncan's classic work found that both the bottom and top sets of arrows trace significant paths of intergenerational status transmission, and that the top path (through education level) was the more significant in 1962. More recent studies find the indirect effect of education (measured as years of schooling) to be increasingly important. This finding fits both the conventional success formula ("To get a good job . . . ") and the macrosociological data about the United States having a more open opportunity structure (because education is gaining importance). Other researchers have added more personal traits such as motivation level and IQ to the status attainment model (Sewell and Hauser, 1975). Some have even measured "cultural capital"—defined as appreciation for painting, opera, and other fine arts—and linked it to family background and school grades (DiMaggio, 1982). But no matter how detailed the model, no matter how many personal traits are inserted among the arrows, only about half of occupational mobility fits the predictions of the

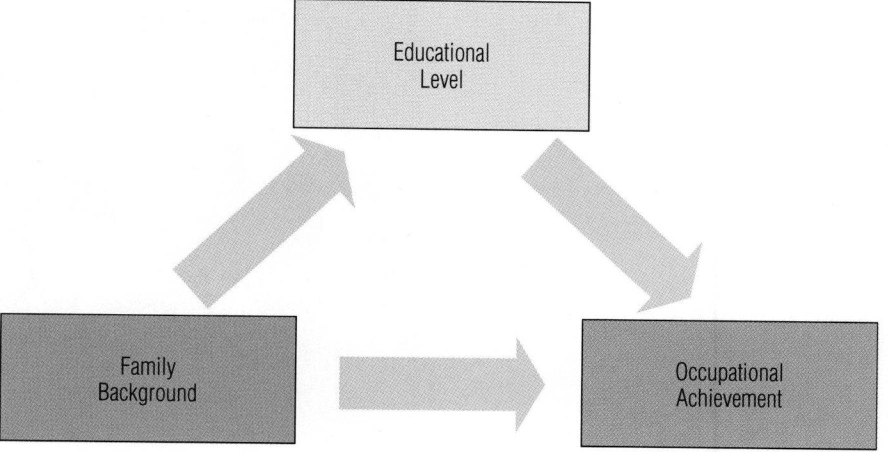

FIGURE 11:2 A STATUS ATTAINMENT MODEL OF INDIVIDUAL ACHIEVEMENT

This is a simplified version of the status attainment mobility model, which focuses upon the traits of individuals. The "Family Background" of a parent has both a direct impact on offspring's "Occupational Achievement" (bottom arrow), and an indirect effect through the "Educational Level" of offspring (top two arrows).

status attainment approach (Jencks et al., 1979). What is the missing coefficient of the success formula?

Social Networks: ". . . with a Little Help from My Friends"

The image in Figure 11:2 is attractive for reasons beyond its scientific status. As we saw in Chapter 7, an ethic of individual achievement lies at the very heart of American culture. This core value infuses our dreams with meaning, and confuses our thoughts with a moral message. The promptings of parents and peers make achievement seem to be a purely personal matter, as though you are literally alone on a ladder on which climbing (or falling from) the rungs depends only upon yourself. This is a seductive notion that is utterly wrong. Now that your value-based assumptions have been noted, can you picture *any* act of achievement performed all alone?

Compare the predicament of the lone rock climber with the coordinated, supportive climbing team. We offer these photos as analogies to the alternative sociological models of social mobility. The status attainment model focuses on individual traits (such as the body weight and arm strength of the woman); the structural model stresses interpersonal ties in the achievement process (like the "ties" holding together the team as they work their way up).

structural model—an approach to occupational mobility that focuses on the structure of social contacts.

A powerful corrective to the individualistic bias of the status attainment approach is the **structural model** of occupational mobility. Instead of viewing you as a bundle of supply packs and equipment about to make the climb alone, this approach posits the obvious: There are other people on the rungs. Picture an army of straining climbers, some rising thanks to helping hands, others slipping off as others tug at their feet. To give this image life, recall the hard evidence presented in Chapter 4. Mark Granovetter's seminal research (1973) established the significance of personal relationships for finding jobs, and suggested the special benefits of "weak ties" (i.e., those on the fringes of the network) for tapping information leading to upper-white-collar positions. Subsequent studies have elaborated this basic finding. One investigation (Jones, 1979) of poor urban males has shown both the strongest and the weakest network ties to be productive job sources. Another study in the United Kingdom indicates the importance of working-class kin bonds in guiding migration decisions and even in influencing employers to hire one's relatives (Grieco, 1987).

Analyses of wider samples have suggested the complexity of the social activity on the ladder. An investigation of occupational contacts in the Detroit Area Study reveals that job-seekers do appeal to their higher-prestige network members, and that higher-prestige contacts do pay off in attaining higher-prestige positions (Marsden and Hurlbert, 1988). Research in other industrialized nations generally confirms this phenomenon cross-culturally. A German study even suggests this refinement: ". . . job shifters with low initial prestige jobs advance by using strong intimate ties, whereas those with high prestige prior jobs advance by employing weak intimate ties" (Wegener, 1991, p. 69).

You have just read about research at the cutting-edge of sociology, with many specifics of the structural mobility model still in dispute. This much, however, is indisputable: The familiar model of the American Dream in Figure 11:2 should be redrawn with network features. Structuralists have already shown, in fact, that the top path through education is not as simple as parents paying tuition. Part of the way education pays off is through opening doors to high-status social contacts, who then can open the door to a job (Lin, Ensel, and Vaughn, 1981). Consider a concrete case:

> When Albert Einstein completed his university studies in 1900, he could not obtain a job appropriate to his training, in part because he had so antagonized his professors that they would neither hire nor help him. After more than a year of searching and temporary employment, Einstein applied for a post at the Swiss Patent Office and was a few months later called to Zurich for an interview with the office director. In spite of an inadequate performance during the interview, Einstein was hired. As it turns out, the director was an intimate friend of the father of Marcel Grossman, a good friend and former classmate of Einstein. The appointment was no doubt a favor from the director to the Grossmans. Einstein's major scientific insights occurred during his several years at the Patent Office . . . (Fischer, 1977, p. 19).

social capital—the social resources for achievement stored in the personal network.

A multitude of such examples and research findings has given rise to a new theoretical idea. **Social capital** is defined as the social resources for attaining one's goals stored in the personal network. The term is distinguished from "human capital," the idea that personally acquired skills—especially education—are an investment directly translatable into individual achievement (see Chapter 17). The case of Einstein shows that human capital is only a partial explanation. Each of us also has an endowment of social resources that can activate or even substitute for our official credentials (Coleman, 1988). As you might suspect, this social capital is not equally distributed in the stratification system of the United States.

SOCIAL CLASSES IN THE UNITED STATES

Earlier, you were asked to poll the meaning of the term "society" within your social network. We predicted that words meaning inequality would pop out of your friends' mouths in their definitions. This prediction is based on the very history of our discipline in the United States. In the 1920s, sociologists began "community studies" designed to reveal the structure of society through detailed scrutiny of a small city: ". . . these turned into studies of stratification, because a complex modern society does not present a simple and unified cultural pattern, but a series of lifestyles and groupings arranged by social class" (Collins, 1988, p. 150). When amateurs or professionals look at our society, they see social classes.

The Meaning of Class

Despite their self-evident reality, there is still dispute among sociologists about the best way to define classes. The situation mirrors the still-heated debates in physics about the fundamental nature of matter. In neither discipline does the theoretical give-and-take prevent working researchers from measuring and analyzing their very tangible subject matter.

It is fitting that a contemporary discussion of this concept begin with Karl Marx. In important respects, Marx revolutionized the understanding of societies by viewing them as structures of classes. A Marxist definition of a "class" is a set of people who share a common relationship to the means of production. In a society such as the United States, this translates into a division between the "bourgeoisie" who control the capital of industrial production (thus, capitalists) and the "proletariat" of workers who sell their labor for wages paid by capitalists (these terms were first defined in Chapter 2). An intermediate class of "petit bourgeoisie" consists of small-scale, self-employed businesspeople. Note that the class positions are rooted in their relations to the economic system, and also in their relationship to each other (e.g., a member of the proletariat is defined as someone bossed by the bourgeoisie).

The Weberian framework for defining classes is already familiar to you from "The Dimensions of Stratification." Weber developed the idea of a multidimensional stratification system by grappling directly with Marx's already famous class analysis. He resisted the Marxist approach of basing the stratification system purely on economic position (i.e., on "the means of production"), and insisted on the independent operation of the other dimensions. Nevertheless, Weber's analysis of status consistency led him to detect common strata within society (like those marked off by the horizontal lines in triangle C of Figure 11:1) whose members share broadly similar "life chances." Sociologists working in this tradition often create an index of **socioeconomic status (SES)**, which is a composite of several dimensions such as income, education, and occupational prestige. This produces an overall score rather than a concrete measure of managing or being managed as in the neo-Marxist tradition.

socioeconomic status (SES)—an index of class position based on a composite of several dimensions such as income, education, and occupational prestige.

TABLE 11:4 Subjective Social Class

SOCIAL CLASS	"If you were asked to use one of four names for your social class, which would you say you belong in: the lower class, the working class, the middle class, or the upper class?"		
Value Label	Value	Frequency	Percent
Upper class	1	43	3.1
Middle class	2	640	47.0
Working class	3	623	45.7
Lower class	4	57	4.2
	Total	1,363	100.0

Main Point: The distribution into social classes in the United States as indicated by respondents' self-identification of class position (i.e., "subjective" social class).

Source: General Social Survey, 1990.

subjective social class—the individual's identification of personal class position in society.

One way to cut through the theoretical disputes is to personalize the issue: *What is your class?* This sort of question measures subjective social class, so called because the individual (rather than a sociologist) identifies personal class position. Table 11:4 displays the subjective class breakdown of the cross-section of the U.S. population drawn for the 1990 General Social Survey. We shall employ these four designations to organize the sociological discussion of social classes in contemporary United States.

The Upper Class

The Superrich. Please return to Figure 11:1. The arrow symbol at the top can now be interpreted: Some people are so rich that if that symbol were drawn to scale, the arrow would have to extend *yards* past the top of the page! We won't name any names, but each October *Forbes* magazine does

This scene evokes the American fascination with "lifestyles of the rich and famous." Part of the reason that we accept *inequality of condition* from the "superrich" down to the "dirt poor" is the American dream of an open-class structure offering equal opportunity based on merit.

just that by evaluating the assets of the 400 richest families in the United States. The "average" person on the list was worth $721 million in 1992, an amount which could buy and sell over 20,000 American families earning the **median income** (i.e., the income point at which half of all families earn more, and half earn less).

median income—the income point at which half of all families earn more, and half earn less.

These staggering figures require a clarification about kinds of money. Turn back to Table 11:1, which displays the distribution of income, composed of pay for work and transfer payments. It excludes the value of property and assets, technically known as **wealth**. The statistics describing the wealth distribution are less detailed than those for income, in part because the superrich tend to be secretive about their holdings ("Old Money doesn't talk"). Even the sketchiest numbers, though, paint a clear picture: Wealth in the United States is even more unequally distributed than is income. The richest 1 percent in our society own over 40 percent of all stocks and bonds and over 80 percent of all trust fund monies. At the other end of the ladder, more than one-tenth of our citizens have a net worth that is zero or negative (i.e., the value of their liabilities outweighs the value of their assets; U.S. Bureau of the Census, 1984, 1991).

wealth—the value of property and assets (distinguished from income).

The Rich. Describing the class spectrum in the United States tests one's prose powers to the limit. It can drive an author to resort to a photographic essay to convey the dramatic range of inequality along one metropolitan route (see photos on pp. 366–367). Too much of a spotlight on the dizzying heights of wealth can dazzle the eyes. The popular preoccupation with "Lifestyles of the Rich and Famous" leads to popular myths about what it takes to belong to the upper class.

How rich is "rich"? This is a slippery question because of varying social standards, but there are relevant objective data. Test your "IQ"—Inequality Quotient—about the following information. What income level defines the top quintile of Table 11:1? According to the most recently available figures, about $60,000 places a family in the highest fifth. Not rich enough? Let's move higher up. The price of admission for the top 5 percent of U.S. families is . . . $100,000 (U.S. Bureau of the Census, 1991). Surprised? Thanks to the superrich, this may seem like a middle-class income, although it is near the apex of the triangle in objective terms. In subjective terms, probably even fewer Americans would define themselves as "rich" than the roughly 3 percent who say they belong to the "upper class" in Table 11:4.

> "She's got an indiscreet voice," I remarked.
> "It's full of—," I hesitated.
> "Her voice is full of money," he said suddenly.
> That was it. I'd never understood before. It was full of money—that was the inexhaustible charm that rose and fell in it, the jingle of it, the cymbals song of it (F. Scott Fitzgerald, *The Great Gatsby*).

Social Life at the Top. Most people suspect that the rich really *are* different, and not just in their bank accounts. Sociologists have proven it. The nature of the proof has been to show that the things that distinguish the elite—including their money—are entangled in social roots.

First, consider the source. Where does the money come from? Certainly, there are well-known success stories of individuals magically converting the rags of childhood into adult riches. Such cases are well known because they are as rare as magic. The realistic formula involves a social connection: Pick the right parents. In the 1986 *Forbes* 400 list, there were 90 families each of whom controlled assets of at least half a billion dollars—*every one of these families inherited all or part of their wealth.* The American Leadership Study drew a sample of 545 of the most elite position holders in the United States and reported that the overwhelming majority had fathers who had owned or managed businesses (Moore and Alba, 1982).

The social organization of socialites goes far beyond passing wealth along family ties. Old Money insider Nelson W. Aldrich, Jr., here describes social structures that had been well established by the day of his great-grandfather (the one who made the Aldrich fortune):

> Old Money exercised guardianship of the distinctive tasks, fashions, and manners of its members in Society, its men's and (far fewer) women's clubs, its boarding schools, and its colonies of country and seashore estates. On these same meeting grounds, it also sought to control its members' friendships and loves (1988, pp. 36–37).

Notice that the exclusivity of such organizations is reinforced by manipulating "friendships and loves"—that is, members' network ties. Aldrich himself was bound within this social orbit, having attended St. Paul's boarding school ("St. Midas'") and Harvard University. Another St. Paul's graduate has turned the instruments of sociological analysis upon his own class. E. Digby Baltzell, with his "insider's heart and outsider's mind" (Schneiderman, 1992, p. 81) coined the term WASP (White, Anglo-Saxon Protestant) to refer to the traditional upper crust of our society. His systematic description of their circle-the-wagons style of association clearly shows that the Midas touch involves the need for extensive social contact (Baltzell, 1964).

Outside the circles of the superrich are less glittering networks, which patrol the top of the ladder. A widely accepted estimate of rags-to-riches mobility is that about 3.4 percent of the children of manual-occupation parents make it into the occupational elite (Szymanski, 1983). Once again it is statistically obvious that network ties matter. As the structural mobility model has already indicated, "Social Life at the Top" is not merely the upscale cocktail parties you'll attend once you arrive; the invitations issued through social networks are a key to your very arrival.

The Middle Class

Given the chance, most Americans will call themselves "middle class." Ask your professor to poll students by saying, "Everyone from a middle-class family, please raise your hand." We have seen this leading question lead to a unanimous show of hands even at colleges populated by the truly rich. Straightforward as it seems, the GSS item composing Table 11:4 is a precision instrument of wording. Previous versions of the question elicited up to 80 percent middle-class respondents in national samples. As these pages have reported, the spectacular range of variation in social rewards makes such a central bulge unbelievable. But it is not unexplainable. Along with the achievement ethic tempting poorer U.S. citizens to identify upward, there is an egalitarian ethic making richer citizens hesitant to call themselves upper class.

These contradictory cultural currents muddy the everyday meaning of middle-class status. Sociologically sophisticated measures of subjective social class (as in Table 11:4) produce some clarification, as do attempts to fill in these categories with objective data. A team of social scientists now studying a sample of 7,300 U.S. households defines the middle class as people earning between $18,500 and $55,000 in 1987 dollars. Their analyses suggest a dynamic class structure, with substantial movement over time across these arbitrary dollar boundaries (Duncan, Smeeding, and Rodgers, 1992). In addition to their arbitrary nature, the multidimensional nature of the class system makes purely monetary definitions seem slightly silly. This is why most sociological approaches turn to the occupational structure for objective data. Turn again to Table 11:3. The "Clerical and Sales" category contains white-collar jobs at intermediate levels of pay, prestige, and power. Many "Professional, Technical, and Managerial" positions receive levels of social rewards not very different from "Clerical and Sales" jobs, although some college presidents and corporate CEOs are supremely rewarded. Given the enormous variation in types of jobs and the remarkable fluidity of the occupational structure, there is no absolute definition of middle class by job category. At the highest rung in Table 11:3 is a grouping that includes Hollywood cosmetic surgeons, astronauts, and teachers who are indubitably middle class (you might politely ask your professors to reveal their salaries—for sociological purposes). The "Craftsmen" category contains foremen, carpenters, and other occupations that are prototypically blue-collar, but whose "life chances" may in some cases match those of their middle-class neighbors.

The Working Class

The cultural premium placed on middle-class status means that the working class is often viewed as a transitional position. A standard version of the American Dream involves a factory worker scrimping to save for children's college tuitions that are their ticket to the middle class. To add a sociological dimension to this personal vision, compare the combined percentages of "Craftsmen" across the generations in Table 11:3. This category included many construction and skilled trades jobs and employed over 20 percent of the fathers, but now employs only about 9 percent of respondents. This attrition occurred over a single generation of workers! The trend is a shrinkage of a blue-collar sector that has been the occupational backbone of the working class.

As with the middle class, shifts in the occupational structure have blurred working-class boundaries. Look at the "Clerical" sector: It contains over one-quarter of all 1990 respondents, up from some 8.7 percent in the previous generation. Clearly there has been a rapid expansion of lower-level, white-collar jobs whose pay, prestige, and power are not clearly superior to blue-collar positions. There has been a parallel growth of the "Service" sector over the generation (in Table 11:3, this is included in the "Operatives, Laborers, and Service" category). These are restaurant employees, janitors, nurses aides—mostly personal service jobs. Many people performing these occupational roles think of themselves as working class, but the social rewards they receive bring them to the brink of the lower class.

The Poor

As impressive a piece of sociological craftsmanship as it is, the GSS is only a sample. Scrutinizing the single set of respondents cannot reveal a full portrait of the class structure, although the trends we have identified are so well documented as to be beyond dispute. Earlier it was noted that the rich are elusive survey respondents. As the merely 4.2 percent of respondents calling themselves "lower class" in Table 11:4 would suggest, the bottom of the class structure also tends to be underrepresented in general purpose surveys. To fill in the picture at the base of the stratification system requires specialized sociological instruments. They view poverty in two dimensions.

The Objective Dimension of Poverty. How poor is "poor"? The difficulties of defining deprivation in a society with billionaires and beggars are suggested by the following exercise. Assume for a moment that you are the head of the household in a nonfarm family of four (yourself, your spouse, and two children living in a metropolitan area). The task is to estimate the *absolute minimum income your family would require for each of the physical needs on the list.* Calculate the smallest monthly dollar total that would provide adequate nutrition, a livable apartment (with utilities), and enough clothes to keep your family warm:

Personal Poverty Budget (nonfarm family of four)

Food	=	
Rent	=	
Clothing	= +	______________ Monthly total
Multiply by 12	=	______________ Annual total

Ask a few of your classmates to make the estimate, then check your amount against those of other students who, hypothetically, have exactly the same family needs as you. Student-to-student variation in calculating the personal poverty budget shows that identifying even the truly needy is no straightforward matter.

"Poverty, like beauty, lies in the eye of the beholder . . . it is not something you can verify or demonstrate, except by inference and suggestion, even with a measure of error. To say who is poor is to use all sorts of value judgments" (Orshansky, 1974, p. 81). These hedging comments were made

These selections from Steven Shames' *Outside the Dream,* a much-praised volume of photographs on poverty in contemporary America, speak much more eloquently than any words about the paradox of poverty in the "Land of Opportunity."

absolute poverty—the state in which material resources are not adequate to provide for minimal physical necessities (defined in the United States by the Federal Poverty Line).

by no less of an authority than Mollie Orshansky, who drew up the first widely accepted Federal Poverty Line (FPL). The FPL is often used as the upper boundary for **absolute poverty**, a state in which families cannot provide for even minimal physical necessities; we say "often used" because many experts believe that the current poverty line—about $14,000 annually, calculated by updating Orshansky's formula—simply is not enough money to feed, house, and clothe four people. The original formula was based on the U.S. Department of Agriculture's economy food plan for temporary emergencies, which their own studies estimated could provide a nutritionally adequate diet for only about 10 percent of the population on a day-to-day basis (Orshansky, 1974). Whether one accepts the assumptions of the formula or not, the FPL is surely a strict measure of real need . . . as your calculations no doubt suggest.

There is something paradoxical about the very existence of poverty within the richest society in human history. We shall probe that paradox with a series of pointed questions: How many are poor, Who are the poor, and finally, Why are they poor?

How many are poor? The objective FPL standard of need permits a straightforward analysis of the secular trend in American poverty. The top line in Figure 11:3 traces the year-by-year numbers of the poor in the United States. Observe the rapid dip in the trend line between 1966 and 1969 (the implementation period for the much-maligned "War on Poverty"), the 1970s decade of no real change, and then a skyrocketing of absolute poverty between 1979 and 1983. Since that reversal of the historical trend, poverty has stabilized at about 30 million, enough persons to stock the 23 largest cities in the United States entirely with poor people. Lest this comparison stir up the stereotype that poverty is a purely a city problem, be aware that the percentage of the rural population who are impoverished actually exceeds the percentage in urban areas (O'Hare, 1988).

In the midst of such mind-numbing numbers, it is worth emphasizing that this vast sea of individuals suffer real deprivation. First, Figure 11:3 has been charted *after* transfer payments have already been added in; that is, these people are poor despite the receipt of government cash grants. Neither are they only missing the occasional meal. According to the Census Bureau, the typical poor family is over $4,000 a year short of the FPL (U.S. Bureau of the Census, 1989), which means that earnings and welfare together fall far short of maintaining even a bare subsistence level. Millions of poor people, of course, are much worse off than what is statistically "typical."

Who are the poor? In looking beyond the headlines to the vast objective data on poverty, one statistic jumps out past all others: the number of children. In the United States, individuals under age 18 constitute some 40 percent of all those under the FPL. Moreover, the special report *Child Poverty in America* (Johnson et al., 1991) has documented that these children are in especially deep deprivation, with millions living in families receiving less than *half* of the FPL. The United States spends the lowest percentage of its Gross Domestic Product (GDP) on income support and, not surprisingly, has the highest proportion of economically deprived children in comparison with Australia, Canada, Germany, Sweden, and the United Kingdom (Smeeding, 1990). For an even more disturbing international comparison, there are more truly hungry children in the United States than the *total* number of children in El Salvador or Cambodia—the sorts of places featured in calls for U.S. citizens to feed the children of the world (Johnson et al., 1991).

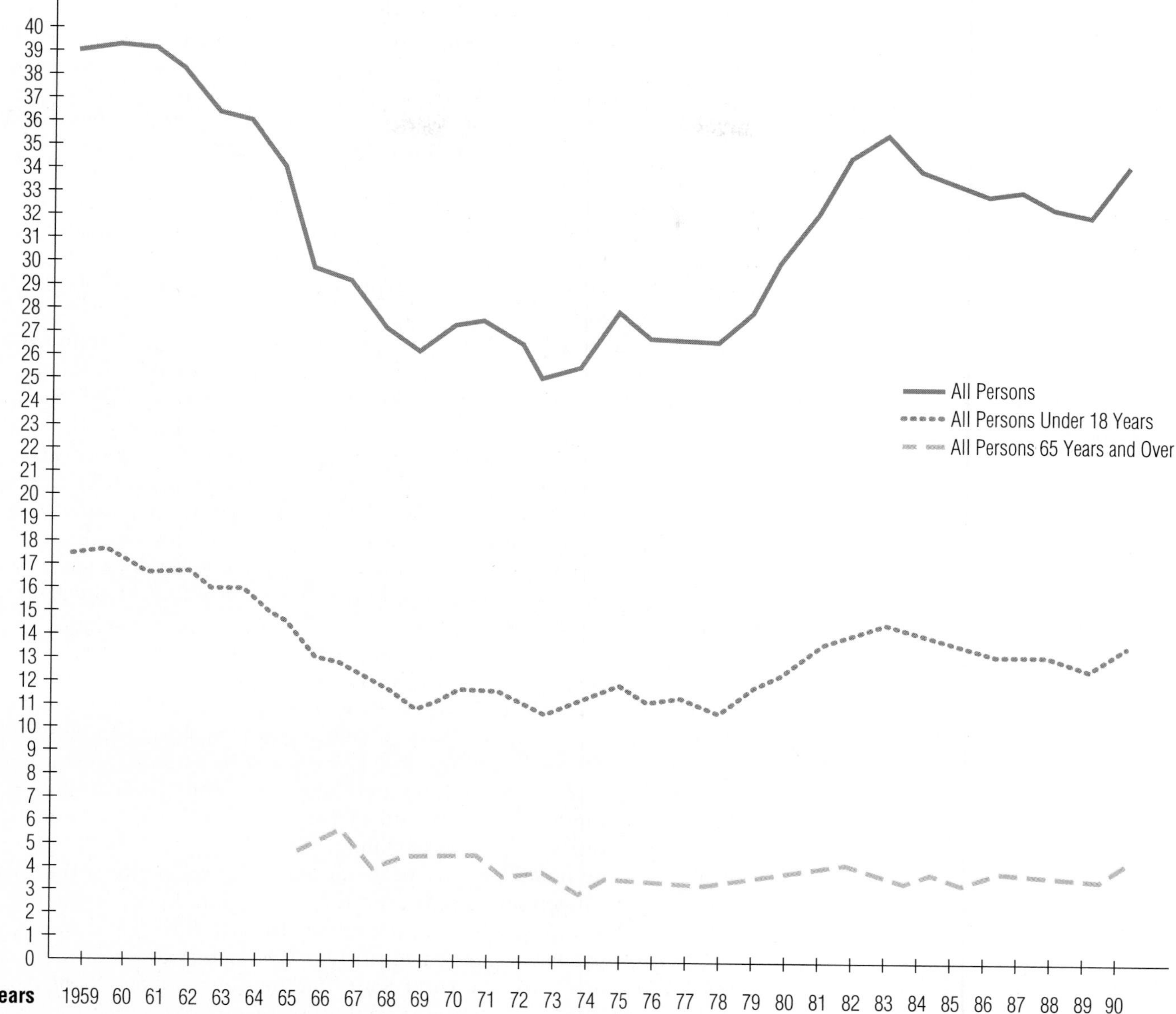

FIGURE 11:3 PROFILE OF POVERTY IN THE UNITED STATES

Numbers of people below the Federal Poverty Line (FPL) in *millions*.

Source: Adapted from U.S. Census, *Current Population Reports,* Series P–60, No. 166, *Money, Income and Poverty Status in the United States: 1988* (Advanced Data from the March 1989 Current Population Survey), U.S. Government Printing Office, Washington, DC, 1989, Tables 18 and 19; *Statistical Abstracts of the United States,* pp. 456–457.

At the opposite end of the age range, about 11 percent of the poverty population is past the culturally accepted retirement age of 65 (note that the poverty of the aged has stabilized at a relatively low level throughout the period shown in Figure 11:3, a point to which we shall return). Over half of the impoverished are thus too young or too old to be in the labor force, and another 11 percent are too ill or disabled to work (O'Hare, 1988); this leaves about a third of the sub-FPL population who are "able-bodied" poor, most of whom *are* in the labor force. Of the 10 million or so "working poor" in 1988, almost half worked full time and still could not break the subsistence barrier of the FPL. To see how this is possible, simply multiply the minimum wage times 40 (hours per week) times 50 (weeks of work per year).

Why are they poor? This quick review of poverty's objective profile is very revealing. One thing it reveals is that simple idleness is not the answer to this paragraph's leading question. Most of the poor cannot work, and most of those who can, do. Aside from eliminating inadequate explanations—like laziness equals poverty—the objective data do not speak for themselves. Proper interpretation of these facts—and the facts of the entire system of inequality—require the illumination of sociological theory. Although that is provided in the sociological theory section later, popular theories of poverty are both sociologically and politically significant.

The Subjective Dimension of Poverty. For a moment, let us put the social science aside. Think about your personal conversations concerning poverty—chatting with a friend after an encounter with a street person, or a family discussion after the nightly news. What images of poor people populate your social network?

National opinion polls reflect much compassion for the destitute, but also a widespread feeling that such people are lazy, stupid, and immoral. Sound familiar? In effect, much of the public views the deficiency of money as caused by a deficiency of character (Jones, 1984). This is not some recent hardening of the national heart. Negative stereotypes of poverty stretch back to the very founding of the United States, and, in fact, back farther still to roots in English society (Katz, 1989). The cultural tenet that this is the "Land of Opportunity" conditions us to view upwardly mobile achievers as winners and the poor as . . . well, losers. Quite naturally, such a view tends to keep poverty on the back burner of social policy in the United States.

As though shocked awake, the United States opened its collective eyes to the reality of poverty in the 1960s. An extensive study of opinion trends since the 1930s found that poverty was first widely identified as a social problem in 1965 (Lauer, 1976). Amazingly, the tide of public opinion rose after an ebbing of the actual number below the FPL. Some 6 million people escaped poverty between 1950 and 1965 (U.S. Bureau of the Census, 1982). Poverty literally burst into subjective awareness when the objective extent of deprivation had been declining. Why?

Begin with the *visibility* of the problem. For large segments of the society, the poor had been out of sight, and therefore out of mind. Sequestered in their rapidly growing suburbs, the middle class had little occasion to see the poor in Appalachia or in the local slum. The mass exodus of indigent African Americans from the rural South to the metropolitan North continued through the 1950s, however, so that by the end of the decade a very large and very deprived population had been deposited on the doorstep of the nonpoor. It is striking that the first appearance in the polls of poverty as a social problem came the year after the first major civil disorder of the decade; namely, the Harlem riot in July of 1964. A riot is an intrinsically dramatic event, especially when media exposure continually reruns violent scenes. Suddenly, poverty had national attention.

Some social historians have called the sixties the "American Decade" because of this society's international supremacy during that period. The United States was the greatest military power on Earth, the world center of medical breakthroughs and technological wizardry, and enjoyed an expanding economy with minimal inflation and unemployment. The sense of societal omnipotence fed rising *expectations* about the imminent solution of human problems. These expectations were further heightened by President Lyndon Johnson's declaration of a War on Poverty in 1964. Just as President Kennedy had publicly challenged us to a (victorious) space race after the Soviet Union's launching of *Sputnik* (the first Earth satellite), President Johnson likened poverty to another beachhead to be taken by the ingenuity and resources of the United States. Despite undeniable objective progress (examine the lines for the sixties in Figure 11:3), poverty was not to be wiped out overnight. The consequence was a growing sense of national frustration because of the existence of so many millions of poor people in the midst of a would-be utopia.

As discussions with the fortysomething generation will confirm, deep cultural currents were stirring in the 1960s. Sociological analysts probing beneath phenomena such as Woodstock and love-ins have identified a shift in *values.* This was the decade of Martin Luther King's "I Have a Dream" speech in which the Civil Rights Act and much race-equalizing legislation was passed. Books such as John Kenneth Galbraith's *The Affluent Society* and Michael Harrington's *The Other America* stressed the paradox of poverty amid affluence, and were best-sellers in the 1960s. Herbert Gans of Harvard speaks of the "Equality Revolution" during this decade, the rising public sentiment that inequality is just unacceptable (Gans, 1973). Quite clearly, a heightened value on equality makes continued inequality seem outrageous. This is why the United States discovered—and was horrified by—poverty in the sixties.

This sociological analysis speaks volumes about the subjective view of poverty in the nineties. Again, check your own opinions. Did it strike you that anything essential to the current scene was missing from the objective sketch of the poor drawn earlier? We guess that you wondered about where "homelessness" fit into the poverty picture. Given their lack of an address, it is not surprising that empirical studies have not settled on a reliable enumeration of this country's homeless population. There is consensus among researchers, though, that the numbers went way up over the past decade. Whatever their exact objective dimension, homeless people are prominent in the public image of contemporary poverty. Although homelessness has existed throughout U.S. history, the *Reader's Guide to Periodical Literature* listed *no* articles on the topic in 1975 (Katz, 1989). Suddenly, in 1982, stories about the homeless were carried in *Newsweek, U.S. News & World Report,* and *The Wall Street Journal.* In 1983 (the year poverty peaked overall), *The New York Times* printed nearly two stories a week on homelessness (Smith, 1988). Why the media blitz on this one poverty subtype? Homeless folks make good copy because their plight is so heartrending. Put another way, homelessness strikes at one of the core *values* of the American Dream: the home as a haven for one's family (see Figure 11:4). It is transformed into a very telegenic nightmare vision when a poor woman sleeps in city streets with her starving children—as many do.

Another freshly spotlighted subtype of the poor is referred to as the underclass. The term first reached a mass audience in a *Time* magazine cover story on August 19, 1977, entitled "The American Underclass." They were called "A Nation Apart" by *U.S. News & World Report* in 1986, stressing their deviance from mainstream U.S. society. Although sociological specialists have not settled on a precise definition, in popular discourse the term generally defines a species of the poor in which illegitimacy, joblessness, crime, and drugs are rampant (Katz, 1989). Because these very traits flaunt mainstream *values,* the public profile of the underclass looms large. At the time of this writing, violent scenes of the 1992 Los Angeles riots are being played and replayed on national television. The breakdown of public order being very *visibly* displayed violates our most basic *expectations* of public decency, and raises the subjective spectre of the underclass.

Social scientists have paid much more attention to the objective conditions surrounding the underclass. In his presidential address to the American Sociological Association, William Julius Wilson (1991) has argued that special poverty problems have grown in 10 cities with true "ghettos"; that is, concentrations of similar (in this case, very disadvantaged) people. As in his earlier work *The Truly Disadvantaged* (1987), Wilson focuses upon the

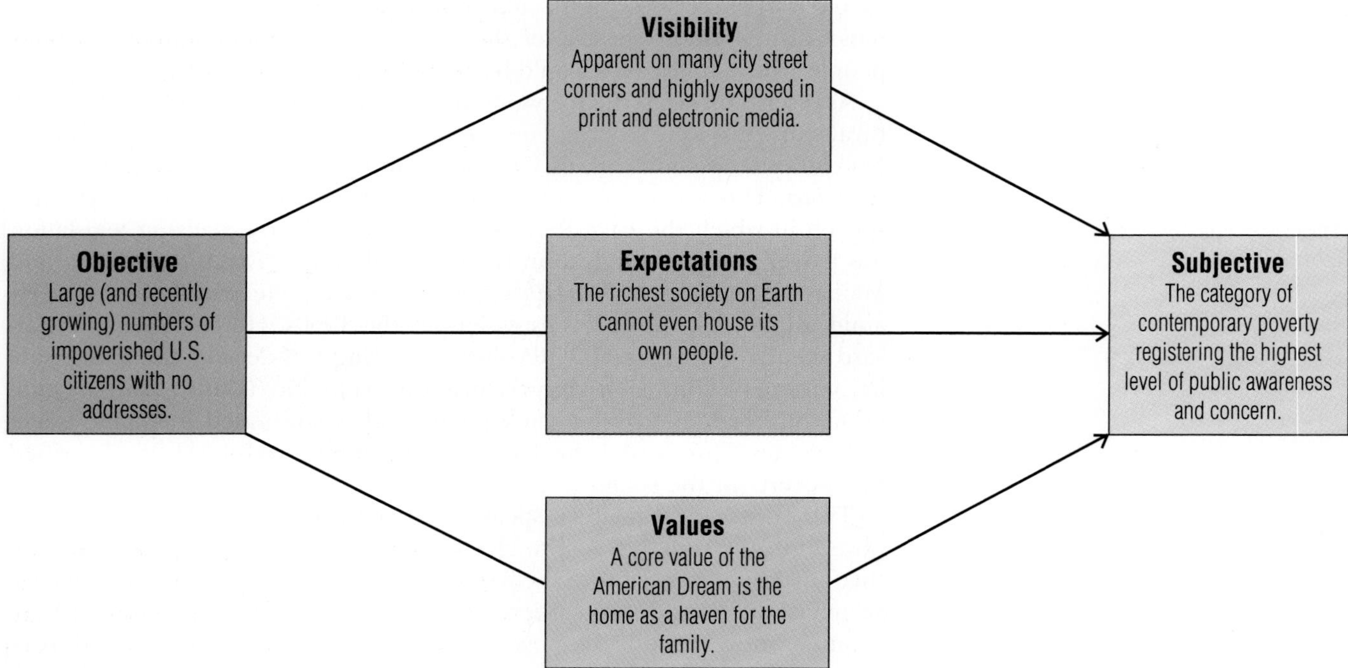

FIGURE 11:4 SUBJECTIVE AND OBJECTIVE DIMENSIONS: THE HOMELESS POOR PROBLEM

demographic, racial, and employment forces generating poverty. While scholars and politicians continue to address issues of the underclass (Jencks and Peterson, 1991), it is important to take Wilson's cue and to see the wider scope of poverty. It is a chilling fact that the chance of descending into poverty has always been a real one for the vast majority of Americans. Return to Figure 11:3. Before the historic shift in 1979, nearly 1 million families living below the FPL were headed by individuals who had professional/managerial occupations, some college education, or both (U.S. Bureau of the Census, 1982). As the ominously rising lines after 1979 would suggest, the chances of virtually any type of person in the United States becoming impoverished have increased. A special study commissioned by the Department of Commerce in the mid-eighties found that the *majority* of Americans descending into poverty fell from incomes well above the FPL (U.S. Bureau of the Census, 1989). Like disease, poverty is not an equal opportunity tragedy (see Chapter 18); however, it clearly can strike anyone, especially during an epidemic.

THEORETICAL PERSPECTIVES ON SOCIAL STRATIFICATION

The story of social stratification in the United States is not a simple one. As in any complex tale, there are many linked plot lines. The real protagonist in this tale has not been a person. Billionaires and beggars are both mere bit players next to the real star: social structure. In each scene, we (the narrators) have been careful to point out the methodical but mysterious machinations of the stratification *system.* This star now takes center stage.

To set the final scene, we flashback to earlier evidence about the social structure of inequality in the United States. You will recall our remarking on the amazing feats performed by this stratification "star." The annual allocation of trillions of dollars to hundreds of millions of people has been

TABLE 11:5 The Redistribution of Income in the United States

	PERCENT DISTRIBUTION OF FAMILY INCOME[a]	
INCOME QUINTILE	1984	1990
Highest fifth	42.7	44.3
Fourth fifth	24.4	23.8
Middle fifth	17.1	16.6
Second fifth	11.1	10.8
Lowest fifth	4.7	4.6

[a]Income includes earnings from employment and transfer payments (such as Social Security and welfare) but excludes wealth (such as stocks and bonds).

Sources: Adapted from United States Bureau of the Census, "Money Income of Households, Families, and Persons in the United States: 1980," *Current Population Reports,* Series P-60, No. 149. Washington, DC: U.S. Government Printing Office, March 1985; *Statistical Abstract of the United States: 1991,* p. 455.

executed with dazzling consistency in the face of wars, business cycles, riots, and even attacks on the system itself. Recall also that income is only the showiest part of the performance. Arranged behind the piles of dollars are matching piles of prestige, power, education, "life chances," art appreciation . . . We have trailed off in the recitation to save space. The truth is, virtually every facet of everyone's life follows the contours of the stratification system. If you doubt it, consult the "Inequality and the Inner Self" section of Chapter 1 presenting an encyclopedic look at how class position controls your experience as documented in *every chapter* of this book!

But there is a plot twist at the end of Table 11:5. As you can see in this extension of Table 11:1, the perfect performance of our protagonist appears to have broken down of late. Note that the richest quintile gained nearly two additional percentage points of the income pie—a huge amount by historical standards—and that *every* other quintile lost from its slice over 1984–1990. In other words, the rich got richer and everybody else got relatively poorer. This sudden shifting of resources toward the very top of the system raises questions about the system itself. However virtuoso its performance, what motivates our "star"? Who writes the script for the system, and why has the script changed? It is time to seek answers in sociological theory.

Functionalism

Social inequality is the single most-studied subject in all of sociology. This is the reason it is featured throughout the book, and the reason we used it to introduce you to the very idea of social structure in Chapter 1. As you have seen in this chapter, much of the intellectual work has been devoted to describing the fantastic patterns of social reward. Now we consider the most intriguing and, arguably, most important issue of all: *Why?*

By definition, functionalists explain social phenomena by their functions. Social inequality, then, must be a cause rather than an effect, performing some good service rather than just divvying up goods and services. How does the stratification system serve the larger social system of the United States? A standard functionalist answer is well posed in terms of college salaries. According to the latest comprehensive survey, the average full professor is paid about $62,000 a year (*Academe,* 1992); according to a noncomprehensive author survey, the typical college staff worker gets about

The remarkable range of "life chances" reflecting the class system of United States society is here revealed in a series of photos following a single metropolitan thoroughfare: Lancaster Avenue originates in inner-city Philadelphia and leads outward to the opulent "Main Line" suburb occupied by the co-authors' university.

LEGG MASON
Members New York Stock Exchange, Inc.

Plymouth
CHRYSLER
MG
USED CARS
Jaguar
PHILPENN
ACME

$20,000. One argument from functionalist theory says that professors perform a more essential function for the college social system than do secretaries or janitors, hence their greater rewards. This is difficult to defend since all employees are in some sense "essential"; if all secretaries and janitors go home, the phones go unanswered, the report cards go unreported, and the students go to the hospital due to disease from uncollected trash.

A more sophisticated functionalist argument stresses talent, training, and trouble. Only some few people have the "right stuff" to pass through the academic wringer of tests and drudgery that can span up to a decade of graduate training. Then, these precious few must be dedicated enough to put up with the trouble of teaching people such as yourself while slaving over research papers. Why do professors do it? The functionalist response is differential social rewards. The (relatively) big bucks, prestigious letters (PhD), and classroom powers are necessary if society is to entice the academically talented to profess for a living.

Now magnify these case examples in the prism of Table 11:5. Across the tens of thousands of occupational statuses that make up the U.S. labor force cuts the functional demand for talent, training, and trouble. The stratification system works as it does because it *works,* producing the right match of persons to positions. From the functionalist perspective, the recent redistribution of rewards upward may have negative consequences—dysfunctions—for those at the bottom, while serving the greater needs of an increasingly high-tech society. This functionalist argument presupposes open mobility so that people can flow to where they do the most good. The opposite is a "caste system," in which one's stratification position is fixed at birth at the level of one's parents (see Chapter 6 for a cross-cultural illustration). Society's elite may slam the doors to its cocktail parties and marriageable daughters, thus excluding upwardly mobile outsiders, and becoming a closed caste (Baltzell, 1964). Alternatively, the "best and brightest" may be admitted to the social circles of the "rich and famous," thus improving the steering of the ship of society.

Functionalist arguments have likewise been applied to the bottom quintile of Table 11:5. Consider the unsettling point of view of "The Positive Functions of Poverty." In this classic article, Herbert J. Gans (1972) lists many of the ways hurtful deprivation helps the nondeprived. Without the poor, who would pick crops, clean toilets, and otherwise do society's "dirty work"? Without the poor, how would social workers, bookies, pawnbrokers, and police find work? Without the poor, with whom would we fill the ranks of the armed services to fight—and die—in society's wars?

Conflict Theory

These are provocative comments to make about "The Land of Opportunity." The whole subject of stratification, in fact, has provoked heated, even nasty, sociological debate both inside and outside of the United States. This is not a dull academic game. At stake is the plunder of society—and who should get it.

As their name would suggest, conflict theorists start from the fundamental premise of opposed human interests. Most fundamentally, it is in my interest to take as many of society's goodies from your pile as I can keep; your interest, quite naturally, is the opposite. This premise dissolves the functionalist picture of society as a system served by its stratification subsystem. Go directly to Table 11: 5. Why do those at the top get a bigger pile? Because they can take it from those at the bottom. Go back to

Figure 11:3. Why is the poverty of aged Americans bottoming out, whereas poverty has climbed in other subpopulations? Because the rising number of senior citizens described in Chapter 20 means political muscle for the old to pull resources away from the young.

The preeminent figure in conflict theory is Karl Marx. All Marxist explanations of stratification systems begin with his single, dazzling insight: At the core of complex societies is a simple class structure. If one looks beneath the bewildering surface phenomena of life in this society—malls, mortgage rates, Mastercards, and much more—there lies a social division of bourgeoisie (the owners of industrial capital) versus the proletariat (the paid laborers of the bourgeoisie). Did you notice the versus? This is not a mere division into haves and have-nots, but a structure of opposed interests—each dollar bargained away from workers in a wage settlement is another dollar for the factory owner. Neo-Marxists have refined this simple two-tiered picture of an industrial system, but still focus on class divisions as the basis for societal conflict. Professors do not own the college like a capitalist owns a factory, but they still successfully bargain for higher salaries than do secretaries within a limited college budget. Neither is such "bargaining" a simple matter of functional merit to society. Can the average CEO in the United States really be worth about $2 million per year in service to the social system—the price of at least 20 engineers—or do CEOs just have corporate clout?

Questions like this one are rhetorical for the conflict theorist. A tougher question is the one that follows: As you stare at Figure 11:1, *why aren't you angry?* The gross disparities in social rewards documented throughout this chapter, the gross deprivations suffered by the deprived in the richest society on the planet . . . all would seem to be fuel for an outrage you probably do not feel. The authors can be reasonably sure of reader apathy not because of your insensitivity, but because of hard sociological data. Lots of polls have shown strong resistance to any radical restructuring of the income distribution, even among the respondents with the most to gain. What lies behind this resistance appears to be ". . . the prevailing beliefs that economic inequality in principle is necessary and beneficial (i.e., just) and that ultimately all Americans are individually responsible for their economic fate" (Kleugel and Smith, 1986, p. 291). This widespread perception that the "system" really is a meritocracy (see Chapter 17) chills any outrage about inequality. But how does most of a nation come to buy the functionalist party line—especially in the face of all the conflicting evidence?

Refer to the famous phrase of Karl Marx: "The ideas of the ruling class are in every epoch the ruling ideas." To whit, whichever class controls the *material means* of production also controls the *mental means* of production. The latter includes TV time, newspaper space, school curricula, congressional speeches—none of which are free and all of which work on the public mind. In a Marxist analysis, the myth of the meritocracy planted in that mind is an "ideology," an idea that justifies the interests of a particular group (Chapter 1). Which group? To a conflict theorist, the answer is obvious.

Symbolic Interactionism

In general, symbolic interactionist theory disapproves of the very concept of "system." Grand processes like the one represented in Figure 11:1 are to be seen from within rather than from above. Instead of a telescope aimed at the whole big structure of stratification, this approach uses a microscope to reveal real people interpreting their own little niches of inequality.

In the rich United States, the most troublesome niche is that occupied by the poor. Among the various theories devised to explain this paradox, perhaps the best known is the **culture of poverty**. In a nutshell, the theory states that the poor are different from you and me—in their beliefs and values—and that is why they remain poor. The phrase emerged from the works of Oscar Lewis (1966), who described the everyday lives of real impoverished people. It gained the status of a theory as warriors in the War on Poverty confronted the "cycle of dependency," in which welfare families were seemingly passing on the habit of welfare from generation to generation. Certainly, the notion that deprived people pass anti-employment attitudes to each other like a kind of work-phobia disease fits popular stereotypes of poverty.

culture of poverty—the theory that the poor have a distinctive set of subcultural beliefs and values that promote poverty.

The trouble with the culture of poverty is simple: No one has found the evidence. Decades of surveys sifting for poor–nonpoor differences in attitudes (especially toward work) have come up pretty empty (Covello, 1980; Goodwin, 1972). Moreover, its "cycle of dependency" premise appears to be a myth. Long-term studies of income status have discovered that most of the poor dip below the FPL only temporarily, and that most children of poor parents are upwardly mobile away from the FPL (Hill, 1985). Discrediting this theory does not discredit the whole symbolic interactionist approach to poverty. Indeed, ethnographic accounts of living in poverty such as Carol B. Stack's (1975) *All Our Kin* (see Chapter 3) have been a source of piercing insights into the human realities of coping with the condition.

Some of the most fascinating symbolic interactionist work concerns the *Interaction Ritual* between social unequals. The term in this book title was coined by pioneering researcher Erving Goffman (1967), who charted the strained relations between superiors and inferiors in a society of supposed equals. He observed the subtle ways in which bosses, customers, and professionals command respect from workers, salespeople, and clients, who as subtly express deference to their higher-status interaction partners. Using the analogy of the theater, Goffman's analysis distinguishes the "frontstage" or official performances of these partners from the "backstage," in which the boss can shed his or her suit of authority and workers can develop demeaning or hostile attitudes toward the boss (Goffman, 1959).

Later research in Goffman's tradition has elaborated the details of inequality interactions. Breaches of etiquette such as staring, touching, groaning, and interrupting are the prerogative of the higher-status partner (Karp and Yools, 1986). In your personal talk with a professor, who watches whom for subtle signs of irritation, and who says "Now wait a minute!" if there is a problem? You are the one more likely to frown only *after* the encounter, and then talk openly about the "jerk" in the backstage haunts of the student subculture.

Integrating the Theories

The heat of the theoretical debate on stratification has kept light from falling on points of common interest. Recently, however, sociological theorists have been working to integrate the insights of these warring approaches (Collins, 1988). To dramatize the fact that these are principles of stratification *systems* and are not unique to the United States today, we shall put the theories together around the strange world glimpsed in Box 11:2.

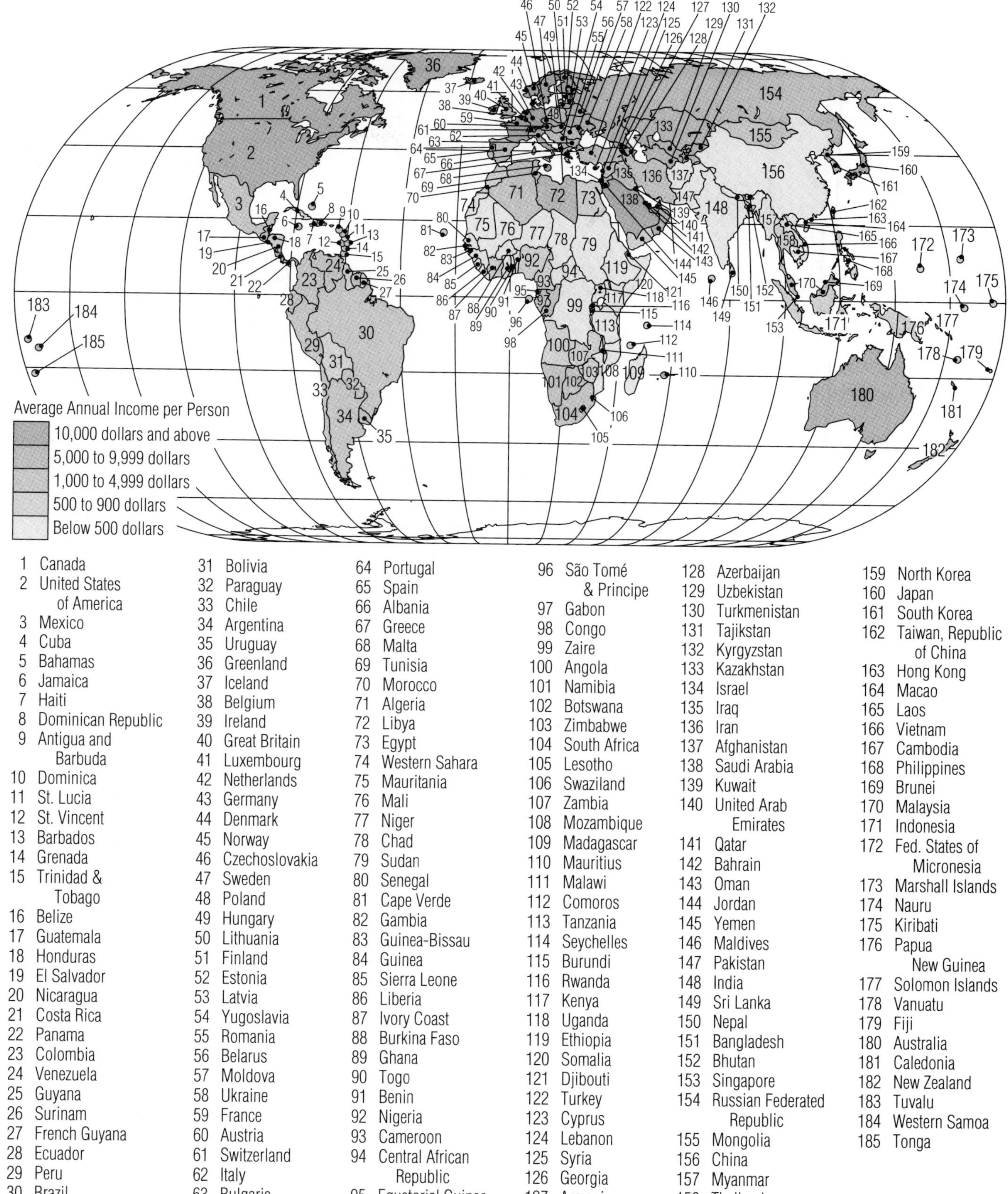

FIGURE 11:5 GLOBAL STRATIFICATION

The unequal distribution of per capita income specifically (and "life chances" generally) is pictured around the planet. Megastructural relations among societies are proposed as explanations for this distribution in Chapter 6.

BOX 11:2 SOCIOLOGICAL IMAGINATION IN FICTION

Lessons about Deprivation

The Dosadi Experiment is set in a far future in which human beings interact with numerous species in an arrangement known as the ConSentiency. The Gowachin are a frog-like species that have confined some of their own with humans on an inhospitable planet Dosadi with a restricted food supply. The purpose of this illegal experiment is to observe the vicious structure of inequality that arises under these conditions and its consequences for behavior. Two scenes are excerpted. In the first, a representative of the Dosadi power structure is observed making a calculating, brutal decision about who shall starve. The second scene follows an agent of the ConSentiency power structure as he moves at large through this cruelly unequal society.

A bullet went *spang!* against the window behind Keila Jedrik's desk, ricocheted and screamed off into the canyon street far below her office. Jedrik prided herself that she had not even flinched. The Elector's patrols would take care of the sniper. The patrols which swept the streets of Chu every morning would home on the sound of the shot. She held the casual hope that the sniper would escape back to the Rim Rabble, but she recognized this hope as a weakness and dismissed it. There were concerns this morning far more important than an infiltrator from the Rim.

Jedrik reached one hand into the corner of early sunlight which illuminated the contact plates of her terminal in the Master Accountancy computer. Those flying fingers—she could almost disassociate herself from them. They darted like insects at the waiting keys. The terminal was a functional instrument, symbol of her status as a Senior Liaitor. It sat all alone in its desk slot—grey, green, gold, black, white and deadly. Its grey screen was almost precisely the tone of her desk top.

With careful precision, her fingers played their rhythms on the keys. The screen produced yellow numbers, all weighted and averaged at her command—a thin strip of destiny with violence hidden in its golden shapes.

Every angel carries a sword, she thought.

But she did not really consider herself an angel or her weapon a sword. Her real weapon was an intellect hardened and sharpened by the terrible decisions her planet required. Emotions were a force to be diverted within the self or to be used against anyone who had failed to learn what Dosadi taught. She knew her own weakness and hid it carefully: she'd been taught by loving parents (who'd concealed their love behind exquisite cruelty) that Dosadi's decisions were indeed terrible.

Jedrik studied the numbers on her computer display, cleared the screen and made a new entry. As she did this, she knew she took sustenance from fifty of her planet's Human inhabitants. Many of those fifty would not long survive this callous jape. In truth, her fingers were weapons of death for those who failed this

Most prominent in this piece are principles of social conflict. The Senior Liaitor sits in her elevated perch looming above people so desperate that they fight to eat garbage. The class conflict is palpable: The "rabble" shoot at Jedrik while she makes "hard decisions" that will starve some of them to death. Lest this seem too science-fictional, recall the vivid scenes of violence in the Los Angeles riots, and realize that city officials really do have to make decisions that close homeless shelters and slash infant feeding funds and program budgets. (Read about a student encounter with this reality in Box 11:3.)

Dosadi is an experiment in inequality, an exploration of what can happen under conditions of extreme want. The system that has evolved allows

BOX 11:2 SOCIOLOGICAL IMAGINATION IN FICTION *continued*

test. She felt no guilt about those she slew.

* * *

All sentient beings are created unequal. The best society provides each with equal opportunity to float at his own level.
—The Gowachin Primary

Bahrank, meanwhile, nosed their machine out of a narrow passage onto a wider street which was crowded by carts, each piled with greenery. The carts moved aside slowly as the armored vehicle approached, hatred plain in the eyes of the Humans who moved with the carts. The press of people astonished McKie; for every cart (and he lost count of them within a block) there were at least a hundred people crowding around, lifting arms high, shouting at the ring of people who stood shoulder to shoulder around each cart, their backs to the piled contents and obviously guarding those contents.

McKie, staring at the carts, realized with a shocked sense of recognition that he was staring at carts piled with garbage. The crowds of people were buying garbage.

Again, Bahrank acted the part of tour guide.

"This is called the Street of the Hungry. That's very select garbage, the best."

The passing scene compelled McKie's attention: hard faces, furtive movements, the hate and thinly suppressed violence, all of this immersed in a normal commercial operation based on garbage. And the numbers of these people! They were everywhere around: in doorways, guarding and pushing the carts, skipping out of Bahrank's path. New smells assaulted McKie's nostrils, a fetid acridity, a stink such as he had never before experienced. . . . It required a moment after Bahrank drove away for McKie to recover his sense of purpose. The buildings rose tall and massive over him, but through a quirk of this Warren's growth, an opening to the west allowed a spike of the silvery afternoon sunlight to slant into the narrow street. The light threw hard shadows on every object, accented the pressure of Human movement. McKie did not like the way people looked at him: as though everyone measured him for some private gain.

Slowly, McKie pressed through the passing throng to the arched entry, observing all he could without seeming to do so. After all those years in BuSab, all of the training and experience which had qualified him for such a delicately powerful agency, he possessed superb knowledge of the ConSentiency's species. He drew on that knowledge now, sensing the powerful secrecy which governed these people. Unfortunately, his experience also was replete with knowledge of what species could do to species, not to mention what a species could do to itself. The Humans around him reminded him of nothing more than a bomb about to explode.

Moving with a constant readiness to defend himself, he went down a short flight of stairs into cool shadows where the foot traffic was lighter but the smells of rot and mold were more pronounced.

Critical Thinking Questions

1. How would you develop a conflict theory comparison between Dosadi and Earthly colonialism, as described in the "Development Theory" section of Chapter 6?
2. What are the elements of Dosadi society that might appear in the "megacities" exploding with population in desperately deprived portions of the Third World? Again, use Chapter 6.

Source: Frank Herbert, *The Dosadi Experiment* (1972). New York: Ace Books, pp. 8, 9, 31, 146–47, 160–61.

almost perfect equality of opportunity: Those who rise to the rank of Liaitor are the most crafty, calculating, and ruthless. It is a kind of gangster meritocracy that sharpens the abilities of all. There is a functionalist element in that the system would degenerate into one massive food riot without the brutal control imposed by the upwardly mobile. This dramatizes realities of our own system, in which professionals who have risen to the top sometimes use force to preserve the social order. Think of the huge investments in police forces, security systems, and barbed wire to protect private property.

The final, symbolic interactionist piece of the theoretical puzzle is apparent in the "Street of the Hungry" scene. As a visitor from the power

BOX 11:3 COLLEGE EXPERIENCE

How I Spent My Summer Vacation

What follows is the account of Joseph Burke, a Notre Dame junior who worked for the Philadelphia Committee for the Homeless (PCH) in the summer of 1991.

Working in Philadelphia this summer with the Philadelphia Committee for the Homeless, I experienced many ups and downs, but the most pervasive feeling had to be frustration. I found myself constantly frustrated that there are people in our community who do not have a place to call their own, who do not have food to eat, who do not have access to medical care, and who do not have someone to love them or to love. When I think back on all the opportunities, support, and love that I have grown up with (and usually take for granted), I feel a deep sorrow for and empathy with those who find hugs and kind words to be so few and far between.

During my eight weeks at PCH, there were numerous times when, after a good conversation or a special moment, I would feel so good inside that I thought I would burst. Unfortunately, however, there are many more times when I was reminded how limited my ability to help is, and that, despite my best intentions, I cannot move mountains.

A recurring frustration that occurred at least once a week was trying to get someone into a shelter. There were several times when someone would approach me, tell me they were sick of their situation, and ask for help in getting off the streets. If it was a Sunday, all I could do was tell them to walk over to the Ridge Avenue shelter and ask for an overnight bed. If the person had been red-carded, however (denied shelter services for a violation ranging from breaking curfew to fighting), then my hands were tied. On a weekday night I could call the Outreach Coordination Center and get transportation to a drug and alcohol detox unit, but problems often arose if the person had been red-carded from the city shelter system. I often found myself talking with someone who was fed up with their life, who wanted to make a fresh start, but all I could do was say in a too well-rehearsed fashion, "Sorry, there is nothing I can do to help you."

Nothing, however, has been more frustrating than dealing with City Government. For four weeks I worked to get a drinking fountain fixed at 16th and the Parkway. My efforts came to no avail. During that four week time, I heard every reason imaginable as to why the fountain couldn't be fixed. During these hot and humid days of summer, clean drinking water is essential to the health of the people who live on the street, not to mention joggers and tourists. I started off with a wonderful dream of the city building drinking fountains across Center City with water flowing from every street corner. As I quickly learned that the city did not share my dream, I settled for just getting this one broken drinking fountain fixed. It seemed like such a small thing, and it really bothers me that it was not fixed. At the start of each phone call I kept thinking, "if people only knew, they would help." I'm not sure what to think now.

Reflecting back on my arrival at PCH, I felt called to act to work to alleviate some of the pain that is rampant on the streets. Now that I have left Philadelphia and will soon go back to school, I feel that I must continue that fight. I am fortunate for the opportunities that the Summer Services Project, PCH, and the Notre Dame Alumni have given me, and depart with a sense that I will be back, even if only to check on my water fountain.

Critical Thinking Questions

1. Briefly explain the "water fountain problem" by "Integrating the Theories." Specifically, what bearing do functionalism, conflict theory, and symbolic interactionism have on Joe Burke's difficulties getting this small service fixed?
2. Although he performed no formal study, how might Joe's experiences reflect the limitations of participant observation research as described in Chapter 3?

Source: Joseph Burke, "How I Spent My Summer Vacation" (Summer 1991). In *Philadelphia Streets,* a publication of the Philadelphia Committee for the Homeless.

structure above the Dosadi rabble, McKie is struck by the interpersonal experience on this street. In this place away from the deliberations of the mighty, the faces openly radiate hatred and menace. This is a human aspect of inequality absent from abstract analyses of the system's conflicts or functions. It is also chillingly reminiscent of the secret feelings of suburbanites as they ride subways through our own "Streets of the Hungry."

SUMMARY

1. Human societies are "stratified" into levels as distinct and ordered as the layers of the Earth.
2. According to Max Weber, a stratification system such as the United States is built from a set of related but distinct social rewards. Practically every part of personal life differs by one's social position, but the three most essential dimensions for understanding the social structure of inequality are income, prestige, and power.
3. In the abstract, each generation can begin at the same level regardless of the social ranking of the previous generation. In reality, inequality of condition inevitably means some inequality of opportunity. Weber defined position in the stratification system by the "life chances" people in that position share at birth, and saw these life chances as determinants of occupational mobility.
4. The status attainment approach tries to account for occupational mobility by linking it with the effects of personal traits; a powerful corrective to the individualistic bias of this approach is the structural model, which sees occupational mobility in the light of social network ties.
5. There is still debate among sociologists about the best way to define classes. The Weberian framework offers one approach. Alternatively, Karl Marx defined a class as a set of people who share a common relationship to the means of production. In the United States, this translates into a division between the bourgeoisie and the proletariat, and an intermediate class of petit bourgeoisie, with the class positions rooted in their relations to the economic system and to each other.
6. Subjective social class, as identified by each individual, can be usefully broken down into the four designations used for the 1990 General Social Survey: the rich, the middle class, the working class, and the poor.
7. The different sociological theories can be applied to explain the existence of these classes within the social stratification system. According to functionalist theory, inequality exists so that the "best and brightest" will be motivated to serve society by the prospect of high income, prestige, and power, while the poor are needed to perform society's "dirty work."
8. Conflict theorists see class division as the basis for societal conflict, serving not the greater good, but the interests of the powerful—interests that are justified by the control of the ruling class over ideology.
9. Symbolic interactionism disapproves of the very concept of "system," and instead attempts, through study of the details of inequality interactions, to reveal how real people interpret their own niches of inequality.

Chapter 12

Personal Perspective

BEING black at "Villanova," hmmm . . . sounds kind of oxymoronic, if not a bit difficult. As African-American female twins we, Yolanda Carter and Yana Carter, can say with certainty that Villanova has left us with at least one legacy—never before have we been more conscious of our racial identity. Having been reared and educated in predominantly white communities, Villanova was definitely not a new experience. Yet, there was something *qualitatively* different, though subtle, about Villanova. Because of the circumstances of our rearing, we were able to occupy a peculiar and unique position within the 'Nova landscape. It was almost as if we existed on this invisible line. The brown color of our skin made us undeniably African American and therefore necessarily preconditioned how people saw us—especially those unfamiliar with African Americans, like many at Villanova. At the same time, our upbringing in predominantly white areas made us somehow "not black." As one of our white friends put it; we didn't fit the "black" stereotype, as defined by white society: we didn't live in the ghetto, we weren't poor, we didn't have any kids—so of course we weren't "really black." Thus we were no longer a threat. Our nonthreatening status made us privy to information and conversations of our white friends that would not have taken place in the company of other African Americans, or even in our company had they seen us as "really black." In this capacity, we heard things laced with racist overtones. For example, a fellow activity member "warned" our good friend not to take a particular Western Civilization course taught by an African-American professor because the teacher taught the class from a "black" point of view; that is, he began his lessons starting from the civilizations of Africa (how dare he insinuate that there was life and culture elsewhere besides the white European world?!), rather than medieval Europe.

Race and Ethnicity

There were numerous other conversations to which we were witness. In one particularly ugly argument, a white dormmate insinuated that the only reason that her African-American roommate was at Villanova was to fill a quota. The message implicit in her stinging words was loud and clear to us—African Americans did not belong at Villanova. It is why many African-American male friends were followed by campus security. It is why a white woman walking to the Law School clutched her purse more tightly and quickened her steps when she noticed our African-American female friend walking behind her.

Although many of our racial encounters were experienced vicariously—through friends, classmates, and hallmates—we remember quite vividly one incident that we experienced directly. It happened during our senior year while we were attending a university-sponsored career fair where various corporate recruiters came to distribute company literature and scope out prospective employees. Students patiently waited in line to speak with each company representative and hand out copies of carefully constructed résumés. In several of the lines, we were blatantly ignored by the recruiters. Where our white fellow students were pursued aggressively *by* the recruiters themselves, *we* had to pursue the representatives' attention ourselves. It was not until they looked at our résumés, which gave proof of our academic and extracurricular accomplishments, that we were even perceived as serious candidates.

We guess we shouldn't be surprised that at a university dedicated to liberal education and multiculturalism, racism still flourishes among the student body. After all, Villanova is simply a microcosm of the world at large. As African-American women at the university, we live in a dual reality. We share a world and a life with our white counterparts, and at the same time we are separated and negated by their racist stereotypes and generalizations. In effect, we are thrown into a paradoxical nonexistence, a nonexistence from which we must constantly struggle to emerge.

YC and YC

Race and Ethnicity

WINTER, 1991. The safe confines of a selective suburban university. Take a walk around campus. Sit in a classroom. What do you see? Content sons and daughters of upper-middle-class people taking notes and fretting about mid-term exams. Some are anticipating that night's basketball game or the next party. Some have thoughts about troops in the Persian Gulf War. They speak strongly of the need to confront Saddam Hussein. They tie yellow ribbons around trees and drape U.S. flags from their dorm windows.

What is missing in this picture? Young African Americans, many of whom are not college students because they were born into an underprivileged environment. At colleges like this, only a small number of African Americans have the luxury of being part of the intellectual and social climate of campus life. Of course, at many colleges African American students are common. However, as a group, they are less likely to attend college than whites. Statistically, many have not even had much chance of a decent job. So they joined the army to "see the world." And indeed they did. Along with that trip came an unexpected stop in the land of the grim reaper. He appeared regularly on the group tour through Saudi Arabia, Kuwait, and Iraq.

Why college for some people and the army for others? There are many answers to that question. But a person's race is one of them. This is what the authors and many other college professors see as a regular part of white "college life." It is not an opinion. It is a fact. And it is a statistically visible fact. The overrepresentation of African Americans and Hispanics in the military is shown clearly in Table 12:1.

Doesn't it sound foolish to ask which is better—a cocker spaniel or a beagle? A greyhound or a golden retriever? Most people would say that it's

TABLE 12:1 Racial and Ethnic Differences in the Military and in College[a]

WHO S IN THE MILITARY?		WHO S IN COLLEGE?	
Race	Percent	Race	Percent
Black	20.8	Black	9.8
Hispanic	4.6	Hispanic	5.8
White	70.4	White	85.2

[a] Main Point: The General Accounting Office (GAO) found that in 1990 African Americans made up 20.8 percent and Hispanics 4.6 percent of the armed forces, compared with 11.1 percent and 3.6 percent respectively in 1972 under the draft. African Americans made up about 12 percent and Hispanics about 8 percent of the total U.S. population in 1990. In the Persian Gulf, the GAO found that as of mid-December 1990, African Americans were 29.8 percent of the Army, 21.3 percent of the Navy, 16.9 percent of the Marines, and 13.5 percent of the Air Force.

Source: General Accounting Office and U.S. National Center for Education Statistics, 1990.

White supremacist groups are active throughout the United States and the world. These "boys" from Alabama are "skinheads," a movement that peaked in the 1970s as a punk style statement. Now it is a racial stance, which supports violence against African Americans and Jews, to name a few of their favorite targets. These people may appear to be fringe lunatics just looking for attention, but their very presence poses a threat to personal freedom. Among other acts, they have murdered in every corner of the United States.

preposterous to rate the value of different dog breeds. And it is certainly even less rational to rate people on the basis of race or national origin. But one of the fundamental principles of sociology is that human behavior is not always rational. The world today is rife with volatile situations driven by racial, ethnic, and religious divisiveness. It is not a problem limited to the United States. It rears its head in Northern Ireland between Catholics and Protestants, in the Middle East between Arabs and Jews, and in Germany between natives and foreigners, to name just a few places. In fact, it is so widespread that there is no part of the world where some group is not despised and despising.

Racial and ethnic membership are some of the master determinants of an individual's life experience. They affect power and wealth, crime, and health. And they make an impact on a host of other things that translate into happiness or misery. What is race? What is ethnicity? What is prejudice? What is discrimination? What are the consequences of each? These and related questions are the focus of this chapter. In many ways this is a negative chapter which documents a sad fact of life—that part of what a person can become is already fixed at birth. Race and ethnicity are part of the structures of social inequality in the United States (see Chapter 11) and globally (see Chapter 6), and also part of the most unstructured of human activities—violence (see Chapter 10). They can also form the basis for the more refreshing experience of harmonious integration. Here we will take a look at the many forms of race and ethnic relations, as well as some theoretical explanations as to how things got to where they are.

THE MEANING OF RACE

race—biologically, a group of people with a common genetic heritage. Legally, an arbitrary concept often constructed to define who is not white. Socially, a subjective perception of what a person says it is.

Among the some 5 billion people in the world today there is an amazing diversity of physical traits such as skin color, hair texture, nose structure, head form, brain size, lip form, facial shape, and physical stature. *Homo sapiens* has spread to every corner of the world throughout the past 10 millennia. As a result, numerous societies have evolved, each with its own unique sense of identity. Part of this identity is known as **race**. Race is an ambiguous concept with mysterious origins. Some trace the term to the "race of Abraham" from the Bible, while others pin it to the Spanish *as,* meaning "origin."

As you will see, race can be defined in biological, legal, and social ways. However, the sociological meaning of race is *a group of people who are seen as socially distinct because of obvious physical characteristics.* But what are *obvious* physical traits? These are largely determined by the subjective whims of the perceivers. In the United States, for instance, skin color differences are considered obvious. We typically refer to people as "black" or "white." In Brazil, skin color distinctions are even more varied, resulting in such categories as *cabra, mulato, escuro, moreno,* and *branco.* Yet, in other parts of the world, skin color has no social meaning at all.

Some of the physical differences among races are the results of interesting adaptations to certain environments. Dark skin provides protection from damaging sun rays in the tropics. Large lung capacity aids breathing in high-altitude climates. But, by and large, physical characteristics used to define races are not the simple unadulterated result of climatic adaptations. There are no "pure" races, just opinions as to what races are. In the nineteenth century, biologists classified three major racial groupings: *Caucasoids* (light skin, light hair), *Negroids* (dark skin, coarse hair), and *Mongoloids* (yellow skin, eyelid folds). Throughout history, a wide variety of human groups have been referred to as races, including the English, French, Scots, Welsh, Arabs, Basques, Jews, Indians, Gypsies, Nordics, Irish, Eskimos, Blacks, Wild Hindus, Latins, and Celts.

In 1990, the Census Bureau dealt with the complicated issue of race by breaking it down into the categories of "Black," "White," "Negro," "American Indian," "Asian or Pacific Islander," "Eskimo," "Aleut," "Spanish/Hispanic," and "Other." Even these categories are controversial since many people are not content with groupings that include people from diverse backgrounds. Not only are they diverse, but they have a profound impact on group life and have led to a cavalcade of social problems including war. The numerous conflicts among American Indian tribes are testimony to that. Another problem with the categories is the labels themselves. For instance, some prefer the term "black" whereas others feel more comfortable with "African American." Some people still prefer "colored" and some "people of color." Although the Census Bureau and many people still use the term "black," in this book we use the term "African American."

Biological Definitions

Throughout time, race has been defined along biological, legal, and social lines. Each of these approaches has its own set of limitations. Biologically, the term *race* refers to a "breeding population," a group of people sharing a common genetic heritage and within which there is inbreeding. The three-way classification system of Caucasoids, Mongoloids, and Negroids is a reflection of biologically connecting the concept of race with inbreeding. But, because different human "races" have always interbred, there is no pure race.

Biologists and physical anthropologists who have tried to classify races have been frustrated by a problem comparable to categorizing snowflakes by geometric structure. The estimates range from as few as three races to over 200, depending on who is doing the estimating. Some classifiers use broad definitions ("lumpers") and others use minute categories ("splitters"). Regardless of the approach taken, classifying race biologically is an impossible task because races are not distinct populations based on physi-

White supremacists like those in the previous photograph do not have a monopoly on racial hatred. Some black Muslim groups have supported the idea that white people are evil. This wall painting shows Malcolm X, a well-known black Muslim activist during the 1960s, who was admired by some for fighting bigotry. After repudiating some of his earlier fundamentalist views, he was assassinated by other Muslim activists. In the 1990s, Mohammed Khalid preaches a hatred of whites and Jews. In 1994, fellow Muslims attempted to assassinate him as well.

cal differences. Racial intermingling has obliterated the genetic distinctions among races. In the case of African Americans, for example, about 75 percent have some white ancestors (Roberts, 1975).

Since Negroids and Caucasians have combined over many generations, and since Mongoloid traits have also spread widely through the American population, the terms themselves have little genetic meaning. As a result, many people defy fixed classification. Even Carleton Coon, an avid supporter of biological classification of races, admits "Not every person in the world can be tapped on the shoulder and told 'You belong to such and such a race'" (Coon, 1965, p. 7). Quite literally, race is not a black-and-white issue, and biology offers little evidence to classify people neatly into distinct groups. If race isn't biological, what then is it? To some degree it's a legal issue, but, for the most part, it's a social fact.

Legal Definitions

Race has also been defined administratively by establishing racial categories through laws or bureaucratic practices such as those employed by the Census Bureau. Obviously, these are social creations. In 1990, census labels were the subject of widespread controversy, particularly the "black" category since, as mentioned earlier, many so-called blacks today prefer to be called "African Americans." Throughout American history, legal definitions of race have been devised to determine who is not white. This perspective promoted the separation and differential treatment of certain groups and was especially evident during the colonial period, when more than one-half million blacks were legally enslaved solely on the basis of color. As one African American federal judge who is also a sociologist put it, the legal status of blacks was actually one of non-status since, "Under the colonial rule of law . . ., blacks who sought the same freedom that was now demanded as the inalienable right of whites could be scalped, mutilated, or even killed" (Higginbotham, 1978, p. 390).

After the slavery period, laws assigned people to all-black or all-white railroad cars, seats on a bus, and tables in a restaurant. Most of the laws centering on race were not really designed to define race but to prevent African Americans from serving on juries, attending white schools, or holding certain jobs. State laws specifically designed to *define* race were variable and arbitrary. For example, Missouri defined black as one-eighth or more of Negro blood. And Louisiana classified people as black if they had more than one-thirty-second of Negro blood! It was not until 1983 that the Louisiana legislature, embarrassed over the standard, finally repealed the law.

Social Definitions

Clearly, biology and the law have failed to provide a satisfactory definition of race. This is because race is a social concept, not a biological or legal one. Race is simply what people say it is. It is a subjective perception by a group or an individual of a group or a single individual. Take the case of Jews. Jews do not constitute a race in biological terms. Yet many people *consider* Jews a race, and many Jews agree.

According to other social definitions of race, individuals are what they tell others they are. Race is self-defined. Mark Linton Stebbins used this concept to his advantage. He successfully ran for city council in Stockton, California, in 1983 by telling the sizable African-American community that he was African American. He is a pale-skinned, blue-eyed man with kinky hair. His birth records show that his parents and grandparents are white. Stebbins claims that he was raised white. However, he conveniently regarded himself as African American when he moved to Stockton. In other words, he defined his own race.

In its everyday usage, the term "race" implies that groups differ along physical lines and have corresponding personality differences. Although there is no evidence that humankind can be divided into such distinct groups, the belief is widespread and consequential. On the positive side, a sense of racial pride helps African-American families enjoy emotional stability and occupational success. The flip side is the nightly world news, with regular reports from Africa and Eastern Europe where divisions based on race have led to bloodshed and death. It is scary that a subjective perception can have such extreme consequences. Race is just such a perception and it has an enormous effect on the lives of individuals and even the conditions of nation-states.

ETHNIC AND MINORITY GROUPS

ethnic group—often used interchangeably with country of origin, but most commonly refers to cultural features that are handed down from one generation to the next.

Like race, there is wide variation in the meaning of the term **ethnic group**. It ranges from small, isolated "kin and culture" groups to large categories of people defined as similar on the basis of one or two shared characteristics (Caplow, 1991). Ethnicity is often used interchangeably with country of origin, but it most commonly refers to cultural features that are handed down from one generation to the next. These may include dress, religion, language, food preferences, historical identity, *and* national origin.

Ethnic groups share a sense of "peoplehood" within a larger society. They are not necessarily a numerical minority within the larger society, although the term is sometimes used that way. It is, most importantly, a sense of group identity, an identity based on distinctive cultural patterns *acquired* through socialization in a particular psychosocial environment (Yinger, 1985).

Race and ethnicity are different. Race is essentially more of a biological concept, whereas ethnicity is a cultural one. Sometimes the two are confused with each other, as in the case of Jews (an ethnic and religious group but not a race); and sometimes the two go hand in hand, as in the case of Asian Americans, who have distinct physical characteristics as well as common cultural traits. This is also true of African Americans and Native Americans. Religion is sometimes a qualifying factor in ethnic identification. Irish Protestants, for instance, are ethnically different from Irish Catholics, and Hungarian Catholics differ from Hungarian Jews.

Ethnic nationalism is the belief that a particular ethnic group constitutes an entity that is distinct from the larger society. Sometimes the larger society is only a temporary system. For instance, the threads that stitched together an unwieldy federation of rivalrous ethnic groups in Eastern Europe and Asia after World War II have been unraveling for years. The process has been a railing crisis, which has shattered that part of the world. Struggles based on ethnic nationalism are not confined to specific geographical zones. American Jews, for instance, have been affected by Zionism in Palestine, and African Americans have been devastated by the sights and sounds of Apartheid in South Africa on the nightly news.

minority group—a subordinate group whose members have significantly less control or power over their own lives than the members of a dominant or majority group.

Many racial and ethnic groups also constitute what is known as a **minority group** within societies. Identifying a minority is not a simple mathematical task because it does not necessarily mean being outnumbered. Rather, a minority group "is a subordinate group whose members have significantly less control or power over their own lives than the members of a dominant or majority group" (Schaefer, 1988, p. 5). Being superior in numbers does not guarantee that a group has control over its destiny. Indeed, there are many instances where the numerical majority is dominated by the numerical minority. We see many instances of such deprivation and subordination around the world. The white minority in South Africa dominates the black majority. Similar social structures also exist in Caribbean islands where European minorities subjugate the indigenous population. Those in the United States do not have to look far for examples of deprivation and not mere numbers constituting minority group status. Witness counties in southern states and northern cities where African Americans are the numerical majority but are clearly subordinate to the white population in terms of life chances such as life, liberty, and the pursuit of happiness.

Sociologists have identified five basic characteristics of a minority group:

1. Physical or cultural characteristics different from the dominant group, including traits that are socially visible such as language or religion.
2. The experience of unequal treatment as in the case of limited access to jobs and decent housing.
3. An ascribed status—people who are born into the group rather than joining it voluntarily.
4. A strong sense of social cohesion among members of a minority group; this "consciousness of kind" may increase as members become more persecuted.
5. Marriage within the group (endogamy); this pattern results from being stigmatized by the dominant group and from the minority group's sense of solidarity (Vander Zanden, 1983).

Generally, minority groups are stratified along racial or ethnic lines, but these are not the only points of demarcation. Since the central meaning of minority group is subordinate status and deprivation of power, there are other examples of minority group status, that are neither racial nor ethnic. These include women, homosexuals, handicapped people, and the elderly population.

African Americans

The 1990 Census counted 29,986,060 black Americans in the population, nearly 3.5 million more than in 1980. Blacks represented 12.1 percent of the estimated 248.7 million Americans, up from 11.7 percent in 1980. The percentage of black Americans in the U.S. population in 1990 was the largest since 1880, when blacks accounted for 13.1 percent of the population, but much lower than the 20 percent figure reported at the birth of the nation.

The Census Bureau figures may have undercounted the African American population by as many as 2 million. Why? African Americans are among the most difficult population groups to count in a census. Because they are more likely than others to live in impoverished urban neighborhoods, they are difficult to enumerate. Some inner-city African Americans also have strong antigovernment feelings and do not want to cooperate with census takers.

Aside from their actual numbers, many African Americans feel invisible. There is a long, violent history of their second-class status in the United States, a history that dates back to slavery. In 1619, the first 20 blacks were unloaded at Jamestown, Virginia. Like millions after them, they had been captured by other Africans and brought to the West African coast where they were purchased by white traders. The two-month trip across the Atlantic consisted of hell on sea—hundreds of tightly packed humans, shackled to each other, lying in their own blood and excrement, hoping that starvation would end their torture; mercifully, it did for some. But for most the voyage was simply an introduction to hell on Earth.

The official status of blacks in the United States was the familiar story of slavery. The blacks who survived the passage were sold as slaves at public auction to slaveowners to meet their increased demand for labor. The slaves' lives were shattered by inhumane treatment including sexual as well as economic exploitation. Family life was devastated by slave breeding and the sale of husbands away from their wives, and children away from their mothers by white owners. Any remnants of African culture, with the most notable exception of some music and religious customs, simply disappeared.

Slavery set the stage for interaction between blacks and whites for centuries to come. Some stereotypes about African Americans today (stupid, promiscuous, happy "in their place") undoubtedly stemmed from an early rationalization used to justify the cruelty of slavery. The Civil War may have marked the official end of slavery, but unequal treatment of blacks continued. This ran the gamut from KKK lynchings to "Jim Crow" laws (named after a black minstrel routine, which satirized blacks) designed to enforce official segregation. Here is a well-known statement from this period:

> I will say, then, that I am not, nor have ever been, in favor of bringing about in any way the social and political equality of the white and black races; and that I am not, nor ever have been, in favor of making voters or jurors of negroes, nor of qualifying them to hold office,

Joseph Mallford William Turner's 1839 painting, *The Slave Ship,* is more than a spectacular vision; it represents the ultimate disregard for black people. In this particular incident, an epidemic broke out on a slave ship. The captain jettisoned his "human cargo" because he was insured against the loss of slaves at sea, but not by disease.

> nor to intermarry with white people; and I will say, in addition to this, that there is a physical difference between the white and black races which I believe will forever forbid the two races living together on terms of social and political equality. And inasmuch as they cannot so live, while they do remain together there must be the position of superior and inferior, and I as much as any other man am in favor of having the superior position assigned to the white race.

The person who uttered these words was the anti-slavery crusader Abraham Lincoln; his words show the durability of prejudice even as Lincoln fought to end slavery.

It is true that segregation has been banned since the late 1960s by federal, state, and local public accommodation laws, but Jim Crow's spirit still lives on in the South. Walk into some bars in New Orleans. Notice the separate quarters for blacks and whites, and it becomes readily apparent that there's a little touch of South Africa still with us today.

There were some significant events for African Americans during the first half of the twentieth century. One was a demographic change in their distribution—an exodus northward (Lemann, 1991). World War I also had consequences for African Americans. Almost half a million served in the armed forces. African Americans from different areas were brought together, shared a common experience, and began to demand their full rights as citizens. World War II furthered the movement toward equality, and some African Americans became officers for the first time. In addition, presidents Roosevelt and Truman issued executive orders favorable to African Americans. So did the Supreme Court. In 1954, it handed down the famous decision in the matter of *Brown* v. *Board of Education,* which outlawed segregation in schools and paved the way for the systematic dismantling of an educational system that had oppressed African Americans.

Although these changes were designed to promote equality, they also led to widespread resentment and violence. The 1960s, for instance, were a powderkeg of racial turmoil. Efforts to gain equality, often referred to as the Civil Rights Movement, were frustrated by the slow pace of school integration, widespread noncompliance with acts of Congress, and the everyday misery of life as a despised people. Many cities witnessed a number of violent riots, and, to add insult to injury, the FBI was exposed as systematically infiltrating civil rights groups. It was in such an atmosphere that the Voting Rights Act was passed in August of 1975, but even that positive event was overshadowed by the torching of Watts in the same week.

Some African American scholars contend that African Americans are an especially *unique* minority as evidenced by an excessively high amount of

BOX 12:1 COLLEGE EXPERIENCE

The School Days of A. Leon Higginbotham, Jr., Federal Judge and Famous Sociologist

In 1944, I was a 16-year-old freshman at Purdue University—one of twelve black civilian students. If we wanted to live in West Lafayette, Indiana, where the University was located, solely because of our color the twelve of us at Purdue were forced to live in a crowded private house rather than, as did most of our white classmates, in the university campus dormitories. We slept barracks-style in an unheated attic.

One night, as the temperature was close to zero, I felt that I could suffer the personal indignities and denigration no longer. The United States was more than two years into the Second World War, a war our government had promised would "make the world safe for democracy." Surely there was room enough in that world, I told myself that night, for twelve black students in a northern university in the United States to be given a small corner of the on-campus heated dormitories for their quarters. Perhaps all that was needed was for one of us to speak up, to make sure the administration knew exactly how a small group of its students had been treated by those charged with assigning student housing.

The next morning, I went to the office of Edward Charles Elliot, president of Purdue University, and asked to see him. I was given an appointment.

At the scheduled time I arrived at President Elliot's office, neatly (but not elegantly) dressed, shoes polished, finger nails clean, hair cut short. Why was it, I asked him, that blacks—and blacks alone—had been subjected to this special ignominy? Though there were larger issues I might have raised with the president of an American university (this was but ten years before *Brown* v. *Board of Education*) I had not come that morning to move mountains, only to get myself and eleven friends out of the cold. Forcefully, but nonetheless deferentially, I put forth my modest request: that the black students of Purdue be allowed to stay in some section of the state-owned dormitories; segregated, if necessary, but at least not humiliated.

mistreatment (Sowell, 1983). They entered the United States as slaves, were institutionally disenfranchised for centuries, and, in a sense, have only recently arrived at the port of opportunity. That's the optimistic view. The pessimistic view is that African Americans have experienced far more social inequality than any other minority group because of deeply ingrained biases against a people who are so easily identified by physical characteristics. If that is true, social progress for African Americans will be especially slow in coming (Dewart, 1991). What *has* happened is something in-between; a small but growing segment of the African American population (the so-called "black bourgeoisie") has experienced notable socioeconomic achievement. There was even dramatic progress in jobless rates among disadvantaged African American youths during the economic recovery period of the late 1980s. However, the bulk of African Americans still live life on the poverty line. This is particularly true in older industrial cities. In fact, three-fourths of the increase in ghetto poverty during the 1970s was accounted for by only 10 cities (Wilson, 1991). In effect, there are two black Americas: one small segment moving up, and the other stuck at the bottom. The picture is especially bleak for African American women, who are the objects of dual discrimination—racial and female. See Box 12:2 for an African American woman's perception. It is clearly a disgruntled perception and one with which many conservatives would disagree.

BOX 12:1 COLLEGE EXPERIENCE *continued*

Perhaps if President Elliot had talked with me sympathetically that morning, explaining his own impotence to change things but his willingness to take up the problem with those who could, I might not have felt as I did. Perhaps if he had communicated with some word or gesture, or even a sigh, that I had caused him to review his own commitment to things as they were, I might have felt I had won a small victory. But President Elliot, with directness and with no apparent qualms, answered, "Higginbotham, the law doesn't require us to let colored students in the dorm, and you either accept things as they are or leave the university immediately."

As I walked back to the house that afternoon, I reflected on the ambiguity of the day's events. I had heard, on that morning, an eloquent lecture on the history of the Declaration of Independence, and of the genius of the founding fathers. That afternoon I had been told that under the law the black civilian students at Purdue University could be treated differently from their 6,000 white classmates. Yet I knew that by nightfall hundreds of black soldiers would be injured, maimed, and some even killed on far flung battlefields to make the world safe for democracy. Almost like a mystical experience, a thousand thoughts raced through my mind as I walked across campus. I knew then I had been touched in a way I had never been touched before, and that one day I would have to return to the most disturbing element in this incident— how a legal system that proclaims "equal justice for all" could simultaneously deny even a semblance of dignity to a 16-year-old boy who had committed no wrong. Shortly thereafter, I left Purdue University and transferred to Antioch College. Ultimately, I chose the law as my vocation, and in 1952 I graduated from Yale Law School.

Critical Thinking Questions

1. Consider the general changes in interracial attitudes that have occurred since 1944 that have been documented in this chapter, and how they have changed interracial experiences on campus.
2. Now consider the general changes in social structures that have occurred since 1944 that have been discussed in this chapter, and how *they* have changed interracial experiences on campus.

Source: A. Leon Higginbotham, Jr., *In the Matter of Color: Race and the American Legal Process,* New York: Oxford University Press, 1978, pp. VII–IX. By permission of the publisher.

Hispanic Americans

A crime is committed by a gang that apparently believes in ethnic diversity. Police issue descriptions of the suspects: a white, an African American, and a Hispanic. A what? In most cases, a victim who gets a halfway decent look at the assailant can tell whether he (or she) was white or African American. But what does a Hispanic look like? There is no universal "look," and the very term "Hispanic" is a label with a nebulous meaning, applied by the general population to an ever-changing group of U.S. residents.

Indeed, a Hispanic may be of any race. For example, many Filipinos identify themselves as Hispanic, and many black Dominicans and Puerto Ricans in the United States are Hispanic, but of African ancestry. According to some, Hispanics may even be of any ethnic origin because, more than anything, the word describes a culture, or a group of cultures, with a common sense of identity (Valdivieso and Davis, 1988). The link occurs among people whose declared ancestors or who themselves were born in Spain or in Latin American countries. Consequently, "Hispanic," which was originally a term of convenience for administrative agencies, roughly translates into "Spanish-speaking people" or "people with a Spanish surname" (Portes and Truelove, 1987; Schick and Schick, 1991).

Hispanics represent the largest ethnic minority in the United States. They are also one of the fastest growing. In 1990, the Census Bureau reported that the Hispanic population increased by more than 50 percent since 1980—from 14.6 million to 22.4 million. The largest subgroup is Mexican-Americans, also known as Chicanos (12.6 million), followed by Puerto Ricans (2.5 million), Cubans (1.1 million), and people from different nations in Central America (2.5 million). Another 3.7 million have other origins. Large portions of the Hispanic population live in California and a handful of other states, but the 1980s also saw a wave of movement into virtually every state—a phenomenon referred to in the popular literature as the "Browning of America."

Each Hispanic group has some special feature or historical fact surrounding its presence in the United States. Many Mexican-Americans are

Migration to the United States comes from all over the world and takes many forms. It is not unusual for people to attempt to escape from the squalor and repression of their homeland to the United States. These "boat people" from Haiti were caught by the Coast Guard and sent to internment camps.

descended from residents of territories annexed by the United States after the Mexican–American War of 1848. Countless others have entered the United States as illegal aliens in more recent times. Puerto Ricans were made full citizens of the United States in 1917. Unlike other migrants, they serve in the U.S. military and have easy access to relatively inexpensive air travel back to their country of origin. Many migrated to New York and other eastern cities but, in the past 20 years, there has been a reverse migration resulting from serious poverty experienced on the mainland. Cubans arrived en masse after the Castro revolution of 1959. The original migrants were typically well-educated, middle-class people but, since the early 1980s, the migrants tend to be poor Cubans fleeing oppression. Known as "boat people," oftentimes they reach the Florida coast cheering, and sometimes they arrive dead. Haitians have had similar experiences as well as being returned en masse by U.S. authorities.

There was a time when different Hispanic groups were substantially varied and represented many voices. That is less true today because differences have blurred, along with a growing feeling of unity and a shared sense of culture, which has not only broken out of the barrio but literally exploded into the American cultural mainstream.

Asian Americans

Although Asian Americans, like Hispanics, are usually discussed as an entity, Asian Americans are the most diverse ethnic group in the United States. They come from over two dozen different countries and do not share a common religion or language or even a common cultural background (O'Hare and Felt, 1991). More than 80 percent of Asian Americans trace their roots to one of five countries: the Philippines, China, Japan, India, and Korea. However, between 1980 and 1989 over 40 percent of Asian immigrants came from Vietnam, Cambodia, and Laos. Recent immigration has significantly changed the composition of this sector of the American population. Not only is the meaning of "Asian American" complicated by so many and changing conventional subgroups, it is further confused by the inclusion of Pacific Islanders in the 1990 census. This is especially odd in light of the fact that some Pacific Islanders, such as Hawaiians and Guamanians (from Guam), are born already possessing U.S. citizenship.

Asian Americans constitute the fastest-growing minority in the United States today. In 1990 they numbered 3.5 million, up from 1.4 million in 1970. The Asian American population grew by 80 percent in the 1980s alone—twice the growth rate of Hispanics, six times the rate of African Americans, and 20 times that of whites. This is a phenomenal increase among a group with radically different histories.

The first major influx of Chinese occurred between 1850 and 1880. Then, some 300,000 immigrants were lured to California by job prospects in gold mining and railroad building. They were not met with open arms but instead were subjected to a great deal of harassment. This included the Chinese Exclusion Act of 1882, which severely limited the number of Chinese immigrants. Hostility toward the Chinese could be traced in part to the belief that they took jobs away from whites. By the early 1900s Chinese immigration was totally prohibited and anti-Chinese riots in "Chinatown" areas of major cities were common. Today's Chinese immigrants also come from Taiwan and Hong Kong. These groups differ in terms of their self-identity as well as their attitude toward the People's Republic of China.

Gene Sogioka was hired by the Bureau of Sociological Research to depict the lives of Japanese Americans who were confined to internment camps during World War II. His watercolor, *Loneliness of Poston,* conveys an image of desolation imposed on the people confined to one such camp in Poston, Arizona. The Third Reich was not the only organization with "camps" during the war. Camps in the United States were less violent, but they were also based on discrimination by ethnicity.

The Japanese immigrated to the United States later than the Chinese. They also have their own special experiences of mistreatment, particularly after the bombing of Pearl Harbor, the reason the United States entered World War II. Fearing espionage and attacks from within, the federal government ushered some 110,000 Japanese (including 70,000 who were U.S. citizens) into special "relocation camps." The camps were really prisons. It is curious to note that no such internment "camps" were established for German Americans or Italian Americans, even though their countries of origin were two of the Allies' largest foes. This comparison suggests that racism rather than national security was the motivating factor. In 1983, the injustice was recognized when the American government issued a national apology and $1.5 billion for the 60,000 surviving Japanese-American internees.

Immigrants from Indochina came to the United States as refugees on the run at the end of the Vietnam War. Most Americans did not favor giving them sanctuary. It was a difficult time for a displaced people, and things continue to be difficult for them. Never fully accepted in the United States, few expect to be able to return to their own country for visits, let alone permanent residence. Compared with other Asian Americans, these people are of low social and economic status. Some of this is due to their recent arrival, and some of it is related to the burning hatred that some Americans harbor toward the Vietnam War. This stands in stark contrast to the history of the movement of people from Korea and the Philippines. Their immigration has been less fraught with drama and hostility. Both Koreans and Filipinos came in "waves" throughout the twentieth century and settled in ways less visible. But, like Asian Americans as a group, they have not been integrated completely into American society.

The data in Table 12:2 show that Asian Americans are clearly a segment of our population that is growing by leaps and bounds. Indeed, they are projected to number close to 10 million by the year 2000 (Bouvier and Agresta, 1992). What is less clear is how well they will fare economically and socially. The Population Reference Bureau presently reports a "mixed picture." Many Asians now residing in the United States are relatively new immigrants and, as a result, have low incomes. On the other hand, the aver-

TABLE 12:2 Asians and Pacific Islanders by Ancestry (1980) and Immigration Flows by Country of Origin (1980 to 1989)

ANCESTRY OR COUNTRY OF ORIGIN	POPULATION 1980		IMMIGRATION[a] 1980 TO 1989		POPULATION 1989
	Number	Percent	Number	Percent	
China[b]	812,178	22	433,031	15	1,245,209
Philippines	781,894	21	473,831	17	1,255,725
Japan	716,331	19	41,739	1	758,070
India	387,223	10	253,781	9	611,004
Korea	357,393	10	338,891	12	696,284
Vietnam	245,025	7	679,378	24	924,403
Samoa/Tonga/Guam	76,441	2	6,214	—	82,655
Laos[c]	52,887	1	256,727	9	309,614
Thailand	45,279	1	59,638	2	104,917
Cambodia	16,044	—	210,724	7	226,768
Pakistan	15,792	—	55,900	2	71,692
Other	219,953	7	55,485	2	275,438
Totals	3,726,440	100	2,865,339	100	6,591,779

Key: A Dash (—) represents less than 0.5 percent.
[a] Includes refugees.
[b] Includes Taiwan, Hong Kong, Macau.
[c] Includes Hmong.

Source: Bureau of the Census, Subject Reports, Asian and Pacific Islander Population in the United States: 1980, PC80–2–1E (Washington, DC: Government Printing Office, 1983), Table 2; and Immigration and Naturalization Service, 1989 *Statistical Yearbook* (Washington, DC: Government Printing Office, 1990), Tables 3 and 27.

age family income for higher-class Asian Americans in 1989 was $35,900. This was higher than the $35,000 average income of white U.S. families. Paradoxically, the poverty rate of less fortunate Asian Americans has been increasing and is now nearly twice the rate of whites. This group is "bifurcated," as statisticians would say. In short, one group of Asian Americans has done well economically, and another group has not. This situation is similar to the aforementioned one among African Americans. One small segment thrives, and one large segment struggles to survive.

Because Asian Americans are both racially and ethnically different from most other people in the United States, their assimilation into mainstream society will be slower than that experienced by, for example, European immigrants. But it should be noted that full assimilation is not usually a high priority goal for first-generation immigrants.

Native Americans

Although no racial or ethnic group has a monopoly on abuse and mistreatment, certainly Native Americans (American Indians) rank high in the hierarchy of the oppressed. The arrival of the colonists initiated the demise of Native Americans through theft of land, trickery, deceit, and genocide. By 1900, their number had dwindled from 1.5 million when the first settlers arrived from Europe to 250,000 through acts as extreme as deliberate extermination. To say that they were pushed westward is inaccurate; they were pushed *every* which way, particularly straight down.

The War Department was the logical choice to organize the Bureau of Indian Affairs (BIA) in 1824. The BIA was ineffectual then and remains so

BOX 12:2 GENDER AND SOCIAL CHANGE

Black Women—Myth and Reality

In this chapter, as well as in the chapter on gender, it is apparent that African Americans and women are often at a disadvantage. What about the person who is both—the African American woman? Some describe her as a case of "double jeopardy." Certainly the following piece supports that view. This issue is hotly debated in some circles. Some contend that it is a blatant case of both prejudice and discrimination. Others, on the other hand, feel that it is just an exaggerated opinion of the objective position of black women in the United States today.

You've seen her. She's coiffed, manicured and cool, leaps tall male egos at a single bound, gets jobs faster than a speeding bullet. Her title is long, but her paycheck short. Her skin tone ranges from milk white, to coffee, to rich Godiva chocolate brown.

She's the much touted and despised "double statistic," scooping up jobs from deserving males all across the nation—yes, you've guessed it. It's the African American woman.

It came as no surprise that some profit-conscious employers, who had no sincere commitment or vested interest in economically empowering blacks or women, would use black women to fulfill job quotas during the post-60s token-employment era. Hence, black women became known as the "twofer" or "double statistic," as a reference to the fact that they can be counted as both a minority and a female in the affirmative-action hiring game.

This bogus status has created much tension between the sexes at a time when black men and women need to be working together to address the problems in the black community. (It's also caused a rift with white women who wrongly perceive black women as having some unfair advantage because of their black skin. But that's another story.)

Well, it is time for a cold splash of reality. It knocks me off my mythological power pedestal to begin to entertain the thought that we have risen from the slave ranks of the doubly oppressed to become the ones twice as likely to enter corporate heaven. I mean let's get serious. Women just got the right to vote in this century, an Equal Rights Amendment is unlikely in the near future, and we will need a new civil rights act to reassure

today as evidenced by the large number of social problems endured by Native Americans such as high rates of infant mortality, suicide, and alcoholism. Misunderstanding between Native Americans and whites has resulted in ethnocentric portrayals of native people as savage, scalp-seeking beasts in historical accounts of American society.

Today there are approximately 2 million Native Americans, about 800,000 of whom live on approximately 300 reservations. The remainder reside in cities or are scattered through the eastern United States. In many ways they are worse off than other minority groups. Not only are they at the bottom of the American socioeconomic ladder, but also they suffer multiple forms of discrimination. Their median level of education is only 5.2 years, and the quality of that education is often inferior, mainly because reservation schools are poorly staffed and generally underfinanced. On the

BOX 12:2 GENDER AND SOCIAL CHANGE *continued*

us that discrimination in the workplace can be litigated.

The fact is that at no time did the median income of black women suggest that we could be staging an economic coup to take control of our own personal lives, with time left over to overthrow male privilege and ego. The 1980 census reveals that although black women have a higher median educational level than black males, black men's earnings are 41 percent higher.

Black men's resentment of black women grows in part because the men feel they are pitted against us in the workplace for corporate advantage, much the same as illegal labor unwittingly undermines the minimum rate to keep the labor price down.

Since the administration of "Roll-back Ronald" Reagan, a conservative high court has whittled away the slim civil rights gained in the '60s, particularly with regard to affirmative action, so the argument that "double statistical" black women are grabbing up the nation's best jobs loses steam. Indeed the 1980 census reports that the unemployment rate for black women is higher than for black males as well as [for] the rest of the population.

Granted, we have seen an increased number of sleek black beauties splashed across the pages of print media and electronically flashed to our living rooms in prime time slots. But the fact of the matter is that America's doubly oppressed black woman continues to be just that.

Consider this: In the same era that we have the "double statistics," we also have "the feminization of poverty," a term that became popular with the growth in the number of poor black female-headed households. The myth of the "double lucky" cannot coexist with the reality of female poverty.

Angela Davis, in her new book *Women, Culture and Politics,* writes: "Two out of three poor adults are women. . . . Women head half of all poor families and more than half the children in female-headed households are poor. . . . Sixty-eight percent of black and Latino children in female-headed households are poor. Among black women over 65 who live alone, the poverty rate is 82 percent."

For that matter, the entire black family is in jeopardy. But blaming the black woman is a sad case of victimizing the victim.

Critical Thinking Questions

1. How does the "double jeopardy" status of black women vary by social class?
2. Which of the major sociological theories best explains the present position of black women in the United States? Why?
3. If in fact there is evidence that African American women are in an especially disadvantaged position, how much of this problem is due to racism and how much to sexism?

Source: Marian Lee Smothers, "Black Women: Myth and Reality," *The Philadelphia Inquirer,* March 10, 1990, p. 7-A. By permission of the publisher.

Navajo reservation, over half the adults are unemployed or working only part-time, and virtually *all* the residents live lives of poverty in substandard housing. Laws were also passed to retard the cultural identity of Native Americans. The "Reorganization Act" of 1934, for example, allowed Indian tribes to elect a council with a chairperson, thereby imposing foreign values and corporate-like structures.

On the positive side, there has been a recent significant increase in the numbers of people who identify themselves as Native Americans. This is not simply a demographic phenomenon but one that is largely based on a growing sense of pride in Native American ancestry among those who previously disavowed it. This switch in self-identification began in the 1960s and has contributed to a tripling of the official size of this population. In all, hundreds of thousands of people in the United States have decided in

In the 1990s climate of "political correctness," infractions abound, including the names of sports teams. The Washington "Redskins" have been the target of special criticism. The lyrics to the Redskins' fight song reads: "Scalp 'em, swamp 'em, big score. Read 'em, weep 'em, touchdown, we want heap more." Other examples include the Atlanta Braves and the Redmen of St. John's University. Denis Mercier, a communications and popular culture professor at Rowan College in New Jersey, is shown in his office with pennants he created to show how Native Americans might feel. The top three are for teams called the Pittsburgh Negroes, the Kansas City Jews, and the San Diego Caucasians.

recent years that they are Native Americans. Aside from ethnic pride, eligibility for affirmative action programs is a motivating factor for this change. California has the highest number of Native Americans (250,000), but, oddly enough, the biggest increases in the 1990 Census show up in places like New Jersey and Alabama, states that have no large tribal groups, tribal lands, or reservations.

Other Groups

It is important to note that numbers do not necessarily translate into power. Neither is power fed by numbers. This is especially true of white Anglo-Saxon Protestants (WASPs) who, though they represented less than 17 percent of the population in 1990, have the greatest political and economic power in the United States. From English, Scottish, or Welsh origin, they have been in the United States the longest (except for Native Americans) and have established deeply entrenched roots in mainstream society. Although they are a numerical minority, they hold the majority of top government and corporate positions and are often referred to as members of the dominant culture. As such they are often credited with the values upon which the United States was built (Brookhiser, 1990). Under their inspiration, forests were cleared, resources developed, universities founded, and the Constitution and the Bill of Rights written.

That is the positive part. The negative part is that, contrary to the principles of democracy and freedom underlying the Constitution, immigrant groups who arrived after British Protestants were met with rejection and hostility. We have mentioned some of these groups earlier—African Americans, Hispanics, and Asian Americans. They are not the only ones on the list of mistreatment. Waves of immigrants from southern and eastern Europe arrived throughout the nineteenth century with hopes of opportunity that were frequently dashed. Of course, WASPs were not solely responsible for the hostile treatment of immigrants. Some of it occurred between immigrant groups, as in the case of the Irish and the Italians. Additionally, many immigrant groups were encouraged to come by businesses that needed their skills and/or inexpensive labor.

In the U.S. population there were 131,128,000 people in 1990 who identified themselves as having Irish, French, Italian, German, or Polish backgrounds. Such groups of people are referred to as "white ethnics." They arrived in the United States as predominantly Catholic peoples. They settled in specific areas of cities that became powderkegs of anti-Catholic rioting. Their religion and unfamiliarity with the English language strongly contrasted with WASP lifestyle. Today these conflicts have subsided almost entirely, although some white ethnics still cling to the "old lifestyle" and live in predominantly ethnic neighborhoods such as "Germantowns" and "Little Italies." As a group, white ethnics continue to be underrepresented at the top of the social class hierarchy.

Jews

Although "Jewish" is not an official category in the 1990 Census, it is estimated that Jews constitute about 2 percent of the American population. That is a difficult estimate to make because there is so much controversy over the elementary question: Who's a Jew? To some, Jews are a race, but that assessment is problematic because of their physical diversity. Others see Jews as a religious group although many Jews do not practice Judaism. In the final analysis, it is apparent that what makes Jews a people is their sense of cohesion as members of an ethnic group (Heilman, 1982).

The question "What is Jewish?" has raised some ire in the United States. The *Concise Oxford English Dictionary,* for example, has caused a long-standing firestorm in the American Jewish community by defining the term as a slur. In 1989, the dictionary offered a "compromise" in its quarrel with Jewish groups, but it still connects the term with "usurers" and "people who drive hard bargains."

Such unflattering, stereotypical verbiage is only one thing Jews have endured. It pales in comparison with the blatant acts of hatred and violence that have been heaped upon Jews throughout time and around the world. Anti-Semitism reared its head at least two thousand years ago when Jews played a role in the crucifixion of Jesus Christ, who was a Jew. It reached its apex in the hellish nightmares of concentration camps in Nazi Germany during World War II. In the United States today it takes the form of anti-Semitic propaganda and violent acts against Jewish institutions. Jewish synagogues are favorite targets of anti-Semites, some of whom are organized hate groups such as the Ku Klux Klan. Anti-Semitism also takes more subtle forms, as when Jews are quietly not considered for membership in social clubs or business corporations.

Some argue that Jews have not achieved occupational equality in the United States (Schaefer, 1988). That may be more true in some fields such as major corporate executive work, and less true in areas such as law and medicine. Since the census is forbidden by law from asking about religious affiliation, it provides no data on the economic status of Jewish Americans. However, common sense would dictate that the notion that Jews have not achieved occupational equality is about as real as the idea that the Holocaust never happened. Whatever the occupational scorecard may be, it is testimony to the character and endurance of the Jewish people that they have had relatively more success than other groups in pulling themselves up the socioeconomic ladder. Much of their occupational success comes from the fact that they are the most highly educated minority group in the United States.

THE CHANGING RACIAL AND ETHNIC COMPOSITION OF THE UNITED STATES

Racial and ethnic diversity has been a hallmark of the United States since colonial times. Waves of immigrants from different parts of the world, and the fact that these groups have had different levels of fertility and mortality, means that the racial and ethnic composition of the United States has been changing constantly (Rothenberg, 1992). Indeed, if present demographic trends continue, white non-Hispanics eventually will become a minority group in the United States, perhaps by the second half of the twenty-first century. While most U.S. residents now trace their ancestry to Europe, by 2050 the projected majority will trace its ancestry to Latin America, Asia, Africa, the Middle East, or the Pacific Islands. Figure 12:1 depicts the main patterns of global population shifts since 1500.

African Americans are still the most numerous U.S. minority group, but they now account for less than one-half of the total minority population. Because of greater immigration and higher fertility, Hispanics will outnumber African Americans early in the twenty-first century, becoming the nation's largest minority group; and Asians will move from a trace

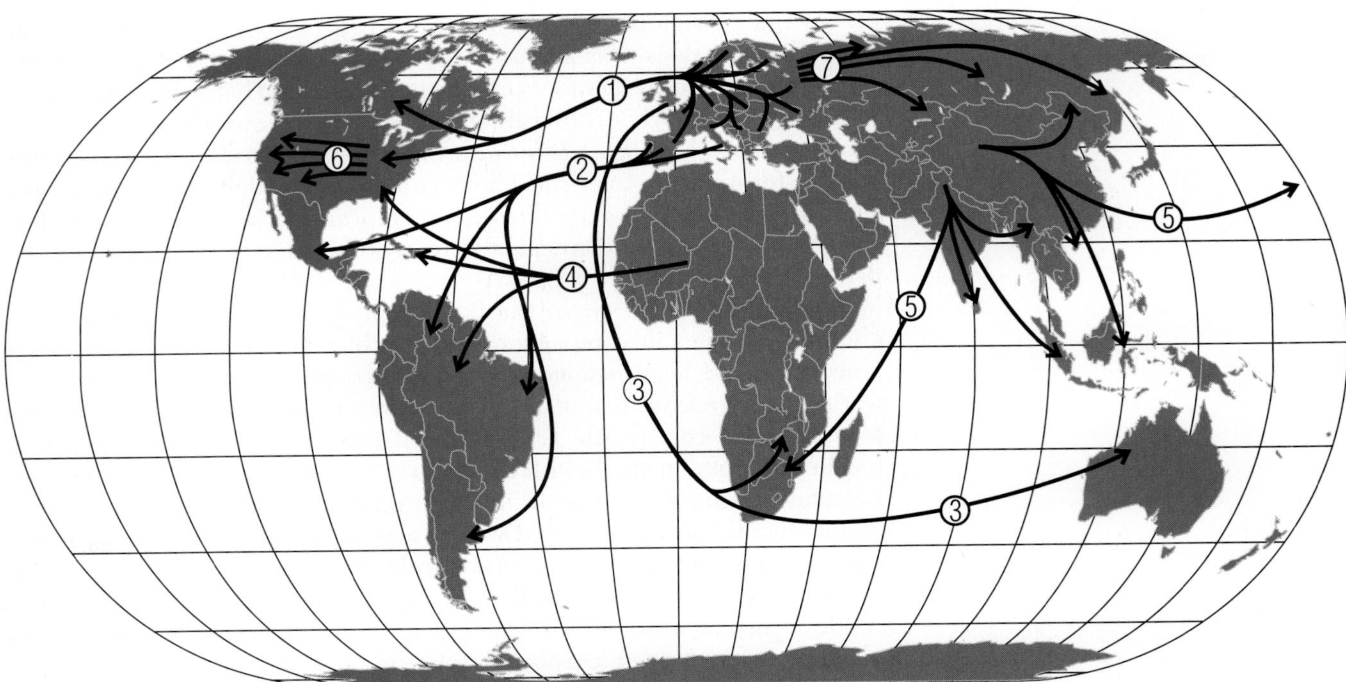

FIGURE 12:1 MAIN CURRENTS OF INTERCONTINENTAL MIGRATION, 1500–1950

Main currents of intercontinental migration have followed many patterns, including 1) from Europe to North America, 2) from Latin countries of Europe to Central and South America, 3) from Great Britain to Africa and Australia, 4) from Africa to America, and 5) from China and India to South Africa, the South Pacific, and America. Intranational migration patterns include 6) westward movement in the United States and 7) the eastward movement in Russia.

Source: W.S. and E.S. Woytinsky, 1953, *World Population Production* (New York: The Twentieth Century Fund), p. 68. © 1953 by The Twentieth Century Fund, New York. Reprinted with permission.

element to a sizable minority. It is unlikely that any single racial or ethnic group will outnumber white non-Hispanics in the very near future, but white non-Hispanics will probably fall from being the majority group to being the largest of several large racial/ethnic minority groups.

Evolving ethnic composition is already having a profound impact on almost every aspect of American society, from social values and popular culture to education, politics, and industry (Alba, 1991). More public schools

In art circles, John Singleton Copley is credited with creating the first positive portrayal of an African American in a U.S. painting. Copley's *Watson and the Shark* (1778) places African Americans in the apex of a real-life experience: holding out the lifeline to a man wallowing helplessly to avoid a shark attack.

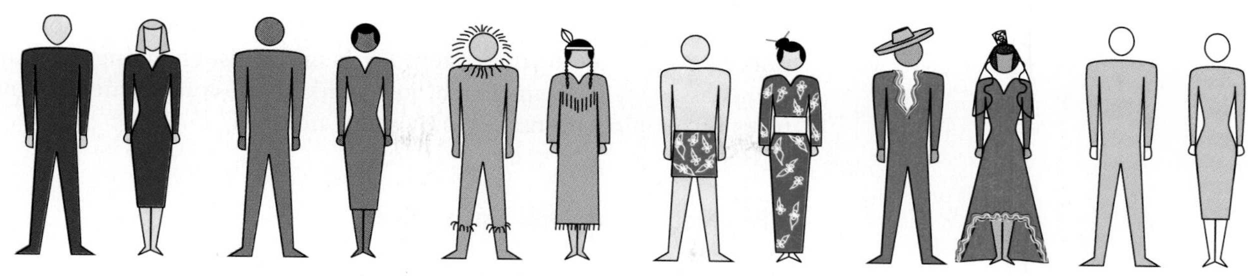

	White	Black	American Indian, Eskimo, Aleut	Asians and Pacific Islanders	Spanish Origin	Other
1970	178,098,000	22,580,289	792,730	1,538,721	9,072,602	516,673
1980	195,571,000	26,903,000	1,429,000	3,834,000	14,803,000	5,283,000
1990	209,326,000	30,788,000	1,737,000	6,881,000	20,528,000	8,647,000
% increase	**7.0**	**14.4**	**21.6**	**79.5**	**38.7**	**63.7**

FIGURE 12:2 RACIAL AND ETHNIC ORIGINS OF AMERICANS, 1970, 1980, AND 1990

There has been a tremendous change in the racial and ethnic origins of Americans over recent decades. This is especially visible in the growth rate of Asian and Hispanic groups.

Source: Census Bureau, 1983 and *Current Population Reports,* series P-25, No. 1045, 1990.

teach non–English-speaking students, and in many big-city school districts, white non-Hispanics are already a minority. Consider the effects on higher education. Political pressure has already begun to alter core humanities curricula at many universities, replacing some of the traditional "canon" of Greek, Latin, and Western European humanities with works reflecting the cultures of Asia, Africa, and other parts of the world. In colleges throughout the United States, Asian faculty members doubled their number to more than 20,000 between 1975 and 1990. And some universities have been charged with having covert racial quota systems for admissions, a phenomenon that serves as a reminder that building and sustaining a multiracial society is difficult and fraught with social problems.

The day may come when white Americans will become a minority group. Long before that day arrives, the presumption that the "typical" U.S. citizen is someone who traces his or her descent in a direct line to Europe will be part of the past. Take a look at Figure 12:2. It depicts the rapidly changing landscape of race and ethnicity in the United States today.

PREJUDICE, DISCRIMINATION, AND RACISM

We often throw around terms such as prejudice and discrimination as if they were interchangeable. Are they? No. In fact, while they are connected, prejudice, discrimination, and racism are different parts of a problem that is commonly referred to as *bigotry.*

The Nature of Prejudice

prejudice—a rigid predisposition to respond to a certain group in a specific way.

Prejudice literally means prejudgment, but it would be foolish to think of prejudice as an operation of the mind involving logic, comparison, and good sense. *Prejudice* is a rigid predisposition to respond to a certain group in a specific way, which emphasizes only selective "facts" and ignores others. Prejudice almost always involves negative feelings such as hatred and aversion. It is easy to find many examples of prejudice in American society. Prejudice manifests itself in such notions as the oversexed black male, the pushy Jew, the dirty Chicano, and dumb Poles. Many people are emotionally committed to these stereotypes and resist changing their attitudes. If this assessment seems harsh, just think about conversations about other types of people within your own social network.

The Nature of Discrimination

discrimination—unequal treatment of members of a minority group.

Prejudice is an attitude. It does not involve overt action. **Discrimination** does. To dislike a group of people is one thing (prejudice), but to treat those people in a less than equal way is another (discrimination). The distinction between attitude and action is important from a social policy perspective, because it is possible to enact legislation to prevent discrimination without necessarily reducing prejudice. However, from a sociological perspective, prejudice and discrimination are highly interrelated. Prejudice typically causes discrimination, which, in turn, increases prejudice, perpetuating the situation.

The relationship between prejudice and discrimination is complex and varies considerably from person to person and from group to group. Robert Merton (1949) described four types of people in terms of the way they express prejudice and discrimination: prejudiced and discriminatory ("active bigots"), unprejudiced and nondiscriminatory ("all-weather liberals"), unprejudiced and discriminatory ("fair-weather liberals"), and prejudiced and nondiscriminatory ("timid bigots"). Active bigots and all-weather liberals require little explanation; they are simply individuals who act on their beliefs. People who vote with the conviction that African Americans are unfit for political office, for example, are active bigots. Many people fall somewhere between these two extremes and act against their feelings, whether bigoted or not, when faced with countervailing social pressures. An example of a fair-weather liberal is a real estate agent who does not personally dislike Hispanics but refuses to sell to them because of fears that it can hurt "property values." Conversely, realtors who hate Asians but do business with them for fear of legal reprisal or simply to make money are timid bigots. Merton's typology is useful not simply because it provides a breakdown of the various ways in which prejudice and discrimination are related but also because it shows how people's thoughts and behaviors can be highly inconsistent. This is especially evident in the case of the person who is not prejudiced but acts in discriminatory ways.

Forms of Discrimination

Discrimination takes many forms, from a joke about being Jewish to a racially motivated murder to the fact that white males get the majority of available transplant organs. It may also underlie a host of economic differences among groups. Table 12:3 displays a number of educational, economic, and lifestyle characteristics that differ among groups.

There is also a distinction between verbal and behavioral discrimination. This was first noted in a classic study by La Piere in 1934. He traveled with a Chinese couple as they stopped at some 250 restaurants and hotels across the United States. They were refused service only once. Later, La Piere sent letters to each of the establishments, asking whether they would serve "members of the Chinese race." Half did not reply, but more than 90 percent of those that did claimed they did not accommodate Chinese guests. While many *said* they discriminate against Chinese people, almost none

TABLE 12:3 A Comparison of Social and Economic Conditions among Whites, Blacks, Asians, and Hispanics: 1980 and 1990

CHARACTERISTICS	WHITES			BLACKS			ASIANS[i]			HISPANICS		
	1980	1990	% Change	1980	1990	% Change	1980	1990	% Change	1980	1990	% Change
Four or more years of high school[a]	70.5	79.1	+12.2	51.2	66.2	+29.3	74.8	80.4	+7.5	45.3	50.8	+12.1
Four or more years of college[a]	17.1	22.0	+28.7	8.4	11.3	+34.5	32.9	39.9	+21.3	7.6	9.2	+21.1
Median family income[b]	$34,743	$36,915	+6.3	$20,103	$21,423	+6.6	$22,713	$36,784	+62.0	$23,342	$23,431	+0.4
Person below poverty level[c]	10.2	10.7	+4.9	32.5	31.9	−1.9	12.3	14.1	+14.6	25.7	28.1	+9.3
Unemployed[d]	4.0	4.7	+17.5	8.7	11.3	+29.9	4.7	5.1	+8.5	8.9	8.0	−10.1
Families — two parents[e]	82.9	77.4	−6.6	48.1	39.4	−18.1	84.4	81.2	−3.8	74.1	66.8	−9.9
Families — mother w/child[e]	15.1	18.8	+24.5	48.7	56.2	+15.4	10.8	12.2	+13.0	24.0	29.3	22.1
% Occupied households (owner)[f]	68.6	67.4	−1.8	43.9	42.9	−2.3	52.0	52.2	+.4	42.4	40.3	−5.0
Average value of home[g]	$48,600	$80,000[h]	+65.0	$27,200	$51,404	+89.0	$83,900[j]	$209,700[j]	+150.0	$44,700	$76,298	+70.7

Figures shown as percentages except where the dollar value is indicated. Notes indicate the source of the information.

[a] *Educational Attainment in the United States: March 1990 and 1991.* U.S. Dept. of Commerce, Bureau of Census and *Current Population Report,* series P-20.

[b] Figures supplied by the U.S. Dept. of Commerce, Bureau of Census. Both 1980 and 1990 figures are in 1990 dollar values.

[c] Figures supplied by the U.S. Dept. of Commerce, Bureau of Census, and *Current Population Report,* series P-60, No. 168.

[d] *Current Population Report,* series P-20, No. 441 and P-60, No. 162 and 166 and *Employment and Earnings,* U.S. Dept. of Labor, Bureau of Labor Statistics, Vol. 38, No. 1, January, 1991.

[e] *Current Population Report,* series P-20, No. 447, *Household and Family Characteristics: March 1990 and 1989.*

[f] Figures supplied by the U.S. Dept. of Commerce, Bureau of Census. The most recent figures available are for 1989.

[g] Figures supplied by the U.S. Dept. of Commerce, Bureau of Census, and *The 1980 Census of Housing,* Vol. 1.

[h] This figure represents the median value of homes owned by whites. The mean value was not available.

[i] *We, the Asian and Pacific Islander Americans.* U.S. Dept. of Commerce, Bureau of Census, and U.S. Dept. of Commerce, Statistical Information Office.

[j] This figure reflects the concentration of Asian and Pacific Islanders in the west and urban areas where housing values far exceed national averages.

actually did. Apparently it is more difficult to discriminate against someone in a face-to-face situation than through the mail.

Violence is a more extreme form of discrimination than simple verbal abuse or avoiding interaction with members of a minority group. Over time, minority group members in the United States have been beaten, whipped, lynched, burned at the stake, or castrated because they were members of a hated group.

Prejudice and discrimination are widespread national problems that have been with us for a long time. However, there are some notable regional differences in the prevalence of these issues. As most people believe, white southerners are especially likely to be prejudiced, particularly in terms of accepting African Americans in equal-status positions. Like alcoholism among the Irish, bigotry among white southerners is a popular subjective stereotype that happens to fit the objective facts. In fact, some parts of the South have been such hotbeds of racial feelings that, in the late 1980s, the American Nazi Party, a lunatic fringe element, declared that the time was ripe to set aside North Carolina as a Carolina Free State, a state for white people only. Today, regional variations in prejudice and discrimination are diminishing. West or east, north or south, stereotypes are stereotypes and prejudice is prejudice. They know no geographical boundaries.

Racism

racism—prejudice or discrimination based on perceived racial characteristics.

individual racism—refers to personally held negative racial attitudes.

institutional racism—sources of discrimination built into the social system.

Racism is prejudice or discrimination based on perceived racial characteristics (Essed, 1991). Although U.S. society has wrestled with the dilemma of dealing with the principle of justice for all and the racist reality of everyday life, racism is not an American issue only. It abounds throughout the world—from anti-Semitism in Austria to gypsy-haters in Italy. Essentially racism takes three forms. One form is **individual racism**, a term often used interchangeably with *race prejudice*. It refers to personally held negative racial attitudes. People who put all Asians into one devalued category are living examples of race prejudice. Sexual racism is one of the components of this type of racism. It is based on the idea that males from certain minority groups are excessively sexual, and preoccupied with particular types of women.

A second form of racism is **institutional racism**, which involves sources of discrimination found outside the individual. For this reason, it is inherently sociological since it is built into the system rather than the individual psyche. Institutional racism includes all the manifest and latent ways in which society's institutions work against the interests of minority groups. It has a long history in the United States and is probably the most widespread form of discrimination. For example, in the South, it used to be illegal to teach blacks how to read and write. During World War II, the Red Cross separated blood from white donors from that donated by blacks. In the 1970s, it was discovered that the United States Public Health Service had approved of a medical experiment in which 425 impoverished African American males were allowed to go untreated for syphilis in order for researchers to understand the long-term effects of the disease.

Some forms of institutional discrimination are illegal in the United States, but exist anyway. For example, admission to a prestigious private school usually is based on ability to pay and personal recommendations. However, if nearly everyone who has the money and influential friends to write the recommendations are majority members, minority group members will have a difficult time gaining admission. The same phenomenon occurs when applying for a white-collar job requires high levels of literacy from someone whose ghetto high school graduates illiterates.

cultural racism—the expression of the superiority of the cultural heritage of one's race over another's.

A third form of racism, **cultural racism**, contains elements of both individual and institutional racism. It is the expression of the superiority of the cultural heritage of one's race over another's. Cultural racism is at work, for instance, when the achievements of a race are ignored in textbooks. It is also at work in black-oriented rap music where "all niggas" are described as believing that all women are "bitches." And racism is at least latently at work when the media treat Japan and particularly its business powers in xenophobic ways (Japan bashing).

Racism knows no international bounds. It is literally everywhere. It is in the hearts and minds of people in Albania as much as it is in the streets of Los Angeles. Box 12:3 testifies to the fact that college campuses are no exception.

PATTERNS OF RACIAL AND ETHNIC RELATIONS

The interplay between different racial and ethnic groups has assumed many sociological patterns throughout history. Basically there are five relational patterns, which run the gamut from genocide to cross-racial friendships.

Genocide

genocide—a purposeful and systematic attempt to exterminate an entire people.

A purposeful and systematic attempt to literally exterminate an entire people is known as **genocide**, although the word is sometimes used to refer to race-based murder, which is not necessarily systematic or purposeful. Clearly this is the most vicious of the relational patterns between groups, and one that is not uncommon. Mass death ran like spreading cancer among blacks in slave ships centuries ago. In the early 1900s racial violence took the more singular form of lynchings in the American South and was a major reason why African Americans migrated to other parts of the country (Tolnay and Beck, 1992).

As we all know, genocide was a nightmarish ordeal in the massacres of Native Americans. But it also occurred in an unintended way when Europeans arrived in the United States and brought smallpox with them. This was a new disease to a people who had no immunity against it. It almost wiped out the Aztecs, Incas, and Blackfeet, to name just a few tribes.

The most systematic and ghoulish of all instances of genocide occurred in Nazi Germany during World War II. Some 6 million Jews were exterminated by gas, bullets, and other forms of mass murder. Identical twins received "special" treatment in the Auschwitz "laboratories" of Josef Mengele. There some 3,000 twins were tested for their reactions to castration, sterilization, and injection of dye into their eyes. Most of them died as a result, and much of the European Jewish population was obliterated by the end of the war.

Genocide still occurs today on a much smaller scale, as in the case of an isolated murder by a Skinhead or the murder of Azeri refugees by Russian soldiers. It does not always take the form of one particular group persecuting another. Such was the case in Yugoslavia in 1992 when Serbs and Bosnians were killing each other in the streets (a civil war). At the same time, numerous people were killed in shootouts between ethnic Romanians and Russians in the former Soviet republic of Moldova.

BOX 12:3 COLLEGE EXPERIENCE

Racial Bias Reemerges on Campuses across the United States

Racism is a fact of life that has no boundaries. As the incidents here detail, college campuses are not immune to the problem.

Among students for whom the Rev. Martin Luther King, Jr., is almost as abstract a figure as George Washington—and nearly as distant—an insidious ugliness seems to be surfacing. Color it racism.

At both elite private colleges and large state universities, racial incidents have occurred with increasing frequency over recent years.

Some have been confined to name-calling and scrawled epithets: the student at Dartmouth College in Hanover, NH, who was taunted as "dark meat" by a group of football players; the message "niggers go home," written on the minority cultural center at Smith College in Northampton, MA; the Ku Klux Klan leaflets and derogatory drawings of black professors that appeared on the state college campus of Pennsylvania State University.

Racist incidents have shocked other colleges around the country. Among the more dramatic:

Dartmouth College, Hanover, NH (1982): *The Dartmouth Review,* an independent student newspaper receiving large alumni contributions, publishes an article "satirizing" black students attending the college, titled "Dis Sho Aint No Jive, Bro." The article reads in part: ". . . Dese boys be sayin' that we be comin' here to Dartmut an' not taking' the classics. . . . We be culturally lightened, too. We be takin' hard courses in many subjects, like Afro-Am Studies . . . and who be mouthin' bout us not being good read? I be practicly knowin' Roots cova to cova, til my mine be boogying to da' words! An I be watchin' The Jeffersons on TV til I be blue in da face. . . ."

University of Michigan, Ann Arbor (1987): WJJX, a campus radio station, receives a call from a student requesting air time to tell some jokes: "What do you get when you cross a black and a groundhog?" asks the caller. "Six more weeks of basketball season." Incredibly, the deejay tells the caller to continue the provocative humor while he searches for a laugh track. "Why do blacks always have sex on their minds?" asks the caller. "Because all their pubic hair is on their head."

Smith College, Northampton, MA (1986): The slogan, "Niggers, Spics, and Chinks quit complaining or get out" is found spraypainted on a campus building.

Indiana University, Bloomington (1988): The dorm room door of black freshman Tim Rey is burned then scrawled with the epithets "nigger" and "KKK."

University of Pennsylvania, Philadelphia (1988): An all-white fraternity is shut down after it hires two black strippers to perform while fraternity members shout racial epithets.

University of Mississippi, Oxford (1988): The Phi Beta Sigma house, the first black fraternity house on Fraternity Row, is gutted by a fire that was started by an arsonist.

. . . Black students at predominantly white schools often report that racial prejudice is a daily fact of college life. This reality is particularly chilling since black students are attending predominantly white colleges in record numbers, while those attending historically black colleges have declined from 44 percent to 16 percent between 1965 and 1985.

"The white kids look at us as if to say, 'You don't belong here, so don't make waves,'" says Sharon, 20, a junior at the University of Maryland. "I just want to get my degree and get out."

The resurgence of campus racism has not been limited to black students. Its ugly tentacles have touched the lives of black professors. Last winter, white students at Dartmouth College published, in the same student newspaper that six years earlier had printed "Dis Sho Aint No Jive, Bro," an article describing the classroom manner of William Cole, a black professor of music, as a cross between a "welfare queen and a bathroom attendant." Following the article's publication, several of the paper's staffers attempted to elicit a response from Professor Cole. "I was accosted by four students after my class in February," says Cole, a professor for 14 years at the ivy league school.

BOX 12: 3 COLLEGE EXPERIENCE *continued*

"They came to me after my class without any invitation, with no appointment, without telling me they were coming, demanding a response, and they accosted me."

As the ugliness of each incident makes clear, America's college campuses are witnessing one of the most turbulent and disturbing periods since the racial unrest of the '60s. The reasons behind the resurgence of campus racism are complex and multilayered, but the consensus among educators, activists, and students is clear: The primary cause of this new bigotry is but a mirror of the nation's larger political climate. The National Institute against Prejudice and Violence describes it as "only a small reflection of the larger society."

Critical Thinking Questions

1. Is racism becoming more common on college campuses? If so, what forces might be at work?
2. What approaches/programs might prove useful in promoting better relations between students from different racial or ethnic backgrounds?

Source: Adapted from *Ebony* (December 1988). By permission of the publishers.

Expulsion

expulsion—the systematic transfer of a group of people.

subjugation—the deliberate, long-run attempt on the part of the socially powerful to maintain their position in society at the expense of others.

An extreme but less violent action that has befallen some racial and ethnic groups is **expulsion**. Actually, it was the first experience of German Jews, who were systematically transferred from their homes to concentration camps designed to carry out the "final solution." Expulsion (sometimes known by the euphemism, *population transfer*) also characterized the movement of Native Americans to "Indian Reservations."

In a way this is what occurred to the mentally ill centuries ago when they were placed in facilities known as insane asylums. The thinking (or lack of it) was the same; if a group of people is an undesirable presence in mainstream society, then put them in a special place. Out of sight—out of mind.

Subjugation

Subjugation is the deliberate, long-run attempt on the part of the socially powerful to maintain their position in society at the expense of others. Yes, the others are members of different minority groups. No, it is not something peculiar to the privileged position of Anglos in the United States. Subjugation is so universally common that some sociologists consider it to be a cross-cultural universal. Witness apartheid in South Africa, the position of Jews in Russia, and the plight of the untouchables in India, and you have traversed much of the globe. It is so widespread around the world and throughout time that it is part of the very fabric of human society.

Racial violence has many faces, which are not always the faces of people of different races. In South Africa, "neck tiring" is a punishment that blacks inflict on blacks who side with whites.

East Los Angeles has been the scene of many a confrontation between Hispanic youths and the police. Artist Frank Romero remembered growing up in L.A. with his painting, *The Closing of Whittier Boulevard.* It portrays extreme residential segregation as police use Gestapo tactics to confine young Hispanics.

Segregation

segregation—any form of separation of races or ethnic groups in a variety of institutional spheres including occupations, political participation, and social memberships.

The word **segregation** appears regularly in the American vocabulary and typically conjures up images of separate housing areas, the most depressed of which are called "ghettos." Figure 12:3 presents data on the level of racial segregation in different U.S. cities. But segregation involves more than residential discrimination. It includes any form of separation of races or ethnic groups in a variety of institutional spheres including occupations, political participation, and social memberships.

City	Index
Gary–Hammond (IN)	91
Chicago	88
Cleveland	87
Detroit	87
Milwaukee	84
Fort Lauderdale	82
New York City	82
Newark	82
Los Angeles	81
Paterson (NJ)	81
St. Louis	81
Atlanta	79
Buffalo	79
Kansas City	79
Philadelphia	79
Boston	78
Dayton	78
Miami	78
Dallas–Ft. Worth	77
Jersey City	77

(Scale: 70, 75, 80, 85, 90)

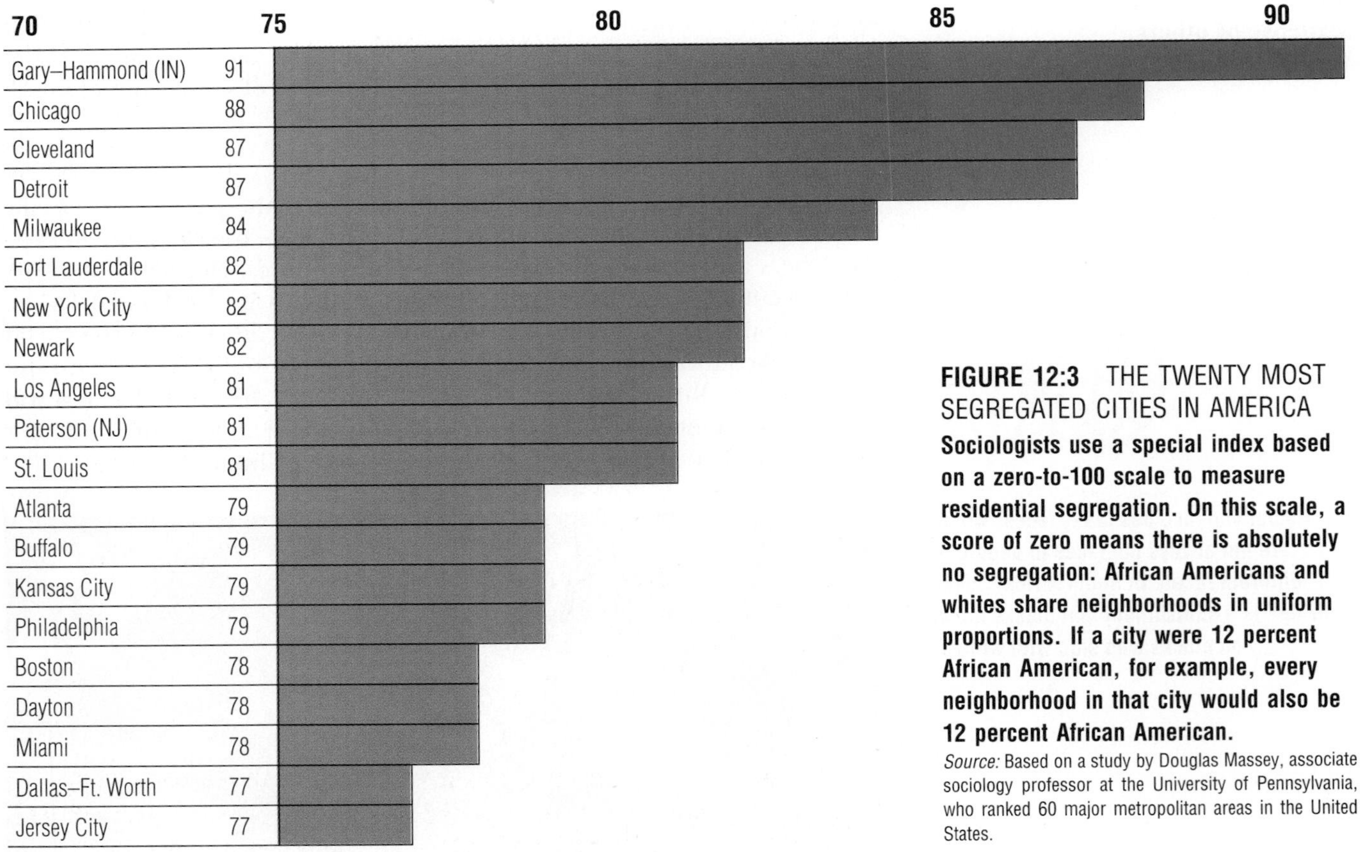

FIGURE 12:3 THE TWENTY MOST SEGREGATED CITIES IN AMERICA
Sociologists use a special index based on a zero-to-100 scale to measure residential segregation. On this scale, a score of zero means there is absolutely no segregation: African Americans and whites share neighborhoods in uniform proportions. If a city were 12 percent African American, for example, every neighborhood in that city would also be 12 percent African American.
Source: Based on a study by Douglas Massey, associate sociology professor at the University of Pennsylvania, who ranked 60 major metropolitan areas in the United States.

Sometimes segregation is a self-imposed act as in the case of the Hutterites, the Amish, and the Hasidic Jews who purposefully separate themselves from others. We see this occurring more frequently around the world today as a rising consciousness of ethnic identity has reformed parts of Eastern Europe into smaller nation–states.

In the United States, segregation has been the experience of many African Americans from womb to tomb. It has crushed their hopes for a life of equal opportunity and, in a sense, made them exiles at home. There is a bright side to all of this, however. It is known as the Civil Rights Movement, a long process of social change that spans close to 400 years. It started slowly with slave revolts and whipped itself into a frenzy during the 1960s. It has been a difficult process riddled with violence, but it has also been a movement of great progress for African Americans. Take a look at Table 12:4 to capture some of the legal activity historically associated with this movement toward equality.

Assimilation

assimilation—the absorption of a minority group into the dominant group.

A minority group may be absorbed into the dominant group through **assimilation**. This could be physical assimilation, as when intermarriage eliminates racial identity over time. It could also take the form of cultural assimilation, as when a minority group relinquishes its cultural traits and adopts those of the dominant group. Assimilation may be forced onto a minority, or the minority may be absorbed into the majority culture at its own pace.

The United States has long been characterized as a "melting pot" society, a place where a merger of ethnic and racial groups into a homogeneous group of people occurs. Has it occurred? It appears to be the case for white ethnics. To be of Irish or Italian background is clearly less of an issue today than it was earlier in the 1900s. But the melting pot theory is still just a theory when it comes to such groups as African Americans. Racial intermarriages do occur, but they are far from the norm (see Chapter 14). California will prove to be an interesting test of the melting pot theory; in 1992, one in five Californians was a foreign-born immigrant, mostly of Hispanic or Asian origin.

At present, we do not seem to be en route to a society of "United Statesians." What seems more likely is that America will be a country of cultural pluralism, a multicultural society, which has been described variously as a tossed salad or a stew, a quilt or a tapestry, a mosaic or a rainbow. Here it is important to note that the history of different racial and ethnic groups in the United States is characterized by assimilation as well as conflict. The data in Figure 12:4 attest to one part of assimilation—changing attitudes of whites toward African Americans. It is also imperative to recognize the many positive contributions that minority groups have made to U.S. culture. The list of these contributions would itself constitute a book.

THEORETICAL PERSPECTIVES ON RACIAL AND ETHNIC RELATIONS

Functionalist Theory

It is clearly awkward and ethically undesirable to walk the straight line of functionalist theory regarding issues of prejudice and discrimination. This is because, as you saw in earlier chapters, functionalists first look for positive

TABLE 12:4 The Civil Rights Movement: Four Centuries of Legal Progress and Setbacks

YEARS	OCCURRENCES
1641–1750	Massachusetts becomes the first colony to recognize slavery as a legal institution. Connecticut follows in 1650; Virginia, 1661; Maryland, 1663; New York and New Jersey, 1664; South Carolina, 1682; Rhode Island and Pennsylvania, 1700; North Carolina, 1715; Georgia, 1750.
1776	Declaration of Independence adopted containing no statement on abolition of slave trade. Continental Congress gives permission to free blacks to enlist in the Revolutionary Army.
1773–1804	By 1773, slavery is prohibited in Massachusetts and New Hampshire; Vermont becomes the first of the newly independent United States to abolish slavery in 1777; Pennsylvania provides gradual emancipation in 1780; Rhode Island and Connecticut ban slavery in 1784; New York partially bans slavery in 1799, New Jersey in 1804.
1863	President Abraham Lincoln signs the Emancipation Proclamation. (Texas slavery emancipation order is signed June 19, and that date is considered Black Independence Day. It is celebrated as Juneteenth Day in Texas and other southern states.)
1866	Civil Rights Act bestows citizenship on black Americans. Congress passes the Fourteenth Amendment, which provides for federal protection of civil rights.
1875	Congress enacts Civil Rights Bill, which provides for equal treatment in public conveyances and places of public amusement.
1881	Tennessee enacts first "Jim Crow" railroad-car law, which forces blacks to sit in separate sections of trains. Booker T. Washington opens Tuskegee Institute in Alabama.
1896	U.S. Supreme Court upholds "separate but equal" doctrine (*Plessy* v. *Ferguson*) when it rules that laws segregating people because of their race do not violate the U.S. Constitution.
1922	U.S. House of Representatives passes Dyer Anti–Lynching Bill, which is later defeated in Senate by southern filibuster.
1927	U.S. Supreme Court overrules Texas law that prevents blacks from voting in "white primaries."
1938	U.S. Supreme Court, in the case of Lloyd Gaines, rules that states must provide education for all its citizens "within the state," leading to creation of professional and graduate schools on all-black campuses.
1941	President Franklin Delano Roosevelt issues Executive Order 8802, which prohibits racial and religious discrimination in war industries and government training programs.
1944	U.S. Supreme Court bans the "white primary," which has effectively prevented blacks from voting in the South.
1946	U.S. Supreme Court bans segregation in interstate bus travel.
1954	U.S. Supreme Court in a unanimous landmark decision (*Brown* v. *Topeka, Kan., Board of Education,* brought by the NAACP) rules that racial segregation in public schools is unconstitutional because "separate educational facilities are inherently unequal."
1955	U.S. Supreme Court, in second Brown decision, orders school boards to draw up desegregation procedures "with all deliberate speed."
1957	Congress passes Civil Rights Act, first since 1875 allowing federal government to bring suit on behalf of anyone denied the right to vote and creating the U.S. Commission on Civil Rights.
1965	The Voting Rights Act of 1965, providing for registration of African American voters by federal examiners, is signed into law.
1967	Thurgood Marshall becomes first African American appointed to Supreme Court. Walter Washington is appointed mayor of Washington, the first African American to head a major U.S. city. African American candidates are elected mayors in the North, including Richard G. Hatcher in Gary, IN, and Carl Stokes in Cleveland.
1968	President's National Advisory Commission on Civil Disorders identifies the major cause of riots in 1967 as the existence of two disparate societies in America,— "one black, one white, separate and unequal"; media culpability is cited. Shirley Chisholm of Brooklyn, NY, becomes the first African American woman member of the U.S. House of Representatives.
1984	The Rev. Jesse Jackson, head of Operation PUSH, makes first serious bid for presidential nomination.
1986	America honors [Martin Luther King, Jr.] with first national holiday for an African American. Edward Perkins is sworn in as the African American U.S. ambassador to South Africa, and says he will make America's "intolerance of racial apartheid" clear to that nation's white minority government.

Do you think there should be laws against marriages between blacks and whites?

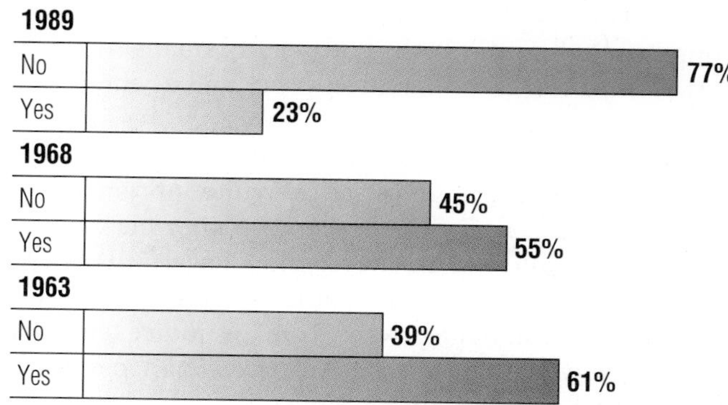

White people have a right to keep blacks out of their neighborhoods if they want to, and blacks should respect that right.

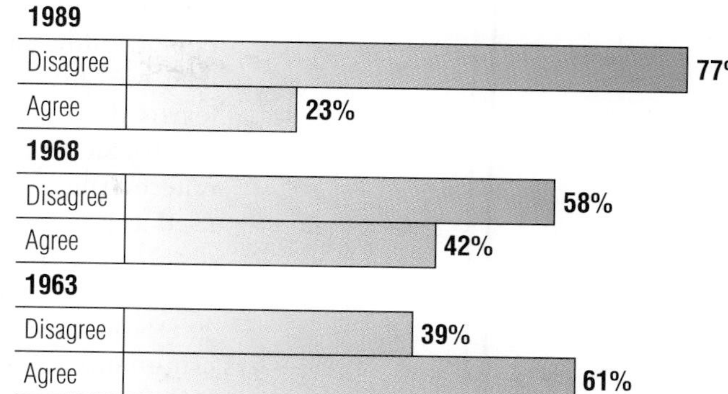

If your party nominated a black for president, would you vote for him if he were qualified for the job?

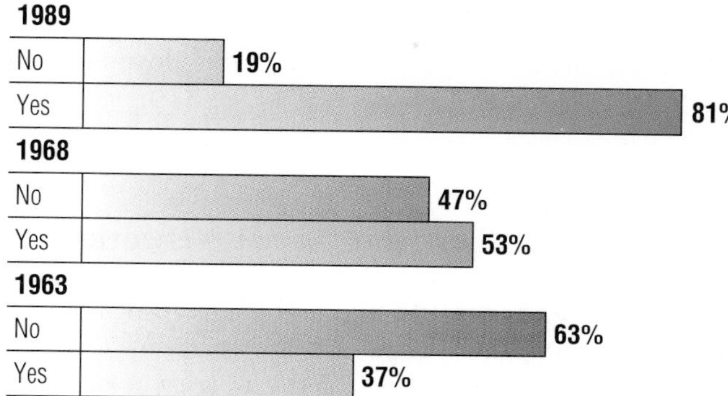

Do you think white students and black students should go to the same schools or to separate schools?

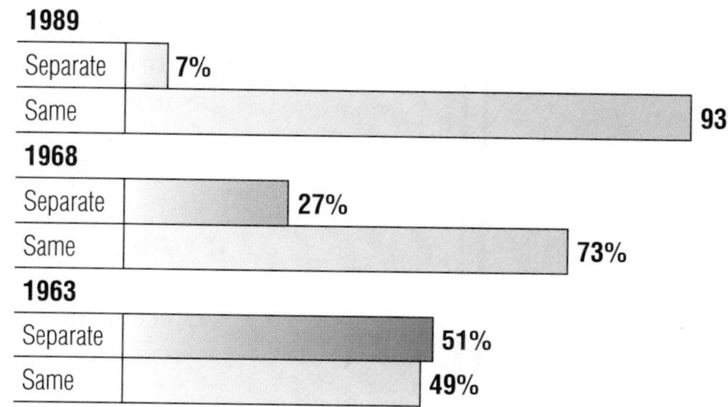

FIGURE 12:4 CHANGING ATTITUDES OF WHITES ABOUT RACE RELATIONS
Opinion polls show a significant increase in positive attitudes of whites about their relations with African Americans.
Source: Responses compiled from surveys by the National Opinion Research Center, University of Chicago, Illinois, 1963, 1968, and 1989.

aspects of sociological realities. Nevertheless, a case can be made that racism serves certain latent functions. The key question is: For whom?

Racist beliefs keep both the dominant and subordinate groups "in their place." If it is widely believed that a race is inherently lazy, for example, why bother with social progress toward full opportunity? This was the kind of thinking that maintained slavery in the South, and it was clearly economically beneficial to whites. That was the short-run "positive" function. The long-run dysfunction, however, was the collapse of an entire social system. Today we witness a similar situation among South African blacks who are oppressed by *apartheid.* It is a situation that benefits the white minority, but what will happen to the social system?

Identification with a race or ethnic group can have very positive social and psychological benefits. The sense of social identity experienced by such membership can promote self-esteem and social cohesion. Even this kind of group solidarity can cut both ways. When it moves beyond a healthy feeling of belongingness and into the realm of ethnocentric in-group/out-group thinking, it then becomes dysfunctional fuel for social conflict.

Conflict Theory

Conflict theorists see nothing positive about prejudice and discrimination. Disputes are not fundamentally about racial or ethnic differences; they are about competition for economic resources. Race and ethnicity are merely other forms of sheep's clothing within which the wolf of exploitation may maraud.

Why are certain groups the objects of economic exploitation? Generally, the most recent group to enter the country is most likely to end up at the bottom of the pile. This was certainly the case in earlier years for a number of immigrant groups, including the Irish, Poles, and Italians. If this is true, we should expect to find less discrimination over time as the group learns the rules of the conflict game in the United States.

African Americans may be a special case because of the unique way they entered the country—as indentured servants or slaves. White supremacy was used as a political issue (particularly in the South) to keep poor blacks from discovering their common class interests in overcoming poverty. This created a deep-seated ideology of black inferiority that is difficult to eradicate.

Dominant groups gain in a number of ways from prejudice and discrimination. Whites in power who hire African Americans can pay them less. Because prejudice also makes it difficult for Hispanics to compete with whites for jobs, they are forced to accept whatever jobs are left over, regardless of how unpleasant or low-paying they may be. College quotas limiting the acceptance of Asians open up slots for other races. These hidden benefits of racism become all too obvious during economic downturns, when minorities inevitably bear the brunt of rising rates of unemployment and poverty.

Symbolic Interactionism: The View from Social Networks

As usual, the symbolic interactionists find the foregoing macrosociological speculations to miss the real point. Where is the nitty-gritty of race and ethnic relations? It is right at the face-to-face level of the neighborhood, the street, and the family dinner table.

Once one zooms in at this level, the symbolic interactionists contend, the origins of prejudice lock into focus. Practically no one thinks that racism—or ethnicism—is genetic. It can only arise from the social environment, and especially that most immediate social environment—the social network. Negative stereotypes of out-groups can quite naturally be passed on from the social modeling (i.e., imitation; see Chapter 4) of significant others within one's in-group. Think of your recent conversations concerning members of other races. Would a symbolic interactionist find evidence of this theory?

One intriguing way to track racial and ethnic progress looks directly at interpersonal relationships. In Chapter 14 ("Family"), patterns of interracial marriages are analyzed. In a nutshell, the rate and social acceptability of marriages between African Americans and whites have increased over the past 20 years, but the changes have been tiny. Instead of asking attitudes about other groups or tracking evidence of socioeconomic discrimination, the interactionist approach counts real interactions. Social network research takes seriously the cliché, "some of my best friends are _______." So, are they? Two separate analyses of the Detroit Area study—which asked approximately 1,000 white men to name their three closest friends—found strong preferences for one's in-group. For every one of the 20 ethnic groups, respondents were much more likely to have friends of the same ethnicity as themselves. Among white males, only a small percentile of "non-whites" were part of their inner friendship circles, and Jews had Jewish members of this circle 80 percent of the time (Laumann, 1973)! Quite clearly, racial and ethnic birds of a feather had flocked together.

Perhaps because of the sensitivity of the issue, more extensive recent data are hard to come by. The General Social Survey does offer two intrigu-

TABLE 12:5 Guess Who Came to Dinner?

WHITE RESPONDENTS	During the past few years, has anyone in your family brought a friend who was a black home for dinner?	
Value Label	Frequency	Percent
Yes	264	29.1
No	642	70.9
	—	—
Total	906	100.0
Valid Cases 1,372	Missing Cases 466	

Main Point: A significant minority of whites invite African Americans to their home.

Source: General Social Survey, 1990.

TABLE 12:6 Blacks with White Close Friends

BLACK RESPONDENTS	How many of your close friends are white?	
Value Label	Frequency	Percent
None	170	33.5
One or two	124	24.4
Three or more	214	42.1
	—	—
Total	508	100.0
Valid Cases 1,372	Missing Cases 466	

Main Point: A majority of African Americans have close friends who are white.

Source: General Social Survey, 1982.

ing glimpses in Table 12:5 and Table 12:6. As evidence of still another racial cliché, observe that nearly three of every 10 white respondents had recently hosted an African American dinner guest who was also a "friend" from the other side, only about one-third of African Americans polled in 1982 had no white "close friends," and over 40 percent had three or more. To the extent that the symbolic interactionists are right in their view that prejudice toward out-groups is hatched in exclusive in-groups, these data about the permeability of racial worlds are crucial.

As you study these tables, think critically about the data and try to answer the following questions.

1. What do these two tables suggest in terms of whether whites or African Americans are more accepting of each other?
2. If the same questions are asked 10 years from now, how will the answers vary?

Integrating the Theories

Despite the polemics, critical thinking demonstrates that, in this case, the analyses of the functionalists and conflict theorists are unusually close. The former emphasize the positive function of social order for the system as long as everyone stays "in their place." The latter point out the dysfunctions of discrimination in the loss of human potential (and the potential for interracial disaster), as well as the selective positive benefits only for those at the top.

The symbolic interactionists spotlight the social machinery by which intergroup relations are created and maintained. It is an unusually sharp shift of perspective down to the microlevel where macrolevel functions and conflicts are forged.

SUBJECTIVE ASPECTS OF INTERGROUP RELATIONS

It is obvious from reading this chapter that different ethnic and racial groups in the United States do not live together in harmony. But have relations improved? Have hostilities lessened? Do groups feel better about each other now compared to recent decades? These are not easy questions to answer because opinion polls are often contradictory. This is why there is no overarching sociological perspective to explain any noted changes in attitudes (Pettigrew, 1985; Shuman and Bobo, 1988). One problem is that polls center almost exclusively on relations between African Americans and whites. However, the consensus does seem to be that there has been *gradual progress* in a number of areas.

Racial issues have become increasingly *visible* during recent decades. From the violent turmoil of the 1960s to the racial harassment policies established in U.S. institutions recently, one thing is clear: This issue has exploded into the public consciousness. Witness its regular role on the nightly news. Owing in part to this increased visibility, prejudice against African Americans has declined throughout the United States, particularly in the South (Firebaugh and Davis, 1988).

More than 40 years of polling on racial attitudes reveals a vastly stronger articulation of the American value that "All men are created equal." For instance, in 1956 half of the whites polled supported the idea of integrated education, according to a National Opinion Research Center (NORC) survey. In 1985, when NORC stopped asking the question, the figure had climbed to more than 90 percent. In a 1963 NORC survey, 40 percent of whites opposed the exclusion of African Americans from particular schools. By 1977, the figure had risen to 60 percent; and by 1989, to nearly 80 percent. Similar progress is displayed in NORC polls on related issues. See Figure 12:5. It displays changing attitudes about race relations but also notes that, while relations have improved, subjective variables account for it being continuously perceived as a major social problem.

What are Americans' *expectations* for the future? In 1989, a Harris poll reported that only a small majority (53 percent) of Americans agreed that more should be done to help disadvantaged African Americans and other minorities in the next administration. As expected, more African Americans than whites saw a need for affirmative action in employment and a willingness to spend money to "attack the causes of crime" through educational and antipoverty programs. All tolled, it is clear that race relations have improved, but the racist foundations of U.S. society are still very much

FIGURE 12:5 SUBJECTIVE AND OBJECTIVE DIMENSIONS: RELATIONS BETWEEN AFRICAN AMERICANS AND WHITES

Although attitude polls show that relations between African Americans and whites have improved, race relations is still perceived as one of our major social problems.

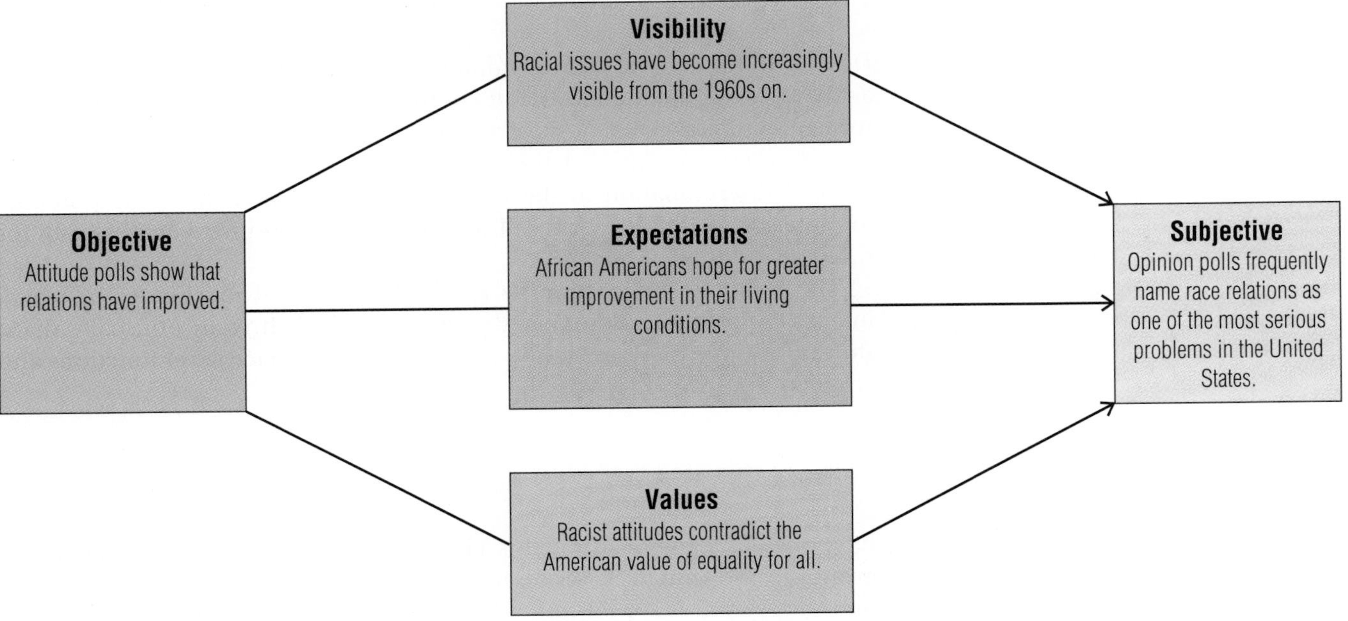

intact. For instance, a 1991 report by the Brookings Institution found that racial stereotypes in the workplace often still interfere with the fair pursuit of a meaningful job (Kirschenman and Neckerman, 1991). But the workplace is just one place where racism rears its ugly head. In 1992, Los Angeles was in flames over an outrage in the criminal justice system. An African American, Rodney King, was severely beaten by police. His attack was videotaped and widely viewed by an American audience. The jury decided that the police were within the law. African Americans claimed that there were two sets of laws: one for whites and one for blacks. In 1993, tensions were reduced somewhat when a new trial put some of the accused cops in prison. The verdict pleased both groups.

SUMMARY

1. Race and ethnicity are complicated concepts: complicated to define; complicated to understand the hostility they generate; and complicated to explain in terms of the driving forces behind intergroup relations. Biological, legal, and social definitions of race are arbitrary and contradictory. Basically, racial membership is a subjective, social perception of what people say it is.
2. The racial and ethnic composition of the United States is in constant flux, although one pattern seems clear—the era of the white majority may soon be coming to an end as the growth rate of African Americans, Hispanics, and Asians continues to swell.
3. Will the time come when these and other so-called minority groups are fully assimilated into U.S. culture? Will their future instead still be riddled with prejudice and discrimination? We only have opinion polls to go by, and presently they report a lessening of interracial tensions. But opinion polls are only a snapshot of the present. With all the expected changes in the twenty-first century, a picture of the future is impossible to develop.
4. One of the more telling aspects about the complexity of the issues of race and ethnicity is the difficulty encountered in writing about it in a book like this. Because of "sensitivities" and the need to be "politically correct," writing it was like walking through a mine field.

Chapter 13

Personal Perspective

I often start my class on gender with a quick description of male–female relations among the Tchambuli people in New Guinea. I never know what to expect from students when I tell them about Margaret Mead's report of what she found there some 60 years ago. She discussed the Tchambuli male as having delicately arranged curls, being *permitted* by his wife to do the shopping, manifesting sexual inhibition, and, in general, as simply passive. Men are kindly tolerated and appreciated, particularly when they put on theatricals for the women. One such courting ritual is the *mwai* dance where men dress like masked women while the real women go amuse themselves with pantomimes of penetration during intercourse. The men submissively wait to be chosen. Most Tchambuli women are dominating, aggressive, robust, and practical. They are also sexually active and especially willing to initiate sex relations. This is the kind of place where it might be possible to see a woman chase a male through the forest and force *him* to submit to sexual intercourse.

The reactions of the students to this exotic society vary. Some look bewildered. Others boast of having heard that old story before. Some of the more-informed students say that Mead's research methods were questionable and that she exaggerated the differences between the sexes (Freeman, 1983). And, invariably, some aspiring male comedian asks for directions to New Guinea.

BJG

Gender

THE story may be well known but its importance is still discussed today. It also illustrates the central theme of this chapter: Differences in patterns of thinking, feeling, and acting between genders are often the result of social learning. These expectations are at the root of a number of everyday problems such as job discrimination, sexual harassment, and domestic abuse. They are also more subtly expressed in lingering stereotypes such as the "dumb blonde" and the "strong, silent type." Female students may confront discrimination in class when professors call on the women less frequently than the men. Male students encounter discrimination when they are required to register for the draft whereas female classmates are not so required.

This chapter examines the meaning of gender roles by focusing on between-gender differences, and various forms of gender discrimination. It also reviews theories explaining why things are the way they are in the United States today. It concludes with a discussion of whether or not relations between the genders have *really* changed, and/or if they are likely to improve in the future.

SEX AND GENDER

sex—the biological characteristics that divide the human species into two fundamental groupings: male and female.

gender—the behavioral and attitudinal traits that are culturally imposed on males and females, and referred to in terms of "masculinity" and "femininity."

There is an important distinction between *sex* and *gender*. **Sex** refers to the biological characteristics that divide the human species into two fundamental groupings: male and female. **Gender** refers to the behavioral and attitudinal traits that are culturally imposed on males and females, and referred to in terms of "masculinity" and "femininity." Sex, in essence, is ascribed at birth. Gender roles, on the other hand, are what you learn to become by virtue of your sex. Many people assume gender traits *naturally* result from an individual's sex. But research shows that gender roles are often not the result of the natural order of things but the result of socially imposed forces.

We are all familiar with the celebrated exclamation that "It's a boy!" or "It's a girl!" This has traditionally been the time when sex assignment begins to develop into gender expectations. Now, with amniocentesis and sonograms, some parents know the baby's sex even before the baby is born, and gender expectations are often initiated in the womb.

What do the concepts of masculinity and femininity mean to you? You have been taught throughout life that certain characteristics are appropriate for males and certain characteristics constitute proper female behavior. For example, when college students in the United States and Europe were asked to consider a number of adjectives and indicate which were more frequently associated with men and which with women (Williams et al., 1977), the results looked like a test of a person's ability to match opposites. Men, for instance, were often seen as courageous, rational, and strong

This carving of an Inuit woman and her baby is germane to the historical process of changing gender roles. Before industrialization and the occupational specialization that accompanied it, a woman assumed various responsibilities on an everyday basis. The woman carries a knife in one hand and a fish in the other, symbolizing that work and child-rearing were not mutually exclusive activities.

whereas women were described as timid, emotional, and weak. This suggests that the term *opposite sex* is no simple accident. It looks suspiciously like a social invention.

Note that the masculine adjectives are more positive than the feminine ones. This suggests lingering subtle prejudice. Collectively, prejudicial attitudes like these are known as sexism—the belief that one sex is inferior to the other. Sexism has a damaging impact on women's lives by limiting their occupational, educational, and political ambitions, by objectifying them as sex objects, and by strangling their opportunity to fashion their lives as they see fit. Sexism has many different social sources (Young, 1988), some of which we discuss here.

BETWEEN-GENDER DIFFERENCES

How different are men and women? Are these differences real or perceived? Are they preordained facts of life that determine some grand design, or does some grand source design determine them? These are questions central to the scientific debate on whether gender differences emerge from within individuals or are imposed on them by society. This controversy is commonly referred to as the *nature versus nurture* question.

In order to examine this question, we turn to research conducted in three other disciplines. Biologists report on physical differences between the sexes. Psychologists examine variations in personality traits. Anthropologists provide us with information concerning how gender roles vary cross-culturally. The bottom line of the combined evidence of these disciplines is that it is foolish to look at the differences between men and women as wholly produced by *either* nature *or* nurture. The answer to the nature–nurture controversy is really a number of answers depending on the issue in question. Some of the answers reflect more nature than nurture. Some reflect more nurture than nature. And some answers do not even exist because the issue is presently a mystery.

Biological Differences

sexism—the belief that one gender is inferior to the other.

Logic would dictate that the biological categories "male" and "female" are discrete and unambiguous. But here logic would lose. For example, in 1979, researchers working in a small area of the Dominican Republic reported an unusual group of children who had been raised as girls but who developed male secondary sex characteristics at puberty. Improper sex assignment at birth was not unusual in this small society because a genetic disorder affecting the children was common. At adolescence, they grew beards, their voices deepened, and they developed adult-size penises and scrotums. Eventually, most of these "girls" made successful adjustments to being male, including marriage and fatherhood (Imperato-McGinley et al., 1979).

There are other cases that make it clear that biological maleness and femaleness are fuzzier categories than they appear to be (Butler, 1993). Such is the case with transsexuals, people who have a total aversion to their biological sex although they are physically normal. Their lives are destined to misery until they undergo sex-change surgery. And the complex, mutilating surgical procedures involved make it clear that these people are truly convinced that their minds are locked inside the wrong kind of body.

transsexuals—people who have a total aversion to their biological sex although they are in all ways physically normal.

hermaphrodites—people whose reproductive organs are so ambiguous that it is difficult to categorize them as either male or female.

Loosely related to transsexualism is the equally fuzzy case of **hermaphrodites**. These are people whose reproductive organs are so ambiguous that it is difficult to categorize them as male or female. They often become defined as male or female according to what parents and physicians *think* they are.

Perhaps the most dramatic examples of the ambiguity of the biological foundation of maleness and femaleness come from observations of children who experience serious physical accidents. Money and Ehrhardt (1972) reported the case of a young rural couple who took their identical twin boys to a physician to be circumcised. During the operation, performed with an electric cauterizing needle, a power surge burned off one baby's penis. The parents were desperate and turned to sex experts who advised them to bring the baby up as a girl. The experiment apparently succeeded. The once normal baby boy grew into a girl who loved to wear dresses and to have "her" hair set. Her twin brother, on the other hand, grew into a rough-and-tumble kid who hated to have his face washed. A follow-up study, however, reported that the altered twin was beset with a host of psychological problems during adolescence (Diamond, 1982). Thus, what appeared to be a case resulting from nurturing may have concluded in favor of nature.

Transsexuals, hermaphrodites, and people who experience traumatic accidents, like the one described, are rare. In other people, there typically are clear-cut biological demarcations between the sexes (Sapiro, 1985). To name a few, women menstruate, gestate, and lactate; men impregnate. Other anatomical dissimilarities include weight, height, musculature, body hair, amount of body fat, and distribution of body fat (thighs and buttocks in women, midriff in men).

sex-linked (traits)—those traits that are carried partially or totally on one of the sex chromosomes.

sex-limited (traits)—those traits carried on genes that are not on either of the sex chromosomes but are typically manifest in only one sex.

Anatomical characteristics and physical development in general are the result of a genetic blueprint whereby females are born with two similar chromosomes (XX) and males are born with two dissimilar chromosomes (XY). Some characteristics are **sex-linked**; that is, they are carried partially or totally on one of the sex chromosomes. These traits are associated with the X chromosome and are typically pathological. Hemophilia is a sex-linked trait. So also is a kidney cancer called Wilms tumor, which is caused by a missing chromosome. In almost all cases the missing chromosome is the mother's, not the father's. Some traits are **sex-limited** rather than sex-linked. These characteristics are carried on genes that are not on either of the sex chromosomes but are typically manifest in only one sex. Baldness in men is such a trait.

Occasional errors in cell division lead to chromosomal abnormalities—extra or missing chromosomes. This is the case in men born with an extra Y chromosome (XYY). It has been speculated that this abnormality, sometimes called the *super male syndrome*, is responsible for aggressive, violent behavior linked to the Y chromosome. While it is true that these men are more likely to be in prisons and institutions for the criminally insane, this may simply be the result of lower intelligence stemming from excess genetic material rather than a greater propensity for violence.

There are clear-cut differences between the sexes in hormones, which are chemicals secreted by various body glands. Testosterone is the principal male hormone and estrogen is the principal female hormone, although both sexes have smaller amounts of the hormone of the other sex. The conventional wisdom is that there is a connection between testosterone and aggression, but biological research offers little support for this idea (Nielsen, 1990).

Sometimes genetic disorders lead to hormonal problems. Such is the case with the *andreno-genital syndrome* (AGS), which causes the adrenal glands of the fetus to malfunction. Girls with AGS are born with masculinized genitalia, although the reproductive organs are female. They are treated with surgery to feminize their genitals and are placed on life-long medication.

Experts' opinions on the influence of hormones on behavior vary widely. Some feel that the influence is direct and significant. Others report that it varies widely between people and even within the same person over time. Another group argues that there is no evidence at all that behavior is determined by hormones (Nielsen, 1990).

On the nature side of the nature–nurture debate stands a new body of research investigating differences in brain lateralization between the sexes. The two hemispheres of the brain are known to be responsible for different functions. In right-handed people, the left hemisphere is connected with capacities such as mathematics and analytical thought. The right hemisphere is the site for more nonverbal processing skills and musical ability. Neurological findings indicate that there is a difference in the way the right and left hemispheres of the brain are organized in men and women, and in how the two halves communicate. It has been suggested that these differences may account for the apparent superiority of women in language and the apparent superiority of men in math (Kimura, 1987). Brain lateralization is another controversial component of the nature–nurture issue. Take the case of the well-established superiority of females in sensing and interpreting sounds. Women pick up nuances of voice and music more readily and are six times as likely as men to sing in tune. This might reflect differences in brain hemispheres, or it might be caused entirely by mothers talking and singing more to girls. Then again, it might be influenced by *both* factors.

Psychological Differences

Closely related to the issue of *brain* is the issue of *mind.* Psychologists study a whole host of phenomena including emotions, role-playing, intelligence, sensation, perception, reasoning, criminality, and self-esteem. Although some of these subjects may have biological or sociological features as well, they are conventionally grouped with psychological research. Throughout history it has been assumed that psychological differences between the genders is simply the way things are. For example, men have been seen as the dominant personality and women as subordinate types. Some believe these differences are a conflict of opposites and others believe they complement each other. These differences are often visible in college classrooms when men ask most of the questions and women passively take notes. That may be an overgeneralization since it does not happen in all classes, but it is one of a string of psychological tendencies that agitate relations between the sexes.

Some experts wonder whether psychological differences between the sexes are real or simply exaggerated *reports.* A more common question is: If the differences are real, do they result from nature or nurture? One place to search for this answer is the first few years of life before individuals have learned their gender roles completely. A number of studies report sex-linked differences among infants. Baby boys are more active and baby girls are more responsive to touch and caring, although there are differences between infants of the same gender. Is this nature's plan? Perhaps, but probably not entirely. Research on the early years of life shows that boys and girls are treated very differently. For example, fathers handling their infant sons for the first time tend to do so more vigorously than they do their infant daughters. And mothers have been found to let their boy toddlers wander much farther away from them in playgrounds than they do their girl toddlers.

In general, parents emphasize physical strength in their sons and delicacy in their daughters. This is evident in early childhood when mothers and fathers bounce baby boys on their knees and coo over baby girls. Numerous reports have documented differential parental treatment of boys and girls in the first six months of life. In various experimental settings, fathers have displayed more punitive behavior toward 12-month-old boys than toward 12-month-old girls; they were also less likely to hold their sons and more likely to engage in toy play with their daughters (Snow et al., 1983). In another study, two groups of mothers described babies Adam and Beth in terms of their appropriate masculine and feminine characteristics, and offered toy trains to Adam and dolls to Beth—even though, unknown to the adults, Adam and Beth were actually the same 6-month-old child (Williams et al., 1977).

This last study illustrates that parents unconsciously react to what they perceive in their children as gender-appropriate characteristics, and then further reinforce those perceived characteristics. Through this self-fulfilling prophecy, parents experience what they expect. Some believe that, if there were not such gender differences in child-rearing, we would not have such a large body of literature analyzing males and females and their tendencies to be respectively assertive or receptive, strong or tender, and rational or intuitive. Without biased child-rearing people might be more **androgynous**; that is, they would have more of a balance of traditional feminine and masculine personality traits. But if this were true, then nature would play no role in the development of differences in the psyches of men and women.

androgynous—having a balance of traditional feminine and masculine personality traits.

Another area of psychological investigation is general intelligence. At one time there were reported differences between male and female performance on IQ tests. Now there are no significant differences because new

Queen Victoria and her family may have "had it all" in terms of power and wealth but they were devastated by health problems. Hemophilia, a sex-linked disease associated with the X chromosome, ran extensively throughout the family. All of the daughters were carriers and some of the sons were afflicted.

tests were designed that eliminated gender-biased questions (Lips, 1988). Incidentally, one interesting finding about intelligence and gender roles is that gender-role nonconformity is positively related to IQ for both sexes. In other words, smarter people are less likely to buy the traditional stereotypes.

Psychologists have also studied male–female differences in sensation and perception. Some curious findings have emerged. From age 4 onward, females outscore males on tests of perceptual speed and accuracy (Antill and Cunningham, 1982). Boys over the age of about 9 show faster reaction times than their female counterparts. But if it is a situation where symbolic information must be processed in order to choose a response, females react faster (Fairweather and Hunt, 1972). Some studies show that females are more intolerant of loud sounds than males (McGuinness, 1972). Others report that females show more sensitivity to touch in the fingers (Weinstein and Sersen, 196l). Difference in touch sensitivity is especially interesting because of the various ways in which it could be interpreted. It could mean, as traditionally thought, that women make better typists and seamstresses than men. On the other hand, it could be argued that women would make better neurosurgeons than men.

Patterns of moral reasoning may also separate the sexes. Reflecting the greater tendency for boys to engage in team sports involving complex rules and roles, males tend to reason according to principles. They see what is right as what is consistent with the rules. Girls, on the other hand, tend to view what is morally right in terms of responsibilities to others. This is a presumed reflection of girls being directed toward small-group games (Gilligan, 1982). The prevailing opinion among social scientists is that moral reasoning differences between the genders result from socialization.

Nature and nurture aside, one highly visible difference between the genders is deviant behavior, particularly crime. Females engage in much less criminal behavior than males. This is a *real* difference. It is not just one

Men and military are no longer synonymous terms, including combat situations. Some 40,000 American women went to war in Operation Desert Storm as technicians, drivers, tanker and helicopter pilots, and dozens of other hazardous occupations. Some were killed, some were captured, and some earned Purple Hearts. It was the defining moment for women in combat. This picture was taken in 1993 when female Air Force pilots began training on the hottest jets in the service.

based on official records, which may be affected by the police treating men differently. It is also found in self-report studies in which people anonymously report their offenses (Nielsen, 1990). And it is found around the world.

It could be argued that men's higher rate of criminality is caused by the psychological tendency for men to be more aggressive. This seems to be a compelling argument when we consider that so much criminal behavior is violent (e.g., rape, homicide, and assault). But it is also possible that men's dominance in the world of crime is but another instance of their dominance in society as a whole. Although some would argue that nature causes men to be more aggressive and hence more criminal, nurture plays an obvious role. Witness the change in rates of criminality between the genders in recent years. As gender roles have changed so also has women's participation in crime. See Box 9:2, Chapter 9 (on deviance), for a report of the dramatic increase in the numbers of women convicted and jailed.

Psychological and behavioral differences between the genders are largely seen as environmental in origin by contemporary social scientists. However, there is much disagreement as to which specific processes cultivate these differences. As detailed in Chapter 8 (on socialization), the human personality is the result of a complex set of interrelated experiences. Children are socialized to behave in the "proper or desirable" way. They imitate role models including parents, heroes, and media figures.

You should note that virtually every explanation of a reported psychological difference between the genders is reported with a particular slant. That slant is based on social learning theory, which centers on concepts involving observable *processes* such as imitation, conditioning, and modeling. That is not the way things have always been explained. At one time, it was popular to assert that these processes had an *unconscious* component. Sigmund Freud, the founder of psychoanalysis, and a sociologist in his own right, postulated that gender role acquisition is the end result of specific experiences during various stages of infancy, childhood, and adolescence. Freud believed that male and female infants at first identify with the mother because she is nurturing and the father is remote. The strong attachment the boy has for his mother is combined with feelings of jealousy and contempt toward his father, who has prior sexual rights to the mother. The boy, realizing his love for his mother is inappropriate, fears his father will discover his feelings and castrate him. This conflict, called the *Oedipus complex* (after the tragic Greek hero who killed his father and married his mother), is resolved only when the boy represses his love for his mother. Then he identifies with his father and internalizes the father's attitudes and behaviors, including those involving norms of masculinity.

Freud suggested a parallel process—the *Electra complex*—for the girl. However, development is less complex for her because she begins life with an identification with the same-sex parent. Part of the theory involves the concept of penis envy on the part of the small girl. This leads her to identify with the father to some extent. Once she realizes these feelings are futile, she develops her own female sex role, modeled largely after her mother.

The notion of penis envy is not only difficult to prove but also very unpopular, not only among feminists but also among mental health professionals, including psychoanalysts (Flax, 1993). Equally unpopular is the psychoanalytic perspective that women's tendency to nurture and self-sacrifice is masochistic. The truth is that the internal psychological processes by which sex roles develop are presently not well understood.

Cross-Cultural Differences

The best evidence concerning biological and psychological differences comes from the cross-cultural level, where we can see variations in sex roles within the same human DNA package. Margaret Mead's research in New Guinea involved more than the unusual Tchambuli described in the "Personal Perspective." She also examined personality differences between the genders in two other preliterate tribes. Among the Arapesh, both men and women behave in ways we would consider "feminine"; they are "cooperative, unaggressive, and responsive to the needs and demands of others" (Mead, 1935/1969, p. 55). The personalities of both sexes are maternal in parental aspects. Men stay "in bed after having a baby" after birth. In this cultural setting it would not be unusual to hear comments on how good-looking a man was before he had his children. By contrast, the head-hunting Mundugumor have standardized the behavior of both men and women as actively masculine. According to Mead, Mundugumor women are "ruthless, aggressive, and positively sexed," as are Mundugumor men (Mead, 1935/1969, p. 90).

Although Mead's research methods and many of her conclusions have been seriously questioned (Freeman, 1983), her cross-cultural research does not stand alone. Since her fieldwork, other anthropologists have reported societies in which gender roles are the opposite of the American version or where differences between the genders are minimal (D'Andrade, 1966). All of this strongly supports the idea that the personalities of men and women are heavily influenced by social conditioning fostered by specific social structures and resultant cultural expectations. Some of this research has been criticized for actively looking for gender roles that contrast with traditional stereotypes. Nonetheless, it has been established that exceptions do exist and that gender roles stem from nurture as well as nature.

The overall cross-cultural pattern has been one of strong male dominance, which is reflected in a division of labor by gender. Occupational specialization by gender is a common feature of societies around the world and through history. Indeed, George Murdock (1955) studied over 200 preindustrial societies and found that most societies viewed certain tasks as appropriate for women and others as appropriate for men. He found that politics, hunting, fishing, and tasks requiring physical strength are typically performed by men, whereas child-rearing and tasks performed close to home are generally assumed by women.

There are some interesting differences in the division of labor by gender according to the evolutionary stage of a society. In hunting-and-gathering societies, hunting is overwhelmingly the province of males and gathering is a female task. Because hunting is associated with more recognition and prestige, the status of men is much higher than that of women. Yet women still play a major role in economic production. Martin and Voorhies' (1975) analysis of Murdock's (1967) voluminous data file on 515 horticultural societies uncovered a clear tendency for women to continue an important economic role in this type of setting as well. But, when social development moves to the agrarian stage, profound changes in technology lead to men controlling production and women being assigned to household and domestic activities. With the advent of industrialism, women have been brought back into the sphere of economic production, but they still do the bulk of the domestic labor and are generally confined to low-paying, low-prestige jobs (Sanderson, 1988).

Women occupy positions of power in the business world with increasing frequency. Though women still have not gained equal status with men in the corporate world, things have improved since the days of "Have my girl call your girl."

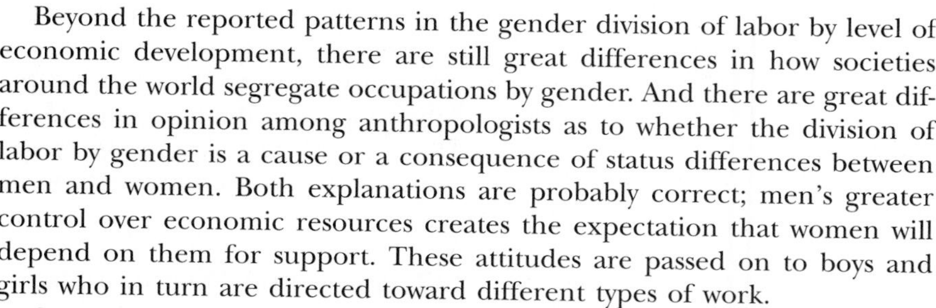

Beyond the reported patterns in the gender division of labor by level of economic development, there are still great differences in how societies around the world segregate occupations by gender. And there are great differences in opinion among anthropologists as to whether the division of labor by gender is a cause or a consequence of status differences between men and women. Both explanations are probably correct; men's greater control over economic resources creates the expectation that women will depend on them for support. These attitudes are passed on to boys and girls who in turn are directed toward different types of work.

Cross-cultural research shows that gender roles are heavily influenced by societal experiences. It also shows that they are influenced by changes in the structure of a society over time. Male dominance is especially prominent in less-developed cultures. In agrarian societies, for instance, women's status reaches its lowest point because of their limited contribution to subsistence tasks such as herding (Martin and Voorhies, 1975). These are the very settings that sometimes dramatically express women's inferior status through footbinding (see Chapter 19) and genital mutilation (see Chapter 7). Feminists around the world have united in horror at these practices and moved to stop such outrageous acts in the offending countries.

Are things much more equitable in modern, industrial societies? They generally *tend* to be as the greater strength of men becomes less important with advances in technology that open old and new types of work to both sexes. But this does not mean that glaring gender inequality does not still exist. In places like Russia, deep-seated, patronizing views of women have been nourished by centuries of sexism and paternalism as evidenced by bride-selling. In the Soviet Central Republic of Turkmeniya some women have burned themselves to death rather than be sold. South Korea is another modern society in which women are relegated to a status so low that they may be convicted of assault for resisting rape (Schoenberger, 1989). Certainly no list of irrational behavior toward women would be complete without Iran. There bands of young men break into private parties and conduct spot checks on cars to be sure that all women are fully covered in black capes called *chadors*. Even in societies where official policy endorses equality—such as China, Sweden, and Israel—it has not been fully realized.

The overall conclusion from cross-cultural research is that gender roles vary widely from society to society (nurture) and cannot be considered a simple result of the biological category of sex (nature). Gender roles also vary throughout history as societies evolve toward more egalitarian structures. But the actual range of gender stratification is asymmetrical; societies range from total male dominance to relative equality between men and women. With rare exceptions, they do not range from total male dominance to equality to total female dominance (Chafetz, 1984). Each society assumes a position along a continuum of gender stratification based on its prevailing assumptions about masculinity and femininity.

The reported biological, psychological, and cross-cultural differences between the genders document the complex origins of gender roles and the difficulty of *objectively* unraveling the nature–nurture controversy. Gender roles are further complicated by *subjective* impressions of what they are and what they should be.

FORMS OF GENDER INEQUALITY

As we will show later in this chapter, there is wide support for the idea of gender equality. But ideas are one thing, behavior is another. Here we examine some of the more deeply embedded forms of discrimination as they appear in the occupational and educational institutions of the United States. With few exceptions, these objective problems are ones that favor men at the cost of fairness to women.

Occupational Discrimination

The rightful place of women in the occupational world has been passionately argued in the boardroom, in the courtroom, and, quite possibly, in your classroom. If the issue has not entered your classroom, perhaps this fact will start a discussion: Over the course of a lifetime, a male college graduate will earn about $1.5 million more than a female college graduate. One reason for this income difference is the fact that many women become homemakers, a role without an income. If you think a second part of the difference is the result of a fundamental form of discrimination, which allows men access to more lucrative jobs, you are partially correct. A third reason is that many women do not even consider certain lines of work, such as engineering, because it has been presented as "men's work" for most of their lives. And a fourth part of the answer is pure, simple prejudice against women as evidenced by the fact that they earn less than men in the same job. This is even true in female-dominated occupations such as nursing. In addition, female college graduates normally make less than males who have finished only high school—$25,544 annually in 1987 compared with $27,293 for men. This earning difference is at the very core of gender roles issues (Abramhamson and Sigelman, 1987; Hess and Feree, 1987). As long as it continues, there is little chance that men and women will ever feel equal in terms of self-esteem and autonomy. Until then, "Equal pay for equal work" will just be a slogan.

In 1990, women who worked full time earned about 68 percent of the annual income of men. This was an improvement from the 60 percent of 1970 when the battle cry of the newborn feminist movement was first

Corporate day care centers have helped enable couples to combine a career and a family. This change has especially benefitted the women who were occupied solely as "housewives" and mothers.

uttered. Experts part company on what these statistics actually reflect. Some say they are evidence of a closing pay gap. Others say that the remaining gap is evidence of discrimination. The 32-percent income disparity was the studied object of heated discussion by every state government (except Delaware, Alaska, Arkansas, Georgia, and Idaho) in 1989 with the goal of achieving equity in public-sector jobs.

There is a positive side to all of this: Women are expected to make great strides in income relative to men by the year 2000 and have already made significant achievements in labor force participation. The fraction of women who work outside the home has increased from 20 percent in 1920 to over 60 percent in 1990. Figure 13:1 portrays a dramatic increase in women's participation in the U.S. workforce over the past century, as well as a merger in the patterns for single and married women. However,

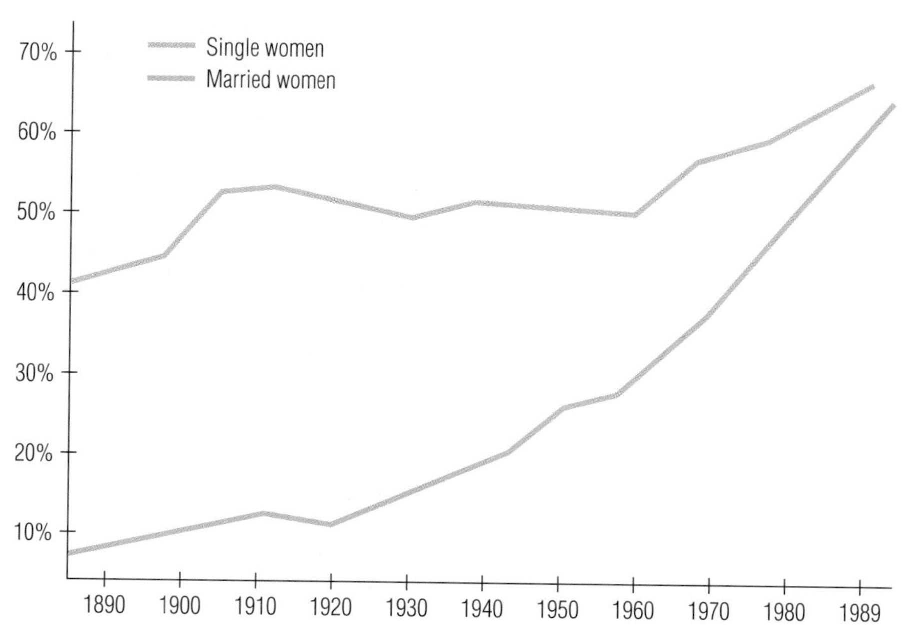

FIGURE 13:1 TRENDS IN WOMEN'S PARTICIPATION IN THE LABOR FORCE, 1890–1989

As the figure shows, in 1989 over 65 percent of single women and 57 percent of married women were U.S. labor force participants.

Source: U.S. Bureau of the Census (1975a): 132, 133; (1987d): 373; (1989): 385.

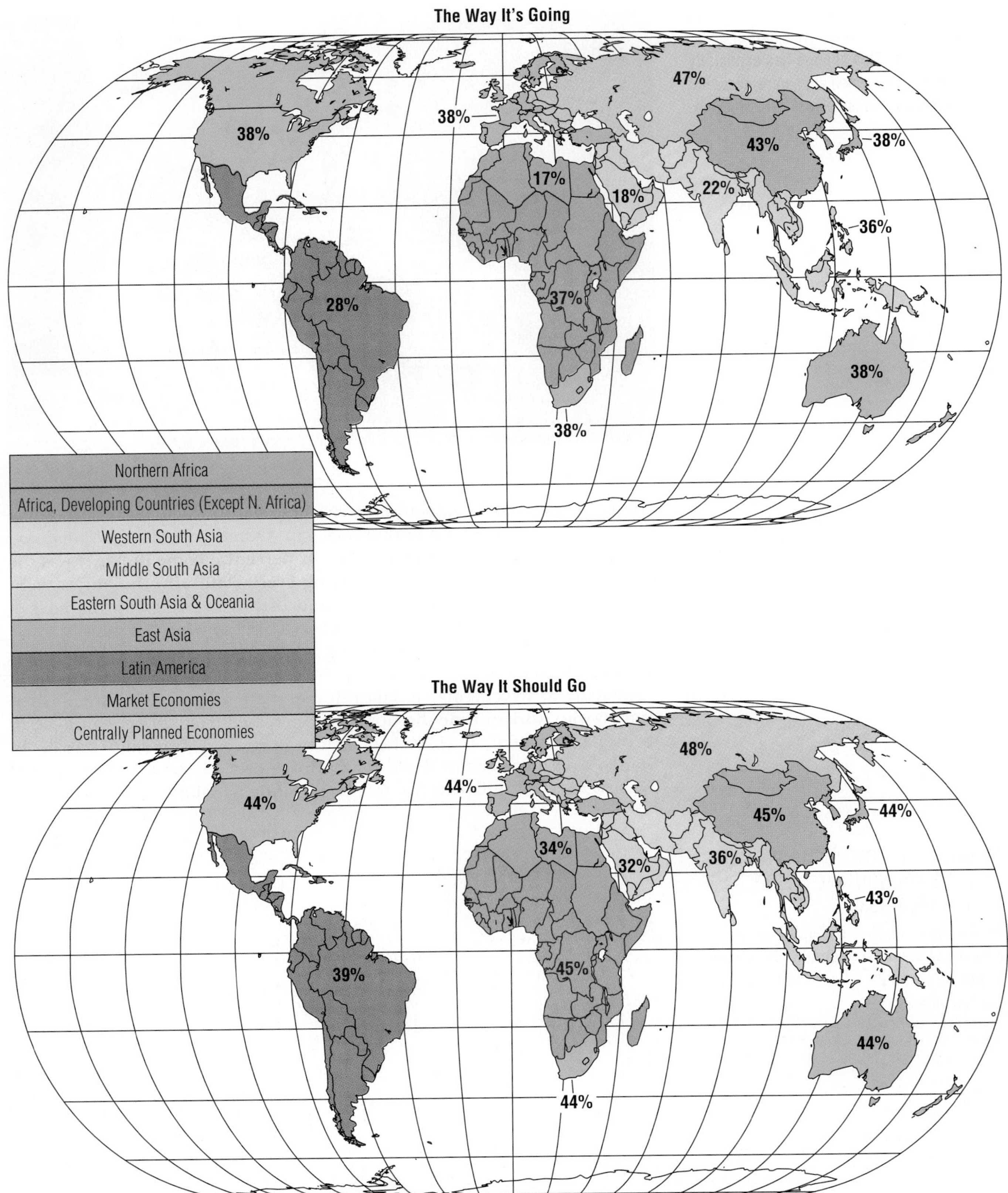
The Way It's Going
38%
38%
47%
43%
38%
17%
18%
22%
36%
28%
37%
38%
38%
Northern Africa
Africa, Developing Countries (Except N. Africa)
Western South Asia
Middle South Asia
Eastern South Asia & Oceania
East Asia
Latin America
Market Economies
Centrally Planned Economies
The Way It Should Go
48%
44%
44%
45%
44%
34%
32%
36%
43%
39%
45%
44%
44%

TABLE 13:1 Women as a Percent of All Workers by Occupation

OCCUPATION	1950	1985	1989
Professional workers	40	49	50.4
Engineers	1	7	7.6
Dentists	N/A	7	8.6
Physicians	7	17	17.9
Lawyers and judges	4	18	22.3
College professors	23	35	38.7
School teachers	75	73	73.3
Registered nurses	96	95	94.2
Managers	14	36	39.8
Sales workers	35	48	49.3
Clerical workers	62	80	80.0
Artisans	3	8	46.4
Operatives	34	40	40.9
Transport operatives	1	8	9.2
Service workers	57	61	62.4

Key: N/A = not available.

Source: Bureau of Census, 1986g. Dept. of Labor, 1980, pp. 10–11. U.S. Bureau of Labor Statistics, Employment-Earnings, January 1990, pp. 183–88.

FIGURE 13:2 FEWER WOMEN WORKING?

The United Nations has set a world goal of ensuring men and women equal opportunity for employment or "economic activity" by the year 2025. If it is to be reached, the total working or economically active population must include certain percentages of female participation by the year 2000 ("The Way It Should Go"). These percentages require significant acceleration in such matters as economic growth and an *increased women's share* of resulting new opportunities (especially industrial opportunities)—as well as in such matters as employment flexibility and child care that help to give women equal economic opportunity. Without such acceleration, present trends result in lower percentages for 2000 ("The Way It's Going")—an overall decline from 36.5 percent in 1985 to 35.5 percent in 2000.

Source: MAPSENSE: Global Comparisons and Trends from World Monitor *Magazine,* 1992, pp. 14–15. By permission of the publisher.

Figure 13:2 indicates that, unless trends change, the female share in the workforce has already peaked in the Western world and will decline globally by the end of the century.

In the United States, growth has been interestingly different in various lines of work. Take a look at Table 13:1, and note the significant improvement in the place of women in specific fields such as law and medicine.

Back to the negative side. Why has the gender–earnings ratio remained unequal? A number of factors contribute. One factor is that women have only recently entered the labor force in large numbers, so many have not had time to work their way into the best-paid jobs. A second factor is that women lose seniority by taking time out to have children. Outright discrimination is another factor. So also is the subjective misimpression that women are less reliable employees because of their higher rates of absenteeism (actually women are absent only one more day a year than men). And so is the historical concentration of women in traditionally low-paid "female" jobs such as clerical work and low-skill service jobs.

Females are highly segregated in "pink-collar" occupations that involve cleaning, nurturing dependents, performing support activities for males—in short, "wifelike" jobs. Even women professionals tend to be concentrated in the so-called "college women's ghetto" of teachers, nurses, social workers, and librarians—all jobs that have lower average salaries than other professional occupations (Blau, 1978). To cite an example close to home, in 1995 only about 1 in 4 college sociology professors is a woman, very nearly the same percentage as in 1972, when the federal government specifically outlawed discrimination in education. This figure highlights the fact that gender barriers in occupations are not dissolved by legislation alone because they are deeply rooted in the social structure. Some occupations may never change. Such is the case with women in the military who want to become Army Ranger Infantry*men* but are not allowed. Many Americans probably believe women don't belong in the Rangers. And perhaps there are not that many women who would want to join in the first place. In other occupations, change has been slow, as with women pilots who fly with the major U.S. airlines. They represent only about 3 percent of the nation's 52,000 working airline pilots and nowhere near the proportion of women entering other occupations once dominated by men.

Workforce Issues

sexual harassment—exists in the workplace if an employee must submit to sexual demands to get a job, keep a job, or be promoted.

Aside from pay inequity and job-typing by gender, other issues have emerged between men and women in the workplace. One of these is **sexual harassment**. This is an ugly problem, and takes many forms from sexual innuendo to outright rape. According to the Equal Employment Opportunity Commission, sexual harassment in the workplace exists if an employee must submit to sexual demands to get a job, keep a job, or be promoted. Although this can happen to either men or women, it usually falls on women because sexual harassment is more a matter of power than a matter of sex.

About 42 percent of all female and 15 percent of all male civil servants report having been sexually harassed. This is particularly alarming in light of the fact that it occurred inside governmental walls where sexual harassment is expressly forbidden. Things are even worse in the military. A 1988–1989 Pentagon survey of 38,000 personnel reported that 64 percent of women in the armed forces said they had experienced some form of sexual harassment! A survey of sexual harassment in the nation's largest companies showed that nearly all the firms had received complaints in 1988, with the most common being verbal abuse and pressure for sexual favors (Klein, 1988). A third of the firms said they had been sued and nearly a quarter had been sued repeatedly. In addition to litigation costs, sexual harassment is estimated to cost Fortune 500 firms an average $7 million a year in absenteeism, low productivity, and employee turnover. In 1987, a record $3.2 million was paid by one company to settle a single case. Some victims have been transformed into staunch crusaders for the protection of women's rights by creating the National Association for the Sexually Harassed (NASH).

Another workforce issue is housework, a job traditionally seen as drudgery and allocated to women. It is drudgery. But as more and more women have entered the workplace, who has assumed the household duties? For the most part, women have continued to do so while spending less time at it, relying more on microwave ovens and cleaning services. The fact that husbands of working women spend 57 minutes a week doing housework compared to 43 minutes of housework by the husbands of "housewives" makes it clear that housework is still "woman's work."

Working wives are another current workforce issue. They try to balance the demands of job and home with little in the way of increased help from their husbands. They are typically paid less than their male counterparts. They are often married to men who become depressed when their wives want more than a homemaker role (Ross, Mirowsky, and Huber, 1983). And, as women succeed in the world of work and earn more money, their husbands see themselves as relatively underpaid (Mirowsky, 1987). These and other factors are responsible for the fact that dual-earner couples spend less time together and may have less satisfactory marriages. Add to that the burden of raising children, a particularly cogent issue in light of the fact that, between the late 1950s and the late 1980s, the proportion of women in the labor force who were mothers of children under age 6 increased from one-fifth to one-half. It is also a burden left to the women to shoulder.

We do not wish to write this chapter as a lengthy litany of the ways in which women are exploited. To some, male exploitation is the only reason

"75% of the people hate their jobs. I hate my wife's."

Men as "househusbands" has been the topic of many a serious conversation. It has also provided fodder for movies and cartoons about men making the transition. In the scene at the right, Michael Keaton engages in battle with a vacuum cleaner in *Mr. Mom.*

for the less-favorable position of women in the world of work. However, there is more to it than that. It is not simply men denying women access to more prestigious and better-paying jobs. It is also a fact that many women do not even consider certain occupations in the first place because they have been directed into "appropriate" lines of work since childhood. This is the result of socialization differences between the genders rather than the result of closed doors at the employment line.

Educational Discrimination

The academic world is filled with varied examples of gender discrimination. Start with the admissions department, where there is heavy reliance on the almighty SAT score. Studies have shown that women score lower than men partly because some questions (12 to 16 percent) are biased in favor of men (Rossner, 1989). They are posed in contexts more familiar to men, such as sports, war, and "boys" camp. The gender gap in college board scores is statistically significant and cuts across all racial and ethnic groups in our society (see Figure 13:3). Biased SAT tests may have cost young

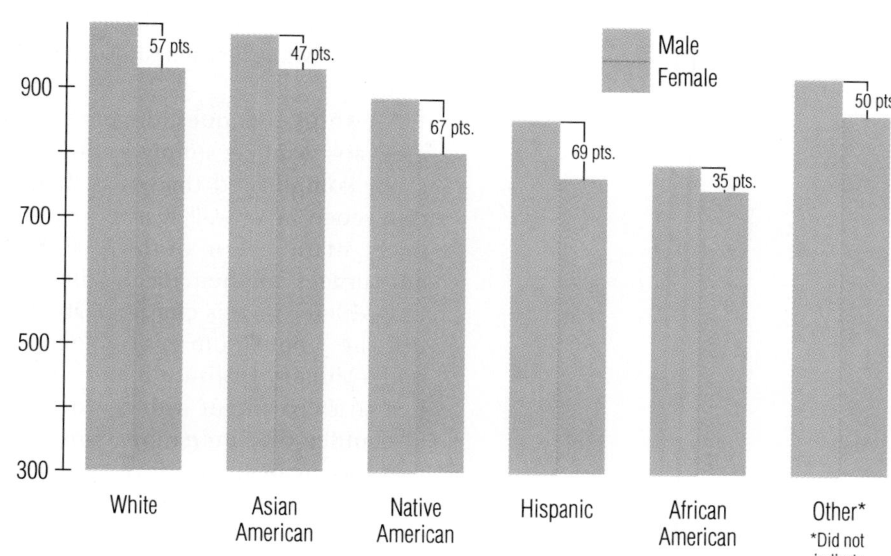

FIGURE 13:3 GENDER GAP IN COLLEGE BOARD SCORES
The average 1987 Scholastic Aptitude Test (SAT) scores of 100,000 high school students by gender and racial/ethnic group depicted.
Source: Center for Women's Policy Studies, Educational Testing Service & Knight-Ridder Graphics Network. By permission of the publisher.

BOX 13:1 COLLEGE EXPERIENCE

Fraternity Gang Rape

This is an excerpt from an anthropological case study and analysis of certain group rituals of male bonding on a college campus. In particular, this study is focused on a phenomenon called "pulling train." According to a report issued by the Association of American Colleges in 1985, "pulling train," or "gang banging" as it is also called, refers to a group of men lining up like train cars to take turns having sex with the same woman. This report labels "pulling train" as gang rape. Bernice Sandler notes more than 75 documented cases of gang rape on college campuses in recent years (*Atlanta Constitution*, June 7, 1988). Sandler labeled these incidents gang rape because of the coercive nature of sexual behavior. The incidents she and Julie K. Ehrhart describe in their 1985 report display a common pattern.

A vulnerable young woman, one who is seeking acceptance or who is high on drugs or alcohol, is taken to a room. She may or may not agree to have sex with one man. She then passes out, or is too weak or scared to protest, and a train of men have sex with her. Sometimes the young woman's drinks are spiked without her knowledge, and when she is approached by several men in a locked room, she reacts with confusion and panic. Whether too weak to protest, frightened, or unconscious, as has been the case in quite a number of instances, anywhere from two to eleven or more men have sex with her. In some party invitations the possibility of such an occurrence is mentioned with playful allusions to "gang bang" or "pulling train."

The reported incidents occurred at all kinds of institutions: "public, private, religiously affiliated, Ivy League, large and small." Most of the incidents occurred at fraternity parties, but some occurred in residence halls or in connection with college athletics. Incidents have also been reported in high schools. For example, in the spring of 1989, news reports described an incident involving the cocaptains of an elite suburban high school football team, who with three schoolmates were charged with sexually assaulting a teenage "mentally handicapped" girl while at least eight other boys watched (*Record* [Hackensack, N.J.], 23 May 1989).

Just a few examples taken from the Ehrhart and Sandler report (1985, 1–2) are sufficient to demonstrate the coercive nature of the sexual behavior.

women millions of dollars in scholarships, particularly the prestigious National Merit Scholarships, as well as slots at the most competitive colleges.

We think it is questionable that the 50-point gap in SAT scores between men and women simply is the result of sexism in the test questions. It is more complicated than that. It involves the fact that a major part of the difference in overall test scores is the result of men scoring much higher in the math section of the SAT. And this stems from early schooling, which encourages mathematical skills more in boys than in girls, an issue discussed later in this chapter. Of course, there are still some schools that do not care about women's SAT scores because they will not admit them. Virginia Military Institute is one such school. In 1990, it was charged by the Justice Department with sex discrimination.

Gender discrimination continues well beyond admission to college. It rears its head in the form of female underrepresentation among faculty, choice of a major, and all-male eating clubs. It can also reach extreme

BOX 13:1 COLLEGE EXPERIENCE *continued*

- The 17-year-old freshman woman went to the fraternity "little sister" rush party with two of her roommates. The roommates left early without her. She was trying to get a ride home when a fraternity brother told her he would take her home after the party ended. While she waited, two other fraternity members took her into a bedroom to "discuss little sister matters." The door was closed and one of the brothers stood blocking the exit. They told her that in order to become a little sister (honorary member) she would have to have sex with a fraternity member. She was frightened, fearing they would physically harm her if she refused. She could see no escape. Each of the brothers had sex with her, as did a third who had been hiding in the room. During the next two hours a succession of men went into the room. There were never less than three men with her, sometimes more. After they let her go, a fraternity brother drove her home. He told her not to feel bad about the incident because another woman had also been "upstairs" earlier that night. (Large southern university)
- It was her first fraternity party. The beer flowed freely and she had much more to drink than she had planned. It was hot and crowded and the party spread out all over the house, so that when three men asked her to go upstairs, she went with them. They took her into a bedroom, locked the door and began to undress her. Groggy with alcohol, her feeble protests were ignored as the three men raped her. When they finished, they put her in the hallway, naked, locking her clothes in the bedroom. (Small eastern liberal arts college)
- A 19-year-old woman student was out on a date with her boyfriend and another couple. They were all drinking beer and after going back to the boyfriend's dorm room, they smoked two marijuana cigarettes. The other couple left and the woman and her boyfriend had sex. The woman fell asleep and the next thing she knew she awoke with a man she didn't know on top of her trying to force her into having sex. A witness said the man was in the hall with two other men when the woman's boyfriend came out of the room and invited them to have sex with his unconscious girlfriend. (Small midwestern college)

Critical Thinking Questions

1. Is fraternity gang rape a sign of our violent times, or is it simply being reported more often now than in the past?
2. How likely would fraternity gang rape be if alcohol and drugs were not present?

Source: Peggy Reaves Sanday, *Fraternity Gang Rape: Sex, Brotherhood and Privilege on Campus* (1990). New York: New York University Press, pp. 1–3. By permission of the publisher.

forms as in the case of fraternity gang rape. Box 13:1 includes some excerpts from Peggy Sanday's book about fraternity rape on campuses today. It is a depressing example of how "regular" guys can sometimes behave beyond the limits of civilization.

In 1980, women earned only 28 percent of all PhDs awarded. While this figure was low, it did reflect a gain over the previous decade. Additionally, from 1988 to 1990, women students made up more than 50 percent of PhDs granted in sociology. To understand the overall situation, however, it is necessary to examine the distribution of those degrees; and the fact is that women are heavily concentrated in a few traditionally female areas such as education, psychology, sociology, and literature, while their numbers remain low in the more technical and higher-paying fields such as engineering and computer science. Female PhDs who teach college find fewer opportunities than their male colleagues as evidenced by the fact that they are more likely to have lower ranks (instructors and assistant professors) than men, who are more likely to be associate professors and full

This graduation picture is worth a thousand words. Although the numbers of women in academia have increased significantly since 1950, college faculties are still male-dominated.

professors. Specifically, 53.6 percent of the men are full professors while only 19.9 percent of the women are full professors. Female professors are also paid less than their male counterparts. In 1990, the average salary for male full professors was $54,340—13 percent more than the average salary of $48,080 for female full professors (*Academe*, 1990). Actually, it may not be accurate to say that female professors have lower rank and salaries than male professors because women have fewer opportunities than men in the academic world. Much of the difference may result from the fact that men have been in their positions longer and are enjoying the benefits that come from seniority. This is but another example of the unknown origins of so many differences between the genders.

The roots of these educational circumstances are complex. Some sprout from seeds planted many years before professional studies commence. To highlight one perspective, consider that most college majors leading to prestigious occupations—in fields such as engineering, medicine, or the sciences—require students to take advanced-level mathematics (Weitzman, 1984). Yet one study showed that only 8 percent of female students entering the University of California at Berkeley had taken enough math in high school to enable them to begin advanced math courses in college (as compared to 57 percent of the men) (Sells, 1978).

The issue of mathematics reflects another unresolved aspect of the whole nature–nurture controversy. Presently the verdict is not yet in on whether males and females differ in "natural ability" in math because the findings of numerous studies on this question are contradictory. What is clear, however, is that a boy and a girl of the same age, studying the same subject, in the same class, in the same school will not share the same educational experience. Although equal percentages of each gender express a liking for math, for example, fewer girls than boys are still doing well in it (or even taking it) by the time they reach high school. Possible explanations are varied. One is that math is labeled a male subject, which may cause female students to fear they will be less popular if they excel in it. It has also been demonstrated that girls are steered away from math by teachers, parents, and guidance counselors who perceive math as a male domain. There is one bright note—the much-trumpeted gap between males' and females' scores on tests of mathematical ability has narrowed significantly since 1975. This change mirrors the gradual decline of sexual discrimination in general.

Other forces in American schooling affect the relative performance of girls and boys. In the lower grades, for example, girls receive negative criticism on the content of their work, while boys are more likely to be chided for sloppiness or lack of effort. The result is that girls believe they lack ability, while boys think they only need to try harder.

The cumulative result of all these gender-relevant influences is that many female adults find it difficult to take themselves seriously as students, since many people around them did not take them seriously in that role earlier in life. Even women with high aspirations feel that earning anything less than A's in college confirms their professors' lower expectations of them, and so they may opt for "safe" majors. They learn from college faculties that are only 25.5 percent female, an imbalance that deprives women students of the role models and mentors so readily available to the male students. All of the "tidbits" of facts offered about gender discrimination in American education add up to one clear picture—the academic world from kindergarten through college is a vital force in reinforcing gender role differences in attitudes and life-long achievement. It has also helped to establish a few of its own.

SUBJECTIVE ASPECTS OF GENDER

Opinion polls indicate some progress in eliminating gender problems. In 1989, for example, a Harris poll reported that educated women over age 40 feel men have become less prejudiced toward women in the past 25 years. They are perceived as less macho-chauvinistic, show greater involvement with their families, accept women as partners and equals, display more interpersonal sensitivity, and are better at communicating their feelings. Nevertheless, in that same year, a Gallup poll reported a shift of opinion concerning which gender had it better. Traditionally, both men and women felt they had the better role. But now, both men and women believe that men have it better. Over the past few decades, gender inequality has become a much more visible problem in the United States. Thus the shift in opinion probably reflects the results of consciousness-raising by feminist groups and concerned others. Indeed, Roper Organization polls of women in 1970 and 1990 document an increase in sensitivity to and awareness of continuing discrimination. Now Shere Hite has solicited intimate confessions from 100,000 American women, making headlines of an alleged dissatisfaction with men as lovers as well.

The rising public profile of gender inequality illustrates how the objective and subjective dimensions of a social issue operate independently of one another. Broadly speaking, the relative position of women has not declined in the past 30 years in terms of education or employment indices or, for that matter, general legal rights. In fact, it has improved in some areas, particularly economically. But the subjective surge in public concern was fueled by sociological factors other than a worsening of women's apparent objective fate. Why was it that social awareness and concern increased while some of the objective issues (occupational, educational, and political discrimination) surrounding sexism may have diminished?

The fact that this problem suddenly appeared in the public's mind when it had been in the public's experience all along can be understood by examining the three determinants of the subjective dimensions of social problems (visibility, expectations, and values) discussed in Chapter 2. Consider how *visibility* bears on the case. Generally speaking, sexism is not intrinsically dramatic. The indignities and denials of self-worth—everyday events keeping women "in their place"—are not very spectacular. But consciousness-raising by feminist groups such as the National Organization for Women (NOW), feminist best-sellers, protest demonstrations, even bra-burnings—all fanned the subjective spark concerning women's place in society.

The subjective dimension has also risen because the *expectations* of women have changed, particularly in regard to equality at the workplace. The 1963 Equal Pay Act, the Civil Rights Act of 1964, and NOW's first convention all fostered an increase in what women expected in the way of workplace equality. Ironically, all of these events occurred after the wide employment gap between the genders began to narrow. But popular magazines regularly documented other aspects of occupational inequality, such as gender typing by job, and the substantially unchanged gender gap in average pay. These seemed all the more intolerable in light of visible progress in other areas and, as a result, women felt even more outrage when full equality did not arrive. This is the familiar cycle of objective improvements raising expectations, and failed expectations raising the subjective dimensions of a social issue.

A third cause of the increased subjective concern over gender inequality is the shift in the *value* placed on equality by both genders. This change began to build in the 1960s as men and women became markedly less tolerant of discriminatory treatment of African Americans, Jews, homosexuals, the impoverished—and women (Gans, 1973). In fact, the rising tide of egalitarianism may already have reached a high-water mark with regard to gender inequality. Analysts of changing gender attitudes over the 1962–1978 period have documented a "tremendous shift" toward more egalitarian perceptions of women (Thornton et al., 1983). The shift in attitudes occurred in the 1960s and 1970s and, as Table 13:2 demonstrates, it remained that way in the 1980s.

The immediate point is that, if the right of women to equal treatment is valued more highly, then continued denial of such treatment is less tol-

TABLE 13:2 Attitudes of Men and Women toward Some Aspects of Gender Roles

QUESTION	RESPONSE	MALE		FEMALE	
		Percent	Frequency	Percent	Frequency
Should women take care of running their homes and leave running the country up to men?	Yes	23.8	144	24.9	189
	No	76.2	461	75.1	570
If your party nominated a woman for president, would you vote for her if she were qualified for the job?	Yes	84.9	512	80.8	606
	No	15.1	91	19.2	144

Main Point: A similar percentage of men and women express egalitarian views toward women.

Source: General Social Survey, 1985.

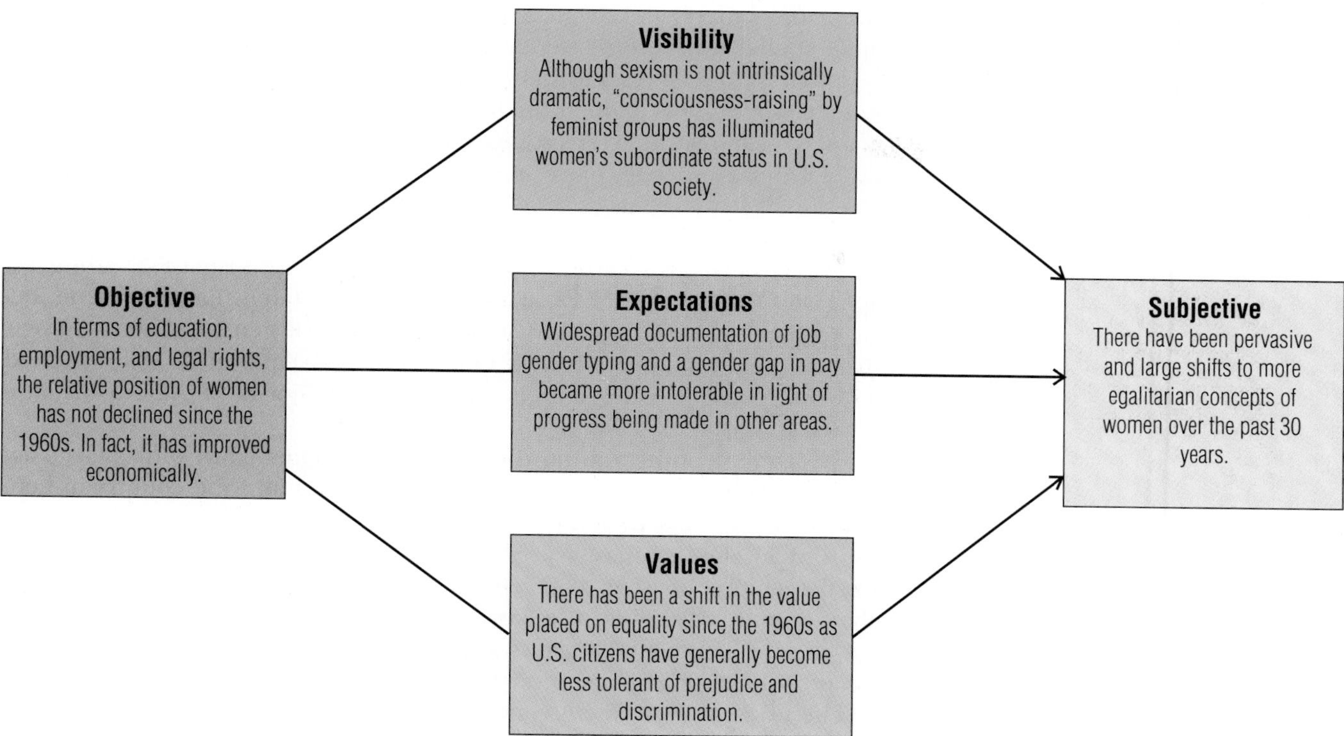

FIGURE 13:4 SUBJECTIVE AND OBJECTIVE DIMENSIONS: THE CASE OF GENDER INEQUALITY

Although the relative position of women has not worsened over recent decades, there is less tolerance of gender inequality.

erable. In fact, the trend toward egalitarian sex-role attitudes is paralleled by the aforementioned growing sense that men simply have it better than women. Figure 13:4 contains the key variables, which partially explain the subjective shifts to more egalitarian concepts of women.

According to a Gallup poll, 49 percent of the American public believe that men have a better life than women, up from 32 percent in 1975 (Gallup, 1990). It is important to note that this change in values is shared by *both* genders. Take a look at Table 13:2, which contains information on how men and women view some of the issues surrounding gender roles. These data from the General Social Survey demonstrate that feminist/egalitarian values are not monopolized by women. They also demonstrate the surprising fact that men are at least as aware of these issues. Thus the problem of gender inequality is not simply a problem of prejudice.

THE WOMEN'S MOVEMENT

There is no concise way to measure how much gender roles have changed through this century, how much of that change was generated by the women's movement, and what the relative position of the genders are today in places like the world of work. It *is* clear, however, that women were worse off in the early 1900s than they are in the 1990s. The first conference of the "Women's Rights Movement" was held in 1844. It centered on the struggle for the right to vote. By 1920, with the passage of the Nineteenth Amendment, that battle was won. But the energy of the women's movement declined and, for some 40 years, collective actions to reduce gender inequality remained dormant. In fact, during the 1950s, they appeared to be altogether dead. The economy was booming and homemakers went about their merry tasks with new cleaning and cooking gadgets. Contentment smiled from every face, and the idea of change seemed unnatural.

Then the 1960s reared their turbulent head. Betty Friedan's *The Feminine Mystique* (1963) fanned the fire of the women's movement as we know it today. Feminist interest groups such as NOW promoted consciousness-raising about women's place in society. It was a time of accomplishment. The Equal Pay Act was passed in 1963. It provided that men and women would receive the same pay for the same job if they were equally qualified.

There were also setbacks for women's groups. In 1972, Congress approved the Equal Rights Amendment, which stated that it shall be illegal to deny a person equality of rights because of gender. After a 10-year struggle, that amendment died. Only 33 of the required 38 states ratified it. Ironically, this happened even though a majority of Americans supported it.

On a more positive note, the women's movement has witnessed a significant amount of progress for both its members and the country in general. It has witnessed Geraldine Ferraro's candidacy for Vice President of the United States. It has clearly affected the microsocial world of interpersonal relations between the genders. Today fewer assumptions are made about people merely on the basis of gender. There is a healthier attitudinal climate within which grows a greater respect for women. In addition, some of the problems mentioned in this chapter are becoming resolved.

The women's movement is not a simple *result* of social change. In many ways it has been the *cause* of extraordinary changes: the explosion of roles for women, their greater political presence, and all of the new options that have replaced the limited life of a homemaker. In a historical context, the women's movement has been a rebellion against a world like that of the 1950s. Clearly there are many battles still to be fought in the years ahead, battles that have emerged as global issues. In 1993, gender violence was such an issue. This issue first received worldwide attention at the United Nations Conference on Human Rights where the floor in front of the podium was covered by stacks of petitions bearing half a million names from 124 countries. It was a global call for halting barbaric treatment of women. In Vienna, women's rights groups from every culture and country came with a unifying theme: Stop the violence! Unlike many diplomats divided along cultural and economic lines, they formed the most organized and cohesive force at the conference. They succeeded in getting their message onto the UN's and the world's agenda.

THEORETICAL PERSPECTIVES ON GENDER INEQUALITY

Functionalist Theory

According to functionalist theory, all societies have gender role differences because they serve a useful purpose. Functionalists note that this was especially true in pre-industrial societies where provision of daily needs was conveniently divided by gender. Desmond Morris (1968) argues that gender roles originated even earlier in the history of human evolution when apes began to hunt. Regardless of the issue of time, functionalists believe that the substance of gender inequality centers around the fact that men are more physically powerful. This in turn leads to a division of labor based on ability. Therefore, the fact that men and women have different occupations is a result of the natural order of things. And it is an order that serves a useful purpose for society as a whole.

Although it is true that women played an economic role in less-developed societies, the biological facts of reproduction account for the fact that these same women often became housebound while men enjoyed wider freedoms. Before the era of effective birth control, women typically experienced frequent pregnancies, which limited their activities. As a consequence of being confined to the home, women naturally assumed responsibility for household duties. Thus it was useful for societal survival for women to center their lives on children and home. In the process, these tasks came to be seen as appropriately, traditionally feminine. Some people today may assume that gender roles are "natural" without understanding their derivation.

Functionalist theory seems logical when applied to pre-industrial societies, but does it make sense in the modern world with its many and complex roles? Feminists would argue that that question is itself a moral outrage. Some functionalists, most notably Talcott Parsons (1951), Robert Bales (1954), and, more recently, Jeffrey Alexander (1980/1983), believe that a division of labor by gender and gender inequality in general still serve positive functions. These sociologists argue that modern families (and, as a result, society) run smoothly when headed by adults who occupy specialized roles. They contend that gender roles are *complementary* not antagonistic. Men's roles are seen as *instrumental*, a reflection of their responsibilities in the labor force. Men emphasize tasks that maintain the external relationship between the family and other social institutions. Thus men are socialized to be rational and aggressive. Women's roles are viewed as *expressive*, a reflection of their responsibilities to manage the internal affairs of the family. This is why they are socialized to provide love, support, and sensitivity to others. These differences are not based on unfairness but on complementarity since women's expressive orientation permits men to be instrumental and vice versa. Parsons and Bales hold that these differences are functional for the family. And, because the family is the most basic social unit, these differences are functional for society as a whole. Margaret Mead (1935/1969) also spoke along these same lines. She made the interesting point that gender differences are functional in that they make the opposite gender more interesting and mysterious. This in turn helps to propagate the species and make life more satisfying.

Functionalism is an increasingly unpopular explanation of gender inequality in the contemporary United States because it smacks of chauvinism and appears to be written specifically to explain an earlier era. The average American woman today has fewer children (two) than her counterpart from the 1700s who had eight. She also lives much longer. The notion of a housebound woman has therefore become irrelevant. The ideas that women cannot function instrumentally and men naturally avoid expressive actions fly in the face of between-gender relations today. Women have clearly made great contributions in the world of occupations. And many men have successfully opted to manage the home. It is noteworthy that functionalists ignore the fact that women are unfairly dominated by men. Their wholesale assignment of men into instrumental roles and women into expressive roles is another instance of their defense of tradition and the status quo. However, from a historical point of view, they do provide a useful explanation of how things got to be the way they are.

Conflict Theory

Conflict theorists see gender inequality as a form of social stratification (see Chapter 11). It is one that occurs at all levels of society and has the deeply embedded features of a caste system. Like racism, it persists over time, benefits the interests of the socially powerful (men), and is maintained through legal means and even physical violence.

According to conflict theory, the reality of the relations between the genders is one of exploitation rather than one of complementary relationships. Nowhere is this more obvious than in the case of the homemaker who is officially classified as "out of the labor force."

Conflict theorists contend that the origin of between-gender inequality was based on such factors as the dominant size and physical strength of men. As noted earlier, these were important in pre-industrial societies but have less relevance to the contemporary world. So, why do they persist? Because men, like any group in a position of dominance, are not likely to relinquish power freely. Thus, the world goes on, and many (especially men) assume it spins around the "natural" order of things.

Karl Marx's analysis of capitalist society centered on the exploitation of the socially powerless by the socially powerful. Marx's writings focused largely on the conflict between the wealthy capitalists (bourgeoisie) and the indigent laborers (proletariat). This conflict also speaks to the struggle between men and women because it is men who possess economic power and women who are deprived of it.

Actually, the specific application of conflict theory to the economic exploitation of women originated with Marx's colleague, Friedrich Engels (1884/1972). The general theme of Engels' writings on the issue of gender stratification is that the problem is incubated by capitalism, an economic structure based on individual opportunity and exploitation of the masses. With capitalism came the development of private property. Men became the owners of property and rose to political dominance. Thus Engels claimed that capitalism extended male dominance through the subordination of women. Capitalism's division of the labor force allows certain groups (minorities, women) to be super-exploited and used as a marginal workforce. This occurs in a number of ways. First, women are socialized to view themselves and their work as a source of convenient and cheap labor. Second, women are often part-time workers and rarely achieve seniority or become eligible for fringe benefits. Third, women are the last to be hired and the first to be fired. Fourth, women have a high rate of unemployment not only because of fewer employment opportunities but also because custom and sentiment favor laying off women rather than men. Finally, add the millions of women encouraged to be homemakers and you add a large chunk of the population who receive no wages at all (Duberman, 1975).

The conflict connection between the plight of women and capitalism is directly consistent with the "feminization of poverty," the fact that an increasing percentage of the impoverished are women, especially minority women (Goldberg and Kremen, 1990). Poverty among women is a complicated situation, which is due to many factors, including high rates of family breakup and unwed childbearing. It is neither limited generally to capitalist societies nor to gender inequality. Gender inequality did not begin in capitalist societies. It has existed for a long time, certainly well before capitalism's introduction in seventeenth-century England. It is also found in socialist societies. Non-Marxian conflict theorists do not believe that capitalism has a monopoly on gender inequality. They believe that women's economic power is a key variable in unraveling the causes of gender discrimination (Blumberg, 1984; Collins, 1988). More specifically, they believe that the relative access of men and women to economic resources runs deeper than the roots of capitalism, extends throughout history, and is found in all parts of the world today.

Symbolic Interactionism

The dependent status of women in the United States appears in many forms—from subtle everyday interactions between genders to formal opinion polls designed to assess change. We see it when women wait for men to open doors, and when women give up their last name in marriage. Social psychologists have documented the fact that men require more personal space than women and that men are far more likely to dominate conversations by talking and interrupting more. In coed colleges, for instance, women speak two and a half times less often than their male college counterparts (Henley, 1977; Kollock, Blumstein, and Schwartz, 1985).

Women's subservient status is a common theme in the media. Turn on the television and you see them presented as being secondary to men. Listen to some rock 'n' roll carefully and you will find many stories filled with men who prowl, dominate, and think of women in terms of appearance

When the *Titanic* sank on April 14, 1912, more than 80 percent of those who drowned were men. Many had relinquished lifeboat seats to women. Today, the dictates of Edwardian civility no longer hold. Recent surveys show that only 35 percent of the men on a "Titanic II" today say they would cede their lifeboats to women.

Housework is the "second shift" for many women who work. African-American artist Jacob Lawrence's *Ironers* (1943) portrays the drudgery of work in Harlem and suggests that the tasks women perform on the job parallel their "responsibilities" at home.

and sexual performance. These are but a few tiny examples of how widespread gender role prejudice is today. Betty Friedan's runaway best-seller *The Feminine Mystique* (1963) called this (then) invisible situation the "problem with no name."

Symbolic interactionism explains the dependent status of women as the result of a socialization process that encourages males and females to develop specific personality traits. These traits have little to do with how society is organized, as functionalists believe. They stem from the microsocial level of everyday behavior and reflect the dominant position of men, as conflict theorists emphasize.

Is there evidence that gender roles are a product of the socialization process? Frankly, it abounds. We see it in studies reporting that women develop negative self-images as they move through school. It is there in the example given when men dominate conversations and regularly interrupt women when they try to speak. Nonverbal forms of communication are also affected by socialization. For example, women keep less distance from others when talking and often stand side by side, whereas men stand farther apart and speak face to face. Women also use more facial expressions, especially smiles. Nowhere is this more apparent than in the case of the perpetually frozen smiles of flight attendants. And socialization is certainly a factor in any serious attempt to explain passivity among women and aggression among men.

Socialization not only fashions the gender-typed behavior of children in a submissive way. It is more than simply programming individuals for behavior appropriate for their gender. According to the *cognitive development* theory of Lawrence Kohlberg (1966, 1969), children engage in *self-socialization*—actively constructing their own gender roles. After a child makes a cognitive judgment that he or she is a boy or girl (between 18 months and age 3), the child seeks values and activities that conform to that self-image. These then become the source of rewards. For a fuller description of differences in gender role socialization, see Chapter 8.

In Chapter 8, we discussed Kohlberg's theory of *moral* development. Some charge that it is sexist because it states that the moral development of women is stunted; they tend to progress only partway up the hierarchy of development. Women get to the point where they make judgments based on caring about others but not on the "higher" level that involves abstract reasoning. The theory may be sexist or it may accurately reflect a sexist socialization process accurately that incubates emotion in women and rationality in men.

Social Networks Perspective

One of the major themes of this chapter is that males and females truly *are* different. They are different on the "inside" in their emotional life, and on the "outside" in that they are treated differently by major societal sectors such as work, school, and family. Spanning the inside and outside of gender roles are microstructures, the networks of personal relationships. As is the case with so much of the sociological data emerging from this intriguingly complex area, network differences appear to be intertwined as both the causes and consequences of male–female differences.

Begin by reviewing what has been said here as it relates to personal relations. The evidential weight in this chapter leads to a straightforward hypothesis: Women should be better at relationships than men. If the "fairer sex" (pun intended) are by nature or by nurture more expressive, more emotionally open, and less aggressive, they should then clearly surpass males in the quantity and quality of their network interactions. As is often the case with sociological research, data both support and twist this hypothesis in unexpected ways.

Perhaps the definitive source on the personal networks of Americans is the 1985 General Social Survey, which asked respondents to identify the people with whom they had discussed "important matters" over the previous six months. In a special analysis of this data set focusing on gender differences, Gwen Moore (1990) drew two basic conclusions about the relationship patterns of men and women. The first and most surprising is that overall network size does not differ significantly by sex. Both men and women have an average of about three network confidants, but this does not mean that who is chosen for the inner circle follows the same pattern. Moore's second conclusion, in fact, is that they do not: Women's networks contain more kin, whereas men's networks contain more friends and coworkers. These network differences persist even within similar social categories; an unmarried working woman with children, for example, is more likely to rely on kin to "discuss important matters" than is a man in the same set of social circumstances.

Why? On the one hand, the kin-centered networks of women can be viewed as a *consequence* of traditional socialization that creates women "family managers" who are in charge of caring for relatives, buying birthday cards, and making dinner party arrangements. On the other hand, gender differences in network composition can be viewed as a cause of further inequality. The research reviewed in Chapter 4 clearly shows that "weak ties" to friends, advisors, and acquaintances are precious sources of information about job opportunities. The predominance of these non-kin relationships in male networks gives a further leg up on a "ladder of success" already top-heavy with males.

This dual cause–consequence aspect of gender networks is also suggested by research on psychological stress. Here there is a difference; as measured by checklists of everyday anxiety and depression symptoms, females register higher levels of stress than do males across a multitude of studies (Pearlin, 1989; Thoits, 1986). In an attempt to cope with these difficult feelings, women may selectively seek out close family members to provide "social support" in sharing their worries; less-stressed males may be more inclined to share personal interests in friendship groups. Daily experience and empirical research both show that women also give the bulk of social support in family matters ranging from the daily care of an aging parent to the hands-on consolation of a sick child.

There is no question that such burdens produce personal stress. The key *sociological* point, however, is twofold: (1) Male and female networks are indeed different and (2) these patterns both reflect and produce the myriad of other differences we sum up in the term "gender roles."

Integrating the Theories

The origin of gender inequality is highly complex. It is rooted in history, conditioned over time, woven into the very fabric of our major institutions, and regularly permeated through the everyday experiences of interpersonal life. As such, no one theory accounts for all facets of gender inequality,

BOX 13:2 GENDER AND SOCIAL CHANGE

The White Male: Victim or Top Dog

The following was inspired by an article in *Newsweek* by David Gates. It was widely read and discussed.

"'The white male is the most persecuted person in the United States,' says Tom Cole," a white man interviewed in 1993 for a magazine story. And "this is a weird moment to be a white man. White American males are surrounded by feminists, multiculturalists, P.C. [politically correct] policepersons, affirmative-action employees, rap artists, Native Americans, Japanese tycoons, Islamic fundamentalists and Third World dictators, all of them saying the same thing: 'You've been a bad boy.' . . . In the words of sociologist and men's activist Michael Kimmel, 'White men feel like they're getting it from all sides.'

"In the world of images and ideas," the white male "is taking a clobbering. On TV, the white male is a boob or a villain, not just on such shows as 'Roseanne,' but in ads, too. In 1987, one researcher found that in the commercials' mini-conflicts between men and women, the woman won out 100 percent of the time. In the movies, he's a target for Thelma and Louise, or a loutish and entirely unwanted suitor for Belle in Disney's 'Beauty and the Beast.'" In real life, too, the white-male-dominated social system is definitely eroding. Consider the following symptoms:

- The proportion of the work force made up by white men is declining rapidly.
- White men with high school degrees saw their incomes chopped by some 25 percent during the 1980s.
- Affirmative action has broken the white male's stranglehold on society's choice occupations.
- Elements of his traditional workplace behavior are being redefined as sexual harassment.
- Certain modes of his traditional dating behavior may now be called rape.

White men are increasingly angry and anxious about this ongoing loss of control, and are although each of the four theories does provide partial insight. Critical thinking allows for a useful blend of the best parts of each theory as well as their weaknesses.

The one limitation shared by all four of the theories is that they fail to include both macrosocial (at the level of organizations and whole societies) *and* microsocial origins (personal interaction patterns). Functionalism and conflict theory spin around ideas such as societal structure and mass oppression. These address the macrosocial but ignore the microsocial. Symbolic interactionism and the social network perspective, on the other hand, provide a richly detailed explanation of how gender inequality is microsocially generated through interpersonal forces but no mention is made of macrosocial factors at work.

There have been recent attempts to explain gender inequality in a broader manner theoretically. The most noteworthy of these theories are those put forth by Joan Huber (1990) and Randall Collins (1988). Bound by a common frustration with existing theories, which seem more descriptive than truly theoretical, both Huber and Collins demonstrate how macrolevel trends relate to people's experiences at the microlevel. Huber uses a historical approach to examine how macrolevel trends during

BOX 13:2 GENDER AND SOCIAL CHANGE *continued*

reacting in many ways. They "voted 60 to 37 percent against Clinton, partly out of fear that his multicultural ecofeminist 'storm troopers' would take away their guns, steaks, cigarettes, V-8 engines—and jobs." Membership in white male interest groups such as the Natural Coalition of Free Men is on the rise, as is the following of pro-white male media personalities such as Rush Limbaugh. Psychiatrists see more white male anxiety cases, and gun sales to white men are increasing, and typically soar immediately after race riots.

"But is the white male truly an endangered species? Hardly. It's still a statistical piece of cake being a white man, at least in comparison with being anything else. White males make up just 39.2 percent of the population, yet they account for 82.5 percent of the Forbes 400 (folks worth at least $265 million), 77 percent of Congress, 92 percent of state governors, 70 percent of tenured college faculty, almost 90 percent of daily newspaper editors, 77 percent of TV news directors. They dominate about everything but NOW and the NAACP; even in the NBA, most of the head coaches and general managers are white guys." Thus, the erosion of the white male's dominant position in American society is not nearly as advanced as many white men think.

But social change is proceeding, and will cause white men increasingly to relinquish their top-dog status. Change in the racial and ethnic composition of the population is just one of the forces propelling this change. As "population researcher William O'Hare writes, 'The United States is undergoing a transition from a predominantly white population rooted in Western culture to a society composed of diverse racial and ethnic minorities.' In the next century, 'minorities' may no longer be in the minority—and half the population, needless to say, will still be women. More women than men are now enrolled in colleges, and by the year 2000, two out of every three new workers will be women or minorities. That's about right, considering white males' share of the population, but it's not the way it was."

Critical Thinking Questions

1. Which of the three perspectives—functionalism, conflict theory, or symbolic interactionism—would be best suited for understanding the situation described above?
2. What do you think the best single indicator of the decline in white male power in the United States would be?

Source: All quoted material from David Gates, "White Male Paranoia" (1993). In *Newsweek*, pp. 48–53.

industrialization have an effect on microtrends. She contends that the macrosocial process of industrialization has had an enormous impact on the personal parts of people's everyday lives, including the abortion issue, child care, rising divorce rates, social security, and even the many and complex tax forms due every April 15. Then all of these personal problems are multiplied over a large population and become social problems.

Collins' theory is a version of stratification theory in general (see Chapter 11). The general principles of stratification apply to the specific issue of inequality by gender. His "political theory of sexual stratification" states that female dominance in everyday life is a result of whether or not a society stresses warfare. Where a need arises for a well-developed military organization, the related emphasis on male physical strength and aggression produces more male domination. Where warfare is not stressed, relations between men and women are more equal. Think of how this might apply globally. Scandinavia, a relatively peaceful area, is known for its endorsement of gender equality. And Iran, a most hostile country, subordinates women to the extreme.

Theories like Huber's and Collins' are a step in the right direction. They are still, however, in the working stage. Someday new theories may unlock the mystery of gender inequality as they continue to press the macro→micro (and micro→macro) buttons (Sanderson, 1988).

SUMMARY

1. Gender and sex are interrelated concepts. Sex is a biological category that includes the anatomical characteristics of men and women. Gender is the self-identification and expectations attached to being a man or a woman. Sex is linked to nature, and gender is mainly linked to nurture.
2. Earlier we noted that the women's movement has made significant progress and also experienced a number of disappointments. For every report of women attaining a more equitable place in a certain sector of society, a new voting result, opinion poll, or scientific study is issued that reports some kind of negative. Much of this difference is the result of the independent movement of the objective and subjective dimensions of the issue. And some of it is the result of the fact that social progress does not occur in a neat, linear fashion.
3. Gender inequality can be explained from a number of different perspectives. Functionalists see such differences as natural and complementary, whereas conflict theorists consider gender inequality to be but one more form of stratification based on exploitation.
4. Symbolic interactionism explains the subordinate status of women as being the result of a socialization process that microsocially operates to encourage males and females to develop specific personality traits. This process is also linked to the fact that the genders are each oriented toward different types of social networks.
5. The final decades of the twentieth century have been a struggle for women. Their endeavors can certainly be called a revolution—in accomplishments, expectations, self-image, and relationships with men. Yes, the place of women in the United States has come a long way, but there is still an enormous amount of new territory to be conquered. Only time will tell if the equality gap between men and women can ever become a closed door.

6. The positive contributions of women to U.S. society are enormous. They run the gamut from running family life to running government. This text offers a further positive note: Compare the number of female scholars cited in sociology texts written in the 1950s with today's numbers. Given the commitment of the United States to equality, you will see that the comparison is indeed refreshing.

University of Bologna students study in the chemistry library at Italy's and Europe's oldest university.

PART FIVE

SOCIAL INSTITUTIONS

In introducing the idea of a "macrostructure," Chapter 5 discussed the elements of those grand groups known as societies. The most fundamental such elements are called institutions.

Family and religion are very personal parts of life, but Chapters 14 and 15 show that they are also penetrated by basic sociological patterns. Political economy (Chapter 16) links two institutions that together inform popular understanding of different "types" of society. Chapter 17 interprets the sociological meaning of what we are doing here in this thing called "education."

Chapter 14

Personal Perspective

My husband's father never changed his son's diaper. The only family meal his father ever cooked was when his mother was in the hospital giving birth to his younger sisters. Those meals were real adventures. His father never washed or dried the dishes, ran the vacuum cleaner, dusted woodwork or furniture, cleaned a bathroom, or did the weekly food shopping. His father did not paint the house or do other maintenance jobs, and his mother, who was never gainfully employed after marriage, took care of the lawnmowing and routine yard work until my husband was old enough to assume those chores. His father did, however, work very hard. His father typically left for work before the family breakfast, and often would not reappear until after dinner. His father spent his weekends and spare time mostly on his antiques hobby, which, fortuitously, was also income-producing.

Unlike his father, my husband has changed many diapers—a few thousand, to be exact. As a college professor, he had several days a week without classes, so he was able to stay home with our preschool children while I pursued my career. And while our children were of school age, he had primary responsibility for them every afternoon after school. During the summer they were all his every day. His duties around the house have included at various times such things as preparing meals, cleaning up after dinner, vacuuming, and food shopping. And he has always taken care of the routine maintenance and yard work. But he has never bathed the children or cleaned the bathrooms in our home. Although he has never said it, I suppose he considers these latter jobs to be "women's work."

MHM

Family

MOST college students know that the family is the basic institution or "building block" of society. That social historical axiom has worked its way into the pool of common knowledge. But what college students generally do not know is that the structure and functions of that building block vary enormously from one society to another, and within a given society over time (Quale, 1988).

Indeed, the family probably is the most flexible and adaptive institution, and gradual change is one constant throughout its history. But ordinarily there is not much short-term change in the family institution because the attitudes of existing families are not very flexible, and new families are formed by individuals whose expectations were forged in existing ones. When new patterns emerge, it usually takes many generations before they are widely adopted (Caplow, 1991).

This is why the rapid changes in the American family that have taken place since the 1950s are so extraordinary. Those changes include a sharp decline in overall childbearing, a huge increase in childbearing among unmarried women, a robust growth of nonmarital cohabiting, a dramatic rise in divorce, and a stunning increase in the labor force participation of married women both with and without children (Cherlin, 1983). These momentous changes in turn have set into motion secondary family changes—such as the changes in the division of labor between husband and wife alluded to in the "Personal Perspective."

This chapter will focus on these changes and other features of the American family. But first it is necessary to step back and to review some basic concepts related to marriage and the family.

THE FAMILY IN SOCIETY

Basic Concepts

family—a relatively permanent group of two or more individuals related by blood, marriage, or adoption who ordinarily live together.

nuclear family—one or two parents living together in a household with their natural and/or adopted children.

Families vary in form the world over, so it is difficult to fashion a definition that fits them all. A fairly standard sociological definition that includes the vast majority of family forms, however, is the following. A **family** is a relatively permanent group of two or more individuals related by blood, marriage, or adoption who ordinarily live together.

Families are generally divided into two organizational types: nuclear and extended. A **nuclear family** consists of one or two parents living together in a household with their natural and/or adopted children. In nuclear families where two parents are present, they are usually married. The nuclear family is the dominant family form in all industrial societies, and is common in many pre-industrial ones as well. As modernization takes place in a society, nuclear families typically proliferate.

This evocative painting, *Folk Family* (1940), is by the African-American artist William H. Johnson. The two-parent family was representative of about 40 percent of African-American families with children in 1991. More than a quarter of all African-American families have incomes surpassing the U.S. median, and about 90 percent of these families have two parents present. Notwithstanding, 60 percent of African-American families with children in 1991 were headed by a single parent, usually the mother. Many of these mothers are unemployed, and their families make up a large part of an underclass that includes about one-third of the African-American population. Economic pressures make it extremely difficult for them to form and maintain two-parent families (Collins and Coltrane, 1991).

extended family—three or more generations living together.

family of orientation—the family into which individuals are born.

family of procreation—the family formed by individuals when they marry and have or adopt children.

marriage—a socially and legally approved mating relationship.

legitimacy—being born to a married couple.

kinship—a social network that links individuals with ties based on blood, marriage, or adoption.

An **extended family** includes three or more generations, often the grandparents, their unmarried children, and their married children, together with the latter's spouses and children. The family members reside together in the same house, in adjacent residences, or in family compounds. Extended families are most common in pre-industrial societies, but are not uncommon in industrial societies. In the United States, for instance, extended families often are found among African Americans, Hispanics, and recently arrived immigrant groups. Many college students already have experienced living in an extended family after a grandparent moved into their family's home.

Families can also be divided into **families of orientation** and **families of procreation**, primarily on the basis of the different roles the individual plays. The family of orientation is the family into which individuals are born or adopted and in which they are socialized. The family of procreation is the family formed by individuals when they marry (typically) and bear or adopt children.

Because of cross-cultural variability it is as difficult to define **marriage** as it is to define family. A minimalist definition is that marriage is a socially approved mating relationship. Marriage formalizes and legitimates a quasi-permanent sexual union between two or more people. Of course, marriages are formalized in different ways in different societies. In some societies a marriage ceremony such as a wedding is performed publicly by a religious or government official or some other community representative. In other societies the union is recognized by a formal exchange of gifts between the partners' parents. But whatever their form, rituals signify the partners' recognition of their new status in the community as well as the community's approval of that status.

You may recall from Chapter 7 (Culture) that men are permitted to marry boys in some pre-industrial societies. But this is unusual in pre-industrial and virtually unknown in industrial societies. In the latter the proper "gender" norm restricts marriage to unions between men and women. Industrial societies also attach a set of expectations to marriage, including an expectation of a sexual relationship and of childbearing, at least in the early stages; an expectation of economic cooperation; and an expectation that the union will endure. In many societies, **legitimacy** is determined by the following: Children born to a married couple are considered legitimate; those born outside of wedlock are labeled illegitimate.

The family is the basic kinship unit. **Kinship** is a specific kind of social network. It links together individuals with ties based on blood, marriage, or adoption. Kinship is the fundamental form of social organization in many pre-industrial societies; the nuclear family assumes that role in industrial ones (Segalen, 1986). Kinship networks can theoretically include hundreds of people depending on how many branches of the family tree are included. But most societies arbitrarily limit kinship structure by ignoring various classes of relatives. In the United States, for example, the average person only interacts regularly with primary relatives—spouse, children, father, mother, and siblings—and the primary relatives of primary relatives (e.g., uncles, nieces, first cousins). Beyond these primary and secondary relatives there is typically little social contact.

Other family concepts are discussed elsewhere in this book generally in a cross-cultural context. Table 14:1 provides a convenient guide to the meaning and location of these concepts. (See also Figure 14:1.)

TABLE 14:1 Family Concepts: A Guide to Concepts Explained in This Book

CONCEPT AND CHAPTER	TYPE	DEFINITION
Number of Spouses (Chapter 7)	Monogamy	A form of marriage in which one man is married to one woman.
	Polygamy	Plural marriage, or marriage involving more than one spouse simultaneously.
	Polyandry	A form of polygamy in which a wife has more than one husband at the same time.
	Polygyny	A form of polygamy in which a husband has more than one wife at the same time.
Partner Preference (Chapter 7)	Exogamy	The custom requiring individuals to marry outside a specific group of which they are members. The exogamous group may be a kinship group such as a family or a clan; a village group; or a group based on religion, race, ethnicity, or class.
	Endogamy	The custom requiring marriage within one's own social group.
Residence Pattern (Chapter 7)	Patrilocal	The custom for a married couple to reside in the husband's parental household or locality.
	Matrilocal	The custom for a married couple to reside in the wife's parental household or locality.
	Neolocal	A custom according to which married couples are normally expected not to live with either family of origin, but to establish a separate or new residence.
Authority Relationships (Chapter 7)	Patriarchal family	A form of family organization in which the father is the formal head and dominant power in the family.
	Matriarchal family	A form of family organization in which the mother is the formal head and dominant power in the family.
	Egalitarian family	A form of family organization in which wife and husband have approximately equal power in the family.
Descent and Inheritance (Chapter 7)	Patrilineal system	Descent (and sometimes inheritance) traced unilaterally through the father and the male line.
	Matrilineal system	Descent (and sometimes inheritance) traced unilaterally through the mother and the female line.
	Bilateral system	Descent (and sometimes inheritance) regarded as determined equally by the mother's and father's lines.
Sex by Marital Status (Chapter 19)	Premarital sex	Sex before marriage.
	Extramarital sex	Sex, while married, with someone other than the spouse.
	Nonmarital sex	Sex between partners who are not married to each other or to any others, including that between or after failed marriages.
Sexual Norms (Chapter 19)	Who norms What norms Where norms When norms Why norms	Sexual norms are divided into categories in much the same way a journalist might organize a story; that is, according to the who, what, where, when, and why of sexual behavior. Chapter 19 has a lengthy cross-cultural discussion of sexual norms.

Source: Theodorson & Theodorson (1969).

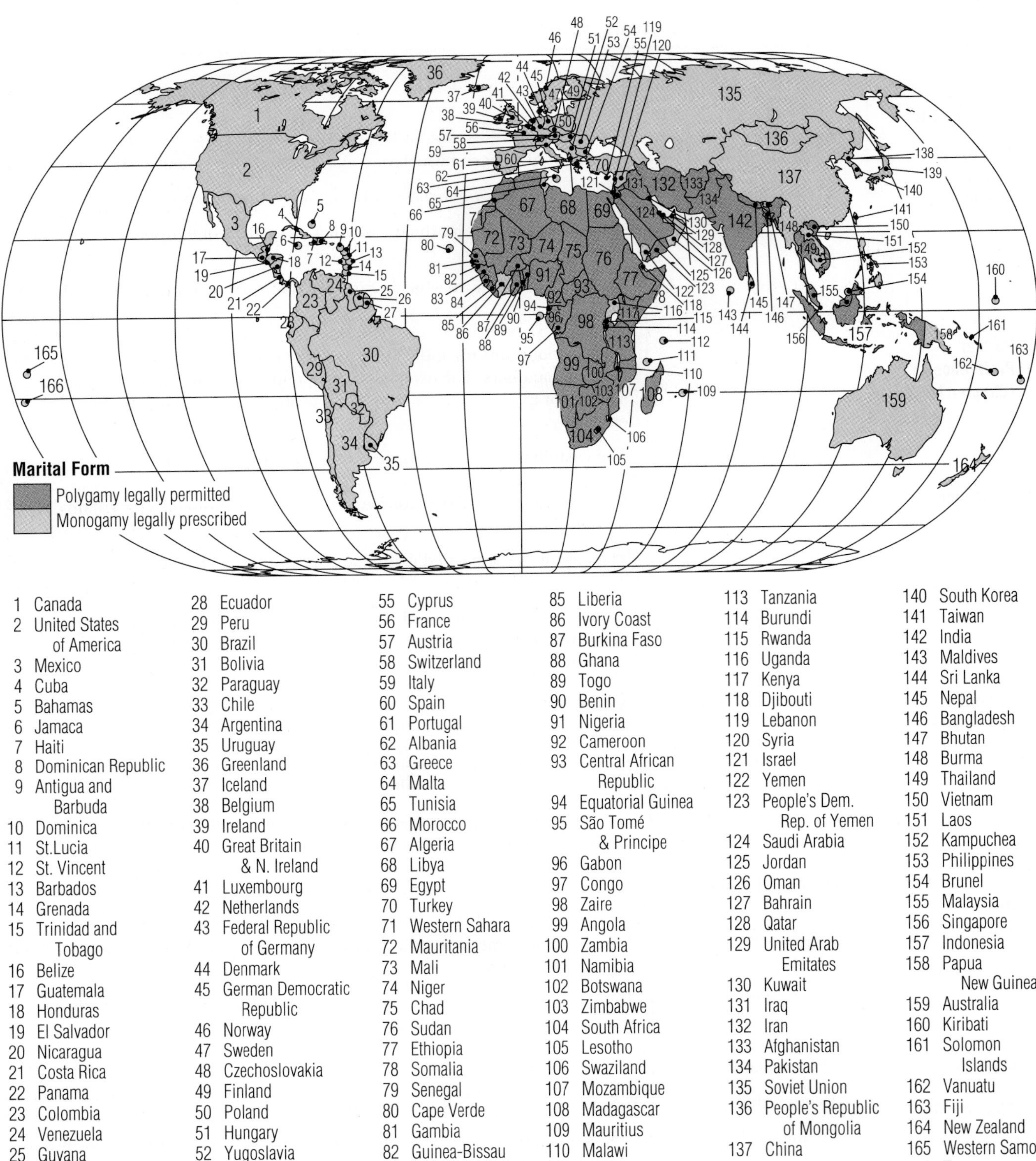

FIGURE 14:1 MONOGAMY AND POLYGAMY AROUND THE WORLD

Polygamy is plural marriage, or marriage involving more than one spouse simultaneously. It is legally permitted in many nations of the world, especially in south Asia and Africa. Monogamy is the only form of marriage permitted in the remaining nations, including all industrial ones and those in the Western Hemisphere.

Source: Peters Atlas of the World, 1990, p. 183. By permission of the publisher.

Functions of the Family

Like the basic concepts, the functions that families perform vary from one society to another. The pre-industrial family performed virtually all of society's basic tasks. It was a self-sufficient economic unit that provided most of its own security, passed on to children necessary knowledge and skills, taught children religion and performed religious rituals, and was host to most recreational activities. But as societies modernize they tend to relinquish functions to more specialized institutions. A father can teach a child how to farm, for example, but not how to be an astrophysicist. Thus, educational, religious, political, and other institutions have evolved in modern societies that perform broad functions previously handled by families. However, the family is still entrusted with a core set of six functions in virtually all societies. These include (1) the regulation of sexuality, (2) reproduction, (3) socialization, (4) material security, (5) social placement, and (6) affection and companionship.

Regulation of Sexuality

As will be discussed in Chapter 19, one thing common to all societies is the cultural regulation of sexual behavior. Even so-called free sex subcultures find it necessary to control aspects of sexuality. This is because sex is so important. Sex is linked to the reproduction of the species, is central to kinship and property rights, is a key component in the emotional lives of individuals, and is inextricably bound up with a cavalcade of problems stretching from abortion to zoophilia. Societies delegate primary responsibility for regulating sex to the family.

The family regulates sex by teaching children the sexual norms of society, by monitoring compliance with those norms, and by punishing deviance. Among the most important of these norms is the culturally universal *incest taboo*, which prohibits sexuality between family members and relatives who are too closely related to marry (Chapter 19). Another important set of norms are the endogamous/exogamous ones mentioned earlier. If you are an unmarried age-typical college student and want to test whether your family of orientation still performs this regulatory function, try this experiment. Announce that you plan to marry someone of a different race who is 10 years older than you, and see what happens. Odds are your family will immediately spring into action and try to change your mind.

Reproduction

For societies to perpetuate themselves, they must find a way to replace their members. A few societies do this in unconventional ways. The Marindanim, for example, a predominantly homosexual New Guinea tribe, help maintain their population by kidnapping children from neighboring tribes (Kottak, 1974). The Shakers, a U.S. religious subculture that prohibited sex, accomplished this replacement task by accepting converts and their children into the community and by adopting orphans (Kephart and Zellner, 1991). The vast majority of societies, however, provide for replacement through reproduction.

To ensure that childbearing at replacement-level (Chapter 20) takes place, a society must create a stable institutional structure with responsibility for this task, and must include within this institution the social roles of mother and father. This institution is the family. Many students are

Ron Taylor Crouch's *Reunion* (1991) includes a young mother and her two children, among other people. The scene not only illustrates the core family function of reproduction, but also portrays the small family in the midst of its supportive social network.

surprised that such an institutional arrangement is necessary. They believe that if you put women and men together in a society, sufficient childbearing will occur automatically. This is not true. Indeed, many societies (e.g., Germany) and social groups (U.S. Jews) today are not having enough children to keep from losing population. Such depopulation occurs when the family institution fails to carry out its fundamental replacement function.

Socialization

In the early 1990s a film appeared called *The Emerald Forest.* It was based on the true story of a 4-year-old American boy who was kidnapped and raised by a Brazilian tribe known as the "invisible people." A number of scenes showed the boy's adoptive father teaching him how to be a proper Indian and how to live in the rain forest environment. The son had become a young man and a full-fledged Indian warrior by the time his biological father finally found him. In the end, despite his biological father's pleading, the son refused to return to the modern world.

This narrative and others like it remind us of two facts: (1) that humans, regardless of their heredity, are highly plastic, and are largely fashioned by the societies in which they grow up; and (2) that, in general, this shaping or socialization process primarily occurs within the family (see Chapter 8). Parents pass along to their children society's values, norms, beliefs, language, artifacts, ideologies, and survival skills. This is a functional arrangement because parents usually have an emotional stake in child-rearing and in the well-being of their children and are thus highly motivated to monitor their children's progress toward full socialization.

It is true that a small number of societies such as some Israeli collective settlements (kibbutzim) and some U.S. subcultures (e.g., the Oneida community) raise children communally rather than primarily in families (Bowes, 1989; Kephart and Zellner, 1991). And, as is discussed in the theory section later, it is also true that in modern societies the family does less socializing of its young than it did in the past, owing to the growing role played by education and the media in the socialization process. Notwithstanding, the family is still the primary socializing agent in the United States and in most societies.

Material Security

In every society there are categories of individuals who cannot survive, subsist, or live comfortably on their own. They are dependent upon others for their basic necessities and comforts of life. Among these categories are infants, young children, the elderly, the sick, the infirm, and the financially destitute. Most societies entrust the task of caring for and supporting such dependent individuals primarily to the family.

Social Placement

When a child is born it has to be placed somehow within the social structure. Virtually all societies entrust the family to perform this function. The family of orientation instantaneously gives the newborn child its ascribed social statuses including class, race, ethnicity, and religion. Because the family is the most important determinant of an individual's social status, a child's legitimacy is considered to be vital in most societies. Legitimacy helps stabilize the social order by permitting the orderly transmission of status and property from the parents' to the children's generation.

Being born into and raised by a family rather than, say, by the community as a whole also gives the individual a set of role relationships based on kinship. These relate not only to immediate family members, but to such relatives as uncles, aunts, and grandparents. Along with these roles, of course, come reciprocal rights and responsibilities.

Affection and Companionship

Another family function is to provide members with affection and companionship. Humans are social beings. Adults and, especially, children have affective and social needs that can only be satisfied through interaction with other people. Responsibility for the lion's share of this interaction typically is given to the family. The family is the generator of characteristically human qualities and traits. Indeed, children who do not experience family life or a close facsimile of it—such as children raised in understaffed orphanages—suffer from personality impoverishment as well as other problems.

Many social scientists believe that a child's early family relationships serve as general models for subsequent ones, and that if these early relationships are absent or problematic, the subsequent ones will be, too. An extraordinary 36-year study, for example, found that hugs and physical affection from parents strongly affect a child's chances for successful marriages, friendships, and careers: Of the children with affectionate parents, 70 percent did well socially, contrasted with only 30 percent of the children whose parents were "cold fish." Interestingly, fathers' hugs turned out to be just as important as mothers' hugs (Schogah, 1992).

Emerging Family Functions

Although the modern family institution has lost some of the functions performed in the pre-industrial era, and is increasingly sharing with other social institutions several of the six core functions discussed, it is gaining

This Pulitzer Prize-winning photo, "Burst of Joy," shows an Air Force officer being greeted by his family after a long absence. Lieutenant Colonel Robert Sterm had been shot down over North Vietnam, and had been a prisoner of war for six years. This photo vividly shows an outpouring of affection, one of the family's core functions.

new functions as well (Benokraitis, 1993). For example, the family now has the function of coordinating the roles that various specialized agencies play in the lives of their children. In this supervisory and management function, parents parse out the time of their children to schools, clubs, sports leagues, religious groups, social-service organizations, and professionals teaching everything from a cappella to Zen (Ishwaran, 1989; Keniston and Carnegie Council on Children, 1977). Similarly, families may be regaining part of their lost recreational function, as the members of at least middle-class and upper-middle-class families are spending more time playing and vacationing together (Nye, 1974).

THE TRANSFORMATION OF THE AMERICAN FAMILY

Before turning our attention to the American family today, let's first take a brief look at the American family in the year 1800, shortly after the birth of the nation (Juster and Vinovskis, 1987). Then we will examine social changes that have occurred in the family since 1800 and particularly over the past three decades. While there were many subcultural variations in family organization during this 200-year span, space permits only a broad sketch of the dominant or "mainstream" family form.

The Family in Early America

Contrary to conventional wisdom, the typical early-American family was not an extended family with three generations residing in the same house or family compound (Demos, 1986). True, extended families were more common at the time of the American Revolution than today, but the nuclear family then as now was far and away the dominant family form (Hareven, 1982). These nuclear families were headed by the husband, who was the primary authority figure. Wives played a subordinate role, disallowed even to be legal guardians of their children or to own property. Children were expected to be extraordinarily obedient, disciplined, and docile (Mintz and Kellogg, 1988).

Unlike today, mate selection was based primarily on practical, economic considerations rather than on romantic love. Also, young adults had to secure parental consent to marry. However, not many men and women married young. The average age at marriage was mid-twenties for men and women, even though the legal age for marriage was 12 for girls and 14 for boys. One reason marriage was relatively late for men was that parents depended on sons for labor on the family homestead until the sons were well into their twenties, and sons depended on parents for help in establishing the sons' homesteads, often by the gift of promised land (Smith, 1973).

Although there were norms against premarital sex, there was actually considerable deviance. Historians report that 30 to 40 percent of brides in the communities studied were pregnant when they took their marriage vows (Demos, 1986). Given that there were relatively few never-married mothers by contemporary standards, premarital pregnancy apparently was an almost automatic marriage producer.

Another big difference between the early-American family and today's family was size, and the size of the household of which the family was part. At the time of the first national census in 1790, the typical American household contained about six members, compared to today's all-time low of 2.6

Amy Tan, the Chinese-American writer and author of *The Joy Luck Club,* is shown standing with, top to bottom, her mother Daisy, sister June, and niece Ming. Asian-American families, including those of Japanese, Chinese, Korean, Vietnamese, Filipino, and East Indian descent, tend to have low fertility, high educational achievement, and a high rate of exogamy, especially for women. Traditional Asian families place family interests above those of the individual. But as native-born Asian immigrants and their children become acculturated and prosper, Asian-American family patterns increasingly resemble those of whites (Collins and Coltrane, 1991).

(U.S. Bureau of the Census, 1992a). One reason for the differential is that early-American households were much more likely to accommodate boarders, strangers, and homeless relatives such as unmarried aunts. In fact, individuals were discouraged from living alone, and some locales levied heavy taxes on those who did so. Another reason for their large size was that these early families had more children than today's families. Women typically had seven children, but these children frequently were not all present in the household at the same time. Many children died during infancy and childhood, and older children were often "put out" into other households to learn a trade.

Families had many children because early America had a pro-childbearing culture. At that time children were members of the workforce from about age 6 onward, and, as such, were economic assets (Hareven, 1982). There were also strong norms against contraception and abortion. Moreover, contraceptive technology was almost totally lacking, and abortion was a life-threatening procedure for women in the pre-antibiotic era.

Another important difference between early-American families and those of today was the low prevalence of divorce. In the past, marriages were considered to be permanent relationships. Although divorce was allowed in the northern colonies, it was strongly discouraged; in the southern colonies, it was actually outlawed. (Indeed, South Carolina did not permit divorce until 1948.) Consequently, in the early nineteenth century only about 5 percent of marriages ended eventually in divorce (Demos, 1974). Divorce was low despite the fact that, judging from court records, extramarital sex was not uncommon (Benokraitis, 1993).

Between 1800 and 1950 many powerful forces played upon the family, including the expansion of the nation from coast to coast (Chapter 20), industrialization (Chapter 21), urbanization (Chapter 6), the early sexual revolution (Chapter 19), and the early women's movement (Chapter 13). Additionally, the federal government and its agencies began to influence the American family during this period. These large-scale social forces and other influential phenomena (like the Great Depression and the world wars) altogether produced enormous changes in the American family by 1950. Among the most important were reductions in household and family size, in parental influence on mate selection, and in the average number of years between the birth of the first and last child. Other important changes include increases in the proportion of husbands and wives working outside the home, in the importance of spousal companionship, in the wife's authority within the family, and in the rate of divorce.

The Family in Transition: 1950–1990

traditional family—a family consisting of a breadwinning husband, a stay-at-home wife, and their dependent children.

The typical 1950s family consisted of a breadwinning husband, a stay-at-home wife, and their dependent children. This organization—labeled here as the **traditional family**—was society's ideal, and about two-thirds of U.S. families conformed to it.

Social change was widespread and rapid in the United States between the 1950s and the early 1990s. No institution remained unaffected, but the traditional family changed the most. Much of this change was due to the continuation of trends toward industrialization, urbanization (and suburbanization), economic growth, individualism, social mobility, and personal freedom. As usual, technological change played a key role (see Box 21:2). The contraceptive revolution, which was based on modern contraceptives and safer methods of sterilization and abortion, is an example from the medical realm. Other med-tech advances led to longer life expectancy, which, among other things, increased the potential duration of marriage, the potential time spouses could play nonparental roles in the empty nest period, and the probability of divorce (Stub, 1982). A nonmedical example is the proliferation of the automobile, a vehicle that removed courtship from the scrutiny of parents and, consequently, greatly facilitated premarital sexuality.

The traditional family was buffeted also by government policies such as those that contributed to the rise of the post–New Deal U.S. welfare state. Conservative critics (e.g., Murray, 1984) contend that many social programs of President Lyndon Johnson's Great Society, for example, contributed to the breakup of families (in addition to rising crime rates, falling educational standards, and other social problems), but liberal analysts disagree (Duncan and Hoffman, 1990; Ellwood and Summers, 1986). There is no doubt, however, that judicial decisions had a profound impact on the family, especially the Supreme Court's legalization of abortion in 1973.

Moreover, virtually all the major social movements of that era—the feminist movement, the sexual liberation movements, the counterculture groups—undermined the traditional family (Jones et al., 1988). Probably

BOX 14:1 SOCIOLOGICAL IMAGINATION IN FICTION

A "Woman's Place" in *The Handmaid's Tale*

Margaret Atwood's novel *The Handmaid's Tale* takes place in a future in which the ultra-fundamentalist right has gained control of society. Women are kept in "their place" in this society because of the threat they had become to men and to traditional family life in the late twentieth century. They are forbidden to be anything but wives, domestics, childbearers, and supervisors of other women. In addition, women are prohibited from having money, owning property, living alone, and reading. In this future society, childbearing once again becomes women's most exalted profession, owing to the fact that only a small proportion of women—the so-called Handmaids—are still able to do it. Most people's reproductive organs have been impaired by pollution.

Offred is a Handmaid assigned to help a powerful man (the Commander) and his sterile wife (Serrena Joy) have a child. Once a month an almost fully clothed Offred must lie between the couple and have perfunctory intercourse with the Commander, as part of a religious ceremony based on the Genesis story about Rachel offering her servant to her husband Jacob so that "she shall bear upon my knees, that I may also have children by her." If Offred is successful and gives birth, she would move on and perform the same duty for another unfortunate couple. The following abridged passage describes part of the mating ceremony.

The Ceremony goes as usual.

I lie on my back, fully clothed except for the healthy white cotton underdrawers. What I could see, if I were to open my eyes, would be the large white canopy of Serrena Joy's outsized colonial-style four-poster bed, suspended like a sagging cloud above us, . . .

Above me, towards the head of the bed, Serrena Joy is arranged, outspread. Her legs are apart, I lie between them, my head on her stomach, her pubic bone under the base of my skull, the most influential was the feminist movement (see Chapter 13), which saw the traditional family as one of the principal obstacles to the goal of liberating women totally. Box 14:1 is an excerpt from a feminist author's satirical novel about a negative utopia, which embodies and exaggerates elements of the traditional family.

Between 1950 and 1990 these social movements and many other phenomena (e.g., major events like the Vietnam War) altered the face of the U.S. family almost beyond recognition. Let's review the more important of these changes.

Decline in the Proportion Currently Married

One of the big changes that occurred between 1950 and 1990 is that people now spend a smaller proportion of their lives in marriage, owing to the following trends (Cherlin, 1992; Thornton, 1989).

Lower Marriage Rates The marriage rate for unmarried women age 15 to 44 dropped by nearly 50 percent between the mid-1950s and 1991, and by 15 percent between 1981 and 1991 (Figure 14:2). The rate for unmarried men also plummeted during these periods (NCHS, 1992b).

BOX 14:1 SOCIOLOGICAL IMAGINATION IN FICTION *continued*

her thighs on either side of me. She too is fully clothed.

My arms are raised; she holds my hands, each of mine in each of hers. This is supposed to signify that we are one flesh, one being. What it really means is that she is in control, of the process and thus of the product. If any. The rings of her left hand cut into my fingers. It may or may not be revenge.

My red skirt is hitched up to my waist, though no higher. Below it the Commander is [having sex with] the lower part of my body. I do not say making love, because this is not what he's doing. Copulating too would be inaccurate, because it would imply two people and only one is involved. Nor does rape cover it: nothing is going on here that I haven't signed up for. There wasn't a lot of choice but there was some, and this is what I chose.

Therefore I lie still and picture the unseen canopy over my head. I remember Queen Victoria's advice to her daughter: *Close your eyes and think of England.* But this is not England. I wish he would hurry up. . . .

Serrena Joy grips my hands as if it is she, not I, who's [having sex]. . . .

What's going on in this room, under Serrena Joy's silvery canopy, is not exciting. It has nothing to do with passion or love or romance or any of those other notions we used to titillate ourselves with. It has nothing to do with sexual desire, at least for me, and certainly not for Serrena. Arousal and orgasm are no longer thought necessary; they would be a symptom of frivolity merely, like jazz garters or beauty spots: superfluous distractions for the light-minded. Outdated. It seems odd that women once spent such time and energy reading about such things, thinking about them, worrying about them, writing about them. They are so obviously recreational.

This is not recreation, even for the Commander. This is serious business. The Commander, too, is doing his duty.

Critical Thinking Questions

1. The fictional premise, that in the future most people's reproductive organs will be impaired by pollution, is not a wholly implausible scenario, given the fact that sperm count actually has dropped precipitously in the twentieth century and pollution is believed to be the main culprit. If reproductive ability does decline substantially in the future, how do you think U.S. society would respond? What social policies do you think a functionalist would recommend?
2. What social policy do you think a conflict theorist would recommend in the same situation?

Source: Excerpted from Margaret Atwood (1986), *The Handmaid's Tale.* Boston: Houghton Mifflin, pages 120–22.

FIGURE 14:2 MARRIAGE RATE, 1940–1990

The marriage rate for unmarried women age 15 to 44 dropped by nearly 50 percent between 1950 and 1990.

Source: Ahlburg and DeVita (1992).

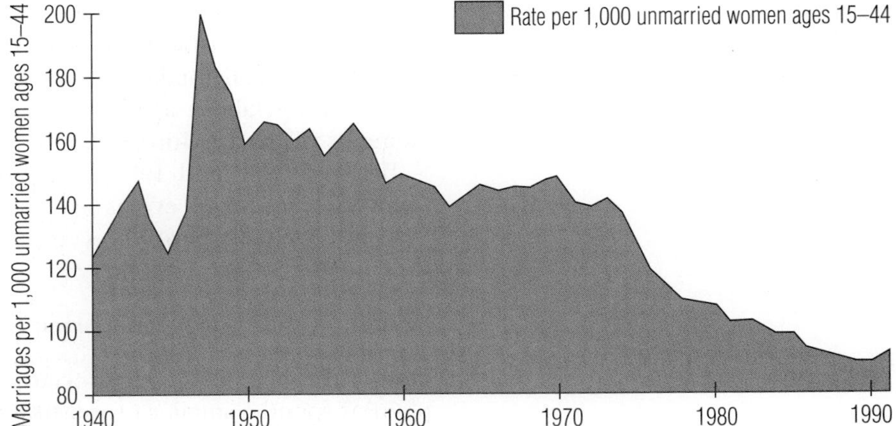

Delayed Marriage. American men and women were also delaying marriage much more in the 1990s than in the 1950s (Saluter, 1989). The median age at marriage for men in 1955 was 22.6; in 1991, 26.3. Similarly, the median age for women was 20.2 in 1955 and 24.1 in 1991 (USBC, 1992b). In the 1950s, young adults were expected to marry and have children as soon as they were financially able to do so (Ryder, 1973). But by the 1990s norms regarding marriage and childbearing had changed.

Decrease in the Proportion Ever Marrying. The changes just described—lower marriage rates and delayed marriage—result in a smaller proportion of the population eventually marrying today than in the 1950s. The proportion of people in a typical generation who never married by age 45 was just 4 percent in the 1950s. Experts now believe that about 14 percent of women who were between age 30 and 34 in 1990 may never marry (Bloom and Bennett, 1990), and the proportion is likely to be even higher for the generations that include age-typical college students today.

Increased Divorce. Divorce rates went through the roof between the 1950s and the 1990s, more than doubling over this period (NCHS, 1992c). If present age-specific divorce rates persist indefinitely, some 52 percent of the marriages that take place today will end in divorce. Divorce is now more common in the United States than anywhere else in the world (Figure 14:3).

Decreased Remarriage. Proportionally far fewer divorced and widowed people remarry today than in the 1950s. The remarriage rate for divorced women has dropped 36 percent just since 1970. Comparable drops for divorced men, widowed women, and widowed men are 46 percent, 48 percent, and 38 percent, respectively. Moreover, for those who do remarry, the average length of time between marriages increased from one to three years over the period; and the divorce rate for these marriages, traditionally higher than those of first marriages, also rose (NCHS, 1991d).

Less Time Spent within Marriage. Despite gains in life expectancy, these aforementioned trends—delayed marriage, increased divorce, and decreased remarriage—mean that those who do marry today spend a much smaller proportion of their lives being married than Americans did in the 1950s (Espenshade, 1985).

Perhaps the best way to appreciate the overall decline in the popularity of marriage is to check out the proportion of persons age 18 and over who are currently married. In 1990, only 61 percent of such persons were currently married compared to 67 percent in the 1950s, a very significant drop of more than 5 percent. Of course, this drop was due not only to the fact that married people now spend less time in marriage, but to the fact that relatively fewer people marry in the first place.

Increased Cohabitation. Cohabitation by definition is living with an individual of the opposite gender in a sexual union without a formal marriage. The prevalence of cohabitation increased enormously between 1950 and 1991. In 1991 there were more than 6 million unmarried adults sharing households with unrelated persons of the opposite gender (USBC, 1992b). This represents more than 5 percent of all couples maintaining a separate household, up from a small fraction of 1 percent in 1950. The age composition of cohabitators also changed drastically over the interval. In the 1950s, more than 70 percent of cohabitators were age 45 or over, but by 1991, only 15 percent were this old (Glick, 1984; USBC, 1992b). Twenty-four percent of cohabitators were under age 25 in 1991, and 66 percent were under age 35. But cohabitation figures for any given year substantially underestimate the percentage of Americans who cohabit at some time during their lives (Thornton and Freedman, 1983). For instance, a 1988 study found that while only 5 percent of women age 15 to 44 were currently cohabitating, one-third had done so at some time in the past (London, 1991).

Changes in Childbearing and Sexuality

The major changes in childbearing since the 1950s are that today women have fewer children, childbearing is delayed, and a higher proportion of children are born outside of marriage. The last is due in part to an increase in premarital and nonmarital sexuality.

Decrease in Childbearing. U.S. women were reproducing at a rate of 3.7 children in the mid-1950s, but the rate had fallen to about two children by 1990. The low fertility of the 1990s has been brought about in large part by the postponement of marriage as discussed, and the widespread use of abortion and contraception, especially sterilization (Westoff, 1986; Williams and Pratt, 1990).

Delayed Childbearing. One reason for the decline in childbearing between the 1950s and the 1990s is the fact that substantial proportions of women are delaying much of their childbearing until relatively late in their reproductive lives, a practice that generally leads to lower completed fertility (McFalls, 1990). The reasons for this pattern of delayed childbearing are later discussed in Box 20:3.

Increased Sexuality among Unmarried Women. Sexual activity among unmarried women increased enormously between the 1950s and the 1990s. Indeed, by the 1980s 75 percent of unmarried women were sexually active compared to 89 percent of married women (see Table 19:2) (NCHS, 1987). Another study found that 80 percent of women who married in the late 1970s did not wait until marriage to begin sexual activity (Bachrach and Horn, 1985). This was a sharp increase from the early 1960s when only 52 percent had had sexual intercourse before marriage.

Increased Childbearing among Unmarried Women. Childbearing among unmarried women grew steadily from 1950 to 1989 (NCHS, 1992c). In

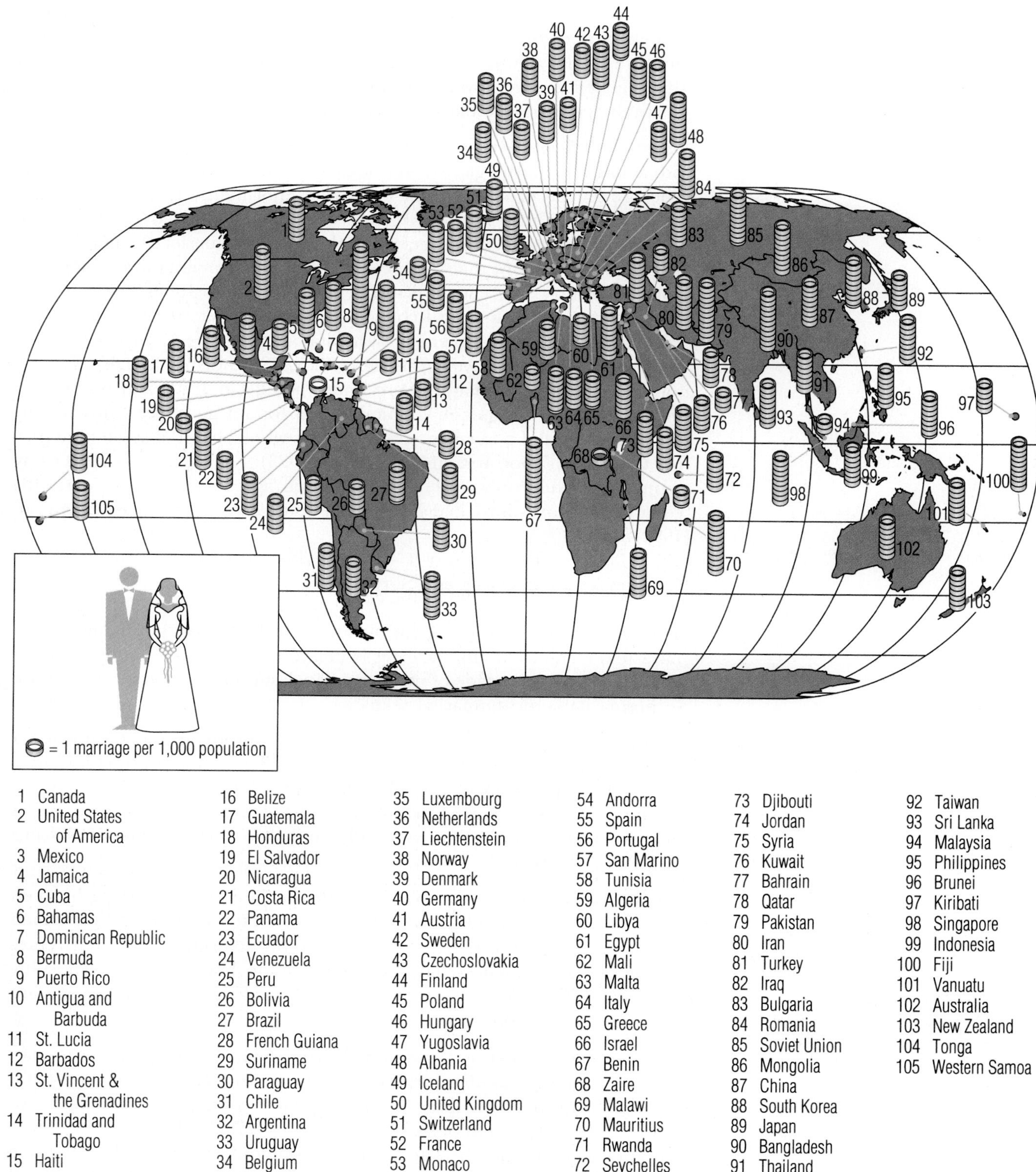

FIGURE 14:3 MARRIAGE AND DIVORCE IN GLOBAL PERSPECTIVE

The ratio of marriages to divorces varies widely by society. In the United States, for example, marriages outnumber divorces by about two to one. By contrast, the ratio is about eight to one in China.

Source: MAPSENSE: Global Comparisons from World Monitor *Magazine*, 1992, pp. 18–19. By permission of the publisher.

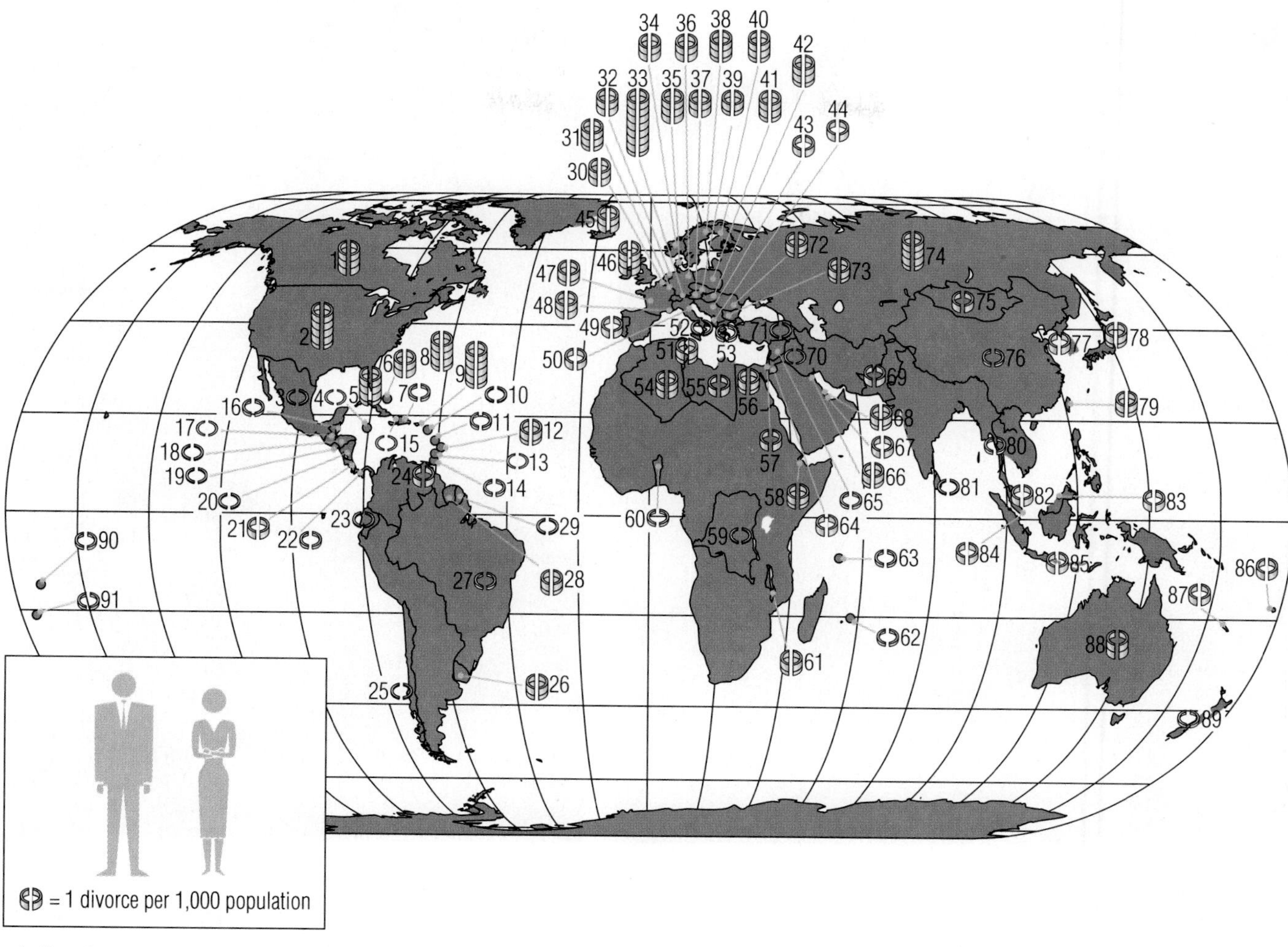

1 Canada
2 United States of America
3 Mexico
4 Jamaica
5 Cuba
6 Bahamas
7 Dominican Republic
8 Bermuda
9 Puerto Rico
10 Antigua and Barbuda
11 St. Lucia
12 Barbados
13 St. Vincent & the Grenadines
14 Trinidad and Tobago
15 Haiti
16 Belize
17 Guatemala
18 Honduras
19 El Salvador
20 Nicaragua
21 Costa Rica
22 Panama
23 Ecuador
24 Venezuela
25 Chile
26 Uruguay
27 Brazil
28 Suriname
29 French Guiana
30 Belgium
31 Luxembourg
32 Netherlands
33 Liechtenstein
34 Norway
35 Denmark
36 Germany
37 Austria
38 Sweden
39 Czechoslovakia
40 Finland
41 Poland
42 Hungary
43 Yugoslavia
44 Albania
45 Iceland
46 United Kingdom
47 France
48 Monaco
49 Portugal
50 San Marino
51 Tunisia
52 Italy
53 Greece
54 Algeria
55 Libya
56 Egypt
57 Israel
58 Djibouti
59 Zaire
60 Benin
61 Malawi
62 Mauritius
63 Seychelles
64 Jordan
65 Syria
66 Kuwait
67 Bahrain
68 Qatar
69 Pakistan
70 Iraq
71 Turkey
72 Romania
73 Bulgaria
74 Soviet Union
75 Mongolia
76 China
77 South Korea
78 Japan
79 Taiwan
80 Thailand
81 Sri Lanka
82 Malaysia
83 Brunei
84 Singapore
85 Indonesia
86 Fiji
87 Vanuatu
88 Australia
89 New Zealand
90 Tonga
91 Western Samoa

In 1991, 1.2 million children were born to unmarried mothers, which is just shy of 30 percent of all births. This phenomenon of single motherhood cuts across social classes. The upper middle class TV character Murphy Brown dramatized this reality in an episode that had political ramifications in the 1992 presidential election campaign. Nevertheless, upscale women have relatively few out-of-wedlock births. For example, single women with college degrees had only 6 percent of all such births in 1991; those with less than a high school education had 48 percent.

1989, more than 4 percent of unmarried women age 15 to 44 gave birth, the highest rate ever observed in the United States. The rise in the proportion of women who are unmarried, the increase in their childbearing rate, and the declining childbearing rate of married women have, since the 1950s, combined to boost the proportion of all U.S. births that are out of wedlock. Indeed, only about 4 percent of all births occurred to unmarried women in 1950, but by 1989 more than 27 percent were out of wedlock, an increase of almost 700 percent (NCHS, 1992c).

Increased Labor Force Participation of Women

As we discussed in Chapter 13 on gender, a veritable revolution occurred in women's work patterns between the 1950s and the 1990s (Figure 14:4). In 1950, only 25 percent of married women were working for pay or looking for a job outside the home. By 1991, more than half (57 percent) were in the labor force. Even more dramatic is the fact that most of this change was due to the movement of married women with preschool children into the world of work. Fully 58 percent of these women were in the labor force in 1991 compared to a mere 12 percent in 1950. Married women with school-age children also entered the workforce in droves. In 1950, just 31 percent were in the labor force; by 1991, the figure was up to 58 percent, and two-thirds of these mothers were employed full-time. As a result of these labor force trends, the proportion of preschool and school-age children who had a full-time mother present in the home plummeted between

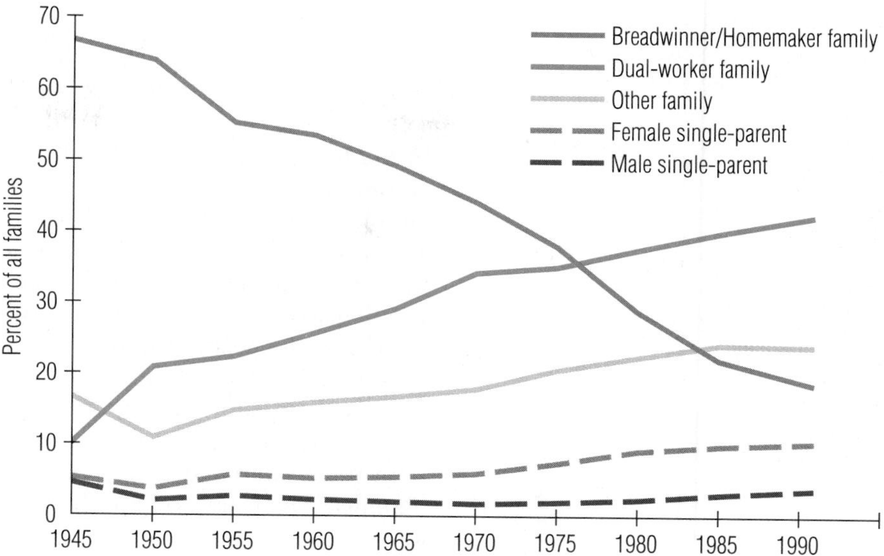

FIGURE 14:4 WOMEN IN THE LABOR FORCE, 1940–1990

A veritable revolution occurred in women's work patterns between the 1940s and the 1990s. By the 1990s most women were in the labor force, and this phenomenon radically changed the nature of the typical American family. Indeed, the proportion of all families that were the breadwinner/homemaker type decreased from nearly 70 percent to about 20 percent during the period.

Source: Ahlburg and DeVita (1992).

1950 and the 1990s. It has been estimated that, by the mid-1990s, only one-third of preschool children and one-fourth of school-age children will have full-time mothers (Hofferth and Phillips, 1987).

In any event, it is almost certain that women and mothers will continue to enter the workforce in the years to come. Indeed, experts predict that upwards of 90 percent of all women will be employed by the turn of the century. David Bloom has called this ongoing trend "the single most important change that has ever taken place in the American labor market" (*U.S. News and World Report,* 1985, p 46).

Decline in Household and Family Size

Another change over this period was that households and families became significantly smaller. The size of the average household continued its 140-year freefall. It declined about 25 percent between 1950 and 1991, from 3.4 to 2.6 persons (USBC, 1975; USBC, 1992a). By 1991, the average family was down to 3.23 members (USBC, 1992a).

Conclusions

In short, by 1991 people were marrying less, divorcing more, remarrying less, and having fewer children. More wives and mothers were in the labor force, more children were growing up without full-time mothers, and more sex and childbearing was taking place outside of the family. The size of households and families continued to decline, and the traditional family form was becoming less and less common.

Remember, in 1950 nearly two-thirds of the nation's families conformed to the traditional family mode. By 1991, only one-fifth continued to do so (USBC, 1992). But even these startling figures underestimate the real decline of the traditional family as the basic building block of U.S. society because there were proportionally far fewer families *of any type* in 1991 than in 1950 (meaning there were proportionally more nonfamily households like a male householder living alone). Another statistic provides a better view of the true enormity of this trend. In 1950, the traditional family constituted about 70 percent of all households; but by 1991, this figure had dropped to a mere 12 percent (USBC, 1992d). So, in a very real sense, the traditional family had become "unusual."

THE AMERICAN FAMILY IN THE 1990s

What Is the American Family?

In the basic-concepts section of this chapter, we gave a somewhat tentative definition of the family, which we labeled "a fairly standard sociological definition." The reason we could not be more definitive is not only that family forms vary enormously the world over, but that there is not even any agreement in the United States among the general public or even among sociologists concerning what constitutes a family. At one extreme are traditionalists for whom the traditional U.S. family (or something close to it) is the only real family form. At the other extreme are non-traditionalists who want the definition to include every conceivable configuration of people who live together.

In the United States today, there is increasing momentum to include as "families" what are commonly called "alternative living groups" or, more sociologically, *families of affinity* (Buunk and van Driel, 1989). Families of affinity are groups who usually live together and consider themselves a family. They include, for example, gay couples, possibly with children (Bozett, 1987); unmarried couples, again possibly with children; or a communal group of unrelated people who share a residence and resources.

The rationale for treating such entities as families is that they often function much the same way as married-couple families, and should be entitled to the same advantages, such as workplace-sponsored health insurance or the ability to make claims on each other's property once the relationship ends. And there has been some social change toward broadening the definition of family at various levels in the United States, with universities in the forefront of that change. For example, such schools as Stanford University, Swarthmore College, the University of Iowa, and the University of Chicago extend all employee benefits to gay and lesbian workers' long-term partners. Nevertheless, many of these universities find it difficult to find health insurance companies willing to extend health insurance benefits to the partners (McCullough, 1993).

There is increasing momentum in the United States today to include as "families" gay couples with children and other so-called alternative living groups.

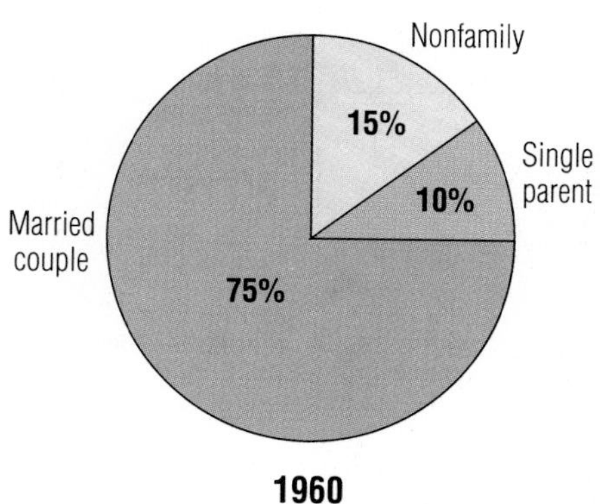

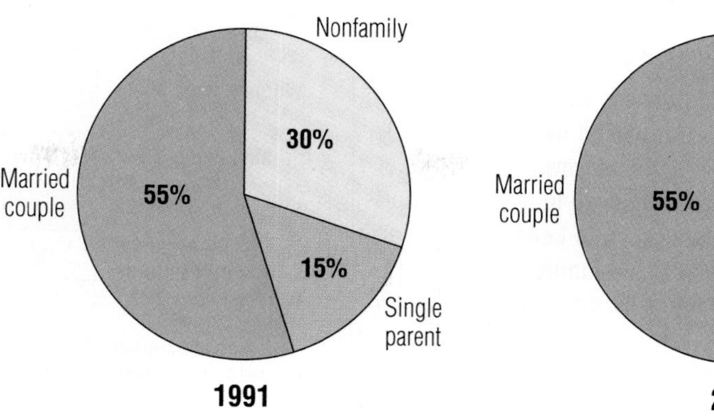

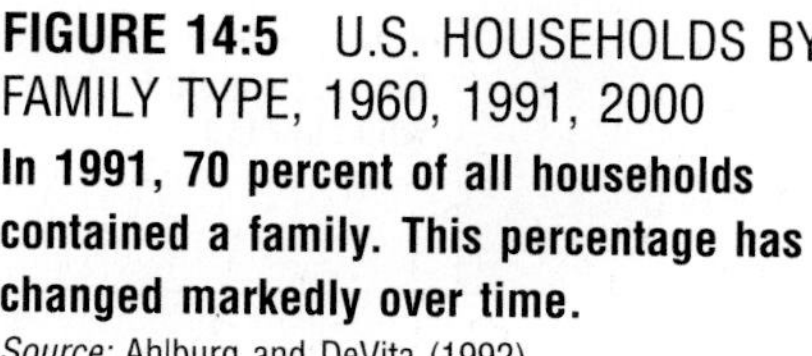

FIGURE 14:5 U.S. HOUSEHOLDS BY FAMILY TYPE, 1960, 1991, 2000
In 1991, 70 percent of all households contained a family. This percentage has changed markedly over time.
Source: Ahlburg and DeVita (1992).

Census Bureau family—a group of two or more persons related by birth, marriage, or adoption and residing together.

household—all persons who inhabit the same housing unit.

householder—the person (or one of the persons) in whose name the housing unit is owned or rented.

Thus, it is clear that the family, like so many other phenomena you have encountered in this book, is a social construction (Gubrium and Holstein, 1990). In the final analysis, the family is what the society says it is.

Even though it seems likely that the definition of the U.S. family will be broadened in the United States eventually, the most commonly used definition in the early 1990s is the Census Bureau's relatively traditional one. A **Census Bureau family** is a group of two persons or more related by birth, marriage, or adoption and residing together. This minimalist family definition is used in the following discussion.

The terms "households" and "families" frequently are used interchangeably in the popular media, but they are very different. A **household** refers to all persons who inhabit a housing unit, such as a house, apartment, single room, or other space used as living quarters. A household may consist of several people who share a dwelling, or one person who lives alone. While all families form households, not all households contain families.

Households typically are divided into two categories: family and nonfamily. A family household must include a **householder** and at least one additional member related to the householder through birth, marriage, or adoption. A nonfamily household is made up of a householder who either lives alone or exclusively with individuals not related to the householder or each other.

In 1991, there were 94 million households in the United States—70 percent of these were family households, and 30 percent were nonfamily households. Families containing married couples comprised 55 percent of all households, while other types of families constituted 15 percent of all households (Figure 14:5).

Nonfamily households include all sorts of individuals and groups. Many of you, for example, live in such households, for they include college students who share a house or an apartment, as well as cohabiting couples. Elderly people living alone also fall into this category. Nonfamily households are becoming ever more common in the United States owing to the aforementioned trends in marriage and divorce (Figure 14:5).

Types of Families

As Figure 14:6 shows, there are five types of families according to the Census Bureau: (1) a married couple with children; (2) a married couple without children; (3) single-parent families headed by a woman; (4) single-parent families headed by a man; and (5) other family types. This latter category includes groupings such as an aging mother living with her adult

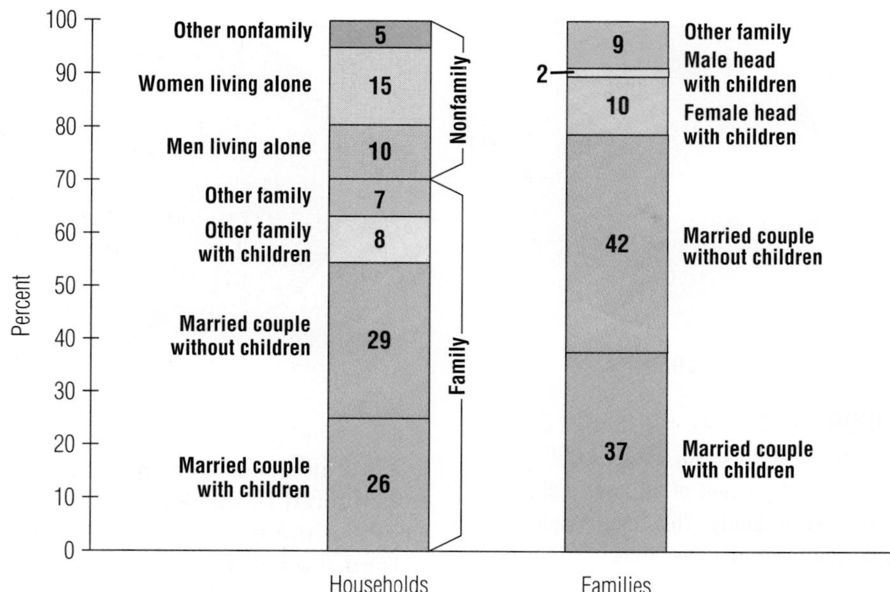

FIGURE 14:6 HOUSEHOLD AND FAMILY COMPOSITION, 1991

The U.S. Bureau of the Census recognizes seven household types and five family types. This figure shows how common each of these types was in 1991. However, it is important to keep in mind that both household and family composition change markedly over time, and that such change has both social causes and consequences.

Source: Ahlburg and DeVita (1992).

son, or grandparents bringing up grandchildren. Note that, in 1991, children were present in fewer than half of all families.

Married-Couple Families with Children

Even though the Ozzie-and-Harriet-style traditional family is fading from the U.S. scene like the vinyl record, married couples with children were still common in 1991, making up 37 percent of all families. Married-couple families with children fall into two categories: (1) intact biological families, including the biological mother and father and their offspring; and (2) step- or blended families.

Although step- or blended families comprise a minority of married-couples-with-children families, about one out of three Americans is presently a stepfamily member such as a stepchild, stepparent, or stepsibling, and this proportion probably will climb to about half by the turn of the century (Larson, 1992). Contrasted with intact biological families, stepfamilies have marriages of shorter duration, fewer children, and lower family income. The latter is true despite the fact that stepfamilies are more likely to have more than one parent in the workforce. Stepfamily marriages have higher divorce rates in part because of greater conflict between members, especially children (Ihinger-Tallman, 1988; Moorman and Hernandez, 1989).

Married-Couple Families without Children

As indicated in Figure 14:6, married-couple families without children are the most common (42 percent) form of family in the United States. This is a radically new situation for the United States, for married-couple families with children were the most prevalent form for our entire history until the 1980s. There are three types of married-couple families without children; namely, preparents, "empty nesters," and nonparents (Mosher and Bachrach, 1982).

Preparents include those married couples who plan to have children but have not done so as yet. Surveys indicate that 80 percent of childless married women in their twenties plan to have children eventually; the proportion for similar women under age 35 is 50 percent (O'Connell, 1991). So, a substantial minority of preparents are destined to become life-long nonparents.

Nonparents, of course, are people who remain childless their entire lives. One of the remarkable recent changes in U.S. family life is that a relatively high proportion of women today will end their reproductive lives childless (or as nonparents). Sociologists can tell this by looking at the proportions of women still childless at various points in their reproductive careers. For example, in the mid-1950s, just 9 percent of women in their late 30s were still childless; in 1990 that proportion (18%) was twice as high. Some people remain nonparents because of infertility problems (McFalls, 1979a; McFalls and McFalls, 1984), but others do so by choice (Veevers, 1980, 1983).

Empty nesters are individuals whose children are grown up and no longer residing in the family home. This group represents about half of all married-couple families without children in the United States. With the aging of the baby boom generation, the relative proportions of empty nesters and, consequently, of married couples without children, will increase significantly.

Single-Parent Families

Figure 14:6 also shows the outcome of another remarkable family trend—the rising prevalence of the single-parent family. In 1970, for example, single-parent families made up only 6 percent of all families. But by 1991, that proportion had climbed to 12 percent. Of these, 10 percent were headed by women and 2 percent by men. Twenty percent of white families with children were headed by a single parent; the proportions for similar African American and Hispanic families were 60 percent and 33 percent, respectively.

Single-parent families are extraordinarily common today compared to the past, owing to many of the aforementioned family-related trends. The most important of these trends are the decline in the proportion currently married (especially as a result of divorce) and the rise in childbearing among unmarried women. As a result, in the early 1990s, nearly 50 percent of young children were reared in a single-parent family during at least part of their childhood (Bumpass, 1990).

Living Arrangements

The powerful forces playing on the family in recent decades have altered greatly the living arrangements of many Americans, especially children, young adults, and the elderly. Many of these now more popular living arrangements are nontraditional in nature.

Children

In 1991, about three-fourths of all children lived with both parents, while one-fourth resided with only one parent. The proportion living with one parent is three times that of the late 1950s.

Sharing a common household or "doubling up" also became much more common in the 1980s and early 1990s, owing to the economic difficulties encountered by many families, particularly single-parent families. Often, young families would move into the home of a grandparent, establishing

BOX 14:2 COLLEGE EXPERIENCE

Show Me the Way to Go Home—Young Adults Refill the Nest

Despite the norm in modern societies since World War II that young adults should establish an independent household prior to marriage (Goldscheider and Goldscheider, 1987), a higher proportion of young adults live at home with their parents today than in recent decades. In 1991, for instance, 54 percent of all 18- to 24-year-olds were still in the family nest compared to just 47 percent in 1970. Contrary to what you might think, adult sons are more likely than daughters to live with their parents. In 1992, for example, nearly two-thirds of the men age 18 to 24 and about half of those age 25 to 29 did so. This phenomenon has come to be called "The Peter Pan Syndrome" (Kiley, 1993).

Analysts cite many reasons why increasing proportions of adult men and women are living with their parents. Several of the reasons are discussed in this chapter, namely (1) the rising age at marriage, which makes the amenities of home especially attractive to young adults; and (2) the high rate of divorce and the declining remarriage rate, which returns legions of economically pressed and emotionally battered survivors to the refuge of the parental home. Other reasons are largely economic. Proportionally more college students stayed at home and went to a local school because the cost of an away-from-home college skyrocketed during the 1980s. Those who did go away often returned home so they could

at least temporary extended families. In half these families both parents are present; in 17 percent, only the mother is; and in 5 percent only the father is. In the remaining 28 percent there are no parents present, and the grandparents rear the grandchildren alone (USBC, 1992b). Often this situation occurs as a result of a drug-related problem of a single parent.

Young Adults

In the not too distant past, a large majority of U.S. adults under age 35 were the head (or spouse of the head) of a separate family household. In 1991, however, fewer than half of young adults that age maintained such a married-couple family household of their own. Young adults today are increasingly either living in the home of their parents (Box 14:2), or are living alone or with roommates (USBC, 1992b). The living arrangement is labeled *cohabitation* when there is a sexual relationship with a roommate of the opposite sex.

The impact of cohabitation on the American family depends primarily on whether it is mostly a prelude or an alternative to marriage (Rindfuss and Vandenheuvel, 1990). In a survey of single individuals who intend to cohabit at some time in their lives, more than 80 percent saw this living arrangement as a test run for marriage. And in 90 percent of cohabiting couples, at least one partner expects this test run to lead to a marriage contract (Bumpass et al., 1991). However, studies show that only about half of first cohabiting unions actually result in marriage (London, 1991). Studies have also reported that married couples who live together first tend to get divorced first (e.g., Schoen, 1992; Thomson and Colella, 1992). For example, the National Survey of Families and Households found that 38 percent of couples who lived together before they married were divorced within 10 years, compared to only 27 percent of couples who married without cohab-

BOX 14:2 COLLEGE EXPERIENCE *continued*

repay huge student loans. Rents and real estate prices also rose sharply during the 1980s; ditto for cars, clothes, and the other consumer goods young adults require. But the salaries of young adults did not grow, and good jobs became more scarce. Young adults tend to remain with their parents longer if the family is an intact biological one as opposed to a step- or single parent one (Goldscheider and Goldscheider, 1989; Mitchell et al., 1989).

Although brief stays are largely problem-free, many analysts believe that adult children should not live with their parents for long periods. The concern is that the young adults will fail to establish a separate adult identity, and can end up with a sense of inadequacy and failure (Kiley, 1993). Another concern is that this phenomenon keeps parents from enjoying financial and personal freedom. Contrary to popular belief, many midlife women greet the departure of their grown children with relief and rising expectations, and marital happiness often increases in the midlife empty nest years (McKinlay and McKinlay, 1986, 1987; Rubin, 1993). Notwithstanding, many parents like having their adult children in the home, and have mostly positive relationships with them (Aquilino and Supple, 1991).

Critical Thinking Questions

1. Do you think the Peter Pan Syndrome poses a serious threat to the family institution? Explain why or why not.
2. What kinds of questions do you think symbolic interactionists are interested in when they study families with adult children?

iting first (Bumpass et al., 1991). Apparently, living together does not help iron out potential marital problems and thus lessen the chance of divorce down the road. But experts caution that cohabitation per se does not cause divorce. Rather, people who choose to cohabit rather than to marry are the kind who are also most likely to call it quits instead of remaining in a less-than-satisfying marriage.

There is a popular perception that young college graduates make up the bulk of cohabiting couples. Not true. It is those individuals who have less education and lower incomes that are most likely to choose this living arrangement, often because they cannot afford to marry. Another perception is that the vast majority of cohabitors live child-free lives. Also not true. About one-half have children, and about one-third have children living with them (Bumpass et al., 1991).

Elderly

Many students believe that the majority of people age 65 and older live in old-age or nursing homes, but this is not true (Mutchler and Burr, 1991). Only a tiny minority (5 percent) lived in such institutions in 1990. Actually, the majority of elderly people live in married-couple households; 54 percent did so in 1991 (Weishaus and Field, 1988). The next most common living arrangement is that of living alone.

But age and gender have a strong influence on the living arrangements of the elderly. About three-fourths of men age 65 to 74 lived with their spouses in 1991, but this proportion dropped to near 60 percent for those age 75 and older. For women, these proportions are much lower: 51 percent and 24 percent, respectively. The difference between men and women is due to the fact that women outlive men by about 7 years. One consequence of this mortality differential is that 34 percent of women age 65 to

Marc Chagall's *Birthday* (1915) captures many of the characteristics of romantic love, especially the feeling of euphoria. Notice that it is the woman who is "sweeping the man off his feet."

74, and 53 percent of those age 75 and older lived alone in 1991. Another consequence is that if one of your parents comes to live with you in their old age, it is twice as likely to be your mother as your father (USBC, 1992a).

Courtship and Marriage

Romantic Love

Most students think that romantic love between males and females is a feature of all societies, but this is not true. In many societies romantic love is unknown, and in others it is regarded as tragic or ridiculous (Jankowiak and Fischer, 1992; Robertson, 1977). Can you understand why some societies consider romantic love to be ridiculous? Think of how your friends act when they are in love. Do they act normally?

Romantic love is difficult to define, but one view of it is that it is a form of mental illness perhaps akin to temporary insanity. Consider the characteristics of romantic love:

1. A strong emotional and physical attachment to the loved one—what a psychiatrist might call "fixation."
2. A feeling of euphoria, not altogether different from "mania."
3. A tendency to idealize the other, to overlook faults and magnify virtues; in short, a form of "irrationality."

Romantic love is, in fact, a form of "derangement." It is an "altered state of consciousness" similar to having mystical experiences, being hypnotized, or "losing your mind" (Wilson, 1985). No wonder people in some societies consider it tragic or ridiculous!

Romantic love is a social creation (Cancian, 1987; Singer, 1987). As Solomon (1987, p. 7) notes:

> Love as we know it is a historically and culturally determined passion, developed only in the last few centuries as the product of socialization and ideas—ideas about sex, marriage, the equality of the sexes, the place of emotion in human life, and the nature and meaning of human life in general. . . . As a product of the history of ideas, love is a passion whose nature changes from century to century, along with the philosophy and theology of the time.

In short, while all humans have an innate genetic capacity for romantic love, societies shape and direct that capacity in different ways (Singer, 1987). This phenomenon is analogous to how societies shape our hunger and sex drives. Thus, the romantic love you experience is different in character from what your grandparents experienced, and is different from what the next generation will experience, especially given the rapid convergence of male and female roles (Cancian, 1987).

Romantic love is found more commonly in industrialized than in preindustrial societies. The latter tend to marry people off for more pragmatic reasons such as the solidification of economic arrangements or political alliances (Xiaohe and Whyte, 1990). But even in industrialized societies practical considerations often are still important, as they are in the U.S. upper class and subcultures like the Amish. As Kephart (1976, p. 31) notes: "Amish youth place minimal importance on romantic love and physical attractiveness, favoring instead those traits which will make for a successful farm life: willingness to work, cheerfulness, reliability, and the like."

But for the most part romantic love is the basis of the U.S. mate selection system (Bailey, 1989; Whyte, 1990). We choose our mates when we are in a "fog" or "deranged" state. And after romantic love runs its course in a year or two, many discover that their mate is not the near "ideal" person they thought they married. Given our high divorce rates, could it be that some other mate selection system might be better? How about arranged marriages with "clear-headed" parents or matchmakers making the selection? Could you put up with such a system? Possibly not. But it is worth

The Kazakh nomads of China play a game called Catch the Maiden before they marry. In this horse-back courting ritual, the man gallops after the woman in pursuit of a kiss. If he succeeds, she then gallops after him and tries to strike him with a riding crop. This ritual has a practical element. On the high plains of Xinjiang Province competent horse riding is essential, and this game is a pragmatic test of a potential spouse's riding skill.

noting that matchmaking is a thriving business in the United States, and many clients are affluent professionals too busy to go mate hunting (Ahuvia and Adelman, 1992; Brand, 1988).

Mate Selection Restrictions

In actuality, romantic love plays far less of a role in mate selection in the United States than most students think. This is due in part to norms concerning suitable age and to sheer geographic limitations or propinquity. It is also due to endogamous norms and homogamous predispositions that act to restrict our choice. Endogamy means marriage between persons having similar social backgrounds such as race or class; its opposite, exogamy, means marriage between persons with dissimilar backgrounds (Table 14: 1). Homogamy refers to marriages between brides and grooms who share personal traits such as personality and appearance. Heterogamy refers to partners with different traits (Kephart and Jedlecka, 1991). If there is no endogamy, exogamy, homogamy, or heterogamy, random mating exists; that is, an individual has an equal probability of marrying all eligible mates. But if these things are present, assortive mating exists; that is, an individual has a higher probability of marrying similar or dissimilar mates than would be the case if random mating were in effect.

random mating—the situation in which an individual has an equal probability of marrying all eligible mates.

assortive mating—the situation in which an individual has a higher probability of marrying similar or dissimilar mates than would be the case if random mating were in effect.

Endogamous Norms

The principal endogamous norms that restrict mate selection in the United States are based on race, ethnicity, religion, and class.

Race. The next time you attend a dance at your school, observe the relative number of interracial couples present. If your school is typical, you will find a relatively low proportion. This is because of norms in U.S. society that say people should date and marry others of the same race (Labov and Jacobs, 1986). And as the mixing of your fellow college mates indicates, this is a powerful norm, eliciting a high level of compliance. In 1991, for example, only 1.9 percent of married couples had interracial marriages, albeit up from a miniscule .7 percent in 1970 (USBC, 1992b). The 1991 proportion is a tiny fraction of what would be expected if random mating existed.

African American/white marriages are particularly suppressed by endogamous norms (Tenzer, 1990). Indeed, if there were random mating, about 10 percent of all U.S. marriages would be between African Americans and whites. In 1991, however, only four-tenths of 1 percent of marriages were African American/white ones, or 25 times fewer than you would expect on the basis of chance (USBC, 1992b). Of these marriages, 75 percent were between African American men and white women; only 25 percent joined white men with African American women. The relatively small proportion of African American/white marriages in 1991 was, however, almost three times greater than that in 1970.

Marriages between whites or African Americans and other racial groups such as Asian Americans, Native Americans, and Eskimos also are suppressed by endogamous norms. In one study about 70 percent of Korean Americans, 60 percent of Chinese Americans, and 40 percent of Japanese Americans married within their own racial group (Krikorian, 1990). Box 12:2, which recounts the story of a young Chinese woman who brings her white fiancé to her parent's home to meet them, illustrates how the family institution influences young adults to comply with these racial norms.

opposite page
Even though endogamous norms restrict mate selection in the United States, interracial and interethnic marriage has increased dramatically in recent years, owing in part to the latest waves of immigration discussed in Chapters 12 and 20. In an effort to dramatize this phenomenon, the editors of *Time* magazine used computerized "morphing" to create the offspring that might result from the mating of seven men and seven women of various ethnic and racial backgrounds. The various combinations of offspring are shown in this fascinating chart. *Time* suggests that this chart is a remarkable preview of the "new faces of America," a country destined to become the twenty-first century's "first multicultural society."

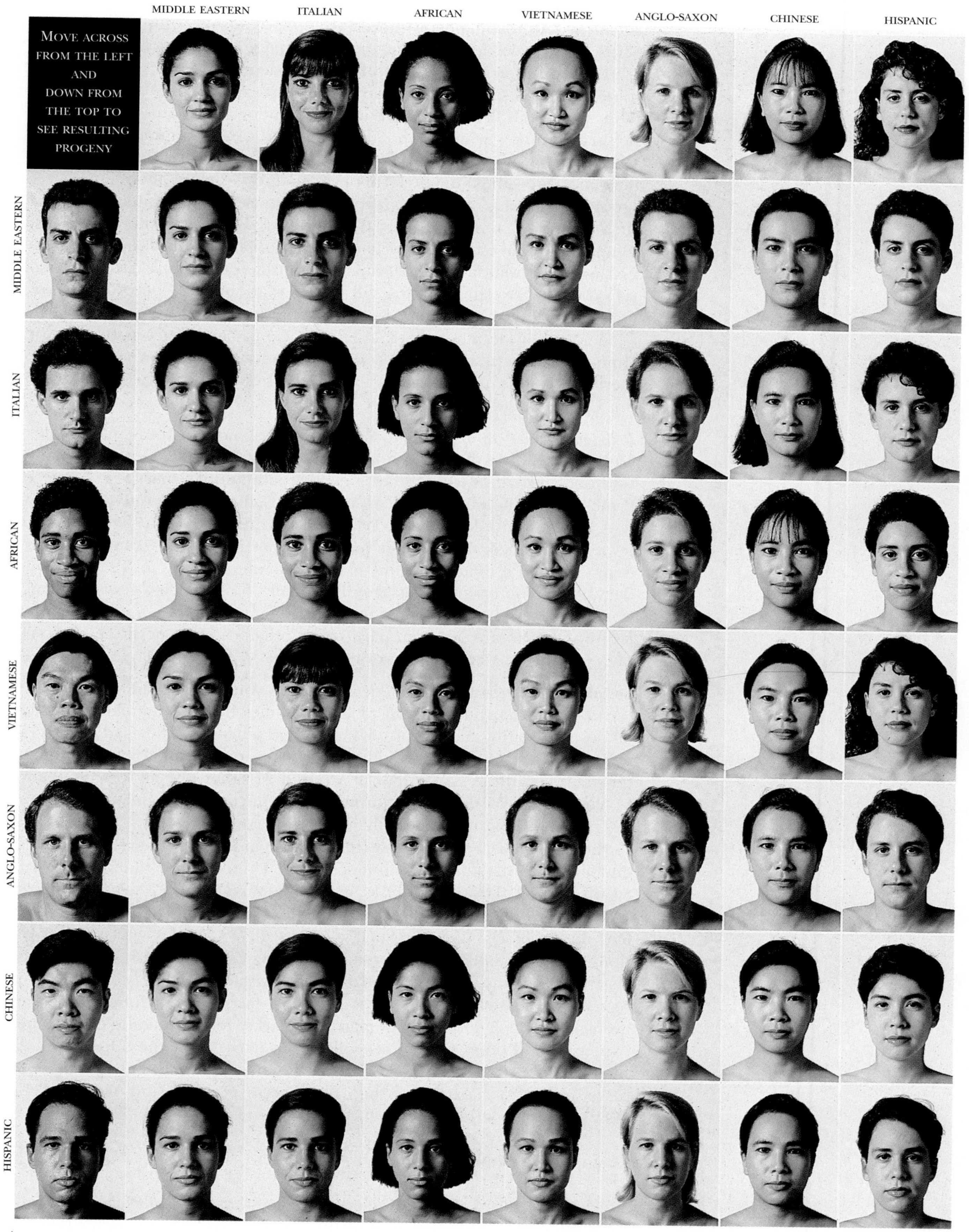

MOVE ACROSS FROM THE LEFT AND DOWN FROM THE TOP TO SEE RESULTING PROGENY

MIDDLE EASTERN | ITALIAN | AFRICAN | VIETNAMESE | ANGLO-SAXON | CHINESE | HISPANIC

MIDDLE EASTERN

ITALIAN

AFRICAN

VIETNAMESE

ANGLO-SAXON

CHINESE

HISPANIC

Ethnicity. Although not as powerful as racial norms, ethnic norms also restrict mate selection (Schoen and Wooldredge, 1989; Spickard, 1989). In 1991, for example, only 16 percent of all married Hispanics were married to non-Hispanics, compared to the 93 percent expected on the basis of random mating (USBC, 1992b). But ethnic endogamy norms are far more powerful among groups who, like Hispanics, have immigrated to the United States most recently. There is a much higher prevalence of ethnic intermarriage—the ultimate form of assimilation—among more established groups. Americans of European ancestry, for example, are intermarrying at such high rates that eventually these groups, as we now know them, will disappear. About 80 percent of Italian Americans and Polish Americans, for instance, who wed in the 1980s married outside their ethnic group (Krikorian, 1990). Nevertheless, this still means that about 20 percent did not, many times the proportion expected if random mating were absolute.

Incidentally, despite racial and ethnic norms that restrict mate selection almost everywhere, the high level of international migration (Chapter 20) inevitably results in increases in the numbers of multicultural marriages in the United States and elsewhere.

Religion. Religion also acts to restrict mate choice. In the United States, Catholics tend to marry Catholics, Protestants tend to marry Protestants (although there is substantial interdenominational marriage between Protestants, such as Episcopalians marrying Lutherans), Jews tend to marry Jews, and so on (Glenn, 1982, 1984; Kalmijn, 1991b). About 60 percent of Jews, for instance, marry other Jews, a proportion about 20 times greater than expected if random mating existed (Cowan and Cowan, 1989; Schneider, 1989). The opening passage of Chapter 15, in which a Jewish college woman expresses a preference for Jewish men, provides a glimpse of why individuals who are not even particularly religious often nevertheless comply with religious endogamy norms.

Social Class. In a 1991 incident in India, a young man and woman were tortured and hanged in front of their families because they had violated taboos segregating higher-caste Hindus from outcastes. They had eloped in defiance of age-old bans forbidding marriage—or any contact for that matter—between these classes. Police arrested 37 other people for complicity in this crime. While these "untouchable" practices were made illegal in 1947, they still persist, especially in rural villages.

Although not nearly as powerful as those in Indian villages, social class endogamy norms still have influence in the United States (Kalmijn, 1991a; South, 1991). The upper class tends to marry within the upper class (Aldrich, 1988), the middle class tends to marry within the middle class, and the lower class tends to marry within the lower class—all in proportions greater than expected if random mating existed. One reason for this class endogamy is the tendency for people with similar levels of education to marry (Kalmijn, 1991b; Mare, 1991). In fact, a latent function of the average college is to provide a marriage market for the middle class; some expensive and often prestigious colleges do likewise for the upper class. A higher proportion of interclass marriages that do occur involve women marrying up in class rather than the reverse (Schoen and Wooldredge, 1989).

Homogamous Predisposition

You have all heard the mate selection adage that "opposites attract." And some famous couples seem to bear this out—consider, for example, brawny Arnold Schwarzenegger and brainy Maria Shriver; or beautiful, unschooled

Marilyn Monroe and homely, bookish Arthur Miller. You probably know of some "odd couples" yourself. But a sociologist would ask whether these couples were the rule or the exception. Of course, the competing hypothesis is that likes attract—that, for instance, aggressive people marry aggressive people and introverts marry introverts. Which is it?

The answer from sociological research is that, unlike magnets, likes attract among people. After doing a review of the literature, Buss (1985) concluded that there is a tendency for people to marry those similar to themselves in almost every physical and personality variable. Tall people tend to marry tall people; obese people tend to marry obese people; blue-eyed people tend to marry blue-eyed people; intelligent people tend to marry intelligent people; aggressive people tend to marry aggressive people; introverts tend to marry introverts, and so on. These tendencies are called **assortive narcissism**. Incidentally, it has been suggested that one reason for their "likeness" is that spouses become more similar in attributes such as personality the longer they live together. However, research indicates that spouses actually become more dissimilar over time (Buss, 1985).

assortive narcissism—the tendency for individuals to marry someone who is similar to themselves in almost every physical and personality variable.

Age

U.S. society has norms that stipulate that people should marry people of approximately the same age (Atkinson and Glass, 1985; Vera et al., 1985). For women, the mate should be the same age or up to a few years older; for men, the same age or within a few years younger. How powerful is this norm? Very! Few people violate it. Only about 5 percent of women, for example, marry men more than 1 year younger than themselves. But, of course, college students are no strangers to this norm—how common is it for freshman men to date senior women on your campus?

Propinquity

propinquity—spatial nearness.

The term **propinquity** is just sociological jargon for spatial nearness. It refers to the fact that people only have social interaction with an infinitesimal fraction of all eligible mates because they never even meet the vast majority of other possibilities. One classic study in the 1940s found that about 80 percent of urban respondents married someone who lived within a radius of five blocks from home. Propinquity is not nearly as powerful a factor in mate selection today as it was in the 1940s, but it is still significant. One fairly common way propinquity works today is that people who move away from their home area are much more likely than chance might dictate to marry someone at the new area who also comes from the same home area.

Discussion

Of course, these mate restriction factors are not independent of each other. Residential neighborhoods are often class-segregated, so a potential mate who lives nearby is also likely to be the same class as you (as well as the same religion, ethnicity, etc.). Similarly, the color of your eyes is not independent of your race or ethnicity. However, although all of these factors are interrelated, they each have their own separate effects on mate selection when the other factors are controlled.

Think of a "pie chart" that represents all possible mates. Propinquity eliminates all but a tiny sliver of that pie. Then age norms subdivide the sliver again, leaving just a tiny sliver of the tiny sliver. In like fashion, race, ethnicity, religion, class, and assortive narcissism successively reduce the dwindling sliver. At the end of this process there are only a handful of possible mates remaining, and at that point romantic love makes the choice. While this scenario may be somewhat exaggerated, the underlying point—that romantic love plays much less of a role in mate selection in the United States than most people think—is still valid. Perhaps that is why arranged marriages are not the abominations most college students believe. After all, in most societies with arranged marriage, parents typically are limited by a similar set of restrictions in making their choice.

DIVORCE

Rates and Causes

It was noted earlier that some 52 percent of the marriages that take place today eventually end in divorce. If separations, desertions, and disrupted long-term cohabitations are considered, the proportion of all marriages and quasi-marriages that are disrupted is higher yet, possibly as high as two-thirds (Martin and Bumpass, 1989). By world and by U.S. historical standards, this is an extraordinarily high level of marital disruption, one that apparently has become an intrinsic part of contemporary U.S. family life (Martin and Bumpass, 1989; Riley, 1991).

The people most likely to divorce include those who marry as teenagers, those who marry after a brief courtship, those who marry as a result of an unintended pregnancy, and those who marry individuals with substance-abuse problems or who themselves have such problems (Morgan and Rindfuss, 1985; NCHS, 1991e). People who do not follow the homogamous norms noted earlier, and who thus marry people with dissimilar social backgrounds, also have relatively high rates of divorce. So do those whose

Americans today place a high value on successful marriages, and divorce is seen as an acceptable alternative to unsuccessful ones. It is generally conceded that some couples are far better off ending conflict-ridden marriages rather than trying to preserve them. Nevertheless, divorce leads to many problems for society and individuals. Edward Munch's *Ashes* (1894) eloquently depicts the anguish often caused by divorce.

spouses failed to receive the approval of the formers' family and friends prior to marriage. Lower-class people have higher rates of divorce than middle-class people, though financially independent women are prone to divorce, not only because they have the financial wherewithal to do it, but often because of the time conflicts and other problems inherent to a dual-career family (Glenn and Shelton, 1985; Vaughan, 1986).

Many Americans believe that more divorces occur around the seventh year of marriage than at any other time, owing in part to the misinformation spread by the classic Marilyn Monroe film, *The Seven Year Itch.* But, in actuality, far more divorces occur in the second and third years of marriage than at any other time. Obviously, these marriages failed almost immediately—it takes the spouses one year to realize they married a "dud," and one or two years to get the divorce. The seventh year does have some significance, however. It is the median duration of failed marriages—half fail before, and half afterward. The early demise of so many marriages is the reason why the divorce rate for both men and women is highest in their late teens and early twenties (Heaton, 1991; NCHS, 1991c).

Reasons for High Divorce Rate

There are many explanations for the high divorce rate in the United States (Preston, 1984; White, 1990). The first is that compared to the past there are now increased incentives and resources to terminate a marriage. Husbands often have an incentive because their disposable income typically rises greatly after the divorce. Many wives also have an incentive because the higher potential earnings of educated women today make it relatively less attractive for them to be a housewife and to rear children. Many spouses have another incentive because it is increasingly possible for them to give up the economic benefits of joint living; by setting up separate residences, each spouse can buy more freedom from the expectations and needs of the other. Similarly, public programs for economically deprived families, particularly Aid to Families with Dependent Children, increase the incentive for divorce because these programs often financially penalize impoverished couples who stay together.

The second reason for higher divorce nowadays is that modernization has concentrated more people in high-density urban areas, has resulted in less gender segregation in the workplace, and has boosted the fraction of jobs that deal with people (service) rather than with raw materials and machines (manufacturing). These developments have brought spouses into contact with a greatly increased number of alternative mates. In short, a much higher proportion of spouses today compared to the past have both the *resources* and the *opportunity* to act on a preference to end a marriage.

The third explanation for the high divorce rates of today is that relatively more people have such a preference to terminate their marriage (Glenn, 1991). Preston (1984, p. 445) notes that divorce has risen dramatically because of "the increased prevalence of a world view that legitimizes calculations based upon individual self-interest." He refers to historical research that documents the rise of **affective individualism** as modernization progresses. Affective individualism is defined as the recognition of the self as a unique being with the right to pursue selfish goals (Cherlin, 1983; Stone, 1982). People who hold such individualistic values are less constrained by the well-being of a spouse or children to remain in an unsatisfactory marriage or even in a satisfactory but less than optimal one (Bumpass, 1990). Public opinion polls, for example, report that, unlike

affective individualism—the recognition of the self as a unique being with the right to pursue selfish goals.

in the past, the vast majority of men and women today believe that divorce is an acceptable solution to mere marital "incompatibility," even if the couple has children (Thornton, 1989; Thornton and Freedman, 1983). (Nevertheless, it should be pointed out that many in the United States still choose to remain in stable unhappy marriages [Heaton and Albrecht, 1991]).

Another reason for the upsurge in divorce is changed attitudes toward it. In the past divorce was considered an act of failure, irresponsibility, and immorality, and divorced people were treated as social outcasts. However, these negative attitudes have decreased greatly over the past several decades. Americans are now much more inclined to view divorce as a solution for bad and even marginal marriages, and divorced people are now less excluded from the normal patterns of social life.

Other reasons for today's extraordinarily high divorce rates include (1) the passage of no-fault divorce laws, which make divorce much easier to obtain; (2) the aforementioned postponement of childbearing and the decline in family size, which facilitates divorce—particularly for women; (3) the decline in the amount of time parents and children work and play together; and (4) increasing sexual permissiveness, which raises the odds that people will look outside their marriages for sexual satisfaction, thus increasing the probability of divorce in the process (Fisher, 1992; Kahn and London, 1991).

THE CHANGING ROLES OF FAMILY MEMBERS

The traditional family of the 1950s contained seemingly clear and well-defined roles: the breadwinner, the homemaker, and the dependent children. But the social changes discussed in this and other chapters (e.g., technological change, the sexual revolution, and gender role changes) have profoundly altered many family roles. The pace of change is so fast that there are no longer any clear guidelines about how to properly play the new and ever-evolving family roles.

Roles of Women

Chapter 13 has already outlined the fundamental changes that have taken place in the lives of women. The widespread participation of women—including wives and mothers—in the labor force, probably the most important of these changes, also has been one of the key forces responsible for the restructuring of the U.S. family (McLaughlin et al., 1989) (see Box 14:3). Working women today have to play many roles simultaneously (e.g., wife, mother, career woman, homemaker), and there simply are not enough hours in the day to do them all to perfection (Googins, 1991). Only about a third of full-time working mothers, for example, feel that they spend enough time with their family (National Commission on Children, 1991). In short, the modern family woman has become a sort of juggler, trying to keep a set of demanding roles in motion all at the same time (Spitze, 1988).

second shift—the other "job" gainfully employed wives and mothers have in the home, doing the bulk of household tasks.

Despite the fact that wives and mothers increasingly work outside the home, they continue to do the bulk of household tasks, a phenomenon known as the **second shift** (Goldscheider and Waite, 1991; Hochschild, 1989). Husbands and children do help with household tasks, but wives do

J. G. Brown's *Meditation* shows a turn-of-the-century housewife stealing away from her arduous duties for a moment of rest and reflection. Traditionally, a wife's role in the family included the provision of virtually all the domestic services. Although family roles have changed substantially in recent decades, wives still do much more housework and child care than husbands do.

In the film, *Terminator 2: Judgment Day,* the android played by Arnold Schwarzenegger becomes nearly human by the movie's end. Pittman (1993) suggests that a similar humanizing process happens to fathers, especially when the men perform the routine tasks of child care when their children are young.

the lion's share of these tasks except for yardwork. The proportion of household tasks performed by husbands and children does increase, however, in families where the wife earns more than $25,000. Family structure also has a bearing on the division of labor within the household. In mother-only families, for instance, children assume more of the load (Goldscheider and Waite, 1991).

Roles of Men

Job descriptions for men also are changing in the modern family (Rubin, 1992; Thornton, 1989). Traditionally, men were merely expected to be family providers, protectors, and peacemakers. Today men increasingly are supposed to play more varied roles (Kimball, 1988; Sanoff et al., 1985). As Furstenberg (1988, p. 193) notes: ". . . fatherhood is in vogue. . . .

BOX 14:3 GENDER AND SOCIAL CHANGE

The New Realities of the U.S. Family

There is really no need for a "Gender and Social Change" box in this chapter because the topic has been touched on at least indirectly on every page. Women in general and the feminist movement in particular have had a profound and pervasive impact on every aspect of the family in recent decades. Here we will simply tick off the major family changes that have occurred since 1950 for which women are in whole or in part responsible:

- the increase in the proportion of women (and, consequently, of men) who never marry;
- the increase in the average age at marriage;
- the decrease in childbearing and the increase in abortion;
- the increase in unmarried childbearing;
- the increase in the proportion of children in child care;
- the increase in the proportion of wives and mothers in the workforce;
- the increase in divorce; and
- the decrease in remarriage.

The last change—the decrease in remarriage—is perhaps least known. But between 1970 and 1988, the rate of remarriage in the United States dropped by more than 40 percent (NCHS, 1991d), and financially independent women have had a lot to do with it. Indeed, Goldscheider (1993) notes that women's lack of interest in remarriage is "the real revolution" of the past two decades.

Women have changed the family so much over the past four decades that it is difficult for them and, probably even more so, for men, to keep up. Making predictions about future family changes is a hazardous business, but one thing for sure is that U.S. women have not yet finished making changes. One likely thrust in the future will be a more equitable "manning" of the second shift.

Critical Thinking Questions

1. Aside from persuading men to do more of the second shift work, what other family changes do you think women will encourage in the future?
2. Sociologists note that societies must reach a proper balance between satisfying its own needs and those of the individual. Is it possible, as some functionalists suggest, that the profound family changes noted above may have shifted the balance too far in the direction of the individual? Is there, for instance, a level of divorce that is too high for a society to be healthy? Similarly, is there a level of childbearing that is too low?

Television, magazines, and movies herald the coming of the modern father—the nurturant, caring, and emotionally attuned parent. . . . Today's father is at least as adept at changing diapers as changing tires" (cited in Ahlburg and DeVita, 1992).

As this chapter's "Personal Perspective" attests, some fathers today do play these expanded roles and are much more involved in child care and parenting than were their own fathers. But such "modern" fathers are still very much in the minority. In the mid-1980s, for example, only 15 percent of fathers played the role of primary child-care provider for children under age 5 in families in which the mother worked (O'Connell and Bachu, 1990).

Most men still perform their traditional role of principal family breadwinner, however, providing on average nearly 70 percent of family income (Presser, 1989). Notwithstanding, a great many fathers who live apart from their children fail to provide adequately for their children's financial well-being (Lester, 1991; Seltzer, 1991).

Roles of Children

Children's lives are much more variable, complex, and uncertain today than they were in the past (Alwin, 1989). Young children in intact biological families often have to adjust to a series of child-care institutions, and older children frequently are forced to take on adult responsibilities earlier (Caplow, 1991; Hill, 1987). Children of all ages in divorced, separated, or blended families face even more adjustments (Hewlett, 1991). They have to adjust to variable family income as they move from one kind of family to another, and they have to cope with a changing cast of family members (Furstenberg and Cherlin, 1991).

Most children in the United States today now experience some form of child care away from parents and the family home (Belsky, 1990). In the 1990s, about two-thirds of children younger than age 6 have some kind of child-care experience, including 56 percent of children younger than age 3. Of course, mothers who work outside the home utilize child care the most. But about one in three full-time homemakers also place their children in child care for at least part of the time (Dawson and Cain, 1990). The latter do so not just to lighten their own child-care responsibilities, but because high-quality child care, especially between the ages of 2 and 5, has been found to benefit children's language and social development (National Research Council, 1990). Poor-quality child care, and possibly child care before age 2, however, can harm a child's development (Belsky and Eggebeen, 1991).

Most children age 5 to 12 receive afterschool supervision either from a parent or from sponsors of organized activities such as sports or music lessons. An increasing number of children in this age bracket, however, have no afterschool supervision at all (Cain and Hofferth, 1989). Such "latchkey children" make up only 3 percent of all 6-year-olds but as many as 40 percent of 12-year-olds (Hofferth, 1991).

Many parents rely on older children, particularly teenagers, to take care of their younger siblings after school (Divine-Hawkins, 1992). Teenagers today are more adult-like than their predecessors of a few decades ago in other ways as well (Gecas and Seff, 1990). For example, they are more socially independent of their parents, and are more likely to have full- or part-time jobs and the financial muscle that accompanies them (Vigoda, 1993). They are also more likely to get pregnant (Dryfoos, 1990).

Stepfamily Roles

Roles in stepfamilies or blended families are particularly complex, ambiguous, and problematic in part because such families are in a sense "incomplete institutions," deficient in clear guidelines for role performance (Cherlin, 1978). Stepparents, for example, do not have the qualifications or the status to play the role of mother or father to their spouse's children (Ambert, 1989). Often they have to be satisfied by fashioning a role that is partly friend, confidant, diplomat, and negotiator (Pasley and Ihinger-Tallman, 1988). Similarly, children often have to make up the role of stepchild as they go (Ochiltree, 1990). It is not at all clear to them how to relate to their parent's new spouse or lover, particularly when there are a succession of them; or how to deal with stepsiblings or a host of other steprelatives (Furstenberg and Cherlin, 1991; Ihinger-Tallman, 1988).

Divorce and remarriage tend to multiply the positions in an individual's family network (see next section), but the role relationships between the individual and these new relatives are weaker than those in an intact nuclear family network (Coleman and Ganong, 1990). Furstenberg and Cherlin (1991, p. 95) describe these step roles as a "thinner form of kinship" because the various parties have less of a stake in each other's well-being. It is unlikely, for instance, that stepchildren will feel the same sense of obligation toward caring for their stepparent in old age as children do with respect to their biological parents.

FAMILY NETWORKS: THE PERSONAL EFFECTS OF INTIMACY

According to Aristotle, isolation is a state reserved for beasts and gods. Although there are disturbing signs that social isolation is on the increase in the United States, most people avoid that state by maintaining regular interpersonal ties with at least some family members. An impressive body of research indicates that these seemingly innocuous contacts with relatives may indeed make lives less bestial.

The literature on the individual impact of family members has emerged from studies of personal networks, which analyze the overall pattern of social contacts, including friends, coworkers, and neighbors as well as relatives (see Chapter 4). While the evidence arrayed in this chapter has shown the significance of the presence—or absence—of an immediate family member, social network research suggests that such effects do not stop at the front door of the family household (Wellerman and Berkowitz, 1988). Each person has a family tree that spreads into the social world, which is selectively pruned by deciding which cousins, grandparents, and aunts *not* to speak to between Christmases. Social factors impose themselves on this social selection process. City-dwellers, for instance, are in regular contact with fewer relatives than are people living in rural areas. Income and education both appear to be inversely related to relative contact; that

Hispanic families in the United States are of many types: Puerto Rican, Cuban, Mexican American, Central American, and South American. These ethnic subgroups differ in family demographics and social class. Cuban families, for instance, tend to be middle class with relatively few children; Mexican-American families tend to be poor with relatively many children; and Puerto Rican families tend to be poor and female-headed. Traditionally, Hispanic families have emphasized family cohesion, and have relied heavily on extended kinship networks for child care, financial assistance, and emotional support (Collins and Coltrane, 1991). Carmen Lomas Garza's *Tamalada* ("making tamales") (1988) shows such a familial social network.

is, those with less of these social resources associate with more relatives. Marital status also affects the selection process (Fischer et al., 1989). For example, divorce often results in less interaction with the noncustodial parent's side of the family, typically the father's parents and relations (Furstenberg and Spanier, 1985). Regardless of the individual's social position, kin are privileged members of the social network in two respects: First, they are generally the object of the strongest emotional ties; second, relatives are the favored source of all forms of material aid.

Families share many kinds of resources. This sharing takes the form of gifts, loans, housing, and services like child- or elder care (Parish et al., 1991). This intergenerational support and assistance occurs in every stage of the life cycle. Children obviously receive family resources, but adults do too (Rossi and Rossi, 1990). Many men and women receive substantial family assistance in their transition from youth to adulthood and throughout the latter period (Rosenzweig and Wolpin, 1990). And adult children, usually daughters, often assume the caregiver role for elderly parents (Abel, 1991; Allen, 1989; Spitz and Logan, 1990). On the other hand, grandparents frequently provide financial help, child care, and other services to their children and grandchildren (Bengtson, 1985; Cherlin and Furstenberg, 1986).

Social networks are related to divorce as both cause and consequence. For example, married couples who move away from family and friends have relatively higher rates of divorce because they receive less support from their social network (Gerstel, 1987; Thornton, 1985). On the other hand, one consequence of divorce is that divorced individuals often experience loneliness and isolation because U.S. social networks are designed primarily with the requirements of married couples in mind. Another consequence is the child's loss of contact with the noncustodial parent's side of the family.

Aside from these somewhat obvious features, kin networks have effects upon us that are a bit more mysterious. Notably, patterns of contact with relatives are reflected in illness patterns. A mass of evidence documents the link between more social support from relatives and better health (see Chapter 18). Even if other disease risk factors are controlled, cohesive kin networks seem to shield people from heart attack, pregnancy complications . . . even death (Pearson, 1986). Research has also revealed a link between kinship and inequality. Lower-class individuals rely very heavily on their kin networks as a kind of social defense against economic uncertainty (USBC, 1992b), and individuals from every class draw heavily on relatives as a source of information leading to jobs. Finally, kin networks are a key to one's level of mental anguish (Umberson, 1992). While relatives can clearly be a source of stress (as in a problem child or the death of a spouse), they also have the proven power to buffer us from stress and to help us cope with "the slings and arrows of outrageous fortune."

THEORETICAL PERSPECTIVES ON FAMILY

Functionalism

As their name indicates, functionalists focus on the aforementioned traditional functions families perform. In particular, functionalists examine the relative ability of different kinds of families to perform these six tasks. They note, for example, that the extended family contains a large pool of potential caregivers for its dependent members: small children, the handicapped, the old, and the infirm. It can, for instance, easily provide support for the wife (with dependent children) of a husband-father who is incapacitated, missing, or dead. By contrast, the nuclear family can be devastated by such an occurrence. Similarly, the extended family provides a secure place and a respected role for the elderly, whereas the nuclear family frequently supplies neither.

Functionalists also focus on the extent to which the U.S. family—in all its forms—performs the six traditional functions. They generally conclude that the U.S. family is increasingly unable to fulfill them (Blankenhorn et al., 1991). Functionalists stress, for example, that the birthrate has been below the replacement rate for the past 20 years; that premarital, extramarital, and nonmarital sexuality are rampant, and increasingly outside of family control; and that many children do not have adequate love or material security (Popenoe, 1991; Preston, 1990).

The family's inability or unwillingness to perform the traditional functions adequately has contributed to one of modern-day's central features—the tendency for the family to gradually give up many of its functions to other more specialized institutions (Popenoe, 1988). For example, the family has given up much of its socialization function to the educational institution, to child-care providers, and to the media. Social security can also be viewed as the government encroaching on the traditional family role of providing material security for the elderly (Carlson, 1988). Indeed, some functionalists believe that the growing welfare state in the United States, which was originally intended to strengthen families, is gradually taking over family functions, and may eventually replace the family in many people's lives as the central institution (Popenoe, 1991).

Conflict Theory

Conflict theorists emphasize that families are not just social machines performing set functions, but are battlegrounds where all sorts of groups compete for dominance. In this last decade of the twentieth century the war over the family has such a high media profile that you probably already know who is fighting whom and why. Husbands and wives wrangle over such matters as gender roles, sex, child care, and the second shift (Pateman, 1988); divorced spouses duel over property and children (Goldberg and Kremen, 1990); parents battle their children over the latter's socialization, autonomy, and marriage choices; groups fight to impose their own vision of the ideal family on society, contesting issues such as abortion and alternative lifestyles; and so on. With all this fighting going on, it's a wonder that the family gets anything accomplished!

Family battles are not always simply metaphorical. Sociological research in recent years has unearthed an astonishing amount of actual violence between husbands and wives, between parents and their children, and between all other possible combinations of family members (Agnew and Huguley, 1989; Knudsen and Miller, 1991; Levinson, 1989). Conflict theorists note that wife battering, for example, occurs in part because of the traditional gender role stereotypes of male dominance and female subservience (Straus and Hotaling, 1980). They also contend that the reasons state and local governments often fail to help battered women is that the interests of women have not traditionally been considered in the design of the political, or for that matter, any other institution (Kurz, 1989; Rothman, 1989).

Jacob A. Riis is famous for his unflinching photographs of tenement life in New York City around the beginning of the twentieth century. His photos of the darkest corners of American life helped the public change its attitude concerning poverty from the Victorian notion that it was an evil to be condemned to the reformer's idea that it was a situation to be remedied (Lacayo, 1989). Riis's stark photographs often focused on family problems. This poignant photo of homeless children finding shelter on a sidewalk grate is testimony to the fact that the phenomenon of homeless children today is nothing new.

Symbolic Interactionism

Interactionist researchers focus on how people actually interact in family-related matters (Aldous, 1977; Menaghan, 1991). For example, much of the sociological research on the initiation of mate selection has an interactionist perspective. Sociologists observe such behavior in all sorts of places, from singles bars in the United States (Givens, 1983; Perper, 1985) to courtship rituals in pre-industrial societies (Donahue, 1985). They have discovered an orderly pattern to "putting the make" on someone that varies surprisingly little cross-culturally. The pattern consists of spoken and unspoken signals, which operate both in heterosexual and homosexual courtship. These signals have been summarized in rough chronological order by Money (1988):

(1) Establishing eye contact
(2) Holding the gaze
(3) Blushing
(4) Averting the gaze, eyelids drooping
(5) Shyly returning the gaze
(6) Squinting and smiling
(7) Vocal intonation animated
(8) Vocal acceleration and breathiness
(9) Vocal loudness
(10) Vocal exaggeration of trivialities
(11) Laughter
(12) Rotating to face one another
(13) Moving closer to one another
(14) Wetting the lips
(15) Garment adjustment exposing more skin
(16) Gesturing and touching, as if inadvertently
(17) Mirroring each other's gestures
(18) Synchronizing body movement

The interactionist perspective has also been used to predict divorce. By watching married couples interact in an experimental situation, one group of researchers was able to predict marital breakups within three years with 94 percent accuracy. The marriage was almost always doomed, for example, if the interaction included criticism, defensiveness, and contempt, and if it resulted in the withdrawal of one spouse from the other. Surprisingly, fighting and expressing anger were not "divorce predictors" (Gottman, 1993).

Integrating the Theories

In their study of the family, functionalists, conflict theorists, and symbolic interactionists *think critically* about different facets of the same phenomena. Consider, for example, wife abuse. As discussed, conflict theorists see wife abuse as a natural outcome of a society that values and teaches male dominance and female subservience. Functionalists argue that violence between husbands and wives is related paradoxically to a family function; namely, the provision of affection and companionship. The family is the most intimate environment, a place where one's emotional needs can be expressed and where they are supposed to be fulfilled. But if these emotional needs are not satisfied entirely, people often feel intensely betrayed and violence can erupt. Finally, symbolic interactionists see much wife abuse as a product of faulty interaction. They contend that wife batterers do not have the requisite social skills for dealing with women. Because they cannot win arguments with their wives verbally, they often resort to "punching them out" (Stacey and Shupe, 1984).

SUBJECTIVE DIMENSION OF FAMILY PROBLEMS

Most people in the United States say that their family is one of the most important facets of their lives, and that they are highly satisfied with their own family (see Table 14:2). Nevertheless, most also believe the family institution itself is in serious trouble—that it is "deteriorating," even "dying" (Caplow, 1991).

The belief that the family is dying is not just a modern or recent one. It was debated, for example, in the Roman Empire toward its end and in the United States during the Great Depression. But the family always seems to survive despite these premature obituaries. Evidently, there is a natural tendency for the subjective dimension of family problems to loom larger than their objective dimension, regardless of how great the latter might be. Why does this tendency exist? The answer revolves around the three factors that determine the subjective dimension: *visibility, expectations,* and *values* (Figure 14:7).

Family problems are extraordinarily visible. There is inherent drama in such phenomena as incest, out-of-wedlock childbearing, gay rights, child abuse, divorce, childlessness, surrogate motherhood, abortion, family role conflicts, and stepfamilies. The media are quick to take advantage of this drama, turning out a steady stream of controversial films and gripping television documentaries, as well as print coverage, on virtually every family problem.

The second factor exaggerating the subjective dimension of family problems is expectations. The more "controllable" a problem appears to be, the more its objective dimension is viewed as outrageous ("Why isn't somebody doing something about this?"). Since families are the most personal and familiar environments in which we live, family problems seem like they

TABLE 14:2 CrossTabulation of Marital Status with the Amount of Satisfaction Derived from Family

FAMILY SATISFACTION	MARITAL STATUS				
Count **COL PCT**	Married **1**	Widowed **2**	Divorced **3**	Separated **4**	Never Married **5**
Very great deal	250 **52.9**	32 **29.6**	34 **29.1**	5 **22.7**	46 **26.0**
Great deal	174 **36.8**	37 **34.3**	41 **35.0**	2 **9.1**	51 **28.8**
Quite a bit	28 **5.9**	14 **13.0**	14 **12.0**	3 **13.6**	35 **19.8**
A fair amount	13 **2.7**	14 **13.0**	10 **8.5**	4 **18.2**	22 **12.4**
Some	6 **1.3**	3 **2.8**	8 **6.8**	5 **22.7**	12 **6.8**
A little	1 **0.2**	5 **4.6**	5 **4.3**	1 **4.5**	5 **2.8**
None	1 **0.2**	3 **2.8**	5 **4.3**	2 **9.1**	6 **3.4**

$n = 897$

Main Point: Married people gain much more satisfaction from their families than those in other statuses. For example, 52.9 percent of married people gain a very great deal of satisfaction compared to only 29.1 percent of the divorced.

Source: General Social Survey, 1990.

FIGURE 14:7 SUBJECTIVE AND OBJECTIVE DIMENSIONS: THE CASE OF THE "DYING" FAMILY

The objective dimension of family problems is distorted by the three intervening variables of visibility, expectations, and values, making the subjective dimension very different from the objective one.

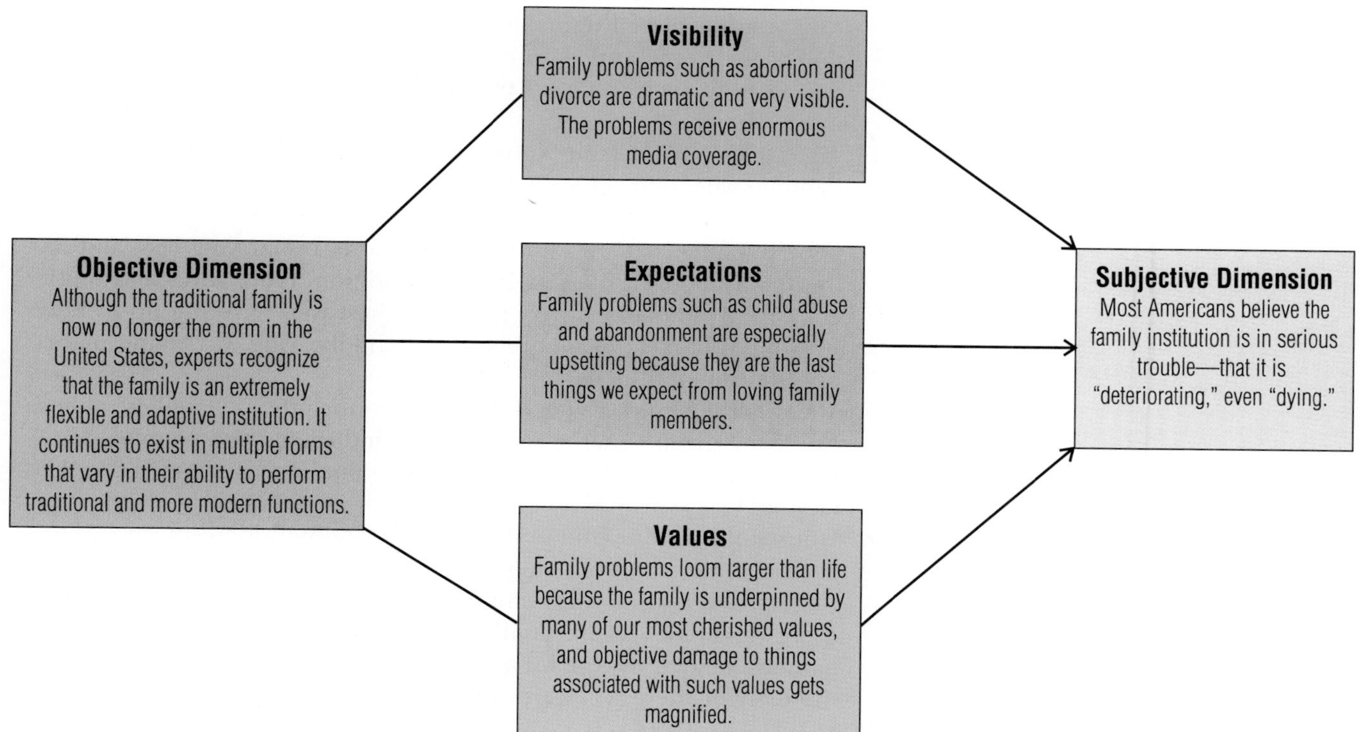

should be easy to solve: "If spouses would just sit down and talk about their differences, there would be less spouse abuse and fewer divorces". Problems like family violence are so upsetting to us in part because they are the last things we expect from loving family members.

In addition, the family is the repository of many of our most cherished values, ones overlaid by tradition and sanctified by religion. Family problems loom larger than life because objective damage done to things associated with such values gets magnified. The reverence for the family as an institution, together with the kindred belief that it is society's building block, means that each statistical addition to such things as divorce and out-of-wedlock childbearing *seems* more ominous than objective slippage in other less-important areas. This is why some of the most fiercely contested public issues like abortion focus directly on central aspects of the family.

SUMMARY

1. A family is a relatively permanent group of two or more individuals related by blood, marriage, or adoption who ordinarily live together. Important family types include the nuclear family, the extended family, the family of orientation, and the family of procreation.
2. Marriage formalizes and legitimates a quasi-permanent sexual union between two or more people. Like the family, marriage's exact form varies widely cross-culturally.
3. The family is usually entrusted with a core set of six functions: reproduction, socialization, material security, social placement, affection and companionship, and the regulation of sexuality.
4. Nuclear families have been the most common family type in the United States since the American Revolution. The early-American family was headed by the husband, whose wife and, ordinarily, many children played subordinate roles.
5. Between 1800 and 1950 powerful forces such as industrialization and urbanization played upon the family, producing increases in such things as divorce and work outside the homestead, as well as decreases in such things as family size and parental influence on mate selection.
6. The typical 1950s family consisted of a breadwinning husband, a stay-at-home wife, and their dependent children. But between 1950 and 1990 this traditional family became less and less common. By 1991, people were marrying less, divorcing more, remarrying less, and having fewer children than in 1950. In addition, more wives and mothers were in the labor force, more children were growing up without full-time mothers, and more sex and childbearing was taking place outside the family.
7. Today there is increasing momentum to include as "families" alternative living groups such as gay couples and unmarried couples because they often function much the same way as married-couple families.
8. Households in the United States are typically divided into two categories: family and nonfamily. Five principal types of families are (a) married couples with children; (b) married couples without children; (c) single-parent families headed by a woman; (d) single-parent families headed by a man; and (e) other family types. The relative numbers of these types are constantly in flux.

9. The powerful forces playing on the family in recent decades have altered greatly the living arrangements of many in the United States, especially children, young adults, and the elderly. Many of these now more popular living arrangements are nontraditional.
10. Romantic love is an altered state of consciousness and a social creation, which plays far less of a role in mate selection in the United States than most people think. Mate selection is restricted by age, propinquity, homogamy, and endogamous norms based on race, ethnicity, religion, and class.
11. By world and by U.S. historical standards, the United States has an extraordinarily high level of marital disruption. Divorce is high for many reasons, including the facts that a much higher proportion of spouses today (a) have both the resources and the opportunity to act on a preference to end a marriage, and (b) are less constrained by the well-being of a spouse or children to remain in a suboptimal marriage.
12. The traditional family of the 1950s contained relatively clear roles. But today there are no longer any clear guidelines about how to properly play the new and ever-evolving family roles.
13. Functionalists focus on the relative ability of different kinds of families to perform the six core functions. Conflict theorists emphasize the struggles that go on within the family, and institutional responses to such conflict. And symbolic interactionists focus on how people actually interact in family-related matters.
14. There is a natural tendency for the subjective dimension of family problems to loom larger than their objective dimension. This is because family problems are highly visible, violate our expectations concerning the behavior of loving family members, and run counter to cherished family values.

Chapter 15

Personal Perspective

So often today one hears that religion is declining, that it has no relevance to contemporary U.S. society. I have tended to accept this view, somewhat complacently. Yet, as I sit on my hillside terrace this warm Sunday morning, I can see, within a few blocks, hundreds of people streaming from *four* different Catholic churches. "Each of these churches seems very well attended," I muse to myself. "What is so important to these people that four Catholic churches can exist in such a tiny urban community? Furthermore," I think, "*each* of these churches supports an active school!" I then recall that, a few months earlier, I had been quite taken aback by a student's response to my statement that religious rituals were rarely performed within the American home today. She countered that, "In my family, religious rituals are very important, especially at holidays. We also pray together each night, and we read the Bible as a family." Other students agreed that religious rituals—prayers, special holiday ceremonies, and even Bible readings—had a prominent place in their homes.

I work with many young people who are contemplating marriage. About a year ago, a very lovely, gregarious young woman was mourning the breakup of a long relationship with a man. She commented, "I think I really need to find a man who is Jewish, too." "Why is that?" I asked, again naively assuming that for young people today religion is not a primary factor in the choice of a marriage partner. She replied, "Well, first, it will please my parents. . . . But, that's not it. I've dated many Gentile men, and there's just not a sense that we know the same world; we don't practice the same ceremonies, share the same heritage or traditions. With a Jewish man, certain things are just taken for granted."

CC

Religion

THESE three incidents force a reconsideration of the role of religion in U.S. society. What does religion mean to the people involved in each of these cases? Is religion actually reemerging as a potent force in the United States? Certainly, religious cults have made a loud noise in recent decades, but they have quieted down of late. And what of mainstream organized religions? Do precarious economic times prompt people to turn to higher powers for help? Does identification with a centuries-old religion offer a sense of immortality to frail humans? Sociology offers us a unique perspective to begin to answer these questions.

faith—when belief is not based on scientific evidence.

As we address these questions and others, we must note that religion is a matter of **faith**. Faith is belief that is not based on scientific evidence. Religion concerns ideas that transcend everyday experience; neither science nor common sense can establish religious truth.

Emile Durkheim presents the single most significant sociological examination of the nature of religion in his book, *The Elementary Forms of the Religious Life* (1912/1965). Here he states that in worshipping God, people are actually worshipping a symbolic image of their society. In this external "God," people invest their wish for omnipotence, their wish to be in control of an uncertain and potentially dangerous world. For any human being, the world presents itself as a very frightening place. Durkheim suggests that prehistoric people created in the concept of "God" or "gods" higher beings who were similar to themselves yet much more powerful.

profane—that part of the world that includes the ordinary aspects of everyday life.

sacred—that part of the world that inspires mystery, awe, respect, and fear in people.

The primary element of any religion, according to Durkheim, is its division of the world into sacred and profane dimensions. The **profane** encompasses all of the ordinary aspects of daily life. The **sacred**, by contrast, inspires awe, respect, mystery, and fear. All societies make these distinctions, though the specific objects defined as sacred and profane vary from culture to culture and even within cultures. It is the respect, accorded to certain objects by a group, that transforms objects from the profane to the sacred. A church or temple becomes a sacred place because it and its contents are *treated* with such awe, not because of an inherent quality of the building materials. Any object—a cow, a tree, a book, any animal, or nonmaterial spirit—can be defined by a people as sacred. The distinction is highlighted in Box 15:1 in which an element of the Christian sacred is suddenly transposed into the realm of the profane.

ELEMENTS OF RELIGION

It is no exaggeration to say that Emile Durkheim laid the foundation for the sociology of religion. Since this intellectual edifice is still under construction, we shall employ Durkheim's definition as the blueprint for our presentation. He defined religion as . . .

BOX 15:1 SOCIOLOGICAL IMAGINATION IN FICTION

The Devil You Know

It is a moment of first contact with an alien species—a much-heralded miracle of the secular, scientific age portrayed in Arthur C. Clarke's *Childhood's End.* The shock of that moment reveals the power of the sacred even in the midst of the most miraculous profane events.

"THIS IS THE DAY!" whispered the radios in a hundred tongues. "This is the day!" thought the cameramen as they checked and rechecked the equipment gathered round the vast empty space upon which Karellen's ship would be descending.

There was only the single ship now, hanging above New York. Indeed, as the world had just discovered, the ships above man's other cities had never existed. The day before, the great fleet of the Overlords had dissolved into nothingness, fading like mist beneath the morning sun.

The supply ships, coming and going far out in space, had been real enough; but the silver clouds that had hung for a lifetime over the capitals of Earth had been an illusion. How it had been done, no one could tell, but it seemed that every one of those ships had been nothing more than an image of Karellen's own vessel. Yet it had been far more than a matter of playing with light, for radar had also been deceived and there were still men alive who swore that they had heard the shriek of torn air as the fleet came in through the skies of Earth.

It was not important: all that mattered was that Karellen no longer felt the need for this display of force. He had thrown away his psychological weapons.

"The ship is moving!" came the word, flashed instantly to every corner of the planet. "It is heading westward!"

At less than a thousand kilometers an hour, falling slowly down from the empty heights of the stratosphere, the ship moved out to the great plains and to its second rendezvous with history. It settled down obediently before the waiting cameras and the packed thousands of spectators, so few of whom could see as much as the millions gathered round their TV sets.

The ground should have cracked and trembled beneath that tremendous weight, but the vessel was still in the grip of whatever forces drove it among the stars. It kissed the earth as gently as a falling snowflake.

The curving wall twenty meters above the ground seemed to flow and shimmer: where there had been a smooth and shining surface, a great opening had appeared. Nothing was visible within it, even to the questing eyes of the camera. It was as dark and shadowed as the entrance to a cave.

Out of the orifice, a wide, glittering gangway extruded itself and drove purposefully towards the ground. It seemed a solid sheet of metal with handrails along either side. There were no steps; it was steep and smooth as a toboggan slide and, one would have thought, equally impossible to ascend or descend in any ordinary manner.

The world was watching that dark portal, within which nothing had yet stirred. Then the seldom-heard yet unforgettable voice of Karellen floated softly down from some hidden source. His message could scarcely have been more unexpected.

"There are some children by the foot of the gangway. I would like two of them to come up and meet me."

There was silence for a moment. Then a boy and a girl broke from the crowd and walked, with complete lack of self-consciousness, towards the gangway and into history. Others followed, but stopped when Karellen's chuckle came from the ship.

"Two will be enough."

Eagerly anticipating the adventure, the children—they could not have been more than six years old—jumped on to the metal slide. Then the first miracle happened.

Waving cheerfully to the crowds beneath, and to their anxious parents—who, too late, had probably remembered the legend of the Pied Piper—the children began swiftly ascending the steep slope. Yet their legs were motionless, and soon it was clear also that their bodies were tilted at right angles to that peculiar gangway. It possessed a private gravity of its

BOX 15:1 SOCIOLOGICAL IMAGINATION IN FICTION: THE DEVIL YOU KNOW *continued*

own, one which could ignore that of Earth. The children were still enjoying this novel experience, and wondering what was drawing them upwards, when they disappeared into the ship.

A vast silence lay over the whole world for the space of twenty seconds—though, afterward, no one could believe that the time had been so short. Then the darkness of the great opening seemed to move forward, and Karellen came forth into the sunlight. The boy was sitting on his left arm, the girl on his right. They were both too busy playing with Karellen's wings to take any notice of the watching multitude.

It was a tribute to the Overlords' psychology, and to their careful years of preparation that only a few people fainted. Yet there could have been fewer still, anywhere in the world, who did not feel the ancient terror brush for one awful instant against their minds before reason banished it forever.

There was no mistake. The leathery wings, the little horns, the barbed tail—all were there. The most terrible of all legends had come to life, out of the unknown past. Yet now it stood smiling, in ebon majesty, with the sunlight gleaming upon its tremendous body, and with a human child resting trustfully on either arm.

Critical Thinking Questions

1. What conclusions can be drawn about the nature of the *sacred* from this imaginative fiction piece?
2. What parallels might be drawn between the story and *The Wizard of Oz*, in terms of people's perception of the *sacred?*

Source: Arthur C. Clarke, *Childhood's End* (1963/1987). New York: Ballantine Books, pp. 66–68. By permission of the publisher.

> a unified system of *beliefs* and *practices* relative to sacred things . . . which unite into one single moral *community* . . . all those who adhere to them (Durkheim, 1912/1965, p. 62, emphases added).

Each of these elements will be spotlighted separately to illuminate the essence of religion in society—and society in religion.

The Talshilhunpo Monastery in Xigaze, Tibet, has been the center for the study of Tantric Buddhism since the 15th century. Like Mahayana Buddhism, which is practiced elsewhere in China, the Tantric sect preaches the concepts of reincarnation and nirvana (the state at which the soul is finally released from mortal existence). However, Tantric Buddhists believe that through vigorous study and meditation, they can bypass reincarnation and reach nirvana in a single lifetime.

Beliefs: The Meaning of Life

belief—a system of meaning that defines the world and explains the mysteries of existence.

Religion offers the individual a **belief** system, which defines the world and helps to clarify the mysteries of existence. All religions—Christianity, Judaism, Eastern sects—seek the meaning of life. Those sharing a common faith that explains human life in relation to the sacred also accept moral norms based on that faith with implications for behavior in the profane world. For example, Catholic doctrine about the soul motivates opposition to abortion legislation.

Practices: The Power of Ritual

In addition to following this moral code based upon their beliefs, religious practitioners are recognized by specific ceremonial activities. Islamic pilgrimages, Catholic confessions, Jewish bar (bas) mitzvahs, even animal sacrifices . . . all are concrete symbols of membership in a religious group. Durkheim discovered in this ceremonial diversity a common sociological thread, which he wove into his theory of religion.

rituals—the formal practices expressing and reinforcing patterns of belief.

Rituals are formal practices expressing and reinforcing patterns of belief. They are devices for drawing the believer out of the profane world and into closer contact with the sacred. A devout Muslim visiting Mecca is not a tourist; he is on a trip with special spiritual meaning. Durkheim clearly saw that such practices not only demonstrate a belief in Allah, they actually *strengthen* that belief. This explains the great importance placed by some religions on ritual participation. With their orientation to the sacred, religious rituals can have a special power. According to contemporary sociologists of religion, they are "an important part of the social cement that holds the American social structure in place" (Hunt and Greeley, 1987, p. 342).

Religious Community Social Networks

By Durkheim's definition, religion links members together into a community. Believers draw common comfort from beliefs that explain life's suffering, and participate as a group in sacred rituals. This theoretical statement has been dramatically demonstrated in another of Durkheim's classic studies, *Suicide* (1897/1951). He observes that the structure of Catholicism and Judaism create a stronger sense of social belonging for their members than does the structure of Protestantism. The first two are older, more traditional religions, have more clearly stated rules for behavior, exert greater demands on the individual to conform to group expectations, and more strongly emphasize the family as the unit of membership in the religion. Protestant churches are more loosely structured; the individual is the unit of membership and is accorded more spiritual freedom.

Durkheim correlates his observation with the finding that Jews and Catholics have lower suicide rates than do Protestants. His conclusion is that religion serves a protective function for the individual by its community-building effect. In a recent reexamination of Durkheim's thesis, Stack (1983) finds that lower church attendance is associated with higher likelihood of suicide; this suggests the significance of ritual in involving church members socially. Martin's (1984) research indicates that affiliation with a religion—*any* religion—reduces the risk of suicide.

As one of the founders of scientific sociology, Emile Durkheim did not have access to the contents and data of modern social network analysis. The breakthrough of *Suicide* was to show that religion's social effects extended even to the extreme of voluntary self-destruction. Contemporary network analysis has explored some of the more basic processes of community formation. Would you insist that your friends be members of the same church? For most people the answer is no, but the social facts say otherwise. Two separate regional samples in the United States have documented the reality of religious homophily (Fischer, 1977; Laumann, 1973); simply put, we are much more likely to have friends of our own religion. The surprising social power wielded by religion is aggressively employed by churches that emphasize face-to-face contact to win converts.

THEORETICAL PERSPECTIVES ON RELIGION

Functionalist Theory

There has probably never existed a society from which religion was completely absent. On this basis, sociologists conclude that religion must be an essential part of social life. What makes it essential? What functions does it serve?

The forerunner of the functionalist perspective was Emile Durkheim, who made explicit the purposes served by religion both for the individual and for the society. First, religion enhances social solidarity by providing norms that members accept and adhere to, thus easing conflict within the community. Precepts such as "Do unto others as you would have them do unto you" provide concrete guidelines for daily behavior that encourage harmonious interactions. Religion further enhances solidarity by imposing strong sanctions (even excommunication or shunning from the group) imposed against those who deviate from the norms, and by offering a means by which to atone for sins or errors. Modern-day reconciliation, for example, is a ritual that restores the deviant Catholic. Functionalists also note that religion helps to consecrate major life events. Nearly every major religion has ceremonies to mark birth, maturity, marriage, and death. Such ceremonies signal the significance of the day for the individual; bind the person strongly into the religious community and, thus, into the larger society; and provide a shared experience common to all members. Religion also helps ease the transition of immigrants into a new society. In the United States, churches based upon those in the immigrants' homeland offer an oasis of traditional beliefs, familiar customs, and a known language (Greeley, 1972). The church becomes a "decompression chamber" (Schaeffer, 1990) to provide relief from the stresses of learning a whole new way of life. For Polish Catholics, Irish Catholics, and Jews, religion has provided an ethnic cohesion and discipline that facilitated upward mobility (Greeley, 1972, 1976).

Religion often serves to legitimate the existing social order and thus ensure conformity with its values and norms. Guy Swanson demonstrated this in his classic 1974 study of 50 non-Western societies. He found that, as Durkheim suggested, each society portrayed itself very clearly in its religion. For example, in societies where elders occupy important positions, ancestors are worshipped. In societies characterized by great economic inequalities, religious beliefs tend to justify large gaps between the wealthy and the nonwealthy. In modern U.S. society, TV Evangelists often exhort their audiences to fulfill their own potential, especially economically, thus endorsing the American emphasis on individual opportunity and achievement motivation. Durkheim's theory and Swanson's data both suggest that religion reinforces the existing social arrangements.

Conflict Theory

Sociologists adopting a conflict perspective, however, argue that religion emphasizes not the overall values and interests of the society, but the interests of the ruling classes. Karl Marx claimed that, in capitalist societies, religion is dominated by those who own the means of production. He argued that religion, by portraying the authority and power of the upper classes as just, helps to pacify the lower classes. By focusing the lower classes on an afterlife in heaven in which they would receive their rewards, Marx contended, Christian religion lulled workers into a false sense of well-being and thus discouraged them from attempting to overthrow their capitalist oppressors. Marx viewed religion as the instrument of the upper classes, "the opium of the people." Marx did acknowledge that religions are sometimes rallying vehicles for the protests of oppressed groups, though a religious movement obscures the true economic nature of its members' plight.

Many conflict theorists today believe that Marx underestimated the degree to which religion can be involved in social justice movements even within a capitalist society. The Reverend Martin Luther King, Jr., and the Southern Christian Leadership Conference, for example, appealed to religious concepts and symbols when they ignited the Civil Rights Movement in the early 1960s. The idea of Christian brotherhood was central to their cause, and they used Bible stories (such as the exodus of the Israelites from Egypt) as models for analyzing their own situations and for planning their actions (Lincoln, 1984; Walzer, 1985). Similarly, in several Latin American countries today, many Catholic bishops and priests view their mission as actively defending impoverished masses against corrupt and exploitative regimes; this is the well-known "liberation theology" movement (Gutierrez,

The name of this Japanese painting, *Jigoku Soshi,* literally means "Hell Scroll." It comes from the Early Kamakura Period, about 1200 A.D. Ideas of heaven and hell were written down with great imagination and vividly painted. The Buddhist priest Genshin told of hells where sinners were forced to attack one another, cutting each other's bodies until only bones remained, or where demons slowly sliced the flesh off the victim. It was a hell of repeated torture.

1983; Hehir, 1981). As these cases illustrate, although established religions usually reflect the social structure and values of the dominant group, they may also suggest a vision of what life could be. These ideals may be the impetus for significant social change.

The role of religion in social class struggles depends on how a people decide to use religion. Christianity can be used as a tool by both the oppressed and the oppressors. In contemporary South Africa, for example, Bishop Desmond Tutu and the Reverend Allan Boesak are leaders of religious groups opposed to the racist apartheid government. They contend that according to Christian beliefs, all people are equal under God; segregation, therefore, is contrary to the Christian sense of justice. At the same time, the white rulers of South Africa have long claimed that apartheid is religiously justified. Each side in this struggle believes that the Bible is divinely inspired, and each cites Bible passages to support its view of relationships between people of different races. Thus, religious ideas can be interpreted in a wide variety of ways, depending on one's social class position.

Symbolic Interactionist Theory

The symbolic interactionist perspective considers all of society to be a human construction. Peter Berger (1967) suggests that religion is a human product that places everyday life within a "sacred canopy" of meaning. Thus, from the symbolic interactionist perspective, marriage as "holy matrimony" is not merely a civil contract between two people; religion imbues marriage with ultimate authority, social authority, and personal meaning.

From this point of view, conversion to a new religion involves a person's active attempt to seek out its meaning (Berger, 1967). People are not merely passive recipients of religion, they are active creators of it. New converts help define their own ties to the new religion. Members of a Fundamentalist Baptist Church studied by James Ault (1987) re-created their religious community each day. This process can be seen in their use of kinship terms to address one another—"brother," "sister," "aunt," and so on, whether or not they were actually related by marriage or blood. Thus, they symbolically established close, enduring ties with one another on a daily basis.

In this Fundamentalist Church the pastor asked the congregation for prayer requests each week, and members responded by telling the group what they wanted the Lord to provide. Over the following weeks, other members would try to fulfill these needs by their own efforts. Rather than attribute this help to themselves, however, they always credited it to God's divine intervention. By essentially generating their own proof of the validity of their religious beliefs, these Fundamentalists strengthened their own religious commitments.

Integrating the Theories

Given the wide range of human spiritual impulses, a single theoretical explanation of religious behavior is probably unrealistic. The daunting complexity of the sociology of religion suggests the benefits of multiple perspectives. Consider the singular finding in Table 15:1, which shows a positive association between religious intensity and happiness—42.4 percent of strongly religious people say they are very happy, compared to 28.9 percent

TABLE 15:1 Crosstabulation of Degree of Happiness by the Degree of Religious Intensity

HAPPY	DEGREE OF RELIGIOUS INTENSITY		
Count	Strong	Not Very or Somewhat Strong	
ROW PCT	1	2	
Very happy	203 **49.3**	209 **50.7**	
Pretty or not too happy	276 **35.0**	513 **65.0**	
			$n = 1201$

Main Point: People with a strong degree of religious intensity are more likely to say that they are very happy, compared to those who have less religious intensity.

Source: General Social Survey, 1990.

of those with less religious intensity. The functionalist interpretation is straightforward: Religiosity is directly beneficial to the individual in society. Conflict theory finds a more sinister purpose lurking behind the same piece of data. If religion indeed is the opium of the people as Marx proposed, one would expect a GSS sample of the nation's masses to show more contentment with a stronger dose of religion. Rather than a passive anesthetic effect, the symbolic interactionist view posits an act of religious creation. If the individual more intensely participates in a religion, that religion will generate greater personal meaning and, consequently, greater personal happiness. This is a case where all three theoretical schemes agree on the facts, but disagree on the underlying sociological mechanisms.

THE SUBJECTIVE DIMENSION OF RELIGION

Regardless of theoretical position, sociologists generally view religion as near to the very heart of society. Religion is the repository of the most central *values* of the social mainstream, a keeper of what gives a society its distinctive identity. As such, it conditions our subjective responses to a wide range of everyday events. The outrage people experience at the news of a murder is magnified by the violation of the moral order ("Thou shalt not kill"), which transcends the viciousness of the act. Part of the reason the public finds cults so unsettling is because cults break the usual kinship between religion and societal values. By definition, cults reject mainstream cultural codes. The whole pattern of cult behavior—from alien doctrines to exotic costumes—seems to be a rebellion against conventional society (Yinger, 1970).

This "halo effect" around the value system also generates stringent standards for religious organizations and professionals. High *expectations* for behavior mean a high risk for hypocrisy. Allegations that a church supports racist politics or is sexist in its clerical selection process seem especially wrong because such organizations are held to a higher standard. Even objectively commonplace "sins" such as sexual impropriety or a high-rolling lifestyle are unacceptable for those who do not practice what they preach.

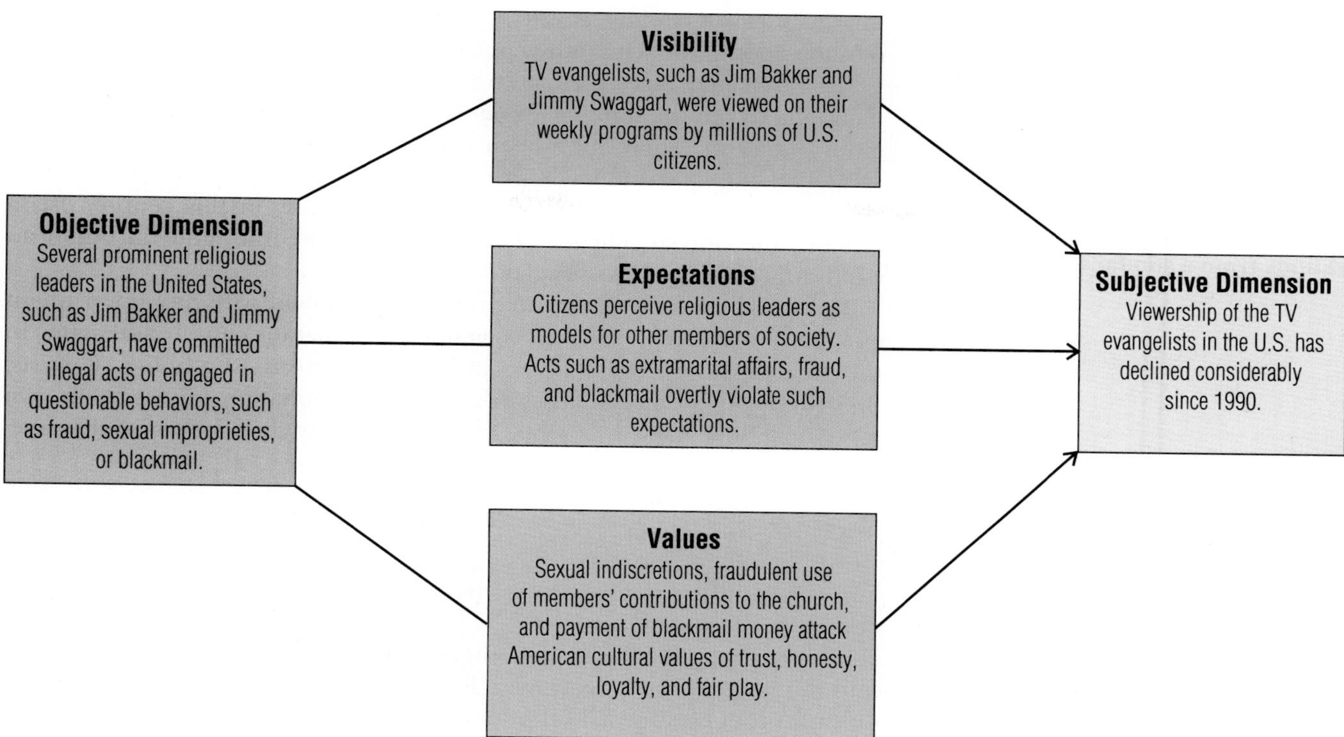

FIGURE 15:1 SUBJECTIVE AND OBJECTIVE DIMENSIONS: THE CASE OF TELEVISION EVANGELISTS
Because of the highly visible immoral behavior of some television Evangelists, viewership has declined. This is a response to the violation of people's expectations and values associated with proper behavior of religious leaders.

Church organizations have always had high *visibility*. From medieval Europe, when Roman Catholic decrees defined public issues, to present-day Iran, where church and state intermingle, the words of religious spokespersons have enjoyed high cultural prestige. In the age of mass media, this means high public exposure of a church's endorsement of a political candidate or its position on the abortion issue. It can also mean a sensational visibility when a minister falls from grace in the public eye. This process is outlined in Figure 15:1.

TYPES OF RELIGIOUS ORGANIZATION

In studying religions, sociologists have found that religious groups can develop a wide range of social structures. These structures are a result of the particular religious community's beliefs, ceremonies, and membership. Over time, the social structure itself can affect the nature of the interaction among members, the relationships of group members to leaders, and the nature of an entire group's relationship to the larger society (Weber, 1922a).

Church

church—a formal religious organization that is well integrated into the society.

The exact form of religious structures varies considerably from society to society and from time to time. Ernst Troeltsch (1931) distinguishes between "church" and "sect." He describes a **church** as a formal religious organization that is well integrated into the society. If it is well established, a church (such as the Catholic Church) can endure for centuries. Churches include all members of a family over many generations. Churches create their own bureaucracies including pastors, priests, and other ordained officials, who develop specific policies and regulations for behavior.

ecclesia—a church that is formally allied with the state.

denomination—a religious organization that is involved in pluralistic competition with other such organizations from a similar tradition.

A church may take one of two forms: an **ecclesia**, a church that is formally allied with the state; or a **denomination**, a church that recognizes religious pluralism. There have been many ecclesias throughout history. The Catholic Church was allied with the Roman Empire for centuries. Confucianism was the state religion in China until early in this century. Islam remains the official religion of Saudi Arabia and Iran, and the Anglican Church is the Church of England.

Denominations, however, are not officially allied with any government and therefore usually exist in societies that separate church and state. In the United States, there are many denominations—Catholics, Baptists, Presbyterians, Lutherans, and so on. Each denomination adheres to its own set of beliefs and practices, while recognizing the right of others to disagree.

Sect

sect—an informal religious structure that is not well integrated into the larger society.

For some differences in three major types of religious organization—churches, sects, and cults—see Figure 15:2. A **sect** differs greatly from a church in that it is an informal religious structure that is *not* well integrated into the larger society. Sects typically have no hierarchy of officials, neither do they produce a formal set of policies and regulations. On this basis Max Weber suggests that a sect can exist for only one generation. Sects highly value personal spiritual experiences, whereas churches rely on more formalized rituals such as the Roman Catholic reconciliation and mass. Members of churches tend to be sedate during services. Sect members seek ecstatic experiences such as loud singing, foot stamping, and even speaking in tongues. Sect members value supernatural feelings as expressions of faith. Often, this transcendence of the here-and-now results in a sense of being cleansed or purified.

Patterns of leadership are also quite different in churches and sects. Churches have formal, trained leaders—priests, rabbis, ministers, and so on. Leaders of sects frequently have no formal religious training. According to Max Weber (1922), they often exhibit "charisma," an aura or mystique that compels certain people to listen to their message. Sect leaders portray themselves as divinely inspired and are able to elicit strong emotions and devoted behaviors from their followers. Jim Jones, for example, a San Francisco self-ordained minister, led hundreds of people to emigrate

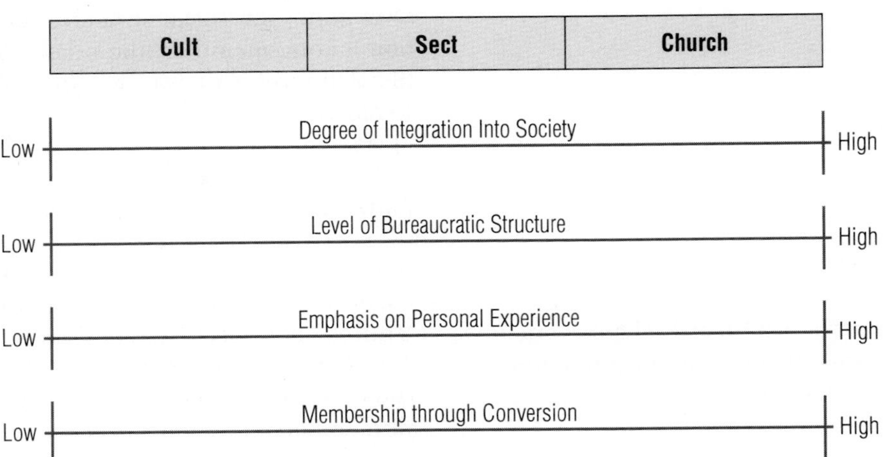

FIGURE 15:2 VARIATION OF RELIGIOUS ORGANIZATIONS

Churches, sects, and cults vary widely in terms of integration into society, bureaucratic structure, emphasis on personal experience, and membership through conversion. Churches and cults are especially dissimilar.

These people in Bali are engaged in a religious ecstatic experience. There are many Hindu temples like this throughout Indonesia. Each temple is dedicated to one of the Hindu deities. The head priest acts as a mediator between the worshippers and the deity inside the temple.

to Guyana in South America in the early 1980s. Jones convinced people to sell their worldly belongings, donate the money to his church, and follow him to South America to establish "Jonestown," the name his religious community would be known as. Jim Jones later directed his followers to drink cyanide-laced punch during a mass suicide that killed both him and his adherents.

Sects, unlike churches, overtly reject the existing social order. Some sects, such as the Amish, withdraw completely and live an isolated existence in order to practice their religion without interference because they view their own beliefs as the *only true* religion. The Amish community in Lancaster County, Pennsylvania, is self-insulated from the surrounding society. The several hundred Amish families there are farmers who use no modern technology. The Amish use no electricity in their farming or in their homes—no televisions or radios—and they do not read any newspapers or magazines. They continue to use the German Bible, which is the only book in most Amish homes. Their children are educated in Amish schools only up to the eighth grade. The Amish use horses and buggies and do not own automobiles. Other than the sale of some of their farm produce to the outside society, the Amish have no interaction with people beyond their own small religious community (Hostetler, 1981).

Troeltsch (1931) also observed that sects are characterized by their asceticism. Their members, such as early Quakers and Puritans, tend to live austere, disciplined lifestyles that discourage participation in worldly events, which are viewed as decadent and sinful. Early Quakers, for instance, wore only gray and black clothing, and called themselves "Plain People." The Amish still wear clothing with no zippers, wear no jewelry, and have no paintings in their homes.

While church membership passes through families from generation to generation, sects rely heavily on conversion of outsiders to their sect, through personal transformation. Because of their rejecting nature, sects attract converts especially from among those who see themselves as misfits and outcasts in general society, and who hope to find personal fulfillment in the sect. Churches are often composed of people of the higher social classes, whereas sects tend to draw from the lower social classes (Niebuhr, 1929).

Because of their emotional intensity, their lack of formal structure, and their breakaway origins, sects tend to be unstable. Many sects, such as the Anabaptists, disappear shortly after their emergence. Sects that do endure, however, become more and more church-like, partly because their emotional pitch flags over time. Also, as a sect moves into its second generation, some bureaucratic mechanisms must be initiated to guide those who are *born* into the group and have *not* participated in the founders' ecstatic experiences. The Quakers, for example, were originally a revolutionary English sect; today they exhibit an established church type of organization, with well-structured lines of authority, published guidelines for conducting religious services, and committees for dealing with problems that may arise.

Cult

cult—a religious movement that is extremely unorthodox vis-à-vis the mainstream society.

A **cult** is a religious movement that is extremely unorthodox vis-à-vis the mainstream society. A sect often rebels against an established church, whereas a cult may spring up seemingly independent of local religious traditions. Cults often develop around a charismatic leader, who brings an unconventional message of salvation. Joseph Smith was such a charismatic leader who began a cult in 1830 in New York, which would become The Church of Jesus Christ of Latter Day Saints—the Mormon Church. Smith claimed to have had a series of visions from God and to have received golden tablets inscribed with the book of Mormon (Marty, 1985). Smith incorporated many conventional Christian ideals but added a number of divergent beliefs and rituals, such as the practice of polygamy.

Reverend Sun Myung Moon is a present-day charismatic leader who formed a cult he calls the Unification Church in Korea in 1956, following his divine vision of being summoned by God. In the United States, this cult is often referred to as "The Moonies," after Reverend Moon's followers. Since moving to the United States in the late 1960s, he has amassed thousands of followers. Reverend Moon has incorporated many Christian beliefs into his doctrine, but he has introduced some more exotic practices, such as group marriages and communal living, into the cult (Barker, 1984). At this writing, the Unification Church continues to number thousands of devotees, even though Reverend Moon is serving time in prison for income tax evasion.

Cults may arise as a result of the diffusion of religious ideals from one culture to another. In Asia, worship of Krishna is a centuries-old meditative religion, Hinduism, practiced primarily by retired men of the upper classes. In the United States, this cult has attracted a youthful, alienated membership, primarily those who have become disillusioned with the norms and values of mainstream America. They symbolize their disaffection by dressing in saffron-colored robes and wearing ponytails on their otherwise shaved heads as they hand out literature in airports (Stark and Bainbridge, 1979).

Steven Tipton (1982) suggests that cults appeal to those who are desperately searching for personal meaning in their lives. Cults can have a very powerful moral and psychological value for the disaffected:

> For some youths the social and ideological stability of these [new religious] movements has meant psychological and even physical survival. For many more, membership in alternative religious movements has meant moral survival and a sense of meaning and purpose. . . . (Tipton, 1982, p. 30).

During their tenure in cults, members frequently adopt radically new lifestyles, which may include communal living, leaving one's worldly family, spending hours chanting, and eating exotic food. These rituals symbolize both rejection of mainstream society and initiation of the person into the cult. They also assign concrete form to the new meanings the person seeks to integrate into his or her life (Barker, 1981; Kilbourne, 1983). Membership in a cult, for the disillusioned individual, is often quite temporary, and serves as an "in-limbo holding chamber" between dropping out of college, quitting an unsatisfying job, and a later reentry into mainstream society (Stark and Bainbridge, 1979).

WORLD RELIGIONS

Thousand of religions—in the form of churches, denominations, sects, and cults—exist throughout the world. Many occupy only a tiny geographical area and have few members. Others, called world religions, include millions of believers across several continents. Six world religions account for 3.5 billion people, about two-thirds of the world's population: Christianity, Islam, Hinduism, Buddhism, Confucianism, and Judaism.

Christianity

Christianity is the most widespread religion, with 1.6 billions members—more than one-fifth of the world's population. About two-thirds of the people in the United States and Canada name Christianity as their religion. Most Christians are Europeans and North Americans.

Early Christianity, with its roots in Middle Eastern Judaism, displayed many characteristics of a cult. The growth of early Christianity was largely a consequence of the teachings of Jesus of Nazareth, a charismatic leader who preached the possibility of personal salvation through **conversion** (the adoption of a new religion, quite different from the religion of one's

conversion—the adoption of a new religion, often quite different from the religion of one's parents.

parents). This notion differed greatly from the Judaic concept of an all-powerful God and traditional membership in the religious community that was passed on within a family. Jesus also preached a radically new message of hope that physical death could be overcome by eternal spiritual life. Judaism contains no concept of an afterlife; Jesus' message was, then, spiritually revolutionary.

monotheism—religious belief in a single divine power or entity.

polytheism—religious belief in which many gods are acknowledged.

Christianity, through **monotheism**, recognizes a single divine entity. This new religion challenged the Roman Empire's traditional **polytheism**; that is, religious beliefs that acknowledge many gods or supernatural entities.

Christians were, at the onset of their cult-like formation, persecuted by the Roman Empire because cults are often felt to be threats to the existing society. Gradually, though, Christianity spread throughout the Mediterranean area. During the fourth century AD, Christianity became the official religion of the Roman Empire—an ecclesia. Thus the process of transformation from cult to church was completed.

Around the fifteenth century, some European Catholic religious leaders, basing their claims on divine inspiration, revolted against established church doctrine and ritual. These rebellions initiated the Protestant Reformation led by John Calvin and Martin Luther, and gave birth to a long period of religious pluralism from which numerous Protestant denominations emerged (Kaufman, 1976; Niebuhr, 1929; Smart, 1969; Stavrianos, 1983). Figure 15:3 illustrates the continued growth of Christianity as measured by worldwide Bible distribution.

Islam

Islam is the second largest religion in the world, with almost 1 billion followers called Muslims (or Moslems or Islamics). A majority of the people in the Middle East and North Africa practice Islam. Most Muslims are non-Arab; the largest concentrations are found in India, Pakistan, and the former Soviet Union. Estimates of the numbers of Muslims in North America range from 1.5 million to 4 million, and are increasing rapidly due to the conversion of many African Americans (Roudi, 1988; Weeks, 1988).

prophet—according to Max Weber, "a purely individual bearer of charisma, who by virtue of his mission proclaims a religious doctrine."

Islam is based on the teachings of the **prophet** Muhammad, born about AD 570 in the City of Mecca (in western Saudi Arabia). A prophet is "a purely individual bearer of charisma, who by virtue of his mission proclaims a religious doctrine" (Weber, 1922a). Muhammad rediscovered the word of God, Allah, in the Qur'an (Koran), which is sacred to Muslims. The Qur'an suggests submission to Allah as the path to personal inner peace. Muslims express this personal devotion through an intense ritual of five prayers each day. The word *Islam* means peace and submission.

Islam spread rapidly after the death of Muhammad although internal divisions arose as they did within Christianity. All Muslims, however, accept the Five Pillars of Islam: (1) recognition of Allah as the one true God and Muhammad as God's messenger; (2) ritual prayers; (3) giving alms to the poor; (4) regular fasting; and (5) making at least one pilgrimage in a lifetime to Mecca, the sacred city of Muhammad's birth (Weber, 1922a; Weeks, 1988).

Muslims are also required to defend their faith against unbelievers, which has justified holy wars. The ideal personality type in Islam, in fact, is the "Warrior." Holy wars *(jihad)* continue into the present, as in Iran and Iraq. Violent internal struggles rage among the three major divisions of Islam: Sunni (the orthodox branch), Shia (who await the coming of a Messiah), and Sufi (the mystical branch). Iran and Iraq presently seek to rid

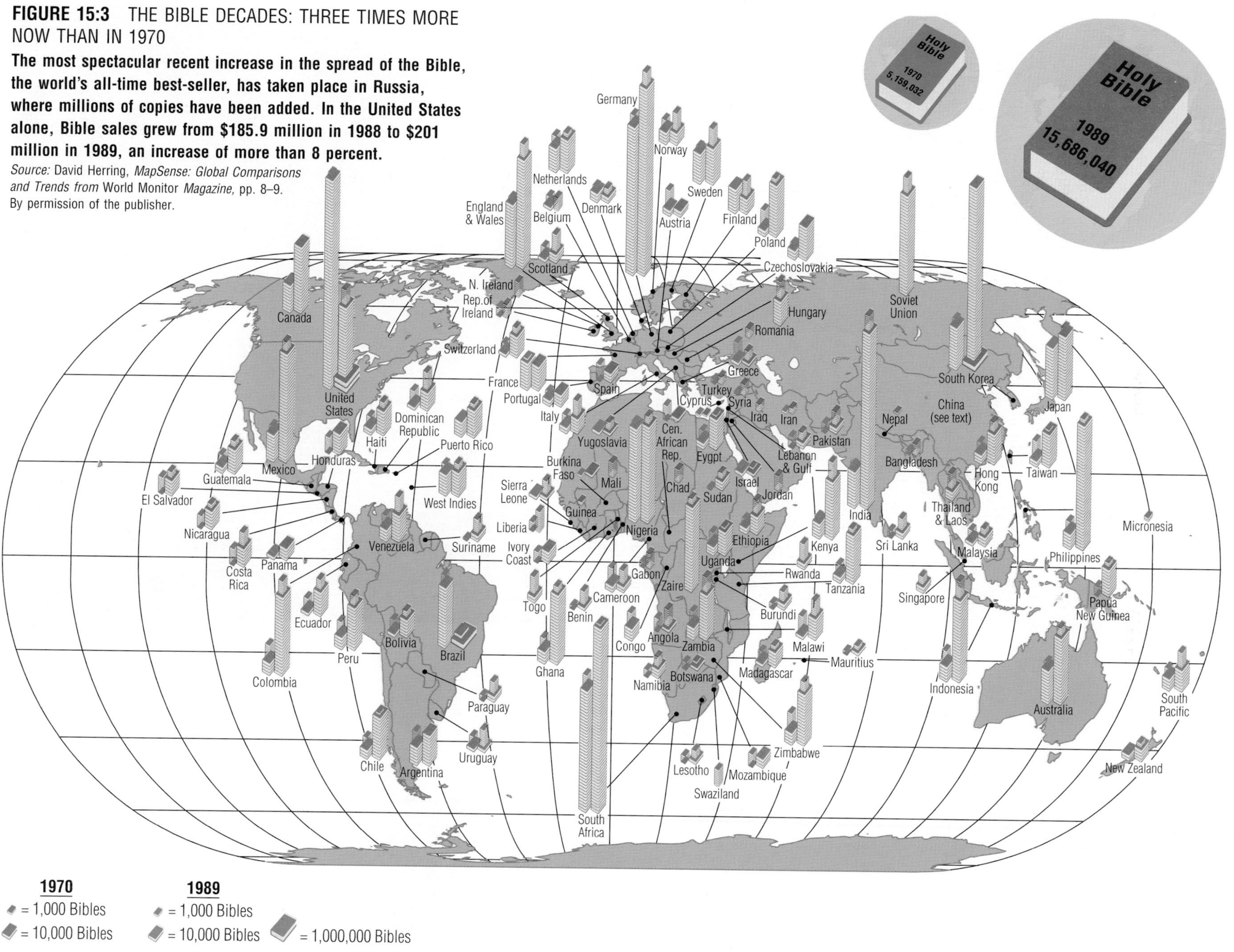

FIGURE 15:3 THE BIBLE DECADES: THREE TIMES MORE NOW THAN IN 1970

The most spectacular recent increase in the spread of the Bible, the world's all-time best-seller, has taken place in Russia, where millions of copies have been added. In the United States alone, Bible sales grew from $185.9 million in 1988 to $201 million in 1989, an increase of more than 8 percent.

Source: David Herring, *MapSense: Global Comparisons and Trends from* World Monitor *Magazine,* pp. 8–9. By permission of the publisher.

their countries of non-Islamic Western influences, which they consider to be immoral (Arjomand, 1988; Martin, 1982; Weber, 1922a).

Hinduism

Hinduism is probably the oldest of world religions, originating in the Indus Valley some 4,500 years ago. Over many centuries, Hinduism and Indian society have become interwoven. Unlike Christianity and Islam, Hinduism diffused very little (Schmidt, 1980). Most of the 664 million Hindus reside in India and Pakistan. North American Hindus number about 885,000.

Hinduism, unlike Christianity and Islam, is not the outgrowth of the life and writing of a single person; neither is there a single book of sacred writings. There are many Hindu texts such as the Vedas, the Upanishads, and Sutras. Although there is considerable variation, Hindus generally believe that each person has fixed moral duties or obligations, called *dharma*. For example, upholding one's position in the traditional caste system (see Chapter 11) is one responsibility that is included in the dharma. Hinduism also embraces *Karma*, a belief in the spiritual progress of each person's soul. Each human action is believed to have a direct spiritual consequence. Proper living ensures spiritual progress, while improper living—not upholding one's dharma—results in spiritual decline. Karma also includes a belief in reincarnation—the belief that a new birth follows each death, and each rebirth is based upon the moral progress achieved in previous lives. Each new incarnation (soul entering a new body) forms a step in the cycle of rebirth, which eventually leads to Nirvana—a paradise of the soul (Kaufman, 1976; Pitt, 1955; Schmidt, 1980).

In Hinduism, there are three primary gods: Brahma, the Creator; Vishnu, the Sustainer; and Siva, the Destroyer. Most Hindus worship either

These Hindus are immersing themselves in the Ganges River as part of a religious ritual. This shot was taken during the *Kumbh Mela,* a public ceremony that occurs every twelve years. At that time, millions of Hindus journey to the Ganges to bathe in its sacred waters.

Siva or Vishnu, though they believe in the existence of all three gods. Hindus generally follow the choice of their parents. Extensive ritual observances are essential to daily life. Some rituals are private, such as the cleansing of the body after contact with a member of a lower caste or a nonbeliever. Others are public, such as the Kumbh Mela, which occurs once every 12 years, in which millions of Hindus journey to the Ganges River to bathe in its sacred, purifying waters (Embree, 1972; Sen, 1961).

Buddhism

Buddhism emerged in India about 2,500 years ago. Today, more than 300 million people, primarily Asians, adhere to the Buddhist religion. Although Buddhism resembles Hinduism in its belief system, its origin is in the life of one charismatic man—Siddhartha Gautama, who was born about 563 BC to a high-caste Indian family. Gautama was devoted to the spiritual life and experienced a radical personal transformation at age 29. Following this, he began traveling and meditating, finally attaining a transcendent state, called *bodhi* or enlightenment. Having reached an understanding of the essence of life, Gautama became a Buddha. His personal charisma enabled Buddha to amass a wide audience who spread his teachings—the *dharma*—throughout India. During the third century BC, the ruler of India became a Buddhist, dispersed missionaries throughout Asia, and declared Buddhism a state religion, or ecclesia.

Buddhists view existence as suffering. They do not deny the experience of pleasure, but believe that joy is transitory. This belief arose, in part, as a reflection of Buddha's own travels in a society ravaged by poverty. Buddhism states that material wealth obstructs spiritual growth and suggests that society's problems can be solved only on an individual level through personal transcendence to an enlightened state. According to Max Weber (1922a), Buddhism embraces world-rejection and is a model of the pursuit of mystical illumination of the person.

Like Hindus, Buddhists subscribe to the idea of reincarnation; only full enlightenment ends the cycle of rebirth and releases the person from earthly suffering. Buddhism contains no god who judges people's lives but, like Hinduism, asserts spiritual consequences for all everyday actions (Schumann, 1974; Thomas, 1975).

Confucianism

From about 200 BC until the beginning of the twentieth century, Confucianism was an ecclesia—the official religion of China. Following the 1949 Communist Revolution, the government of the People's Republic of China has discouraged any religion. Nonetheless, hundreds of millions of Chinese continue to be influenced by Confucianism.

This religion was created by a man named K'ung Fu-tzu, known to Westerners as Confucius, who is believed to have lived between 551 BC and 479 BC. Confucius was extremely concerned with the hardships endured by the Chinese people. Unlike Buddha, who urged spiritual withdrawal from the earthly world, Confucius recommended that his followers seek appropriate moral behavior in this world in their pursuit of salvation. Confucianism rapidly intermeshed with the traditional culture of China, much as Hinduism has merged into Indian life.

Confucianism is based on the concept of *jen* or "humaneness," meaning that morality should always precede self-interest. Especially within one's own family, concern for others is primary; to ensure a strong family, a person must be unfailingly loyal. In Confucianism, one behaves morally in everyday interactions. There is no other-world to come, as in Christianity.

Confucianism does not make a clear distinction between the sacred and the profane elements of the world. Thus, Confucianism might be argued to be a system for a disciplined life, based on Chinese traditions, rather than a religion. Like a religion, however, Confucianism is a body of beliefs and practices that guides behavior and promotes a sense of belonging (Kaufman, 1976; Schmidt, 1980).

Judaism

Judaism is a religion numbering more than 18 million members worldwide. The largest number of Jews reside in North America; others are in Europe and the Middle East, but Jews are very widely dispersed. At its inception

FIGURE 15:4 RELIGIONS OF THE WORLD

The global distribution of world religions.

Source: The New Encyclopedia Britannica, pp. 526–27. Vol. 26, 15th Edition, 1991.

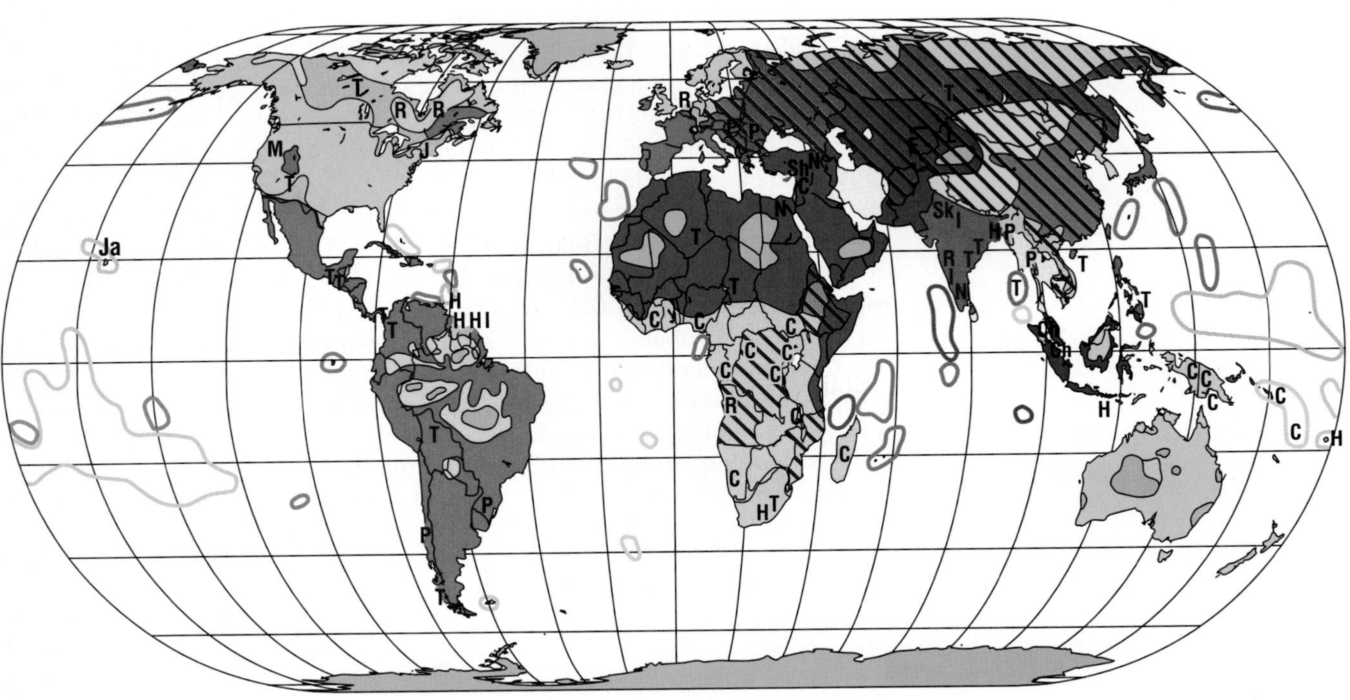

Religions

The majority of the inhabitants in each of the areas colored on the map share the religious tradition indicated. Letter symbols show religious traditions shared by at least 25 percent of the inhabitants within areal units no smaller than one thousand square miles. Therefore minority religions of city-dwellers have generally not been represented.

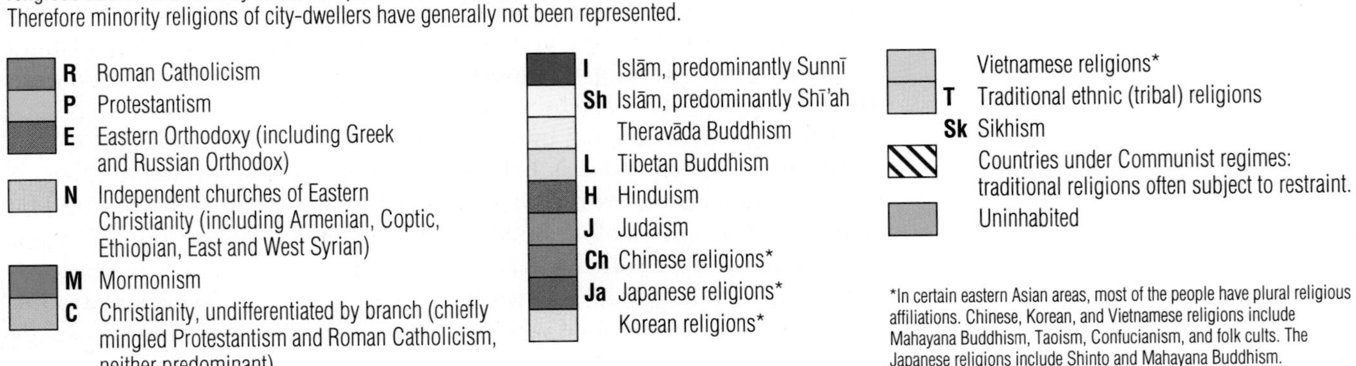

animism—the attribution of a soul or spirit to living things and inanimate objects.

(about 4000 BC) in ancient Mesopotamia and Egypt, Judaism was a religion of worship of animal spirits. **Animism** declined after Jacob, grandson of Abraham, led his people into Egypt. Under Egyptian rule, the Jews endured centuries of enslavement. In the thirteenth century BC, however, slavery ended as Moses, the adopted son of an Egyptian princess, led his people out of that country. Following this exodus, Judaism became monotheistic, honoring one all-powerful God who had led them to freedom.

As Christians are divided into many denominations, Jews form three distinct groups in the United States. The first, Orthodox Jews, include more than 1 million Americans. They strictly observe traditional beliefs and practices, including forms of dress, segregation of men and women at religious services in the synagogue, and eating of only Kosher (i.e., ritually pure) foods. In the mid-nineteenth century, many Jews accommodated to the larger society by eliminating segregation of men and women in the temple and easing dietary restrictions. This group has become known as Reform Judaism (1.3 million in the United States). More recently, a third group, Conservative Judaism (about 2 million Americans), has established a middle ground between the two more extreme positions.

Jewish emigration to America began in the mid-1600s. Large numbers of Jews arrived in the United States during the last decades of the nineteenth century as anti-Semitism increased in Europe. This anti-Semitism reached its height when Nazis annihilated about 6 million people during the 1930s and 1940s (Abzug, 1985). One of the oldest world religions, Judaism has changed considerably over its thousands of years. Like Christianity and Islam, Judaism recognizes a single God. Like Hinduism and Confucianism, Judaism emphasizes behavior in this present world according to traditional moral principles. The history of Judaism also serves as a reminder of the degree to which religious minorities have been subjected to persecution (Bedell, Sandon, and Wellborn, 1975; Greeley, 1989; Schmidt, 1980; Seltzer, 1980; Wilson, 1982). Figure 15:4 illustrates the distribution of major religions worldwide.

RELIGION IN THE UNITED STATES TODAY

Religious Affiliation

Unlike societies in which there is a state religion, the United States is characterized by religious pluralism; Americans can choose from dozens of denominations. Although advances in education, science, and technology threaten to undermine traditional religion, much evidence indicates that religion continues to be a vital element in the lives of many U.S. citizens (Collins, 1982; Greeley, 1989). National surveys indicate, for example, that about 90 percent of Americans claim belief in a particular religion (NORC, 1989). Formal affiliation with a religious organization characterizes about two-thirds of the population; this proportion has remained relatively constant over the past 50 years (NORC, 1989; U.S. Bureau of Census, 1989).

Of the population of the United States, 33 percent associate themselves with one of the many liberal or moderate Protestant denominations. Another 15 percent profess membership in conservative Protestant churches, such as Southern Baptists and Assembly of God. African American Protestant groups account for 9 percent of the population, Catholics for 25 percent, and Jews for 2 percent. The remaining 16 percent are split between those who claim some other religious faith and those who belong to no religious organization.

These simple statistics can camouflage the continuously changing nature of religious affiliation in the United States. One of the major changes, as noted by Robert Wuthnow (1988), is an overall decline in denominationalism. There is much less competition among Protestant denominations such as Methodists versus Presbyterians. Protestant and Catholic leaders are becoming more cooperative. The Catholic Church is experiencing growth; Catholic membership has risen considerably in recent years, due largely to a high birthrate among Catholics as well as to Hispanic immigration to the United States. Fundamentalist Protestant groups such as Pentecostals have also expanded, often at a faster rate than the U.S. population as a whole. On the other hand, liberal Protestant denominations are undergoing slow decline, losing younger members in particular to Fundamentalist churches. The American Jewish population is not on the rise, due to a low Jewish birthrate and a high rate of marriage into other religions. Attendance at Jewish services is up slightly, however. To understand these trends and statistics more completely, we need to examine another dimension of people's relationship to their religion.

Religiosity

Charles Glock (1962a, 1962b) distinguishes five distinct dimensions of religiosity. *Experiential* religiosity refers to a person's perceived emotional tie to a religion. The religious intensity item in Table 15:1 taps this dimension. *Ritualistic* religiosity refers to the frequency of participation in concrete ritual activities, such as prayer, performance of holiday ceremonies, and church attendance. *Ideological* religiosity concerns the intensity of belief in specific religious doctrines (such as Jesus being the Son of God). *Consequential* religiosity reflects evidence of religious belief in a person's everyday behavior: Does a person actually do unto others as they do unto him? *Intellectual* religiosity refers to a person's knowledge of the history, beliefs, and traditions of a religion. People tend to vary along these religious dimensions.

How religious are Americans? Ninety-five percent of Americans claim to believe in a divine power, although only 65 percent say they "know that God exists and have no doubts about it" (NORC, 1989). Ninety percent of Americans identify with a specific religion, and 84 percent say they "feel a closeness to God." Americans score relatively high on measures of experiential religiosity, while they seem to be less religious in ideological terms; only about 70 percent claim to believe in a life after death (NORC, 1989). Americans score even lower on dimensions of ritualistic religiosity. For example, only 50 percent of American adults say they pray at least once a day. Only one-third of Americans report that they attend religious services on a weekly or nearly weekly basis (NORC, 1989).

The pattern of American religiosity, then, is a complex one. Because belief in God is normative in American culture, many people may agree to this belief simply as a matter of conformity. Similarly, people may attend religious services for social interaction opportunities or to enjoy a sense of belonging, rather than out of a sense of true religious devotion. Patterns of religious belief also differ among the specific religious organizations. Stark and Glock (1968) found Catholics to hold their beliefs more strongly than Protestants, and members of sects to believe more intensely than do members of Protestant or Catholic churches.

Correlates of Religious Affiliation

Social Class

Religious affiliation is significantly related to social class position. Wade Roof (1979) reports that Jews and members of certain Protestant denominations—Presbyterian and Episcopalian—have the highest overall social status in the United States. Other Protestant denominations, such as Methodists and Congregationalists, occupy a middle position, while slightly lower social status is found among Catholics, Baptists, Lutherans, and various other sects. More recent studies suggest that Catholics are moving upward in social class standing. Protestant denominations, which enjoy the highest social status, are those of Northern European background. Typically, their ancestors began to establish themselves in the United States more than a century ago, and they encountered little prejudice or discrimination. Roman Catholics are likely to have been more recent immigrants to the United States (Johnstone, 1983). Jews, however, tend to occupy high social classes even though many are very recent immigrants to this country and have often encountered much anti-Semitism. Traditional Jewish culture places great emphasis on educational achievement. Although a large percentage of Jews began their lives in the United States in relative poverty, their intense enthusiasm for learning has encouraged extensive education of children, and facilitated great upward mobility over one or two generations.

Ethnicity and Race

Throughout the world, religion is strongly linked to ethnicity. Both Christianity and Judaism are dispersed among many ethnic groups. In the United States there are, for example, Irish Catholics, Polish Catholics, Italian Catholics; there are German Jews, Russian Jews, and Polish Jews. Nearly every U.S. ethnic group contains several religious denominations. Americans of English descent, for example, include members of many Protestant

Religion is a very engaging and highly emotional experience. In this African-American church in Virginia, mass baptism of adults provides an outlet for religious expression and a sense of personal fulfillment and belongingness.

denominations, such as Episcopalians, Methodists, and Quakers, as well as Roman Catholics and Jews.

The church has historically occupied a central place in the lives of African Americans. After their arrival in this country, many African Americans joined Christian groups but fused the Christian beliefs and practices with elements of their African religions, such as spontaneous singing and personalized ecstatic experiences. These elements continue to exist in some contemporary African American religious organizations (Frazier, 1965; Roberts, 1980). Despite Christianity's professed belief in brotherhood and equality before God, African Americans historically attended all-black churches or worshipped in segregated sections of predominantly white churches. In the present-day United States, middle-class African American churches, such as the African Methodist Episcopal Church, have emerged. Significant numbers of African Americans have also begun to join the Catholic Church.

Political Attitudes

On most issues, American Protestants are more conservative than either Catholics or Jews. Protestants typically support the Republican Party, whereas Catholics and Jews have tended to align themselves with the more liberal Democratic Party (Gallup, 1982; Wilson, 1978). Yet, on the highly controversial issue of abortion, non-Fundamentalist Protestants are more likely to take the liberal Pro-Choice stance, whereas Catholics are more firmly Pro-Life, the conservative view.

Overall, the conservatism of Protestants reflects their higher social class position in U.S. society. Many liberal Catholics and Jews, on the other hand, are ethnic and religious minorities who have suffered discrimination and oppression at the hands of the Protestant majority. Similarly, the African American church has historically been politically active, representing both the long-standing response to prejudicial treatment by a Christian majority, as well as a commitment to basic Christian beliefs, such as equality and brotherly love.

Current Trends in Traditional American Churches

Throughout the 1980s and into the 1990s, Americans have not abandoned their existing churches so much as they have attempted to make them more responsive to changing personal needs. Americans now seek a more intense and ecstatic spirituality, more spontaneous participation by members in religious services, and more active stances on social issues (Gallup Report, 1985; Woodward, 1992). We can examine recent developments within U.S. Catholic Churches, Protestant denominations, and Jewish congregations, all of which illustrate these overall trends.

Catholics

Over the past 30 years, Roman Catholics have experienced radical upheaval in their religious lives. The reforms instituted by Vatican II (1962–1965) marked the almost revolutionary dissent from traditional teachings for Catholics. Vatican II eliminated the Latin mass and meatless Fridays; permitted the laity to receive Communion wafers in their own hands, and to drink wine from the chalice; as well as other significant departures from centuries-old traditions. The church has continued to change after Vatican II, particularly in the United States. Many Catholics openly speak out against church policy on issues such as birth control, divorce, remarriage, and the concept of papal infallibility. Many dissenters still claim to remain solidly Catholic in their views of life, death, and God, and plan to continue their membership in the church, albeit on their own terms (Greeley, 1972).

Other internal and external changes have occurred in U.S. Catholicism. Many descendants of earlier, economically deprived Catholic immigrants have become successful, well-educated, suburban middle- and upper-middle-class Americans. At the same time, however, the number of priests and nuns in the United States has greatly diminished. One-fifth of all Catholic priests have left the ministry; an even greater proportion of nuns have abandoned their religious orders (Marty, 1985). Understaffed parish churches have asked lay people to become more involved in the administrative and liturgical duties, such as the reading of Scriptures and the distribution of Communion.

Despite sweeping changes, the role of women in the Catholic Church is a source of escalating tension. Many Catholic women are deeply distressed by urgings from the Vatican that they remain in traditional roles. Catholic women are becoming more vocal in their opposition to the church's stands against birth control, premarital sex, remarriage, optional celibacy for priests, altar girls, and even the ordination of women. Nuns, who still outnumber priests by two to one, are leading the movement to enlarge the role of women in the Catholic Church. Nuns have also broadened their positions in the larger society, serving as lawyers, lobbyists, and political activists.

On other social issues, the Catholic Church has been acting as a social conscience and advocate for change. In the spring of 1983, the first pastoral letter from Unified Catholic Bishops against nuclear arms was published. In the fall of 1984, another Catholic Bishops' pastoral letter on the U.S. economy urged greater efforts to lessen poverty and unemployment (Marty, 1985; O'Rourke, 1983).

Protestants

From the mid-1960s on, mainline Protestant denominations have been experiencing a drop in membership. Between 1972 and 1982, for example, membership declines were as follows: United Methodist Church—10 percent, Episcopal Church—15 percent, and United Presbyterian Church—21 percent. Over the same years, Fundamentalist Protestant churches were attracting record numbers of new members. Southern Baptist convention membership rose 20 percent, Seventh Day Adventists made a 35 percent gain, and Assemblies of God grew by 62 percent (Roof and McKinney, 1985; Wuthnow, 1988).

Mainline churches are now swinging back toward more traditional elements—more prayers, stronger spirituality, more literal interpretation of scripture, and renewed religious faith. As yet, however, mainline churches have regained little of the lost membership. The revitalized emphasis on fundamental faith and a literal approach to scripture has enhanced the ecumenical movement, which fosters worldwide Christian unity and a merging of Protestant churches (Roof and McKinney, 1985; Wuthnow, 1988).

Religion can be a central stage for issues involving gender and social change. It has only been in recent times, for instance, that women were permitted to become rabbis.

Jews

While the differences among Orthodox, Conservative, and Reform Jews are similar to fundamental distinctions between Fundamentalist and liberal Protestants, the three former groups share concern for the State of Israel and for the well-being of world Jewry.

Many American Jews want a more meaningful religious life than is offered in passive worship in a large, often impersonal congregation. Often these Jews are seeking out "Havurah *(group)*," a movement that promises a more spiritually and personally meaningful religion. A Havurah consists of several families who meet on a regular basis. The meetings may involve study groups, emphasize social service activities to help the infirm or needy, and try to personalize Judaism by bringing families together for worship and celebration of holidays. Havurahs also promote greater participation of women in religious services. Reform synagogues now ordain women rabbis.

Like many mainline Protestant denominations, Jewish groups were very active in the Civil Rights Movement and other social causes of the 1960s and 1970s. Today Jews are looking inward for a more intense spiritual life. Many young Jews are revitalizing religious rituals in their synagogues, observing traditional dietary laws, and studying the Torah, Talmud, and other Jewish scholarship more avidly (Kaufman, 1976).

INVISIBLE OR PRIVATE RELIGION

Some of those who are most critical of mainline organized religion are actually quite religious. They have chosen to practice what Thomas Luckmann (1967) calls "invisible" or "private" religion; that is, many people are creating their own personal religious belief systems without communal support and without participation in traditional institutional religious bodies.

Many of those who embrace a private faith claim no affiliation with any religious organization. The number of such people in the United States rose from 2 percent in 1967 to 8 percent in 1986. Those who practice a private religion do not often discuss their religious beliefs with others, with the possible exception of close network members. They keep their faith, their worship, and spiritual lives to themselves (Hart, 1987). The existence of invisible religions may help explain the seemingly paradoxical finding that although 95 percent of Americans say they believe in God, only 42 percent attend church regularly (Harris, 1987).

The primary goal of private religions is self-fulfillment. Much attention is focused on techniques—mystical, magical, psychotherapeutic, and technological—that can facilitate this sense of fulfillment. This emphasis on techniques is a common denominator of what is termed the "New Age" movement, which includes a wide variety of consciousness-altering methodologies. Biofeedback, meditation, Silva Mind Control, est, yoga, lifespring—all are designed to heighten the person's inner-spiritual sensitivity, increase individual self-discipline, and enhance the potential for a transcendent experience (Bordewich, 1988). The different techniques can be learned and then practiced by oneself almost anywhere, thus facilitating the growth of private religion.

Some theologians are disturbed by the pervasiveness of private religions because they believe this could undermine the importance of the sense of community provided by the organized church. In sociological terms, private religion seems to be an inevitable outgrowth of several U.S. values (Hart, 1987). First, in a democratic society, we value freedom of choice and, historically, selection of a religion has been a matter of personal preference. Second, we often examine several "products" before determining our final choice; such everyday "market" experiences may encourage Americans to view religion as a similarly *personal* matter, not to be shared with or justified to anyone else. Finally, we have access to a great deal of religious doctrine, practices, and information through radio, television, books, and magazines—without having to belong to any religious organization. This encourages people to practice their private religion in whatever ways they wish.

Secularization

secularization—a general decline in the social authority of religion, often associated with technologically advanced societies.

The growth of private religions seems to be an element of a larger and more controversial pattern of change, known as **secularization** of religion. Secularization refers to a general decline in the social authority of religion. Formally, it is the process often associated with technologically advanced societies by which religious institutions and symbols cease to legitimate, support, and justify various dimensions of society and culture. Secularization diminishes religion's sphere of influence (Cox, 1971; O'Dea and Ariad, 1983).

Peter Berger (1979) argues that secularization has occurred in U.S. society for several reasons. First, modernization has spurred the growth of science, which endorses reason and systematic observation as supreme authorities in our knowledge of the world. As people gradually accept the naturalistic perspective offered by science, their capacity for faith in the supernatural may gradually erode. Second, modern societies are much more religiously heterogeneous than are traditional societies. With so many religions from which to select, it becomes increasingly difficult to believe that any single one embodies absolute truth. Thus the traditional authority of religions can be further diminished. Finally, the complex technological nature of modern life with its ubiquitous computers and ever-growing pace may not be a compatible environment for spirituality. "If the angels spoke to us all the time," says Berger (1979), "the business of modern living would grind to a halt."

Berger (1967) also suggests that secularization can be observed on three levels: societal, cultural, and individual. At the societal level, religious institutions no longer exercise significant control over the activities of the government or the public educational system. Patterns of secularization have also affected cultural life. As secularization proceeds, Berger argues, the arts, literature, and philosophy draw less and less frequently from religious sources for inspiration. They turn instead to political or social issues such as abortion, substance abuse, capital punishment, AIDS, or discrimination as the raw materials for contemporary drama, paintings, novels, essays, and so on. Finally, secularization has a personal dimension. In Berger's view, the individual consciousness has become secularized. The modern West, he says, increasingly creates individuals who think about the world and evaluate their own lives without the benefit of a firm religious perspective. In the pre-secular era, religious ideals were accepted as fundamental, unquestionable truths. Theologian Harvey Cox explains the contrast:

> The world looks less and less to religious rules and rituals for its morality or its meanings. For some, religion provides a hobby, for others, a mark of national or ethnic identification, for still others, an aesthetic delight. For fewer and fewer does it provide an inclusive and commanding system of personal and cosmic values and explanations (Cox, 1971, p. 3).

Does this mean that the complete disappearance of religion is inevitable in the foreseeable future? Much of the previous discussion of the present status of mainline religions in America suggests that it does not. As indicated earlier, there has been a recent swell of activity in organized churches, sects, and cults, and in the sphere of private religion in the past few decades.

Secularization is *not* a progressive elimination of religion; rather it is an uneven process of change, in which some aspects of religion may ebb while others flourish. Secularization has brought some religious rituals into closer correspondence with modern societal practice. The Catholic Church, for example, has given up the use of Latin in masses in favor of using the commonly spoken language of the locale. Some religions such as the Episcopalian have also begun to permit the ordination of women.

Civil Religion

Although secularization has brought about a decline in some traditional rituals and beliefs, it has also indirectly spurred the rise of other religious forms (McGuire, 1987). Both processes are operative in what Robert Bellah (1975) has termed **civil religion**—a set of symbols, beliefs, values, and practices that give sacred meaning to a nation and its people.

civil religion—a set of symbols, beliefs, values, and practices that give sacred meaning to a nation and its people.

Because of a strong history of separation of church and state, the United States has never established a national church. The common thread that unites Americans of diverse religious affiliations is its civil religion, what Will Herberg (1955) calls its underlying "culture-religion"—a secular, nonsectarian core that unifies Americans around a public expression of sacred beliefs, symbols, and rituals.

Civil religion gives sacred meaning to a nation and its people. This is the Vietnam Veterans' Memorial, where people come to pray for those who were reported missing or who met tragic death in an unpopular war. This type of shrine gives dignity to the deaths of millions of Americans and a sense of regained honor to their families and friends.

Patriotism and religion often evoke similar emotional and psychological experiences in the individual. Participants in a patriotic celebration on Memorial Day or the Fourth of July often feel the same reverence and awe that is shared by people at religious services (Herberg, 1955). Emile Durkheim suggests that all rituals help people to recognize their collective identity, the power of their belonging to a society. Civil religion is not a specific religious doctrine, but it does incorporate many elements of traditional religion. Many elaborate rituals exist, such as the standing of thousands of people for the playing of the National Anthem before a sports event; or public parades on Memorial Day, New Year's Day, and Thanksgiving. Sacred symbols include the flag, the Statue of Liberty, the Lincoln Memorial, Arlington National Cemetery, and many others, each of which has acquired a mystical quality that is perceived to embody the nation's values. The Vietnam Veteran's Memorial is a more recently created sacred symbol; ritual behaviors include the placing of flowers, flags, and other special objects at the wall where the names of war dead are engraved.

The concept of a U.S. civil religion has generated considerable comment, controversy, and research since Robert Bellah's original formulation of the idea in 1967 (Bellah and Hammond, 1980; Demerath and Williams, 1985; Gehrig, 1979). Empirical studies have demonstrated a widespread acceptance of these beliefs and practices among the American people. However, some writers (including Bellah himself) have questioned whether the assumption of a general agreement on the sacredness of U.S. society can validly be applied to a U.S. society that has become increasingly fragmented and polarized.

Religious Revival

As we have seen, secularization encourages new forms of religious activity. According to Stark and Bainbridge (1985), two trends appear concurrently with secularization: religious revival and religious innovation. Religious revival is an effort to restore more fundamental, spiritual features to established religions. Religious innovation involves efforts to create new religions or to change existing ones to better meet people's needs.

Fundamentalism: Religious Revival and Innovation. In response to the liberalization of beliefs in many mainstream Protestant churches, a growing number of Christians are seeking what they consider the original or "fundamental" beliefs and practices of their faith. This Fundamentalist resurgence is visible both in the *innovation* of new sects, some of which have broken away from established churches; and in *revival* of older, more traditional rites and values within mainstream Protestant churches. Fundamentalists seek to restore religious purity to churches whose doctrines and rituals, they believe, have been denatured and eroded by too much accommodation to the ways of modern society. To counteract such consequences of modernization, Fundamentalists emphasize absolute adherence to the Bible as the ultimate authority on all issues. Fundamentalism's appeal is that it offers certainty in an uncertain world. While some people see this as extremist and dogmatic, others find it very reassuring and comforting.

Fundamentalist Christian groups display four elements (Wilcox, 1989). First, Fundamentalists subscribe to a literal interpretation of the Bible. They view more liberal interpretations offered by establishment churches as simply incorrect. In regard to the creationism issue, for example, Fundamentalists agree that God created the Earth in seven days, exactly as described in the book of Genesis. Second, Fundamentalists are quite intolerant of religious diversity. Because they so strongly embrace their own beliefs as the one true religion, all other beliefs are erroneous by definition. Third, Fundamentalism is sect-like in its focus on members' personal experience of the religion. Fundamentalism encourages members' active participation in services. The transcendent experience of being "born again" serves as a foundation for development of an ongoing personal relationship with Jesus. Fourth, Fundamentalism displays sect-like hostility toward the contemporary world, which is considered to be a source of a secular humanism that threatens their true religious conviction (Wilcox, 1989).

Generally, Fundamentalists belong to conservative Christian organizations, such as Pentecostals, Southern Baptists, Seventh-Day Adventists, and the Assembly of God. If Fundamentalist concepts are defined as those who interpret the Bible literally, about 20 percent of Americans would be termed Fundamentalists (NORC, 1989). Fundamentalism has historically been strongest in rural America, having its greatest growth about a century ago, when modern cities were expanding very rapidly (Wilcox, 1989).

During the 1980s Christian Fundamentalism acquired a political dimension in the form of what has become the New Christian Right (Ostling, 1985; Speer, 1984; Viguere, 1981). Jerry Falwell, a Fundamentalist preacher who catapulted this movement into the national arena, described its goals:

> I am seeking to rally together the people of this country who still believe in decency, the home, the family, morality, the free enterprise system and all the great ideals that are the cornerstone of this nation.

> Against the growing tide of permissiveness and moral decay that is crushing our society, we must make a sacred commitment to God almighty to turn this nation around immediately (Falwell, cited in Speer, 1984, p. 20).

In 1989, Falwell formally disbanded his "moral majority" and turned his energies to his own church in Lynchburg, Virginia. He and other Fundamentalist ministers continue their public opposition to the Equal Rights Amendment, civil rights for homosexuals, and the wide availability of pornographic materials. Also, during the 1980s, Fundamentalists made extensive use of television, the most powerful medium for communication to mass audiences.

The Electronic Church

Millions of Americans have become participants in a new, secularized form of religious activity. Television and radio audiences now form large, diverse congregations as members of the "Electronic Church." The mass media have become essential for generating new converts and contributors to a variety of Fundamentalist religions. This new vehicle for religious communication well fits modern life. In a transient United States, in which people move frequently and may not wish to switch from church to church, participation in a television worship service provides both a sense of continuity and a scheduling convenience. Television religions also create the illusion of face-to-face interaction with the minister.

Evangelistic television and radio programs reach a wide audience. A 1985 Neilsen poll showed that 60 percent of Americans tuned in to at least one religious program weekly. At the outset of the 1980s, this uniquely U.S. religious activity claimed about 1,400 radio stations and 60 TV stations. Aided by electronic churches, religious leaders such as Oral Roberts and Jim and Tammy Bakker became better known than all but a few clergy of the past (Jacquet, 1986). Radio programs, in particular, tend to appeal to the impoverished and less educated segment of society, who feel unable to cope with their problems. Two-thirds to three-fourths of the audiences of both TV and radio religious programs tend to be age 50 or older, and about two-thirds are women. For the elderly and the socially isolated, these radio and television programs replace going out to church services (Jacquet, 1985).

Here is the epitome of the electronic church—a "drive-in church." It is not only a visually striking example of this new secularized form of religious activity but also consistent with some parts of the American lifestyle—quick and convenient—just like a fast-food restaurant or convenience store.

Of course, the electronic media provide an excellently tuned vehicle for the solicitation of contributions to support the ministry. Broadcasting with 3,200 stations in half the countries in the world, Jimmy Swaggart received $180 million in contributions in 1986. In the late 1980s the Electronic Church began to lose some of its authority, however. One of its most widely known preachers, Jim Bakker, was found to be paying blackmail money to a woman with whom he had had a brief affair several years earlier. He was forced to resign his ministry and was eventually found to be defrauding his contributors. Bakker began serving a prison term in 1989 (Jaquet, 1986; Wilcox, 1989). Some Americans have begun to question the integrity of television Evangelists, and disillusionment deepened when Jimmy Swaggart was also found to have committed sexual indiscretions. Thus the Electronic Church has declined somewhat in popularity and influence.

Although television preachers will have to work diligently to restore their lost audiences, the Electronic Church is likely to continue as a significant aspect of religion in the modern United States.

This is the courtyard of the Haram Mosque in Mecca, where a quarter of a million Muslims are paying homage to Allah. In its turmoil, the Middle East lies well this side of paradise. Yet, from the point of view of religion, it offers feasts unrivaled in this contemporary world.

SUMMARY

1. What is the role of religion in the world and in the United States today? This is the underlying question addressed in this chapter. In the process, we have pursued a number of paths.
2. Religion is a matter of faith; it is belief not based on scientific evidence. The primary elements of religion, according to Emile Durkheim, are its division of the world into sacred and profane dimensions. The profane includes all aspects of ordinary, everyday life. The sacred, on the other hand, inspires awe, respect, mystery, and fear.
3. Religion provides a belief system that provides meaning and understanding to the mysteries of life. Rituals are practices that express those beliefs. Further, rituals and beliefs unite adherents into a community, which creates a strong sense of belonging among members.
4. Through this strong community, religion enhances members' sense of connectedness to the larger society. The belief systems of religion also reinforce the norms of the society and impose strong sanctions against those who deviate from those norms. All major religions also celebrate major life events through special ceremonies.
5. From a conflict perspective, religion serves to justify the authenticity of the ruling class and pacify the lower classes. More recently, however, religion has become involved in social justice movements, as demonstrated by the work of Catholic bishops in Latin American

countries. The symbolic interactionist perspective suggests that religion imbues all aspects of life with transcendent meaning.

6. The structure of religious organizations varies greatly from society to society and over time. Ernst Troeltsch (1931) distinguished between a "church," a formal organization that is well-integrated into society, and a "sect," an informal structure that is *not* well integrated into the society. A *cult* is a religious movement that is quite unorthodox vis-à-vis mainstream society. Over time, sects such as the Quakers may evolve into churches.
7. There are thousands of religions throughout the world. However, six major religions can be distinguished: Christianity, Islam, Hinduism, Buddhism, Confucianism, and Judaism. Each has its own distinct set of beliefs and rituals, which unite its adherents into communities.
8. Unlike some other countries, the United States has no state or national religion, and is characterized by religious pluralism. About two-thirds of Americans are affiliated with a religious organization. The pattern of U.S. religiosity is complex and varies according to social class, ethnicity, race, and political attitudes.
9. There are many people who, although not affiliated with any mainstream organized religion, are actually quite religious. They practice what Thomas Luckmann (1967) calls "invisible" or "private" religion. They create their own personal religious belief system without participating in any traditional institutional religious body.
10. The growth of private religions is one element of a larger, more controversial pattern of change, known as secularization—a general decline in religion's sphere of influence in the United States. People presently look less and less to religion for answers to social and personal questions.
11. Another religious form—"civil religion"—has flourished. Civil religion is a secular core that unifies Americans around public expressions of beliefs, symbols, and rituals, such as patriotic celebrations on the Fourth of July and the playing of the National Anthem before sports events.
12. The United States is witnessing a religious revival of original or fundamental beliefs and practices of faith. Fundamentalists seek to restore religious purity to churches whose doctrines and rituals, they believe, have been eroded by accommodation to modern society.
13. Finally, millions of Americans have become participants in a unique, secularized form of religious activity. Television and radio audiences now comprise large, diverse congregations of the "electronic church." This new vehicle for religious communication is a reflection of modern life in the highly mobile United States.

Chapter 16

Personal Perspective

IT was my first job that did not involve the phrase, "Do you want fries with that?"

I still remember the training session. The foreman first handed me the tools of the trade: a bucket of paint thinner and a rag. He then explained my task. "Flip off the machine, dip your rag, wipe off the nozzle, and flip it back on. Move to the second machine, flip, dip, wipe, flip. Repeat on each machine, and then it will be time to return to the first one. Got it?" I muttered something clever ("Pretty important job, huh?"), then got to work. Flip, dip, wipe, flip. By my own conservative estimate, I repeated the sequence 42,000 times during that memorable summer.

Essentially, I was a machine tender. My specialized job was at position 12 of 28 distinct processes on what was known as a "can line." The factory manufactured cans in separate lines that consisted of strings of machines stretching for over a city block. Into one end would be fed sheets of metal, and out the other, barely visible end would pop specially fashioned cylinders for holding soda, tomatoes, or oil.

In the preceding three sentences, I have explained all I really understood about the industrial process I served for eight hours a night (11 PM to 7 AM) over 10 summer weeks.

You may have gathered by now that this job was not completely fulfilling. It was maddeningly boring, to the point that I would mentally compute the number of *minutes* left until (you should excuse the expression) Labor Day. The monotony of repeating four simple movements over and over could not be broken by conversation. For one thing, the roar of the machines was so loud that a shout could not be heard from 10 feet away. For another, the repetition was mindless, but demanding. If I did not keep up with my nozzle-wiping, the conveyor belt moving the cans would clog, and the whole production line would close down with much siren-whooping and embarrassment. I never even learned the name of the woman doing the same job on the line several yards away. The industrially engineered pace of production forced us to work at its preset speed.

The only break in the boredom was the shock of a pink slip. It was taped to the punch-in clock one day informing me that I had been laid off. Mixed with the shame of unemployment—this was, after all, my "master status" for the summer—was a growing curiosity. What had happened? The company gave no reason on the pink slip for its action. While trying to restore my sleep cycle to normal, I actually spent that first night reading the financial pages of the newspaper. For what it was worth, I was not alone. Unemployment had climbed nationwide that month, especially in the manufacturing sector. It was a period of what economists call "stagflation," characterized by high inflation, which the political institution fought with a restrictive monetary policy (cuts in the money supply by the Federal Reserve) that, in turn, drove up unemployment.

This was a rude awakening to the personal significance of politics, a subject I had frankly considered as boring as the can job. Not this time. The political arm of society itself had shaken the economy, which then shook out my pocketbook. I really needed the money. My college tuition had just been raised, and student loans were harder to get—another conspiracy of the political/economic system against me. Fighting down paranoia, I took a job as a gravedigger.

BJJ

Political Economy

While we commonly think of "politics" and "economics" as separate and distinct, the two spheres are actually quite closely related. As the story suggests, political control and economic resources interact with one another in significant ways. Every aspect of our lives is structured to some extent by the nature of the political economy in which we live. From its impact on our decision about what to study in school (What field has job openings?) or even what to do in our spare time (Did the city raise a bond to build the stadium?), the influence of the political–economic system on our lives is often so pervasive as to seem invisible. Beyond the obvious ways in which economic and political systems come to bear on each other—via such entities as government regulatory institutions or through the vagaries of political campaign financing—the state and the economy in the modern world are so tightly bound together that one cannot be properly understood apart from the other.

state—the central political structure of a society.

The political economy that we are familiar with in the United States today is the product of a series of very specific and quite recent historical processes. For example, most of the social benefits provided by the government, such as Social Security and Unemployment Insurance, are developments of the twentieth century. The transition from an economy centered on farming and small businesses to one distinguished by large corporate hierarchies has happened almost entirely since the Civil War. And the first real formation of the nation–state as we know it today, with clearly defined borders and a centralized government, took place less than 500 years ago.

Speculations upon political economy extend at least as far back as Aristotle. However, formal examinations of the political economy in the contemporary sense have their origins in the writings of the eighteenth-century analysts of capitalism. Adam Smith and David Ricardo built their theories of capitalism upon a consideration of "political economy," a term linking this new economic system to the new governmental forms that emerged with it. While they did not foresee the role of the state as entirely passive, the key function of government was to be the "acceptance of the economic laws of capitalism" (Therborn, 1976, p. 85), thus allowing Smith's famous "invisible hand" to benefit all. Commentators since that time have been heavily concentrated in the professional disciplines of political science or economics. Despite the powerful structural connections, sociology has also shown a tendency to disconnect "politics" and "economics" into two mutually exclusive realms for study.

These intellectual divisions are unfortunate because the classical sociologists who laid the foundation of the social sciences were essentially students of these linked institutions. Karl Marx, Max Weber, and Emile Durkheim each placed studies of the political economy at the forefront of their work.

This propaganda poster from China depicts the ideal of a communist political economy. Communism is a particular type of structural connection of the political and economic institutions, and the people shown suggest the relevance of political economy to individual lives.

Marx's approach to political economy is perhaps the best known, as it formed the backbone of his general theory about society. By focusing on the development and dynamics of capitalism, Marx explained the source of the conflicts and divisions in modern society. His now-familiar framing of the concepts of alienation, exploitation, and class conflict were stimulated by looking at the political economy as the center of society. Marx's concentration on the relations between capital and labor involved in the material production of capitalist societies stimulated innumerable studies of the political economy—some developing his ideas, some critiquing them. In both cases, Marx's work has had an enormous effect upon sociological approaches to the political economy, and is a powerful argument for studying it as a single subject.

While Weber assigned the state a more prominent position than did Marx in his theoretical analyses, the former certainly recognized the fundamental importance of the economy as well as the political system in contributing to the distinctiveness of Western capitalist societies. Weber's description of the process of rationalization in modern nations is linked to the process of bureaucratization, which flourishes in the capitalist political economy (see Chapter 2). For Weber, the rising scale of human groups in every sphere of contemporary life gradually stamps out the freedom of people to control their own paltry lives in the shadow of huge bureaucracies. Further, if it were not for the bureaucratic political system of modern nation–states, a capitalist economic system requiring social order and predictability would not even be possible. In Weber's formulation, the economic system also acts back upon the functioning and form of the political system. Politics and economics have a reciprocal relationship, with each helping to cement the rational, bureaucratic structures that today characterize our society.

Durkheim's work is less overtly concerned with an examination of political economy, but it is there nevertheless in his general theory of societal development. Durkheim's ideas about normative development are closely bound to the analysis of the division of labor in modern societies. The laws of a nation help to sustain the smooth functioning of an ever more complex society. Try to imagine the dealings of modern industrial corporations without the protective mechanism of modern corporate law. While the causal arrows connecting the political economy to value systems are somewhat different for Durkheim than they are for Weber or Marx, his work is a testament to the fact that polity and economy are joined at the hip.

Marx, Weber, and Durkheim have dominated sociological theory in part because they differ about the central mechanisms of social life. Despite these differences, all three theorists are noted for examining societal processes with an eye to the impact they have on people's real experience. The study of political economy need not be an abstract exercise about a boring subject, but should ideally show the great power that political *and* economic institutions have to shape the way we live. In particular, the assumptions many of us hold about the United States itself are rooted in the specific political and economic system that is its heart. "Freedom" and "democracy" are commonly heard in reference to the United States, and it is easy to accept these vague terms as real. However, a closer look at the U.S. system reveals that our "freedom" is not unlimited; neither is our government a real democracy in the technical sense (on how many decisions do you get a personal vote?). It is also very easy for a college student to accept the conventional wisdom that this is a middle-class society and that living standards are consistently improving. In actuality, the middle class has recently been *shrinking*, with the ranks of millionaires increasing by the thousands and the ranks of the poor growing by the millions (Barlett and Steele, 1992). In 1985, the share of income going to the top 20 percent of families was the highest ever recorded in U.S. history, whereas the share of income going to the bottom 60 percent of families was the lowest ever recorded (Thurow, 1987, p. 30). This fading of the American Dream motivates the study of the dream factory itself—the political economy.

TYPES OF POLITICAL ECONOMIES

Capitalism

capitalism—a political economy in which the means of production are privately owned.

The system prevalent in most of the West—and, increasingly, the non-West—is **capitalism**. Since its origins in the seventeenth century, the nature of the capitalist state has undergone a number of transformations. The map in Figure 16:1 shows the relative dominance of different types of political economies around the world.

Laissez-faire, roughly translated in Webster's dictionary to mean "Let people do what they consider best," was an early form of capitalism. Its focus was on the importance of individual freedom. This freedom was to be ensured by a minimum of government interference in the private sector. Adam Smith's guiding idea was that the "invisible hand" of the market

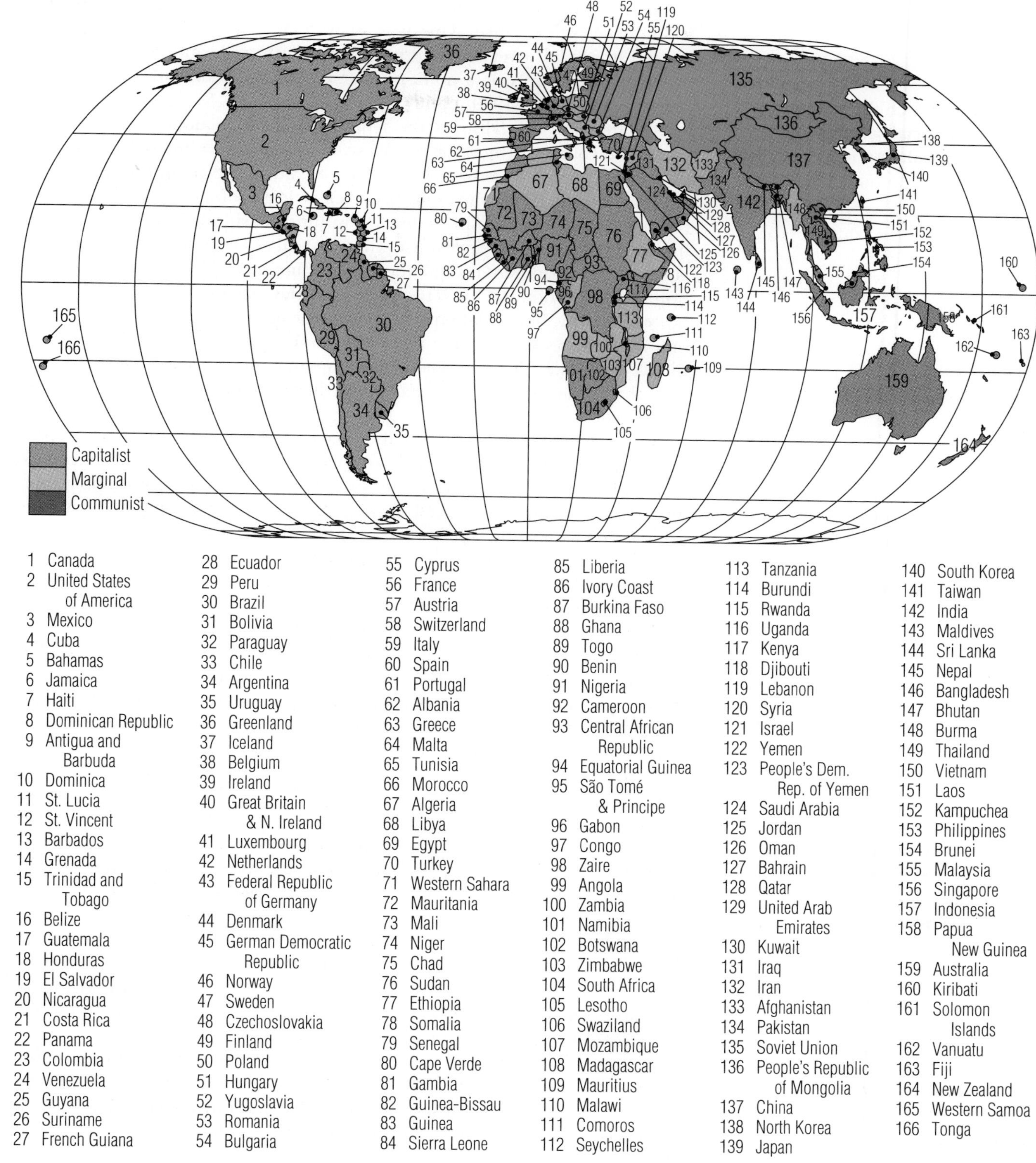

FIGURE 16:1 A GLOBAL VIEW OF POLITICAL ECONOMIES

The color code divides the globe into capitalist, communist, and socialist (marginal) societies *as of 1990.* The text explains that these official classifications of the type of political economy may be more ideology than reality.

Source: Peters Atlas of the World, 1990, pp. 170–171. New York: Harper & Row. By permission of the publisher.

ensures prosperity if businesses compete and consumers buy unimpeded by political interference. This type of wide-open capitalist economy only existed briefly in a very limited number of countries, and it is referred to today mainly to provide a point of historical comparison with **welfare state capitalism** (Gough, 1979, p. 50).

welfare state capitalism—a political economy in which the state provides some social services and economic regulation in a capitalist system.

Welfare state capitalism is the type of political economy that currently prevails throughout most of the West, including the United States. "Welfare" in this sense does not refer merely to aid to the poor, but more generally to the fact that the state provides at least some social services and regulates the economy in at least a minimal fashion. Public education, housing, and unemployment insurance, as well as tax policies, worker safety laws, and environmental regulations are some examples of state intervention in the economy. This intervention is often accompanied by the ideology of equality, but social equality has never been achieved in this (or any other) social system. Despite the government presence in the workings of the welfare state, the economy is fundamentally based on private property, with the private sector having a crucial bearing on the productive power of a nation.

By contrast, countries such as the former USSR have officially abolished private property and the "private sector," while retaining crucial elements of a capitalist economy *within* the government's administrative apparatus. Such societies can be classified as **state capitalist** (Bettelheim, 1976). While they often claim to be "socialist" or "communist," these nations still exploit the labor of the many for the benefit of a small, privileged class of elites. As in the welfare states, declared goals of equality are undermined by social structures that ensure varying levels of inequality. The special privileges of favored bureaucrats in the USSR were well known even in the West, and were widely resented at home. The fact that Eastern Europe is now quickly reverting to an overtly Western-style political economy is an indicator that these nations have been more "capitalist" in character than their public ideology allowed (Knapp and Spector, 1991).

state capitalism—a political economy in which there are capitalist elements within the state-owned means of production.

Socialism

socialism—a political economy in which there is state ownership of the means of production and no private property.

What, then, would a real **socialist** political economy look like? There are several different answers to this question. In the words of V.I. Lenin, "Socialism is merely state-capitalist monopoly *which is made to serve the interest of the whole people* and has to that extent *ceased* to be capitalist monopoly" (quoted in Bettelheim, 1976, p. 465). A socialist society in this classic conception would be characterized by state ownership of the means of production (i.e., the polity would possess all factories and offices) as well as an end to private property. This would mean the elimination of the exploitation of working people by a small elite class.

By this definition, there are certainly no socialist societies in existence today—no state is without class-based activity of some sort. Karl Marx saw socialism as a step in the journey toward communism. He envisioned a socialist state controlled by the working class (proletariat) until the capitalist class (bourgeoisie) disappeared. In a more current definition, socialism is often equated with "economic democracy" (Sherman, 1987). Such a system could provide for every individual to have a voice not only in the election of government officials, but also in decisions about production, the allocation of profits, and the conditions of the work environment. It is difficult to find real-world examples of socialist states even meeting this less

The Israeli community Yotvata in the Negev desert is a *"kibbutz,"* an economic unit in which property is held collectively by the members, who also share in the work and child care. As you read this section, attempt to classify the kibbutz as a type of political economy.

stringent definition. Currently, socialism remains a theoretical alternative to the prevailing political economic system of welfare state capitalism.

Communism

communism—a political economy in which there is collective ownership of the means of production, social equality, and, eventually, no state.

The term communism often stirs images of a rigid, oppressive, increasingly passé form of dictatorship. However, the concept of communism as expressed by Marx and Engels meant something very different from the types of societies recently called "communist." They foresaw not only the abolition of private property and class exploitation, but also the end of countries and nationalism. Marx and Engels thought that "political power . . . is merely the organized power of one class for oppressing another" (Marx and Engels, 1848/1959, p. 31). With the development of a workers' state, class distinctions and inequality would gradually fade away to the point that a state would no longer be necessary.

Is communism another theoretical model like socialism, or is there an example of a communist society in the world today? If the definition of communism is that provided by Marx and Engels, then there are no existing illustrations. In fact, there has been no case of a truly classless society either before or after the upheavals in Eastern Europe. A recent study of China, for example, finds wide income inequalities based on differing property rights (Walder, 1992). Nevertheless, a number of nations bill

BOX 16:1 SOCIOLOGICAL IMAGINATION IN FICTION

Economic Culture Shock

In *The Dispossessed,* two planets with radically different political economies reopen cultural exchange through the visit of a brilliant physicist, Shevek. Shevek's home planet was first populated by exiled revolutionaries, who created a communal, anarchic society with no private property or wages. Urras, the planet Shevek visits, is similar to Earth with its multiple nation–states, individualism, and gross inequalities. The two scenes excerpted here depict Shevek's experiences in the city of Nio Esseia in the capitalist nation A-Io, roughly comparable to contemporary New York City.

Shevek wandered across acres of polished marble under that immense ethereal vault, and came at last to the long array of doors through which crowds of people came and went constantly, all purposeful, all separate. They all looked, to him, anxious. He had often seen that anxiety before in the faces of Urrasti, and wondered about it. Was it because, no matter how much money they had, they always had to worry about making more, lest they die poor? Was it guilt, because no matter how little money they had, there was always somebody who had less? Whatever the cause, it gave all the faces a certain sameness, and he felt very much alone among them. In escaping his guides and guards he had not considered what it might be like to be on one's own in a society where men did not trust one another, where the basic moral assumption was not mutual aid, but mutual aggression. He was a little frightened.

* * *

Saio Pae had taken him "shopping" during his second week in A-Io. . . . The whole experience had been so bewildering to him that he put it out of mind as soon as possible, but he had dreams about it for months afterwards, nightmares. Saemtenevia Prospect was two miles long, and it was a solid mass of people, traffic, and things: things to buy, things for sale. Coats, dresses, gowns, robes, trousers, breeches, shirts,

themselves as "communist," and anti-communism has been the official stance of the U.S. government throughout much of this century.

POWER

Where Is the Power?

Imagine that you and a group of your fellow students decided to protest the most recent hike in tuition and demand a two-year freeze on any further tuition increases. Would anyone listen to you? Is it likely that your demands would be met? Why or why not? Who would decide?

The decision-making process in a university is similar in many respects to the decision-making process in a business or government agency. Those with power in any organization set the "agenda"; that is, what is to be placed on the table for a decision. Their power may also be directly exercised in a variety of ways, including clout over the use of economic resources.

Chances are that a proposed tuition freeze would be met by some pretty strong resistance from the administration of the university that originally proposed it. And this resistance would most likely be successful, which is

BOX 16:1 SOCIOLOGICAL IMAGINATION IN FICTION *continued*

blouses, hats, shoes, stockings, scarves, shawls, vests, capes, umbrellas, clothes to wear while sleeping, while swimming, while playing games, while at an afternoon party, while at an evening party, while at a party in the country, while traveling, while at the theater, while hunting—all different, all in hundreds of different cuts, styles, colors, textures, materials. Perfumes, clocks, lamps, statues, cosmetics, candles, pictures, cameras, games, vases, sofas, kettles, puzzles, pillows, dolls, colanders, hassocks, jewels, carpets, toothpicks, calendars, a baby's teething rattle of platinum with a handle of rock crystal, an electrical machine to sharpen pencils, a wristwatch with diamond numerals; figurines and souvenirs and kickshaws and mementos and gewgaws and bric-a-brac, everything to disguise its use; acres of luxuries, acres of excrement. In the first block Shevek had stopped to look at a shaggy, spotted coat, the central display in a glittering window of clothes and jewelry. "The coat costs 8,400 units?" he asked in disbelief, for he had recently read in a newspaper that a "living wage" was about 2,000 units a year. "Oh, yes, that's real fur, quite rare now that the animals are protected," Pae had said. "Pretty thing, isn't it? Women love furs." And they went on. After one more block Shevek had felt utterly exhausted. He could not look any more. He wanted to hide his eyes.

And the strangest thing about the nightmare street was that none of the millions of things for sale were made there. They were only sold there. Where were the workshops, the factories, where were the farmers, the craftsmen, the miners, the weavers, the chemists, the carvers, the dyers, the designers, the machinists, where were the hands, the people who made? Out of sight, somewhere else. Behind walls. All the people in all the shops were either buyers or sellers. They had no relation to the things but that of possession.

Critical Thinking Questions

1. A basic sociological proposition introduced in Chapter 1 is that surrounding social structures alter one's personality. Based on Shevek's experiences, how might inner selves differ if brought up in a pure capitalist versus a pure socialist society?
2. The "Saemtenevia Prospect" sounds quite like any suburban mall. What would be the differences between functionalist and conflict theory interpretations of such a profusion of consumer goods?

Source: Ursula K. LeGuin, *The Dispossessed* (1974). New York: Avon Books, pp. 106–7, 167.

Boris Yeltsin is shown with Premier Viktor Chernomyrdin at a luxurious vacation estate. Despite its official billing as a communist political economy, the former USSR had an elite class with privileges suggestive of capitalist elites.

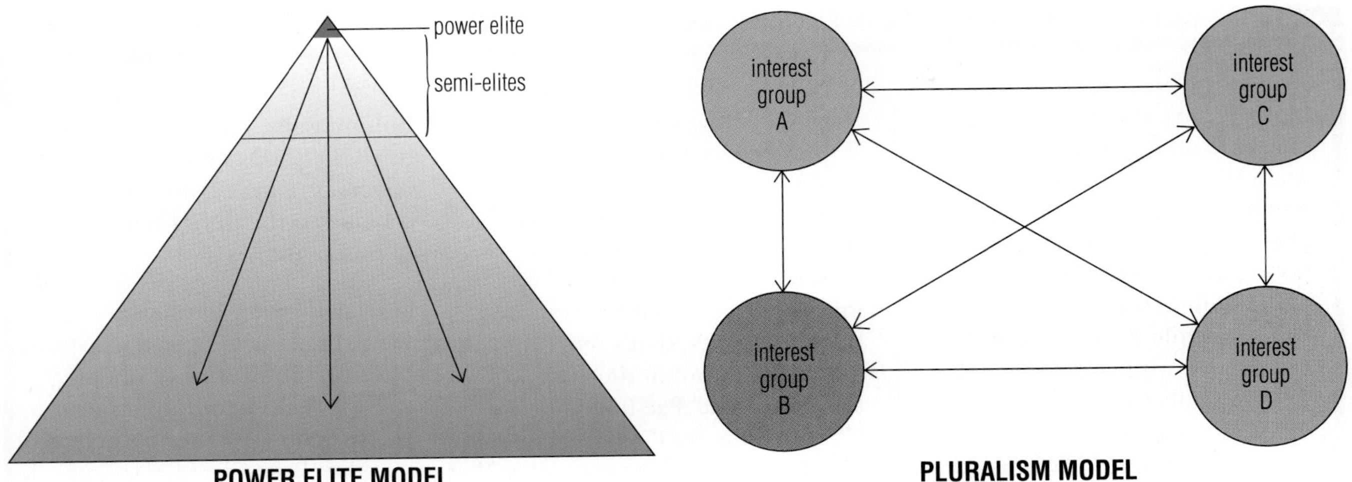

FIGURE 16:2 POWER ELITE VERSUS PLURALISM MODELS OF THE U.S. POWER STRUCTURE
The pyramid figure depicts a tiny, socially connected power elite running the United States from the top down. The contrasting figure depicts multiple, balanced interest groups in the pluralism model.

proven by constantly rising tuition bills. Why is this the case? As you probably know by experience, the college student is in a relatively powerless position. While it is possible for students acting together to change certain limited aspects of school policy, it is generally true that those who control the college budget make policy as they see fit; the same holds true for most other organizations. This power–money connection again shows the wisdom of jointly considering political economy.

What Is the Power Structure?

The Classic Debate

pluralism—a distribution of power that is diffused among many competing interest groups.

power elite—a distribution of power that is concentrated in the hands of a tiny, consolidated elite.

Some of the most bitter and basic disputes in sociology arise over discussions of power. Perhaps the most well-known of these debates is between proponents of the **pluralism** and **power elite** models (see Figure 16:2). Pluralists generally stress the democratic essence of U.S. society, and believe that power is diffused among many competing interest groups. Conversely, power elite theorists claim that power in the United States is highly concentrated within a tiny circle of decision-makers, who have consolidated to make all major decisions that pull the strings in the society.

Robert Dahl is a chief proponent of the pluralist position. He developed this idea by employing a decisional model of community power in *Who Governs?* (1961), a study of the political structure of New Haven, Connecticut. By examining how decisions about such matters as education spending and urban renewal came to be made, Dahl found that power tends to be spread out among a number of people with stakes in different aspects of local government. Depending on the policy measure in question, different groups of people had different levels of influence. There is no longer a small group of "patricians" at the helm of government as there was at the turn of the century, Dahl argues; rather, organized groupings of citizens with specialized concerns about only a single issue have dispersed the exercise of power. In other words, Dahl found that those who cared enough about an issue to devote their energy and resources toward obtaining a particular outcome were likely to be successful. This interpretation informs the exploits of contemporary single-issue groups focusing on abortion, the environment, and AIDS. Absolute measures of economic power or social standing seem to be important only in determining *potential* power. *Actual* power

Gun control is a contemporary issue involving power interests contending over public policy. Which model best fits the facts of this controversial case—pluralism or power elite?

is dependent upon circumstances, including which stakeholders oppose one's aims. This position on the distribution of power sees the political economy of the United States as responsive to a plurality of popular interests.

The power elite theorists see it very differently, claiming that a typical citizen's preferences or interests are irrelevant to the process of state policy making. C. Wright Mills outlined the classic form of this position in *The Power Elite* (1956). He claimed that the political, economic, and military structures were closely intertwined, with the leaders in one sector colluding with those in the other sectors to magnify their power. A relatively unified, cohesive, tiny elite dominates decision making in all areas, relying on middle-level subordinates to carry out their orders, and to make their orders palatable to the population at large. The Executive branch of the federal government, the executives of the largest corporations, and the highest ranking officers of the military thus work in concert to control the United States. A contemporary application would see the Persian Gulf War as engineered by former President Bush, the military Chiefs of Staff, and captains of industry whose firms stood to gain by the conflict (e.g., General Dynamics weapons manufacturers and the oil companies). A second level of semi-elites acts to implement the decisions of the elite; congresspersons and the heads of local governments are often perceived by the ordinary citizen to be the formulators of policy, but in actuality they are merely the servants and "spin doctors" of the power elite. By this argument, the vast majority of U.S. citizens are without any real power, and have no real access to people with power. Mills foresaw an increasingly polarized society in which the great mass of non-elites would have virtually no control over the direction of their "democratic" country.

Contemporary policy analyst G. William Domhoff supports Mills's contention that a small, wealthy elite dominates the politics of the United States, but is careful to note that this elite is not a monolithic entity whose members are in complete agreement with each other. There are both conservative and liberal tendencies among the "governing class." It is important to note, however, that "the limits of most policy disputes in the United States are defined by the limits of differences within the power elite" (Domhoff, 1970, p. 107). Therefore, the debates over policy issues that play themselves out on the network news are reflective of the disagreements within the elite, and are not representative of differences in public opinion as a whole.

Networks, Power, and Markets

Before any new issue is introduced, notice something about the foregoing discussion. Although not phrased in these terms, the pluralism versus power elite debate has really been about the structure of power networks in U.S. society. Specifically, a tiny, elevated set of socially interconnected power brokers (power elite) are opposed to balanced, multiple power centers, themselves internally organized and involved with each other as networks (pluralism). Much recent research has directly examined power networks in both of these traditions (e.g., Perrucci and Potter, 1989). In a real sense, the infusion of network theories and techniques has enriched this debate. The same can be said about the famous engine of enrichment itself—"the market." The distinctions among the "Types of Political Economies" (earlier) are often conceived in terms of this device of capitalism. The current events in Eastern Europe, for example, are interpreted as political transformations of "planned" into "market" economies.

What is a market? To a neo-classical economist, a market is an arrangement of buyers and sellers. Sellers (suppliers) dump their product on the market, and buyers purchase the product from the market; the price is then set by the intersection of supply and demand curves you probably have seen on the board in economics class. It is viewed as a rational process in which all parties are out to maximize their individual self-interests. According to *the* classical economist, Adam Smith, the "invisible hand" of the market guides all of this self-seeking to productive efficiency and consumer satisfaction.

In recent years, sociologists have been crossing disciplinary boundaries and reformulating ideas about how markets actually work. Their fundamental insight is simple: *A market is a social structure* (White, 1981a, b). In still another demonstration of the political-economy link, these analysts point out that markets cannot exist in a sociological vacuum. There is a social foundation, generally established by the state, that sets up the conditions within which markets may function (Baker, 1987); establishing private property, protecting business patents, and giving consumers rights are what a political authority must actually do to move to a market economy. Once a market appears, it is penetrated by network structures. Picture a stock exchange with dozens of floor traders shouting out their bids. A study of the Chicago Options Exchange found that even this apparently individualized, rationalized setting is shot through with personal relationships that affect the trading (Baker, 1983). Mark Granovetter (1985) has generalized such findings into the term "economic embeddedness," which means that economic actions are embedded in networks of relations. People do not buy from an anonymous market of faceless sellers. They get to know the butcher, and hire a stockbroker who knows bond traders to do their bond trading.

What Is Power?

As you might have gathered from the arguments outlined here, a precise definition of "power" is hard to come by. When physical force is applied to coerce criminals or children into behaving a certain way, it is fairly easy to see the exercise of power. However, there are numerous situations in which power is exercised more subtly, through methods such as manipulation or persuasion (Wrong, 1979). The use of power is not mainly associated with negative, destructive outcomes, for it often serves to stimulate production in a society (Dad: "Do your homework!"), as well as to bring disparate individuals together into a community or family—hence the "power of love" (Boulding, 1989).

Nondecision Making

nondecision making—the process by which challenges to those in power are suppressed before power is exercised.

In the 1960s, Peter Bachrach and Morton Baratz wrote a series of influential articles that focused on an angle of power that had previously gone unanalyzed by sociologists. The former noted that powerful people not only have a heavy hand in determining which choices are to be made, but are also able to control the kinds of options that are available to be chosen. This is termed **nondecision making**, the process by which challenges to those who hold power are suppressed by being "suffocated before they are even voiced" (Bachrach and Baratz, 1970, p. 44). To return to the example of the protest against tuition hikes, the administration is likely to respond to student demands by claiming that tuition increases are necessary for the college to function adequately. This sounds like a reasonable response, until we look at the options that are not even being considered, such as why any tuition at all is required. Why not provide a "free" college education to everyone who qualifies, as is done in several European countries? By limiting the debate to options that are not threatening to their positions, those with power are able to ensure that truly threatening demands are kept off the table for discussion (Lukes, 1974).

Authority and Legitimacy

Questions of power often lead to questions of authority: Why do people submit to those with power? How do those in control maintain their power? It is fairly easy to see why people submit to governments who use violence and physical coercion to compel compliance. But such naked force is relatively rare in human affairs, given the great number of orders given and taken. In most instances, power is considered legitimate, so that orders are followed without significant challenge, and the right of a ruler to rule is accepted by those ruled. Max Weber defined power backed by **legitimacy** as **authority**, and he outlined three main types: rational–legal, traditional, and charismatic.

legitimacy—the belief that the exercise of power is proper and acceptable.

authority—legitimated power.

rational–legal authority—legitimacy is based on organizational position and rationalized rules.

Rational–legal authority is based upon a position held within a social structure, usually a bureaucratic one; authority does not rest with the individual but with the office. Most types of political authority that we are familiar with fall under this category. For example, Ronald Reagan was able to wield a great deal of power as President of the United States, which he has since forfeited. His authority was rooted in the organized political order of the United States, and his commands were subject to certain "legal," presumably "rational," limits. Teachers, police officers, and judges are other examples of those with authority based on bureaucratic position. Thus, rational–legal authority is highly impersonal; its increasing prevalence reflects the increasing bureaucratization of modern society. The old-style "boss" is now the "assistant administrative vice-president."

traditional authority—legitimacy is based on long-standing social patterns.

Traditional authority is less common today than in previous history, when kinship ties and religion were the dominant forms of social organization. Kings, queens, and chiefs are some examples of those with traditional authority. Their right to rule is based on tradition, and others respect their position not just because they are legally bound to, but because *it has always been this way.* This is authority built from generations, in which authority is not questioned because it is a part of long-standing social order. Whereas rational–legal authority is noted for its impersonality, traditional authority rests upon personal bonds. It is a "matter of personal loyalty within the area of accustomed obligations" (Weber, 1947, p. 328). While Weber viewed traditional authority as falling in the wake of rational–legal authority's rise, the former has not passed from the social scene. Why do you obey Mom?

charismatic authority—legitimacy is based on extraordinary personal qualities attributed to an individual by followers.

Charismatic authority is perhaps the most interesting and unusual way to legitimate authority. In this case, the power of an individual to command obedience rests neither upon rational rules nor tradition, but upon the sheer force of personality. There seems to be something almost supernatural or preordained about the person who holds charismatic authority that commands obedience all by itself. Examples of charismatic leaders from history range from Jesus to Caesar, and there are more contemporary figures such as Gandhi, Martin Luther King, Jr., and Hitler. Such authority is capable of commanding remarkable—even revolting—acts from followers. By the power of personality, Jim Jones was able to convince hundreds of followers to join him in drinking Kool-Aid® laced with cyanide; more

Charles Le Brun's famous painting *Louis XIV Taking Up Personal Government* (1680) suggests the awesome weight of tradition constituting kingly authority. Louis XIV was king of France from 1643 to 1715, and he is a legendary absolute monarch of the classical age. Consider his authority compared with that of today's president of France.

recently, David Koresh led cult members ("Davidians") to a flaming death near Waco, Texas. Hitler's charismatic legacy is read on the tombstones of millions. Such potent authority often poses a serious threat to authority resting on rational–legal or traditional grounds; consider successful revolutions in countries such as Cuba (under Fidel Castro) and China (under Mao Tse Tung), or the challenge raised by the Civil Rights Movement under the leadership of Martin Luther King, Jr. However, charismatic authority is also the most fragile and rare of the three forms, since it is bound up with the extraordinary personalities of individuals. There have been countless movements based on charismatic authority that have collapsed with the death of the leader. In order for charismatic authority to last in creating legitimacy, it generally must be consolidated under either rational–legal authority or traditional authority. Hence, Christ's charisma survived in the traditional hierarchy of the early Catholic Church.

THE MODERN STATE

States and Nationalism, War and Peace

When we think of the "state," we generally assume it to be a universal, basic entity that exists of its own accord. To picture the world without strong central governments requires an imaginative leap for most of us; current political boundaries and the "national" cultures they encompass are so ingrained in our collective perceptions that they seem to be part of the landscape. However, states are a very recent construction in the history of humankind. In fact, the human race has spent about 99 percent of its existence in stateless societies (Knapp and Spector, 1991). Although most people in the world today live within the confines of a nation–state, this recent trend is not applauded by all. Marx was a virulent opponent of nationalism and the creation of states; he saw them as predicated upon the internal divisions of a class society. The state, in this view, is a means for dominating people rather than a liberating advancement.

Why, then, do states come into being? The answer illustrates the close connection between politics and the economy that is the very reason for the existence of this chapter. Before the capitalist mode of production, there was no compelling need for a true national state to exist. Social ties based on kinship and tradition did not require a centralized government apparatus to enforce them; they were perfectly sufficient to maintain order in a village or even a city–state. Consider the kin structures fictionalized in *Romeo and Juliet* or those of ancient Athens. With the rise of capitalism and its demand for markets, the loose configurations of kingdoms and principalities were gradually transformed into large, centralized forms of government that encompassed a variety of ethnic groups and cultures. Among other things, large armed states guarantee an orderly internal market for peaceful buying and selling, and they also have the armies to create profitable colonies elsewhere. While access to resources and markets may have been the impetus behind state formation, war has been the means by which modern national states have become fully institutionalized (Carneiro, 1978).

Manuel Rodriguez's *The Revolution* (1946) evokes the timeless pathos of violent conflict; that timelessness is graphically reinforced in a recent photo of Salvadoran children turning away from the horrors of modern warfare. Historical sociologists such as Charles Tilly have developed theories of war and revolution tied to the development of states.

Modern national states are characterized by tightly drawn borders with a "buffer zone" around them—like the invisible national limits established at sea. As a state grows more secure in its place, it often attempts to assimilate the old, established buffer zone and create a new buffer zone around the redrawn boundaries (Tilly, 1991). Such expansion inevitably runs into conflict from other states who claim the same buffer zone as their territory, and war ensues. The processes of state making and war are thus intrinsically linked, and are interrelated with the processes of taxation and revolution (Tilly, 1981). Taxation of subject populations is necessary to support the military forces required for the defense and expansion of state territories. The collection of taxes often requires direct or indirect coercion on the part of the rulers. The extraction of war labor in the form of a draft and of armament monies through taxes creates both economic and political disadvantages for the ruled. This, in turn, contributes to conflict and resistance within states. The greater a state's drive for expansion via war making, the greater its monetary needs from subject peoples, and the greater the tendency toward revolution within states (Tilly, 1991). Thus, both internal and external conflict are closely bound up with the processes of state development, which in turn is tied to the needs of the market. Consider how well this theoretical model illuminates fights over the draft and the defense budget in the United States, or the endless tangle of European wars and revolutions between 1750 and 1950.

Ethnic conflicts and nationalist movements are so prevalent today that they seem as if they have always been with us. Whether in the form of open warfare in what used to be Yugoslavia, or demonstrations by African American separatists, ethnically charged issues seem to infuse much of the news we read about today. The conventional wisdom is that ethnic groups pressing for national recognition are basic entities who have always shared a common culture, and have always thought of themselves as belonging to the same community—sort of a big tribe. According to Tilly's theory, ethnic groups are neither basic nor unchanging, but are social constructions tightly linked to the processes of state making and war. He notes that ethnic groups begin to make claims for control over an autonomous state under two conditions: (1) If other groups begin to make claims for statehood that would subordinate the ethnic group, or (2) if the state begins to threaten either the group's identity or its economic position (Tilly, 1992). The former sounds like the Serbs, the latter like America circa 1776. The formation of the modern nation–state thus leads to the *development* of mobilized ethnic groups with nationalist demands. Rather than tribal cultures naturally building their own state, Tilly's framework switches the causal arrow: State making makes ethnic nationalists (Tilly, 1992).

State formation and war making do play a large role in the creation of nationalist sentiments, but they also result in other more concrete conflicts of interest. The "military–industrial complex" refers to the relationship between the Defense Department and private industry in the development and production of weapons. Corporations stand to make huge profits from military spending, and consequently act in concert with the Pentagon to pressure Congress to allocate large sums to the defense budget. As a result, the government often spends huge amounts of money on planes, tanks, and weapons systems of dubious value. You have probably heard stories of the Pentagon spending thousands of dollars for a toilet seat; part of the reason for such wastefulness is the influence wielded by military and economic elites acting together to serve their own interests. A generation ago, C. Wright Mills noted that "Not politicians, but corporate executives, sit with the military and plan the organization of war effort" (1956, p. 276).

This propaganda poster depicts the development of the Strategic Defense Initiative (SDI), popularly known as "Star Wars." If it had not been cancelled, SDI would have been a multibillion-dollar colossal collaboration of the "military-industrial complex."

He believed that the United States was on a "permanent war economy" directed by the members of the power elite, especially those in the highest positions of the military and corporate worlds. It is not only conflict theory critics who share this view. The term "military–industrial complex" was popularized by ex-Supreme Allied Commander and ex-President Dwight D. Eisenhower.

BUSINESS, GOVERNMENT, AND POLICY IN THE UNITED STATES

The influence of business interests on the priorities of the U.S. government extends beyond defense spending to encompass virtually every aspect of state policy making. Laws supposed to serve the public interest also serve the interests of corporations. For example, regulations requiring the producers of various goods to meet certain standards of quality were enacted with the support of large corporations, who appreciated that smaller potential competitors would be unable to implement the expensive regulations (Alford and Friedland, 1985). Since private businesses are perceived as holding the well-being of the economy in their hands ("the business of America is business"), their demands are often given policy priority.

Regulating the Poor

Even seemingly generous social programs such as "welfare" serve functions that are favorable to the growth and development of business. Frances Fox Piven and Richard A. Cloward have argued that welfare programs are the direct result of the government's attempts at *Regulating the Poor* (1971). They argue that "expansive relief policies are designed to mute civil disorder, and restrictive ones to reinforce work norms" (1971, p. xiii). This is a disturbing argument. It says that welfare programs are not a mark of a government's concern for the well-being of its citizens, but are mainly means by which the economic status quo is preserved with a minimum of social unrest.

If large numbers of people are living in abject poverty, unable to feed or clothe themselves, what do they have to lose by rebelling against the system? Government-provided income maintenance can go a long way toward ensuring its legitimacy. When economically deprived people protest the inequality of the U.S. political economy, it is relatively easy for the government to quiet the dissension by funneling benefits to protesting communities. Even though antipoverty policy in the United States is notoriously stingy (see Chapter 11), it provides some stability in a rocking boat. Once the danger of a mass uprising has passed, programs are often cut or scaled back. For example, the Reagan administration slashed Aid to Families with Dependent Children (AFDC), although political support for social welfare programs prevented the cutbacks from being as severe as the business community would have liked (Piven and Cloward, 1987). Piven and Cloward contend that this explains the vacillations in America's welfare policy over this century. Unrest in the 1930s and 1960s was bought off by benefits subsequently eroded by cutbacks. If this interpretation is correct, what should now be occurring in the aftermath of the 1992 Los Angeles riots?

Tax Policy

We have seen that any state requires a rather large degree of sacrifice from its citizens. Whether in the form of taxes, military conscription, or obedience to objectionable laws, members of a state must live lives that are ultimately subordinate to the demands of their government. The amazing aspect of this relationship is that, in most of the West, it exists with relatively little violent coercion on the part of governments. In order for a government to function without the use of constant force, it must be perceived as legitimate in the eyes of those within its territory. Just as authority is based on an individual's perceived right to give an order, the government must gain some right to exercise power. State legitimacy involves the creation of an impression that the government is providing services or functions that are socially important, and that decentralized localities would be unable to provide for themselves. This crucial legitimation is undermined by the state's accumulation of resources through taxation—the IRS does not make Uncle Sam beloved. Legitimacy can be bought back by state administration of entitlement programs such as Social Security. Without some such form of legitimation, states can fall. Again look to Eastern Europe (as we shall do in detail at the end of the chapter).

One of the ways that the U.S. government directly supports the efforts of private businesses is through tax breaks and incentives. Death and taxes may be unavoidable for the average person, but large corporations have found a number of ways to wriggle out of the latter and, thus, not to worry about the former. A variety of special-interest exemptions have allowed certain kinds of companies to operate entirely tax free. For example, Carnival Cruise Lines realized a profit of $502.5 million from 1985 to 1988, yet paid not a single cent in taxes because of a loophole for foreign-based companies (Barlett and Steele, 1992, p. 43). Perhaps even more objectionable is the tax-exempt status accorded to corporate interest payments, or "Net Operating Losses" (Barlett and Steele, 1992). Under this rule, companies that have recently restructured (which generally involves a significant loss of jobs), and incurred large interest payments, may escape *all tax liabilitity,* despite reported profits of millions of dollars. Such exemptions and write-offs cost the government billions in lost revenue, which may then be passed on to the individual taxpayer. Each taxpayer is not affected equally, moreover. Lower-income workers are hit the hardest by Social Security taxes, sales taxes, and excise taxes because these taxes are set at a flat rate, thus siphoning off a bigger relative share of lower incomes. In the 1980s, taxes owed by the wealthiest Americans were actually cut by at least one-third (Barlett and Steele, 1992). Almost everyone across the political spectrum agrees with these facts. The disagreement is about whether they ultimately serve the social system of the United States.

Regulating the Corporate Sector

Chances are you are supportive of many government policies that are in effect to regulate the behavior of businesses. For example, you can be reasonably sure that the steak you have just ordered at a restaurant will be free of bugs and worms (at least big ones), which would not necessarily be the case if the government did not regulate the quality of food items sold to the public. Most people feel safer keeping their life savings in a bank rather than beneath their mattresses, although this was not the case until the federal government insured deposits; just ask someone who lived through the bank collapses of the Great Depression. Government regulations also control the level at which the environment may be polluted, the degree to which companies may combine to form monopolies, and the prices of goods and services in certain industries. Such regulations have come into being out of social necessity; most U.S. citizens will neither tolerate eating rotten food nor breathing filthy air, and the government would quickly lose legitimacy if it were to ignore these feelings. However, regulations have not necessarily been harmful toward business. As we have noted above, such regulations may help existing firms by keeping out new competitors.

In general, government regulations can cut into private-sector profits. This may help to explain why laws restrictive of business are often laxly enforced, particularly concerning such issues as worker safety. Almost 61,000 Americans die each year from work-related illnesses or injuries; this means that about three workers perish due to occupational hazards for every murder that is committed in the United States (Reiman, 1990). Many of these deaths are preventable by well-enforced safety regulations. The Occupational Health and Safety Administration (OSHA) responsible for investigating workplaces is woefully understaffed and is incapable of posing as a real deterrent to unsafe working conditions. Since cleaning up a factory or instituting new safety practices at a plant erodes profits, private industry often fights against stringent worker safety laws and tries to circumvent existing laws by high-priced lobbying in Washington. One result is that your job may be dangerous to your health.

WORK IN THE UNITED STATES

The Division of Labor

A handmade product is considered by many to be a charming, quaint object worth a few extra dollars. The idea that a single individual invested time, effort, and creativity in a useful object is an appealing one that attaches meaning to the final result. However, such individual crafting of raw materials into a finished product is today an extreme rarity, confined mainly to tourist areas and craft shows. This is the case because such labor is just inefficient. In modern economies, it is essential to have highly specialized tasks so that products may be mass produced with a minimal investment in training costs. For example, the thought of driving an individually handcrafted automobile is absurd from an efficiency standpoint. A simple fender job would require craft artistry instead of just picking up a machined part. Contemporary society is too complicated not to have a division of labor, in which each occupation is narrowly specialized and organized with other jobs in a complex web of interconnecting tasks. Consider the "Personal Perspective" can-factory job versus each individual baking personal pottery just to hold liquids.

As the U.S. economy has become increasingly complex with the advent of new technologies and organizational innovations, so have jobs become ever more specialized. The U.S. Census has classifications for tens of thousands of occupations, many of which involve coordinating the activities of other specialists. With the increasing division of labor in the workforce has come increasing **segmentation**, as well. Segmentation involves broad divisions among workers based not only upon the kind of task performed, but also along reinforcing political and cultural dimensions (Gordon, Edwards, and Reich, 1982). Women and minorities perform more of society's "dirty work" and routinized clerical work than do white males. In 1984, clerical and service work, traditionally among the lowest paid and least prestigious of jobs, accounted for about 50 percent of employed women (Power, 1988, p. 40). Professional and managerial positions were occupied in 1980 by 31.4 percent of employed white males, but only 17.4 percent of employed African American males (Allen and Farley, 1986). Such statistics are familiar from elsewhere in this book. They are cited here to show that the division of labor at work is overlaid by other sociological dimensions. Distinct types of work are found in market segments with distinct types of workers.

segmentation—broad divisions among types of workers reinforced by political and cultural dimensions.

Perhaps the most notable change in the occupational structure of the United States since the colonial period has been the shift from an economy based on agriculture and farming (**primary sector**) to one based on heavy industry and wage labor (**secondary sector**). The main trend this century has been away from industrial production toward a rapid growth in the **tertiary sector**, or service sector (see Figure 16:3). Since World War II, the number of higher-wage manufacturing jobs has rapidly declined, while

primary sector—that portion of the workforce devoted to the extraction of raw materials (e.g., agriculture, mining).

secondary sector—that portion of the workforce devoted to the conversion of raw material into made, valued goods (e.g., manufacturing, construction).

tertiary sector—that portion of the workforce devoted to providing services (e.g., education, communication).

Many U.S.-based industrial firms have relocated their operations to Third World countries. This is a factory in Mexico surrounded by the dwellings of workers paid far less than their U.S. counterparts. Technological development and industrial relocation have contributed to shrinkage of the *secondary sector* in the United States.

lower-wage retail and service jobs have grown by the millions (Barlett and Steele, 1992). At the same time, professional and technical occupations have also increased. This shift in the occupational structure has been termed the movement toward a "post-industrial society," due in large part to the advent of new technologies that have rendered a number of traditional working-class jobs obsolete. Automated factories and the prominence of the computer are a part of the reason that assembly-line jobs are decreasing while clerical jobs are increasing. The can-factory job described in the "Personal Perspective" is now performed by a computer chip that requires no human hands. Industrial changes are also responsible, as the growth of business services, social services, and professional staffing have led to an increase in professional, technical, and clerical workers (Kalleberg and Berg, 1987). Additionally, much of the manual labor that had been

FIGURE 16:3 EMPLOYMENT BY SECTOR: 1900 TO 2000

Shifts in the occupational structure of the United States are shown as trend lines. The dominant trend this century is the rise of service occupations (including government); manufacturing jobs have been steadily eroding, and farming continues its occupational shrinkage from the preceding century.

Source: U.S. Bureau of the Census and Bureau of Economic Analysis.

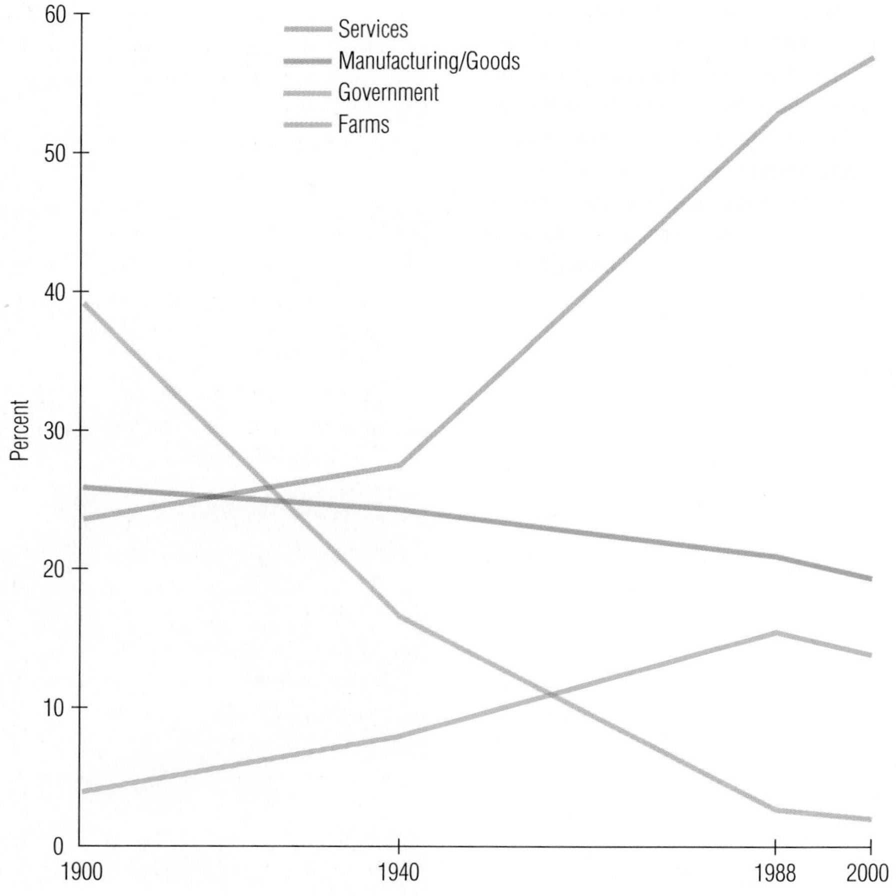

performed by high-wage, unionized workers in the United States is now being relocated to poorer countries where wages are very low. And deep-seated sociological trends such as bureaucratization (Chapter 5) and structural differentiation (Chapter 2) have accelerated the development of the white-collar sector.

Alienation

Increasing specialization and the corresponding routinization of work has had its effects on the psyche of the U.S. worker. Marx noted 150 years ago that "the worker is related to the *product of his labor* as to an *alien object*" (1844/1986, p. 108); hence the term *alienation* (already defined in Chapter 2). While a number of changes in the nature of work have taken place since Marx's time, the gist of his assertion seems even more true today. In most occupations, workers get little sense of personal fulfillment from the final outcome of their labor; often, their part in the work process is very narrow and specialized, and its part in the overall production process is a mystery to them (again, see "Personal Perspective"). The kinds of jobs that have been expanding rapidly in recent decades, such as clerks and food servers, are often too routine and repetitive to provide any real sense of personal accomplishment. And since the "routine" for pushing paper or running the register is usually not designed by the worker, the lack of

TABLE 16:1 Crosstabulation of Concern of Public Officials by Respondent's Occupation

RESPONDENT'S OCCUPATION	PUBLIC OFFICALS ARE NOT INTERESTED IN THE AVERAGE MAN	
Count ROW PCT	Agree	Disagree
Professional, technical, managerial	162 **57.9**	118 **42.1**
Clerical, sales	150 **69.1**	67 **30.9**
Operatives, laborers, service, farm	267 **77.2**	79 **22.8**

$n = 843$

Main Point: Observe that the percentage of respondents who agree that "public officials are not interested in the average man" increases between the "Professional, technical, management" category and the "Clerical, sales" category; agreement is highest (nearly 8 out of every 10 respondents) in the "Operatives, laborers, service, farm" category, which contains the most alienating jobs of all.

Source: General Social Survey, 1990.

autonomy and control can importantly contribute to a sense of worker alienation (Blauner, 1964).

While there has been a growth in professional and managerial jobs that allow for some control over the conditions of one's work, the greatest expansion in jobs has been at the bottom of the corporate hierarchy with precious little freedom or flexibility. A secretary, for example, rarely gets to decide when to show up for work or how to design the company filing system. It has also been shown that the complexity of one's occupation (in addition to degree of control and level of income) are important factors in psychological well-being (Adelmann, 1987). The mind-numbing effects of an alienating job have reverberations that are felt throughout a worker's life, in areas ranging from personal values (see Chapter 1) to the personal sense of political efficacy. Table 16:1 clearly shows that workers in more alienating occupations are in fact more likely to believe that they are ignored by the agents of the political economy.

LACK OF WORK IN THE UNITED STATES

The Objective Dimension of Unemployment

All of this talk about alienation of course presumes that one is employed, yet millions of U.S. citizens are unemployed and looking for work as you read this. Millions more are working at jobs for which they are overqualified (such as the proverbial taxicab driver with a PhD). Official unemployment rates tell only part of the story. They neither include "discouraged workers" who are not actively searching for a job because they have given up, nor those who are employed only part-time because they were incapable of finding full-time work; in 1992, these two types included some 7 million discouraged people. The costs of unemployment to both the individual and the economy as a whole are enormous. Lost output and wasted

BOX 16:2 GENDER AND SOCIAL CHANGE

Unemployment and the Great Depression

Voice of the unemployed: "The other day I answered an ad. When I got there, there were 40 people applying. The man looked us over, picked one out, and said, 'I'll take you and pay you $15 a week.' Another fellow in the crowd called out, 'I'll work for $10' and got the job."

—Unemployed factory worker

Unemployed montage: An average of 350 Americans each day applied for jobs in Russia, and emigration was larger than immigration . . . During the winter of 1932–33, Chicago's public school teachers did not get paid . . . An Arkansas man walked 900 miles looking for work . . . Men set forest fires in the state of Washington so they would be hired to put them out . . . And in big cities men prayed for heavy snow that would provide them with shoveling jobs . . .

Today, unemployment is a problem when one in every 20 workers doesn't have a job. During the Depression, about one-quarter of the working population was unemployed, and that didn't count farmers barely surviving by working seven days a week from sunrise to sunset, or factory workers making ends almost meet by working two days a week.

West Virginia mining towns had unemployment rates of 97 percent, and across the border in Fayette County, Pa., there was a colony of forgotten men living in abandoned coke ovens. In the steel mill town of Donora, Pa., in 1932, only 277 of the 14,000 residents had jobs. There were whole towns in Kentucky's coal-

resources are a drag on the overall functioning of the economy—as well as a drag on persons wasting their talent. The personal havoc wreaked by unemployment has severe social effects; family tension, low self-image, increased health problems, and a greater incidence of mental illness have been found to be associated with unemployment (Hibbs, 1987). Unemployment hits minorities and women with particular ferocity. The unemployment rate for African American youths is generally three to four times the overall rate, and the median time young African American men spend between jobs is six months (Cherry et al., 1987). Women have become an increasingly permanent part of the labor force, yet suffer unemployment rates higher than those of men in the same occupations (Power, 1988); women are more often stuck in part-time positions, unable to obtain a full-time job. Some functionalist theorists believe that unemployment is an unfortunate, but inevitable, feature of modern life. Others—mainly conflict theorists—believe that relatively high unemployment rates are in the interest of capitalists, who then have a reserve army of labor to quiet the wage demands of workers. In either case, unemployment continues to be a serious problem in the political economy of the United States.

The Subjective Dimension of Unemployment

The personal pain of unemployment illustrated in Box 16:2 and in the "Personal Perspective" is reflected in public concern about the issue (please refer to Figure 16:4). Opinion polls in the 1980s often found unemployment to be *the* leading issue of national concern; studies stretching back to the 1930s have consistently indicated its importance in the polls (Jones,

BOX 16:2 GENDER AND SOCIAL CHANGE *continued*

mining area where no person had even a penny of income. They ate blackberries and dandelions, and children chewed their own hands. They planted vegetables but were so hungry they ate them before they were ripe.

There were so many unemployed college graduates, the New York department stores required applicants for the position of elevator operator to have bachelor's degrees. The National Education Association reported in 1931 that 75 percent of all American cities banned the employment of wives—lest they take a job from a man trying to support his family.

The widespread impression that the Soviet Union was "industrializing" led many skilled American workers to seek employment there. When the Soviet Embassy sought Americans to fill 6,000 jobs in 1931, more than 100,000 applications were received.

Critical Thinking Questions

1. Why is this chilling sketch of the Great Depression entitled "Gender and Social Change"? Reread the first two paragraphs with that question in mind, noting how the desperation is consistently described in male terms. These news snippets suggest very different *values* placed on gender equality in the 1930s. Now, how might those different values have affected the subjective dimension of some social problem (other than unemployment) during this era in the United States?
2. Focus on this quote: "The National Education Association reported in 1931 that 75 percent of all American cities banned the employment of wives . . ." How would the functionalist and conflict theories' interpretations of such laws differ?

Source: William Ecenbarger, "Cheer Up, It Could Be Worse" (August 25, 1991). In *Philadelphia Inquirer.*

McFalls, and Gallagher, 1989). While the objective significance of unemployment has just been documented, it is still legitimate to wonder why this issue is collectively considered so serious. After all, there are competing problems such as war, AIDS, drugs . . . it is a long and disturbing list.

What is especially disturbing about unemployment is that it strikes at the "master status." As is explained in Chapter 4, work is viewed as the

FIGURE 16:4 SUBJECTIVE AND OBJECTIVE DIMENSIONS: UNEMPLOYMENT IN THE UNITED STATES

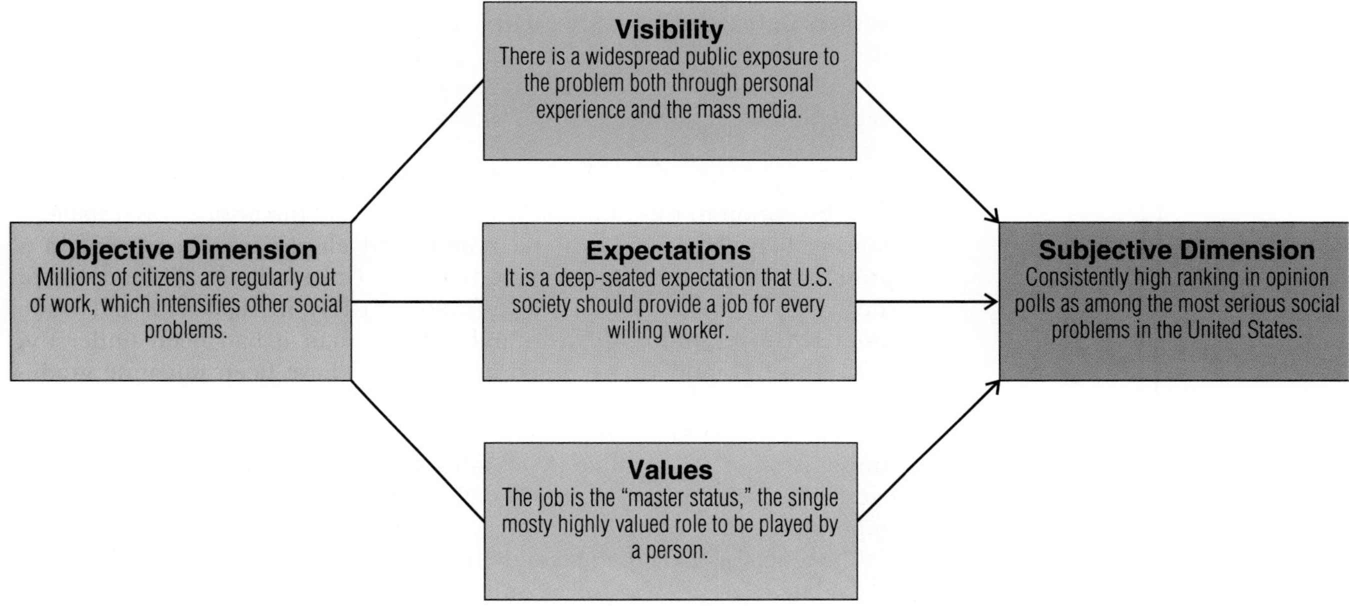

centerpiece of the status set, the single most highly *valued* role to be played. This ideal increasingly extends to career-minded women as well as to men. When both sexes are deprived of their master status by the millions, this violates deep-seated public *expectations* that U.S. society should be able to provide jobs for willing hands. Political economist Douglas A. Hibbs, Jr., has shown that political administrations failing to meet this basic expectation will be voted out (Hibbs, 1987).

The heightened cultural consciousness of unemployment is further raised by high *visibility*. Virtually everyone knows someone who has been recently laid off. In addition to this personal reminder, unemployment rates are regularly reported on the evening news. Plant closings are the subject of in-depth journalistic accounts. In part, unemployment gets so much publicity because the violation of popular expectations and values make it so "newsworthy." The resultant media exposure then rams home the problematic nature of the "Lack of Work in the United States."

UNIONS

When you hear someone mention the term "union," does the image spring to mind of a smoke-filled room and the deal making of thugs? If unions suggest scenarios such as this, you are certainly not alone. Unions have become identified in the minds of many with corruption and fraud. This was not always the case; unions came into being in the United States as forces genuinely responsive to the needs of the workers they represented. Where did the unsavory public image come from?

The first trade unions in the United States were established around 1830 in New York and Philadelphia, although they did not survive the economic crisis of 1837. The emergence of unions as significant organizations occurred in the 1860s, as industrial expansion was rapidly increasing the number of wage earners—many of whom endured abhorrent working conditions. After a series of successful strikes, the Knights of Labor rose to prominence in the 1880s. However, they then suffered several setbacks and quickly declined in membership as the American Federation of Labor (AFL) expanded. The AFL was based largely on the traditional craft unions (i.e., shoemakers, printers, etc.), which restricted their membership to workers with specialized skills. They also abandoned broader political struggle based on class lines in favor of "pure and simple" unionism (Harrington, 1970). This meant concentrating on "bread and butter" issues such as wages and benefits rather than attacking the inequality of the capitalist labor system.

Although some unions (such as the Industrial Workers of the World) took exception to this philosophy of compromise, the business-as-usual bargaining between leaders of the unions and employers was to remain a prominent feature of work relations in the United States. The advent of the Congress of Industrial Organizations (CIO) in the 1930s led trade unionism to be more inclusive and militant than it had been under the AFL. The AFL and CIO merged in 1955, and have been pursuing gradualist programs of collective bargaining through the present day. Business and labor leaders have reached a sort of gentlemen's agreement whereby unions refrain from militant, class-based political struggle in return for occasional wage increases and benefit packages. While unions have made important gains both in improving working conditions and in gaining material benefits for their members, their power has drastically waned since the glory days of the 1930s. Today, only about 15 percent of the U.S. workforce is unionized (Walton and Rockoff, 1990). Unions have experienced important setbacks that have inhibited their ability to make any substantive demands on business at all; these include the breaking of the air traffic controllers' strike in the early 1980s and the Champion Paper Company strike in the mid-1980s.

iron law of oligarchy—Robert Michels' term for the tendency of democratic organizations to come to be dominated by a self-protective elite.

While the union movement has had its origins in legitimate concerns for the rights of workers, unions in the United States have tended to become hierarchical, conservative structures. Radical working-class political parties in Europe have frequently met the same fate. Robert Michels explained such transformations with his **iron law of oligarchy**. Michels claimed that an oligarchical tendency is built into the evolution of a democratic organization, regardless of its stated principles or philosophy. Stating that oligarchy is "a preordained form of the life of social aggregates" (1915/1958, p. 407), he argued that even the most idealistic of democratic movements tends to form a small ruling elite that will lose touch with the masses it leads and become protective of its power (i.e., an oligarchy). Part of the mechanism is that grass-roots movements must become bureaucratic or else be crushed by management with its specialized bureaucrats in labor law, economics, and public relations; unprofessional unions would be ignored like a typical student protest about tuition hikes. Bureaucracies are by their very nature hierarchical (Chapter 5) and are all too easily transformed into top-down, elite-controlled structures. In light of current voter dissatisfaction in the United States, it is tempting to view the whole political process in this sociological light. The perceived control of the two major political parties by an oligarchy of entrenched bosses and lobbyists has fueled the candidacy of Ross Perot and numerous proposals for campaign reform.

IS THE UNITED STATES A DEMOCRACY?

An outrageous question? Let us consider the objective facts. The very legitimacy of the U.S. government is based in large part on the democratic election of its leaders. The "fact" that the United States is a democracy is taken for granted; it has been ingrained in our subjective consciousness since early childhood. Most of us have also been taught that this true democracy is superior to other nations in the world that do not share our emphasis on freedom and individual rights. Yet how democratic is the United States? Do we really choose our leaders? Are these leaders truly responsive to public opinion? These are questions you have probably not even considered asking yourself, but they are certainly worth thinking about.

Voting

Open and fair elections for the participation of every citizen are the bottom line for a democratic society. The United States prides itself on putting choices before its citizens, so that "we the people" can rationally decide upon the course of action our government should follow. However, the only choice offered to most voters—between Democrats or Republicans—is not really much of a choice at all. Termed "The Greatest Show on Earth" (Parenti, 1983), both Democrats and Republicans make a public display of their minor points of disagreement, yet on most substantive questions of political philosophy the two parties are strikingly similar. The support and development of private industry is fundamental to the platforms of both parties.

Although the Democrats are popularly conceived to be the party of labor and minorities, they have been just as likely as Republicans to crack down on protestors on our own soil and to intervene against working-class revolutionaries abroad (Parenti, 1983). This situation is quite different from the political circumstances in European democracies, where voters have a clear choice between at least three qualitatively different positions, such as those of the Tory, Liberal, and Labour parties in the United Kingdom.

In the 1988 presidential elections, only 51 percent of U.S. citizens cast a ballot; the United States consistently has the lowest turnout rates for national elections among 24 democratic nations (with the exception of Switzerland, where national elections are relatively unimportant because decisions of real political import are made at the local level; Piven and Cloward, 1989). Additionally, the social composition of active voters here is no cross-section of the U.S. population; it is overwhelmingly white, affluent voters who participate in elections. While the lack of a substantive choice between candidates is a part of this low turnout rate, voter registration laws in the United States seem to conspire against the electoral participation of poor and minority populations. In 1980, about 40 percent of the U.S. electorate was not even registered, with two-thirds of unregistered households having incomes below the median (Piven and Cloward, 1989, p. 17). This is a drastically different situation from that encountered in European countries with high turnouts, where everyone is either automatically registered to vote when they come of age, or where government canvassers register voters before major elections (Wolfinger, 1991). The United States is the only democracy that places the burden of voter registration upon the individual rather than upon the government.

Public Opinion and Public Policy

Public opinion in a democracy is supposed to be a guidepost for policymakers, but there is currently a heated debate as to what impact, if any, the opinions of average U.S. citizens have on politicians and lawmakers. While it would be unreasonable to expect government leaders to respond to every blip in a tracking poll with a radical restructuring of policy, it is nonetheless assumed that large, significant changes in the subjective dimension will make a policy difference. Large, relatively uniform changes in public preferences about an issue have, in fact, been interpreted as having an impact by some analysts (Page and Shapiro, 1983). They cite decreased defense spending after mass disapproval of the Vietnam War as an example of the power of public opinion to shape public policy, especially on prominent issues (Abramson and Penner, 1990).

Other studies have found that large swings in public opinion concerning the spending priorities of the federal government have had no detectable effect on official policies. Despite volatile public sentiments about a host of issues, government spending priorities have remained pretty constant (Knapp and Spector, 1991). It has also been argued that mass opinion does have an effect on government action, but the content of public sentiments and the means by which they are expressed are limited by those in power (Ginsberg, 1986). Public opinion may thus appear to have a direct effect, but this effect is steered by the power brokers. The actual influence that the public has on the decisions of its leaders is difficult to measure. It is perhaps safe to say only that mass sentiment has *some* effect in setting the limits of public policy in the political economy of the United States (see Burstein, 1991).

THEORETICAL PERSPECTIVES: FOCUS ON EASTERN EUROPE

The massive upheaval that erupted in Eastern Europe and the Soviet Union in 1989 took most people, including social theorists, by surprise. Suddenly, the lines separating the world into "us" and "them" became blurred. The conventional dichotomy that had provided the foundation for the cold-war mentality had vanished, seemingly overnight. The relatively peaceful revolutions that surfaced throughout Eastern Europe were immediately heralded as the triumph of the "people" over the iron hand of dictatorship. However, the initial euphoria has given way to ethnic violence, economic instability, and an uncertainty about the future. Sociology's theoretical perspectives help one to make sense of the apparent suddenness of the large-scale changes, and of the radical transformations of an entire region of the world.

Functionalism

A functionalist explanation of the Eastern European revolutions would stress the dysfunctions built into the "communist" systems that were overthrown (there are quotation marks because these societies never fit the definition of the term given earlier in this chapter). Totalitarian governments may have served the purpose of keeping order during and after a time of war (e.g., World War II), as well as of accelerating the process of industrialization in the so-called command economies (e.g., the USSR). However, the flexible economies of democratic, capitalist societies are the most productive—hence the most functional—in the contemporary world economy. As long as the fruits of rapid economic development could be used to support the military and ideological apparatus, the Eastern European system functioned without serious disturbance. This does not mean that everyone was in happy agreement over that status quo; but the military and police were able to quash any serious attempts to change the political economy. The modest economic success that the Soviet Union and its satellites enjoyed for decades was not, however, eternal. When factors largely external to Eastern Europe caused the economy to falter, the standard of living was further squeezed. Attempts at economic restructuring by introducing more "freedoms" were a signal to the people that the familiar system they had known was dying of dysfunctions. The sweeping wave of demonstrations was the final gasp of political economies that had ceased to operate as "systems" at all.

Conflict Theory

A conflict perspective interprets these momentous events very differently. While the ideology underlying the "communist" governments was one that emphasized equality and cooperation, in actuality there was serious inequality within both the Soviet Union and the rest of Eastern Europe. The inequality was much less than what we are used to in the West, but the West was not founded upon socialist principles preaching the eventual elimination of class distinctions. The parallel existence of government elites wearing tailored suits in their limos and working people who often had to wait in notoriously long lines just to buy a loaf of bread made it clear to almost everyone that there was a serious tension between propaganda and reality.

Scenes from the sudden spectacular shifts in political economy across eastern Europe: The Berlin wall is being dismantled by a jubilant throng, and an individual boy pilots a Western-style skateboard beneath a looming portrait of Lenin.

Conflict between the masses and the elites had been present in Eastern European societies since the emergence of a privileged stratum, called *apparatchiks,* in the Soviet system. The revolutions occurring in 1989 were an open expression of this conflict that had existed all along. However, the toppling of the old has not immediately ushered in an egalitarian new system. Conflicts among groups within the former communist bloc have escalated; bitter ethnic rivalries have been sharpened like sabers. The socialist ideology appears to have been replaced by the naked struggle for ethnic dominance predicted by Tilly's theory of nationalism. Further, the desire to plunge into a free-market economy is bound to create more class conflict in the time to come.

Symbolic Interactionism

A symbolic interactionist would not be as concerned with the macrostructure of the Eastern European political economy, but would instead focus on the microstructures linking individuals. Regardless of the big structures at work in a society, the real truth is that people make revolutions. Why were the death-knell demonstrations against the communist governments able to swell to CNN proportions? Face-to-face recruitment within networks of fed-up individuals. When people mutually discovered from conversations with each other that they were dissatisfied with things as they were, and that it was now possible to act together to change conditions without fear of certain death, the protest movements exploded. As the opposition "made its way from underground literature to the television screen" (Konrad, 1990, p. 18), people picked up from each other the sense that their protests were making a difference. Expressions of dissatisfaction with the government snowballed into a successful revolution, as individuals sensed their collective power. The symbolic interactionist thinks that the seeds of revolution are not to be found in the overarching structural conditions, but germinate within the day-to-day meanings shared among ordinary people.

Integrating the Theories

Functionalism, conflict theory, and symbolic interactionism are all useful for analyzing social changes in Eastern Europe—or anywhere else. Each perspective offers different insights, and an integration of the three can provide a nuanced picture of fundamental shifts in political economy.

Let us put the pieces of the theoretical puzzle together around the special case of China. Widely viewed as a mysterious giant among human societies, China's mysteries are translatable by the three theoretical perspectives of sociology. On the surface, the passionate and terrifying events in Tienanmen Square—also in 1989—manifested processes well known to symbolic interactionists. The seemingly spontaneous street demonstrations bespeak the rising value of democracy transmitted from person to person. Beneath the surface, daring to hope for a government "by the people" is drawn in part from the sense that dysfunctions are overwhelming the present Maoist system. Deeper yet, part of that decay may be the rot of class inequalities contradicting communist ideals.

Many sinologists—China experts—predict major changes paralleling those in Eastern Europe. If so, see them through the complementary lenses of sociological theory.

SUMMARY

1. Political control and economic resources interact with each other in significant ways. Every aspect of our lives is structured to some extent by the nature of the political economy in which we live.
2. Karl Marx looked at the political economy as the center of society in framing his concepts of alienation, exploitation, and class conflict.
3. For Max Weber, politics and economics have a reciprocal relationship, with each helping to cement the rational, bureaucratic structures that characterize our society today.
4. While Emile Durkheim is less overtly concerned with political economy, his ideas about normative development are closely bound

to the analysis of division of labor in modern societies, which in turn depend for their smooth functioning on the laws of nations.

5. Welfare state capitalism and state capitalism are the two types of political economies prevailing in the world at present. Two alternative systems, socialism and communism, exist only in theory.
6. Some of the most bitter and basic disputes in sociology arise over discussions of power. Pluralists generally stress the democratic essence of U.S. society and believe that power is diffused among many competing interest groups, while power-elite theorists claim that power in the United States is highly concentrated within a tiny circle of decisionmakers. This classic debate can be viewed as a discussion about the structure of power networks in U.S. society.
7. The political–economy link can be clearly seen in the interrelationship of state making and war. Both internal and external conflict are closely bound up with the processes of state development, which is tied to the needs of the market.
8. Business interests in the United States strongly influence defense spending, as well as virtually every aspect of state policy making. Even seemingly generous social programs such as welfare serve functions favorable to the growth and development of business by legitimating the government and preserving the economic status quo with a minimum of social unrest.
9. As the United States becomes a post-industrial society, increasing specialization and the corresponding routinization of work contribute to a growing sense of worker alienation.
10. Even worse off than someone in an alienating job is someone with no job at all. Widespread loss of people's most highly valued role violates deep public expectations that U.S. society should be able to provide jobs for willing hands. The heightened cultural consciousness of unemployment is further raised by its high visibility.
11. U.S. citizens hope to solve such pervasive national problems as unemployment by participating in the democratic process. Voters' choices are limited, however, because the support and development of private industry is fundamental to the platforms of both major political parties. Further, while some studies detect an impact of public opinion on public policy, others indicate that this impact is steered by those in power, thus limiting the effect of mass sentiment on the setting of policy in the political economy of the United States.

Chapter 17

Personal Perspective

My seventh-grade science teacher, Mr. Gulick, appreciated neither my taste in clothes, nor the cultural icons of another country. I was wearing a tee-shirt emblazoned with one of Belgium's most beloved figures—a young boy urinating. Proudly referred to by Belgians as the "Mannekin-Pis," countless Flemish fountains and paintings revolve around this young lad and his unremitting stream. My friends found the shirt amusing and even interesting after I explained its cultural significance. My teachers expressed no opinion on the matter—until I got to science class. Mr. Gulick demanded to know if my parents knew about this disgusting shirt. I told him it was a gift from them. After I accused him of impinging on my First Amendment rights, he exploded and threatened to fail me if I didn't go down to see the Dean of Discipline and get a ruling on my attire. This had me a bit worried since the Dean was a physical education teacher who proved Woody Allen's adage: "Those who can't, teach; those who can't teach, teach gym." Surprisingly, Mr. Futterman was amused at the whole incident and sent me back to class. To this day, I am certain that my grade in seventh-grade science suffered because of this affair.

At the time, this seemed like just another example of my getting into trouble at school. Despite having excellent grades, I was always being screamed at for something. For another example, in fifth grade we were supposed to take a field trip to a neighboring school to see a production of *The Sound of Music.* Well, I had just seen the movie and hated it. I announced this to my teacher and said that I would prefer spending the day in the library reading. I was even willing to write some sort of report rather than subject myself to another two hours of the Von Trapp family. When I said out loud that I would "forget" to have my permission slip signed, I was whisked to the principal's office where Mr. Olander quickly grew rabid and

Education

frothed at the mouth. He was uninterested in my reasons and focused only on whether I had the "right" to even question my participation. He said if I didn't get my slip signed I would have to sit all day in a first-grade classroom rather than read in the library. Well, I went on the field trip and hated every minute of it. But my principal was happy that I did what I was supposed to do, even though it was not educational.

RE

When most people think of schools, they think of places where students learn knowledge and skills. But schools do many more things than simply impart a formal curriculum. Schools have so-called hidden curricula, which teach students such things as what to value and how to behave. The "Personal Perspective" recounts one professor's experiences with this hidden curriculum, experiences probably similar to those you have had over the years. Think of the instances in school (even in college) where there was more emphasis on obedience, following rules, and conformity than on learning trigonometry, exploring something, or grappling with life's meaning. Did you ever miss 20 minutes of class getting a late pass when you were 30 seconds late for homeroom? How often were you discouraged from coloring outside the lines? Did you ever have to memorize a speech or a poem without the slightest idea as to its meaning? Finally, remember the sure ticket to the principal's office and possible suspension: bringing 30 pieces of gum to class, chewing one piece loudly and, when asked by your teacher if "you brought enough for the class," saying yes and giving a piece to everyone.

There is of course no obvious connection between chewing gum in class and learning how to conjugate verbs, and there is a lot more about education that is far from obvious as well. This chapter discusses both the obvious and non-obvious aspects of education, and we return to the topic of curricular content in a later section. Let's first examine the relationship between education and the American Dream, which, as you will discover, is also not nearly as obvious as most people think.

EDUCATION AND THE AMERICAN DREAM

American Dream—the ideals of freedom, equality, and especially opportunity traditionally stressed as available to individuals in the United States.

The traditional **American Dream** says that people are likely to be successful if they have certain natural talents, the proper skills and values, and a good educational degree. This formula is expressed in Figure 17:1 as Success = Innate Talents + Learned Skills + Education. Success refers not just to wealth, but to the amount of power and prestige individuals have relative to others. In short, the formula suggests that individual factors are the most important determinants of achieving social success.

Innate talent refers to biological aptitude including intelligence and certain motor skills. Some individuals are good at sports, some at chess, and some at calculating cube roots. According to popular thinking about the formula, "natural" intelligence is especially important in determining which individuals will be successful.

There are two related types of learned skills: (1) technical skills and knowledge, and (2) achievement values. According to the American Dream scenario of success, individuals must master certain basic skills such as mathematics, grammar, and physics. People must also internalize the

SUCCESS	=	**INNATE TALENTS**	+	**LEARNED SKILLS**	+	**EDUCATION**
		intelligence aptitude athleticism		1. Technical Skills and Knowledge math spelling physics 2. Achievement Values study and work hard just say no to drugs stay in school		years of schooling degrees

FIGURE 17:1 EDUCATION AND THE AMERICAN DREAM

The traditional American Dream states that people are likely to be successful if they have certain natural talents, the proper skills and values, and a good education.

correct values; that is, they must learn to work hard, to strive for excellence, to "just say no" to drugs, and to recognize the importance of education itself.

In this formula for success, innate talents and learned skills have an additive relationship. This means that the more a person has of each, the more successful he or she is likely to be. It also suggests that a relative abundance

Two hundred years ago most education of children took place in the home. In *Interior Scene* (c. 1835) by Jane Stuart, a dutiful mother has put aside her sewing to listen to her son recite his lessons. Home education at least in the upper classes typically began around the age of 2 and continued for many years. Had there been alternatives, many parents would have gladly given up this demanding and often problematic duty.

One hundred years ago, most schools in the United States resembled more the one-room schoolhouse depicted in Winslow Homer's *The Country School* (1871) than the large bureaucratic schools found in most communities today. Actually, there are still more than 600 one-room public schoolhouses left in the United States, and the students in such schools do as well or better in achievement tests than their counterparts in large bureaucratic schools.

of either innate talents or learned skills (including attitudes and values) can make up for a deficiency in the other. In a simple arithmetic equation, both 3 + 8 and 9 + 2 equal 11. The same result is possible when one factor is smaller as long as the other factor is larger. Thus the American Dream of success claims that certain learned skills and achievement values can compensate for a lack of natural talent. For example, basketball players with limited innate talents (e.g., shortness) can still excel by counteracting this with superior technical skill (e.g., knowledge of the game's strategy) and solid achievement values (e.g., hustle). Off the court, individuals with limited intelligence can still be successful if they study extra hard and avoid distractions such as drugs.

Education is a relative "constant" in this American Dream formula for success. According to this vision, everybody has equal access to quality education through grade 12 and beyond. Therefore, schooling's effect on success is also additive. The more education you get, the more likely you are to be successful. It is up to individuals to maximize their chances for success by getting as much education as they can.

Education is also the primary institutional mechanism that sifts and sorts people into various social statuses. The complex division of labor in the United States requires different talents, skills, and motivational levels, depending upon location in the social hierarchy. For example, we expect a Supreme Court Justice to have more talent and more motivation than the Zamboni driver at the local ice rink. Within this allocation process, schools play a dual role. On the one hand, they impart the skills, knowledge, and values necessary for this complex division of labor. On the other hand, schools test and measure how much aptitude individuals possess and how well they have learned their skills. By assessing natural talents, technical skills, and motivational levels, schools help allocate "human resources" into the proper statuses in society.

This success formula has not been plucked out of the sociological air. It is a distillation of many studies documenting national attitudes about how

Allan Rohan Crite's *School's Out* (1936) shows children streaming from a large bureaucratic school typical of the type most U.S. students attend today. It is apparent that this particular neighborhood school serves minority students almost entirely. Residential segregation and "separate but equal" school policies were in effect prior to the 1954 Supreme Court decision, *Brown* v. *the Board of Education,* which outlawed the racial segregation of students within school systems. Nevertheless, by the mid-1990s, *de facto* racial segregation in school systems is still common in the United States, particularly in urban areas.

the success system works. The conventional view is that people are accurately judged on their intelligence and motivation, have equal access to education, and eventually occupy social statuses commensurate with their personal merit. The widespread assumption is that successful people have the "right stuff" while unsuccessful people do not, and that all people thus end up in their proper social slots. In other words, the American Dream formula for success posits that the allocation of social rewards (e.g., wealth, power, and prestige) is based on an individual's **achieved status** rather than an **ascribed status** (e.g., race, class, gender). The role of education in the success system is a key element of the populist vision of **meritocracy**, not too unlike the idealized version of schooling described in Box 17:1.

achieved status—a position acquired by an individual through his or her own efforts.

ascribed status—a position that is not based on individual ability, skill, effort, or accomplishment, but on a position inherited in the society.

meritocracy—a society in which persons make their way on their own ability and talent rather than because of class privileges.

Sociologists, however, do not accept this American Dream formula of success at face value. The idea of meritocracy sounds wonderful, but empirical studies indicate that it is as much fiction as fact. Most sociologists agree that schools sort people into various social locations. But they disagree about how fairly schools sort, and about how fairly social resources are allocated to members of society. While not ruling out the importance of merit, sociologists also look for explanations of social success that have nothing to do with it. For example, sociologists examine how boys and girls are treated differently in schools, and how this affects their chances of success. Similarly, sociologists compare the curricular and extracurricular resources of schools in diverse neighborhoods to see if differential resources exist and, if so, whether or not they affect success.

There is no consensus within sociology on just what components of education are most important to study, or on just how fairly schools help allocate social success. Some sociologists focus their studies on student–teacher interaction, whereas others look at school curricula. Some sociologists examine if what we learn in school really helps us succeed, whereas others

BOX 17:1 SOCIOLOGICAL IMAGINATION IN FICTION

An Equal-Opportunity Society

In his novel, *The Rise of the Meritocracy,* Michael Young envisions a social division of labor based strictly on an individual's skills and talents. Schools play a preeminent role in this meritocracy.

This society will give a new meaning to equality of opportunity. This . . . should not mean equal opportunity to rise up the social scale, but equal opportunity for all people, irrespective of their "intelligence," to develop the virtues and talents with which they are endowed, all their capacities for appreciating the beauty and depth of human experience, all their potential for living to the full. The child, every child, is a precious individual, not just a potential functionary of society. The schools should not be tied to the occupational structure, bent for turning out people for the jobs at any particular moment considered important, but should be devoted to encouraging all human talents, whether or not these are of the kind needed in a scientific world. The arts and manual skills should be given as much prominence as science and technology. The hierarchy of the schools should be abolished and common schools established. These schools should have good enough teachers so that all children should have individual care and stimulus. They could then develop at their own pace to their own particular fulfillment. The schools would not segregate the like but mingle the unlike; by promoting diversity within unity, they would teach respect for the infinite human differences. The schools would not regard children as once and for all shaped by Nature, but as a combination of potentials which can be cultivated by nurture.

Critical Thinking Questions

1. In the real world, is a near absolute meritocracy ever really possible?
2. Should schools be designed to primarily serve the needs of the individual or the needs of society?

Source: Michael Young, *The Rise of the Meritocracy, 1870–2033.* (1959). New York: Random House.

study how specific schools seem to regularly channel certain kinds of students into particular social slots. Despite these and other differences, most sociologists agree that, contrary to the formula, there is no simple additive relationship between education and social success. Most important, sociologists believe that understanding education's role in social success necessitates looking beyond individual aptitudes and attitudes.

EDUCATION AND THE AMERICAN REALITY

Although the gap in earnings between those with and without college degrees increased substantially over the 20 years prior to 1990, the severe economic recession of the early 1990s challenged the validity of the American Dream. Many young people with good grades, excellent skills, high motivation, and impressive degrees were unable to find work. While a college degree traditionally has been an almost sure ticket to success, it no longer seemed to guarantee anything except, in many cases, a big loan debt. Even the accounting profession, which hired almost every available

The social class of the family into which children are born has a profound effect on their opportunity to achieve educational success and the American Dream. Upper-class children can use family wealth, power, and prestige to secure elite private school educations that in turn reinforce their existing class advantages. Many lower-class children have a lower average educational achievement in part because they attend schools with inferior resources. Thus, the U.S. educational institution helps perpetuate already existing social inequalities.

accounting major in the 1980s, cut back drastically on job offers during this period. Young women and men with BAs often found themselves waiting longer for a "decent" job, or simply waiting tables.

With the legitimacy of the American Dream in question, it is important to understand the sociological relationship between education and success. In the United States, people tend to view success (or the lack of it) as a purely individual phenomenon. Why did you fail? Maybe you didn't study enough for that big chemistry test or maybe you should have resisted peer pressure to "party hardy" the night before SATs. Perhaps becoming more proficient at calculus would help ensure your dreams of being a great pancreatic surgeon, or at least would have gotten you into Harvard University instead of Podunk College. This attitude reflects a national tendency to "psychologize" our lives; that is, to ignore the complex interrelationships among larger social factors and how these factors influence our personal lives. But success is more complicated than just assessing one's own grades.

Education and Innate Talents

As with other biological explanations for human behavior, sociologists do not dismiss outright that differences in natural intelligence exist, and that these differences partially explain an individual's success. However, sociologists emphasize that biology is not destiny, and that social factors also play an important part in explaining individual success. Nevertheless, the notion of a single, innate "intelligence factor," and the IQ score that supposedly measures it, has become one of the most powerful ideas in modern life (Gould, 1981). Unequal distribution of social resources is commonly legitimized on the basis of this similarly unequal distribution of natural intelligence. Smarter people will be more successful. Schools help determine an individual's "smartness" rank by administering IQ tests and achievement tests (sometimes called proficiency tests), and by assigning grades based on academic proficiency.

There is a strong empirical correlation among IQ score, educational achievement, and social success as measured by income (Blau and Duncan, 1967). People with higher IQ scores get better grades, reach higher levels of education (graduate school), and make more money than people with lower IQ scores. Some scholars argue that this supports a genetic explanation for social success (Allen, 1992). For example, the fact that African

Americans consistently score lower on IQ tests (Jensen, 1969) has led psychologist Richard Herrnstein to conclude that "the major cause of [African Americans'] intellectual and social deficits is hereditary and genetic in origin, and thus not [affected by changes] in the environment" (Allen, 1992; Herrnstein, 1973). According to these explanations, unsuccessful parents pass on inferior genes to their children, which almost assures that their children will also be inferior and unsuccessful. From this perspective, schools and IQ tests perform the invaluable social function of identifying the most able and weeding out the least able.

Most sociologists do not accept this dominant role of inherited intelligence in a meritocratic sorting of social rewards (Collins, 1988). Rather, they argue that innate factors explain only about 17 percent of the variance in IQ scores, with the remaining difference caused by social factors (Taylor, 1980). Indeed, even defenders of a dominant genetic basis of intelligence claim that no more than 50 percent of an IQ score is explained by heredity (Allen, 1992). This means at least half of a person's IQ score is not biological. Solely genetic explanations linking intelligence and success also have difficulty explaining why women have much lower incomes than men despite insignificant differences in IQ (Collins, 1988).

It is also worth noting two other factors about IQ tests. First, IQ tests themselves have been frequently criticized for measuring *learned* knowledge skills rather than *innate* intelligence (Gould, 1981; Marlaire and Maynard, 1990). Second, some historical analyses of IQ tests suggest that they may have been developed to lend "scientific" legitimacy to social inequalities based on gender, race, and ethnic origin (Gould, 1981; Myrdal, 1944).

In short, instead of the single most important component of social success, most sociologists view intelligence as merely one element of a larger calculus that considers social factors more important. These sociologists see innate intelligence as "parameters" for social success. Within these parameters, then, social factors such as educational opportunity, social class, race, and gender play the major role in affecting an individual's success (Jencks, 1985). Therefore, two individuals with exactly the same level of innate intelligence (however measured) may end up with vastly differing amounts of success, depending on each individual's specific social context.

Education and Learned Skills

The second component of the American Dream formula for social success concerns things people learn from their social surroundings, namely, knowledge and values. Above and beyond any biological inheritance, people must also learn technical competence—along with certain values—to accrue wealth, power, and prestige. All the "smarts" in the world will only go so far if a person has bad grammar and a bad attitude. In fact, even those with relatively modest natural talents supposedly can experience upward social mobility if they work harder than their more talented peers.

As already mentioned, schools maintain a dual institutional responsibility for teaching these cultural elements and measuring whether an individual has correctly learned them. While schools are normally associated with imparting knowledge and technical skills, they are also important conduits of dominant social values and beliefs—even belief in the American Dream formula itself. Think about how many times teachers told you that making a solid effort was as important as getting good grades. It is no coincidence that report cards often have two sections, one for grades and one for effort. In phys-ed classes, people who cannot walk and chew gum at the same time are encouraged to "keep trying" athletic things that cause them pain and embarrassment. The apparent rationale is that falling off the climbing ropes a 10th time builds character and contributes to long-term success.

How people regard education itself is perhaps the most important value associated with the American Dream formula for success. Consider how contemporary discussions about the "problems" in American education focus on this particular value of appreciating education. According to the American Dream formula, people must be willing to put forth the effort to attend and succeed in school. If not, they have nobody to blame but themselves for their failure. Here, social success is affected not only by uncontrollable biological capacities, but by a very controllable willingness to work hard and avoid distractions from school. If they want to be successful, young people must *want* to be successful.

Success and Human Capital

human capital—the amount individuals invest in themselves, which may determine their own social success.

Human capital is the idea that how much individuals "invest" in themselves largely determines their own social success. As with financial capital, a little bit of initial human capital investment is seen as a sure ticket to later bounties. The more individuals invest in developing their personal stock, the more they will achieve later in life (measured by wealth, power, and prestige). This "personal investment portfolio" has many components, the two most important of which are skills and values. Human capital theories about success stipulate that it is up to each person to cultivate her or his own skills and values, and that the most important mechanism for this development is education. In a sense, schools are seen as the "marketplace" where people acquire the personal resources necessary to be socially successful.

technocracy—a society whose social system operates according to the dictates of technology and engineering.

In terms of developing skills, some social scientists believe that the United States is becoming more of a **technocracy**, a society where very sophisticated capabilities are needed to satisfy increasingly specialized slots in the division of labor (Bell, 1973; Galbraith, 1967). Therefore, individuals must invest much time in their schooling; otherwise they might not have

Children who attend high-quality preschool programs have, later in life, higher earnings, fewer arrests, fewer out-of-wedlock births, and more commitment to marriage. However, though each dollar spent on the preschool children saves many dollars later on then-unnecessary social services, such programs are expensive. They cost about twice what the average Head Start program does. Because of inadequate funding, Head Start programs like the one shown here have trouble obtaining qualified staff and adequate facilities. Moreover, there are few continuation programs to nurture Head Start graduates later on, and the academic and social gains made by children in ordinary Head Start programs are often lost within a few years.

TABLE 17:1 Percent of High School Dropouts by Race, 1970–1989

	YEAR				
RACE	1970	1980	1985	1989	% Change
White	10.8	11.3	10.3	10.5	−2.8
Black	22.2	16.0	12.6	11.4	−48.6

Source: U.S. Bureau of the Census (1992c), *Statistical Abstract of the United States: 1992,* Washington, D.C., p. 160.

the tools necessary to be successful in our highly complex society. This increased personal investment in human capital supposedly leads to higher social productivity, higher wages, and a healthier overall economy (Mincer, 1974; Rosenbaum, 1979). Finally, human capital theory insists that people are judged increasingly on their achieved rather than ascribed statuses.

Education is seen as a critical component for building an individual's "portfolio" of human capital since that is where complicated skills are learned. Schools must prepare students for the technical requirements of a post-industrial, corporate society. The recent call for improved national testing of American students assumes that schools are not adequately teaching these skills, and that this failure is significantly responsible for many social problems. The recent decline in standardized test scores such as the SAT is often cited to demonstrate this failure (see Table 17:5). In 1991, former president Bush and his Secretary of Education proposed a new standardized test for students. They argued this would show how well students were learning and how well schools were teaching. Such tests would parallel the standardized tests of other industrialized countries. The idea of a national proficiency test based on some core body of knowledge and skills has been much debated among both policymakers and scholars.

Education and Values

In the early 1990s, the mass media were full of stories on current efforts to stress "value education" in the nation's schools. This reflects the growing belief that social problems such as America's lack of global economic competitiveness stem from improper motivation and poor values. The argument goes that many schools and families no longer teach "basic" values such as discipline, hard work, sexual abstinence, and civic pride. This results in less virtuous people, many of whom seem more interested in selling drugs on the street than in selling computer software to global companies. To succeed personally and as a society, the argument goes, people must stop squandering their intellectual capital. This argument is similar to the discussion about technical proficiency, except attitudes and values rather than skills are at issue.

The relative absence of these attitudes also is used to explain why certain racial and ethnic groups do worse in school and, hence, why they are less socially successful. For instance, dropout rates are higher among African American students and Hispanic students than among white students (see Table 17:1). Similarly, college enrollments of African Americans and Hispanics have decreased since the mid-1970s but have increased for whites. According to this perspective, success among members of these minority groups is lagging because they don't realize the value of education. This is similar to an argument that explains why early-twentieth-century Jewish immigrants to the United States were more successful than

TABLE 17:2 Average Scholastic Achievement Test (SAT) Math Scores by Race, 1976–1991

	YEAR							
RACE	1976	1985	1987	1988	1989	1990	1991	% Change
White	493	490	489	490	491	491	489	−4
Black	354	376	377	384	386	385	385	+31

Source: U.S. Bureau of the Census (1992), *Statistical Abstract of the United States: 1992,* Washington, D.C., p. 159.

non-Jewish immigrants. It held that Jews showed a relatively greater willingness to attend school, study hard, and finish degrees than other immigrant groups. Jewish families supposedly had better values about education than, say, Italian and Irish immigrant families. Consequently, Jews better developed their human capital and were able to achieve more than other immigrant groups.

EVIDENCE ON THE AMERICAN DREAM FORMULA

A generation ago, biological factors (i.e., talent and intelligence) were emphasized as the most important components of the American Dream formula for success. Today, however, learned skills and values are viewed as the most important components. But as with the old genetic explanations, many scholars challenge this newer view that developing "human capital" is the primary factor in determining social success. This is because there is little evidence (1) that success is correlated with learned skills, (2) that schools actually provide learned skills, and (3) that societies with high overall amounts of human capital are the most productive (Collins, 1988).

There is strong evidence that the more years of education you have, the more successful you will be as measured by income (Jencks et al., 1972). A human capital perspective would maintain that education increases your level of learned skills and thus makes you more able to fill an important, highly rewarded social role. It is unclear, however, if this increased success is caused strictly by a person's learned skills or whether more ascriptive factors like race and gender are also at work. It seems obvious that a person's degree should indicate mastery of important skills and knowledge. Those with more advanced degrees, therefore, should be more successful regardless of any ascribed statuses. Indeed, the degree–success relationship holds true when all Americans are looked at together: Those with high school diplomas make significantly more money (and have higher prestige jobs) than those who dropped out, and college-educated people earn more than those with a high school diploma.

The evidence also shows, however, that this relationship between attained degree and success does not hold constant across ascribed social categories. For example, recent census data show that white males with college degrees earn about 25 percent more per year than African American males with college degrees. (It should be noted that some of this difference is also due to the difference in the average quality of the colleges whites and African Americans attend). Also, white males who drop out of high school still earn more on average than African American or Hispanic males with high school degrees. Finally, women with college degrees earn on average about the same as men with high school diplomas. While some

TABLE 17:3 Average Reading Proficiency Test Scores of 17-Year-Olds by Race, 1979–1988

RACE	YEAR			
	1979	1983	1988	% Change
White	293	296	295	+0.68
Black	243	264	274	+12.8

Source: U.S. Bureau of the Census (1992), *Statistical Abstract of the United States: 1992,* Washington, D.C., p. 160.

of this discrepancy comes from such factors as differences among groups in average number of years in the labor force and differences in the average quality of the colleges various groups attend, much of it is due to racism, sexism, and other forms of discrimination.

Trends in standardized test scores also challenge a simple human capital explanation for social success. Table 17:2 shows changes in SAT math scores by race between 1976 and 1991, and Table 17:3 shows changes in reading proficiency tests scores by race between 1979 and 1988. In both measures of learned skills, average scores of African Americans have increased significantly while average scores of white students have remained about the same. According to the standard formula for success, you might expect this increase in performance among African Americans to be reflected by increased college attendance and increased income. However, over this same time period, college enrollment rates for African Americans have actually declined while enrollment rates for whites have increased. In addition, Labor Department data show that the median income of African American families has remained virtually unchanged since 1979, while the median income of white families has increased by about 3 percent during that time (Bovee, 1991).

This problematic relationship between human capital and success is also illustrated in Table 17:1, which shows dropout rates for African Americans and whites. While these data indicate a slightly higher dropout rate for African Americans, they also show that this difference is negligible and that since 1970 the dropout rate of African Americans has declined significantly while the rate for whites has stayed about the same. Assuming that this reflects an increased commitment to education by African Americans, a simple human capital explanation of social success would predict a relative increase in their median income compared to that of whites. This, however, is not the case. In short, while schools and education do play some role in distributing social resources based on learned skills, the meritocratic payoff of school performance is constrained by ascribed social forces.

Social Class and Schooling

A fundamental problem with simple human capital explanations is that they focus mainly *inside* the individual student's experience. But many factors *outside* the student's personality have strong educational effects as well. For example, African American and white dropout rates are identical when both attend school in affluent suburbs; this is also true in poorer urban and rural areas (Griffith, Frase, and Ralph, 1989). This suggests that social class provides common educational capital whatever a given student's personal investment (see Table 17:4).

Victor Mays's painting of the 1902 Harvard–Yale crew races at New London shows a crack Yale eight outrowing a fast Harvard boat. According to reports, there were so many yachts with Harvard and Yale alumni that it took nearly an hour for the fleet to file through a nearby drawbridge after the race. Aboard the white-hulled yacht *Dolphin,* the largest in the scene, is President Theodore Roosevelt, who graduated from Harvard in 1880. Mays's painting indicates the close connections between wealth, power, and elite universities. Graduates of such universities have traditionally taken advantage of powerful and influential networks of alumni to further their own quests for the American Dream.

The educational effects of social class were powerfully established by sociologist James Coleman (1966) in a landmark study commissioned by the U.S. government. The first "Coleman Report" documented the unequal distribution of resources to the nation's schools, but Coleman argued that such resources (e.g., teachers' salaries, physical plant) exercised surprisingly little influence over student achievement. Coleman's findings shifted

TABLE 17:4 Crosstabulation of Education by Social Class

RESPONDENT'S CLASS	EDUCATIONAL LEVEL		
Count **ROW PCT**	Less than High School	High School	Greater than High School
Lower class	24 **42.1**	26 **45.6**	7 **12.3**
Working class	161 **25.9**	367 **59.0**	94 **15.1**
Middle class	90 **14.2**	313 **49.2**	233 **36.6**
Upper class	3 **7.0**	17 **39.5**	23 **53.5**

$n = 1{,}358$

Main Point: The relationship between social class and education is clear. The proportion of each class having more than a high school education rises from a mere 12.3 percent in the lower class to a robust 53.5 percent in the upper class.

Source: General Social Survey, 1990.

the focus of the sociology of education—and public policy—toward the significance of "family background." The term itself suggests the relevance of the home environment of the student and, in particular, the social class of that home. Coleman's data clearly support this suggestion: The social class of a student's family affects school achievement independently of race, IQ, school budget, and many other factors.

Although the "Coleman Report" altered our understanding of the human capital model, it has been criticized for missing social class effects at the institutional level. Replications of his research draw stronger conclusions about the impact of schools than did Coleman (Giddens, 1991; Hurn, 1985; Rutter and Giller, 1984). Moreover, critics contend that schools *can* have a larger impact than they observably did in the "Coleman Report" if their financial resources were expended in a more productive way (Ferrante, 1991; Pedersen and Faucher, 1978).

A contemporary contribution to this argument is offered by Jonathon Kozol (1991), who has documented vast differences among U.S. public schools depending upon the social class composition of their students. Kozol examined dozens of decaying public schools, primarily in large cities. While many of these schools have predominantly African American and Hispanic students, the same dreary conditions were found in schools attended by impoverished whites. Kozol found, for example, that in poverty-stricken schools in East St. Louis, 110 students in four history classes share only 26 books. On the South Side of Chicago, chemistry teachers in one school use popcorn poppers as Bunsen burners. PS 261 in the South Bronx (New York) was found to have 400 more students than is legally (fire) safe. The school was originally converted from a skating rink and has no playground, few classroom windows, and classes with both sixth and second graders sharing the same desk. In stark contrast, just a few miles away from these schools can be found other public institutions with remarkable resources. One suburban Chicago school has seven gyms, an olympic-size pool, and separate rooms for fencing, wrestling, and dance instruction.

But such disparities are not merely geographic in nature; that is, not just based on differences between impoverished inner cities and affluent suburbs. Kozol also found vast differences in the quality of educational

Vast differences reflect the financial resources available to public schools. Schools in affluent neighborhoods have the resources to support huge physical plants including impressive athletic complexes complete with large stadiums. Schools in poor urban neighborhoods often have cramped, decaying physical plants and many do not even have playgrounds or athletic fields.

resources available to students from different social classes within the same school district. For instance, PS 24 in the wealthy Riverdale section of the Bronx, only a few bus stops from aforementioned PS 261, has class sizes well below the city average, and excellent educational and recreational facilities.

Thus it is clear that the American ideal of equal opportunity through equal access to education is not a reality across neighboring communities or even within them. Such vast educational inequities result primarily from the way that schools generate revenues. Public schools in the United States are highly decentralized. This means that local citizens play a major role in the specific characteristics of their schools, and that these characteristics reflect the community. However, this also means that local economic resources are the most important source of educational revenues, and that poorer areas have relatively less money available for education than do wealthy areas. In most places, almost half of all public school revenues are generated by local property taxes. Most of the remaining funds come from the state government, with only a small fraction coming from the federal government. Thus, poor communities, especially those in economically deprived states, have far less money to spend on education than wealthy ones, especially those in affluent states. In Texas, for example, the most affluent districts spend about three times more per pupil than the poorest districts.

This inequality of revenue and the corresponding differences in expenditures per student have become greater during the past decade as the federal government has cut educational spending. This has forced states and communities to pick up a greater portion of the tab. And, since state and local taxes are generally regressive (i.e., take a higher proportion of income from impoverished people compared to affluent ones), relatively nonwealthy communities are finding it increasingly difficult just to maintain schools at present levels. Indeed, some state courts have recognized this inequity and ordered legislatures to restructure the formula with which local public schools generate their funding. For example, Kentucky recently was forced to restructure its funding formula. By 1991, each public school in the state spent about $3,200 of public funds for each student. Before the court ruling, the richest schools spent $4,200 per student while the poorest schools spent about $1,700 per student. Given the fact that impoverished communities spend far less money on education than wealthier ones, it is easy to understand why polls show that dissatisfaction with public schools is much less common among the middle class than among the poor.

Despite all the debates in the sociology of education and in the political realm, several facts about social class and schooling are well established. First, the social "investment" in each student is dramatically unequal. Second, school quality as measured in expenditures does affect achievement, although the extent of the effect is uncertain and may be relatively low. Third, family background strongly influences a typical student's success in any school, although the reasons for this influence are also uncertain.

Social Networks and Schooling

In addition to the 1966 *Coleman Report,* James Coleman continues to influence sociological perspectives on education. In *High School Achievement* (1982), Coleman contends that private schools (especially religiously based ones) are much more effective than public schools. Based on his own sample of both types of schools and using selected standardized measures, Coleman cites clear differences in homework completion, dropout rates, and academic performance. The superior education of private schools is made possible, he argues, because of the interpersonal connections among the students, their parents, and school professionals. A caring and concerned nexus of social networks, then, is largely responsible for the relative superiority of private education. Coleman calls this cluster of interpersonal relationships social capital. Essentially, this is the set of *interpersonal* resources overlaying the *personal* investments of the American Dream formula.

social capital—the set of interpersonal resources overlaying the personal investments of the American Dream formula.

Coleman's argument has not been immune to criticism from other social scientists. For one thing, there is the matter of social class differences between private school students who pay tuition and public school students who do not. Some sociologists, using Coleman's original data but different theoretical models about schools, have even drawn conclusions contradictory to Coleman's (Knapp, 1994). Bordieu and Passeron (1977) also talk about social capital (calling it cultural capital) but in a very different way than Coleman. They argue that the "tastes" associated with upper-class culture are an important mechanism for transmitting social inequalities between generations. Personal preferences such as an appreciation of expensive French wines, interest in opera, and a phony British accent can all be traced to the basic social unit referred to as "family background" (DiMaggio, 1982; McClelland, 1990).

Social network research also raises questions about the individualistic American Dream formula for success. One intriguing study of primary school children has focused on the interaction patterns of "aggressive" kids or bullies. To the investigators' surprise, such children are not shunned and actually have as many "best friends" as do less-aggressive children (Cairns, 1988). Such findings snap us out of the trance induced by the formula through recall of the rich—and sometimes painful—interpersonal experiences of our own school days. For example, the dramatic suggestion at college orientations to "look left, then look right; one of the three of you won't make it" is supposed to instill personal motivation. *Interpersonal* motivation clearly matters; even after ability levels, grades, and a host of individual traits are controlled, the social influences of peers affect that likelihood of dropping out (Bank, Slavings, and Biddle, 1990).

A final demonstration of network effects involves a 13-year panel study of suburban high school students, which identified a "delinquency subculture" oriented to stealing, breaking things, and fighting, as well as a "party subculture" oriented to partying, rock concerts, and drinking (Hagan, 1991). Sound familiar? Such subcultural groupings are well-known features of the social life at many high schools. What is startling is their long-term effects. Hagan traced these people into their twenties and thirties when they had become generally established in their occupations. The data clearly indicated that "party subculture" participants became *more* successful than the "delinquent subculture" participants and their more orthodox classmates, possibly because the "party people" acquired social skills applicable to their occupational networks. Such studies should remind us that education and schooling is a complex *social* process not easily reduced to simple formulas about hard work, good study habits, and other conventional values.

EDUCATION AND THE CLASSROOM

Sociologists are also interested in the day-to-day action within schools. Research in this area attempts to look inside the "black box" of the educational process itself instead of treating school as something that just happens. In unpacking this black box, sociologists are interested in both the *content* of education (i.e., the actual material taught) and the *form* of education (i.e., how the material is taught). Even at this micro level, a sociological perspective sheds light on the conventional belief that the United States is a meritocracy, and that education is the institutional conduit for fairly sorting society's members into their proper social locations.

Curriculum and Content

Most people acquire skills and knowledge at school. They learn how to read, write, count, and speak well. They also learn about history, nature, art, literature, music, and volleyball. This is a primary or *manifest* function of education—imparting skills and transmitting cultural knowledge from one generation to the next (i.e., socialization). But sociologists also are interested in the secondary or *latent* functions of education—those things that are not part of education's "official" mission. These are part of a so-called **hidden curriculum**, which exists simultaneously with the more *formal curriculum* of course matter.

hidden curriculum—that part of education that embodies latent functions such as the transmission of social values and norms.

As noted earlier, the hidden curriculum emphasizes such things as obedience, following rules, and conformity rather than acquiring knowledge and skills. Indeed a college professor once noted that 12 years of schooling creates not students but lobotomy patients, barely capable of critical thinking, but superb at following orders. A sociologist has even likened the school experience—especially kindergarten—to boot camp where children "learn to go through routines and to follow orders with unquestioning obedience, even when these make no sense to them" (Gracey, 1972). Indeed, research indicates that grades often reflect a student's conformity more than academic achievement, especially among students who are viewed as less intelligent (Brophy and Good, 1974; Gravenberg and Collins, 1976).

Values such as ethnocentrism and patriotism are also part of the hidden curriculum. Although students often learn to understand and perhaps to appreciate other cultures and languages, they also learn at least indirectly that the United States is better than other countries. This frequently leads to a contradiction in the values children learn. On the one hand, schools teach that fighting is wrong (and punishable); while, on the other hand, they teach how the United States is always right when it fights other countries. Similarly, the presence of ROTC and Junior ROTC at colleges and high schools may reflect the "nationalistic" component of the hidden curriculum.

Values favoring competition and winning are also part of the hidden curriculum (Box 17:2). In addition to battling for grades, these values are also reflected in school attitudes toward athletic teams. A study of a Texas high school football team is an extreme case in point. The study found strong links among the success of the team, the daily travails of the school, and the self-image of the surrounding community (Bissinger, 1990). While the English department at this school spends in total about $5,000 per year on supplies, the football team annually spends $70,000 on chartered air flights and plays home games in a $6 million stadium. The intensity to beat opposing teams is so strong that homicides have occurred around big games. Once high school is over, however, these lionized athletes frequently find themselves in dead-end jobs with little opportunity for upward social mobility. In a real sense, the hidden curriculum in this school that stresses winning is more powerful than the manifest curriculum of learning skills and gaining knowledge. This same contradiction is also evident at many colleges where coaches earn a great deal more than professors and administrators.

BOX 17:2 COLLEGE EXPERIENCE

Student Athletes or Athlete Students?

Perhaps you enjoy spending a noisy evening cheering on your school's sports teams. You are glad when your college recruits the finest athletes because they are more fun to watch and more likely to win, giving the school and yourselves added prestige. However, you may also notice how many of these same athletes frequently cut class and do poorly on exams, yet still manage to stay in school. You may even wonder if recruiting the best athletes is unfair to the majority of students who do not get any special academic or financial treatment. Must academic standards and fairness be abandoned if college athletics are to remain popular?

This seeming paradox has been repeatedly addressed by the National Collegiate Athletic Association (NCAA), the organization that oversees college athletics in the United States. In 1983, the NCAA adopted "Proposition 48," which set minimum admissions standards for incoming student athletes. Proposition 48 required a total minimum SAT score of 700 and a 2.0 average in a set of 11 core courses taken during high school in order for students to play varsity sports and, more important, receive athletic scholarships. In 1991, the NCAA raised these standards to a 900 SAT score and a total of 13 core courses during high school.

Supporters of these requirements argue that standards should be more or less equal for all students regardless of their athletic ability. If the term "student athlete" is to have any real meaning, colleges must admit varsity athletes who can compete in the classroom as well as in the gym. Some proponents accuse big-time college programs of exploiting the abilities of young athletes by promising them a college education despite their frequent lack of basic skills. After four years of helping draw sell-out crowds and TV revenues, the "student athlete" is cast aside by the school without ever having received even the semblance of an education. Raising academic standards, it is argued, would help lessen such abuses.

Opponents of this rule change claim that it relies too heavily on standardized tests, which are biased against certain groups of people. In addition, these rules are insensitive to the social conditions that spawn lower high school achievement and to the fact that an athletic scholarship is the only chance these individuals have to actually attend college and receive a degree. Moreover, once removed from deficient educational environments, some academically poor high school students become good college students who need no special treatment in completing their education. From this perspective, athletic scholarships are a kind of affirmative action program that helps disadvantaged people attain equal footing with those who have had more positive social experiences.

Both of these positions have their good points. Sociologically speaking, it would be helpful if there were some empirical information that could show that one side's position was better overall. For instance, how many student athletes with scores around 700 actually graduate, and does this differ from the graduation rate of those athletes with higher initial scores? If the scores did not predict future college success, they would not be important and would serve only to make college impossible for certain groups of people. If, on the other hand, there was a significant difference in college success, higher initial standards would help ensure higher graduation among student athletes. Until such data are available these rules will continue to be debated "in theory" on the basis of anecdotes and personal experiences rather than on more convincing systematic evidence (Laderman, 1992).

Critical Thinking Questions

1. Do you think tougher admissions standards for student athletes would encourage them to do better academic work in high school? Would such higher standards also likely improve the performances of the many other students who aspire to but fail to receive college athletic scholarships?
2. How would a conflict theorist and a functionalist differ with respect to their appraisal of NCAA Division One athletic programs in colleges?

Classroom Learning

self-fulfilling prophecy—a prediction that leads to behavior that fulfills the prediction.

Sociologists are also concerned with actual classroom behavior (Bates and Murray, 1975). Here, it is the actions and interactions of students and teachers that illuminate the actual process of education. Within this particular microsociological perspective, the most important idea is that of the self-fulfilling prophecy. This is when someone's expectations and assumptions cause behavior that fulfills those expectations. Within the sociology of education, the self-fulfilling prophecy usually refers to children achieving and accomplishing certain results due more to the expectations of the teacher rather than according to their own abilities. In one classic study of this phenomenon (Rosenthal and Jacobson, 1968), teachers were told that students had been separated into different ability groups when, in fact, they had been randomly assigned to the groups. At the end of a year those in the supposedly "smarter" group showed more academic improvement than those in the supposedly "less smart" group. This appears to be a clear case of expectations creating unfair achievement differences. William Ryan (1982) relates another story in which a teacher developed similar expecta-

BOX 17:3 GENDER AND SOCIAL CHANGE

Gender Differences in Test Scores

Undoubtedly, almost all of you reading this book have taken either a Scholastic Aptitude Test (SAT) or an American College Testing (ACT) exam. The conventional wisdom says that these tests show how well you will do in college and are thus a critical factor in determining if and where you attend college, how well you do in college, and how successful you will be in the future. As with their IQ counterparts, your numerical score on these tests can have a significant impact on your life. Indeed, a few points can make a difference on where you go to college or whether you attend college at all.

However, there is growing concern that these standardized exams do not predict college success very well. Some colleges have actually stopped using standardized test scores for admitting students. Bates College in Maine, for example, concluded that SAT scores have little if any predictive effect on how a student does in college. High school grades were much more closely related to college success. Other small, highly respected, liberal arts colleges have drawn similar conclusions, and have reduced greatly the role of SAT/ACT scores in the admissions process.

In addition, there is concern among some educators that ascribed social factors such as social class and gender substantially affect scores on these tests. For instance, over the past two decades males have scored higher than females on SATs and PSATs. In the late 1960s, girls had higher verbal scores than boys, but that advantage had disappeared by 1972. A strict genetic explanation for intelligence and success would posit that boys are innately smarter than girls, which explains why they are more successful in these tests. A strict human capital theory would argue that boys score better because they have learned more and they put more effort into the tests.

Most sociologists, however, view these test score differentials in a more complex way. First, they point out that rather than simply reflecting a difference in innate intelligence or learned skills and values, boys do better than girls because teachers and parents disproportionately encourage boys to excel in school. Elementary school girls actually start off with higher standardized test scores than boys, an advantage that declines throughout their formal education (Conroy, 1988). Sociologists contend that boys and girls are socialized under different sets of norms and expectations that contribute to differences in later test scores.

Sociologists also view these higher male scores partly as a function of bias in the standard-

tions based on what she thought were IQ scores. Later, it was discovered that these supposed IQ scores were actually locker numbers!

Self-fulfilling prophecies also are related to expectations based on ascribed status. For example, teachers often group students on the basis of perceived learning potential. But in one study, rather than using results from certain reading tests, elementary school teachers based these groupings on their identification of a student's social class (Rist, 1970). While race was not a factor in this case (all the students were African American), another study showed how class and race influence teachers' perceptions about students' learning potential. Here, teachers were shown pictures of totally anonymous students and asked to rate their potential for educational success. White children and those thought to be of a higher social class (based on clothing) more often were chosen to be potentially successful in school (Harvey and Slatin, 1975). These studies further undermine the argument that schools sort people fairly based on natural skills and achieved abilities. Rather, they suggest the concrete processes by which schools help perpetuate the traditional social inequalities of class, race, and gender (Box 17:3).

BOX 17:3 GENDER AND SOCIAL CHANGE *continued*

ized tests themselves. Studies have found that boys do better than girls on some standardized tests because they are less hesitant to make guesses (Conroy, 1988). Also, the text in reading comprehension and word problems contains more male characters and topics such as sports with which boys are more familiar. Finally, boys may be better prepared for the pressure associated with these standardized tests. This is consistent with the fact that boys do better on these tests but receive lower grades in school.

These differences in test scores have critical ramifications for the possibilities of social success. Many college scholarships are awarded not on grades but on standardized test scores. According to the National Center for Fair and Open Testing, 67 percent of all Empire State Scholarships in New York went to boys in the 1980s (Conroy, 1988). While New York and Massachusetts are the only two states that base state scholarships primarily on SAT scores, such gender gaps are even more widespread with other awards. National Merit Scholarships, for example, are based primarily on PSAT scores. In 1986, high school girls received only 36 percent of the $23 million in National Merit Scholarship money (Conroy, 1988). Despite growing skepticism by some colleges, standardized test scores remain an important admissions criterion at most universities. Coupled with the effect on scholarships, lower scores on these tests greatly reduce girls' chances of achieving social success by limiting their ability to attend the "best" colleges or any college at all.

In short, sociologists argue that differences in test scores by gender are not only due to innate talent or human capital differences but to the organization of our social institutions and how these institutions treat males and females differently. Achieving the American Dream of success is definitely harder if you are female. Women's groups and feminist scholars have worked hard to identify and eliminate these biases over the past two decades. For example, in 1992 the American Association of University Women (AAUW) released a comprehensive report that argued that educational discrimination against women begins in kindergarten and continues through higher education (Roser, 1992). The AAUW offered 40 proposals, including improved teacher training, to make the educational institution less biased against female students.

Critical Thinking Questions

1. Given that most elementary school teachers are women, how would a sociologist explain why a mostly female teaching core would discriminate against girls from kindergarten through elementary school?
2. How would the differences between the genders discussed in Chapter 13 contribute to gender differences in test scores?

Students taking a course in automotive shop generally are members of a vocational track, and are not likely to go on to college. A relatively large proportion of students from poor neighborhoods are channeled into this lower track, which limits their opportunity to achieve the American Dream.

These self-fulfilling prophecies often have an antimeritocratic nature. For example, one study took "average" elementary school students—including many from economically deprived families—and placed them in an enrichment program normally reserved for "gifted" students. Remarkably, after only a few months, the average students dramatically improved their math scores. Such an improvement would have been highly unlikely without this extra educational attention. Once again, it's clear that the American Dream formula for success is at best an incomplete explanation for social reality.

The self-fulfilling prophecies often become institutionalized through a process called *tracking*. Here, different expectations of student abilities lead to dramatically different curricula within individual schools. For example, many schools have a "college prep" track, a "vocational" track, and a "jail" track. Those in the first group take arts and science courses; those in the second group take practical business courses (i.e., bookkeeping and typing) and perhaps industrial arts; and those in the third group take courses primarily designed to keep them off the streets for a few more years. The groups rarely interact with each other, almost as if there were three separate schools under one roof.

Tracking can take place between schools as well. The earlier examples of unequal spending on different schools illustrate the frequent relationship between these interschool tracks and ascribed statuses such as social class and race. Those from more advantaged neighborhoods are likely to attend schools that have high expectations of their educational potential and chances for social success; those from disadvantaged neighborhoods do not. Clearly, these partially preordained outcomes challenge the conventional belief that schools fairly allocate social success based strictly on an individual's natural talents, technical skills, and approved values.

THEORETICAL PERSPECTIVES ON EDUCATION

Functionalism

Education is a critical component in the functionalist view of society since it is one of the main institutional mechanisms for transmitting a society's culture to future generations. In other words, education is partly responsible for properly socializing individuals, thus contributing to overall social equilibrium. A society can remain stable only if its members share key norms, values, and beliefs, and if important technical knowledge is passed from one generation to the next. Functionalists also argue that education contributes to social stability by selecting those individuals with the greatest technical and intellectual talents, and channeling them into strategic social locations. As it became universally available, education was a major part of American society's reallocation of social rewards based on achieved rather than ascribed statuses.

In this pure form, functionalism is not very influential in contemporary sociological research on education, although it was the foundation of almost all educational sociology until the early 1960s. Instead, functionalism survives as the buttress of the human capital perspectives discussed earlier. These perspectives link education to the economic and technical skills that allow American society to continue modernizing. But even these human capital perspectives are rarely used in sociological research on education; they are much more prevalent within economics and political science (Karabel and Halsey, 1977). Regardless of which academic discipline employs functionalist ideas, it undoubtedly influences our everyday explanations of education in the United States. Most people believe that schools serve the purposes of teaching basic skills (including intellectual skills) and deciding which people have learned these skills best. More important, the average American believes that "people get what they deserve"; and that the present allocation of human resources is fair and contributes to society's overall health. In other words, the majority in the United States believe in the validity of the American Dream formula, which is consistent with functionalist theory.

Conflict Theory

Conflict theory is much more influential than functionalism in the contemporary sociology of education. Contradicting functionalism, conflict theory argues that U.S. society is not, and has never been, a meritocracy where people are fairly rewarded for their natural talents and learned skills. Instead, education is just another institutional mechanism that perpetuates social inequalities from generation to generation. The transmission of skills and values, while certainly important, is secondary to education's primary role of maintaining inequalities of wealth, power, and prestige.

Conflict theory has influenced many of the sociological perspectives already discussed. Marx's emphasis on capitalism's class struggle has spawned research on how someone's ascribed social class can severely limit the educational opportunities available, and how these limited opportunities perpetuate capitalist class domination (Bowles and Gintis, 1976).

Credentialism

Some sociologists challenge the human capital idea that people are judged and rewarded according to the *content* of their educational experiences. They argue that the perceived prestige of certain *credentials*, such as college diplomas and teaching certificates, are more important than the actual knowledge and skills the individual acquires in the process of gaining the credential. This position runs counter to the conventional idea that meritocracy drives the U.S. system of social rewards, and that education fairly assigns people to the social slots where their substantive talents are most necessary (Berg, 1970; Cohen and Pfeffer, 1986; Collins, 1979; Olneck and Kim, 1989). These ideas are rooted in the conflict theories of Max Weber.

The credentialism perspective suggests that job skills are innate, are acquired in the course of daily living, or are learned on the job rather than in school. The popular 1992 film *Don't Tell Mom the Babysitter's Dead* is based on this perspective. In that film, an 18-year-old, played by Christina Applegate, falsifies her age and her credentials on her résumé in order to secure an executive position in the fashion industry. Her ability to function well, even spectacularly, in that position suggests that it is a person's basic abilities rather than credentials that really matter on the job. Similarly, sociological research often draws the same conclusion. For example, a study of engineers found that knowledge from college classes had very little to do with the actual demands of being an engineer (Zussman, 1985). Notwithstanding, employers continue using degrees to judge a person's capabilities and to decide whether or not to hire that person. The credentialism perspective holds that degrees primarily reflect conformity to the norms and rules associated with certain professions rather than learned skills per se (Collins, 1979; Zussman, 1985). Employers view degrees as proof that job candidates know how to "behave" like executives or professors. Substantive skills are seen as far less important at this initial hiring stage.

Today's students may recognize the importance of credentials over substance. In 1991, a college student wrote the infamous book *Cheating 101,* which suggests many dishonest ways to get good grades without necessarily knowing the course material well (O'Reilly, 1991). Many students bought the book secure in the knowledge that future employers or professional schools would judge them on the basis of grade credentials rather than substantive knowledge. Similarly, students are increasingly falsifying transcripts and diplomas (Rockoff, 1991). Rather than castigating these students for having "bad values," one college registrar remarked that the larger society has helped create this behavior with its emphasis on raw grades, a view consistent with the credentialist perspective.

The credentialism perspective also acknowledges some of the social class factors mentioned earlier. People with degrees from prestigious universities, for example, usually are more successful than those with ones from less-distinguished institutions (Collins, 1979; Ladinsky, 1967; Useem and Karabel, 1991). Rather than reflecting the superior education offered at elite universities, the credentialism perspective argues that it is the inflated *perception* of this elite education that often leads to success. Another classic film, *Working Girl* (1988), dramatizes this point. In that film Melanie Griffith plays the part of a talented young woman with a "night school" college degree who repeatedly fails to gain entry into her New York firm's management trainee program because the slots are given automatically to "Ivy League" types. However, while impersonating her incapacitated boss, she shows her ability by masterminding a major business deal with a high-powered businessman played by Harrison Ford. The credentialism perspective also points out that since elite institutions are usually expensive, relatively wealthy people find it easier to purchase this superior credential. Therefore, rather than sorting people according to achieved skills in a completely fair and accurate way, universities contribute to the perpetuation of social inequality from generation to generation (Hearn, 1990; Karabel and Astin, 1975).

gatekeeping—the supervision and restriction of the flow of people through often arbitrary or unfair barriers to socially advantageous positions in society.

Gatekeeping

Another sociological theory that challenges the American Dream formula for success is called **gatekeeping**. This perspective is similar to the credentialism and social network perspectives in emphasizing the nonmeritocratic

Arthur C. Guyton, M.D., one of the best-known names in American medicine, is a Harvard University graduate. So are all ten of his children, all of whom are also physicians. Arthur's wife, Ruth, is a physician too, and a Phi Beta Kappa graduate from Wellesley. With two very intelligent parents, it is not surprising that the Guyton children are all also bright. But brightness, excellent grades, and impressive activities alone are not always sufficient to gain admission into Harvard. It usually takes something more—for example, a special talent, a unique background, or a parental legacy. Children of graduates of prestigious universities have a much better chance of gaining admission to such universities than other applicants, all other things being equal.

factors that often influence educational and social success. For instance, a gatekeeping perspective might look at the actual organizational mechanisms used by elite schools in selecting their students that, in turn, restrict the allocation of prestigious credentials. Many prestigious universities, for example, have admissions quotas for legacies—those individuals whose parent attended the school. Due to high costs, those with superior resources have always been more likely to enter the gates of such universities and acquire their prestigious degrees. Social class advantages are thus institutionalized through legacy preferences (Karen, 1990).

This gatekeeping process is reflected particularly in the preference prestigious universities give to students graduating from elite boarding schools. These boarding schools are very expensive and provide little financial assistance to economically disadvantaged students who wish to attend. Getting through a boarding school gate may be critical to getting through the gate of a prestigious university, and such access has more to do with ascribed characteristics like social class than with actual educational prowess (Persell and Cookson, 1990).

Symbolic Interactionalism

Symbolic interactionalism is also very influential in contemporary sociological research on education. Studies of the form and content of education are rooted in a theoretical model that stresses human interaction and how humans define their social world. This type of sociological research is interested particularly in the aforementioned "black box" of schools—what actually goes on inside them—rather than in the more macrolevel structural concerns of functionalism and conflict theory.

The self-fulfilling prophecy-type studies discussed in the section titled "Classroom Learning" often utilize the interactionist model. The Rosenthal and Jacobson (1968) study, in which teachers' expectations concerning ability led to unfair achievement differences in their students, is a good case in point. Studies on tracking also usually adopt an interactionist approach. Of particular note is the dissimilar and often unequal ways teachers interact with students in different tracks.

Education at the primary level in China is now nearly universal, but only about a third of Chinese primary school students go on to high school and only about 2 percent continue on to universities. Nevertheless, China's gross national product increased 350 percent in the 1980s, and its vast unskilled and semi-skilled labor force with its relatively low wages is competing ever more successfully for jobs in the global economy.

Integrating the Theories

As the sociology of education has matured, the disputes among these theoretical schools have mellowed. While functionalism's practical impact on actual research has declined, one of its core propositions is generally accepted by most sociologists: Education transmits the dominant social norms, values, and skills from one generation to another without which our society could not maintain integration and stability. Contemporary research influenced by conflict theory also accepts this. However, conflict theory would make the important distinction that the dominant values, such as the primacy of private property, are not necessarily the best values with which to achieve social integration. Moreover, conflict theories focus on how education legitimizes and rationalizes the perpetuation of social inequality by making individuals feel wholly responsible for their own failure or success. The symbolic interactionist position often accepts these larger macrosociological premises, but prefers focusing on the actual behavior of individuals within the educational institution. Research in this area is interested typically in exactly *how* norms, values, and skills are transmitted, and *how* teacher/student interaction helps maintain an absolute meritocratic ideology about U.S. society despite evidence to the contrary. As is always the case, all three theoretical perspectives yield distinctive insights into the same social phenomena, and two perspectives are always standing ready as *critical thinking* counterpointers to chasten any sociologist who acts as if the other one is the only way to understand a phenomenon.

SOCIOLOGICAL RESEARCH AND PUBLIC POLICY

The sociological perspective can be quite useful for understanding contemporary educational problems, and for suggesting how these problems might be addressed. Sociologists employ theoretical ideas and empirical research to unravel the social forces shaping American education. Although they do not agree on how to understand every educational issue, most sociologists agree that there is usually more to an issue than immediately meets the eye, and that public opinion and educational policy decisions more often are rooted in ideal models like the American Dream than in objective reality.

Standardized Test Scores and Public Policy

Since 1980, Americans have become increasingly concerned about how their children rank against students in other developed nations in terms of educational achievement. This is because there is a growing recognition that these foreign students represent the competition for jobs in the ever more global twentieth-century economy. The populations of both developed and developing nations are becoming increasingly literate and educated (see Figure 17:2), and are already syphoning off semi-skilled and highly skilled jobs from the U.S. labor market.

Particularly worrisome are recent studies showing that U.S. students receive relatively low scores on proficiency tests compared to their counterparts in other developed countries. In one test American seventh graders finished near last among 15 nations in math and science, even though the

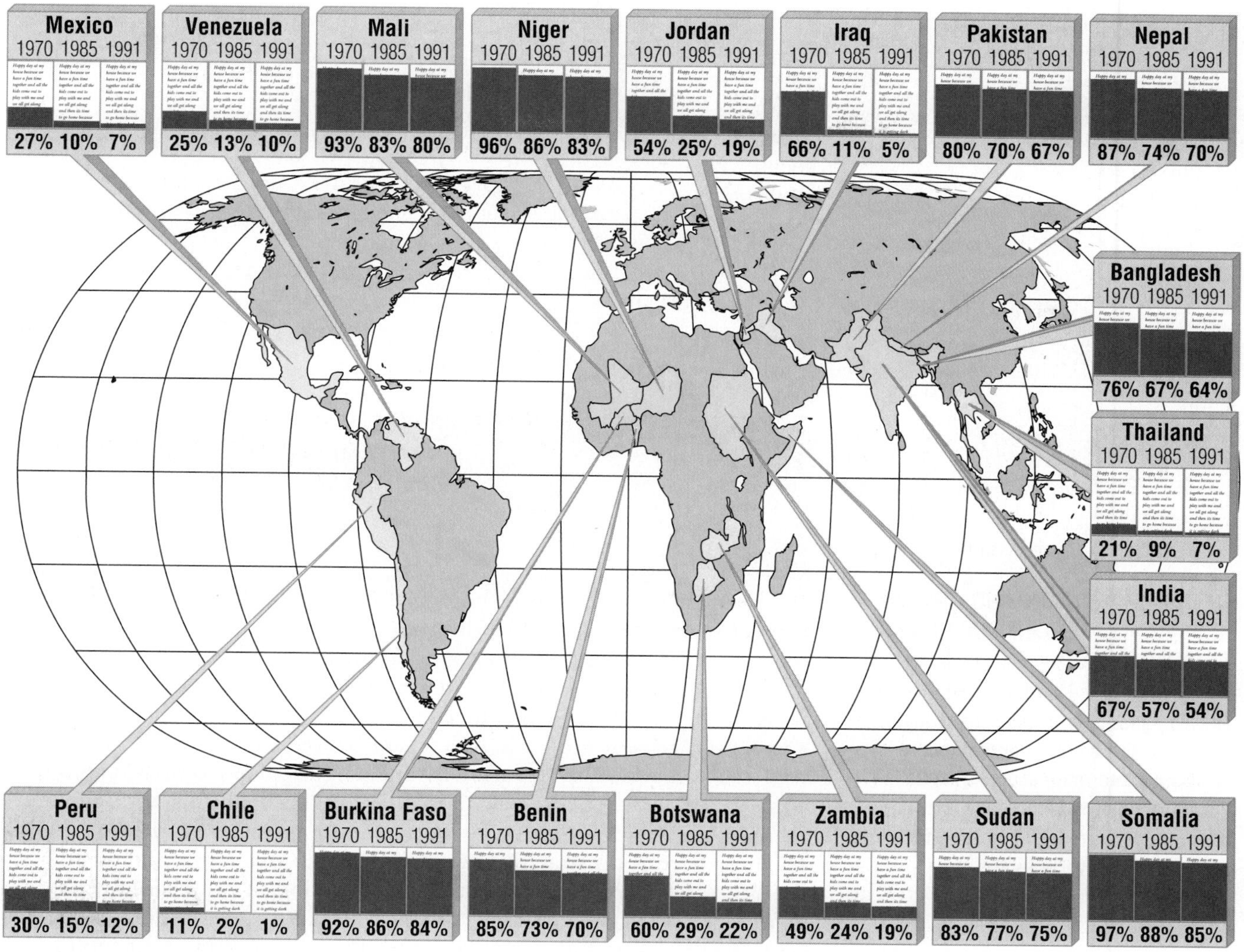

Country	1970	1985	1991
Mexico	27%	10%	7%
Venezuela	25%	13%	10%
Mali	93%	83%	80%
Niger	96%	86%	83%
Jordan	54%	25%	19%
Iraq	66%	11%	5%
Pakistan	80%	70%	67%
Nepal	87%	74%	70%
Bangladesh	76%	67%	64%
Thailand	21%	9%	7%
India	67%	57%	54%
Peru	30%	15%	12%
Chile	11%	2%	1%
Burkina Faso	92%	86%	84%
Benin	85%	73%	70%
Botswana	60%	29%	22%
Zambia	49%	24%	19%
Sudan	83%	77%	75%
Somalia	97%	88%	85%

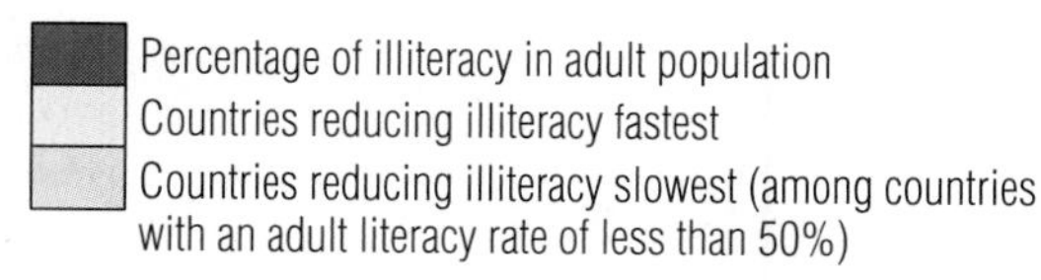

FIGURE 17:2 THE DECLINE OF ILLITERACY IN DEVELOPING COUNTRIES

In the industrial world, about 4 percent of adults are illiterate. Conversely, in some developing countries more than 90 percent of adults remain illiterate. But, as this map indicates, the shadow of illiteracy over the developing world is shrinking, meaning stiffer global competition for American workers.

Source: MAPSENSE: Global Comparisons and Trends from World Monitor *Magazine*, 1992 (pp. 10–11). By permission of the publisher.

United States is near first in per capita spending on education (see Figure 17:3). The United States also recently lost its edge in the proportion of young adults who complete high school (see Figure 17:4) Part of the blame for the increasingly poor relative showing of U.S. students has been attributed to the poor performance of U.S. schools.

Although the empirical evidence does show that U.S. students lag behind their counterparts in many other advanced nations, the evidence cited is sometimes either exaggerated or misleading. For example, one often-cited indicator for the eroding U.S. position is the decline among U.S. students in standardized tests scores such as the SAT. Average SAT scores from 1967 to 1991 are presented in Table 17:5. While there is a clear decline in scores between certain years, these data could actually also be used to make a different argument: Since 1981, SAT scores in the United States have increased 6 points, perhaps indicating that U.S. education is

Percent of GDP spent on education		Average percent of correct answers in science testing		Average percent of correct answers in math testing	
Israel	10.2	South Korea	78	South Korea	73
United States	7.5	Taiwan	76	Taiwan	73
Canada	7.4	Switzerland	74	Switzerland	71
Jordan	7.1	Hungary	73	Soviet Union*	70
Soviet Union*	7.0	Soviet Union*	71	Hungary	68
Ireland	6.7	Slovenia	70	France	64
France	6.1	Italy	70	Italy	64
Hungary	5.7	Israel	70	Israel	63
Scotland	5.2	Canada	69	Canada	62
Switzerland	4.8	France	69	Scotland	61
South Korea	4.5	Scotland	68	Ireland	61
Italy	4.0	Spain	68	Slovenia	57
Taiwan	3.6	United States	67	Spain	55
Slovenia	3.4	Ireland	63	United States	55
Spain	3.2	Jordan	57	Jordan	40

*Russian-speaking schools in 14 republics

FIGURE 17:3 MATH AND SCIENCE SCORES AND PERCENT OF GROSS DOMESTIC PRODUCT SPENT ON EDUCATION IN 15 COUNTRIES

Thirteen-year-olds in the United States rank near the bottom internationally in science and math scores despite the United States being near the top internationally in spending for education.

Source: Educational Testing Services.

improving slightly or at least holding steady while the country's economic problems are worsening. Two diverse conclusions can thus be drawn from the same data depending on what point the policy analyst is trying to make.

The relationship between standardized test scores and educational quality is further challenged by other empirical data. For instance, Table 17:6 shows average scores on the ACT exam between 1967 and 1991. Average ACT scores have remained virtually unchanged since 1970, although there was a sharp decline between 1967 and 1970. This confusing and sometimes contradictory evidence suggests that, contrary to the views of many policymakers, there is no straightforward and simple relationship between standardized test scores and the quality of education in the United States.

In fact, the decline in some standardized test scores may be related in part to other factors that have little to do with the overall quality of U.S. education. For example, while the Vietnam War was raging in the late sixties and early seventies, college deferments were a way for young people to avoid the draft. High school students without prior college aspirations probably found themselves taking the SAT or ACT hoping to obtain a four-year college deferment. If these people tended to score lower on the exams—for whatever reason—it would drag down overall national averages. Thus, any apparent change in the educational prowess of U.S. students or in the quality of schools may be due in part to a change in the demographic composition of those taking college entrance examinations between 1967 and 1975.

FIGURE 17:4 PERCENT OF 1989 POPULATION WHO COMPLETED HIGH SCHOOL IN 8 INDUSTRIAL COUNTRIES

The United States has recently lost its edge in the proportion of young adults who complete high school.

Source: Time Magazine, "Losing an Edge," July 20, 1992 (p. 19).

Age 25 to 64		Age 25 to 34	
Country	Percent	Country	Percent
United States	82.0	Germany	91.5
Switzerland	78.8	Japan	90.6
Germany	78.4	Switzerland	88.4
Canada	71.4	United States	86.6
Japan	69.7	Canada	83.5
Britain	64.5	Britain	76.7
France	48.1	France	63.0
Italy	25.7	Italy	41.1

TABLE 17:5 Average SAT Scores, 1967–1991

YEAR	SCORE
1967	958
1968	956
1969	956
1970	948
1971	943
1972	937
1973	926
1974	924
1975	906
1976	903
1977	899
1978	897
1979	894
1980	890
1981	890
1982	893
1983	893
1984	897
1985	906
1986	906
1987	906
1988	904
1989	903
1990	900
1991	896

Source: U.S. Bureau of the Census (1994), *Statistical Abstract of the United States: 1994,* Washington, D.C., p. 159.

TABLE 17:6 Average ACT Scores, 1967–1989

YEAR	SCORE
1967	19.9
1970	18.6
1975	18.5
1980	18.5
1983	18.3
1984	18.5
1985	18.6
1986	18.8
1987	18.7
1988	18.8
1989	18.6

Source: U.S. Bureau of the Census (1992), *Statistical Abstract of the United States: 1992,* Washington, D.C., p. 159.

More recent declines in SAT scores might reflect in part similar shifts in the population of test takers. For example, there was a substantial increase during the seventies and eighties in the numbers of women and minorities taking college entrance exams. If members of these groups scored lower on standardized tests, this also would drag down overall national averages. Many of these individuals are also from poorer social classes, which constrains their ability to spend $700 on Stanley Kaplan type courses, which can increase SAT scores by as much as 60 points.

A sociological perspective does not reject possible links between education and social problems, or imply that public policy is incapable of dealing with these issues. Rather, it suggests that blaming real or imagined social problems on the educational system is often overly simplistic and may lead to rash policy decisions that exacerbate rather than solve these problems. For instance, laws have been proposed that would increase the number of schooldays in the United States from 180 per year to the levels in Japan (240) or Germany (210). The logic here is that people in these countries are better educated and more productive because of the longer school year. However, children in the former Soviet Union went to school for 210 days, yet the Soviet economy failed miserably. Similarly, if the number of schooldays were the key, Thailand (200 days) would have a more robust economic system than either England (180 days) or France (192 days).

Clearly, the relationship among the number of schooldays, educational attainment, and national economic strength is complex, and defies simple policy solutions.

The Call for National Testing

The supposed deterioration of U.S. education has led many policymakers to advocate a national test that would measure what students know, and would indicate how schools and teachers could provide better education. Many advocates of this national test point to the aforementioned relatively low scores U.S. students receive on proficiency exams compared to their counterparts in other countries.

But a large body of research questions the accuracy and usefulness of standardized tests. The American Educational Research Association argues that the multiple-choice tests used in the United States were designed to rank and track students inexpensively rather than as a mechanism to strengthen instruction (Darling-Hammond and Lieberman, 1992; Erickson, 1984; Ferrante, 1992). Ironically, the misuse of standardized tests harms those students who need the most help by stigmatizing them or by directing them into remedial tracks, which further emphasize multiple-choice tests. Also, schools might be more reluctant to accept or retain low-scoring students if, as might happen, their funding were tied to their overall standardized test scores (Darling-Hammond and Lieberman, 1992). For example, students who have learned other languages before English (a rapidly growing proportion of the U.S. population) are at a severe disadvantage on these exams. Schools with a greater proportion of such students will likely have lower aggregate test scores that could lead to a decrease in funding rather than the increased funding needed to deal with this challenge (Ferrante, 1992).

THE SUBJECTIVE DIMENSION OF EDUCATION

In 1991, President Bush told graduates at the University of Michigan that "political correctness" threatened to destroy U.S. colleges and universities. Bush stated that colleges were becoming more interested in fomenting social revolution than in teaching the knowledge and skills that make the United States more economically competitive. Again, this is an attempt to make a causal connection between education and economic strength, and then to base public policy decisions on this relationship.

Former president Bush's position reflects a growing concern that U.S. universities are becoming dominated by professors and administrators who see college education as a way to impose their "politically correct" opinions on students. According to those concerned, this growing emphasis on political correctness, frequently called "PC," is expressed in many ways. For instance, some colleges now restrict "hate speech" directed at certain social groups, and others are making extraordinary efforts to diversify their student and faculty populations. Finally, and perhaps most importantly, universities are allegedly eliminating courses rooted in traditional Western culture and replacing them with "multicultural" courses that stress the differences rather than similarities among Americans. It is argued by critics that many aspects of the PC movement are harming America's ability to thrive in the global economy.

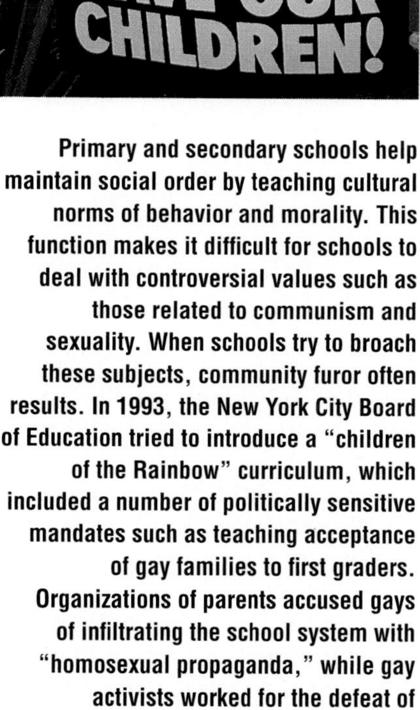

Primary and secondary schools help maintain social order by teaching cultural norms of behavior and morality. This function makes it difficult for schools to deal with controversial values such as those related to communism and sexuality. When schools try to broach these subjects, community furor often results. In 1993, the New York City Board of Education tried to introduce a "children of the Rainbow" curriculum, which included a number of politically sensitive mandates such as teaching acceptance of gay families to first graders. Organizations of parents accused gays of infiltrating the school system with "homosexual propaganda," while gay activists worked for the defeat of "conservative homophobes" such as Mary Cummins, a Queens School District board member who led the eventually successful fight against the Rainbow curriculum.

This growing concern with political correctness can be evaluated best by examining the three forces that determine the subjective dimensions of all social problems: visibility, expectations, and values (Figure 17:5). Since the mid-1980s, the issue of political correctness has become increasingly *visible.* Popular magazines ran cover stories on it, and best-selling books have also called attention to this phenomenon. In addition, political correctness violates certain *expectations* that Americans have about colleges and education. People expect professors and administrators not to substitute their personal beliefs for facts and not to penalize students for disagreeing with them. Moreover, the rise of political correctness is seen as a threat to certain core *values* such as free speech and individuality. Emphasis on a "multicultural" society also challenges the traditional value that all Americans should blend together in a "melting pot" of common cultural beliefs. Requiring courses on racism and sexism suggests that such problems may be a prominent feature of U.S. society rather than just the deviant behavior of specific individuals.

But there is some evidence that the high subjective dimension of political correctness is not matched by its objective dimension. The American Council on Education and the Carnegie Foundation for the Advancement of Teaching, for example, found that less than 10 percent of all colleges experienced any conflict over "political correctness" during the 1990–1991 school year (Collins, 1991). Similarly, the Modern Language Association discovered that the vast majority of history and literature classes still rely on the "classics," but that many have also begun to supplement these texts with less standard readings (Mooney, 1991).

Incidentally, the whole PC controversy reflects in part the deeper demographic changes involved in the "browning" of the United States. As Chapter 12 makes clear, the relative growth of African American, Hispanic, and Asian American subpopulations is transforming the United States into a *de facto* multicultural society. Political correctness is a predictable consequence of this change in the nation's racial and ethnic composition. PC is also an inevitable by-product of the growing power of women in U.S. society (Chapter 13).

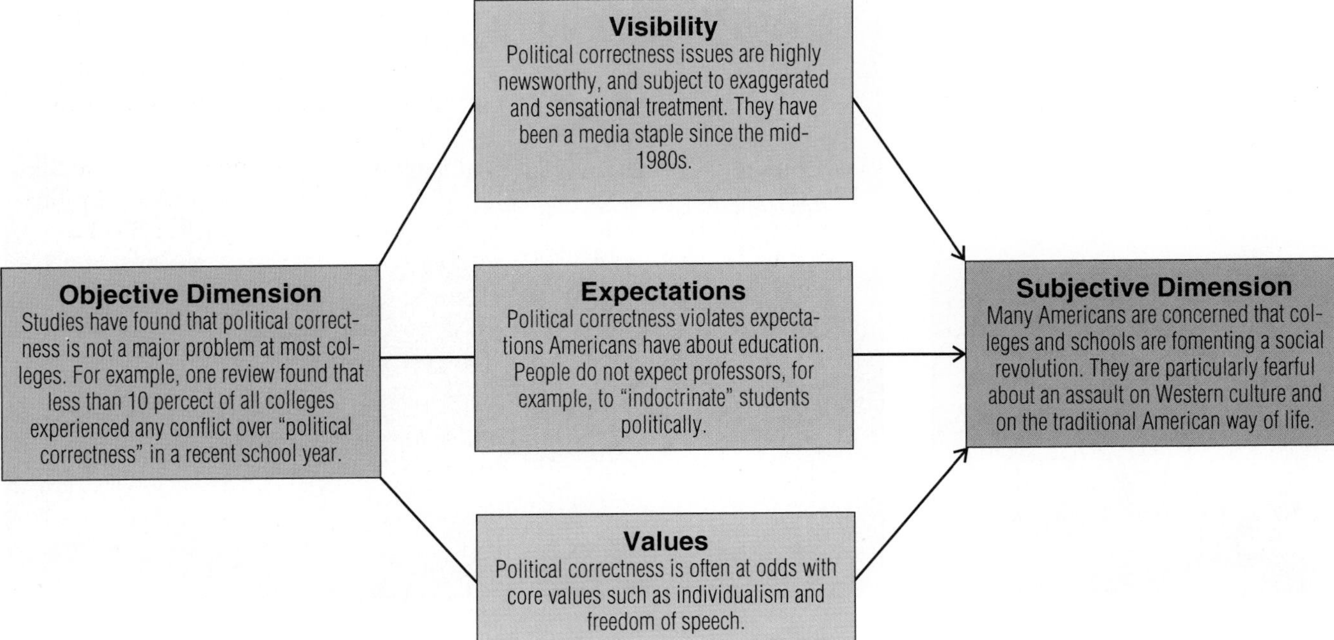

FIGURE 17:5 SUBJECTIVE AND OBJECTIVE DIMENSIONS: THE CASE OF POLITICAL CORRECTNESS
The subjective dimension of political correctness differs from the objective dimension, owing to the operation of the intervening variables—visibility, expectations, and values.

SUMMARY

1. The traditional American Dream holds that individuals are likely to be successful in life if they have natural talents, the proper skills and values, and a good education.
2. The conventional view is that in U.S. society individuals are judged accurately on their intelligence and motivation, have equal access to education, and eventually occupy social statuses commensurate with their personal merit.
3. Sociological research shows that this American Dream formula of success is as much fiction as fact. The educational institution does sort people into various social locations, but it frequently does not do it fairly.
4. Sorting is often based on an individual's ascribed statuses (e.g., race, gender, class) rather than on achieved statuses.
5. Average educational achievement does differ by race, class, and gender, but these differences are due at least in part to differences in such social factors as cultural background, family expectations, discrimination, and erroneously self-fulfilling expectations on the part of teachers.
6. The educational institution has both manifest and latent functions. The former involve the transmitting of skills and cultural knowledge from one generation to the next. The latter involve such things as imparting behavioral rules and values, and various screening and selection functions.
7. The conflict perspective emphasizes that education reinforces existing inequalities through such processes as gatekeeping and credentialism.

8. Symbolic interactionism primarily focuses on the behavior of individuals within the educational institution.
9. Most sociologists agree that public opinion and educational policy decisions more often are rooted in ideal models like the American Dream than in objective reality.
10. The high subjective dimension of political correctness is not matched by its objective dimension. The whole PC controversy reflects in part changes in the nation's racial and ethnic composition and in the power of women in U.S. society.

This photograph is a reminder of the *status quo* before "The Great Transformation." The Giles Family Register is an embroidery in silk on linen stitched by Mary (Polly) Giles early in the nineteenth century. This type of needlework picture is called a "mourning sampler," and was typically crafted by girls during the period. Notice the ineffably sad demographics of the Giles's family history. Polly's parents, John and Mary Giles of Townsend, Massachusetts, lost five of their first six children. Their only daughter, Susan, died in 1798 while an infant, and their sons John, Samuel, Abner, and Joel perished in August and September of 1800. The boys were probably victims of an epidemic such as dysentery or of a childhood disease such as measles. Only the Giles's first-born child, Daniel, who was then 10, survived the epidemic. John and Mary Giles went on to have three more children, Polly (1801), Joel (1804), and John (1806). Note also that John Giles's first wife, Susan Baldwin Giles, died at age 24, that his first son, Daniel, eventually died at age 37, and that Daniel's wife, Betsy, died at age 35.

The Giles Family Register is testimony to the extremely high mortality that existed prior to "The Great Transformation," and this high mortality is germane to all four chapters in Part Six. Chapter 18 discusses changing patterns in the chief causes of death, from the infectious diseases that decimated the Giles family to the chronic diseases holding sway today. Chapter 19 notes that rampant infectious diseases, especially those that can be sexually transmitted, contributed to the restrictive sexual norms prior to "The Great Transformation." Syphilis, for instance, was a major cause of death in the nineteenth century. Chapter 20 makes the point that the large families of the past came about in part owing to the high mortality rate. In the Giles's case, for instance, nine births yielded only four children who survived to adulthood. Finally, the technological change discussed in Chapter 21, especially in medicine, was largely responsible for greatly decreasing infant and childhood mortality and for yielding the high life expectancy of today.

PART SIX

SOCIAL CHANGE

Sociology was born in a turbulent, terrible time—the nineteenth century. The theoretical giants of our field were attempting to grasp "The Great Transformation" of traditional into modern societies.

Today's headlines also seem to describe "a turbulent, terrible time." The sociological concepts first developed for understanding the nineteenth century, in fact, help to explain the transformation producing the twenty-first century. Chapters 18 ("Health and Medicine") and 19 ("The Sociology of Sexuality") show changing social patterns that touch you "in the flesh." Chapter 20 ("Population") examines the social causes and consequences of the raw amount of human flesh. Chapter 21 exposes the sociological dynamics of technological change.

Chapter 18

Personal Perspective

IT was just another hot August day in 1991 when my 11-year-old daughter, Jeanne Marie, complained of a stomach pain. When it persisted I took her to the family doctor, who immediately diagnosed appendicitis. Jeanne Marie was rushed to a nearby hospital and was on the operating table within an hour. Even at that the surgeon found that her appendix had already ruptured, spewing its toxic contents into the nooks and crannies of her abdominal cavity. Fortunately, the surgeon was highly skilled, and Jeanne Marie's operation took place in an excellent American hospital with vast human and institutional resources. Otherwise, she might have died. Fortunately, too, I had good health insurance. If not, I would have been saddled suddenly with a $20,000 medical bill, which would have been a severe shock to the family finances of a college professor.

JAM

Health and Medicine

health—a state of complete mental, physical, and social well-being.

maximum life span—the oldest age to which a human being can live.

SOCIOLOGY is concerned with the social causes and consequences of nearly everything, and health and illness are no exceptions. This chapter explores both the impact of society on health and illness, and the impact of health and illness on society. It also discusses the social institution of medicine and the social aspects of health and illness.

The World Health Organization defines **health** as "a state of complete mental, physical, and social well-being." But this positive concept is difficult to measure. Instead, sociologists usually focus on the negative concept of illness to assess health conditions in a society. But even the concept of illness is difficult to pin down because it is partly social in nature, and the social part is culturally variable. However, one outcome of illness—death—is relatively easy to define and measure, and mortality is an unequivocal indicator of a society's health status. Consequently, sociologists often use mortality as a substitute for illness in general, and this chapter relies heavily on that approach (Mosley and Cowley, 1991).

GENETIC, ENVIRONMENTAL, AND SOCIAL CAUSES OF ILLNESS AND DEATH

The 1980s film *The Boy in the Bubble* told the story of a boy with a severe immunodeficiency disease who was required to live in a plastic bubble room. This sterile hospital room shielded him from environmental causes of death such as illness-causing bacteria and, incidentally, from social causes of death such as automobile accidents as well. However, people with this genetic disease still die very young, usually before age 2, even if they live in bubble rooms, arguably the most healthful places on Earth.

But how long could the average person, perhaps someone like yourself, live in such an ideal environment? The answer to that question would depend mostly on the quality of the person's genes that govern longevity. Such genes determine an individual's *life span,* the number of years a person could live under the best social and environmental circumstances.

Researchers believe there is an upper limit to the human life span; that is, a **maximum life span**, because humans have an only slightly alterable genetic clock that eventually orders the body to shut down (Hayflick, 1970). Just how long can humans live? Well, there have been reports of Americans living as long as 137 years. And there are also accounts of mountain populations in Ecuador, the Soviet Caucasus, and the Pakistani Kashmir containing large numbers of remarkably old inhabitants, including some supercentenarians more than 150 years old. But the very old often exaggerate their age, and the recording of birth dates was haphazard when these centenarians were born and remains so today in developing countries (Garson, 1985). The oldest person in the world whose age has been authenticated was 120 years of age at the time of death, and each time the world's oldest person dies they almost invariably are replaced by someone who dies at the same age or younger. Hence, experts believe the maximum human life span is around 120 years (although there is disagreement about whether it will be possible to push the age to higher levels through ultramodern medical technology or bioengineering) (Coale, 1991; Gavrilova and Gavrilova, 1991). This means that in all likelihood no one would live more than 120 years even in the bubble's super-healthful environment.

But not everyone has the longevity genes to live to age 120 or even to age 100 for that matter. Indeed, even with bubble rooms and other advanced forms of medical technology in use today, only about 1 in 100 persons in industrialized countries lives beyond the age of 100 (USBC, 1988a). It is becoming increasingly clear that human beings as a *group* have

Medics tend to a possible homicide victim shot during a robbery in Tacoma, Washington. Homicide, a primarily social phenomenon, is the tenth leading cause of death in the United States. It is the social component of death and illness that places them within sociology's realm.

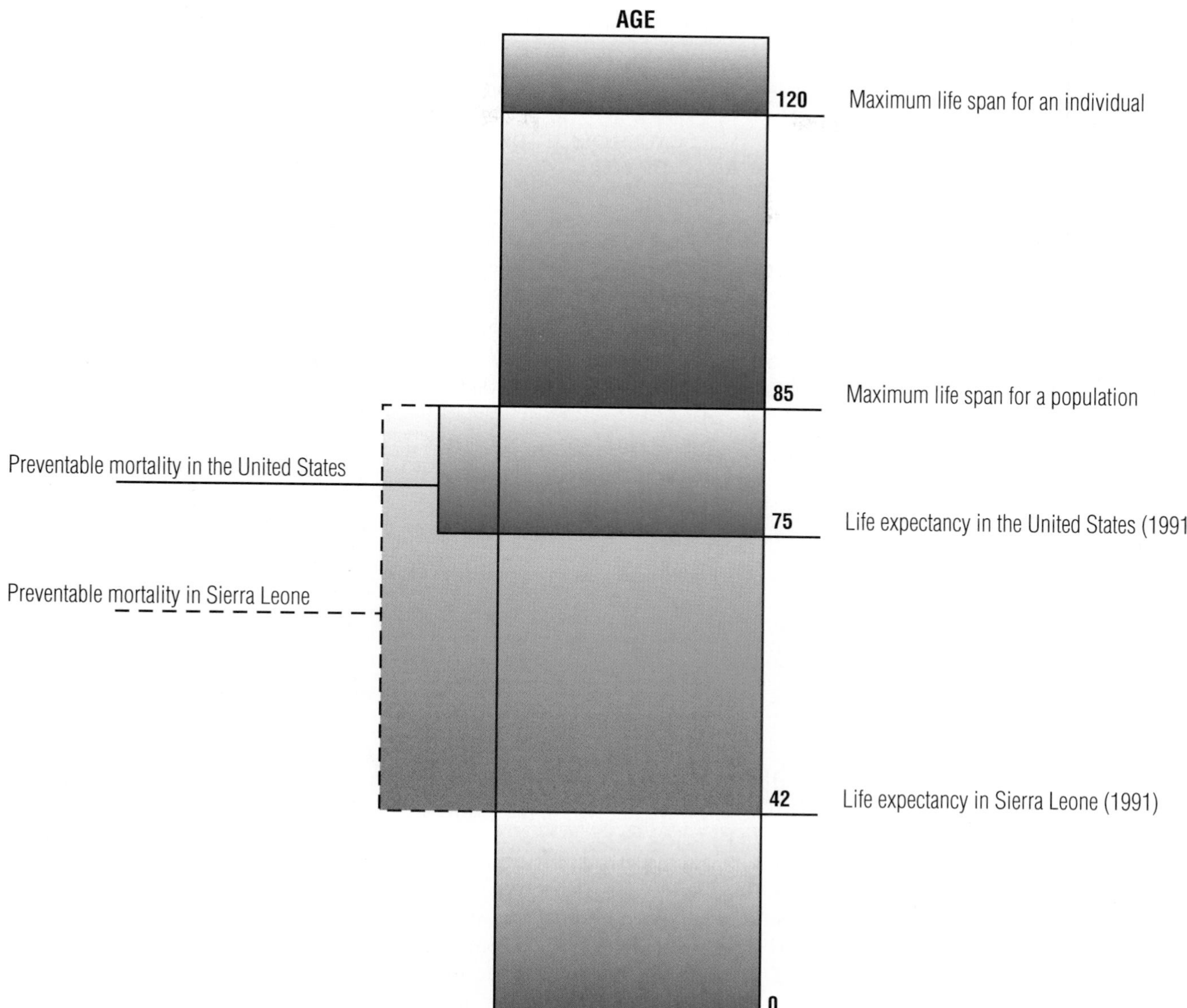

FIGURE 18:1 LIFE SPAN, LIFE EXPECTANCY, AND PREVENTABLE MORTALITY

The amount of preventable mortality in a society is variable. As this figure indicates, the inhabitants of Sierra Leone experience proportionally about four times as much preventable mortality as those residing in the United States.

maximum average life span—**the average age at death for a population under ideal health circumstances.**

a biologically fixed average life span of about 85 years (Fries, 1980; Olshansky, 1990). Therefore, while some individuals would live to age 120 in the bubble and others would die during infancy, the mean age at death for *all* bubble dwellers would be about 85 years. Age 85 is thus the **maximum average life span** for a *group* of people; that is, the average age at death under ideal "bubble room" circumstances.

But the average person does not live in a bubble and thus does not live to age 85. Life expectancy in all societies is in fact lower than 85 years. The difference between age 85 and a population's actual life expectancy at birth is a good indicator of the extent of potentially avoidable or premature death in a society (see Figure 18:1) (Fries, 1980). For example, life expectancy at birth in the United States in 1991 was 75 years, which means that the average American is being deprived of 10 years of life owing largely to potentially avoidable environmental and social causes of death. It is this social component of death and illness that places these topics within sociology's realm.

TABLE 18:1 The 10 Major Causes of Death: United States, 1991

RANK	CAUSE OF DEATH	DEATHS PER 100,000	PERCENT OF ALL DEATHS	RATIO OF RATES: MALE: FEMALE	RATIO OF RATES: AFRICAN AMERICAN: WHITE
1	Heart disease	286	33.2	1.9	1.5
2	Cancer	204	23.7	1.5	1.4
3	Stroke	57	6.6	1.2	1.9
4	Lung disease	36	4.2	1.7	0.8
5	Accidents	35	4.1	2.6	1.3
6	Pneumonia/ Influenza	31	3.6	1.7	1.5
7	Diabetes	19	2.3	1.1	2.4
8	Suicide	12	1.4	4.4	0.6
9	AIDS	12	1.4	7.4	3.4
10	Homicide and legal intervention	11	1.2	3.8	6.8
	All other causes	157	18.3	—	—
	All causes of death	860	100.0	1.7	1.6

Source: National Center for Health Statistics (1993a), *Monthly Vital Statistics Report*, Advance report of final mortality statistics, 1991, 42, 2, Supplement.

SOCIAL FACTORS AS A CAUSE OF ILLNESS AND DEATH IN THE UNITED STATES

Table 18:1 lists the 10 leading causes of death in the United States during 1991. These causes account for 82 percent of all deaths. Table 18:1 is the source of the common knowledge that heart disease and cancer are the two biggest killers. Indeed, these two diseases are in a league by themselves. The odds are that one or the other will be your killer.

There are a few surprises on this list that may have caught your attention. For example, few students realize that accidents (rank no. 5) and pneumonia and influenza (rank no. 6) have such lofty positions. The next time you get the flu, treat it with respect, because it is a potent killer. It takes the lives of between 15,000 and 50,000 Americans a year, depending on the severity of the annual epidemic. Similarly, most students are surprised to find that suicide (rank no. 8) is so high on the list, and that it is higher than homicide. You might find it unsettling to think that the person most likely to take your life is not some homicidal maniac or jealous lover, but the person you look at in the bathroom mirror each morning.

AIDS—an acronym for the disease caused by the immunodeficiency virus (Acquired Immuno-Deficiency Syndrome).

Of particular note is the position of human immunodeficiency virus infection (AIDS) on the list, ranked number 9. Virtually unknown in 1980, AIDS has stormed up the causes-of-death list with frightening and unprecedented speed. It broke into the "10 major causes of death" list in 1987, claiming the number 10 spot, and had accelerated to the number 9 position by 1991. In the near future this sexually transmitted disease (STD) will move farther up the list and will probably settle around the number 7 position. Thus, in the space of about two decades, AIDS will have left in its wake virtually all of the most prolific killers of humankind.

Obviously, no one is immortal and everyone eventually must die of something. But what is striking about the list is that so many deaths are premature, unnecessary, and, in short, socially avoidable. This fact is clearest with respect to such causes as accidents, suicide, and homicide. But in actuality, controllable social behavior is heavily involved in bringing about virtually all causes of death.

In the bubble room metaphor above, the causes of death were divided neatly into three types: (1) genetic, (2) environmental, and (3) social. But in the real world the three causes are very difficult to separate and often interact to produce their health effects. For example, the Pima Indians of Arizona have the highest prevalence of noninsulin-dependent diabetes in the world because their ancestors preferred to dine solely on big game such as bison and often went lengthy periods between kills. Consequently, the tribe developed genes that permitted them to endure long periods of fasting. But today the Pima are no longer hunters. They live a sedentary lifestyle, and have abundant food. As a result, those same socially engineered genes now predispose them to diabetes. Why then do the Pima have the highest prevalence of diabetes? Because of their genetic makeup and because of social change (*Insight*, 1991). Similarly, although AIDS has an immediate environmental cause (i.e., the AIDS virus), it is also caused by such social behavior as the use of contaminated needles for injecting drugs, the practice of unsafe sex, and flawed medical procedures. While this chapter focuses primarily on the social causes of death and illness, it is prudent to keep in mind that these social causes often are bound up inextricably with genetic and/or environmental causes as well.

The social causes of illness and death can be divided into two subtypes; namely, lifestyle causes such as dietary behavior, and health-care-system causes such as inadequate health insurance. Figure 18:2 is a schematic diagram showing the four relevant factors. Applying the diagram to the case of cancer, it can be seen that the risk of death is affected by whether a parent had cancer ("Genetics," rectangle A), inhalation of airborne carcinogenic material ("Environment," rectangle B), by the timeliness of detection and the quality of treatment of any tumor ("Health Care System," rectangle C), and by the habit of smoking cigarettes ("Lifestyle," rectangle D).

FIGURE 18:2 CAUSES OF ILLNESS AND DEATH

The causes of illness and death can be divided into four types, namely: (A) genetic; (B) environmental; (C) lifestyle; and (D) health care system.

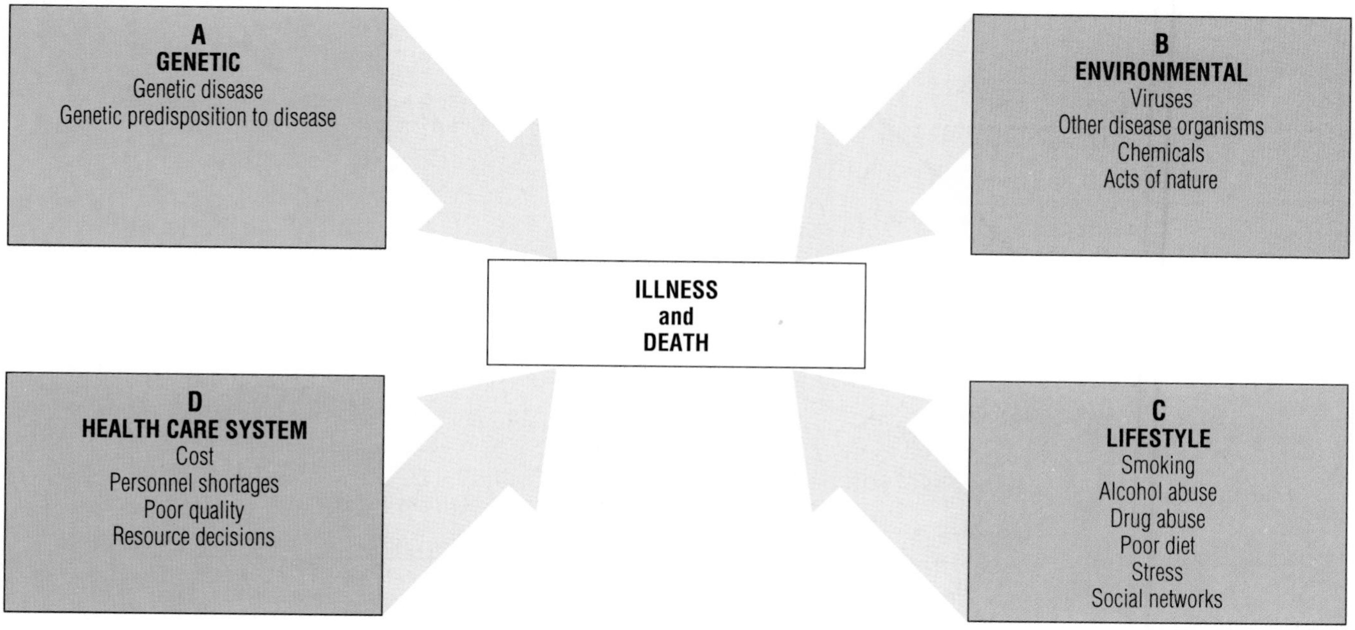

A
GENETIC
Genetic disease
Genetic predisposition to disease

B
ENVIRONMENTAL
Viruses
Other disease organisms
Chemicals
Acts of nature

ILLNESS and DEATH

D
HEALTH CARE SYSTEM
Cost
Personnel shortages
Poor quality
Resource decisions

C
LIFESTYLE
Smoking
Alcohol abuse
Drug abuse
Poor diet
Stress
Social networks

Moreover, the rectangle forces interact in complex ways to multiply mortality risks. An individual whose parent had coronary disease and who overeats while living in a stressful environment has many times the average likelihood of a heart attack.

LIFESTYLE FACTORS

lifestyle factors—preventable causes of death such as smoking, alcohol and drug abuse, poor diet, lack of exercise, stress, and inadequate social networks.

As noted above, the average American now loses about 10 years of potential life owing to preventable causes of death. How much of this loss is due to **lifestyle factors** such as poor diet cannot be known precisely. But a Centers for Disease Control (CDC) study estimated that unhealthy lifestyles accounted for about 50 percent of the mortality attributable to the leading causes of death. Health care system problems contributed only 11 percent, and environmental and genetic factors were responsible for the remaining 39 percent (Mosley and Cowley, 1991). This section reviews the principal unhealthy lifestyle factors (Figure 18:3).

Smoking

Over the last millennium humanity has been devastated by fearsome plagues including the Black Death, smallpox, malaria, yellow fever, Asiatic cholera, and tuberculosis. Now another plague can be added to this "who's

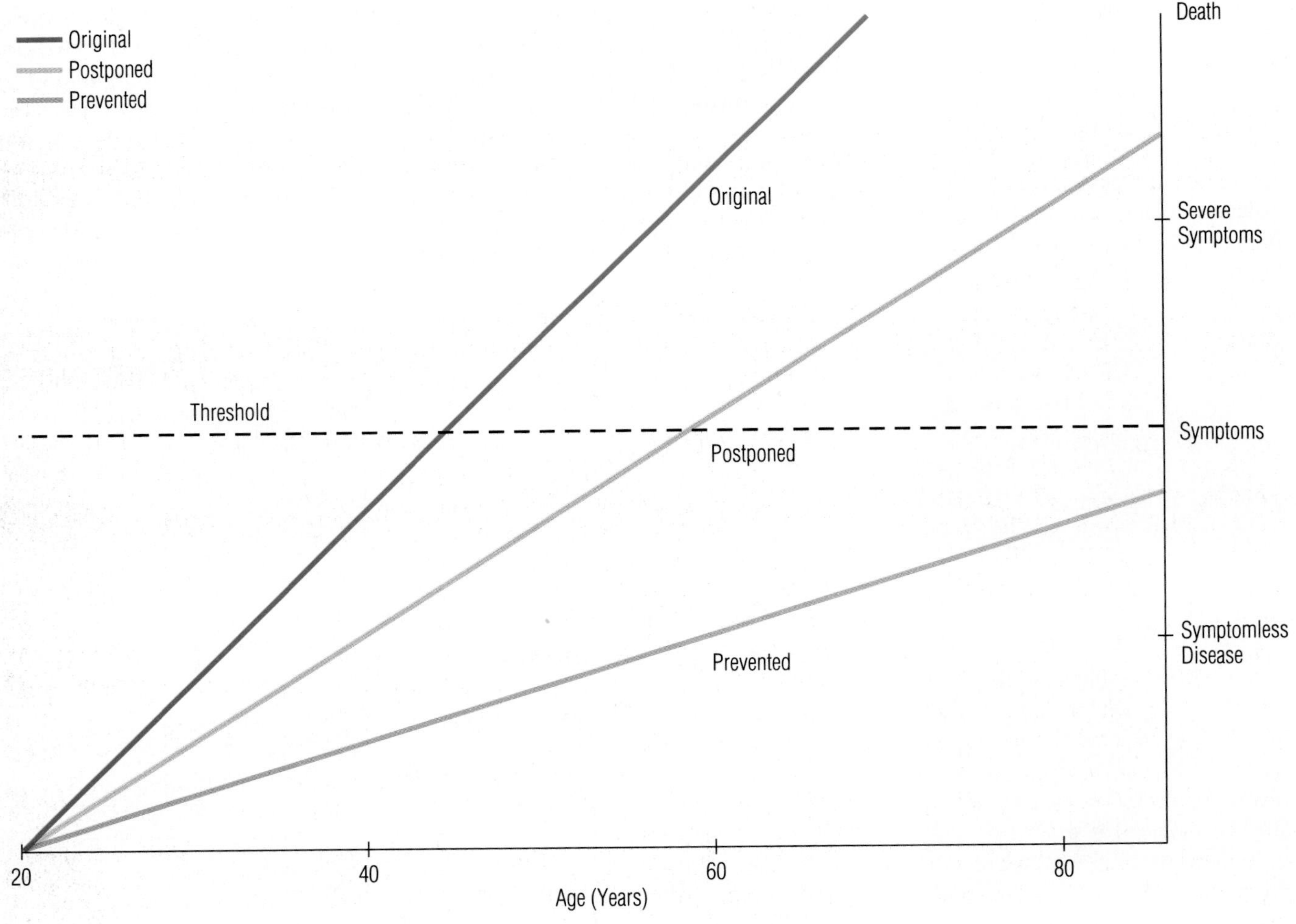

tobaccosis—a class of diseases resulting from the smoking, chewing, and/or snuffing of tobacco.

who" list of mega-killers, namely, tobaccosis, which includes all those diseases resulting from the smoking, chewing, and/or snuffing of tobacco. The onset of this plague began in 1492 with Columbus's discovery of the New World, but its effects went largely undetected for more than four centuries thereafter. As a result, like a silent snowfall in the long "epidemiological night," tobaccosis heaped illness and death upon an unsuspecting humanity for hundreds of years. By the mid-twentieth century, when its malignant nature became clearly understood, it had already become the world's foremost plague. The United States has suffered more than other nations from the tobaccosis pandemic, owing to its preeminent role in the production, marketing, and use of tobacco products. Indeed, by the mid-twentieth century tobaccosis had replaced the white plague—tuberculosis—as the chief underlying killer in the United States, and in much of the rest of the modern world as well (Ravenholt, 1990).

The main form of tobacco use in the United States (and the world) is cigarette smoking. Cigarette smoking is a form of drug abuse. Although the public does not consider tobacco smoke as a drug, experts do because it meets all the necessary criteria. The active ingredient in tobacco, nicotine, is classified as a stimulant because of its initial effects: raised blood pressure, increased heartbeat, glandular stimulation, and so forth. And cigarette smoke is habit-forming. Cigarette smokers are true addicts who display withdrawal effects if smoking is stopped, and recidivism is common among smokers who quit. The fact is that cigarette smoking is the most prevalent and the most debilitating and deadly form of drug addiction in the United States and in the world (Pollin, 1984; Pollin and Ravenholt, 1984).

Moreover, tobacco smoke contains thousands of chemicals such as hydrogen cyanide, carbon monoxide, and nicotine, as well as the radioisotope polonium 210, which is many times more mutagenic, and hence more cancer-causing or carcinogenic, than equivalent amounts of gamma radiation. The combination of smoking's addictive properties and its toxic and mutagenic ones make it the foremost human poison of the twentieth century. Smoking exposes the entire human body—every tissue and every cell—to its poison, thus causing or accelerating the broad spectrum of degenerative diseases and cancers that make up tobaccosis (Ravenholt, 1990).

Tobaccosis took the lives of approximately 500,000 Americans annually during the 1980s, and consequently is responsible for about 20 percent of all deaths. To put that fact into perspective, consider this: Tobacco kills more Americans *every year* than did all the battles of World War II. Tobacco use plays an important role in precipitating death from most of the major causes listed in Table 18:1, especially heart disease and cancer. For example, tobacco is responsible for approximately 30 to 40 percent of all U.S. cancer deaths (Ravenholt, 1985).

It is especially noteworthy that tobacco use is the leading *preventable* cause of death in the United States. More people die from tobaccosis than from the combined toll of AIDS, automobile accidents, cocaine, heroin, alcohol, suicide, homicide, and fires. Indeed, it has been estimated that people who begin to smoke during adolescence and who smoke a pack a day for life lose on average more than eight years of life.

Cigarette smoking hit a peak in the United States in 1965 when fully 42 percent of adults had the addiction. The prevalence of the habit has been declining since then. By 1988 only 28 percent of Americans were smokers. This decline has been due to the operation of social forces. The first step was education, starting with the Surgeon General's landmark advisory against smoking published in 1964. Then came a change in public opinion,

FIGURE 18:3 LIFESTYLE FACTORS AND CHRONIC DISEASE DEVELOPMENT: PATTERNS OF DISEASE DEVELOPMENT

(On facing page) It is important to understand the basic nature of chronic illnesses such as heart disease, emphysema, arthritis, and even cancer. First, these diseases are universal; individuals differ only in how rapidly the tendency toward actual illness increases in their bodies. Second, these conditions progress, literally for decades, in a presymptomatic state. The conditions may begin in an individual's 20s, 30s, or 40s and may not be detected until perhaps 40 years later. Third, these diseases are slowly progressive unless prevented. Fourth, these diseases have lifestyle risk factors such as stress; lack of exercise and/or social support; and the use of tobacco, alcohol, and illicit substances. The presence of these risk factors causes the progression of disease to become more rapid. These risk factors may not always cause the disease, but they at least affect the rate of development. The essence of prevention is to change the rate of development of disease. The goal is to change the rate of unseen progression from the steepest lines in the figure to a less-rapid progression. This can be done primarily by minimizing the risks from the lifestyle factors.

and a rise in smoking's subjective dimension. This was followed by social pressure and, eventually, anti-smoking legislation.

Alcohol Use

alcoholism—an addiction to the drug alcohol.

Alcohol use is another lifestyle factor that leads to much illness and premature death. Like tobacco, alcohol is a mind-altering substance. It is a highly valued, even glorified, drug in many societies including the United States because of its ability to relieve tension, to alleviate pain, and to produce a feeling of well-being, sedation, intoxication, or unconsciousness. **Alcoholism**, an addiction to the drug, involves drinking that exceeds societal norms and that negatively affects the drinker economically, socially, and/or physically. The National Commission on Marijuana and Drug Abuse labeled alcoholism as the most serious drug problem in the United States (other than tobacco use). Approximately 100 million Americans consume alcohol, and about 18 million have serious drinking problems.

Alcohol is a poison that has a harmful effect on virtually every body organ. Chronic heavy drinking increases the chances of heart attack, cancer, stroke, cirrhosis of the liver, automobile accidents, pneumonia, mental illness, and sexual dysfunction, to name just the best-known adverse effects. Even moderate drinking during pregnancy can produce miscarriages and birth defects, and is a principal cause of mental retardation in American children. Because alcohol attacks the body's immune system, AIDS can accelerate in infected carriers who drink.

Not surprisingly, therefore, alcohol is a major killer, claiming the lives of about 100,000 each year in the United States. Like tobacco, alcohol plays a direct or indirect role in bringing about death from virtually all the major causes. It kills (1) by acute intoxication; (2) by the debilitating effects of chronic consumption (e.g., alcohol-induced cirrhosis of the liver accounts for more than half of liver disease deaths); (3) by causing infant mortality

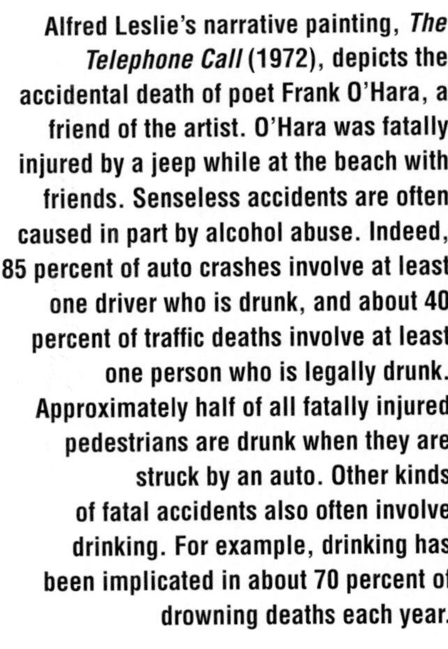

Alfred Leslie's narrative painting, *The Telephone Call* (1972), depicts the accidental death of poet Frank O'Hara, a friend of the artist. O'Hara was fatally injured by a jeep while at the beach with friends. Senseless accidents are often caused in part by alcohol abuse. Indeed, 85 percent of auto crashes involve at least one driver who is drunk, and about 40 percent of traffic deaths involve at least one person who is legally drunk. Approximately half of all fatally injured pedestrians are drunk when they are struck by an auto. Other kinds of fatal accidents also often involve drinking. For example, drinking has been implicated in about 70 percent of drowning deaths each year.

via the fetal alcohol syndrome; and (4) by facilitating homicides, suicides, and fatal accidents as a result of impaired judgment and altered behavior (Ravenholt, 1984). An example of this last pathway is the fact that alcohol is a factor in 30 to 50 percent of suicides.

The combined effects of drinking and smoking enormously increase the probability of acquiring many life-threatening illnesses. For example, the risk of cancer of the mouth and throat is 15 times greater for smokers who drink than for those who are free of both these lifestyle factors. In general, alcoholics live 10 to 12 years less than nonalcoholics, partly because of a poor diet, which, among other things, makes them more susceptible to disease.

Alcohol consumption and its carnage hit a peak in the United States in the 1970s. During the 1980s alcohol-related deaths fell about 12 percent, owing in large part to social changes brought about by an anti-alcohol social movement. These changes include the proliferation of tougher state laws penalizing drunk driving, increased enforcement of these laws, older legal drinking ages, and increased public intolerance for problem drinkers, especially drunk drivers (Ross, 1984). Nevertheless, U.S. drunk driving penalties are still not very severe compared to those in many other countries. In El Salvador, for example, the penalty for a first-time drunk driving conviction is execution by firing squad.

Drug Use

Chapter 9 on deviance discusses the various forms of legal and illegal psychoactive drugs. These drugs kill in many of the same ways that alcohol does. They take life (1) through acute drug overdose (related especially to intravenous use of heroin and cocaine); (2) through debilitative, carcinogenic, and psychic effects of chronic drug abuse; (3) through drug-caused misjudgments and behavioral changes resulting in suicides, homicides, and accidents; and (4) through disease picked up via intravenous drug injections. Most notable among the latter are AIDS and hepatitis B. Moreover, drug abusers often live in overcrowded and unsanitary conditions and do not maintain proper nutrition and health habits. This outlaw lifestyle together with the aforementioned toxic and behavioral effects means that drug abuse contributes to virtually every major cause-of-death category. All told, it has been estimated that drug abuse contributes to about 35,000 deaths in the United States each year (Ravenholt, 1984, 1990).

Despite declines in the proportion of the population using drugs during the 1980s, illness and death associated with drug use have continued to rise. For instance, the death rate for drug-induced causes alone increased by 32 percent from 1983 to 1989 (NCHS, 1992a). This increase can be tied directly to a number of worsening social problems, particularly those with social inequality at their root (Jones et al., 1988).

Diet

Diet is another lifestyle factor that can cause illness and death. Americans generally have poor diets. The Surgeon General's *Report on Nutrition and Health* (1988), the most comprehensive review of the connection between diet and health, concludes that Americans not only eat too much food, but also eat too much of the wrong foods, particularly the saturated fats found chiefly in meat and dairy products.

It is fair to say that the foods you eat may kill you. Indeed, our nutritional habits are strongly implicated in many of the nation's top killers, including the top three: heart disease (e.g., foods elevating serum cholesterol); cancer (e.g., fats and specific substances such as saccharin); and stroke (e.g., salt intake related to hypertension). To cite just one of many other examples, diet is an important factor in the development of diabetes (rank no. 7 on the list), a condition affecting about 11 million people and contributing to the deaths of over 40,000 people each year.

Obesity itself is a potent killer, owing to the pervasive health hazard it poses for many systems of the body. Studies have found that obese people have higher rates of virtually all the major killers and, consequently, a lower life expectancy. Some 23 percent of U.S. adults over age 19 are obese (defined as 20 percent or more above the desirable weight), and about one-third of those qualify as severely obese (National Institutes of Health, 1985).

Altogether, poor nutrition helps account annually for more than two-thirds of deaths in the United States. As the Surgeon General's report notes, "aside from drinking or smoking, diet is the one personal choice that more than any other influences long-term health prospects."

As the national obsession with dieting suggests, Americans are concerned about dietary lifestyle issues. Many are moving to prevent ill health by changing their diets. Over the past three decades, for instance, there has been a marked decline in the consumption of dairy and meat products and a concomitant drop in cholesterol levels in both women and men (Fries, 1989).

Exercise

The United States is a nation of couch potatoes. Seventy percent of Americans do not get enough exercise, which is problematic since inactivity is a major risk even after other lifestyle factors have been factored out (Blair, 1989; Ekelund et al., 1988; Paffenbarger et al., 1986; Slattery, 1989).

Exercise is one of the most effective means of staving off health problems. Even a small amount of exercise grants a significant protection not only against heart disease but also against cancer, stroke, accidents (by, for example, reducing osteoporosis), diabetes, and a host of other debilitators and killers. Individuals who engage in more vigorous exercise experience more pronounced health effects such as having only half the likelihood of heart attack characteristic of sedentary persons (Peters, 1983). Vigorous exercise may even postpone major symptoms and death from AIDS among those infected. In short, people who exercise stay healthier and live longer lives.

Exercise confers this protection through a variety of physical and behavioral mechanisms. For example, it is thought that exercise cuts down on heart disease by limiting blood-vessel blockages, and that it reduces colon cancer by increasing the speed of waste materials through the bowels. Behaviorally, exercise decreases stress and often increases an individual's social network. Walking, jogging, running, aerobic dancing, and other exercise activities get people out of their houses and offices, and afford them the opportunity to be with old friends and to make new ones (Hayes and Ross, 1986).

The health-through-fitness social movement in the United States has succeeded in getting a sizable minority of people to exercise regularly. But most Americans still are not active enough, including most children and young people. Apparently, nachos and Nintendos are winning out over two-hand-touch and hide-and-go-seek (Loupe, 1989).

Stress

The evidence is strong that people with stressful lives have relatively high rates of many diseases. In fact, such people have two to four times as much illness as other people independent of all other risk factors. Chronic stress increases the risk of such major causes of death as heart disease, cancer, suicide, homicide, and accidents (Susser, 1991). Moreover, stress has been related to many non-life-threatening forms of suffering. For example, it is the cause of the majority of sexual dysfunctions such as impotence, and has been linked to other ailments such as headaches, ulcers, colitis, and the common cold (Cohen et al., 1991). Indeed, some medical authorities consider that at least one-half of all physical disorders are at least partially caused or worsened by emotional disturbances (McFalls, 1979b).

Though it is not known exactly how stress makes people ill, experts believe that it interferes with one of the general integrating systems of the body such as the nervous, hormonal, or immune systems. Additionally, stress also leads to psychological disorders including depression and exhaustion, to medication for these conditions, and to tobacco, alcohol, and drug use—all of which are linked to other illnesses. Finally, stress contributes to accidents, suicide, and homicide through behavioral mechanisms such as concentration impairment, and through the aforementioned psychological disorders such as depression.

Stress is endemic to the social structure of U.S. society. Many Americans find themselves increasingly stressed out by the joint demands of work and family life (Schor and Leete-Guy, 1992). Severely stressful "traumatic life events" are surprisingly commonplace. The General Social Survey reports, for example, that in any given year about 36 percent of Americans live through at least one such event (e.g., the death of a relative, divorce, unemployment, or hospitalization) (see Table 18:2) (NORC, 1990).

People with stressful lives have relatively high rates of disease. Research has shown that pets reduce stress and help maintain health. Some people keep pigs as pets. Once a pig realizes that a person provides the food supply, it shows that person great affection.

TABLE 18:2 Crosstabulation of the Number of Traumatic Events Happening to Respondent by Race, 1990.

RESPONDENT'S RACE	NUMBER OF TRAUMATIC EVENTS			
Count **ROW PCT**	Zero	One	Two	Three
White	448 **63.9**	213 **30.4**	32 **4.6**	8 **1.1**
Black	70 **68.0**	29 **28.2**	4 **3.9**	—
Other	24 **54.5**	16 **36.4**	4 **9.1**	—
Total	542 **63.9**	258 **30.4**	40 **4.7**	8 **1.0**

$n = 848$

Main Point: About 36 percent of respondents experienced a traumatic event (death, divorce, unemployment, hospitalization-disability) during the previous year.

Source: General Social Survey, 1990.

Social Networks

It has long been known that the quantity and quality of social ties are factors in maintaining health (Cohen and Willis, 1985; Pearson, 1986). Frequent interaction with family, friends, community members, supportive coworkers, self-help support groups—even pets—leads to better health and less illness (Allen and Blascovich, 1991; Karasek and Theorell, 1990). Persons integrated into cohesive social networks are less likely to suffer from heart disease, accidents, and many of the other major causes of death. In fact, one major study found that those who were relatively isolated had a two- to threefold higher death rate than those with more extensive ties (Berkman and Syme, 1979). Isolated individuals also have higher rates of non-fatal illnesses and complications such as arthritic joint swelling, ulcers, and psychiatric disorders (Caplan, 1981).

Indeed, social support has effects on health throughout an individual's life course—from conception to the moment of death. For example, premature infants thrive in direct proportion to the time and affection lavished upon them by their mothers and other network members. Infant and childhood mortality rates are higher for children without two parents. And, according to the National Center for Health Statistics, children living in single-parent or stepparent families have higher rates of illness and emotional distress than those living with both biological parents. College students who interact with their relatives report fewer illness symptoms than those who do not (see Box 4:1) (Jones et al., 1988). Married people live longer than unmarried people. Divorced people have the highest death rate among all unmarried groups. The death rate for divorced and widowed people in their twenties and thirties is as much as 10 times greater than that of their married counterparts (Hu and Goldman, 1990). Individuals who migrate (and thus "uproot") have a relatively high level of ill health and psychological impairment, at least until that time when new social networks are developed (Kuo and Tsai, 1986). And the social isolation of older people (especially older men) accounts in part for the fact that they have the highest rate of suicide of any age group (Sattin, 1991).

Social networks influence health through several mechanisms. One mechanism involves stress (discussed above). In this explanation, network members serve as de-stressors; that is, supporters who may soften the impact of life's shocks on the mind and body of the individual (Jacobson, 1986). Another mechanism relates to the fact that people who have social support networks in place are more likely to follow medical advice to do such things as alter their diet, stop drinking or smoking, or take medication (Williams et al., 1992). Supporters either pressure them to do such things, or the ill change their behaviors in part for the benefit of family members and other supporters. This explains in part why alcoholics with families are more likely to stop drinking, and why 43 percent of divorced and separated Americans smoke compared to only 27 percent of married Americans. Yet another mechanism mediating the effect of social support on health is that socially supported ill people are more likely to have someone around to assist them during their illnesses—to nurse them, to shop for them, and to take them to medical care facilities (Williams et al., 1992).

Not necessarily apparent in the above discussion is the fact that relatives and friends can be a mixed blessing. Relationships may cushion stress, but they also may cause stress. Many of the traumatic events of our lives—the death of a spouse, divorce, the death of a close family member or friend, sexual difficulties, a change in health of a family member—involve shocks to or through members of our social networks. Thus not all social relations are pro-health (Mechanic and Hansell, 1989; Wellman, 1981).

More Americans than ever have thinned-out social networks. One reason for this is that today many more Americans of all ages live alone than in the past. In 1990, for example, 25 percent of all households consisted of just one person compared to only 17 percent in 1979 (McFalls, 1991). In general this trend does not bode well for the health of Americans because being "home alone" is definitely hazardous to one's health.

The Social Roots of Lifestyle Factors

Lifestyle factors in illness and death do not simply flow from the freely chosen personal actions of an individual. They are also products of the nature of the society in which the individual lives. Take, for example, high blood pressure, a condition that is a major risk factor in both heart disease and stroke. Since nearly everyone knows a person with high blood pressure, you probably are aware that personal choices such as smoking or high salt consumption contribute to the disease. But social forces also push up the blood pressure gauge. Like many other illnesses, high blood pressure is worsened, for example, by social stress and is improved by social support.

Moreover, even so-called personal choices such as smoking or salt intake are products in large part of social forces. Individuals do not make the choice to smoke in a social vacuum. Smoking is common in the United States for many social reasons. One is the fact that U.S. tobacco companies encourage smoking through innovative advertising and promotional campaigns (Ravenholt, 1990). These campaigns are increasingly aimed at the less educated and the young, and are so effective that many preschoolers already recognize logos representing cigarette brands (DiFranza et al., 1991; Fischer, 1991). As a result of these campaigns many Americans view smoking as an acceptable pastime rather than as a dangerous path to addiction, illness, and early death. Similarly, U.S. society socializes Americans to consume alcohol. Television, movies, and advertisements associate drinking with fun, wealth, and attractiveness rather than with fatal traffic accidents, rapes, murders, drownings, and family violence. Indeed, it has been estimated that before the age of 21, the average American has been exposed to tens of thousands of beer-glorifying commercials. Likewise, few Americans have carefully developed their food preferences with health in mind. People are taught to like—even crave—certain foods by their parents. But the traditional U.S. diet turns out to be ill conceived, and even those Americans who try to improve their eating habits often fail. It is difficult, for instance, to keep salt intake low given the high salt content in processed (and "convenient") foodstuffs typically available to U.S. consumers.

In short, lifestyle factors do not merely refer to the bad habits and choices of individuals, but to the lifestyle of a society. As David Mechanic (1986) puts it:

> Health is shaped fundamentally by culture, society, and environment. . . . Physical and psychological illness, however influenced by inheritance and biology, arise in no small way from conditions in the family, at work, and in the community generally (p. 203).

Consequently, societies with different lifestyle factors have different patterns of illness and death. Colon cancer, for example, the second most common form of cancer (after lung cancer) in the United States, is 10 times more common than in most Asian countries. Predictably, Chinese immigrants to the United States who adopt the typical American diet and lifestyle are up to 7 times more likely to develop colon cancer than those Chinese who remain in the homeland. Rich American foods containing saturated fats along with a lack of exercise make the difference (Whittemore, 1990; Willet, 1991).

THE AMERICAN HEALTH CARE SYSTEM

health care—an activity intended to improve one's state of health.

The **health care** system is the second major social determinant of the level of premature mortality (and illness) in a society (see Figure 18:2).

The average American loses about 10 years of potential life owing to preventable causes of death. The average Romanian loses 15 years and has a lower life expectancy, in part because toxic environmental pollution is worse. This photo was taken in Copsa Mica, a Romanian town that has been called the "blackest town in the world." Its industries spew out noxious, coal-based clouds that cover everything—including hands, faces, houses, cars, trees, and grass—with clinging soot. The health of children is particularly compromised by these environmental poisons.

New technologies such as this helicopter-based, Medi-Vac unit have reduced the death rate from most of the major causes of death. The homicide rate, for example, would be about three times higher today were it not for such speedy, competent rescue teams and for improvements in the quality of medical care (especially shock trauma and emergency care), which have taken place over the last thirty years.

Performance of the Health Care System

How well does the health care system in the United States perform its task of preventing premature death and illness? The answer to that question is mixed. In one respect, the system has performed extraordinarily well. Premature death and illness have been reduced dramatically, and Americans now live decades longer than they did just 100 years ago. This progress was brought about mostly by the accumulation of medical knowledge about how infectious diseases spread, and the consequent application of these research findings in public health and personal hygiene practices (Preston, 1987).

Similarly, over the past three decades new technologies and treatments have reduced the death rate from most of the major causes of death listed in Table 18:1. For example, the death rate from heart disease has been cut by more than one-third; and from stroke, by more than one-half; and the survival rate from cancer has increased about 50 percent—from about one in three during the 1960s to about one in two by 1990 (Price, 1988). Continued research, especially into such promising areas as bioengineering, undoubtedly will lead to further progress and medical miracles.

But the health care system does have serious shortcomings, probably the most important of which is its inability to give everyone in the society equal access to good quality health care. This lack of access comes about for many reasons.

Access to Physicians

The first reason has to do with access to physicians. Although the United States has one of the highest physician-to-patient ratios in the world, the fact remains that as many as 43 million Americans have little or no access to doctors (Vernaci, 1992). This is particularly the case in rural areas where there is an extreme shortage of doctors. In fact, 111 rural counties had no doctor at all as of the late 1980s. Doctors shun rural areas in part because relatively more rural than urban people are poor and lack insurance coverage (Herrin 1991). Needless to say, this situation leaves many rural people in dread of a sudden illness, a heart attack, or a traffic accident. Resourceful rural communities go to great lengths today trying to attract doctors, including supporting their future doctors as they go through medical school, which, as many of you probably recognize, is the idea behind the TV series *Northern Exposure.* Although not as extreme as in rural areas, many inner cities face a severe shortage of doctors as well.

Specialization versus Primary Care

The second hurdle standing between many individuals and proper medical care is that there are too few general practitioners. The health care system—and U.S. communities—presently lack about 35,000 general practitioners.

Over the past 50 years there has been a virtual stampede of medical school graduates into the specialties. In the 1930s, there were five general practitioners for each medical specialist; by the 1990s that ratio had reversed. One reason for this choice is monetary. Physicians typically elect to go into more lucrative practices as specialists because these can command two to three times as much income as that of the average family practitioner. More glamour and prestige are associated with specialties as opposed to general practice, particularly if the specialty involves exotic operations like organ transplants. But the trend toward specialization is also due to the explosion of medical knowledge and the desire of physicians to apply this knowledge within the specialized fields of modern medicine.

While the specialization of medicine has many obvious advantages, too much specialization means too little primary care. According to one national study (cited in Jones et al., 1988), most people visit doctors for primary care; that is, for such everyday symptoms as a cough, muscle ache, or abdominal discomfort. Moreover, people employ general practitioners to monitor their own and their dependents' overall health, and to refer them to the appropriate specialists if a need arises. Without access to general practitioners, people's health suffers, as do their wallets. Left to find their own way through a costly and complex medical system, people often end up using the high-priced skills of a specialist when those of a general practitioner would have sufficed (Greenfield et al., 1992).

Discrimination

Another obstacle to proper health care occurs when physicians refuse to perform certain medical services such as abortion or to provide services for certain groups such as the homeless drug addicts (Strauss et al., 1991).

AIDS provides a particularly pertinent case in point. Thousands of physicians in the United States systematically avoid or refuse to care for AIDS patients (Gerbert et al., 1991). This behavior is due not only to concerns about contagion, but reflects the larger societal prejudice against homosexuals and drug abusers, two groups at high risk of contracting the infection. Medical students are also apparently shunning AIDS patients, since hospitals in cities with large AIDS populations are experiencing an eroding ability to attract U.S. medical school graduates (Ness et al., 1991).

Medicaid—a government program of medical aid for the impoverished.

Medicare—a government program of medical aid for the elderly.

Another type of discrimination is the refusal of many physicians to provide medical services to indigent **Medicaid** patients or elderly **Medicare** patients. Fees paid by these federal programs often are much less than the physician's usual fee and result in a loss of potential income. As a result,

Resourceful rural communities without physicians sometimes support future doctors as they go through medical school with the agreement that the individual will set up practice in the community after graduation. The *Northern Exposure* TV character Dr. Joel Fleischmann got his medical degree this way. The federal government has responded to the regional shortage of physicians. The National Health Service Corps scholarship program supports physicians during their medical training in exchange for their working for a period after graduation in rural areas, inner cities, Indian reservations, or prisons. But the program is too small to have much of an impact on the shortage problem, and 17 percent of the graduates refuse to do the promised service.

only about half of the nation's physicians accept the Medicare allowance as an adequate fee and, consequently, many of these patients are turned away.

Incompetence and Lack of Social Control

A fourth obstacle to good quality health care is medical error and incompetence. Despite its impressive ability to heal illness and prevent premature death, the U.S. health care system kills thousands and harms millions of people who come seeking help. Estimates are that more than 100,000 Americans are injured or killed each year in hospitals because of medical error, unnecessary surgery, or outright negligence (Wolfe et al., 1991). Nearly 1 in 25 hospital patients suffers injuries at the hands of a doctor, and more than one-fourth of those injuries are the result of substandard care (Bedell et al., 1991; Brennan et al., 1991).

One cause of this is physician incompetence. The Federation of State Medical Boards estimates that about 5 percent of the nation's physicians are definitely incompetent (Jones et al., 1988). At least part of this incompetence can be attributed to physicians' drug abuse. It is conservatively estimated that during some period of their careers 1 percent of physicians are drug dependent, and 6 percent are alcohol abusers (Morrow, 1982).

Physician incompetence and drug dependency are not just due to human weakness, but occur within a professional arena woefully lacking in social controls. There is no formal extra-medical machinery in place to weed out unfit physicians. The medical profession's peer review process (self-policing) is notorious for failing to blow the whistle on malpracticing physicians, or for frequently failing to take serious disciplinary action against "problem" doctors (Wolfe, 1991).

It is worth noting that the first four obstacles to health care—geographic access, specialization, discrimination, and incompetence—have focused mostly on physicians largely because of space-constricting factors. The reader should understand that many of these obstacles apply as well to other components of the health care system such as hospitals—it is not just physicians who frequently provide substandard care. It is estimated that more than a third of U.S. hospitals fail to meet quality standards for procedures such as surgery, blood transfusions, and coronary and intensive care units. These are the management decisions of autonomous social organizations, not of doctors alone. Hospitals are scarce in rural areas, discriminate against AIDS patients, refuse to provide abortion services, and devote too much of their resources to high-tech specialties and too little to primary care services.

The High Cost of Medical Services

The extraordinarily high cost of health services also restricts access to them. The "Personal Perspective" experience—a $20,000 medical bill for an appendectomy—is a case in point. A $50,000 coronary bypass operation for a 50-year-old man is another. Totaling up all such bills on a national basis for 1991 yields the sum of $738 billion, or about 13 percent of the U.S. Gross National Product. It is ironic that the health care system, which was designed to solve the social problem of poor health, has itself become a social problem.

The United States currently pays its health care costs via a mixed national health care insurance system, consisting of employment-based insurance, other private insurance, the health care system for veterans,

Medicare coverage for the elderly, and Medicaid coverage for those unable to afford care. In general, this mixed private and public insurance system has woven a safety net for covering health care prices. But only 86 percent of the U.S. population is covered by this system, and the system only pays for roughly 70 percent of all medical bills. This means that in 1991 nearly 36 million Americans did not have public or private health insurance, and that 30 cents of each of those 738 billion health care dollars came out of people's pockets (NCHS, 1991b).

How is it possible for 36 million Americans to lack health insurance in a society with huge governmental programs providing medical care for the needy? The answer is that these programs do not cover all impoverished people. In dollar terms, Medicaid is the largest single welfare program in the United States, and the program does pay a portion of the health bills of about 10 percent of the population. But states differ widely in their eligibility requirements for people and services, and consequently millions of other indigent and borderline indigent Americans are not covered. Still others are only partially covered.

In addition, Social Security's health care program, Medicare, which automatically serves the vast majority of Americans age 65 and over, only covers a portion of health care bills. The (often economically deprived) elderly citizen is required to pay the difference. In fact, owing to this incomplete coverage, skyrocketing medical costs, and their generally fixed incomes, the elderly currently spend about the same percentage (20 percent) of their income on health care as they did before the enactment of Medicare!

Similarly, private insurance plans generally do not pay 100 percent of health costs. Insurees end up paying a portion of the costs because of preconditions or uncovered deductibles (i.e., insurance pays nothing until a certain threshold dollar amount is reached); co-insurance (i.e., insurance pays only a fraction of all costs) beyond the deductible dollar amount; lifetime cumulative limits on the dollar amount of services provided; and restrictions on such things as office visits, length of hospital stay, and diagnostic tests.

catastrophic illness—a serious medical affliction, which can crush an individual or a family financially.

Moreover, few Americans are completely safe from so-called **catastrophic illness** such as serious debilitating forms of cancer and stroke. Catastrophic illnesses can crush an individual or a family financially, especially when the victim requires nursing home care or home health care. Contrary to what most people think, nursing home care (which cost an average of $30,000 a year in the early 1990s) is not covered by typical private health insurance or Medicare. Most people must pay for it themselves and consequently become impoverished soon after entering a private nursing home. When persons are declared destitute, Social Services can accept them as welfare clients, and then Medicaid generally pays for a suboptimal level of nursing home care.

In short, about 36 million Americans are in an insurance "no man's land," with too much income to qualify for public health care and too little income to afford insurance; and for those who are covered by the insurance net, many major expenses still drop through as personal burdens.

The high cost of health services in the United States is due in part to the "third party" nature of the insurance structure. The financial guarantees of the insurer mean that the first two parties—the patient and the physician—have very little incentive to cut costs. Since their bills will be paid, patients naturally seek the best (and often most expensive) care available. And physicians can actually triple their incomes by adding on defensible but often unnecessary procedures and tests (Gray, 1991; Moloney and Rodgers, 1979). Doctors have further financial motives to practice costly defensive medicine to avoid medical malpractice suits (which amount to $5 billion a year), and to minimize their own costly premiums for malpractice insurance (Williams, 1983). A Rand Corporation study found that 20 percent of all medical procedures and treatments are completely unnecessary; and the Aetna Insurance Company estimates that another 30 percent consists of discretionary care, which may not be effective. Another 10 percent of the nation's health bill is due to physician and hospital fraud, and an additional 12 percent is due to health care providers' complex and often wasteful system of recordkeeping (Castro, 1991). In short, about half the staggering health care budget of the United States is spent on unnecessary, wasteful, and fraudulent practices, while millions of Americans go without basic health care.

But the insurance system and its accompanying waste and fraud are not the only reasons health care costs are soaring. About half the growth in spending results from external social forces such as population growth and general inflation. Of the other half, two-thirds can be attributed to the increased volume and intensity of health care demands stemming from such societal factors as an aging population, the AIDS epidemic, crack babies, and trauma caused by random violence (Hellinger, 1991; Schneider and Guralnik, 1990). The remaining third is due to medical price growth above general inflation, arising from such sources as new high-priced technology (Samuelson, 1988) and the dramatic increase in nurses' salaries brought about by nurse shortages (Coughlin, 1991).

Resource Decisions

Fueled by these many forces, medical costs are literally out of control, and attempts at medical cost containment initiated in the 1980s have been a stunning failure (Schwartz and Mendelson, 1991). These cost control programs generally limit some of the fees received by physicians or hospitals, or the reimbursement of the costs paid by patients. Their impotence stems partly from the disorganized and fragmented nature of the health care system itself. The organizational complexity of this system makes it extremely hard to devise fair and workable financial limits. In addition, the system has too many loosely connected parts to try to apply any one financial remedy. Placing dollar limits on Medicaid and Medicare, for example, would result only in higher costs for those patients whose medical bills often already contain a hidden surcharge used to pay for the health care of the impoverished. Even if hospital costs were to be controlled effectively, physicians remain unencumbered to charge whatever the market will bear in their unregulated offices (Williams, 1983).

Reform of the health care system in the United States will likely occur in two stages. The first stage will be one of incremental change. Health care will be expanded to cover more of the uninsured, primarily by such tactics as broadening the eligibility standards of Medicaid and by requiring all employers to insure workers. But while this first-stage reform will solve the problem of some people being totally uninsured, it will not solve the problem of skyrocketing health care costs. In fact, it will worsen it. Many health-care policy analysts believe that this first-stage reform, like the cost control programs of the 1980s, will be ineffectual because it will treat symptoms rather than the underlying disease (McCue, 1989). They argue that only a complete redesign of the entire health care system has any hope of slowing escalating health costs.

Analysts believe that this second stage of reform will occur around the turn of the century. By then health care costs will be so burdensome that

Angered by high medical costs, disturbed over shrinking health insurance benefits, and frustrated by the health care system in general, many Americans were in favor of health care reform in the mid-1990s. Hillary Clinton spearheaded the Clinton administration efforts to bring about that reform. The controversial issues that she, the government, and the American people have dealt with are the very ones (like resource decisions) discussed in this chapter.

a groundswell of public concern will force a transformation. In all probability, the new system will be similar to that of Canada, which sets an upper limit for health care spending, and which allocates the subsequent limited resources by government authority on the basis of commonly agreed-upon principles. Part of the problem with the present disorganized health care system in the United States is that there is no general authority making such resource decisions and no consensus concerning the allocation of resources.

During the 1990s, consensus will have to be reached on a number of value-laden issues as a precondition for second-stage reform. The most important of these issues are: (1) What proportion of the GNP should be spent on health care? (2) What limitations should be placed on the right to health care? (3) How should health care funds be divided between prevention and illness? and (4) How much, and what type of, medical research should be funded by the government?

A Limit on Health Care Spending

Health care is a social budget item. It competes with other budget items such as food, education, defense, and entertainment for a share of the GNP. Between 1970 and 1991 health care spending has been an extraordinarily successful competitor, increasing its share of the GNP from 7 percent to 13 percent, an 85 percent jump. Experts predict that the present health care system would account for 16 percent of the GNP by the year 2000, and would gobble up a staggering 37 percent by 2030. For the federal government, health care costs are the fastest growing major item, and are already crowding out spending for other urgent needs (Castro, 1991). Clearly, the U.S. health care system is headed for a "meltdown" in the not too distant future. Given finite resources, this escalation cannot go on indefinitely, and a decision concerning an upper limit for health care spending will have to be made.

The Right to Health Care

The stage-one reform will be based on the premise that health care, like education, is a basic individual right. But the right to education is not limitless—it generally applies to primary and secondary education but not to college or graduate education. Similarly, the right to health care would be limited by the cap on spending just discussed. Unfortunately, financial limits force resource decisions, which means some people will live while others will die (Colen, 1986; Plough, 1986). In the present system, resources often are allocated on ability to pay, or even the degree of subjective support drummed up for a given disease by celebrities in the mass media (e.g., Elizabeth Taylor for AIDS or Jerry Lewis for muscular dystrophy). But in the stage-two transformation, it is likely that resource decisions will be made on the basis of more rational cost/benefit analyses.

Perhaps Oregon's proposed health plan provides a glimpse into the future of how these decisions will be made in the United States as a whole. Oregon's plan ranks 709 health care conditions and their treatments according to seriousness and the probability that treatment will return the patient to long-term good health. Given limited state financial resources, it is estimated that only the first 587 conditions on the list would be eligible for treatment. In general, the elderly and the terminally ill are not entitled under this system to highly expensive medical care. A chronic alcoholic, for example, would not be eligible for a liver transplant, but a child would be (see Box 18:1).

Needless to say, the rationing of health care is an emotionally charged "right-to-life" issue, but one that must be met head on (Dougherty, 1988; Strosberg et al., 1989). Indeed, since all present systems ration health care at least indirectly via limitations on resources or by price, the controversial issue is not rationing per se, but the basis of that rationing. More controversy is likely to ensue in the future as computers decide the level of care an individual will receive. By 1992, a database existed that was designed to make life-and-death decisions about appropriate care of patients in intensive-care units and emergency rooms. Indeed, there is a good chance that sometime in the future a cold-hearted computer will tell doctors whether they should try to save your life or to let you die straightaway.

Prevention versus Treatment

One problem with the present health care system is that it devotes too many resources to curing full-blown illnesses and too few resources to the more mundane realm of preventive medicine, where many illnesses could be avoided altogether. Less than 4 percent of the nation's expenditures for health are devoted to any form of preventive activity.

There are several reasons for the present pro-treatment bias of the U.S. health care system, all having deep sociological roots. An intellectual basis for this approach is **germ theory**, which has been called "the most powerful single idea in the history of medicine" (Twaddle and Hessler, 1977, p. 11). Essentially, the discovery that microorganisms could produce acute disease has focused the attention of the medical profession on killing germs after they have attacked a patient. While this focus on stopping the contracted infection has generated miraculous cures, it has also retarded efforts to ward off or eliminate the offending germs in the first place. The organization of physician training around this germ model means the neglect of potent—but nongerm-oriented—models of disease.

germ theory—the belief that acute disease is caused by microorganisms.

BOX 18:1 SOCIOLOGICAL IMAGINATION IN FICTION

Sydney van Scyoc's "A Visit to Cleveland General" is a story about a powerful hospital in a future in which resource decisions have been made in favor of such practices as enforced sterilization of the impoverished and involuntary euthanasia of the elderly. This segment focuses on enforced family planning and contraception, and on the use of consciousness-altering drugs to gain patient compliance under the guise of care and therapy. Albin Johns is a reporter being given a tour of the hospital by senior social worker Miss Kling.

"First stop: Maternity. Don't worry—everybody's decent."...

Miss Kling halted before a glowing cubicle, cocked her head shrewdly at the unmaternal little figure within. "Good morning, Edna," she boomed.

The girl splashed against the glass, an overripe little plum with flaming hair and feral black eyes. "You! Where's my kid? Three days you've told me you'd get him up here next day for sure. Ten days, and I haven't seen him yet. First that campaign to get me to sign adoption papers. Ha! Then you're keeping him till I'm strong enough to hold him—you say. Now for three days this yack about him being deformed."

Miss Kling chuckled blandly. "Now you know we've been waiting to see if he could survive, Edna. We wanted to spare you seeing the little thing if he couldn't live."

"Look, granny, I told you—I wasn't so dopey I didn't see the kid down in delivery. I got a good look. Nine pounds plus and everything where it belongs. Lungs like a pair of bellows. A natural born fullback. The doctor said so himself. I—"

Miss Kling rasped prevailingly, "Now, Edna, be calm. I'll have Dr. Dover explain the cause of death to you in person. I want you to consider it God's mercy—"

"Death!" the girl shrilled.

"—the little fellow didn't live to suffer. A single girl couldn't hope to care for such a terribly handicapped child all by herself. The expenses alone . . ."

Miss Kling's stubby fingers crawled over the control panel. Rainbow fog seeped into the cubicle.

The girl's face discolored with rage. "I sure don't need any *man* to pay my way! I'm nineteen years old! I make good dollars dancing the nudie circuit. I come and go as I please. It's nothing to me Gordy ran out with that freak Gandi before I got him down to Marriage Hall."

Miss Kling smiled. "Dear, I wouldn't presume to judge your morals. I'm just Kling, your old granny in your time of trouble."

The girl's tirade ended abruptly. She blinked stupidly and sank to her knees in the swirling rainbow fog. "What did you say? About my baby?"

"Now, you saw the poor little fellow yourself, Edna. Poor guy."

Edna sobbed thickly. "Poor lit-

A second factor promoting treatment over prevention in the United States is the structure of social rewards. Most doctors practice on a fee-for-service basis that pays off on the amount of treatment performed, not the amount of suffering avoided. In addition, social prestige in medical research as well as grant money is showered on those involved with such exotic treatment techniques as organ transplants and laser surgery, not on those preaching healthful habits.

A closely related third factor is the American culture's love affair with high technology (see Chapter 21). Americans believe in the desirability of dominating nature through technology, and view innovations in treatment hardware as technological fixes, painless solutions brought about by the magic of science. Our cultural admiration for high technology explains why hospitals spend millions of dollars on high-tech equipment, much of

BOX 18:1 SOCIOLOGICAL IMAGINATION IN FICTION *continued*

tle kid. And it's all Gordy's fault! He's the one made our baby deformed. He's the one ran off—"

"Now, Edna, one of our pretty little nurse machines will come," Miss Kling cooed. "You're going to have an injection. It's just a little something we give all our unwed mothers. It won't hurt at all, and you won't have to worry about babies for years and years."

"Won't have to worry?" Edna murmured.

"No more about babies. Not for five years. Why, by then you might be married. You might even *want* another baby in five years."

Edna smiled softly, curled up on the floor. Her hair piled scarlet over her face.

Johns stared at her, peacefully asleep on the glassy floor, awash in pastel fog. Then he noticed Miss Kling had trundled away. . . . She halted before a cubicle containing a slight, pale girl in her twenties. "Good morning, Trenda. I'm Mable Kling, your social caller. How do you feel?"

The girl looked up listlessly. "I'm all right, thank you." She touched a tear off her cheek.

Miss Kling beamed. "The nurse will bring your brand new son in just a moment. Don't you want to pretty up a little, for your first visit?"

"My—son?" the girl said gropingly.

Miss Kling's fingers crawled over the control panel. The cubicle began to fog. Miss Kling chuckled reassuringly. "He's a real football player. Scaled nearly ten pounds this morning—you'd swear he was a couple of weeks old already. Lungs like a pair of bellows. And he has a mop of red hair. Just like your husband."

The girl sat up, confused. . . . "You mean the baby's really all right? He wasn't born too early?"

"You can see for yourself in a couple of minutes. You feel up to hefting a ten-pounder?"

"Oh, yes!" The cubicle was densely fogged. The girl's face flushed with excitement. "Why I—I even thought I heard someone say it was a girl!"

They left her excitedly dabbing her lips with color, lost in lavender fog.

Johns sobbed brokenly, overwhelmed.

"Now there's a case to make my job worthwhile," Miss Kling rumbled. "That sweet little girl lying there heartbroken, and I fixed everything up smart. By the time she gets the baby home, she won't even remember her sad hours."

Critical Thinking Questions

1. In this 1968 short story, van Scyoc correctly anticipated such phenomena as the introduction (in 1991) of NORPLANT, a contraceptive that lasts five years, as well as efforts to coerce poor women into using it. How would a functionalist and a conflict theorist interpret a social policy aimed at encouraging or forcing impoverished women to accept such long-lasting contraceptives?
2. In an Oregon-type health care plan, it is likely that a terminal AIDS patient, for example, would be entitled only to "comfort care," not to "heroic" measures. What would be the social consequences of a health care system that makes such rationing decisions?

Source: Sydney van Scyoc, "A Visit to Cleveland General," 1968. In Martin H. Greenberg, John W. Milstead, Joseph D. Olander and Patricia Warrick (Eds.), 1975, *Social Problems Through Science Fiction,* pp. 339–56. New York: St. Martins.

which is underutilized, while proven but low-tech prevention programs are underfunded.

In any event, the stage-two transformation of the U.S. health care system undoubtedly will involve a reappraisal of the proper mix of resources directed toward both prevention and treatment. There is already momentum building among analysts to give preventive programs a much larger share of health-care resources. This is because prevention of illness is unquestionably cheaper, more efficient, and, in many ways, better than treatment.

Experts calculate that health promotion and preventive programs can postpone *up to 70 percent of premature deaths,* whereas the curative and rehabilitative approach can postpone no more than about 15 percent of such deaths (Koop, 1992). Lifestyle illnesses—those associated with such things

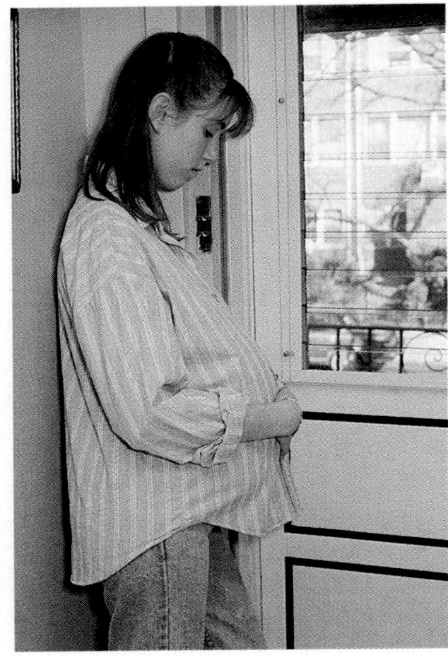

The prevention of illness is unquestionably less costly, more efficient, and better in many other ways than treatment. Consider the case of prenatal care. In the United States, each year about 200,000 pregnant teenagers receive no prenatal care, increasing the risk of having low-birth-weight infants. Despite expensive efforts to save them, many of these babies die in their first year of life, pushing infant mortality to one of the highest rates in the industrialized world. Others are kept alive by modern medical technology, which can cost as much as $250,000 per child. The survivors are more likely to have other diseases throughout their lives requiring costly medical treatment. Owing to resultant low IQ's and other difficulties, many of these individuals also require other forms of public assistance. Analysts agree that it would be much less expensive to make sure that every pregnant woman gets prenatal care than to fund treatment after birth as well as the other assistance programs.

as smoking, drinking, illicit drugs, poor diet, and lack of exercise, are prime targets for health promotion and preventive programs. Also typically included in this category are health problems due to reckless driving, nonuse of seatbelts or motorcycle helmets, and sexually transmitted diseases, particularly AIDS (Strauss et al., 1991).

One reason health costs are so high is that people expect the health care system to repair the consequences of their bad health habits, usually at little or no financial cost to themselves. But in a future Oregon-type health care rationing system, the consensus might be that so-called self-inflicted problems should receive low priority scores and, consequently, little or no treatment. One corporation that has already moved in this direction is the Circle K Corporation, the nation's second largest chain of convenience stores. Circle K denies health insurance benefits to employees who suffer from medical problems resulting from certain "personal lifestyle decisions," including drug and alcohol abuse, self-inflicted wounds, and AIDS proven not to have been contracted from blood transfusions (Will, 1988). Whether you agree with such a value tradeoff or not, such hard choices are coming.

Medical Research

There are a number of issues concerning medical research that will have to be addressed as part of the stage-two reform: (1) How much of the health care system budget should be devoted to research as opposed to prevention programs and treatment? (2) What proportion of the research budget should be devoted to basic research and what proportion to research on specific illnesses? (3) Of that portion allocated to specific illnesses, how should the budget be divided up among them? Presently, these issues are not being addressed by the U.S. health care system in terms of a cost/benefit analysis or in any other systematic fashion.

The situation with respect to AIDS illustrates these issues. When the AIDS epidemic first became evident in the early 1980s, the federal government's funding response was sluggish. Critics contended that it was slow because AIDS victims were primarily gay men who were considered social outcastes (Shilts, 1987). But by the 1990s the federal government devoted a robust $1.6 billion to AIDS funding. That was nearly three times more than the budget for heart disease—which killed 17 times as many people; and more than the budget for cancer—which killed 12 times as many (Ravenholt, 1990). AIDS was elevated to the top of the nation's public health agenda, not because it caused the most death or illness, but because gay men became a highly organized interest group. AIDS activism has also been very successful because it has raised AIDS' subjective dimension. This was facilitated by the fact that many AIDS victims are young, creative, and famous, and their deaths are particularly poignant, public, and visible. The facts that AIDS is contagious and apparently 100 percent fatal also helped boost its subjective dimension, particularly as it became evident to the general public that homosexuals were not its only victims.

Another AIDS issue swirls around the relative proportion of AIDS funds used for medical research versus prevention. Prevention is the most effective means of suppressing a communicable epidemic. But AIDS activists pushed for the rapid development of treatments for AIDS victims rather than for prevention, and, consequently, twice as much has been spent on drug research than on preventive programs. Some analysts believe that this overemphasis on cures comes at the expense of educating those who remain at risk, most notably African Americans and Hispanics living in the nation's inner cities.

AIDS research is also bound up with another general research issue; that is: What portion of the overall medical research budget should be spent on broad, basic research programs, and what portion should be devoted to research on specific target diseases? Analysts argue that, in the long run, basic research is more productive than specific disease research, and that the generous funding of AIDS research has come in part at the expense of this more beneficial basic research. Many researchers argue that the ultimate solution to AIDS, as well as to other afflictions, will be found through basic research in fields such as immunology (Denhardt, 1990).

Aside from AIDS, there are many other research issues that must be sorted out in the stage-two transformation. For example, society will have to decide about the value and efficacy of a whole range of "brave new world" biomedical research projects ranging from human reproduction to the postponement of death via artificial hearts and other body parts (Fox, 1976). Perhaps the most cost-effective research strategy of all would be to underwrite aging research, given the current rapidly increasing average age of the U.S. population and the enormous costs associated with the treatment of such catastrophic illnesses of the elderly as Alzheimer's disease.

The two-stage transformation described above will be no panacea. There are no simple, painless answers to the problems of the health care system. The oft-touted Canadian health care system has resulted in long delays for services, and many Canadians come to the United States to take advantage of advanced, high-quality care. The Canadian system, like other nationalized systems, also relies heavily on U.S. medical research and technology. Former U.S. Surgeon General C. Everett Koop (1992) cautions that "experience the world over has shown that when government economic controls are applied to health, they prove in time to be detrimental, and eventually there is an erosion of quality, of productivity, and then of innovation and of creativity." Nevertheless, such programs can provide universal health care and relatively high life expectancy for society's members (Mosley and Cowley, 1991).

SOCIAL CATEGORIES

Chapter 20 discusses the fact that life expectancy and mortality rates vary substantially by social categories such as age, gender, socioeconomic status, race, and ethnicity. These mortality (and underlying illness) differentials come about as a result of the differential operation of the four causal categories depicted in Figure 18:2; namely, genetic, environmental, lifestyle, and health care system causes.

Age differences in mortality are due principally to genetic factors. But the observed between-ages mortality differentials are influenced by nongenetic causes as well. The differential between the elderly and those age 15 to 24, for example, is not as large as it might be because relatively more young people than old people die from socially preventable lifestyle causes linked to alcohol and drug abuse, risk taking, crime, stress, and social network deficiencies (Box 18:2).

Similarly, women live longer than men (see Table 18:1) due in large part to genetic factors, but environmental, lifestyle, and health care system causes also play important roles. Indeed, males and females in the United States differ markedly with respect to all the major lifestyle factors. For example, women traditionally use tobacco and alcohol less than men but suffer from more stress (Ravenholt, 1990; Verbrugge, 1989). And the health care system contributes to these mortality and illness differences generally in ways favoring men over women (see Box 18:3).

BOX 18:2 COLLEGE EXPERIENCE

Violent Death—A Specialty of Young Adults

Compared to most age groups, age-typical college students have relatively low serious illness and death rates. Young adults have barely a 1 percent chance of dying between age 15 and 24. But that 1 percent attrition means that 40,000 individuals in each successive group of 15-year-olds never reach their 25th birthday. Most of you probably know tragic individual cases behind these statistics, and are aware that the vast majority of such deaths are socially preventable. Indeed, the rank order of causes of death for 15- to 24-year-olds is very different from that shown in Table 18:1 for the entire population. Accidents (46 percent), homicide (17 percent), and suicide (13 percent) are ranked respectively one, two, and three, and account for a disturbing 76 percent of all deaths in recent years (NCHS, 1992a). Homicide is by far the chief cause of death for African American youths, whereas automobile accidents are the major cause of death for white youths.

Between 1960 and 1990, the death rate for Americans as a whole declined by 23 percent, but that of young adults age 15–24 fell only 2 percent (NCHS, 1991a). Why? A dramatic rise in violent deaths from accidents, homicide, and suicide

BOX 18:3 GENDER AND SOCIAL CHANGE

Women: Stepchildren of the Health Care System

Women have been traditionally the stepchildren of medical research. Virtually all the classic heart disease studies—the number one cause of death in women as well as in men—have been conducted exclusively on men. Similarly, this for-men-only bias is evident in studies concerning nearly all the major causes of death and illness, and is particularly present in research tests on new drugs that routinely leave out women. Moreover, too little research funding is devoted to health problems specific to women such as ovarian cancer and endometriosis. In 1990, for instance, the National Institutes of Health spent only 13 percent of its budget studying women's health, even though women represent more than 50 percent of the population.

This one-sided nature of medical research and testing is in part a reflection of long-standing sexism in the U.S. health care system (Apple, 1990). But it is also due to valid, though in this case shortsighted, scientific concerns. For example, a study that includes both women and men generally must be substantially larger than one dealing only with men to have the same degree of statistical validity. The reproductive and hormonal cycles of women also complicate the research design. And women in their reproductive period often are excluded from drug testing for fear of harming future offspring.

Studies also demonstrate that women have less access than men to major diagnostic and therapeutic interventions (Ayanian and Epstein, 1991; Pfeffer et al., 1991). For example, women with serious heart disease get far less aggressive medical treatment than men with the same condition. Women are also less likely to receive kidney dialysis or transplantation or even diagnosis of lung cancer. This situation too is due in part to gender bias in the health care system, but it is also a function of known disease differences between the sexes. For example, women with chest pains are less likely than men to actually have

BOX 18:2 COLLEGE EXPERIENCE *continued*

over the period has offset general population reductions in other causes.

This dramatic rise in violent deaths has social roots in the lifestyle factors. The explanations typically involve family and social network breakdowns, academic and career competition (stress), urban poverty, and alcohol and drug abuse (Fingerhut et al., 1992). To cite just one example, in 1990, 42 percent of college students reported having engaged in high-risk drinking (defined as imbibing quickly five or more drinks in a row) within the previous two weeks (Johnston et al., 1990). This fact explains in part why more than 8,000 teenagers and young adults die in alcohol-related accidents every year. It is also worth noting that another lifestyle factor, unsafe sex, increasingly is taking dead aim at young people. By 1989, AIDS had already accelerated into the number six cause-of-death position for those age 15–24, and threatens to move still higher during the 1990s (NCHS, 1992a).

Finally, many of the health problems of middle- and old-age have their roots in lifestyle habits established during the age-typical college years. For example, 37 percent of the deaths of American women in middle-age can be attributed to smoking, and most of those women started smoking in their late teens.

Critical Thinking Questions

1. Over recent decades, what factors account for the dramatic rise in violent deaths among young adults?
2. How would a conflict theorist explain the relatively high rate of homicide among African American youths?

BOX 18:3 GENDER AND SOCIAL CHANGE *continued*

heart disease, and bypass surgery is more risky for women (Pfeffer et al., 1991).

Nevertheless, there is general consensus that women have not received their fair share of medical research and treatment, and during the early 1990s women began to mobilize to deal with this inequity. Breast cancer, a disease that strikes 175,000 women and kills 45,000 women each year, was the first major focus of this activity. Activist groups battling for more attention to this disease sprung up across the country, and in 1991 joined a number of political, health, and more traditional groups fighting breast cancer—140 in all—to form the Breast Cancer Coalition (BCC).

One factor fueling this rise of activism is the success of groups fighting for greater funding of AIDS research and treatment. Breast cancer activists point out that AIDS killed only about half as many people as breast cancer in 1990 but got 19 times as much federal research funding. While not opposed to the level of AIDS funding per se, breast cancer activists want their disease to get a fair share of the nation's health funding. By 1992, some progress had already been made. For example, in response to pressure from the BCC, Congress ordered the National Institutes of Health to boost by 48 percent spending on breast cancer research. While this was a major improvement, the AIDS funding allocation that year was still nine times greater.

Progress has been made in other areas as well. In 1991, NIH announced the creation of a major long-term study that will track the health of women over many years. It is the most definitive, far-reaching study of women's health ever undertaken. In addition, pharmaceutical companies were in the process of developing 263 medicines to battle diseases that primarily afflict women. And research on women's diseases of all kinds was on the upswing. So sensitive had this new women's issue become that one medical researcher said, "You cannot write a federal research grant [now] unless you include women. Women are the science issue of the '90s" (Fitzgerald, 1991).

Critical Thinking Questions

1 How would a conflict theorist explain why women traditionally have been the stepchildren of medical research?
2. How would a conflict theorist explain why women themselves waited until the late 1980s to organize and fight against this inequitable situation?

Matuschka is a 39-year-old artist who had a mastectomy in 1991. On August 15, 1993 her self-portrait, *Beauty Out of Damage,* appeared on the *New York Times Magazine* cover to draw attention to a story about the political crusade for more breast cancer money and better research on women's illnesses. Even though it had the gauzy beauty of a fashion photo, such a bold picture had never before appeared in a mainstream publication, and it provoked enormous attention and interest. That is one of the purposes of radical art—to raise the subjective dimension of social problems such as breast cancer.

Mortality also varies by social class. High income deflates an individual's risk of just about every major and minor disease. Even the so-called diseases of affluence—heart disease, cancer, and stroke—actually afflict the nonwealthy more than the wealthy residents in developed countries (Mosley and Cowley, 1991). Genetics play only a negligible role in creating these mortality differentials; and environmental factors have a modest impact, owing to the fact that economically deprived communities experience greater than average exposure to environmental poisons, including lead, air pollutants, toxic waste, and tainted fish (Environmental Protection Agency, 1992). Lifestyle factors are especially important. Compared to the nondeprived, the deprived have high rates of tobacco and "hard" drug use, high rates of homicide, AIDS, and unhealthy diets, and low rates of exercise. Finally, the U.S. health care system has always drawn sharp class distinctions between those who could pay and those who could not (Stevens, 1989). The indigent have less access to the health care system, and the quality of the care that is available to them is worse than that used by higher-income persons (Braveman et al., 1991; Rivo et al., 1989).

Racial and ethnic differences in mortality and morbidity are due for the most part to these socioeconomic factors (Table 18:1) (Rodgers, 1992; Starfield et al., 1991). Take, for instance, the fact that African Americans have a lower cancer survival rate than whites. This comes about because relatively more African Americans than whites are economically deprived. Impoverished people have the lowest cancer survival rates for many class-related reasons, including the fact that their cancers are diagnosed at typically later, less-treatable stages because of their relative lack of access to the health care system (Freeman, 1987).

But it would be a mistake to conclude that socioeconomic factors explain racial and ethnic mortality differentials entirely. There are genetic differences among groups linked to illness (Ekelund et al., 1989). And longstanding, systematic, institutionalized racism in society and, more specifically, in the health care system accounts for a significant part of these mortality differentials. One example suffices to illustrate this point. Proportionally, four times as many older whites receive heart bypass surgery than older African Americans, even with Medicare coverage (Hartz et al., 1992).

THEORETICAL PERSPECTIVES ON HEALTH CARE

Functionalism

Institutions carry out necessary social tasks. One of these tasks is to preserve health and to care for those who become sick and infirm. This task is not entrusted to any single institution in the United States. Rather, it is divided up in a piecemeal fashion among society's primary institutions. Examples of health-related activities performed by the various institutions are easy to list. The family institution provides basic preventative and nursing care to its members. The political institution furnishes funding for health care and medical research, and enacts laws and sanctions against drunk driving and smoking in public places. The educational institution disseminates health-related knowledge, provides teaching hospitals, trains physicians, and carries out medical research. The economic institution operates most hospitals, and produces medicine, medical equipment, and health insurance services. And, finally, the religious institution runs religious-affiliated hospitals, and supplies medical personnel as well as charitable funding. The fact that health activities are scattered so widely over

Alice Neel's *T.B., Harlem* (1940) shows an African-American man suffering from tuberculosis, a disease prevalent in the airless and lightless tenements of urban ghettos like Harlem in the first half of the twentieth century. Neel paints the man's pain-wracked and mangled body without false pity or sentimentality, drawing attention to the bandage covering the wound left after the removal of eleven ribs. Since Emancipation, African-American men have been at the bottom of the race/gender totem pole, lagging far behind African-American women, white men, and white women in life expectancy.

society's basic institutions means that health care in the United States is more fragmented than it would be if a single institution had control over all these activities. Many dysfunctions of the system can be attributed to the lack of functional integration available in a single, specialized system.

As noted above, the social causes of death and illness can be divided into two types; namely, lifestyle causes and health care system causes. Family-based health care activities (and risk factors) fall into the first category, and operate principally through social networks. The complex of official medical activities is generally referred to as the health care system (see rectangle C in Figure 18:2).

The health care system can be divided usefully into two segments; namely, health care skills and health care delivery. The health care skills segment is unquestionably the finest in the world. Not so for the system segment delivering these skills to the public. Consider the case of hepatitis B, for example. About a million Americans are chronic carriers of the viral infection, and face potentially fatal complications. But despite the development of an effective vaccine in 1982, the incidence of this infection has not declined significantly in the United States. Why is the vaccine not slowing the spread of the disease in the United States, as it is in some countries such as China? Because it has not been *delivered* to all Americans or even to all high-risk Americans. The main reason for this situation is its cost—up to $120 per dose. In contrast, this U.S.-developed vaccine is administered to all infants in China at a cost of $1 per dose. This case demonstrates the fact that while the United States has many superb healing and preventative skills, these are not delivered efficiently. Thus sociologists conclude that the health care delivery system is socially disorganized—another way of saying it lacks functional integration.

One of a society's basic tasks is to provide care for members who become sick or injured. During health care emergencies in the former Soviet Union, for example, this cure was often provided by brigades of nurses. This photograph shows one such brigade in Gorno Altaisk marching and singing patriotic songs as a prelude to practicing procedures for large-scale civil emergencies such as wars, epidemics, earthquakes, and floods.

The U.S. health care delivery system is huge and complex. Owing to space constraints the focus here can only be on its most prominent institutional setting—the hospital. The more than 7,000 hospitals in the United States form the organizational center of modern medicine, collectively housing about 1 million patients every day and grossing several billion dollars annually. But there is precious little coordination of services across hospitals. It is not unusual for two hospitals in the same community to acquire the expensive equipment needed for certain operations, when one facility would be more than sufficient for the region. Wasteful duplication of services is just one reason why U.S. hospitals on average are operating at only 65 percent of capacity (Castro, 1991).

Lack of interhospital cooperation costs more than money—it costs lives. For example, the consolidation of several hospital maternity units into one larger, well-equipped center can reduce maternal mortality by two-thirds (Rushmer, 1975). The reason why many such life-saving opportunities are squandered is because hospitals are not part of an overall, organized system cooperating to serve public health care needs. On the contrary, hospitals generally are independent units competing against each other for patients' dollars and medical status.

From the functionalist perspective, these hospital organizational problems are symptomatic of a faulty functional system. This perspective views each part of the health care delivery system—including hospitals and their components—in terms of its overall contribution to the goal of minimizing illness and premature death. If a hospital ward, for example, serves the positive function of helping a number of people but diverts twice that many from preventive therapy, its net health effect is negative, or dysfunctional. Social policy based on this functionalist perspective would attempt to integrate all the parts together into a well-organized medical system, which would take the place of the present loose collection of people and organizations dispensing health services.

Conflict Theory

From the conflict perspective, the reason why the U.S. health care delivery system is not an efficient, organized structure delivering health is because various groups are pursuing maximum profit rather than maximum public health (Gray, 1991; Stevens, 1989). Private, for-profit hospitals compete with each other, not just because no authority has arranged them into a better functional system, but because they each want to garner the largest possible share of the billions in hospital revenues. The conflict theory's emphasis on profit explains why many hospitals in underserved rural and inner-city areas have closed in recent years despite a pressing public need. Such hospitals have lost in the competition for profits.

The conflict of maximizing profit versus maximizing public health also applies to physician behavior. Many of the access problems noted above have profit at their root. For example, physicians predominantly locate in suburban, specialized practices because that is where the money is. Similarly, the faulty decisions physicians make leading to illness and premature death often come about because of the haste involved in cramming as many fee-paying patient services into the day as possible. Since time literally is money for physicians, quick surgery and fast-acting drugs are overutilized despite their documented dangers. The fact that the American Medical Association, until the early 1990s, has opposed virtually every public policy that might bear negatively on the economic interests of doctors—including Medicare and Medicaid—is easy to understand from the conflict perspective. Social policy enlightened by conflict theory would attempt to terminate the professional dominance of physicians and other powerful interest groups (Friedson, 1970), and to restructure the system so that the health care needs of consumers are balanced with the profit-seeking motives of producers.

Symbolic Interactionism

This perspective is also useful for understanding health care delivery obstacles. One of these concerns the quality of face-to-face interaction between physician and patient. Many of the physician shortcomings already discussed can be traced in part to the organization of hospital-based medical education that concentrates on technical training and often fails to provide physicians with key doctor–patient interaction skills. The latter have been shown to affect everything from the success of treatment to the likelihood of a malpractice suit (Bush, 1983). Most physicians receive no serious training in these crucial skills and, in fact, tend to grow more distant and authoritarian as they progress through their education and careers. As a result, many physician errors are made because of simple misunderstandings (Davis and Cohen, 1981).

Similarly, the symbolic interactionist perspective helps illuminate why physicians are so loath to discipline incompetent doctors. While physicians are willing to identify their colleagues' errors in small group discussions among their own kind, a "recognition of common interests" prevents them from doing so at official meetings or in public (Millman, 1976).

Integrating the Theories

The three theoretical perspectives can be trained simultaneously on health topics to yield a more complete understanding. Take, for instance, the fact that socioeconomically deprived people have the worst health. According to functionalism, some people end up with poor health because the health care delivery system is socially disorganized and inefficient. In a market economy, impoverished people typically bear the brunt of this inefficiency, but the functionalist point is that the impoverished would get better care if the system could somehow be better organized. The conflict perspective explains that economically deprived people have the worst health because the U.S. health care delivery system is designed to maximize profit rather than public health. Lower classes get the worst health care because they have relatively less money to pay for that care. Finally, symbolic interactionism stresses the fact that nonaffluent people have poor health in part because they approach and use doctors and hospitals less effectively than do the affluent. Socioeconomically deprived people have less control over their lives in general (Kohn, 1969) and, consequently, are less likely to believe that they can control their health by adopting health-producing behaviors (Ross et al., 1983) or by becoming involved in their own treatment, which generally leads to more favorable outcomes (Cockerham, 1988).

SOCIAL CONSEQUENCES OF ILLNESS

Death has a profound impact on an individual's social network. The loss of a breadwinning husband, for example, is particularly devastating for a homemaking widow, because she seldom can reconnect to the network from which her remaining family's income had previously derived. Ben Shahn's *Miners' Wives* (1948) reminds the viewer of the desperate plight of wives and families precipitously cut off from their livelihood. Seen through the doorway are the receding mine owners, who probably brought news of the death, and the seemingly ever-more distant mine, a view symbolizing the loss of that economically vital segment of the family's social network.

This chapter so far has focused mostly on the social *causes* of illness and death. This section turns the tables and examines their social *consequences.*

Illness and death have the power to affect whole societies negatively, especially when they occur on a grand scale. Indeed, historically, disease has been blamed for destroying entire civilizations. For instance, in the sixteenth century, the Aztec civilization was decimated by the Spaniards' introduction of an Old-World disease: smallpox. Many Native American tribes as well as other pre-modern peoples met similar fates as the result of "foreign" diseases for which they had no natural immunity. Short of causing annihilation, diseases can also bring about enormous social change. The Black Death, a plague that killed a third of Europe's population in the fourteenth century, seriously undermined the political, economic, and religious institutions of the medieval world (Kearl, 1989). In short, diseases such as syphilis, cholera, smallpox, and malaria have devastated human societies for many centuries, have played a central role in human affairs, and have changed the course of history (McNeil, 1976).

But it is not just the macrostructure of a society that is damaged. Illness and death have a profound impact on the microstructures as well. Consider, for example, their impact on social networks. Each person's death leads to the partial death of all the deceased's significant others. The death of a close friend, for example, leads to the destruction of a portion of an individual's own self that can never again be reactivated. Similarly, the death of the oldest member of a family (usually a grandmother) can result in the family's disintegration, especially if the only time the siblings, cousins, and different generations come together and interact is at the oldest member's home during holidays or vacations (Kearl, 1989).

In the United States, illness is a major social problem. Many social indicators can be used to probe the problem. Consider first the loss of the most precious resource of all: life. Preventable or postponable illness annually steals about 1.3 million lives and about 23 million years of life from the United States population (Fries, 1989). While the value of lost life to the individuals suffering premature death, to their loved ones, and to society in general is incalculable, the costs of preventable and postponable illness to society have been estimated in dollar terms. The bill now totals about half a trillion dollars annually, an amount greater than the U.S. defense budget.

Another U.S. social indicator of the health-related social problem is the morbidity of the living. Many people are saddled with chronic conditions for years or even decades. Such diseases as multiple sclerosis and arthritis sentence millions of Americans to long-term suffering (NCHS, 1988). The activity of 14 percent (35 million) of the U.S. population is limited by some ill-health condition (NCHS, 1991f). And over 30 million Americans live with chronic, sometimes incapacitating, pain that does not respond to surgery and/or medication (Kotarba, 1983). The very old in particular often endure long, lingering illnesses before they die that tax social and emotional resources (Young and Olson, 1991). The everyday burden of disease can strain—and even sever—the social relationships of patients with their spouses, family members, and friends (DiMatteo and Hays, 1982). Those institutionalized because of their medical conditions face relatively high rates of divorce. Other ill people, who no longer qualify for health insurance on their own, suffer predicaments known as "marriage lock" and "job lock"—that is, they are dependent on their spouse's or employer's insurance plan and, therefore, cannot afford to divorce or change jobs. No wonder health status is the single best predictor of an American's life satisfaction (Fernandez and Kulik, 1981)!

Perhaps the best way to appreciate the social consequences of illness is to focus on specific illnesses. AIDS is of particular interest to sociologists because of its pervasive social consequences (Kaplan et al., 1987). The disease's impact on the gay community has been extraordinary. As Henry (1992, p. 36) notes:

> The [AIDS] crisis turned an often hedonistic male subculture of bar hopping, promiscuity and abundant "recreational" drugs—an endless party centered on the young and restless—into a true community, rich in social services and political lobbies, in volunteerism and civic spirit.

AIDS' impact on U.S. society as a whole also has been profound. Indeed, AIDS has affected virtually all U.S. institutions. Many of these effects are due to AIDS' stigma, which flows from the facts: AIDS is fatal, usually sexually transmitted, and concentrated in two non-mainstream groups; namely, homosexual men and intravenous drug abusers (NCHS, 1989d). The result has been irrational fear, ignorance, and discrimination (Rosenberg, 1989). The fact that thousands of laws have been passed at the federal and state level addressing various AIDS-related issues—both favorable and unfavorable to AIDS-infected individuals—is a clear indicator of massive institutional change. The issues addressed by these laws include antibody testing, blood bank confidentiality, employment, housing, informed consent, insurance, marriage, prisons, and reporting of the disease (Rothstein, 1989). AIDS undoubtedly will produce further change in the United States as the disease continues to spread. One possible institutional repercussion, for instance, might be a revival of otherworldly religions that provide personal consolation for victims and their families, and the assurance of life after death (Platt, 1987).

As shown in Figure 18:4, AIDS also is spreading throughout the world, owing to the increased volume of travelers and immigrants. As it inundates the global village, it elicits responses from national and international institutions.

But it is not strictly illness alone that has consequences for society. The institutional response to illness also has significant social effects. One of

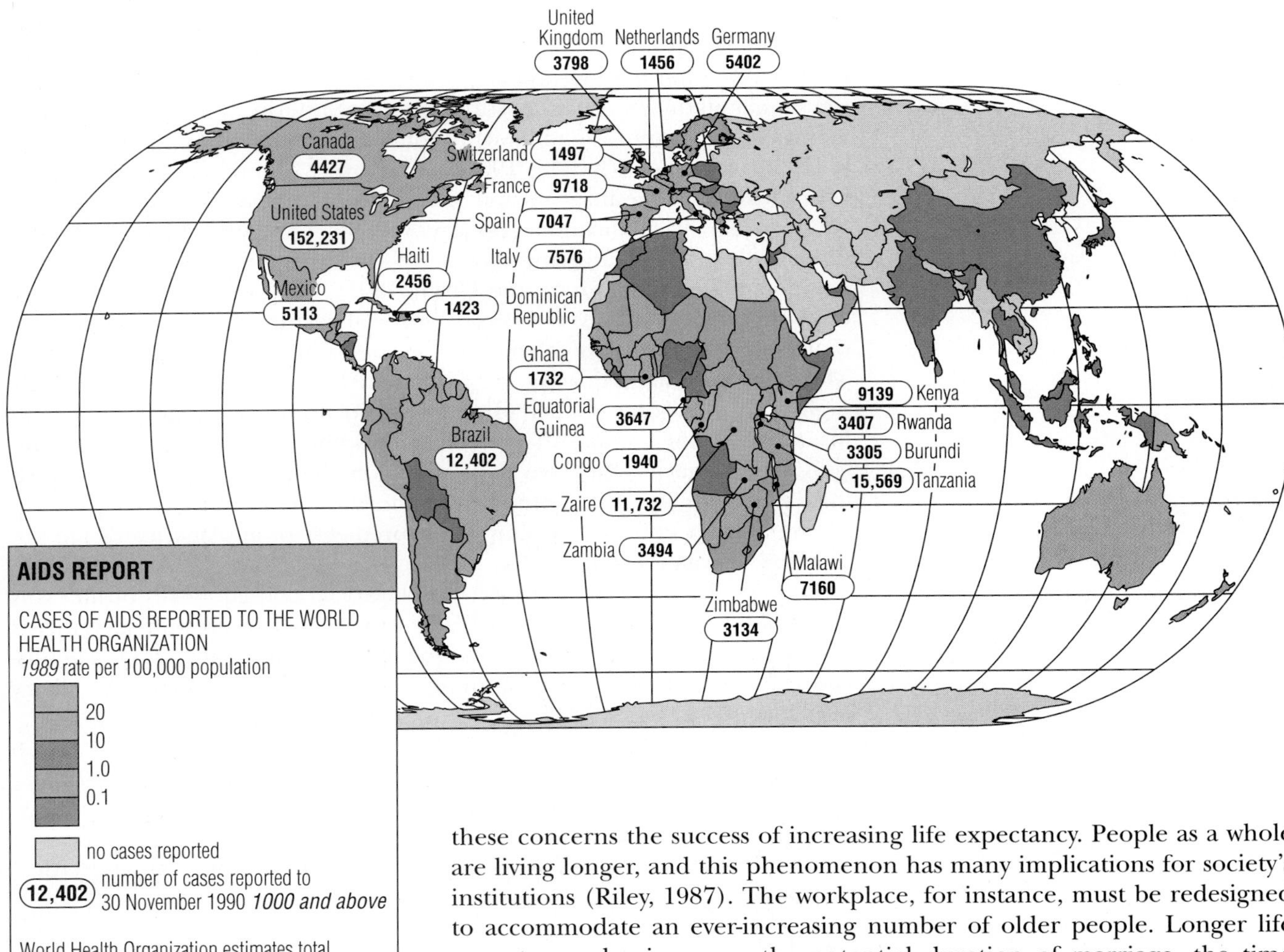

FIGURE 18:4 WORLDWIDE PREVALENCE OF HIV INFECTION
The distribution of the HIV virus at present is very uneven, with the United States and subSaharan Africa greatly overrepresented. However, more than 100 countries have reported AIDS cases, and experts believe that the virus is now present in all nations. Eventually hundreds of millions of people worldwide will be infected with the HIV virus, and the AIDS pandemic almost certainly will have profound social and demographic effects on many societies and on the world's population as a whole.
Source: Michael Kidron and Ronald Segal (1991). *The New State of the World Atlas.* New York: Simon & Schuster, pp 42–43.

these concerns the success of increasing life expectancy. People as a whole are living longer, and this phenomenon has many implications for society's institutions (Riley, 1987). The workplace, for instance, must be redesigned to accommodate an ever-increasing number of older people. Longer life expectancy also increases the potential duration of marriage, the time spouses play nonparental roles, and the probability of divorce (Stub, 1982). In addition, longer life expectancy has increased dramatically the number of physically and mentally disabled people in the population. One study found, for instance, that 19 percent of those age 75 to 84 and 47 percent of those who live past 85 have Alzheimer's disease (Evans, 1989).

THE SOCIAL DEFINITIONS OF ILLNESS

To this point this chapter has dwelled on the social causes and consequences of illness. But there are many other social aspects of health and illness that intrigue sociologists. For example, here is a common student experience:

> You wake up in the morning and notice you do not feel quite right. But in the rush to get to school, you do not have time to dwell on the queasiness that, you reason, will probably go away once you get going and get something in your stomach. But midway through your first class, it dawns on you that you really don't feel good, and you say to yourself, "I must be sick." You may even tell classmates about the situation, and one might suggest that you stop by the campus infirmary. There a physician diagnoses the flu.

This common student experience illustrates the essential distinction between the objective and subjective dimensions of illness. While the virus was in your body making you feel bad (i.e., objectively present) long before you decided that the condition must be illness, you avoided seeing the symptoms as sickness (i.e., a subjective definition) until they interfered with the performance of your student role. From your own experience you probably also know that in the face of an important social event—a final exam or a big party—there is a tendency to delay the subjective definition of sickness much longer than would otherwise be the case. Thus, it is clear that the objective and subjective features of your illness are related, but not in any simple way.

This scenario also suggests a second point: Illness is a sociological as well as a biological phenomenon. Each element of the scenario has a social aspect. You discount the symptoms initially to fulfill the *social* expectations of a student, and you cease overlooking them when you can no longer satisfactorily perform that social role; a *social* friend encourages you to go to the infirmary where a physician confers the official *social* title of "patient." Moreover, you probably contracted the flu in the first place through *socializing* with a schoolmate or family member. In short, illness is a pattern of behavior that is socially sensitive at every stage.

Indeed, social influences operate at even the most basic physiological levels. Consider, for instance, the sensation of pain. Reaction to pain varies by social context. One classic study found that volunteers block out more pain in a pain tolerance test when they think they are competing against another group than when there is no mention of another group (Lambert et al., 1960). Two groups known for their amazing ability to block out pain while performing their respective social roles are football players and combat soldiers.

Another tipoff to the fact that the reaction to pain is not a simple physiological response to excited nerve endings but is in part socially determined is that it varies by ethnic group (Angel and Gronfein, 1988). For instance, Jewish and Italian hospital patients respond to pain in an emotional way, WASP patients are more stoic, and Irish patients try

Social influences have a bearing on the sensation of pain. For example, professional football players are renowned for their amazing ability to block out pain while performing their game roles.

extraordinarily hard to deny the discomfort (Zborowski, 1952). Reaction and sensitivity to pain also varies by age, gender, and the strength of social support networks (Mechanic and Angel, 1987). Thus, the *way* we feel about *what* we feel is fashioned by social groups, social situations, and social roles (Morris, 1991).

Of course, it is not just reaction to pain that has a social component. Other physiological stimuli, which we may or may not call illness, are also in part socially defined (Angel and Thoits, 1987). Native American groups ignore physical states that other Americans define as serious illness, and vice versa. Medical concern about particular symptoms also varies appreciably by socioeconomic group.

One of the general findings of medical sociology that surprises students is that virtually everyone has health problems. Indeed, studies of supposedly healthy populations reveal that over 90 percent of all individuals have physical disorders. Nevertheless, only a small fraction of that number define themselves as sick. You probably think that the seriousness of the disorder is what leads to that definition. But, again, it is not that simple. As in the fictional case of your in-school flu attack, sickness is often defined less by physical "feelings" and more by socially visible "failings." A college professor with chronic, painful arthritis may meet his classes routinely and not consider himself sick, but may call in sick if an effusive head cold makes him look or sound "awful." In short, symptoms that disrupt everyday activities dramatically increase the odds of a "sickness" definition and of medical action (Mechanic, 1978).

Social considerations also are involved in the process of officially labeling illness. A physician's diagnosis is often based on more than just biological knowledge of symptoms. Physicians perform an indisputably social role, and therefore are subject to social demands. For instance, company doctors must adapt their diagnoses to the dual social pressures of the individual's desire to be released from work and management's desire to keep the individual working (Walters, 1982). In evaluating the sanity of a violent criminal, court-appointed psychiatrists must balance the interests of society for justice and security against the criminal's legal and human rights. Even parents factor in their own work schedules and other social obligations in deciding whether or not to declare a child too sick to go to school. The sick label is thus more than a matter of physical symptoms or scientific diagnosis. Even the objective state of death can be medically ambiguous (e.g., when can a person in a coma be considered legally dead?), and is therefore socially defined by state death statutes.

sick role—**a pattern of behavior expected of someone who is ill.**

Once the social label of sickness is affixed, the labeled individual faces a revised set of social expectations (Parsons, 1951). The **sick role** confers the right to be excused from one's ordinary social responsibilities such as attending class or going to work. The sick role additionally entitles the individual to sympathy and coddling. In exchange, the individual must concede the unwelcome nature of the disability, and do whatever is necessary to expedite recovery and the resumption of normal social duties.

An individual who is ill but who does not receive the official social label of being sick faces another set of social consequences. For example, an obese person can be stigmatized and unpopular for violating cultural norms of appearance and, at least apparently, of self-control, even though the overweight may be due to a glandular disorder (DeJong, 1980). Public knowledge of such disorders can lessen such negative consequences. Thus the public definition of illness has crucial consequences for attitudes toward an ill individual.

SUBJECTIVE DIMENSIONS OF HEALTH AND ILLNESS

This chapter has cited many statistics that show that overall health in the United States has improved dramatically in recent decades. Yet public opinion polls find that the proportion of Americans who feel satisfied with their health has fallen sharply over the same period. People now report far more symptoms and episodes of illness as well as greater disability and more days in bed owing to disease than they did in the past (Barsky, 1988; Glassner, 1988). In short, the healthiest people in history are haunted increasingly and inordinately by the possibility of sickness. Why?

Americans are overly concerned about their health in part because the media constantly bombards them with alarming news reports of such hazards as pesticides and carcinogens in food, of pollutants in tap water, and of asbestos fibers falling from ceilings. As a result of the high *visibility* of disease phenomena, people are more afraid then they need be about the risks encountered in daily lives.

The mass media's publicizing of real or potential medical breakthroughs not only heightens the visibility of health issues, but also creates an *expectation* of imminent cure. The attention given such reports explains the optimism shared by more than 75 percent of Americans that the cure for cancer is just around the corner. Past medical successes also play into these heightened expectations. The virtual elimination of polio, for example, has saved the lives of hundreds of thousands while convincing millions of the omnipotence of medical science. Given our apparent capacity to conquer diseases, unconquered killers like AIDS seem all the more an outrage (Figure 18:5).

FIGURE 18:5 OBJECTIVE AND SUBJECTIVE DIMENSIONS: THE CASE OF AIDS

The subjective dimension of the AIDS epidemic is much greater than its objective dimension, owing to the operation of the intervening variables—visibility, expectations, and values.

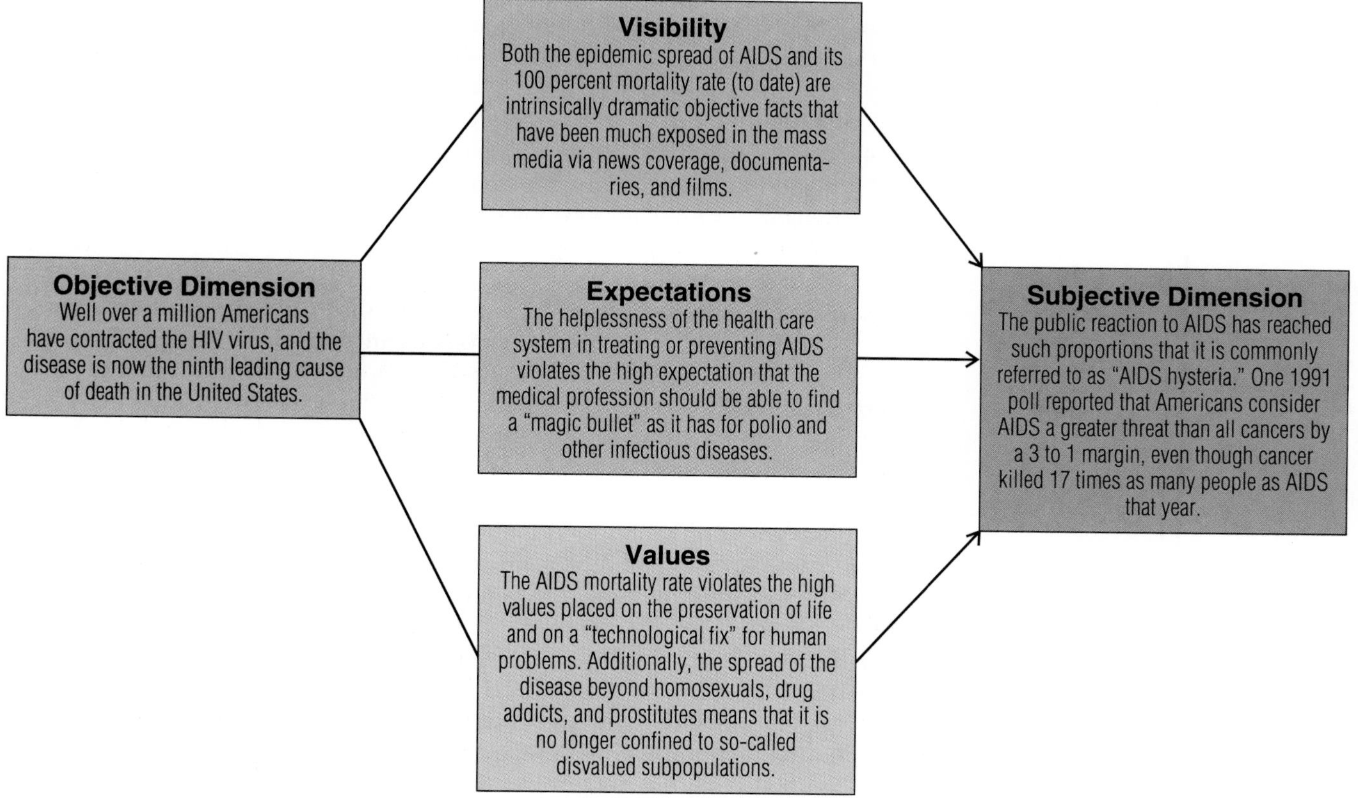

The increased subjective dimension of health problems also comes about because more things are defined as illness today than in the past (Barsky, 1988). Such conditions as baldness, insomnia, snoring, interpersonal violence, even aging—which used to be considered simply as unfortunate miseries of life—have all been redefined as diseases. Given that these things are now "medical" phenomena, the assumption is that physicians can diagnose, treat, and cure them. These heightened expectations fly in the face of the fact that there is usually no medical panacea for these conditions.

The expectation that all our health problems should be curable arises in part from the fundamental U.S. *value* that humans should dominate nature. It also is related to the U.S. value of self-determination, which in this context means the ability to control one's own health. Good health itself has assumed a moral dimension, and proper eating and exercise have been turned into "moral acts." Indeed, for many Americans keeping fit has become a "quasi-religious" quest, and illness is defined not as a natural process but as the outcome of some "immoral" action. If you get sick, you are to blame because you should have exercised or eaten properly. Given these values it is not surprising that insurance companies are now questioning their coverage of "self-inflicted" illness such as lung cancer in smokers and brain injury to unhelmeted motorcyclists.

SUMMARY

1. Sociology is concerned with the social causes and consequences of health and illness. Health is a state of complete mental, physical, and social wellbeing. Illness is the absence of health.
2. Life expectancy in all societies is lower than that which is biologically possible owing to social factors.
3. Causes of death can be divided into three types: (a) genetic, (b) environmental, and (c) social. Social causes can be further divided into two subtypes: (e) lifestyle causes and (f) health care system causes.
4. The principal unhealthy lifestyle factors include those related to tobacco, alcohol, and drug abuse and diet, exercise, stress, and social networks. Other lifestyle factors such as sexual behavior (see Chapter 19) and environmental pollution (see Chapter 21) are discussed elsewhere in this text.
5. Lifestyle factors causing illness and death do not simply flow from the freely chosen personal actions of an individual. They are also products of the nature of the society in which the individual lives.
6. The health care system in the United States has performed extraordinarily well over the past century. Premature death and illness have been reduced dramatically, and Americans now live decades longer. But the system does have serious shortcomings, probably the most important of which is its inability to give everyone in U.S. society equal access to quality health care. This inability stems partly from the disorganized and fragmented nature of the health care system itself.
7. Reform of the health care system will likely occur in two stages. In the first stage health care will be expanded to cover more of those people not now insured. In the second stage, a new system will set an upper limit for health care spending, and allocate the subsequent limited resources by government authority on the basis of commonly agreed-upon principles.

8. Life expectancy varies substantially by social categories such as age, gender, socioeconomic status, race, and ethnicity. These differences come about as a result of the differential operation of genetic, environmental, lifestyle, and health care system factors.
9. Functionalists note that health care activities are scattered widely over society's institutions, and that many dysfunctions can be attributed to the lack of functional integration available in a single, specialized institution.
10. From the conflict perspective, the reason the U.S. health care system is not an efficient, organized structure delivering health is that various groups are pursuing maximum profit rather than maximum public health.
11. Symbolic interactionists focus on such things as the quality of interaction between physician and patient, and how this relates to the effectiveness of the health care system.
12. Illness and death have the power to affect whole societies negatively, and also have a profound impact on microstructures like social networks.
13. Social phenomena are not just causes and consequences of illness. There are many other aspects of health and illness that have a sociological component, including the very definition of illness itself.
14. Although overall health in the United States has improved dramatically in recent decades, public opinion polls find that the proportion of Americans who feel satisfied with their health has fallen sharply. Sociological analysis can explain this paradox by throwing the spotlight on the three determinants of illness' subjective dimension: visibility, expectations, and values.

Chapter 19

Personal Perspective

I remember when I first found out about intercourse. It occurred in the 1950s when I was about 10 years old. I was sitting in my backyard with my best friend, Edward, when he asked me in a challenging way: "What's the dirtiest word you know?" That was a very interesting question to a 10-year-old, and required some thinking. I mentally ticked off the possibilities in my dirty-word repertoire (boob, ass, prick, etc.) and finally settled on "shit." "I know one dirtier than that," Edward blurted out. "What is it?" I said. "F——!" I didn't know what that word meant, but I did know the instant he said it that he had me beat. Maybe it was just the way he said it, but the word had a certain ring to it. I asked him what it meant, but he didn't know either. He just knew it was really dirty. Needless to say, I made it my immediate business to find out what the word meant by asking older kids until I found one who knew. "That's when you get up real close to a girl," the older kid said, "and knee her hard in the groin." I thanked him for "cluing me in," and I remember thinking that the act did sound kind of erotic. Being the proud bearer of this fascinating knowledge, I quickly transmitted it to my age mates until I eventually ran into a guy who knew the word's real meaning and told me. I remember being thunderstruck. I could not have been more surprised. For me, intercourse came totally from "out of the blue."

JAM

The Sociology of Sexuality

COLLEGE students are often surprised to learn that human sexuality is a sociological topic. They generally consider sexuality to be essentially a biological, genetic, or "natural" phenomenon rather than a social one. To them sex is something studied in a health course. But research on sexuality indicates that it is both a biological and social phenomenon, and that sociological factors are at least as important as biological factors in determining the nature of sexual behavior.

heterosexuality—sexual orientation toward the opposite sex.

homosexuality—sexual orientation toward the same sex.

bisexuality—sexual orientation toward both sexes.

Take, for example, **heterosexuality**. Because most people are attracted to members of the opposite sex, it is commonly thought that heterosexuality is hard-wired within human genes. But this view ignores the fact that many people are attracted to the same sex (**homosexuality**), to both sexes (**bisexuality**), to other species *(beastiality)*, and to such inanimate objects as statues *(pygmalionism)* and fires *(pyromania)*. Still other people are attracted sexually to no one and nothing. This wide variance in sexual preferences indicates that sexual preference is highly flexible and to a very large extent learned (Gregersen, 1982).

But it is not just sexual preference that is flexible and learned. Virtually all human sexual behavior is taught by society. Indeed, sociologist Kingsley Davis (1976) notes that without learning about sexuality, "human beings would not even know how to copulate."

Most college students find this all hard to believe, right? But think back to the time when you first learned about intercourse. Weren't you surprised? Didn't you react with shocked disbelief the way child characters on television often do, who typically say, "That's disgusting" or "My parents

Children learn a lot about sexuality from their friends. This is true in the United States and in other cultures, such as the environment of Rome's Piazza di Spagna.

Sexual behavior varies enormously from one society to another. Premarital sexual "horsing around" is easier in the United States than it is in Poltava, a province in the northwestern part of the former Soviet Union. Indeed, to kiss a young woman in Poltava, a young man must have considerable riding skills. In this photo, Nicholai Zazula makes his move in mid-gallop in the traditional festival game "Kiss a Girl." Once she has been caught, the frightened Anzhela Klalimova tries to slow the pace.

would never do that." Did knowledge about intercourse come to you completely "from out of the blue," as it did for the 10-year-old in the "Personal Perspective"? If you answered no to these questions, it may be because you are a relatively young college student who grew up in the sex-satiated 1970s and 1980s. You probably got little doses of sexual information from the time you were very young, mostly from television, in the form of rock videos and PG and R rated films. Moreover, many of your childhood homes probably contained men's magazines such as *Playboy* and other overtly sexual material. You learned about sex gradually, almost the same way you learned language.

But if you answered yes to the above questions, you are probably a nontraditional college student whose childhood, like that of the authors, took place before the 1970s. Prior to the 1970s there was a conspiracy on the part of society to keep children ignorant about sex for as long as possible (Gagnon, 1977; Money, 1988). And it worked. Remember, in the 1950s there were no hard-core porn movies either in the theaters or on videocassette, no mass-market men's magazines (*Playboy* magazine was in its infancy and didn't have full frontal nudity until the late 1960s), no cable television with its uncut films, and virtually no sex of any sort on regular television.

In short, without sexuality being taught, it is possible for human beings to have no idea about intercourse until well into adolescence and even beyond. Indeed, in the past (and in some present-day cultures such as rural China) many women only learned about intercourse around the time of their marriage (Pearsall, 1969). King Henry VIII's fourth wife, Ann of Cleves, for example, was so ignorant about sex that she thought her never-consummated marriage had been consummated by merely sleeping in the same bed as Henry on their wedding night (Reuters News Service, 1991). Even in the United States today some adults are incredibly ignorant about sex (Kinsey Institute, 1990). For example, in one medical study of 1,000 married women having difficulty achieving pregnancy, fully 5 percent were found to be virgins who thought they had been having intercourse (McFalls, 1979b).

All of this is evidence that intercourse is not instinctual but socially learned. As Davis (1971) suggests, if human beings were raised in a social vacuum and never taught about intercourse, they might never know about copulation. Of course performing such an experiment on humans would be unethical. But similar experiments have been conducted on higher primates. For example, Rhesus monkeys raised in isolation never spontaneously achieve the proper positioning for intercourse and fail to reproduce once they are removed from isolation. Moreover, it is then too late even to teach most male monkeys how to copulate (Goldfoot et al., 1984; Harlow and Mears, 1979). Thus the premise that sexual behavior is largely a learned process comes not just from sociological research but from research in such fields as zoology, psychology, sexology, and the medical sciences.

Perhaps the best sociological evidence for sexual behavior being a learned phenomenon comes from observations that sexual behavior varies enormously from one society to another. We examine this variation both cross-culturally and historically later in this chapter. It is worth noting here, however, that one thing common to all societies is the cultural regulation of sexual behavior (Davenport, 1978; Davis, 1976). Even "free sex" subcultures find it necessary to control aspects of sexual behavior. For example, in the Oneida community, a nineteenth-century American subculture where marriage was forbidden and adults were encouraged to mate with many different partners, a committee served as an intermediary between the propositioners and the propositioned members, set time limits for sexual encounters, and made sure members did not monopolize other members (Kephart and Zellner, 1991). The fact that all societies regulate sexual behavior is a dead giveaway concerning its adaptable and learned nature. After all, if we were all programmed by our genes to behave in a certain sexual way, there would be no need for social regulations to ensure that we did so. Genetically programmed behavior would be more or less automatic.

Incidentally, this illustrates another relevant sociological principle; that is, that societies do not regulate human activities that are not going to occur very often anyway. When societies do regulate some activity, it is usually because there is a real social need to do so. Incest is a case in point. Societies have both formal and informal regulations against incest because the behavior, contrary to conventional wisdom, is not precluded by our genes. That is, humans are not innately disinclined toward it. Societies must teach their inhabitants that incest is improper, and societies must institute regulations to ward off and punish deviance.

As noted above, sexual behavior has a biological as well as a social component. The social learning process is superimposed upon the biological component of sexuality, which is responsible for the nature of human anatomy and the basic, undirected human sex drive. This sex drive is evident in human beings even before birth. Male fetuses, for example, have erections, and children of all ages participate in a variety of sexual play activities such as masturbation, playing "doctor," and "strip poker" (Gagnon, 1977; Greenwald and Leitenberg, 1989; Knudsen, 1987).

The basic human sex drive can be compared to the hunger drive (Gregersen, 1982; Robertson, 1987). Humans have a biologically based hunger drive, but are taught through socialization what items are appropriate to eat. The learning child is steered away not only from inedible things but from edible things that are "improper" to eat. These lessons vary from society to society. You, for instance, probably do not consider caterpillars to be food. But to caterpillar lovers in countries such as Zambia, they taste just fine, especially if they are big, firm, and hairy. Monkeys, pythons, and rats are also a part of the diet in Zambia (Zucchino, 1988), as are spiders, puppies, and lizards in other parts of the world. Indeed, human flesh is part of the (at least ritual) diet in some societies (Harner, 1977; Harris, 1988), but in most other societies people would rather die than eat another human's flesh, which is what happened to a group of soccer players whose plane crashed in the Andes during the 1970s. Some of them starved to death rather than eat the frozen bodies of their dead comrades. You probably would retch if forced to eat caterpillars or puppies, to say nothing about humans, and you would probably argue vigorously that you had a "natural" or instinctive dislike for such food. But it is clear from the examples above that your squeamishness would not be a genetic instinct but a learned pattern superimposed on a biological need. The same is true of sexuality. Society takes the basic undirected sex drive and, through socialization, directs it toward socially approved sexual behavior and away from potentially sexual but socially forbidden behavior.

Thus human sexuality illustrates yet another sociological principle: Much of the human behavior that people generally assume is "natural" or instinctual is really socially programmed. We have encountered instances of this principle elsewhere in this book, such as in Chapter 14, where it was noted that romantic love is a social creation, although, like sex and hunger, one for which humans have an innate potential (Singer, 1987).

Before moving on it is important to note that some scholars argue that basic sexual orientation—whether a person is a homosexual or a heterosexual—might be due to genetic or other biological factors (Gallagher et al., 1993). Although there is no conclusive evidence supporting this position, the latest research increasingly suggests that sexual orientation may be an innate trait, at least in some individuals (Hamer et al., 1993). Nevertheless, even if this possibility eventually proved true, the fact would remain that *most* sexual behavior is learned.

In sum, while the potential for sexual behavior is provided by human biology, social factors largely determine how that potential is expressed (Davenport, 1977; DeLamater, 1981). Thus sexual behavior is for the most part a social creation.

THE SOCIAL IMPORTANCE OF SEXUAL BEHAVIOR

Sexual behavior is not merely a social creation—it is an exceptionally important social creation. Indeed, some sociologists contend that sexual behavior may be the most important of all human activities. This is because, as Smith (1990, p. 1) notes:

> It is the process by which the species is reproduced, is the central behavior around which families are formed, and is a key component in the emotional lives of individuals. It is also central to a number of social and medical problems: marital difficulties and divorce; the crimes of rape, incest, and child molestation; the reproductive issues of infertility, sterility, contraception, unwanted pregnancies, and abortion; and sexually transmitted diseases (STDs).

Another expert (Robinson, 1976, p. vii) notes that "sex has always been a great issue, as important to the human experience as making a living, conquering nature, or maintaining social order." In fact, some social scientists (e.g., Freud, 1961; Katchadourian, 1972) contend that social order and sexuality are so inextricably linked that society itself is not possible without the regulation (or as Freud would say, the repression) of sexuality. This is one reason that, as noted above, all societies regulate sexual behavior.

Writing in a college text that sex is important may be a clear violation of the rule, "Don't preach to the converted." College men, after all, think

TABLE 19:1 Frequency of Sexual Intercourse during the Past Year among the Sexually Active Crosstabulated by Marital Happiness and Race

FREQUENCY OF SEX	MARITAL HAPPINESS								
	WHITE			NON-WHITE			TOTAL		
Count **ROW PCT**	Very Happy	Pretty Happy	Not too Happy	Very Happy	Pretty Happy	Not too Happy	Very Happy	Pretty Happy	Not too Happy
Once a week or less	102 **60.7**	61 **36.3**	5 **3.0**	7 **46.7**	8 **53.3**	—	109 **59.6**	69 **37.7**	5 **2.7**
More than once a week	64 **80.0**	16 **20.0**	—	10 **62.5**	5 **31.3**	1 **6.3**	74 **77.1**	21 **21.9**	1 **1.0**

$n = 279$

Main Point: Married people who have sex more than once a week tend to be much happier than those who do not.

Source: General Social Survey, 1990.

about sex about once every 10 minutes (Nastasee, 1990). But even college students do not fully appreciate the important and extensive role sexuality plays in their lives. For example, when asked, "What is the most important objective in life?" most college students usually answer "happiness." Yet few of them are aware of the strong positive relationship between frequent sexual intercourse and, say, marital happiness, as revealed by the GSS data in Table 19:1. Similarly, few college students are aware that one out of every 200 college men is infected with the sexually transmitted AIDS virus (Gayle, 1990), or that the disease is the fifth leading cause of death for women of childbearing age. In short, few students are aware that sexual behavior is bound up inextricably with so many of their most important goals such as life, liberty (sexual regulations restrict liberty), and the pursuit of happiness.

RESEARCH ON SEXUAL BEHAVIOR

Despite its incredible importance, less systematic social scientific research has been carried out on sexual behavior than on any other important topic (Smith, 1990). This is due in part to the fact that sexual behavior is not easy to study, for it is difficult to observe sexual activities directly, and many people are unwilling to discuss them with an outsider. Moreover, research on some topics such as child sexuality is virtually taboo (Money, 1988). Nevertheless, enough research has been carried out to inform us about sexual behavior both in the United States and elsewhere. Each sociological research strategy has contributed to this body of knowledge.

Experimental Research

pornography—written or visual materials intended chiefly to arouse sexual excitement.

Experimental research on sexual behavior is typified by the work of Malamuth and Donnerstein (1984) on the relationship between viewing violent **pornography** and subsequent aggression against women. Their research indicates that it is the violent rather than the sexual aspect of violent pornography that produces adverse effects. For example, in one set of experiments Donnerstein (1983) showed that films containing sexual violence against women increased male viewers' acceptance of such myths as "Women really want to be raped and may actually enjoy it," and also boosted the percentage of viewers who admitted that they would rape women if they were certain they would not be apprehended. In another set of laboratory experiments, viewing sexually violent films reduced men's sympathy toward rape victims and increased men's aggressive behavior against women (Donnerstein and Linz, 1984).

Participant Observation

A famous example of participant observation research on sexual behavior is the work of Laud Humphreys (1970). Humphreys, a sociologist and a Protestant minister, wanted to gain knowledge about that subgroup of homosexual men who frequent public places such as bathhouses and porno shops (or "tearooms") for the purpose of engaging in anonymous sex. To conduct this research, Humphreys went to a men's room that served as a tearoom in the middle of a St. Louis park. There he took the role of the "watchqueen" or lookout, the person who stands in the doorway and alerts participants inside to police raids, the approach of juveniles, and other problems. The watchqueen role also permitted Humphreys to observe the sexual behavior within the tearoom without having to reveal his identity as an outsider.

Assuming the role of watchqueen also permitted Humphreys to note the license plate numbers of participants and subsequently to trace their names and addresses. About a year later he visited and interviewed many of these men, supposedly about subjects having nothing to do with homosexual behavior. In the process he learned a good deal about their general social characteristics. One surprising finding was that the majority of these men were married with children and, from all outward appearances, were indistinguishable from heterosexuals.

Human Relations Area Files—an extensive compilation of ethnographic data on sexuality as well as on other topics such as subsistence, material culture, and social structure.

Participant observation methods have been relied upon heavily for the study of sexual behavior in other cultures. Much of this research is ethnographic fieldwork carried out by anthropologists who often live in the society under study for substantial periods of time. The cross-cultural examples used in this chapter come primarily from the **Human Relations Area Files** (Murdock, 1957), and from a number of other compilations, most notably those of Ford and Beach (1978), Davenport (1978), Gregersen (1982), and Frayser (1985).

While cross-cultural research clearly shows the amazing diversity of human sexual behavior, one research limitation stems from the fact that sexual activity occurs in private in most societies. Although anthropologists do enter into many intimate areas of the lives of their subjects, sexual behavior often remains off limits. Anthropologists must usually rely on what non-Western people tell them about sexual behavior, and this information is obviously subject to some distortion. Moreover, because most anthropological research has been conducted by males (Margaret Mead is a notable exception) who got their information from talking to male informants, these accounts of sexual behavior have a two-layer masculine bias. Knowledge about how women experience, interpret, and communicate about sex is often missing, and hence our knowledge about sexual behavior in these non-Western societies is incomplete (Gray and Wolfe, 1988).

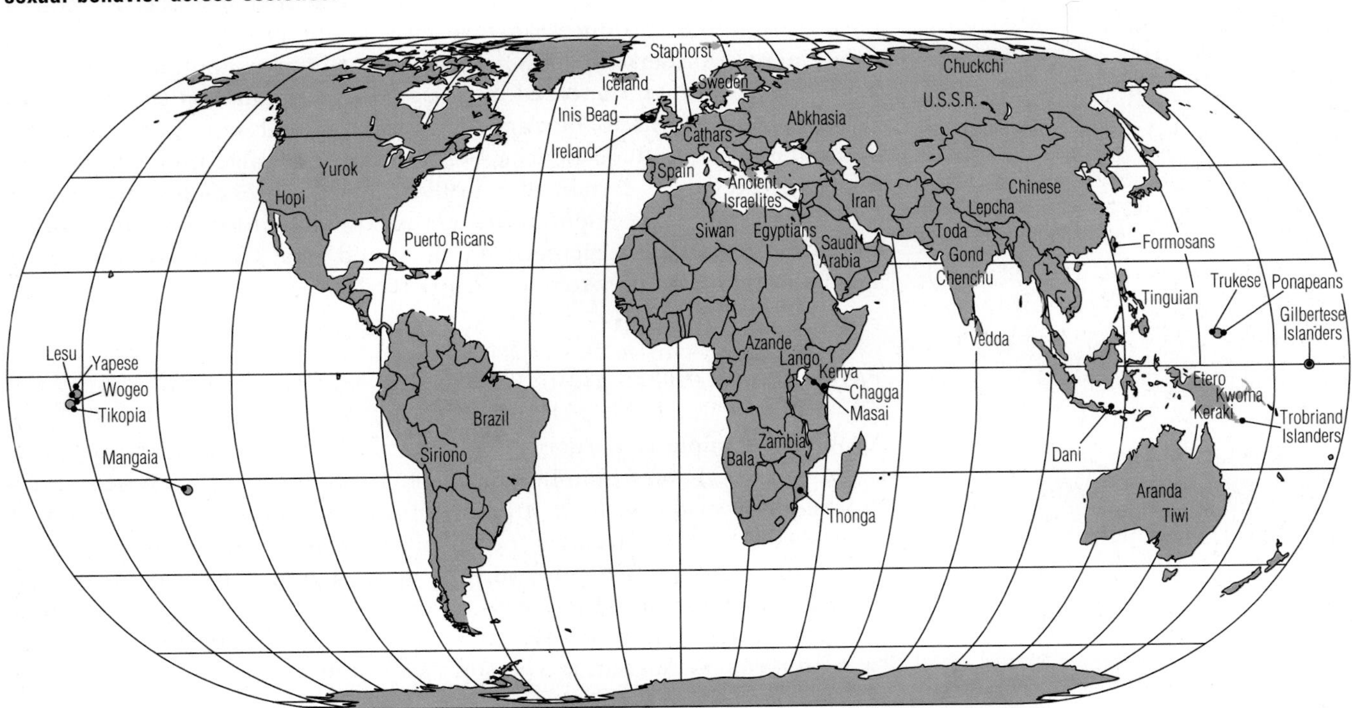

FIGURE 19:1 SOCIOLOGY OF SEXUALITY IN GLOBAL PERSPECTIVE: LOCATIONS OF SOCIETIES DISCUSSED IN CHAPTER 19

Our discussion highlights the diversity of sexual behavior across societies.

Standards of female beauty vary greatly over time. Marilyn Monroe, a film star in the U.S. during the 1950s, had a much fuller figure than is fashionable in the 1990s. Today, extremely slender supermodels like Kate Moss are popular.

ethnocentrism—**the belief in the inherent superiority of one's own group and culture.**

Survey Research

Survey research is the major source of data on contemporary sexual behavior. Fifty years ago sex surveys were almost unimaginable, but are now commonplace. One problem with these surveys, however, is that their findings are often conflicting (Elson, 1990). For example, in one 1988 survey by Abigail Van Buren (alias, "Dear Abby") 15 percent of wives said they had been unfaithful to their spouses, but in another survey by Shere Hite (1987) 70 percent of women married five years or more said they were having sex outside of their marriages. Obviously, both these findings cannot be accurate. And in this instance probably neither is because both surveys employed fundamentally unscientific and flawed methodologies (Smith, 1988). The fact is that most sex surveys, especially popular magazine surveys, use techniques that virtually guarantee unrepresentative and biased results.

Fortunately, however, questions about sex have been asked by national surveys that focused primarily on other topics, and data from these high-quality surveys are utilized in this chapter wherever possible. Of particular value are the data obtained from a battery of questions incorporated into the 1989 General Social Survey.

SEXUAL BEHAVIOR: A CROSS-CULTURAL PERSPECTIVE

One benefit of studying sociology is that it tends to minimize ethnocentrism. You are almost certainly ethnocentric when it comes to understanding sexual behavior because you probably have only encountered sexuality as it is expressed in U.S. culture. But as this section reveals, sexual behavior is culturally diverse and there is no agreed-upon "best" or "natural" pattern. Even such things as sex appeal and beauty vary greatly across cultures and over time (see Box 19:1).

The Restrictive/Permissive Continuum

The most fundamental question all societies must answer about sexuality is just *how sexual* the society should be. For the United States in the 1990s the answer to that question is "very sexual." We believe almost every individual should be sexually active at the appropriate times in the life cycle. We are generally opposed to sexual self-denial and celibacy. We pressure people to marry and remarry. We see abstinence as an intolerable form of contraception. We are, in short, a relatively pro-sex or sexually "permissive" society. If you want to place that fact on a personal level, think about what the reaction of your parents, friends, or spouse would be if you were to announce that you planned to be celibate for the rest of your life!

Of course all societies are not sexual to the same degree as our culture is. Some societies are rabidly anti-sex, whereas other societies are even more pro-sex than U.S. society. One way to visualize this variation is through the use of the simplified continuum in Figure 19:2, which extends from the most super-restrictive, anti-sex societies at one pole to the most permissive, pro-sex societies at the other. All societies can be placed somewhere along this continuum depending on the nature of their sexual values and norms. Social scientists have found that societies tend to be consistent with respect to these norms. Those that have restrictive attitudes toward premarital sex, for example, tend to forbid activities such as extramarital sex as well as homosexuality (Gray and Wolfe, 1988).

FIGURE 19:2 THE PERMISSIVE/RESTRICTIVE CONTINUUM OF SEXUAL NORMS

Societies differ in general attitudes toward sexuality. Some societies are anti-sex, whereas others are much more pro-sex than the United States today.

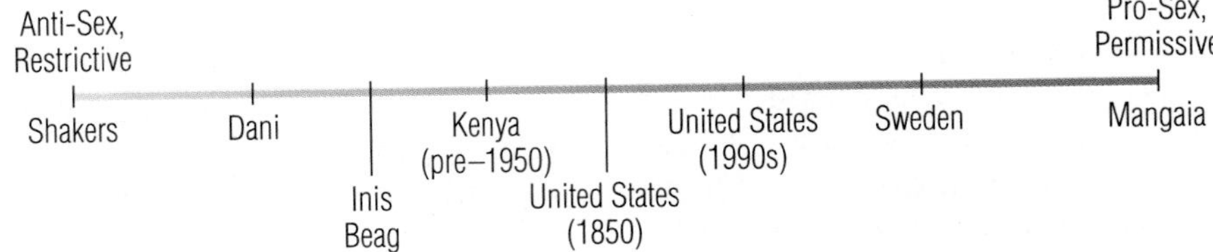

The Shakers and the Father Divine Movement, both U.S. religious subcultures, are good examples of the most anti-sex societies. In fact, the Shakers are probably the most anti-sex group of all time. Like the Cathars who lived in medieval Europe, the Shakers believe that the flesh is evil and that having children just creates more innocent spirits embedded in the flesh (Gagnon, 1977). Since sex is the root of this evil, they prohibit it as well as all other physical contact between men and women. Similarly, the Father Divine Movement believes sex is unclean and a mark of depravity. Married couples who join the group are physically separated, and each spouse lives a celibate life apart from the other. Without childbearing both the Shakers and the Father Divine Movement rely on the acquisition of converts, but the number of converts has dwindled in recent decades and both groups are dying out (Kephart and Zellner, 1991).

BOX 19:1 SOCIOLOGICAL IMAGINATION IN FICTION

Cultural Variation in Standards of Beauty

An excellent example of cultural variation in sexuality concerns the way the body, particularly the female body, is eroticized (Gregersen, 1982). Standards of female beauty vary greatly over time and across cultures (Davenport, 1978; Frayser, 1985). In modern societies today, forces such as advertising and entertainment produce vivid notions of sexualized beauty that continue to change, placing stress on women to assume the body image or type currently in style (Mazur, 1986; Wolf, 1991). Some women overconform, leading to health problems and even death. Hysteria, which was common among women early in the twentieth century, was an exaggeration of that era's fragile feminine ideal. "Bosom anxieties" afflicted many small-breasted women in the 1950s and 1960s when having large breasts was desirable. Even today, despite potentially severe adverse complications, more than a million U.S. women have had breast enlargement operations. Anorexia and bulimia, conditions barely heard of two decades ago, are pathological responses to the "trim hips, slender body" ideal of beauty prevalent in the 1990s.

The following passage, taken from James Clavell's novel *Tai Pan* (1966), accurately describes a standard of beauty in China in vogue as recently as a half century ago. Not incidentally, it is also another example of how such standards can be harmful to women.

May-May had bound feet. They were only three inches long. When Struan had bought her five years ago he had cut off the bandages and been horrified at the deformity that ancient cus-

The Shakers are probably the most anti-sex group of all time. Their anti-sex stance determines many of the features of Shaker society. For example, Shaker buildings typically have separate doors, stairs, and living quarters for men and women, and wide halls to prevent even their clothes from brushing those of the opposite sex. If a pregnant woman joined the sect and subsequently gave birth to a girl, that child might live her whole life without ever touching a male.

BOX 19:1 SOCIOLOGICAL IMAGINATION IN FICTION ***continued***

toms had decreed was a girl's essential sign of beauty—tiny feet. Only a girl with bound feet—lotus feet—could be a wife or concubine. Those with normal feet were peasants, servants, low-class prostitutes, amahs or workers, and despised. . . .

Struan had asked her then, using Gordon Chen as interpreter, how it was done. She had told him proudly that her mother had begun to bind her feet when she was six. "The bindings were bandages two inches wide and twelve feet long and they were damp. My mother wrapped them tightly around my feet—around the heel and over the instep and under the foot, bending the four small toes under the sole of the foot and leaving the big toe free. As the bandages dried they tightened and the pain was terrible. Over the months and years the heel closes near to the toe and the instep arches. Once a week the bandages are taken off for a few minutes and the feet cleaned. After some years the little toes become shriveled and dead and are removed. When I was twelve I could walk quite well, but my feet were still not small enough. It was then that my mother consulted a woman wise in the art of the foot binding. On my twelfth birthday the wise woman came to our house with a sharp knife and ointments. She made a deep cut across the middle of the soles of my feet. This deep slit allowed the heel to be squeezed closer to the toes, when the bandages were replaced."

"What cruelty! Ask her how she stood the pain." Struan remembered her quizzical look as Chen translated the question and as she replied in charming singsong. "She says, for every pair of bound feet there is a lake of tears. But what are tears and pain? Now I am not ashamed to let anyone measure my feet." . . .

"Ask her if her feet hurt her now." "They will always hurt her, sir. But I assure you it would pain her much more if she had big, disgusting feet."

Critical Thinking Questions

1. How would a conflict theorist explain why societies typically place more importance on the shape of women's bodies as opposed to men's bodies?
2. How would a conflict theorist explain why women try to conform to cultural standards of beauty even at the expense of their own health.

Source: Excerpted from *Tai Pan* by James Clavell (1966). New York: Dell, pp. 118–19.

Moving rightward along the continuum, we encounter groups like the Dani, a primitive Indonesian society that, while not anti-sex, is relatively indifferent about it. Husbands and wives sleep in separate men's and women's houses, often not even in the same village, and may go for as long as five years without having sex.

Next along the continuum come societies such as Inis Beag, a society situated on an island off the coast of Ireland, whose sexual script is probably somewhat reminiscent of that of Western societies of the past (Gagnon, 1977). Inis Beag is an economically deprived, Roman Catholic society, one in which only some people are expected to be sexual. This is because resources such as farmland are scarce, only a fraction of the men inherit property, and only they are expected to marry and raise families. The remaining men (and women) are expected to remain celibate for their entire lives owing to strong norms against all forms of sexuality outside of marriage. Within marriage only intercourse is permitted, and that is infrequent. Even nudity in the presence of a spouse is taboo (Messenger, 1969).

Moving farther rightward along the continuum we find societies like Kenya in which men, until a few decades ago, traditionally did not marry and begin their sexual lives until around age 30, after they had proven themselves by killing a lion or an enemy and had acquired enough cattle and land to support a wife. Moreover, during the time his wife breast-fed a child, a period that could last up to five years, a Kenyan man was expected to live apart from her and to abstain from sex.

Most modern societies fall on the continuum around the same place as the United States in the 1990s, although there is some scatter. Countries such as Ireland and Spain fall to the left of the United States, while those such as Sweden and Iceland fall to the right (Linner, 1972). Communist societies, such as the former Soviet Union and China, and fundamentalist Islamic nations, such as Saudi Arabia and Iran, are much more sexually restrictive than capitalist societies.

At the extreme right or permissive pole of the continuum are the hypersexual societies of the world. The Mangaians, who inhabit one of the Polynesian islands, are a good example (Gagnon, 1977). Sexual pleasure for both genders is a high priority among the Mangaians, and most forms of sexuality are encouraged. Public nudity is common. There is no formal courtship such as exists in the United States, and premarital intercourse occurs spontaneously and virtually indiscriminantly. In fact, there is a practice called "night crawling" in which an adolescent boy enters another family's hut and has intercourse with an adolescent girl while her parents politely ignore it. These young men go from hut to hut and have sex with several young women on a given night. Adults also engage in frequent and exceptionally vigorous coital activity. In general, norms favoring such practices as adult–child sex, polygamy, extramarital sex, and spouse-borrowing tend to be found in such ultra-permissive societies (Gray and Wolfe, 1988).

Given our apparently sex-saturated culture, it may have come as a surprise to you that the United States is not one of the most pro-sex societies. True, we do have our own group of sexual "maniacs." In fact, about 6 percent of the U.S. population have been characterized as sex addicts; that is, people so obsessed with sex that they have allowed it to be the governing principle of their lives (Carnes, 1983, 1988). No doubt you have encountered a few. But it must be remembered that our traditional culture has many anti-sex elements that are still influential. This explains in part why many Americans are not active sexually. Indeed, according to GSS data, fully 22 percent of adult Americans had no sex partners during 1989, and those who did indulged in intercourse on average only about once a week

sexual dysfunction—problems affecting sexual performance such as impotence and lack of sexual desire.

(Smith, 1990). Also telling is the widespread sexual dysfunction in U.S. society, which affects as many as half of all couples sometime during their lives (Ende et al., 1984; Frank et al., 1978; Masters and Johnson, 1970).

Sexual Norms

In this section we review some of the sexual norms of mainstream U.S. society and contrast them with the sexual norms of other societies and select U.S. subcultures. Sexual deviance and nonconformity in the United States are also considered because no society's control of behavior is ever perfect.

Sexual norms are standards of sexual conduct. Societies teach the sexual norms through the process of socialization. There are many sexual norms because virtually all aspects of sexuality are socially regulated. One way to organize the sexual norms is to divide them into categories in much the same way a journalist might organize a story; that is, according to the who, what, where, when, and why. The specific prescriptions (what is allowed) and proscriptions (what is not allowed) vary from society to society, but the headings remain the same. Learning and internalizing these sexual rules is part of growing up in any society (Gagnon, 1977).

Who Norms

Who one should have sex with is socially defined. The principal "who" sexual norms in the United States would include the following: Sex should be with someone other than oneself (as opposed to masturbation); with the opposite gender (as opposed to homosexuality); with other adults (as opposed to pedophilia); with non-blood relatives (as opposed to incest); with spouses (as opposed to extramarital sex); and only with those who want to have sex (as opposed to sexual harassment and rape). A number of other "who" sexual norms—those related to race, ethnicity, religion, social class, and adult age differences—are also key mate selection norms and are discussed in Chapter 14. Let's examine variations in some of these norms.

Adult–Non-Adult Sex. Consider, for example, the cross-cultural range of norms dealing with adults having sex with children and adolescents. There are quite a few societies in which sex between adults and non-adults is normative. Among the Azande and the Siwan of Africa, the Aranda of Australia, and the Keraki of New Guinea men have sex with boys, often the sons of friends (Evans-Prichard, 1970). Old men among the Tiwi of Australia have sex with pre-teen girls (the men actually promise to marry the girls before the girls are conceived) (Lindholm and Lindholm, 1980), while adult women among the Chuckchi of Siberia have sex with pre-teen boys (the women marry the boys when the boys are 2 years old). Perhaps that's where the expression "robbing the cradle" originated.

Again, despite the norm against adult–non-adult sex in the United States, deviance is epidemic. Surveys by Finkelhor (1979) and Russell (1984) have found that about 20 to 30 percent of women are sexually victimized during childhood or adolescence. The proportion for men is much lower, yet still substantial. Fifteen percent of reported child sexual abuse victims are males, and boys are the target of both heterosexual and homosexual abuse. The 1987 National Survey of Children reported that about 5 percent of women and 0.3 percent of men experienced at least one episode of nonvoluntary sexual intercourse while they were children (Moore et al., 1989).

Homosexuality. As discussed in Chapter 7, social norms concerning homosexuality are culturally variable. Some societies prefer homosexuality to heterosexuality, while others forbid and condemn homosexual behavior. However, most societies fall in between these extremes of preference and condemnation, and approve or at least accept homosexual behavior (Gray and Wolfe, 1988).

U.S. society has a norm against homosexual behavior. The consensus view is that gender role, erotic preference, and sexual behavior should all be consistent. Biological males should act like men, lust after women, and perform heterosexual acts; females should be similarly consistent. Males who engage in homosexual behavior are considered more feminine than men who do not; similarly, lesbians are defined as more masculine than non-lesbians. These views exist notwithstanding the fact that the vast majority of homosexual behavior in this country is homophilic; that is, practiced by adults without any gender role changes (see Chapter 7). The norm against homosexual behavior is also reinforced by lingering convictions that homosexuality is due to mental disease and/or moral depravity (McFalls et al., 1992).

Needless to say, many Americans violate the norm against homosexuality, especially during adolescence. Evidence for this comes from a national probability survey of sexual behavior conducted by the Kinsey Institute in 1970. Roughly one-fifth of adult males had at least one lifetime homosexual experience, mostly as adolescents. The best data on the prevalence of homosexual behavior among adults after age 18 come from the General Social Survey (Smith, 1990), which found that about 7 percent of the adult population have had at least one homosexual contact since age 18, though less than 1 percent have been exclusively homosexual since that age. The GSS also found that 1.5 percent of sexually active adults had a homosexual experience in the previous year (1989), a figure in line with the best other available estimate, which comes from the Kinsey Institute's 1970

One of the distinguishing features of Western societies during the last twenty-five years has been the emergence and widespread influence of the homosexual subculture and its products, such as art. Even non-gay artists can now paint homosexual subjects as a matter of course. In *Leather Bar,* Beryl Cook depicts in a somewhat humorous way an incident at a well-known London pub. A would-be patron gets ejected because he is not wearing the proper leather outfit obligatory at that kind of gay bar.

national survey (Fay et al., 1989), and much lower than the 10 percent estimate typically cited by gay rights organizations. However, it should be pointed out that these high-quality national probability surveys still provide only the lower bounds of homosexual behavior because homosexual experiences undoubtedly are underreported even when the best methodology is used.

Extramarital Sex. Cross-cultural variation with respect to norms concerning extramarital sex is also considerable. A sizable minority of societies approve or condone some form of extramarital relations. Societies that permit polygyny have higher rates of this behavior than monogamous societies (Broude and Greene, 1976), possibly because it is difficult for the husband to keep tabs on several wives. The practice of husbands permitting brothers or other close kinsmen to have sex with their wives in some polygynous societies is also a factor (Gray and Wolfe, 1988). In other societies extramarital sex takes the form of reciprocal "wife lending" or "wife exchange." Those stories you have heard about Eskimo men offering travelers their wives as a kind of after-dinner treat are not just old wives' tales. They actually do it, as do other groups such as the Chuckchi of Siberia. Another group of societies permits extramarital sex only on certain special occasions when everyone is expected to have sex with someone other than their spouse. Finally, a few societies approve of extramarital sex without limitation. The Toda of India, for instance, have no word in their language for adultery, and consider it immoral for a person to wish to withhold a spouse from another (Ford and Beach, 1978).

At the other extreme lie societies that have stronger norms against extramarital sex than even those of the United States. Often the penalties for breaking the norm are extremely harsh. Islamic societies sometimes stone adulterers to death. In China, while adulterous women are no longer weighed down with stones and drowned, some are sent to reeducation prisons (Burton, 1988). In parts of Brazil, adulterous wives are routinely beaten severely and killed by their husbands, most of whom are never tried or convicted for "defending their honor" in this way. It is not incidental that these examples are all about women. Restrictive societies are typically more tolerant of sexual transgressions and experimentation on the part of men than women. This is an aspect of the much-discussed sexual *double standard.*

The United States has widely shared norms against extramarital sex. The 1988 GSS found that 91 percent of Americans believe that it is "always or almost always wrong to have extramarital relations" (Greeley et al., 1990). Moreover, despite the reports from popular studies about the widespread prevalence of extramarital relations, the best studies indicate that Americans conform to the norm of fidelity fairly well. The GSS, for example, found that less than 2 percent of married people had a sex partner(s) other than their spouse in 1988. Surprisingly, men and women had about the same rate of infidelity (Smith, 1990). In another national survey with a longer-term focus, 90 percent of wives and husbands said they had never been unfaithful to their spouses (Elson, 1990). Thus what emerges from good-quality survey results is the conclusion that Americans are a "most monogamous people" (Greeley et al., 1989).

Masturbation. Masturbation provides another example of cultural diversity. Among the Lesu of New Ireland there is no prohibition of masturbation, and men, women, and children engage in the practice without regard to privacy (Powdermaker, 1933). On the other hand, the Kwoma of New Guinea strongly oppose the practice; in fact, they supposedly never touch their genitals even while urinating.

Despite norms against it, masturbation is a common form of deviance in the United States (Atwood and Gagnon, 1987; Kinsey et al., 1948, 1953). Indeed it is probably a more common form of sexual activity than intercourse (Marcus and Francis, 1975).

What Norms

Societies establish norms concerning the whole range of sexual acts that humans can perform. From social sources, people learn what can be done and the proper order of doing it (Gagnon, 1977). Of course, the lessons taught vary significantly from society to society. There are even significant differences among societies as to the range and content of behaviors that are classified as "sexual." In some tribal societies, for example, eating is considered a mildly erotic act. Husband and wives can eat together, but not brothers and sisters (Davenport, 1978). In short, societies define the cultural boundaries between what is sexual and non-sexual (Ford and Beach, 1978).

foreplay—**sexual stimulation intended as a prelude to sexual intercourse.**

In virtually every society sexual intercourse is preceded by **foreplay** (Ford and Beach, 1978). But both the amount and kinds of foreplay vary greatly cross-culturally. Some peoples, such as the Ponapeans of the Pacific, indulge in foreplay for hours; whereas others, such as the Lepcha, move immediately to intercourse itself (Gorer, 1938). Kissing, a very common prelude to sex in many societies, is not practiced by the Siriono or the Thonga who find it revolting. Even "kissing" itself varies by culture. The Tinguian people, for example, put their lips near their partner's face and suddenly inhale. Sexual nudity is culturally approved in most but not all societies. The Inis Beag abhor nudity, and intercourse takes place at night without light, under covers, and with clothes on, a practice, incidentally, that Kinsey found to be common among U.S. couples as late as 1950 (Kinsey et al., 1948). Stimulation of the genitals, breasts, or other sexually sensitive zones, manually or orally, is practiced in many cultures, though such contact is forbidden by a few societies such as the Wogeo and the Tikopia who live on Pacific islands. Anal intercourse is part of the approved homosexual and/or heterosexual practices of some societies, but is condemned by others. The Mohave Indians practice anal and vaginal intercourse interchangeably, while the Kwoma consider the former unnatural and disgusting. **Sadomasochism** is a regular feature in some societies. This approved violence takes many forms including scratching, biting, pulling the hair, poking fingers into eyes, and rough intercourse. In other societies, violent stimulation is unknown or condemned.

sadomasochism—**the infliction of physical pain during foreplay or sexual intercourse.**

Another cultural variable is the position in which intercourse occurs. The most common position around the world is the face to face, man on top position (Gregersen, 1982). Contrary to what has been written in sociology texts for years, the widespread popularity of this so-called missionary position probably is not the result of zealous, ethnocentric missionaries suppressing native intercourse positions. Indeed, among those societies in which the missionary position is not the most popular, there are surprisingly few other positions favored. No societies, for example, favor the "rear entry" or "woman above" positions, though many societies view these and other positions as acceptable alternatives (Gray and Wolfe, 1988).

In the United States "what" norms favor such practices as nudity, kissing, manual foreplay, oral sex, and vaginal intercourse, but oppose anal intercourse and sadomasochism. Just how many Americans violate these norms is, despite all the pop surveys about sex, simply unknown. Nevertheless, despite the absence of reliable data it is certain that there is a significant amount of sexual deviance in the United States. Studies by *Redbook* (1987), *Cosmopolitan* (Wolfe, 1981), and *Playboy* (Hunt, 1974) magazines, for example, found that about 20 percent–40 percent of their responding readership have engaged in anal intercourse. Similarly, one Kinsey study (1948) estimated that at least 3 percent of women and 10 percent of men were sexually responsive to sadomasochistic stimuli, and more recent magazine surveys concur (Weinberg, 1987). In addition, popular culture such as John Cougar Mellencamp's hit song "Hurt So Good" reflect the presence of such deviance in the United States:

Sink your teeth right through my bones, baby
Let's see what we can do.
Hurt so good,
Come on baby make it hurt so good,
Sometimes love don't feel like it should,
You make it hurt so good

Where Norms

Most societies include the "where" norm of privacy, which means that individuals are expected to seek seclusion for sexual acts. But a few societies lack this norm. Formosan natives and the Yapese, for example, copulate in public. Similarly, unmarried youths among the Gond have sex within sight of other youth with whom they share a communal dormitory (Elwin, 1968).

However, some societies that include the privacy norm have trouble living up to it. For most of human history, whole families slept in the same cave, tent, hut, or room, indeed, in the same bed (where beds existed). In

Data from sex surveys indicate that conformity to sexual norms varies by social class in the United States. In his 1933 painting *Shore Leave,* Paul Cadmus captures the sensuality of working-class dating in a public place. Incidentally, this is also an example of covert gay art, painted at a time when gay subject matter was deemed improper. Note that while his shipmates frolic with women in the foreground, a sailor cruises a young man in the left background.

historical western European societies, for example, children often learned about sex while sleeping in the same bed as their parents (Gagnon, 1977). Privacy is still difficult to obtain in many societies today. In the former Soviet Union and China young people do not have their own apartments and cannot go to hotels together. Getting away from prying eyes is so difficult that at nightfall courting pairs flood the parks, and lovers couple on the ground (Kimelman, 1990; Leo, 1986). The apartments that do exist are usually small, and families often share a single bedroom. Lack of privacy also plagues many developing societies, which is why their inhabitants often have sex out of doors in the forest or the bush.

Some societies include norms prescribing outdoor sex for reasons other than privacy. The Gond and the Yurok believe that coitus indoors will lead to poverty. On the other hand, the Hopi and Lango insist that indoors is the only legitimate place to copulate. They prescribe that norm because it better enables them to suppress premarital and extramarital relations.

U.S. society has norms favoring both indoor sex and privacy, usually the privacy of the bedroom. Sex does occur in other places, however, but it is usually considered a bit risque. As a matter of expediency "where" deviance is more common in premarital and extramarital relations than in marital sex. Popular irregular places for illicit sex are automobiles and budget motels (Bailey, 1988).

When Norms

"When" can be construed many different ways—when in relation to the human life cycle and to marriage; and when in a temporal, cyclical, or frequency sense.

When Sexual Life Begins. Most societies include norms that specify at what ages or at what phases of the life cycle sex is appropriate. Some of these norms deal with the appropriate age or time to begin one's sexual life, since most societies take an intense interest in the sexual behavior of their young. Many societies encourage children and adolescents to participate in sexual activity, including the Gond, the Trobriand Islanders, the Trukese, and the Lepcha. Indeed, the latter are convinced that without sex girls would not mature. Even some industrialized societies, like the Staphorst, a community in The Netherlands, prescribe premarital sex for the young. To court a young woman a young Staphorst man typically crawls through her bedroom window three times a week and spends the night with her. In a nearby room, her parents are aware and approve of this activity, for in that society young women must be pregnant prior to marriage (Newton, 1978). Premarital sex is also socially approved in Iceland, where unmarried women account for three-fourths of all births (Tomasson, 1980).

In other societies, the norms discourage young people from engaging in sexual activity prior to marriage. This is particularly true in many parts of the Mediterranean world where a girl's virginity is zealously guarded until marriage. The Egyptians in the village of Silwa, for example, expect brides to be virgins (Ammar, 1954). Parents attempt to guarantee this by keeping their daughters away from boys, by dressing them in figure- and face-concealing garments, and by cutting off their clitorises when they are age 7 to reduce their desire for premarital sex. The Gibertese Islanders have such strong norms against premarital sex that they sometimes invoke the death penalty for both parties. The Vedda of Ceylon may kill a man for even chatting with an unmarried woman. Clearly you have to choose your romance-seeking vacation spots carefully.

Most young women and men in the United States engage in premarital sexual activity. Mary Ryan's *White Horse Nights* (1983) shows a couple necking in an automobile at a drive-in movie, a popular place for premarital sex from the 1950s to the early 1980s. The automobile itself helped remove such activities of young adults out from under the scrutiny of their elders, and contributed to higher rates of premarital sexuality.

Broude and Greene (1976) studied attitudes toward female premarital sexual behavior in 141 societies. They found that 25 percent approved, 37 percent tolerated discreet premarital sex provided it did not result in pregnancy, 13 percent disapproved (except for a woman and her fiancé) but had only mild sanctions, and 25 percent strongly disapproved of premarital sex. While societies that prohibited premarital sex for women generally did so for men as well, men indulged in premarital sex much more than women in societies where a double standard existed (Barry and Schlegel, 1984, 1985). For example, in Puerto Rico unmarried men are expected to conform to a macho image of sexuality, whereas unmarried women are supposed to uphold a pious standard of chastity (Ritzer et al., 1979).

The United States falls in between the almost-anything-goes norms of the most permissive societies and the virginity cults of the most restrictive. Some elements of U.S. culture such as the entertainment industry promote premarital sex, whereas other elements such as traditional religious organizations repress it (Gagnon, 1977). In any event, according to the GSS about 64 percent of Americans now tolerate premarital sex (Greeley et al., 1990), and most male and female Americans now engage in premarital activity (Forrest and Singh, 1990).

When Sexual Life Ends. Cross-cultural findings about sex and aging are comparatively rare (Frayser, 1985). But one survey of 106 societies found that the elderly were expected to remain sexually active in 70 percent of them. Indeed, in 22 percent of these societies women are actually expected to become less inhibited about sexuality as they grow old (Winn and Newton, 1980). Societies that include norms favoring sex in old age tend to be those that value older people (Crooks and Baur, 1990). The mountain people of Abkhasia (former Soviet Union) are a case in point. The elderly there continue to have heterosexual relations well beyond the ages typical of their counterparts in industrialized societies (Beach, 1978). The African Bala also maintain a high degree of approved sexual activity in the older years (Merriam, 1971). But many other societies limit sexuality in old age, especially for women. In traditional Kenya, for example, a woman's sex life was limited to about 20 years. Indeed it was considered scandalous for a woman to bear another child after her oldest child had married.

U.S. society has norms against the elderly having sex. This cultural negativism toward sex (and romance) on the part of the elderly is a form of **ageism**. Sexual ability and interest are supposed to decline with advancing age, and people are supposed to gradually become **asexual** as they age. If older people are not asexual, their interest in sex is seen, at best, as inappropriate and, at worst, as unnatural and disgusting. The gist of these cultural attitudes is expressed in jokes about "dirty old men." But older women are actually more restricted than are older men. If an older man marries a younger woman, it is often viewed with amusement. But relationships between older women and younger men are much less likely to be winked at or accepted (Frayser, 1985). Incidentally, this form of ageism is characteristic among homosexuals as well as heterosexuals (Berger, 1982).

ageism—discrimination and prejudice against persons of a certain age, especially the elderly.

asexual—lacking sexual interest and activity.

General Social Survey data indicate that most Americans conform to the norm specifying increasing sexual abstinence with age (Smith, 1990). Intercourse frequency declines sharply with age from about 78 times per year for those under age 40 to 8 times per year for those over age 70. While this decline is related in part to the fact that the proportion of people without spouses increases with age (Mooradian and Greiff, 1990), it is noteworthy that the decline also occurs among the currently married. Conformity to the norm exists despite the fact that sexual interest and ability can extend beyond the age of 100 (Bretschneider and McCoy, 1988).

Coital Frequency. How often people have "approved" intercourse is related to cultural norms and varies enormously by society. The Dani, as noted earlier, have sex about once every few years, while Chagga men have sex many times a night with their multiple wives. In some societies very frequent intercourse is thought to be weakening and debilitating. Other cultures believe that a man has a limited number of lifetime ejaculations and must use them sparingly (Ford and Beach, 1978). The Thonga believe that "hot people" (or those who engage in too much intercourse) are dangerous because they upset the fragile balance of nature with their activities and harm the sick and the elderly who are already in a weakened state (Junod, 1927).

Americans generally believe that adults in their prime, particularly those currently married, should have intercourse several times a week. Data from the National Survey of Family Growth (NCHS, 1987) indicate that about 42 percent of currently married American women age 15–44 conform to the norm (see Table 19:2). The 5 percent who have sex at least once a day

TABLE 19:2 The Frequency of Intercourse

Number of women who ever had sexual intercourse, and percent distribution of women who had intercourse in the last three months by frequency of sexual intercourse, according to marital status and age: United States, 1982

MARITAL STATUS AND AGE	Number of Women Who Ever Had Sexual Intercourse (in thousands)	Percent Who Had Intercourse in the Past Three Months	FREQUENCY OF INTERCOURSE (percent distribution)					
			Total	Once a Month	Two to Three Times a Month	Once a Week	Several Times a Week	Every Day
All Marital Statuses								
15–44 years	46,684	89.7	100.0	8.2	20.5	28.2	37.7	5.4
15–19 years	4,467	85.2	100.0	17.5	27.0	24.1	24.3	7.1
20–24 years	9,080	88.4	100.0	9.4	19.9	27.1	35.4	8.2
25–29 years	9,929	92.3	100.0	5.7	17.4	23.6	47.2	6.1
30–34 years	9,189	91.6	100.0	6.9	19.4	29.8	39.5	4.4
35–39 years	7,725	90.7	100.0	6.1	21.2	31.6	37.9	3.3
40–44 years	6,293	87.1	100.0	8.5	22.6	33.7	31.7	3.5
Currently Married								
15–44 years	28,231	99.5	100.0	4.3	17.8	30.5	42.0	5.4
15–19 years	612	100.0	100.0	6.3	13.9	17.9	43.6	18.2
20–24 years	4,130	99.8	100.0	3.1	12.4	28.4	43.6	12.5
25–29 years	6,442	99.7	100.0	2.9	16.0	26.4	49.5	5.2
30–34 years	6,482	99.7	100.0	5.3	16.5	31.4	42.6	4.1
35–39 years	5,783	99.7	100.0	4.6	21.4	31.9	39.2	2.9
40–44 years	4,783	98.2	100.0	5.1	23.1	36.3	32.6	2.8
Not Currently Married								
15–44 years	18,452	74.9	100.0	16.1	25.8	23.6	29.1	5.5
15–19 years	3,855	82.8	100.0	19.7	29.5	25.3	20.6	4.9
20–24 years	4,950	78.8	100.0	16.0	27.8	25.7	26.7	3.7
25–29 years	3,487	78.6	100.0	12.4	20.5	16.9	41.8	8.4
30–34 years	2,707	72.1	100.0	12.1	29.2	24.3	29.2	5.3
35–39 years	1,943	64.0	100.0	12.9	20.3	30.0	31.8	5.0
40–44 years	1,510	51.7	100.0	29.3	19.1	18.1	26.1	7.4

Source: National Survey of Family Growth (National Center for Health Statistics, 1987).

are considered "sex maniacs," while those having sex once a month or less (4.3 percent) are viewed as "frigid" or undersexed. Actually, many of the latter suffer from Inhibited Sexual Desire, which is the formal term for abnormally low interest in sex (Ende et al., 1984; Frank et al., 1978). Note also that coital frequency is lower among those not currently married, which is in line with U.S. norms concerning nonmarital sex.

Coital Restrictions. Many societies include norms that limit when intercourse can occur within marriage and other sexual unions. These norms are much more common in pre-industrial than in industrial societies. There are four principal types of restrictions: **gestational**, **postpartum**, **menstrual**, and **occasional** (Davis and Blake, 1956).

gestational restrictions—**norms against sex during pregnancy.**

postpartum restrictions—**norms against sex during a specified period of time immediately following a birth.**

menstrual restrictions—**norms against sex during the woman's menstrual period.**

occasional restrictions—**infrequent norms against sex at certain times.**

Most societies have some form of gestational restriction; that is, coitus is forbidden during some part of pregnancy. Postpartum abstinence is mandated in nearly all societies, although the time period varies greatly—from two weeks in the United States to about five years in traditional Kenya. In some societies postpartum abstinence is determined by the length of the breastfeeding period or by some developmental stage of the child (for example, when the child begins teething or walking). The prohibition of coitus during menstruation and sometimes for a few days after is almost universal. One New Guinea tribe believes that contact between a man and menstrual blood—or even with a menstruating woman—would corrupt the man's vital juices, permanently dull his wits, and eventually lead to his death. Killing the woman for this offense is sanctioned behavior.

Some societies have other kinds of coital restrictions such as forbidding the sick (and sometimes their relatives) to have sex, forcing widows and widowers to abstain from intercourse, or limiting sex to either the nighttime or the daytime. For instance, the Chenchu of India have norms against nighttime sex because they believe that a nighttime conception would result in a blind child. Conversely, the Masai of Africa are convinced that daytime sex would cause the man's blood to flow into the woman's womb, leaving him dead (Ford and Beach, 1978).

U.S. society includes some of these norms, and although they are relatively mild compared to many pre-industrial societies, they are not socially insignificant. Gestational restrictions, for example, are undoubtedly linked to extramarital sex and prostitution.

Why Norms

The "why" norms specify the culturally approved reasons for engaging in sexual activities. There are all sorts of reasons for engaging in sex: for love, reproduction, pleasure, relaxation, achievement, aggression, rebellion, degradation, or economic gain. But not all these reasons are approved in every society (Gagnon, 1977). Indeed, there are some societies (such as the Shakers) that do not have any approved reasons for sex.

Let's examine cross-cultural variation with respect to one of these reasons: pleasure. Societies that have strong norms favoring sexual pleasure include two mentioned before, the Mangaians and the Icelanders. The Mangaians believe that sexual pleasure is the birthright of both men and women. All women are taught how to achieve orgasm, and men are socialized to believe that their partner's pleasure is an essential ingredient of their own sexual enjoyment. Sexual pleasure for men and women is also highly valued in Iceland, where casual sex is an accepted part of the culture.

At the other extreme are societies that have strong norms against sexual pleasure. Usually the double standard exists and the pleasure prohibition applies only to women. In these societies sex is seen as a man's pleasure but a woman's duty. Women who enjoy sex too much are labeled as immoral, "loose" women, animals, "loca" (crazy, in Mexican), or victims of black magic. Girls are socialized to be modest and reserved about sex, and even to fear it. In the most anti-pleasure cultures female circumcision or genital mutilation is practiced to blot out even the potential for pleasure. "Honeymoons" in anti-pleasure societies are often traumatic experiences, and a marriage may not be consummated immediately after the wedding. Grooms appreciate modest, sexually fearful brides because such behavior is an indicator that their spouses married as virgins and are not oversexed. Indeed, in these societies a husband is often reluctant to sexually arouse his wife, fearing that she might "get to like it too much." Not surprisingly, such women learn well, and look upon sex with detachment, revulsion, or as a form of abuse. In some of these cultures, husbands focus their own sexual energies on "loose women" and prostitutes.

U.S. culture approves of sexual pleasure for both men and women, although the degree of approval for women varies by social group. The denial of women's right to pleasure is, for example, more common among the working class and some conservative religious groups. Similarly, pleasure is not an approved reason for sex in certain U.S. subcultures such as MOVE, a Philadelphia area contraculture that sees procreation as the only legitimate reason for sex (Klibanoff, 1985). The mainstream U.S. culture also approves of sex for procreation and as a way of expressing love and intimacy.

rape—forcible sexual intercourse perpetrated against the will of the victim.

prostitution—the relatively indiscriminant exchange of sexual acts for economic benefits.

There are many reasons for sex that are not sanctioned in the United States either as a primary or secondary purpose. A partial list of such proscriptive "why" norms would include the following. Sex should not be for aggression (there are norms against rape); for degradation (there are norms against sadomasochism); for vicarious power and status (there are norms against "groupie" sex with rock stars, politicians, and professional athletes); and for economic or personal gain. This latter proscriptive norm applies not only to prostitution but to such phenomena as marrying for wealth, having sex with a powerful person to further one's career, using (and possibly withholding) sex to wring a concession out of a spouse, and even the insistence on an "expensive evening" as a precondition for "putting out" on a date. Needless to say, many Americans deviate from these norms. Prostitution, for example, is commonplace in the United States.

Discussion

The cross-cultural perspective reveals clearly that society determines how individuals experience and express sexuality. It also shows how different social norms produce extraordinarily diverse kinds of sexual behavior. When humans are born they are more or less like computers coming off an assembly line. Even with their biological hardware, they need a sexual program or script in order to function. Different societies read in different programs, and most people carry out their programmed instructions. In this sense, people are socio-sexual "robots." If you do not believe this, think about what your sexual behavior would be like if, as an infant, you had been lost by your parents in the African jungle and were subsequently found and raised by the Azande people (see Chapter 7). If you are a guy under age 20, you might now be the homosexual wife of an Azande military man. What's more, if you refused that role, you would be stigmatized as deviant. And if you were told about some of the sexual norms of your present American classmates (such as their norm against homosexuality), you would find them astonishing (Frayser, 1985; Money, 1988).

Nevertheless, most American students continue to think that some of the sexual behavior of other societies is just plain disordered or senseless. There is an ethnocentric tendency to forget that sexual behavior takes its meaning from the culture in which it occurs and the role it plays in that culture (Gagnon, 1977). This is the principle of cultural relativity you encountered in Chapter 7. A society's rules about premarital sex, for example, are not made in a social vacuum, but are related to factors such as technology, wealth, social relations, and social organization (Gray and Wolfe, 1988). If a society is permissive with respect to premarital sexuality, for instance, it must make some sort of institutional arrangement for the inevitable children born outside of marriage.

Indeed, one of the most fundamental lessons of cross-cultural research is that "even practices that sound crazy make sense." For example, the aforementioned genital mutilation of girls is a demonstration of male authority and power. Similarly, marrying someone who has not yet been conceived is eminently sensible in Tiwi society because it helps forge beneficial family alliances "in advance." It is a form of "buy now, pay later." Among the Chuckchi the marriage between a 14-year-old girl and a 2-year-old boy, whom she then raises, not only fosters strong marriages, since the couple ultimately will have both a marital and a maternal bond, but reduces problematic population growth by reducing the girl's childbearing years.

As a matter of fact, many of the sexual practices in premodern societies were designed at least in part to minimize childbearing and, hence, population growth. Remember the traditional Kenyan males who married late, abstained from sex for five years after the birth of a child, and married a woman who ceased engaging in sex once her first child married? And the Etero who had 295 intercourse-restricted days a year, and norms favoring homosexuality? These practices clearly suppress population growth.

There are many other things that we can learn about sexuality using the cross-cultural perspective. We can determine, for instance, which sexual activities are universal and which are culturally variable. Apparently, there are few important norms—if any—that are culturally universal. Some norms are extraordinarily common, though, such as the expectations that at least some members of the society are heterosexual and that some will practice sex within a marital context. Those norms are near universal because they help societies carry out two basic functions: reproduction and the regulation of sexuality. Despite the wide variety of sexual behavior discussed in this chapter, it is important to note that throughout history the vast majority of adults were married heterosexuals, and the same is true today.

incest taboo—**a norm that prohibits sexual activity between relatives.**

Some sort of incest taboo is the only sex-related cultural universal. Societies differ, however, concerning which relatives or fictive kin (i.e., relatives created through such conduct as sharing food, land, or common activities) are considered too close for sexual behavior. Why some sort of incest taboo is universal is a much-debated topic and there are three major schools of thought: biological explanations, sociological explanations, and cultural explanations (Gray and Wolfe, 1988).

The biological explanations argue that social norms against incest are superimposed on a primate genetic tendency to avoid sex with close relatives (Shepher, 1983). Most non-human primates (apes, monkeys, lemurs) exhibit inbreeding avoidance. Sociological theories hold that incest taboos are necessary to allow societies to operate smoothly. One such theory emphasizes the role incest taboos play in forging alliances between families or groups by forcing out-group marriage, thus helping them to survive either economically or militarily (White, 1969). Another sociological theory suggests that the incest norm is necessary to keep the roles within the family from overlapping, and thus to prevent major role conflicts, confusion, and the resultant society-threatening family instability (Davis, 1948). Finally, the cultural explanations emphasize how different societies conceptualize incest, the social definition of "relative," and the ways societies manipulate the taboo to serve their own purposes (Heritier, 1982; Wagner, 1972). The best explanation, as you no doubt can guess, is a mixture of all three sets of explanations because each contributes to our overall understanding of the phenomenon.

Incidentally, the universality of the incest taboo does not make it immune to violation. Due to its morally offensive nature, reliable information about its prevalence in the United States is unavailable. However, one study found that 16 percent of females contacted had been sexually abused by some relative before age 18, including 5 percent who had been victimized by either their biological fathers or stepfathers (Russell, 1986).

Another lesson derived from cross-cultural research is that virtually all forms of human sexual behavior are condoned in some societies and condemned in others, including such practices as bestiality, sex with certain close relatives, and sadomasochism. The conclusion you should draw from this fairly leaps off the page: *Sexual deviance, like all deviance, is socially defined.* It is what most people in a society say that it is. Consider some of the implications of this situation for our society. It means, for example, that our sexual social problems such as homosexuality and even our sexual mental disorders such as pedophilia are at least in part arbitrarily defined within the society. Such conclusions should give us pause concerning any rigid attitudes we may have toward various forms of sexual behavior.

The cross-cultural perspective is also valuable in helping us evaluate some of the contemporary issues swirling around sexual behavior. For instance, you read in Chapter 7 that in some pre-industrial societies males pass through a stage of regular homosexuality activity without compromising the development of their adult heterosexual identity and behavior. This fact certainly has relevance to the debate in the United States concerning the roles homosexual experimentation and proximity to avowed homosexuals (such as parents and teachers) play in determining the sexual identity of youths.

In short, the cross-cultural perspective calls on you to think about your own sexual attitudes and experiences and how they have been fashioned by your socialization.

THE SEXUAL REVOLUTION IN THE UNITED STATES

The term "sexual revolution" usually refers to changes in sexual attitudes and behavior during the past several decades in the United States. But that is a shortsighted perspective. The revolution really started during the middle of the nineteenth century.

Sexuality in Nineteenth-Century America

As shown in Figure 19:2, the United States was a much more sexually restrictive society in 1850 than it is today (Frayser, 1985). Most important, the dominant "why" norm was that sex should always be reproductive. This norm determined the nature of many other norms. It meant that sex was limited to heterosexual, vaginal intercourse; and that all forms of nonmarital, nonprocreative sexual activity were prohibited, including such

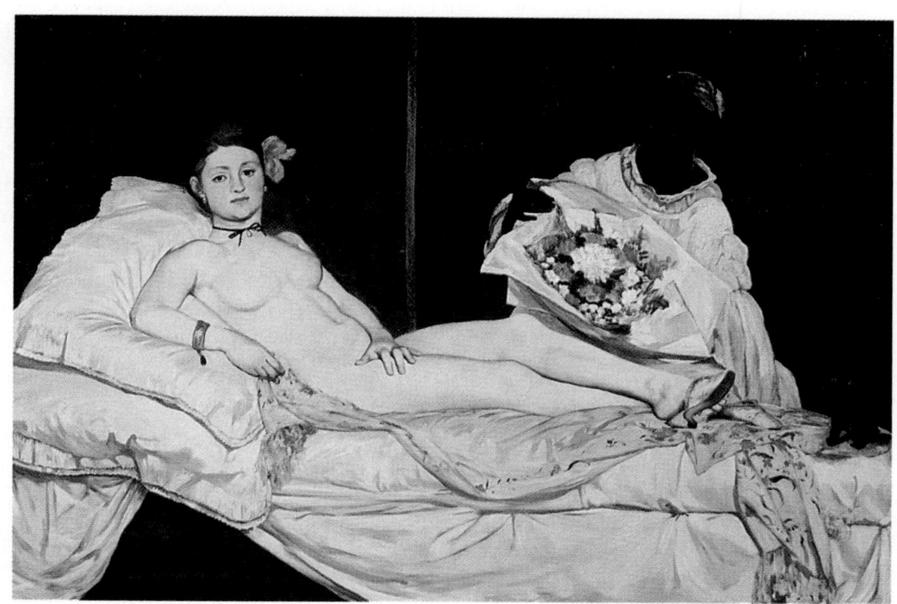

Eduoard Manet's masterpiece, *Olympia*, was considered scandalous when it first appeared in 1865. The painting pictured an obvious courtesan lying on an unmade bed, showing no sign of modesty as her servant presents her with flowers from an admirer. Manet's painting was badly received by the public owing in part to the sexual prudishness of nineteenth-century Europe (and the United States).

things as homosexuality, masturbation, premarital sex, and extramarital sex. Celebrations of birth and marriage reinforced these norms, as did related norms that restricted activities such as divorce and birth control. Indeed, the ultra-prudishness of the era might best be illustrated by Lady Gough's *Book of Etiquette* (1863), which advised hostesses to reorganize their bookshelves by separating female authors from male authors (unless they were married)—presumably to prevent the authors from taking literary license.

It is worth emphasizing, however, that the United States in 1850 was not at the restrictive extreme of the continuum (see Figure 19:2). For one reason, punishment for violation of the restrictive norms was not severe. Remember, the most restrictive societies often punish deviants with death. And, contrary to our stereotypical view of this "Victorian" period, there was considerable deviance. In New England towns, for instance, one bride in five was pregnant when she married (Larkin, 1988), and prostitution was commonplace in the United States (and even in Victorian England itself) (Gagnon, 1977). Of course, with respect to deviance, the double standard was alive and well. For example, men apprehended visiting prostitutes were not publicly censured, but women caught engaging in deviant sexual acts were ostracized and redefined as "fallen women." The double standard was practiced in part to assure that the biological fathers of children could be identified, as it is in most societies that link sex exclusively to reproduction.

The restrictive sexual norms of this era were fashioned in part by religious traditions. The Catholic Church and conservative Protestant and Jewish groups traditionally have held that sex should be restricted to heterosexual intercourse between spouses. The Puritans in particular believed strongly that sex was only appropriate within a reproductive, marital context. These and other religious groups believed that the purpose of sexual activity was reproduction, not physical pleasure, and these beliefs were elaborated into norms that forbade such things as masturbation, oral and anal sex, homosexuality, and child sexual activity. Likewise, intercourse during menstruation, pregnancy, and old age was prohibited because conception was not possible during those periods. In addition, since these religious traditions have strong family values, any activity that menaced the family unit such as adultery and incest was strictly prohibited (DeLamater,

1981). Victorian morality superimposed upon these religious values an additional notion that there was something intrinsically unhealthy about sex (Katchadourian, 1972).

But why did such restrictive religious traditions come about in the first place? Two of the many possible reasons stand out, one having to do with population growth, and the other with disease (DeLamater, 1981). The former has to do with the fact that in many historical societies life expectancy was under 30 years and women had to average bearing at least six children just for the society to maintain its population size (and to avoid extinction) and more than six children for the population to grow (increase). Growth was important because many societies such as the ancient Israelites had to protect themselves from fierce enemies, and more people meant more security. Thus procreation often became the single cultural justification for sex in such societies. All sexual acts that were not procreative were considered antisocial perversions.

The second reason for restrictive traditions has to do with disease, especially sexually transmitted diseases (STDs). Prior to 1950, there were no effective medications against infection, such as antibiotics, and STDs were fearsome threats to individuals and societies. Syphilis, for example, was not only a killer but could cause such things as blindness and insanity throughout its course. Consequently, it was reprehensible for, say, a man to engage in extramarital sex because he not only threatened his own health and life, but also those of his innocent spouse and unborn children. It was also socially irresponsible because most STDs can lower reproductive ability (McFalls and McFalls, 1984), a fact that relates to the population growth concerns discussed above.

In sum, it was necessary in the past for many societies to adopt restrictive sexual values for population and health reasons. Religious institutions generally lend their support to such necessities by according those values a religious justification as well. Often, there is also a purely religious rationale for the value, such as the doctrine that sex is basically sinful, and celibacy is the safest course to avoid "hellfire." In addition, there may be other kinds of values inextricably linked to the population, health, and religious ones, such as the gender role value that virility and femininity are directly proportional to the number of children one has.

Sociocultural Change

In the latter half of the nineteenth century the sexual revolution commenced and the United States began to move gradually along the continuum toward the permissive pole. The pace of this transformation was not even. It accelerated twice: once during the period that stretched from World War I through the "roaring 1920s"; and again in the post–World War II period, particularly from the mid-1960s to the late 1970s.

The famous Kinsey studies (Kinsey et al., 1948; Kinsey et al., 1953) took place after about two-thirds of the sexual revolution period had run its course. The Kinsey studies not only revealed that sexual behavior in the 1940s was already much more permissive than it had been in the mid- to late nineteenth century, but, by looking at the behavior of different generations, the studies showed that the movement toward permissiveness had been continuous over the entire period. The Kinsey studies also revealed that in the 1940s changes in the sexual norms had lagged well behind changes in sexual behavior. Indeed, the amount of sexual deviance reported by Kinsey shocked the American public, and the revelation of widespread sexual deviance actually helped to accelerate change toward permissive sexual norms (Frayser, 1985).

The sexual revolution from about 1850 to the present came about as a result of a series of social and cultural changes, many of which are discussed elsewhere in this book. Offir (1982, p. 25) summarizes the most important of these changes as follows:

1. Industrialization has brought relative affluence to millions and has caused a change in values from thrift and self-control to consumerism and self-gratification (and, some critics would say, self-indulgence). Indeed, our economy depends on increasing demand for the products and experiences that bring "the good life." Affluence also gives people the leisure time to seek fun and pleasure in their lives.
2. An emphasis on scientific answers to human problems has undermined traditional religious approaches and belief in an absolute standard of morality. In addition, science tempers our notions of what should be by providing us with information about what is. And as we have learned more about our own sexuality—for example, that women like men are sexual beings—this information has enabled us to rethink attitudes and to change behavior.
3. The changing status of women has allowed modern women to question the double standard and to consider their own right to sexual satisfaction.
4. Increased mobility has made it difficult for people to establish long-term friendships and commitments, and, as a result, people have become more dependent on their spouses for emotional support and companionship. In this context, sex becomes more than a procreative duty or commodity that women reluctantly provide for their husbands; it is a pleasure to be mutually enjoyed and a way of maintaining a close bond between marital partners.
5. The development of effective birth control has permitted the separation of sex and reproduction. The result is the legitimization of other motives for sex and the removal of pregnancy as a barrier to nonmarital sexual activities.

Other changes over the period that have influenced sexual behavior include the decline in respect for established authority, and extraordinary increases in divorce, abortion, and sterilization.

Sexuality in the United States Today

The United States today is situated much closer to the permissive pole of the continuum than it had been at the beginning of the sexual revolution (Frayser, 1985). Most notably, there is now far less overlap between sexuality and reproduction. Prevailing social norms no longer demand that sex be procreative, and many nonprocreative and solely pleasure-oriented activities are tolerated. Attitudes toward such sexual phenomena as premarital sex, homosexuality, cohabitation, pornography, and sexual equality for women are much more favorable than in the past, and so too are those having to do with sex-related phenomena such as abortion, contraception, and sterilization. Moreover, these changes in norms and attitudes have been echoed by behavioral changes. All of the practices mentioned are at or near their all-time highs in terms of amount or availability.

FIGURE 19:3 ATTITUDE TOWARD PREMARITAL AND EXTRAMARITAL SEXUAL RELATIONS: GSS ANNUAL SURVEY, 1972–1988

Only about 36 percent of Americans now disapprove of premarital sex. But almost all Americans still oppose extramarital relations.

Source: Greely et al. (1989).

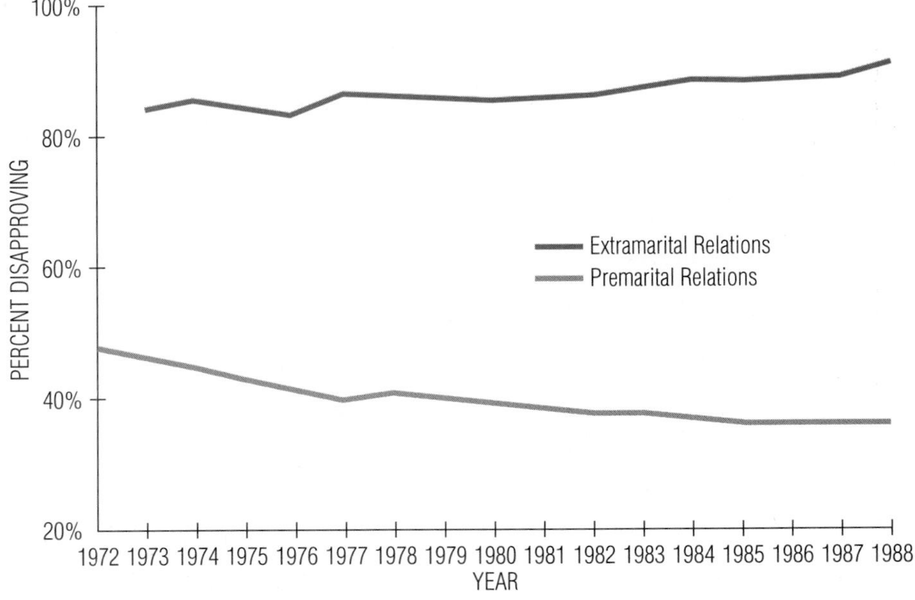

Probably the greatest change has occurred in attitudes and behavior concerning premarital sexuality. Figure 19:3 depicts public attitudes toward premarital sexuality measured by the GSS from 1972 to 1988. The downward trend in disapproval shown in the figure is just the tail end of a much longer decline stretching back into the nineteenth century. As noted earlier, only 36 percent of Americans now disapprove of premarital sex. But the social change is not just confined to attitudes. In 1988, the National Survey of Family Growth found that 53 percent of all females age 15 through 19 had intercourse. Moreover, 58 percent of those sexually active had had sex with two or more partners (Forrest and Singh, 1990). There are no similar reliable statistics on American males, but it is certain that a much higher proportion of males than females engage in premarital sex. Indeed, that proportion for males had risen to 85 percent as early as the 1940s at least in certain groups (Kinsey et al., 1948), and probably exceeds

In sexually permissive societies such as the United States, sex is commonly used to market products. Although both men and women are portrayed in advertisements as sex objects, women are overwhelmingly featured. It has long been a staple of the advertising industry to associate smiling or seductive women with the ownership of products that appeal to men. The overt use of men such as Marky Marks as sex objects in ads is a relatively recent manifestation of the sexual revolution.

BOX 19:2 COLLEGE EXPERIENCE

College Students and AIDS

Age-typical college students are no strangers to the issues discussed in this chapter. Consider premarital sex, for instance. GSS data show that 87 percent of those age 18 to 29 had at least one sex partner in 1989, and those in this age group reported an average of six lifetime sex partners (Smith, 1990). Data from smaller studies just on college students reveal similar levels of premarital sexual behavior. One such study found that the percentage of sexually experienced college women was about 88 percent in all three time periods investigated (namely, 1975, 1986, and 1989) (DeBuono et al., 1990). College students also share general social norms about such sexual variance as extramarital sex. In a recent national poll of Americans age 18 to 24, 100 percent of women and 97 percent of men said that faithfulness was an essential requirement for a spouse (Gibbs, 1990).

College life is fairly awash in sexual issues such as date rape, fraternity gang rape, sexual harassment, dormitory visitation rights, gay bashing, even prostitution rings (at Brown University in 1986). But perhaps the most serious sexual issue to confront college students in the 1990s is AIDS.

College students have failed to heed the call for safer sex, despite the emergence of AIDS and other STDs such as herpes and chlamydia. As noted above, college students continue to have sex and to have multiple partners—an AIDS risk—at about the same rates they did before the AIDS epidemic struck (DeBuono et al., 1990). Moreover, only a minority of college students always use a condom during intercourse, a safer sex technique (DeBuono et al., 1990). Finally, many students at least occasionally practice the most dangerous form of sex, anal intercourse (DeBuono et al., 1990; MacDonald et al., 1990). The Kinsey Institute reports that at least one in four college students have tried it at least once (Weiss, 1988).

If you think that asking a prospective sexual partner about their health or sexual history is a reliable way of avoiding AIDS, think again. Researchers have found that many college students lie to prospective sex partners. In one survey of Southern California college students, 10 percent of the women and 34 percent of the men admitted they had told a lie in order to have sex. Moreover, 4 percent of the women and 20 percent of the men stated that they would lie about being HIV positive, if that were the case, and 42 percent of the women and 47 percent of the men indicated that they would understate the numbers of prior sex partners (Cochran and May, 1990). Consequently, to mix a metaphor, you would be wise to take "sweet nothings" with a "grain of salt."

All of this has led to serious concern about the spread of AIDS among college students. This concern is justified given the aforementioned statistic that one in every 200 college men is already infected with this dreaded disease (Gayle, 1990).

Critical Thinking Questions

1. Many students are surprised when they learn that one in every 200 college men is already infected with AIDS. But why should this figure not surprise anyone familiar with the risk factors associated with AIDS infection?
2. Which of the three perspectives—functionalism, conflict theory, or symbolic interactionism—would be most useful in studying (and trying to minimize) the dishonesty exhibited by many college students concerning their sexual history? Please explain your answer.

90 percent today. Another feature of the premarital trend is the fact that, since the 1970s, teenage women and men have become sexually active at younger and younger ages (Kahn et al., 1988). A lot of premarital sex takes place in serious, committed relationships, often with an intended spouse; but much is of the casual variety as well, much more than in the past (see Box 19:2).

The social products of the sexual revolution are interlinked. For example, premarital sex is also a facet of cohabitation, which is much more common today than in the past (Chapter 14). Another example is the connection between premarital sex and the sexual double standard discussed earlier. The fact that women are rapidly closing the premarital sex gap with men is evidence that the double standard has eroded significantly.

But despite the movement toward permissiveness generated by the sexual revolution, the United States is still far from being one of the most sexually permissive societies (Frayser, 1985). Some traditional restrictive norms still have force, such as the norm against extramarital sex (see Figure 19:3) and the norm favoring monogamy (Greeley et al., 1989; Smith, 1990). Moreover, the sexual revolution just moved some activities out of the disapproved category into the condoned or tolerated, not into the approved category. For example, many parents condone premarital sex, but few openly encourage their adolescent children to engage in it, as is the case in some ultra-permissive societies. Similarly, many of those who now tolerate homosexuality do not see it as an alternative lifestyle on an equal footing with heterosexuality. Also, many parents still do not discuss sex with their children, or have difficulty doing so; much sexually oriented material is still labeled and prosecuted as pornography; and sex education is still a controversial topic (The Alan Guttmacher Institute, 1989). Even in the 1990s, advertisements for contraceptive products are not accepted readily by the mass media, extramarital sex is illegal in about half of the 50 states, and oral and anal sex among heterosexuals and homosexuals alike are impermissible in many states (Sachs, 1990). Indeed, even commonly used four-letter words, such as the F-word in the "Personal Perspective," are typically printed without all their letters and much of their impact because of lingering allegiance to restrictive norms of the past.

These lingering sexual restrictions are due in part to the fact that the sexual revolution was not waged by all groups to the same extent. As a result there are now significant age, income, educational, religious, urban/rural, and regional differences in sexual attitudes. Older people in particular tend to favor restrictive sexual norms (Smith, 1990).

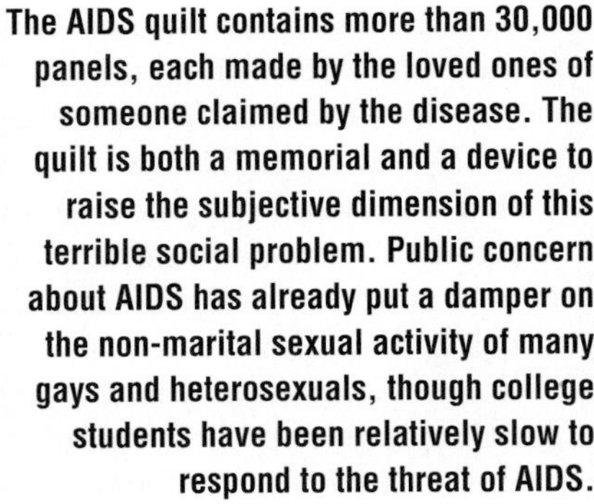

The AIDS quilt contains more than 30,000 panels, each made by the loved ones of someone claimed by the disease. The quilt is both a memorial and a device to raise the subjective dimension of this terrible social problem. Public concern about AIDS has already put a damper on the non-marital sexual activity of many gays and heterosexuals, though college students have been relatively slow to respond to the threat of AIDS.

Many believe that the violent subordination of women implicit in sexual harassment, rape, and pornography springs from the more powerful position of men in society. The buttons in this photo were produced by feminists who are crusading to change society's attitudes about such problems in the short run, and to change the gender-based nature of society itself in the long run.

The sexual revolution actually stalled somewhat during the 1980s. While there has been little retreat since 1980 from the new more permissive norms (Smith, 1985), there has not been any significant additional movement toward the permissive pole of the continuum either. Rather, the 1980s through the early 1990s was a period of relative stability with respect to sexual norms and behavior. There are probably many reasons for this. Interest groups favoring the more traditional, restrictive norms (e.g., anti-gay groups and anti-abortion groups) may have finally dug their heels in deeply enough to slow or halt at least temporarily the revolution's advance. STDs such as AIDS and genital herpes put the damper on the nonmarital sexual activity of many individuals, a kind of reincarnation of the aforementioned disease/sexuality relationship of the past. Indeed, there is evidence that both gays and heterosexuals curtailed their nonmarital sexual behavior in response to these diseases (Greeley et al., 1989, 1990). Finally, many people were harmed psychologically by the rampant promiscuity and casual sex of the 1970s, and are retreating to sexual relationships that offer love, care, commitment, and companionship (Blumstein and Schwartz, 1983).

But the period since 1980 was also one that saw interest groups favoring permissive norms attempting to solidify and institutionalize the gains they made over the past several decades. For instance, gays tried to capitalize on the increased tolerance for homosexuality by pressing for gay civil rights: the right to marry, join the military and the clergy, and be free of occupational and housing discrimination. Women's groups spearheaded campaigns to transform growing concern about women's issues such as sexual harassment into social control mechanisms (e.g., regulatory agencies, laws, etc.) (see Box 19:3).

Which way the United States will go in the future is uncertain. While there is a tendency on the part of students (and the media) to believe that the United States will become ever more permissive, that is not necessarily the case. Periods of permissiveness in the past have been followed by repressive ones and vice versa. For example, the American colonies were more sexually permissive than the United States during the Victorian period (Larkin, 1988). Moreover, there have been many societies in the distant past, such as ancient Rome, that had increasingly permissive norms even while facing evermore fierce enemies and diseases. Actually, however, it is diseases, particularly AIDS, that may hold the key to the immediate sexual future of the United States. If AIDS continues to make inroads into the heterosexual population, it is conceivable that the United States could move back toward the restrictive pole in a major way. On the other hand, as the older more restrictive generations gradually die out, pressure could build to move once again toward the permissive pole or at least to rid U.S. society of much of its present cultural ambivalence about sexuality.

In the meantime, the relatively permissive sexual values of U.S. society are spreading to many other cultures. This is due in part to the worldwide consumption of American films, television, music, and other cultural products that contain and often promote these permissive sexual values. Needless to say, this globalization of U.S. sexual values has an important bearing on such major megastructural problems as the AIDS pandemic and the population explosion.

SOCIAL NETWORKS AND SEX

Few human acts are as personal as sex. One reason you may have read this chapter even before it was assigned is to find out about *other* people's sexuality. Behind the veils of mystery, privacy, and cross-cultural barriers lie a

BOX 19:3 GENDER AND SOCIAL CHANGE

The Feminist Counterattack on Sexual Exploitation

In the early 1970s, when a radical feminist consciousness pulled incest out of the closet, we thought we were engaged in an unprecedented discovery. In fact, charity volunteers and social workers a century earlier dealt with incest cases daily, understanding them to be a standard, expected part of the caseload of a child protective agency such as the Society for the Prevention of Cruelty to Children.

Throughout the sexual revolution, female writers, activists, and groups have spearheaded social change on sexual issues, especially those having to do with the exploitation of women. As Linda Gordon's (1988, p. 56) statement above indicates, women activists were dealing with child sexual abuse and incest as early as the 1870s. Indeed, Gordon argues that the sympathy generated for these child victims and the subsequent reductions in the incidence of incest was one of the major achievements of nineteenth-century feminists. Over the past three decades, modern feminists have not only helped raise public concern over the remaining incest, which is still relatively common in the United States (Armstrong, 1990; Russell, 1986), but about such other exploitation issues as rape, sexual harassment, pornography, and prostitution.

Feminists have been successful particularly in helping the public understand that rape is not primarily a crime of lust, but a crime of violence and that the principal objective of rape is the humiliation and subjugation of the victim and the consequent affirmation of the power of the rapist (Brownmiller, 1986; Russell, 1975, 1984). Feminists have also been instrumental in puncturing the myth that most rapes are committed by strangers. In fact, acquaintances commit most rapes, including even spouses and dating partners (Finkelhor and Yllo, 1985; Russell, 1982). Feminists have not only raised public consciousness about marital rape and date rape, but have been influential in the creation of policies and laws to deal with these offenses. In addition, they have pushed through laws protecting the rights of rape victims in court proceedings.

Feminists also have been successful in changing attitudes, policies, and laws regarding sexual harassment. Sexual harassment involves uninvited, unwanted, coerced, and usually repeated sexual attention or advances. It generally takes place in situations in which the perpetrator has power over the victim. Indeed, feminists point out that it is the ability to exercise power

"fact of life" about sex: It is a social act. The whole weight of evidence in this chapter has shown the stamp of society on every form of sexual expression. But society is not some remote abstraction; it brushes up against your life through the workings of your social network. Consider the fact that a couple can be viewed as a bond between two flesh-and-blood "nodes" in the wider web of society. Other nodes may have introduced the lovers and encouraged their sexual union; still other nodes may even be temptations to infidelity, which eventually breaks up that union. Sex is personal, but it is also interpersonal.

But even before social networks affect our sexual relationships, they play an important role in our sexual development. For example, where do you get your information—and misinformation—about sex? As the "Personal Perspective" "knee to the groin" incident suggests, much "official information" about sex is processed through the conversational channels of the network before it becomes part of the individual's behavior. Similarly, the

BOX 19:3 GENDER AND SOCIAL CHANGE *continued*

rather than the actual sex per se that is the primary motive for sexual harassment (Gutek and Nakamura, 1983). Sexual harassment is common in the workplace and on college campuses where, for example, approximately 30 percent of all female college students report experiencing it during their academic careers (Hughes and Sandler, 1986). Recently, feminists have also thrown the spotlight on less-known forms of exploitive sex such as physicians and psychiatrists having sexual contact with their trusting, vulnerable patients (Rutter, 1989).

Similarly, feminists have raised consciousness about the exploitive nature of prostitution (Dworkin, 1981; Giobbe, 1990). Like rape and sexual harassment, feminists emphasize that prostitutes are generally troubled, minority, economically deprived or otherwise disadvantaged women who principally serve the interests of more powerful men. Feminists have also made some progress in bringing about legal reform on behalf of prostitutes.

Finally, many feminists have objected strenuously to exploitive, particularly violent, pornography (Dworkin, 1981; Griffin, 1982; Leidholdt, 1990). Some feminist groups have protested the commercial degradation of women evident in pornographic scenes where women are stripped, bound, raped, tortured, mutilated, and/or murdered. These groups contend that such scenes foster sexism by making men feel sexually superior to women, a feeling that generalizes to nonsexual relationships in the home and workplace (Jeffreys, 1990). They also argue that pornography deprives women of their civil rights and may even lead to rape. Along with other anti-pornography groups, feminists have had some success in having specific types of pornography banned in various cities and counties. But in general their main objective has been to raise consciousness about the sexist nature of pornography.

The progress feminists have made in changing attitudes about these and other forms of sexual exploitation is readily evident in national public opinion polls. For example, in 1970, 66 percent of American women said they resented being looked upon as a sex object; by 1990, that figure had risen to 80 percent. Similarly, when asked "Are you annoyed by pictures of nude women in men's magazines?" the proportions saying "yes" for 1970 and 1990 were 43 percent and 61 percent, respectively (Roper Organization, 1990). Date rape and sexual harassment regulations at many colleges are also examples of the changes in the sexual climate spearheaded mainly by women.

Critical Thinking Questions

1. It is not uncommon for elderly women to be raped by young men. Why do you think that happens?
2. Not all feminist groups oppose pornography per se. Why do you think feminists split on this issue? Does pornography serve any useful function for society?

waves of change making up the sexual revolution have not been invented spontaneously by individuals in each new generation. Rather, they have been borne by a complex process of experimentation, discussion, and attitudinal change along the strands of the social network.

THE SUBJECTIVE DIMENSION OF SEXUAL SOCIAL PROBLEMS

There are many social problems associated with sexuality in the United States. Public concern about these problems is a function of values, visibility, and expectations.

Values are the most important determinant of the degree of public concern about sexual problems. As U.S. society moved toward the permissive pole during the sexual revolution, it adopted more pro-sexuality values.

DUGAS (Gaétan)

Au C.H.U.L. le 30 mars 1984, à l'âge de 32 ans, est décédé M. Gaétan Dugas, commissaire de bord pour Air Canada, fils de M. Arthur Dugas et de dame Lorette Perry. Il demeurait à l'Ancienne-Lorette. Les funérailles auront lieu le

In his 1987 book, *And the Band Played On,* Randy Shilts outlined the history of the early days of the AIDS epidemic in the United States. His conclusion was that the federal government and the gay community focused more on ideological preaching than on prudent public health measures, thus letting the epidemic spiral out of control at a cost of millions of lives. Shilts's book was also the first to identify "Patient Zero," the man who possibly introduced the disease to the homosexual community in the United States. That man turned out to be Gaétan Dugas, a gay flight attendant who, by his own estimate, had sex with 250 partners a year, and continued to do so unrepentantly even after he was told he was endangering his partners. Dugas was able to spread the disease so widely, owing in part to his membership in gay social networks associated with gay bars and bathhouses in Los Angeles, New York, and eight other cities frequented by his airline. Both Dugas and Shilts have since died as a result of AIDS.

Since such issues as homosexuality became gradually less inconsistent with these new values, public concern about it declined significantly. Other phenomena such as premarital sex and pornography (Figure 19:4) became so commonplace, owing to the new values, that these behaviors lost nearly all of their status as social problems. On the other hand, the increasing support for values against sexual exploitation and violence, especially toward women, have raised public concern about such problems as rape and sexual harassment. Extramarital sex, prostitution, and incest remain problems with high subjective dimensions because they run counter to revered family values.

Sexual problems may be the most *visible* of social problems. There is intrinsic drama in such phenomena as extramarital sex, homosexuality, rape, and prostitution. Always on the watch for a story that will capture the public's interest, the media are quick to capitalize on this real-life drama. Sexual problems are featured regularly in highly emotional films (e.g., *The Accused*), gripping television documentaries, and popular talk shows. They are also the subject of in-depth coverage in the print media.

Expectations also influence public concern about sexual problems. In general, the more controllable or unthinkable a problem seems to us, the more we tend to view it as outrageous when it occurs. Problems like incest, extramarital sex, and marital rape are relatively more upsetting to us because they are the last things we expect from loving, caring parents and spouses. Similarly, "rough sex" murders such as the one involving preppies Robert Chambers and Jennifer Levin (Wolfe, 1989), serial sex murders such as the case of the Hillside Stranglers (O'Brien, 1987), and brutal gang rapes such as the infamous "wilding" rape of a New York City investment banker in 1989 are especially shocking because they violate our expectations about normal human behavior.

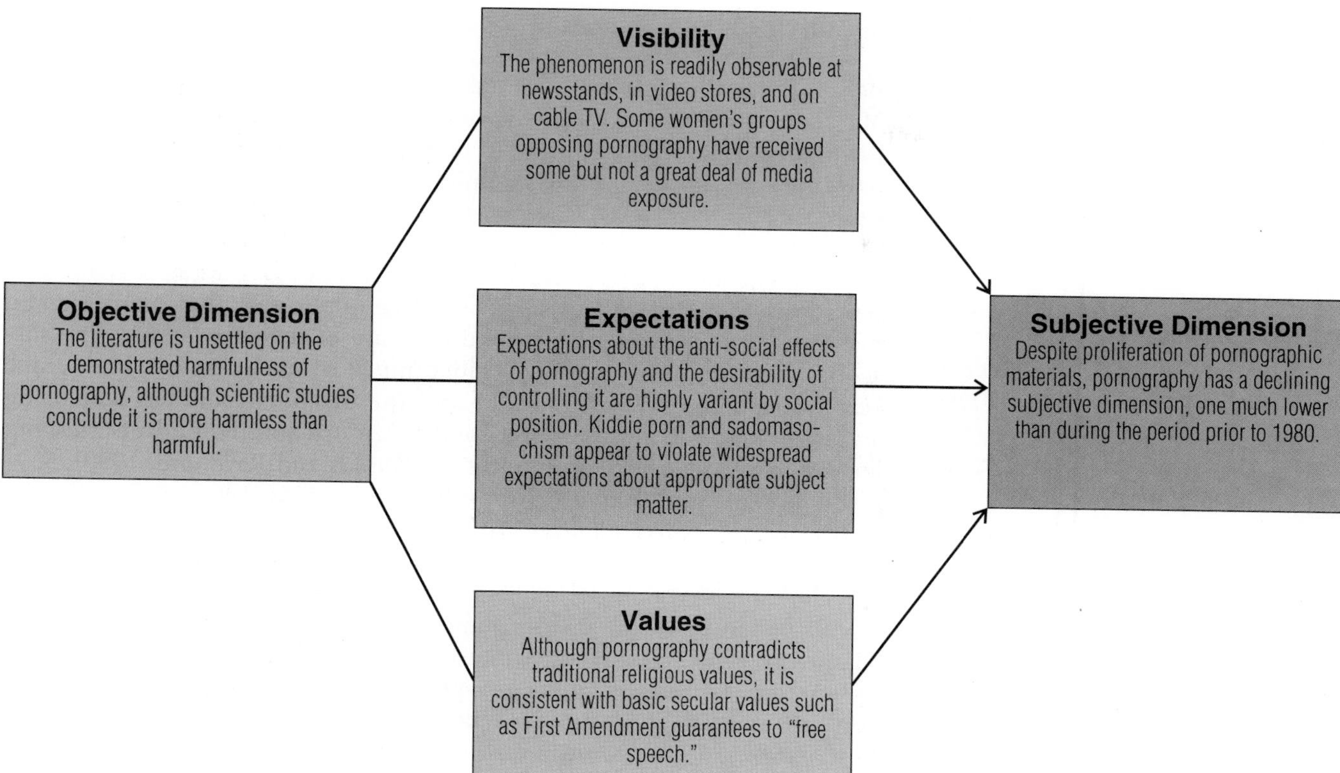

FIGURE 19:4 SUBJECTIVE AND OBJECTIVE DIMENSIONS: THE CASE OF PORNOGRAPHY

The subjective and objective dimensions of pornography are not very different in scale. This situation is due to the fact that all three intervening variables—visibility, expectations, and values—exert both positive and negative forces on the subjective dimension.

THEORETICAL PERSPECTIVES ON SEXUAL BEHAVIOR

Functionalism

Throughout this chapter you have encountered insights about sexual behavior, which are the products of sociologists applying the functionalist perspective. Remember the basic functionalist proposition: Regular social practices—even those as private as sex—can serve the society in many ways. For example, a function mentioned earlier is the ability of restrictive sexual norms to generate desired population growth by maximizing fertility and minimizing mortality from disease. Similarly, prostitution can have the function of holding marriages (and families) together by providing sexual services not available within an otherwise satisfactory marriage. Finally, restrictive norms concerning homosexuality force many homosexuals to remain "in the closet" where they often marry heterosexuals, a situation that leads to the dysfunction of marital unhappiness and disruption. Incidentally, one excellent reason for heterosexual college students not to harass homosexuals is that driving gays into the closet raises the probability that each heterosexual student will eventually marry a gay person, with all the problems that would entail for both parties.

Functionalism is particularly useful in understanding unusual sexual customs in pre-industrial societies. Intercourse taboo days, the marriage between adolescents and infants, delaying marriage and sex to long after puberty, and like customs often have a positive manifest or at least latent population control function at their root. Similarly, incest taboos have the latent positive function of helping families operate effectively and of helping groups form alliances for economic and military survival.

Conflict Theory

Before the sexual revolution in the United States, patriarchy was the rule. Men controlled sex within the society, and husbands did the same within the family. Wives were expected to be submissive and to perform their sexual duties on demand. Little attention was given to their sexual needs or desires (Shorter, 1982). One way sociologists explain this situation is through conflict theory, which emphasizes the conflict inherent in such power inequality between the sexes. Conflict theorists argue that the sexual revolution came about in part owing to the fact that many women increasingly recognized the exploitive nature of sexual relations. The subsequent alienation of women provided much of the energy for the sexual revolution throughout its course, and for the open conflicts still being waged today—not only between women's groups and their adversaries, but among women's groups themselves (Leidholdt and Raymond, 1990).

But it is not just women's groups that are fighting over sexual issues. Gay rights organizations, religious groups, anti-pornography movements, prostitution protest committees, and civil liberties groups, to name just a few, are all wrangling about sexual issues and the control of sexual behavior. Conflict theorists focus on this jumble of conflicts, noting in the process that it is not just class conflict that is socially significant.

One aspect of the conflict perspective concerns the benefits of social conflict. An example related to sexual issues is the fact that the traditional hostility toward gays contributes to the social cohesion (solidarity) of the gay community.

Symbolic Interactionism

Interactionist researchers focus on how people actually interact sexually. For example, the interactionist perspective has been used to understand how a sexually suggestive situation such as woman having a pelvic exam can be socially managed to make all involved parties feel more comfortable. This is accomplished through the use of stage settings (e.g., waiting room, examination room, doctor's office), props (hospital gowns, sheets, book-lined shelves), and roles ("patient," "competent doctor," "sympathetic nurse") (Henslin and Briggs, 1971).

The symbolic interactionist perspective also helps decode the hidden or referential meaning of such behavior as the choice of a coital position, which, of course, involves more than just the spatial mechanics of joining two bodies (Arnold, 1977). Similarly, an analysis of sexual stereotypes about forms of sexual variance can profit from the symbolic interactionist approach. The existence and prevalence of such stereotypes are reinforced by pejorative terms (e.g., "fag," "whore"), jokes about sexual variance, and various other by-products of everyday interaction.

Integrating the Theories

In their study of human sexuality, functionalists, conflict theorists, and symbolic interactionists *think critically* about different facets of the same phenomena. Consider, for example, prostitution. Prostitution can be functional in a society if it allows families to survive by providing a safety valve for sexual desires and activities that cannot be fulfilled within marriage. Conflict theory emphasizes that prostitution is a form of exploitation against women by men who hold the power in society. Finally, interactionist theory focuses on the day-to-day interaction among prostitutes, and between prostitutes and others (e.g., clients, pimps, and criminal justice system personnel) (Hobson, 1987).

SUMMARY

1. Sexuality is both a biological and social phenomenon, and sociological factors are at least as important as biological factors in determining the nature of sexual behavior.
2. Virtually all human sexual behavior is taught by society. Perhaps the best evidence for sexual behavior being a learned phenomenon comes from observations that sexual behavior varies enormously from one society to another.
3. Some sociologists contend that sexual behavior may be the most important of all human activities. Yet less systematic research has been carried out on sexual behavior than on any other important social topic.
4. Survey research is the major source of data on contemporary sexual behavior.
5. The most fundamental question all societies must answer about sexuality is just how sexual the society should be. Some societies are rabidly anti-sex, while others are extremely pro-sex. Most societies lie somewhere in between these extremes.
6. Sexual norms are taught through the process of socialization and govern virtually all aspects of sexuality. These norms can be divided into categories according to the who, what, where, when, and why of sexual behavior.
7. The cross-cultural perspective reveals that the society determines how individuals experience and express sexuality. It also shows how different norms produce extraordinarily diverse kinds of sexual behavior.
8. Virtually all forms of sexual behavior are condoned in some societies and condemned in others. Sexual deviance is thus socially defined.
9. The sexual revolution in the United States began during the middle of the nineteenth century. In 1850, the United States was a much more sexually restrictive society than it is today.
10. The pace of the sexual revolution was uneven. It accelerated twice—once during the "roaring 1920s," and again in the post-World War II period up to the present.
11. By the 1990s, the United States was a relatively permissive society, particularly in such areas as premarital sexuality. But despite the movement toward permissiveness generated by the sexual revolution, the United States is still far from being one of the most sexually permissive societies.
12. Social networks play an important role in our sexual development, and affect our sexual relationships as well.
13. Sexual social problems have relatively low objective and subjective dimensions.
14. When considering sexual behavior, functionalists focus on the manifest and latent functions carried out by these behaviors. Conflict theorists emphasize the conflict inherent in sexual relations between individuals who have unequal power. Symbolic interactionists focus on how people actually interact sexually.

Chapter 20

Personal Perspective

THE personal perspective of this chapter focuses on you. Consider the following questions:

- When and where were you born? How many others were born the same year?
- What is your probability of getting married or divorced?
- Do you have children or do you ever plan to? If so, how many, and how far apart?
- How many jobs will you have? What kind? What are your chances of promotion? When will you retire?
- How many times will you move? Where are you likely to go?
- How long will you live? What are the chances of your dying within a year? Within 10 years? What is likely to cause your death?

JAM

Population

Most students think demography is just math in disguise, all numbers, a sort of dry social accounting. But once immersed in the subject many students change their minds. Indeed, most students find demography fascinating because the discipline's topics are so personally relevant. All the questions in the "Personal Perspective" are in part demographic questions, illustrating the fact that nearly all of life's major events have demographic features. What this means, therefore, is that if you are not interested in demographic phenomena, you are not interested in yourself.

In addition, once students learn about demography, they come to appreciate its enormous social importance. Indeed, demographic forces have always had a profound impact on societies, and this has never been more true than during the past half-century, a period in which the United States and other societies have experienced unprecedented change in social and demographic structures. Since these demographic forces have not been resheathed, they will continue to be major players in causing social change and in shaping social policies and programs for the balance of our lives and beyond. Most students quickly recognize that an understanding of demographic forces, their interrelationships, and their effects on social institutions will help them deal more effectively with these forces in the future.

demography—the study of human populations, including their size, composition, and distribution, as well as the causes and consequences of changes in these factors.

Demography or population studies is a subdiscipline of sociology because population phenomena have important social causes and consequences (Stycos, 1987). Here is the key definition. **Demography** is the study of human populations, including their *size, composition,* and *distribution,* as well as the causes and consequences of changes in these factors. The three immediate causes of demographic change are *fertility, mortality,* and *migration.* The six italicized words above are demography's core subjects and this chapter is organized around them.

FERTILITY

Fecundity and Fertility

fecundity—the physiological ability of individuals and couples to have children.

Fecundity refers to the *physiological ability* of individuals and couples to have children. Some individuals are unable to have children throughout their lives due to genetic dysfunction. Others are super-fecund, the world record for female fecundity (and fertility) being held by a nineteenth-century Russian woman who reputedly produced 69 children in 27 pregnancies (McWhirter, 1985). Although this claim is suspect, there is no doubt that some women have given birth to more than 30 children. Thus individual female fecundity varies from zero to more than 30 children. (Male fecundity can range much higher but is generally limited by their mate's fecundity.) *Maximum fecundity* for a whole population falls somewhere between these extremes. Most authorities estimate that maximum population fecundity is about 15 children per woman (e.g., Bongaarts, 1978; Petersen, 1975). In other words, a population of women who engaged in regular intercourse from menarche to menopause without using any form of birth control would, under the most favorable reproductive circumstances, average about 15 children per woman (McFalls, 1979a).

fertility—the number of births that actually occur to an individual or a population.

Fertility refers to the number of births that *actually occur* to an individual or a population. The fertility of national populations ranges from about 1.3 (Italy) to 7.9 (Gaza) children per woman, with about 3.3 being the worldwide average in 1992 (PRB, 1993). The difference between this performance and the 15-child estimate of maximum fecundity is due to a variety of social, economic, cultural, and health factors (Davis and Blake, 1956). You can probably identify any number of these factors, including those related to cultural childbearing values (Does the society value large or small families?); social roles (Is a wife primarily a mother and childrearer?); economic realities (Do parents rely solely on children to look after them in old age?); and sexually transmitted diseases (How common are fecundity-impairing diseases such as gonorrhea and chlamydia?) (McFalls

Each year about 22 million babies are born in China, a number greater than the populations of Australia and New Zealand combined. Owing in part to so many births, China became the world's first "demographic billionaire" in the 1980s. Its population stood at 1.2 billion in 1993. China has over a fifth of the world's population and more than a quarter of that of the developing world. Presently the Asian nation is making a Herculean effort to reduce its birth rate. One tactic is to limit married couples to just one child.

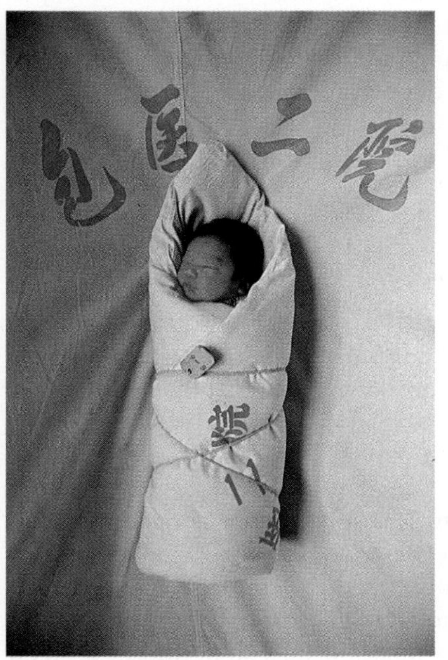

TABLE 20:1 The Intermediate Variables that Affect Fertility

I. FECUNDITY VARIABLES (those governing reproductive ability)
 1. Ability to have intercourse
 2. Ability to conceive
 3. Ability to carry a pregnancy to term and to give birth

II. SEXUAL RELATIONSHIP VARIABLES (those governing the proportion of the reproductive period in which intercourse occurs)
 A. Variables governing the formation and dissolution of heterosexual relationships (i.e., marriage, consensual unions, short-term affairs, etc.)
  4. Lifelong celibacy: proportion who never enter a heterosexual relationship
  5. Amount of the reproductive period spent before first heterosexual relationship
  6. Amount of reproductive period spent after or between heterosexual unions
   a. When long-term relationships are disrupted by divorce, separation, or desertion
   b. When long-term relationships are severed by the permanent institutionalization or death of the mate
   c. When short-term relationships are terminated for any reason
 B. Variables governing the continuity and frequency of intercourse within heterosexual relationships
  7. Voluntary sexual abstinence
  8. Involuntary sexual abstinence
   a. Due to temporary separation
   b. Due to intercourse taboos
  9. Frequency of intercourse (excluding periods of abstinence)

III. BIRTH CONTROL VARIABLES (those governing whether intercourse is allowed to result in a birth)
  10. Contraception
   a. By mechanical and chemical means
   b. By behavioral means (especially withdrawal)
   c. By breastfeeding for contraceptive purposes
  11. Voluntary sterilization
  12. Induced abortion

Source: Davis & Blake (1956); modified by McFalls and McFalls (1985) and McFalls (forthcoming). By permission of the publisher.

and McFalls, 1984). Societies differ with respect to these and a host of other fertility-related factors, and the level of their fertility varies accordingly.

But these factors cannot affect fertility directly; they first must work through one or more *intermediate variables* (Davis and Blake, 1956) (see Table 20:1). Although each of the 12 variables listed in the table influences the fertility of every society, differences in fertility between societies are determined primarily by the four most powerful ones: no. 2, ability to conceive (which can be decreased most by breastfeeding); no. 5, the amount of the reproductive period spent before the first sexual relationship; no. 10, contraception; and no. 12, induced abortion (Bongaarts, 1982). Thus, West Germany achieved the lowest fertility rate on record for a nation (1.28 births per woman in 1985) in large part due to relatively high rates of contraception and abortion (Haub, 1989). Conversely, the Hutterites, a North American Anabaptist subculture, which holds the childbearing world record (12 children per woman in the 1930s), accomplished this feat in large part by eschewing contraception, abortion, and unmarried life (Eaton and Mayer, 1954).

In general, modern societies have relatively low fertility. Women in such societies reproduced at a lifetime rate of 1.8 children in 1992. In contrast, their counterparts in developing societies, excluding China, reproduced at a lofty rate of 4.4 children per woman in that year.

Total Fertility Rate

With the exception of the 12-child Hutterite average, all the rates in the previous section are total fertility rates. What do they mean? Think about it for a moment. If you wanted to measure the *current* rate of childbearing in a society for a given year, say 1995, how would you go about it? You cannot look at what, say, 21-year-old women are doing because you would get only the rate for 21-year-olds. How about measuring the lifetime fertility of women who had completed their reproductive periods in 1995, say, women age 49? True, this is a useful measure of fertility called the "completed fertility rate." But it really does not tell you much about fertility in 1995—only a bit about the fertility of 49-year-olds when they were 49. Almost all their childbearing took place in the past, some of it as long as 35 years ago when the society was very different. You need something better to measure the overall rate of childbearing in a single target year. That something better is the *total fertility rate* (TFR).

Whose fertility does the TFR measure? No one really—at least no *real* group of women. It is a measure of the fertility of an *imaginary* group of women who pass through their fictitious reproductive lives subject to the actual rates of childbearing experienced by real women of all ages in the target year. To help you understand this better, refer to the TFR for 1991 calculated in Table 20:2.

The TFR is based on statistics about real women in a given target year such as U.S. women in 1991 above (Haupt and Kane, 1991). Column (1) indicates the number of women in each age group, and column (2) shows the total number of actual births women in each age group had in 1991. Column (3) gives the *average* number of children women in each age group had in 1991. For example, the women age 20–24 averaged .111 children in 1991. Summing the rates in column (3) (and multiplying that sum by 5) results in the number of children "imaginary" women would have by age 44 if they passed through their lives subject each year to the rates in column (3) that applied to real women in 1991. The reason it is necessary to

TABLE 20:2 Calculating the U.S. Total Fertility Rate (TFR), 1988

AGE OF WOMEN	(1) NUMBER OF WOMEN	(2) BIRTHS TO WOMEN IN AGE GROUP	(3) AGE-SPECIFIC BIRTHRATE (2) ÷ (1)
15–19	8,890,000	488,941	.055
20–24	9,574,000	1,067,472	.111
25–29	10,928,000	1,239,256	.113
30–34	10,903,000	803,547	.074
35–39	9,660,000	269,518	.028
40–44	8,155,900	40,776	.005
		Sum	.386
		TFR = Sum × 5	1.930

Source: Arthur Haupt and Thomas Kane, *Population Handbook*, 3rd. Edition (Washington, DC: Population Reference Bureau, 1991).

multiply the sum of column (3) by 5 is because the imaginary women would spend 5 years in each age group, and thus be subject to the risk of birth 5 times in each 5-year age group. For example, they would have .111 children when they were 20; another .111 when they were 21, and so forth.

TABLE 20:3 What Women Feel Is the Ideal Number of Children Crosstabulated with Race

IDEAL NUMBER OF CHILDREN	RESPONDENT'S RACE			
Count **ROW PCT**	White	Black	Other	All
Zero	4 **0.9**	—	—	4 **0.8**
One	10 **2.3**	—	—	10 **2.0**
Two	238 **55.7**	23 **38.3**	15 **71.4**	276 **54.3**
Three	106 **24.8**	14 **23.3**	4 **19.0**	124 **24.4**
Four	42 **9.8**	11 **18.3**	1 **4.8**	54 **10.6**
Five	5 **1.2**	1 **1.7**	—	6 **1.2**
Six	3 **0.7**	1 **1.7**	—	4 **0.8**
Seven or more	1 **0.2**	—	—	1 **0.2**
As many as wanted	18 **4.2**	10 **16.7**	1 **4.8**	29 **5.7**

$n = 508$

Main Point: Regardless of race, most women desire two or three children. Few desire one or none.

Source: General Social Survey, 1990.

FIGURE 20:1 UNITED STATES BIRTH RATES BY AGE OF MOTHER, 1955–1991

Each line in this graph represents the level of childbearing of women in a specific age group over time. Note that the rate of childbearing has declined at all ages.

Source: National Center for Health Statistics (1993b).

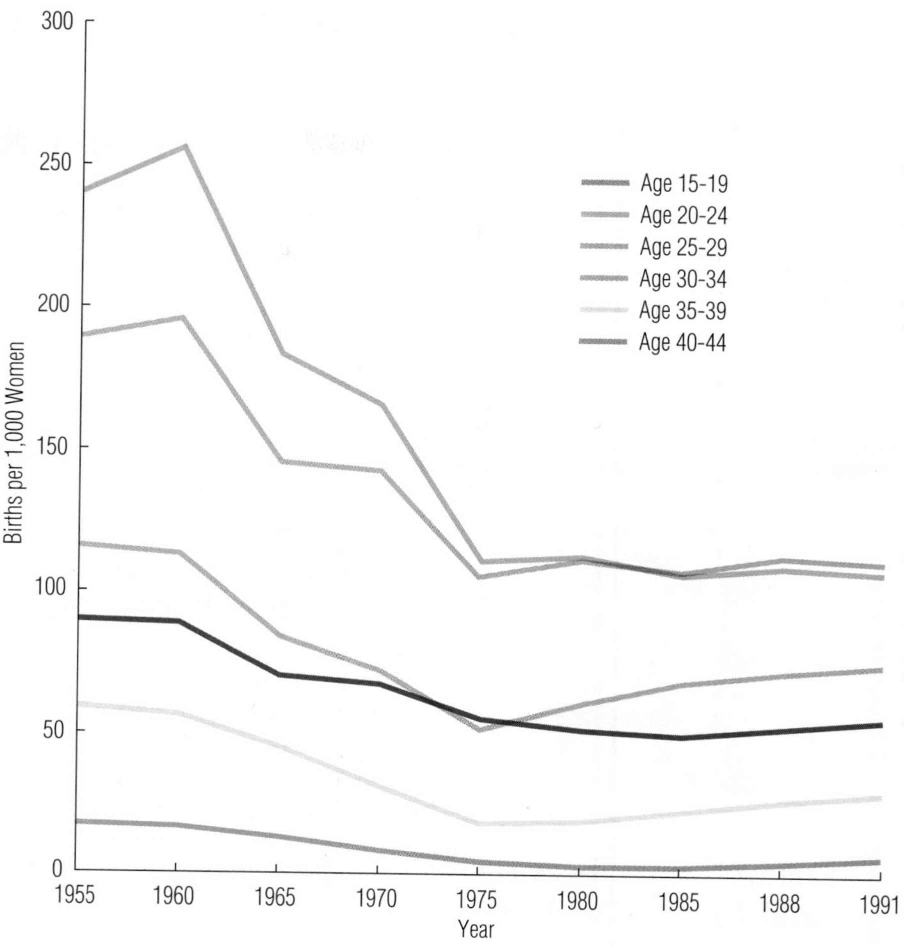

Fertility in the United States

Fertility Trends

American women averaged more than 7 children each until the early decades of the nineteenth century. Average fertility declined gradually after then, interrupted only by the post–World War II "baby boom." It reached an all-time low of 1.74 children in 1976, and has remained relatively low ever since. This "baby bust" has come about because of a dramatic reduction in childbearing at all ages (see Figure 20:1).

The current low fertility has been brought about in large part by a postponement of marriage and by the widespread use of abortion and contraception (Westoff, 1986), especially sterilization, now the most common method of contraception in the United States (Pratt et al., 1984). Judging by the long-term fertility trend and the near absence of incipient social trends favoring higher fertility, it is likely that this low level of fertility will persist indefinitely (McFalls, 1981).

Despite the fact that few American women believe childless or one-child families are ideal (see Table 20:3), one feature of the present baby bust is that many women (and couples) will actually have only one child or no children at all, including many of these who want two or more children (Baldwin and Nord, 1984). Indeed, Bloom (1982) estimated that as many as 20 percent of women in various age groups born since 1950 could finish their reproductive careers either intentionally or unintentionally childless. Perhaps you or your mate will be one of them.

Fertility Differentials

Age. Birthrates vary substantially by age (see Figure 20:1). Since 1983, women age 25–29 have had the most births, slightly more than women age 20–24, the perennial leaders. Another age-related phenomenon can be discerned in Figure 20:1. Notice the upturn in childbearing among women age 30–44, which began during the 1970s and 1980s, owing principally to the decisions made by many women to postpone childbearing (see Box 20:1). Incidentally, delayed childbearing is also a major cause of the aforementioned increased rates of childlessness (McFalls, 1990). Finally, Figure 20: 1 reveals that, despite the fact that teenage girls (and boys) lost their virginity at increasingly early ages (Hofferth et al., 1987), the rate of

BOX 20:1 GENDER AND SOCIAL CHANGE

Delayed Childbearing and Fewer Children than Desired

A notable feature of the present baby bust is the fact that substantial proportions of women are delaying much of their childbearing until relatively late in their reproductive lives, a practice that generally leads to lower completed fertility (McFalls, 1990). One facet of this delayed childbearing trend is that women are putting off the birth of their first child until later and later into their reproductive period. But the delayed childbearing trend is not confined to older women having first children. Women are also postponing their second and higher-order births as well (NCHS, 1989b; Ventura, 1989).

The reasons for this pattern of delayed childbearing, which is common in European countries as well (Toulemon, 1988), are wide-ranging and complex. The desire of increasing numbers of women to pursue education and to establish themselves in careers before embarking on motherhood is probably the most important reason (Bloom and Trussell, 1984; Ventura, 1982, 1989). Deferred marriage also plays a role, because many more women now postpone that event until sizable portions of their reproductive lives have elapsed. Another factor is the high divorce rate among American couples. Given the common knowledge that about 50 percent of recent first marriages are projected to end in divorce, many women undoubtedly delay childbearing until they are certain their marriages are stable. Other factors that account for the upswing in delayed childbearing include economic problems confronting the jumbo-sized baby boom cohorts involved, the availability of legal abortion and effective contraception, which make the postponement decisions of women more feasible, and the host of basic changes in the family institution (see Chapter 14) and in the relations between men and women within and outside of marriage (see Chapter 13; Levy and Michel, 1985). Whatever the reasons for the upswing in delayed childbearing, there are no signs that American women—including the age-typical college women reading this text—will turn away from this childbearing pattern anytime soon (Baldwin and Nord, 1984).

Critical Thinking Questions

1. Women who postpone childbearing run a risk of completing their reproductive lives childless or with fewer children than desired. What social and biological events could contribute to such an outcome?
2. How do the basic changes in the family institution and in the relations between men and women within and outside marriage (see Chapters 13 and 14) account in part for the upswing in delayed childbearing? How would a conflict theorist view this response to these changes?

teenage childbearing has held relatively steady over the past two decades due largely to the availability of legalized abortion (NCHS, 1993b; Smollar and Ooms, 1987).

Race and Ethnicity. The total fertility rate for white women in 1991 was 2.0; for African American women, 2.5; and for Hispanic women, about 2.9 (NCHS, 1993b; USBC, 1989a). African American women have a higher fertility rate than white women primarily because of dramatically higher fertility rates between age 15 and 24. While the African American and Hispanic rates are substantially higher than the white rate, they are relatively low by world standards, which means that neither group is having stereotypical "huge families." However, there are large group differences in the proportion of children born out of wedlock—56 percent for African Americans, 26 percent for Hispanics, and 15 percent for whites (USBC, 1989a). The fertility of Asian Americans (1.9) is slightly lower than that of the U.S. population as a whole, although some groups such as the Chinese Americans (1.6) and the Japanese Americans (1.4) have exceptionally low fertility (Retherford and Levin, 1989). While there are fertility differences between white ethnic groups (Irish Americans, Italian Americans, etc.), these are becoming less distinguishable over time (Lieberson and Waters, 1988). In short, it is apparent that the social, economic, and cultural assimilation of racial and ethnic groups into the U.S. mainstream leads to assimilation in fertility behavior as well.

Socioeconomic Status. The middle and upper classes in the United States have much lower fertility than the lower class regardless of race or ethnicity. In general, fertility is negatively related to income, educational attainment, and the occupational prestige of women and their mates. In 1988, for example, women age 35–44 with five or more years of college averaged 1.6 children compared to 2.3 births for women who completed high school only, and nearly 3 births for non-high school graduates (USBC, 1989a). The so-called yuppies are noted for small families, especially the subset known as DINKS, an acronym for double-income, no kids couples (Smilgis, 1987). Also, contrary to prevailing public opinion, women on welfare have fewer children than women in general (Rank, 1989).

MORTALITY

Life Span, Life Expectancy, and Premature Mortality

life span—the maximum age that human beings could reach under optimum conditions.

The second cause of population change is mortality. Like fertility, mortality has both biological and social determinants (see Chapter 18). Researchers believe there is a limit to human longevity; that is, a maximum **life span** of about 120 years. But people who live that long have superlongevity genes (Olshansky et al., 1990). Indeed, it is becoming increasingly clear that human beings as a *group* have a biologically fixed life span of only about 85 years. Therefore, the mean age at death would be about 85 if all potentially avoidable causes of death were eliminated. The difference between age 85 and a population's life expectancy at birth is a good indicator of the amount of potentially avoidable or premature death in a society (Fries, 1980). Such premature mortality is due to both biological causes (e.g., the AIDS virus) and social causes (e.g., suicides).

Life expectancy and its complement, premature mortality, vary by society. In 1992, the inhabitants of developing nations (excluding China) had an average life expectancy of 60 years, and an average loss of 25 years of potential life. Comparable figures for advanced nations were 74 years and 11 years, respectively. Japan, with the world's highest life expectancy (79 years), had the least premature mortality; Sierre Leone, with the lowest life expectancy (42 years), had the most premature mortality. Indeed, the inhabitants of Sierre Leone typically lose more life (43 years) than they experience (PRB, 1993).

Despite the existence of premature mortality worldwide, human beings in both advanced and developing societies live much longer now than in the past. The average length of life in the world at the turn of this century was less than 30 years; by 1992, it was 63 years (PRB, 1993). This means that since the origin of the human species some 2 million years ago, the vast majority of progress in conquering premature mortality has taken place in the minute slice of time since 1900. Contrary to earlier scholarly opinion that these gains were primarily due to improvements in living standards, the increased life expectancy worldwide reflects mostly the accumulation of knowledge concerning disease, especially infectious disease, and the systematic application of this information through public and personal health practices (Preston, 1987).

Mortality in the United States

Life expectancy in the United States was 77 years in 1992, up spectacularly from 47 years in 1900 (PRB, 1993). But, given the genetically fixed average life span of 85 years, Americans on average are still being deprived of 8 years of potential life.

The leading causes of death in the United States are discussed in Chapter 18. Most of these "modern" causes—including the two biggest killers, heart disease and cancer—strike primarily after age 50 rather than during childhood; that is why life expectancy at birth has increased. But no one is immortal, not even college men whose frequent risk-taking behavior suggests they believe otherwise. Something is going to get everyone later if not sooner.

Shown here is life's last moment for race car driver Gordon Smiley as his car bursts into flames and disintegrates around him during the Indianapolis 500 qualifying trials in 1982. The cause of death, that is, death by accident, was placed on his death certificate, and eventually became part of the 1982 national cause of death statistics compiled by demographers at the National Center for Health Statistics. In 1982, accidents were the fifth most common cause of death in the United States, and they remain so today.

Also, as discussed in Chapter 18, the Grim Reaper is not an "equal opportunity" slayer. Death rates vary in the United States by everyday social categories such as age, sex, socioeconomic status, race, ethnicity, and religion.

Life Expectancy

life expectancy—an estimate of the average number of additional years people of a specified age can expect to live if current mortality rates were to continue.

Life expectancy, the best measure of mortality, is a concept many people use but few really understand. Stop for a moment and think: What does the aforementioned U.S. life expectancy in 1992 of 77 years mean, and to whom does it apply? Some students know that the term "life expectancy" as used in this section is really a shorthand way of expressing "life expectancy at birth." They therefore conclude that the figure above means that those born in 1992 are expected to live to an average age of 77. Not true. The 1992 birth cohort is bound to experience future changes in mortality that are impossible to predict. Will there be nuclear wars, devastating plagues, or fantastic medical advances? Possibly. Typically some students then suggest that life expectancy in 1992 comes from the average age at death of the most recent birth cohort in which everyone is now dead—say, the cohort born in 1872 whose last survivor died at age 120 in 1992. But most of this cohort's mortality occurred in the distant past when mortality rates were much higher than those that will be experienced by people born in 1992.

The plain fact is that life expectancy at birth in 1992 applies to no real group, not even to real people born in 1992. Like the total fertility rate, life expectancy applies to a hypothetical group who would pass through their imaginary lives subject to the mortality rates at each age in a single year such as 1992. Life expectancy is thus the best measure of mortality in a single year.

MIGRATION

migration—the movement of people across a specified territorial boundary for the purpose of changing residency.

immigration—the process of entering one country from another to take up permanent residence.

emigration—the process of leaving one country to take up residence in another.

residential mobility—any change of address within a country.

internal migration—population movement between different areas within a country.

Migration, the third component of population change, is the movement of people across a specified territorial boundary for the purpose of changing residence. There are two types: *internal migration* and *international migration.* The terms *in-migration* and *out-migration* are used for internal migration, movement between different areas within a country. The terms **immigration** and **emigration** are used for international migration, which is movement between countries (Haupt and Kane, 1988).

Residential Mobility and Internal Migration

Residential mobility is any movement within a country; **internal migration** is residential movement that crosses a specified territorial boundary such as a county line. Residential mobility is a feature of most societies, particularly advanced ones, but the U.S. population is extremely mobile by world standards. For example, each year about four times as many Americans change residence as do the inhabitants of Ireland (Long, 1988).

The residential mobility rate is the proportion of a population who have moved during the past year. The U.S. rate has varied between 16 percent and 21 percent since 1960. Almost two-thirds of this movement involved

In Chapter 6 the question was posed, Why do rural young people in the Third World migrate to the squalid squatter shantytowns that surround Third World cities? The answer is that despite the horrid conditions in Third World slums, these places afford better access to jobs, education, health care, good diets, and recreation than are available in rural communities. The same was true in the United States when cities were dreadful places in many ways. Andrew Wyeth's *Christina's World* (1948) eloquently conveys the oppressive loneliness of farm life and its lack of opportunities, especially for physically handicapped people. By contrast, George Bellow's *Cliff Dwellers* (1913) captures the vitality and dynamism of urban places. Together these two scenes help us appreciate the relentless pressures pushing young people out of rural areas and the truth in the old saying, "How are you going to keep young people down on the farm once they have seen the lights of the city."

moves within the same county. Intra-county movers generally are making housing adjustments or responding to life cycle changes such as separation from parents, marriage, divorce, or births. Long distance (i.e., at least inter-county) movers do so primarily for economic reasons such as seeking a new job or accepting a corporate or military transfer. Others move long distances to attend school, to change climate or lifestyle, or for family reasons (USBC, 1989c). Residential mobility can become a social problem when too much occurs, or when it has strong adverse effects on the places of origin or destination (Jones et al., 1988; O'Hare, 1988).

Residential Mobility Differentials

Age. Figure 20:2 presents residential mobility rates by age for the United States and four other advanced countries *circa* 1980. Notice that the shapes of the curves are similar, although their amplitude (the percent moving at given ages) varies considerably. In each country residential mobility is relatively high for children under age 5; relatively low for mid-teens; and extraordinarily high for persons in their early 20s. Thereafter mobility rates decline, rapidly at first, and then more gradually with age (Long, 1988). Mobility data for the United States in more recent years reveal the same age patterns (USBC, 1989b). From inspecting such data you now know that the age-typical college student is the prime mover, if not yet shaker, of U.S. society.

The similarity of the curves in Figure 20:2 supports the life-cycle approach to explaining residential mobility (Long, 1988). Mobility is high between the late teens and the early thirties as individuals leave their parents' home to attend college, find jobs, get married, and begin families. Naturally, the young children of these young parents also have high rates of mobility. As older parents settle into neighborhoods and careers, their mobility and that of their older, often teenage, children decline. The elderly tend to stay put, though a sizable minority become transplanted retirees often in Sunbelt states, while others move out of their family homes into smaller residences and life-care facilities.

Gender. There is not much difference between males and females either in the amount of movement (men move slightly more, 18.4 percent versus

FIGURE 20:2 RESIDENTIAL MOVERS BY AGE: UNITED STATES AND SELECTED COUNTRIES, *CIRCA* 1980

This graph shows residential mobility rates by age for different countries. Notice that the shapes of the curves are similar, though the percent moving at given ages varies considerably. The similarity of the curves supports the life-cycle approach to explaining residential mobility.

Source: Modified from Long (1992).

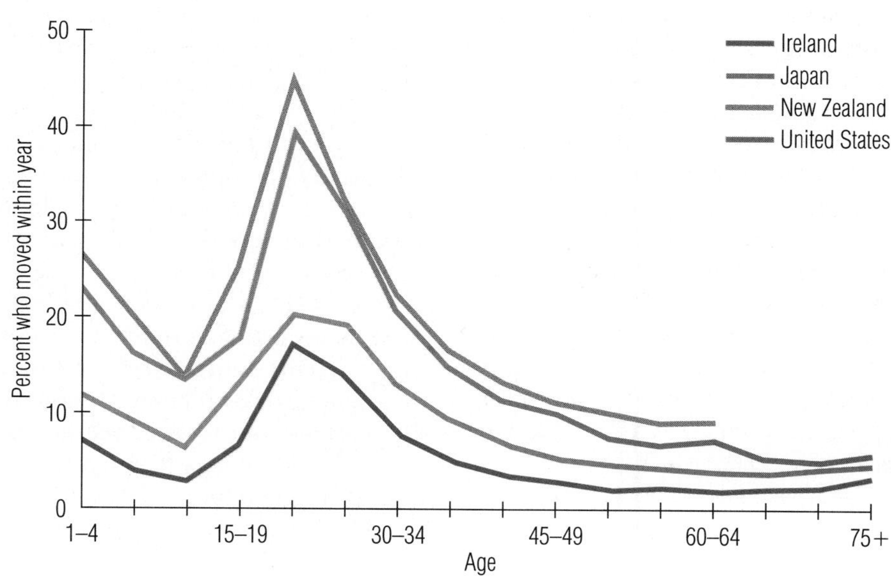

17.8 percent in 1986) or in their mobility age profiles (USBC, 1989b). The age-specific mobility rates of both sexes, when plotted, resemble the curve for the entire U.S. population in Figure 20:2. However, the curve for females is shifted slightly to the left of that for males. The rapid increase in mobility that begins in the late teens begins somewhat earlier for women than for men, owing to the fact that women tend to marry at a younger age than do men (Long, 1988).

Race and Ethnicity. Whites have lower rates of mobility than minority groups. In 1986, for instance, the proportion of whites who moved was 18 percent compared to 20 percent for African Americans and 23 percent for Hispanics (USBC, 1989b). Whites typically have higher long-distance rates and lower local rates than African Americans. In addition, African American movement is less highly concentrated during age 18–30. These racial differences are attributable to the fact that African Americans are more likely to be economically deprived and to be renters than whites and, consequently, find it more difficult to achieve the same level of residential and occupational stability that characterizes whites after age 30 (Long, 1988).

Socioeconomic Status. Residential mobility does not vary in any simple way with occupation or income. Among professionals, for instance, doctors, lawyers, or others with local bases of operation have low rates of mobility; top business executives, on the other hand, are highly mobile. Only educational attainment is clearly related to mobility, and that relationship is U-shaped. The most frequent movers are individuals at the educational extremes. Those who complete high school but do not go on to college have the lowest mobility rate. While those at the educational extremes move at about the same high rate, the character of that movement is different. The best educated make relatively more long-distance moves; the least educated make relatively more local moves (Long, 1988).

Lifetime Residential Mobility

Most national data on residential mobility are derived from questions asked by the U.S. Census ("Where did you live on this date five years ago?") or by the Census Bureau's periodic Current Population Survey ("Where did you live on this date one year ago?"). This type of data is used to calculate the age-specific rates for the United States in Figure 20:2. But how can this type of data be used to answer such socially significant questions as: How many moves does the average person make in a lifetime? How often does the average person move? Given only the age-specific rates available, how would you go about answering such questions?

As with fertility and mortality, it is not possible to answer these questions for real people. But it is possible to answer them for imaginary people using the life table approach. This is done by estimating the number of moves a hypothetical cohort will make in its lifetime if it is subject to the mobility rates (and mortality rates) of all age groups in a given target year. Long (1988) used this approach on 1982 data and found that the average hypothetical individual would experience 10.52 changes of residence over a lifetime. This is the source of the oft-quoted statement in newspaper and magazine articles that the average American moves about 11 times over a lifetime. But you know from the above that this number does not apply to actual people; it is really merely the best measure of the overall rate of residential mobility in a given year, in this case, 1982. Similarly, the other oft-quoted statistic in the popular literature, the average number of years between moves, can be calculated by dividing life expectancy (74 years in 1982) by the number of lifetime moves (10.52). The answer, 7.03, suggests that the average American moves once every seven years.

International Migration

international migration—population movement between countries.

Like internal migration, international migration is a worldwide phenomenon. Indeed, in recent years, international migrations of one sort or another were making headlines around the world—the dramatic stampede of East Germans into West Germany; white South Africans "taking the chicken run," as South Africans derisively call it, out of that nation; the emigration of Jews from the former Soviet Union to Israel; and the international movement of refugees who are the victims of civil wars in many parts of the world (Kismaric, 1989). These migrations occurred for the traditional reasons: The migrants either wanted to upgrade their lot in life or escape from difficult, often intolerable, circumstances. In short, migrants are "pushed" from their homeland by difficult conditions and/or "pulled" to a new country where conditions appear better (Bouvier and Gardner, 1986). International migration, of course, contributes to globalization by spreading and blending various ethnic and national cultures throughout the world.

The United States has traditionally received more immigrants than any other country, and presently receives twice as many immigrants as all other countries combined. No one knows exactly how many immigrants enter the United States each year, largely because illegal immigration is inadequately documented. But a good estimate is that in recent years about 1 million newcomers have annually immigrated to the United States, the highest level since the mass migration of Europeans at the turn of the century. During the 1980s legal immigration including refugees and those granted asylum averaged about 700,000 persons a year (Immigration and Naturalization Service, 1990), and illegal immigration probably averaged somewhere between 200,000 and 600,000 persons per year (Bouvier and Gardner, 1986). The numbers seeking to enter the United States are likely to increase in the future owing to the mounting population and economic pressures in the Third World, particularly in Mexico and the Caribbean Basin (Merrick, 1986).

About 100,000 U.S. residents emigrate each year. Most are older immigrants who are returning to their country of origin to spend their last years; others are simply looking for a country with a low cost of living. Indeed, emboldened by a flurry of publications touting Mexico's low cost of living and other advantages, many retired Americans have said *adios* to bad weather, high rents, skyrocketing utility and medical bills, rising crime, and humdrum lives in the United States, and have migrated to Mexico, which now has more U.S. Social Security beneficiaries than any other foreign country (Walton, 1990).

International Migration Differentials

Age. Traditionally, the immigrant flows have been composed disproportionately of young adults, who are most likely to migrate because they are in the stage of their life cycle when adaptability is greatest and attachments are fewest. Although the present immigration policy with its guiding principle of family reunification (i.e., giving preference to relatives of previous immigrants) has diminished somewhat the proportion of young adults among recent immigrants, young adults still predominate (Bouvier and Gardner, 1986).

Sex. Males have traditionally outnumbered females among migrants. An extreme example of this phenomenon was the 27 to 1 male-to-female ratio among Chinese immigrants at the turn of this century (Petersen, 1978). (These immigrants came to work on railroad and other labor-intensive projects.) However, today the ratio is close to unity (1.02 males for each female), at least for legal immigrants, due again to the selection principle of family reunification (Bouvier and Gardner, 1986). The male-to-female ratio is substantially higher, however, for refugees, those granted asylum, and illegal aliens (Passel, 1985).

Race and Ethnicity. The vast majority of immigrants to the United States between the early 1800s and the mid-1960s were of white, European stock. By 1985, Europeans accounted for a mere 11 percent of immigrants. About 46 percent of legal immigrants came from Asia, and 39 percent from Latin America. Africa contributed only 3 percent. The vast majority (80 percent) of all illegal immigrants come from Latin America (Bouvier and Gardner, 1986). Included among the remaining 20 percent are groups such as the Irish, 100,000 of whom live in the fearful shadow world of the illegal alien (Haub, 1987).

Socioeconomic Status (SES). Legal immigrants as a whole have higher socioeconomic status than natives in their country of origin, but a somewhat lower status than U.S. residents. Some immigrant groups arrive better equipped than others. With respect to education, for example, census data show that 67 percent of the total population age 25 and over had at least completed high school compared to only 53 percent of immigrants. But the proportion was much higher for immigrants from Africa (82 percent), and from Asia (73 percent), especially from India (89 percent); and lower for immigrants from Latin America (41 percent), particularly from Mexico (21 percent; U.S. Bureau of the Census, 1980). Statistics on occupation and income show a similar relationship between U.S. residents and legal immigrants as well as among the various immigrant groups. In general, Asians have a relatively high SES and Hispanics a relatively low SES. This indicates that a two-tiered society may be evolving, with Asians competing with whites and well-educated African Americans for positions in society's upper strata, and Hispanics competing with poorly educated African Americans for positions in the lower strata (Bouvier and Gardner, 1986).

Social Networks and Migration

Migration, like social structure, is a multi-tiered phenomenon. It can be analyzed in terms of the interrelationships between whole societies (e.g., What role does illegal immigration play in relations between the United States and Mexico?), through the linkages of institutions and social organizations (e.g., What is the impact of residential mobility on institutions in the community of origin or destination?), or through the patterns of social relations among individuals (e.g., To what extent is migration a social process that is mediated by long-standing family, friendship, and community ties?). This last microstructural approach can be used to understand the role played by social networks in facilitating migration.

Migrants typically want to upgrade their lot in life or escape from difficult, often intolerable circumstances. In 1991, lack of hope for a better life pushed more than 100,000 Albanians into joining an exodus from their country of 3.5 million people. About half the migrants fled across the Adriatic Sea to Italy, only to be refused entry and turned back.

Studies of the migration process have found that individuals usually neither choose to uproot themselves at random, nor do they choose their place of destination by going "eenee, meenee, minee, mo" (Borrie, 1954; Juliani, 1981; Lochore, 1951; Price, 1963). Rather, migration is a social process involving social networks that connect the place of origin to the place of destination. The movement of individuals takes place through *chain migration,* defined as movement in which prospective migrants learn of opportunities, secure transportation, and acquire initial housing and employment in the place of destination by means of primary social relationships with previous migrants (MacDonald and MacDonald, 1964; Petersen, 1975).

Chain migration operates in international and internal migration. In the former, a few bold immigrants blaze a trail to a new country, establish a foothold, and then send for friends and family to join them. These individuals form small ethnic communities, such as the Chinatowns in many American cities, which act as magnets (or "pull" factors) to others in the

place of origin. The bulk of immigration to the United States in the twentieth century has had this character, and it still operates powerfully today among Hispanics and Asians who, upon arrival, join established colonies of their compatriots such as Little Saigon in Orange County, California. Moreover, the new emphasis on family reunification in U.S. immigration policy encourages chain migration.

Chain migration also played an important historical role in rural to urban migration within the United States. The presence of a network of relatives and friends in a particular city attracted rural out-migrants to that city and helped ease the problems associated with relocation. While chain migration is not as important today as it was in the past, moving "to be closer to families and friends" is still one of the main reasons given by individuals for internal migration (Long, 1988).

But it should be noted that when it comes to social networks, migration is a two-edged sword. Migration often tears individuals loose from social networks with deleterious effects. Migrants must give up their familiar home and often their network of relatives and lifelong friends who usually provide valuable financial, health, and other benefits. They also must relinquish established relationships with neighbors, churches, and other institutions (Horton and Leslie, 1981). No wonder that much migration is movement back to the embrace of such personal networks.

POPULATION SIZE AND GROWTH

The size of a population can be altered only through the three immediate causes of demographic change discussed above: fertility, mortality, and migration. This situation is expressed by the following demographic equation:

$$\text{POPULATION GROWTH} = (B-D) + (I-O)$$

where for any time period, B, D, I, and O are, respectively, the numbers of births, deaths, people moving in, and people moving out of the population. The expression (B–D) is called **natural increase**; and (I-O), **net migration**. Thus, **population growth** is the sum of natural increase and net migration. Population growth can be positive, as in a growing population; negative, as in a population that is actually declining in size; or zero, as in a population that is neither gaining nor losing size. This last case is called zero population growth or ZPG. Population *doubling time* is the number of years until the population will double assuming a constant rate of growth. It can be calculated by dividing the number 70 by the growth rate expressed as a percentile. For example, a population with a 2 percent growth rate would double in 35 years.

natural increase—the difference between the total number of births and the total number of deaths in a population.

net migration—the difference between the total number of people migrating into an area and the total migrating out.

population growth—the sum of natural increase and net migration.

Demographers keep track of the size and growth of many types of populations—from the population of the world to that of a residential block in your hometown (cf., e.g., White, 1987).

World and National Populations

World population in 1991 exceeded 5.5 billion and was growing at a rate of about 1.8 percent annually. Note the relevant contributions to growth of births and deaths in the demographic balancing equation for the world (see Table 20:4). World population is growing today because births exceed deaths by a wide margin. Net migration, of course, is not a world popula-

TABLE 20:4 The Demographic Balancing Equation for the World and the United States, 1990[a]

	STARTING POPULATION, 1990	+	(BIRTHS – DEATHS) NATURAL INCREASE	+	(IMMIGRANTS – EMIGRANTS) NET MIGRATION	= ENDING POPULATION, 1991
World[b]	5,245,071	+	(142,959 – 50,418) 92,541	+	(NA[c] – NA)	= 5,337,612
United States[b]	248,168	+	(4,179 – 2,162) 2,017	+	(853 – 160) 693	= 250,878

[a]Numbers in thousands.
[b]The demographic equations for the world and for the United States are calculated above. Approximations are used where exact data are unavailable.
[c]NA = not applicable.
Source: McFalls (1991).

tion growth factor, and will never be unless space colonization becomes a reality. The Earth's population will increase during the 1990s by another billion, and will continue to grow rapidly during the twenty-first century.

How do we know how large the Earth's population will be in the 1990s and thereafter? Once again, we really don't know. But demographers can make educated guesses called *population projections* (Haub, 1987). One way to do this is to make assumptions about the future numbers of births and deaths (and immigrants and emigrants for non-global populations) for each future year and to plug these numbers into the demographic equation. Summing the resultant population growth for each year and adding that sum to the current population size yields the projected population size for any desired future year. For example, using a similar methodology, the United Nations recently projected that world population in the year 2025 will reach 8.5 billion, if the UN's most reasonable assumptions about future fertility and mortality prove correct. The UN also gave less likely lower and higher projections of 7.6 billion and 9.4 billion, respectively (United Nations, 1989).

China is the world's most populous nation. Its population in 1992 of nearly 1.2 billion inhabitants was 60,000 times larger than that of San Marino, the southern European nation with the world's smallest population (20,000). But India, with a growth rate nearly twice as high as China's, is bearing down on China and could surpass that country as the world's most populous nation in the next 60 years. Gaza is presently the world's fastest growing nation, with a 5.0 percent growth rate and a 14-year doubling time. Hungary is the world's slowest growing nation. In fact, with its negative growth rate (−0.2 percent), Hungary's population is actually becoming smaller (PRB, 1993).

The Population of the United States

The United States is the third most populous nation in the world, trailing only China and India. The 1990 demographic equation for the United States is calculated in Table 20:4. It shows that the population increased by 2.7 million people during 1990, owing to the fact that the numbers of births and immigrants exceeded the numbers of deaths and emigrants by that amount. Note the relative contribution made to growth by natural increase and net migration. The latter, which includes both legal and illegal immigration, accounted for more than 25 percent of population growth. U.S. population reached 258 million in 1992.

According to Census Bureau (1989) projections, the U.S. population could reach a peak of 309 million around 2040, and then start to decline, falling back to 292 million by 2080. But this is just one of 30 projections made by the Census Bureau, and its accuracy is only as good as the accuracy of the Bureau's assumptions about future fertility, mortality, and migration.

POPULATION COMPOSITION

population composition—the characteristics of a population, such as age, sex, and ethnicity.

Population composition refers to its characteristics. Here the focus is on age and sex composition. Other compositional characteristics such as religion, race, ethnicity, and marital status are discussed elsewhere in this book.

Age Composition

Age and Shape of Societies

The age composition of a society can be depicted by a *population pyramid,* a figure that shows the proportion of the population in each age group. The sum of the proportions in all age groups equals 100 percent of the population.

There are three general types of population pyramids: rapid growth, slow growth, and zero growth. Figure 20:3 gives an example of each. A rapid growth population is the only one that really looks like a pyramid, owing to the fact that each age cohort is larger than the one born before it. Rapid-growth populations come about primarily because of high fertility. Think about it. If couples in one generation average six children (as they do in Kenya), their children's generation will be about three times larger than their own generation. Thus, the pyramid would be about three times as wide at the base as in the middle. Rapid growth populations also get their distinctive shape because they had high mortality in the past, which means that the older age groups have relatively few surviving members and are thus relatively small. Conversely, they have lower mortality presently than in the past, particularly lower infant mortality, which means the younger age groups have relatively more survivors and are thus relatively large.

FIGURE 20:3 AGE PATTERNS OF POPULATIONS

These population "pyramids" show the proportion of the population in each age/sex group. It is clear that populations can have very different age/sex compositions.

Source: McFalls (1991). By permission of the publisher.

Age Patterns of Population

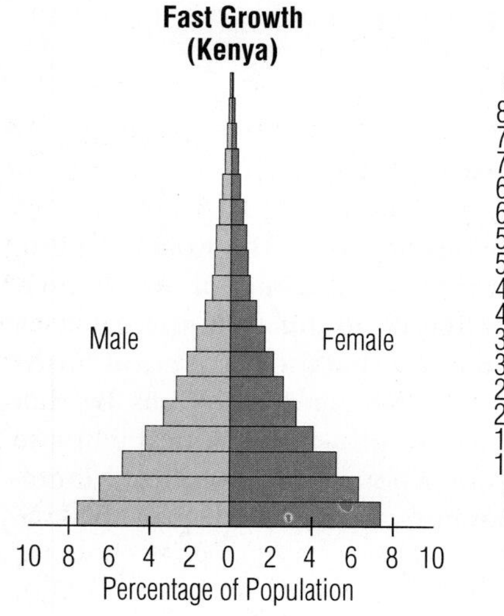

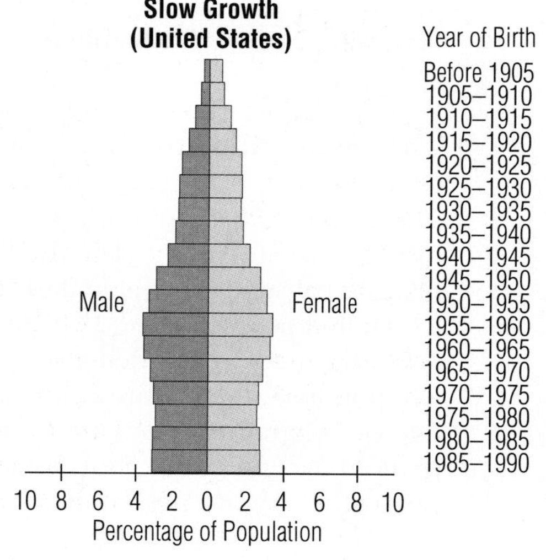

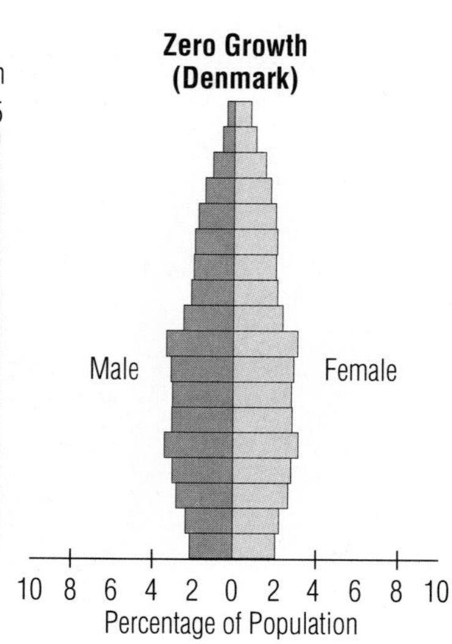

Because the vast majority of people in rapid growth populations are young and capable of present or future childbearing, these populations are called "young."

Near-zero-growth populations such as that of Sweden look more like rectangles than pyramids (see Figure 20:3). Each cohort is about the same size as every other one owing to the fact that the birthrate and the death rate have been low and relatively constant for a long time. This means that each age group is about the same size at birth and, since few people die before old age, the cohorts remain close in size until late in life when mortality rates must rise and erode the top of the rectangle. Because a relatively high proportion of people in near-zero-growth populations are old, these populations are called "old" or "stationary."

A slow-growth population is generally in the process of changing from a rapid-growth to a zero-growth shape in response to changes in fertility and mortality. The United States is typical of these "middle age," slow-growth societies (see Figure 20:3).

Population pyramids can also be shaped by migration. Since migration is age-selective, it alters the shape of both the place-of-origin and place-of-destination pyramids. In general, since migrants tend to be disproportionally young, the place-of-origin pyramid grows older, and the place-of-destination pyramid grows younger. But there are exceptions to this rule such as the state of Florida, whose pyramid has grown older owing to the influx of retirees.

The United States

The age structure of the United States looks more like a bowling pin than a pyramid (see Figure 20:3). This shape is due to drastic swings in the average number of births that have occurred in the twentieth century from the then-historic low of the 1930s to the baby boom peak of 1957, down to the baby bust low of the 1970s to 1990s (Bouvier, 1980). The pyramid's middle age bulge is composed of the baby boom cohorts who are making their way up the structure as time passes. Such a bulge has been likened to a swallowed pig moving through a python (McFalls et al., 1986). The narrower base is made up of the baby bust cohorts born since the late 1960s (see Box 20:2). Each year the population gets older, owing primarily to the aging of the baby boomers and the continuation of the baby bust. Rising life expectancy also gets an assist. The U.S. median age was 33 in 1992, up from 28 in 1970, and 16 in 1800 (USBC, 1989b). During your lifetime the median age could be as high as 46 (cf. Soldo and Agree, 1988).

Effects of Age Composition

The age structure of a society has a profound impact on its demographic and social situation. Some of these impacts have been noted already; for example, the effect of age structure on population growth, on the average age of a society (and hence, its character), and on the relative well-being of different birth cohorts (cf. Bianchi, 1990). Particularly noteworthy is the ongoing aging of U.S. society, which will have wide-ranging effects on everything from education to health care, the job market, and even funeral industry stocks (USBC, 1988a). For example, since baby boomers are now moving into middle-age and their parents into old age, it is inevitable that the baby boomers' "elder care" cause will gain momentum and will compete for scarce resources with the baby busters' "child care" cause. Indeed, dealing with the aging of America may be the most significant challenge this country faces in the next half-century (Dychtwald and Flower, 1989).

BOX 20:2 COLLEGE EXPERIENCE

College Students: Boomers and Busters

Virtually all young adults are either boomers or busters—if not behaviorally, at least demographically. This means they are probably members of either a baby boom or a baby bust cohort. Baby boomers include those born between 1945 and 1964; busters include those born after 1964. Does it matter which type of cohort individuals are in? Absolutely. It matters a lot. An individual's prospects in life are determined in part by the relative size of his or her birth cohort. People compete with other people in their age group for the desirable things in life—education, jobs, promotions, housing, health care, and other resources. In general, baby boomers are worse off than busters because boomers face far more competition from the relatively numerous other boomers (Kennedy, 1989).

But this is hardly news to you boomers. You have already experienced your share of educational, occupational, and housing problems. Many of you found yourselves in crowded primary and secondary school classrooms; others were not admitted to the college of their choice because of record numbers of applicants. Once in a college, many of you have forsaken what really interests you to major in a "practical" field you hope will help you compete with your numerous age mates for the too-few good jobs. No doubt you have been stunned already by the cost of housing, which has been driven up by the high demand created by boomers. And you will continue to face scarcities and fierce competition for such things as promotions and health care for the balance of your lives. That is enough bad news. The good news is that your sheer numbers add up to political power, which can help you obtain certain resources and cultural influence, thus allowing you to disproportionally determine the nature of U.S. society.

You busters know all about that cultural muscle. Your generation bemoans being overshadowed by the bulging generation that went before yours. You complain about the incessant nostalgia; you winced at TV programs like "Thirtysomething" and "The Wonder Years," and at retro-designed cars like the Mazda Miata. You bristle at the fact that your music is crowded off the air by "oldies" older than you are.

But being culturally overshadowed by boomers is one of the few group-size problems busters have (another would be a higher chance of being drafted if the draft were ever reinstituted). In general, baby busters have been and will continue to be blessed with a relative surplus of goods and services and by a relative lack of peer competition. Some demographers (e.g., Easterlin, 1980) believe that this advantaged status could lead to dramatic social change, including, perhaps, another baby boom. It was the baby busters of the 1930s, after all, who were the parents of the present baby boomers.

Critical Thinking Questions

1. How would a functionalist view a population situation in which adjacent generations are vastly different in size?
2. How would a conflict theorist view the same situation?

Age composition is especially relevant to social problems that rarely have causes or consequences independent of age. The individuals enmeshed in such problems often come disproportionately from particular age groups. For example, the chronically ill are disproportionally elderly, whereas criminals are mostly young adults. What this means is that changes in the age composition can alter the severity of a social problem even if there is no change in the underlying social causes.

The United States has different proportions of people at various ages. All things being equal, the larger the adult age group, the more power it has to divert society's resources to its own use. Traditionally, elderly people have formed a relatively small group and, consequently, a relatively poor one. In 1960, for example, about 35 percent of people aged 65 or over lived below the poverty line, and this percentage was several times higher for minorities. Ben Shahn's *Willis Avenue Bridge* evocatively depicts traditional social marginality. By the mid-1990s, however, the poverty rate for elderly Americans had fallen by about two thirds, owing to their increasing political power, which is certain to increase further once the baby boom generation moves into that age category.

Sex Composition

Determinants and Variation

The sex composition of a population can be summarized best by the sex ratio, the ratio of males to females in a given population. This ratio is usually multiplied by 100 to yield a whole number, and is expressed as the number of males for every 100 females. The world's sex ratio in the late 1980s was 101, or 101 males for every 100 females. The ratio for advanced societies was 94; for developing nations, 104. The country with the highest sex ratio was the United Arab Emirates (218); the lowest was Monaco (87) (United Nations, 1989).

Inquisitive students are probably now wondering why there are so many males in the United Arab Emirates and so few in Monaco. So are your authors. We do not know either without doing research on those countries. But we do know that these unusual sex ratios, like all sex ratios, can only be determined by our now familiar forces—fertility, mortality, and migration. Before we go on, think for a moment! What would be the impact of high fertility on the sex ratio? of high mortality? or of any type of migration? The last question is relatively easy. The answer depends on which sex is more common among the migrants. If more males than females move into an area, for example, the sex ratio rises.

To answer the questions about fertility and mortality, it is first necessary to understand that a population's sex ratio is the weighted average of the sex ratios of all age groups. The sex ratio varies enormously by age. In the United States, for example, about 150 males are conceived for every 100 females, but by birth the sex ratio is down to 106 owing to the much higher death rate for male as opposed to female fetuses. The sex ratio at each age continues to get progressively lower due to the aforementioned fact that the death rate of males is higher than that of females at every age. Indeed, centenarians have a stunningly low sex ratio of 33. Any force, such as high fertility, that increases the relative proportion of young people in a society raises the overall sex ratio of the society, because young people have a relatively high sex ratio. Conversely, any force, such as high mortality, that decreases the relative proportion of young people lowers the society's overall sex ratio. (Paradoxically, high mortality tends to make a population older because its associated infectious and parasitic diseases kill relatively more infants and children than older people.)

Most nations follow the sex ratio pattern just described for the United States, though their actual ratios may be somewhat different. Some nations have substantially different patterns, however, especially those such as India in which females have low status and are discriminated against in terms of the allocation of food, medical care, and love (Miller, 1981). Many such nations practice sex-selective female abortion and infanticide, and women in general have higher death rates than men in those nations. As a result, these nations have extraordinarily high overall sex ratios. This is why the sex ratio for a region such as southern Asia is 107 compared to 95 for Europe and the United States.

Population pyramids like those in Figure 20:3 show sex composition as well as age composition. If you look closely, you can see the features described above for the United States; for example, more boys than girls in the youngest age groups, and more women than men in the oldest age groups.

Effects of Sex Composition

When you were reading about sex ratio imbalances above, did you begin thinking about the relative availability of unmarried men and women, and the plight of individuals who cannot marry simply because there are not enough members of the opposite sex to go around? Most students do. But being unable to marry is not merely a personal problem for those without potential mates. The sex ratio has profound social, psychological, and economic effects on the basic structure of society (Guttentag and Secord, 1983). It affects the comparative status and power of women and men, norms of sexual behavior, marriage rates, family stability, and childbearing practices. In the United States, for example, the growing surplus of women is related to many family-related trends of the past three decades, including increasing numbers of single women, rising age at marriage, falling marital fertility, increasing rates of divorce, growing rates of out-of-wedlock childbearing, rising female employment, and increasing female earnings (Goldman et al., 1984). In this vein, Wilson (1988) argues that it is the shortage of marriageable African American males in lower socioeconomic areas that is largely responsible for the dramatic increase in out-of-wedlock births and female-headed families. Similarly, the sex composition of immigrant groups has a bearing on the speed and ease with which they are assimilated into the receiving society. A group with surplus males, for instance, is viewed as a threat to the mate-securing abilities of native males and, consequently, invites social disorganization (Bouvier and Gardner, 1986).

POPULATION DISTRIBUTION

population distribution—how individuals and their population-related activities are spatially dispersed.

Population distribution refers to how the people and their population-related actions are spatially dispersed. Demographers are especially interested in distributions by world regions, by country, by country subdivisions such as regions and states, by urban and rural area, and by segments of metropolitan areas (e.g., central city, suburb, neighborhood, etc.). Population distribution at any level is determined—once again—by fertility, mortality, and migration.

Distribution of the World Population

Population is unevenly distributed among the world's regions. The developing regions contained approximately 66 percent of the world population in 1950 and 78 percent in 1992. Given their higher growth rate driven mainly by higher fertility, these regions will have five-sixths of world population by 2025 (United Nations, 1989). Indeed, these regions are growing so fast that by the year 2100 the population of the Third World will outnumber that of developed countries by a staggering 18 to 1 (United Nations, 1979).

Although fertility is paramount, migration does play a role in world population redistribution. Indeed, international migration is presently at an all-time high. Movement occurs from the less-affluent developed nations to the more affluent ones (e.g., from Portugal to France), and from the most destitute developing nations to the relatively more prosperous ones (e.g., from Colombia to Venezuela) (Bouvier, 1984). But the most significant movement now is that from Third World nations to developed nations. Nevertheless, though migration is at an all-time high, only about 1 percent of the Third World's population growth—just the growth, not the population itself—is absorbed by the developed nations through this process (Kols, 1983).

A major feature of population redistribution in the Third World is urban growth (see Chapter 6). The urban population of these nations rose from 275 million to more than 1.5 billion between 1950 and 1992 (United Nations, 1989; PRB, 1993). About 60 percent of this urban growth was caused by natural increase, the difference between the numbers of births and deaths of current city dwellers (both those born in the city and those who have migrated there). The remaining urban growth occurs because of rural-to-urban migration (Kols, 1983). One conspicuous consequence of this growth is the proliferation of jumbo-sized cities in the Third World as shown in Figure 20:4.

Distribution of the U.S. Population

Like world population, the U.S. population is unevenly distributed. *Population density,* the number of inhabitants per square mile, ranges from 64,000 in Manhattan to 1 in Alaska, the loneliest place in the United States (PRB, 1992). More than 50 percent of the population lives within 50 miles of a coastal shoreline (Long, 1990), so it is likely that you will settle someday "down by the sea" as well. The heartland of the United States is sparsely populated in many areas. For example, the region stretching from northern Texas to Montana is virtually an American empty quarter (see Figure 20:6). Wyoming has only 460,000 people, a lower population than 24 U.S. cities, including Cleveland. Parts of Minnesota are so eager to populate that they offer free parcels of 40 acres to individuals willing to settle (Kagan, 1989). The most populous region of the country is the South, with 35 percent of the population, followed by the Midwest (24 percent), the West (21 percent), and the Northeast (20 percent) (PRB, 1992).

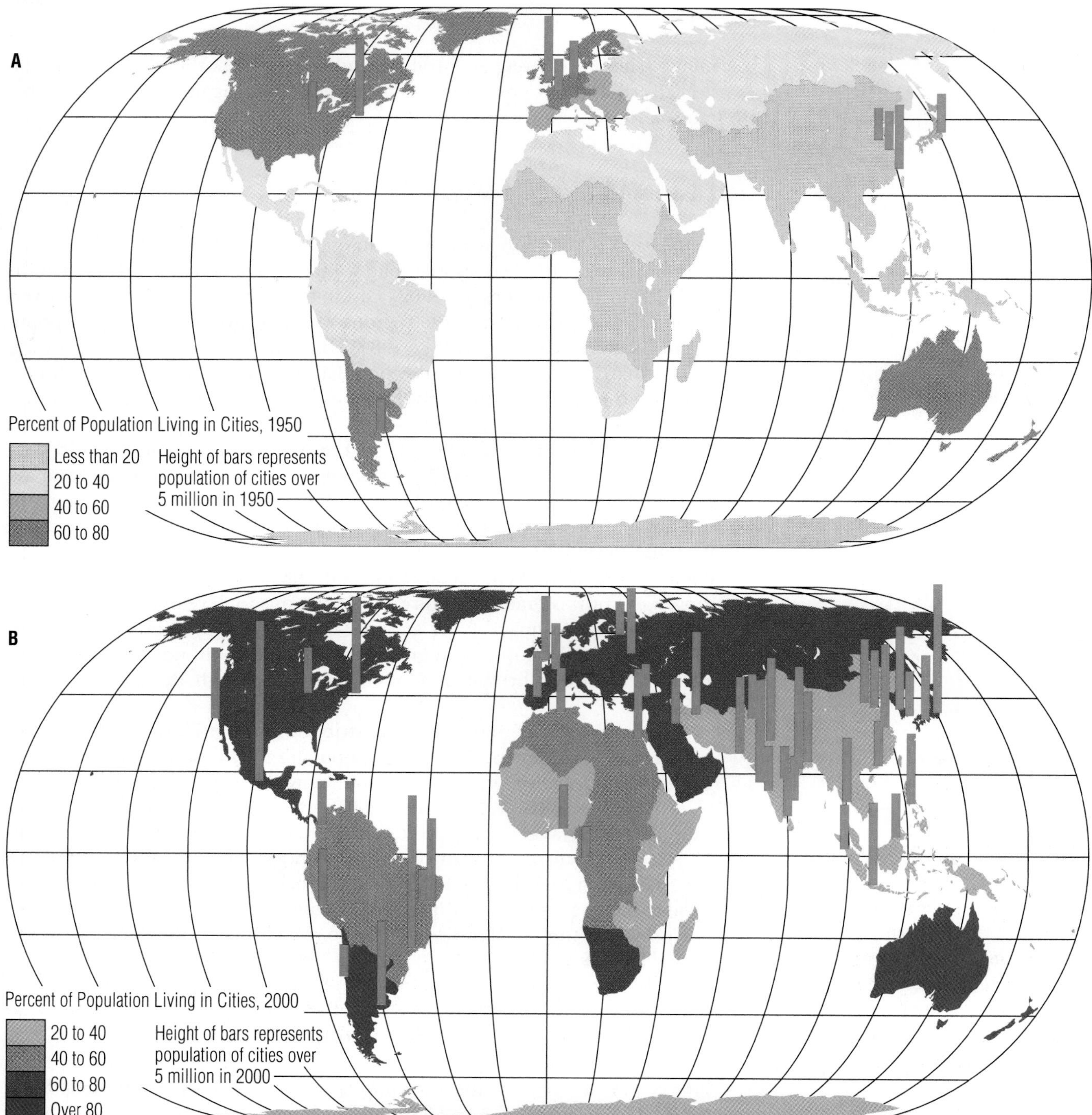

FIGURE 20:4 (A) WORLD URBAN POPULATION, 1950 (B) WORLD URBAN POPULATION, 2000

These maps show the percentage of urban population by world region in 1950 and 2000. The worldwide rapid transition from rural- to urban-based societies is evident. So too is the growth in the number of people living in extremely large metropolitan areas.

Source: Population Images, United Nations Fund for Population Activities, 1988, pp. 10–13.

Population distribution is constantly changing in the United States owing to geographic differences in natural increase and net migration (see Figure 20:5) . International and internal migration have always been the main determinants of redistribution, but the effects of natural increase are far from negligible. For example, Alaska's rate of natural increase (1.73 percent) is 12 times greater than that of West Virginia (.15 percent) (PRB, 1992).

International migrants do not distribute themselves evenly throughout the United States. They settle disproportionally in certain states and communities. Indeed, about two-thirds of all newly arrived immigrants live in

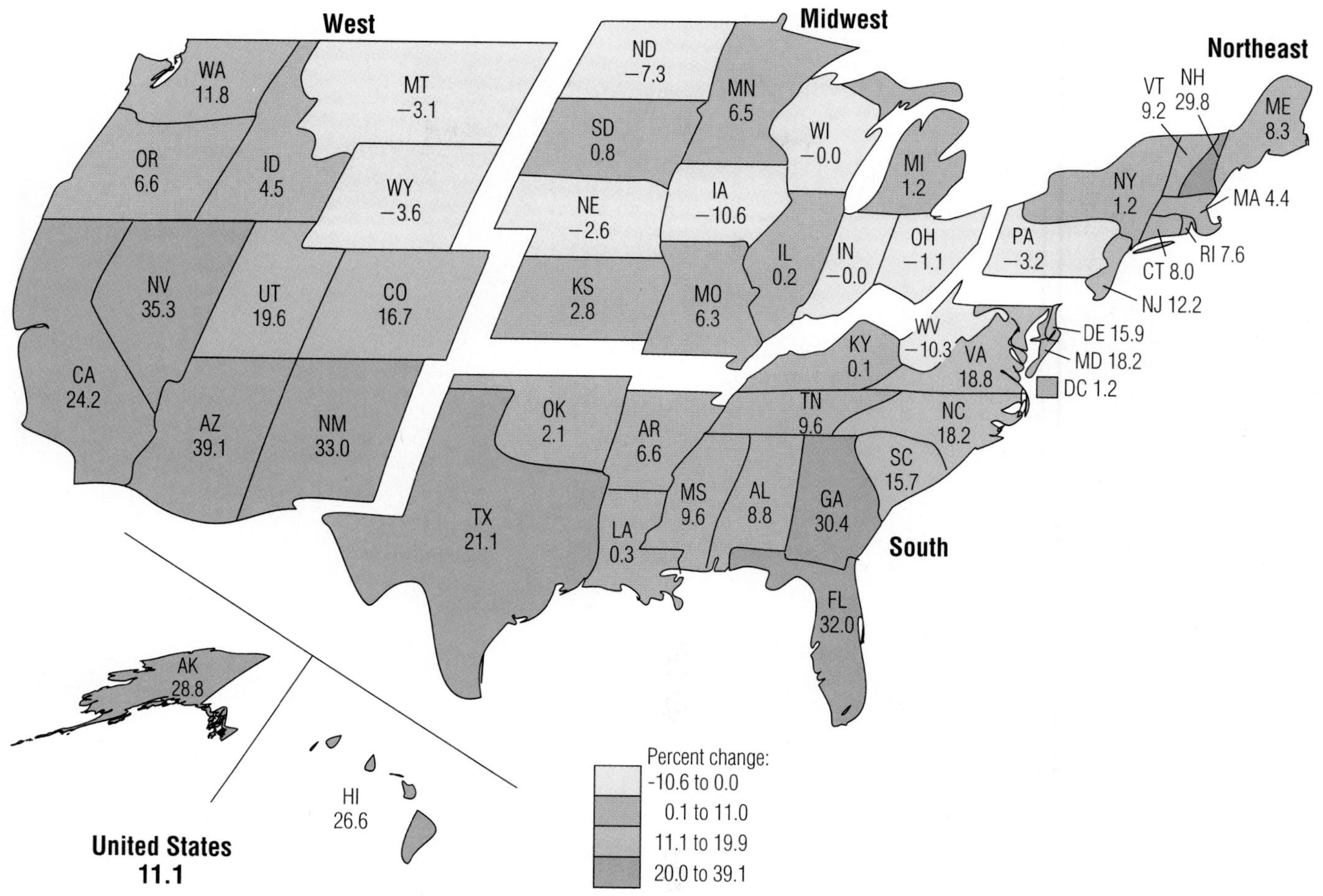

FIGURE 20:5 PROJECTED PERCENT CHANGE IN POPULATION FOR STATES, 1986 TO 2000

Population distribution in the United States is constantly changing. As the map indicates, the western and southern regions are presently growing much faster than the Northeast and Midwest. Thus the former regions are gaining and the latter regions are losing population share.

Source: U.S. Bureau of the Census (1989b).

just five states: California, Texas, New York, Florida, and Illinois, with 40 percent living in California and Texas alone (Bouvier and Gardner, 1986).

Historically, internal migration has redistributed population via several major migration streams (Frey and Speare, 1988). The first stream is movement from the Eastern Seaboard states westward, a demographic process that ultimately pushed the American frontier into the Pacific Ocean. This process has yet to completely ebb. The second stream is migration from rural to urban areas (Frey, 1990). By 1992, about 75 percent of the U.S. population lived in urban areas (see Figure 20:6) (PRB, 1993). One such area is Los Angeles, which, by the year 2000, will be an unofficial supercity 100 miles long with the largest population concentration in the country. The third major stream was the migration from the South to the Northeast and North Central states, particularly among African Americans. However, in recent decades, more people, including African Americans, have migrated into rather than out of the South, a phenomenon that is part of the fourth and now dominant stream—the movement from the "Snowbelt" states to the "Sunbelt" states (Biggar, 1979).

The distribution of population within and around metropolitan areas is another focus of demographic study. The Census Bureau has specific and continually changing definitions for many metropolitan parts (such as central city) and combinations of parts (such as Consolidated Metropolitan Statistical Area [CMSA]) (Haub, 1985; USBC, 1989b). You should familiarize yourself with these concepts if you plan to do research or reading in this area. But for introductory sociology, it is sufficient to understand that

The first major migration stream in the United States was the movement of whites westward, the demographic force behind the cultural principle of "Manifest Destiny." Albert Bierstadt's *Emigrants Crossing the Plains* (1867) helped create the heroic image of this national conquest. Whites saw the Western territories as virtually empty, "promised" lands. Notice the golden floods of light from the westerning sun symbolizing the implicit approval of God; notice also the absence of opposing Native Americans. By contrast, Robert Lidneux's *Trail of Tears* (1942), which appeared nearly a century later, contradicts the cultural myths implicit in Manifest Destiny. It shows the forced migration of Native Americans to western reservations to make room for the in-migrant whites. The actual population transfer depicted here occurred in 1838, when 16,000 Cherokees were forced to make an arduous 1,000-mile trek during the winter. Four thousand Cherokees perished along the way.

(1) metropolitan growth has been faster than growth in nonmetropolitan areas for all of U.S. history, except for the anomalous 1970s, when more people, especially young college graduates, left than entered metropolitan areas (Fugitt, 1985); (2) within metropolitan areas suburban areas are growing more rapidly than central cities (indeed, many central cities like Philadelphia have been losing population for several decades) (Frey, 1987); and (3) metropolitan areas are like giant "Pac Men," continually expanding outward from original central cities, gobbling up additional cities and

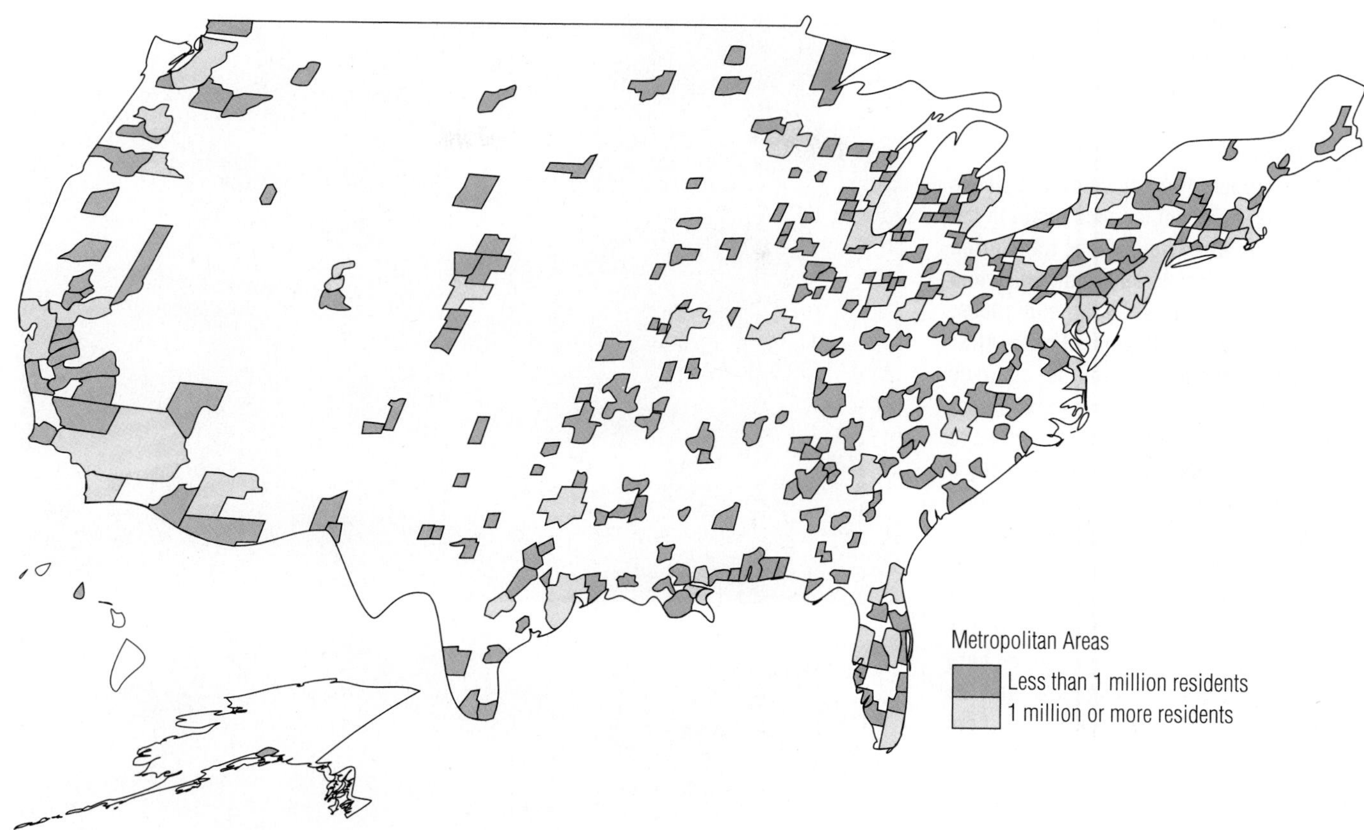

FIGURE 20:6 DISTRIBUTION OF METROPOLITAN AREAS IN THE UNITED STATES, 1990

Approximately 75 percent of the United States population resides in the urban areas designated in this map. Note the clumping together of many adjacent urban areas into giant megalopolises. Note also the relative concentration of urban areas near seacoasts and also around the Great Lakes.

Source: McFalls (1991). By permission of the publisher.

counties in their path (Interchange, 1987). Los Angeles, for instance, has more incorporated cities within its sprawl than some states.

Population distribution and redistribution affect the demographic composition of the areas involved with many social consequences (Frey and Speare, 1988). For example, the flight from central cities to the suburbs is predominantly a movement of the middle and upper classes, thus leaving behind groups that are disproportionally impoverished. With respect to African Americans, Wilson (1988) argues that the African American underclass came about in part because over the past three decades middle-class and upper-class African Americans abandoned their inner-city neighborhoods, leaving behind the impoverished and removing an important element in the social fabric of these African American communities.

POPULATION GROWTH PROBLEMS

Population Explosion

Modern history's most devastating explosion took place in 1883 when Krakatoa, a volcanic island in Indonesia, blew apart. The bang was so loud it was heard 3,000 miles away. Five cubic miles of rock fragments were catapulted into the air; islands 50 miles away were bombarded with fiery boulders as heavy as 70 pounds. Giant tidal waves, some 120 feet high, radiated outward, sweeping over coastal towns on neighboring islands, killing tens of thousands of people. All life on Krakatoa itself perished. One moment there was a mountainous island teeming with life; in the next, a lifeless 1,100 foot hole, 7 miles wide in the ocean floor.

Suburbanization is the most irresistible demographic trend of the past 50 years. It began in earnest shortly after World War II, accelerated during the 1960s and 1970s when suburban malls drained shoppers from downtown business districts, and shot up once again in the 1980s when businesses transferred millions of jobs to suburban office and industrial parks. By the mid-1990s, approximately 50 percent of the U.S. population resided in suburbs, and only about 25 percent lived in central cities. The fifty-year flight from central cities to suburbs has been predominantly a movement of the middle and upper classes, thus leaving behind groups that are disproportionately poor and non-white. The result is an America that is essentially divided into two worlds, the lower class urban one represented here by South Central Los Angeles, and the middle class suburban one typified here by Silver Firs, Seattle.

The word *explosion* is so commonplace that it has lost much of its impact. The story of Krakatoa is presented here to emphasize what an explosion really is; that is, a cataclysmic departure from the pre-explosion status quo. As such, the term "explosion" is an apt one for characterizing what has been happening to population growth. The world is now in the midst of a titanic *population explosion*, which began *circa* 1650, and has yet to reach its peak. The cataclysmic nature of this population phenomenon can be seen in Figure 20:7; notice how world population, like Krakatoa in 1883, is rocketing skyward.

Figure 20:7 should help you appreciate the character of the population explosion by placing it in historical perspective. During the first 2–5 million years of human history, world population never exceeded 10 million people, owing to a rate of population growth scarcely above zero. Just as

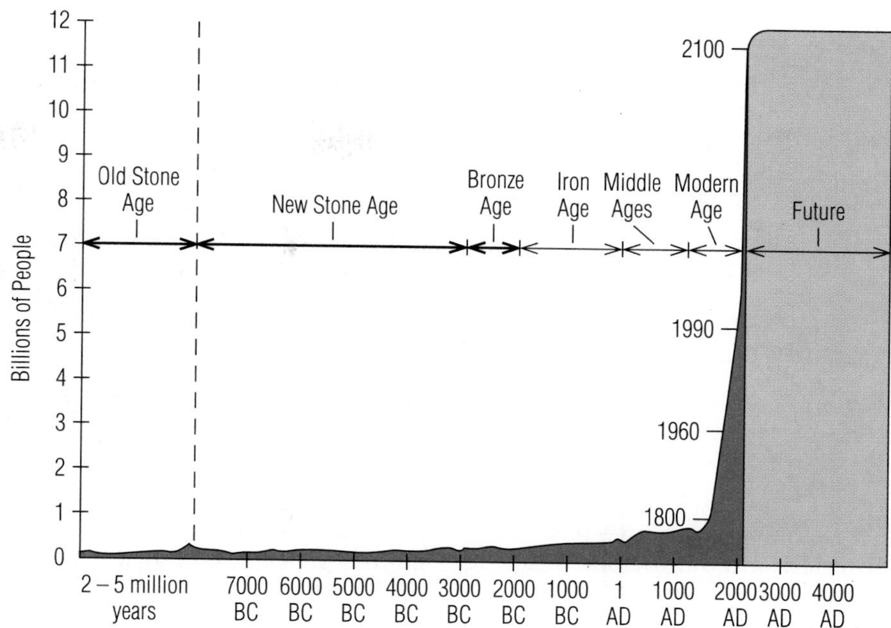

FIGURE 20:7 HISTORICAL WORLD POPULATION GROWTH

This graph illustrates population growth from the beginning of time to the present in what has come to be called the "J"-shaped curve. Notice it took the human species as long as 5 million years to reach a population of 1 billion, and that humankind is now accomplishing that in less than a decade.

Source: McFalls (1991). By permission of the publisher.

minor eruptions generally precede monstrous volcanic blasts, a relatively small population explosion preceded today's gigantic one. The smaller explosion began about 8000 BC with the first domestication of animals and the initiation of agriculture. By 1650, it had expanded world population about 50 times: from 10 million to 500 million. Then the big explosion detonated. World population shot up another 500 million people in only 150 years, reaching its first billion around 1800. It added a second billion by 1930, in just 130 years; a third billion by 1960, in just 30 years; a fourth billion by 1975, in just 15 years, and a fifth billion by 1986, in just 11 years.

Today, the population explosion continues, and has yet to reach its peak ferocity. Each year a new 12 month population increase record is set (about 93 million in 1993), only to be eclipsed by the following year's growth. Indeed, the net increase in world population in the year 2000 will be about 13 percent higher than the former record levels of the 1980s. A sixth billion will be added to world population sometime during the 1990s, probably in less than 10 years; and massive growth will continue at least well into the twenty-first century.

Take another look at Figure 20:7 and at the awesome dimensions of the ongoing population explosion depicted there. Notice that it took the human species as long as 5 million years to reach a population of 1 billion. Humankind is now doing that in less than a decade.

But the population explosion is not just an awe-inspiring demographic phenomenon; it is a major social problem (cf. Goliber, 1989; Hendry, 1988; Jones et al., 1988; Repetto, 1987). You have already encountered some of its troublesome repercussions in this and other chapters, such as the unleashing of massive international migration and the proliferation of gigantic cities with their mammoth shantytowns (see Figure 20:4). Indeed, while a few population scholars downplay the negative impact of population growth (Drucker, 1986; Simon, 1981, 1989; Wattenberg, 1987), most believe that population growth is an exceptionally important problem because it is a multiplier of the damage created by other world problems (cf. Brown and Jacobson, 1986; Jones et al., 1988). For example, population growth exacerbates environmental degradation and resource depletion, and puts unmanageable pressures on governmental institutions, national economies, and virtually all natural resources (Ehrlich and Ehrlich, 1990; National Academy of Sciences, 1986; PRB, 1990).

It is important to note, however, that population growth is not solely responsible for these other social problems. For example, environmental degradation is brought about not only by numbers of people, but by how much they consume and the degree to which their consumption generates environmental degradation (Bean, 1990). Thus, the reduction of rapid population growth alone would not be enough to solve such problems, though it certainly would contribute to their solution.

Demographic Transition

demographic transition—the historical shift of birth and death rates from high to low levels in a population.

The population explosion came about owing to a change in the ratio of births to deaths. Prior to the explosion, the birthrate and the death rate fluctuated at a relatively high level (see Figure 20:8). This situation is the first stage of a process called **demographic transition.** The death rate was high in pre-explosion societies because of poor health and harsh living conditions. In fact, life expectancy at birth was less than 30 years owing in large part to extremely high rates of infant and child mortality. The birthrate was high because women had to average at least six children to offset this high mortality. A society would otherwise simply die out—and many did! To generate a high birthrate, pre-explosion societies created cultures that impelled individuals to have many children. For example, the religious institution generally encouraged people to "be fruitful and multiply," and a man's virility and a woman's status were frequently linked to their number of children. But large families served many important functions in preexplosion societies other than offsetting high mortality, including furnishing parents with the labor force needed for family enterprises (such as family farms) and with care and security during old age. Large families also were functional because they increased the economic, political, and military power of such larger entities as the tribe or nation.

Social change, principally modernization, set stage two of the demographic transition into motion by causing the death rate to drop. Mod-

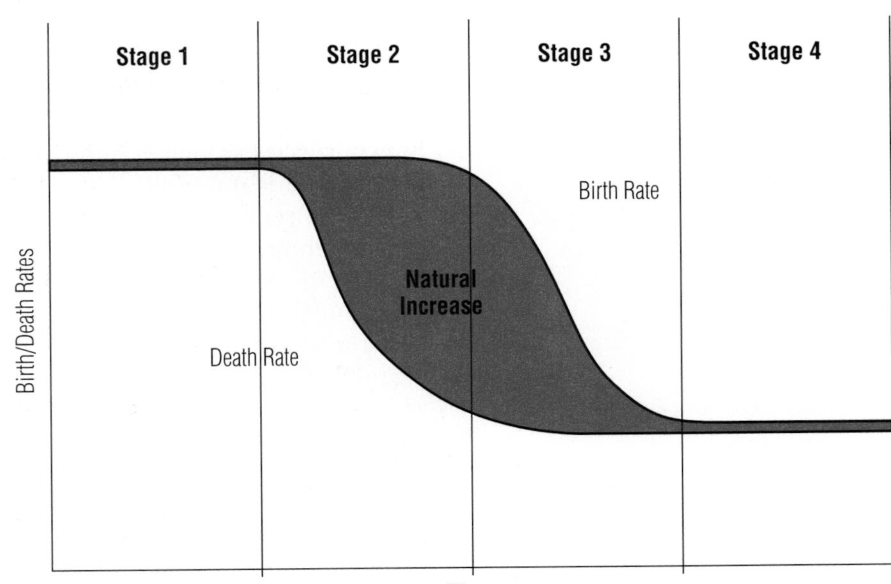

FIGURE 20:8 THE STAGES OF DEMOGRAPHIC TRANSITION

The population explosion came about owing to change in the ratio of births to deaths. The shaded area of this figure is directly proportional to the rate of population growth at various points of time during the transition.

Source: McFalls (1991). By permission of the publisher.

ernization accomplished this by improving living conditions and increasing control over disease. Unlike the death rate, the birthrate continued at or near its previous level during stage two, thus igniting the population explosion. Note that the population explosion came about more as a result of lower mortality rather than higher fertility as is commonly thought.

Why didn't the birthrate fall in tandem with the death rate? The reason is that the technological, medical, and other elements of modernization, which reduce mortality, are eagerly accepted by most pre-explosion societies because of their obvious utility against the universal enemy: death. However, high fertility values are embedded and enmeshed in the social system, and often remain useful for other functions such as furnishing security for aging parents. Cultural lag also plays a role. It takes considerable time for people to recognize that lower death rates create population pressures that can be eased by having fewer children. It can take generations to recognize, for instance, that it is no longer necessary to have eight children to be assured that four will survive to adulthood.

In the third stage of the demographic transition the birthrate plunges downward, catching up with the death rate by the end of the stage. Population growth remains relatively high during the early part of the third stage, but falls to near zero in the latter part. The birthrate declines for many reasons, including the fact that large families gradually become seen as problematic in modernizing societies. In the fourth and final stage of the demographic transition the birthrate and the death rate are now close together again, but this time they fluctuate around a relatively low level.

Developed nations such as the United States have largely completed the demographic transition and, with an overall annual natural increase rate of 0.4 percent, are now minor players in the ongoing population explosion. On the other hand, many developing nations are still in stage two and early stage three of the transition and are growing rapidly (Watkins, 1987). Excluding China, the growth rate for developing societies in 1992 was 2.3 percent; and population doubling time was only 30 years. Indeed, the population explosion is still building in intensity worldwide principally because that 2.3 percent growth rate is being multiplied each year against the huge population base of the Third World.

Future Prospects

If the present rate of population growth were to persist, world population would rocket to 10 billion by 2030, 20 billion by 2070, 40 billion by 2110, 80 billion by 2150, and so on. Indeed, owing to geometric progression, humanity would outweigh the Earth and then the solar system in remarkably short periods of time if the present high rate of growth continued indefinitely. But the fact is, no rate of growth can be sustained indefinitely. A tiny positive rate of +.00001 ultimately would yield a population whose mass would expand at the speed of light, while a tiny negative rate of −.00001 ultimately would carry humanity back past Adam and Eve (Preston, 1987). Thus, zero population growth, which has been a characteristic of the human population for more than 99 percent of its history, must be reachieved eventually at least as a long-term average.

But ZPG cannot be attained immediately for two reasons. First, it requires time for fundamental social change regarding childbearing behavior to take place. Second, the world's present age composition will generate massive growth even if a relatively small family size becomes the worldwide norm in the near future. About half of the developing world's inhabitants presently are below age 15, and they inevitably will parent the

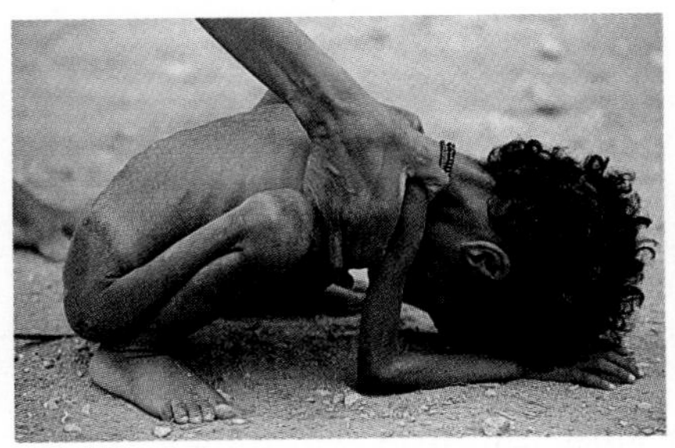

The first photograph in this chapter shows a healthy, well-nourished Chinese baby whose birth contributed to the population explosion in China and in the world as a whole. This photo of a Somali child shows what can happen to children when a population approaches or exceeds a region's carrying capacity. Children are among the first to die in famines, and it is estimated that the 1992 Somali famine killed one fourth of all children under age 5. The Somali famine was caused in part by one of the highest total fertility rates (7.0) and growth rates (3.2 percent) in the world. But non-demographic factors such as political instability also contributed to the horrific conditions there in 1992.

largest birth cohorts in history. But like any explosion, the population explosion will eventually fizzle out, probably by the end of the twenty-first century. By then, the demographic transition will have run its course.

Estimates of how large the world population will actually be when it stops growing range from 8 to 11 billion (see Figure 20: 7) (Bogue and Tsui, 1979; United Nations, 1979, 1989; Zachariah and Vu, 1979). Whether Earth can support such huge populations indefinitely or at all is uncertain. Earth's ultimate carrying capacity is unknown, in part because carrying capacity is a dynamic concept whose specifications are constantly changing as discoveries are made, as new technologies are devised, and as resource management techniques are improved. Despite these estimation problems, the National Academy of Sciences concluded that a world population of 10 billion "is close to (if not above) the maximum that an intensely managed world might hope to support with some degree of comfort and individual freedom" (National Academy of Sciences, 1969). The Council on Environmental Quality and the U.S. Department of State (1980) concurred with this assessment.

But other scholars are highly critical of the 10 billion estimate. The Worldwatch Institute, for example, believes that the world's basic biological systems (i.e., forests, grasslands, croplands, and fisheries) and its oil resources are insufficient even to reach, let alone maintain, a population of 10 billion. The institute argues that these systems are already overtaxed at the current 5 billion population level, and that continued population growth eventually will lead to major systems failures long before the 10 billion mark is attained. Indeed, the institute contends that the Earth's carrying capacity is much lower than 10 billion, and that societies will be forced to restrict individual childbearing and to adopt policies to quickly stabilize population size once they brush up against this lower limit. If societies are unable to do this, the major biological systems—and Earth's carrying capacity—could collapse. Thus, the institute argues that the nations of the world must mount a "concerted effort to slam on the demographic brakes" now. This would halt population growth by about 2015 and yield a long-term population of about 6 billion people (Brown, 1979; Brown et al., 1984). However, there is no precedent for such concerted effort, and it is unlikely to be successful even if it were attempted (van der Tak et al., 1979).

Whatever the carrying capacity of Earth really is, peak stabilized world population probably will settle and remain uncomfortably close to it because carrying capacity constraints are likely major determinants of the ultimate size of the human population. Like microorganisms in a culture dish, humanity seems intent on growing to the limits of its finite environment instead of leaving a prudent reserve. Unfortunately, there are prohibitive costs—both human and ecological—attached to this population/resources behavior (see Box 20:3) (Jones et al., 1988).

Zero and Negative Population Growth

Once positive population growth ceases and ZPG is reached, there is no self-regulating mechanism that maintains a society at ZPG. Societies can easily pass through ZPG and slip into negative population growth (NPG). Indeed, many population experts (e.g., Brown, 1990) and interest groups (e.g., NPG, Inc. [New York]; ZPG, Inc. [Wash.]) would welcome such a population implosion, and some countries have already established negative population growth as a goal. For example, China wants to reduce the size of its population by half over the next several decades (Tien, 1983; 1992).

BOX 20:3 SOCIOLOGICAL IMAGINATION IN FICTION

The Population Explosion

Enormous numbers like those associated with the population explosion—8 billion, 10 billion, 12 billion, or more—have a certain numbing quality. Beyond some point, additional increments of humanity have little meaning to us. Even charts like Figure 20:7 showing world population rocketing upward do not adequately convey the social consequences of continued population growth. But science-fiction can stretch social fabric over population projection bones, giving us vivid and often poignant scenarios of the possible social worlds that could emanate from immense growth. Science-fiction writers tend to have two visions of grossly overpopulated worlds: (1) a brutal, impoverished anti-utopian one, and (2) a dubiously triumphant technological one.

The anti-utopian fiction offers a thoroughly dismal future in which runaway population growth unleashes one or more of the Four Horsemen of the Apocalypse—pestilence (often pollution or nuclear waste), war (often between the rich and the nonrich), famine, and death. Paul Theroux's *O-Zone* (1986) is typical of this genre, as is his description of an American world that is cheek by jowl with people:

> It was a meaner, more desperate and worn out world. It had been scavenged by crowds. Their hunger was apparent in the teethmarks they had left, in the slashes of their claws . . . its cities were either madhouses or sepulchres (p. 11).

One feature of such worlds is lack of sheer space and, of course, privacy. In Robert Sheckley's "The People Trap" (1968), humans lived 10 persons to a room, and virtually no one had ever seen an unencumbered acre of property, much less dreamed of possessing one. Space was even tighter in J.G. Ballard's "Billenium" (1962), a society in which humans were confined to 3 square meters of living space in cities because all available nonresidential space had to be devoted to production.

Another common feature of anti-utopian societies is their failure to assimilate racial and ethnic minorities. For example, in Strieber and Kunetka's *Nature's End* (1986), a native American character observes:

> The huge population of the L.A. Metroplex—Indo-Chinese, Vietnamese, Mexican, African—is not unlike that of Calcutta in the way it acts and looks. Except, of course, we are here, the Born Americans. In our gleaming cars, with our houses full of robot servants, we have become imperialists in our own land (p. 64).

In other works, conflict between the dominant class and the subordinate class (usually either the impoverished, minorities, or aliens) erupts into armed struggle. This remark from an "owner" class person in *O-Zone* (1986) is typical:

> There is no more terrifying image than a hairy filthy alien—an Arab, an African, an illegal Hispanic—poised in the darkness clutching a heat-seeking missile; it was an ape with a deadly weapon (p. 30).

The solutions to overpopulation and its consequences in anti-utopian fiction are often worse than the problems themselves. In *Nature's End* (1986), for example, the international government ordered a random lottery to determine which third of humanity would be exterminated.

The second science fiction vision of grossly overpopulated worlds, the dubiously triumphant technological one, proceeds from the premise that science has conquered such problems as hunger, resource scarcities, and environmental degradation, and that gigantic populations can physically inhabit Earth and

(continued on next page)

BOX 20:3 SOCIOLOGICAL IMAGINATION IN FICTION ***continued***

other planets. (An example of such a world is Isaac Asimov's *Trantor* [1966], a densely populated, industrially advanced world in which 40 billion people lived in a city that stretched over a planet's entire land surface.) This genre focuses on changes in social organization that result from such gigantic populations or that permit them to function. Another example is Philip Jose Farmer's "The Sliced-Crosswise Only-on-Tuesday World" (1971). This society's solution to overpopulation was to divide the population into seven groups, and to assign each group one day of the week in which to "live." The group would spend the other six days in suspended animation in transparent coffin-like containers. The plot centered on the plight of a Tuesday man who fell in love with a Wednesday woman:

> He looked [into] Jennie Marlowe's [container]. He felt sick again. Out of his reach: never for him. Wednesday was a day away (p. 26).

Farmer's story of temporal stratification gives us a glimpse of how huge populations may negatively impact on human fredom, even on such basic rights as the freedom to be active an entire life or to associate with anyone in society.

Science-fiction writers rarely envision small population futures. Their view is almost always coincident with that of population projectionists; that is, that gigantic populations are in store for much of humanity at least for the next several centuries. Thus, these tales often have a self-conscious cautionary quality, saying in a sense, "Don't let these kinds of worlds happen to you or your descendants!"

Critical Thinking Questions

1. Which of the science-fiction visions of grossly overpopulated worlds—the brutal impoverished anti-utopian, or the dubiously triumphant technological—do you think has the greatest probability of becoming a reality in the United States? Why?
2. Why do you think so many science-fiction writers envision anti-utopian societies that fail to assimilate racial and ethnic minorities? Will the present racial problems likely get better or worse in the future if population continues to grow in the United States and the world? Explain.

But ZPG and NPG have their own set of problems. One is that the population ages markedly; that is, the proportion of the population made up of older people rises dramatically. Another problem is that labor force shortages develop. Consequently, such things as social support programs for the elderly are strained. The consensus opinion among population scholars is that if a nation slowly declines in size the negative effects of such problems are manageable. But if the down-sizing is rapid, the social and economic problems can be severe (Teitelbaum and Winter, 1985).

Nevertheless, regardless of the actual damage brought about by NPG, concern about it is enormous in countries at or below ZPG. Natural decrease (more deaths than births) is a reality in Hungary, Bulgaria, Estonia, Latvia, and Germany, and 18 of the other 22 European countries are at or near ZPG (PRB, 1993). Assuming this phenomenon continues, one Council of Europe demographic study projects that there will be only half as many Europeans in 100 years as there are today (Rosenblum, 1987). Many European leaders fear that their falling populations may threaten their economies, their defense systems, even their national identities. Various economic pronatalist incentives such as grants to induce women to stay home and have babies have been attempted in some European countries, but have not managed to boost fertility enough to ward off population decline. And immigration is not viewed as a feasible solution. Indeed, virtually all European countries have imposed strict controls limiting immigration, and have initiated programs in an attempt to stimulate return migration of former residents (David, 1982; van de Kaa, 1987). In the face of population decline, some feminists are concerned that women will be pressured into having more children at the expense of their recent educational, occupational, and other gains. But population experts believe that only policies compatible with the shift to individualism so characteristic of modern societies have any chance to slow or reverse the fertility decline in these societies (Huber, 1990; van de Kaa, 1987). Even these policies are considered long shots, and long-term population decline—or what has been termed "the second demographic transition"—appears inevitable for most of Europe (and for the United States, too, if immigration levels were to be cut substantially) (van de Kaa, 1987).

THE SUBJECTIVE DIMENSION OF POPULATION PROBLEMS

As you read through this chapter you no doubt noticed that many social problems emanate from the population processes of fertility, mortality, and migration. These include, to name just a few, the scarcity and waste of social resources caused by baby booms and busts; premature death, especially in certain demographic subgroups; the concentration of people in some places (such as gigantic cities) and depopulation elsewhere (especially in rural areas), with all that these processes imply for the quality of life in both areas; social disturbances owing to changes in a population's racial and ethnic composition; and population growth that undermines the quality of life for present and future generations. The objective damage such problems produce is indisputable.

Americans in general are mildly concerned about some population problems. They do have general opinions concerning such issues as the desirability of population growth, the appropriate level of immigration, and the "ideal" racial and ethnic composition of the population. Moreover, subjective concern about such issues does flare up occasionally. For example, during the 1980s subjective concern rose sharply over the flow of legal and illegal immigrants into the United States. Polls indicated that Americans strongly favored imposing limitations on immigration and completely terminating illegal movements into the country (Bouvier and Gardner, 1986). This heightened concern was due in part to the weak economy in the early 1980s, which raised fears of increased job competition, and to the media attention (*visibility*) invariably focused on such emotionally charged situations.

Nevertheless, despite mild concern about population problems in general and the occasional flare-up of particular demographic issues, population problems are not subjectively viewed by most Americans as being among our most serious social problems. One reason for this is their overall low visibility. Population problems typically lack the dramatic event—the startling calamity or outrageous incident—that galvanizes attention and action. Rather, they develop inconspicuously from the gradual accumulation of individual births, deaths, and migrations.

Another reason for the relative lack of concern about population problems is that the experts themselves have often disagreed on their severity. Debate about overpopulation, for instance, has been going on at least since Aristotle, who cautioned that populations could outstrip their subsistence base, leading to poverty and social discord (Preston, 1987). Malthus (1798, 1965) reached a similar conclusion in the early nineteenth century. He argued that the natural consequences of population growth are poverty and misery because the food supply cannot grow as fast as the population. On the other hand, Marx and Engels (1844, 1986) rejected this Malthusian view. They blamed poverty not on the impoverished or overpopulation but on the evils of social organization in capitalist societies. Overpopulation in their view was a natural feature of capitalism, and would not exist in socialist societies because the latter would provide enough resources for each person or the motivation to reduce family size when resources were scarce (Weeks, 1986). Today, the debate over overpopulation continues. Although scholars (e.g., Simon, 1981) who do not believe that the rapid growth of the world's population is a major social problem are, as noted, a distinct minority, their iconoclastic dissent is well publicized and leads to confusion. Moreover, the tone of media articles on world population growth vacillate from doomsday hysteria to complacent unconcern, depending on which experts are used as the source.

The subjective dimension of the population explosion is low but has been moving upward in recent years owing to its obvious connection to the world's mounting and increasingly visible environmental problems (cf. Brown, 1990; Jones et al., 1988) (see Figure 20:9). Commitment to the environment is the most deeply and widely held value among Americans, according to Gallup research (Thompson, 1985). This *value* is a key determinant of the subjective dimension of environmental problems, and by association, influences the subjective dimension of the population explosion as well.

Expectations also play a role in determining the subjective dimension of population problems. For example, when concern about the population explosion or depopulation flares up, people tend to believe that the rate of growth—whether positive or negative—will continue until people are

FIGURE 20:9 SUBJECTIVE AND OBJECTIVE DIMENSIONS: THE CASE OF THE POPULATION EXPLOSION
The subjective dimension of the population explosion is much lower than its objective dimension owing to the operation of the intervening variables visibility, expectations, and values.

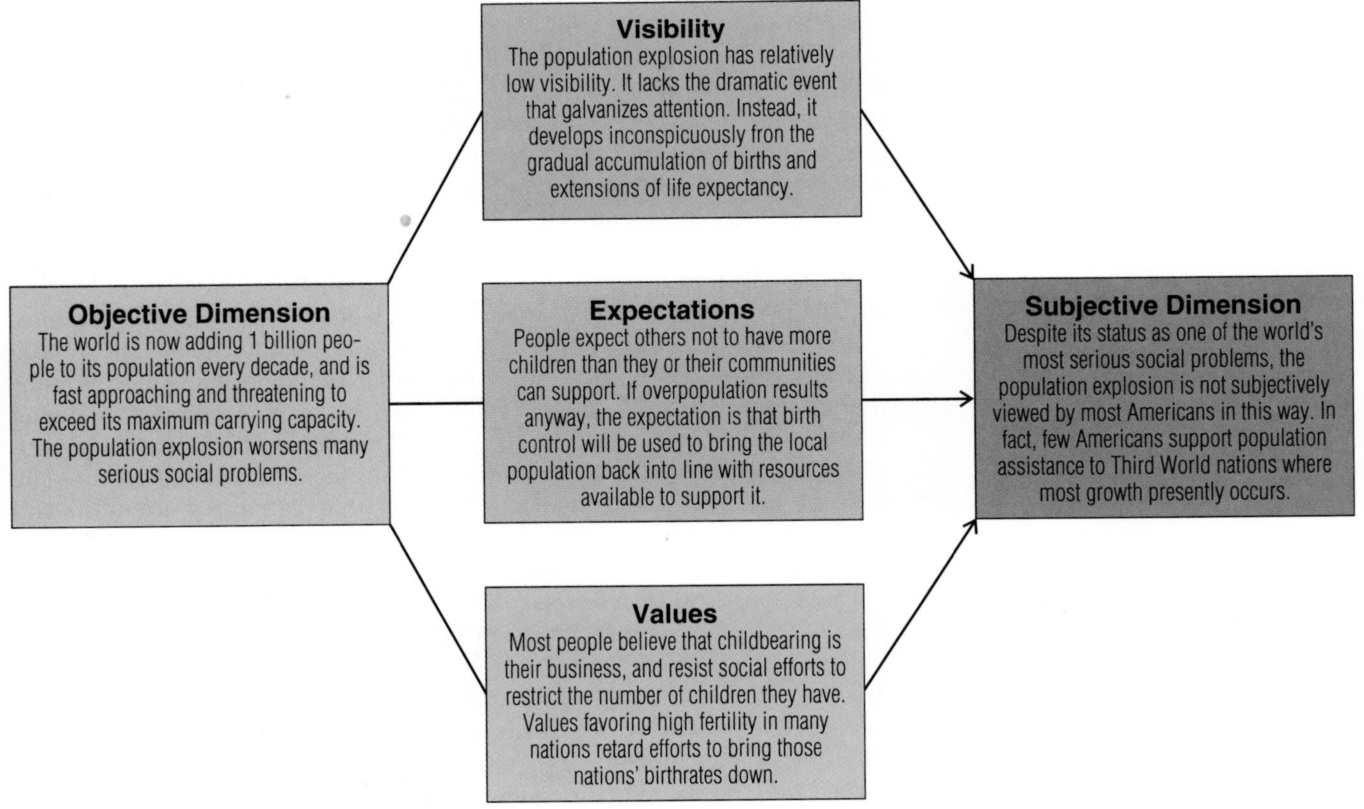

standing on each other's shoulders or until no one is left (Preston, 1987). Such expectations, however, underestimate a society's ability to solve problems through social change.

SUMMARY

1. Demography is the study of human populations, including their size, composition, and distribution, as well as the causes and consequences of changes in these factors.
2. Fertility varies enormously from one society to another, but all societies fall far short of the biological maximum for childbearing, owing to the operation of a set of 12 intermediate variables.
3. Mortality also varies enormously from one society to another, and, again, no population approaches its maximum possible life expectancy because of both biological and social reasons.
4. Migration is the movement of people across a specified territorial boundary for the purposes of changing residences. There are two types: internal migration and international migration. Migrants are usually pushed from their place of origin by difficult conditions and/or pulled to their place of destination where conditions appear to be better.
5. Population growth is equal to the number of births minus deaths plus the number of people moving in less the number moving out. Population growth can be positive, negative, or zero.
6. A population pyramid is a geometric figure that shows the proportion of the male and female populations in each age group. The age and sex compositions of a society have profound impacts on its demographic and social situation.
7. The distribution of a population is how the people and their population-related actions are spatially dispersed. Demographers are interested in distributions by world regions, by country, by regions and states, by urban and rural area, and by segments of metropolitan areas.
8. The world is now in the midst of a population explosion, which began about the year 1650, and has yet to reach its peak. Each year a new 12-month population record is set only to be eclipsed by the following year's growth. Most population scholars believe that world population growth is an exceptionally important problem because it is a multiplier of the damage created by other serious social problems such as environmental degradation and resource depletion.
9. Although the objective damage population problems produce is indisputable, Americans in general are only mildly concerned. One reason for this is the low visibility of these problems. Another is the lack of complete agreement among experts concerning the severity of these problems. Where public concern about population problems does flare up, it is usually because of erroneous expectations about their consequences, or because the connection between population and other more disvalued problems such as environmental degradation is made clear at least momentarily by interest groups or the media.

Chapter 21

Personal Perspective

I have a friend named Bill. When he and his wife Carolyn got married 12 years ago, he wanted to have just two children, a girl and a boy. His first child was a girl and so was his second. Bill loved both of these daughters very much, but he still wanted the experience of having a son as well. So even though Bill and his wife had only wanted two children, they decided to have another in hopes that it would be a boy. But they had another girl! — and then another, and another, and another. Today Bill has six lovely daughters and cherishes all of them. But he still yearns to have a son.

JAM

Technology, Science, and Environment

Someday soon the inevitable will become reality. Scientists in Japan and elsewhere are presently working on developing the technology that will allow individuals like Bill to choose the sex of their children. It is already possible to increase the chances of having a child of one sex or the other to about 60 percent. It is just a matter of time before a method will be perfected that raises those odds to near 100 percent When Bill reads the morning headline trumpeting the discovery of such sex selection technology, he will probably leap to his feet, thrust both fists high above his head, and shout for joy! But just because a technology is developed does not necessarily mean people like Bill will have access to it. To cite one example, the abortion pill was still outlawed in the United States in 1994 despite its proven effectiveness. Sex selection technology would have to be approved, too, sooner or later. If it eventually comes to a vote, how would you cast your ballot? Would you vote to let Bill select for the son he so desperately wants?

When asked this question in class a few students usually accuse Bill of sexism and say no. Most students empathize with Bill and say yes, at least initially. After a moment to reflect on the consequences of approving this technology, however, students typically begin to express reservations. Some students bring up the fact that parents in the United States have a preference for sons. Would couples who want only one child disproportionately choose sons? Having had a boy and a girl already, would couples who want just three children disproportionately opt for a second son rather than a daughter? Would sex selection technology ultimately lead to a sex ratio imbalance within society; that is, would there be significantly more boys than girls in future generations? Quite possibly. Indeed, sometimes a student brings up the fact that nations such as China and India already have such generational sex ratio imbalances arising from sex-selective abortion and infanticide (Tien, 1992).

It is usually at this point in the discussion that male students, who at the outset almost invariably supported Bill's right to use sex selection technology, begin to abandon him in droves. This occurs as they realize that sex selection of children eventually means a shortage of women and, consequently, of sexual mates for men. You do not need to be a mathematician to realize that a swing of just 10 percentage points in the generational sex ratio—from nature's approximate 50–50 ratio to 60–40—means that fully one-third of men (20 out of every 60) would be "leftover."

Being unable to find a mate or to marry is not just a personal disappointment for individuals who want to mate or marry. As noted in Chapter 20, an unbalanced sex ratio has profound negative social, psychological, and economic effects on the basic structure of society (Goldman et al., 1984). Thus, while unregulated sex selection technology may be in the individual's (and Bill's) immediate self-interest, it may not be in their long-term

In frontier areas such as parts of Alaska during the oil pipeline construction project or the towns of the American "Old West" shown here, men generally outnumber women by a wide margin. Unbalanced gender ratios have many negative effects on frontier societies, contributing, for example, to unusually high rates of alcohol abuse, prostitution, crime, and violence.

self-interest. (Does Bill really want a son who cannot find a mate?) And it certainly is not in society's best interest.

In short, technology, whether new or already existing, is not a thing apart from society. Technology profoundly impacts on society and is, in fact, one of the most important—if not the most important—cause of social change. Similarly, technology does not come about in a social vacuum. Technology is a social creation—one that must be understood in terms of its social and cultural dimensions. The fact that the scientists who are hard at work on sex selection technology come from Japan rather than from the !Kung tribe of southern Africa is not happenstance. Unlike the !Kung society, Japan is the kind of society that gives rise to such sophisticated technological research. In sum, technology has both social causes and consequences, and it is subject to social policy and control. This is why you encounter technology in a sociology text.

THE NATURE OF TECHNOLOGY

When most students think of technology they usually think just about machines, tools, devices, and various bits of hardware. But technology also consists of the ways of manipulating such hardware. In fact, the Greek root for the word technology *(techne)* means "skill," "art," or "craft." The purpose of technology is to do things not otherwise doable, or to do them in a better way. Technology comes about through the application of knowledge, which has its source in human intelligence. Humans rely on technology not only to make their lives better but for their very survival. Technology is thus intrinsic to the human condition.

But technology is more than just hardware and skills. It requires organization because the development, production, and application of a technology necessitates effort on the part of many people. All but the most simple technologies rely on an intricate network of such groups as material suppliers, toolmakers, service providers, and interested consumers. The development and application of a technology necessitates an organizational framework to coordinate all these network activities, and to focus them on the attainment of a specific technological goal.

Thus, technology is best seen as a system of hardware, skills, and organizational structures. The first railroad locomotive, for example, was of little use by itself. It required rights-of-way, track, specialized rolling stock, stations, engineers, schedules, management, mechanics, fuel facilities, freight, passengers, even destinations, to mention just a few of the interconnected elements in the railroad system that allowed the locomotive to operate effectively. All the elements of such technological systems do not materialize simultaneously. It usually takes time for various hardware components, skills, and organizational structures to develop. Moreover, because technological change often causes considerable human pain and social disruption, support for the technological system may be delayed further until requisite social adjustments can be made.

technology—a system based on the application of knowledge, manifested in physical objects, related skills, and organizational forms, for the attainment of specific goals.

By definition, then, a **technology** is a system based on the application of knowledge, manifested in physical objects, related skills, and organizational forms, for the attainment of specific goals (Volti, 1992).

THE SOCIAL CAUSES OF TECHNOLOGY

All societies have technologies. Even "Stone Age" societies had tools that required considerable skill and practice to produce. Students typically believe that technologically advanced societies became that way solely

Most Americans believe that technological change will improve their lives overall. Indeed, technology has been called "the opiate of the educated public today," for no other single entity is so universally invested with high hopes for the betterment of humankind and of society. The average American's love affair with new technology may have reached a peak in the first half of the twentieth century, a period described as the golden age of technological enthusiasm. This love and enthusiasm is captured in the paintings of Jack Juratovic, which, like *Teague's Duesie* (1990), often pair the voluptuous grace of a big classic car with the streamlined sweep of a steam locomotive. This is an apt double image for our study, as the automobile is undoubtedly the most romanticized form of technology, and railroad technology will be a theme throughout this chapter.

In this Japanese painting from the Edo-Tokugawa period (1600–1853), beaters drive boars, deer, and rabbits into an enclosure filled with hunters. Animals are prevented from escaping by secondary enclosures surrounding the primary one. This hunting system taken as a whole is a form of technology just like a railroad. Both require hardware, skills, and an organizational framework.

because an unusually large number of great inventors, such as Thomas Edison, and/or great technology appliers, such as Henry Ford, just happened to have lived in them. But a sociologist would ask: How come technology seems to flourish in some societies and not in others? Why is it that some societies such as the United States, for instance, seem to have far more than their fair share of great inventors, scientists, and technologically savvy entrepreneurs (Hughes, 1989)? Clearly, the nature of the society—and of its values and institutions—has a strong influence on which type of technology the society possesses (McGinn, 1991).

Values

The most important value question for a society vis-à-vis technology is: What should be the relationship between human beings and the natural world? There are only three possible answers to that question: (1) Humans should submit to nature; (2) humans should live in harmony with nature; and (3) humans should dominate nature.

Clustered around the focal value that humans should dominate nature is a constellation of secondary values favoring such things as materialism, progress, rationalism, and hard work (see Figure 21:1). Material things like automobiles and billiard tables fundamentally come from nature. The more materialistic a society is, the more nature is forced to relinquish its raw materials. Similarly, progress means ever greater success at improving the natural condition of humans through better substances, chemicals, processes—in short, through increased mastery of the physical environment. Rationalism leads to a better understanding of nature, allowing it to be conquered most efficiently, and nature cannot be conquered without hard work. Societies that wish to dominate nature favor advanced technologies because these technologies will help to achieve this focal value and its secondary values.

FIGURE 21:1 THE TECHNOLOGY-RELATED VALUE, HUMANS SHOULD DOMINATE NATURE, AND THE SECONDARY VALUES THAT ARISE FROM IT

Clustered around the technology-related value that humans should dominate nature is a constellation of secondary values favoring such things as materialism, progress, rationality, and hard work.

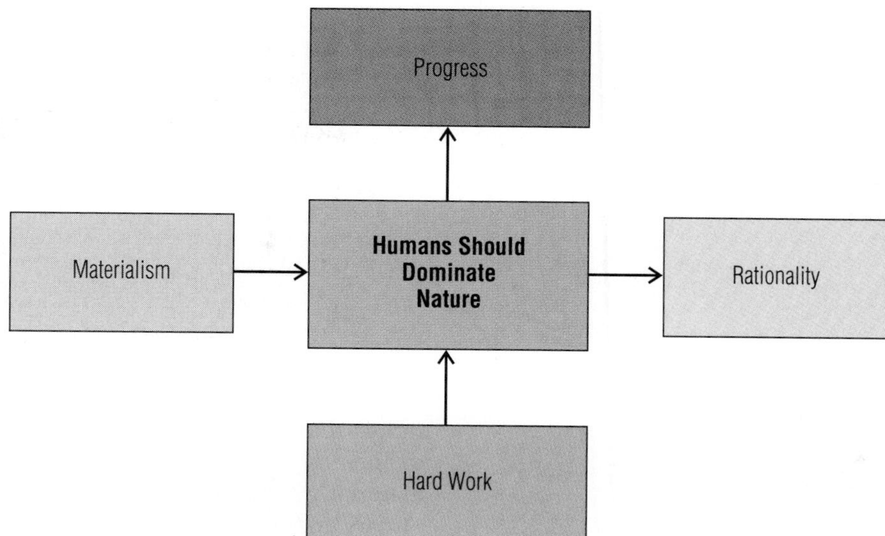

Societies that try to live in harmony with nature, on the other hand, have secondary values such as spiritualism (anti-materialism) and traditionalism (anti-progress), and, consequently, these societies possess simpler technologies. A hunting-and-gathering society such as the !Kung, who live in Africa's Kalahari Desert, developed simple technologies that do not put excessive pressure on their environment. They are not interested in progress or in material things and, unlike people in technologically advanced societies, do not work very hard. The !Kung are able to provide for their basic needs working about 15 hours a week. They spend their remaining time on such leisurely activities as visiting their friends or participating in spiritual trance-inducing dances. Thus, the !Kung value such things as leisure and recreation over material goods and hard work, and their simple technology is a reflection of such value choices (Lee, 1968).

Conversely, technologically advanced societies, like that of the United States, believe in dominating nature (Porter, 1992). We believe it is

People in hunting and gathering societies like the !Kung or this Ugandan tribe do not work as much as those in technologically advanced ones. They typically work only about 15 hours a week and spend a good deal of their remaining time participating in such recreational pursuits as singing and dancing.

possible—even desirable—to overcome natural obstacles to satisfy our needs. For example, rather than turning to ambitious conservation programs, our attitude toward threatened energy shortages is that we will solve the problem eventually by dominating nature in some other way—by, for instance, harnessing nuclear, wind, geothermal, wave, or solar power. Such solutions, of course, require advanced technology. Indeed, technologically advanced societies have a virtual love affair with technology, and cherish the progress and material things technology makes possible (Hughes, 1989). But technological progress does not result in less work per capita in such societies even though it does generate labor-saving devices. The reason for this paradox is that advanced technology also produces a steady stream of new or better material goods—the latest gadget or the faster car—which people in technologically advanced societies crave. In short, rather than technology being used to reduce the hours of work, it is used to increase income to accommodate the desire for and consumption of material goods (Sahlins, 1968). The fact that hard work per se is also secondary to the "dominate nature" focal value makes this paradox all the more inevitable (see Figure 21:1).

Sometimes an inventor comes up with a technology that is at odds with the basic values of a society. Ordinarily, such a technology is rejected, at least initially. It might be accepted later, but usually only if society's values have changed to accommodate it.

Institutions

Institutions also have profound impacts on the kinds of technology possessed by a society. The educational institution can provide knowledge and skills that ultimately are used in the creation, development, or application of technology. Less obviously, the recreational institution can also foster technological development. Many inventions owe their origin to hobbies and to "play" activities rather than simply to work. Societies that are unable to provide people with the leisure time necessary to pursue hobbies or simply to "tinker" are at a relative technological disadvantage compared to those that can.

Religious Institution

The religious institution of a society can have a positive impact on technological development. For example, Merton (1973) argues that Puritanism gave science (and technology) a boost in the sixteenth century by recognizing that there is an underlying order in the universe, that there must be universal laws to account for this order, and that it is the duty of human beings to know God by learning about the natural world he created. Similarly, Weber (1904–1905/1958) maintained that capitalism (and its technological underpinnings) arose in part owing to the Protestant belief in predestination and to their values of hard work and frugality.

At least as often, however, a society's religious institution has impeded the development of technology, particularly in the past. This is especially true of religions such as Catholicism that believe in "natural law." By definition, natural law demands that humans live in harmony with or submit to nature rather than dominate it. As a result, many basic technologies (e.g., medical ones such as vaccination, pain suppression, and birth control) were attacked over the centuries by traditional churches as unholy interventions into areas humans had no right to enter (Cohen and Cohen, 1989). The Catholic Church today still resists unnatural or "artificial" technology related to contraception.

Economic Institution

The economic institution also has a strong bearing on which type of technology is created and applied in a society (Volti, 1992). Market economies are by their very nature conducive to technological advances. The great technological innovations that began during the fifteenth century such as advances in ocean navigation and ship construction were related closely to the ascent of capitalism and the appearance of a market system. Indeed, the technological dynamism of capitalist society was noted with grudging respect by two of its archenemies, Karl Marx and Friedrich Engels (1848/1959), in *The Communist Manifesto.*

The type of market economy that exists in the United States today creates the most receptive environment for technological innovation for three reasons. First, because it offers monetary rewards to individuals who can satisfy consumer needs, a market economy provokes inventive efforts. Second, businesspeople and entrepreneurs in a market economy have a strong incentive to develop and apply new technologies to produce superior and/or cheaper products because of the presence of numerous competitors. Finally, as noted earlier, a technology is a system composed, in part, of many auxiliary goods and services. A market system is especially able to elicit the production of these complementary goods and services.

In contrast, centrally planned economies such as that of China or of the former Soviet Union do not stimulate technological advance very well. This is due in part to a basic incompatibility between the requirements of technological innovation and a centrally planned economy's system of management. Technological innovation is an unpredictable activity, one that cannot be "planned" by central bureaucracies in the same way they can

Tom Lovell's *Rescue at Sea* shows a motor launch from a nearby steam-powered ocean liner attempting the daring rescue of a damaged zeppelin. The motor launch, steamship, and the dirigible, as well as the locomotives seen elsewhere in this chapter, were technological products of nineteenth-century capitalist societies. Indeed, the technological dynamism of such societies was noted with grudging respect during the nineteenth century by two of capitalism's archenemies, Karl Marx and Friedrich Engels, in *The Communist Manifesto:* "The bourgeoisie, during its rule of scarce one hundred years, has created more massive and colossal productive forces than have all preceding generations together. Subjection of Nature's forces to man, machinery, application of chemistry to industry and agriculture, steam-navigation, railways, electric telegraphs, clearing of whole continents for cultivation, canalization of rivers, whole populations conjured out of the ground—what earlier century had even a presentiment that such productive forces slumbered in the lap of social labour?" (cited in Volti, 1992:47).

plan the routine production of, say, light bulbs. In addition, centrally planned economies typically have reward systems that create disincentives for technological innovation. Managers and workers get rewarded for meeting or exceeding quotas for existing products, not for creating, developing, or applying new technologies. Further, rewards for improved technology generally are short-term ones, and the improved technology just leads in the long term to higher production quotas. Finally, centrally planned economies do not have the same ability as market economies to furnish auxiliary items necessary to a technology.

Political Institution

The type of technology created and applied in a given society is also influenced by the political institution. Governments in particular have many ways to facilitate technological advance. A government can be involved in the generation of new technologies directly through its support of research and development. It can also provide a supportive economic framework for technological development by encouraging capital investments that embody new technologies. This can be done, for example, by lowering taxes derived from investment income, by allowing the accelerated depreciation of capital equipment, or by offering tax credits to investors in new technologies. The government can also furnish a supportive legal framework for technological development by, for example, granting patents to those who create new technologies, or by providing courts and laws to resolve issues engendered by technological change. Governments can additionally affect technological development through their support of education in general, and of science and technology education in particular. Moreover, governments can supply the essential auxiliary goods and services that make up a technological system. For instance, air travel and transport necessitate air traffic control, safety inspections, weather forecasts, customs regulation, and government-supported airports and airlines.

The United States leads the world in technological development, in part because its government traditionally has recognized that its military security and economic prosperity are linked closely to its ability to advance technologically. The federal government underwrites the cost of the National Aeronautics and Space Administration, as one example, for this reason. In *Columbia at Booster Separation* (1981), Bob McCall portrays the space shuttle in heroic fashion. Commissioned by NASA, this painting is intended in part to help ensure continued public support for the space program. That support cannot be taken for granted because some critics contend that the scientific and technological payback from the space shuttle is tiny compared to the billions of dollars it burns up.

Governments vary in their ability and willingness to perform these and other technology-related functions. The United States leads the world in technological development in part because our government has traditionally recognized that our military security and economic prosperity are linked closely to our ability to advance technologically (U.S. Congress, 1991). During the 1980s, for example, the federal government financed two-thirds of the nation's basic research and nearly half of its total expenditure on research and development. Other modern nations have increasingly followed the U.S. example in this regard, especially Japan, whose Ministry of International Trade and Industry has aggressively sponsored the development of high-tech industries as well as synergistic, joint research efforts within and between these industries (Freeman, 1987). Indeed, by the early 1990s the United States was being challenged strongly by Japan and Europe in the area of technological leadership (Raloff, 1992), and many analysts warned that the United States would lose its lead eventually if its government did not do more to support science and technological development (Council on Competitiveness, 1991; Elmer-DeWitt, 1989; Holmes, 1991).

Science Institution

The institution of science is composed of social arrangements whose principal function is to discover reliable knowledge (Merton, 1973). Although this text does not have a separate chapter on science, it is a major institution in modern industrial societies and has an immense influence on their technology and development (Ben-David, 1971). Obviously, the stronger a nation's scientific institution is, the more advanced its technology will be.

The nature of the connection between science and technology, however, is not so obvious. Most students incorrectly think technology is just applied science. Certainly, many technologies are influenced strongly by basic scientific discoveries. Breakthroughs in physics, for instance, have lead to whole new industries. Television, microwaves, radar, X-rays, semiconductors, computers, lasers—technologies that presently generate about 25 percent of the gross national product of the United States—are derived from discoveries in quantum physics, which took place in the early twentieth century (Lemonick, 1990). But many other technologies do not at all stem from scientific research. Indeed, as Volti (1992, p. 55) notes, "When the full history of technology is surveyed, it is apparent that most technologies have been developed and applied with little scientific input." This includes the "Stone Age" tools and the simple technologies of the !Kung mentioned above, as well as many modern technologies, such as the roller ball pen used to write the first draft of this chapter.

It is also worth noting that the converse is often true; that is, that technological advances lead to scientific discoveries rather than the reverse. For instance, the technological invention of the steam injector in the mid-nineteenth century eventually led to the abandonment in physics of the then-popular caloric theory of heat and to its replacement by the kinetic theory of heat (Kranakis, 1982).

Thus, rather than seeing technology as merely applied science, it is better to view science and technology as distinct enterprises that have developed along separate paths that frequently intersect. Each can contribute significantly to the other's development at these cross points. Scientific knowledge can precipitate technological advances, and technologies can produce both the opportunities and the stimuli for new scientific inquiries. The dynamism of both science and technology is enhanced by this reciprocal feedback loop (Layton, 1976).

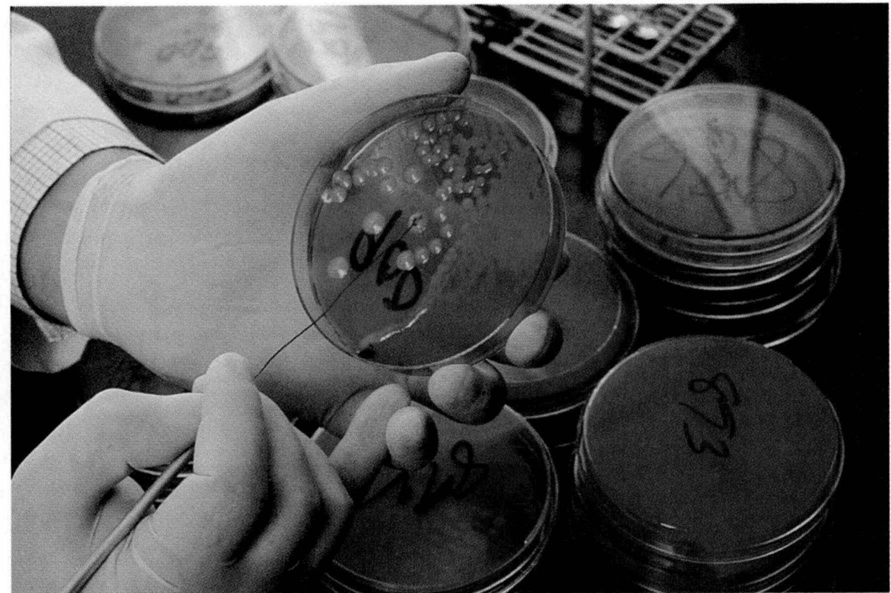

Of the two types of scientific research, basic research involves the pursuit of knowledge for its own sake. A classic example is the study of bacteria growing in a Petri dish to learn the secrets of biochemistry and genetics. By contrast, applied research has an explicit social goal. It uses basic research knowledge to create a new technology. Applied science may use what is learned about microbes in the Petri dish to create new medicines and biotechnologies. The link between technology and basic and applied research is embodied in the labor-saving robots that help build automobiles. The robots are a technological product of applied research, especially in the computer sciences, which in turn is a product of basic research in physics and mathematics.

The science institution is underpinned by many of the same values that foster technological advance, including the aforementioned value that it is desirable to dominate nature and, especially, its secondary values of progress and rationalism. Rationality is an intrinsic element of the scientific methodology. The rational approach allows the questioning of traditional ideas; resolves questions through experimentation, testing, and observation; and fosters the development of exact measurement methods (Mathias, 1972). The scientific institution is also influenced strongly by the other social institutions for better or for worse. For instance, in the United States during the early 1990s some forms of biological research such as that having to do with fetal tissue were discouraged by the U.S. government and by the Catholic Church. On the other hand, the economic and political institutions provided virtually all of the funding for other scientific research.

Scientific work is governed by the four norms of universalism, communism, disinterestedness, and organized skepticism (Merton, 1968). *Univer-*

salism specifies that science should be universal in nature, and that scientific findings must be judged solely on their intrinsic merit and not on the basis of the personal characteristics of individual scientists proposing them. *Communism* stipulates that scientists should share their findings with the entire scientific community, and that scientists should not own their scientific contributions or keep them secret. *Disinterestedness* requires that scientists place scientific truth above their own professional self-interest. Finally, *organized skepticism* demands that scientific findings and theories should be evaluated critically by other scientists before achieving acceptance. Like most norms, these scientific norms are violated at times, but the scientific community's tough disciplinary response to such transgressions is telling proof that the norms exist. As is generally true of deviance, violations of scientific norms occur because of pressures to be successful in the scientific world without sufficient access to the means to that success.

technological diffusion—the movement of a technology from one society or group to another.

Although science and technology are distinct phenomena, it is fair to say that science is an increasingly important generator of technology. Scientific–technological progress took off around 1650 and has been consistent, continuous, cumulative, and irreversible ever since (Caplow, 1991). The United States has the world's most advanced technology in part because it has the world's finest and most prolific science institution. One indicator of this is the fact that U.S. scientists have garnered far more Nobel prizes in science than scientists of any other nation.

Diffusion

The technological development of a society is also dependent on its willingness and ability to utilize technology invented and developed in other societies. The movement of a technology from one society (or group) into another is called **technological diffusion**. All technologically dynamic societies need the infusion of ideas, tools, and materials from other societies, coupled with the expertise to exploit them.

China had the world's most advanced technology in the year 1500. By that year the Chinese had invented not only porcelain "china" but

During the period stretching from 1600 to 1850, Japanese rulers kept foreigners and foreign influence out of Japan. But in 1853, four large, black U.S. warships commanded by Commodore Matthew C. Perry arrived to demand the opening of the country to trade. Once the trade treaties were signed, selected treaty harbors rapidly filled with "black ships," as most foreign trading vessels were called. These ships brought traders, missionaries, diplomats, and adventurers of all kinds, and cultural and technological diffusion ensued. Among the first gifts the Americans gave to the Japanese were a telegraph instrument, a camera, and a completely operating steam locomotive along with rails, tender, and passenger cars. The period painting below and the cover illustration show the port of Yokohama. Once it was opened to foreign trade, Yokohama became Japan's most important foreign port.

gunpowder, paper, the magnetic compass, the differential gear, the chain drive transmission, the spinning wheel, and watertight bulkheads for ships (Temple, 1989). But the Chinese were not willing to accept and adopt technologies that originated elsewhere. This reluctance persisted with brief interruptions well into the twentieth century. Even the communists who took power in 1949 did not accept wholeheartedly foreign ideas and procedures (although China recently has exhibited an increased openness to outside technology). Consequently, China slid from the apex of the technological totem pole in 1500 to somewhere near the middle today in part because of their lack of in-bound technological diffusion.

By 1500, European societies had their own technological triumphs, particularly in cathedral building and mining, but they still placed a distant second to China in overall development. The European societies, however, were willing to accept technologies that were invented elsewhere, including the Chinese ones mentioned above (Hall, 1957). Their adoption of the watertight bulkhead and the magnetic compass, for example, dramatically improved transoceanic navigation, thus permitting European economic and military power (aided also by the use of China's gunpowder) to extend throughout the world. In short, European societies after 1500 became much more technologically advanced than China owing in part to the fact that technological diffusion proceeded mostly in a one-way direction.

One reason for the advanced technological status of the United States throughout its history is that it, too, has been extraordinarily open to the adoption of foreign technology (Morison, 1977). Indeed, many of the technologies thought to be quintessentially "American"—for example, the automobile, the television, and the jet airplane—were, in fact, pioneered in other societies. In addition, U.S. technological development always has benefited from its unusually liberal immigration policies (see Chapter 20) because immigrants have been and continue to be responsible for many of the nation's greatest technological accomplishments. For example, Enrico

China had the world's most advanced technology throughout most of recorded history and was renowned for its clay and ceramic products, some of which came to be known as "China." One overwhelmingly awesome example is the six thousand life-size pieces of pottery that represented Emperor Qin Shihuang's guardian army. These sculptures were entombed with the emperor for the purpose of protecting him in the afterlife. Each figure is a complete and differentiated model of the real people in full regalia who had protected him during his life.

Fermi, an immigrant from Italy, was one of the leaders of the Manhattan Project, which developed the atomic bomb and, ultimately, other forms of nuclear power. But it was not only the immigrant inventors and scientists who advanced U.S. technology. The immigrant waves have also included legions of highly skilled workers who helped develop, manufacture, and market the inventions (Volti, 1992).

Similarly Japan became a technological giant during the past 150 years owing in part to the process of diffusion (Maddison, 1969). The progress of Japan over this period has relied heavily on the infusion of foreign technologies and technical advice. Today, Japan is well-known for its ability to copy and to improve technologies invented elsewhere and to do so at a lower cost. Most U.S. college students own one or more of the resultant products, such as cameras and audio/video equipment. Of course, as noted above, Japan today is not just a clever copyist, but is one of the world's leaders in technological innovation.

It should be noted that societies vary in their ability to advance technologically through diffusion. Remember, technologies are best viewed as systems, and require an array of complementary inputs, which the recipient society may not possess. A society can acquire and dissect a piece of technologically advanced hardware to see how it is made. But it may not have the human skills and organizational patterns to reproduce it on a large scale. Societies that profit most from imported technologies are those that have high levels of indigenous technological capability and of research and development (Blumenthal, 1979). This means that societies with high levels of indigenous technological innovation are also the societies that make the best use of technologies originated elsewhere (Freeman, 1982).

Developing countries in particular have difficulty adopting sophisticated technologies originating in modern societies, not just because they lack the aforementioned complimentary components, but because the modern technologies are often fundamentally incompatible with the needs of the recipient country (Volti, 1992). Many of these sophisticated technologies are capital-intensive rather than labor-intensive. In other words, these technologies reduce the numbers of workers required by substituting expensive capital equipment for people. But developing countries with their large and growing populations have not only a surplus of workers but a shortage of capital. Thus, the sophisticated technologies are not always **appropriate technologies**, and often lead to social problems such as increased unemployment and social inequality (Toth, 1978). These problems occur because generally the capital-intensive technology disproportionately benefits the capital-holding privileged groups in the society, while the underprivileged groups bear the brunt of the increased unemployment. Developing societies thus probably benefit more from **intermediate technologies**, which are more sophisticated than traditional ways of doing things but less sophisticated than the most modern ways (Schumacher, 1973). For example, it may be better in India to build 40 small sugar mills that are labor-intensive, rather than one giant mill filled with capital-intensive machinery (Wells, 1973).

appropriate technology—technology well-suited to the capital and labor characteristics of a society.

intermediate technologies—technology that is more sophisticated than traditional ways of doing things but less sophisticated than the most modern ways.

Of course, technological diffusion also occurs among advanced societies. Indeed, U.S., European, and Japanese firms are increasingly joining together in global alliances, impelled by the monumental cost of developing important new technologies and by the necessity of securing access to global markets. A state-of-the art microchip plant, for example, costs more than half a billion dollars. These globe-girdling strategic alliances are natural conduits for technology transfer.

Innovation Networks and Diffusion

Imagine that every brand-new technology—what we shall call *innovation*—glows with a brilliant, laser light. A film taken from a satellite Earth orbit would clearly show the shining trails of technology diffusion across international lines. Such transfers involve mechanisms such as patent sales, trade relations, "brain drains" (technocrats from one society moving to another), and cultural exchanges (including exchanges of college students). In sociological terms, this is evidence of megastructure, patterns of relations linking whole societies. The satellite photography would also reveal lines of illumination between large organizations within national boundaries. The cooperative agreement between Apple and IBM forged in the early 1990s would show a shining path of shared innovation; lesser lights would involve business technology councils, university–corporate partnerships, and even high-tech espionage. These lighted links are macrostructures.

More delicate but much denser traceries of light would connect individuals at the microstructural level. Recall the discussion in Chapter 1 of "invisible colleges," personal and academic relations among researchers in various group settings that together make up a real "scientific community"—that is, an interpersonal network whose shared information adds up to a discipline such as physics or sociology. The focus here is on the process by which technological innovations are diffused or passed along once the breakthrough has occurred.

Perhaps the most widely cited study in this literature was conducted by sociologist James S. Coleman and his associates among doctors in four moderate-sized communities (Coleman et al., 1966). Coleman's survey asked the doctor respondents to name the three doctor friends whom they saw most often socially. It turned out that unscientific friendship activities,

Because new technologies, especially the fusion of computers and telecommunications, greatly increase the capability of firms like MGM to operate anywhere in the world, globalization is becoming a necessity for almost all companies that have products or services that can be marketed internationally. Firms without global operations lack economies of scale and scope in vital areas such as research, product development, and manufacturing. Aided by the new technology, global companies can exploit relatively small niches in national markets that collectively yield efficient scale. The new technologies also permit scarce skills and resources from many parts of the world to be marshalled together to solve company problems wherever they occur (Page, 1993).

such as cocktail parties and ball games attended together, facilitated the passage of new medical techniques from doctor to doctor to doctor. In other words, interpersonal networks speeded up the diffusion of innovations through the medical community and thus to patients.

Microstructural diffusion does not operate only among technocrats. The lines of light passing along innovations do connect the suppliers of new technologies, but they also link consumers in familiar ways. The wide applications of the silicon chip in the 1970s led to rapid replacement of adding machines by calculators, and of mechanical watches by digital watches. Much of the impetus driving such diffusion came from people showing off the new wonders they had bought to friends and acquaintances. You probably will be the "show off" or the "shown" as this process repeats itself in the next decade with the introduction of high-resolution TV.

THE SOCIAL CONSEQUENCES OF TECHNOLOGY

The previous section dwelled on the social forces that influence technological change. This section examines the opposite relationship—technological change as an inducer of social change (Buchanan, 1992). We have already discussed one example of this phenomenon in conjunction with this chapter's opening "Personal Perspective." Remember we noted that ungoverned sex selection technology would cause a sex ratio imbalance, which in turn would lead to profound negative social, psychological, and economic effects.

One form of technology, whose impact on society already has occurred, is the railroad. Indeed, some scholars argue that the railroad, more than any other single force, shaped modern societies as we know them today (Faith, 1992; Martin, 1992). The railroad was the first large-scale and perhaps the most impressive creation of the Industrial Revolution. According to Nicholas Faith (1992),

> . . . the modern world would begin with the coming of the railways. They turned the known universe upside down. They made a greater

The railroad was the first large-scale, and perhaps the most impressive, creation of the Industrial Revolution. Consider the scope and power of just one railroad: the Pennsylvania Railroad (PRR). The PRR was the first modern business organization and billion-dollar firm. At its zenith in the 1930s, the PRR had enough track to circle the globe, and it employed nearly 300,000 of the 50 million workers in the U.S. labor force. "Do not think of the Pennsylvania Railroad as a business enterprise," wrote *Fortune* magazine in 1936. "Think of it as a nation." Dean Cornwell's *Serving the Nation* (1943) captures the power of this railroad and the vital role it played during World War II. Representing the nation itself, Uncle Sam rises allegorically in grand scale behind the PRR and the smoky steel mills that represent the resources and productivity of the United States.

and more immediate impact than any other mechanical or industrial innovation before or since.

Some of the changes created or made possible by railroads include total war, the modern corporation, precise time-keeping, capital markets, the urban proletariat, the suburbs, mass merchandising, corporate lawyers, fresh vegetables in winter, middle-class vacations—even cheap "paperback" novels designed initially for reading on trains. In short, the wrenching changes brought about by railroads were responsible in large part for transforming the rural, agricultural, animal-based, slow-paced life of the eighteenth century into the urban, industrial, mechanical, hurried life of the twentieth century.

While you can marvel at the fantastic social change that can be traced to technologies such as sex selection and railroads, it is important to keep in mind that these social changes are always a joint product of the technological change *and* the "initial social conditions" that led to the technological change in the first place (McGinn, 1991). The technological change/social change relationship is thus circular in character; that is, social change leads to technological change, which in turn leads to social change, and so on. For example, the emerging Industrial Revolution led to the invention and development of the railroad, which subsequently provided the impetus for further industrialization. The erroneous belief that technology acts as a force independent of its social context is called **technological determinism**.

technological determinism—the belief that technology acts as a force independent of its social context.

The impact of technology on society is a vast topic. After all, technological change plays a role in virtually all the megastructural trends associated with modernization: industrialization; urbanization; militarization; continuous population growth; increases in mechanical energy, goods, and services; the destruction of pre-modern cultures; and environmental degradation and resource depletion (Caplow, 1991). Moreover, at the macrostructural level technological change has helped bring about profound changes in all the major institutions of modern society (McGinn, 1991). Consider, for example, the impact of TV on the political institution. Finally, at the microstructural level, technological change fashions the fundamental contours of your life—everything from how you work, to what you eat and drink, to the manner in which you are entertained (see Box 21:1) (Volti, 1992). We will discuss here some of the consequences of technology on just three forms of social behavior: work, communications, and warfare.

Work

Work is important in both economic and noneconomic ways. With respect to the latter, work has a major bearing on a person's sense of individual identity and self-esteem. But the economic function of work is even more important because it is the principal form of social activity through which the individual and the society subsist. In fact, societies are often classified according to the kinds of **subsistence technology** involved in their principal activities. Lenski and Lenski (1982) provide a typical typology:

subsistence technology—the principal form of economic activity through which a society exists.

Hunting and gathering societies
Simple horticultural societies
Advanced horticultural societies
Simple agrarian societies
Advanced agrarian societies
Industrial societies

BOX 21:1 COLLEGE EXPERIENCE

Technology: A College Student's Best Friend

Technological advances over the past three decades have made life for college students much less burdensome. Consider for a moment how much easier you have it compared to two of your book's authors, who were in college during the mid-1960s. Some of the educational technologies you enjoy, which we had to do without, include the computer with its word processing, calculating, and other abilities; copying machines to reproduce reference materials and class notes; computerized searches, indexes, and bulletin boards; electronic calculators, spellers, dictionaries, and thesauruses; roller ball, felt tip and throwaway ballpoint pens; and computerized libraries and registrar offices. Think how much more hectic your life would be without these technologies.

Technology, of course, continues to change the lives of college students. Recently, for example, the microcomputer has mated with the video disk to produce a flexible and encompassing learning tool that promises to create an educational revolution. The big news in the classics world, for instance, is Perseus 1.0, an interactive database program that contains the equivalent of 25 volumes of ancient Greek literature by 10 authors, roughly 4,000 entries in an on-line classical encyclopedia, a 35,000-word on-line Greek lexicon, a 6,000-image photographic database, and hundreds of drawings and descriptions of archeological and art objects. With this system, you—if you choose to study Greek—can read a text side by side with its translation, and you can call up at any time a thumbnail sketch of a mythical figure, an analysis of any word, a relevant map, and/or a picture of art related to the text. Other interactive video programs are available in languages, law, and medicine, and eventually this technology will find its way into all fields (much to the dismay of some college professors who fear this new technology will make them redundant) (Birkerts, 1992).

Of course, your life as a college student also differs from that of your authors owing to technological changes unrelated to education per se. Consider, for example, how recreation has changed. We not only did not have compact discs (CDs), but the audio cassette was unavailable, and even FM radio was still in its infancy. In fact, much of the very music you listen to—songs like "Radio Waves" (Roger Waters) and "I Robot" (The Alan Parsons Project)—could not have been produced using mid-1960s technology. The same is true of the intensely technological fantasy films that college students love—from *Star Wars* through *Jurassic Park.* A short list of other forms of recreational technology unavailable to college students in the mid-1960s would include music videos, computer games, the VCR, astroturf, composite tennis racquets, high-tech athletic shoes, answering machines (to screen dates), and the Pill (which did not become widely available until the late 1960s).

Critical Thinking Questions

1. The technological changes that have eased the burdens of college life have been offset somewhat by the explosion of knowledge in most fields that has occurred since the mid-1960s. Is it possible that college work, like housework, has changed more in character than in quantity over the past few decades?
2. What would concern a conflict theorist about many of the technological advances that have made it possible for a college student to be much more productive?

This list is rank ordered in terms of the degree of overall technological development, with hunting-and-gathering societies representing the least development and industrial societies the most development. Various hybrid forms could be interspersed throughout the list, and it can be argued that another category, post-industrialized society, should be added to the bottom of the list. In any event, subsistence technology is the most powerful single variable influencing the social and cultural characteristics of societies (Lenski and Lenski, 1982). As the subsistence technology of a society changes, fundamental social and cultural characteristics change as well.

Let's turn our attention to some of the technological changes that have occurred over the past two centuries in the United States and that have transformed both the economic and noneconomic aspects of work (see McGinn, 1991).

Occupational Profile of the Workplace

Industrialized societies like the United States have three kinds of industries:

- **Primary industries**—those that produce raw materials such as farming, fishing, and mining.
- **Secondary industries**—those that process the raw materials and convert them into finished products, such as factories and mills.
- **Tertiary industries**—those that provide the services found in industrial societies such as health care, education, retail trade, and government and social services.

During the early stages of industrialization, workers move out of the primary and into the secondary industries. But during the later stages of industrialization, growth in the secondary industries slows and then reverses, and tertiary industries become the largest sector of the economy.

This process transformed the labor force in the United States over the past two centuries. In 1800 about 95 percent of the U.S. labor force was engaged in farming, but by 1990 the proportion had dropped to about 2 percent. The proportion of the labor force involved in secondary industries rose to about 40 percent by 1910, but fell to about 28 percent by 1990. Approximately 70 percent of U.S. workers now work in tertiary industries, performing service-type jobs.

This striking transformation of the U.S. labor force was made possible in large part by technological development. Advances in agricultural technology and science in areas such as machinery, seeds, fertilizers, and herbicides vastly increased productivity using fewer and fewer farmworkers to provide food for the general population, and enabling subsequently freed-up workers to move into secondary manufacturing-type industries. Similarly, advances in manufacturing technology such as new machines, processes, and materials eventually reduced the demand for labor in the secondary industries. Finally, present growth in the tertiary industries is being driven by technological developments such as the computer and advanced telecommunications.

These macrostructural changes in the proportion of the labor force employed in various industrial sectors have a microstructural counterpart in the kinds of jobs people have. In 1800, the average man had a choice of only a few hundred jobs; the average woman had far fewer choices. Today workers can choose from about 25,000 occupational titles, including about 3,000 titles that did not exist 20 years ago (U.S. Employment Service, various dates). Again, technological change is responsible in large part for this expanding range of choices (see Box 21:2).

BOX 21:2 GENDER AND SOCIAL CHANGE

Technology and the Liberation of Women

"Let me tell you what I think of bicycling," said suffragist Susan B. Anthony in an interview for *New York World* in 1896. "I think it has done more to emancipate women than anything else in the world. I stand and rejoice every time I see a woman ride on a wheel. It gives women a feeling of freedom and self-reliance" (Mullenneaux, 1992, pp. F1, F4).

Technological change has had a profound impact on U.S. women's lives over the past two centuries. In 1800, virtually all women worked in the home doing domestic and agricultural tasks. The technological change that probably changed women's domestic lives the most was electrification, particularly electrification of the countryside. This new technology lifted many burdens from women. For example, it powered water-well pumps, freeing women from the arduous task of lifting and carrying great quantities of water. It also partially lifted the burdens of loneliness and of ignorance by making radio and, later, television possible.

During the twentieth century a whole cavalcade of technological developments radically altered the nature of housework, including a new technological infrastructure such as new household fuels (oil and gas) and their delivery systems, running water, and telephones; labor-saving appliances such as the vacuum cleaner, electric iron, washing-machine, dryer, dishwasher, refrigerator, and microwave oven; and convenience items such as canned, concentrated, frozen, and fast-foods, as well as drip-dry clothes and throw-away diapers (McGinn, 1991). In short, technology helped liberate women from the drudgery of housework, gradually making it ever more possible for them to gain paid employment outside the home. However, it must be noted that some scholars (e.g., Bose et al., 1984; Schwartz-Cowen, 1976) believe this technology-as-liberator thesis is given too much credit for the liberation of women at the expense of important concurrent nontechnological changes.

Technological change also has had a profound effect on women's roles in the workplace over the past two centuries. Between 1800 and 1900, new technology such as the typewriter, telegraph, telephone, and steel-framed office building furnished new gender-typed employment opportunities for women. Although only a small proportion of women took advantage of these opportunities in the nineteenth century, the new jobs created, such as secretary and telephone operator, made it evident to all women that alternatives existed to their homemaker role and to traditional low-tech women's jobs, such as being a domestic servant. Indeed, it was the movement of women out of domestic service into these new jobs that provided part of the impetus for the development of the aforementioned labor-saving appliances.

During the twentieth century, new technology helped enable a steadily increasing proportion of women to join the workforce. Technological marvels like the nineteenth-century typewriter and the twentieth-century computer went far to eliminate differential strength as a basis for female and male work roles, and made it possible for women to qualify for an increasing share of all jobs (Teich, 1990b; Walshok, 1990). Nevertheless, in some work situations—especially situations traditionally segregated by gender—new technologies have actually reinforced existing sexist divisions of labor. For example, office automation in some industries has favored male rather than female workers (Volti, 1992; Weinberg, 1990). In the insurance industry, for instance, low-level clerical jobs are increasingly filled by women, whereas high-level, data processing, management positions are almost exclusively held by men (Feldberg and Glenn, 1983).

Of course, non-work-related technological developments also have profoundly influenced women's lives and helped enable

(continued on next page)

BOX 21:2 GENDER AND SOCIAL CHANGE *continued*

them to join the labor force. Perhaps chief among these have been advances in medical technology that, by dramatically reducing infant mortality, allowed women to have fewer children to achieve a given family size; and advances in birth control technology, which increased the ability of women to control reproduction. Similarly, women benefited greatly from the increased mobility afforded by transportation technologies—from bicycles, to trolleys and trains, to automobiles, the quintessential freedom machine.

Technological change is also changing women's lives in the Third World. In New Guinea, for instance, rural men who traditionally hold their society's high-status position of hunter–warrior are in turn both mystified and mortified when they are forced to deal with women as equals, if not superiors, in the modern sector (Linden, 1990). But, as in developed nations, new technology does not always help women. The modernization of agriculture in the Third World, for example, has often left women increasingly dependent on men because mechanization and training have been devoted almost exclusively to male activities, increasing men's power and wealth relative to women (Sivard, 1985).

Critical Thinking Questions

1. In the second paragraph of Box 21:1, it is noted that some scholars believe that technology is given too much credit for the "liberation" of women. What concurrent nontechnological changes do these scholars believe are often given too little credit?
2. Why do you think well-intentioned economic development programs sponsored by the United States and international agencies often end up helping men more than women in Third World nations?

Locus, Content, and Process

Technological development over the past 200 years has also changed radically the locus and content of work (McGinn, 1991). The locus of work changed from the farm to the factory, and then to the office building and to a host of other service locales. Job content also changed, from the hand-operation of farming tools to the manipulation of industrial machinery and of information, although many service jobs such as hairdressing still involve hand-operated tools. In general, technological change over the past two centuries has made the content of work less physical and more perceptual/mental in character in primary, secondary, and tertiary industries.

Time

Technological change has altered the relationship between work and time in two ways: It increased the amount of time expended on work and it led to the precise scheduling of work (O'Malley, 1992; Volti, 1992). Technologically simple hunting-and-gathering societies like the aforementioned !Kung expend relatively little time on work; people in post-industrial societies devote relatively large amounts of time to work. In addition, pre-industrial work typically was not conducted on a regular daily schedule, and was often characterized by a period of intense activity followed by a period of non-work. In the industrial workplace, an individual is scheduled to work a fixed number of hours each day (even if there is little work to do) in part because of the ability of large technology-intensive industrial factories to work continually and the need for them to do so in order to be profitable. Indeed, the artificial method of marking time that you take for granted today—Standard Time and the four U.S. time zones—first came into being in 1883 in response to the scheduling needs of a then-new technology: the railroads.

The Modern Business Firm

In the middle of the nineteenth century, new transportation and communications technologies such as the railroad, steamship, telegraph, and the trans-Atlantic cable emerged that dramatically increased the ease and speed of product distribution. This made mass-production attractive, and new mass-production technologies were developed. These new distribution and production technologies stimulated a transformation in the structure of the business firm—away from the small, single unit, informally run, family-owned and managed firm, which could not take full advantage of these new developments, toward the kind of firm that could. Most of you will someday work for this kind of large multiunit, horizontally and vertically integrated, professionally managed, hierarchically organized firm (Chandler, 1987; McGinn, 1991).

Unions

The mass-production and distribution technologies of the modern business firm often led to a number of problems for workers, including grim and dangerous working conditions, tedium owing to ever finer divisions of labor and to assembly-line work, and a higher level of worker–management estrangement. This estrangement resulted from the replacement of the relatively personal relations workers had with pre-industrial bosses by the impersonal rigid discipline meted out by the new industrial bosses. Consequently, unions were organized to help labor deal with these problems posed by large-scale organizations growing out of technological change (Heibroner and Singer, 1984).

Incidentally, one of the major successes of unions over the years has been the shortening of the work week. In 1860, the work week was about 67 hours long in the manufacturing industries; today it is only about 42 hours. But the unions probably would not have been so successful unless technology had advanced to the point where allowing a shorter work week and increasing wages would still permit increased productivity and greater profitability.

Communication

Printing

For almost all of human history, people lived their lives in abject ignorance. They knew little of the world outside their own local area, and knew only that much of their own histories that could be passed down orally from generation to generation. Only a tiny percentage of the world's languages were ever given written form and in those few societies that did have a written language only a small segment of the population (usually the political and religious elite) could read. But even such elites had access to relatively few books because manuscripts had to be copied by hand and were exceedingly expensive. This social order began to dissolve in Europe with the fifteenth-century invention of the printing press with movable type, one of the most influential technological innovations of all time (Volti, 1992).

Printing and the subsequent vastly expanded production and circulation of books had profound social consequences for European societies. The spread of information through print media promoted the rational modes of thought discussed above that are an essential property of modern societies. A critical spirit developed because people no longer relied solely on the judgment or pronouncements of intellectual elites but were instead able to choose between multiple and often conflicting printed sources.

Printing also led to changes in people's perceptions of the physical and natural world. It permitted the widespread distribution of ever-more accurate maps and allowed the publicizing of geographic discoveries, both of which stimulated further exploration of the empty spaces on the maps (Mumford, 1934). Printing also fostered science by increasing the circulation of scientific information (as is the case with this book) and by providing an intellectual feedback system to judge the validity of scientific work (which is why the first draft of this book was critiqued by other sociologists before it was allowed to reach your hands) (Eisenstein, 1984).

Printing also had an enormous impact on people's views of the spiritual world. In the pre-printing-press European world, Catholicism prevailed, and challenges to the authority of the centralized church remained local and isolated. Printing allowed protesters to circulate their dissident views and to recognize that other distant groups held similar unorthodox interpretations of Christian beliefs. These groups then formed alliances and mounted a unified, formidable attack on the dominant Catholic order, a rebellion known as the Protestant Reformation. In addition, the Protestant belief that individuals should read and interpret the Bible for themselves led to the printing of Bibles in people's own languages, not Latin. This not only prompted the expansion of literacy, but also undermined the unity of the medieval Catholic world, and gave a boost to the development of the nation–state (Volti, 1992).

Printing and the subsequent growth of literacy in Europe undermined not just the dominant religious institution but the entire medieval social order. It also set the stage for the Industrial Revolution and is now a necessary feature of post-industrial society. The social consequences of printing have yet to be fully expressed in many Third World societies where illiteracy rates are high.

The Electronic Media

Radio and television, developed in the twentieth century, are the principal forms of electronic media. And, although it is clear that their impact on society is as great as that of printing, we have yet to fully understand the nature of their effects (Meyrowitz, 1985). Television is the dominant and most influential form of media in the United States today. Ninety-eight percent of American households contain one or more television sets, and a TV is on about seven hours a day. Americans spend more time watching TV than on any other activity except sleeping and working. In fact, TV viewing is the principal leisure activity of Americans, consuming 40 percent of the average person's free time (Schogol, 1990).

Television has co-opted many of the cultural activities and ceremonies of people's lives. Many Americans primarily experience such things as sports, art, religion, literature, and politics not firsthand, but via the tube (Kubey, 1990). In fact, some scholars (e.g., Bianculli, 1992) argue that television is our culture, that the memories of television past rather than, say, the knowledge of great literature, are what most Americans share as a culture and as a collective consciousness. While this might be an exaggeration, it is certain that television increasingly performs important social functions such as socializing children and determining which events deserve news coverage and hence receive public attention.

There is considerable debate about whether the social benefits of electronic media outweigh their negative effects (Murray, 1992). Concern exists, for instance, that television violence causes aggressive behavior in viewers

Congolese artist Trigo Piula's painting, *Ta Tele* (1988) or "Your television" in French, shows at its center a Nganga or traditional healer. But rather than holding the customary ancient mirror that once enriched many such power figures and that was intended to capture distant spirits, the Nganga holds the new symbol of power, a television set. The TV screens in the background display the dreams and escapist fantasies that television satisfies. The TV-spawned personal dreams of each patient in the audience appear inside their own heads. The diffusion of Western-style consumer electronics and programming is making the world's peoples increasingly Western and homogeneous. In a rural town in China, teenagers zap alien creatures in a video game owned by a savvy curbside entrepreneur.

(Centerwall, 1992; Freedman, 1984), and that programming and news are "socially constructed" by media "bigwigs" advancing their own social, political, or commercial interests (Medved, 1992; Montgomery, 1989). On the other hand, the electronic media help compensate for the disruption of enduring community ties that occurs in highly mobile, modern societies. The common culture created by the media serves as a partial antidote to the loneliness resulting from the weakening of community ties and from the consequent increasing tendency of post-industrial people to spend their time in the privacy and security of their homes (Volti, 1992; Williams, 1965).

The electronic media have also significant megastructural effects via cultural diffusion. The international communications market is dominated by fewer than 100 firms, most of which are located in the United States (Lyon, 1988). These firms export the American and/or Western worldview through television, films, commercials, and music. This so-called electronic cultural imperialism undoubtedly alters the values and institutions of Third World and other nations, and is literally making the world's peoples increasingly homogeneous.

Warfare

For most of human history, technology limited the death and damage wrought by warfare. Clubs, knives, spears, rocks, and other thrown objects were inefficient weapons, and remain so in the pre-modern societies that continue to do battle with them. But as societies became more technologically advanced, they invariably applied their technological know-how to the improvement of weapons. Indeed, weapon improvement was in the first place often the stimulus for the technological advances (Szuic, 1990).

Warfare in the ancient world was revolutionized by the production of metals used to make stronger and more deadly weapons and the body armor to defend against them; by the development of the bone-and-sinew laminated bow that had superior power and accuracy compared to primitive all-wood bows; by the invention of the horse-drawn chariot that increased the mobility and overall offensive capabilities of armies; and by the development of siege machinery such as catapults to attack fortifications (Finch, 1951). With these weapons, nations like Persia and Rome were able to invade and conquer neighboring states and to create political and military empires.

The stirrup, introduced into Europe in the sixth century, was another technological development that revolutionized warfare. It secured a rider to a horse and allowed the two to fight as a unit, which immensely increased the lethal power of an individual soldier. The stirrup eventually gave rise to the mounted knight, a figure as awesome to foot soldiers on the feudal battlefield as today's tank is to infantrymen.

The mounted knight changed the social structure of Europe. It was exceedingly expensive to train and maintain an army of knights, their horses, and their staffs, even for monarchs (Laffont, 1968). So rulers financed knights by allotting to them huge tracts of land, along with the power to govern and tax the residents. Thus arose the feudal order, which, throughout the Middle Ages, constituted the principal form of political organization in Europe. The mounted knight also gave rise to the culture of chivalry, which tended to confine warfare to a warrior class of knights and other combatants (noncombatants were relatively safe), and which generated a code of specific battle rules that limited the manner in which warfare took place. In addition, feudal knights built castles for defensive security, borrowing construction technology from their Moslem opponents in the Crusades.

Just as feudalism came about in part owing to new weapons technology, it came apart for the same reason. Toward the end of the Middle Ages, infantry soldiers became more than a match for knights and calvary with the help of the pike, a 19-foot-long wooden staff with a steel point (Oman, 1898); the long-bow, a nearly 6-foot-long bow capable of rapidly firing armor-piercing arrows over the length of two football fields (Preston et al., 1956); and the crossbow—a high-tech, mechanically pulled device able to hurl a half-pound bolt at high velocity (Foley et al., 1985). Knights reacted to these weapons by increasing the gauge of the armor used by both the knight and his steed. The added weight, however, made them too slow and cumbersome to be effective, and eventually the mounted knight vanished from the battlefield. Additionally, the castle—once virtually impregnable—became vulnerable in this era to a new technological engine of war, the trebuchet, a mechanically improved catapult capable of projecting a 300-pound missile as far as 300 yards (van Crefeld, 1989).

By the early fourteenth century, the pike, longbow, crossbow, and trebuchet had the European feudal system reeling, and new weapons based on gunpowder developed in that century delivered the *coup de grâce*. Gunpowder was first used to power artillery pieces, and technological developments in cannon barrels and in gunpowder itself over the next two centuries made even the then-fortified castles vulnerable to attack. However, these castles and forts were reinforced further to withstand cannon fire, and were equipped with their own cannons. Consequently, they

This aerial photograph of the medieval French town Carcassonne clearly shows the double-walled fortifications devised by feudal societies to withstand attack from increasingly potent assault weapons. The ability of fortified castles and small towns to hang on against ever-improving weapons until the end of the eighteenth century greatly helped small states to maintain their independence, and thus retarded the political consolidation of Europe into large nation states.

continued to yield considerable security until the late eighteenth century, when they could no longer resist the massed fire power from mobile artillery units. However, the ability of fortified castles to hang on against ever-improving artillery until the end of the eighteenth century greatly helped small states maintain their independence, and thus retarded the political consolidation of Europe into large nation–states (McNeill, 1982).

(Facing page) This illustration shows what would happen to New York City if a one-megaton nuclear bomb were detonated 6,500 feet above the Empire State Building. Panel 1 shows that during the first few seconds following the detonation, the initial flash of thermal radiation from the fireball starts primary fires all over the city. But as the spherical blast wave (black arcs) and its accompanying high winds speed outward (Panel 2), they snuff out many of these fires while destroying most of the city's structures. A large number of secondary fires then begin. The secondary and remaining primary fires grow together and form major conflagrations (Panel 3), which are walls of fire spread by surface winds as far as there is combustible material to sustain them. These conflagrations eventually coalesce (Panel 4) and may give rise to a firestorm (Panel 5), which is a massive self-fanning stationary fire. A firestorm can cover 100 square miles, generate temperatures of up to 2,000 degrees Fahrenheit (enough to melt metal), create howling 200-plus mile-an-hour winds (capable of flinging cars about), and burn for days. The smoke and dust generated by the nuclear explosion and its aftermath would stay in the atmosphere for a considerable period, blocking the sunlight and reducing the surface temperature of Earth (Panel 6).

The above description of the effects of a one-megaton explosion over New York City is horrifying enough, but it is a minimum damage scenario. Both the United States and some former states of the Soviet Union have warheads ranging up to 50 megatons. A single 20-megaton bomb would disintegrate or burn up every structure within 450 square miles and kill everything within a radius of 20 miles. To make matters worse, the most probable scenarios for nuclear war call for massive, multiweapon strikes. In such attacks, New York City alone would likely be hit with twenty to thirty-five nuclear weapons.

The development of handguns and rifles trailed that of cannons by about a century (Howard, 1976). Early firearms required numerous loading procedures before they could be fired. Because these loading procedures could be easily bungled in the heat of battle, they had to be impressed into soldiers through incessant drills until the loading procedures became almost automatic even in the midst of an enemy onslaught. Soldiers were organized into formations in part to coordinate the loading and firing of firearms, and they were subjected to a rigid chain of command that, among other things, told them when to shoot. Thus, unlike the knight, who was a free-riding, autonomous warrior, the gun-toting soldier of the eighteenth century was a battlefield robot: a mere replaceable part of a great military machine (McNeill, 1982). The importance of these new military machines—with their emphasis on obedience to impersonal authority, standard procedures, and constant repetition—goes far beyond the military realm. These hierarchical, regimented, and routinized armies were prototypes of civilian organizations such as factories and schools (Volti, 1992).

Naval warfare has also been transformed by technology. Before the development of the cannon, a warring ship would try to ram an enemy ship and/or land a boarding party of seamen–soldiers who would fight the enemy crew. Shipboard cannons revolutionized naval warfare by allowing ships to bombard each other from afar. Similarly, naval ships became immensely larger and more powerful in the nineteenth century with the incorporation of two new technologies: steel construction and the steam engine. These technological developments completely changed the day-to-day life and culture of seamen, transforming them into little more than floating technicians and factoryworkers who spent their time tending machines and stoking coal (Morison, 1977).

Speaking of coal, unlike their sail-powered predecessors, steam-powered ships needed fuel and hence coaling stations to operate throughout the world. The establishment of these naval coaling stations in turn provided part of the impetus for the imperial conquest of foreign territories. This conquest had a relatively low military cost for the then-technologically advanced European nations because of the vast superiority of their high-tech weapons compared to the more primitive weapons utilized by native defenders. In the Battle of Omdurman in the Sudan, for instance, a British force of a few hundred soldiers and a gunboat on a nearby river engaged 40,000 Muslims in battle. The victorious British forces lost just 40 soldiers; the Muslims lost 11,000. But it was not just high-tech warships, artillery, and firearms that made low-cost imperial conquest possible. Other forms of technology such as medicines, railroads, merchant steamships, and telegraphs increased the effective military power of European nations to such an extent that they were able to dominate 85 percent of the world's territory by the year 1914 (Headrick, 1981).

During the twentieth century, new technologies such as the machine gun, submarine, airplane, missiles, and nuclear weapons continue to transform warfare. One important social consequence of modern weapons has been the blurring of the distinction between combatant and noncombatant. Civilian populations are now often considered legitimate targets of warfare (Volti, 1992).

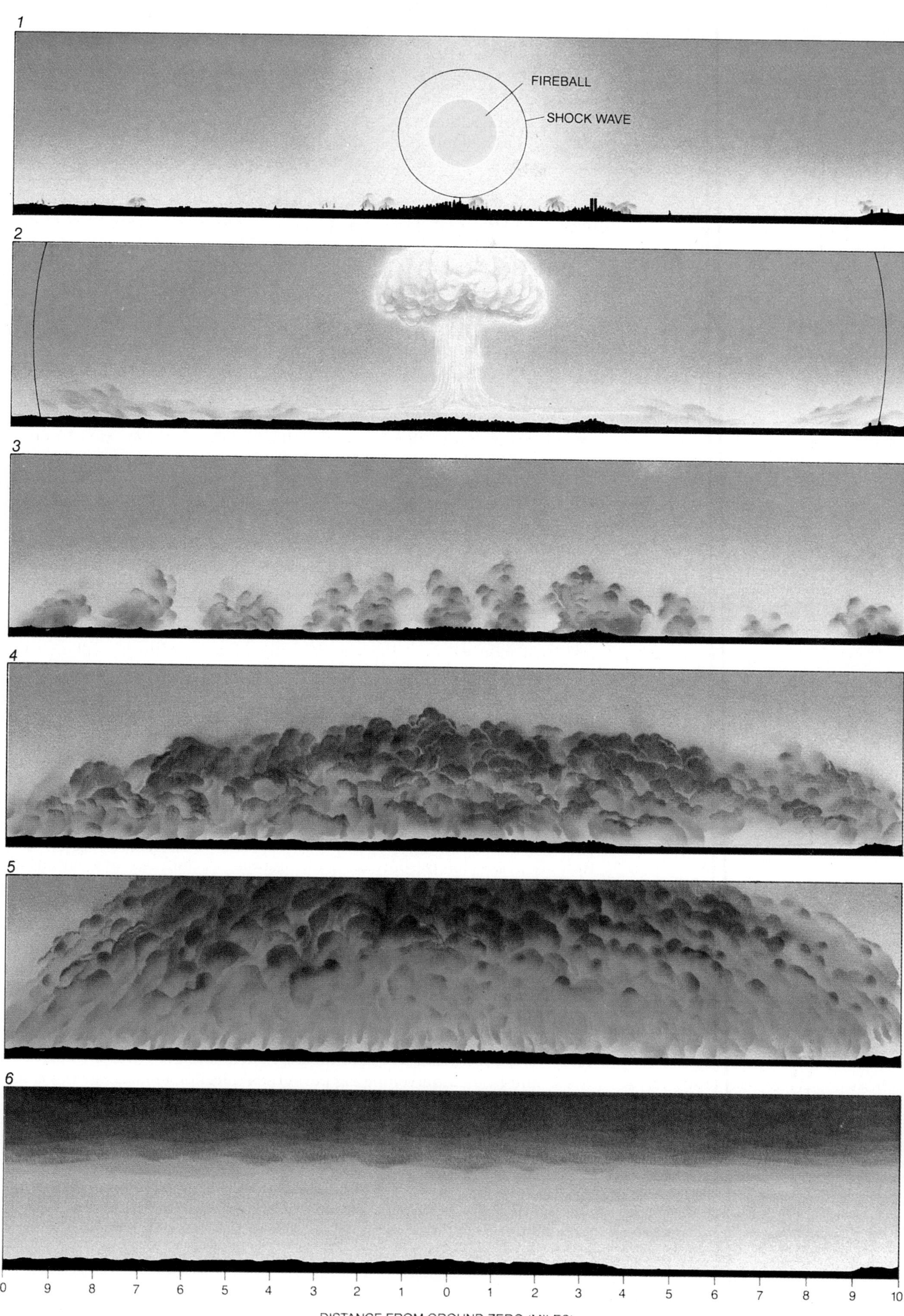
1
FIREBALL
SHOCK WAVE
2
3
4
5
6
10
9
8
7
6
5
4
3
2
1
0
1
2
3
4
5
6
7
8
9
10
DISTANCE FROM GROUND ZERO (MILES)

The technology embodied in nuclear weapons in particular has many profound consequences for society and for relations between societies (Jones et al., 1988). Indeed, Alexander King contends that "the nuclear bomb . . . has had more influence on international relations than any other single happening of the past century, including the rise of Marxism" (cited in McGinn, 1991, p. 196). An all-out nuclear war between superpowers would destroy modern society itself (Bergstrom, 1983; Lenski and Lenski, 1982), and industrial civilization might never be restored (Boulding, 1964; Weisskopf, 1981). Some experts even maintain that such a war could lead to the extinction of humanity itself (Ahern, 1985).

Problems Caused by Technology

Humankind has benefited greatly from technological development and its social consequences over the millennia. Technology has lengthened our lives, boosted prosperity, reduced many burdens, and improved the quality of our lives in many other ways. To elaborate briefly on just one of its positive effects, technology has been the single most important source of economic growth in history. It has increased the production and quality of goods and services, and has parented a vast number of new ones. But technology is a double-edged sword, playing a central role in many of humankind's greatest problems (Raymo, 1993). Indeed, it is a major cause of overpopulation, environmental degradation, resource depletion, and the threat of nuclear annihilation (see Figure 21:2) (Jones et al., 1988).

Technology creates problems in many ways. One of the most obvious ways is through sheer failure of a technological system. Spectacular technological failures since 1980 include the Chernobyl nuclear plant catastrophe in the former Soviet Union, the Bhopal chemical plant calamity in India in which poisonous gas was released into the neighboring community, and the *Challenger* space shuttle disaster in the United States. As noted in Chapter 5, these failures are examples of "normal accidents" that inevitably occur in the operation of sophisticated technological systems (Perrow, 1984).

Another way technology causes problems is through the latent consequences of some manifest technological change. For instance, unintended problem effects of the automobile include traffic fatalities, pollution, depletion of petroleum resources, deterioration of central cities, suburban sprawl, and the destruction of valuable farmland by the road system (Womack et al., 1991).

Technology also causes problems via cultural lag. Take the example used earlier of the sex selection of children. That technological development when it occurs will be introduced precipitously, and will probably be used immediately, with the aforementioned negative social consequences. Eventually the government may pass laws to regulate sex selection, perhaps by licensing the process to ensure that the same number of boy and girl permits are issued. But it will take time for such social structural changes to occur, and in the intervening lag period sex selection technology will cause the aforementioned social problems.

Cultural lag is ever more common in modern societies because of the rapid pace of technological innovation. This rapidity is due to the fact that technological development has a snowballing effect; the more technology there is in a culture, the more new technology is generated and the faster the whole process proceeds. Consequently, modern societies and their inhabitants frequently get hit with a new wave of technological change

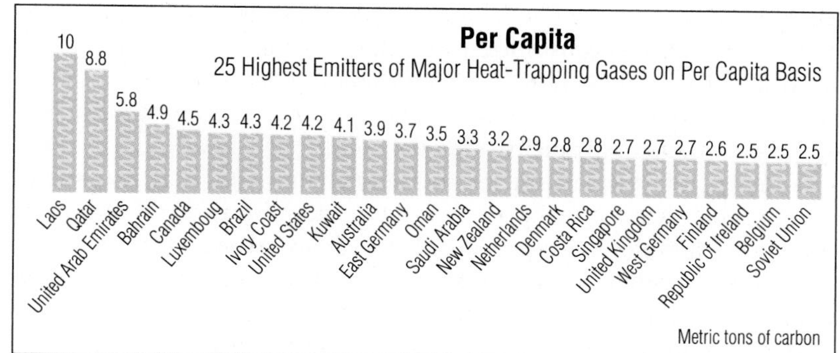

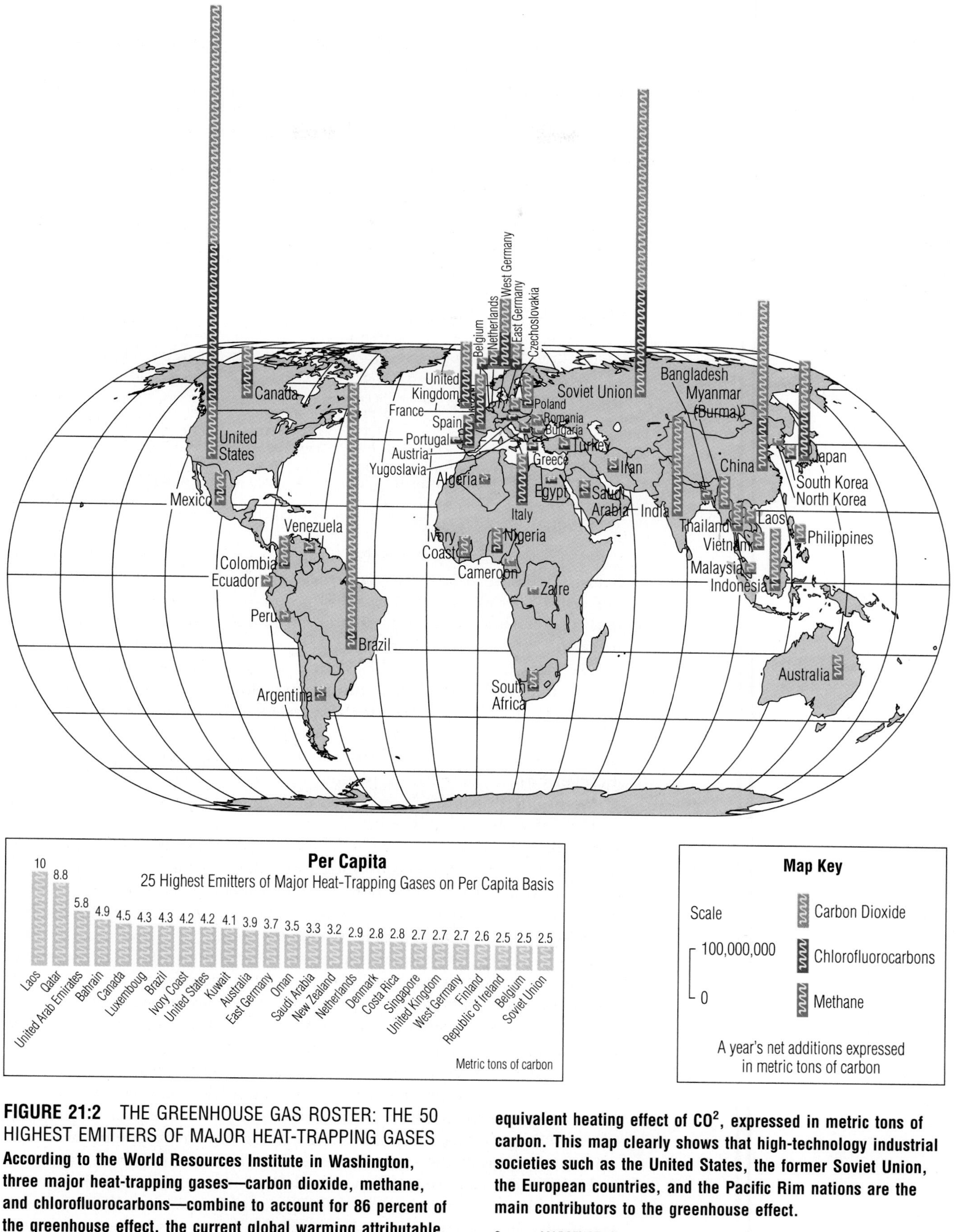

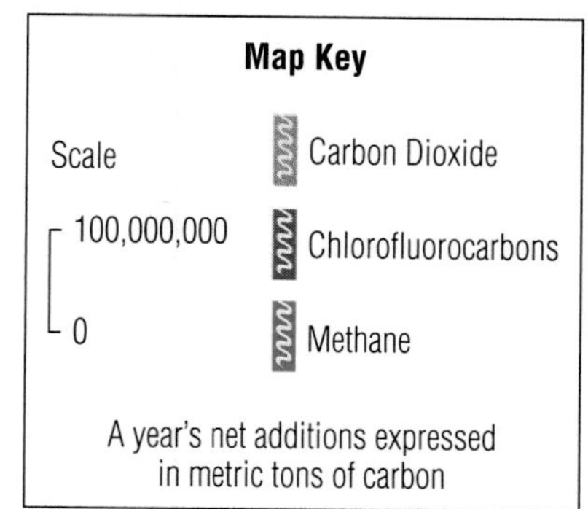

FIGURE 21:2 THE GREENHOUSE GAS ROSTER: THE 50 HIGHEST EMITTERS OF MAJOR HEAT-TRAPPING GASES **According to the World Resources Institute in Washington, three major heat-trapping gases—carbon dioxide, methane, and chlorofluorocarbons—combine to account for 86 percent of the greenhouse effect, the current global warming attributable to human activity. All the gases are described in terms of the equivalent heating effect of CO^2, expressed in metric tons of carbon. This map clearly shows that high-technology industrial societies such as the United States, the former Soviet Union, the European countries, and the Pacific Rim nations are the main contributors to the greenhouse effect.**

Source: *MAPSENSE: Global Comparisons and Trends from* World Monitor *Magazine*, 1992, p. 30. By permission of the publisher.

TABLE 21:1 Crosstabulation of the Feelings People Have about Science, by Race

Item # 357: "Would you tell me if you tend to agree or disagree with this statement: One trouble with science is that it makes our way of life change too fast."

RESPONDENT'S RACE	RESPONDENT'S FEELINGS ABOUT SCIENCE	
Count **ROW PCT**	Agree	Disagree
White	470 **38.9**	738 **61.1**
African American	85 **46.7**	97 **53.3**
Other	40 **67.8**	19 **32.2**
Total	595 **41.1**	854 **58.9**

$n = 1{,}449$

Main Point: A large minority of Americans believes science makes our life change too fast.

Source: General Social Survey, 1988.

before they have adjusted to and solved the problems posed by the previous one (see Table 21:1). The rapid pace of technological change is thus itself problematic because it leads to chronic and pervasive social disorganization.

The fact that technological change is a major cause of social change means that technology is a fundamentally subversive force, powerful enough to destroy communities and societies (Caplow, 1991). For example, the community of Caliente, Nevada, which had a single industry—servicing steam locomotives—turned into a virtual ghost town after the diesel-electric locomotive supplanted the steam locomotive in the middle of the twentieth century.

This example—railroad workers losing their jobs—is an instance of economic dislocation, a common problem produced by technological development. Automation, the substitution of machines for workers, is a major cause of workers losing their jobs and even their careers. Although automation typically creates new occupations elsewhere in the economy, these jobs are rarely filled by the displaced workers.

automation—**the substitution of new or improved machines for workers.**

Technology is not just a cause of social problems, for it is commonly used to help "fix" them (Teich, 1990a). The administration of the drug methadone, for example, helps to control heroin addiction; and the airbag cuts down on the number of automobile injuries and fatalities. Indeed, the list of technologies that have been used to help fix social problems is very long. But technologies that solve one problem often create new or different problems in the process. For example, pesticides can take a heavy toll on insect populations and drastically reduce insect-borne problems such as illness or crop damage. But once released into the environment, these powerful poisons gradually make their way into human tissues, causing other forms of illness requiring different and often new medical technologies to deal with them. Moreover, while existing pesticides kill virtually every insect exposed, a few bugs in a given species escape, owing to some genetic quirk. These survivors become the ancestors of a new breed of resistant insects, which eventually dominate the species. New pesticides must then be developed to deal with the "improved" version of the bug. In the long run, pesticides are simply a very efficient way of creating tougher, hardier insects. Thus, a **technological fix** for a problem often leads to a series of secondary problems often more troublesome than the original problem, and which require more complicated and more risky technological fixes (Weinberg, 1990).

technological fix—attacking a technological or social problem with a technological solution.

CONTROL OF TECHNOLOGICAL CHANGE

It would be socially desirable to control technological change, given the profound and pervasive social consequences produced. It would be in a society's best interest not only to try to avoid or at least minimize the problems created by new technology, but to be able to influence the direction of technological change so that it furthers high-priority social goals. Given society's limited technological resources, it probably would be better, for instance, to devote those resources to the development of more fuel-efficient automobile engines rather than to powerful engines for 200 mile-per-hour-plus super cars. Although a few scholars take the position that technology develops autonomously and is in some sense outside of human control, most scholars see technology as a social construction that can be controlled by humans (McGinn, 1991) (see Box 21:3). The only question for them is: Which humans?

It is possible to argue that government agencies and large corporations disproportionally determine the character of the technology developed in the United States. As noted above, during the 1980s the federal government financed two-thirds of the nation's basic research and nearly half of its total expenditure on research and development. Since World War II three agencies—the Department of Defense, NASA, and the Atomic Energy Commission—determined the allocation of 90 percent of these expenditures (Volti, 1992). There is no doubt that we would have a different mix of technologies today if these allocation decisions were made by a different set of government agencies or by other groups and organizations. If a large portion of those decisions had been entrusted to organizations more interested in social problems than in military ones, we might be farther along in solving such problems as environmental degradation.

Many interest groups argue that the control of technology should be in the hands of the public rather than in those of relatively small groups of government agency officials, business executives, scientists, and engineers (Mazur, 1990). The problem with this ideal is that most people are technological ignoramuses (Brennan, 1989; Schwartz, 1992). Most Americans are unable to program their VCRs, let alone understand the technology lying behind them. People are techno-dolts in part because of the enormous expansion of knowledge that has occurred over the past two centuries. In fact there are now more than 900 scientific and technical specialties, and over 20,000 scientific journals. Even scientists and engineers have little knowledge about scientific and technological developments outside of their own narrow areas of expertise. This knowledge situation severely limits the ability of people and their elected representatives to determine the direction of technological development. Public choices are increasingly based on information supplied and evaluated by a small group of experts. The more this happens in a society, the closer the society moves toward **technocracy** or rule by technical experts (Barnes, 1985; Habermas, 1971). Democracy is undermined to the extent that elected representatives

technocracy—the rule of society by technical experts.

BOX 21:3 SOCIOLOGICAL IMAGINATION IN FICTION

The Half-Hour War

This passage from Michael Crichton's novel *Congo* deals with a common science-fiction theme; that is, technological machines operating outside the control of human beings.

For thirty years, military thinkers had been awed by intercontinental ballistic missiles. But [General] Martin said that "ICBMs are crude weapons. They do not begin to approach the theoretical limits imposed by physical laws. According to Einsteinian physics, nothing can happen faster than the speed of light, 186,000 miles a second. We are now developing high-energy pulsed lasers and particle beam weapons systems which operate *at the speed of light.* In the face of such weapons, ballistic missiles traveling a mere 17,000 miles an hour are slow-moving dinosaurs from a previous era, as inappropriate as cavalry in World War I, and as easily eliminated."

Speed-of-light weapons were best suited to space, and would first appear in satellites. Martin noted that the Russians had made a "kill" of the American spy satellite VV/02 as early as 1973; in 1975, Hughes Aircraft developed a rapid aiming and firing system which locked onto multiple targets, firing eight high-energy pulses in less than one second. By 1978, the Hughes team had reduced response time to fifty nanoseconds—fifty billionths of a second—and increased beam accuracy to five hundred missile knockdowns in less than one minute. Such developments presaged the end of the ICBM as a weapon.

"Without the gigantic missiles, miniature, high-speed computers will be vastly more important in future conflicts than nuclear bombs, and their speed of computation will be the single most important factor determining the outcome of World War III. Computer speed now stands at the center of the armament race, as megaton power once held the center twenty years ago."

Elliot recognized at once the most serious consequence of the speed-of-light weapons—they were much too fast for human comprehension. Men were accustomed to mechanized warfare, but a future war would be a war of machines in a startlingly new sense: machines would actually govern moment-to-moment the course of a conflict which lasted only minutes from start to finish.

In 1956, in the waning years of the strategic bomber, military thinkers imagined an all-out nuclear exchange lasting 12 hours. By 1963, ICBMs had shrunk the time course to 3 hours. By 1974, military theorists were predicting a war that lasted just 30 minutes, yet this "half-hour war" was vastly more complex than any earlier war in human history.

rely on the judgments of such experts rather than those of citizens. Moreover, in a technocracy the public is reduced to hoping that the experts are right (Volti, 1992).

But the "rightness" of a technological judgment is not merely a function of the technical merit of the technology at issue. Value judgments also have to be made owing to the many social consequences the technology will produce. Returning to the sex selection example, technical experts might conclude that a future sex selection technology is safe and effective. But given the sex ratio problems such a technology would cause, the decision to pursue and/or introduce such a technology is one best made by the general public who, after all, would have to live with the consequences. Moreover, the fact that technological changes do not impact on everyone equally—that is, that some groups benefit while others lose—makes it all the more desirable for important technological decisions to be made as part of a

BOX 21:3 SOCIOLOGICAL IMAGINATION IN FICTION ***continued***

In the 1950s, if the Americans and the Russians launched all the bombers and rockets at the same moment, there would still be no more than 10,000 weapons in the air, attacking and counterattacking. Total weapons in interaction events would peak at 15,000 in the second hour. This represented the impressive figure of 4 weapons interactions every second around the world.

But given diversified tactical warfare, the number of weapons and "systems elements" increased astronomically. Modern estimates imagined 400 million computers in the field, with total weapons interactions at more than 15 billion in the first half hour of war. This meant there would be 8 million weapons interactions every second, in a bewildering ultrafast conflict of aircraft, missiles, tanks, and ground troops.

Such a war was only manageable by machines; human response times were simply too slow. World War III would not be a push-button war because as General Martin said, "It takes too long for a man to push the button—at least 1.8 seconds, which is an eternity in modern warfare."

This fact created what Martin called the "rock problem." Human responses were geologically slow, compared to a highspeed computer. "A modern computer performs 2,000 calculations in the time it takes a man to blink. Therefore, from the point of view of computers fighting the next war, human beings will be essentially fixed and unchanging elements, like rocks. Human wars have never lasted long enough to take into account the rate of geological change. In the future, computer wars will not last long enough to take into account the rate of human change."

Since human beings responded too slowly, it was necessary for them to relinquish decision-making control of the war to the faster intelligence of computers. "In the coming war, we must abandon any hope of regulating the course of the conflict. If we decide to 'run' the war at human speed, we will almost surely lose. Our only hope is to put our trust in machines. This makes human judgment, human values, human thinking utterly superfluous. World War III will be war by proxy: a pure war of machines, over which we dare exert no influence for fear of so slowing the decision-making mechanism as to cause our defeat."

Critical Thinking Questions

1. Crichton's passage might be a preface to the Arnold Schwarzenegger films *The Terminator* (1984) and *Terminator II* (1991) in which, once the machines were given control, they tried to annihilate humanity. Is increasingly ceding control of our lives to computerized machines an inevitable feature of post-industrial society? Why or why not?
2. More generally, is it possible for a modern society to control the development of technology? Explain.

Source: Michael Crichton, *Congo* (1980). New York: Avon Press, pp. 276–77.

democratic political process in which the technical and social consequences are made explicit (Volti, 1992).

Preparing the electorate for meaningful participation in such a complicated political process is one of the greatest challenges facing today's high-tech democracies, including the United States (Teich, 1990a). One place for such preparation to occur is in college. Critics argue that today's undergraduate university education does not properly prepare students to become "good citizens" in democratic technological–scientific societies. Most college graduates are largely illiterate in the fields of science and technology because college curriculums are still under the sway of nineteenth-century anachronistic notions concerning what students should be taught. Thus, in yet another example of cultural lag, the educational institution has failed to keep pace with American society's rapid technological development (McGinn, 1991).

Ashanti DeSilva and Cynthia Cutshall now occupy a prominent place in the history of medicine. They are the first patients ever to be treated by human-gene therapy, an awesome new technology that could revolutionize medicine. The two girls suffered severe immunodeficiency, the same genetic disease that afflicted David, the famous "boy in the bubble" discussed in Chapter 18. Using genetic engineering, scientists replaced the girls' defective genes with normal ones and now they are well. However, as with most important new technologies, gene therapy and more generally, genetic research, pose scores of ethical dilemmas. For example, who has the right to know a person's genetic fingerprint? Or, should employers have the right to screen job applicants for possible genetic flaws?

SUBJECTIVE DIMENSION OF TECHNOLOGY

Public concern about technology is as old as technology itself. In early-eighteenth-century England, for example, militant workers known as Luddites smashed the machines that were to take their jobs. In the United States, technological innovations such as vaccination, the telegraph, the railroad, and the automobile faced some public opposition when first introduced. But overall public concern about technology has varied over time (McGinn, 1991; Teich, 1990a). Public concern was relatively low in the United States during the latter half of the nineteenth century and the first half of the twentieth century, a period Hughes (1989) describes as a golden century of technological enthusiasm. During the period surrounding World War II concern about technology began to rise, touched off by the development of atomic weapons in the United States and the participation of German scientists and engineers in the Nazi war effort. Public concern subsided during the 1950s as a result of the federal government's high-profile funding of technological and scientific work, and owing to the affluence of the period brought about in part by technology and science.

The 1960s and 1970s were decades of growing public concern about technology. Public awareness of environmental degradation and social protest over the Vietnam War were the major drivers of this concern since science and technology were seen by many as important causes or at least contributors to both problems. The energy crisis and alternative fuel debates, the Three Mile Island near meltdown, the national defense computer system malfunctions, the proliferation of nuclear weapons, test-tube babies, and genetic engineering were just some of the controversial scientific and technological developments that kept concern relatively high throughout the 1970s. Indeed, during the 1960s and 1970s, a substantial minority of Americans viewed technology and science "as a threat, a Frankenstein monster out of control, carrying humanity headlong toward destruction" (Teich, 1990a, p. iv). An anti-technology movement emerged, which called for increased controls on technology, and for more Earth-friendly technological systems.

During the 1980s, concern about technology and science declined. The public and policymakers alike began to see technology as a way to counter economic and military challenges from abroad, and as a means to raise the competitiveness of U.S. industry. There were, of course, provocative technological issues during the decade like the "Star Wars" Strategic Defense Initiative (SDI) and continuing automation-caused unemployment, as well as a string of techno-disasters—from Bhopal to *Challenger* to Chernobyl. But these issues and events were unable to dispel the overall atmosphere of technological and scientific boosterism, a public mood that has extended into the 1990s.

But even in periods when concern about technology was relatively high, it was still relatively low compared to concern about such things as crime or health care. The relatively low subjective dimension of technology comes about in large part as a result of the operation of the first two of the now-familiar forces—values, expectations, and visibility. *Visibility* is relatively unimportant, for high visibility successes such as the *Apollo* moon landing are offset by high visibility failures such as the *Challenger* space shuttle disaster.

Americans are pro-technology because they have *values* that favor dominating nature, materialism, progress, and rationalism. Americans are drawn to the miracles technology offers, to the new products like cellular telephones and microwave ovens that boggle the mind and make life eas-

On December 21, 1988, the shattered remains of the bombed Pan American Flight 103 fell on Lockerbie, Scotland. All 259 people aboard the plane and 11 others on the ground were killed. Investigators pieced together the remains of the plane. Eventually, it was concluded that Libya sabotaged the plane. One of the problems with such high technology as nuclear power plants, skyscrapers, and jumbo jets is that they place many people at risk while, at the same time, they are vulnerable to terrorist attack.

ier. While specific technologies such as nuclear power may elicit major public concerns, the positive aspects of technology as a whole outweigh the negative ones. Even when people are opposed to one form of technology such as nuclear power, they generally are in favor of a competing technology like solar power. Thus, in power struggles between the technological "establishment" and anti-technology activist groups, national polls indicate that most people take the establishment's side (Mazur, 1990; Volti, 1992).

Public concern about technology is also relatively low because in modern societies, as opposed to traditional ones, there are *expectations* that continual change will occur, and that technology will be both a cause and a manifestation of that change. Most Americans expect that the change will be positive overall. Indeed, one author (McDermott, 1990) calls technology "the opiate of the educated public today, for no other single entity is so universally invested with high hopes for the betterment of humankind and of society" (p. 100).

Another reason for technology's low subjective dimension is the American expectation that technology is a self-correcting process, that any problems it creates are temporary and will be solved by a later round of technological innovation (McDermott, 1990). It is expected, for instance, that technology inevitably will provide a safe place to store nuclear waste and a safe means of disposing of toxic waste. In short, Americans still have great faith in "technological fixes," not only for purely technological problems but for social problems as well, despite evidence that technological fixes are often illusory. Americans' expectations are reflected in the common saying that "if we can put a man on the moon, we should be able to solve any problem" (see Figure 21:3).

Although the overall subjective dimension of technological change is relatively low at the national level, public concern often flares up at the local level as part of the "not in my back yard" phenomenon. For instance, people generally are in favor of nuclear power, but frequently raise a storm of protest if a nuclear power plant is planned for their neighborhood (Volti, 1992).

THEORETICAL PERSPECTIVES ON TECHNOLOGICAL CHANGE

Functionalism

Functionalists emphasize that technology and science are major causes of social change at every level of society (Merton, 1970). They stress that all of these changes have functional and dysfunctional consequences for society. Functional consequences include, for example, material wealth and a longer and healthier life. Dysfunctional consequences include such things as overpopulation, environmental degradation, resource depletion, and possible nuclear war—all potentially doomsday problems for humankind (Jones et al., 1988). Technology often creates these functions and dysfunctions simultaneously, as in the case where automation creates new jobs for some individuals and chronic unemployment for others.

Conflict Theory

Conflict theorists stress that society is full of conflicts and unequal distributions of power, and that these power differences determine in part the pattern of technological change (Volti, 1992). They contend that specific technologies are invented and developed because they benefit powerful groups. The conflict perspective explains why, for example, ultramodern hospital technologies are developed and installed to serve the middle and upper classes in communities that lack basic medical services for the impoverished. More generally, conflict theorists point out that in directing technological development established institutions are particularly responsive to large, well-organized bodies, such as industries, labor unions, and other special interests.

Conflict theory also puts into perspective humanity's historical resistance to some forms of technological innovation and the struggles of various groups to control technology (Mazur, 1990; Rybczynski, 1983). It helps explain the actions of the machine-smashing Luddites in early-nineteenth-century England as well as today's Teamster union truck drivers who oppose new railroad technologies. The common point is that new technologies encounter such opposition because they threaten a group's important interests (Johnston, 1992).

(Facing page) Technology is a fundamentally subversive force, powerful enough to destroy industries, communities, and even societies. Thus, it is no wonder that public revolt against new technology is as old as technology itself. In early eighteenth-century England, for example, militant workers known as Luddites smashed machines that were to take their jobs. Theodor Kaufmann illustrates another such example in *Westward, the Star of Empire* (c. 1871). Native Americans understood all too well that the new railroads opened up their territories to settlers much more efficiently than horses and buckboards. In addition to derailing trains, Native American tribes such as the Sioux of the Plains attacked railroad survey parties and construction gangs even though these groups were armed and often had military escorts. In the end the railroads won, and the Native Americans lost, not just the struggle to stop the "iron horse," but their very societies.

Symbolic Interactionism

Symbolic interactionism also sheds light on the social causes and consequences of technological change (McGinn, 1991). Symbolic interactionists focus, for example, on the changes in interaction that take place between

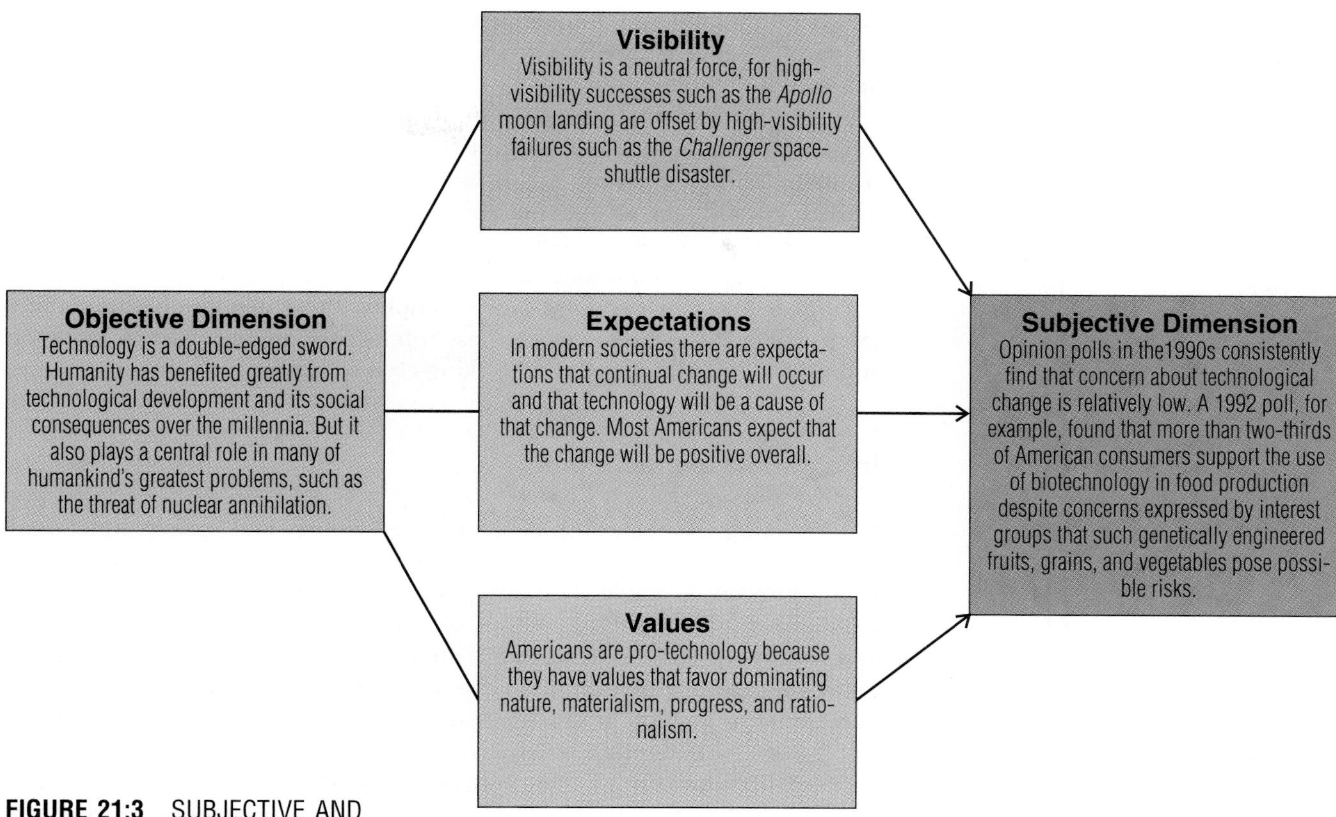

FIGURE 21:3 SUBJECTIVE AND OBJECTIVE DIMENSIONS: THE CASE OF TECHNOLOGY

The subjective dimension of technological change is much lower than its objective dimension, owing to the operation of the largely pro-technology intervening variables visibility, expectations, and values.

managers and workers in the wake of a technological change. It was noted above, for instance, that the mass-production technologies of the modern business firm led to a number of problems for workers, one of which was an increased level of worker–management estrangement. This estrangement resulted from the replacement of the relatively personal interaction workers had with pre-industrial bosses by the impersonal rigid discipline

meted out by the new industrial bosses. This change in the character of interaction in turn was one of the reasons for the development of labor unions.

Symbolic interactionists also note that, ironically, continuing technological change has been an important cause of union decline in recent years (Caplow, 1991). And once again interaction has played a key role in this decline because recent technological changes have reduced the quantity and character of worker-to-worker interaction. For example, in a cross-cultural study of automobile factories, Form (1976) found that as the production technology becomes more complex, there are fewer workers at a given workstation. This leads to less interaction among workers both on and off the job, which reduces working-class solidarity and weakens unions.

Integrating the Theories

In examining the relationship between technology and society, functionalists, conflict theorists, and symbolic interactionists often critically think about different facets of the same phenomena. Consider, for example, the relationship between technological change and the recent decline of labor unions. As just discussed, symbolic interactionists would look at how technological change weakens unions by reducing worker-to-worker interaction. Functionalists looking at the same subject would focus on the fact that new technology such as the containerization of goods on ships and trains is adopted because it is efficient and profitable to replace labor with capital intensive technology. Unions decline in this case simply because there are fewer workers to join. Finally, conflict theorists would concentrate on the fact that the use or threatened use of advanced technology to deskill or replace workers has shifted the balance of power in recent years in favor of management. From this perspective, unions decline because they have less power with which to fight management at the bargaining table.

SUMMARY

1. Technology has both social causes and consequences, and it is subject to social policy and control.
2. Technology is a system based on the application of knowledge, manifested in physical objects, related skills, and organizational forms, for the attainment of specific goals
3. All societies have technologies. The nature of the society and of its values and institutions has a strong influence on what type of technology the society possesses.
4. The most important value question for a society with respect to technology is, What should be the relationship between human beings and the natural world?
5. The religious, economic, political, science, and educational institutions have profound impacts on the kind of technology possessed by a society.
6. Science and technology are distinct enterprises. Scientific knowledge can precipitate technological advances, and technologies can produce both the opportunities and the stimuli for new scientific inquiries.
7. The technological development of a society is dependent upon its willingness and ability to utilize technology invented and developed in other societies.

8. Technological change is a prime inducer of social change, but these social changes are always a joint product of the technological change and the initial social conditions that led to the technological change in the first place.
9. Technological change has had profound effects on many forms of social behavior including work, communications, and warfare.
10. Technology is a double-edged sword. Humankind has benefited greatly from technological development, but technology has also played a central role in many of humanity's greatest problems.
11. Although no modern society can control technology completely, many interest groups argue that control should be in the hands of the public rather than in those of government agency officials, business executives, scientists, and engineers.
12. Public concern about technology has varied over time. The level of public concern is driven primarily by the public's values and expectations.
13. Functionalists see technology primarily as a cause of positive and negative social change. Conflict theorists emphasize that the unequal distribution of power in a society determines in part the pattern of technological change. Symbolic interactionists focus on the changes in interaction that take place between individuals in the wake of a technological change.

References

Abel, Emily. (1991). *Who Cares for the Elderly? Public Policy and the Experience of Adult Daughters.* Philadelphia: Temple University Press.

Abeles, Ronald P. (1976). Relative deprivation, rising expectations, and black militancy. *Journal of Social Sciences,* 32:119–137.

Aberle, David F. (1966). *The Peyote Religion among the Navaho.* Chicago: Aldine.

Abramhamson, Mark, and Lee Sigelman. (1987). Occupational sex segregation in metropolitan areas. *American Sociological Review,* 52:588–597.

Abrams, G. (November 26, 1992). Survey sees ethics lapses as pervasive. *The Philadelphia Inquirer,* p. G1.

Abramson, Alan J., and Rudolph G. Penner. (1990). Special interests, public opinion and public policy. *American Enterprise,* 1:79–80.

Abzug, Robert H. (1985). *Inside the Vicious Heart: Americans and the Liberation of Nazi Concentration Camps.* New York: Oxford University Press.

Academe. (March–April, 1990). The Annual Report on the Economic Status of the Profession, 1989–1990. Some dynamic aspects of academic careers: The urgent need to match aspirations with compensation, pp. 3–27.

Academe. (March–April, 1992). The Annual Report on the Economic Status of the Profession, 1991–1992. Vol. 78.

Achebe, Chinua. (1958). *Things Fall Apart.* Portsmouth, NH: William Heinemann Limited.

Addams, Jane. (1895). *Hull House Maps and Papers.* New York: Crowell.

Adelmann, Pamela K. (1987). Occupational complexity, control, and personal income: Their relation to psychological well-being in men and women. *Journal of Applied Psychology,* 72:529–537.

Ageton, Suzanne S., and S. Delbert Elliott. (1979). The incidence of delinquent behavior in an irrational probability sample of adolescents. *Project Report No. 3,* Boulder, CO: Behavioral Research Institute.

Agnew, Robert, and Sandra Huguley. (1989). Adolescent violence toward parents. *Journal of Marriage and the Family,* 51:699–711.

Ahern, T. (March 15, 1985). Nuclear winter and arms buildup. *The Philadelphia Inquirer.*

Ahlburg, Dennis A., and Carol J. DeVita. (1992). New realities of the American family. *Population Bulletin,* 47(2). Washington, DC: Population Reference Bureau.

Ahuvia, Aaron C., and Mara B. Adelman. (1992). Formal intermediaries in the marriage market: A typology and review. *Journal of Marriage and the Family,* 54:452–463.

Alan Guttmacher Institute, The. (1989). *Risk and Responsibility: Teaching Sex Education in America's Schools Today.* New York: Alan Guttmacher Institute.

Alba, Richard D. (1991). *Ethnic Identity: The Transformation of White America.* New Haven, CT: Yale University Press.

Albert, Judith C., and Stewart Albert. (1984). *The Sixties Papers: Documents of a Rebellious Decade.* New York: Praeger.

Albrecht, Terrance L., and Vickie A. Ropp. (Summer 1984). Communicating about innovation in networks of three U.S. organizations. *Journal of Communication,* 78–91.

Aldous, Joan. (1977). Family interaction patterns. *Annual Review of Sociology,* 3:105–135.

Aldous, Joan. (1978). *Family Careers: Developmental Change in Families.* New York: John Wiley & Sons.

Aldrich, Nelson W., Jr. (1988). *Old Money.* New York: Knopf.

Alexander, Jeffrey C. (1980–1983). *Theoretical Logic in Sociology* (4 volumes). Berkeley: University of California Press.

Alexander, Jeffrey C. (1989). The new theoretical movement. Pp. 77–101 in *Handbook of Sociology,* Neil J. Smelser, ed. Newbury Park, CA: Sage Publications.

Alford, Robert R., and Roger Friedland. (1985). *Powers of Theory: Capitalism, the State, and Democracy.* Cambridge: Cambridge University Press.

Allen, C. (January 13, 1992). Gray matter, black and white controversy. *Insight.*

Allen, Karen, Jim Blascovich, and Joe Tomaka. (October 1991). Presence of human friends and pet dogs as moderators of autonomic responses to stress in women. *Journal of Personality and Social Psychology*, 61:582–589.

Allen, Katherine R. (1989). *Single Women/Family Ties: Life Histories of Older Women.* Newbury Park, CA: Sage.

Allen, Steve. (1975). The public hating. Pp. 316–321 in *Social Problems through Science Fiction*, J.W. Milstead, J.D. Olander, and P. Warrick, eds. New York: St. Martin's Press.

Allen, Vernon L. (Winter 1970). Toward understanding riots: Some perspectives. *Journal of Social Issues*, 26:1–18.

Allen, W.R., and R. Farley. (1986). The shifting social and economic tides of black America. *Annual Review of Sociology*, 12:247–346.

Allon, Natalie. (1979). The interrelationship of process and content in fieldwork. *Symbolic Interaction*, 2:63–78.

Allport, Gordon W., and Leo Postman. (1947). *The Psychology of Rumor.* New York: Holt.

Alwin, Diane F. (1989). From obedience to autonomy: Changes in traits desired in children, 1924–1978. *Public Opinion Quarterly*, 53:99–106.

Ambert, Anne Marie. (1989). *Ex-Spouses and New Spouses: A Study of Relationships.* Greenwich, CT: JAI Press.

American Psychiatric Association. (1980). *Diagnostic and Statistical Manual of Mental Disorders* (3d ed.). Washington, DC: American Psychiatric Association.

Ammar, Hamid. (1954). *Growing Up in an Egyptian Village.* London: Routledge and Kegan Paul.

Anderson, Barbara A., B.D. Silver, and P.R. Abramson. (1988). The effects of the race of the interviewer on race-related attitudes of black respondents in SRC/CPS national election studies. *Public Opinion Quarterly*, 52:289–324.

Andriolo, K.R. (1989). Masked suicide and culture. Pp. 165–186 in *The Relevance of Culture*, Morris Freilich, ed. New York: Bergin and Garve.

Ang, Ien. (1985). *Watching Dallas: Soap Opera and the Melodramatic Imagination.* London: Methuen.

Angel, Ronald, and William Gronfein. (1988). The use of subjective information in statistical models. *American Sociological Review*, 53:464–473.

Angel, Ronald, and Peggy Thoits. (1987). The impact of culture on the cognitive structure of illness. *Culture, Medicine, and Psychiatry*, 11:465–494.

Antill, John K., and John D. Cunningham. (1982). Sex differences in performance on ability tests are a function of masculinity, femininity and androgyny. *Journal of Personality Psychology*, 42:718–728.

Antrobus, J.S., R. Dobbelaer, and S. Salzinger. (1988). Social networks and college success or grade point average and the friendly connection. In *Social Networks of Children Adolescents and College Students*, S. Salzinger, J. Antrobus, and M. Hammer, eds. Hillsdale, NJ: Lawrence Erlbaum.

Apple, Rima D. (ed.). (1990). *Women, Health, and Medicine.* Hamden, CT: Garland Publishing.

Aquilino, William S., and Khalil R. Supple. (1991). Parent-child relations and parent's satisfaction with living arrangements when adult children live at home. *Journal of Marriage and the Family*, 53:13–27.

Arjomand, Said A. (1988). *The Turban for the Crown: The Islamic Revolution in Iran.* New York: Oxford University Press.

Armstrong, Louise. (1990). Making an issue of incest. Pp. 45–55 in *The Sexual Liberals and the Attack on Feminism*, Dorchen Leidholdt and Janice Raymond, eds. New York: Pergamon Press.

Arnold, K. (1977). The introduction of poses to a Peruvian brothel and the changing images of male and female. Pp. 179–197 in *The Anthropology of the Body*, J. Blacking, ed. London: Academic Press.

Asimov, Isaac. (1966). *Foundation.* New York: Avon Books.

Atkinson, Maxine P., and Becky L. Glass. (1985). Marital age heterogamy and homogamy, 1900 to 1980. *Journal of Marriage and the Family*, 47:685–691.

Atwood, J., and John Gagnon. (1987). Masturbating behavior in college youth. *Journal of Sex Education and Therapy*, 13(2):35–42.

Atwood, Margaret. (1986). *The Handmaid's Tale.* Boston: Houghton Mifflin.

Ault, James. (1987). Family and fundamentalism: The Shawmut Valley Baptist Church. In *Disciplines of Faith: Studies in Religion, Politics and Patriarchy,* J. Obelkevich, L. Roper, and R. Samuel, eds. London: Routledge & Kegan Paul.

Ayanian, John Z., and Arnold M. Epstein. (1991). Differences in the use of procedures between men and women hospitalized for coronary heart disease. *The New England Journal of Medicine,* 325:221–230.

Bachman, Jerald, et al. (1978). *Adolescence to Adulthood: Change and Stability in the Lives of Young Men.* Ann Arbor, MI: Institute for Social Research.

Bachrach, Christine, and Marjorie Horn. (1985). Marriage and first intercourse, marital dissolution, and remarriage. NCHS, *Advanced Data,* April 12:107.

Bachrach, Peter, and Morton S. Baratz. (1970). *Power and Poverty: Theory and Practice.* New York, London: Oxford University Press.

Bailey, Beth L. (1989). *From the Porch to the Back Seat: Courtship in Twentieth Century America.* Baltimore: Johns Hopkins Press.

Baker, W. (1983). Floor trading and crowd dynamics. In *Social Dynamics of Financial Markets,* P. Adler and P. Adler, eds. Greenwich, CT: JAI Press.

Baker, W.K. (1987). What is money? A social structural interpretation. In *Intercorporate Relations: The Structural Analysis of Business,* M.S. Mizruchi and M. Schwartz, eds. Cambridge: Cambridge University Press.

Baldwin, Wendy, and Christine Nord. (1984). Delayed childbearing in the U.S.: Facts and fictions. *Population Bulletin,* 39(4). Washington, DC: Population Reference Bureau.

Bales, Robert F. (1954). The equilibrium problem in small groups. In *Working Papers in the Theory of Action,* T. Parsons et. al., eds. Glencoe, IL: Free Press.

Ballard, J.G. (1962). *Billenium.* Pp. 37–52 in *Social Problems through Science Fiction,* Martin H. Greenberg, John W. Milstead, and Joseph Warrick, eds. New York: St. Martin's Press.

Baltzell, Edward Digby. (1964). *The Protestant Establishment.* New York: Vintage.

Banks, Barbara, Ricky Slavings, and Bruce Biddle. (1990). Effects of peer, faculty and parental influences on students' persistence. *Sociology of Education,* 63:208–225.

Baran, Paul. (1957). *Political Economy of Growth.* New York: Monthly Review Press.

Barber, James. (1975). *Clear and Present Dangers.* New York: Praeger.

Barker, Eileen. (1981). Who'd be a Moonie? A comparative study of those who join the Unification Church in Britain. Pp. 59–96 in *The Social Impact: of New Religious Movements,* B. Wilson, ed. New York: The Rose of Sharon Press.

Barker, Eileen. (1984). *The Making of a Moonie: Brainwashing or Choice?* Oxford England: Basil Blackwell.

Barlett, Donald L., and James B Steele. (1992). *America: What Went Wrong?* Kansas City: Andrews and McMeel.

Barlow, Hugh D. (1993). *Introduction to Criminology.* New York: Harper Collins College Publishers.

Barnes, Barry. (1985). *About Science.* New York: Basil Blackwell.

Barry, Herbert, and Alice Schlegel. (1984). Measurements of adolescent sexual behavior in the standard sample of societies. *Ethnology,* 23:315–329.

Barry, H., and A. Schlegel. (1985). Culture customs that influence sexual freedom in adolescence. *Ethnology,* 25:151–162.

Barsky, Arthur J. (1988). *Worried Sick: Our Troubled Quest for Wellness.* Boston: Little, Brown.

Bates, F., and V. Murray. (1975). The school as a behavior system. *Journal of Research and Development in Education,* 17:223–233.

Beach, Frank. (1978). *Human Sexuality in Four Perspectives.* Baltimore: The Johns Hopkins Press.

Bean, Frank D. (April 1, 1990). Too many, too rich, too wasteful. *The New York Times,* p. 27.

Becker, H.S. (1953). Becoming a marijuana user. *American Journal of Sociology,* 59:235–242.

Bedell, George C., Leo Sandon, Jr., and Charles T. Wellborn. (1975). *Religion in America.* New York: Macmillan.

Bedell, Susan, David Deitz, David Leeman, and Thomas Delbanco. (1991). Incidence and characteristics of preventable iatrogenic cardiac arrests. *Journal of the American Medical Association,* 265:2815–2820.

Bell, Alan P., Martin S. Weinberg, and Susan K. Hammersmith. (1981). *Sexual Preference: Its Development in Men and Women.* Indianapolis: Indiana University Press.

Bell, Derrick. (1973). *The Coming of Post Industrial Society.* New York: Basic.

Berg, Ivar. (1970). *Education and Jobs.* New York: Praeger.

Bellah, Robert N. (1975). *The Broken Covenant.* New York: Seabury Press.

Bellah, Robert N., and Phillip E. Hammond. (1980). *Varieties of Civil Religion.* New York: Harper & Row.

Bellah, Robert N., M.R. Neelly, W.M. Sullivan, A. Swidler, and S.A. Tipton. (1985). *Habits of the Heart: Individualism and Commitment in American Life.* Berkeley: University of California Press.

Belsky, Jay. (July/August 1990). Infant day care, child development, and family policy. *Society:* 10–13.

Belsky, Jay, and David Eggebeen. (1991). Early and extensive maternal employment and young children's socioemotional development. *Journal of Marriage and the Family,* 53:1083–1110.

Ben-David, Joseph. (1971). *The Scientist's Role in Society.* Englewood Cliffs, NJ: Prentice-Hall.

Bengston, Vern L. (1985). Diversity and symbolism in grandparental roles. In *Grandparenthood,* V.L. Bengston and J.F. Robertson, eds. Beverly Hills, CA: Sage Publications.

Benokraitis, Nijole V. (1993). *Marriages and Families.* Englewood Cliffs, NJ: Prentice-Hall.

Bequai, August. (1978). *White Collar Crime: A 20th Century Crisis.* Lexington, MA: Lexington Books.

Berg, Ivar. (1970). *Education and Jobs.* New York: Praeger.

Berger, Peter. (1967). *The Sacred Canopy: Elements of a Sociological Theory of Religion.* Garden City, NY: Doubleday.

Berger, Peter. (1979). *The Heretical Imperative: Contemporary Possibilities of Religious Affirmation.* Garden City, NY: Doubleday/Anchor.

Berger, Peter L., and Brigitte Berger. (1979). Becoming a member of society. In *Socialization and the Life Cycle,* P. Rose, ed. New York: St. Martin's Press.

Berger, Peter L., and Thomas Luckmann. (1967). *The Social Construction of Reality.* New York: Anchor Books.

Berger, Raymond Mark. (1982). *Gay and Gray: The Older Homosexual Male.* Urbana: University of Illinois Press.

Bergstrom, S. (March 1983). Effects of nuclear war on health and health services. Report submitted to the World Health Organization, Thirty-Sixth World Health Assembly, Geneva.

Berk, Richard A. (1974). *Collective Behavior.* Dubuque, IA: Wm. C. Brown.

Berkman, Lisa, and S. Leonard Syme. (1979). Social networks, lost resistance, and mortality—A nine year followup study of Alameda County residents. *American Journal of Epidemiology,* 109:186–204.

Bernstein, Basil. (1971). *Class, Codes, and Control* (Vol. 1). London: Routledge & Kegan Paul.

Bernstein, Basil. (1977). *Class, Codes, and Control* (Vol. 3: rev. ed.). London, England: Routledge & Kegan Paul.

Bernstein, Basil. (1981). Codes, modalities, and the process of cultural reproduction: A model. *Language in Society,* 10:327–363.

Best, Joel. (1987). Rhetoric in claims-making: Constructing the missing children problem. *Social Problems,* 34:101–121.

Best, Joel, and G. Horiuchi. (1985). The razor blade in the apple: The social construction of urban legends. *Social Problems,* 32:488–499.

Best, Raphaela. (1983). *We've All Got Scars. What Boys and Girls Learn in Elementary School.* Bloomington: Indiana University Press.

Bettelheim, Charles. (1976). *Class Struggles in the USSR* (B. Pearse, Trans.). New York: Monthly Review.

Bianchi, Suzanne M. (1990). America's children: Mixed prospects. *Population Bulletin,* 45(1). Washington, DC: Population Reference Bureau.

Bianculli, David. (1992). Teleliteracy: Taking television seriously. New York: *Continuum.*

Bielby, William T., and James N. Baron. (1986). Men and women at work: Sex segregation and statistical discrimination. *American Journal of Sociology,* 91:759–799.

Bierstaker, Thomas J. (1981). *Distortion or Development?* Cambridge, MA: Harvard University Press.

Biggar, Jeanne. (1979). The sunning of America: Migration to the sunbelt. *Population Bulletin,* 34(1). Washington, DC: Population Reference Bureau.

Birkerts, Sven. (November 1992). Perseus unbound. *Harvard Magazine,* pp. 57–60.

Bissinger, H.G. (1990). *Friday Night Lights.* Reading, MA: Addison-Wesley.

Blackman, A., E. Taylor, and J. Willwerth. (Fall 1990). The dreams of youth. *Time, Women: The Road Ahead,* 10–14.

Blair, Steven N., Harold Kohl III, Ralph Paffenberger, Debra Clark, Kenneth Cooper, and Lavvy Gibbons. (1989). Physical fitness and all cause mortality: A prospective study of healthy men and women. *Journal of the American Medical Association,* 262(17):2395–2401.

Blankenhorn, David, Steven Bayme, and Jean Elshtain. (1991). *Rebuilding the Nest.* Milwaukee, WI: Family Service America.

Blau, Francine. (1978). Women in the labor force. Pp. 29–62 in *Women Working: Theories and Facts in Perspective,* A. Stromberg and S. Harkees, eds. Palo Alto, California: Mayfield.

Blau, Peter M. (1963). *The Dynamics of Bureaucracy.* Chicago: University of Chicago Press.

Blau, Peter, and Otis Dudley Duncan. (1967). *The American Occupational Structure.* New York: John Wiley & Sons.

Blau, Peter M., and W.M. Marshall. (1987). *Bureaucracy in Modern Society.* New York: Random House.

Blauner, Bob. (1964). *Alienation and Freedom: The Factory Worker and His Industry.* Chicago: University of Chicago Press.

Bloom, David E. (1982). What's happening to the age at first birth in the United States? A study of recent cohorts. *Demography,* 19:351–370.

Bloom, David E., and Neil G. Bennett. (1990). Modeling American marriage patterns. *Journal of the American Statistical Association,* 85(412):1009–1017.

Bloom, David E., and James Trussell. (1984). What are the determinants of delayed childbearing and permanent childlessness in the United States? *Demography,* 21:591–611.

Blumberg, Rae L. (Ed.). (1984). A general theory of gender stratification. In *Sociological Theory.* San Francisco: Jossey-Bass.

Blumenthal, Tuvia. (1979). A note on the relationship between domestic research and development and imports of technology. *Economic Development and Cultural Change,* 27:303–306.

Blumer, Herbert. (1951). Collective behavior. In *New Outline of the Principles of Sociology,* A.M. Lee, ed. New York: Barnes and Noble.

Blumer, Herbert. (1969). *Symbolic Interactionism.* Englewood Cliffs, NJ: Prentice-Hall.

Blumstein, Phillip, and Pepper Schwartz. (1983). *American Couples: Money, Work, Sex.* New York: William Morrow.

Bogue, Donald, and A. Tsui. (Spring 1979). Zero world population growth. *The Public Interest,* 99–113.

Bongaarts, J. (1978). A framework for analyzing the proximate determinants of fertility. *Population and Development Review,* 4:105–132.

Bongaarts, John. (1982). The fertility inhibiting effects of the intermediate fertility variables. *Studies in Family Planning,* 13:179–189.

Bordewich, F. (May 1, 1988). Colorado's thriving cults. *The New York Times Magazine,* pp. 16–18, 23, 32.

Bordieu, Pierre, and Jean-Claude Passeron. (1977). *Reproduction: In Education, Society, and Culture.* Beverly Hills: Sage.

Borrie, W.D. (1954). *Italians and Germans in Australia.* Melbourne, Australia: Cheshire.

Bose, Christine, Phillip Bereano, and Mary Malloy. (1984). Household technology and the social construction of housework. *Technology and Culture,* 25:53–82.

Bott, Elizabeth. (1971). *Family and Social Network.* London: Tavistock.

Boulding, Kenneth E. (1964). *The Meaning of the 20th Century.* New York: Harper.

Boulding, Kenneth E. (1989). *Three Faces of Power.* Newbury Park, CA: Sage.

Bourdieu, P. (1980). Le capital social notes provisoires. *Actes de la Recherche en Sciences Sociales,* 3:2–3.

Bourdieu, P. (1984). *Distinction: A Social Critique of the Judgement of Taste.* Cambridge: Harvard University Press.

Bouvier, Leon. (1980). America's baby boom generation: The fateful bulge. *Population Bulletin,* 35(1). Washington, DC: Population Reference Bureau.

Bouvier, Leon. (1984). Planet Earth 1984–2034: A demographic vision. *Population Bulletin,* 39(1). Washington, DC: Population Reference Bureau.

Bouvier, L.F., and A. Agresta. (1992). Projections of the Asian American population, 1980–2030. In *Asian and Pacific Immigration to the United States,* J.T. Fawcett and B. Carino, eds.

Bouvier, Leon, and C. Davis. (1982). *The Future Racial Composition of the United States.* Washington, DC: Population Reference Bureau.

Bouvier, Leon, and Robert W. Gardner. (1986). Immigration to the U.S.: The unfinished story. *Population Bulletin,* 41(4). Washington, DC: Population Reference Bureau.

Bovee, T. (September 20, 1991). Blacks continue to trail whites at the pay window. *The Philadelphia Inquirer.*

Bowes, A.M. (1989). *Kibbutz Goshen: An Israeli Commune.* Prospect Heights, IL: Waveland Press.

Bowlby, John. (1965). *Child Care and the Growth of Love.* Middlesex, England: Penguin.

Bowlby, John. (1973). *Separation: Anxiety and Anger.* New York: Basic Books.

Bowlby, John. (1979). *Attachment.* New York: Basic Books.

Bowles, Samuel, and Herbert Gintis. (1976). *Schooling in Capitalist America.* New York: Basic Books.

Boyd, Robert, and Peter J. Richerson. (1985). *Culture and the Evolutionary Process.* Chicago: University of Chicago Press.

Bozett, Frederick. (1987). *Gay and Lesbian Parents.* New York: Praeger.

Brand, David. (November 28, 1988). Make me a perfect match. *Time,* pp. 14–15.

Braveman, Paula, Susan Egerter, T. Bennett, and Jonathan Showstack. (1991). Differences in hospital resource allocation among sick newborns according to insurance coverage. *Journal of the American Medical Association,* 266:3300–3308.

Brennan, Richard P. (1989). *Levitating Trains and Kamikaze Genes: Technological Literacy.* New York: John Wiley & Sons.

Brennan, Troyan, Lucian Leape, Nan Laird, Liesi Hebert, Russell Localio, Anis G. Lawthers, Joseph P. Newhouse, Paul C. Weiler, and Howard Hiatt. (1991). Incidence of adverse events and negligence in hospitalized patients. *New England Journal of Medicine,* 324:370–376.

Bretschneider, Judy G., and Norma McCoy. (1988). Sexual interest and behavior in healthy 80 to 102 year olds. *Archives of Sexual Behavior,* 17(2):109–120.

Brewer, John, and Albert Hunter. (1989). *Multimethod Research: A Synthesis of Styles.* Newbury Park, CA: Sage Publications.

Brinton, Crane. (1960). *The Anatomy of Revolution.* New York: Random House.

Brookhiser, Richard. (1990). *The Way of the Wasp.* New York: Free Press.

Brophy, Jere, and Thomas Good. (1974). *Teacher-Student Relationships: Causes and Consequences.* New York: Holt, Rinehart, and Winston.

Broude, Gwen J., and Sarah J. Greene. (1976). Cross-cultural codes on twenty sexual attitudes and practices. *Ethnology,* 15:409–429.

Brown, Julia S. (1952). A comparative study of deviations from sexual mores. *American Sociological Review,* 167:135–146.

Brown, Lester. (1979). Resource trends and population policy: A time for reassessment. Worldwatch Paper 29. Washington, DC: Worldwatch Institute.

Brown, Lester. (1990). *State of the World.* New York: W.W. Norton.

Brown, Lester, W. Chandler, C. Flavin, S. Postel, L. Starke, and E. Wolf. (1984). *State of the World 1984.* New York: W.W. Norton.

Brown, Lester, and Jodi Jacobson. (1986). Our demographically divided world. Worldwatch Paper 74. Washington, DC: Worldwatch Institute.

Brownmiller, Susan. (1986). *Against Our Will* (Rev. ed.). New York: Bantam Press.

Brunvand, Jan H. (1981). *The Vanishing Hitchhiker: American Urban Legends and Their Meaning.* New York: W.W. Norton.

Brunvand, Jan H. (1984). *The Choking Doberman and Other New Urban Legends.* New York: W.W. Norton.

Brunvand, Jan H. (December 24, 1988). Letter to the Editor. *The New York Times.*

Buchanan, Robert Angus. (1992). *The Power of the Machine.* New York: Viking.

Bumpass, Larry L. (1990). What's happening to the family? Interactions between demographic and institutional change. *Demography,* 27:485–495.

Bumpass, Larry L., James A. Sweet, and Andrew Cherlin. (1991). The role of cohabitation in declining rates of marriage. *Journal of Marriage and the Family,* 53(4):913–927.

Burawoy, Michael. (1990). Marxism as science: Historical challenges and theoretical growth. *American Sociological Review,* 55:775–793.

Burke, Joseph. (1991). How I spent my summer vacation. *Philadelphia Streets* (pamphlet). Philadelphia Committee for the Homeless.

Burris, Val. (1983). Who opposed the ERA? An analysis of the social bases of antifeminism. *Social Science Quarterly,* 64:305–317.

Burstein, P. (1991). Policy domains: Organization, culture and policy outcomes. *Annual Review of Sociology,* 17:327–350.

Burt, Ronald S., K.P. Christman, and H.C. Kilburn, Jr. (1980). Testing a structural theory of corporate cooptation: Interorganizational directorate ties as a strategy for avoiding market constraints on profits. *American Sociological Review,* 45:821–841.

Burton, Sandra B. (September 12, 1988). The sexual revolution hits China. *Time,* p. 65.

Bush, David. (1983). Interpersonal dimensions of the consultation: Recent trends in American research on doctor-patient communication. In *Communication and the Consultation,* D.A. Pendleton, and D.F. Bush, eds. Oxford: Oxford University Press.

Buss, David M. (1985). Human mate selection. *American Scientist,* 73:47–51.

Butler, Judith. (1993). *Bodies That Matter: On the Dissuasive Limits of Sex.* New York: Routledge.

Button, James W. (1978). *Black Violence.* Princeton, NJ: Princeton University Press.

Buunk, Bram P., and Barry Van Driel. (1989). *Variant Lifestyles and Relationships.* Beverly Hills, CA: Sage.

Cain, Virginia S., and Sandra L. Hofferth. (1989). Parental choice and self-care for school-age children. *Journal of Marriage and the Family,* 51:65–77.

Cairns, Robert. (1988). Social networks and aggressive behavior: Peer support or peer rejection? *Developmental Psychology,* 24(6):815–823.

Callender, C., and L.M. Kochems. (1986). Men and not-men-male gender mixing statuses and homosexuality. Pp. 165–178 in *Anthropology and Homosexual Behavior,* E. Blackwood, ed. New York: Haworth Press.

Cameron, William B. (1966). *Modern Social Movements: A Sociological Outline.* New York: Random House.

Campbell, A., and H. Schuman. (1968). Racial attitudes in fifteen American cities. *Supplementary Studies for the National Advisory Commission on Civil Disorders.* Washington, DC: U.S. Government Printing Office.

Campbell, Donald T. (1975). On the conflicts between biological and social evolution and between psychology and moral tradition. *American Psychologist,* 30:1103–1126.

Cancian, Francesca M. (1987). *Love in America: Gender and Self-Development.* New York: Cambridge University Press.

Cantor, Murial, and Suzanne Pingree. (1983). *The Soap Opera.* Beverly Hills, CA: Sage Publications.

Caplan, Gerald. (1981). Mastery of stress: Psychosocial aspects. *American Journal of Psychiatry,* 138:413–420.

Caplan, Nathan, Marcella Choy, and John Whitmore. (February 1992). Indochinese refugee families and academic achievement. *Scientific American,* pp. 36–42.

Caplow, Theodore. (1991). *American Social Trends.* Orlando, FL: Harcourt Brace Jovanovich.

Carlson, Allan. (1988). *Family Questions: Reflections on the American Social Crisis.* New Brunswick, NJ: Transaction Press.

Carneiro, R.L. (1978). Political expansion as an expression of the principle of competitive exclusion. In *Origins of the State: The Anthropology of Political Evolution,* R. Cohen and E.R. Service, eds. Philadelphia: Inst. for the Study of Human Issues.

Carnes, Patrick. (1983). *Out of the Shadows.* Minneapolis: Compare Publication.

Carnes, Patrick. (November 13, 1988). Sexual addiction. Paper presented to the National Council on Family Relations Conference, Philadelphia, PA.

Castro, Janice. (November 25, 1991). Condition critical: Ten ways to cure the health care mess. *Time,* pp. 34–42.

Cater, Douglass, and Stephen Strickland. (1975). *TV Violence and the Child: The Evolution and Fate of The Surgeon General's Report.* New York: Russell Sage Foundation.

Center for Studies in Criminology and Criminal Law. (1983). University of Pennsylvania, Philadelphia. The seriousness of crime: Results of a national survey, as reporter in U.S. Department of Justice, Report to the Nation on Crime and Justice. Washington, DC: U.S. Government Printing Office.

Center for Women's Studies. (1987). Gender Gap in College Board Scores. Princeton, NJ: Educational Testing Service.

Centerwall, Brandon. (1992). Television and violence. The scale of the problem and where to go from here. *Journal of the American Medical Association,* 267:3059–3063.

Centra, J.A. (1973). *SIR Report No. 3.* Princeton, NJ: Educational Testing Service.

Chafetz, Janet S. (1984). *Sex and Advantage: A Comparative, Macrostructural Theory of Sex Stratification.* Totowa, NJ: Rowman and Allankeld.

Chagnon, Napoleon. (1977). *Yanomamo: The Fierce People.* New York: Holt, Rinehart and Winston.

Chandler, Alfred E. (1987). Technology and transformation of the industrial organization. Pp. 56–82 in *Technology, Economy, and Society,* J. Colton, and S. Bruchy, eds. New York: Columbia University Press.

Chase-Dunn, Christopher. (1991). *Global Formation.* New York: Basil Blackwell.

Chavez, Lydia. (July 17, 1987). Women's movement, its ideals accepted, faces subtler issues. *The New York Times.*

Cherlin, Andrew A. (1978). Remarriage as an incomplete institution. *American Journal of Sociology,* 84:634–644.

Cherlin, Andrew A. (1992). *Marriage, Divorce, and Remarriage.* Cambridge, MA: Harvard University Press.

Cherlin, Andrew J. (1983). Changing family and household: Contemporary lessons from historical research. *Annual Review of Sociology,* 9:51–66.

Cherlin, Andrew J., and F.F. Furstenberg. (1986). *The New American Grandparent: A Place in the Family, a Life Apart.* New York: Basic Books.

Cherry, R. et al., eds. (1987). *The Imperiled Economy, Book 1.* New York: The Union for Radical Political Economics.

Chess, Stella, and A. Thomas. (1987). *Know Your Child.* New York: Basic Books.

Chomsky, Noam. (1957). *Syntatic Structure.* The Hague: Mouton.

Chu, Susan Y., James W. Buehler, and Ruth L. Berkelman. (1990). Impact of human immunodeficiency virus epidemic on mortality of women of reproductive age, United States. *Journal of the American Medical Association,* 264, 226.

Chua, Eoan. (April 9, 1990). Strangers in paradise. *Time,* pp. 32–35.

Circirelli, Victor. (1980). A comparison of college women's feelings toward their siblings and parents. *Journal of Marriage and Family*, 42:111–118.
Clavell, James. (1966). *Tai Pan*. New York: Dell.
Coale, Ansley. (1991). People over age 100: Fewer than we think. *Population Today*, 19:6–8.
Cochran, Susan D., and Vickie M. Mays. (1990). Sex, lies, and HIV. *The New England Journal of Medicine*, 322:774.
Cockerham, William. (1988). Medical sociology. Pp. 575–599 in N. Smelser (ed.), *Handbook of Sociology*. Newbury Park, CA: Sage.
Cohen, Albert K. (1966). *Deviance and Control*. Englewood Cliffs, NJ: Prentice-Hall.
Cohen, E.B., and E.H. Cohen. (July 18, 1989). Choosing your ethnicity and the development of social engineering. Paper presented at Future View.
Cohen, Sheldon, David Tyrell, and Andrew P. Smith. (1991). Psychological stress and susceptibility to the common cold. *New England Journal of Medicine*, 325:606–612.
Cohen, Sheldon, and Thomas Ashby Willis. (1985). Stress, social support, and the buffering hypothesis. *Psychological Bulletin*, 98:310–357.
Cohen, Yinon, and Jeffrey Pfeffer. (1986). Organizational hiring standards. *Administrative Science Quarterly*, 31:1–24.
Coleman, James S. (1966). *Equality and Educational Opportunity*. Washington, DC: U.S. Government Printing Office.
Coleman, James S. (1982). *High School Achievement*. New York: Basic.
Coleman, James S. (1988). Social capital in the creation of human capital. *American Journal of Sociology*, 94 (Supplement):95–120.
Coleman, James S. (1990). Commentary: Social Institutions and Social Theory. *American Sociological Review*, 55:333–339.
Coleman, James S., Elihu Katz, and Herbert Menzel. (1966). *Medical Innovation: A Diffusion Study*. Indianapolis: Bobbs-Merrill.
Coleman, Marilyn, and Lawrence H. Ganong. (1990). Remarriage and stepfamily research in the 1980's: Increased interest in an old family form. *Journal of Marriage and the Family*, 52:925–940.
Colen, B.D. (1986). *Hard Choices: Mixed Blessings of Modern Technology*. New York: G.P. Putnam's Sons.
Collins, H. (July 29, 1991). Study: Few politically correct disputes. *The Philadelphia Inquirer*.
Collins, Randall. (1979). *The Credential Society*. New York: Academic Press.
Collins, Randall. (1982). *Sociological Insight: An Introduction to Nonobvious Sociology*. New York: Oxford University Press.
Collins, Randall. (1988). *Theoretical Sociology*. New York: Harcourt Brace Jovanovich.
Collins, Randall, and Scott Coltrane. (1991). *Sociology of Marriage and the Family*. Chicago: Nelson Hall.
Compact Edition of the Oxford English Dictionary, The. (1971). New York: Oxford University Press.
Comte, Auguste. (1854). *System of Positive Policy*. New York: Burt Franklin Series.
Conklin, John E. (1992). *Criminology*. New York: Macmillan.
Conroy, M. (February 1988). Sexism in our schools. *Better Homes and Gardens*, pp. 44–47.
Cooley, Charles H. (1902/1956). *Human Nature and the Social Order*. New York: Free Press.
Cooley, Charles H. (1909/1956). *Social Organization: A Study of the Larger Mind*. Peoria, IL: Free Press.
Coon, Carleton S. (1965). *The Living Races of Man*. New York: Knopf.
Corsaro, William A. (1985). *Friendship and Peer Culture in the Early Years*. Norwood, NJ: Ablex.
Corsaro, William A., and Thomas Rizzo. (1988). Discussion and friendship: Socialization processes in the peer culture of Italian nursery school children. *American Sociological Review*, 53(6):879–894.
Coser, Lewis. (1956). *The Functions of Social Conflict*. New York: The Free Press.

Coughlin, Lawrence. (October 1991). Washington newsletter on health care. United States House of Representatives, Washington, DC.

Council on Competitiveness. (1991). Gaining new ground: Technology priorities for America's future. Washington, DC.

Council on Environmental Quality & the U.S. Department of State. (1980). The global 2000 report to the President. Washington, DC: U.S. Government Printing Office.

Covello, V.T. (ed.). (1980). *Poverty and Public Policy: An Evaluation of Social Science Research.* Cambridge: Schenkman.

Cowan, Paul, and Rachel Cowan. (1989). *Mixed Blessings: Marriage Between Jews and Christians.* New York: Doubleday.

Cox, Harvey. (1971). *The Secular City* (Rev. Ed.). New York: Macmillan.

Cox, Harvey. (1977). *Turning East: The Promise and Peril of the New Orientalism.* New York: Simon & Schuster.

Crane, Diana. (1972). *Invisible Colleges.* Chicago: The University of Chicago Press.

Cressey, Donald R. (1971). *Other Peoples' Money: A Study in the Social Psychology of Embezzlement.* Belmont, CA: Wadsworth.

Crichton, Michael. (1980). *Congo.* New York: Avon.

Crooks, R., and K. Baur. (1990). *Our Sexuality.* Redwood, CA: Benjamin Cummings.

Crowne, Douglas P., and D. Marlowe. (1964). *The Approval Motive.* New York: John Wiley & Sons.

Crozier, Michael. (1964). *The Bureaucratic Phenomenon.* Chicago: University of Chicago Press.

Culbert, L.R., J.R. Lachenmeyer, and J.L. Good. (1988). The social networks of the commuting college student. In *Social Networks and College Students,* S. Salzinger, J. Antrobus, and M. Hammer, eds. Hillsdale, NJ: Lawrence Erlbaum.

Dahl, Robert Alan. (1961). *Who Governs? Democracy and Power in an American City.* New Haven, CT: Yale University Press.

Dahrendorf, R. (1959). *Class and Class Conflict in Industrial Society.* Stanford, CA: Stanford University Press.

Dalton, M. (1959). *Men Who Manage.* New York: John Wiley & Sons.

Damon, William. (1983). *Social and Personality Development.* New York: W.W. Norton.

D'Andrade, Roy G. (1966). Sex Differences and Cultural Institutions. In *The Development of Sex Differences,* E.E. Macoby, ed. Palo Alto, CA: Stanford University Press.

Darling-Hammond, L., and A. Lieberman. (January 29, 1992). The shortcomings of standardized testing. *The Chronicle of Higher Education,* p. B1.

Davenport, William. (1978). Sex in Cross-Cultural Perspective. In *Human Sexuality in Four Perspectives,* F. Beach, ed. Baltimore: Johns Hopkins University Press.

David, Henry. (1982). Eastern Europe: Pronatalist policies and private behavior. *Population Bulletin,* 36(6). Washington, DC: Population Reference Bureau.

Davies, James. (1974). The J-curve and power struggle theories of collective violence. *American Sociological Review,* 39:607–619.

Davies, James C. (1962). Toward a theory of revolution. *American Sociological Review,* 27:5–19.

Davies, Mark, and Denise Kandel. (1981). Parental and peer influences on adolescents' educational plans: Some further evidence. *American Journal of Sociology,* 87(2):363–387.

Davis, James Allan. (1987). *Social Differences in Contemporary America.* San Diego: Harcourt Brace Jovanovich.

Davis, James Allan, and Tom W. Smith. (1985). *General Social Surveys, 1971–1985.* Chicago: National Opinion Research Center.

Davis, James Allan, and Tom W. Smith. (1989). *General Social Surveys, 1972–1989* (machine-readable data file). Principal investigator, James A. Davis; Director and Co-Principal Investigator, Tom W. Smith. NORC ed. Chicago: National Opinion Research Center, producer, 1989; Storrs, CT: The Roper Center for Public Opinion Research, University of Connecticut, distributor.

Davis, Kingsley. (March 1947). Final note on a case of extreme isolation. *American Journal of Sociology*, 52(5):432–437.

Davis, Kingsley. (1948). *Human Society.* New York: Macmillan.

Davis, Kingsley. (1976). Sexual behavior. Pp. 313–360 in *Contemporary Social Problems* (3d ed.), R. Merton, and R. Nisbet, eds. New York: Harcourt Brace Jovanovich.

Davis, Kingsley, and Judith Blake. (1956). Social structure and fertility: An analytical framework. *Economic Development and Cultural Change*, 4:211–235.

Davis, Nanette J., and Clarice Stasz. (1990). *Social Control of Deviance.* New York: McGraw-Hill.

Davis, Neil M., and Michael R. Cohen. (1981). *Medication Errors: Causes and Prevention.* Philadelphia: George F. Stickley.

Dawson, Deborah A., and Virginia S. Cain. (October 1990). Child care arrangements. *Advance Data from Vital and Health Statistics*, 187. Hyattsville, MD: National Center for Health Statistics.

DeBuono, Barbara A., Stephen H. Zinner, Maxim Daamen, and William M. McCormack. (1990). Sexual behavior of college women in 1975, 1986, and 1989. *New England Journal of Medicine*, 322:821.

De Graaf, Nan Dirk, and Hendrik Derk Flap. (1988). With a little help from my friends: Social capital as an explanation of occupational status and income in the Netherlands, the United States and West Germany. *Social Forces*, 67:452–472.

DeJong, William. (1989). The stigma of obesity: The consequences of naive assumptions concerning the cause of physical deviance. *Journal of Health and Social Behavior*, 21:75–87.

DeLamater, John. (1981). The social control of sexuality. *Annual Review of Sociology*, 7:263–290.

Della, P.S. (1980). Patterns of American Jewish fertility. *Demography*, 17:261–273.

Demerath, M.K. III, and R. Williams. (1985). Civil religion in an uncivil society. *The Annals of the American Academy of Political and Social Science*, 480.

Demos, John. (1974). The American family in past time. *American Scholar*, 43(3):422–446.

Demos, John. (1986). *Past, Present, and Personal: The Family and Life Course in American History.* New York: Oxford University Press.

Denhardt, David T. (October 6, 1990). Funds for research, not AIDS. *The Philadelphia Inquirer*, p. 25A.

Denzin, Nathan K. (1989). *The Research Act.* Englewood Cliffs, NJ: Prentice-Hall.

Deutchman, Iva E., and Sandra Prince-Embury. (1981). Political ideology of pro- and anti-ERA women. *Women and Politics*, 1:39–55.

Dewart, J. (ed.). (1991). *The State of Black America 1991.* New York: National Urban League.

Diamond, Milton. (1982). Sexual identity, monozygotic twins reared in discordant sex roles and a BBC follow-up. *Archives of Sexual Behavior*, 11:181–185.

DiFranza, Joseph, John Richards, Paul Paulman, Nancy Wolf-Gillespie, Christopher Fletcher, Robert Jaffe, and David Murray. (1991). RJR Nabisco's cartoon camel promotes Camel cigarettes to children. *Journal of the American Medical Association*, 266(22):3149–3153.

DiMaggio, Paul. (1982). Cultural capital and school success: The impact of status culture participation on the grades of U.S. high school students. *American Sociological Review*, 47:189–201.

DiMaggio, Paul J., and Walter W. Powell. (1983). The front cage revisited: Institutional rationality and collective rationality in organizational fields. *American Sociological Review*, 48:147–160.

DiMatteo, M. Robin, and Ron Hays. (1982). Social support and serious illness. In *Social Networks and Social Support*, B.H. Gottleib, ed. Beverly Hills, CA: Sage.

Divine-Hawkins, Patricia. (1992). Latchkey in context: Family, community, and self/sib arrangements for the care of school-age children. PhD dissertation, Graduate School of Education, Harvard University.

Domhoff, G.W. (1970). *The Higher Circles: The Governing Class in America.* New York: Vintage Books.

Domhoff, G.W. (1978). *Who Really Rules: New Haven and Community Power Reexamined.* New Brunswick, NJ: Transaction.

Donahue, P. (1985). *The Human Animal.* New York: Simon & Schuster.

Donnerstein, E. (November 1983). Massive exposure to sexual violence and rape. Paper presented at the 26th Annual Meeting of the Society for the Scientific Study of Sex, Chicago.

Donnerstein, E., and D. Linz. (1984). Sexual violence in the media: A warning. *Psychology Today,* 18(1):14–15.

Dougherty, Charles J. (1988). *American Health Care.* New York: Oxford University Press.

Drucker, Peter F. (Spring 1986). The changed world economy. *Foreign Affairs,* 768–791.

Dryfoos, Jay G. (1990). *Adolescents at Risk: Prevalence and Prevention.* New York: Oxford University Press.

Duberman, Lucille. (1975). *Gender and Sex in Society.* New York: Praeger Publishers.

Dubin, Murray. (January 10, 1992). National Center for Health Statistics study links social ills and absent fathers. *Philadelphia Inquirer.*

Duncan, Greg J., and Saul D. Hoffman. (1990). Welfare benefits, economic opportunities, and out-of-wedlock births among black teenage girls. *Demography,* 27(4):519–536.

Duncan, Greg T., Timothy M. Smeeding, and Willard Rodgers. (1992). The incredible shrinking middle class. *American Demographics,* 14:34–38.

Durkheim, Emile. (1893/1964). *The Division of Labor in Society.* New York: Free Press.

Durkheim, Emile. (1895/1964). *The Rules of Sociological Method.* New York: Free Press.

Durkheim, Emile. (1897/1951). *Suicide: A Study of Sociology* (J.A. Spaulding and G. Simpson, Trans.). New York: Free Press.

Durkheim, Emile. (1912/1965). *The Elementary Forms of Religious Life* (J.W. Swain, Trans.). New York: Free Press.

Dworkin, Andrea. (1981). *Pornography: Men Possessing Women.* New York: Putnam.

Dychtwald, Kenneth, and Joe Flower. (1989). *Age Wave.* Los Angeles: Tarcher.

Easterlin, Richard A. (1980). *Birth and Fortune.* New York: Basic Books.

Eaton, Joseph, and Albert Mayer. (1954). *Man's Capacity to Reproduce.* Glencoe: Free Press.

Ecenbarger, William. (August 25, 1991). Cheer up, it could be worse. *Philadelphia Inquirer* (Sunday magazine).

Ehrlich, Paul R., and Anne H. Ehrlich. (1990). *The Population Explosion.* New York: Simon & Schuster.

Eisenstein, Elizabeth. (1984). *The Printing Revolution in Early Modern Europe.* New York: Cambridge University Press.

Ekelund, Lars-Goran, C.M. Suchrindran, R.P. McMahon, G. Heiss, A.S. Leon, D.W. Romhilt, C.L. Rubenstein, J.Z. Probstfield, and J.F. Runwitch. (1989). Coronary heart disease morbidity and mortality in hypercholesterolemic men predicted from an exercise test. *Journal of the American College of Cardiology,* 14(3):556–563.

Eldefonso, Edward. (1978). *Law Enforcement and the Youthful Offender.* New York: John Wiley & Sons.

Elder, Glen H. (1987). Families and lives: Some developments in life course studies. *Journal of Family History,* 12(1–2):170–199.

Elkin Frederick, and Gerald Handel. (1984). *The Child and Society: The Process of Socialization* (4th ed.). New York: Random House.

Elliott, Delbert S., and Suzanne S. Ageton. (1980). Reconciling race and class differences in self-reported and official estimates of delinquency. *American Sociological Review,* 45:95–110.

Elliott, Delbert S., David Huizinga, and Suzanne S. Ageton. (1985). *Explaining Delinquency and Drug Use.* Beverly Hills, CA: Sage Publications.

Ellwood, David T., and Lawrence H. Summers. (1986). Is welfare really the problem? *The Public Interest,* 83:57–78.

Elmer-DeWitt, Phillip. (January 16, 1989). Battle for the future. *Time*, pp. 42–43.

Elsinger, P.K. (1973). The conditions of protest behavior. *Science Review*, 67(1):11–28.

Elson, John. (February 19, 1990). America's new fad: Fidelity. *Time*, p. 91.

Elwin, Verrier. (1968). *The Kingdom of the Young*. Oxford: Oxford University Press.

Embree, Ainslie T. (1972). *The Hindu Tradition*. New York: Vintage Books.

Empey, Lamar T. (1982). *American Delinquency*. Homewood, IL: Dorsey.

Encyclopedia of Associations. (1994). Volume I. Detroit, MI: Gale Publishers.

Ende, J., S. Rockwell, and M. Glasgow. (1984). The sexual history in general medicine practice. *Archives of Internal Medicine*, 144:558–561.

Engels, Friedrich. (1844/1953). Outlines of a critique of political economy. Reprinted in R.L. Meek, *Marx and Engels on Malthus*. London: Lawrence and Weshart.

Engels, Friedrich. (1884/1972). *The Origin of the Family, Private Property and the State*. New York: International Publishers. Englewood Cliffs, NJ: Prentice-Hall.

Environmental Protection Agency. (1992). *Environmental Equity*. EPA Task Force.

Erickson, Bonnie H. (1988). The relational basis of attitudes. In *Social Structures: A Network Approach*, B. Wellman and S.D. Berkowitz, eds. Cambridge: Cambridge University Press.

Erickson, Frederick. (1984). School literacy, reasoning, and civility: An anthropologist's perspective. *Review of Educational Research*, 54:525–546.

Erikson, Erik Hamburger. (1963). *Childhood and Society* (2d ed.). New York: Norton.

Erikson, Kai T. (1966). *Wayward Puritans: A Study in the Sociology of Deviance*. New York: John Wiley & Sons.

Erikson, Kai T. (1976). *Everything in Its Path: Destruction of Community in the Buffalo Creek Flood*. New York: Simon & Schuster.

Escholz, P.A., and A.F. Rosa. (1984). Student slang for college courses. Pp. 69–76 in *Conformity and Conflict*, J.P. Spradley and D.W. McCurdy, eds. Boston: Little, Brown.

Espenshade, Thomas J. (1985). Marriage trends in America: Estimates, implications and underlying causes. *Population and Development Review*, 11(2):193–245.

Essed, Philomena. (1991). *Understanding Everyday Racism*. Newbury Park, CA: Sage Publications.

Etzioni, Amitai. (1975). *A Comparative Analysis of Complex Organizations*. New York: Free Press.

Etzioni, Amitai. (November 15, 1985). Shady corporate practices. *The New York Times*.

Evans, Dennis A. (1989). Prevalence of Alzheimer's disease in a community population of older persons. *Journal of the American Medical Association*, 262:2551–2556.

Evans-Pritchard, E.E. (1970). Sexual inversion among the Azande. *American Anthropologist*, 72:1428–1434.

Fairweather, H., and S.J. Hunt. (1972). Sex differences in a perceptual motor skill in children. In *Gender Differences: Their Ontogeny and Significance*, C.O. Ounsted and David C. Taylor, eds. Edinburgh: Churchill Livingstone.

Faith, Nicholas. (1992). *The World Railways Made*. New York: Carroll and Grof.

Farley, Reynolds, and Walter R. Allen. (1987). *The Color Line and the Quality of Life in America*. New York: Russell Sage Foundation.

Farmer, Philip J. (1971). The sliced-crosswise only-on-Tuesday world. Pp. 21–36 in *Social Problems through Science Fiction*, Martin H. Greenberg, John W. Milstead, Joseph D. Olander, and Patricia Warrick, eds. New York: St. Martin's.

Farnworth, Margaret., and Michael J. Leiber. (1989). Strain theory revisited. *American Sociological Review*, 54:263–374.

Fay, Robert E., Charles F. Turner, Albert D. Klassen, and John N. Gagnon. (1989). Prevalence and patterns of same gender sexual contact among men. *Science*, 243:338–348.

Feld, Scott L. (1982). Structural determinants of similarity among associates. *American Sociological Review*, 47:797–801.

Feldberg, Roslyn L., and Evelyn N. Glenn. (1983). Technology and women's degradation: Effects of office automation on women clerical workers. In

Machina ex Dea: Feminist Perspectives on Technology, J. Rothchild, ed. New York: Pergamon Press.

Fernandez, Roberto, and Jane C. Kulik. (1981). A multilevel model of life satisfaction: Effects of individual characteristics and neighborhood composition. *American Sociological Review,* 46:840–851.

Ferrante, Joan. (1992). *Sociology: A Global Perspective.* Belmont, CA: Wadsworth.

Festinger, Leon, Henry Riecken, and Simon Schachter. (1956). *Lunch Prophecy Fails.* New York: Harper & Row.

Finch, James K. (1951). *Engineering and Western Civilization.* New York: McGraw-Hill.

Fine, Gary A., and Sheryl Kleinman. (1979). Rethinking subculture: An interactionist analysis. *American Journal of Sociology,* 15:1–20.

Fingerhut, Lois, Deborah D. Ingram, and Jacob J. Feldman. (1992). Firearm and nonfirearm homicide among persons 15 through 19 years of age. *Journal of the American Medical Association,* 267:3048–3058.

Finkelhor, David. (1979). *Sexually Victimized Children.* New York: Free Press.

Finkelhor, David, and K. Yllo. (1985). *License to Rape: The Sexual Abuse of Wives.* New York: Holt, Rinehart, and Winston.

Finkelstein, Neal W., and Ron Haskins. (1983). Kindergarten children prefer same color peers. *Child Development,* 54(2):502–508.

Firebaugh, Glenn, and Kenneth E. Davis. (1988). Trends in antiblack prejudice, 1972–1984: Region and cohort effects. *American Journal of Sociology,* 94:251–272.

Fischer, Claude S. (1977). *Networks and Places: Social Relations in the Urban Setting.* New York: The Free Press.

Fischer, Claude S. (1982). *To Dwell among Friends.* Chicago: The University of Chicago Press.

Fischer, Claude S. (1984). *The Urban Experience.* New York: Harcourt Brace Jovanovich.

Fischer, Judith L., Donna L. Sollie, Gwendolyn T. Soffell, and Shelley K. Green. (1989). Marital status and career stage influences on social networks of young adults. *Journal of Marriage and the Family,* 51:521–534.

Fischer, Paul M., Meyer P. Schwartz, John W. Richards, Jr., Adam O. Goldstein, and Tina H. Jojas. (1991). Brand logo recognition by children aged 3 to 6 years. *Journal of the American Medical Association,* 266(22):3145–3148.

Fisher, Helen. (1992). *Anatomy of Love: The Natural History of Monogamy, Adultery, and Divorce.* New York: Norton.

Fitzberald, F. Scott. (1920). *The Great Gatsby.* New York: Macmillan.

Fitzgerald, Susan. (April 21, 1991). Medical research belatedly discovers women. *The Philadelphia Inquirer,* p. 2A.

Flax, Jane. (1993). *Disputed Subjects: Essays on Psychoanalysis, Politics and Philosophy.* New York: Routledge.

Fogelson, Robert M. (1970). Violence and grievances: Reflections on the 1960's riots. *Journal of Social Issues,* 26:141–163.

Foley, Vernard, George Palmer, and Werner Soedel. (1985). The crossbow. *Scientific American,* 252:104–110.

Ford, Clellan, and Frank A. Beach. (1951/1978). *Patterns of Sexual Behavior.* New York: Harper Colophon.

Ford, R.L. (1988). *Work, Organization and Power.* Boston: Allyn and Bacon.

Fordyce, M.W. (1988). A review of research on the happiness measures: A sixty section index of happiness and mental health. *Social Indicators Research,* 20:355–381.

Forer, L.K. (1976). *The Birth Order Factor: How Your Personality Is Influenced by Your Place in the Family.* New York: David McKay.

Form, William. (1976). *Blue Collar Stratification.* Princeton, NJ: Princeton University Press.

Fox, Renee. (1976). Advanced medical technology: Social and ethical implications. *Annual Review of Sociology,* 2:231–268.

Fox, Richard J., Melvin Crask, and Jonghoon Kim. (1988). Mail survey response rate: A meta-analysis of selected techniques for inducing response. *Public Opinion Quarterly,* 52:467–491.

Frank, Andre G. (1972). *Lumpenbourgeoisie: Lumpendevelopment.* New York: Random House.

Frank, Ellen, Carol Anderson, and Debra Rubinstein. (1978). Frequency of sexual dysfunction in normal couples. *New England Journal of Medicine,* 299:111–115.

Frayser, Suzanne G. (1985). *Varieties of Sexual Experience.* New Haven: HRAF Press.

Frazier, E. Franklin. (1965). *Black Bourgeosie: The Rise of a New Middle Class.* New York: Free Press.

Freedman, Jonathan L. (1984). Effects of television violence on aggressiveness. *Psychological Bulletin,* 96:234–235.

Freeman, Christopher. (1982). *The Economics of Industry and Innovation.* Cambridge: Cambridge University Press.

Freeman, Christopher. (1987). *Technology Policy and Economic Performance: Lessons from Japan.* London: Pinter.

Freeman, Derek. (1983). *Margaret Mead and Samoa: The Making and Unmaking of an Anthropological Myth.* Cambridge, MA: Harvard University Press.

Freeman, Harold. (February 27, 1987). Cancer among the poor: Results of a major American Cancer Society study. Paper presented at the University of Pennsylvania Faculty Club.

Freeman, Jo. (1973). The origins of the women's liberation movement. *American Journal of Sociology,* 78:792–811.

Freeman, Jo. (1979). *Resource Mobilization and Strategy. Dynamics of Social Movements.* Cambridge, MA: Winthrop.

Freeman, Linton C., and C.R. Thompson. (1989). Estimating acquaintanceship volume. In *The Small World,* M. Kochen, ed. Norwood, NJ: Ablex.

French, M.A. (January 17, 1993). A practice some call mutilation. *The Philadelphia Inquirer,* pp. Fl and F6.

Freud, Sigmund. (1961). *Civilization and Its Discontents.* New York: W.W. Norton.

Frey, William. (1987). Migration and depopulation of the metropolis: Regional restructuring or rural renaissance? *American Sociological Review,* 52:240–257.

Frey, William. (1990). Metropolitan America: Beyond the transition. *Population Bulletin,* 45(2). Washington, DC: Population Reference Bureau.

Frey, William, and Alden Speare. (1988). *Regional and Metropolitan Growth and Decline in the United States.* New York: Russell Sage Foundation.

Friedan, Betty. (1963). *The Feminine Mystique.* New York: W.W. Norton Co.

Friedlander, Dov, and Calvin Goldscheider. (1984). Israel's population: The challenge of pluralism. *Population Bulletin,* 39(2). Washington, DC: Population Reference Bureau.

Fries, James. (1980). Aging, natural death, and the compression of morbidity. *New England Journal of Medicine,* 303:130–135.

Fries, James. (1989). *Aging Well.* Reading, MA: Addison-Wesley.

Fuguitt, Glenn V. (1985). The nonmetropolitan population turnaround. *Annual Review of Sociology,* 11:259–280.

Furstenberg, Frank F. (1988). Good dads—bad dads: Two faces of fatherhood. In *The Changing American Family and Public Policy,* A.J. Cherhn, ed. Washington, DC: The Urban Institute Press.

Furstenberg, Frank F., and Andrew J. Cherlin. (1991). *Divided Families: What Happens to Children When Parents Part?* Cambridge, MA: Harvard University Press.

Furstenberg, Frank F., and Graham B. Spanier. (1985). *Recycling the Family: Marriage After Divorce.* Beverly Hills, CA: Sage Publications.

Gaensbauer, T., and S. Hiatt. (1984). *The Psychobiology of Affective Development.* Hillsdale, NJ: Lawrence Erlbaum.

Gagnon, John H. (1977). *Human Sexualities.* Glenview, IL: Scott, Foresman.

Galbraith, John Kenneth. (1966). *The Affluent Society.* Boston: Beacon.

Galbraith, John Kenneth. (1967). *The New Industrial State.* Boston: Houghton Mifflin.

Gallagher, Bernard J. III. (1974). An empirical analysis of attitude differences between three kin-related generations. *Youth and Society,* 5:327–349.

Gallagher, Bernard J. III. (1979). Attitude differences across generations: Class and sex components. *Adolescence,* 14:503–516.

Gallagher, Bernard J. III. (1995). *The Sociology of Mental Illness.* Englewood Cliffs, NJ: Prentice-Hall.

Gallagher, Bernard J. III, Joseph A. McFalls, and Carolyn Vreeland. (1993). Preliminary results from a national survey of psychiatrists concerning the etiology of homosexuality. *Psychology*, 30:1–3.

Gallup, George. (1982). *Religion in America.* Princeton, NJ: Princeton Religion Research Center.

Gallup Organization. (February 1989). Unlike 1975, most Americans think men have it better. *Gallup Poll Monthly.*

Gallup Report. (May 1985). *Fifty Years of Gallup Surveys on Religion.* (Report No. 236).

Gates, David. (March 29, 1993). White male paranoia. *Newsweek*, pp. 48–53.

Gans, Herbert J. (1972). The positive functions of poverty. *American Journal of Sociology*, 78:275–288.

Gans, Herbert J. (1973). *More Equality.* New York: Pantheon.

Gans, Herbert J. (1980). *Deciding What's News: A Study of CBS Evening News, NBC Nightly News,* Newsweek *and* Time. New York: Vintage.

Ganzeboom, H.B.G., R. Luijkx, and D.J. Treiman. (1989). International class mobility in comparative perspective. *Research in Stratification and Mobility*, 9:3–79.

Ganzeboom, H.B.G., D.J. Treiman, and W.C. Ultee. (1991). Comparative intergenerational stratification research: Three generations and beyond. *Annual Review of Sociology*, 17:277–302.

Gardner, Robert, Bryant Robey, and Peter Smith. (1985). Asian Americans: Growth, change, and diversity. *Population Bulletin*, 40(4):1–44. Washington, DC: Population Reference Bureau.

Garfinkel, Harold. (1967). *Studies in Ethnomethodology.* Englewood Cliffs, NJ: Prentice-Hall.

Garson, Lea. (1985). The centenarian question: Old age mortality in the Soviet Union 1897–1970. PhD dissertation, Princeton University.

Gates, David. (1993). White male paranoia. *Newsweek*, pp. 48–53.

Gavrilova, Leonid A., and Natalia S. Gavrilova. (1991). *The Biology of Lifespan: A Quantitative Approach* (V.P. Skulachev, Ed.; John and Liliya Payne, Trans.). New York: Harwood.

Gay, J. (1986). Mummies and babies and friends and lovers in Lesotho. Pp. 97–116 in *Anthropology and Homosexual Behavior*, E. Blackwood, ed. New York: Haworth Press.

Gayle, Helene D., Richard P. Keeling, Moguel Garcia-Tunon, Barbara W. Kilbourne, John P. Narkunos, Fred R. Ingram, Martha F. Rogers, and James W. Curran. (1990). Prevalence of the HIV among university students. *New England Journal of Medicine*, 323:1538–1541.

Gecas, Victor, and Monica A. Seff. (1990). Families and adolescents: A review of the 1980's. *Journal of Marriage and the Family*, 52:941–958.

Gehrig, G. (1979). American Civil Religion: An Assessment. Monograph Series 3, Storrs, CT: Society for the Scientific Study of Religion.

Gentry, Cynthia. (1988). The social construction of abducted children as a social problem. *Sociological Inquiry*, 58:413–425.

Gerbert, Barbara, Bryna T. Maguire, Thomas Blecker, Thomas J. Coates, and Stephen J. McPhee. (1991). Primary care physicians and AIDS. *Journal of the American Medical Association*, 266:2837–2842.

Gerstel, Naomi. (1987). Divorce and stigma. *Social Problems*, 43:172–186.

Gerth, H.H., and C. Wright Mills (eds.). (1972). *From Max Weber: Essays in Sociology.* New York: Oxford University Press.

Geschwender, James A. (1964). Social structure and the Negro revolt: An examination of some hypotheses. *Social Forces*, 43:248–256.

Gibbons, Tom. (February 24, 1985). Justice not equal for poor here. *Chicago Sun-Times.*

Gibbs, N. (1990). The dreams of youth. Special issue, *Time*, pp. 10–14.

Giddens, Anthony. (1991). *Introduction to Sociology.* New York: W.W. Norton.

Gilligan, Carol. (1982). *In a Different Voice: Psychological Theory and Women's Development.* Cambridge, MA: Harvard University Press.

Gilligan, Carol. (1990). Teaching Shakespeare's sister. In *Making Connections: The Relational Worlds of Adolescent Girls at Emma Willard School,* C. Gilligan, N. Lyons, and T. Hammer, eds. Cambridge: Harvard University Press.

Gilligan, Carol. (August 25, 1990) Adolescence: A Critical Period for Critical Thinking? Paper presented at the biennial meeting of The Society for Research on Adolescence, Atlanta, GA.

Gilmore, David. (1990). *Manhood in the Making.* New Haven: Yale University Press.

Ginsberg, Benjamin. (1986). *The Captive Public: How Mass Opinion Promotes State Power.* New York: Basic Books.

Ginzberg, Eli. (1991). Access to health care for Hispanics. *Journal of the American Medical Association,* 265:238–241.

Giobbe, Evelina. (1990). Confronting the liberal lies about prostitution. Pp. 67–82 in *The Sexual Liberals and the Attack on Feminism,* Dorchen Leidholdt and Janice Raymond, eds. New York: Pergamon Press.

Givens, D. (1983). *Love Signals.* New York: Crown Press.

Glassner, Barry. (1988). *Bodies: Why We Look the Way We Do (and How We Feel About It).* Putnam.

Glenn, Norvall D. (1982). Interreligious marriage in the United States. *Journal of Marriage and the Family,* 44:555–566.

Glenn, Norvall D. (1984). A note on estimating the strength of influences for religious endogamy. *Journal of Marriage and the Family,* 46:725–727.

Glenn, Norvall D. (1991). The recent trend in marital success in the United States. *Journal of Marriage and the Family,* 53:261–270.

Glenn, Norvall D., and B.A. Shelton. (1985). Regional differences in divorce in the United States. *Journal of Marriage and the Family,* 47:641–652.

Glick, Paul C. (1984). American household structure in transition. *Family Planning Perspectives,* 16:205–211.

Glock, C.Y. (1962a). On the study of religious commitment. *Religious Education,* 62(4):98–110.

Glock, C.Y. (1962b). The religious revival in America. Pp. 24–52 in *Religion and the Face of America,* Jane Zahn, ed. Berkeley, CA: University of California Press.

Goffman, Erving. (1959). *The Presentation of Self in Everyday Life.* Garden City, New York: Anchor.

Goffman, Erving. (1961). *Asylums: Essays on the Social Situation of Mental Patients, and Other Inmates.* Garden City, NY: Anchor.

Goffman, Erving. (1963). *Stigma: Notes on the Management of Spoiled Identity.* Englewood Cliffs, NJ: Prentice-Hall.

Goffman, Erving. (1967). *Interaction Ritual.* New York: Doubleday.

Goffman, Erving. (1981). *Forms of Talk.* Philadelphia: University of Pennsylvania.

Goldberg, Gertrude, and Eleanor Kremen (eds.). (1990). *The Feminization of Poverty: Only in America?* Westport, CT: Greenwood Press.

Goldfoot, David A., Kim Wallen, Deborah Neff, Mary C. McBrair, and Robert W. Goy. (1984). Social influences upon the display of sexually dimorphic behavior in rhesus monkeys: Isosexual rearing. *Archives of Sexual Behavior,* 13:395–412.

Goldman, Noreen, and M. Montgomery. (1989). Fecundability and husband's age. *Social Biology,* 36:146–166.

Goldman, Noreen, Charles Westoff, and C. Hammerslough. (1984). Demography of the marriage market in the United States. *Population Index,* 50:5–25.

Goldscheider, Calvin. (1983). Modernization, migration and urbanization. In *Population Movements,* P. Morrison, ed. Liege, Belgium: Ordina.

Goldscheider, Calvin, and Francis K. Goldscheider. (1987). Moving out and marriage: What do young adults expect? *American Sociological Review,* 52:278–285.

Goldscheider, Francis K. (1993). Statement in *The New York Times,* cited secondarily in Suzanne Fields, "Not buying the stories of divorcees' happiness." *Insight,* Jan. 11, pp. 18–19. [Goldscheider notes her statement was based on the Francis. K. Goldscheider (1990) article, "The aging of the gender revolution," *Research on Aging,* pp. 531–545.]

Goldscheider, Francis K., and Calvin Goldscheider. (1989). Family structure and conflict: Nest-leaving expectations of young adults and their parents. *Journal of Marriage and the Family,* 51:87–97.

Goldscheider, Frances K., and Linda J. Waite. (1991). *New Families, No Families?* Berkeley and Los Angeles: University of California Press.

Goleman, Daniel. (June 19, 1984). Order found in the development of emotions. *The New York Times,* pp. C1, C8.

Goleman, Daniel. (May 28, 1985). Spacing of siblings strongly linked to success in life. *The New York Times,* pp. C1, C4.

Goleman, Daniel. (December 2, 1986). Major personality study finds that traits are mostly inherited. *The New York Times,* pp. C1, C2.

Goliber, Thomas. (1989). Africa's expanding population: Old problems, new policies. *Population Bulletin,* 44(3). Washington, DC: Population Reference Bureau.

Goode, Erich. (1978). *Deviant Behavior: An Interactionist Approach.* Englewood Cliffs, NJ: Prentice-Hall.

Goode, Erich. (1992). *Collective Behavior.* New York: Harcourt Brace Jovanovich.

Goode, Stephen. (October 9, 1989). On the outs over who gets in. *Insight,* pp. 8–15.

Goodwin, L. (1972). *Do the Poor Want to Work?* Washington, DC: The Brookings Institution.

Googins, Bradley K. (1991). *Work/Family Conflicts: Private Lives—Public Responses.* New York: Auburn House.

Gorer, Geoffrey. (1938). *Himalayan Village.* New York: Basic Books.

Gordon, David M., Richard Edwards, and Michael Reich. (1982). *Segmented Work, Divided Workers.* Cambridge: Cambridge University Press.

Gordon, Linda. (January 1988). The politics of child sexual abuse. *Feminist Review,* pp. 56–64.

Gottman, John M. (1993). *What Predicts Divorce?* Hillsdale, NJ: Lawrence Erlbaum.

Gough, Ian. (1979). *The Political Economy of the Welfare State.* London: Macmillan.

Gould, Stephen J. (1981). *The Mismeasure of Man.* New York: W.W. Norton.

Gracey, Harry L. (1972). *Curriculum or Craftsmanship: Elementary School Teacher in a Bureaucratic System.* Chicago: University of Chicago Press.

Granovetter, Mark. (1973). The strength of weak ties. *American Journal of Sociology,* 78:1360–1380.

Granovetter, Mark. (1985). *Capitalism and the American Political Ideal.* Armonk, NY: M.E. Sharpe.

Gravenberg, O., and G. Collins. (1976). Grades: Just a measure of conformity. *Humboldt Journal of Social Relations,* 3:58–62.

Gray, Bradford. (1991). *The Profit Motive and Patient Care.* Cambridge, MA: Harvard University Press.

Gray, J. Patrick, and Linda D. Wolfe. (1988). An anthropological look at human sexuality. Pp. 650–678 in *Human Sexuality,* W. Masters, V. Johnson, and R. Kolodny, eds. Glenview, IL: Scott Foresman.

Greeley, Andrew. (1972). *The Denominational Society.* Glenview, IL: Scott, Foresman.

Greeley, Andrew. (1976). The ethnic miracle. *The Public Interest* 45.

Greeley, Andrew, Robert Michael, and Tom Smith. (1989). A most monogamous people: Americans and their sexual partners. NORC *Topical Report No. 17.* Chicago: Norc.

Greeley, Andrew, Robert T. Michael, and Tom W. Smith. (1990). Americans and their sexual partners. *Society,* 27(5):36–42.

Green, Mark. (February 5, 1981). Urban overcrowding threatens stability in less developed countries. *Intercom.*

Greenfield, Sheldon, Eugene C. Nelson, Michael Zubkoff, Willard Manning, William Rogers, Richard L. Kravitz, Adam Keller, Alvin R. Tarlov, and John E. Ware, Jr. (1992). Variations in resource utilization among medical specialties and systems of care. *Journal of the American Medical Association,* 267:1624–1630.

Greenwald, Evan, and Howard Leitenberg. (1989). Long-term effects of sexual experiences with siblings and nonsiblings during childhood. *Archives of Sexual Behavior,* 18(5):389.

Gregersen, Edgar. (1982). *Sexual Practices: The Story of Human Sexuality.* London: Mitchell Beazley.

Grieco, Margaret. (1987). *Keeping It in the Family: Social Networks and Employment Chance.* London: Tavistock Publications.

Griffin, Susan. (1982). *Pornography and Silence.* New York: Harper Colophon Press.

Griffith, Jean, Mary Frase, and John Ralph. (1989). American education: The challenge of change. *Population Bulletin,* 44(4). Washington, DC: Population Reference Bureau.

Grossman, Lawrence. (1984). Jewish population growth. *The William Petschels National Jewish Family Center Newsletter,* 4(1):1–4.

Gubrium, Jaber F., and James A. Holstein. (1990). *What Is Family?* Mountain View, CA: Mayfield Publishing.

Gurr, Ted R. (1970). *Why Men Rebel.* Princeton, NJ: Princeton University Press.

Gutek, B., and C. Nakamura. (1983). Gender roles and sexuality in the world of work. In *Changing Boundaries and Sexual Behavior,* E. Allgeier and N. McCormick, eds. Palo Alto, CA: Mayfield Press.

Gutierrez, Gustavo. (1983). *The Power of the Poor in History.* Maryknoll, NY: Orbis.

Guttentag, Marcia, and Paul Secord. (1983). *Too Many Women?* Newbury Park, CA: Sage.

Habermas, J. (1971). *Toward a Rational Society.* London: Heinemann.

Hacker, Andrew. (Ed.). (1983). *U/S, A Statistical Portrait of the American People.* New York: Viking.

Hagan, John. (1991). Destiny and drift: Subcultural preferences, status attainments, and the risks and rewards of youth. *American Sociological Review,* 56:567–582.

Hahn, Jeffrey, and Kathleen P. King. (1982). Client and correlates of patient attrition from an inpatient alcohol treatment center. *Journal of Drug Education,* 12:75–86.

Hale, Christine. (1990). Infant Mortality: An American Tragedy. *Population Trends and Public Policy,* 18. Washington, D.C.: Population Reference Bureau.

Hall, A. Rupert. (1957). The rise of the West. In *A History of Technology,* C. Singer et al., eds. Oxford: Clarenden Press.

Hall, Richard H. (1987). *Organizations: Structures, Processes, and Outcomes.* Englewood Cliffs, NJ: Prentice-Hall.

Hamer, Dean H., Stella Hu, Victoria Magnuson, Nan Hu, and Angela M.L. Pattatucci. (1993). A linkage between DNA markers on the X chromosome and male sexual orientation. *Science,* 261:321–327.

Hanley, C.J. (December 9, 1992). Superpowers fed Somalia's chaos. Associated Press.

Hannan, M.T., and J.H. Freeman. (1977). The population ecology of organizations. *American Journal of Sociology,* 82:929–964.

Hanson, Sandra L. (1983). A family life cycle approach to the socioeconomic attainment of working women. *Journal of Marriage and the Family,* 45(2):323–338.

Hareven, Tamara. (1982). American families in transition: Historical perspectives on change. Pp. 446–466 in *Normal Family Processes,* F. Walsh, ed. New York: Guilford Press.

Hareven, Tamara. (1982). The life course and aging in historical perspective. Pp. 1–26 in *Aging and Life Course Transitions: An Interdisciplinary Perspective,* T. Hareven and K. Adams, eds. New York: Guilford Press.

Harlow, Harry, and Margaret Harlow. (November 1962). Social deprivation in monkeys. *Scientific American,* pp. 137–146.

Harlow, Harry, and Clara Mears. (1979). *The Human Model: Primate Perspectives.* New York: Wiley Press.

Harner, Michael J. (1977). The ecological basis for Aztec sacrifice. *American Ethnologist,* 4:117–135.

Harrington, M. (1962). *The Other America.* New York: Macmillan.

Harrington, M. (1970). *Socialism.* New York: Saturday Review.

Harris, Louis. (1987). *Inside America.* New York: Vintage.

Harris, Louis and Associates. (1989). Men improving. *Lears Magazine.*

Harris, Marvin. (1974). *Cows, Pigs, Wars and Witches: The Riddles of Culture.* New York: Vintage Books.

Harris, Marvin. (1988). *Culture, People, Nature: An Introduction.* New York: Harper & Row.

Hart, Stephen. (1987). Privatization in American religion and society. *Sociological Analysis,* 47(4):319–334.

Hartz, Arthur J., Kenneth C. Goldberg, Steven J. Jacobsen, Henry Krakauer, and Alfred A. Rimm. (1992). Racial and community factors influencing coronary artery bypass graft surgery rates for all 1986 Medicare patients. *Journal of the American Medical Association,* 267:1473–1477.

Harvey, Dale, and Gerald Slatin. (1975). The relationship between a child's SES and the teacher's expectations: A test of the middle class bias hypothesis. *Social Forces,* 54:140–159.

Haub, Carl. (1985). The last metro (definition)? *Population Today,* 11:6–8.

Haub, Carl. (1987). Understanding population projections. *Population Bulletin,* 42(4). Washington, DC: Population Reference Bureau.

Haub, Carl. (1989). Take a number. *Population Today,* 17(6):10.

Haupt, Arthur, and Thomas Kane. (1988). *Population Handbook.* Washington, DC: Population Reference Bureau.

Hayes, Diane, and Catherine Ross. (1986). Body and mind: The effect of exercise, overweight, and physical health on psychological well-being. *Journal of Health and Social Behavior,* 27:387–400.

Hayflick, Leonard. (1970). Aging under glass. *Experimental Gerontology,* 5:291–303.

Headrick, Daniel R. (1981). *The Tools of Empire: Technology and European Imperialism in the Nineteenth Century.* New York: Oxford University Press.

Hearn, Jeffrey. (1990). Pathways to attendance at elite colleges. In *The High Status Track,* P. Kingston and L. Lewis, eds. Albany, NY: SUNY Press.

Heaton, Tim B. (1991). Time-related determinants of marital dissolution. *Journal of Marriage and the Family,* 53:285–295.

Heaton, Tim B., and S. Albrecht. (1991). Stable unhappy marriages. *Journal of Marriage and the Family,* 53:747–758.

Hehir, J. (April 10, 1981). The bishops speak on El Salvador. *Commonweal,* pp. 199–223.

Heibroner, Robert L., and Aaron Singer. (1984). *The Economic Transformation of America: 1600 to the Present.* New York: Harcourt Brace Jovanovich.

Heilman, S.C. (1982). The sociology of American Jewry: The last ten years. *Annual Review of Sociology,* 6:135–160.

Helsing, Knud J., Moyses Szklo, and GeorgeW. Comstock. (1981). Factors associated with mortality after widowhood. *American Journal of Public Health,* 71:802–809.

Helson, Ravenna, and Geraldine Moore. (1984). Personality change in women from college to mid-life. *Journal of Personality and Social Psychology,* 53:126–186.

Hendry, Peter. (1988). Food and population: Beyond five billion. *Population Bulletin* 43(2). Washington, DC: Population Reference Bureau.

Henley, Nancy M. (1977). *Body Politics: Power, Sex and Nonverbal Communication.* Englewood Cliffs, NJ: Prentice-Hall.

Henry, W.A. (August 3, 1992). An identity forged in flames. *Time,* pp. 35–37.

Henry, William A. (April 9, 1990). Beyond the melting pot. *Time,* pp. 28–31.

Henslin, James, and Mae A. Briggs. (1971). Dramaturgical desexualization: The sociology of vaginal examination. Pp. 151–164 in *Studies in the Sociology of Sex,* J. Henslin, ed. New York: Appleton-Century-Crofts.

Herberg, Will. (1955). *Protestant, Catholic, Jew.* Garden City, NY: Anchor Books.

Herbert, Frank. (1965). *Dune.* New York: Ace Books.

Herbert, Frank. (1977). *The Dosadi Experiment.* New York: Ace Books.

Herdt, Gilbert. (1981). *Guardians of the Flutes: Idioms of Masculinity.* New York: McGraw-Hill.

Herdt, Gilbert. (1982). *Rituals of Manhood.* Berkeley, CA: University of California Press.

Heritier, F. (1982). The symbolics of incest and its prohibition. Pp. 152–179 in *Between Belief and Transgression: Structural Essays in Religion, History, and Myth,* M. Izard and P. Smith, eds. Chicago: University of Chicago Press.

Herrin, Angelea. (March 13, 1991). Rural areas lack doctors, study finds. *Philadelphia Inquirer.*

Herrnstein, Richard. (1973). *IQ in the Meritocracy.* Boston: Little, Brown.

Herzog, A. Regula, and Willard L. Rodgers. (1988). Interviewing older adults: Mode comparison using data from a face-to-face survey and a telephone resurvey. *Public Opinion Quarterly,* 52:84–99.

Hess, Beth B., and Myra M. Feree (eds.). (1987). *Analyzing Gender: A Handbook of Social Science Research.* Beverly Hills, CA: Sage Publications.

Hewith, John P. (1989). *Dilemmas of the American Self.* Philadelphia: Temple University Press.

Hewlett, Sylvia. (1991). *When the Bough Breaks: The Cost of Neglecting Our Children.* New York: Basic Books.

Hibbs, Douglas A. (1987). *The American Political Economy.* Cambridge, MA: Harvard University Press.

Higginbotham, A.L., Jr. (1978). *In the Matter of Color: Race and the American Legal Process: The Colonial Period.* New York: Oxford University Press.

Hill, Malcolm. (1987). *Sharing Child Care in Early Parenthood.* London: Routledge and Kegan Paul.

Hill, M.S. (May 1985). The changing nature of poverty. *Annals of the American Academy of Political and Social Science,* 31–47.

Hite, Shere. (1987). *Women and Love: A Cultural Revolution in Progress.* New York: Knopf.

Hobson, Barbara M. (1987). *Uneasy Virtue: The Politics of Prostitution and the American Reform Tradition.* New York: Boser Books.

Hochschild, Arlie. (1989). *The Second Shift: Working Parents and the Revolution at Home.* New York: Viking.

Hodge, Marie, and Jeff Blyskal. (October 1989). Who says college campuses are safe? *Readers Digest,* pp. 141–148.

Hodge, Robert, and David Tripp. (1986). *Children and Television: A Semiotic Approach.* Cambridge, England: Polity Press.

Hofferth, Sandra L. (1991). *National Child Care Survey, 1990.* Washington, DC: The Urban Institute Press.

Hofferth, Sandra L., Joan R. Kahn, and Wendy Baldwin. (1987). Premarital sexual activity among U.S. teenage women over the past three decades. *Family Planning Perspectives,* 19:46–53.

Hofferth, Sandra L., and Deborah A. Phillips. (1987). Child care in the United States, 1970 to 1995. *Journal of Marriage and the Family,* 49:559–571.

Hofstede, Geert. (1984). *Culture's Consequences: International Differences in Work-Related Values.* Newbury Park, CA: Sage.

Holmes, John. (September 16, 1991). Dollars and science. *Insight,* pp. 34–37.

Holmes, T., and R.H. Rahe. (1967). The social readjustment scale. *Journal of Psychosomatic Scale,* 11:213–218.

Horner, M.S. (1972). Toward an understanding of achievement-related conflicts in women. *Journal of Social Issues,* 28:157–176.

Horton, Paul, and Gerald Leslie. (1981). *The Sociology of Social Problems* (2d ed.). Englewood Cliffs, NJ: Prentice-Hall.

Hostetler, John Andrew. (1981). *Amish Society.* Baltimore: Johns Hopkins University Press.

House, James S., D. Umberson, and K.R. Landis. (1988). Structures and processes of social support. *Annual Review of Sociology,* 14:293–318.

Hout, Michael. (1988). More universalism, less structural mobility: The American occupational structure in the 1980's. *American Journal of Sociology,* 93(6):1358–1400.

Howard, Michael. (1976). *War in European History.* London: Oxford University Press.

Hu, Yuan Reng, and Noreen Goldman. (1990). Mortality differentials by mental status: An international comparison. *Demography,* 27:233–250.

Huber, Joan. (1990). Macro-micro links in gender stratification. *American Sociological Review,* 55:1–10.

Hughes, J., and B. Sandler. (1986). *In Case of Sexual Harassment, a Guide for Women Students.* Washington, DC: Association of American Colleges.

Hughes, Thomas P. (1989). *American Genesis: A Century of Invention and Technological Enthusiasm.* New York: Viking.

Hugick, Larry. (1989). Women play the leading role in keeping modern families close. *Gallup Report,* 286:26–34.

Hulldobler, Bert, and Edward O. Wilson. (1990). *The Ants.* Cambridge, MA: Belknap Press of Harvard University Press.

Humphreys, Laud. (1970). *Tearoom Trade: Impersonal Sex in Public Places.* Chicago: Aldine.

Hunt, Morton. (1974). *Sexual Behavior in the 1970s.* New York: Dell.

Hunter, J. (1983). *American Evangelism: Conservative Religion and the Quandry of Modernity.* New Brunswick, NJ: Rutgers University Press.

Hurn, Christopher. (1985). *The Limits and Possibilities of Schooling: An Introduction to the Sociology of Education.* Boston: Allyn and Bacon.

Hyman, Herbert H. (1942). The psychology of status. *Archives of Psychology,* 269:1–94.

Ihinger-Tallman, Marilyn. (1988). Research on stepfamilies. *Annual Review of Sociology,* 14:25–48.

Imperato-McGinley, Julianne, Ralph E. Peterson, Teofilo Gautier, and Erasmo Sturla. (1979). Androgens and the evolution of male gender identity among male pseudohermaphrodites with 5-Alpha-Reductase deficiency. *New England Journal of Medicine,* 310:839–840.

Inkeles, Alex, and David A. Smith. (1974). *Becoming Modern.* Harvard University Press.

Insight. (July 27, 1987). Gypsy underclass: A Hungarian dilemma, p. 7.

Insight, (March 11, 1991). Indian diabetes tied to hunter heritage, p. 53.

Interchange. (1987). Where is metropolitan U.S.? 16(4):1–3.

Ishwaran, Karlgoudor. (Ed.). (1989). *Family and Marriage: Cross-Cultural Perspectives.* Toronto: Wall and Thompson.

Jackson, Robert M. (1977). Social structure and process in friendship choice. Pp. 59–78 in *Networks and Places,* C.S. Fischer et al., eds. New York: Free Press.

Jackson, Robert M., Claude S. Fischer, and Lynne M. Jones. (1977). The dimensions of social networks. Pp. 39–58 in *Networks and Places,* Claude S. Fischer et al., eds. New York: Free Press.

Jacobson, David E. (1986). Types and timing of social support. *Journal of Health and Social Behavior,* 27:250–264.

Jacquet, C.M. (ed.). (1986). *Yearbook of the American and Canadian Churches, 1985.* Nashville: Abington Press.

Jankowiak, William, and Edward Fischer. (1992). A crosscultural perspective on romantic love. *Journal of Ethnology,* 31, 149–156.

Janowitz, Morris, and Edward A. Shils. (1948). The cohesion and disintegration of the Wehrmach in World War II. *Public Opinion Quarterly,* 12:280–315.

Jeffreys, Sheila. (1990). Eroticizing women's subordination. Pp. 132–132 in *The Sexual Liberals and the Attack on Feminism,* Dorchen Leidholdt and Janice G. Raymond, eds. New York: Pergamon Press.

Jencks, Christopher. (1985). Who must we treat equally for educational opportunity to be equal? *Ethics,* 98:518–533.

Jencks, Christopher, et. al. (1972). *Inequality. A Reassessment of the Effect of Family and Schooling in America.* New York: Basic Books.

Jencks, Christopher., Susan Bartlett, M. Corcoran, J. Crouse, D. Eaglesfield, G. Jackson, K. McClelland, P. Meuser, M. Olneck, J. Schwartz, Sh. Ward, and J. Williams. (1979). *Who Gets Ahead? The Determinants of Economic Success in America.* New York: Basic Books.

Jencks, Christopher, and P.E. Peterson (eds.). (1991). *The Urban Underclass.* Washington, DC: The Brookings Institution.

Jensen, Arthur R. (1969). How much can we boost IQ and scholastic achievement? *Harvard Educational Review,* 39:1–123.

Jiao, Shulan, G. Ji, and Qicheng Jing. (1986). Comparative study of behavioral qualities of only children and sibling children. *Child Development,* 57:357–361.

Johnson, C. M., L. Miranda, A. Sherman, and J.D. Weill. (1991). *Child Poverty in America.* Washington, DC: Children's Defense Fund.

Johnston, David. (November 23, 1992). Truckers trying to stack the deck against railroad upgrade. *The Philadelphia Inquirer,* p. ID.

Johnson, John M. (1975). *Doing Field Research.* New York: Free Press.

Johnston, Lloyd, Patrick O'Malley, and Jerald Bachman. (1990). Drug use, drinking, and smoking: National survey results in high school, college, and young adult populations. Final report prepared by the National Commission on Drug-Free Schools.

Johnstone, Ronald L. (1983). *Religion in Society: A Sociology of Religion* (2d ed.). Englewood Cliffs, NJ: Prentice-Hall.

Jones, Brian J. (1979). *Work and Network.* Unpublished PhD dissertation, University of Pennsylvania.

Jones, Brian J. (1984). Toward a constructive theory of antipoverty policy. *American Journal of Economics and Sociology,* 43(2):247–256.

Jones, Brian J., Bernard J. Gallagher III, J.M. Kelley, and T. Arvanites. (1992). The mental health make-up of a forensic population. *Sociological Practice Review,* 2:803–812.

Jones, Brian J., Bernard J. Gallagher, and Joseph A. McFalls. (1988). *Social Problems.* New York: McGraw-Hill.

Jones, Brian J., Joseph A. McFalls, and Bernard J. Gallagher. (1989). Toward a unified model for social problems theory. *Journal for the Theory of Social Behavior,* 19:337–356.

Jones, Elise F. (1986). *Teenage Pregnancy in Industrialized Countries.* New Haven, CT: Yale University Press.

Jones, Elise, and Charles Westoff. (1979). The end of Catholic fertility. *Demography,* 16:209–217.

Jones, Ernest. (1961). *The Life and Work of Sigmund Freud.* New York: Basic Books.

Jones, L.Y. (January 29, 1990). Busted by the baby boom. *Time,* p. 36.

Jones, Mary Cover. (1965). Psychological correlates of somatic development. *Child Development,* 36:899–911.

Juliani, Richard. (1981). *The Social Organization of Immigration: Italians in Philadelphia.* New York: Arno Press.

Junod, Henri Alexandre. (1927). *The Life of a South African Tribe* (2d ed.). London: Boyd and Bolger.

Juster, Susan M., and Maris A. Vinovskis. (1987). Changing perspectives on the American family in the past. *Annual Review of Sociology,* 13:193–216.

Kagan, Daniel. (February 6, 1989). Free acres in northern wonderland. *Insight,* pp. 56–57.

Kagan, Jerome. (1984). *The Nature of the Child.* New York: Basic Books.

Kahn, Joan R., William D. Kalsbeck, and Sandra L. Hofferth. (1988). National estimates of teenage sexual activity: Evaluating the comparability of three national surveys. *Demography* 25:189–204.

Kahn, Joan R., and Kathryn A. London. (1991). Premarital sex and the risk of divorce. *Journal of Marriage and the Family,* 53:845–855.

Kalleberg, Anne L., and Ivar Berg. (1987). *Work and Industry: Structures, Markets, and Processes.* New York: Plenum.

Kalmijn, Matthijs. (1991a). Status homogamy in the United States. *American Journal of Sociology,* 97:496–523.

Kalmijn, Matthijs. (1991b). Shifting boundaries: Trends in religious and educational homogamy. *American Sociological Review,* 56:786–800.

Kammeyer, Kenneth C., and Helen Ginn. (1986). *An Introduction to Population.* Chicago: Dorsey.

Kandel, Denise B. (1978). Homophily, selection and socialization in adolescent friendships. *American Journal of Sociology,* 84:427–436.

Kandel, Denise B., and Israel Adler. (1982). Socialization into marijuana use among French adolescents: A cross-cultural comparison with the United States. *Journal of Health and Social Behavior,* 23:295–309.

Kandel, Denise B., Mark Davies, and Victoria H. Ravies. (1985). The stressfulness of daily social roles: Marital, occupational, and household roles. *Journal of Health and Social Behavior,* 26:64–78.

Kanter, Rosabeth M. (1972). *Commitment and Community.* Cambridge, MA: Harvard University Press.

Kanter, Rosabeth M. (1977). *Men and Women of the Corporation.* New York: Basic Books.

Kaplan, Howard B., Robert J. Johnson, Carol A. Bailey, and William Simon. (1987). The sociological study of AIDS: A critical review of the literature and suggested research agenda. *Journal of Health and Social Behavior,* 28:140–157.

Karabel, Jerome, and A. Astin. (1975). Social class, academic ability, and college 'quality.' *Social Forces,* 53:381–398.

Karabel, Jerome, and A.H. Halsey. (1977). *Power and Ideology in Education.* New York: Oxford University Press.

Karasek, Robert, and Thores Theorell. (1990). *Healthy Work: Stress, Productivity, and the Reconstruction of Working Life.* New York: Basic Books.

Karen, David. (1990). Toward a political organizational model of gatekeeping: The case of elite colleges. *Sociology of Education,* 63:227–240.

Karp, David A., and William C. Yoels. (July 1976). The college classroom. *Sociology and Social Research,* 60:421–438.

Karp, D.A., and W.C. Yoels. (1986). *Sociology and Everyday Life.* Itasca, IL: F.E. Peacock Publishers.

Katchadourian, H. (1972). *Human Sexuality.* New York: Norton Press.

Katz, Michael B. (1989). *The Undeserving Poor.* New York: Pantheon Books.

Kaufman, W. (1976). *Religions in Four Dimensions: Existential, Aesthetic, Historical and Comparative.* New York: Readers' Digest Press.

Kearl, Michael. (1989). *Endings.* New York: Oxford University Press.

Kelly, Raymond. (1977). *Etoro Social Structure: A Study in Cultural Contradiction.* Ann Arbor: University of Michigan Press.

Kelly, Rita Mae, and Jane Bayes. (1988). *Comparable Worth, Pay Equity, and Public Policy.* Westport, CT: Greenwood Press.

Kendall, M.G., and B.B. Smith. (1939). *Tables of Random Sampling Numbers.* Cambridge: Cambridge University Press.

Keniston, K., and the Carnegie Council on Children. (1977). *All Our Children: The American Family Under Pressure.* New York: Harcourt Brace Jovanovich.

Kennedy, Robert E. (1989). *Life Choices: Applying Sociology.* New York: Holt, Rinehart and Winston.

Kephart, William M. (1982). *Extraordinary Groups: The Sociology of Unconventional Lifestyles.* New York: St. Martin's Press.

Kephart, William M., and Davor Jedlecka. (1991). *The Family, Society, and the Individual.* New York: Harper Collins.

Kephart, William M., and William Zellner. (1991). *Extraordinary Groups.* New York: St. Martin's Press.

Kilbourne, B. (1983). The Conway and Siegelman claims against religious cults: An assessment of their data. *Journal for the Scientific Study of Religion,* 22(4):380–385.

Kimball, Gayle. (1988). *50/50 Parenting: Sharing Family Rewards and Responsibilities.* Lexington, MA: Lexington Books.

Kimelman, Donald. (July 11, 1990). No room for sex: A constant in Soviet life. *The Philadelphia Inquirer,* p. 1A.

Kimura, Doreen. (1987). Are men's and women's brains really different? *Canadian Psychology,* 28:133–147.

Kingkade, Ward. (1990). USSR ethnic composition: Preliminary 1989 census results. *Population Today,* 3:6–7.

Kingston, Paul, and Lionel Lewis. (1991). *The High Status Track.* Albany, NY: SUNY Press.

Kingston, Paul W., and Steven L. Nock. (1987). Time together among dual-earner couples. *American Sociological Review,* 53:391–400.

Kinsey, Alfred C., et al. (1948). *Sexual Behavior in the Human Male.* Philadelphia: W.B. Saunders.

Kinsey, Alfred C., et al. (1953). *Sexual Behavior in the Human Female.* Philadelphia: W.B. Saunders.

Kinsey Institute. (1990). *The Kinsey Institute New Report on Sex.* New York: St. Martin's Press.

Kirschenman, J., and K. Neckerman. (1991). *The Urban Underclass.* Washington, DC: The Brookings Institution.

Kismaric, Carole. (1989). *Forced Out: The Agony of the Refugee in Our Time.* New York: Random House.

Klein Ethel. (1984). *Gender Politics: From Consciousness to Mass Politics.* Cambridge, MA: Harvard University Press.

Klein, F. (December 1988). Sexual harassment. *Working Woman.*

Klibanoff, Hank. (May 22, 1985). An insider's view of life within MOVE. *The Philadelphia Inquirer.*

Kluegel, James R., and Eliot R. Smith. (1986). *Beliefs about Inequality: Americans' Views of What Is and What Ought to Be.* New York: Aldine De Gruyter.

Knapp, Peter. (1994). *One World—Many Worlds: General Sociological Theory in Contemporary Research.* New York: Oxford University Press.

Knapp, Peter, and A.J. Spector. (1991). *Crisis and Change.* Chicago: Nelson Hall.

Knudsen, Dean D. (1987). Sex in childhood: Aversion, abuse or right? *Journal of Sex Education and Therapy,* 13(1):16–24.

Knudsen, Dean, and Joan Ann L. Miller (eds.). (1991). *Abused and Battered: Social and Legal Responses to Family Violence.* Hawthorne, NY: Aldine.

Kochen, Manfred. (ed.). (1989). *The Small World.* Norwood, NJ: Ablex Publishing.

Koenig T., and T. Boyce. (1985). Corporate financing of the Christian Right. *Humanity and Society,* 9(1):13–28.

Kohlberg, Lawrence. (1966). A cognitive-developmental analysis of children's sex-role concepts and attitudes. In *The Development of Sex Differences,* E.E. Macoby, ed. Stanford, CA: Stanford University Press.

Kohlberg, Lawrence. (1969). Stage and sequence: The cognitive developmental approach to socialization. In *Handbook of Socialization Theory and Research,* D.A. Goslin, ed. Chicago: Rand-McNally.

Kohlberg, Lawrence. (1976). Moral Stages and moralization: The cognitive developmental approach. In *Moral Development and Behavior,* T. Lickona, ed. New York: Holt, Rinehart and Winston.

Kohlberg, Lawrence, and Carol Gilligan. (Fall 1971). The adolescent as philosopher: The discovery of self in a postconventional world. *Daedalus,* 100:1051–1086.

Kohn, Melvin L. (1959). Social class and parental values. *American Journal of Sociology,* 64:337–351.

Kohn, Melvin L. (1969). *Class and Conformity.* Homewood, IL: Dorsey.

Kohn, Melvin L. (1976). Occupational structure and alienation. *American Journal of Sociology,* 82:111–130.

Kohn, Melvin L. (1977). *Class and Conformity: A Study in Values* (2d ed.). Homewood, IL: Dorsey Press.

Kohn, Melvin L. (1981). Personality, occupation, and social stratification: A frame of reference. Pp. 276–279 in *Research in Social Stratification and Mobility: A Research Annual,* D.J. Treiman and R.V. Robinson, eds. Greenwich, CT: JAI Press.

Kohn, Melvin L., and Carmi Schooler. (1978). The reciprocal effects of the substantive complexities of work and intellectual flexibility: A longitudinal assessment. *American Journal of Sociology,* 84:24–52.

Kohn, Melvin L., and Carmi Schooler. (1983). *Work and Personality: An Inquiry Into the Impact of Social Stratification.* Norwood, NJ: Ablex.

Kollock, Peter, Philip Blumstein, and Pepper Schwartz. (1985). Sex and power in interaction: Conversational privileges and duties. *American Sociological Review,* 50:34–46.

Kols, Adrienne. (1983). Migration, population growth, and development. *Population Reports* M7.

Konrad, G. (1990). Chance wanderings. *Dissent,* 189.

Koop, C. Everett. (May 3, 1992). Our health care system needs sweeping changes. *The Philadelphia Inquirer,* p. A15.

Kotarba, Joseph A. (1983). *Chronic Pain: Its Social Dimensions.* Beverly Hills, CA: Sage.

Kottak, C. (1974). *Anthropology: Exploration of Human Diversity.* New York: Random House.

Kramer, Ronald C. (1983). Controlling corporate crime through strategies of organizational intervention: A critical evaluation. *Policy Perspectives,* 3:181–215.

Kranakis, Eda F. (1982). The French connection: Gifford's injector and the nature of the heat. *Technology and Culture,* 23:3–38.

Krauthammer, Charles. (October 13, 1992). Somalia is dying not from a lack of food or medicine but from an absence of order. *The Philadelphia Inquirer.*

Kraybill, Donald. (1989). *The Riddle of Amish Culture.* Baltimore: Johns Hopkins University Press.

Krikorian, Mark. (March 25, 1990). Ethnic intermarriage stirs the melting pot. *The Philadelphia Inquirer.*

Kubey, Robert. (1990). *Television and the Quality of Life. How Viewing Shapes Everyday Experience.* Hillsdale, NJ: Lawrence Erlbaum.

Kübler-Ross, Elisabeth. (1969). *On Death and Dying.* New York: Macmillan.

Kuo, Wen, and Yung-Mei Tsai. (1986). Social networking, hardiness, and immigrants' mental health. *Journal of Health and Social Behavior,* 27:133–149.

Kurtines, William, and Esther Blank Greif. (August 1974). The development of moral thought. *Psychological Bulletin,* 81:453–470.

Kurz, Demie. (1989). Social science perspectives on wife abuse. *Gender and Society,* 3:489–505.

Labov, Teresa, and Jerry Jacobs. (1986). Intermarriage in Hawaii, 1950–1983. *Journal of Marriage and the Family,* 48:79–88.

Lacays, Richard. (1989). Conscience. *Time* (special Fall edition), pp. 22–23.

Laderman, D. (January 1992). Easy passage expected for proposals to raise academic standards. *The Chronicle of Higher Education,* 8:43.

Ladinsky, J. (1967). Higher education and work achievement among lawyers. *Sociological Quarterly,* 8:222–232.

Laffont, Robert. (1968). *The Ancient Art of Warfare.* Greenwich, CT: New York Graphic Society.

Lambert, Wallace E., E. Libman, and E. Poser. (1960). The effect of increased salience of a membership group on pain tolerance. *Journal of Personality,* 28:350–357.

Langlois, Judith H., and Cookie Stephen. (1977). The effects of physical attractiveness and ethnicity on children's behavioral attributes and peer preferences. *Child Development,* 48:1694–1698.

Larkin, Jack. (1988). *The Reshaping of Everyday Life in the United States, 1790–1840.* New York: Harper & Row.

Larson, Jan. (1992). Understanding stepfamilies. *American Demographics,* 36–40.

Lauer, Robert H. (1976). Defining social problems: Public opinion and textbook practice. *Social Problems,* 24:122–130.

Laumann, Edward O. (1973). *Bands of Pluralism: The Form and Substance of Urban Social Networks.* New York: John Wiley & Sons.

Layton, Edwin T. (1976). American ideologies of science and engineering. *Technology and Culture,* 17:688.

Leahy, Robert L. (1983). The development of self and the problems of social cognition: Identity formation and depression. In *Review of Personality and Social Psychology* (Vol. 4), L. Wheeler and P. Shaver, eds. Beverly Hills, CA: Sage.

Leahy, Robert L., and Stephen Shirk. (1985). Social cognition and the development of self. In *The Development of Self,* R.L. Leahy, ed. New York: Academic Press.

LeBon, Gustav. (1895/1960). *The Crowd: A Study of the Popular Mind.* New York: Viking.

Lee, Richard B. (1968). What hunters do for a living, or how to make out on scarce resources. In *Man the Hunter,* R.B. Lee and I. DeVore, eds. Chicago: Oldine-Atherton.

Lee, Valerie, and Kenneth Frank. (1990). Students' characteristics that facilitate the transfer from two-year to four-year colleges. *Sociology of Education,* 63:178–193.

LeGuin, Ursula K. (1969). *The Left Hand of Darkness.* New York: Ace Science Fiction Books.

LeGuin, Ursula K. (1974). *The Dispossessed.* New York: Avon.

Leidholdt, Dorchen. (1990). When women defend pornography. Pp. 125–131 in *The Sexual Liberals and the Attack on Feminism,* Dorchen Leidholdt and Janice G. Raymond, eds. New York: Pergamon Press.

Leidholdt, Dorchen, and Janice G. Raymond. (1990). *The Sexual Liberals and the Attack on Feminism.* New York: Pergamon Press.

Lemann, Nicholas. (1991). *Promised Land: The Great Black Migration and How It Changed America.* New York: Knopf.

Lemert, Edwin. (1951). *Social Pathology.* New York: McGraw-Hill.

Lemonick, Michael D. (April 16, 1990). The ultimate guest. *Time,* pp. 50–56.

Lenski, Gerhard, and Jean Lenski. (1982). *Human Societies.* New York: McGraw-Hill.

Leo, John. (February 10, 1986). Some stirrings on the mainland. *Time,* p. 77.

Lester, Gordon H. (1991). Child support and alimony, 1989. *Current Population Reports,* P-60, no. 173.

Lester, Marilyn. (1980). Generating newsworthiness: The interpretive construction of public events. *American Sociological Review,* 45:984–994.

Lever, Janet. (1978). Sex differences in the complexity of children's play and games. *American Sociological Review,* 43(4):471–483.

Levinson, Daniel. (1978). *The Seasons of a Man's Life.* New York: Knopf.

Levinson, David. (1989). *Family Violence in Cross Cultural Perspective.* Newbury Park, CA: Sage Publications.

Levy, Frank, and Richard Michel. (April 1985). Are baby boomers selfish? *American Demographics,* 38–41.

Lewis, Michael, Catherine Stanger, and Margaret W. Sullivan. (1989). Deception in 3-year-olds. *Developmental Psychology,* 25:439–443.

Lewis, O. (1966). The culture of poverty. *Scientific American,* 215:19–25.

Lewis-Beck, Michael S. (1979). Some economic effects of revolution models, measurement and the Cuban evidence. *American Journal of Sociology,* 84:1127–1149.

Lieberson, Stanley, and Eleanor O. Bell. (1992). Children's first names: An empirical study of social taste. *American Journal of Sociology,* 98:511–554.

Lieberson, Stanley, and Mary Waters. (1988). *From Many Strands: Ethnic and Racial Groups in Contemporary America.* New York: Russell Sage Foundation.

Light, Donald W. (1980). *Becoming Psychiatrists: The Professional Transformation of Self.* New York: W.W. Norton.

Lin, Nan, A. Dean, and Walter M. Ensel. (1986). *Social Support, Life Events and Depression.* Orlando, FL: Academic Press.

Lin, Nan, W.M. Ensel, and J.C. Vaughn. (1981). Social resources and occupational status, attainment. *Social Forces,* 59:1163–1181.

Lincoln, Charles Eric. (1984). *Race, Religion and the Continuing American Dilemma.* New York: Hill and Wang.

Linden, Eugene. (June 11, 1990). Dashed hopes and bogus fears. *Time,* p. 58.

Linden, Eugene. (January 11, 1993). Megacities. *Time,* pp. 28–38.

Lindholm, C., and C. Lindholm. (September 10, 1980). Mating power among the Tiwi. *Science Digest,* pp. 79–83, 114.

Linner, Birgitta. (1972). *Sex and Society in Sweden.* New York: Harper Colophon.

Linton, Ralph. (1937). *The Study of Man.* New York: D. Appleton Century.

Lips, Hilary M. (1988). *Sex and Gender: An Introduction.* Mountain View, CA: Mayfield Publishing.

Lipset, Seymour M., and Richard Bendix. (1959). *Social Mobility in Industrial Society.* Berkeley: University of California Press.

Liska, Allen E. (1987). *Perspectives on Deviance.* Englewood Cliffs, NJ: Prentice-Hall.

Lochore, R.A. (1951). *From Europe to New Zealand.* Wellington, Australia: Institute of International Affairs.

London, Kathryn A. (1991). Cohabitation, marriage, marital dissolution, and remarriage: United States, 1988. *Advance Data from Vital and Health Statistics,* 194. Hyattsville, NM: National Center for Health Statistics, pp. 1–3.

Long, Larry. (1988). *Migration and Residential Mobility in the U.S.* New York: Russell Sage Foundation.

Long, Larry. (1990). Population by the sea. *Population Today,* 18(5):6–8.

Lorence, Jon, and Jeylan Mortimer. (1985). Job involvement through the life course: A panel study of three age groups. *American Sociological Review,* 50:618–638.

Lorenz, Konrad. (1966). *On Aggression.* New York: Harcourt, Brace and World.

Loupe, D. (1989). U.S. youth gaining weight, losing stamina. *Science News,* 136:199.

Low, C. (January 4, 1988). Ultraright clamoring in Europe. *Insight,* pp. 34–35.

Luckmann, Thomas. (1967). *Invisible Religion.* New York: Macmillan.

Lukes, Steven. (1974). *Power: A Radical View.* London: Macmillan.

Lyon, D. (1988). *The Information Society: Issues and Illusions.* Cambridge: Polity Press.

Maccoby, Eleanor E., Margaret E. Snow, and Carol N. Jacklin. (1984). Children's dispositions and mother-child interactions at twelve months and eighteen months: A short-term longitudinal study. *Developmental Psychology,* 20:459–472.

MacDonald, John S., and Leatrice D. MacDonald. (1964). Chain migration, ethnic neighborhood formation and social networks. *Milbank Memorial Fund Quarterly,* 42:82–91.

MacDonald, Noni E., George A. Wells, William A. Fisher, Wendy K. Warren, Matthew A. King, Jo-Anne Doherty, and William R. Bowie. (1990). High-risk STD/HIV behavior among college students. *Journal of the American Medical Association,* 263:3155–3159.

Maddison, Angus. (1969). *Economic Growth in Japan and the USSR.* New York: W.W. Norton.

Magnuson, Edward. (March 20, 1989). The re-greening of America. *Time,* p. 30.

Mahmoody, Betty, and W. Hoffer. (1988). *Not Without My Daughter.* New York: St. Martin's Press.

Malamuth, Neil M., and Edward Donnerstein. (1984). *Pornography and Sexual Aggression.* Orlando, FL: Academic Press.

Malthus, Thomas R. (1798/1965). *An Essay on Population.* New York: Augustus Kelly, Bookseller.

Marcus, I.M., and J.J. Francis (Eds.). (1975). *Masturbation: From Infancy to Senescence.* New York: International University Press.

Mare, Robert D. (1991). Five decades of educational assortive mating. *American Sociological Review,* 56:15–32.

Marlaire, Courtney, and Douglas Maynard. (1990). Standardized testing as an educational phenomenon. *Sociology of Education,* 63:83–101.

Marsden, Peter V., and Jeanne S. Hurlbert. (1988). Social resources and mobility outcomes: A replication and extension. *Social Forces,* 66:1038–1059.

Marshall, Susan E. (1985). Ladies against women: Mobilization dilemmas of antifeminist movements. *Social Problems,* 32(4):348–362.

Martin, Albro. (1992). *Railroads Triumphant.* New York: Oxford University Press.

Martin, Linda. (1989). The graying of Japan. *Population Bulletin,* 44(2). Washington, DC: Population Reference Bureau.

Martin, M. Kay, and Barbara Voorhies. (1975). *Female of the Species.* New York: Columbia University Press.

Martin, R.C. (1982). *Islam: A Cultural Perspective.* Englewood Cliffs, NJ: Prentice-Hall.

Martin, Teresa C., and Larry L. Bumpass. (1989). Recent trends in marital description. *Demography,* 26:37–52.

Martin, W. (1984). Religiosity and U.S. suicide. *Journal of Clinical Psychology,* 40:1166–1169.

Marty, M. (1985). Transpositions: American religion in the 1980's. *The Annals of the American Academy of Political and Social Science,* 480.

Marx, Karl. (1978). Preface to A Contribution to the Critique of Political Economy. In *The Marx-Engels Readery,* R. Tucker, ed. New York: W.W. Norton.

Marx, Karl. (1844/1986). *The Economic and Philosophic Manuscripts of 1844,* D.J. Struik, ed. New York: International.

Marx, Karl. (1867/1977). *Capital,* Vol. 1 (B. Foukes, Trans.). New York: Vintage.

Marx, Karl, and Friedrich Engels. (1957). *Marx and Engels on Religion.* New York: Schocken Books.

Marx, Karl, and Friedrich Engels. (1848/1959). *The Communist Manifesto.* In *Marx and Engels: Basic Writings on Politics and Philosophy,* L. Fever, ed. New York: Doubleday.

Maslow, Abraham H. (1943). A theory of human motivation. *Psychological Review,* 50:370–396.

Masters, William H., and Virginia E. Johnson. (1970). *Human Sexual Response.* Boston: Little, Brown.

Mathias, Peter. (1972). Who unbound Prometheus? Science and technical change, 1600–1800. In *Science and Society 1600–1900,* P. Mathias, ed. Cambridge: Cambridge University Press.

Mazur, Allan C. (1986). U.S. trends in feminine beauty and overadaptation. *Journal of Sex Research,* 22(3):281–303.

Mazur, Allan C. (1990). Controlling technology. In *Technology and the Future,* A.H. Teich, ed. New York: St. Martin's Press.

McAdam, Doug. (1982). *Political Process and the Development of Black Insurgency.* Chicago: University of Chicago Press.

McAdoo, Harriette P. (1993). *Family Ethnicity.* Newbury Park, CA: Sage.

McCarthy, John D., and Meyer N. Zald. (1973). *The Trend of Social Movements in America.* Morristown, NJ: General Learning Press.

McCarthy, John D., and Meyer N. Zald. (1977). Resource mobilization and social movements: A partial theory. *American Journal of Sociology,* 82:1212–1241.

McClelland, Katherine. (1990). Cumulative advantage among the highly ambitious. *Sociology of Education,* 63:102–121.

McCrary, Lacy. (December 17, 1989). More women landing in jail. *The Philadelphia Inquirer.*

McCue, Jack D. (1989). *The Medical Cost-Containment Crisis.* Ann Arbor, MI: Health Administration Press Perspectives.

McCullough, M. (January 30, 1993). Campuses debate extending benefits to domestic partners. *The Philadelphia lnquirer.*

McDermott, John. (1990). Technology: The opiate of the intellectuals. Pp. 100–125 in *Technology and the Future,* A.H. Teich, ed. New York: St. Martin's Press.

McDougall, W. (1908). *An Introduction to Social Psychology.* London: Metheun.

McFalls, Joseph A. (1979a). Frustrated fertility: A population paradox. *Population Bulletin,* 34(2). Washington, DC: Population Reference Bureau.

McFalls, Joseph A. (1979b). *Psychopathology and Subfecundity.* New York: Academic Press.

McFalls, Joseph A. (1981). Where have all the children gone? The future of reproduction in the U.S. *USA Today,* 109:30–33.

McFalls, Joseph A. (1990). The risks of reproductive impairment in the later years of childbearing. *Annual Review of Sociology,* 16:491–519.

McFalls, Joseph A. (1991). Population: A lively introduction. *Population Bulletin,* 46(2). Washington, DC: Population Reference Bureau.

McFalls, Joseph A., Bernard J. Gallagher, and Brian J. Jones. (1986). The social tunnel versus the python: A new way to understand the impact of baby booms and baby busts on a society. *Teaching Sociology,* 14:129–132.

McFalls, Joseph A., Bermard J. Gallagher III, and Brian J. Jones. (Forthcoming). Political orientation and occupational values of college youth: Changes over a 20 year period. *Adolescence.*

McFalls, Joseph A., Bernard J. Gallagher III, and Carolyn N. Vreeland. (October 1992). The etiology of male homosexuality: Preliminary results from a survey of psychiatrists. Paper presented at the Annual Meetings of the Pennsylvania Sociological Society, Oxford, PA.

McFalls, Joseph A., and Marguerite H. McFalls. (1984). *Disease and Fertility.* Orlando, FL: Academic Press.

McFarland, Mary. (November–December 1989). 200 years and counting. *Social Education,* 53.

McGinn, Robert E. (1991). *Science, Technology and Society.* Englewood Cliffs, NJ: Prentice-Hall.

McGuinness, Diane. (1972). Hearing: Individual differences in perceiving. *Perception,* 1:465–473.

McGuire, Meredith B. (1987). *Religion: The Social Context* (2d ed.). Belmont, CA: Wadsworth.

McKinlay, John B., Sonja M. McKinlay, and Donald Brambila. (1987). The relative contributions of endocrine changes and social circumstances to depression in mid-aged women. *Journal of Health and Social Behavior,* 28:345–63.

McKinlay, Sonja M., and J.B. McKinlay. (1986). Aging in a healthy population. *Social Science and Medicine,* 23:531–535.

McLaughlin, Steven D., Barbara M. Melber, John O. Billy, Denise M. Zimmerle, Linda D. Wenges, and Terry R. Johnson. (1989). *The Changing Lives of American Women.* Chapel Hill: University of North Carolina Press.

McLean's. (January 23, 1989). A growing menace: Violent skinheads are raising urban fears, pp. 43–44.

McNeil, William. (1976). *Plagues and People.* Garden City, NY: Doubleday.

McNeill, William H. (1982). *The Pursuit of Power: Technology, Armed Force, and Society Since A.D. 1000.* Chicago: University of Chicago Press.

McWhirter, Norris. (1985). *Guiness Book of World Records.* New York: Bantam Books.

Mead, Geroge H. (1934). *Mind, Self and Society.* Chicago: University of Chicago Press.

Mead, Margaret. (1935/1969). *Sex and Temperament in Three Primitive Societies.* New York: William Morrow.

Meadows, Donnella H., et al. (1972). *The Limits to Growth.* New York: New American Library.

Mechanic, David. (1978). *Medical Sociology.* New York: Free Press.

Mechanic, David. (1986). Correcting misconceptions in mental health policy. *Milbank Quarterly,* 2:203–230.

Mechanic, David, and R. Angel. (1987). Some factors associated with the report and evaluation of back pain. *Journal of Health and Social Behavior,* 28:131–139.

Mechanic, David, and Stephen Hansell. (1989). Divorce, family conflict, and adolescents' well-being. *Journal of Health and Social Behavior,* 30:105–116.

Medalia, Nehum, and Otto Larson. (1958). Diffusion and belief in a collective delusion: The Seattle windshield pitting epidemic. *American Sociological Review,* 23:221–232.

Medved, Michael. (1992). *Hollywood vs. America.* New York: Harper Collins.

Mellen, S.L. (1981). *The Evolution of Love.* San Francisco: W.H. Freeman.

Menaghan, Elizabeth G. (1991). Work experiences and family interaction processes: The long reach of the job? *Annual Review of Sociology,* 17:419–444.

Mensch, Barbara S., and Denise B. Kandel. (1988). Underreporting of substance use in a national longitudinal youth cohort: Individual and interviewer effects. *Public Opinion Quarterly,* 52:100–124.

Merriam, A. (1971). Aspects of sexual behavior among the Bala. In *Human Sexual Behavior: Variations in the Ethnographic Spectrum,* D. Marshall and R. Suggs, eds. Englewood Cliffs, NJ: Prentice-Hall.

Merrick, Thomas. (1986). Population pressures in Latin America. *Population Bulletin,* 41(3). Washington, DC: Population Reference Bureau.

Merrick, Thomas, and Stephen Tordella. (1988). Demographics: People and markets. *Population Bulletin,* 43(1). Washington, DC: Population Reference Bureau.

Merton, Robert K. (1949). Discrimination and the American creed. In *Discrimination and National Welfare,* R.H. Maclver, ed. New York: Harper & Row.

Merton, Robert K. (1968). *Social Theory and Social Structure.* New York: The Free Press.

Merton, Robert K. (1970). *Science, Technology and Society in Seventeenth-Century England.* New York: Harper & Row.

Merton, Robert K. (1973). *The Sociology of Science: Theoretical and Empirical Investigations.* Chicago: University of Chicago Press.

Merton, Robert K., and A.S. Rossi. (1968). Contributions to the theory of reference group behavior. In *Social Theory and Social Structure,* R.K. Merton, ed. New York: The Free Press.

Messenger, John C. (1969). *Inis Beag: Isle of Ireland.* New York: Holt, Rinehart & Winston.

Mestrovic, Stjepan G., and Helene M. Brown. (1985). Durkheim's concept of anomie as *dereglement. Social Problems,* 33:81–99.

Meyrowitz, Joshua. (1985). *No Sense of Place: The Impact of Electronic Media on Social Behavior.* New York: Oxford University Press.

Michels, Robert. (1915/1958). *Political Parties* (E. Paul and C. Paul, Trans.). Glencoe, IL: The Free Press.

Milgram, Stanley. (1963). Behavioral study of obedience. *Journal of Abnormal and Social Psychology,* 67:371–378.

Milgram, Stanley. (1975). *Obedience to Authority: An Experimental View.* New York: Harper & Row.

Milgrom, P., and J. Roberts. (1988). An economic approach to influence activities in organizations. *American Journal of Sociology,* Supplement Vol. 94, S154–S179.

Mill, John Stuart. (1891). *A System of Logic* (Vol. I). NY: Harper & Row.

Miller, Barbara D. (1981). *The Endangered Sex.* Ithaca, NY: Cornell University Press.

Millman, Marcia. (1976). *The Unkindest Cut: Life in the Backrooms of Medicine.* New York: Morrow Quill.

Mills, C. Wright. (1956). *The Power Elite.* New York: Oxford University Press.

Mills, C. Wright. (1959). *The Sociological Imagination.* New York: Oxford University Press.

Mincer, Jacob. (1974). *Schooling, Experience, and Earnings.* New York: National Bureau of Economic Research.

Mintz, Beth, and Michael Schwartz. (1981). Interlocking directorates and interest group formation. *American Sociological Review,* 46:951–968.

Mintz, Steven, and Susan Kellogg. (1988). *Domestic Revolutions: A Social History of American Family Life.* New York: Free Press.

Mirowsky, John. (1987). The psycho-economics of feeling underpaid: Distributive justice and the earnings of husbands and wives. *American Journal of Sociology,* 92:1404–1434.

Mirowsky, John, and Catherine R. Ross. (1989). *Social Causes of Psychological Distress.* New York: Aldine de Gruyter.

Mitchell, Barbara A., Andrew V. Wister, and Thomas K. Burch. (1989). The family environment and leaving the parental home. *Journal of Marriage and the Family,* 51:605–613.

Moloney, Thomas W., and David E. Rogers. (1979). Medical technology: A different view of the contentious debate over costs. *New England Journal of Medicine,* 301:1413–1419.

Money, John. (1988). *Gay, Straight, and in Between.* New York: Oxford Press.

Money, John, and A.E. Ehrhardt. (1972). *Man and Woman, Boy and Girl.* New York: New American Library.

Montgomery, Kathryn C. (1989). *Target: Prime Time: Advocacy Groups and the Struggle Over Entertainment.* New York: Oxford University Press.

Mooney, C. (November 6, 1991). Study finds professors are still teaching the classics, sometimes in new ways. *The Chronicle of Higher Education,* 1.

Mooradian, Arshag D., and Vicki Greiff. (1990). Sexuality in older women. *Archives of Internal Medicine,* 150:1033–1038.

Moore, Gwen. (1990). Structural determinants of men's and women's personal networks. *American Sociological Review,* 55:726–735.

Moore, G., and R.D. Alba. (1982). Class and prestige in the American elite. In *Social Structure and Network Analysis,* P.V. Marsden and N. Lin, eds. Beverly Hills, CA: Sage.

Moore, Kirstin A., Christine W. Nord, and James L. Peterson. (1989). Nonvoluntary sexual activity among adolescents. *Family Planning Perspectives,* 21(3):110–114.

Moorman, Jeanne E., and Donald J. Hernandez. (1989). Married-couple families with step, adopted, and biological children. *Demography,* 26(2):267–277.

Morgan, S. Philip, and Ronald R. Rindfuss. (1985). Marital disruption: Structural and temporal dimensions. *American Journal of Sociology,* 90:1055–1077.

Morison, Elton E. (1977). *From Know-How to Nowhere: The Development of American Technology.* New York: New American Library.

Morris, Desmond. (1968). *The Naked Ape.* New York: McGraw-Hill.

Morris, David B. (1991). *The Culture of Pain.* Berkeley, CA: University of California Press.

Morrow, Carol. (1982). Sick doctors: The social construction of professional deviance. *Social Problems,* 30:92–109.

Mortimer, Jeylan, Jon Lorence, and Donald Kumka. (1986). *Work, Family and Personality: Transition to Adulthood.* Norwood, NJ: Ablex.

Mortimer, Jeylan, and Roberta Simmons. (1978). Adult socialization. Pp. 415–454 in *Annual Review of Sociology* (Vol. 4), R.H. Turner, J. Coleman, and R.C. Fox, eds. Palo Alto, CA: Annual Reviews.

Mosher, William D., and Christine A. Bachrach. (1982). Childlessness in the United States. *Journal of Family Issues,* 3(4):517–543.

Mosher, William D., and Geary Hendershot. (1984). Religious affiliation and the fertility of married couples. *Journal of Marriage and the Family,* 46:671–677.

Mosley, Wiley H., and Peter Cowley. (1991). The challenge of world health. *Population Bulletin,* 46(4). Washington, DC: Population Reference Bureau.

Mueller, Carol, and Thomas Dimieri. (1982). The structure of belief systems among contending ERA activists. *Social Forces,* 60:657–675.

Mullenneaux, Lisa. (November 9, 1992). Her bikes ease strain for women. *The Philadelphia Inquirer,* pp. F1, F4.

Müller, Ronald. (1974). (More) on multinationals. *Foreign Policy,* 13:70–103.

Mumford, Lewis. (1934). *Technics and Civilization.* New York: Harcourt, Brace and World.

Murdock, George P. (1945). The common denominator of cultures. In *The Science of Man and the World Crisis,* Ralph Linton, ed. New York: Columbia University Press.

Murdock, George P. (1955). Comparative data on the division of labor by sex. *Social Forces,* 15:551–553.

Murdock, George P. (1957). World ethnographic sample. *American Anthropologist,* 59:664–688.

Murdock, George P. (1967). *Ethnographic Atlas.* Pittsburgh: University of Pittsburgh Press.

Murdock, George P. (1979). *Social Structure.* New York: Macmillan.

Murray, Charles. (1984). *Losing Ground: American Social Policy, 1950–1980.* New York: Basic Books.

Murray, Michael. (1992). *Review of Research on the Impact of Television on Society.* Washington, DC: American Psychological Association.

Mutchler, Jan, and Jeffrey Burr. (1991). A longitudinal analysis of household and nonhousehold living arrangements in later life. *Demography,* 28:375–390.

Myrdal, Gunnar. (1944). *An American Dilemma.* New York: Harper.

Nastasee, Susan A. (1990). The illustrated man. *Men's Health,* 6(1):70–71.

National Academy of Sciences. (1969). *Resources and Man.* San Francisco: Freeman.

National Academy of Sciences. (1986). *Population Growth and Economic Development: Policy Questions.* Washington, DC: National Academy Press.

National Center for Health Statistics [NCHS]. (1983). National Ambulatory Medical Care Survey: Summary. *Advance data from Vital and Health Statistics,* 88.

NCHS. (1987). Married and unmarried couples, United States, 1982. Vital and Health Statistics, 23,15.

NCHS. (May 24, 1988). Prevalence of selected chronic conditions, United States, 1983–1985. *Advance Data,* 155.

NCHS. (1989a). Annual summary of births, marriages, divorces, and deaths: United States, 1988. *Monthly Vital Statistics Report,* 37, 13.

NCHS. (1989b). Advance report of final natality statistics, 1987. *Monthly Vital Statistics Report,* 38, 3.

NCHS. (1989c). Advance report of final mortality statistics, 1987: Monthly Vital Statistics Report 38, 5, 1–48.

NCHS. (August 24, 1989d). Characteristics of persons dying from AIDS. *Advance Data,* 173.

NCHS. (1991a). Annual summary of bitmaps, marriages, divorces, and deaths: United States, 1990. *Monthly Vital Statistics Report,* 39(13).

NCHS. (June 18, 1991b). Characteristics of persons with and without health care coverage: Unites States 1989. *Advance Data,* 201.

NCHS. (May 21, 1991c). Advance report of final divorce statistics, 1988. *Monthly Vital Statistics Report,* 39, 12, 52.

NCHS. (August 26, 1991d). Advance report of final marriage statistics, 1988. *Monthly Vital Statistics Report,* 40, 4,5.

NCHS. (September 30, 1991e). Exposure to alcoholism in the family: United States, 1988. *Advance Data,* 205.

NCHS. (May 21, 1991f). Disability and health: Characteristics of persons by limitation of activity and assessed health status, United States, 1984–1988. *Advance Data,* 197.

NCHS. (1992a). Advance report of final mortality statistics, 1989. *Monthly Vital Statistics Report,* 40(8), Supplement 2.

NCHS. (September 30, 1992b). Annual summary of births, marriages, divorces, and death: United States, 1991. *Monthly Vital Statistics Report,* 40, 13.

NCHS. (December 12, 1992c). Advance report of final natality statistics, 1989. *Monthly Vital Statistics Report,* 40, 8, 5.

NCHS. (August 31, 1993a). Advance report of final mortality statistics, 1991. *Monthly Vital Statistics Report,* 42, 2, Supplement.

NCHS. (1993b). Advance report of final natality statistics, 1991. *Monthly Vital Statistics Report,* 42, 3, Supplement, 1–48.

National Institutes of Health (February 25, 1985). Press conference of Jules Hirsch, Chairman of the panel on obesity and health.

National Institute of Mental Health. (1982). Television and behavior: Ten years of scientific progress and implications for the eighties. (Vols. 1 & 2), Washington, DC: U.S. Government Printing Office.

National Opinion Research Center [NORC]. (1985). *General Social Survey.*

NORC. (1985). *General Social Surveys 1972–1985* [machine-readable data file]. Chicago: National Opinion Research Center.

NORC. (1987). General Social Survey: Questions and Answers.

NORC. (1989). *General Social Surveys, 1972–1989: Cumulative Codebook.* Chicago: National Opinion Research Center.

National Research Council. (1990). Who cares for America's children? Hayes, Cheryl D., Palmer, John L., and Zaslaw, Martha J., eds. Washington, DC: National Academy Press, 108–144.

Ness, Roberta, Joyce Kelly, and Charles Killian. (1991). House staff recruitment to municipal and voluntary New York City residency programs during the AIDS epidemic. *Journal of the American Medical Association,* 266(20):2843–2846.

Neuman, E. (February 24, 1992). Cancer: The issue feminists forgot. *Insight,* pp. 7–34.

New Encyclopaedia Britannica, The. (1991). Vol. II. Chicago: Encyclopaedia Britannica, Inc.

New Republic. (April 13, 1989). Nazi retreat, pp. 10–11.

Newcomb, Theodore. (1950). *Social Psychology.* New York: Holt, Rinehart and Winston.

Newton, Gerald. (1978). *The Netherlands: A Historical and Cultural Analysis.* Boulder, CO: Westview.

Niebuhr, Helmut Richard. (1929). *The Social Sources of Denominationalism.* New York: Henry Holt.

Nielsen, Joyce. (1990). *Sex and Gender in Society: Perspectives on Stratification.* Prospect Heights, IL: Waveland Press.

Norvsic, Marija. (1988). *SPSS-X User's Guide* (3d edition). Chicago, IL: SPSS, Inc.

Nussbaum, Paul. (January 31, 1989). The night stalker. *The Philadelphia Inquirer.*

Nye, F. Ivan. (1974). Emerging and declining family roles. *Journal of Marriage and the Family,* 36:238–244.

O'Brien, Darcy. (1987). *Two of a Kind: The Hillside Stranglers.* New York: Signet.

Ochiltree, Gay. (1990). *Children in Stepfamilies.* Brookvale, Australia: Prentice-Hall.

O'Connell, Martin. (1991). Late expectations: Childbearing patterns of American women for the 1990s. Studies in American Fertility. *Current Population Reports,* P-23.

O'Connell, Martin, and Amara Bachu. (1990). Who's minding the kids? Child care arrangements: Winter, 1986–87. *Current Population Reports,* P-70.

O'Connor, J.R. (1973). *The Fiscal Crisis of the State.* New York: St. Martin's Press.

O'Dea, Thomas F., and J.O. Ariad. (1983). *The Sociology of Religion* (2d ed.). Englewood Cliffs, NJ: Prentice-Hall.

Offir, Carole W. (1982). *Human Sexuality.* New York: Harcourt Brace Jovanovich.

Ogburn, William Fielding. (1922). *Social Change with Respect to Culture and Original Nature.* New York: Huebsch.

O'Hare, William P. (1985). Poverty in America: Trends and new patterns. *Population Bulletin* 40(3). Washington, DC: Population Reference Bureau.

O'Hare, William P. (1988). *The Rise of Poverty in Rural America.* Washington, DC: Population Reference Bureau.

O'Hare, W.P, and J.C. Felt. (1991). *Asian Americans: America's Fastest Growing Minority Group.* Washington, DC: Population Reference Bureau.

Olneck, Michael, and Ki-Seok Kim. (1989). High school completion and men's incomes: An apparent anomaly. *Sociology of Education,* 62:193–207.

Olshansky, S. Jay, Bruce A. Carnes, and Christine Cassel. (1990). In search of Methuselah: Estimating the upper limits of human longevity. *Science,* 250:634–640.

O'Malley, Michael. (1992). *Keeping Watch: A History of American Time.* New York: Penguin.

Oman, Charles W. (1898). *A History of the Art of War: The Middle Ages from the Fourth to the Fourteenth Century.* London: Methuen.

O'Reilly, D. (December 5, 1991). A students credo: Cheat or perish. *The Philadelphia Inquirer.*

O'Rourke, David K. (1983). Revolution and alienation in the American church. *Commonweal,* Cx, 76–79.

Orru, Marco. (1987). *Anomie: History and Meanings.* Boston: Allen & Unwin.

Orshansky, M. (1974). How poor is measured. In *The Sociology of American Poverty,* J. Huber and H.P. Chalfant, eds. Cambridge: Schenkman.

Ostling, R.N. (September 2, 1985). Jerry Falwell's crusade. *Time,* pp. 48–52, 55–57.

Ostling, R.N. (May 23, 1988). Americans facing toward Mecca. *Time,* pp. 49–50.

Oved, Iaacov. (1988). *Two Hundred Years of American Communes.* New Brunswick, NJ: Transaction Press.

Paffenbarger, Ralph S., Jr., Robert T. Hyde, Alvin L. Wing, and Chung-Chen Hsieh. (1986). Physical activity, all cause mortality, and longevity of college alumni. *New England Journal of Medicine,* (314):615–613.

Page, Benjamin I., and Robert Y. Shapiro. (1983). Effects of public opinion on Policy. *American Political Science Review,* 77:176.

Page, Dan. (June 1993). Globalization, technology, and competition. *HBS Bulletin,* pp. 10–12.

Palazzolo, Charles S. (1981). *Small Groups.* New York: D. Van Nostrand Co.

Palen, John J. (1992). *The Urban World.* New York: McGraw-Hill.

Parenti, Michael. (1983). *Democracy for the Few.* New York: St. Martin's Press.

Parish, William L., Lingxin Hao, and Dennis P. Hogan. (1991). Family support networks, welfare, and work among young mothers. *Journal of Marriage and the Family,* 53:203–215.

Parsons, Talcott. (1951). *The Social System.* Glencoe: Free Press.

Parsons, Talcott. (1971). *The System of Modern Societies.* Englewood Cliffs, NJ: Prentice-Hall.

Pasley, Kay, and Marilyn Ihinger-Tallman (eds.). (1988). *Remarriage and Stepparenting: Current Research and Theory.* New York: Guilford.

Passel, Jeffrey S. (September 11, 1985). Testimony before the U.S. House of Representatives Subcommittee on immigration, refugees, and international law.

Pateman, Carole. (1988). *The Sexual Contract.* Stanford, CA: Stanford University Press.

Pattnayak, Satya. (1992). Integrating liberal pluralist and dependency perspectives of specific levels of state capacity. *International Review of Modern Sociology,* 22:62–78.

Pearlin, Louis I. (1989). The sociological study of stress. *Journal of Health and Social Behavior,* 30:241–256.

Pearsall, R. (1969). *The Worm in the Bud: The World of Victorian Sexuality.* Toronto: Macmillan Press.

Pearson, Judith E. (1986). The definition and measurement of social support. *Journal of Counseling and Development,* 64:390–395.

Pedersen, Eigil, and Therese Faucher. (1978). A new perspective on the effects of first grade teachers on children's subsequent adult status. *Harvard Educational Review,* 48(1):1–31.

Pennings, Johannes M. (1980). *Interlocking Directorates.* San Francisco: Jossey-Bass.

Perper, Timothy. (1985). *Sex Signals: The Biology of Love.* Philadelphia: ISI Press.

Perrow, Charles. (1984). *Normal Accidents: Living with High-Risk Technologies.* New York: Basic Books.

Perrucci, Robert, and Harry R. Potter (eds.). (1989). *Networks of Power.* New York: Aldine de Gruyter.

Persell, C., and P. Cookson, Jr. (1990). Chartering and bartering: Elite education and social class. In *The High Status Track,* P. Kingston and L. Lewis, eds. Albany, NY: SUNY Press.

Peters, Ruth K. (1983). Physical fitness and subsequent myocardial infarction in healthy workers. *Journal of the American Medical Association,* 249:3052–3056.

Petersen, William. (1975). *Population.* New York: Macmillan.

Petersen, William. (1978). Chinese Americans and Japanese Americans. In *Essays and Data on Americana Ethnic Groups,* T. Sowell, ed. Washington, DC: The Urban Institute.

Peterson, James. (October 27, 1992). Problems of urban America revert to back burner. *The Philadelphia Inquirer,* p. A16.

Petranek, Charles F. (January/February 1988). Recruitment and commitment. *Society,* 48–51.

Pettigrew, T.F. (1985). New black-white patterns: How best to conceptualize them? *Annual Review of Sociology,* 11:329–346.

Pfeffer, Marc, Lemuel A. Moye, Eugene Braunwald, Lofty Basta, Edward J. Brown, Thomas E. Cuddy, Giles R. Dagenais, Gregory C. Flaker, Edward M. Geltman, Bernard J. Gersh, Steven Goldman, Gervasio A. Lamas, Milton Packer, Jean L. Rouleau, John D. Rutherford, Richard M. Steingart, and John H. Wertheimer. (1991). Selection bias in the use of thrombolytic therapy in acute myocardial infarction. *New England Journal of Medicine,* 266:528–532.

Phillips, Bernard. (1985). Sociological Research Methods. Homewood, IL: The Dorsey Press.

Piaget, Jean, and B. Inhelder. (1969). *The Psychology of the Child.* New York: Basic Books.

Pines, Maya. (September 1981). The civilization of Genie. *Psychology Today,* pp. 28–34.

Pitt, M. (1955). *Introducing Hinduism.* New York: Friendship Press.

Pittman, Frank. (1993). *Man Enough: Fathers, Sons, and the Search for Masculinity.* New York: Putnam.

Piven, Frances Fox, and Richard A. Cloward. (1971). *Regulating the Poor: The Functions of Public Welfare.* New York: Vintage.

Piven, Frances Fox, and Richard A. Cloward. (1987). The contemporary relief debate. In *The Mean Season,* F. Block, et al., eds. New York: Pantheon.

Piven, Frances Fox, and Richard A. Cloward. (1989). *Why Americans Don't Vote.* New York: Pantheon.

Platt, John. (November–December 1987). AIDS 2000: The future of AIDS. *The Futurist,* 10–17.

Plough, Alonzo. (1986). *Borrowed Time: Artificial Organs and the Politics of Extending Lives.* Philadelphia: Temple University Press.

Pollard, S., and C. Holmes (eds.). (1968). Documents in European Economic History. Pp. 534–536 in Vol. 1. *The Process of Industrialization 1750–1870.* New York: St. Martin's Press.

Pollin, William. (1984). Why people smoke cigarettes. Paper based on testimony presented to the U.S. Congress, March 1982, and published by the National Institute on Drug Abuse.

Pollin, William, and R.T. Ravenholt. (1984). Tobacco addiction and tobacco mortality: Implications for death certification. *Journal of the American Medical Association,* 252:2849–2854.

Pontell, Henry N. (ed.). (1993). *Social Deviance.* Englewood Cliffs, NJ: Prentice-Hall.

Popenoe, David. (1988). *Disturbing the Nest: Family Change and Decline in Modern Societies.* New York: Aldine de Gruyter.

Popenoe, David. (May 1991). Breakup of the American Family: Can we reverse the trend? *USA Today Magazine.*

Population Today. (1985). Demographics force Soviets to begin inducting women. p. 5.

Population Today. (January 1993). Take a number, p. 10.

Population Reference Bureau [PRB]. (1990). *America in the 2lst century: Environmental Concerns.* Washington, DC: Population Reference Bureau.

PRB. (1992). *The United States Population Data Sheet.* Washington, DC: Population Reference Bureau.

PRB. (1993). *The World Population Data Sheet.* Washington, DC: Population Reference Bureau.

Porter, Alan L. (1992). An introduction to technology assessment and impact analysis. Pp. 153–158 in *Technology and the Future,* A.H. Teich, ed. New York: St. Martin's Press.

Portes, A., and C. Truelove. (1987). Making sense of diversity: Recent research on Hispanic minorities in the United States. *Annual Review of Sociology,* 13:359–385.

Post, David. (1990). The social demands for education in Peru: Students' choices and state autonomy. *Sociology of Education,* 63:258–271.

Postman, Neil. (1979). *Teaching as a Conserving Activity.* New York: Delacorte.

Powdermaker, H. (1933). *Life in Lesu.* New York: Norton.

Powell, Walter W. (1985). *Getting Into Print: The Decision-Making Process in Scholarly Publishing.* Chicago: The University of Chicago Press.

Power, M. (1988). Labor market restructuring and women's economic experience since 1970. In *The Imperiled Economy, Box II,* R. Cherry, et al. eds. New York: Union for Radical Political Economics.

Pratt, W.F., William D. Mosher, Christine A. Bachrach, and Marjorie C. Horn. (1984). Understanding U.S. fertility. *Population Bulletin* 39(5). Washington, DC: Population Reference Bureau.

Presser, Harriet B. (1989). Can we make time for children? The economy, work schedules, and child care. *Demography,* 26(4):523–544.

Preston, Richard A., Sydney F. Wise, and Herman O. Werner. (1956). *A History of Warfare and Its Interrelationships with Modern Society.* New York: Praeger.

Preston, Samuel H. (1984). Children and the elderly: Divergent paths for America's dependents. *Demography,* 21:435–457.

Preston, Samuel H. (1987). The social sciences and the population problem. *Sociological Forum,* 2:619–644.

Preston, Samuel H. (Spring 1990). The vanishing American family. *University of Pennsylvania's Arts and Sciences Magazine,* pp. 8–10.

Price, Charles Archibald. (1963). *Southern Europeans in Australia.* Melbourne, Australia: Oxford.

Price, J. (September 5, 1988). Advances keep America on its feet. *Insight,* pp. 54–55.

Quale, G. Robina. (1988). *A History of Marriage Systems.* Westport, CT: Greenwood.

Quann, C.J. (1984). *Grades and Grading: Historical Perspectives and the 1982 AACRAO Study*. Washington, DC: American Association of Collegiate Registrars and Admissions Officers.

Quinn, D. (1992). *Ishmael*. New York: Bantam Books.

Quinney, Richard. (1974). *Criminal Justice in America*. Boston: Little, Brown.

Quinney, Richard. (1980). *Class, State and Crime*. New York: Longman.

Raloff, Janet. (1992). Tackling R & D stagnation. *Science News*, 142:190–191.

Rank, Mark. (1989). Fertility among women on welfare: Incidence and determinants. *American Sociological Review*, 54:296–304.

Ravenholt, R.T. (1984). Addiction mortality in the United States 1980: Tobacco, alcohol, and other substances. *Population and Development Review*, 10:697–724.

Ravenholt, R.T. (1985). Tobacco's impact on twentieth-century U.S. mortality patterns. *American Journal of Preventive Medicine*, 1:4–17.

Ravenholt, R.T. (1990). Tobacco's global death march. *Population and Development Review*, 16:213–240.

Raymo, Chet. (1993). *The Virgin and the Mousetrap. Essays in Search of the Soul of Science*. New York: Penguin.

Redbook. (September 1987). Special sex survey results.

Reiman, Jeffrey. (1990). *The Rich Get Richer and the Poor Get Prison: Ideology, Class, and Criminal Justice*. New York: Macmillan.

Rensberger, B. (February 29, 1988). Sexual competition and violence. *The Washington Post*.

Repetto, Robert C. (1987). Population, resources, environment: An uncertain future. *Population Bulletin*, 42(2). Washington, DC: Population Reference Bureau.

Retherford, R.D., and M.J. Levin. (1989). Is the fertility of Asian and Pacific Islander Americans converging to the U.S. norm? *Asian and Pacific Forum*, 3:21–29.

Reuters News Service. (May 1, 1990). Israel sees greater increase in its non-Jewish population.

Reuters News Service. (January 4, 1991). Henry VIII's sex life found less than royal. *The Philadelphia Inquirer*.

Riley, Glenda. (1991). *Divorce: An American Tradition*. New York: Oxford.

Riley, Matilda. (1987). On the significance of age in sociology. *American Sociological Review*, 52:1–14.

Riley, M.W., A. Foner, and J. Waring. (1988). Sociology of age. Pp. 243–290 in *Handbook of Sociology*, N.J. Smelser, ed. Newbury Park, CA: Sage Publications.

Rindfuss, Ronald R., and Audrey Vandenheuvel. (1990). Cohabitation: A precurser to marriage or an alternative to being single? *Population and Development Review*, 16:703–725.

Rist, Roy. (1970). Student social class and teacher expectations: The self-fulfilling prophecy in ghetto education. *Harvard Educational Review*, 40:411–450.

Ritzer, George, Kenneth C. Kammeyer, and Norman R. Yetman. (1979). *Experiencing a Changing Society*. Boston: Allyn and Bacon.

Rivo, M.L., V. Kofie, E. Schwartz, M.E. Levy, and R. Tuckson. (1989). Comparisons of black and white smoking-attributable mortality morbidity and economic costs in the District of Columbia. *Journal of the National Medical Association*, 81(11):1125–1130.

Roazen, Paul. (1974). *Freud and His Followers*. New York: Meridian.

Robbins, S.J. (1989). *Organizational Behavior*. Englewood Cliffs, NJ: Prentice-Hall.

Roberts, D.F. (1975). The dynamics of racial intermixture in the American Negro: Some anthropological considerations. *American Journal of Human Genetics*, 7:361–367.

Roberts, J. (1980). *Roots of a Black Future: Family and Church*. Philadelphia, PA: The Westminster Press.

Robertson, Ian. (1978). *Sociology*. New York: Worth.

Robertson, Thomas S. (1980). Television advertising and parent-child relations. In *The Effect of Television Advertising on Children*, R.P. Adler et al., eds. Lexington, MA: Lexington Books.

Robey, Bryant. (April 1989). Two hundred years and counting: The 1990 Census. *Population Bulletin*, 44. Washington, DC: Population Reference Bureau.

Robinson, Paul. (1976). *The Modernization of Sex: Havelock Ellis, Alfred Kinsey, William Masters, and Virginia Johnson.* New York: Harper Colophon.

Rockoff, J. (July 6, 1991). Better credentials are a steal. *The Philadelphia Inquirer.*

Rodgers, Richard G. (1992). Living and dying in the U.S.A.: Socio-demographic determinants of death among blacks and whites. *Demography*, 29:287–305.

Roethlisberger, Fritz J., and William J. Dickson. (1939). *Management and the Worker.* Cambridge, MA: Harvard University Press.

Rogot, Eugene, Paul Sorbie, Norman Johnson, Claudia Glover, and David Treasure. (1988). *A Mortality Study of One Million Persons by Demographic, Social and Economic Factors: 1979–1981 Follow Up.* Washington, DC: U.S. Department of Health and Human Services.

Roof, Wade Clark. (1979). Socioeconomic differentials among white socioreligious groups in the United States. *Social Forces*, 58(1):280–289.

Roof, Wade Clark, and W. McKinney. (1985). Denominational America and the new religious pluralism. *AAPSS Annals*, 480:24–39.

Roper Organization. (April 26, 1990). Women's opinions of men take [a] turn for the worse. *The Philadelphia Inquirer.*

Rose, Arnold M. (1967). *The Power Structure.* New York: Oxford University Press.

Rose, Gerry B. (1982). *Outbreaks.* New York: Free Press.

Rosenbaum, J. (1979). Organizational career mobility: Promotion chances in a corporation during periods of growth and contraction. *American Journal of Sociology*, 85:21–48.

Rosenberg, Charles E. (1989). What is an epidemic? AIDS in historical perspective. *Daedalus*, 10:21–35.

Rosenblum, M. (February 15, 1987). As birthrates drop, Europe worries about its future. *The Philadelphia Inquirer*, p. A3.

Rosenfeld, Anne, and Elizabeth Stark. (May 1987). The prime of our lives. *Psychology Today*, pp. 62–72.

Rosenhan, David L. (1973). On being sane in insane places. *Science*, 179:250–258.

Rosenthal, Robert, and Lenore Jacobson. (1968). *Pygmalion in the Classroom.* New York: Holt Rinehart and Winston.

Rosenzweig, Mark R., and Kenneth I. Wolpin. (1990). Paternal and Public Transfers to Young Women and Their Children. Mimeo. Department of Economics, University of Minnesota.

Roser, M.A. (February 12, 1992). Report sees sex bias in schools. *The Philadelphia Inquirer*, p. B3.

Rosnow, Ralph L., and G A. Fine. (1976). *Rumor and Gossip: The Social Psychology of Hearsay.* New York: Elsevier.

Ross, Catherine E., John Mirowsky, and William Cockerham (1983). Social class, Mexican culture, and fatalism: Their effects on psychological distress. *American Journal of Community Psychology*, 11:383–399.

Ross, Catherine E., John Mirowsky, and Joan Huber. (1983). Dividing work, sharing work, and in-between marriage patterns and depression. *American Sociological Review*, 48:809–823.

Ross, H.L. (1984). Social control through deterrence: Drinking-and-driving laws. *Annual Review of Sociology*, 10:21–35.

Rossi, Alice, and Peter Rossi. (1990). *Of Human Bonding: Parent–Child Relations across the Life Course.* New York: Aldine de Gruyter.

Rossner, Phyllis. (1989). *The SAT Gender Gap: Identifying the Causes.* Washington, DC: Center for Women's Policy Studies.

Rostow, Walt W. (1960). *The Stages of Economic Growth.* Cambridge, MA: Harvard University Press.

Rothenberg, Paul S. (1992). *Race, Class, and Gender in the United States.* New York: St. Martin's Press.

Rothman, Barbara K. (1989). *Recreating Motherhood: Ideology and Technology in a Patriarchal Society.* New York: W.W. Norton.

Rothstein, Mark A. (Fall 1989). Medical screening: AIDS, rights, and health care costs. *National Forum*, pp. 7–10.

Roudi, Nazy. (1988). The demography of Islam. *Population Today,* 16(3):6–9.

Ruan, Fang F. and Yung-Mei Tsai. (1988). Male homosexuality in contemporary mainland China. *Archives of Sexual Behavior,* 17:2.

Rubin, Lillian B. (1992). Changing expectations: New sources of strain. In *Contemporary Issues in Society,* Hugh F. Lena, William B. Helmreich, and William McCord, eds. New York: McGraw-Hill.

Rubin, Lillian B. (1993). The empty nest. In *Sociology: Windows on Society.* Los Angeles, CA: Roxbury Publishing Co.

Rupp, Leila J., and Verta Taylor. (1987). *Survival in the Doldrums: The American Women's Rights Movement, 1960s.* New York: Oxford University Press.

Rushmer, Robert E. (1975). *Humanizing Health Care: Alternative Futures for Medicine.* Cambridge, MA: MIT Press.

Russell, Diane E. (1975). *The Politics of Rape: The Victim's Perspective.* New York: Stein and Day.

Russell, Diane E. (1982). *Rape in Marriage.* New York: Macmillan.

Russell, Diane E. (1984). *Sexual Exploitation: Rape, Child Sexual Abuse and Workplace Harassment.* Beverly Hills, CA: Sage.

Russell, Diane E. (1986). *The Secret Trauma: Incest in the Lives of Girls and Women.* New York: Basic Books.

Rutter, Michael, and Henri Giller. (1984). *Juvenile Delinquency: Trends and Perspectives.* New York: Guilford.

Rutter, P. (1989). *Sex in the Forbidden Zone.* Trenton, NJ: Jeremy Tarcher Press.

Ryan, William. (1982). *Equality.* New York: Vintage.

Rybczynski, Witold. (1983). *Taming the Tiger: The Struggle to Control Technology.* New York: Penguin.

Rybczynski, Witold. (1991). *Waiting for the Weekend.* New York: Viking.

Ryder, Norman B. (1973). Recent trends and group, differences in fertility. Pp. 57–68 in *Toward the End of Growth Population in America,* C.F. Westoff, et al., eds. Englewood Cliffs, NJ: Prentice-Hall.

Sachs, A. (October 1, 1990). Handing out scarlet letters. *Time,* p. 98.

Sadoff, M. (1990). *America Gets MADD.* Irving, TX: Mothers Against Drunk Driving.

Sahlins, Marshall. (1968). Notes on the original affluent society. In *Man the Hunter,* R.B. Lee and I. De Vore, eds. Chicago: Aldine Atherton.

Saluter, A.F. (1989). Singleness in America. *Current Population Reports,* P-23, 162.

Samuelson, Robert J. (December 15, 1988). Why health care is out of control. *The Philadelphia Inquirer,* p. 27A.

Sanchirico, Andrew. (1991). The importance of small business ownership in Chinese American educational achievement. *Sociology of Education,* 64:293–304.

Sanday, Peggy. (March 1974). Penn anthropologist faults environment for low IQ. *Pennsylvania Gazette.*

Sanday, Peggy R. (1990). *Fraternity Gang Rape: Sex, Brotherhood and Privilege On Campus.* New York: New York University Press.

Sanderson, Stephen K. (1988). *Macrosociology: An Introduction to Human Societies.* New York: Harper & Row.

Sankar, A. (1986). Sisters and brothers, lovers and enemies: Marriage resistance in southern Kwangtung. Pp. 69–81 in *Anthropology and Homosexual Behavior,* E. Blackwood, ed. New York: Haworth Press.

Sanoff, Alvin P., Steve L. Hawkins, Gordon Witken, Sarah Peterson, Steve Huntley, and Michael Bose. (June 3, 1985). The American male. *U.S. News & World Report,* pp. 44–51.

Sante, Luc. (1991). *Low Life: Lures & Snares of Old New York.* New York: Random House.

Sapir, Edward. (1929). The status of linguistics as a science. *Language,* 5:207–214.

Sapir, Edward. (1949). Selected writings of Edward Sapir. In *Language, Culture and Personality,* D.G. Mondelbaun, ed. Berkeley: University of California Press.

Sapiro, Virginia. (1985). *Women, Biology, and Public Policy.* Beverly Hills, CA: Sage Publications.

Sattin, Richard, Patrick Meehan, and Linda Saltzman. (1991). Suicide among older U.S. residents. *American Journal of Public Health,* 81(9):1198–1200.

Schaeffer, Richard T. (1988). *Racial and Ethnic Groups.* Glenview, IL: Scott, Foresman.

Schaeffer, Richard T. (1989). *Sociology.* New York: McGraw-Hill.

Schaeffer, Richard T. (1990). *Racial and Ethnic Minorities.* Boston: Little, Brown.

Scheff, Thomas J. (1966). *Being Mentally Ill: A Sociological Theory.* Chicago: Aldine.

Schein, Edgar. (1978). *Occupational Socialization.* New York: Norton.

Schick, Frank L., and R. Schick (eds.). (1991). *Statistical Handbook on U.S. Hispanics.* Phoenix: Oryx Press.

Schiff, Michel, Michel Duyme, Anrick Dunaart, John Stewart, Stanislaw Tankiewicz, and Juse Feingold. (1978). Intellectual status of working class children adopted early into upper middle class homes. *Science,* 200(30):1503–1504.

Schmidt, Roger. (1980). *Exploring Religion.* Belmont, CA: Wadsworth.

Schneider, Edward, and Jack Guralnik. (1990). The aging of America: Impact on health care costs. *Journal of the American Medical Association,* 263:2335–2340.

Schneider, Susan W. (1989). *Intermarriage: The Challenge of Living with Differences Between Christians and Jews.* New York: Free Press.

Schneiderman, Howard G. (1992). Out of the golden ghetto. *Society,* 29:78–83.

Schoen, Robert. (1992). First unions and the stability of first marriages. *Journal of Marriage and the Family,* 54:281–284.

Schoen, Robert, and John Wooldredge. (1989). Marriage choices in North Carolina and Virginia, 1969–71 and 1979–81. *Journal of Marriage and the Family,* 51:465–481.

Schoenberger, K. (1989). Women relegated to second-class status in South Korea. *The Philadelphia Inquirer,* p. M6.

Schogol, Mark. (August 29, 1990). Glued to the tube. *The Philadelphia Inquirer.*

Schor, Juliet, and L. Leete-Guy. (1992). *The Overworked American.* New York: Basic Books.

Schumacher, Ernst Friedrich. (1973). *Small is Beautiful: Economics as if People Mattered.* New York: Harper & Row.

Schuman, Howard, and Lawrence Bobo. (1988). Survey-based experiments on white racial attitudes toward residential integration. *American Journal of Sociology,* 94:273–299.

Schumann, H.W. (1974). *Buddhism: An Outline of Its Teachings and Schools.* Wheaton, IL: The Theosophical Publishing House, Quest Books.

Schwartz, Joseph. (1992). *The Creative Moment. How Science Made Itself Alien to Modern Culture.* New York: Harper Collins.

Schwartz-Cowen, Ruth. (1976). The "industrial revolution" in the home: Household technology and social change in the 20th century. *Technology and Culture,* 17:13.

Science News. (July 6, 1991). Phone glitches and other computer faults, *Science News,* 7.

Segalen, Martine. (1986). *Historical Anthropology of the Family.* New York: Cambridge University Press.

Segall, Marshall H., Pierre R. Dasen, John W. Berry, and Ype H. Poortinga. (1990). *Human Behavior in Global Perspective: An Introduction to Cross-Cultural Psychology.* New York: Pergamon Press.

Sells, Lucy. (February 28–29, 1978). Mathematics—a critical filter. *Science Teacher.*

Seltzer, Judith. (1991). Relationships between fathers and children who live apart: The father's role after separation. *Journal of Marriage and the Family,* 53:79–101.

Seltzer, Robert M. (1980). *Jewish People, Jewish Thought: The Jewish Experience in History.* New York: Macmillan.

Sen, K.M. (1961). *Hinduism.* Baltimore, MD: Penguin.

Sewell, William Hamilton, and Robert M. Hauser. (1975). *Education, Occupation and Earnings: Achievement in the Early Career.* New York: Academic Press.

Shaffir, W.B., R.A. Stebbins, and A. Turowetz (eds.). (1980). *Fieldwork Experience: Qualitative Approaches to Social Research.* New York: St. Martin's Press.

Sheckley, Robert. (1968). The people trap. Pp. 3–20 in *Social Problems through Science Fiction,* Martin H. Greenberg, John W. Milstead, Joseph D. Olander, and Patrica Warrick, eds. New York: St. Martins Press.

Sheehan, Thomas. (October 1976). Senior esteem as a factor in Socioeconomic complexity. *The Gerontologist,* 16(5):433–440.

Shepher, Joseph. (1983). *Incest: A Biosocial View.* New York: Academic Press.

Sherif, M. (1956). Experiments in group conflict. *Scientific American,* 54–58.

Sherman, Howard J. (1987). *Foundations of Radical Political Economy.* Armonk, NY: M.E. Sharpe.

Shilts, Randy. (1987). *While the Band Played On: Politics, People, and the AIDS Epidemic.* New York: St. Martin's Press.

Shorter, Edward. (1982). *A History of Women's Bodies.* New York: Basic Books.

Shrum, Wesley. (1991). Critics and publics: Cultural mediation in highbrow and popular performing arts. *American Journal of Sociology,* 97:347–375.

Simmel, Georg. (1904). The sociology of conflict. *American Journal of Sociology,* 9:490 ff.

Simmel, G. (1950). *The Sociology of Georg Simmel* (K.H. Wolff, Trans. and Ed.). New York: The Free Press.

Simon Herbert A. (1976). *Administrative Behavior.* New York: Free Press.

Simon, Herbert A. (1977). *Models of Discovery.* Boston: D. Reidel.

Simon, Julian L. (1981). *The Ultimate Resource.* Princeton, NJ: Princeton University Press.

Simon, Julian L. (1989). On population and economic development. *Population and Development Review,* 15(2):323–332.

Simpson, Ida Harper. (1979). *From Student to Nurse: A Longitudinal Study of Socialization.* New York: Cambridge University Press.

Singer, Dorothy. (1983). A time to re-examine the role of television in our lives. *American Psychologist,* 38(7):815–816.

Singer, Irving. (1987). *The Nature of Love.* Volume 3: *The Modern World.* Chicago: University of Chicago Press.

Singer, Jerome, and Dorothy Singer. (1983). Psychologists look at television: Cognitive, developmental, personality and social policy implications. *American Psychologist,* 38(1):825–834.

Sivard, R. (1985). *Women—a World Survey.* Washington, DC: World Priorities.

Skinner, B.F. (1948). *Walden Two.* New York: Macmillan.

Skinner, B.F. (1974). *About Behaviorism.* New York: Alfred A. Knopf.

Skocpol, Theda. (1979). *States and Social Revolutions: A Comparative Analysis of France, Russia and China.* New York: Cambridge University Press.

Skogan, Wesley G. (1987). The impact of victimization on fear. *Crime and Delinquency,* 33:135–154.

Skolnick, Arlene. (1986). *The Psychology of Human Development.* New York: Harcourt Brace Jovanovich.

Slattery, Martha L., and D.R. Jacobs, Jr. (1988). Physical fitness and cardiovascular disease mortality: The U.S. Railroad study. *American Journal of Epidemiology,* 127:571–580.

Smart, Ninian. (1969). *The Religious Experience of Mankind.* New York: Charles Scribner's Sons.

Smeeding, T.M. (1990). Social thought and poor children. *Focus,* 12(3):11–14.

Smelser, Neil J. (1962). *Theory of Collective Behavior.* New York: Free Press.

Smilgis, Martha. (April 20, 1987). Here come the DINKs. *Time,* p. 75.

Smith, C.J. (1988). *Public Problems: This Management of Urban Distress.* New York: The Guilford Press.

Smith, David A., and D.R. White. (1992). Structure and dynamics of the global economy: Network analysis of international trade, 1965–1980. *Social Forces,* 70:857–893.

Smith, Daniel Scott. (1973). Parental power and marriage patterns: An analysis of historical trends in Hingham, Massachusetts. *Journal of Marriage and the Family,* 35:419–428.

Smith, Tom W. (1985). Trends in attitudes on sexual and reproductive issues. *GSS Social Change Report* No. 23. Washington, DC: NORC.

Smith, Tom W. (Spring 1988). Speaking out: Hite vs. Abby in methodological messes. *AAPOR News,* pp. 3–4.

Smith, Tom W. (1990). Adult sexual behavior in 1989: Number of partners, frequency, and risk. *GSS Topical Report* No. 18.

Smollar, Jacqueline, and Theodora Ooms. (1987). *Young Unwed Fathers.* Washington, DC: U.S. Government Printing Office.

Smothers, Marion Lee. (March 10, 1990). Black women: Myth and reality. *The Philadelphia Inquirer,* p. A7.

Snow, David A., Louis A. Zurcher, and Robert Peters. (1981). Victory celebrations as theater: A dramaturgical approach to crowd behavior. *Symbolic Interaction,* 4(1).

Snow, Margaret E., Carol N. Jacklin, and Eleanor E. Maccoby. (1981). Birthorder differences in peer sociability at thirty-three months. *Child Development,* 52:580–595.

Snow, Margaret E., Carol N. Jacklin, and Eleanor E. Maccoby. (1983). Sex-of-child differences in father-child interaction at one year of age. *Child Development,* 54:227–232.

Sobel, Dava. (October 28, 1980). Siblings: Studies find rivalry, dependency revive in adulthood. *The New York Times,* p. C1.

Soldo, Beth, and Emily Agree. (1988). America's elderly. *Population Bulletin,* 43(3). Washington, DC: Population Reference Bureau.

Solomon, Robert C. (1987). *About Love: Reinventing Romance for Our Times.* New York: Simon & Schuster.

South, Scott J. (1991). Sociodemographic differentials in mate selection preferences. *Journal of Marriage and the Family,* 53:928–940.

Sowell, Thomas. (1983). *The Economics and Politics of Race.* New York: Morrow.

Speer, J.A. (1984). The new Christian Right and its parent company: A study in political contrasts. Pp. 19–40 in *New Christian Politics,* D.A. Bromley and A. Shupe, eds. Macon, GA: Mercer University Press.

Spenner, Kenneth T. (1988). Social stratification work and personality. *Annual Review of Sociology,* 14:69–97.

Spickard, Paul R. (1989). *Mixed Blood: Intermarriage and Ethnic Identity in Twentieth Century America.* Madison: University of Wisconsin Press.

Spilerman, S. (1977). Careers, labor market structure and socioeconomic achievement. *American Journal of Sociology,* 83:551–593.

Spitz, Rene D. (1951). The psychogenic diseases of infancy: An attempt at their etiological classification. *Psychoanalytic Study of the Child,* 6:255–275.

Spitze, Glenna. (1988). Women's employment and family relations: A review. *Journal of Marriage and the Family,* 50:595–618.

Spitze, Glenna, and John Logan. (1990). Sons, daughters and intergenerational social support. *Journal of Marriage and the Family,* 52:420–430.

Squire, Peverill. (1988). Why the 1936 Literary Digest poll failed. *Public Opinion Quarterly,* 52:125–133.

Srinivas, M.N. (1971). *Social Change in Modern India.* Berkeley: University of California Press.

Stacey, William, and Anson Shupe. (1984). The family secrets: Domestic violence in America. *Journal of Marriage and the Family,* 46(2):155–156.

Stack, Carol B. (1975). *All Our Kin.* New York: Harper & Row.

Stack, S. (1983). The effect of the decline in institutionalized religion on suicide, 1954–1978. *Journal for the Scientific Study of Religion,* 22.

Stahl, Sidney, and Marty Lebedum. (1974). Mystery gas: An analysis of mass hysteria. *Journal of Health and Social Behavior,* 15:44–50.

Staines, Graham L., and Joseph H. Peck. (1983). *The Impact of Work Schedules on the Family.* Ann Arbor: Institute for Survey Research, University of Michigan.

Star, Susan H. Leigh. (1988). Introduction: The sociology of science and technology. *Social Problems,* 35:197–205.

Starfield, B., S. Shapiro, J. Weiss, K.Y. Liang, K. Ra, D. Paige, and X.B. Wang. (1991). Race, family income, and low birth weight. *American Journal of Epidemiology,* 134:1167–1174.

Stark, Rodney. (1984). The rise of a new world faith. *Review of Religions Research,* 26.

Stark, Rodney. (1985). *Sociology.* Belmont, CA: Wadsworth.

Stark, Rodney, and W. Bainbridge. (1979). Of churches, sects, and cults: Preliminary concepts for a theory of religious movements. *Journal for the Scientific Study of Religion*, 18:117–133.

Stark, Rodney, and W. Bainbridge. (1985). *The Future of Religion: Secularization, Revival and Cult Formation.* Berkeley, CA: University of California Press.

Stark, Rodney, and C. Glock. (1968). *American Piety: The Nature of Religious Commitment.* Berkeley, CA: University of California Press.

Stavrianos, L.S. (1983). *A Global History: The Human Heritage* (3d ed.). Englewood Cliffs, NJ: Prentice-Hall.

Steinberg, Stephen. (1989). *The Ethnic Myth.* Boston: Beacon.

Sternlieb, Gary, and James Hughes. (1986). Demographics and housing in America. *Population Bulletin*, 41(1). Washington, DC: Population Reference Bureau.

Stevens, Rosemary. (1989). *In Sickness and in Wealth: American Hospitals in the Twentieth Century.* New York: Basic Books.

Stone, Lawrence. (1982). The historical origins of the modern family. *The Fifth Annual O. Meredith Wilson Lecture of History.* Salt Lake City: Department of History, University of Utah.

Stone, Robyn, Gail Lee Cafferia, and Judith Sangl. (1982). Caregivers of the frail elderly: A national profile. *The Gerontologist*, 27:622.

Stoner, C., and J. Parke. (1977). *All God's Children.* Radnor, PA: Chilton Book.

Stouffer, Samuel A., E.A. Suchman, L.C. DeVinney, S.A. Star, and R.M. Williams, Jr. (1949). *The American Soldier.* Princeton, NJ: Princeton University Press.

Straus, Murray A., and Gerald T. Hotaling. (1980). *The Social Causes of Husband–Wife Violence.* Minneapolis: University of Minneapolis Press.

Strauss, Anselm, Shizuko Fagerhaugh, Barbara Suczek, and Carolyn Wiener. (July–August 1991). AIDS and health care deficiencies. *Society*, 63–72.

Strieber, Whitley, and Jay Kunetka. (1986). *Nature's End.* New York: Warner Books.

Strosberg, Martin, Alan Fein, and James Carroll. (1989). *Rationing Medical Care for the Critically Ill.* Washington, DC: The Brookings Institution.

Stub, Holger. (1982). *The Social Consequences of Long Life.* Springfield, IL: Thomas.

Stycos, J. Mayone. (1987). Demography as an interdiscipline. *Sociolog.cal Forum*, 2:616–617.

Sullivan, Harry S. (1953). *The Interpersonal Theory of Psychiatry.* New York: W.W. Norton.

Surgeon General, United States. (1988). *Surgeon General's Report on Nutrition and Health.* Washington, DC: U.S. Government Printing Office.

Susser, Mervyn, Maureen C. Hatch, Sylvan Wallenstein, Jan Beyea, and Jeri W. Nieves. (1991). Cancer rates after the Three Mile Island nuclear accident and proximity of residence to the plant. *American Journal of Public Health*, 81(6):719–724.

Sutherland, Edwin H. (1940). White collar criminality. *American Sociological Review*, 5:1–12.

Swanson, G. (1974). *The Birth of the Gods.* Ann Arbor: University of Michigan Press.

Szasz, Thomas S. (1961). *The Myth of Mental Illness.* New York: Hoeber.

Szuic, Tad. (1990). *Then and Now: How the World Changed Since World War II.* New York: William Morrow.

Szymanski, A. (1983). *Class Structure: A Critical Perspective.* New York: Praeger.

Talbott, S. (December 14, 1992). Dealing with anti-countries. *Time.*

Tan, Amy. (1989). *The Joy Luck Club.* New York: George Putnam's Sons.

Taylor, Howard. (1980). *The IQ Game.* New Brunswick, NJ: Rutgers University Press.

Teich, Albert H. (ed.). (1990a). *Technology and the Future.* New York: St. Martin's Press.

Teich, Albert H. (1990b). Reshaping technology. Pp. 221–222 in *Technology and the Future*, A.H. Teich, ed. New York: St. Martin's Press.

Teitelbaum, Michael, and Jay Winter. (1985). *The Fear of Population Decline.* New York: Academic Press.

Temerlin, Maurice K. (1975). *Lucy: Growing Up Human.* Palo Alto, CA: Science and Behavior Books.

Temple, Robert. (1989). *The Genius of China: 3,000 Years of Science, Discovery, and Invention.* New York: Simon & Schuster.

Tenzer, Lawrence R. (1990). *A Completely New Look at Interracial Sexuality.* Jersey City, NJ: Scholars Publishing House.

Theodorsen, George A., and Achilles G. Theodorson. (1969). *Modern Dictionary of Sociology.* New York: Thomas Crowell.

Therborn, G. (1976). *Science, Class and Society.* London: NLB.

Theroux, Paul. (1986). *O-Zone.* New York: George Putnam's Sons.

Thoits, Peggy A. (1986). Multiple identities: Examining gender and marital status differences in distress. *American Sociological Review,* 51:259–272.

Thomas, Alexander, and Stella Chess. (1977). *Temperament and Development.* New York: Bruner and Mazel.

Thomas, Alexander, and Stella Chess. (1980). *The Dynamics of Psychosocial Development.* New York: Bruner and Mazel.

Thomas, E.J. (1975). *The Life of Buddha as Legend and History.* London: Routledge & Kegan Paul.

Thompson, G.P. (1985). The environmental movement goes to business school. *Environment,* 27(4):7–11.

Thompson, Kenneth. (1986). *Beliefs and Ideology.* New York: Tavistock Publications.

Thomson, Elizabeth, and Ugo Colella. (1992). Cohabitation and marital stability: Quality or commitment. *Journal of Marriage and the Family,* 54:259–267.

Thornton, Arland. (1985). Changing attitudes toward separation and divorce: Causes and consequences. *American Journal of Sociology,* 90:856–872.

Thornton, Arland. (1989). Changing attitudes toward family issues in the United States. *Journal of Marriage and the Family,* 51:873–893.

Thornton, Arland, D.F. Alwin, and D. Camburn. (1983). Causes and consequences of sex-role attitudes and attitude change. *American Sociological Review,* 48:711–727.

Thornton, Arland, and Deborah Freedman. (1983). The changing American family. *Population Bulletin,* 38(4). Washington, DC: Population Reference Bureau.

Thurow, L. (1987). A Surge in Inequality. *Scientific American,* 256:30–37.

Tien, H. Yuan. (1983). China: Demographic billionaire. *Population Bulletin,* 38(2). Washington, DC: Population Reference Bureau.

Tien, H. Yuan. (1992). China's demographic dilemmas. *Population Bulletin,* 47(1).Washington, DC: Population Reference Bureau.

Tilly, Charles. (1973). Revolutions and collective violence. In *Handbook of Political Science,* F.I. Greenstein and N.W. Polsby, eds. Reading, MA: Addison-Wesley.

Tilly, Charles. (1978). *From Mobilization to Revolution.* Reading, MA: Addison-Wesley.

Tilly, Charles. (1981). *As Sociology Meets History.* New York: Academic Press.

Tilly, Charles. (1991). Changing forms of revolution. In *Revolution and Counter-Revolution,* E.E. Rice, ed. Cambridge, MA: Basil Blackwell.

Tilly, Charles. (1992). States and nationalism in Europe since 1600. The Working Paper Series, 128. New York: Center for Studies of Social Change, New School for Social Research.

Time. (March 5, 1990). Research for men only, p. 59.

Time. (January 11, 1993). Megacities, pp. 34–36.

Tipton, Steven M. (1982). *Getting Saved from the Sixties: Moral Meaning in Conversion and Cultural Change.* Berkeley: University of California Press.

Tischler, H., P. Whitten, and D. Hunter. (1986). *Introduction to Sociology.* New York: Holt, Rinehart, and Winston.

Tittle, Charles R., Wayne J. Villemez, and Douglas A. Smith. (1978). The myth of social class and criminality. *American Sociological Review,* 43:643–650.

Tobin, Joseph J., David Y.H. Wu, and David H. Davidson. (1989). *Preschool in Three Cultures: Japan, China and the United States.* New Haven, CT: Yale University Press.

Tocqueville, Alexis de. (1852/1955). *The Old Regime and the French Revolution.* Garden City, NY: Doubleday.

Tomasson, Richard. (1980). *Iceland: The First New Society.* Minneapolis: University of Minnesota Press.

Tönnies, Ferdinand. (1887). *Community and Society.* East Lansing: Michigan State University Press.

Torrey, Edwin Fuller. (1988). *Nowhere To Go: The Tragic Odyssey of the Homeless Mentally Ill.* New York: Harper & Row.

Toth, Robert C. (June 18, 1978). Fitting technology to need held critical in the Third World. *Los Angeles Times.*

Toulemon, L. (1988). Historical overview of fertility and age. *Maturitas.* Supplement 1, pp. 5–14.

Traugott, Mark. (1978). Reconceiving sexual movements. *Social Problems,* 26:38–49.

Treiman, Donald J. (1977). *Occupational Prestige in Comparative Perspective.* New York: Academic Press.

Treiman, D.J., and K.B. Yip. (1991). Educational and occupational attainment in 21 countries. Pp. 373–394 in *Cross-National Research in Sociology,* M. Kohn, ed. Newbury Park, CA: Sage.

Tripp-Reimer, T., and S.E. Wilson. (1991). Cross-cultural perspectives on fatherhood. Pp. 1–27 in *Fatherhood and Families in Cultural Context,* F.W. Bozett and S.M.H. Hanson, eds. New York: Springer.

Troeltsch, Ernst. (1931). *The Social Teaching of the Christian Churches.* New York: Macmillan.

Turner, Jonathan H. (1981). Returning to social physics: Illustrations from the work of George Herbert Mead. *Current Perspectives in Social Theory,* 2:187–208.

Turner, Jonathan H. (1985). *The Structure of Sociological Theory.* Homewood, IL: Dorsey.

Turner, Ralph H., and Lewis M. Killian. (1972). *Collective Behavior* (2d ed.). Englewood Cliffs, NJ: Prentice-Hall.

Twaddle, Andrew C., and Richard M. Hessler. (1977). *A Sociology of Health.* St. Louis, MO: F.S. Mosby.

Umberson, Debra. (1992). Relationships between adult children and their parents: Psychological consequences for both generations. *Journal of Marriage and the Family,* 54:664–674.

United Nations. (1979). Prospects of population: Methodology and assumptions. *Population Studies* 67, New York.

United Nations. (1989). *World Population Prospects 1988.* New York.

United Nations Development Programme. (1992). *Human Development Report.* New York: Oxford University Press.

United States Bureau of the Census. [USBC]. (1975). Historical Statistics of the United States, Colonial Times to 1970. Part 1. Series A 291 and A 335–349.

United States Department of Health and Human Services. (1991). *Healthy People 2000: National Health Promotion and Disease Prevention.* Washington, DC: U.S. Government Printing Office.

USBC. (1982). Characteristics of the U.S. Population Below the Poverty Level: 1980. Washington, DC: U.S. Government Printing Office.

USBC. (1984). Statistical Abstract of the United States. Washington, DC.

USBC. (1985). Money income of households, families, and persons in the United States: 1980. *Current Population Reports,* P-60, No. 149.

USBC. (1988). Department of Labor 1980, 10–11.

USBC. (1988). America's centenarians. *Current Population Reports,* P-23, No. 153.

USBC. (1989). Current Population Reports, Series P-60, No. 166. Monthly Income and Poverty Status in the United States. U.S. Government Printing Office, Washington, DC.

USBC. (1989). Current Population Reports Series P-70, No. 5-RD-1. Transitions in Income and Poverty Status: 1984–1985. U.S. Government Printing Office, Washington, DC.

USBC. (1989). Statistical Abstract of the United States, 1989. Washington, DC: U.S. Government Printing Office.

USBC. (1989a). Fertility of American women: June 1988. Current Population Reports P-20, 436.

USBC. (1989b). Current Population Reports, Series P-23, No. 159, Population Profile of the United States: 1989, Washington, DC: U.S. Government Printing Office.

USBC. (1990). Employment Earnings, January, 183–188.

USBC. (1991). Statistical Abstract of the United States. Washington, DC.

USBC. (1992a). Household and family characteristics: March 1991. Current Population Reports, Series P-20, No. 458.

USBC. (1992b). Marital status and living arrangements: March 1991. Current Population Reports, Series P-20, No. 461.

USBC. (1992c). Statistical Abstract of the United States: 1992 (112th edition), Washington, DC.

USBC. (1992d). How we are changing: Demographic state of the nation: 1992. Current Population Reports, Special Studies, Series P-23, No. 177, February.

U.S. Congress. (1991). *Federally Funded Research: Decisions for a Decade.* Office of Technology Assessment. Washington DC: U.S. Government Printing Office.

U.S. Department of Justice (1984). *Sourcebook of Criminal Justice Statistics.* Washington, DC: U.S. Government Printing Office.

U.S. Department of Justice, Federal Bureau of Investigation. (1987). *Crime in the United States* (uniform crime reports). Washington, DC: U.S. Government Printing Office.

U.S. News & World Report. (September 2, 1985). Changing profile of the U.S. labor force, pp. 46–47.

Useem, Michael, and Jerome Karabel. (1991). Pathways to top corporate management. In *The High Status Track,* P. Kingston and L. Lewis, eds. Albany, NY: SUNY Press.

Vaillant, George. (1977). *Adaptation to Life.* Boston: Little, Brown.

Valdivieso, Rafael, and Cary Davis. (1988). *U.S. Hispanics: Challenging Issues for the 1990's.* Washington, DC: Population Reference Bureau.

Van Baal, J. (1966). *Dama: Description and Analysis of Manindanim Culture (South New Guinea).* The Hague: M. Nijhoff.

van Crefeld, Martin. (1989). *Technology and War: From 2000 B.C. to the Present.* New York: The Free Press.

van de Kaa, Dirk J. (1987). Europe's second demographic transition. *Population Bulletin,* 42(1). Washington, DC: Population Reference Bureau.

van der Tak, Jean, Carl Haub, and Ellen Murphy. (1979). Our population predicament: A new look. *Population Bulletin,* 34(5). Washington, DC: Population Reference Bureau.

van Scyoc, Sydney. (1975). A visit to Cleveland General. Pp. 339–356 in *Social Problems through Science Fiction,* Martin H. Greenberg, John W. Milstead, Joseph D. Olander, and Patricia Warrick, eds. New York: St. Martin's Press.

Vander Zanden, James W. (1983). *American Minority Relations.* New York: Knopf.

Vanfossen, Beth Ensminger. (1979). *The Structure of Social Inequality.* Boston: Little, Brown.

Vaughn, Diane. (1986). *Uncoupling Turning Points in Intimate Relationships.* New York: Oxford University Press.

Veevers, Jean. (1980). *Childless by Choice.* Toronto: Butterworth.

Veevers, Jean. (1983). Researching voluntary childlessness. In *Contemporary Families and Alternative Lifestyles,* E. Macklin and R. Rubin, eds. Beverly Hills, CA: Sage.

Ventura, Stephanie J. (1982). Trends in first births to older mothers, 1970–79. *Monthly Vital Statistics Report,* 32(2), Supplement 2. Washington, DC: NCHS.

Ventura, Stephanie J. (1989). Trends and variations in first births to older women, 1979–86. *Vital Health Statistics,* 21(47). Washington, DC: NCHS.

Vera, Herman, Donna H. Berado, and Felix M. Berado. (1985). Age heterogamy in marriage. *Journal of Marriage and the Family,* 5:553–566.

Verbrugge, Lois. (1989). The twain meet: Empirical explanations of sex differences in health and mortality. *Journal of Health and Social Behavior,* 30:282–304.

Vernaci, Richard L. (February 28, 1992). Study finds poor access to physicians. Associated Press.

Veysey, L. (January/February 1988). Ideological sources of American movements. *Society,* 58–61.

Vigoda, Ralph. (February 10, 1993). More full-time college students are working full-time jobs. *The Philadelphia Inquirer.*

Viguere, R.A. (1981). *The New Right: We're Ready to Lead.* Falls Church, VA: The Viguere Co.

Vobejda, Barbara. (November 11, 1988). Asian-American quotas suspected at Harvard, UCLA. *The Philadelphia Inquirer,* p. D12.

Volti, Reidi. (1992). *Society and Technological Change.* New York: St. Martin's Press.

Vreeland, Carolyn, Bernard J. Gallagher III, and Joseph A. McFalls, Jr. (1993). The attitudes of mental health professionals on the etiology of male homosexuality: A national survey. *Psychology,* 30:1–4.

Wachs, E. (1988). *Crime-Victim Stories: New York City's Urban Folklore.* Bloomington: Indiana University Press, 1988.

Wagner, R. (1972). Incest and identity: A critique and theory on the subject of exogamy and incest prohibition. *Man,* 7:601–613.

Waite, Linda J. (1980). Working wives and the family life cycle. *American Journal of Sociology,* 86:272–294.

Walder, Andrew G. (1992). Property rights and stratification in socialist redistributive economies. *American Sociological Review,* 57:524–539.

Wallerstein, Immanuel. (1974). *The Modern World System: Capitalist Agriculture and the Origins of the European World Economy in the Sixteenth Century.* New York: Academic Press.

Wallerstein, James S., and Clement J. Wyle. (1947). Our law abiding law-breakers. *Probation,* 25:107–118.

Walshok, M. (1990). Blue collar women. Pp. 288–296 in *Technology and the Future,* A.H. Teich, ed. New York: St. Martin's Press.

Walters, Vivienne. (1982). Company doctors' perceptions of and responses to conflicting pressures from labor and management. *Social Problems,* 30:1–13.

Walton, Gary M., and Hugh Rockoff. (1990). *History of the American Economy.* San Diego: Harcourt Brace Jovanovich.

Walton, Mary. (January 7, 1990). Got it made in Mexico. *Inquirer Magazine,* pp. 14–31.

Walzer, M. (1985). *Exodus.* New York: Basic Books.

Ward, R.A., S.R. Sherman, and M. La Gory. (1984). Subjective network assessments and subjective well-being. *Journal of Gerontology,* 39:93–101.

Washburn, S.L. (1978). What we can't learn about people from apes. *Human Nature,* 1:70–75.

Watkins, Susan C. (1987). The fertility transition: Europe and the Third World compared. *Sociological Forum,* 2(4):645–673.

Watson, John B. (1925/1970). *Behaviorism.* New York: W.W. Norton.

Wattenberg, Benjamin J. (1987). *The Birth Dirth.* New York: Pharos.

Weber, Max. (1904–5/1958). *The Protestant Ethic and the Spirit of Capitalism.* New York: Scribner's.

Weber, Max. (1922a). *Economy and Society.* New York: Bedminster Press.

Weber, Max. (1922b). *The Sociology of Religion.* Boston: Beacon Press.

Weber, Max. (1947/1968). *The Theory of Social and Economic Organization* (A.M. Henderson and T. Parsons, Trans.). New York: The Free Press.

Weber, Max. (1949). *The Methodology of the Social Sciences* (Translated and edited by Edward A. Shils and Henry A. Finch). New York: The Free Press.

Weed, F.J. (1987). Grass-roots activism and the drunk driving issue: A survey of MADD chapters. *Law & Policy,* 9:259–78.

Weeks, John R. (1986). *Population.* Belmont, CA: Wadsworth.

Weeks, John R. (1988). The demography of Islamic nations. *Population Bulletin,* 43(4). Washington, DC: Population Reference Bureau.

Weeks, John R. (1992). *Population.* Belmont, CA: Wadsworth.

Wegener, Bernd. (1991). Job mobility and social ties: Social resources, prior job, and status attainment. *American Sociological Review,* 56:60–71.

Weinberg, Sandy. (1990). Expanding access to technology: Computer equity for women. Pp. 277–287 in *Technology and the Future*, A.H. Teich, ed. New York: St. Martin's Press.

Weinberg, Thomas S. (1987). Sadomasochism in the United States: A review of recent sociological literature. *Journal of Sex Research*, 23(1):50–69.

Weinstein, Sidney, and Eugene A. Sersen. (1961). Tactual sensitivity as a function of handedness and laterality. *Journal of Comparative and Physiological Psychology*, 54:665–669.

Weishaus, Sylvia, and Dorothy Field. (1988). A half century of marriage: Continuity or change? *Journal of Marriage and the Family*, 10:763–774.

Weiss, Rick. (1988). Desperately seeking sexual statistics. *Science News*, 136:28.

Weisskopf, V. (1981). A Soviet inquiry. *Worldview*, 24, 8.

Weitzman, Lenore J. (1984). Sex-role socialization: A focus on women. In *Women: A Feminist Perspective*, J. Freeman, ed. Palo Alto, CA: Mayfield.

Weller, Jack M., and E.L. Quarantelli. (November 1973). Neglected characteristics of collective behavior. *American Journal of Sociology*, 79:665–685.

Wellman, Barry. (1981). Applying network analysis to the study of support. In *Social Networks and Social Support*, B.H. Gottlieb, ed. Beverly Hills, CA: Sage.

Wellman, Barry, and S.D. Berkowitz (eds.). (1988). *Social Structures: A Network Approach.* New York: Cambridge University Press.

Wellman, Barry, P.J. Carrington, and A. Hall. (1988). Networks as personal communities. Pp. 130–184 in *Social Structures: A Network Approach*, B. Wellman and S.D. Berkowitz, eds. New York: Cambridge University Press.

Wells, Louis T. (1973). Economic man and engineering man. Choice and technology in a low-wage country. *Public Policy*, 21:319–342.

Westoff, Charles F. (1986). Fertility in the United States. *Science*, 234:554–559.

Wheeler, S. (1966). The structure of formally organized socialization settings. Pp. 112–120 in *Socialization After Childhood*, O.G. Brim and S. Wheeler, eds. New York: John Wiley & Sons.

White, Burton, Barbara Kaban, and Jane Attanucci. (1979). *The Origins of Human Competence.* Lexington, MA: D.C. Heath.

White, Harrison C. (1981a). Production markets as induced role structures. Pp. 1–57 in *Sociological Methodology*, S.L. Leinhardt, ed. San Francisco: Jossey-Bass.

White, Harrison C. (1981b). Where do markets come from? *American Journal of Sociology*, 87:517–547.

White, Harrison C. (1988). Varieties of markets. Pp. 226–261 in *Social Structures: A Network Approach*, B. Wellman and S.D. Berkowitz, eds. New York: Cambridge University Press.

White, Harrison C. (1992). *Identity and Control.* Princeton, NJ: Princeton University Press.

White, Leslie A. (1969). *The Science of Culture.* New York: Farrar, Straus & Giroux.

White, Lynn K. (1990). Determinants of divorce: A review of research in the eighties. *Journal of Marriage and the Family*, 52:904–912.

White, Michael. (1987). *American Neighborhoods and Residential Differentiation.* New York: Russell Sage Foundation.

Whitehead, Harriet. (1981). The bow and burden strap: A new look at institutionalized homosexuality in native North America. Pp. 80–115 in *Sexual Meanings: The Cultural Construction of Gender and Sexuality*, S.B. Ortner and H. Whitehead, eds. New York: Cambridge University Press.

Whittemore, A.S., A.H. Wo-Williams, M. Lee, Z. Shu, R.P. Gallagher, J. Deng-ao, et al. (1990). Diet, physical activity, and colorectal cancer among Chinese in North America and China. *Journal of the National Cancer Institute*, 82(11):915–926.

Whorf, B.L. (1956). The relation of habitual thought and behavior to language. In *Language, Thought and Reality*, B.L. Whorf, ed. Cambridge, MA: MIT Press.

Whyte, Martin K. (1990). *Dating, Mating, and Marriage.* New York: Aldine de Gruyter.

Whyte, William Hollingsworth. (1957). *The Organization Man.* Garden City, NY: Doubleday.

Wiegand, Ginny. (November 22, 1992). Woman of the streets. *The Philadelphia Inquirer Magazine,* pp. 12–29.

Wilcox, C. (1989). Support for the Christian Right old and new: A comparison of supporters of the anti-communism crusade and the Moral Majority. *Sociological Focus,* 22(2):87–97.

Wiley, Norbert. (1979). Notes on self-genesis: From me to we to I. *Studies in Symbolic Interaction,* 2:87–105.

Will, George. (August 11, 1988). If a disease is preventable, why should insurance pay for it? *The Philadelphia Inquirer,* p. A24.

Willet, W., M. Stampfer, G.A. Colditz, et al. (1991). Postmenopausal estrogen therapy and cardiovascular disease. *New England Journal of Medicine,* 325(11):756–762.

Williams, John, Howard Giles, John R. Edwards, Deborah L. Best, and John T. Daws. (1977). Sex-trait stereotypes in England, Ireland, and the United States. *British Journal of Social and Clinical Psychology,* 16:303–309.

Williams, Linda B., and William F. Pratt. (1990). Wanted and unwanted childbearing in the United States, 1973–1988. *Advance Data from Vital Statistics,* 189. Hyattsville, MD: National Center for Health Statistics.

Williams, Raymond. (1965). *The Long Revolution.* New York: Penguin Books.

Williams, Redford B., J.C. Barefoot, R.M. Califf, T.L. Haney, W.B. Saunders, D.B. Pryor, M.A. Hlatky, I.C. Siegler, and D.B. Mark. (1992). Prognostic importance of social and economic resources among medically treated patients with angiographically documented coronary artery disease. *Journal of the American Medical Association,* 267(4):520–524.

Williams, Robin M., Jr. (1970). *American Society: A Sociological Interpretation.* New York: Knopf.

Williams, William. (1983). Health Care Cost Containment and Cost Shifting. Unpublished pamphlet. Provident Mutual Insurance Co.

Wilson, Brian. R. (1982). *Religion in Sociological Perspective.* New York: Oxford University Press.

Wilson, Edward O. (1975). *Sociology.* Cambridge, MA: Belknap Press.

Wilson, Edward O. (1979). *On Human Nature.* New York: Bantom.

Wilson, John. (1973). *Introduction to Social Movements.* New York: Basic Books.

Wilson, John. (1978). *Religion in American Society: The Effective Presence.* Englewood Cliffs, NJ: Prentice-Hall.

Wilson, Stephen. (1985). Personal communication.

Wilson, William J. (1987). *The Truly Disadvantaged: The Inner City, the Underclass, and Public Policy.* Chicago: University of Chicago Press.

Wilson, William J. (1991). Studying inner-city social dislocations: The challenge of public agenda research. *American Sociological Review,* 56:1–14.

Wingrove, David. (1990). *Chung Kuo: The Middle Kingdom.* New York: Dell Publishing.

Winn, Marie. (1985). *The Plug-In Drug: Television, Children and the Family.* New York: Penguin.

Winn, Rhonda, and Niles Newton. (1980). Sexuality in aging: A study of 106 cultures. *Archives of Sexual Behavior,* 11:293–298.

Wirth, Louis. (1938). Urbanism as a way of life. *American Journal of Sociology,* 44:3–24.

Wolf, Naomi. (1991). *The Beauty Myth.* New York: Morrow.

Wolfe, Linda. (1981). *The Cosmo Report.* New York: Arbor House.

Wolfe, Linda. (1989). *Wasted: The Preppie Murder.* New York: Simon & Schuster.

Wolfe, Sidney M., P. Boyle, D. Callahan, J.J. Fins, et al. (1991). Sources of concern about the Patient Self-Determination Act. *New England Journal of Medicine,* 325(23):1666–1671.

Wolfinger, Raymond E. (July–August 1991). Voter turnout. *Society,* 23–26.

Womak, James P., Daniel T. Jones, and Daniel Roos. (1991). *The Machine that Changed the World.* New York: Macmillan.

Woodward, K. (January 6, 1992). Talking to God. *Newsweek,* pp. 39–44.

World Population Conference. (1974). World Population Plan of Action, August. Washington DC: U.S. Agency for International Development.

Wright, Stuart. (1978). *Crowds and Riots: A Study in Social Organization.* Beverly Hills, CA: Sage.

Wrong, Dennis H. (1961). The oversocialized conception of man in modern sociology. *American Sociological Review,* 26:183–193.

Wrong, Dennis H. (1979). *Power: Its Forms, Bases and Uses.* New York: Harper & Row.

Wuthnow, Robert. (1985). The growth of religious reform movements. *AAPSS Annals,* 480:106–116.

Wuthnow, R. (1988). *The Restructuring of American Religion.* Princeton, NJ: Princeton University Press.

Xiaohe, Xu, and Martin K. Whyte. (1990). Love matches and arranged marriages: A Chinese replication. *Journal of Marriage and the Family,* 52:709–722.

Yakoubian, V., and F.J. Hacker. (1989). Reactions to disaster at a distance: The first week after the earthquake in Soviet Armenia. *Bulletin of the Menninger Clinic,* 53:331–339.

Yankelovich, David. (1981). *New Rules: Searching for Self-Fulfillment in a World Turned Upside Down.* New York: Random House.

Yinger, J. Milton. (1970). *The Scientific Study of Religion.* London: Macmillan.

Yinger, J. Milton. (1985). Ethnicity. *Annual Review of Sociology,* 11:151–180.

Young, Michael. (1961). *The Rise of the Meritocracy.* Baltimore, MD: Penguin.

Young, Rosalie F., and Elizabeth A. Olson (eds.). (1991). *Health, Illness, and Disability in Later Life.* Newbury Park, CA: Sage.

Young, T.R. (1988). The social sources of gender oppression. *Newsletter of the Society for the Study of Social Problems,* 19:20–22.

Zablocki, B. (1980). Alienation and Charisma: A Study of Contemporary American Communities. New York: Free Press.

Zachariah, K., and My Vu. (July 1979). Population projections 1975 and long term (stationary population), unpublished tables. Washington, DC: World Bank.

Zanker, A., R. Knight, R. Chesnoff, and D. Stanglin. (March 31, 1986). Europe's immigration battles. *U.S. News & World Report,* pp. 25–27.

Zborowski, Mark. (1952). Cultural components in responses to pain. *Journal of Social Issues,* 8(4):16–30.

Zimbardo, Philip G. (1972). Pathology of imprisonment. *Society,* 9:4–6.

Zindell, D. (1988). *Neverness.* New York: Bantam Books.

Zucchino, David. (January 1, 1988). Feasting on a seasonal delight: Caterpillar. *The Philadelphia Inquirer.*

Zussman, Robert. (1985). *Mechanics of the Middle Class: Work and Politics Among American Engineers.* Berkeley: University of California Press.

Glossary

absolute poverty—the state in which material resources are not adequate to provide for minimal physical necessities (defined in the S.O. by the Federal Poverty Line).

acculturation—the process of taking norms and values from one culture and incorporating them into another culture.

achieved status—a position acquired by an individual through his or her own efforts.

affective individualism—the recognition of the self as a unique being with the right to pursue selfish goals.

ageism—discrimination and prejudice against persons of a certain age, especially the elderly.

AIDS—An acronym for the disease caused by the immunodeficiency virus (Acquired Immuno-Deficiency Syndrome).

alcoholism—an addiction to the drug alcohol.

alienation—a sense of estrangement from self and others in society.

altruistic suicide—caused by excessive social integration.

American dream—the ideals of freedom, equality, and especially opportunity traditionally stressed as available to individuals in the United States.

androgynous—having a balance of traditional feminine and masculine personality traits.

animism—the attribution of a soul or spirit to living things and inanimate objects.

anomie—the weakening of moral regulation of the sect associated with personal and social disorder.

anticipatory reference group—a group whose standards are internalized in advance of personal membership.

anticipatory socialization—a process of learning directed toward gaining a desired membership in a peer group.

appropriate technologies—technology well-suited to the capital and labor characteristics of a society.

ascribed status—a position that is not based on individual ability, skill, effort, or accomplishment, but on an inherited position in the society.

asexual—lacking sexual interest and activity.

assimilation—the absorption of a minority group into the dominant group.

assortive mating—the situation in which an individual has a higher probability of marrying similar or dissimilar mates than would be the case if random mating were in effect.

assortive narcissism—the tendency for individuals to marry someone who is similar to themselves in almost every physical and personality variable.

authority—legitimated power.

automation—the substitution of new or improved machines for workers.

belief—a system of meaning, which defines the world and explains the mysteries of existence.

bias—a distortion introduced into a study by improper sampling, measurement procedures.

bisexuality—sexual orientation toward both genders.

bivariate relationship—a statistical association relationship between two variables.

bounded rationality—a simplified model of a decision-making problem based on selected sources of information.

bourgeoisie—the capitalist class in industrial society who derive their incomes through ownership of profit-making enterprises.

bureaucracy—according to Max Weber, the distinctively modern group form characterized by specialization, hierarchy, regulations, impersonality, and technical qualifications.

bureaucratic ritualism—bureaucratic regulations being treated as more important than bureaucratic goals.

capitalism—a political economy in which the means of production are privately owned.

caste system—a hierarchical arrangement of social strata in which an individual's status is fixed at birth.

catastrophic illness—a serious medical affliction that can crush an individual or a family financially.

causality—a situation in which a change in one variable (the independent variable) produces a change in another variable (the dependent variable).

Census Bureau family—a group of two or more persons related by birth, marriage, or adoption and residing together.

charismatic authority—legitimacy is based on extraordinary personal qualities attributed to an individual by followers.

choice/constraint model—people making social choices within the constraints imposed by larger social structures.

chronic offenders—the people who regularly violate the law.

church—a formal religious organization that is well integrated into the society.

circulation mobility—the shifts in occupational position that occur within a given occupational structure.

civil religion—a set of symbols, beliefs, values, and practices that give sacred meaning to a nation and its people.

class—a set of individuals sharing a common relationship to the means of production.

class consciousness—an awareness among the members of a given class of their common interests in the class struggle.

closed-ended item—a survey question in which available answer choices are provided to the respondent in pre-coded form.

closeness—the degree of emotional intimacy in a network tie.

communism—a political economy in which there is collective ownership of the means of production, social equality, and, eventually, no state.

compliance theory—explanation of the mechanisms by which organizations gain the compliance of their members.

concept—an abstract category for classifying aspects of reality.

conflict theory—a major theoretical approach in sociology that focuses on the conflict among the social structures in a society.

conformist—a person who accepts both cultural goals and socially accepted means of achieving those goals.

conscience collective—Emile Durkheim's term for a common set of ideas and moral sentiments shared by individuals.

conservative movement—a movement that seeks to retain the status quo and resist possible change.

control group—subjects in an experiment not exposed to the experimental stimulus of the independent variable.

conversion—the adoption of a new religion, often quite different from the religion of one's parents.

core—the set of technologically advanced, developed countries with a dominant position within the world system.

counterculture—a subculture that actively challenges the norms and values of mainstream society.

crosstabulation—a table that "crosses" the frequencies of different variables to look for statistical relationships.

cult—a religious movement that is extremely unorthodox vis-à-vis the mainstream society.

cultural constants—the elementary social structures found in every society.

cultural racism—the expression of the superiority of the cultural heritage of one's race over another's.

cultural relativism—an open-minded way of thinking, which holds that there is no universal standard by which to evaluate cultures.

cultural universals—the specific practices found in every culture.

culture—the socially standardized ways of thinking, feeling, and acting that a person acquires as a member of a particular society.

culture lag—the period of social maladjustment during which non-material culture is adapting to changes in material culture.

culture lead—a social strain generated by a change in non-material culture that calls for a new material break-through.

culture of poverty—the theory that the poor have a distinctive set of subcultural beliefs and values that promote poverty.

culture shock—a feeling of disorientation engendered by moving from one culture to another.

data—the information gathered through scientific study of a phenomenon.

deinstitutionalization—the mass release of patients from mental hospitals into the community.

demographic transition—the historical shift of birth and death rates from high to low levels in a population.

demography—the study of human populations, including their size, composition, and distribution, as well as the causes and consequences of changes in these factors.

denomination—a religious organization that is involved in pluralistic competition with other such organizations from a similar tradition.

density—the degree of interconnection among network members.

deviant behavior—any behavior that fails to conform to the norms or rules of the group.

deviant person—someone who regularly violates society's most valued norms, particularly those norms established by socially elite groups.

diffusion—the spread of cultural elements from one culture to another.

discrimination—unequal treatment of members of a minority group.

dramaturgical school—Those analyzing social life as a "theatrical production."

duration—the time span over which a network tie has endured.

dysfunction—a negative consequence of a social part for the system of society.

ecclesia—a church that is formally allied with the state.

egalitarian—family authority and decision making is shared by both genders.

egoistic suicide—caused by too little social integration.

emigration—the process of leaving one country to take up residence in another.

empirical—based on the analysis of real-world experience.

enculturation—another term for socialization.

endogamy—choosing a spouse from within a particular group.

escapist/retreatist movement—a movement that withdraws from what it perceives as a corrupt society.

ethnic group—often used interchangeably with country of origin, but most commonly refers to cultural features that are handed down from one generation to the next.

ethnocentrism—the belief in the inherent superiority of one's own group and culture.

ethnomethodology—the study of common sense practical reasoning.

exchange theory—an approach to social structure that views social relations as transactions within which resources are given and taken.

exogamy—a custom requiring that marriage partners be chosen from outside a defined group.

experimental group—subjects in an experiment exposed to the experimental stimulus of the independent variable.

experimentation—a research strategy that creates an artificial situation in order to simplify reality and highlight variables of interest.

expulsion—the systematic transfer of a group of people.

extended family—three or more generations living together.

face-to-face interview—the survey format in which the items are presented to respondents in a personal conversation.

faith—when belief is not based on scientific evidence.

family—a relatively permanent group of two or more individuals related by blood, marriage, or adoption who ordinarily live together.

family of orientation—the family into which individuals are born.

family of procreation—the family formed by individuals when they marry and have or adopt children.

fecundity—the physiological ability of individuals and couples to have children.

fertility—the number of births that actually occur to an individual or a population.

focus group—an open-ended discussion among several respondents guided by the interviewer.

folkways—the norms governing everyday behavior whose violation causes little concern.

foreplay—sexual stimulation intended as a prelude to sexual intercourse.

frequency distribution—a display of the numbers and percentages of respondents for each value of a variable.

functionalism—a major theoretical approach in sociology that focuses on how social parts contribute to society as a system.

gatekeeping—the supervision of the flow through often arbitrary or unfair barriers to socially advantageous positions in society.

gemeinschaft—("community") a place of personalized relationships based on mutual acquaintanceship.

gender—the behavioral and attitudinal traits that are culturally imposed on males and females, and referred to in terms of "masculinity" and "femininity."

generalizability—the degree to which conclusions can be extended to the population outside of study participants.

generalizations—the statements typifying the behavior of large numbers of people in a social structure.

generalized belief—a widely shared explanation of strain experienced by members of a society.

genocide—a purposeful and systematic attempt to exterminate an entire people.

germ theory—the belief that acute disease is caused by microorganisms.

gesellschaft—("society") a place of impersonality based on a lack of mutual acquaintanceship.

gestational restrictions—norms against sex during pregnancy.

group—a set of persons with 1) social boundaries, 2) internal structure, and 3) common expectations.

health—a state of complete mental, physical, and social well-being.

health care—an activity intended to improve one's state of health.

hermaphrodites—people whose reproductive organs are so ambiguous that it is difficult to categorize them as either male or female.

heterosexuality—sexual orientation toward the opposite gender.

hidden curriculum—the knowledge gained by students as a consequence of going to school, though it is not intentionally taught.

homosexuality—sexual orientation toward the same gender.

household—all persons who inhabit the same housing unit.

householder—the person (or one of the persons) in whose name the housing unit is owned or rented.

human capital—the amount individuals invest in themselves, which may determine their own social success.

Human Relations Area Files—an extensive compilation of ethnographic data on sexuality as well as on other topics such as subsistence, material culture, and social structure.

hypotheses—the predictions drawn from theory that can be empirically tested.

ideal type—Max Weber's term to describe a given social phenomenon in its conceptual purity in order to reveal its essential features.

ideology—a set of ideas justifying the interests of a class.

immigration—the process of entering one country from another to take up permanent residence.

incest taboo—a norm that prohibits sexual activity between relatives.

income—all monies received as employment pay and government transfer payments.

individual racism—refers to personally held negative racial attitudes.

inequality of condition—the unequal allocation of social rewards.

inequality of opportunity—the unequal access to social rewards.

inferential statistics—the formulas used to draw a generalization about a population on the basis of sample values.

innovator—one who accepts cultural goals, but pursues them in socially unacceptable ways.

institutional racism—sources of discrimination built into the social system.

institutions—large-scale social structures that address basic societal needs.

interaction frequency—how often a network tie is activated by personal communication.

interlocking directorate—members of the executive board of one organization also sitting on the board of other organizations.

intermediate technologies—technology that is more sophisticated than traditional ways of doing things but less sophisticated than the most modern ways.

internal migration—population movement between different areas within a country.

international migration—population movement between countries.

iron law of oligarchy—Robert Michels' term for the tendency of democratic organizations to come to be dominated by a self-protective elite.

isomorphism—the structural similarity of organizations.

items—the questions asked in survey research.

kinship—a social network that links individuals with ties based on blood, marriage, or adoption.

law—a formal sanction.

legitimacy—the belief that the exercise of power is proper and acceptable.

level of analysis—the higher the level, the larger the social structure under study.

life expectancy—an estimate of the average number of additional years people of a specified age can expect to live if current mortality rates were to continue.

life span—the maximum age that human beings could reach under optimum conditions.

lifestyle factors—preventable causes of death such as smoking, alcohol and drug abuse, poor diet, lack of exercise, stress, and inadequate social networks.

mail questionnaire—the survey format in which the items and available responses are prewritten for respondents, who must answer and return the instrument by mail.

marriage—a socially and legally approved mating relationship.

master status—the individual's role that is given the greatest societal significance.

material culture—the total tangible items in society.

matriarchal—a society in which women assume the dominant positions of power and authority.

maximum average life span—the average age at death for a population under ideal health circumstances.

maximum life span—the oldest age to which a human being can live.

means of production—Karl Marx's term for the economic structure of society.

mechanical solidarity—the human attraction generated by common moral sentiments, typical of tribal societies.

median income—the income point at which half of all families earn more, and half earn less.
Medicaid—a government program of medical aid for the impoverished.
medicalization—people's abnormal behavior being viewed as a medical problem requiring treatment by physicians.
Medicare—a government program of medical aid for the elderly.
megacities—cities with at least 5 million inhabitants.
menstrual restrictions—norms against sex during the woman's menstrual period.
meritocracy—a society in which persons make their way on their own ability and talent rather than because of class privileges.
mesostructures—social relations that link higher to lower levels of social structure.
migration—the movement of people across a specified territorial boundary for the purpose of changing residence.
minority group—a subordinate group whose members have significantly less control or power over their own lives than the members of a dominant or majority group.
mob—a cohesive, emotionally aroused crowd that often engages in violent disruptive acts.
monogamy—a marriage consisting of one spouse of each gender.
monotheism—religious belief in a single divine power or entity.
mores—the norms that are sanctioned strongly.
multi-factor theory—an explanatory approach identifying multiple sources of social change.
multidimensional stratification system—the approach associated with Max Weber that analyzes the several distinctive, key, related dimensions of social inequality.
multimethod approach—the use of several research techniques in the same research project.
multinational corporations—large firms operating beyond the macrostructure of a single society.
multiple reference groups—an individual's membership in several reference groups at one time.
multiplex—a social tie with more than one relationship type.
multivariate analysis—an examination of statistical relationships among more than two variables.
natural increase—the difference between the total number of births and the total number of deaths in a population.
natural selection—the Darwinian concept based on the idea of the survival of the fittest.
negative reference group—a group by which an individual is heavily influenced, primarily because the individual does *not* want to become a member of this group.
negative relationship—a statistical association in which a higher level of one variable is associated with a lower level of another variable.
net migration—the difference between the total number of people migrating into an area and the total migrating out.
non-material culture—the ideas, beliefs, attitudes, and values of a society.
nondecision making—the process by which challenges to those in power are suppressed before power is exercised.
normal accidents—breakdowns that are an inherent property of certain kinds of tightly coupled complex organizations.
norms—those established standards of behavior that reflect societal values.
nuclear family—one or two parents living together in a household with their natural and/or adopted children.
objective dimension—the concrete, measurable human harm associated with a societal phenomenon.
objectivity—the real qualities of a thing outside the mind of the researcher observing it.
occasional restrictions—infrequent norms against sex at certain times.
open-ended items—the survey questions that allow a respondent to phrase his or her own answers.
organic solidarity—social integration based on functional dependence of specialists, typical of modern societies.
organizational environment—the larger social setting of an organization, including other organizations.
panic—the relatively rapid spread of fear from one person to another.
paradigm—an intellectual model for selecting crucial concepts and forms of evidence.
participant observation—the researcher participates in the group process in order to observe its natural functioning.
patriarchal—the societies in which men have the greatest power and make most of the family decisions.
periphery—the set of less-developed countries providing labor and raw materials to the core within the world system.
pluralism—a distribution of power that is diffused among many competing interest groups.
polyandry—one woman married to two or more men.
polygamy—marriage involving more than two parties.
polygyny—one man married to two or more women.
polytheism—religious belief in which many gods are acknowledged.
population composition—the characteristics of a population, such as age, sex, and ethnicity.
population distribution—how individuals and their population-related activities are spatially dispersed.
population growth—the sum of natural increase and net migration.
pornography—written or visual material intended chiefly to arouse sexual excitement.
positive functions—the positive consequences of social parts for the system of society.
positive relationship—a statistical association in which a higher level of one variable is associated with a higher level of another variable.
postpartum restrictions—norms against sex during a specified period of time immediately following a birth.
power—the ability to influence other people, even against their resistance.
power elite—a distribution of power that is concentrated in the hands of a tiny, consolidated elite.
prejudice—a rigid predisposition to respond to a certain group in a specific way.
prestige—"social honor," one of Weber's key dimensions of stratification systems.
primary deviance—the original deviant act.

primary group—a group characterized by intimate, multiplex, expressive relations.

primary sector—that portion of the workforce devoted to the extraction of raw materials (e.g., agriculture, mining).

probability sampling—a procedure in which the chance of a unit's selection is known in advance and can therefore estimate the rate of sampling error.

profane—that part of the world that includes the ordinary aspects of everyday life.

proletariat—the laborer class in industrial society who derive their income from wages paid by the bourgeoisie.

prophet—according to Max Weber, "a purely individual bearer of charisma, who by virtue of his mission proclaims a religious doctrine."

propinquity—spatial nearness.

prostitution—the relatively indiscriminant exchange of sexual acts for economic benefits.

race—biologically, a group of people with a common genetic heritage. Legally, an arbitrary concept often constructed to define who is not white. Socially, a subjective perception of what a person says it is.

racism—prejudice or discrimination based on perceived racial characteristics.

random mating—the situation in which an individual has an equal probability of marrying all eligible mates.

random sample—a procedure in which all population units have an equal probability of being selected.

randomization—the method by which subjects are assigned to either the experimental or control group according to the rules of chance.

rape—forcible sexual intercourse perpetrated against the will of the victim.

rate—the number of occurrences of a phenomenon for a constant base of population.

rational-legal authority—legitimacy is based on organizational position and rationalized rules.

rationalism—the systematic application of standardized means to predetermined ends.

reactionary movement—a movement that seeks to restore society, or a large part of it, to a former condition.

reactivity—artificial alterations in behavior created by an awareness of being studied.

rebels—the people who reject cultural goals and means and replace them with their own.

reference group—a group whose standards one applies to the self.

reformative movement—a movement oriented toward partial or moderate change in society.

reification—the fallacy of treating an abstraction as real.

relative deprivation/rising expectations—after a long-disadvantaged group begins to experience a slight improvement in conditions, its members see that a better life is possible, their expectations soar, and the remaining deprivation feels greater than ever, even though actual conditions have improved.

reliability—the degree to which a measurement procedure yields consistent results.

replication—the duplication of a research procedure to verify the results.

residential mobility—any change of address within a country.

resocialization—the learning and internalization of a new set of norms, values, and skills.

respondent—a participant in a survey.

response rate—the percentage of the sample actually responding to the survey.

retreatists—the people who reject cultural goals and socially accepted ways of achieving goals.

revolutionary movement—a movement that seeks large-scale, sweeping social change.

riot—a violent, active crowd composed of a large number of people and developing over long periods of time.

ritualists—the people who have given up on pursuing cultural goals but still go through the motions of achieving the goals.

rituals—the formal practices expressing and reinforcing patterns of belief.

role—a pattern of behavior appropriate for a given status.

role conflict—the inconsistency of demands across the positions of an individual's status set.

role expectations—the specific behaviors a status occupant is supposed to exhibit.

role set—a pattern of complementary roles linked to a single status.

role strain—inconsistent expectations within the role set.

ruling class—the class that controls the means of production of a given society.

rumor—an often unreliable story that circulates quickly from person to person, and is accepted as true, though its source may be unknown.

sacred—that part of the world that inspires mystery, awe, respect, and fear in people.

sadomasochism—the infliction of physical pain during foreplay or sexual intercourse.

sample—a set of people systematically selected from the larger population about which the researcher wishes to generalize.

sampling frame—the list of population units from which a sample is drawn.

sanctions—a reward or punishment for adhering to or violating norms.

satisfice—a decision that is satisfactory and sufficient, rather than a perfect decision based on complete rationality.

second shift—the other "job" gainfully employed wives and mothers have in the home, doing the bulk of household tasks.

secondary analysis—the re-use of datasets already compiled by public or private organizations.

secondary deviance—the deviant acts that result from a person being labeled a deviant.

secondary group—a group characterized by impersonal, uniplex, instrumental relations.

secondary sector—that portion of the workforce devoted to the conversion of raw material into made valued goods (e.g., manufacturing, construction).

secondary socialization—the socialization that occurs during adulthood.

sect—an informal religious structure that is not well integrated into the larger society.

secularization—a general decline in the social authority of religion, often associated with technologically advanced societies.

segmentation—broad divisions among types of workers reinforced by political and cultural dimensions.

segregation—any form of separation of races or ethnic groups in a variety of institutional spheres, including occupations, political participation, and social memberships.

self-fulfilling prophecy—a prediction that leads to behavior that fulfills the prediction.

semi-periphery—the set of countries intermediate between the core and periphery within the world system.

sex—refers to the biological characteristics that divide the human species into two fundamental groupings, male and female.

sex-limited (traits)—those traits carried on genes that are not on either of the sex chromosomes but are typically manifest in only one sex.

sex-linked (traits)—those traits that are carried partially or totally on one of the sex chromosomes.

sexism—the belief that one gender is inferior to the other.

sexual dysfunction—problems affecting sexual performance such as impotence and lack of sexual desire.

sexual harassment—exists in the workplace if an employee must submit to sexual demands to get a job, keep a job, or be promoted.

sick role—a pattern of behavior expected of someone who is ill.

social capital—the social resources for achievement stored in the personal network; the set of interpersonal resources overlaying the personal investments of the American Dream formula.

social category—an aggregate of individuals who share a common trait.

social control—a set of methods designed to ensure that people abide by the norms and rules of the empowered group.

social facts—Emile Durkheim's term for the supra-individual phenomena that are the subject matter of sociology.

social integration—the forces binding society together.

social movement—a conscious, collective, organized attempt to bring about or resist large-scale change in the social order by non-institutionalized means.

social network—the patterns of ties among the units of a social system.

social strain—a social setting receptive to collective action, due to sudden disruption, long-term social change, or ongoing value conflicts, which generate feelings of tension.

social support—emotional and practical help provided by network members.

socialism—a political economy in which there is state ownership of the means of production and no private property.

socialization—a basic social process through which an individual becomes integrated into a social group by learning the group's rules as well as his or her role in that group.

society—a large number of people who live in the same territory and are relatively independent of others outside their area.

socioeconomic status (SES)—an index of class position based on a composite of several dimensions such as income, education, and occupational prestige.

sociological imagination—C. Wright Mills' famous term for the discipline's ability to show the relationship between social and personal patterns.

sociology—the scientific study of the relationship between social structure and human behavior.

squatter settlements—areas surrounding cities, populated by masses of migrants lacking access to city services.

state—the central political structure of a society.

state capitalism—a political economy in which there are capitalist elements within the state-owned means of production.

statistically significant—a conclusion (on the basis of an inferential statistic) that a relationship exists in the population beyond a reasonable doubt.

status—a structural position in a social system.

status attainment model—an approach to occupational mobility that focuses on individual-level traits.

status consistency—the common situation of relatively similar rankings of a status in terms of the differing dimensions of inequality.

status set—the multiple social positions occupied by an individual.

stigma—a mark of social disgrace inflicted upon a deviant person.

structural conduciveness—certain aspects of a society that facilitate collective action.

structural differentiation—Emile Durkheim's theory tracing the increasing complexity and specialization of social structures.

structural mobility—the shifts in occupational position that occur within a given occupational structure.

structural model—an approach to occupational mobility that focuses on individual-level traits.

structural strain—the distress in people's lives that can cause them to deviate.

subculture—a group that stands apart from the larger society by supporting different values, language, religion, traditions, and the like.

subjective dimension—the general level of concern about that phenomenon registered in public opinion.

subjective social class—the individual's identification of personal class position in society.

subjects—participants in an experiment.

subjugation—the deliberate, long-run attempt on the part of the socially powerful to maintain their position in society at the expense of others.

subsistence technology—the principal form of economic activity through which a society exists.

superstructure—the various forms of social life built upon the means of production.

symbolic interactionism—a major theoretical approach in sociology that focuses on the meanings that arise from the interactions among individuals in a society.

symbols—the mechanisms necessary for the storage and transmission of the large quantities of information that constitute culture.

technocracy—a society whose social system operates according to the dictates of technology and engineering; the rule of society by technical experts.

technological determinism—the belief that technology acts as a force independent of its social context.

technological fix—attacking a technological or social problem with a technological solution.

technology—a system based on the application of knowledge, manifested in physical objects, related skills, and organizational forms, for the attainment of specific goals.

telephone interview—the survey format in which the items are presented to respondents over the telephone.

tertiary sector—that portion of the workforce devoted to providing services (e.g., education, communication).

theory—a proposition about the relationship between two or more concepts.

tobaccosis—a class of diseases resulting from the smoking, chewing, and/or snuffing of tobacco.

total institutions—organizations that exercise nearly complete control over the lives of their members.

traditional authority—legitimacy is based on long-standing social patterns.

traditional family—a family consisting of a breadwinning husband, a stay-at-home wife, and their dependent children.

transsexuals—people who have a total aversion to their biological sex although they are in all ways physically normal.

validity—the degree to which a procedure measures what it is supposed to measure.

value—a socially shared standard about what is good, desirable, and right in a particular culture.

value-free—Weber's term for the "ethically neutral" procedures of sociology that would, ideally, allow an objective view of social reality untainted by personal values.

variable—a measured concept whose values can vary.

verstehen—Max Weber's term for the attempt to understand the intentions of social actors on their own terms.

wealth—the value of property and assets (distinguished from income).

welfare state capitalism—a political economy in which the state provides some social services and economic regulation in a capitalist system.

Copyright Acknowledgments

For permission to reprint copyrighted materials, the publisher is grateful to the following.

FIGURES AND TEXT

Figure 1:2—Adapted from Melvin L. Kohn and Kazimierz M. Slomczynski. 1990. *Social Structure and Self-Direction: A Comparative Analysis of the United States and Poland,* pp. 186–187. Reprinted by permission of Basil Blackwell. Cambridge, MA. Reprinted by Permission.

Box 2:1—From *Chung Kuo* by David Wingrove. Copyright © 1990 by David Wingrove. Used by permission of Delacorte Press, a division of Bantam Doubleday Dell Publishing Group, Inc.

Box 2:2—Excerpted from Ginny Wiegand. "Woman of the Streets," *The Philadelphia Inquirer Magazine.* November 22, 1992, pp. 12–29. Reprinted with permission by the Philadelphia Inquirer, 11/22/92.

Box 3:1—Excerpted from Philip G. Zimbardo. "Pathology of Imprisonment," *Society* 9: 4–6. Copyright © by Transaction Publishers, 1972. Used by permission of the publisher.

Box 3:2—Excerpted from Carol B. Stack. *All our Kin.* pp. 27–29, xi, 14–16. Copyright © by Harper & Row Publishers, 1975. Used by permission of the publisher.

Box 3:4—Excerpted from Harvey M. Choldin. "A Briefing on the Census," *Footnotes,* March 1990, p. 4. Used by permission of the author.

Table 3:1—Excerpts from *All Our Kin: Strategies for Survival in a Black Community* by Carol B. Stack. Copyright © 1974 by Carol B. Stack. Reprinted by permission of HarperColllins Publishers Inc.

Figure 4:4—Claude S. Fischer. 1982. *To Dwell Among Friends.* P. 40. Adapted by permission of The University of Chicago Press.

Box 4:2—Excerpted from Frank Herbert, *Dune,* pp. 286–288. Copyright © by Ace Books, 1975. All rights reserved. Used by permission of the publisher.

Figure 5:5—Table from *Normal Accidents: Living with High-Risk Technologies* by Charles Perrow. Copyright © 1984 by Basic Books, Inc. Reprinted by permission of BasicBooks, a division of HarperCollins Publishers, Inc.

Box 5:2—From *Jurassic Park* by Michael Crichton. Copyright © 1990 by Michael Crichton. Reprinted by permission of Alfred A. Knopf, Inc.

Figure 5:6—Adapted from Ronald S. Burt, Kenneth P. Christman and Harold C. Kilburn. 1980. "Testing a Structural Theory of Corporate Cooptation: Interorganizational Directorate Ties as a Strategy for Avoiding Market Constraints on Profits." *American Sociological Review,* 45 (October): 827. Reprinted by permission of the American Sociological Association.

Figure 5:7—Adapted from Richard H. Hall. 1987. *Organizations: Structure, Processes and Outcomes,* Englewood Cliffs, N.J., p. 237. Reprinted by permission of Prentice-Hall, Inc.

Acetate Section—MADD: A Study of Social Structure. MADD® logo used by permission of Mothers Against Drunk Driving (MADD). Text reviewed by Media Relations Office, MADD.

Box 6:1—From *Ishmael* by Daniel Quinn. Copyright © 1992 by Daniel Quinn. Used by permission of Bantam Books, a division of Bantam Doubleday Dell Publishing Group, Inc.

Box 6:2—Excerpted from M. N. Srinivas, *Social Change in Modern India.* Copyright © by University of California Press, 1971. All rights reserved. Used by permission of the publisher.

Table 6:6—J. Palen. 1992. *The Urban World 4E,* Copyright © 1993 McGraw-Hill, Inc. All rights reserved. Reprinted by permission of the publisher.

Figure 6:1—Adapted from R. White and R. Cortes. 1992. "Measure of Misery," *The Philadelphia Inquirer,* p. E3, Reprinted by permission of The Philadelphia Inquirer.

Box 7:1—Excerpted from Garry Abrams, "Survey sees ethics lapses as pervasive". *The Philadelphia Inquirer.* November 26, 1992, p. E1. Copyright © by The Philadelphia Inquirer. Used by permission of the publisher.

Figure 7:1—From *New Rules* by Daniel Yankelovich. Copyright © 1981 by Daniel Yankelovich. Reprinted by permission of Random House, Inc.

Box 7:2—Excerpted from Mary Ann French, "A Practice Some Call Mutilation," *The Philadelphia Inquirer.* (Philadelphia: January 17, 1993, pp. F1, F6.) Copyright © by The Washington Post, 1993. Used by permission of the publisher.

Box 7:3—Excerpted from Betty Mahmoody and William Hoffer, *Not Without My Daughter,* (New York: pp. 99–101). Copyright © by St. Martin's Press, 1988. Used by permission of the publisher.

Box 8:1—Excerpted from B. F. Skinner, *Walden Two* (New York: MacMillan, pp. 96–117). Copyright © by MacMillan, 1948/1970. Used by permission of the publisher.

Table 9:1—Julia S. Brown, 1952. "A Comparative Study of Deviations from Sexual Mores," *American Sociological Review* (April 1952, 167: 138). Reprinted by permission of the author.

Box 9:1—Excerpted from Steve Allen, "The Public Hating," in *Social Problems Through Science Fiction,* eds. Greenberg et al., (New York, pp. 323–328). Copyright © by St. Martin's Press, Inc., 1975. Used by permission of the publisher.

Box 9:2—Excerpted from Lacy McCrary, "More Women Landing in Jail," *The Philadelphia Inquirer,* (December 17, 1989, p. 15). Reprinted with permission by The Philadelphia Inquirer, 12/17/89.

Table 9:2—Center for Studies in Criminology and Criminal Law. University of Pennsylvania, Philadelphia. *The Seriousness of Crime: Results of a National Survey,* as reported in U.S. Department of Justice, Report to the National on Crime and Justice (Washington, D.C.: U.S. Government Printing Office, October, 1983), pp. 4–5. Reprinted by permission of the publisher.

Table 11:2—Donald J. Treiman, 1977. *Occupational Prestige in Comparative Perspective* (New York: p. 155–156). Copyright © 1977 Academic Press. Reprinted by permission of the publisher.

Box 11:1—Reproduced, with permission, from the Annual Review of Sociology, Volume 17, © 1991, by Annual Reviews Inc.

Box 11:2—Excerpted from Frank Herbert, *The Dosadi Experiment.* (New York: pp. 8, 9, 31, 146–7, 160–1). Copyright © by Ace Books, 1977.

Box 11:3—Excerpted from Joseph Burke, "How I Spent My Summer Vacation," *Philadelphia Streets.* (Summer 1991, pp. 3–4). Copyright © by Philadelphia Committee for the Homeless, 1991. Used by permission of the publisher.

Box 12:1—Excerpted from Marian Lee Smothers, "Black Women: Myth and Reality," *The Philadelphia Inquirer* (p. 7a). 1990. Used by permission of the publisher.

Box 12:3—Excerpted from "Racial Bias Re-Emerges on Campuses Across the U.S.," *The Philadelphia Inquirer,* (March 10, 1987, p. 86), Reprinted with permission by The Philadelphia Inquirer, 3/10/87.

Figure 12:2—Adapted from Douglas Massey, Kirk Montgomery, and Nancy Denton. 1987. "Trends in Residential Segregation of Blacks, Hispanics and Asians," *American Sociological Review,* 52(6): 802–25 (Figure 12:2—The Twenty Most Segregated Cities in America). Copyright © by American Sociological Review. Reprinted by permission.

Table 12:4—Tanya Barrientos, 1989. "A Memorial to the Civil Rights Movement," *The Philadelphia Inquirer,* (November 5, 1989, pp. 1E and 4E). Reprinted with permission by The Philadelphia Inquirer, 11/5/89.

Box 13:1—Excerpted from Peggy Reeves Sanday, *Fraternity Gang Rape."* (New York: pp. 1–3). Copyright © by New York University Press, 1990. Used by permission of the publisher.

Box 14:2—Excerpts from *The Handmaid's Tale* by Margaret Atwood. Copyright © 1985 by O. W. Toad, Ltd. First American Edition 1986. Reprinted by permission of Houghton Mifflin Co. All rights reserved.

Figure 14:1—Dennis Ahlburg and Carol De Vita, "New Realities of the American Family," Population Bulletin 47, No. 2, p. 12. (Washington, D.C.: Population Reference Bureau, 1992).

Figure 14:2—Dennis Ahlburg and Carol De Vita, "New Realities of the American Family," Population Bulletin 47, No. 2, p. 25. (Washington, D.C.: Population Reference Bureau, 1992).

Figure 14:3—Dennis Ahlburg and Carol De Vita, "New Realities of the American Family," Population Bulletin 47, No. 2, p. 5. (Washington, D.C.: Population Reference Bureau, 1992).

Figure 14:4—Dennis Ahlburg and Carol De Vita, "New Realities of the American Family," Population Bulletin 47, No. 2, p. 6. (Washington, D.C.: Population Reference Bureau, 1992).

Box 15:1—Excerpted from Arthur C. Clarke, *Childhood's End.* (New York, pp. 66–68). Copyright © by Ballantine Books, 1953. Used by permission of the publisher.

Figure 15:3—Adapted from David Herring. 1992. "The Bible Decades," *Map Sense: Global Comparisons and Trends from World Monitor Magazine.* (p. 8). Reprinted by permission of The Christian Science Monitor.

Box 16:1—Excerpted from Ursula K. Leguin, *The Dispossessed,* (New York, pp. 106–107, 167). Copyright © by Avon Publisher, 1974. Used by permission of the publisher.

Figure 16:2—Adapted from Population Reference Bureau, 1989. *America in the 21st Century: Human Resource Development,* p. 3. Reprinted by permission of the Population Reference Bureau, Inc. Reprinted by permission.

Figure 17:2—Adapted from David Herring. 1992. "The Decline of Illiteracy in Developing Countries," *Map Sense: Global Comparisons and Trends from World Monitor Magazine,* p. 9. Reprinted by permission of The Christian Science Monitor.

Box 18:1—Excerpted from *Aging Well* (pp. 18–19), © 1989 by James F. Fries. Reprinted by permission of Addison-Wesley Publishing Company, Inc.

Box 18:2—Excerpted from Sydney van Scyoc, "A Visit to Cleveland General," in Greenberg, et al., *Social Problems Through Science Fiction,* p. 347–349. Copyright © by St. Martin's Press, 1975. Used by permission of the publisher.

Box 18:3—Excerpted from Michael Kidron and Ronald Segal, *The New State of the World Atlas,* (New York: pp. 42–4). Copyright © by Simon and Schuster, 1991. Used by permission of the publisher.

Box 19:1—From *Tai-Pan* by James Clavell. Copyright © 1966 by James Clavell. Used by permission of Delacorte Press, a division of Bantam Doubleday Dell Publishing Group, Inc.

Figure 19:2—Adapted from Andrew Greeley, et al. 1989. "A Most Monogamous People," GSS Tropical Report No. 17, p. 39. Copyright © by NORC. Reprinted by permission of NORC.

Box 20:1—Excerpted from Arthur Haupt and Thomas Kane, *Population Handbook,* 3rd Edition. (Washington, D.C.: Population Reference Bureau). Copyright © by Population Reference Bureau, 1991. Used by permission of the publisher.

Figure 20:2—Adapted from Joseph McFalls, "Population: A Lively Introduction," *Population Bulletin,* 46, No. 2, (Washington, D.C.: Population Reference Bureau, 1991).

Table 20:3—Adapted from Joseph McFalls, "Population: A Lively Introduction," *Population Bulletin,* 46, No. 2, (Washington, D.C.: Population Reference Bureau, 1991).

Figure 20:3—Adapted from Joseph McFalls, "Population: A Lively Introduction," *Population Bulletin,* 46, No. 2, (Washington, D.C.: Population Reference Bureau, 1991).

Figure 20:4—Adapted from Robert W. Fox. 1988. *Population Images,* pp. 10–13. Copyright © by United Nations Fund for Population Activities. Reprinted by permission.

Figure 20:6—Adapted from Joseph McFalls, "Population: A Lively Introduction," *Population Bulletin,* 46, No. 2, (Washington, D.C.: Population Reference Bureau, 1991).

Figure 20:7—Adapted from Joseph McFalls, "Population: A Lively Introduction," *Population Bulletin,* 46, No. 2, (Washington, D.C.: Population Reference Bureau, 1991).

Figure 20:8—Adapted from Joseph McFalls, "Population: A Lively Introduction," *Population Bulletin,* 46, No. 2, (Washington, D.C.: Population Reference Bureau, 1991).

Box 21:3—Excerpted from Michael Crichton, *Congo.* (New York: pp. 276–277). Copyright © by Avon Publisher, 1980. Used by permission of the publisher.

PHOTOS

Chapter 1 Pp. 2–3, © Anthony Suau/Gamma Liason; P. 6–Top, Superstock; P. 6–Bottom, © Gerd Ludwig, From *A Day In The Life of China*—Collins Publishers; P. 7, © Robert McCall; P. 22, Bettmann Archives.

Chapter 2 P. 23, 27, 29, © Bob Daemmrich; P. 36, Giraudon/Art Resource; P. 39, © Bert Caputo/Stock Boston; P. 40–Top Left, © P. Durand-Sygma; P. 40–Top Right, © Bill Gallery/Stock Boston; P. 40–Bottom Left, © Photo Edit; P. 40–Bottom Right, © Alan Oddie/Photo Edit; P. 41, © Paul Conklin/Photo Edit; P. 45, AP/Wide World; P. 49, © David Young-Wolff/Photo Edit; P. 51, © Dana Fineman/Sygma; P. 55, UPI/Bettman; P. 57, Reuters/Bettman; P. 58, Soviet Life Magazine.

Chapter 3 P. 64, NASA Goddard Space Flight Center, P. 66, Harry Koprowski, M.D.; P. 70, UPI/Bettman; P. 71, Gamma-Liaison; P. 72, The Phillips Collection, Panel 1: During the World War There was a Great Migration North by Southern Negroes. 1940–41. Tempera on masonite. 11″ × 17″. *The Phillips Collection.* Washington, D.C.; P. 77, Jan Staller/The Stock Market; P. 80, © Courtesy CBS News; P. 84, © 1992 Michael Kowal/Custom Medical Stock Photo; P. 92–Top, School of Engineering and Applied Science, University of Pennsylvania; P. 92–Bottom, © 1992 Frank Siteman/Stock Boston.

Chapter 4 Pp. 96–97, © Tom Saunders/Aerial Focus; P. 100, © 1991 Chlaus Lotscher/Stock Boston; P. 101, © Bob Daemmrich/Stock Boston; P. 103, 1927. Oil on canvas 28″ × 36″, Des Moines Art Center, James D. Edmundson Fund; P. 107, © Lynn Johnson/Black Star; P. 108, © Fredrik D. Bodin/Stock Boston; P. 110, UPI/Bettmann; P. 113, © 1991 Richard Falco/Black Star; P. 118, AP/Wide World; P. 127, Megan Jones.

Chapter 5 P. 131, © Richard Hutchings/Photo Edit; P. 134, David Young-Wolff/Photo Edit; P. 137, Joseph Schuyler/Stock Boston; P. 138, Bob Daemmrich/Stock Boston; P. 144–Top, Custom Medical Stock Photo; P. 144–Bottom, Metropolitan Museum of Art, George A. HearnFund, 1956 P. 149, © Charles Feil/Stock Boston; P. 155, Top Left, Art Resource; Top Right, Superstock; Center, Borromeo/Art Resource, N.Y.; Bottom Left, Erich Lessing/Art Resoure; Bottom Right, Superstock; P. 158, P. Durand/Sygma; P. 159, © Sergio Dorantes/Sygma.

Chapter 6 P. 163, © 1993 Carlos Hunter, RTO-TDC/Contact Press; P. 166, Ken Murray Collection; P. 168, © Terry E. Eiler/Stock Boston; P. 174, © Bruno Barbery/Magnum; P. 175, Asian American Free Labor Institute; P. 177, Owen Franken/Stock Boston; P. 179, 1950. Egg tempera on composition board. sight:18⅛ × 36⅛ inches. (46cm x 91.8cm). Collection of Whitney Museum of American Art, New York. Purchased with funds from the Juliana Force Purchase Award; P. 183, Reuters/Bettmann.

Chapter 7 Pp. 186–187, © AP/Wide World; P. 191, © 1988 Stacy Pick/Stock Boston; P. 194–Top, © Paul Conklin/Photo Edit; P. 194–Bottom, © Daniel Brody/Stock Boston; P. 195, © Michael Newman/Photo Edit; P. 198, © Jack Stein Grove/Photo Edit; P. 199, © Gerd Ludwig from *A Day In The Life of China*—Collins Publishers; P. 205, Lynn Johnson/Salt Lake City Tribune; P. 210–Left, © Thomas Abercrombie/National Geographic; P. 210–Right, © Cosmopolitan Magazine; P. 212–Top, Rick Stewart/Allsport; P. 212–Bottom, © Thomas Abercrombie/National Geographic; P. 218, © John Launois/BlackStar; P. 226, Winfield Parks/National Geographic.

Chapter 8 P. 235, The Bettman Archive; P. 239–Left, © Ben Blankenburg/Stock Boston; P. 239–Right, © Michael Newman/Photo Edit; P. 241, Art Institute of Chicago, Robert A. Waller Fund; P. 243, © Sisse Brimberg/National Geographic; P. 245, Hampton University Museum; P. 250, Al Bello/Allsport; P. 253, UPI/Bettmann; P. 257, © Seny Norasingh from *A Day In The Life of the Soviet Union*—Collins Publishers; P. 258, © Phil McCarten/Photo Edit; P. 262, © 1993 Nicole Bengiveno/Matrix.

Chapter 9 P. 269, © 1965 by Stanley Milgram. From the film "Obedience" distributed by the Pennsylvania State University, Audio Visual Services; P. 273, Chuck Nacke/Woodfin Care; P. 276, Historial Pictures/Stock Montage, Inc.; P. 279, Bettmann; P. 281, Reuters/Bettmann; P. 286, Reuters/Bettmann; P. 290, Ted Thai/Time Magazine; P. 293, Photos by UPI/Bettmann; P. 294, UPI/Bettmann; P. 297, Kotoh-Zefa/H. Armstrong Roberts; P. 299, Zalesky-Clemmer/Black Star; P. 301, National Museum of American Art/Art Resource, N.Y.

Chapter 10 P. 304–Top, AP/Wide World Photos; P. 304–Bottom Left, © Barbara Alper/Stock Boston; P. 304–Bottom Right, © Jim Whitmer/Stock Boston; P. 308, © John Filo; P. 309, J. Rettaliata/Allsport; P. 310, Giraudon/Art Resource, New York; P. 311, Aimar-Joffet/Sipa; P. 315, Express Newspapers/Archive Photos; P. 316, AP/Wide World; P. 320, Sergei Karpukhin-AP/Wide World Photos; P. 321, Reuters/Bettmann; P. 325, Rapho/Black Star; P. 330, Panel 50 from the series *The Migration of the Negro.* (1940–41). Tempera on gesso on composition board, 18″ × 12″. The Museum of Modern Art, New York. Gift of Mrs. David M. Levy. Photograph © 1994, The Museum of Modern Art, New York.; P. 331, Art Resource, New York.

Chapter 11 Pp. 334–335, Photo courtesy of the Norman Rockwell Museum at Stockbridge. Repoduced by the permission of the Norman Rockwell Family Trust. © 1964 Norman Rockwell Family Trust; P. 339, "Caste and Ecology in the Social Insects" (Monographs in Population Biology #12) by Oster & Wilson, Princeton University Press; P. 344, Joyce Paul; P. 345, © David Bramley/Tony Stone Worldwide; P. 350–Top, © Michael Grecco/Stock Boston; P. 350–Bottom, © Michael Newman/Photo Edit; P. 352–Top, P. Royer/H. Armstrong Roberts; P. 352–Bottom, © Joe Bensen/Stock Boston; P. 355, Wilson McLean/The Picture Plane; P. 359–Left & Right, Stephen Shames/Matrix; P. 366, 367, © Sal DiMarco.

Chapter 12 P. 379, © 1993 Alan Jakubek; P. 381, Ron Tarver/Philadelphia Inquirer; P. 384, © 1994 All Rights Reserved. The Museum of Fine Arts, Boston; P. 388, Susan Greenwood/Liaison.; P. 390, From collection #3830 N3676 Division of Rare and Manuscript Collections, Carl A. Kroch Library, Cornell University; P. 394, Bob Hill; P. 396, Ferdinand Lamont Belin Fund, © 1994 National Gallery of Art, Washington D.C.; P. 403, © David Turnley/Detroit Free

Press/Black Star; P. 405, Courtesy of Robert Berman Gallery/Santa Monica, California.

Chapter 13 P. 414, Courtesy of John K.B. Robertson; P. 417, Historical Pictures/Stock Montage, Inc.; P. 418, Herman Kokojan/Black Star; P. 421, © Tom McCarthy/Photo Edit; P. 423, © 1990 Seth Resnick/Stock Boston; P. 427–Left, © Cresci/Rothco; P. 427–Right, Photofest; P. 430, © Costa Manos/Magnum Photos; P. 437, UPI/Bettmann; P. 438, Private Collector. Photo Courtesy of The Terry Dintenfass Gallery N.Y.

Chapter 14 Pp. 444–445, Robin Moyer from *A Day in the Life of Italy*—Collins Publishers; P. 448, National Museum of American Art/Art Resource; P. 452, Ron Taylor Crouch; P. 453, Sal Veder-AP/Wide World; P. 455, Bob Footherap; P. 462–Left, © David Young-Wolff/Photo Edit; P. 462–Right, CBS; P. 470, Limor Imbar; P. 470, *Birthday* (l'Anniversaire). (1915) Oil on cardboard, 31¾″ × 39¼″. The Museum of Modern Art, New York. Acquired through the Lillie P. Bliss Bequest. Photograph © 1994 The Museum of Modern Art, New York.; P. 471, Jay Dickman from *A Day In The Life of China*—Collins Publishers; P. 473, Photos by Ted Thai/ Time Magazine. Computer Morphing by Kin Wah Lam. Design by Walter Bernard and Milton Glaser; P. 476, Scala/Art Resource, N.Y.; P. 479–Left, Photofest; P. 479–Right, Metropolitan Museum of Art, George A. Hearn Fund, 1979; P. 483, © 1987 Carmen Lomas Garza. Collection of Leonilla Ramirez, Dan Ramon's Restaurant, San Francisco, California. Photo by Wolfgang Dietze; P. 485, The Jacob A. Riis Collection, #123, Museum of the City of New York.

Chapter 15 P. 493, Steve McCurry/Magnum; P. 496, National Museum, Tokyo; P. 501, © Gilbert M. Grosvenor/National Geographic; P. 506, © Marcello Bertinetti/Photo Researchers; P. 511, © David Harvey/National Geographic; P. 514, A. BenaiNous-E. Bakel/Gamma Liaison; P. 517, © Susan Meiselas/Magnum; P. 519, © Douglas Burrows/ Gamma Liaison; P. 521, Thomas Abercrombie/National Geographic.

Chapter 16 P. 525, © Richard Nesdale-Art/Cam Video; P. 529, © Richard Nowitz; P. 531, D. Sokolow/Itar-Tass/ Sovfoto; P. 533, © David Woo/Liaison; P. 536, Giraudon/ Art Resource, N.Y.; P. 537-Left, Laurie Platt Winfrey, Inc.; P. 537–Right, © James Nachtwey/Magnum; P. 539, Photri Inc.; P. 543, Bettmann; P. 552–Top, J. Langevin/Sygma; P. 552–Bottom, © Tom Stoddart/Katz/Saba; P. 553, Torin Boyd from *A Day In The Life of the Soviet Union*—Collins Publishers.

Chapter 17 P. 558, Courtesy of Joseph A. McFalls, Photo by George Sistrovich; P. 559, St. Louis Art Museum; P. 560, National Museum of American Art, Washington, D.C./Art Resource, N.Y.; P. 562–Left, © 1989 Amy Etra/Photo Edit; P. 562–Right, © 1994 David Burnett/Contact Press Images; P. 564, © N.R. Rowan/Stock Boston; P. 568, © 1992 Victor Mays/Mystic Seaport Museum; P. 569, © Bob Daemmrich; P. 576, © Billy E. Barnes/Photo Edit; P. 579, Susan Guyton; P. 585–Left, © Chris Brown/and Right, Saba.

Chapter 18 Pp. 588–589, Private collection. Embroidery in silk on linen by Mary (Polly) Giles. Groton Female Seminary, Groton, Massachusetts, c. 1825; P. 592, © 1993 Geff Hinds/The News Tribune, Tacoma, Washington; P. 592, Alfred Leslie; P. 501, William Campbell/Time Magazine; P. 504, V. Leloup-Figaro/Gamma-Liaison; P. 605, © 1984 Del Mulkey/Photo Researchers; P. 610, Robert F. Kusel/Sygma; P. 614, © 1991 Robert Brenner/Photo Edit; P. 618, © 1993 Matuschka/Skarratt; P. 619, National Museum of Women in the Arts, Gift of Wallace and Wilhelmina Holladay; P. 620, James Balog from *A Day In The Life of the Soviet Union*—Collins Publishers; P. 622, Philadelphia Museum of Art: Given by Wright S. Lindington; P. 625, Mike Cooper/ Allsport.

Chapter 19 P. 631, Mike Davis from *A Day In The Life of Italy*—Collins Publishers; P. 632, Jay Dickman from *A Day In The Life of the Soviet Union*—Collins Publishers; P. 637–Top, Bettmann; P. 637–Bottom, Daniel Simon/Gamma Liaison; P. 639, John Loengard-Life Magazine. © Time Warner, Inc.; P. 642, From "Art in the Seventies" by Phaidon Press, Ltd., Produced by arrangement with Rogers, Coleridge & White Ltd. London; P. 645, Oil on canvas. 33 × 36 inches. (83.8cm × 91.4cm). Collection of Whitney Museum of American Art. Gift of Malcolm S. Forbes; P. 647, Mary Ryan; P. 653, Art Resource, N.Y.; P. 656, © Jon Levy/The Gamma Liaison Network; P. 658, Jeffrey Markowitz/Sygma; P. 659, Churchill & Klehr for Insight Magazine; P. 662–Left, Stephen Ferry/Gamma Liaison; P. 662–Right, Gamma Liaison.

Chapter 20 P. 668, Nick Kelsh from *A Day In The Life of China*—Collins Publishers; P. 674, Bettmann; P. 676–Top, Tempera on gessoed panel, 32¼ x 47¾″. The Museum of Modern Art, New York. Purchase. Photograph © 1994 The Museum of Modern Art, New York; P. 676–Bottom, Los Angeles County Funds, © Los Angeles County Museum of Art; P. 681, © Michel Setboun/JB Pictures; P. 683, Tempera on paper over composition board, 23 × 31⅜″. The Museum of Modern Art, New York. Gift of Lincoln Kirstein. Photograph © 1994 The Museum of Modern Art, New York; P. 692–Top, National Cowboy Hall of Fame and Western Heritage Center, Oklahoma City; P. 692–Bottom, Woolaroc Museum, Bartlesville, Oklahoma; P. 694–Top, © 1993 Rick Rickman/Matrix; P. 694–Bottom, © 1889 Dan Lamont/Matrix; P. 698, Coutausse/Contact Press.

Chapter 21 P. 706, American Stock/Archive Photos; P. 707, Jack Juratovic; P. 708, Laurie Platt Winfrey, Inc.; P. 709, © George F. Hobley/National Geographic; P. 711, Tom Lovell/Illustration House; P. 712, N.A.S.A; P. 714–Top, © Hank Morgan/Photo Researchers; P. 714–Bottom, © George Haling/Photo Researchers; P. 715, Laurie Platt Winfrey, Inc.; P. 716, China Pictorial; P. 718, © David Young-Wolff/Photo Edit; P. 719, Ken Murray Collection; P. 727–Top, Courtesy of the Artist, Trigo Piula and the Center for African Art New York; P. 727–Bottom, Rick Rickman, from *A Day In The Life of China*—Collins Publishers; P. 729, © Jonathan Blair/National Geographic; P. 731, Scientific American; P. 738, Ted Thai/Time Magazine; P. 739, Rex Features, London P. 741, *Westward, The Star of Empire* (CA. 1871) by Theodor Kaufman, from the St. Louis Mercantile Library.

Name Index

Subject Index